VISUAL BASIC® 5 SUPERBIBLE

VOLUME 1

D1568574

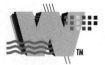

WAITE
GROUP
PRESS ™

A Division of
Macmillan Computer
Publishing

Corte Madera, CA

Eric Winemiller
David Jung
Pierre Boutquin
John Harrington
Bill Heyman
Ryan Groom
Todd Bright
Bill Potter

PUBLISHER • Mitchell Waite
ASSOCIATE PUBLISHER • Charles Drucker

ACQUISITIONS MANAGER • Susan Walton

EDITORIAL DIRECTOR • John Crudo
PROJECT EDITOR • Laura E. Brown
DEVELOPMENTAL/TECHNICAL EDITORS • Chris Stone, Wei Li
PRODUCTION EDITORS • Kelsey McGee, Marlene Vasilieff
COPY EDITORS • Merrilee Eggleston, Debi Anker, Deirdre Greene,
Michelle Goodman, Ann Longknife/Creative Solutions

MANAGING EDITOR • Brice P. Gosnell
INDEXING MANAGER • Johnna L. VanHoose
RESOURCE COORDINATORS • Deborah Frisby, Charlotte Clapp
EDITORIAL ASSISTANTS •Carmela Carvajal, Carol Ackerman, Andi
Richter, Rhonda Tinch-Mize, Karen Williams

SOFTWARE SPECIALIST • Dan Scherf

DIRECTOR OF MARKETING • Kelli S. Spencer
PRODUCT MARKETING MANAGER • Wendy Gilbride
ASSOCIATE PRODUCT MARKETING MANAGER • Jennifer Pock
MARKETING COORDINATOR • Linda B. Beckwith
MARKETING ASSISTANT • Charles Kemper

PRODUCTION MANAGER • Cecile Kaufman
PRODUCTION TEAM SUPERVISORS • Brad Chinn, Andrew Stone
COVER DESIGNERS • Tim Amrhein, Regan Honda
BOOK DESIGNER • Jean Bisesi, Karen Johnston, Sandra Schroeder

PRODUCTION • Karen Johnston, Carol Bowers, Jenny Dierdorff,
Cyndi Davis-Hubler, Chris Livengood

Printed in the United States of America
  98 99 • 10 9 8 7 6 5 4 3 2

Library of Congress Cataloging-in-Publication Data
Visual Basic 5 SuperBible / Eric Winemiller ... [etal.].
       p.   cm.
    Includes index.
    ISBN 1-57169-111-1 9vol.10. -- isbn 1-57169-112-x (vol.2) --
ISBN 1-57169-102-2 (set)
    1. BASIC (Computer program language) 2. Microsoft Visual BASIC.
I. Winemiller, Eric, 1969-
    QA76.73.B3V567   1997
    005.13'3--dc21

97-21822
CIP

VISUAL BASIC ALPHABETICAL CONTROL TABLE

VISUAL BASIC ALPHABETICAL JUMP TABLE

VISUAL BASIC TASK JUMP TABLE

ActiveX Controls

Adding a user defined control to a project: **UserControl**, 1793-1794

Aligning to a container's edge: **Alignable**, 1815

Allowing or denying focus: **CanGetFocus**, 1816

Assign and capture an access key: **AccessKeyPress**, **AccessKeys**, 1814, 1813

Behave as a default or cancel button: **DefaultCancel, DisplayAsDefault**, 1817, 1409

Binding to a data source: **Bindable**, 1373

Containing other controls: **ControlContainer**, 1776

Create property pages: **Property Page Wizard**, 78, 1729, 2047

Creating an ActiveX document: **UserDocument**, 76-77, 1893-1894, 1901-1905

Edit at design time: **EditAtDesignTime**, 1818

Enumerating constants: **Enum**, 172

Fire events: **Events, RaiseEvent**, 1749, 542-543

Get remote property values: **AsyncProperty**, 1864

Host a control in a browser: **Object tag**, 1883

Making an invisible control: **InvisibleAtRuntime**, 1824

Navigate the Web: **GoBack, GoFoward, NavigateTo**, 1863, 1864

Providing a toolbox picture: **ToolboxBitmap**, 1825

Reading and writing properties: **PropertyBag, ReadProperties, WriteProperties**, 1833-1835

Clipboard

Transfer text or graphics data between windows or applications: **Clipboard** (object), 206

Find out whether the clipboard has graphics or text: **GetFormat**, 1241

Get graphics from the clipboard: **GetData**, 1240

Get text from the clipboard: **GetText**, 1242

Send graphics to the clipboard: **SetData**, 1243

Send text to the clipboard: **SetText**, 1244

Clear the contents of the clipboard: **Clear**, 1239

Communicate with DOS windows: **SendKeys**, 1187

Controls

Display an indicator of progress: **ProgressBar**, 1936

Display notebook-style tabs: **TabStrip, Tabbed Dialog**, 1945

Display an icon-filled bar: **ToolBar**, 1948

Display a hierarchical view of a set of data: **TreeView**, 1951

Store or display a collection of images: **ImageList**, 1924

Display a graphical view of data: **ListView**, 1928

Display a slider control: **Slider**, 1938

Create a status bar to display information: **StatusBar**, 1941

Associate control values with a database: **Data, DBGrid, DBCombo, DBList**, 219, 223, 228, 235

Controls (General)

Examine attributes of active control: **ActiveControl**, 673, 1814

Respond to user changes in contents: **Change**, 53, 654, 1011

Manipulate controls in a control array: **Index**, 676

Identify a particular control: **Tag**, 683

Find form that contains the control: **Parent**, 681

Label a control on a form: **Label**, 261

Create a new instance in a control array: **Load**, 150-151, 714-719

Specify 3D or "flat" look: **Appearance**, 603

Database

Use multiple databases: **WorkSpaces** (collection), **CreateWorkspace**, 1349

Perform database maintenance: **CompactDatabase**, 1547 **RepairDatabase**, 1547

Control database security: **Permissions**, 1550

Use SQL, DML, and DDL queries: **Querydef, Database** (property), 1360

Abort a transaction set: **RollbackTrans**, 1467

Commit the transaction set to the database: **CommitTrans**, 1467

Manipulate a set of records: **Recordset**, 1366-1367

Specify the source of data for a data bound control: **DataSource, DataField**, 1375-1376, 1381-1382

Debugging

Halt program execution: **Stop**, 568

Output program values for debugging: **Debug** (object), 562

Set and clear breakpoints: **Toggle Breakpoint, Clear All Breakpoints**, 562, 569

Step out of a sub or function: **Step Out**, 567

Step through code including procedures: **Step Into**, 567

Step through code without showing procedures: **Step Over**, 568

Step to the cursors location: **Step To Cursor**, 568

Set or show next statement to be executed: **Set Next Statement, Show Next Statement**, 565, 566

Show the calling order of subroutines: **Calls**, 125, 130

Use conditional compilation: **#If...#Else...#End If, #Const**, 1984, 1985

Dialog Boxes (and Related Controls)

Display a message in a box with standard icons: **MsgBox** (function and statement), 450, 455

Get text from a user by displaying a box: **InputBox**, 448

Specify choices that can be on or off: **CheckBox** (control), 200

Define a group of choices of which only one can be selected: **OptionButton** (control), 284

Create a group of related controls: **Frame** (control), 256

Label part of a dialog box: **Label**, 261

Display a button that executes a specified action: **Command button** (control), 213

Display a common dialog box: **CommonDialog**, 457

Drive, Directory, and File List Boxes

Set up boxes for working with the disk:
DriveListBox, DirListBox, FileListBox
(objects), 241, 238, 245

Set or read the current drive in a Drive list box: **Drive**, 1045

Set or read the name of the currently selected file:
FileName, 1047

Set or read the search path for a Directory or File list box:
Path, 1058

Specify what happens when the search path is changed:
PathChange, 1059

Set or read the file search pattern for a list box: **Pattern**, 1060

Specify what happens when file search pattern is changed:
PatternChange, 1062

Specify DOS attributes of files to be displayed in list: **Archive,
Hidden, ReadOnly, System**, 1044, 1048, 1063, 1067

Obtain items in a Drive, Dir, or File box's list: **List, ListCount,
ListIndex**, 1050, 1053-1054

Dynamic Data Exchange (DDE)

Specify type of link (hot/cold and server status):
LinkMode, 1293

Specify actions to take when a link is opened: **LinkOpen**, 1296

Get information from a linked application: **LinkRequest**, 1300

Specify item and topic to be used in a link: **LinkItem,
LinkTopic**, 1289, 1304

Send contents of a picture box to a linked application:
LinkSend, 1301

Send a command to a linked application: **LinkExecute**, 1286

Send information from a client to a server: **LinkPoke**, 1289,
1295

Deal with errors or timeouts during link: **LinkError,
LinkTimeout**, 1283, 1303

Specify what happens when a link is closed: **LinkClose**, 1282

Errors

Enable error trapping: **On Error Goto...**, 532

Disable error trapping: **On Error Goto 0**, 532

Retrieve a string expression containing a description of the
error: **Description**, 537

Associate a position within a help file with this error:
HelpContext, HelpFile, 538, 539

Retrieve the numeric value of an error: **Number**, 541

Retrieve the name of the object or application that generated an
error: **Source**, 543

Clear the error object after an error has been handled: **Clear**,
536, 1239

Generate a runtime error: **Raise**, 542

Focus

Specify which application gets the focus: **AppActivate**,
509, 1254

Specify which form or control gets the focus: **SetFocus**, 1265

Specify what happens when a form or control gets the focus:
GotFocus, 1262

Specify what happens when a form or control loses the focus:
LostFocus, 1264

Specify whether a control can respond to user input: **Enabled**,
1258, 1819

Control use of Tab key to move between controls:
TabIndex, TabStop, 1267, 1268

Fonts

Set or get name of current font: **Name**, 985

Find out what fonts are available: **FontCount, Fonts**, 977, 979

Set point size of font: **Size**, 987

Set typestyle: **Bold, Italic, Strikethrough, FontTransparent,
Underline**, 970, 981, 983, 989, 991

Forms (General)

Position form on screen: **Left, Top**, 769, 781

Set dimensions of form on screen: **Height, Width**, 766, 783

Display form title: **Caption**, 1174, 1256

Set up button to perform a specified action: **Command button**
(control), 1174, 1256

Set color and style: **BackColor, BorderStyle, ForeColor**, 605,
609, 617

Allow resizing of form: **ControlBox, MaxButton, MinButton**,
711, 719, 723

Respond to user actions: **Icon, MousePointer, Resize,
WindowState**, 729, 738

Show or hide form: **Hide, Show, Visible**, 712, 733,
1822, 1825

Load form without showing: **Load** (statement), 717

Refer to forms in code: **Name**, 671, 679-681, 985-987

Examine attributes of active form: **ActiveForm**, 675

Specify actions to take place when form is loaded: **Load**
(event), 714

Remove form: **Unload**, 737

Create an MDI main form: **New MDI Form**, 721-723

Create MDI child forms: **MDIChild**, 721

Trap keyboard input: **KeyPreview**, 1183

Graphics (Drawing)

Set Colors: **RGB, QBColor**, 816, 815

Specify style and width for shape boundary line: **DrawStyle,
DrawWidth**, 874, 877

Specify color and fill pattern for drawing: **FillColor, FillStyle**,
878, 881, 1096

Specify how drawing will interact with background:
DrawMode, 871

Draw shapes on a graphics object: **Circle, Line, PSet**, 860,
863, 869

Clear a drawing area: **Cls**, 801

Load graphics from a file: **LoadPicture**, 804

Determine graphics object initially appearing in a form:
Picture (property), 926

Determine color of a point: **Point**, 1458

Get handle to manipulate a graphics image: **Image**, 802-804

Control redrawing of graphics: **AutoRedraw, Paint**, 797, 806

Save graphics to a file: **SavePicture**, 818

Graphics (Setup)

Create a graphic object: **Picture** (control), 1260

Set measure to use for graphics coordinates: **ScaleMode**, 776

Establish graphics coordinates: **Scale, ScaleHeight, ScaleLeft, ScaleTop, ScaleWidth,** 771, 773, 775, 778, 779

Determine current position for drawing: **CurrentX, CurrentY,** 764

Position a graphic object: **Left, Top,** 769, 781

Set dimensions of a graphic object: **Height, Width,** 766, 783

Change layering of controls: **ZOrder, ClipControls,** 800, 820

Grids

Set up a grid: **Grid** (control), 258

Add rows to a grid: **AddItem, Rows,** 1077, 1094

Add columns to a grid: **Cols,** 1094

Change information in a grid: **Text, Clip,** 1087, 1110,

Change column width: **ColWidth,** 1095

Change row height: **RowHeight,** 1095

Create fixed rows and columns: **FixedRows, FixedCols,** 1098

IDE (Integrated Development Environment)

Install or remove add-ins: **Add-In Manager,** 73

Access the properties of Visual Basic itself: **User-Interface manipulation objects,** 1737

Access the properties of a form, module, or class module: **Component manipulation objects,** 1737

Access the properties of a control or form: **Form manipulation object,** 1736

Access the menus and menu choices: **CommandBars,** 1752

Access the properties of the whole project: **Project manipulation objects,** 1737

Access the available properties: **Properties, Property,** 1777

Access the group of currently selected components: **SelectedVBControls,** 1779

Keys

Link Enter or Escape keys to a button: **Cancel, Default,** 920, 923

Read status of keys including function and other special keys: **KeyDown, KeyUp,** 1177, 1184

Get ASCII value of a pressed key: **KeyPress,** 1181

Send keystrokes to control another Windows application: **SendKeys,** 1187

Trap form-level keyboard input: **KeyPreview,** 1183

Communicate with DOS windows: **SendKeys,** 1187

Language

Set the scope and lifetime of a variable: **Private, Public, Static,** 161

Repeat a group of instructions until or while a condition is true: **Do...Loop,** 140-141

Exit from a specific block of code: **Exit...,** 143-144

Repeat a group of instructions for each member of an array or collection: **For Each...Next,** 140-141

Repeat a group of instructions a specified number of times: **For...Next,** 139-141

Branch to a subroutine, then return: **Gosub...Return,** 136

Branch without return to a portion of code: **Goto,** 136

Perform a simple conditional execution of code: **If...Then...Else,** 137-138

Perform a complex conditional execution of code: **If...Then...ElseIf,** 137-138

Branch based on a supplied numeric value, then return: **On...Gosub,** 136-137

Branch based on a supplied numeric value without return: **On...Goto,** 136-137

Perform conditional execution based on the value of one expression: **Select Case...,** 1405

Halt execution for debugging: **Stop,** 568-569

Refer to object members without repeating parent name: **With...End With,** 144

Repeat a group of instructions while a condition is **True: While...Wend,** 143

Use your own subroutines and functions: **Call, Declare, Exit, Function...End Function, Sub...End Sub,** 526-527

Create your own properties: **Property Let...End Property, Property Get...End Property, Property Set...End Property,** 2146, 2148

Retrieve command-line arguments: **Command** (function), 507-511

Retrieve environment variables: **Environ,** 507-512

List, Combo, and DropDown Boxes

Set up a list box: **List box** (control), 265-269

Set up a combo box: **Combo box** (control), 208-213, 574, 946

Set style of a combo box; add drop down feature: **Style,** 1033, 1035

Specify what happens when a DropDown box is opened: **DropDown,** 1016

Set or return the items in a list: **List,** 1019-1020

Find out how many items are in a list: **ListCount,** 1020-1021

Add an item to a list: **AddItem,** 1009-1010

Remove an item from a list: **RemoveItem,** 1025-1026

Refer to a list by number: **ListIndex,** 1021-1022

Get the item that the user has selected: **Text,** 1386

Sort a list: **Sorted,** 1032

Enable more than one selection: **MultiSelect,** 1023, 1055

Determine what items are selected: **Selected,** 1027, 1066

Cross reference list item to something else: **ItemData, NewIndex,** 1018, 1024

Menus

Create a popup menu: **PopupMenu,** 725

Mouse

Determine if user has clicked the mouse: **Click, DblClick,** 921, 922, 1126, 1129

Determine if user has pressed or released mouse button: **MouseDown, MouseUp,** 1131, 1137

Specify actions to take place when user has moved the mouse: **MouseMove,** 1134

Set whether dragging will begin automatically: **DragMode,** 871, 1158

Begin or end dragging under program control: **Drag,** 1149

Specify icon to be shown while a control is dragged: **DragIcon,** 1155

Specify actions to be taken while dragging over a form or control: **DragOver,** 1160

Specify actions to be taken when mouse is released over a form or control: **DragDrop,** 1152

Numerical Expressions

Find the absolute value of a numerical expression: **Abs**, 351

Use mathematical functions on a numerical expression: **Atn, Cos, Exp, Log, Sin, Sqr, Tan**, 352

Change the type of a numerical expression: **CInt, CLng, CSng, CDbl, CCur, CBool**, 387

Change the format of a numerical expression: **Fix, Hex, Int, Oct**, 353, 392

Use a random number: **Randomize, Rnd**, 356, 357

Determine the sign of a numerical expression: **Sgn**, 358

Financial functions: **DDB, FV, IPmt, IRR, MIRR, NPer, NPV, Pmt, PPmt, PV, Rate, SLN, SYD**, 368-379

Object-Oriented Programming

Create your own class: **ClassModule, Set** (statement), **New** (keyword), 204, 565

Get class properties: **Property Get**, 2146

Set class properties: **Property Let**, 2148

Hide or expose data within your classes: **Private, Public**, 161

Define Initialization and Termination procedures for your classes: **Initialize, Terminate**, 714, 735, 2145, 2150

Establish a class hierarchy: **Collection, Parent**, 207, 681

Use a custom class: **Instancing, Public**, 161, 2177

OLE

Create an embedded or linked object: **OLE** (control), **Action**, 279, 1617

Activate an object: **Action, AutoActivate**, 1617, 1620

Use the clipboard with OLE objects: **Action**, 1617

Use OLE automation: **GetObject, CreateObject**, 1677, 1679

Determine what actions an object supports: **Verb, ObjectVerbsCount, ObjectVerbFlags, ObjectVerbs**, 643, 1662

Paste or insert an object: **Action**, 1617

Printer

Set units to be used for printing: **ScaleMode**, 776

Set page dimensions: **ScaleHeight, ScaleLeft, ScaleTop, ScaleWidth**, 773, 775, 778, 779

Set or get current print position on page: **CurrentX, CurrentY**, 764

Draw graphics for printing: **Circle, Line, PSet**, 860, 863, 869

Determine dimensions needed to print a string: **TextHeight, TextWidth**, 906

Print string at current position in current font: **Print**, 899, 1215

Print a Visual Basic form: **PrintForm**, 1216

Get the current page number: **Page**, 1210

Start a new page (form feed): **NewPage**, 1208

Send contents of printer object to Windows for printing: **EndDoc**, 1206

Kill a current print job: **KillDoc**, 1207

Set the number of copies to be printed: **Copies**, 1203

Set the printer orientation: **Orientation**, 1209

Set the print quality: **PrintQuality**, 1218

Set the paper source and size: **PaperBin, PaperSize**, 1210, 1212

Set or get the printer port: **Port**, 1214

Set or get information on the printer device and driver: **DeviceName, DriverName**, 1204

Set the printer output size: **Zoom**, 1221

Resources

Determine if your application is running on a Far East version of Windows: **IMEStatus**, 1995

Load data from a resource file: **LoadResData**, 1997

Load a bitmap, icon, or cursor from a resource file: **LoadResPicture**, 1999

Load a string from a resource file: **LoadResString**, 2000

Scroll Bars

Set up scroll bars: **Scroll bars** (control), 297

Set up scroll bars for a Text box: **ScrollBars** (property), 581, 1394, 1899

Set maximum and minimum values to be represented by a scroll bar: **Max, Min**, 936-937

Set or return current value represented by scroll bar: **Value**, 928, 939, 1527, 1862

Specify change in scroll bar's value when user clicks on arrow: **SmallChange**, 938

Specify change in scroll bar's value when user clicks on bar: **LargeChange**, 935

Strings

Extract a part of a string: **Left, Mid** (function), **Right**, 330, 333, 336, 769

Work with the ASCII value of a character: **Asc, Chr**, 326, 327

Convert the case of a string: **LCase, UCase**, 329, 342

Find one string within another: **InStr**, 328

Justify a value in a string: **LSet, RSet**, 331, 337

Compare two strings: **Like, Option Compare, StrComp**, 335, 339

Deal with spaces: **LTrim, RTrim, Space, Trim**, 332, 337, 338, 341

Switch between strings and numbers: **Format, Str, Val**, 388, 394, 395

Determine the length of a string: **Len**, 331

Text

Determine dimensions needed for a text string: **TextHeight, TextWidth**, 906

Display text string on form, picture box, or printer: **Print**, 899, 1215

Text Boxes

Set up multiline text box: **MultiLine**, 579, 949

Add scroll bars to a text box: **ScrollBars** (property), 951, 1394, 1899

Set or find out what text has been selected: **SelLength, SelStart, SelText**, 953, 954, 956

Set or get the text inside a text box: **Text**, 957, 1386

Time and Timers

Get or set system date: **Date$** (function and statement), 404, 406

Transaction Server

Dedication

To my wife who has, fortunately for me, learned to live with a lot less attention than she deserves. **–Eric Winemiller**

To my uncle, Masa Samura. **–David Jung**

To my wifey, Sandra. **–Pierre Boutquin**

For Barbara, whose encouragement is my inspiration, and for VB programmers everywhere. **–John Harrington**

To my very patient and understanding wife, Jodi, and my wonderful infant daughter, Cassie. **–Bill Heyman**

For Kristy. **—Ryan Groom**

To my mother and meemaw, who taught me all the basics of being successful. And to my ex-boss, the Sharkman, who got me started. **–Todd Bright**

About the Authors

Eric Winemiller is a principal software developer for Visteon Corporation in Maitland, Florida where he builds Back Office and Visual Basic-based medical applications. The project he helped develop for Orlando Health Care Group and Visteon Corporation placed 10th in *Info World's* 1995 top 100 client/server sites. Eric has previously published in *Visual Basic Developer* and *SQL Server Professional* magazines. He has a bachelor's degree in computer science from the University of Central Florida and is currently pursuing his master's degree. His family considers the Commodore 64 they gave him for his 13th birthday the best 200 bucks they ever spent. In his spare time, he can be found trying to be a digital artist, puttering around his woodshop, or renovating his old house.

David Jung has been developing programs in BASIC ever since he discovered personal computers back in the early 1980s. A graduate of California State Polytechnic University, Pomona, David has a degree in computer information systems. His development expertise is in designing and constructing cross-platform client/server and distributed database solutions using Visual Basic, Access, SQL Server, Oracle, DB2, and Internet technology. He is a member of the Pasadena IBM Users Group's technical staff and leads its Visual Basic Special Interest Group. He is a frequent speaker at seminars and users groups showing how Visual Basic, Java, and the Internet can be integrated into business solutions. He is the Windows 95/NT sysop on PC World's PC Tech Forum on CompuServe. David is co-author of several Waite Group Press books, including *Visual Basic 5 Client/Server How-To, Visual Basic 4 Objects and Classes SuperBible*, and *Visual Basic 4 OLE, Database and Controls SuperBible*. When he's not writing, programming, on-line, or presenting, David can be found on the bike trials in the San Gabriel Valley in Southern California, on the golf course, or spending time with friends and family (including two dogs that he pretends to like <g>).

Pierre Boutquin is a senior analyst in the corporate treasury of a major Canadian bank where he develops leading-edge market risk management software. He has over ten years of experience implementing PC-based computer systems with in-depth knowledge of object-oriented analysis and design, Visual C++, Visual Basic, and SQL. When not reading (or writing) computer books, Pierre occupies himself with researching which pure-bred cats make the best owners, finance, chess, and keeping up with news from Belgium, his native country. You may reach him at `boutquin@istar.ca`.

Bill Heyman is an independent consultant who specializes in architecting and developing applications using C++, Java, and Visual Basic. With his roots back in Apple][6502 development in the early '80s, Bill has expanded his systems building skills to the development of cross-platform distributed applications on Windows, OS/2, and UNIX, for IBM, Andersen Consulting, and other companies. He can be reached at `heyman@heymansoftware.com` and `http://www.heymansoftware.com/~heyman/`.

Like many in the computer business, **John Harrington** has enjoyed a checkered career. After selling life insurance, building houses, teaching electronics, and building a practice in hypnotherapy, he has settled into consulting and contracting as a Visual Basic programmer. His first computer was a home-built Cosmac Elf, but it was Microsoft Extended Basic on the TRS80 Model 1 that really got him hooked. After forays into half a dozen other programming languages, he is back to BASIC. He is currently a partner in Tampa Programming Group, programming business applications in Visual Basic. In his spare time, he writes for The Waite Group. His previous effort was as lead author of *Visual Basic 5 Interactive Course*.

Ryan Groom is President of Gulliver Software, a company that specializes in Internet content filtering. He has been programming since the age of 12 and works extensively in Visual Basic, Access, and Java. He can be reached at `ryan@gulliver.nb.ca` and `http://www.gulliver.nb.ca`.

Todd Bright graduated in 1993 from Northeast Louisiana University and has since worked in the imaging technology arena with Visual Basic and Visual C++. He is a partner in a consulting firm and also works in a full-time contract programming position. His hobbies include physical fitness and being outdoors. He can be reached at `toddb@sisonline.com`.

Bill Potter is President of Potter, Saylor & Associates, a consulting firm in Seattle, Washington. He uses Visual Basic to write large client/server and executive information systems, as well as smaller commercial and shareware programs. He started programming Basic in 1979, and made Visual Basic his primary tool in the ancient days of the VB 1.0 beta. He graduated from the University of Michigan. Bill was lead author of *Visual Basic 4 Objects and Classes SuperBible* and a co-author of *Visual Basic 4 OLE Database Controls SuperBible* and *Visual Basic SuperBible, Second Edition*, all Waite Group publications.

Table of Contents

Contents

Contents

VOLUME II

Contents

Contents

Acknowledgments

Eric Winemiller thanks Richard Wright, of *OpenGL SuperBible* fame, for saying, "Hey, you wanna write a book?" Eric also thanks Laura Brown and all the others at Waite Group Press who put up with the silly questions and provided much hand-holding for a neophyte book author. He especially thanks his wife, Judy, whose support and love carried him through the late nights and lack of weekends. And most of all, Eric thanks his family for that first computer that got it all started.

David Jung thanks Waite Group Press and Mitchell Waite for providing the opportunity to write, and Laura Brown for her perseverance in assembling the mountain of writing material and putting up with, "I just need one or two days," excuses. Thanks also to the other editors, including Wei Li and Chris Stone; they help keep our work honest. David especially thanks the staff at Moss Micro, LLC for their support; his friends and family for their support and encouragement; his wife, Joanne, for always understanding that "I can't take the dogs for a walk just yet," and his uncle, Masa Samura, for sparking his interest in computers and always being a positive influence in his computer career and life.

Pierre Boutquin thanks Laura Brown, Kurt Stephan, Susan Walton and all the other Waite Group associates for the opportunity to participate in this project. Wei Li, Kelsey McGee, Chris Stone and Marlene Vasilieff are all appreciated for their help in making him look like an accomplished writer. Most important, he must acknowledge the enthusiastic encouragement provided to him by his wife, Sandra. Without her, and the occasional help from Jennifer, he surely would have faltered in this lengthy effort.

John Harrington thanks everybody who made his part of this project happen. Thanks to Barbara, who tolerated all of the loneliness that is the wont of a writer's mate. Thanks, also, to his partner, Les, who practically ran the business without him as he worked on these volumes. And thanks especially to the Waite Group and the team they gave him to do this, especially Laura Brown, who somehow managed to sort it all out. Finally, thanks to the hundreds of Visual Basic programmers who post questions and answers on the Usenet newsgroups. You do more good than you know.

For **Bill Heyman**, the co-authoring of this book represents a milestone in his career. As a result, he thanks all his friends and colleagues who have helped him get to where he is today. The list is way too long to mention here, but to all his colleagues past and present, thank you; he has not forgotten you. In particular, Bill Ciarfella of IBM started him out in his professional software development career and gave him the perspective and insights into what it takes to engineer great software. But most of all, he acknowledges the patience and support that his wife, Jodi, has given him in his career. She has been and continues to be his cheerleader, coach, and inspiration to achieve their common goals in life.

Ryan Groom thanks his parents, Bill and Betty, for their eternal support. To Kristy for her patience: "Now we can have a long weekend away." Thanks to Chris Flemming for his adeptness with the written word. Thanks to Csaba for listening and tolerating his rants and raves.

PREFACE

Visual Basic 1.0 revolutionized the development of Windows programs by allowing easy access to what was once the daunting task of mastering the many controls and messages of the Windows environment. Visual Basic also provided the first example of a successful component object model for programming in which third-part, reusable components (VBXs) could be dropped into your programs to provider extra functionality. For the first time, one could create legitimate Windows applications without getting down to the "bare metal" of the Windows API. Versions 2.0 to 4.0 continued to add features and power, but 5.0 is where Visual Basic grew up. With a native code compiler and the ability to create heavy-duty transaction and Internet components, Visual Basic is playing with the big boys now, while still providing the easiest way to develop for Windows.

This two-volume set takes *Visual Basic 4 Objects and Classes SuperBible* and *Visual Basic 4 OLE Database Controls SuperBible*, the two books of the previous edition, and adds coverage to take you from neophyte to guru. Parts I-VIII provide beginning and intermediate Visual Basic programmers with an encyclopedic coverage of the basic features of the Visual Basic language. When you are ready to move on or if you're already familiar with the structure and syntax of Visual Basic, Parts IX-XVII tackle the more advanced features of Visual Basic, such as databases and ActiveX.

No special hardware requirements are assumed in this book, and any machine that can run Windows 95 or Windows NT 4.0 and Visual Basic 5.0 will be able to run the Visual Basic projects presented at the end of the chapters in this book. Some projects may require additional software specific to the subject matter such as Microsoft Transaction Server or Microsoft Internet Explorer.

For quick reference, you can easily look up any function, statement, method, property, or event in the Alphabetical Jump Table in the front of this book. To find out what language features are related to a specific task you want your program to perform, use the Task Jump Table. To see an alphabetic listing of all controls (including icon figures representing each control), use the Controls Jump Table.

Do you want to learn more about a particular aspect of Visual Basic? Just turn to the table of contents, find the chapter that deals with your topic, and begin reading. Each chapter in these books is a self-contained presentation on one aspect of the Visual Basic language: Many chapters include a chapter project demonstrating many of the techniques outlined in that chapter.

Ordinarily, consistent with the Visual Basic 5.0 convention on line continuation, we use the underscore character (_) to indicate program lines that are too long to fit on a single line. In this book, however, we have used a code continuation character ⇐. You may either replace ⇐ in your code with the underscore character, in which case

Visual Basic will consider the line following the underscore a continuation of the previous line, or you may simply concatenate the lines into a single, long line of code, in which case you should remove but not replace the ⇐ character in your program listing.

We believe you will find this book to be very useful in your work with Visual Basic. Much of the success of Visual Basic can be attributed to the fun which the language brings to Windows programming. We hope that using this book will make your Visual Basic programming easier, richer, and more fun. Happy programming!

PART I
OVERVIEW

1

WHY VISUAL BASIC?

In the years since its introduction, Visual Basic has revolutionized Windows programming and familiarized many thousands of programmers with an object-based, event-driven approach to software design. Visual Basic 5.0 brings Visual Basic to the forefront of modern programming languages by providing an array of sophisticated features that make the language truly object-oriented and interface it with the latest in database technology. Over the past few years, it has become the fastest and easiest way to make robust applications for Microsoft Windows. This chapter will point out some of the important new features in Visual Basic 5.0 and describe how you can use the *Visual Basic 5.0 SuperBible* as a powerful learning and reference tool.

About Visual Basic

Visual Basic's object-based nature requires a variety of programming perspectives—more so than with its procedural predecessors, such as QuickBASIC. For instance, you may be designing a new application from scratch. You might begin by visualizing the application in your mind's eye as the user will see it. Think of it as working from the outside in. You start work on the screen layouts by selecting the appropriate forms, objects, and controls needed to communicate with the user. You then write the BASIC statements that make up the "engine" of the program: the code that performs calculations, formats text, or draws images.

Another situation might be porting an existing DOS program that needs a Windows interface. Here you may work from the inside out. First, you look at the kind of input the application needs, and then you design your screens to provide the most efficient and comfortable way for the user to interact with your program. You may also want to use Visual Basic's powerful form and printer facilities to improve the appearance of the program's output.

Increasingly, you will be called on to use Visual Basic to create customized programming solutions in the modern Windows environment. For example, you may need to work with data in both a Microsoft Access database and a Microsoft Excel spreadsheet (or with one of many other applications). For a simple application you may use the new data bound controls to bring the external database into Visual Basic. For more sophisticated applications, you can draw on the Jet database engine (in the Professional Edition) and obtain a variety of 32-bit ActiveX controls that add "snap in" functionality to your program.

As a development tool for the Internet, Visual Basic 5.0 has the capability to take advantage of ActiveX documents that will allow you to customize your solutions to be browser-centric rather than form-centric.

Whatever your objective, designing a Visual Basic program is an interactive process, and your perspective may well change from "outside in" to "inside out," even during the same project. This means that the kind of information you need from a reference book will also change. You may need to review the characteristics and properties of Visual Basic's built-in objects, explore a particular property, event, or statement in more detail, or match up a desired program function with appropriate Visual Basic techniques.

The *Visual Basic 5.0 SuperBible* is designed with these shifts of perspective in mind. We combine a detailed, systematic reference with a variety of access methods for getting at the information you need. Wherever you're coming from, we'll make sure you get where you need to go.

What's New in Visual Basic 5.0

Visual Basic 5.0 represents a major development in the evolution of Microsoft's visual programming languages for the Windows operating systems. Visual Basic 5.0 steps forthrightly into the world of full 32-bit programming.

The structure of the Visual Basic language has been changed to accommodate the latest developments in programming. With its powerful class libraries and polymorphism, Visual Basic 5.0 goes a long way toward being a fully object-oriented language. You are encouraged to design your own classes, provide them with the properties that allow controlled access to your data objects, and write methods that carry out tasks. In Visual Basic 5.0, custom classes work hand in hand with OLE servers and the ActiveX controls that supplant the old VBX standard. As you get more advanced in the creation of objects, you will want to look further into object-oriented development. Object-oriented development has been enhanced in this version of Visual Basic by introducing polymorphism. Polymorphism means that many classes can provide the same property or method, and a calling application does not have to know what class an object belongs to before calling the property or method. This is explained in greater detail in Part XVII, "New Object-Oriented Programming."

A number of key features are summarized in the sections that follow. We start with features common to the Learning and Professional Editions, covering new general features and changes to the code development environment. We conclude with new features found only in the Enterprise Edition.

New, Key General Features

Like previous releases, Visual Basic 5.0 is available in three editions. Each is geared to meet a specific set of development needs. The three editions are Learning,

Professional, and Enterprise. A brief description of each edition is summarized in Table 1-1.

Table 1-1 The three editions of Visual Basic 5.0

Edition	Development Need
Learning	Allows developers to create 32-bit Windows applications.
Professional	32-bit Windows application development, plus ActiveX technology components and Crystal Report Writer.
Enterprise	Allows developers to create distributed 32-bit applications in a team environment. Includes Automation Manager, Component Manager, database management tools, and Visual SourceSafe.

Rather than going into a laundry list of new features within Visual Basic, we will describe some of the new, key features that make Visual Basic 5.0 a premier development environment. These features are summarized in Table 1-2.

Table 1-2 New general features in Visual Basic 5.0

Use This...	To Do This...
ActiveX technology	Create ActiveX controls and documents
Code editor enhancements	Use improved IntelliSense technology, whereby the development interface assists with automatic code completion
Wizards	Development assistants that automate some of difficult and redundant tasks
Multiple projects	Work on multiple projects in the same instance of Visual Basic
Native code	Compile your Visual Basic projects to native code for faster execution

ActiveX Technology

Before Visual Basic 5.0, you needed to be a C/C++ or Pascal programmer to create ActiveX components. With the Professional and Enterprise Editions, you can now create your ActiveX components for your distributed systems without leaving the comfort of your Visual Basic development environment. You can create ActiveX controls for your applications or the Internet and ActiveX documents. Refer to Part XIV, "Creating ActiveX Controls and ActiveX Documents" for more information.

Code Editor Enhancements

IntelliSense technology, first seen in Microsoft Office products, dramatically improves a developer's productivity by building intelligence in the code editor. Through IntelliSense, the code editor featuring Complete Word and QuickInfo technology. With Complete Word, the code editor will attempt to figure out the keyword or variable you are trying to use. For example, if you type "PR" and press the CTRL key and Space bar, Complete Word will fill in PRINT. With QuickInfo, when you enter the name of a control, such as "Label1.", the Code Editor will present you with a dropdown list of properties for the control. If you enter a function, such as "Tan()", the Code Editor will show a balloon message that will describe the syntax, which is

"Tan (Number As Double) As Double)." This feature is a great help—because I always forget the parameters for a function.

Development Wizards

In the Microsoft Office products, wizards are tools to enable users to get through difficult startup processes more quickly. Development wizards are no different. They allow developers to create functional shells for their applications. An Application Wizard and Setup Wizard are available in the Learning Edition. ActiveX technology wizards are available in the Professional and Enterprise Editions. Chapter 6, "Using Wizards," covers this in more depth.

Multiple Projects

Like Microsoft Word, in which you can have several documents open within the same instance, Visual Basic 5.0 allows you have multiple documents open within the same instance. A project that contains multiple documents is called a group. This can be useful when developing and debugging ActiveX components. Chapter 5, "Program Groups and Projects," covers this in more depth.

Native Code

The Professional and Enterprise Editions now allow you to compile your project to native code. By compiling your projects to native code, you will no longer need to rely on a runtime module to translate your pseudocode (or p-code) to native code. This will result in faster program execution. Chapter 7, "Using the Native-Code Compiler," covers this in more depth.

Using the *Visual Basic 5.0 SuperBible*

The *Visual Basic 5.0 SuperBible* is a versatile reference that you can use to expand and refine your knowledge of Visual Basic. It is a complete reference to Visual Basic 5.0. It combines topical organization by part and chapter with direct access to the elements of Visual Basic alphabetically, by entry name, and by programming task.

What's in a Chapter?

Each chapter of the *Visual Basic 5.0 SuperBible* (except for chapters that are organized as overviews) generally consists of three parts: a topic discussion and one or more summary tables, alphabetically arranged reference entries, and, frequently, a chapter project.

Topic Discussion and Summary Tables

The first section of each chapter provides a brief general introduction to the topic, and a discussion of any crucial programming issues related to the topic. It concludes with concise tables listing the properties, events, and methods, statements, and so forth, that will be covered in the chapter. Many of the chapters also contain tables listing the Visual Basic constants used as property settings.

Reference Entries

The main body of each chapter consists of alphabetically arranged reference entries for each Visual Basic element that is relevant to the chapter topic. For example, Chapter 41, "Displaying Text," has a reference entry for each method and function that directly influences the display of text. Many chapters contain reference entries for all the items listed in the summary table, but because some elements are relevant to more than one topic, and the reference entry for any given element generally appears only once in the book, some chapters will have more table entries than reference entries. If an element in a table is not covered in a particular chapter's reference entries, consult the Alphabetical Jump Table for the location of the description of that element.

The reference entries are designed to put the most concise information first: what this feature does and the rules (syntax) for using it. The reference entries of most chapters in the *Visual Basic 5.0 SuperBible* follow a format similar to that shown in Figure 1-1.

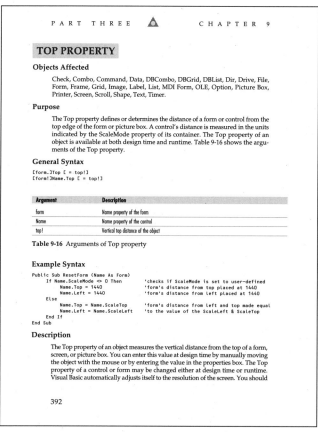

Figure 1-1 Parts of a reference entry

In general, each reference entry includes the following parts:

■ Name. The name of the object, property, event, or statement. The detailed table of contents and the Alphabetical Jump Table list the entry by this name.

■ Objects Affected. A list of all the Visual Basic objects that contain the element. In some cases, statements don't affect any objects directly; in such cases, this section is omitted. Events (such as mouse or keyboard events) are usually relevant to many different objects.

■ Purpose. A short statement summarizing the function of the item. It answers the question "What is this used for?" Details are given later in the entry.

■ General Syntax. A template showing how to use the item in program code. Where appropriate, the BASIC data declarations are given to show what type of data (integer, double, string, and so on) is required for each argument. Arguments that are in square brackets ([ ]) are optional. Either/or options are separated by a pipe; for example, Public|Private. A table generally provides a summary description of each argument.

■ Example Syntax. A code listing illustrating how the item might be used in a program, using real arguments.

■ Description. Gives the details of the item's usage and behavior, and relationship to other elements of Visual Basic. For complex items, the description is broken down into individual topics.

■ Example. This section tells you how the item is used in the chapter project.

■ Comments. Optionally points out some special circumstances or quirks of the object, property, method, event, or statement.

The reference entries in Chapter 16, "Objects and Collections," are organized somewhat differently from those in the rest of the book. Since the focus in Chapter 16 is on objects, the entry for each object brings together the properties, events, and methods used with that object. These are summarized in tables. Note that each property or event has its own entry elsewhere in the book. (To find the entry, use the Alphabetical Jump Table, described later.) Each object reference entry consists of the following parts:

■ Purpose. Briefly states what the object does.

■ Properties, Events, and Methods. Summarizes in tables the properties that the object possesses, the events to which the object can respond, and the methods through which your program can use the object's functionality.

■ Description. Summarizes the use of the object and the considerations involved in programming with it.

Chapter Projects

Many chapters in this book conclude with a Visual Basic project that illustrates features discussed in the chapter, as shown in Figure 1-2.

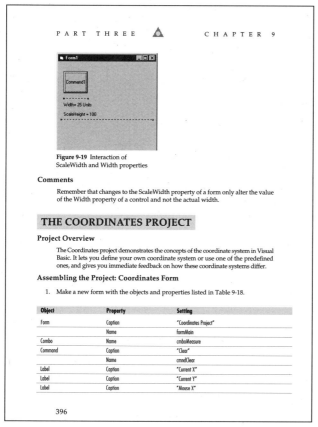

PART THREE ▲ CHAPTER 9

Figure 9-19 Interaction of
ScaleWidth and Width properties

Comments

Remember that changes to the ScaleWidth property of a form only alter the value
of the Width property of a control and not the actual width.

THE COORDINATES PROJECT

Project Overview

The Coordinates project demonstrates the concepts of the coordinate system in Visual
Basic. It lets you define your own coordinate system or use one of the predefined
ones, and gives you immediate feedback on how these coordinate systems differ.

Assembling the Project: Coordinates Form

1. Make a new form with the objects and properties listed in Table 9-18.

Object	Property	Setting
Form	Caption	"Coordinates Project"
	Name	formMain
Combo	Name	cmboMeasure
Command	Caption	"Clear"
	Name	cmndClear
Label	Caption	"Current X"
Label	Caption	"Current Y"
Label	Caption	"Mouse X"

396

Figure 1-2   Many chapters have a project that ties
together all the details of that chapter

Each project is a complete, ready-to-run Visual Basic program. In the interest of
space, and because of the need to focus on particular aspects of Visual Basic, these
projects are not full-fledged applications. Each project section contains the following
elements:

■ Project Overview. Discusses what the project does and what Visual Basic features it
illustrates.

■ Assembling the Project. A step-by-step tutorial, including tables showing form elements and complete code listings.

■ How It Works. Discusses the details of the project and explains some of the behind-
the-scenes tricks and techniques.

Some people find that they learn better if they actually type in the code from the
listings provided in the book. Others prefer to study the code that they cut and paste
from the project CD.

Finding What You Need

Now that you know how the book is organized, let's look at the many ways you can access this wealth of information.

Looking Up Reference Entries

Suppose you are designing your program's user interface and you decide that you need to get text input from the user (perhaps the user's name). If you know that the InputBox function can do the job, you can turn to the Alphabetical Jump Table, shown in Figure 1-3, and skim until you find the entry for InputBox.

The Alphabetical Jump Table lists all the reference entries in the book, with the page number on which each entry begins. When you know what object, property, event, method, statement, or function you want, and simply desire more information about it, the Alphabetical Jump Table is the fastest way to get to it.

VISUAL BASIC ALPHABETICAL JUMP TABLE

Action (property),	Change (event),	CreateWorkspace (method),	DrawMode (property),
Activate (event),	Check (object),	CrystalReport (control),	DrawStyle (property),
Activate (property),	CheckBox (class),	CurrentX (property),	DrawWidth (property),
ActiveControl (property),	CheckBox (control),	CurrentY (property),	Drive (object),
ActiveForm (property),	Checked (property),	Data (class),	DriveListBox (class),
ActiveProject (property),	Circle (method),	Data (control),	DriveListBox (control),
Add (method),	Class (property),	Data (object),	DriverName (property),
AddInMenu (property),	Class Module (object),	Data (property),	DropDown (event),
AddItem (method),	Clear (method),	Database (class),	Duplex (property),
AfterColUpdate (event),	Clear (property),	Database (property),	EditMode (property),
AfterDelete (event),	Click (event),	DatabaseName (property),	Enabled (property),
AfterInsert (event),	Clip (property),	DataChanged (property),	EndDoc (method),
AfterUpdate (event),	Clipboard (object),	DataField (property),	EOFAction (property),
Align (property),	ClipControls (property),	DataMode (property),	Err (Object),
Alignment (property),	Close (method),	DataSource (property),	Error (event),
AllowAddNew (property),	Cls (method),	DataText (property),	Exclusive (property),
AllowDelete (property),	Col (property),	DBCombo (class),	EXEName (property),
AllowRowSizing	ColAlignment (property),	DBCombo (control),	EXEName (property),
(property),	ColContaining (method),	DBCombo (object),	FetchVerbs (method),
AllowUpdate (property),	ColIndex (property),	DBEngine (object),	Field (class),
AniPushButton (control),	Collection (class),	DBGrid (class),	File (object),
App (object),	Collection (object),	DBGrid (control),	FileControl (property),
Appearance (property),	Color (property),	DBGrid (object),	FileDescription (property),
AppIsRunning (property),	ColorMode (property),	DblClick (event),	FileListBox (class),
Application (object),	ColResize (event),	DBList (class),	FileListBox (control),
Application (property),	Cols (property),	DBList (control),	FileName (property),
Archive (property),	ColumnHeaders (property),	DBListBox (control),	FileNumber (property),
Arrange (method),	Columns (property),	Deactivate (event),	FileTitle (property),
AutoActivate (property),	ColWidth (property),	Deactivate (property),	FillColor (property),
AutoReDraw (property),	Combo (object),	Debug (object),	FillStyle (property),
AutoShowChildren	ComboBox (class),	Default (property),	Filter (property),
(property),	ComboBox (control),	DefaultExt (property),	FilterIndex (property),
AutoSize (property),	Command (object),	DefaultPassword (property),	FirstRow (property),
AutoVerbMenu (property),	CommandButton (class),	DefaultUser (property),	FixedAlignment (property),
BackColor (property),	CommandButton (control),	DefColWidth (property),	FixedCols (property),
BackStyle (property),	Comments (property),	Delete (method),	FixedRows (property),
BeforeColUpdate (event),	CommonDialog (control),	Description (property),	Flags (property),
BeforeDelete (event),	CompactDatabase (method),	DeviceName (property),	Font (class),
BeforeInsert (event),	CompanyName (property),	DialogTitle (property),	Font (object),
BeforeUpdate (event),	Component (property),	Dir (object),	Font (property),
BOFAction (property),	Connect (property),	Directory List Box (control),	FontBold (property),
Bold (property),	Container (class),	DirListBox (class),	FontCount (property),
Bookmark (property),	Container (property),	DisplayType (property),	FontItalic (property),
BorderColor (property),	ControlBox (property),	Document (class),	FontName (property),
BorderStyle (property),	Controls (collection),	DoVerb (method),	Fonts (property),
BorderWidth (property),	ControlTemplate (property),	Drag (method),	FontSize (property),
BoundColumn (property),	Copies (property),	DragDrop (event),	FontStrikeThru (property),
BoundText (property),	Copy (method),	DragIcon (property),	FontStrikeThru (property),
Cancel (property),	Count (property),	DragMode (property),	FontUnderline (property),
CancelError (property),	Creatable (property),	DragOver (event),	ForeColor (property),
Caption (property),	CreateEmbed (method),	Draw (method),	Form (object),
CellSelected (property),	CreateLink (method),		Format (property),

i

Figure 1-3   The Alphabetical Jump Table, at the beginning of the book, lets you quickly look up reference entries

Looking Up Complete Topics

While the Alphabetical Jump Table is the fastest method for finding the reference entry, the index at the end of this book is far more complete. The index gives a complete listing of the page numbers throughout the book where a topic (such as "forms") or a particular item (such as "Change event") is discussed. This lets you learn about a programming topic from many different angles.

Finding Out How to Do Something in Visual Basic

When you're in the middle of developing a program, you often think in terms of tasks. That is, you know what you need your program to do, but you may not know exactly how to accomplish it. For example, you may know that you need to get some text from the user, but you're not sure what methods Visual Basic provides for the purpose. This is where the Task Jump Table comes in. This table, shown in Figure 1-4, is organized by programming task. In our example, you skim along the table until you find "Text Boxes," which tells you where associated methods are discussed.

VISUAL BASIC 4.0 OBJECTS & CLASSES

VISUAL BASIC TASK JUMP TABLE

Clipboard

Transfer text or graphics data between windows or applications: **Clipboard** (object), xx
Find out whether the clipboard has graphics or text: **GetFormat**, xx
Get graphics from the clipboard: **GetData**, xx
Get text from the clipboard: **GetText**, xx
Send graphics to the clipboard: **SetData**, xx
Send text to the clipboard: **SetText**, xx
Clear the contents of the clipboard: **Clear**, xx
Communicate with DOS windows: **SendKeys**, xx

Controls (General)

Examine attributes of active control: **ActiveControl**, xx
Respond to user changes in contents: **Change**, xx
Manipulate controls in a control array: **Index**, xx
Identify a particular control: **Tag**, xx
Find form that contains the control: **Parent**, xx
Label a control on a form: **Label**, xx
Create a new instance in a control array: **Load**, xx
Specify 3D or "flat" look: **Appearance**, xx

Dialog Boxes (and related controls)

Display a message in a box with standard icons: **MsgBox** (function and statement), xx, xx
Get text from a user by displaying a box: **InputBox$**, xx
Specify choices that can be on or off: **Checkbox** (control), 68
Define a group of choices of which only one can be selected: **Option button** (control), xx
Create a group of related controls: **Frame** (control), xx
Label part of a dialog box: **Label**, xx
Display a button that executeS a specified action: **Command button** (control), xx
Display a common dialog box: **CommonDialog**, xx

Drive, Directory, and File List Boxes

Set up boxes for working with the disk: **Drive list box, Directory list box, File list box** (objects), xx, xx, xx
Set or read the current drive in a Drive list box: **Drive**, xx
Set or read the name of the currently selected file: **FileName**, xx
Set or read the search path for a Directory or File list box: **Path**, xx

Specify what happens when the search path is changed: **PathChange**, xx
Set or read the file search pattern for a list box: **Pattern**, xx
Specify what happens when file search pattern is changed: **PatternChange**, xx
Specify DOS attributes of files to be displayed in list: **Archive, Hidden, ReadOnly, System**, xx, xx, xx, xx
Obtain items in a Drive, Dir, or File box's list: **List, ListCount, ListIndex**, xx, xx, xx

Focus

Specify which application gets the focus: **AppActivate**, xx
Specify which form or control gets the focus: **SetFocus**, xx
Specify what happens when a form or control gets the focus: **GotFocus**, xx
Specify what happens when a form or control loses the focus: **LostFocus**, xx
Specify whether a control can respond to user input: **Enabled**, xx
Control use of Tab key to move between controls: **TabIndex, TabStop**, xx, xx

Fonts

Set or get name of current font: **FontName**, xx
Find out what fonts are available, **FontCount, Fonts**, xx, xx
Set point size of font: **FontSize**, xx
Set typestyle: **FontBold, FontItalic, FontStrikethru, FontTransparent, FontUnderline**, xx, xx, xx, xx, xx

Forms (General)

Position form on screen: **Left, Top**, xx xx
Set dimensions of form on screen: **Height, Width**, xx, xx
Display form title: **Caption**, xx
Set up menu for a form: **Menu** (control), xx
Set up button to perform a specified action: **Command button** (control), xx
Set color and style: **BackColor, BorderStyle, ForeColor**, xx, xx, xx
Allow resizing of form: **ControlBox, MaxButton, MinButton**, xx, xx, xx
Respond to user actions: **Icon, MousePointer, Resize, WindowState**, xx, xx, xx, xx
Show or hide form: **Hide, Show, Visible**, xx, xx, xx
Load form without showing: **Load** (statement), xx

iv

Figure 1-4   The Task Jump Table is organized by programming task

Finding a Control by Its Icon

Sometimes you may want quick access to a particular control, looking it up either by
name or by its button icon. You can do this conveniently using the Alphabetical
Control Table, shown in Figure 1-5.

Reviewing Visual Basic in Depth

If you decide you want to review an area of Visual Basic programming in depth, simply
look at the detailed table of contents and browse the topic headings there. You can
then proceed to read individual reference entries or entire chapters, using the introductory discussion, reference entries, and chapter project to sharpen and complete
your understanding of the topic presented.

**VISUAL BASIC
ALPHABETICAL
CONTROL TABLE**

Icon	Name	Page
	CheckBox	73
	ComboBox	80
	CommandButton	84
	CommonDialog	87
	Data	92
	DBCombo	95
	DBGrid	98
	DBList	103
	DirListBox	106
	DriveListBox	110
	FileListBox	113
	Frame	124
	Grid	126
	Image	130
	Label	132
	Line	134
	ListBox	135
	OLE	144
	OptionButton	149
	PictureBox	152
	Shape	164
	TextBox	166
	Timer	169

Figure 1-5   The Alphabetical Control Table lets you look
up controls by visually scanning button icons

We recommend that you read the chapters in Part I, "Overview," to review your understanding of Visual Basic, and follow up by reading each chapter's introductory discussion. If you find that you aren't sure of your understanding of a particular topic, you may want to study its chapter in depth. Chapter 10, "Program Design," offers a good introduction to Visual Basic program design and development methodologies.

2

OVERALL ELEMENTS OF A VB PROGRAM

Like many other object-based development environments, Visual Basic organizes your programs into *projects*. A project consists of the source files required for your application, plus specifications for building your application. With Visual Basic 5.0 Professional and Enterprise Editions, you can work on more than just application projects and OLE automation projects. New to Visual Basic 5.0, you can also create ActiveX controls for applications, the Internet, and ActiveX documents. This chapter introduces the key components of a project.

Components of an Application Project

A Visual Basic application project—standard, ActiveX EXE, and ActiveX DLL—utilizes standard modules, form modules, class modules, ActiveX controls, OLE automation servers, insertable objects, object libraries, and resource modules. A simple project may consist of a single form module, while an advanced project may contain several of each of these components. Form modules, standard modules, class modules, and resource modules are listed as separate items in the Project window. Figure 2-1 shows a sample Project window.

In addition to maintaining a list of the components that make up a particular project, Visual Basic also stores information in a project file that keeps track of environment options, .EXE options, project options, and any system references associated with the project. All this information is contained in a single project file that has a .VBP extension. Visual Basic 3.0 and earlier versions used the extension .MAK, but this confused some developers, because C/C++ programs also used the .MAK extension and they were not compatible with Visual Basic's .MAK files.

Because each part of a project is saved in a separate file, you can store common classes or procedures in a single file that can be added to multiple projects. For example, almost every Windows program has an About dialog box. You could save time by

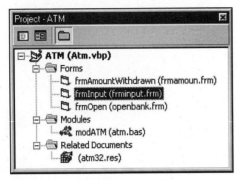

Figure 2-1   The Project window

designing a generic About box and saving it in a single file that can be incorporated into many different Visual Basic projects.

The components that can be included in an application Visual Basic project are summarized in Table 2-1.

Table 2-1 Component parts of a Visual Basic project

Use This...	Extension	To Do This...
Standard module	.BAS	Contain project code, generally accessible throughout your project
Form module	.FRM, .FRX	Design and code your user interface
Class module	.CLS	Define methods and properties for a custom object
ActiveX control	.OCX	Add additional functions to the Toolbox
ActiveX server	.EXE, .DLL	Add functionality of OLE 2.0 (out-of-process and in-process objects)
Insertable objects		Add objects from an OLE 2.0–compliant application to the Toolbox or a form
Object library	.OLB, .TLB	Obtain information about OLE automation objects
Resource module	.RES	Store string, bitmap, and other compiled data
ActiveX designers	.DSR, .DSX	Add visual interfaces for tasks that might require a great deal of coding

Figure 2-2 shows how these project components fit together conceptually. The standard module, which has a .BAS or .GLB extension, is at the "highest" level, containing declarations of constants, variables, and procedures that can be accessed throughout the program. The form and class modules contain code that defines forms and custom-defined objects, respectively. ActiveX controls are usually developed separately (often by a third-party vendor). They represent functionality that can be "imported" into your application. ActiveX servers, formerly known as OLE automation servers, provide ways of creating your object that can contain functions such as business rules. Insertable objects are similar to ActiveX controls, but they represent objects provided by other applications (such as spreadsheets or graphs). An object library contains information (such as constants and object names) made available by other applications. Finally, a resource module provides compiled data resources that are available to your project.

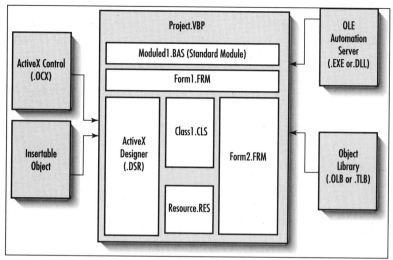

Figure 2-2   Components of a Visual Basic application project

Standard Modules

Standard modules, with the extension .BAS, contain declarations of constants, types, and variables, as well as procedures and functions. Unlike form modules, which contain both code and descriptions of all attached controls, standard modules contain only code. Module-level declarations and definitions in a standard module are by default public, which means that constants, variables, and procedures declared within a standard module are by default accessible by code in other modules and forms. Standard modules were referred to as code modules in versions of Visual Basic prior to version 4.0.

Previous versions of Visual Basic also had global modules, with the extension .GLB. A global module is similar to a standard module, but it stores only constant, type, and variable information. It defines no functions or procedures. The practice of using a global module is no longer encouraged, because many global variables are now included in object and type libraries.

Some items that you may want to put in a standard module are API declarations, constants, user-defined types, variables, and general and external procedures. When writing a program with Visual Basic 5.0, you should use the keyword Public rather than the keyword Global to explicitly make variables accessible outside of a module.

Form Modules

Form modules, with the extension .FRM, are the foundation of your application's user interface. They contain all of your text fields and controls, including any property settings of these controls. Forms can also contain constant and variable declarations, procedures, and event procedures for the various form and control events. More complex applications may have several forms, each with its own form module.

Declarations in a form module default to private, which means that constants, variables, and procedures in a form module are not available to code outside that form unless you explicitly declare them as public.

Form modules that house controls other than the standard ActiveX controls, text boxes, labels, list boxes, and frames, require a secondary file to contain all the properties of the ActiveX controls. This file, with the extension .FRX, is a binary file that contains binary property information. For example, it will contain the embedded picture in a Picture control, or it will contain the grid layout of the MSFlexGrid control.

Class Modules

Class modules, with the extension .CLS, are similar to form modules, except that they have no visual component. You can use class modules to create your own objects. Class modules can include code for methods and properties associated with an object that you define, but they cannot include their own events. With the Professional and Enterprise Editions of Visual Basic 5.0, you can compile class modules into distributable OLE automation servers. Part XII, "Object Embedding and Automation," will provide complete instructions and examples for creating and using your own classes within OLE automation servers.

ActiveX Controls

ActiveX controls, with the extension .OCX, contain information Visual Basic needs to provide new features and controls to your application's toolbar. An ActiveX control can be a variation on an existing Microsoft Windows control, such as a modified version of the gauge control, or it can be a completely new category of control, such as a graphics import filter that lets you import many types of graphical images.

You can only use VBX (Visual Basic Extension) controls with the 16-bit version of Visual Basic. When Visual Basic 5.0 opens a project containing a VBX control, it replaces the VBX control with an OCX control, if an OCX version of the control is available.

An ActiveX control is just another term for an OLE object. It is based on Microsoft COM (Component Object Model) architecture and is a self-registering object. You can use ActiveX controls in both 16-bit and 32-bit versions of Visual Basic; however, you need to use 16-bit ActiveX controls with the 16-bit version of Visual Basic, and 32-bit ActiveX controls with the 32-bit version of Visual Basic. In general, almost all new ActiveX controls are 32-bit.

You add ActiveX controls to or remove them from the Toolbox by using the Components dialog box, as shown in Figure 2-3. In the Components dialog box, the Controls tab shows within a list box all the available controls that are registered on your system. To add a control to your project, select the check box to the left of the control name. To remove a control, deselect its check box. If the control is in use within your project, which means that the control is placed on a form, you cannot remove it from the Toolbox.

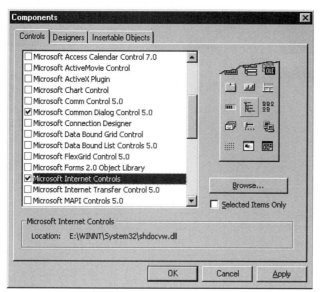

Figure 2-3 Components dialog box illustrating the available ActiveX controls

ActiveX EXEs

ActiveX EXEs, with the extension .EXE, were formerly known as OLE automation servers. They allow you to use the methods and properties exposed by OLE 2.0 objects in your projects. All editions of Visual Basic 5.0 come with powerful sets of OLE server objects. You can also create your own objects or obtain them from third-party developers. All Visual Basic editions can *use* an object application file, even though only the Professional and Enterprise Editions can *create* them. You'll need to add a reference to the object application to your project before you can use any of its classes. Use the Projects→References menu command to bring up the References dialog box shown in Figure 2-4. If your object application doesn't appear in the list yet, click the Browse button and use the File→Open common dialog box to navigate to the correct directory. Choose Executable Files from the List Files of Type combo box, and select the correct EXE or DLL file. This will add the object name and description to the References dialog box. Click the object name to select it, and press the OK button to add the reference to your project.

ActiveX DLLs

Using Visual Basic 5.0, you have the ability to make in-process OLE servers, or ActiveX DLLs. These were formerly known as OLE DLLs. An ActiveX DLL offers the same benefits of true dynamic link libraries (DLLs), with the exception of making Declare statement calls against them. In order to take advantage of them, use the DLL through OLE automation. Once an ActiveX DLL is properly registered in your

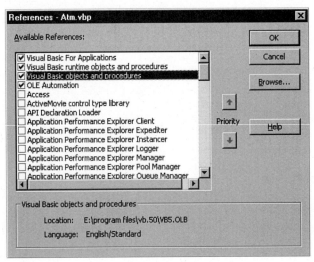

Figure 2-4   Use the References dialog box to add
references to object applications to your project

Windows registry, it can be added to your application like any other OLE object. Any
OLE-compliant application can take advantage of this DLL as well. The advantage of
an ActiveX DLL over an out-of-process OLE server is that an ActiveX DLL loads itself
in the processing space of the client application. Be cautious, however; an unstable
ActiveX DLL can cause instability within the application.

Insertable Objects

Insertable objects do not have file extensions. They exist within object applications—
such as Microsoft Excel or Microsoft Word for Windows—that support a visual user
interface. As with controls, you can add these insertable objects directly onto your
Visual Basic form to create an integrated solution. In fact, you can even add these
insertable objects to your Toolbox. An *integrated solution* is a programming solution
that contains information from different sources, for example, spreadsheets, charts,
and databases created by different applications.

You add insertable objects to or remove them from the Toolbox by using the
Components dialog box's Insertable Objects tab, as shown in Figure 2-5. In the
Components dialog box's Insertable Objects tab, the list box shows all the available
insertable objects in your system registry. To add an insertable object, select the check
box to the left of the insertable object's name. To remove an insertable object, deselect
its check box. If the insertable object is in use within your project, you cannot remove
it from the Toolbox.

The frame at the bottom of the Components dialog box shows the location of the
file in which the control or insertable object resides. By marking the Selected Items
Only check box, you will only be able to select objects and controls that are used

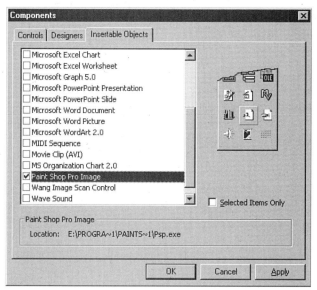

Figure 2-5   Components dialog box illustrating
insertable objects you can add to your project

within your current project. To add a control or insertable object to the list, use the
Browse button on the References dialog box.

An insertable object is added to the Windows registry when an OLE 2.0–compliant
application is installed into your Windows environment. For example, Microsoft Excel
is an OLE 2.0–compliant application. Its charts and worksheets are objects of Excel,
and they are valid insertable objects. OLE custom controls are, by nature, OLE
2.0–compliant objects and are added to the Windows registry when you install them
on your system. In Windows 95 and NT, the registry is an integral part of the environment, because it is a database that not only contains object information, but also has
information for the plug-and-play features. The Windows 95 and NT registry consists
of two files—SYSTEM.DAT and USER.DAT—stored in the Windows subdirectory.

Object Libraries

An object library file, with the file extension .OLB or .TLB, provides information about
available OLE automation objects to OLE automation controllers, such as Visual Basic
applications. Executable files (.EXE) and dynamic link libraries (.DLL) can also contain object libraries. When you use objects from other applications with your Visual
Basic application, you establish a reference to the object libraries of those applications.

To add an object library to your Visual Basic development environment, use the
References dialog box (Figure 2-4), found under the Project menu. To add a reference
to your project, select the check box next to the reference's name. To remove a reference, deselect its check box. If the reference is in use within your project, Visual Basic

will not allow you to deselect its check box. You can use the priority buttons to move references up and down the Available References list, prioritizing your object references if two or more objects have the same name. In cases like this, the first object on the list is referenced first. The Visual Basic objects and procedures frame displays the path and language version of the object. There is no easy way to determine whether a file has an object library. If you are not sure, try adding the file to the reference by using the Browse button. If the reference fails, the file does not contain an object library.

To view the referenced object libraries, use the Object Browser by selecting it from the View menu or from the toolbar (or by pressing F2). The Object Browser is discussed in greater detail in Chapter 3, "The VB Programming Environment."

Resource Files

A resource file, with the extension .RES, can contain bitmaps, text strings, and other data. Using a resource file increases your application's performance and capacity because it allows you to load strings, images, and data into memory when needed, rather than when the form or module is loaded. Resources are useful for isolating strings and images from source code, which makes it easier to localize an application for foreign markets.

Resource files are compiled resource code; therefore, when you add a resource file to your program, the View Form and View Code buttons in the Project window are disabled when the file is selected. You cannot create or edit a resource file using Visual Basic. To create a resource file, you need to use a development product that has a resource editor and compiler, such as Microsoft Visual C++.

ActiveX Designers

An ActiveX designer, with the extension .DSR, provides a visual design interface for tasks that might require a lot of coding. An ActiveX designer is like a form module or class module. ActiveX designers are based on the Component Object Model (COM). The COM is what all ActiveX and OLE technologies are based on. It is a standard that defines how applications expose objects.

An ActiveX designer was formerly known as an OLE embedding server that has a programmable interface and dedicated visual designer. It is an in-process server, like an ActiveX DLL, which means that it is loaded in the same memory address as the application that uses it. Similar to a resource file, an ActiveX designer is loaded only when it is needed. When it is no longer needed within the application, Visual Basic will release the ActiveX designer's resources and create another ActiveX designer object when it is needed again.

Included with version 5.0 are two ActiveX designers: the Microsoft Forms 2.0 Form and Microsoft UserConnection. To include them in your project, select the Designers tab from the Components dialog box, as illustrated in Figure 2-6.

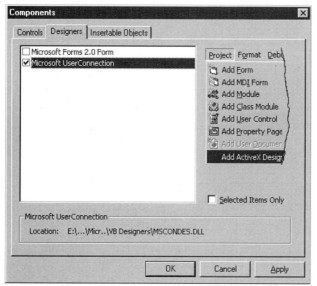

Figure 2-6   Components dialog box showing the
ActiveX designers you can add to your project

Components of an ActiveX Control and Document

A Visual Basic ActiveX control and ActiveX document project utilizes all the components that an application project can, as well as a few new components. The additional
components that can be included in a Visual Basic ActiveX control and document project are summarized in Table 2-2.

Table 2-2 Component parts of an ActiveX control and document

Use This...	Extension	To Do This...
User-defined control modules	.CTL, .CTX	Define the appearance and interface of the control
Property page	.PAG	Alternate way to display your control's property values
User document module	.DOB, .DOX	Define the appearance and interface of the document

New to the Visual Basic 5.0 Professional and Enterprise Editions is the ability to
create ActiveX controls. In the past, you could create these controls only in C/C++ or
Pascal with the Windows Software Development Kit. And as part of the ActiveX technology, you can also create applications based on the ActiveX Document Model with
Visual Basic. This allows you to develop applications that can be viewed through a
Web browser, such as Microsoft's Internet Explorer or Netscape's Navigator, as well as
through products such as Microsoft Office Binder. The process of developing ActiveX
controls and documents is discussed in Part XIV, "Creating ActiveX Controls and
ActiveX Documents."

User-Defined Control Modules

User-defined control modules, with the extension .CTL, are similar to form modules. Most ActiveX controls provide components that the developer can place on a form, such as a text box or a grid. The user-defined control file contains this information. Any object you draw on the interface will appear in your form module when you use the control. It can also contain constant and variable declarations, procedures, and event procedures for the various form and control events that can be called by other procedures.

More complex controls may have several forms, which provide different sets of functionality. For example, you might have a control that provides trigonometric graphics for sine, cosine, and tangent. You would develop three different user-defined control files for each control. Modules with the extension .CTX are like .FRX files. They contain binary information that are to be used by the .CTL.

Property Page

Property page modules, with the extension .PAG, are similar to form modules in that you draw controls onto an interface. A property page module is used to present a control's Properties in a dialog box manager. For example, when you use the ActiveX control StatusBar, there are properties associated with it that appear in the Properties windows, as seen in Figure 2-7. The properties are not grouped in any distinct logical manner. The developer of this control does provide an alternate way to work with properties. This is through the property page. You right mouse click on the control, and select Properties for the context menu that appears. The layout of the StatusBar's properties is more logical. Figure 2-8 is an example of the StatusBar's properties page. Each property tab across the top is the equivalent of a property page module; therefore, you can have more than one property page module for each user-defined control module.

User Document Modules

User document modules, with the extension .DOB, are similar to form modules. As you do in form modules, you draw objects on the layout, which can contain constant and variable declarations, procedures, and event procedures for the various form and control events that can be called by other procedures. Like a form module, a user document module has a counterpart in the extension .DOX, which stores any binary information that is affiliated with the .DOB file.

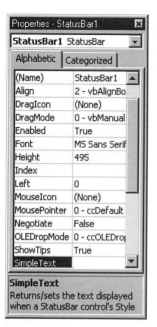

Figure 2-7   StatusBar's Properties window

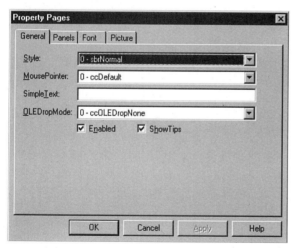

Figure 2-8   StatusBar's Property Pages dialog box

3

THE VB PROGRAMMING ENVIRONMENT

Since its introduction, Visual Basic has made it easier for developers to become more productive by integrating development, debugging, and compiling features into one environment. In a traditional development environment, there are three distinct stages: writing the code, compiling it, and testing the application. In such an environment, the code editors you program in do not have any code-checking intelligence. If there are any errors in your code, you do not find them until you compile it. At that point, the editor performs a syntax check and a logic check. If both processes pass, it compiles your program. Then you test your application to ensure that it works. If any errors are found, you have to go back to your editor, correct your mistakes, and go through the compile and test stages again until your application works.

Visual Basic, like most Windows development environments, seamlessly puts all these components into an Integrated Development Environment (IDE). As you type the code for your program, the editor performs syntax checking to ensure that you are entering valid code. When you compile your code, the IDE will perform a logic check, and if an error arises, an error flag will notify you and place you in the code in which the error occurred. When it compiles, you are in a "runtime" mode. In this mode, your application takes control and you can interact with it. If an error occurs, you will be notified by a dialog window and you will then be placed in the code that caused the error. Essentially, you can code, test, and debug your application all within one environment.

This chapter introduces the key components of the IDE, demonstrates some techniques to use to effectively work within the environment, and describes some of the new features in Visual Basic 5.0 that can make it easier to develop applications.

Integrated Development Environment

One of the most significant changes in Visual Basic 5.0 is the IDE. The IDE found in Visual Basic 5.0 is that same IDE that is used in the Visual Basic 5.0 Custom Control Edition, Visual InterDev (formerly known as Internet Studio), and Visual Basic for Applications (VBA) used with Microsoft Office products and VBA licensed products, like Visio. This interface, illustrated in Figure 3-1, is known as Development Studio.

In a Windows development environment, you have the ability to work on application code and your user interface, then test and debug your application without leaving the IDE. As you can see in Figure 3-1, you have access to your code, the user interface, properties windows, your ActiveX control toolbar, and more. This differs from the previous Visual Basic IDE in that prior to Visual Basic 5.0, the IDE was designed as a Single-Document Interface (SDI). In an SDI, each window is a free-floating window that is not contained within a main window and can move anywhere on the screen as long as Visual Basic is the current application. Microsoft Notepad is an example of an SDI application. Figure 3-2 is an example of the same application that appears in Figure 3-1, but it is open with the IDE in an SDI format.

New to Visual Basic 5.0 is the capability to have the IDE in a Multiple-Document Interface (MDI) format. In this format, the windows associated with the project will stay within a single container, known as the parent. Code- and form-based windows will stay within the main container form. Project, Properties, Toolbox, and Intermediate windows can be moved outside the MDI environment, "docked" within

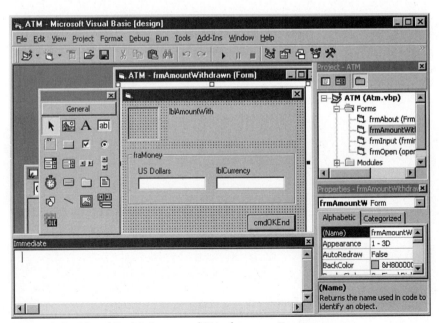

Figure 3-1 Visual Basic's Integrated Development Environment

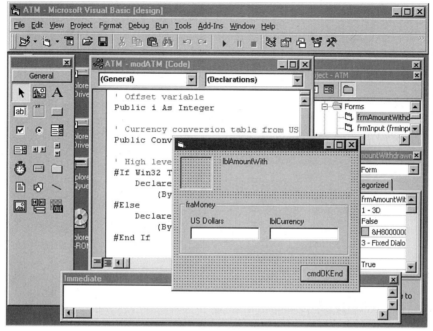

Figure 3-2   Visual Basic's IDE as a Single-Document Interface

the parent, or linked with one another. *Docked* means that the windows can be connected to the parent. *Linked* windows means that you can place two windows together
and move them around as if they were one window. In Figure 3-1, the Project,
Properties, and Immediate windows are docked and linked.

TIP

The screen shots shown in Figures 3-1 through 3-4 were taken on a 640×480 resolution setting. If the
environment looks cramped to you, that's because it is. It is a good idea to have your development
environment resolution set at 800×600 or greater.

Menu Bar and Toolbar Extensibility

As all Windows products do, Visual Basic has a menu and toolbar. In the
past, the only way to extend either was by writing add-in components or
writing an application that linking itself to the IDE through Windows API
(Application Programming Interface) calls. This method of adding to the IDE
is still true, but customization is built into the environment. Customizing
your menus and toolbar can help make you more productive.

You can customize the menu and toolbar by right mouse clicking to either the menu bar or toolbar. From the context menu, select the Customize item. Select the Commands tab from the Customize dialog window. From here you can add, change, or remove any menu or toolbar item you choose. In Figure 3-3, Comment Block is a command that is not in any menu item or toolbar. To add it to either the menu or toolbar, select the item and drag it to the menu item you would like to place it in or drag it to a position on the toolbar, and drop it on that location. Figure 3-4 shows what the Comment Block command looks like in the Edit menu.

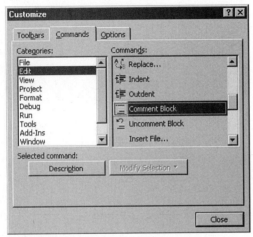

Figure 3-3 Customize dialog window

Figure 3-4 Comment Block within the Edit menu

Form Layout

One of the most frustrating things that confront developers has been to develop for different screen resolutions. The general rule has been to always develop your applications to the screen resolution your clients most commonly have. In most cases, this is VGA (640 pixels × 480 pixels). A pixel is a visible dot of light on a monitor. But most developers use resolutions of SuperVGA (800×600) or higher. Consequently, in the past, this meant that the developer had to change screen resolution to ensure that, once finished, the application would fit within the screen; otherwise, a form might be too big and the user might not see the whole form.

New to Version 5.0 is the capability to view the position of the form on a screen without having to change video resolution. This feature is called Form Layout, and Figure 3-5 is an example of what it looks like if your development environment is at a resolution of 1024×768. As you can see in the figure, Form1 is well within the 640×480 boundary. When you resize a form, it will be visually represented in the Form Layout window. This way you can always tell if your form will fit within the desired resolution.

To view the Form Layout window, select the Form Layout option from the View menu.

Environmental Settings

Visual Basic lets you customize your environment to suit your development needs. You can do everything from changing your programming environment to changing executable settings. Prior to Visual Basic 4.0, you had limited control over your code format, environmental settings, and project settings. When you generated an executable file of your program, you also had limited options. Visual Basic 5.0 has expanded the environment and project settings into six different tool areas: Editor, Editor Format, General, Docking, Environment, and Advanced. These options are found within the Options tabbed dialog box, available from the Tools menu.

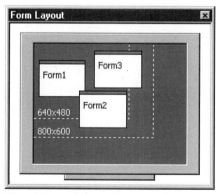

Figure 3-5   Form Layout window displaying Form1 within the 640×480 resolution area

Editor

In Visual Basic 5.0, you use the Editor tab of the Options dialog, shown in Figure 3-6, to specify how the editor interacts with you and your code. This tabbed dialog contains two frames, Code Settings and Window Settings. The Code Settings frame consists of the following settings:

■ Auto Syntax Check. By marking this, Visual Basic will check the structure of your code line after you move to the next line.

■ Require Variable Declaration. By marking this, you need to declare all constants and variables in modules or forms. If you do select this option, Visual Basic adds the Option Explicit statement to general declarations in any new module or form.

■ Auto List Members. By marking this, Visual Basic will display a list box of information to assist you in completing your statement. Figure 3-7 illu155strates this.

■ Auto Quick Info. By marking this, Visual Basic will display, in a tooltip window, information about the function and its parameters. Figure 3-8 illustrates this.

■ Auto Data Tips. By marking this, when you are in break mode, Visual Basic will show the value of the variable the mouse is placed on. Figure 3-9 illustrates this.

■ Auto Indent. By marking this, when you tab the first line, all subsequent lines will start at the tab position.

■ Tab Width. The value you set will determine how many spaces the tab key will use. The default value of the Tab Width is 4. The range of the Tab Width is 1 to 32 spaces.

The Window Settings frame consists of the following settings:

■ Drag-and-Drop Text Editing. By marking this, you will be able to drag and drop variables from within a code window into the Immediate debug window or variable Watch window.

■ Default to Full Module View. Marking this gives you the ability to view all of your code within your code window.

■ Procedure Separator. Marking this causes a horizontal line to separate each procedure in the code window when the Default to Full Module View option is marked. If the check box is not marked, the code window displays only the logic relevant to the procedure you are currently viewing.

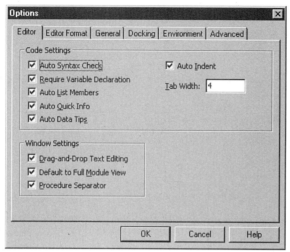

Figure 3-6   Editor tab in the Options dialog

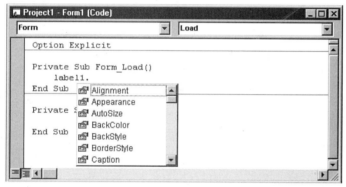

Figure 3-7   Auto List Members displaying available properties for a text box object

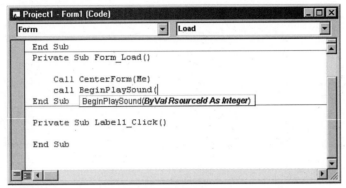

Figure 3-8   Auto Quick Info displaying function information on the BeginPlaySound function

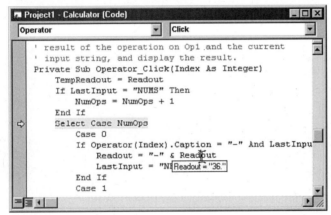

Figure 3-9   Auto Data Tips displays the value of the variable Readout

Editor Format

Using the Editor Format tab of the Options dialog, you specify the appearance of your Visual Basic code in your development environment. This tabbed dialog lists the types of text found in code, and lets you specify attributes for selected text types, as shown in Figure 3-10. The settings within the Code Colors frame are as follows:

■ Text list. A list of text items you can customize.

■ Foreground. This specifies the color of the actual code text.

■ Background. This specifies the background color of the code text.

■ Indicator. This specifies the indicator color in the code window's margin. This is not applicable for all text items.

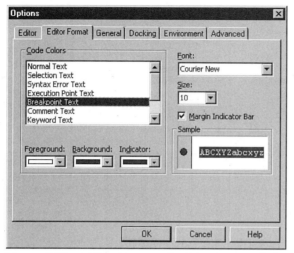

Figure 3-10   Editor Format tab of the Options dialog

The other properties support the following:

- Font. This specifies which font will be used for all the code.

- Size. This specifies the font size of the code.

- Margin Indicator Bar. Marking this will make the Margin Indicator Bar appear in the Code window.

- Sample. Displays a sample of the font, size, color, and Margin Indicator Bar settings.

General

With the General tab of the Options dialog shown in Figure 3-11, you customize the settings, error handling, and compile settings for your development environment. This tabbed dialog contains three frames: Form Grid Settings, Error Trapping, and Compile. The Form Grid Settings are used to determine the grid appearance and interaction of the form window. The Form Grid Settings frame consists of the following settings:

- Show Grid. By marking this, you will be able to see the dotted grid on your form in design mode.

- Grid Units. The unit of measure the grid spacing is in.

- Width and Height. Use these to set the width and height of the grid. The range is 24 to 1188 twips.

- Align Controls to Grid. By marking this, when you draw an object on your form, its edges will snap to the grid lines.

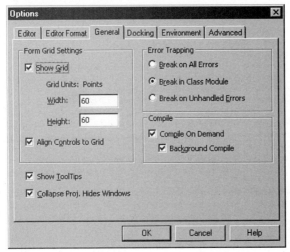

Figure 3-11 General tab of the Options dialog

In the Error Trapping frame, you can determine how the Visual Basic environment handles errors in runtime mode. The Error Trapping frame consists of the following settings:

■ Break on All Errors. Selecting this option will cause all error-handling routines (for example, On Error statements) to be ignored when an error occurs.

■ Break in Class Module. Selecting this option will cause any unhandled error in a class module to stop runtime mode and put you into break mode.

■ Break on Unhandled Errors. Selecting this option will cause Visual Basic to break execution only when an error occurs that you have not explicitly trapped in your code (using the On Error statement).

The Compile frame options deal with how Visual Basic compiles your application. The Compile frame consists of the following settings:

■ Compile On Demand. By marking this, Visual Basic will only compile those sections of code that are needed at the time the application is running. This will allow you to start your application sooner, because the compiler does not inspect and compile every module in your application.

■ Background Compile. By marking this, Visual Basic will compile the project in the background during any idle time. This option is only available if the Compile On Demand option is marked.

The other properties support the following:

■ Show Tooltips. Tooltips are brief messages that describe a tool when you place the mouse pointer over it. By marking this, tooltips are displayed for the Toolbar and Toolbox buttons.

■ Collapse Proj. Hides Windows. By marking this, if you collapse a project in the Project window, all the code and form windows open in the IDE will be closed. This is useful if you are working with projects in a group fashion. Group projects will be explained in Chapter 5, "Program Groups and Projects."

Docking

With the Docking tab of the Options dialog, shown in Figure 3-12, you can determine which windows can be dockable. Dockable windows allow you to attach or link a window to another window or the IDE container if you are in MDI mode. To make any of the listed windows dockable, mark the check box to the left of window name.

Environment

Use the Environment tab of the Options dialog box, shown in Figure 3-13, to set attributes of your Visual Basic development environment. You can set how Visual Basic starts, how it interacts with the project files, and which templates are available and where they are located.

The options in the When Visual Basic starts frame determine how Visual Basic starts each time. By marking Prompt for project, you will be prompted by the New Projects dialog window each time you start Visual Basic. If you mark Create default project, Visual Basic will assume you want to make an application project (EXE) each time you start Visual Basic. You can have Visual Basic save your project before executing it from the Visual Basic development environment. By selecting the Save Changes, Prompt To Save Changes, or Don't Save Changes radio button, you will save any changes made to a project before entering runtime mode automatically, be prompted by a dialog box and asked if you would like to save any changes before entering runtime mode, or not save the changes at all and just enter the runtime mode.

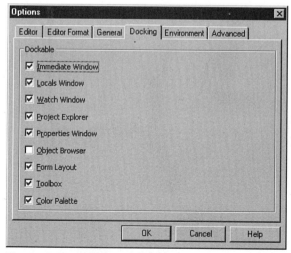

Figure 3-12   Docking tab of the Options dialog

> **TIP**
> It would be wise to have the When a program starts setting set to either Save Changes or Prompt To Save Changes. You may make many changes to your code, and it's always safer to save your changes, or be given the option to save them, before going into runtime mode. You never know when your system might lock up on you and not save the latest version of your program.

Visual Basic has template forms that help speed up your development process, similarly to how letter templates help speed up your letter writing. The Show Templates For frame lists all the types of templates you have available. By marking any of them, you will make them visible in the Add dialog box when you add an item to your project. Examples of template files are About boxes, Option boxes, and Splash screens. The field Templates Directory designates the location of the template files.

Advanced

Use the Advanced tab of the Options dialog, shown in Figure 3-14, to customize miscellaneous advanced settings for your Visual Basic development environment.

Marking the Background Project Load option allows you to have the project load in the background while you begin work in Visual Basic. This option may save you time when loading a very large project.

Marking the Notify when changing shared project items option will cause the IDE to notify you when you change a project item shared with other projects. As mentioned in Chapter 2, "Overall Elements of a VB Program," you can have forms and

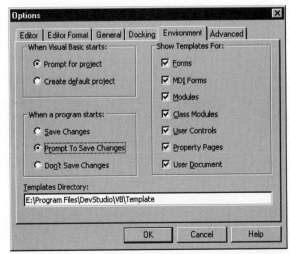

Figure 3-13 Environment tab of the Options dialog

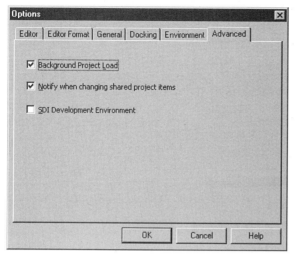

Figure 3-14   Advanced tab of the Options dialog

modules in a common directory that all applications use. If you have two projects open with a Visual Basic group, this option can be useful. Each project has a link to the physical project item, and each project loads a copy of it in memory when the projects are loaded. Visual Basic will prompt you to see if you would like to update the other project item loaded in memory as well. Figure 3-15 is an example of the dialog box that prompts you.

By marking SDI Development Environment, you will make the IDE look like previous versions of Visual Basic. All the windows will be free floating and the form and module windows will not be contained within a parent window. Refer to Figure 3-1 and Figure 3-2 at the beginning of this chapter.

Make Project Options

When you are ready to make an executable file out of your project, you select the Make *<filename>*.EXE File choice from the File menu. This option will vary depending on the type of project you are working on. If you are working on an ActiveX DLL or ActiveX document DLL, the selection will be Make *<filename>*.DLL File. If you are

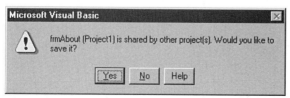

Figure 3-15   Notification of updating another project that shares that same project item

working on an ActiveX control, the selection will be Make *<filename>*.OCX File. You enter a filename or select an existing filename to replace, as shown in Figure 3-16, on the Make Project dialog box. Click on the Options button to display the Project Properties dialog box, shown in Figure 3-17. Use this dialog box to set detailed attributes and compilation settings for the executable file you make for your project. The two tabs, Make and Compile, are the same two tabs found in the Project Properties dialog box that appears when you select Project Properties from the Project window as described in Chapter 2. By changing any of these settings, you will override any options stored in your project file, VBP.

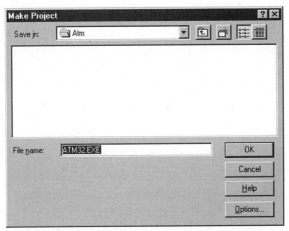

Figure 3-16   Make Project dialog box

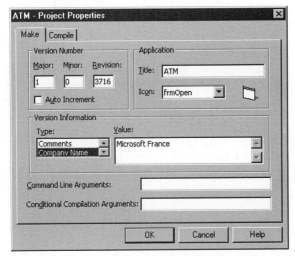

Figure 3-17   Project Properties Make tab

All files made with Visual Basic 5.0 are 32-bit. To make any 16-bit Visual Basic applications, you will need to use Visual Basic 4.0 or an earlier version. ActiveX DLLs are known as in-process OLE servers, or OLE DLLs. These dynamic link libraries (DLLs) are different from the ones you would create in languages like C or Pascal and should be referred to as *in-process OLE servers*. They work like true DLLs, allowing other applications to share their compiled modules. Unlike true DLLs, however, they cannot be called with a Declare statement. The advantage offered by in-process OLE servers is performance. Calling an in-process OLE server can be significantly faster than calling an out-of-process OLE server. An out-of-process OLE server, or ActiveX EXE, runs in its own memory address space, while the in-process OLE server runs in the memory address space of the client.

Most software developers like to keep track of what version they have created. Rather than relying on the date and time stamps that accompany files, you can embed an internal version number. In the Version Number frame, you can set the appropriate Major, Minor, and Revision numbers. If you mark the Auto Increment check box, your project's revision number will increase automatically each time you make an executable file. In the Application frame, you can give your application a title that Windows uses when displaying a Task List of programs that are currently running in memory. Here you can also embed an icon into your application by using an icon that is assigned to one of your forms. In the Version Information frame, you can enter version-specific comments about your application, such as general comments, a company name, a file description, and the like. To view the version information within the file, view the file's Properties and select the Version tab.

The arguments you place in the Command Line Arguments text box are only valid when you choose to execute your program from the Run item in the File menu. This emulates the application picking up arguments in the way a DOS program gets arguments (such as a filename or option switch) from the command line.

The Conditional Compilation Arguments text box allows you to enter constant declarations your program uses for conditional compilation. Conditional compilation arguments would look like the following:

```
conRDO=-1:conDebug= -1:conDAO=0
```

Conditional compilation usage will be discussed later in this chapter.

The Compile tab of the Project Properties dialog is used to set how your program will compile. Figure 3-18 illustrates this dialog box. Prior to Visual Basic 5.0, when you compiled your application into an executable file, it wasn't compiled into a true executable format, like a compiled C or Pascal program. It was compiled into what is known as p-code, or pseudocode. When your application was executed, it was linked to a runtime module—like VBRUN300.DLL, VBRUN432.DLL, or MSVBVM50.DLL— and it executed as if it were native code. This is why the speed of a Visual Basic application in runtime is not much improved over that of its compiled counterpart. With Visual Basic 5.0, you can now compile your application into a true executable; however, this does not eliminate the need for the MSVBVM50.DLL. This DLL will still

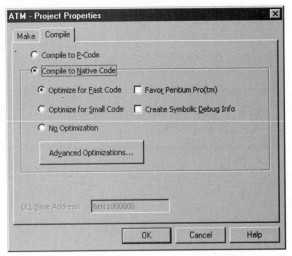

Figure 3-18   Project Properties Compile tab

need to be shipped with your application because it provides services like startup and shutdown code for your application, functionality for forms and intrinsic controls, and run-time functions like Format and CLng.

By marking Compile to P-Code, you compile your application into p-code, just as you have done in past versions of Visual Basic. By marking Compile to Native Code, you are able to select how your code will be optimized. The optimization settings are as follows:

■ Optimize for Fast Code. Use this setting if you want the compiler to make your application as fast as it can be. The compiler will not pay attention to how large it makes your application.

■ Optimize for Small Code. Use this setting if you want the compiler to make your application as small as possible.

■ No Optimization. The compiler will not attempt to optimize your application.

■ Favor Pentium Pro™. By marking this option, you want the compiler to optimize the code for the Pentium Pro processor. This option should only be marked if your application is going to run on that platform. The application will still run on earlier versions of the Pentium processor line, but not as efficiently.

■ Create Symbolic Debug Info. Marking this option will have the compiled application generate the symbolic debug information. This means that an executable file compiled with this option can be debugged using Visual C++'s CodeView, or any other debugging tool that can handle CodeView debugging information.

The command button, Advanced Optimizations, displays another dialog box, as shown in Figure 3-19, with more advanced settings for optimizing your compiled program. The parameters you can use are as follows:

■ Assume No Aliasing. Aliasing provides a name that refers to a memory location that is already being used under a different name. By selecting this option, you are allowing the compiler to apply optimizations it could not otherwise use, such as storing variables in registers and performing loop optimizations. However, you should be careful not to check this option if your program passes arguments ByRef, since the optimizations could cause the program to execute incorrectly.

■ Remove Array Bound Checks. By default, Visual Basic checks to make sure a reference to an array is within the array's boundaries. By selecting this option, you are removing this fail-safe, which could cause your application to crash because a reference was made to an invalid array reference. For example, with this option selected, a reference to vArray(12), when the array was defined by REDIM vArray(10), will cause your application to crash, because you are referring to reference that does not exist. For more information on arrays, refer to Chapter 14, "Variables."

■ Remove Integer Overflow Checks. By default, Visual Basic checks to make sure that every calculation of an integer-based data type—byte, integer, and long—is within the range of that data type. By selecting this option, you are removing this fail-safe, so if a calculation is larger than the data type capacity, no error will occur, meaning you could receive incorrect calculated values. For more information on integer data types, refer to Chapter 14.

■ Remove Floating Point Error Checks. By default, Visual Basic checks to make sure that every calculation of a floating-point data type—single or double—is within the range of that data type and that there will not be any "division by zero" operations. By selecting this option, you are removing this fail-safe, so if a calculation is larger than the data type capacity, no error will occur, meaning you could receive incorrect calculated values. For more information on floating-point data types, refer to Chapter 14.

■ Allow Unrounded Floating Point Operations. By default, Visual Basic checks to make sure that every calculation of a floating-point expression is rounded off to the correct degree of precision—single or double—before comparisons are performed. By selecting this option, you are removing this fail-safe, therefore, allowing the compiler to compare floating-point expressions without first rounding them to the correct precision.

■ Remove Safe Pentium™ FDIV Checks. Remember when the Pentium microprocessor first came out and there was a flaw in the floating-point division (FDIV) process? By selecting this option, you remove the check to ensure the calculations used by the FDIV are correct. Your values may be slightly incorrect if your application is run on a system with a flawed Pentium.

NOTE

Be cautious setting some of these parameters. Some settings, based on your code, might cause your programs to not execute properly.

The text box labeled DLL Base Address represents the address you wish the DLL to occupy in memory. The default memory location is &H11000000. If the DLL cannot load itself into the preferred memory address, it will automatically find a memory address that it can occupy. This could cause a performance decrease, because the calling program will not immediately find the DLL in its designated memory address. By specifying a preferred memory address, you improve performance of the DLL by avoiding conflicts with other DLLs already in memory. The address range is between &H1000000 (16 megabytes) and &H80000000 (2 gigabytes). The base address must be a multiple of 64K. The memory used by your component begins at the initial base address and is the size of the compiled application, rounded up to the next multiple of 64K.

> **TIP**
> It is highly recommended that you change this base address because if you leave it at the default value, it is very probable that it will conflict with another in-process server. If your application is using multiple in-process servers, you may want to choose a base address for your main component and calculate each address from there. This avoids conflicts with another developer or another company's component.

Conditional Compilation

As a software developer, you may want to make your program platform independent. With conditional compilation, you can embed platform-specific code segments into your application and selectively display components based on their development status. Here is an example of conditional compilation arguments:

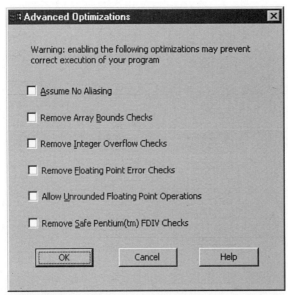

Figure 3-19   Advanced Optimizations dialog box

```
#If conDebug Then            ' Run-Time Message
    Call MsgBox("Debugging The Calculation Module.", _
                vbInformation, "Run-Time Mode")
#End If
#If conRDO then         ' RDO Logic
    Set rs = cn.OpenResultset("Select * from Authors", rdOpenStatic)
#Else                   ' DAO Logic
    Set rs = cn.OpenRecordset("Select * from Authors",dbReadOnly)
#End If
```

Using Add-Ins

In versions of Visual Basic prior to 4.0, there was no easy way to add functionality to your development environment. To add new functions, you had to write your own DLL that could subclass itself to Visual Basic. Visual Basic 4.0 changed that through add-ins. An *add-in* is an object application that adds capabilities to the Visual Basic development environment. To add an add-in to or remove one from your environment, you use the Add-In Manager dialog box, as shown in Figure 3-20. Select the Add-Ins menu item found under Tools in the main menu.

All available add-ins are listed in the Available Add-Ins list box. For an add-in to be listed there, it must be registered in your system registry when you install it. If you mark the check box and click OK, you have added the add-in to your Visual Basic environment. To remove it, simply clear the check box. Once an add-in is added, it is loaded every time you start Visual Basic. Add-ins put menu items in your Add-Ins menu under Tools, and Visual Basic saves the reference to the add-ins in your registry.

The sample project that comes with Visual Basic 5.0, TabOrder, is a good example of how to create an add-in tool. This add-in lets you change the tab order of the objects on your form without having to change the property of each object. The tab order of objects is based on when they were placed on the form. The first item will have a tab order of zero (0), and the last item placed on the form will have the greatest value. This is assuming the object has a TabOrder property. The project is made up of a standard module, class module, user document module, and resource module. The

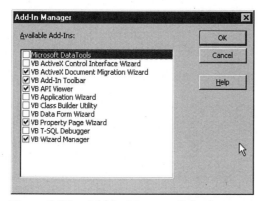

Figure 3-20   Add-In Manager dialog box

standard module contains API code specific for add-ins. The class module contains methods and properties to handle the objects on the form it will interact with. The user document module provides the user interface for the add-in and the code that references methods and properties in the class module. The resource file contains the tooltip messages used on the user document. To generate the project into an add-in, use the Make *filename*.DLL from the File menu.

After the add-in has been created into a DLL, the add-in does not automatically appear in the Add-In Manager. You need to register the add-in in the registry. Open up a command prompt window, and at the MS-DOS prompt, type REGSVR32 TABOR-DER.DLL and press (ENTER). You should receive a message notifying you that the DLL was successfully registered. After the add-in is registered, you will need to add an entry to the [Add-Ins32] in the VBADDIN.INI file about the add-in. To do this, while the TabOrder project is loaded, type AddToINI in the Immediate window. You should receive a value of 1 if the call was successful. Now you are ready to use the add-in.

To use the add-in, select the Add-In Manager from the Add-Ins menu and mark the VB TabOrder Window add-in. Figure 3-21 illustrates what the Add-In Manager looks like with the VB TabOrder added. After you press OK, this add-in will add an icon to your standard toolbar, as shown in Figure 3-22. When you click the TabOrder button on the toolbar, you will see the TabOrder tool window. Figure 3-23 depicts the TabOrder tool showing the tab order of the controls on the frmAmountWithdrawal of the ATM project.

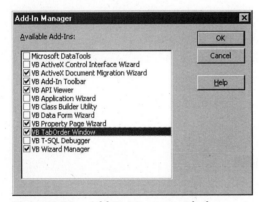

Figure 3-21   Add-In Manager with the TabOrder add-in

Figure 3-22   The TabOrder add-in on the standard toolbar

Figure 3-23 The TabOrder
add-in tool

Object Browser

The Object Browser presents a three-level hierarchical display of all the classes, properties, methods, events, and constants available to your application from Visual Basic, other OLE components, and object libraries, as shown in Figure 3-24. It allows you to easily select objects and cut and paste them into your code. The Object Browser is not available at runtime.

To access the Object Browser, choose the Object Browser option from the View menu, click the Object Browser Toolbar button, or press F2. The Project/Libraries drop-down list box displays the object libraries and modules (forms, classes, standard, and so on) available to your project. To add or remove object libraries from this list, use the Reference dialog box, as described in Chapter 2. The Classes list box displays all of the available classes in the library or project selected in the Project/Libraries box. The Members list box displays all the methods, properties, events, and constants of the class selected. If you select a class and do not specify a member, you will get the default member if one is available. The default member is identified by an asterisk (*) or by the default icon specific to the member.

At the bottom of the Object Browser, a description of the class or member is displayed, along with procedure information. For example, in Figure 3-24, the Class Constants is selected. In the description area, you can see that Constants is a member of the VBA object library and that it contains predefined constants.

The Object Browser has the ability to look up the name of a function, procedure, method, property, or constant. Enter the string value in the Search drop-down list box and press the Search button. The Search drop-down list box contains the last four search strings that you entered until you close the project. You can use the standard Visual Basic wildcards when typing a string. Figure 3-25 illustrates what the Object Browser looks like after finding a result of a search.

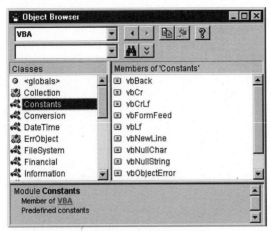

Figure 3-24   Object Browser dialog box

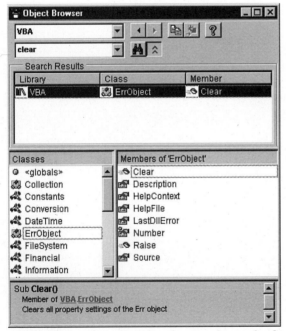

Figure 3-25   Object Browser showing the result of
a search on the word "Clear"

4

GETTING STARTED: YOUR FIRST VB PROGRAM LANGUAGE BASICS

Developing programs in Visual Basic is not that different from developing in other languages. As mentioned in Chapter 2, "Overall Elements of a VB Program," a Visual Basic program consists of various modules—forms, standard, class, and so on. In Chapter 3, "The VB Programming Environment," you were introduced to the environment in which you will be developing your programs. When you first sit down and study the Visual Basic Integrated Development Environment (VBIDE), it can be a bit overwhelming. With its new user interface, it can be intimidating to seasoned developers as well. But once you start working with the VBIDE, all your fears and anxieties will be allayed.

In this chapter, we will put the knowledge from the previous two chapters into a working Visual Basic program.

Creating the Form and Controls

By default, when you first start Visual Basic, you will be prompted with a New Project window. From here, you can select which type of project you wish to build. For the project at the end of this chapter, you will select the Standard EXE. If you set your Visual Basic environment not to prompt you for this dialog window, the default project will be a Standard EXE project.

You will see a window captioned Form1. At this point, if you click on Start under the Run menu, Form1 will function like a standard window in Windows; it can be maximized, minimized, moved, or resized.

The form is one of the many intrinsic objects in Visual Basic. Objects have characteristics called properties. One of the properties on a form is its Caption, which appears in the title bar of the form. Right now the caption is the default, Form1.

Properties can be changed at design time, when you are designing your application as we are doing now, or at runtime, when your program is running. To change the properties at design time, you will use the Properties window, or with some ActiveX controls, you will change properties through the property page. If an ActiveX control has a property page, it will have a property called (Custom) after the (About) property in the Properties window. Figures 4-1 and 4-2 illustrate the Properties window and Property Pages window. This chapter's project will change the Caption property of the Label control at runtime.

Events

In this chapter's project, the text box's Change event will be used to display, in the caption of the Label control, the number of characters in the TextBox control. This event is described in detail following Table 4-1.

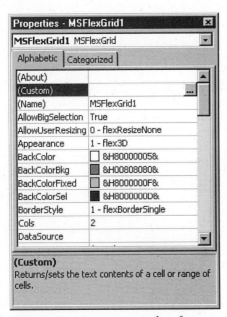

Figure 4-1 Properties window for MSFlexGrid

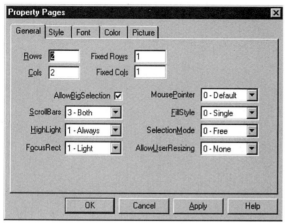

Figure 4-2 Property Pages window for
MSFlexGrid

Visual Basic 5.0 recognizes 58 different events. Some events are recognized by
many objects, some by only a few or even just one object. Table 4-1 lists the events
and their meaning. To locate the reference section that covers a specific event, refer to
the Alphabetical Jump Table or the index of this book.

Table 4-1 Visual Basic events

Event	Meaning
Activate	Form just received focus
AfterAddFile	File added to current project
AfterChangeFileName	Filename changed
AfterCloseFile	File closed
AfterRemoveFile	File removed from project
AfterWriteFile	File saved
BeforeLoadFile	Before a file is added
Change	Control's value just changed
Click	Control just got clicked
ConnectAddIn	Add-in added to Visual Basic
DblClick	Control just got double-clicked
Deactivate	Form just lost focus
DisconnectAddIn	Add-in removed from Visual Basic
DoGetAddFileName	User selected Add File
DoGetNewFileName	User saving file or project
DoGetOpenProjectName	User opening a new project

continued on next page

continued from previous page

Event	Meaning
DragDrop	Control just got dropped
DragOver	Another control just got dragged over this control
DropDown	User clicked the down arrow on combo box
Error	Externally caused database error
GotFocus	Control just received the focus
Initialize	Object created
KeyDown	User just pressed a key
KeyPress	User just pressed a key
KeyUp	User just released a key
LinkClose	DDE link just closed
LinkError	DDE link has an error
LinkExecute	DDE link just received an external command
LinkNotify	DDE link data has changed in a Notify style link
LinkOpen	DDE link has just opened
Load	Form has just loaded
LostFocus	Control just lost focus
MouseDown	User just pressed mouse button
MouseMove	User just moved mouse
MouseUp	User just released mouse button
ObjectMove	OLE object moved or resized
OLECompleteDrag	Source object is notified that drop action occurred
OLEDragDrop	Source object is dropped onto a control
OLEDragOver	Source object just got dragged over this control
OLEGiveFeedback	Provides a drag icon feedback to the user
OLESetData	Sets data when a Source object is dropped
OLEStartDrag	Sets the type of data format and drop effect the source object supports when drag is started
Paint	Control just got uncovered
PathChange	Path property just changed
PatternChange	Pattern property just changed
QueryUnload	Form is about to unload
Reposition	Current record just changed
RequestChangeFileName	User specified new filename
RequestWriteFile	Prompt before project saved
Resize	Form just changed size
RowColChange	Grid's active cell just changed
Scroll	Scrollbar thumb just moved
SelChange	New cell selected in grid
Terminate	Object was destroyed

Event	Meaning
Timer	Timer interval finished
Unload	Form unloading
Updated	OLE object changed
Validate	Current record about to change

Change Event

Objects Affected ComboBox, DBCombo, DBGrid, DirListBox, DriveListBox, FileListBox, HScrollBar, Label, PictureBox, TextBox, VScrollBar

Purpose The Change event initiates an action when the user changes the value of an object's primary property, such as by making a selection or entering data. Table 4-2 summarizes the arguments used for the Change event.

General Syntax `Sub Name_Change ([Index As Integer])`

Table 4-2 Arguments of the Change event

Argument	Description
Name	Name of the control
Index	An integer that uniquely identifies an element of a control array

Example Syntax

```
Public OldText As String

Private Sub Text1_Change ()
    OldText = Text1.Text              ⇐
'update ThisText any time the text in Text1 is changed
End Sub
```

Description Many of the objects in Visual Basic have a primary property. For instance, the TextBox control's primary property is the Text property. Use the Change event to respond to any changes in an object's primary property. This event occurs regardless of the manner in which the property is changed; it initiates if the property changes by a user action, the program's code, or dynamic data exchange (DDE) events. The Change event doesn't trigger if you assign a value to an object's primary property that is the same as its current setting.

Table 4-3 lists all the objects that use the Change event, and the properties on which it is based.

Table 4-3 Objects that activate the Change event, and their primary properties

Use Change with This object...	To React to a Change in This Property...
ComboBox	Text
DBCombo	Text
DBGrid	Value
DirListBox	Path
DriveListBox	Drive
FileListBox	Path (use the PathChange event)
FileListBox	Pattern (use the PatternChange event)
Label	Caption
PictureBox	Picture
HScrollBar	Value
VScrollBar	Value
TextBox	Text

Be careful not to code circular Change events. Writing code in one control's Change event that triggers a change in another control's primary property, which in turn changes the original control's primary property, leads to an uncontrollable series of Change events that only end when Windows gives an error message after it runs out of stack space. For instance, imagine a program that has two labels, with the following Change events:

```
Private Sub Label1_Change ()
    Label2.Caption = Str(Val(Label1.Caption) + 1)
End Sub

Private Sub Label2_Change ()
    Label1.Caption = Str(Val(Label2.Caption) + 1)
End Sub
```

The Label1_Change event modifies the Caption property of the Label2 object. This causes Label2's Change event to occur. That event modifies Label1's Caption property, which will again cause its Change event to occur. As you can see, this will result in both events calling each other endlessly.

Combo Boxes and Data Bound Combo Boxes
Changes made to a combo box's Text property trigger its Change event. The Text property only applies when a combo box's Style property is set to 0 or 1 (drop-down or simple combo); therefore, the Change event can only occur with these styles. If a combo box's Style property is set to 2, no Change event could ever be initiated.

Users may change the Text property of a combo box by doing one of two things. First, they can type text directly in the edit portion of a combo box. Since the text changes with each keystroke, the Change event occurs every time the user presses another key. For example, if the user types the word HELLO, the Change event will be called five times, once for each keystroke. Second, the user can change this property by selecting any of the list entries in the combo box. A list entry is selected anytime the user presses the up or down arrow keys, or clicks on one of the entries with the mouse.

Setting the combo box's Text property within a program's code also triggers the Change event. For instance:

```
Combo1.Text = "Hello"
```

In the above line of code, the Text property of a combo box is set to "Hello." After this is performed, Visual Basic initiates the combo box's Change event. When that event has finished, execution will resume at the line following this one. Chapter 46, "List and Combo Boxes," contains more detailed information about combo boxes.

DBGrid

The primary property for the DBGrid control is Value. The Change event will occur anytime this property changes. You must set the AllowUpdate property of the DBGrid to True to allow users to change DBGrid data. Once AllowUpdate is set to True, users may then update data directly in the grid triggering the Change event. You can also change the Value property via code. See Chapter 48, "Grid Controls," for more information on the DBGrid control.

DirListBox, DriveListBox, and File List Boxes

The primary property for the directory list box is the Path property. The Change event will occur anytime this property changes. The user may change this property by double-clicking on any entry listed in the directory box. This sets the Path property to the path specified by the entry chosen by the user. Setting the Path property to a new value within a program's code also causes the Change event to occur.

The primary property for the Drive list box is the Drive property. This property can be changed by choosing a new drive letter from the object's drop-down list, or by assigning a value to the property within the program's code.

The File list box has two primary properties: Path and Pattern. Because of this it also has two Change events: PathChange and PatternChange. The PathChange event occurs when the Path property of a File list box has been changed. The PatternChange property occurs when its Pattern property has been modified. Both of these events are explained in detail in Chapter 47, "File, Directory, and Drive Boxes."

Label

The primary property for the Label object is the Caption property. The Caption property can be changed by assigning it a string value within your program's code, or as the result of a DDE operation.

Picture Boxes   The primary property for the Picture object is the Picture property. The Picture property can be changed by assigning it a value within your program's code, or as the result of a DDE operation.

HScrollBar and VScrollBar   The primary property for the ScrollBars object is the Value property. This property indicates the relative position of a scrollbar's thumb on the bar. The Value property of a scrollbar can be changed in four ways. First, the user can click on either arrow. This causes the Value property to increment or decrement by the amount indicated by the bar's SmallChange property. Second, clicking the gray area of the scrollbar updates the Value property in a manner similar to clicking an arrow, but the amount of change is indicated by the bar's LargeChange property. Third, the user can click and drag the thumb to a specific position on the bar. This causes the Value property to be set according to the position of the thumb on the bar. Finally, your code can directly set the Value. Chapter 43, "Scrollbars," uses the Change event with the Scroll Bars object in its sample project.

Text Boxes   When used with the TextBox object, the Change event occurs when any change is made to the box's Text property. Since the text changes with each keystroke, the Change event occurs every time the user presses a key that generates an ASCII character. For example, if the user types the word HELLO, the Change event happens five times, once for each keystroke. Assigning a string value to this property within your program will also initiate a Change event. A DDE conversation may also create a change in a text box, causing a Change event.

Chapter 44, "Text Boxes," uses the Change event along with the TextBox object.

Comments   Although some objects do not have an associated Change event, you may code your program to react to a change in these objects' primary properties by using other events for the same purpose. For example, the Click event may be used to react to a change in the CheckBox, OptionButton, and ListBox objects.

Event Procedure

Although each control recognizes a predefined set of events, you determine if it responds to those events by writing code in event procedures. Much like regular sub procedures, event procedures contain code that performs specific actions. For example, clicking a command button with the mouse triggers its Click event; code you write for this event procedure might confirm that the user wants to end the application.

A reference to an event begins with the name of the object that triggers the event, followed by an underscore (_) and the name of the event:

```
Private Sub Command1_Click ()
    MsgBox "You've just clicked Command1"
End Sub
```

Forms are the exception: Rather than using the name of the form, the event subroutine uses the keyword Form (or MDIForm for the main MDI form of an application).

```
Private Sub Form_Load ()
    List1.AddItem "Red"
    List1.AddItem "Blue"
    List1.AddItem "Green"
End Sub

Private Sub MDIForm_Load ()
    Form1.Load
    Form2.Load
    Form3.Show
End Sub
```

Many events pass arguments to the procedure that your code can use. For example, the MouseDown event passes information about which mouse button was pressed, which control keys (if any) were held down, and exactly where the mouse is positioned:

```
Private Sub Picture1_MouseDown (Button As Integer, Shift As Integer, ⇐
    X As Single, Y As Single)

    'button argument checks which mouse button
    If Button = LEFT_BUTTON Then
        'X and Y are current mouse position
        Picture1.Line (x1!, y1!)-(X, Y)
    End If
End Sub
```

Control arrays have just one event procedure for the entire array. This makes it easy to write generic code that applies to related controls that are grouped in the array. Event procedures in control arrays always have an Index argument that determines which control in the array triggered the event. This next example shows a menu control array with four elements. The Select Case uses the Index property to take appropriate action depending on which menu choice the user clicked.

```
Private Sub menuWindowArrange_Click (Index As Integer)
    Select Case Index
        Case 0: MDIForm1.Arrange vbCascade
        Case 1: MDIForm1.Arrange vbTileHorizontal
        Case 2: MDIForm1.Arrange vbTileVertical
        Case 3: MDIForm1.Arrange vbArrangeIcons
    End Select
End Sub
```

The Change Project

Project Overview

The Change project demonstrates the use of the Change event. As explained earlier and in more detail in Chapter 13, "Program Flow," an event is an action recognized by a form or control, such as a mouse click or a keystroke. Event-driven languages like

Visual Basic let the user control program flow. When the user does something (or the system causes an event, like a shutdown message), the program responds to that action. This is in contrast to a traditional program, which starts at the beginning and controls all aspects of program flow to the end. By permitting the user flexibility in using the program, event-driven languages, like Visual Basic, permit far more flexible user interfaces than are possible under the traditional approach.

In this project, you will create a form with a TextBox control and a Label control. The text box's Change event will be used to display the number of characters in the box. Although this project uses only one of the controls that have a Change event, the concept behind using the Change event is similar for all other controls.

Assembling the Project: the Change Form

    1. Create a new Standard EXE project called Change.VBP. On the default form, place on it the controls specified in Table 4-4.

Table 4-4 Property setting for the Change project's form

Object	Properties	Setting
Form	Name	Form1
	BorderStyle	3-Fixed Dialog
	Caption	"Change Project"
	Height	2325
	Width	4770
TextBox	Name	Text1
	BorderStyle	0—None
	Height	1605
	Left	0
	MultiLine	True
	ScrollBars	2—Vertical
	Text	(no text)
	Top	0
	Width	4670
Label	Name	Label1
	BackColor	Light Gray—&H00C0C0C0
	BorderStyle	1—Fixed Single
	Caption	no characters
	Height	315
	Left	0
	Top	1620
	Width	4670

    2. Check the appearance of your form against Figure 4-3.

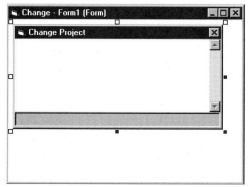

Figure 4-3 The Change project

3. Enter the following code into the Text1_Change event. In this event the number of characters that reside in the text box is determined with the Len function.

```
Private Sub Text1_Change ()
    Dim nCount As Integer
    Dim sMsg As String

    nCount = Len(Text1.Text)
    sMsg = " characters"
    Select Case nCount
        Case 0
            sMsg = " no characters"
        Case 1
            sMsg = " one character"
        Case Else
            sMsg = Format$(nCount, " ### ")
            sMsg = sMsg & "characters"
    End Select
    Label1.Caption = sMsg
End Sub
```

How It Works

To run the project, select Start from the Run menu. Visual Basic will compile your project. If there are any errors due to typos or minor syntax problems, you will be notified by the IDE. Otherwise, your application will execute.

When the user enters some text in the text box, the Change event triggers. The Caption property of Label1 is set in the Text_Change event's code, based on the number of characters found. Because this event occurs anytime a change is made to the text in Text1, the label caption gets updated immediately. Figure 4-4 illustrates how the project looks with some text entered into the text box.

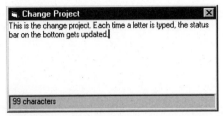

Figure 4-4   The label caption is updated based on the text entered in the form's text box

5

PROGRAM GROUPS AND PROJECTS

Versions of Visual Basic prior to 5.0 allowed developers to work on only one project per VBIDE (Visual Basic Integrated Development Environment). This could be frustrating, because many developers work on more than one project at a time. In order to work on more than one project, you had to open different VBIDEs for each project. Prior to version 4.0, you had to make copies of the VB.EXE files and rename them, for example, VB.EXE, VB1.EXE, VB2.EXE. It could be confusing toggling between projects, not to mention very resource intensive.

In Visual Basic 5.0, you are provided with the ability to work on several projects within one VBIDE. This is called a project group. It is similar to the Binder in Microsoft Office, which allows you to work on several Office documents within one environment while the binder file keeps track of where the documents are located. A project group provides you with a similar model that allows you to work on several Visual Basic projects within one interface.

This chapter will cover project files and their properties, as well as discuss reasons for using project groups.

Projects

As discussed in Chapter 2, "Overall Elements of a VB Program," a Visual Basic application is called a project. A project is defined as a collection of files made up of forms and code modules. The information about the project is kept in a project file. A project file contains the location and reference information for the following items:

- Form modules (.FRM)
- Standard modules (.BAS)
- Class modules (.CLS)

■ Resource file (.RES)

■ ActiveX controls (.OCX)

■ Project properties

If the project is for the development of an ActiveX control or ActiveX document, it can also include the following files:

■ User control modules (.CTL)

■ Property page files (.PAG)

■ User document modules (.DOB) (for ActiveX documents)

The project file is not stored in a special format. It can be viewed with any text editor, such as Windows Notepad. The following listing is an example of the contents of a project file (.VBP). Some of the parameters listed might not make any sense to you right now, but as you learn more about the project properties, these parameters and their settings should start to make sense.

```
Type=Exe
Form=frmMain.frm
Class=CDataObjects; CDATAOBJ.Cls
Module=bError; bError.Bas
Reference=*\G{00020430-0000-0000-C000-000000000046}#2.0#0# _
    E:\WINNT\System32\STDOLE2.TLB#Standard OLE Types
Reference=*\G{EE008642-64A8-11CE-920F-08002B369A33}#1.0#0# _
    E:\WINNT\System32\MSRDO20.DLL#Microsoft Remote Data Object 1.0
Object={5E9E78A0-531B-11CF-91F6-C2863C385E30}#1.0#0; MSFLXGRD.OCX
```

■ Type. Defines the type of project you are developing, such as EXE for Standard EXE or CONTROL for an ActiveX control.

■ Form. Defines the location and filename of the form that it is equal to. If there is no directory noted in the "Form=," then the form is located in same directory as the project file. There will be an entry for every form in the project.

■ Module. Defines the location and filename of the module that it is equal to. If there is no directory noted in the "Module=," then the module is located in the same directory as the project file. There will be an entry for every module in the project.

■ Reference. In order to guarantee uniqueness for an object library or type library, each one is assigned a GUID, which stands for Globally Unique Identification Key. GUIDs are a mechanism defined by the Component Object Model. The value within the braces is a GUID. The value after the first pound sign is major version number, or high byte, of the object library. The value after the second # is the minor version number, or low byte, of the object library. Then the location of the object library is listed with the object library's name.

■ Object. The property refers to any ActiveX control that you are using within your project. It contains a GUID, major and minor version information, and the filename of the ActiveX control.

```
IconForm="frmMain"
Startup="frmMain"
HelpFile=""
Title="qbe"
ExeName32="qbe.exe"
Path32="..\..\..\VBCS-HowTo\cs505\5-06"
Command32=""
Name="Project1"
HelpContextID="0"
CompatibleMode="0"
MajorVer=1
MinorVer=0
RevisionVer=1
AutoIncrementVer=1
ServerSupportFiles=0
VersionCompanyName="Waite Group Press"
VersionFileDescription="VB5CS-HowTo 5-6 Example"
CompilationType=-1
OptimizationType=0
FavorPentiumPro(tm)=0
CodeViewDebugInfo=0
NoALiasing=0
BoundsCheck=0
OverflowCheck=0
FlPointCheck=0
FDIVCheck=0
UnroundedFP=0
StartMode=0
Unattended=0
ThreadPerObject=0
MaxNumberOfThreads=1
```

The rest of the properties correspond with settings you will learn later in this chapter. If a property has the value of zero (0), then it means the value is not marked and the option is not used. When a property is set to minus one (–1), then it means the property is true and the option is used.

The contents of the Project window can be displayed two different ways. It can be viewed in the traditional hierarchy, in which all the files are listed in alphabetical order grouped by forms, standard and class modules, and resource files, respectively, as illustrated in Figure 5-1. The alternate way to view the files within the Project window is by viewing them in an Explorer model. Each group—forms, standard and class modules, and resource files—has its own folder. You can expand or collapse any folder to view its contents, as Figure 5-2 shows the Project window with all the folders expanded. You can toggle between the two formats by clicking on the Folder button on the Project window's toolbar.

Figure 5-1 Project window in the traditional view

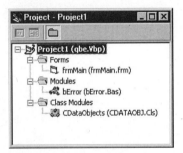

Figure 5-2 Project window displaying components grouped in folders

Project Properties

In previous versions of Visual Basic, there really were not a lot of properties to set for a project other than general settings, such as what form the project started with, what the project's name was, and so forth. Because projects are getting more complex, their settings are no longer considered just environmental settings. Using Visual Basic 5.0, to get to a project's property settings, select the *<projectname>* Properties item from the Project menu item. You can also select the project name in the Project window with the right mouse button and choose *<projectname>* Properties from the context menu.

General Properties

The General tab of the Project Properties window is used to specify settings for the active Visual Basic project. When you first define your application, its type is filled in the Project Type drop-down list box. For example, in Figure 5-3, the project was defined as a Standard EXE. In the process of development, you might realize that it would be better developing this project as an ActiveX EXE. In that case, change the Project Type to ActiveX EXE, and the VBIDE will check your project for any invalid properties. If any errors arise, the VBIDE will give you a message suggesting that you should not make the change.

You can determine which of your project's forms is to be loaded first when the application starts. Select the form by choosing it in the Startup Object drop-down list box. You can also set the Startup Object to be a Sub Main procedure, which you can set up to load several forms at once, initialize objects, display a message while processes are running, and so on.

Under Project Name, enter a name for your project that will appear in the Object Browser and Windows registry. It is important that this name be unique. This name cannot contain a period or spaces, and it cannot begin with a number. The project name will be used in the *type library* for your ActiveX component. A type library, also known as a TypeLib, contains the description of the objects and interfaces available in your component.

In the Help File Name text box, enter the name of the help file associated with your application, if one is available. If you do not know the name and location of the help file, you can look for it using the browse button, which is the button with the ellipsis (...). The Project Help Context ID text box is used to identify the specific help topic that will be called when a user selects the Help button, while the application's object library is selected in the Object Browser.

The Project Description text box describes your application when it appears in the References and Object Browser dialog boxes. If you are creating an ActiveX control, this text will appear in the Components dialog box.

There are two project load settings for a project. This means that when your Visual Basic project is loading into the VBIDE, certain processes need to be executed. The first one is Upgrade ActiveX Controls. Marking this property means that as the project is loading, if the system has a newer version of an ActiveX control than the one used in your project, the VBIDE will upgrade your project to the new ActiveX control. The other setting is Require License Key. This setting is available only if you are developing an ActiveX control. Visual Basic will create a license file (.VBL) when you compile your application. The VBL file must be registered on a developer's machine for the components to be used in the design environment. The Application Setup Wizard will build a setup program that properly registers the information in the VBL file on the target user's machine when the setup program is run.

The frame titled Unattended Execution is available only in the Enterprise Edition and is used to support the development of scalable ActiveX components using multi-threading technology. The term *unattended execution* means that a project is intended to run without user interaction. An unattended project does not have an interface element. The frame itself will not become enabled unless you have class modules defined with the Instancing property set to Multiuse. The Thread per Object setting indicates that each instance of a class marked as Multiuse in the Instancing property will be created on a thread from the thread pool. The threads setting determines the maximum number of threads created for the thread pool. When a Multiuse class is instantiated, threads are created as needed up to the number set in the text box. When the maximum number of threads is reached, Visual Basic begins to assign new instances to the existing threads.

Two new features support building scalable ActiveX components using multithreading technology. Building ActiveX components for unattended execution (no user interface elements) in distributed applications allows the components to be used in multithreaded environments. ActiveX DLL components marked for unattended execution support the ActiveX/COM Apartment threading model. ActiveX EXE components marked for unattended execution will allocate object instances across multiple threads for better scalability as instances are created.

Make Properties

Most software developers track their application release by their version number, rather than relying on the date and time stamps that accompany files. You can embed an internal version number and version information inside your EXE or DLL. Figure 5-4 shows the Make tab of the Project Properties window. Date and time stamps can be changed because they are just a field on the storage media's file allocation table, while version numbers are embedded within the application.

In the Version Number frame, you need to set the appropriate Major, Minor, and Revision numbers. If you mark the Auto Increment check box, your project's revision number will increase automatically each time you compile your project into an executable. An example of the version scheme would be 1.0.95, which means it's the 95th build of the first release of your application. You might be thinking, "When would I change the major and minor numbers, then?" A lot of developers use the minor version number to indicate minor changes such as simple bug fixes in calculations or process handling. You might consider changing the major version number when you add some significant features to your existing application. The range of all the version numbers is 0 to 9999.

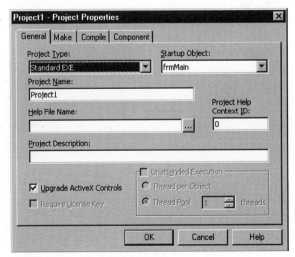

Figure 5-3   General properties

In the Application frame, you can give your application a title that Windows will use when displaying a Task List of program that is currently running in memory. You can also embed an icon into your application by using an icon that is assigned to one of your forms.

In the Version Information frame, you can enter version-specific comments about your application, such as general comments, your company name, a file description, and the like. To view the version information of a file, select the file in Windows Explorer and use the Properties item from the File menu or the file's context pop-up menu. Once the file's properties appear in a dialog box, select the Version tab. The Version tab will display the version information you entered in from this Project Properties tab, as illustrated in Figure 5-5.

Compile Properties

The Compile tab of the Project Properties window is used to determine how your program will be compiled. Figure 5-6 illustrates this dialog box. Prior to Visual Basic 5.0, when you compiled your application into an executable file, it was not compiled into a true executable format, such as a compiled C or Pascal program. It was compiled into what is known as p-code, or pseudocode. When your application was executed, it was linked to a runtime module—such as VBRUN300.DLL, VBRUN4xx.DLL (xx equals 16 or 32), or MSVBVM50.DLL—and it executed as if it were native code. The runtime module translated the compiled Visual Basic into native code to be executed. This is why the speed of a Visual Basic application in runtime is not much improved over that of its compiled counterpart.

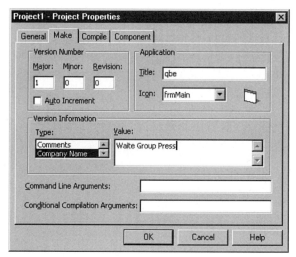

Figure 5-4 Make tab

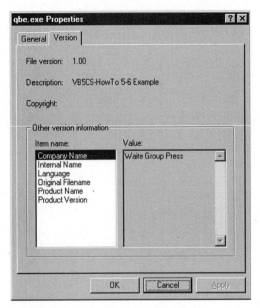

Figure 5-5 Application version information
viewed in the properties of a file

When you press Start from within the Visual Basic IDE, the IDE compiles your project into a temporary executable file and links it with the runtime module. The main difference is that you can watch your code execute during this processing by setting breakpoints, or "step" through it using the Step function of the IDE. With Visual Basic 5.0, you can now compile your application into a true executable, which is native code. Therefore, you will no longer need a Visual Basic runtime module to run your application. In terms of running your application, writing in Visual Basic 5.0 is the equivalent of writing your application in C/C++, Pascal, or Assembly.

On the Compile tab of the Project Properties window, you can determine if you would like your project to be compiled as p-code or native code. By marking Compile to P-Code, you compile your application into p-code, just as you have done in past versions of Visual Basic. If you mark this choice, you will need to include the Visual Basic runtime module, or virtual machine module, with your application.

By marking Compile to Native Code, you can choose how you would like your code to be optimized. When Visual Basic compiles your program to native code, it uses the same optimization compile engine that Microsoft Visual C++ uses. The optimization settings, or "switches," as they are commonly referred to by C programmers, are discussed in greater detail in Chapter 7, "Using the Native-Code Compiler."

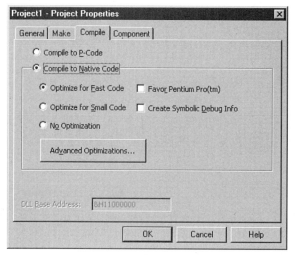

Figure 5-6 Compile tab

Component Properties

The Component tab of the Project Properties window is enabled only when you are developing ActiveX servers (EXE or DLL); therefore, it is available only in the Professional and Enterprise Editions. Figure 5-7 illustrates the Component tab. This tab is used to determine how your ActiveX component executes.

The Start Mode frame contains option buttons that indicate how your application will start—either as a standalone application or as an ActiveX component. If the Start Mode is set to ActiveX Component and you have not defined any public classes in your project, you must use the End statement or choose End from the Run menu or toolbar to end the application. If you choose Close from a form's Control menu, the form closes but the project continues to run.

The Remote Server frame contains a check box that, when marked, creates a Windows registry file, *<projectname>*.VBR, for your project. This file contains the registry information needed for the server to run on a remote system. It is available only in the Enterprise Edition.

The Version Compatibility frame contains option buttons to set the level of version compatibility to which your ActiveX component will need to comply. When developing in a client/server or component-based environment, ensuring version compatibility needs to be considered as part of your development strategy for backward compatibility. As an example of ensuring backward compatibility, suppose you have in a Calculator object a financial calculation method, DividendsPaidOut, that requires one argument, Numerator. If you distribute a new version of the ActiveX component in which you changed the DividendsPaidOut method to include the argument Denominator, you will cause a runtime error in applications that use the Calculator object. If backward compatibility is enforced, the error can be avoided, because the ActiveX component will flag the user that more information is required.

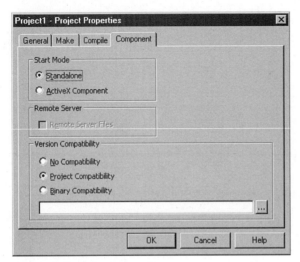

Figure 5-7 Component tab

There are three levels of version compatibility that can be set for an ActiveX server. They are No Compatibility, Project Compatibility, and Binary Compatibility. No Compatibility means that backward compatibility is not enforced at all. Using this property guarantees that you will start with a clean slate of identifiers, and that existing applications will not mistakenly try to use the incompatible version. The two caveats that go along with this property are that you first will have to change the filename of your ActiveX component so that the incompatible version will not overwrite earlier versions on your clients' systems. You will also have to change the project name to ensure that the ActiveX object has a different program ID (CLSID) and type library than the incompatible component.

The Project Compatibility setting should be used when you are developing the first version of an ActiveX component. This property preserves the type library, so that you are not continually setting references from your test projects to your component projects. This property also makes it easier to switch between the component project and the compiled component when you are testing.

Binary Compatibility should be used when you begin work on the second version of any ActiveX component, if you want applications compiled using the earlier version to continue to work using the new version. A caveat with this property is that if you are using multiple interfaces in your ActiveX component and the Implements statement to provide backward compatibility, you should not use this setting. If you enhance any of the interfaces in your component, Visual Basic will change the interface ID. The technique of evolving component software by adding interfaces depends on *interface invariance*. This means that an interface, once defined, is never changed, and this includes the interface ID.

The file location box is used to display the filename and location of the file the project should be compatible with. If you do not know the filename and its location, you can look for it using the browse button, which is the button with the ellipsis (...).

Project Groups

A philosophy for developing systems is to develop them by building your application in components. These components can be in the form of ActiveX EXEs (out-of-process servers), ActiveX DLLs and ActiveX controls (both are in-process servers). Out-of-process servers are applications that execute in a memory space different from that of the application that calls it. In-process servers execute within the same memory space of the application that uses them. As you start to build these types of systems, the method by which you manage these projects can be very complex.

Traditionally, you would have to build these components in different environments, or in different VBIDEs. Debugging these different components in different environments was very time-consuming and not interactive. For example, if you were working on an ActiveX DLL, you would have to run the application in one VBIDE, and run the test application in another. In order to debug the ActiveX DLL, you would have to put message box messages in your ActiveX DLL code to notify you where you were in that code. If an error arose, you would have to figure out where the error occurred based on your message box messages. You would have to stop your test application, stop your ActiveX DLL, and hope you could find the error. You could not interact with your code as you could if you were just writing a Standard EXE application.

A project group helps take a level of this complex process away. By using a project group, you can effectively work on several projects within the same environment. They can all be Standard EXE projects, ActiveX DLL projects, and so forth. The most common way of using project groups is to develop ActiveX DLLs and controls. You can have several ActiveX projects in the group along with a test application. In Figure 5-8, you see the VBIDE with two projects open at the same time. One project is an ActiveX control, and the other is Standard EXE, which is being used as a test application for the control. Working on projects like this, you can add the ActiveX control to your test application and test and debug the control without having to compile the control. The advantage of this is that you can interactively debug the control. If an error occurs within the control, you can go straight to the code that is causing the error, correct it, and continue your test. The same can be done with an ActiveX DLL, because ActiveX controls and DLLs are both in-process servers. In order to test an ActiveX EXE, you cannot interactively debug it in the same VBIDE. You can have the ActiveX EXE project as part of your project group, but in order to debug it, you will need to run it from a different instance of Visual Basic, as you did in Visual Basic 4.0, because it needs to run in a separate memory space from that of the calling application.

You can add a new or existing project to your VBIDE at any time. By doing so, your Project window becomes a Project Group window. You can save the project group as a Visual Basic Group (.VBG) file and work with it in subsequent development sessions. Although you have saved these projects as a group, you are not limited to working on them as a group. You can still work on each project independent of the other projects within the group. You can work on them within the group. You can even have the same project in multiple groups. The actual content of a VBG file is a list of all the VBP files and their locations. If you open a VBG file and a project that is referenced within it cannot be found, you will receive a File Not Found error message, the project name,

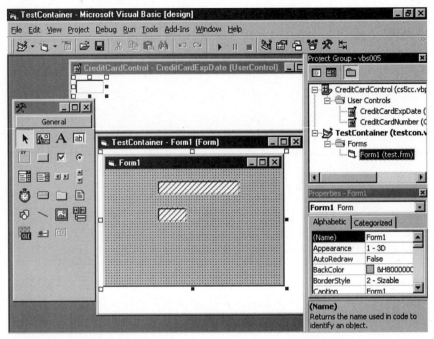

Figure 5-8 VBIDE with an ActiveX control and Standard EXE test project open

and information about where it was supposed to be. The message will also ask if you wish to continue loading the project group or not. If you choose Yes, Visual Basic will attempt to load the rest of the projects within the VBG file. If you choose No, the VBIDE will stop loading where the error occurred.

When you are working with a project group, only one project can be executed. By default, the last project added is the one that will execute when you select Start from the Run menu. Visually, you can see which project is the startup project, because the project name is in bold within the project group window. To change which project is the startup project, select the project name in the project group window with the right mouse button. From the context menu, select the Set as Startup menu item. ActiveX control projects are the only projects that cannot be startup projects.

To add a new or existing project to a project group, select Add Project from the File menu. The Add Project dialog box will appear, giving you the option of which type of project you wish to add to your project. The Learning Edition will allow you to add only a new Standard EXE or existing Standard EXE project to your project group. To add an existing project, select the Existing or Recent tab to find the project.

To remove a project from a group, select the project in the Project Group window. Then select Remove Project from the File menu or from the Project window's context menu.

6

USING WIZARDS

In medieval times, wizards were people who could conjure up magical creatures and make items appear out of thin air with a few special components. Microsoft wizards can seem equally magical, but rather than conjuring up creatures, they create projects or components for projects with a few basic commands from you.

Over the past few years, wizards have been finding their way into a lot of Microsoft products. They have become increasingly popular because they are designed to make long, tedious tasks easier. They lead you step by step through a series of screens, which in turn are converted into the programming you would have had to do yourself.

In previous versions of Visual Basic, the only wizard available to you was the Application Setup Wizard. In the Learning Edition of Visual Basic 5.0, you also get the Application Wizard. This wizard provides a framework for you to build your applications. In the Professional and Enterprise Editions, not only will you get the Application Wizard and Application Setup Wizard, you will have the ActiveX Control Interface Wizard, ActiveX Document Migration Wizard, Data Form Wizard, and Property Page Wizard. In the Enterprise Edition, you get all the above-mentioned wizards and you get the T-SQL Debugger. To help you manage the wizards, the Professional and Enterprise Editions come with a Wizard Toolbar. To assist you in creating your own wizards, there is the Wizard Manager.

This chapter will describe the basic features of each wizard and how to interact with it. For a more detailed description of wizards, refer to Part XVI, "Wizards and Helper Tools."

Wizards and the IDE

The basic management of wizards within the Visual Basic IDE (Integrated Development Environment) is through the Add-In Manager. All the available wizards are displayed in the Available Add-Ins list box, as shown in Figure 6-1. To enable a wizard or wizards in your environment, mark the check box next to the name of each wizard you wish to enable and press the OK button. To remove a wizard, simply clear its check box and press the OK button. Once a wizard has been enabled, it is bound to your environment every time you start Visual Basic. To use a wizard, select it from the Add-Ins menu. Figure 6-2 illustrates what your Add-Ins menu will look like with some wizards enabled.

Add-In Toolbar

An alternate way to access the wizards is through the Add-In Toolbar. In order to use the Add-In Toolbar, you need to enable it through the Add-In Manager. Figure 6-3 illustrates what the Add-In Toolbar looks like. The +/- is used for adding or removing Wizards on the toolbar. Each wizard you enable through the Add-In Toolbar is displayed through a toolbar icon. To use a wizard, simply click on the wizard's toolbar icon. This toolbar acts like any other toolbar in that it can be docked to any side of the IDE or used as a floating toolbar.

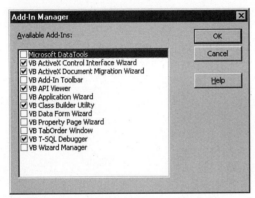

Figure 6-1 Add-In Manager dialog box

Figure 6-2 Add-Ins
menu with several wizards
enabled

Figure 6-3 Add-In Toolbar

Wizard Basics

Navigating is the same in all wizards. Each wizard starts with an Introduction screen that describes the function of the wizard, and the last step is the Finished screen. This step indicates that you are done and asks you to enter a name for the module the wizard is about to generate.

Along the bottom of all wizard windows are navigation buttons. The Help button will get you context-sensitive help information about the step you are on. The Cancel button will abort the wizard. The Previous and Next buttons will navigate you back one step or forward one step, respectively. The Finish button will cause the wizard to begin processing the information you have given it.

Application Wizard

With the Application Wizard, instead of having to develop a program from scratch, you can generate a basic project framework by answering seven basic questions from the following screens:

- Interface Type. You can choose the type of user interface you would like your program to have. You can choose from MDI (Multiple-Document Interface), SDI (Single-Document Interface), or an Explorer-like interface.

- Menus. One of the most common components of a Windows-based application is its menu items. You can choose which menu items will be part of your project. The menu items are File, Edit, View, Window, and Help. The basic file structure will be included with the menu item you select. For example, File will include Open, Close, Send to, and Exit.

- Resources. If you plan to use a resource file that contains your icons or strings values, you can select to add the resource file to your project here. If you decide not to add the resource file here, you can always add it to your project at a later time.

- Internet Connectivity. Allows your program to access the World Wide Web by using an Internet browser ActiveX control. You can also assign a default URL (uniform resource locator) address.

- Standard Forms. Most programs have a lot of forms in common, like a Splash screen, which displays information about the program as it loads or a dialog screen to log onto your database. In this step, you can choose the following forms to be added to your project: Splash screen, login dialog, Options dialog box, and About box. These files reside in the Template directory, and you can customize them at your own discretion.

- Data Access Form. Generate forms based on a database.

Application Setup Wizard

The Application Setup Wizard is the only wizard that is used outside of the Visual Basic IDE. To use this wizard, find Application Setup Wizard in the Microsoft Visual Basic 5.0 Start menu. As with previous Application Setup Wizards, you are asked a series of questions that will help you build the distribution diskettes needed to ship your program to your user community. The Professional and Enterprise Editions support the capability to distribute ActiveX components across the Internet, as well as the installation of remote server components using Distribute COM (DCOM) and remote automation.

ActiveX Control Interface Wizard

With the Professional and Enterprise Editions, you have the ability to create ActiveX controls (OCX files). This wizard is designed to help you create and assign the public and custom properties, methods, and events to your control's user interface. The steps you will go through with this wizard are as follows:

- Select a Control. This step only appears when you have more than one user control in the current project group. Otherwise this screen is skipped.

- Select Interface Members. This step is used to select property, method, and event names you want to assign to the control. The property, method, and event names under the Selected Names list box are common to all ActiveX controls. Select any property, method, or event names you wish to add to your control from the Available Names list box and move them to the Selected Names list.

- Create Custom Interface Members. This step allows you to name custom property, method, or event names to the control. You will have to develop them later but at least you have their placement in the control predefined.

- Set Mapping. This step is designed for you to assign the functionality of the property, method, or event in your control the members in the fundamental control.

- Set Attributes. This step allows you to assign default values for any member you assigned in the previous step.

ActiveX Document Migration Wizard

With the Professional and Enterprise Editions, you have the ability to create ActiveX document applications. This wizard is designed to help you change your existing Visual Basic form into ActiveX user document modules. ActiveX document applications allow your applications to either be used through an Internet Web browser that is ActiveX enabled, through the Microsoft Binder that comes with Microsoft Office 97, or within another application.

To use this wizard, you need to be in a project that you wish to convert. The steps you will go through with this wizard are as follows:

- Form Selection. In this step, you select which forms in the current project you want to convert to user document modules.

■ Options. In this step, you specify how you want the wizard to handle unsupported code, if you want to remove the converted form from the project, and whether you want the converted project made into an ActiveX document EXE or DLL. Unsupported code is code that is valid in a Standard EXE project but not available in ActiveX documents. An example of unsupported code would be the Show or Hide methods.

Class Builder

With the Professional and Enterprise Editions, this utility is designed to help you build an object model of classes and collections for your project. For classes and collections you design with the Class Builder, it will keep track of their hierarchy and generate the appropriate properties, methods, and events into your project. You can use the Class Builder on classes and collections that were not designed with the Class Builder, but it will not retain any hierarchical information at first. All the classes and collections elements are stored at the root of the hierarchy. You will need to arrange them into a hierarchical order by dragging and dropping them into the correct Properties, Methods, and Events tabs. When you save the changes, the hierarchy will be retained. Figure 6-4 is an example of the Class Builder. This wizard is a lot more interactive than the other wizards.

The pane on the left side of the Class Builder is called the Object Model Pane. It contains a visual hierarchy of the classes and collections that go with the current project. The pane on the right side is the Properties, Methods, and Events Pane. It contains all the properties, methods, and events defined for the selected class or collection.

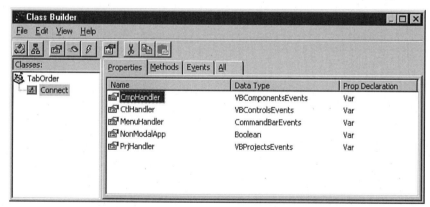

Figure 6-4   Class Builder showing the properties of the Connect class

Data Form Wizard

With the Professional and Enterprise Editions, you can use the Data Form Wizard to help you make forms to display data or to be used for data entry. The steps you will go through with this wizard are as follows:

- Database Type. Select the type of database you will be connecting to.

- Connect Information. This step will only appear if you are connecting to an ODBC database. You will set up your ODBC connection with information such as DSN, User ID, and password.

- Form. This step allows you to choose how the data will be displayed on the form. The layout types are single records, grid or Access datasheet-like layout, or Master/Detail. An invoice is an example of a Master/Detail form. The Master information is the customer information, and the Detail information is the items the customer purchased. The information is tied together by the Customer number.

- Master Record Source. In this step, you will assign the table you wish to base the form on and the columns you wish to use.

- Detail Record Source. This step will only appear if you selected Master/Detail in the Form step. You will assign the table you wish to base the detail form on and the columns you wish to display.

- Record Source Relation. This step will only appear if you selected Master/Detail in the Form step. You will assign how the Master form is related to the Detail form. Using the example of a customer invoice, the Customer has a Customer ID that contains all of his or her billing information. The order contains all the items the customer is purchasing and is referenced by the Customer ID. Therefore, the record source relationship is the Customer ID.

- Control Selection. In this step, you will design which data control commands you want to add to the form. The controls to choose from are Add Record, Delete Record, Refresh, Update, Close form, and Show Data Control.

Property Page Wizard

Property pages are an alternate way to modify an ActiveX control's property information. Prior to ActiveX controls, the only way to modify properties at design time was through the Property window. Embedded within an ActiveX control can be a series of property pages. Not all ActiveX controls have them. Property pages allow you to group similar properties into a single tabbed form. This gives the developer who is using your control a central place to modify any property information rather than having to look around the Property window. For example, you might want to group all the font information on one page. To view the property pages of any ActiveX control, select the control with the right mouse button and select Properties from the context menu. If the control has property pages, they will appear in a Properties dialog box; otherwise, you will have to work with the Properties window. Figures 6-5 and 6-6 are examples of a property page of an ActiveX control and a property page at design time.

This wizard is designed to help you add property pages to the ActiveX control you are developing. You can either design your property page modules first or create them within the wizard. The steps you will go through with this wizard are as follows:

■ Select a User Control. If you have more than one control in your ActiveX control project, you will specify which user control module you want to assign the property page for.

■ Select the Property Pages. There are three standard property pages defined. They are StandardColor, StandardFont, and StandardPicture. The StandardColor page is designed to have color settings. The StandardFont page is designed for all font settings. The StandardPicture is used to set a picture within a control. You will select which standard property pages you would like associated with your control. You can also add new property pages at this point.

■ Add Properties. On this screen, you assign which available properties you want to be displayed on each property page. The standard property pages cannot be modified. The list of available properties are the properties you exposed on the control when you used the ActiveX Control Interface Wizard or any properties that you raised in your code.

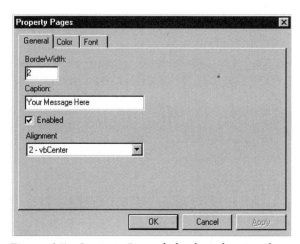

Figure 6-5   Property Pages dialog box showing the General tab

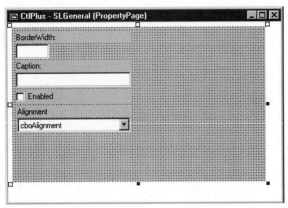

Figure 6-6 Property page of the General tab at design time

T-SQL Debugger

The T-SQL Debugger, which comes with the Enterprise Edition, allows you to debug stored procedures written in Microsoft SQL Server's Transact SQL dialect without having to leave the Visual Basic IDE. It is integrated as part of the UserConnection ActiveX designer described in Chapter 2, "Overall Elements of a VB Program." In the past, if you had to develop stored procedures for SQL Server, you would have to use ISQL or SQL Server's Enterprise Manager. With T-SQL Debugger, you can

■ Display the SQL call stack

■ View and modify local variables and parameters

■ Control and manage breakpoints within the transaction

■ View global variables

T-SQL Debugger currently works with SQL Server 6.5 with Service Pack 1 installed. There are two basic components of the T-SQL Debugger. One is a client-side component that gets installed when you install all the Enterprise tools for Visual Basic. The other component is a server-side component that is located on your Visual Basic CD-ROM. The server-side component will install on both Microsoft Windows NT 3.51 and 4.0. You should refer to the Visual Basic Books Online for more details on how to install the server-side component.

To use the T-SQL Debugger, there are three different methods. They are used at design time, from within the UserConnection ActiveX designer, and during runtime debugging.

To use T-SQL Debugger at design time, you first need to add the T-SQL Debugger to your Add-Ins menu by selecting it in the Add-In Manager window. Select it from your Add-Ins menu, and the T-SQL Debugger window will launch. Figure 6-7 is an example of what the T-SQL Debugger looks like testing a store procedure.

To use T-SQL Debugger with the UserConnection ActiveX designer, right mouse click on the Query object and select the Debug Stored Procedure from the context menu. This will bring up the T-SQL Debugger with the store procedure that was in the Query object.

To use T-SQL Debugger during runtime, you will need to set some properties in the T-SQL Debugger Options under the Tools menu.

For a more detailed explanation of how to use the T-SQL Debugger, see Chapter 71, "Using T-SQL Debugger."

Wizard Manager

The Wizard Manager is a utility designed to assist you in creating your own wizards. It creates a framework of steps for your wizard and helps you manage the order in which the steps will appear. The Wizard Manager uses only one form for the entire wizard. All the different steps are a series of frame controls that get moved into the visible area of the form.

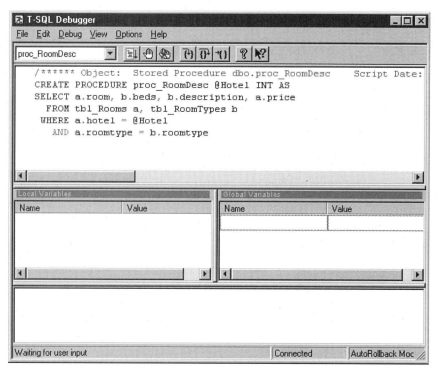

Figure 6-7 T-SQL Debugger testing a stored procedure

With the Wizard Manager window, there are a series of toolbar buttons and a list box. The buttons are navigation buttons to help manage the *step* frames. A step frame is the equivalent of a screen within a wizard. The list box contains all the steps the wizard will use. They are in the order of Introduction screen, Step *n* (where *n* is the step number), and Finished!. When you first start the Wizard Manager, it will create a wizard project similar to the one displayed in Figure 6-8. By default, the number of step frames created is four. Each frame consists of three controls: an image control, a label, and a text box. You can modify the contents of these frames just like you can with any other form. Almost all wizard steps contain these elements; therefore, the default wizard project provides these for you for template purposes. This way you do not have to re-create the frame for each step you plan to develop.

The toolbar buttons are designed to help you manipulate the positions of your Wizard steps. The buttons consist of the following:

- Move Step. This button moves the current visible step out of the visible screen frame. Use this button as your last task when creating your wizard. You do this because you want the frame area to be clear when your wizard is generated. Otherwise, the last frame you worked on will remain visible in the frame area.

- Add New Step. This will allow you to add a new step into your project. It will be inserted between the last step and the Finished! step.

- Insert Step. This will insert a new step before the step that is selected in the Wizard Manager.

- Move Step Up One Position. This will move the selected step up one position in the Wizard Manager's list box.

- Move Step Down One Position. This will move the selected step down one position in the Wizard Manager's list box.

- Refresh Step List. This will refresh the Wizard Manager's list box to reflect any changes made.

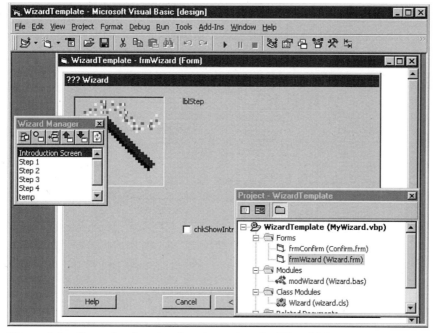

Figure 6-8   Example of a wizard project using the Wizard Manager

7

USING THE NATIVE-CODE COMPILER

BASIC has traditionally been known as an interpreted language. This means that a middle component translates each line of code into an instruction set that the computer can understand—machine language. An advantage to this is that the interpreter can test your code as you write it. Another advantage of an interpreted language is that the language itself usually sounds very much like English. But because each line of code is translated, your application's performance can suffer.

Compiled languages, like C/C++ or Pascal, convert English-like code directly into machine-readable code. No translation is involved; therefore, your programs will execute a lot faster.

Visual Basic incorporates elements from both interpreted and compiled languages. Visual Basic interprets each line of code as you write it into a set of instructions known as p-code, or pseudocode. At runtime, the p-code interpreter goes through your program to translate and execute your compiled instruction set. The result of a compiled p-code project is a small, compact, executable project. The disadvantage is that your program must be linked with a Visual Basic runtime module that your project links to. So what does this mean? Some of your instructions are compiled into p-code that can be executed without going through a Visual Basic runtime module, while other instructions are linked to a Visual Basic runtime module or other DLL (dynamic link library).

With Version 5.0 of Visual Basic Professional and Enterprise Editions, you are able to compile applications into *native code*. Native code is the instruction set that a computer understands without any translation or interpretation.

Compile Tab

The Compile tab of the Project Properties window is used to set how your program will compile. Figure 7-1 illustrates this dialog box. Prior to Visual Basic 5.0, when you compiled your application into an executable file, it wasn't compiled into a true executable format, like a compiled C or Pascal program. It was compiled into what is know as p-code, or pseudo-code. When your application was executed, it was linked to a runtime module—such as VBRUN300.DLL, VBRUN4xx.DLL (xx equals 16 or 32), or MSVBVM50.DLL—and it executed as if it were native code. The runtime module translated the compiled Visual Basic into native code to be executed. This is why the speed improvement of a Visual Basic application in runtime is not much improved over that of its compiled counterpart.

When you press Start from within the Visual Basic IDE, the IDE compiles your project into a temporary executable file and links it with the runtime module. The main difference is that you can watch your code execute during this processing by setting breakpoints, or "step" through it using the Step function of the IDE. With Visual Basic 5.0, you can now compile your application into a true executable, that is, native code. In terms of running your application, writing in Visual Basic 5.0 is the equivalent of writing your application in C/C++, Pascal, or Assembly. However, even though your application will not rely on the MSVBVM50.DLL for interpreting the pseudo-code into native code, you will still need to ship it with your application because it provides services like startup and shutdown code for your application, functionality for forms and intrinsic controls, and runtime functions like Format and CLng.

On the Compile tab, you can determine if you would like your project to be compiled as p-code or native code. By marking Compile to P-Code, you compile your application into p-code, just as you have done in past versions of Visual Basic.

By marking Compile to Native Code, you can choose the method of how you would like your code to be optimized. When Visual Basic compiles your program to native code, it uses the same optimization compile engine that Microsoft Visual C++ uses. The optimization settings, or "switches," as they are commonly referred to by C programmers, are discussed in the following sections.

Optimize for Fast Code

An advantage of a native code application is the speed with which it executes. For most things, there are usually several different methods to use to achieve the same goal. Programming is no different. Marking Optimize for Fast Code will cause the compiler to convert your Visual Basic statements into the most efficient code it can, allowing your application to execute in the quickest manner possible. One caveat about this setting: What you gain in speed, you may lose in increased size. This means that even though your code may execute faster, the algorithm might be more complicated; therefore, the size of your compiled program might be larger.

Optimize for Small Code

Marking Optimize for Small Code will cause the compiler to examine each Visual Basic statement and determine which is the smallest algorithm to use to make your compiled program the smallest possible. The caveat about this setting is that you might sacrifice the speed with which your application executes, because the smallest algorithm might not be the most efficient.

No Optimization

The No Optimization option will cause the compiler to not attempt to optimize your application. This will result in a straight translation of your Visual Basic statements into native code. It will not attempt to speed up any algorithm or produce a small executable.

Favor Pentium Pro™

A lot of application developments have moved into the 32-bit arena. With the introduction of the Intel Pentium Pro™ microprocessor, 32-bit performance has drastically increased. This is mostly due to its built-in secondary cache internal architecture and it's ability to execute 32-bit instructions in parallel.

By using this option, the compiler will optimize your native code for the Pentium Pro processor. Please note that you should use this option only if your application is going to run exclusively on that platform. The application will still work on other Intel-based computers, but performance will significantly suffer. For example, you have a program that scrolls frames across your screen. If you compile your application with the Favor Pentium Pro switch enabled on any system other than a Pentium Pro–based system, the scrolling will be very jagged and unprofessional looking.

Create Symbolic Debug Info

By marking the Create Symbolic Debug Info option, you will be able debug your native code application by using Microsoft Visual C++ Debugger or another compatible debugger utility, like Pure Atria's Purify or Nu-Mega's BoundsChecker. The compiler will create a *<projectname>*.PDB file program database. This file contains type information and symbolic debugging information for use with the debugger. The symbolic debugging information includes the names and types of variables, as well as functions.

DLL Base Address

The DLL Base Address text box is only enabled when you are creating an ActiveX DLL. The value you enter represents the address you wish the ActiveX DLL to occupy in memory. The default memory location is &H11000000. If the ActiveX DLL cannot load itself into the preferred memory address, it will automatically find a memory address that it can occupy. This could cause a performance decrease, because the

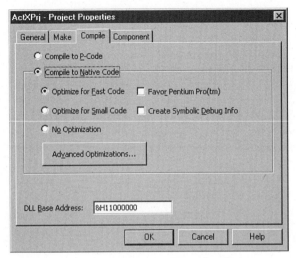

Figure 7-1 Project Properties Compile tab

calling program will not immediately find the ActiveX DLL in its designated memory address. By specifying a preferred memory address, you improve performance of the ActiveX DLL by avoiding conflicts with other DLLs already in memory. The address range is between &H1000000 (16 megabytes) and &H80000000 (2 gigabytes). The base address must be a multiple of 64K. The memory used by your component begins at the initial base address and is the size of the compiled application, rounded up to the next multiple of 64K.

TIP

It is highly recommended that you change this base address because if you leave it at the default value, it is very probable that it will conflict with another in-process server. If your application is using multiple in-process servers, you may want to choose a base address for your main component and calculate the each address from there. This way avoids conflict with another developer or another company's component.

Advanced Optimizations

The command button Advanced Optimizations will display another dialog box, as shown in Figure 7-2, with more advanced settings for optimizing your compiled program. The parameters you can use are as follows:

Assume No Aliasing

Marking the Assume No Aliasing option notifies the compiler that your program does not use *aliasing*. An alias is a name that refers to a memory location that is already referred to by a different name. Using this option allows the compiler to apply optimizations it could not otherwise use, optimizations like storing variables in registers and performing loop optimizations. Loop optimization removes unvarying subexpressions from the body of a loop. A caveat: You should not consider using this optimization method if your project passes arguments using ByRef, because the optimizations could cause your project to execute incorrectly.

Remove Array Bounds Checks

By default, Visual Basic checks to make sure that a reference to an array is within the array's boundaries. By selecting the Remove Array Bounds Checks option, you are removing this fail-safe and could cause your application to crash because a reference was made to an invalid array reference. For example, with this option selected, a reference to vArray(12), when the array was defined by REDIM vArray(10), will cause your application to crash, because you are referring to an array that does not exist. For more information on arrays, refer to Chapter 14, "Variables."

Remove Integer Overflow Checks

By default, Visual Basic checks to make sure that every calculation of an integer-based data type—byte, integer, and long—is within the range of that data type. By selecting the Remove Integer Overflow Checks option, you are removing this fail-safe. If a calculation is larger than the data type capacity, no error will occur, meaning you could receive incorrect calculated values. For more information on integer data types, refer to Chapter 14.

Remove Floating Point Error Checks

By default, Visual Basic checks to make sure that every calculation of a floating-point data type—single or double—is within the range of that data type and that there will not be any "division by zero" operations. By selecting the Remove Floating Point Error Checks option, you are removing this fail-safe. If a calculation is larger than the data type capacity, no error will occur, meaning you could receive incorrect calculated values. For more information on floating-point data types, refer to Chapter 14.

Allow Unrounded Floating Point Operations

Floating-point calculations are normally rounded off to the correct decimal precision before any comparisons are made. By marking the Allow Unrounded Floating Point Operations option, you are allowing the natively compiled code to compare results of floating-point calculations without first rounding the results to the correct decimal place. This can result in improved speed of some floating-point operations, but it may also result in calculations being maintained at a higher decimal precision than programmed for, resulting in values that might not equal one another when normally they would.

Remove Safe Pentium™ FDIV Checks

Remember when the Pentium microprocessor first came out and there was a flaw in the floating-point division (FDIV) process? By default, the compiler will implement some mathematical algorithms to produce safe code that tests for the processor bug and calls runtime routines to generate correct floating-point results, rather than using the native instructions of the processor. By selecting the Remove Safe Pentium™ FDIV Checks option, you remove the fail-safe that ensures that the calculations used by the FDIV are correct. The resultant size of your code and the speed with which it executes will increase, but your values may be slightly incorrect if your application is run on a system with a flawed Pentium.

> **NOTE**
> Be cautious setting some of these parameters. Some settings, based on your code, might cause your programs to not execute properly, or in the manner you anticipated.

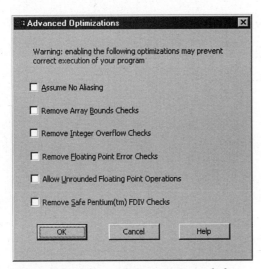

Figure 7-2 Advanced Optimizations dialog box

Interpreted Versus Compiled Applications

Visual Basic developers have long been taunted by developers who use C/C++, Pascal, or Assembler, because Visual Basic did not create true executable programs, which is to say Visual Basic developers did not create native-code applications. Now, with version 5.0, this is no longer an issue. The main argument against Visual Basic has been that native-code applications execute faster than applications that require a runtime interpreter. But in an event-driven environment such as Microsoft Windows, is this really an issue? The majority of applications being written today have a user interface that requires considerable user interaction, like mouse navigation, data entry, and so forth. How fast does one form really need to be in order to launch another form?

As more and more developers and companies move into a distributed environment in which applications are built on components, the distinction between compiling applications using interpreted p-code versus native code becomes a little clearer. When building components that are designed to do a lot of calculations, you should compile the components as native code. The applications can be optimized to execute in the most efficient manner and other components will not have to wait as long.

In the process of developing applications that require a lot of Windows API (Application Programming Interface) procedure calls, the speed difference between p-code and native-code applications is negligible. This is mainly due to the fact that such applications require a lot of linking to external sources, and it is the links to external sources that slow down an application.

When developing components for the ActiveX controls (OCXs), this can get pretty tricky. Usually ActiveX controls are considered self-contained business components or objects that can assist your application by adding functionality to it. The question of whether the component should be native code or p-code is generally not an issue. Most people would argue that native code is how the component should be compiled; this way the user does not have to rely on a runtime module. In reality, a lot of native-code–compiled projects do require some runtime modules. In this case, they require Microsoft Foundation Class (MFC) modules. The project is still compiled in native code; it's just that some of the functions are contained in the MFC modules, just as some Windows API calls are in the kernel.

In a single workstation environment or within an enterprise network, using native-code–compiled applications really is not especially important, because you can leave a lot of the MFC runtime modules on a server that all the workstations share. It is when you develop components for the Internet or a company's intranet that this can be an issue. It becomes an issue of speed. Not the speed of controls execution, but the speed with which the control gets downloaded to an individual's workstation. On a 14,400bps line, a 60KB file takes about 60 seconds to download. If your natively compiled ActiveX control is 120KB, then it will take approximately two minutes for your control to download to the individual's workstation. Granted, it only needs to download once, and as long as you do not update the control or the individual does not delete it, that person will never have to download it again. But if you have more than one control on your HTML document and they all are around 120KB, the person will have to wait quite a while before being able to use your HTML document. You might consider compiling your ActiveX control in p-code rather than native code. By compiling it as p-code, the redundant code that is built into native code will stay within the MSVBVM50.DLL runtime module. The p-code application will stay small, making the download time shorter. Also, the MSVBVM50.DLL will only have to be downloaded once in order for it to be used with your controls.

As you can see, having the ability to compile your applications into native code is not necessarily as advantageous as the debates over the years have made it sound. You should consider your target audience when determining the most effective way to get your application to them.

8

EXTENDING THE IDE WITH ACTIVEX CONTROLS

The standard controls that load as part of your basic Toolbox give you a solid start for building applications. However, in almost every application, you will want to develop some controls that are not directly supported by Visual Basic, or not supported at all by the underlying Windows controls.

The Visual Basic standard controls form a group of controls that provide common components of a Windows standard GUI (for example, command buttons, text boxes, option buttons). In addition, Microsoft provides ActiveX controls with all three editions of Visual Basic. These custom controls provide common components of the Windows 95 standard GUI (for example, sliders, progress bars, Windows 95 status bars).

This chapter includes both an overview of ActiveX controls and a thorough discussion of how to use them to enhance your applications. For more information about a particular ActiveX control that comes with Visual Basic 5.0, you can refer to later chapters in this book. To learn more about creating your own ActiveX controls, refer to Part XIV, "Creating ActiveX Controls and ActiveX Documents."

What Is an ActiveX Control?

Since the advent of Visual Basic 1.0, extending your development environment through custom controls has always been possible. The first type of custom control was a VBX, which stands for Visual Basic Extension. These controls were 16-bit, tied very closely to the Windows 16-bit architecture, and were designed to work very closely with Visual Basic. This dependency made VBX controls difficult to port over to a 32-bit environment such as Microsoft Windows 95 or Microsoft Windows NT, other development environments, such as Microsoft Visual C++, or other platforms, such as MIPS or Alpha environments.

As Microsoft's cross-platform strategy evolved, the technology of OLE (object linking and embedding) version 1.0 emerged. It was originally intended as a tool for creating and working with compound documents. But as the OLE model was first implemented, it quickly became apparent that this model only addressed the tip of the iceberg. A more pressing issue was defining a mechanism for software components to provide services to one another. This led to the creation of Microsoft's Component Object Model (COM). COM laid the foundation for OLE version 2.0. Not only does OLE 2 provide services for compound documents to work together, it also defines a common way to access software services.

OLE controls, or OCXs, were developed in response to the need for simpler, yet more powerful access to the control and OLE functionality. OLE controls can be either 16-bit or 32-bit. The original specification for an OLE control was quite strict, requiring a COM object to implement a large set of interfaces. Each control was required to display its own user interface, send events to a control container, let a container set its own properties, and more. For many controls, this was a lot of overhead. If OLE controls were to be used over the Internet, many of these requirements would not be necessary. Also, the OLE controls would take longer to download because of all the unnecessary code built into the control.

ActiveX controls are based on the OLE control model, but the ActiveX model contains a less rigid set of requirements. The minimum services an ActiveX control needs to provide are support of IUnknown and the capability to self-register. The IUnknown is the most fundamental COM interface. Self-registering means that a control is able to create its own entries in the registry when requested to do so.

In a nutshell, OLE controls are ActiveX controls, but not all ActiveX controls are OLE controls. For more background on OLE, COM, and ActiveX, refer to Section XIV.

ActiveX Controls and the Toolbox

ActiveX controls become an extension to your Visual Basic Toolbox. You use ActiveX controls just as you would use any of the built-in Toolbox controls, such as the Text Box and Command Button controls. When you add ActiveX controls to your Visual Basic IDE (Integrated Development Environment), they become part of your project's Toolbox. Figure 8-1 illustrates the default Toolbox.

You add ActiveX controls to or remove them from the Toolbox by using the Components dialog box, as shown in Figure 8-2. To display the Components dialog box, select Components from the Project menu item on the main menu, right mouse click the Toolbox, and select Components from the context menu, or press the hot key, CTRL+T.

In the Components dialog box, the Controls tab shows within a list box all the available controls that are registered on your system. To add a control to your project, select the check box to the left of the control name. To remove a control, deselect its check box. If the control is in use within your project, which means that the control is placed on a form, you cannot remove it from the Toolbox.

Figure 8-1 Default Toolbox

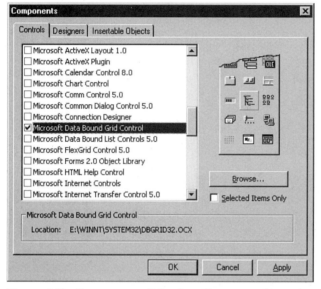

Figure 8-2 Components dialog box illustrating the
available ActiveX controls

NOTE

Unlike previous versions of Visual Basic, in Visual Basic 5.0 you can now resize the Toolbox. If you add
more controls to your Toolbox than can be displayed, they will scroll off the screen. Because of an over-
sight on Microsoft's part, there is no scrollbar.

To add ActiveX controls to the Components dialog box, click the Browse button.
This will bring up an Add ActiveX Control dialog that will allow you to search your
system to locate files with the .OCX filename extension. These files are commonly

installed in your System or System32 directory under your Windows directory. When you add an ActiveX control to the list of available controls, Visual Basic automatically selects its check box in the Components dialog box.

Registering ActiveX Controls

When Visual Basic's Professional and Enterprise Editions are installed, all their ActiveX controls are automatically installed in the System or System32 directory and registered in your system registry.

Frequently during a group development project, you might receive ActiveX controls from other developers. In order for you to use them, their information should be placed in your registry in order for you take advantage of them. To register a control, you can use the REGSVR32.EXE program from a DOS prompt. A dialog box will notify you as to whether you successfully registered the control. For example, if you were registering a credit card ActiveX control someone developed, the command you would type at the DOS prompt would look something like the following:

```
regsvr32 crdtcard.ocx
```

To remove the ActiveX control from your system registry, you would use the /U parameter with the REGSVR32 command. You would type the following at the DOS prompt:

```
regsvr32 /u crdtcard.ocx
```

Another technique to register ActiveX controls is to create a shortcut to REGSVR32.EXE on your Windows 95 or NT desktop. To register a control, simply drag it from the Windows Explorer and drop it on the REGSVR32 shortcut. Please note that since REGSVR32 is a command-line program, it does not have a Windows icon associated with it. In Figure 8-3, the REGSVR32 shortcut is using an icon that can be found in the SHELL32.DLL.

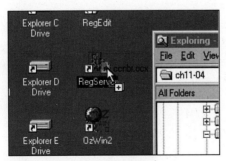

Figure 8-3 Dropping an ActiveX control onto a REGSVR32 shortcut

VBX/16-Bit OCX Controls to ActiveX Controls

Visual Basic 5.0 has the capability to migrate older Visual Basic projects into the 32-bit environment. During this process, the IDE will go through your project and inspect it for any custom controls. If it finds any 16-bit controls, VBX or OCX, the IDE will check your registry to see if you have installed their 32-bit counterparts. If they are installed and registered, the IDE updates your project accordingly. If the 32-bit counterparts are not found, it is because they are either not installed or not registered properly. In this case, the IDE will notify you that there was a problem loading any forms that might be using that control. The notification will ask you if you wish to continue to load the project or not. If you choose to continue to load, then any controls it could not find will be replaced with the PictureBox control. This serves as a placeholder letting you know where a control should have been.

There are a number of VBX and OCX controls that were available in previous versions of Visual Basic that are no longer supported. The controls that are no longer supported are the following:

- AniButton
- Gauge
- Graph
- KeyState
- MSGrid
- Outline
- Spin
- ThreeD

If you upgraded from version 4.0 to 5.0, these controls are probably still located on your system and in your registry. If you need these controls for any reason, they are included on your Visual Basic 5.0 CD-ROM in the \TOOLS\CONTROLS directory. To install these controls, you will need to register them using RegSvr32, which is the 32-bit registration program.

Grouping Controls

In past versions of Visual Basic, when you added controls to your Toolbox, the controls were added to the Toolbox in sequential order. In version 5.0, you can group your controls. This is useful if you're using a lot of controls and would like to keep your controls organized.

To group controls together, create tabs to the Toolbox. To do this, right mouse click the Toolbox and select Add Tab from the context menu. Figure 8-4 illustrates the context menu. A dialog box will appear, and in the text box, type in the name of the tab.

To place controls on a tab, click on the tab to make it the active tab, then add the control to the Toolbox as described earlier. If you wish a control to be moved from one tab to another, you can move it by clicking and dragging. Click the control you wish to move and drag it to where you wish to place it. When dragging from one tab to another, the target tab will become active when the control is placed over it, and you can place it in the target tab. The Toolbox may look like it is placing the controls in some random order, but it isn't. The IDE is placing them in the Toolbox in the order in which you added them to your project. Figures 8-5 and 8-6 portray the Toolbox without and with tabs, respectively.

The Toolbox tabs can be changed at any time. You can change their order, and rename or delete them. To change any of the properties of the tab, select the tab by clicking on it with the right mouse button. From the context menu, as shown in Figure 8-7, you can select to rename or delete a tab, or move its position up or down in the Toolbox. When you delete a tab, all the controls on that tab get moved back to the General tab. When moving the tabs around, the General tab is one tab you cannot change.

The tabs you create reside within the IDE, not the Visual Basic Project file. What this means is that if you add a control to a tab, it will always appear underneath that tab, unless you remove that tab. It also means that when you open a project that does not use any of the controls in a tab, the tabs will not contain any controls. This will be confusing at first, but as time goes on, you will understand how to use this feature more effectively.

Figure 8-4 Toolbox context menu

Figure 8-5 Toolbox without tabs to organize the controls

Figure 8-6 Toolbox with tabs

Figure 8-7 Context menu for the Toolbox tab

Types of ActiveX Controls

There are a couple of types of ActiveX controls: general purpose and data bound.

General Purpose ActiveX Controls

A general purpose ActiveX control is the most common type of ActiveX control you will develop with. They are used to allow for data input, to display information, to provide a method to access Windows properties, and more.

Data Bound ActiveX Controls

A data bound ActiveX control is one that can be linked to a Data or Remote Data (MSRDC) ActiveX control. Data bound ActiveX controls can display field values for the current record in a data set or group of values in a list box or grid. Developers familiar with Microsoft Access are very familiar with the concept of data bound controls.

Data bound ActiveX controls that come with Visual Basic are the following:

■ Masked Edit control

■ Rich Textbox control

■ Data Bound Grid control

■ Data bound list controls (List and ComboBox)

■ FlexGrid control

Creating, Running, and Distributing Executable Files

After you have finished developing your application and have compiled it, the ActiveX controls are needed by your application so that it can work properly outside of the Visual Basic IDE. To make sure it does, you need to distribute those ActiveX controls with your application when you create your distribution diskettes.

When distributing your application, if you forget to include the ActiveX controls or any files that are associated with them, you will receive an error.

Required ActiveX Control Files

Table 8-1 lists all the ActiveX control files that need to ship with your application should you decide to use them.

Table 8-1 ActiveX controls filenames

Control	Required Files	Note
Animation	COMCT232.OCX	Microsoft Windows common control
Communications	MSCOMM32.OCX	Microsoft serial port control
ImageList	COMCTL32.OCX	Microsoft Windows common control

Control	Required Files	Note
Internet Transfer	MSINET.OCX	Retrieves either HTML or a file via HTTP and FTP respectively
ListView	COMCTL32.OCX	Microsoft Windows common control
MAPI	MSMAPI32.OCX	Requires Microsoft Mail, Exchange, or Outlook installed
Masked Edit	MSMASK32.OCX	Provides restricted data entry
MSFlex Grid	MSFLEXGRID.OCX	Replaces the GRID.OCX
Multimedia MCI	MCI32.OCX	Requires a multimedia-based PC
PictureClip	PICCLP32.OCX	For displaying parts of a graphic image
ProgressBar	COMCTL32.OCX	Microsoft Windows common control
RichTextBox	RICHTX32.OCX	Allows advanced text formatting
Slider	COMCTL32.OCX	Microsoft Windows common control
Microsoft Chart	MSCHART.OCX	Graphic charts
Microsoft Tabbed		
Dialog	TABCTL32.OCX	Group tabs to contain controls
StatusBar	COMCTL32.OCX	Microsoft Windows common control
TabStrip	COMCTL32.OCX	Microsoft Windows common control
Toolbar	COMCTL32.OCX	Microsoft Windows common control
TreeView	COMCTL32.OCX	Microsoft Windows common control
UpDown	COMCTL32.OCX	Replaces the SPIN.OCX
Winsock	MSWINSCK.OCX	Provides TCP and UDP connectivity for networking and the Internet

9

MICROSOFT REPOSITORY

Objects, code reusability, information models, and component libraries describe what make up the Microsoft Repository. Rapid Application Development (RAD) tools, Computer Aided Software Engineering (CASE) tools, and structured development life-cycle (SDLC) methodologies like IBM's AD/Cycle and Ernst & Young LLP's Navigator System Series have all been preaching the use of repositories for years. Microsoft, through a joint effort with Texas Instruments, has developed the Microsoft Repository. The Microsoft Repository is part of the Professional and Enterprise Editions of Visual Basic.

To understand what the Microsoft Repository can do, let's first look at what makes a repository. The minimum a repository must do is support the storage of detail about data structures, data elements, and process logic that is cross-referenced to a graphical model. Its intent is to provide shared access to a large number of objects or data elements. It provides a uniform and flexible organization to the shared objects and surrounding systems. Object-oriented databases are the ideal technology for system-wide repositories, because they support object identity, semantic information, complex data types, and version control.

This chapter will serve as an overview of what constitutes a repository, and describe the Microsoft Repository and how you can use it. For more in-depth information about the Microsoft Repository, you can refer to Visual Basic Books Online. Detailed information about the Microsoft Repository is beyond the scope of this book.

Elements of a Repository

A basic prerequisite for software reuse is a code library or software repository. Over the past 10 years, many CASE tools and Integrated Project Support Environments (IPSEs) have recognized the need for repositories but have failed to fully implement them. The repository provides a common place to update information about relationships between objects. Listed below are the benefits of using a repository in application development:

■ Any number of applications may access the repository, supporting extendability.

■ Changes to data are reflected immediately and are available to all applications.

■ Applications are integrated with the repository, not with each other.

■ The repository hides the implementation detail of the shared information and associated access methods.

Since applications are linked together through the repository, the repository becomes the central component resource. This allows the applications themselves to be isolated from one another. And since all these resources are shared, it may provide significant reduction in the complexity of the overall system and the individual application. Figure 9-1 illustrates a high-level look at this concept.

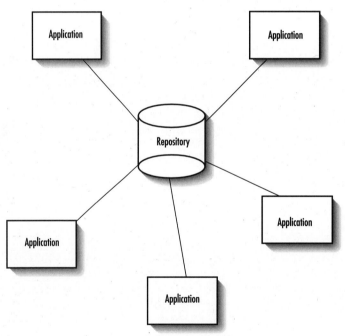

Figure 9-1   Repository-centric development

Of course, with benefits, there are always consequences. The consequences of using a repository are

■ Changes in the repository can have a system-wide impact.

■ You need to provide for concurrency control in the data access layer.

■ There is no way to provide or receive notification of data changes.

■ Accessing shared data may be expensive due to external location.

When a lot of applications use the repository, any changes to a component that is commonly used will be felt by any application relying on that component. This means that testing a repository component becomes a high priority in software development. If a change is made to an object within the repository, it will have a ripple effect through your system. So any changed object should be well thought out and tested outside the repository before its implementation.

Most repositories do not have a mechanism, similar to a version control system like Microsoft Visual SourceSafe, for notifying developers when a change has been made to the system. If an object has been changed or updated, the repository will not notify the application development community. It will be up to your standards team to develop a strategy for deploying information about component changes to the rest of the development community.

Microsoft's Repository

The Microsoft Repository is more than just a mere code database; it is an integrated product upon which tools are built. It has the following characteristics:

■ It contains information to help you maintain your applications across the enterprise.

■ It is extensible.

■ It is object oriented.

■ It contains information models to let you manipulate objects.

■ It supports both COM (Component Object Model) and ActiveX development.

The version of the Microsoft Repository that is included with the Professional and Enterprise Editions comes with some basic information to help you maintain your applications. As you and your organization become more comfortable using the Repository in your development process, you will find that you can develop your own user support tools. Such tools can analyze, report, or present information about your projects, similar to a code cross-referencing tool, but with great detail about the objects used and how they are used with other applications.

Since the Repository is fairly boundless, it can be used to extend existing information about an object, capture information based on your information model, or be a hybrid of both. This flexibility allows you to adapt it to your organization's development methodology, rather than having to alter your methodology to suit its constraints.

The Repository recognizes an object as a unit of persistence, in which the identity, state, and description of the properties are stored as part of the object. For object-oriented programmers, it makes it easy for you to manage your persistent data. If the Repository were merely a database of objects, you would need to be concerned with where the object was located within the database and how it should be used. The Repository handles this for you by the use of its object model engine, which will be discussed later in this chapter.

You can store the classes of your object model in the Repository, retrieve them from it, and use its general data manipulation facilities on them. This is accomplished by defining your data in information models. This will be discussed later in this chapter under "Tool Information Models."

Finally, as with all Microsoft products, it supports COM and ActiveX interfaces to make accessing objects in the Repository more uniform.

Components of the Microsoft Repository

The Microsoft Repository is broken down into the following components:

- The repository database and engine
- The Repository Browser
- Information models

The repository database is a relational database that runs on either Microsoft SQL Server or Microsoft Access. You can query the database directly with SQL queries, but you should not write directly to the database. The repository engine best handles appropriate management of the Repository. It is designed to manage data in the Repository and provide the basic functions to store and retrieve repository objects and the relationships among them.

A function of a repository is its ability to provide a developer with a means of "visualizing data." This is the function of the Repository Browser. As you can see from Figure 9-2, the Repository Browser looks a lot like the Windows registry. This is not by coincidence, because the Windows registry is also a repository. It's the central repository for hardware and software information for your Windows 95 and NT operating system. The Repository Browser will be described in greater detail later in this chapter.

There are two different information models in the Repository. The first is the *Type Information Model* and the other is the *Tool Information Model*. One of the reasons the Microsoft Repository is so extensible is because it is self-describing. The Type Information Model is the fundamental information model used to define all information models that are stored in the Repository. The methods and properties exposed by

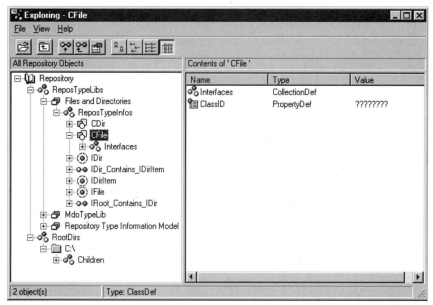

Figure 9-2   Visual Basic's Repository Browser

the various interfaces of the Type Information Model are what you use to define your information model. The Type Information Model is automatically stored in the Repository when you create a repository database.

A Tool Information Model is an object model for a software tool or set of tools. It specifies the types of information of interest, like classes, collection types, interfaces, methods, property definitions, and relationship types, for one or more tools.

Repository Engine Object Model

The Repository Engine Object (REO) Model contains data in the form of objects and relationships. The values of each object are also stored. In a relational database model, you have tables that are related to other tables, and each table stores values. The REO Model is similar to it. For example, you have an object for your development resources, an object for all your projects, and an object for business rules. The objects themselves are separate objects with values stored in them. They are linked together by relationships. Your development resource (for this example we'll refer to him as Bill) works on a business object for amortizing loan information. The business object is included in a project, which is included in an application. Figure 9-3 is a visual representation of this example.

In order for your application to use the REO Model, you will need to establish a connection to it. The REO can be accessed either through automation or COM (Component Object Model). When accessing the REO through automation, you will use methods similar to those you would use to access any other object model. When accessing the REO through COM, you are going to use the Repository's COM Interface

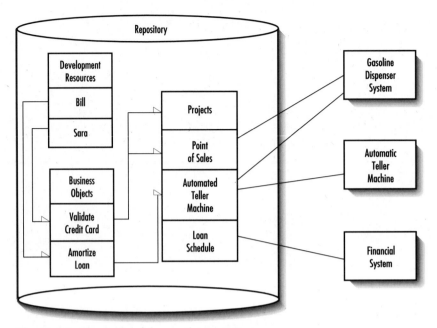

Figure 9-3   Example of data in the Repository

model. Table 9-1 lists the methods and objects you need to use to access the REO through automation. Table 9-2 lists the Repository Transaction object properties and methods used to interact with the REO. Table 9-3 lists the COM Interfaces for the REO, and Table 9-4 lists the COM Interface methods for the IRepositoryTransaction to be used when interacting with the REO.

Table 9-1 Methods and objects to access the REO through automation

Use This...	Type	To Do This...
Create	Method	Create a new repository database and open it
CreateObject	Method	Create a new repository object
Open	Method	Open an existing repository database
Err	Method	Retrieve repository error information

Table 9-2 Repository Transaction object properties and methods

Use This...	Type	To Do This...
Status	Property	Get the transaction status of the repository
Abort	Method	Cancel the currently active transaction

Use This...	Type	To Do This...
Begin	Method	Begin a new transaction
Commit	Method	Commit the active transaction
Flush	Method	Clears uncommitted changes made to the repository database
GetOption	Method	Get various transaction options from the repository
SetOption	Method	Set various transaction options in the repository

Table 9-3 Repository Interface methods to access the REO through COM

Use This...	To Do This...
IRepository::Create	Create a repository database
IRepository::CreateObject	Create a new repository object
IRepository::Open	Open a repository database
IRepositoryErrorQueue	Error handling

Table 9-4 Repository Transaction Interface methods

Use This...	To Do This...
IRepositoryTransaction::get_Status	Get the status of a transaction
IRepositoryTransaction::Abort	Cancel the currently active transaction
IRepositoryTransaction::Begin	Begin a new transaction
IRepositoryTransaction::Commit	Commit the active transaction
IRepositoryTransaction::Flush	Clear uncommitted changes made to the repository database
IRepositoryTransaction::GetOption	Get various transaction options
IRepositoryTransaction::SetOption	Set a transaction option

For more information about the REO and accessing it through automation or COM, refer to the "Repository Reference" section in Visual Basic Online Books.

Repository Browser

The Repository Browser presents a hierarchical view of the contents of the Repository. It was developed through a joint effort between Microsoft Corporation and Crescent Software, a division of Progress Software. As described earlier, a repository needs to display its contents in a visual manner. This is the purpose of the Repository Browser. The Browser is also useful for dynamic data retrieval. As a repository database grows, dynamic data retrieval enables optimal performance and resource utilization.

To load the Repository Browser, you will need to locate the Repository subdirectory under the Visual Basic directory, or find it under the VB directory on your Visual Basic CD. The Repository Browser is the REPBROWS.EXE file within the BIN directory. If the program is not on your hard drive, and you plan to use the Browser, it would be a good idea to copy the Repository directory to your hard drive and then make a shortcut to it.

The Browser itself works on the same model as the Windows Explorer. The windowpane on the left displays the main hierarchical structure of all the objects in the Repository database. The structure starts with the Repository Root, from which all objects, interfaces, and collections descend. The windowpane on the right displays the contents—name, type and value—of a selected branch. The data displayed in the Browser is managed in a transitive pattern:

- Interfaces have collections.

- Collections have repository objects.

- Repository objects have interfaces.

By default, the Repository Browser shows collections in the repository objects. To change which objects are shown in the Repository Objects pane, select the Filters menu item from the View menu. Click on the Type tab on the Repository Filters window to display the interface shown in Figure 9-4. If you would like to see the Repository Interfaces because you are accessing the Repository through COM, mark the Interfaces check box. To show the destination to origin relationship, mark the other check box.

Tool Information Models

One of the two information models that make up the Repository is the Tool Information Model (TIM). It is an object that specifies the types of information that a tool or set of tools can manipulate. For example, a database program can make changes to tables, table columns, and rows. A spreadsheet program can make changes to rows, columns, and cells of a worksheet.

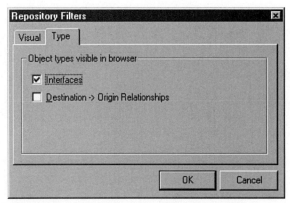

Figure 9-4   Repository Filters dialog window

A TIM is made up of classes, relationship types, interfaces, property definitions, methods, and collection types. A *class* is a template structure that the stored object must conform to. This is similar to designing columns in a database. For example, you develop a Car class. When you store an object representing a car, it can have a make and model number, but it cannot have a dealer's name, because that information would be listed as a relationship type. A *property definition* is a template to which stored property values must conform. This is similar to designing the data type of a column. Using the Car class, when you store the make of a car, you store a name like "Ranger" or "Supra." A *relationship type* is a template to which stored relationships must conform. For example, you create a "manufacturing" relationship type that defines that a manufacturing company makes cars. "Ford" manufactures "Rangers" is a valid relationship type for manufacturing, whereas "Eddie Car" sells "Rangers" would not be valid relationship type for manufacturing. It would be a valid relationship type for "dealer" or "resell." Collections, interfaces, and methods will be described in more detail under "Type Information Models."

The Professional and Enterprise Editions of Visual Basic 5.0 come with a TIM called the Microsoft Development Objects (MDO) Model. It is a TIM specifying the types of data of interest to you, a Visual Basic programmer. It lets you use repository-aware tools to analyze the structure of your Visual Basic projects. It is named MdoTypeLib and is found in the ReposTypeLibs collection. To learn more about how to use MDO, refer to "The Microsoft Development Object Model" section under the Repository Programmer's Guide in the Visual Basic Books Online.

Type Information Models

The Type Information Model is the second information model that makes up the Repository's information model. It is the object model the Repository uses to store tool information models. Since the Type Information Model stores TIM information, type information models consist of classes, interfaces, properties, methods, relationship types, and collection types.

When developing each object through class modules, you expose its properties, collections, and behaviors through *interfaces*. An interface can have a set of class objects that it implements. Conversely, each class can have a set of interfaces that it implements. Using the Car object example as described earlier, a Car object consists of Make and Model. The interfaces it implements would be IMake and IModel. If you had a Motorcycle object, it too could implement the interfaces of IMake and IModel. The user does not need to know how to use separate interfaces for each object, because different objects use the same interfaces. The information is stored in whichever object the application instantiated.

With each interface the Type Information Model exposes, there is a property or properties that it exposes. Using the IModel interface, an example of some properties might be Package and Options. An interface can also expose one or more *methods*. A method for IModel might be Refinance or Lease. Each interface can also expose one or more *collection types*. The relationship type associated with a collection relative to the role of the object determines a collection type. Using the Manufacturing relationship type described earlier and the Car object, a collection type could be defined as "Manufacturer of Cars" or "Cars of Manufacturer"; therefore, a relationship is a member of two collections.

Using the Repository with Visual Basic

As mentioned in the discussion of the Repository Engine Object Model, there are two ways you can access the Repository. You can access it either through automation objects or through COM interfaces. When using the Repository with Visual Basic, there are two type libraries that you can use to reference it in your project. The type libraries are the Microsoft Repository and Microsoft Repository Add-In Type Library. To add these type libraries, select them from the References window, found under the Project menu. Figure 9-5 shows which two type libraries need to be selected.

The Microsoft Repository Type Library exposes the automation and COM objects so you can access the Repository. The Microsoft Repository Add-In Type Library exposes the Microsoft Development Object Model and Repository Add-In Objects (RepVB). If you decide to access the Repository through automation or COM, you are controlling the way information is being manipulated into the Repository. For an analogy, think of accessing the Repository through automation or COM as being similar to accessing a database through ODBC. Using ODBC, you have to handle every aspect of data connectivity, including making the connection, managing the data, updating references, and so on. Accessing the Repository through the Microsoft Repository Add-In Type Library is like accessing a database through the Data Access Object (DAO). You have

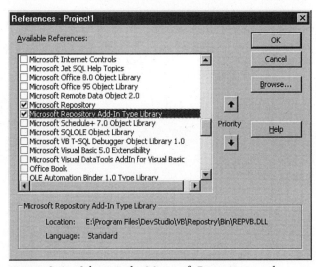

Figure 9-5   Selecting the Microsoft Repository and Microsoft Repository Add-in Type Library from the References window

an object model that helps you manage your connections, manage your data, and so on. You do not have to be concerned with every little detail, because the object model takes care of some of the detail elements for you.

The Object Browser will allow you to view the classes, properties, and methods available to you when you add the Microsoft Repository Type Library, the Microsoft Repository Add-In Type Library, or both. The Microsoft Repository Type Library is labeled RepositoryTypeLib. The Microsoft Repository Add-In Type Library is labeled RepVBTypeLib. Figure 9-6 shows the Project/Library drop-down list box showing the type libraries in the Object Browser.

The two type libraries and their use are described in greater detail in "Using the Repository with Visual Basic" in the Repository Programmer's Guide in the Visual Basic Books Online.

The Future of the Repository

The Microsoft Repository version 1.0 is the first step into a larger development frame of mind. It paves the way for a more integrated method of development. By allowing developers to access objects that are stored within the Repository, it will promote code reusability across the enterprise. Scheduled for the next release of the Microsoft Repository is an object model that will include versions and configurations control. This will allow you to control versions of objects and code within the Repository, and to store system configuration information. The next logical step will be to integrate the Repository into Visual SourceSafe, Microsoft's version control product.

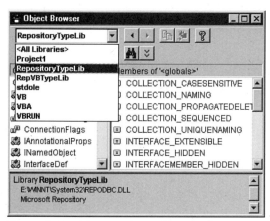

Figure 9-6   Object Browser showing the two type libraries in the Project/Library drop-down list box

As you can see, the Repository is based on something new and something old. Most of all, it will become an integral part of Microsoft's Developer Studio of products as well as an integral part of Microsoft's development strategy. Products such as Rational Software's Rational Rose for Visual Basic is already designed to be integrated with the Repository, and future products from other independent software vendors are in the works. Whether the Repository is right for you currently or in the future, only you can decide. For the most current information about the Microsoft Repository, refer to the Microsoft Repository Web site at http://www.microsoft.com/repository.

10
PROGRAM DESIGN

> **NOTE**
> "I cannot imagine any condition which could cause this ship to founder. I cannot conceive of any vital disaster happening to the vessel. Modern shipbuilding has gone beyond that." *E.I. Smith, captain of the RMS* Titanic *in 1912.*

Whether you are the captain of the most modern vessel or the developer of a mission-critical business system, unless someone has thought out the design of the system thoroughly, you will probably run into a snag of some sort along the way. As the saying goes, the chain is only as strong as the weakest link.

Visual Basic was one of the first tools that brought drag-and-drop components to Windows application development. Prior to Visual Basic, you had to draw your form completely in code. You didn't have any idea how your Windows form would look until you compiled and ran it, and changing the layout was very tedious.

With Visual Basic, you can build a prototype of your application in a matter of hours rather than days. You no longer need to be fluent in the Microsoft Windows Software Development Kit. Visual Basic is commonly referred to as a Rapid Application Development (RAD) tool. But what many RAD developers overlook is the fact that with quick development, they still need a good application design.

There is a lot more to Visual Basic 5.0 than just being a RAD tool. It is now an integral part of Microsoft's client/server and Internet/intranet strategy. This chapter will discuss how to design Visual Basic applications, from standalone executables to ActiveX components to the Internet.

Application Design

If the proper amount of time is not spent on general application development design prior to beginning work on development, you can expect to pay the price down the road. Whether you are developing your application in Visual Basic, C/C++, Pascal, or COBOL, you should take the time to consider application design. Unless you are developing an application like a stopwatch or a calculator, application design is almost always overlooked or scheduled the least amount of time. That is because most programmers look at design as boring, and they would rather start developing as soon as they get their assignments.

There used to be a common myth among developers that users never really know what they want. How could a user possibly know how the system should work? Sometimes this is true, but other times users do know what they want and developers misunderstand the requirements.

Generally, applications that developers start writing just because they want to finish quickly take longer to complete than a properly designed and clearly specified application. Applications in which time was invested up front will be easier to maintain and will work much better than applications that were thrown together hastily. Everyone who has developed applications for any period of time has horror stories to tell about development projects that failed.

Keep Your User Interface Simple

The user interface (UI) is the portion of the application that the user sees. It is critical that the interface be designed properly and that it be intuitive. There are many good books on UI design, so we are not going to teach it in this book. But there are a few rules that you should follow:

■ Keep the design really, really simple. Cutting edge controls are great, but you will be the only one who knows how they work. Unless you enjoy support calls, keep the cool and obscure controls to a bare minimum.

■ Stick to the basics. Do not go overboard on controls moving around, changing sizes, and so forth. Again, keep it simple.

■ Use a role model. One of the advantages of a graphical user interface (GUI) is a common look and feel. By making your applications look like and function similarly to other GUI applications, the time it takes your users to learn your application will be minimal. Look at Microsoft Word, Excel, and other successful applications for GUIs to use as patterns in your applications.

■ Do not use a bunch of crazy colors. Think back to when you used your first word processor. The first document you created probably had bold and italic print everywhere, and ten different fonts displayed on each page. It was probably difficult to read and not very appealing to look at. User interfaces tend to suffer from the same disease. If you are going to use color, make sure it is effective, and get input early in the UI design from other developers and your target audience.

■ There are times when it is desirable and highly appropriate to deviate from the norm. It might be appropriate to completely break the Windows user interface standards. Your task might be to create an application that is designed around a long-standing manual process or form, such as a check writing or employee expense report. It can be advantageous to create an interface that mimics the manual process of the form. It will give your users instant identification and comfort with the application. Even though you might digress from the norm, you should also try to include as many Windows standards as possible, such as tab stops, accelerator keys, and so forth. By incorporating some of the Windows standards, the users will feel comfortable because they will not have to learn a new way of navigating through the application, like getting to the menus or selecting information from a list. Be smart about your UI design, and it will improve the usability of the application. Remember that the UI is the only thing the user will ever see.

Lowest Common Denominator

As part of a development group, your computing power is probably just short of a Cray Supercomputer with super-high-quality graphics and almost unlimited hard drive space. Your application runs at light speed on your system, but when you deploy your application to the enterprise, your application runs as slow as a turtle.

You need to consider your audience. Just because you have the latest and greatest computers in your area, that does not mean the rest of your company does. If you're developing an application for a group that only has VGA display capabilities, then do not develop your UI to be larger than their screen capabilities.

Use a Coding Standard

Another myth among developers is that their code is self-documenting; therefore, there is no need to comment their code. This is very common among programmers of high-level languages. High-level languages often use English-like programming syntax for code. If the code is English-like, why should you have to comment your code? Because what makes sense to you right now might not make sense to you six months from now, or even six minutes from now.

Coding standards are a necessary evil, in the eyes of many developers. They are valuable and help with consistency among developers and between projects. There are quite a few good published coding standards available on the market, and chances are you or your company has already adopted one.

You should choose a coding standard and then implement it. You should not feel it has to be fully defined before the standards are used. It should only take you a day to define variable and control naming standards, as well as the method by which you declare procedures and functions. Other decisions might take longer, such as function naming standards and where it's important for the noun to preface the verb, and so on. The thing to remember is that you should not dwell on the standards or defining them. Choose a small team and let them work on them, but do not spend nine months talking about a coding standard. The goal is to program cohesively; spending millions and millions of hours defining standards will not help you reach that goal.

Always Include an Error Handler

Part of your coding standards should be to include error handlers. Every function should have, at a bare minimum, something that handles and displays errors to the user. Do not wait until the end of your application development to put in error handling. It is very tempting to cut corners to get the project completed, but error handling is best written with each function while the purpose of the function is fresh in your mind. Error handling is typically a hated chore and is not adequately implemented by most developers. However, your application's success can hinge upon how well error handling is written.

A caveat with error handling is that there are times certain functions should not have an error handler at all. This is the rare case when you are calling the function from within another function, and you want any errors to "bubble up" and be handled by the calling function. An example of an error-handling routine is as follows:

```
Function MDIChildCount() As Integer

    On Error GoTo MDIChildCount_Err

    Dim nFrm As Integer
    Dim nChildCount As Integer

    ` Count the number of open MDI child
    ` window forms in this app.
    For nFrm = 0 To Forms.Count - 1
        If Forms(nFrm) Then
            nChildCount = nChildCount + 1
        End If
    Next nFrm

MDIChildCount_Exit:
    MDIChildCount = nChildCount
    Exit Function

MDIChildCount_Err:
    GenericError " MDIChildCount()", Err
    Resume MDIChildCount_Exit

End Function

Public Sub GenericError(sProcedure As String, lErr As Long)
    On Error Resume Next

    MsgBox sProcedure & " " & Error$(lErr) & ". " & CStr(lErr)

Exit_ GenericError:
    Exit Sub
End Sub
```

If an error occurs during the MDIChildCount function, it is going to call the GenericError routine. This routine will display the function or sub procedure the error occurred in along with a description of the error.

Code Review and System Testing

Something that is commonly overlooked in systems development is properly testing a system before deploying it to the user community. In the publishing world, a common adage is "never proofread your own mistakes." This means that the person who wrote or typeset a manuscript should not proofread it. That person will not be as objective in looking over his or her own material as someone else might be. The same holds true with application development. Two things that you should consider as part of your development strategy are code review sessions and system testing.

A code review session is not a new concept to a systems development life cycle (SDLC). Many development methodologies have this as part of the development requirements. The purpose of a code review is not to go through the developer's code line by line. It is designed to ensure that the developer designed a module, component, interface, or application to meet the business specifications. It is better to catch errors in the general structure of an application this early on rather than after the application has been put into production.

With development tools like Visual Basic, it is easy for developers to perform functional testing as they code. This means they can ensure that their code compiles and that it meets the required business specifications. The developer may understand the fundamental business logic he or she is developing for, but might not understand the context in which it will be used in the completed system. Therefore, it is important that someone who understands the system requirements test the application or component(s) before the system gets put into production.

Historically, most systems do not get thoroughly tested before they reach the user community. By performing your own testing first, you can catch a lot of the minor errors and bugs up front. Also, testing can help ensure that the business rules are implemented correctly or are at least functionally correct according to the design specifications.

Regression testing is also something you should look into when developing an application testing strategy. This is usually accomplished by using an automated testing tool like Rational Software Corporation's SQASuite or Mercury Interactive's WinRunner. Regression testing is important because when it comes to maintaining an application, it can help ensure that you did not introduce new bugs into areas of code that were working before. The last thing a developer wants to do is break something that was working just fine.

Holding code review sessions and implementing system testing can help you reduce the embarrassment of distributing a bad system.

Client/Server Concepts

When developing database applications that are going to be distributed throughout your enterprise, you should consider the three-tier client/server architecture concepts and implement them into your projects. Three-tiered architecture defines a strategy in which User Services, Business Services, and Data Services are located and isolated in individual layers to make the application easier to develop and maintain. Recently, many books and articles have been written about three-tiered architecture, such as The Waite Group's *Visual Basic 5 Client/Server How-To* (Waite Group Press, 1997). Figure 10-1 illustrates the three-tiered concept.

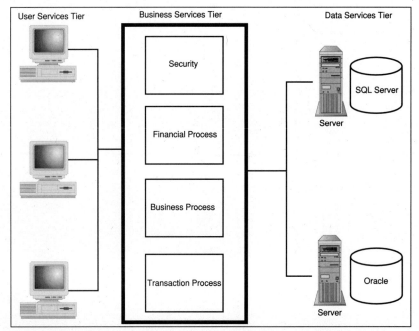

Figure 10-1 Three-tiered architecture depicting the separate layers and how they are linked.

The following is a brief description of three-tiered architecture. It covers the bare minimum, so do not let this be your only investigation into three-tier concepts. You will be well served by spending time finding out more about the intricacies, advantages, and methods of implementation of this architecture.

■ User Services are the visual component and serve as the interface with the user. This tier is the visual link that ties the user to the rest of your application. Its primary function is to retrieve and display information. User Services frequently perform data validation and control the current state of the application in conjunction with the Business Services tier.

■ Business Services are a central repository for functions and classes (in Visual Basic 4.0 and 5.0) that perform calculations and implement actual processing of data. This is where the algorithms perform the "magic stuff." Business Services usually publish an interface so that the User Services component can call a business service as needed. Business Services frequently need to access Data Services to store, change, or retrieve persistent data.

■ Data Services manage persistent data often located in a database such as SQL Server or Oracle. Its primary task is to maintain the correct state and integrity of the data. Data Services interfaces are generally queries or stored procedures that are called directly from the Business Services.

With this defined architecture, these three tiers enable very carefully defined business rules to be developed in either Visual Basic (3.0/4.0) standard modules or in Visual Basic (4.0/5.0) class modules. These business rules should be well thought out and publish very specific functional procedures. These interfaces can be called by any form module or other visual component as needed to perform a task. Remember that the interfaces you publish are links to the User Services tier and should not be changed in any circumstance. A change would require all clients of the service to be notified of the change and require workarounds in the calling code. A better choice is to create another function to implement the change. Then slowly phase out the old procedure, as it is no longer needed.

It is not always sensible, or economically feasible, to do all of your work in a three-tiered concept. Three-tiered architecture can require more planning and work than the normal two-tier applications for a small project. However, you should always strive to adhere to a clean model for breaking out functions that can be encapsulated as business rules and reused at another time. This will take a bit of getting used to, but it will help your applications as you go forward.

The Internet/Intranet

It is difficult to pick up a trade journal or listen to the news without hearing at least one reference to the Internet. Like it or not, it has become part of the business model, and it's here to stay. When considering how your application is going to be deployed, you should keep this in mind. Many companies are trying to use the Internet as a way to extend their own network. For example, say your company has offices all around the world, and most of them are connected to your WAN (wide area network). With your database servers located in New York, transactions from your offices in Sydney, Australia, are probably very slow, and the cost of maintaining their connection to your WAN is probably very high. By using the Internet and with the right security in place (firewalls), you can have that office connect to an Internet service provider (ISP) through an ISDN connection and use the Internet as your data transportation layer.

Lots of companies are considering putting their applications on the Internet as well as running them on their own intranet. They want their applications to have the same look and feel on both. This helps reduce training and it eliminates the need to design two different applications to support two different environments. The Internet and an intranet use the same technology—browsers, TCP/IP, and so forth. The main difference is that the intranet is within a company's security firewall, while the Internet is outside.

Object-Oriented Programming

When developing your applications with Visual Basic, you cannot help but think about objects. Microsoft has begun embracing the idea of object-oriented programming (OOP) throughout all their development products. There are many books on OOP, such as *Doing Objects with Microsoft Visual Basic 5.0* (Ziff-Davis Press, 1997). OOP is also covered later in this book in Section XVII, "New Object-Oriented Programming." One thing to keep in mind about OOP is that a solid understanding of its theory and a structured implementation method is needed in order to make an OOP project a success. There have been too many horror stories of how an OOP project failed because the developers were so caught up with developing the perfect objects that the objects were unusable. OOP is not for everyone, but it can be useful when implemented properly.

Use Version Control Software

When working on large projects, you will usually be developing in teams. Since a Visual Basic project is composed of different modules, it is possible to have developers working on different modules at the same time. You want to make sure that all the developers are using the latest versions of every form and module and that they are not modifying the code someone else is working on. In order to do that, you should consider using version control software, like Microsoft Visual SourceSafe.

Version control software is nothing new to a lot of software developers. It has been used on mainframe and mid-range computers for years. By using version control, you can ensure that only one person is working on a component at a time. You can also share components across applications so that if you make a change to a shared component in one application, the other applications will also see the change. Trying to do this manually without the assistance of software can get out of hand in a hurry.

For information on how to use Visual SourceSafe within Visual Basic, refer to Chapter 103, "Visual SourceSafe."

11

STRUCTURAL ELEMENTS

As you start designing your application, you should consider how your code is going to be structured and modularized. One of the main elements of structured programming involves defining and using self-contained areas of a program called *procedures*. Most often, these procedures perform a single task. Such a procedure can be called any number of times from within a program to perform that task. Coding in this manner provides three distinct advantages. First, once the procedure is coded and debugged, it can be used any number of times without having to recode it. Second, using separate procedures makes a program modular, organizing the code to match the functional structure of the program. This makes it easier to track down and eliminate any logic errors in an application. Finally, because these procedures are entirely self-contained, any variables declared within a procedure become local variables that cannot be changed from outside the procedure. This eliminates any logic errors that might occur if the programmer inadvertently uses the same variable name for two different purposes in different areas of a program.

Another element of structured programming is the way your code is laid out within each procedure or function. It may not seem like much now, but for code readability, maintainability, and reusability, it can make a big difference. This chapter will discuss what procedures are and how to define them within your application.

Programmer-Defined Function, Sub, and Property Procedures

For many years the BASIC languages did not have the capability to define or use procedures. That is no longer the case. In fact, all the events that are linked to objects in Visual Basic are procedures. Visual Basic, along with other modern BASIC languages, includes function and sub procedures. A third type of procedure, the property procedure, was introduced with Visual Basic 4.0. All three types of procedures are used to perform specific tasks defined by the programmer. Functions can return a value, along with performing their task. The new property procedures can create and manipulate custom properties for forms and modules.

Table 11-1 lists the statements used to define and use programmer-defined functions and sub procedures.

Table 11-1 Statements that control functions and procedures

Use This...	Type	To Do This...
Call	Statement	Execute a programmer-defined or DLL sub procedure
Declare	Statement	Inform Visual Basic of external DLL procedures
Exit	Statement	Exit a programmer-defined sub procedure or function
function...End Function	Statements	Define a programmer-defined function
Property Get...End Property	Statements	Return the value of a property
Property Let...End Property	Statements	Set the value of a property
Property Set...End Property	Statements	Set a reference to an object
Sub...End Sub	Statements	Define a sub procedure

Scope of Functions, Subs, and Property Procedures

Like variables, function, sub, and property procedures have scope. The scope of a function, sub, or property procedure defines the procedure's accessibility to other portions of your program and even to other programs as part of an exposed object. These procedures can be placed in a form, a standard module, or a class module. If you declare procedures in a form as Public in Visual Basic 5.0, they can be accessible to other forms and modules. Procedures that are placed in forms no longer need to be in the private domain of that form. They can now be called from anywhere else in your program. Of course, you can still restrict access to a particular procedure or form by declaring it Private.

Defining and Using Programmer-Defined Sub Procedures

Before a sub procedure can be used, you must first define it. You do this with the Sub and End Sub statements. These statements surround the code inside the sub procedure and define the beginning and end of the procedure. Create a sub procedure by typing the Sub keyword followed by the name of the procedure:

```
Sub procedureName
```

Visual Basic will automatically create a new procedure for you, and will terminate the procedure block with the End Sub statement. You can define procedures so that they accept arguments that provide information to act on. If you do not specify the procedure as Public, Private, or Friend, Visual Basic will assume that the procedure is a public procedure. The following is an example of a Private sub procedure that accepts a string argument:

```
Private Sub printMessage(msg$)
    Cls
    Print msg$
End Sub
```

In this example, we have defined a sub procedure that accepts a string. It clears the form and prints the string on the form, then exits the sub procedure. Once the procedure has been designed, it can then be executed by calling it as follows:

```
Call printMessage("Print this!")
```

Alternatively, you can omit the Call keyword and simply have

```
printMessage "Print this!"
```

When you omit the word Call, you must also omit the parentheses around the procedure arguments. For readability purposes, it is recommended that you use the Call statement when executing a sub procedure. In examining code, when you see the Call statement, you will immediately know that you are looking at a sub procedure.

Defining and Using Programmer-Defined Functions

As stated above, a function is very similar to a sub procedure. The big difference is that a function returns a value, while a sub procedure does not. Functions are defined in a manner similar to sub procedures. Instead of using Sub and End Sub statements, however, functions are defined with Function and End Function statements. Create a function in the same way you create a sub procedure: Simply type in the keyword Function followed by the function name. Visual Basic creates a new function block for you, and ends the block with the End Function statement. If you do not specify the procedure as Public, Private, or Friend, Visual Basic will assume that the procedure is a public procedure.

An extra step is also involved in defining a function. Because functions return a value, you need to specify what type of value (single-precision, integer, string, and so on) the function is to return. You also need to tell the function exactly what value to return before exiting. This example shows a function definition:

```
Private Function BTrim (T$) As String
    T$ = Trim(T$)
    For i = 1 to Len(T$)
        If Asc(Mid(T$, i, 1)) = 0 Then
            T$ = Left(T$, i) & Mid(T$, i + 1)
        End If
    Next i
    BTrim = T$
End Function
```

In this example, we've defined a function that accepts one string argument. Because the function is declared As String, we know that it will return a string value. The purpose of this function is to return a copy of its passed argument with both leading and following spaces removed, and without any embedded nulls (ASCII character 0). Notice that the function's code ends with the statement BTrim = T$. Assigning a value to the function name (BTrim) gives the function its return value.

Defining and Using Programmer-Defined Properties

Property procedures are a powerful tool in the Visual Basic programmer's arsenal. Properties attached to objects have always been available as a part of the Visual Basic environment as something you could either set or read. An example of this would be the Enabled property of command buttons or the Font property of text controls. Now the programmer can create custom properties that are part of a module, form, or object. There are three property procedures: Property Get, Property Let, and Property Set.

The Property Get statement creates the name, arguments, and code that provide the value of an object's property. The example below shows a Property Get definition:

```
'setup of example
Private Badswitch as variant            'variant for error number
Private InnerState as Byte              'variant for State value
InnerState = 1                          'set test value of InnerState
Public Property Get MyState (Switch As Integer)
    BadSwitch = 8686                            'set error number

    If Switch => 0 or Switch < 8 Then   'check for valid switch
        MyState = InnerState and 2^Switch 'set property equal to State ⇐
                                          value (true or false)
    Else
        Mystate = CVErr(BadSwitch)      'switch number invalid
    End If
End Property

'test of example
If IsError(Module1.MyState(value)) Then 'if value not between 0 and 7 ⇐
                                        then an error is returned
    MsgBox "ERROR"                      'if value = 0 then a True is returned
Else                                    'any other value returns false for the current
    MsgBox CBool(Module1.MyState(value)) 'value of InnerState.
End If
```

Property procedures are used to manipulate custom properties and to create them. A custom property is a characteristic of an object, usually some sort of data. In Visual Basic 5.0, properties are usually implemented in pairs of procedures, one to set the value of a property and the other to get the value of a property. In the example above, the Property Get procedure illustrates how to get the value of a particular switch (or bit) of the MyState property. If this procedure was in a module called Module1, it would then become a property of that module. It could also be used in a form or in a class module, thus becoming a property of those objects. Used without a matching Property Let or Property Set, the property named in a Property Get statement becomes a read-only property. To allow other objects or projects to manipulate the value of a property, you must provide a matching Property Let or Property Set statement.

The Property Let statement is used to set the value of a non-object's property, like an integer or variable. The example below shows a Property Let definition:

```
Public Property Let MyState (Switch as Integer, SetState as Boolean)
    If Switch => 0 and Switch < 8 then          'make sure Switch is within⇐
                                                bounds
        If SetState then                        'if True then set bit
            InnerState = InnerState Or 2 ^ Switch 'in InnerState.
        Else                                    'if False then
            Innerstate = Innerstate And (255 - 2 ^ Switch) 'clear specified bit.
        End if
```

```
    End If
End Property

Module1.Mystate 1, False                          'clears bit one of MyState ⇐
property
Module1.Mystate 0, True                           'sets bit 0 of Mystate Property
```

In this example, the Property Let procedure illustrates how to set the value of a particular switch (or bit) of the MyState property. If this procedure was in a module called Module1, it would then become a property of that module. It could also be used in a form or in a class module, thus becoming a property of those objects. This example is the matching Property Let to the example used in the Property Get description. Note that they use the same name, MyState, in the examples. This is what links them as a matched pair.

The Property Set is used to set a property's reference to an object. It is very similar to the Property Let procedure. The example below shows a Property Set definition:

```
'declaration of demo
Public Property Set RecordSource(xRS As Recordset)'Sets the object's recordset to the ⇐
caller's
    Set MyRS = xRS                          'recordset then checks for populated ⇐
record set.
    If MyRS.Recordcount <> 0 then           'if populated then move to first record ⇐
and
        MyRS.MoveFirst                      'display it.
        ShowRecord
End Property

'use of Property Set demo
Dim MyRecordset as Recordset
Dim Navigator as New NavControl
Set MyRecordset = Mydb.OpenRecordset(SQL$)      'sets a recordset object
Set Me.Navigator.Parent(Me)                     'sets the navigator's Parent property ⇐
to the form
Set Me.Navigator.RecordSource(MyRecordset)      'sets the object's recordset to the ⇐
form's recordset
```

The Property Set statement allows the application to pass an object reference to another object. When you declare a Property Set statement in a form or module, you are giving that form or module an object property that can be set in code elsewhere. The name you give the Property Set statement becomes the name of the property object of the form or module. In the example above, a Form is opening a Recordset object as MyRecordset and passing the reference of that Recordset to an object called Navigator, which is an instance of a NavControl object class. (NavControl is a user-defined class module and not part of Visual Basic.) When this reference is set, the Navigator object internally sets its own reference to the same Recordset, then calls a procedure that displays the record on the parent form. The capability to create object-level properties is a fundamental part of the object-oriented programming (OOP) capabilities of Visual Basic 5.0.

When developing property procedures, you will usually develop them in pairs, a Property Get and Property Let, or Property Get and Property Set. By default, if you select the Add Procedure menu item from the Tools menu, it will create the Property

Get and Property Let procedure layout for you. If you want to make the property read-only, then you will only use a Property Get. And as it does with all procedures, if you do not specify the procedure as Public, Private, or Friend, Visual Basic will assume that the procedure is a public procedure.

To add a property procedure, you need to be in a Code View mode. Select the module you wish the property procedure to be placed in, and select Add Procedure from the Tools menu. In the Add Procedure dialog box, as seen in Figure 11-1, enter the name of the property you wish to create, select the Property option, and whether you wish to make it a public or private property. You can also determine if you wish to make the value of the property static or not. When you're finished, press the OK button, and a Property Get and Property Let will be inserted into your Code View window, as illustrated in Figure 11-2.

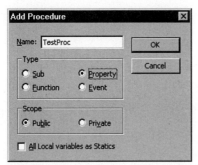

Figure 11-1   Add Procedure dialog defining a property procedure

Figure 11-2   Property Get and Property Let generated from the Add Procedure dialog box

Using Exit to Leave a Procedure

There might be times when you need to exit a procedure before you reach the End Sub, Function, or Property line in your code. To do this, you can use the Exit statement. The Exit statement, followed by Sub, Function, or Property, allows you to immediately exit the procedure at the point it appears in your code. Some developers might think this could lead to badly structured code, because in theory, you should never have to leave a procedure prematurely if the procedure is designed correctly. But there are instances in which this is not the case. For example, in cases where error-handling routines are used, you might use subroutines, and if you do, you need to use the Exit statement to exit the procedure, as illustrated in the example below:

```
Private Sub TestSubject()

    On Error Goto Err_TestSubject

ExitTestSubject:
    Exit Sub

Err_TestSubject:
    Call afx_GenericError("TestSubject", Err)
    Resume ExitTestSubject
End Sub
```

In the example above, the Exit Sub statement is used to leave the procedure when either the program finishes and continues through the ExitTestSubject subroutine label, or if an error occurs and the Resume ExitTestSubject statement is invoked.

Procedures Have Friends

In addition to being able to declare procedures as Public, Private, or Static, you can declare them as *Friend*. A Friend procedure works just like a Public procedure in that it appears to be available to the rest of your application, but it is not available to anyone outside. Essentially, a Friend procedure fits between a Public and a Private procedure. Public procedures can be called from anywhere within the application, as well as by any other application using the application's object. Private procedures prevent applications outside the object from calling the procedure, but also prevent the procedure from being called from within the project in which the class itself is defined. A Friend procedure makes the procedure visible throughout the application, but not to the outside world. Friend procedures can only appear in class modules, and can only modify procedure names, not variables or types. Procedures in a class object can access the Friend procedures of all other class objects in a project. Friend procedures do not appear in the type library of their class and they cannot be late bound.

Where to Define Procedures

Since the introduction of all these procedures in Visual Basic 4.0, many non–object-oriented programmers have been confused as to where the procedures should be defined. Prior to Visual Basic 4.0, it was pretty clear where procedures needed to be defined, because you only had two choices, form or standard modules.

As a basic rule of thumb, if the procedure relates to the user interface, it should be defined in a form module. If the procedure pertains to the events, methods, or properties, it should be defined in a class module. All other procedures, like Windows API calls or procedures that do not relate to an object, should be defined in a standard module. As you get more efficient with these procedures, you will learn which module is appropriate for which procedure. This will become very helpful as you begin to introduce object-oriented development techniques into your project life cycle.

Windows API Declarations

The Microsoft Windows environment includes many functions that are tied directly into the operating system. These functions are referred to as API (Application Programming Interface) functions. Visual Basic provides built-in features that emulate many but not all of the Windows API functions. This section will show you how to call a Windows API function directly from Visual Basic.

Visual Basic 5.0 Professional and Enterprise Editions provide information on the Windows API in several files: WIN32API.TXT (32-bit Windows API functions), and MAPI32.TXT (32-bit Windows Messaging API functions). It also provides an API Viewer for examining the files, enabling you to copy and paste Windows API function declarations into your Visual Basic code.

Here is a sample Windows API function declaration:

```
Declare Function CloseMetaFile Lib "gdi32" Alias "CloseMetaFile" (ByVal hMF As Long) As
Long
```

This declaration tells Visual Basic that we will be using the CloseMetaFile function from the GDI32 library. It also specifies that one long argument is required (passed by value) and that the function returns a long value. You can declare a Windows API function in the general declarations area of a form, standard, or class module. However, it is good practice to declare API functions in a standard module with a name such as APIDECL.BAS, because it is easier to debug API function declarations if they are all located in the same place.

When using Windows API functions, you must be very careful to provide the correct argument data types; otherwise, you may cause a General Protection Fault (GPF) at runtime. Therefore, it is a good idea to save your project frequently.

Object-Oriented Methods

The phrase "object-oriented methods" means several different things to the software development community, as does the term "object-oriented." In the context of this chapter, it will refer to the object-oriented functions that belong to a class. After all, the term "method" means "function that belongs to a class."

Object-oriented programming is not a new idea. It was pioneered about 30 years ago on the Simula-67. To understand object-oriented methods, you should have an understanding of its four key principle concepts. They are

■ Abstraction

■ Encapsulation

- Inheritance
- Polymorphism

Abstraction

Abstraction is the process of eliminating the unimportant details of an object. This way, only the appropriate characteristics that describe an object remain. This results in data abstracts. All mainstream programming languages provide a way to store pieces of related data together. This helps make complex systems easier to deal with. In a way, you can think of data abstraction the way you think of data normalization, which is the act of removing redundancy within a database design. Through data abstraction, when you remove redundant data, you are removing unnecessary information about the object that does not pertain to it.

Encapsulation

Encapsulation is a concept that is closely related to abstraction, because it allows for the isolation of an object's internal complexity from the object's use and operation within the greater application. It is also the capability to contain and hide information about an object's internal implementation.

An ActiveX control is a good example of encapsulation. A lot of its functions and operations are hidden from you. When you modify its properties, some of the operations might act differently from the default method. You as a developer don't need to be concerned with the exact method in which the operation executes, only that the result is accurate according to your input and the properties you set. As when you validate a credit card number, when you change the property of a control or access a method, you don't have to know exactly how it is accomplished, just as long as you receive the results.

Inheritance

Inheritance is the capability to make new, more versatile objects from existing objects without changing the original object. This allows you to build more complex systems based on existing components. Inheritance in object-oriented programming is much like inheritance in human biology: it is what you acquire from past generations. For example, with automobiles, the base object states that it has four wheels, a frame, a chassis, a motor, and so on. As you built upon that object, you can refine the objects as sports car, truck, and passenger vehicle. These objects inherit all the components of the "automobile" object. You can further define each object into more complex objects, and they will all inherit the original characteristics of the objects on which they were built. The same holds true with programming objects.

NOTE
Visual Basic, unlike other object-oriented programming languages, does not support inheritance. This is important to note because other OOP languages use inheritance to provide polymorphism.

Polymorphism

Polymorphism means that many different objects might contain methods that have identical names, such as a GetSecurity method. Even though they may do the same thing, the way each method is implemented can be different. Through polymorphism, you are allowed to reuse the same name for a related concept on different types of objects. The system will choose which method you are trying to use either by "early binding" or "late binding." In versions of Visual Basic prior to 4.0, late binding is the common way of accessing objects. Late binding occurs when Visual Basic cannot determine at compile time which object a method belongs to. The following code is an example of late binding:

```
Public Sub GetSecurity(ByVal oEmployee As Object)
    Dim nLName As Integer
    Dim nSSN As Integer
    Dim rc As Integer

    nLName = CInt(oEmployee.LastName)      ' Late Bound
    nSSN = oEmployee.SSN                   ' Late Bound

    ' Calculate Security CheckSum
    rc% = CalcSecurity(nLName + nSSN)
    If rc% = True Then
        Debug.Print "Has Authority"
    Else
        Debug.Print "Has No Authority"
    End If
End Sub
```

In the above example, the oEmployee.LastName and oEmployee.SSN are considered late bound because oEmployee, which is the object, needs to be determined at runtime. This could affect your application's performance, because it needs to figure out the object's structure before proceeding.

Early binding means that Visual Basic will know what the object's structure is at compile time and can determine if the properties and methods you are accessing are valid. The following code example will be almost identical to the one you just looked at, with one exception: rather than oEmployee being defined as an Object, it will be defined by the object's name.

```
Public Sub GetSecurity(ByVal oEmployee As Employee)
    Dim nLName As Integer
    Dim nSSN As Integer
    Dim rc As Integer

    nLName = CInt(oEmployee.LastName)      ' Early Bound
    nSSN = oEmployee.SSN                   ' Early Bound

    ' Calculate Security CheckSum
    rc% = CalcSecurity(nLName + nSSN)
    If rc% = True Then
        Debug.Print "Has Authority"
    Else
        Debug.Print "Has No Authority"
    End If
End Sub
```

By defining the object by its name, Visual Basic is able to resolve which object is being used and can prepare the structure ahead of time. This can provide improved performance, because Visual Basic will not have to resolve anything up front, the way it did with a late bound object.

12

PROCESS CONTROL

One of the reasons computers are more than just advanced calculators is that they have the capability to control the order and flow of the execution of their operations. This control over execution is called process control. Process control can be broken down into three main elements: branching, iteration, and conditional execution.

Branching is the most basic of the process control elements. It involves simply jumping from one area of code to another. In Visual Basic there are two types of branching. The first of the two merely jumps to another part of your program. It does nothing to help you return to your original starting point. The second type saves its place in the program's code before branching. This allows the program to return to where it came from once its task is finished.

Iteration involves the repetition of program instructions. There will be many times in your programs when you will wish to execute a set of instructions a number of times, or continually while (or until) a certain condition exists. Visual Basic provides three techniques for performing iteration.

Conditional execution allows your programs to execute a set of instructions only if a certain condition is true. This gives your programs the ability to make decisions based on the values of data.

This chapter will cover how the three forms of process control are used with your Visual Basic applications.

Branching

Branching is the direct transfer from one process to another process within your application. There are two forms of branching:

- Unconditional branching, where the process transfers control to another process.

- Conditional branching, where the process transfers control to another process based on a value it is testing for.

Table 12-1 lists the statements available in Visual Basic that perform branching.

Table 12-1 Statements that perform branching

Use This...	Type	To Do This...
Gosub...Return	Statements	Unconditional branch to a subroutine then return
Goto	Statement	Unconditional branch without return to a portion of code
On...Gosub	Statements	Branch based on a supplied numeric value, then return
On...Goto	Statements	Branch based on a supplied numeric value without return

Visual Basic has two statements that perform unconditional branching: Gosub and Goto. The Gosub statement also branches to a specified label, but it saves its place before doing so. Your program can then return to its original position in the code by executing a Return statement. You will probably never need to use a Gosub statement in your Visual Basic programs. Subprocedures and user-defined functions offer a more powerful and elegant alternative; Gosub has been retained only for backward compatibility with older BASIC programs.

The Goto statement branches to the specified label. It does not save its place before branching, so once it has branched, there can be no going back. The Goto statement is generally considered an unstructured command, and its use generally obscures the clarity of your programming. You should in almost all cases use structured programming constructs (like subprocedures, user-defined functions, and loops) rather than resorting to the Goto statement. The Goto statement, however, is commonly used for branching in error-handling code. For examples of this, refer to Chapter 30, "Error Handling."

Both Gosub and Goto must specify a label that exists in the same procedure as the branching instruction. A label is a unique name that ends with a colon. For example:

```
Goto lbl_Error
```

jumps execution to the part of the program that begins with the label lbl_Error. (Visual Basic also allows you to use line numbers instead of labels. Line numbers are a cumbersome feature of early versions of BASIC and are seldom used today.)

The two conditional statements in Visual Basic are the On Gosub and On Goto statements. These statements put a twist on the branching commands Gosub and Goto. Instead of specifying one label as the target of the branch operation, you supply these statements with a numeric value and a list of labels. Depending on the value supplied, the program will branch to one of the listed labels:

```
On winner Gosub First, Second, Third
    :
    :
First:
    B$ = "Your horse won!"
    Prize = 1000 * wager
Return

Second:
    B$ = "Your horse placed!"
    Prize = 100 * wager
```

```
Return

Third:
    B$ = "Your horse showed!"
    Prize = 10 * wager
Return
```

Note that the On Gosub and On Goto statements automatically assign sequential integers to the specified variable. That is, in the above example, when winner is 1, the instructions at the label First: are executed; when winner is 2, the instructions at Second: are executed; and so on. On Goto works in the same way, except that there is no return from the branch.

Conditional Execution

Conditional execution defines a set of instructions that will execute only if a certain condition (defined by you) is True. In other words, conditional execution allows your program to make decisions and perform specific tasks based on the outcome of these decisions. Table 12-2 lists statements that perform the conditional execution.

Table 12-2 Statements that perform conditional execution

Use This...	Type	To Do This...
If...Then...Else...	(Single-line If)	Perform a simple conditional execution of code
If...Then...Elself...	(Multiple-line If)	Perform a complex conditional execution of code
Select Case...	Statements	Perform conditional execution based on the value of one expression
Stop	Statements	Halt execution for debugging

If...Then...Else... and If...Then...Elself...

The simplest of Visual Basic's decision-making statements is the single-line If statement. This statement simply says, If the condition is True, do a task. Optionally, you can also specify a second task for the If statement to perform when the condition is False: If the condition is True, do a task; otherwise do a different task. The following is an example of a single-line If statement:

```
If A = B Then C = True Else C = False
```

The single-line If statement is limited to one line of instructions. To execute a whole block of instructions based on the outcome of a condition, use a block If statement. This statement requires you to end the statement with an End If. The block If statement allows you to execute an entire block of code based on the outcome of the If:

```
If GarmentColor = Green Then
    GreenShirts = GreenShirts + 1
    Cost = Cost + 1
Else
    RedShirts = RedShirts + 1
    Cost = Cost + 2
End If
```

The multiple-line If statement lets you group seemingly unrelated tests in the same If statement:

```
If GarmentColor = Green Then
    GreenShirts = GreenShirts + 1
    Cost = Cost + 1
ElseIf GarmentSize = Large Then
    LargeShirts = LargeShirts + 1
End If
```

In this example, the variable GarmentColor is tested to see if it equals the value in Green. If it does, the block of code under the test executes. If it does not, the GarmentSize variable is tested.

Select Case

If you need to test a single variable for several different values, you can use the Select Case structure. The Select Case structure makes many tests on the same value. Most programmers prefer to use Select Case rather than a multiple-line If because they feel it is more readable. The following examples show a multiple-line If statement and the equivalent Select Case statement:

```
If ThisColor = Blue Then
    CtrBlue = CtrBlue + 1
ElseIf ThisColor = Red OR ThisColor = Green Then
    CtrNotBlue = CtrNotBlue + 1
Else
    CtrOther = CtrOther + 1
End If

Select Case ThisColor
    Case Blue
        CtrBlue = CtrBlue + 1
    Case Red, Green
        CtrNotBlue% CtrNotBlue% + 1
    Case Else
        CtrOther = CtrOther + 1
End Select
```

The above examples are functionally equivalent. However, the Select Case is clearer and easier to understand. The Select Case statement can also be used as a substitute for On Gosub and On Goto. Below is what an On Gosub conditional statement would look like and what it would look like using Select Case.

```
On winner Gosub First, Second, Third
    :
    :
First:
    B$ = "Your horse won!"
    Prize = 1000 * wager
Return

Second:
    B$ = "Your horse placed!"
    Prize = 100 * wager
Return
```

```
Third:
    B$ = "Your horse showed!"
    Prize = 10 * wager
Return

Select Case winner
    Case 1
        B$ = "Your horse won!"
        Prize = 1000 * wager
    Case 2
        B$ = "Your horse placed!"
        Prize = 100 * wager
    Case 3
        B$ = "Your horse showed!"
        Prize = 10 * wager
End Select
```

The Select Case structure is both clearer and shorter than the unstructured On...Gosub statements.

Iteration

Visual Basic, as with all programming languages, provides the user with a plethora of ways of looping through processes. This section will describe these looping statements, shown in Table 12-3.

Table 12-3 Statements that perform iteration processes

Use This...	Type	To Do This...
Do...Loop	Statements	Repeat a group of instructions until or while a condition is True
Exit...	Statements	Exit from a specific block of code
For...Next	Statements	Repeat a group of instructions a specified number of times
For Each...Next	Statements	Repeat a group of instructions for each member of an array or collection
With...End With	Statements	Refer to object members without repeating parent name
While...Wend	Statements	Repeat a group of instructions while a condition is True

Loops

There are four types of loop instructions you can use to perform iteration in Visual Basic. These are For...Next, For Each...Next, Do...Loop, and While...Wend. Each kind of loop has its own features and is useful in particular circumstances.

The For...Next Loop

The For...Next loop performs a block of instructions a set number of times. You specify as arguments to the For statement a starting value, an ending value, and a numeric variable name that will be used as a counter. When the For statement is first encountered, the counter variable is initialized to the starting value. The block of code is then executed until the counter variable exceeds the ending value. Figure 12-1 shows the flow of a For...Next loop. The following statements count from 1 to the value of Num%, summing the numbers in between:

```
Total = 0
For N% = 1 To Num%
     Total = Total + N%
Next N%
```

Note that you can specify that the counter be incremented by a number other than 1, by using the Step keyword. You can decrement a counter by using a negative value as the Step value. The following loop counts downward from the value of Num% to 1 by threes.

```
For N% = Num% To 1 Step -3
```

The For Each...Next Loop

The For Each...Next loop performs a block of instructions just like the For...Next loop, except that it repeats a group of statements for each element in a collection of objects or an array rather than repeating the statements a specified number of times. This approach is very useful when you don't actually know how many elements are in a collection or an array. Figure 12-2 shows the flow of a For Each...Next loop. The loop starts with the first element in the collection or array. The block of code in the structure is repeated once for each element. This is an example of how to use this new structure with an array:

```
Dim MyArray(12) As String
Dim element As Variant
Dim x%
For Each element in MyArray()
    MyArray(element) = "Hello"
Next element
```

Another example using a collection is the following:

```
Dim MyDS As Recordset
Set MyDs = MyDB.CreateRecordset("Authors")
For Each Field in MyDS
    Combo1.Additem MyDS.Field.Name
Next Field
```

This example fills a combo list with the names of each field in the Authors table. When using the For Each...Next structure, certain limitations must be observed:

■ For collections, the element can only be a variant variable, a generic object variable, or an object listed in the Object Browser.

■ For arrays, the element can only be a variant variable.

■ An array of the user-defined type cannot be used with the For Each...Next structure.

Varieties of the Do...Loop Structure

The Do...Loop is the most versatile and hence the most useful loop structure in Visual Basic. The statements that comprise a Do...Loop allow you to repeat a block of code as long as a certain condition (which is defined by you) exists, or until a certain condition becomes True. It also lets you specify whether to check the condition at the top or

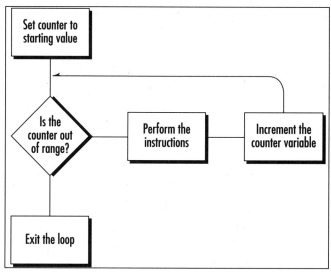

Figure 12-1   The flow of a For...Next loop

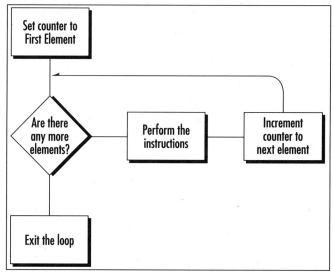

Figure 12-2   The flow of a For Each...Next loop

bottom of the loop. This gives you four unique styles of loops: Do While, Do Until, Loop While, and Loop Until.

Both the Do Until and Do While loops check the condition at the top of the loop. This means that if the exit condition is met before the loop is entered, the instructions within the Do...Loop will not execute. The following are examples of the Do While and Do Until loops:

```
Open "TEST.DAT" For Input As #1
Do Until EOF(1)
     Line Input #1, A$
Loop

Open "TEST.DAT" For Input As #1
Do While Not EOF(1)
     Line Input #1, A$
Loop
```

These two loops are actually equivalent: Both make sure that the end of the file has not been reached before attempting to input any data. Since reading beyond the end of a file generates an error, it is important that checking be done at the top of the loop. Figure 12-3 shows the flow of processing in the Do Until and Do While loops. Notice that the only difference is that the Do Until loop checks whether the condition is False, and the Do While loop checks whether the condition is True.

The Loop Until and Loop While loops check the exit condition at the end of the loop, so the statements within the loop are always executed at least once. The following are examples of these styles of loops:

```
Do 'this is a Do Until loop:
     'Code within loop will repeat until the user enters something
     Person$ = InputBox("Please enter your name")Person$ = Trim(Person$)
Loop Until Person$ > ""

Do 'this is a Do While loop:
     'Code within loop will repeat as long as the variable
     'Person$ is empty
     Person$ = InputBox("Please enter your name")
     Person$ = Trim(Person$)
Loop While Person$ = ""
```

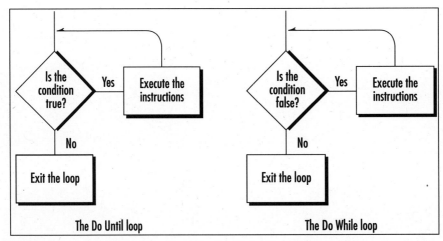

Figure 12-3   The flow of the Do...Until and the Do...While loops

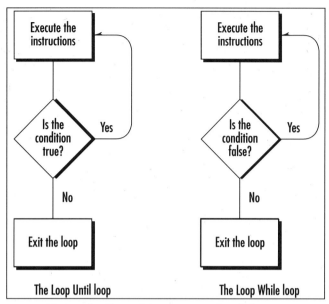

Figure 12-4   The flow of the Loop Until and the Loop
While loops

The flow of these loops is illustrated in Figure 12-4. Notice that here, too, the only
difference between the loops is that Loop Until checks whether the condition is False,
while the Loop While loop checks whether it is True. In both cases, the code executes
once before the check is made, since at least one iteration is needed for the user to
enter the data.

The While...Wend Loop

The last of the four types of loops is the While...Wend loop. This loop structure is left
over from older BASIC languages. It performs the same function in the same manner
as the Do While loop:

```
Open "TEST.DAT" For Input As #1
While Not EOF(1)
     Line Input #1, A$
Wend
```

Exiting Loops

You may have a situation that calls for exiting a loop prematurely. For example, this
loop counts up the winnings in a game. The user has a slight chance of "breaking the
bank," which requires separate handling:

```
msg$ = "Congratulations, you've won!"
For i = 1 to numChances
     winnings = Int(Rnd * 1000)
     If winnings = 999 Then
```

continued on next page

continued from previous page

```
        Beep
        totalWinnings = 1000000
        msg$ = "Congratulations! You've broken the bank!"
        Exit For
    End If
    totalWinnings = totalWinnings + winnings
Next i
Print msg$
Print "Your total winnings are: " _
    & Format(totalWinnings, "$###,###,###")
```

This iterates through the loop numChances number of times. It normally just adds a random amount of money into the totalWinnings. One time in a thousand it will "break the bank." After setting totalWinnings to a million dollars, execution resumes at the line immediately following the Next statement, which in this case is Print msg$.

You may use Exit For in For...Next loops and For Each...Next loops. You can use Exit Do in Do...Loops and Do...While loops.

With...End With

The With...End With statement allows you to perform a series of operations on an object's properties or procedures without having to specify the object's name for each property. The following example illustrates the With...End With statement:

```
With MyNavigator
    .DbName = "c:\Biblio.Mdb"
    .RecordSource = "Authors"
    .State = "Mystate"
End With
```

This code sets the specified properties of the MyNavigator object. You can also nest With...End With statements by placing With...End With blocks within each other. If, while nesting the With...End With statements, you refer to an outer With...End With block that is masked by an intervening With...End With, you must provide a fully qualified object reference to the object:

```
With MyObject
    .centered = yes
    .border = 3
    .top = 100
    With Style
        .3d = true
        .Opaque = true
        'second and subsequent nests need full path to object
        With Myobject.Style.Font
            .Name ="Arial"
            .Size = 12
        End With
    End With
End With
```

This statement reduces the need to type out the object's path for every property setting and encourages the programmer to set the object's properties in one place, which makes for more readable code.

13

PROGRAM FLOW

Visual Basic is an event-driven language. An event is an action recognized by a form or control, such as a mouse click or a keystroke. Event-driven languages like Visual Basic let the user control program flow. The application spends most of its time idly waiting for the user to act on it. When the user does something (or the system causes an event, such as a shutdown message), the program responds to that action. This is the essence of a graphical user interface: Create a flexible environment that the user can control.

Contrast this approach with traditional programming methods. A traditional program starts at the beginning and controls all aspects of program flow. The user can certainly give the program input, but cannot alter program flow other than in limited, narrowly defined ways. Traditional programming languages have usually had inflexible user interfaces because of this approach.

Each object in Visual Basic has a number of specific events it recognizes. You can make your application respond to events by writing code in an event procedure. Much like regular sub procedures, event procedures contain code that performs specific actions. For example, clicking a command button with the mouse triggers its Click event; code you write for this event procedure might confirm that the user wants to end the application. Although each control recognizes a predefined set of events, you determine if they respond to those events by writing code in the event procedures. Each object has its own set of event procedures that are independent of any other objects in the application.

Visual Basic recognizes 58 different events. This chapter summarizes those events.

Event-Driven Programming

A hurdle over which all non-Windows programmers need to jump is working with the event-driven programming model. In traditional or "procedural" applications developed in languages like COBOL, the application itself controls which portions of code execute and in what sequence. Execution starts with the first line of code and follows a predefined path through the application, calling procedures as needed. This type of development is also known as "top-down programming," because it is easy to determine where a program starts and stops. There is only one entry point and usually only one exit point.

In an event-driven application, the code does not follow a predetermined path. It executes different code sections in response to events. Events can be triggered by the user's actions, by messages from the system or other applications, or even from the application itself. The sequence of these events determines the sequence in which the code executes; therefore, the path through the application's code differs each time the program runs.

Because you can't predict the sequence of events, your code must make certain assumptions about the "state of the world" when it executes. When you make assumptions about the state of an object or control, you should structure your application in such a way as to make sure that the assumption will always be valid. An example might be that you want to make sure a text field contains a valid entry before allowing the user to submit his or her request. You will want to disable the Submit or OK button if a valid entry is not in the text field.

You can also have your code trigger events during their execution. For example, when you type a new value into the text box, the Change event gets triggered if there is code within the procedure. Within the Change event procedure, you can have it call other procedures and events. By adding code to the Change event, any time the text value changes, the Change event will trigger, whether the user changed the value or not. It could change because the user entered in a new value or because a value was retrieved from a database query. Either way, the Change event will trigger.

If you assumed that the Change event would only be triggered by user interaction, you might see unexpected results. As described in the above example, the Change event may occur because the value was changed as the result of information retrieved from the database. You might not have wanted or expected the Change event to be triggered other than by user input, but because of the nature of the Change event, there is no way to prevent it from being triggered by other things as well. It is for this reason that it is important to understand the event-driven model and keep it in mind when designing your application.

Event Procedures

An event procedure is different from other procedures in a couple of respects. Event procedures are triggered by an event associated with a control or form, while other procedures are called by another process. All event procedures are provided by Visual Basic and are associated with a particular control or form. A reference to an event begins with the name of the object that triggers the event, followed by an underscore (_) and the name of the event:

```
Private Sub Command1_Click ()
    MsgBox "You've just clicked Command1"
End Sub

Private Sub textPatientName_GotFocus ()
    textPatientName.BackColor = QBColor(7)
    textPatientName.ForeColor = QBColor(1)
```

```
    textPatientName.SelLength = Len(textPatientName.Text)
End Sub
```

Forms are the exception: Rather than using the name of the form, the event subroutine uses the keyword Form (or MDIForm for the main MDI form of an application).

```
Private Sub Form_Load ()
    List1.AddItem "Red"
    List1.AddItem "Blue"
    List1.AddItem "Green"
End Sub

Private Sub MDIForm_Load ()
    Form1.Load
    Form2.Load
    Form3.Show
End Sub
```

Many events pass arguments to the procedure that your code can use. For example, the MouseDown event passes information about which mouse button was pressed, which control keys (if any) were held down, and exactly where the mouse is positioned:

```
Private Sub Picture1_MouseDown (Button As Integer, Shift As Integer, X As ⇐
Single, Y As Single)
    If Button = LEFT_BUTTON Then            'button argument checks which⇐
mouse button
        Picture1.Line (x1!, y1!)-(X, Y)     'X and Y are current mouse ⇐
position
    End If
End Sub
```

Control arrays have just one set of event procedures for the entire array. This makes it easy to write generic code that applies to related controls that are grouped in the array. Event procedures in control arrays always have an Index argument that determines which control in the array triggered the event. This next example shows a menu control array with four elements. The Select Case uses the Index property to take appropriate action depending on which menu choice the user clicked.

```
Private Sub menuWindowArrange_Click (Index As Integer)
    Select Case Index
        Case 0: MDIForm1.Arrange vbCascade
        Case 1: MDIForm1.Arrange vbTileHorizontal
        Case 2: MDIForm1.Arrange vbTileVertical
        Case 3: MDIForm1.Arrange vbArrangeIcons
    End Select
End Sub
```

Finally, event procedures are normally stored within form modules only. Because event procedures have a one-to-one correspondence with an object on a form or the form itself, they cannot exist outside the form module. The event procedure can, of course, call other procedures within or outside the form module, as illustrated in the following code:

```
Private Sub Form_Load
    Me.WindowState = vbNormal
    Call CenterForm(Me)
End Sub
```

The above code, called the forms Load event, first sets the form window to a non-maximized state, then calls a sub procedure that centers the form within your screen. Using an option new to Visual Basic 5.0, you can now create your own event procedures and assign them to a form module. This is done through the use of the WithEvents keyword. The use of the keyword and how to create your own event procedures is described in greater detail in Chapter 34, "Events."

You should also note that an event procedure is always in the form of a sub procedure. It can never be a function. If you try to make it a function you will receive an error.

Visual Basic Events

Visual Basic 5.0 has 58 events, which are listed in Table 13-1. Some events are recognized by many objects, some by only a few or even just one object. These events are covered in detail in various chapters throughout this book.

Table 13-1 Visual Basic events

Event	Meaning
Activate	Form just received focus
AfterAddFile	File added to current project
AfterChangeFileName	Filename changed
AfterCloseFile	File closed
AfterRemoveFile	File removed from project
AfterWriteFile	File saved
BeforeLoadFile	Before a file is added
Change	Control's value just changed
Click	Control was just clicked
ConnectAddIn	Add-in added to Visual Basic
DblClick	Control was just double-clicked
Deactivate	Form just lost focus
DisconnectAddIn	Add-in removed from Visual Basic
DoGetAddFileName	User selected Add File
DoGetNewFileName	User saving file or project
DoGetOpenProjectName	User opening a new project
DragDrop	Control was just dropped
DragOver	Another control was just dragged over this control
DropDown	User clicked the down arrow on combo box
Error	Externally caused database error
GotFocus	Control just received the focus
Initialize	Object created
KeyDown	User just pressed a key
KeyPress	User just pressed a key

Event	Meaning
KeyUp	User just released a key
LinkClose	DDE link just closed
LinkError	DDE link has an error
LinkExecute	DDE link just received an external command
LinkNotify	DDE link data has changed in a Notify style link
LinkOpen	DDE link has just opened
Load	Form has just loaded
LostFocus	Control just lost focus
MouseDown	User just pressed mouse button
MouseMove	User just moved mouse
MouseUp	User just released mouse button
ObjectMove	OLE object moved or resized
OLECompleteDrag	Source object is notified that drop action occurred
OLEDragDrop	Source object is dropped onto a control
OLEDragOver	Source object was just dragged over this control
OLEGiveFeedback	Provides a drag icon feedback to the user
OLESetData	Sets data when a Source object is dropped
OLEStartDrag	Sets the type of data format and drop effect the source object supports when drag is started
Paint	Control was just uncovered
PathChange	Path property just changed
PatternChange	Pattern property just changed
QueryUnload	Form is about to unload
Reposition	Current record just changed
RequestChangeFileName	User specified new filename
RequestWriteFile	Prompt before project saved
Resize	Form just changed size
RowColChange	Grid's active cell just changed
Scroll	Scrollbar thumb just moved
SelChange	New cell selected in grid
Terminate	Object was destroyed
Timer	Timer interval finished
Unload	Form unloading
Updated	OLE object changed
Validate	Current record about to change

You have two ways of seeing an event procedure's code. You can either double-click on an object or form, which will open the Code window and display the default event procedure, or select an object or form and press the F7 key.

Order of Events

The order in which events get triggered in a Windows environment is one of the things traditional top-down developers have a difficult time grasping. Even seasoned Windows developers sometimes forget the order of execution.

When you're debugging your code, it is common to "step through" the code line by line or by procedure ([F8] or [SHIFT]+[F8], respectively). Using breakpoints to stop logic is also a common technique used to find out what events are executed. Unfortunately, none of these three methods always paints a clear path of the event order. For example, in order for a form's Activate event to trigger, the form needs to be the topmost active form. If you step through the code window, the Form1_Activate event will never trigger, because the code window is the topmost active form.

Another misleading order of events that a lot of beginners overlook occurs when you reference a control on a form that is not yet loaded into memory. The form's Load event first must trigger to load the form into memory before the code concerning the control can execute. In some development instances, this might not be a problem. For example, suppose you have a procedure that retrieves a substantial amount of data, and the retrieved information populates a form's text boxes. The form is not loaded in memory yet. When the control on the form is referenced, the form must first load into memory so the application will know where to put the information. This causes the form's Load event to trigger. If there is a lot of code in the Load event, the user may think that the system is slow and inefficient. In reality, the problem is that an additional step, the form's Load event, first must occur before the step that populates the form can execute. One solution is to use the Load statement before referencing the control. Figure 13-1 illustrates a form's Load event triggering within the middle of a process. Figure 13-2 shows the flow of events with the form being explicitly loaded.

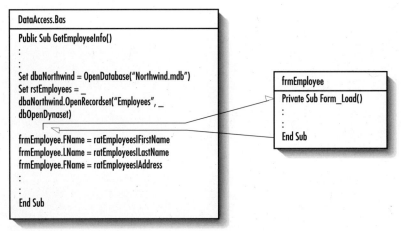

Figure 13-1 Referencing a form before it is loaded

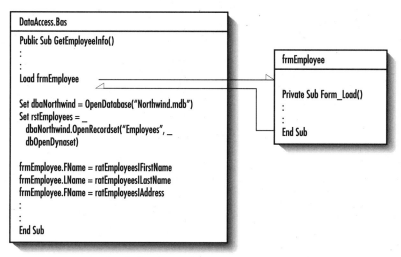

Figure 13-2 Explicitly loading a form
before referencing it

DoEvents Function

If your event procedure's code causes an event to happen, when will that event occur? Will it necessarily occur before the subsequent lines in the calling procedure? This is not a trivial question, because Windows is a multitasking, event-driven environment. You may be depending on the relative timing of certain event procedures with respect to certain lines of code.

The DoEvents function passes control to the operating system kernel. Control is returned after the operating system has finished processing the events in its queue and all keys in the SendKeys queue have been sent. This does not cause the current application to give up the focus, but it does enable background events to be processed. DoEvents returns an integer representing the number of open forms in standalone versions of Visual Basic. DoEvents returns zero in all other applications.

The results of yielding to the operating system may not always be what you expect. For example, the following Click-event code normally will continue to draw until the Do...While loops 1,000 times. However, due to the DoEvents function within the loop, if the cmdCancel_Click event is triggered before 1,000 loops are completed, the program will end. If the DoEvents function is not within the loop, triggering the cmdCancel_Click event will not end the application before the 1,000 loops are completed because the application will not allow any other input from the user until the loop has completed. Figure 13-3 is a visual representation of how DoEvents works.

```
Private Sub cmdStartPrint_Click()

    Dim XPos AS Long
    Dim YPos as Long
    Dim nCounter as Integer
```

```
' Set current position to the center
' of the form
CurrentX = Me.ScaleWidth / 2
CurrentY = Me.ScaleHeight / 2

' Clear form and set size of dot
Me.Cls
Me.DrawWidth = 50

Do While nCounter < 1000

    ' Set the point coordinates
    XPos = Rnd ' Me.ScaleWidth
    Ypos = Rnd ' Me.ScaleHeight

    ' Draw the point
    PSet (XPos, YPos), QBColor(Rnd ' 15)

    ' Increment counter
    NCounter = nCounter + 1

    ' Execute pending events if any
    DoEvents
Loop

End Sub

Private Sub cmdCancel_Click()
    End
End Sub
```

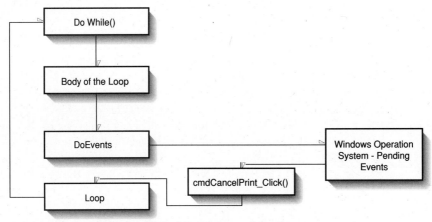

Figure 13-3   A flow diagram of DoEvents within a loop

You may want to prevent an event procedure that gives up control with DoEvents from being called again before DoEvents returns. Otherwise, the procedure might end up being called endlessly, until system resources are exhausted. You can prevent this from happening either by temporarily disabling the control that triggered the event or by setting a static flag variable so you know when the event has finished. If you do not take this into consideration, you can end up with events misfiring because your users might think they executed a process and continue to click on the Submit button. This will cause several events to fire that can either overflow the process buffer or cause events to execute out of turn.

14

VARIABLES

Within your application, there will be times when you will need to store values either temporarily when performing calculations or for reference purposes. Variables allow you to do this. They are how a programming language refers to the various types of data that can be held in the computer's memory. A variable has both a *name* that you use to refer to it in your code, and a *data type* that indicates what kind of information it stores. Variables also have a *scope* of operation that defines where they're available, and have a *lifetime* that defines how long they retain their value.

To use variables successfully, you must know how you can name a variable, what types of data a variable can represent, and how to assign and use the value of a variable. This chapter discusses these things in detail.

Variable Names

A variable's name must start with a letter, it may be up to 40 characters long, and it must consist of only letters, numbers, and the underscore (_) character. You cannot use a reserved word like For or If. You can use variables *implicitly* by just using them without ever declaring them, as in the following example:

```
Private Sub Command1_Click ()
    T$ = Text1.Text
    Print LCase(T$)
End Sub
```

You can also *explicitly* declare a variable before using it. This can dramatically reduce programming errors in large projects. Use the Dim or Static keyword to declare a variable that is local to a subroutine or function. Use the Private or Public keyword to declare a variable in the declaration section of a form, module, or class module.

```
Private Sub Command1_Click ()
    Dim T As String
    T = Text1.Text
    Print LCase$(T)
End Sub
```

You can enforce the need to explicitly declare all of your variables by placing the Option Explicit statement in the declarations section of a form or module:

```
Option Explicit          'this forces you to explicitly declare
                         'all variables
```

You can also set the Visual Basic 5.0 environment to automatically add this line to each new project. Do this by selecting the Tools menu, then the Options submenu, and mark the "Require Variable Declaration" check box on the Editor tab.

Rules for Defining Variables

Visual Basic has some rules regarding how you may set up a variable name. These rules help Visual Basic tell the difference between your variables and other elements of the language. These rules are

1. A variable name may not be longer than 255 characters.

2. The first character of a variable name must be a letter (A through Z). This letter can be uppercase or lowercase.

3. The remaining characters can be letters (A through Z, or a through z), numbers (0 through 9), or underscores (_).

4. The last character can be one of these type declaration characters (explained later): %, &, !, #, @, $, or nothing.

5. The variable name cannot be a Visual Basic reserved word. Reserved words include the names of Visual Basic properties, events, methods, operators, statements, and functions.

Variable names in Visual Basic are not case sensitive. That is, Visual Basic makes no distinctions between uppercase and lowercase characters in a variable name. In the code fragment below, all three lines refer to the same variable.

```
invoicetotal = 100
INVOICETOTAL = 100
InvoiceTotal = 100
```

When declaring and using variable names, it is helpful to use a name that can be easily read and that describes the purpose of the data it contains, rather than a cryptic abbreviation such as N or T1. This makes it much easier for you to understand how a program works. Proper use of capitalization can help make variable names more readable. For instance, although the three lines in the example above refer to the same variable, the third format is much easier to read and understand because the first letter of each word in the variable name is capitalized. You can also use the underscore character (_) to help make a variable more readable. For example:

```
Invoice_Total = 100
```

This variable name is made more readable because the underscore character separates different words in the variable name. Underscores, however, have the potential to make your Visual Basic program actually less readable: Visual Basic uses underscores in its event procedures (for example, Command1_Click), so using underscores in your variable names might make them difficult to distinguish from events.

You can also use proper capitalization to help you identify the scope of a variable. Although Visual Basic does not enforce any particular convention, you will find it convenient to consistently apply capitalization. A common programming practice makes the first letter of a local variable lowercase, the first letter of a module-level or global variable uppercase, and user-defined constants all uppercase. In Visual Basic 4.0 and 5.0, object library constants are upper- and lowercase (intercapped), with a lowercase prefix representing the library name.

```
invoiceTotal        'local variable
InvoiceTotal        'module-level or global variable
INVOICETOTAL        'constant
vbMaximized         'object library constant
```

Variable Data Types

In most languages, variables represent not only the value of data, but the type as well. Each type of variable views its contents in a different way. In Visual Basic there are 12 variable types: fixed-length string, variable-length string, byte, Boolean, integer, long, single-precision, double-precision, currency, Object, date, and variant. String variables represent data as ASCII characters. The seven numeric variable types each implement a different method for storing a numeric value. The numeric type you choose determines the range of the values you can place in that variable, and how accurately these values can be stored. The date type contains a date-time value in the form of a double-precision number, but it can receive any valid date string as an argument. The variant type can represent any of the other kinds of data, and is the default type for variables that are not otherwise declared.

The String Variables (fixed and variable length) are essentially the same. The only difference is a fixed length, defined by:

```
Dim FixVar * 10 As String
```

While Variable length is defined as:

```
Dim VariableLengthVar As String.
```

Specify the data type of a variable either with a special character appended to the variable name, as in T$, or by a type declaration, as in Private T As String. It is good programming practice to explicitly declare all variables, and we recommend that you use explicit variable declaration exclusively. How you declare your variables is described later in this chapter. Table 14-1 lists Visual Basic's variable data types, their type identifiers, if any, a sample of each, a description, and an example of the kind of value each type contains.

Table 14-1 Variable types in Visual Basic

Type Name	Character	Sample Variable	Description	Example
String	$	Msg$	String of characters	Hello, World!
Byte	(none)	Ouch	1-byte unsigned integer	65335
Boolean	(none)	IsItTrue	2-byte unsigned integer	True or False
Integer	%	Count%	2-byte signed integer	−3598
Long	&	recordNum&	4-byte signed integer	39849890
Single	!	xPos!	4-byte floating-point	9483.345
Double	#	distanceToGalaxy#	8-byte floating-point	829855903.009938994093
Currency	@	nationalDebt@	8-byte, fixed-decimal	9389403883.9383
Object	(none)	MyObj	4-byte address to OLE object	an object instance
Date	(none)	ThisDay	Contains a valid date	11/23/1994
Variant	(none)	varValue	any of the above types	

Table 14-2 lists Visual Basic's variable types, their storage requirements, and the range, if any, that can be held in that type.

Table 14-2 Types and ranges of variables in Visual Basic

Variable Type	Storage Required	Range of Variable
String	Length of string + 4	To almost 65,535 characters
Byte	1 byte	0 to 255
Boolean	2 bytes	True or False
Integer	2 bytes	−32,768 to +32,767
Long	4 bytes	−2,147,483,648 to +2,147,483,647
Single	4 bytes	−3.402823E+38 to −1.401298E−45 and +1.401298E−45 to +3.402823E+38
Double	8 bytes	−1.797693134862315D+308 to −4.94066D−324 and +4.94066D-324 to +1.797693134862315D+308
Currency	8 bytes	−922337203685477.5808 to +922337203685477.5807
Object	4 bytes	Any object instance
Date	8 bytes	Jan 1, 100 to December 31, 9999 and 0:00:00 to 23:59:59 hours
Variant	Varies + 22 bytes	Any of the other data types

String variables hold text or alphanumeric information. Strings can be of fixed or variable lengths. A *fixed-length string* is assigned a specific length when it is created, and that length cannot be changed. When you attempt to assign a value to a fixed-length variable that has a character length larger than specified, the information that is greater than the length is truncated. Fixed-length strings are best used when you need to store values in a database or flat file with a specific number of characters. *Variable-length strings* continually shrink and grow as values are assigned to them. Theoretically, a string can be up to 65,535 characters long in earlier versions of Windows, and it can be as long as about two billion in Windows 95 and NT. However, strings require overhead in memory (4 bytes per string) for some control information, so the actual maximum length is a little less than that.

Byte variables are number values stored in one 8-bit unsigned byte. They can range in value from 0 to 255. The byte type is the simplest kind of numeric data and requires only 1 byte for storage. If you attempt to place a value greater than 255 or a value of less than zero into a byte variable, you will generate an overflow runtime error. If you place a fractional value into a byte variable, it will round the value to the nearest whole number. It is best to use this data type when you are exchanging information that is in some binary format, between Visual Basic and another environment, or when you are directly accessing a file with binary information.

The Boolean type is a 16-bit number, but it can only return a True or False. You can use the keywords True and False to set a Boolean type's value. You can also set the value to False with a numeric value of 0 or to True with any nonzero value. The Boolean type will only return a False (0) or True (–1) when you are trying to convert it to a numeric type, regardless of the original value you assigned to it. It is best to use this data type when you plan to represent information with two, and only two, values; for example, to determine if a message was or was not received.

The integer variable type is the simplest kind of numeric data. This variable type requires 2 bytes of memory for storage, and can hold any whole number in the range –32,768 to +32,767. Because integers can only store whole numbers, any fractional portion of a number is rounded off to the nearest whole number when it is assigned to an integer variable. It is best to use this data type for most incremental counters and average number-based information, as long as it is not larger than 32K.

The long integer variable type is closely related to the integer. The long type, however, uses 4 rather than 2 bytes of storage. Because of this, its range is much greater than the integer variable, allowing you to store whole numbers from –2,147,483,648 to +2,147,483,647. It is best to use this data type for incremental counters greater than 32K and large numbers like a city's population.

Both the single-precision and double-precision variable types store numbers that might have a fractional portion. These variables store values in a floating-point number format. Representing numbers in floating-point format is very much like using scientific notation. Like scientific notation, floating-point numbers have a sign, a mantissa, and an exponent. The main difference between the two is that scientific notation is a base 10 system (decimal), and floating-point numbers work on a base 2 (binary) system. The advantage of representing a number in this fashion is that it allows the variables to store a fairly large range of numbers in a limited amount of memory. However, there are disadvantages to using floating-point numbers. Along with the limits on range, a floating-point number is also limited to the number of digits it can represent accurately. As a result of this, rounding floating-point numbers sometimes produces a result that may be insufficiently precise for your application. Finally, math operations on a floating-point number are not as fast as when performed on an integer or long integer variable.

A single-precision, or single, variable requires 4 bytes of storage, and has a range of –3.37E+38 to –1.40E–45 for negative values. Positive values range from +1.40E–45 to +3.37E+38. It can accurately hold numbers up to seven digits long. It is best to use this data type for any non-whole number that can fit within its range. In business applications, it is rare that you will require a number larger than a single-precision.

The double-precision, or double, variable uses 8 bytes of memory. It can represent negative numbers from –1.80D+308 to –4.94D–324 and positive numbers from +4.94D–324 to +1.80D+308—a huge range of values, with an accuracy of 16 digits. It is best to use this data type for very large numbers, such as those used in like scientific applications.

> **NOTE**
> The exponential indicator for the double-precision literal is D rather than E. The D indicates that the number should be interpreted as double-precision rather than single-precision.

The currency variable type is a modified integer. What sets it apart from an integer is that it has an implied decimal point. This allows numbers represented by a currency variable to have up to four digits to the right of the decimal point. Because it is stored as an 8-byte integer, math operations are faster on it than on floating-point numbers. The range of a currency variable is from –9.22E+14 to +9.22E+14, and it can accurately represent any number of digits that fall into that range. It is best to use this data type in financial applications, because it eliminates small rounding errors that might occur with the single-precision and double-precision data types. You should be aware that some development environments like C/C++ do not support the currency data type; therefore, if your application interacts with such an environment, you should convert your currency value to a single.

The Object variable type requires 4 bytes for storage that references objects. It is best to use this data type when you are referring to a control or form for OLE automation. Refer to Chapter 74, "OLE Overview," for a more thorough explanation of how to use the Object data type.

The date variable type stores a value that represents a date between January 1, 100, and December 31, 9999, and a time between 0:00:00 and 23:59:59. It is stored internally as an 8-byte IEEE 64-bit (8-byte) floating-point value. Values to the left of the decimal point are date values, and values to the right of the decimal point represent time values. You can use any valid date string as an argument for the date type. "#Jan.1,1994#", "#1/1/94#", or "#12:15 AM#" will all translate into a valid date/time value as long as you enclose them with the number sign (#). All of the date and time manipulation functions that accepted the date variant type as an argument in versions of Visual Basic prior to Visual Basic 4.0 will also accept the new date type.

The Variant variable type is a data type for all variable types that are not explicitly declared for. Its memory requirement varies depending on the data type it is storing plus another 22 bytes of overhead. As a developer, you should really try to stay away from using this data type as much as possible due to its resources overhead and performance issues. The 22 byte overhead might not sound like a lot right now, but if you have over a hundred data types defined as variants, that is more than 2K of memory wasted just because you were too lazy to define your variables' data types. Performance is an issue because Visual Basic will need to stop and figure out what the data type of the variable is before it can continue to process it.

Scope and Lifetime of Variables

When a variable is declared in Visual Basic, the placement of its declaration determines how accessible that variable will be to certain portions of the program. The visibility of a variable to the program is referred to as a variable's *scope*. The scope in Visual Basic is set up in a tiered format. Each tier has rules associated with it that govern how variables declared within it can be accessed. These tiers are set up in a hierarchical manner. The lifetime of variables ranges from the lifespan of a procedure call to the lifespan of an application instance.

The coding area of Visual Basic 5.0 has four major module objects: forms, MDI forms, modules, and class modules. These areas are broken down into a declarations area and a procedural area. The scope of your declarations is directly affected by where in these two lower divisions you place them. While Visual Basic 5.0 is backward compatible with prior versions, there have been changes in the way a variable's scope is defined. While you can still use the global declaration to create application-wide variables, the public declaration has completely different connotations and gives you much greater control over just how *public* the variable will be. You can make form- and MDI form–level variables and procedures available to other modules and forms. The scope of your variables and procedures in class modules can even be made available to other applications.

In the declarations area of your module or form objects you can declare variables as either private or public. Private variables have a scope limited to the module or form in which they are declared. Public variables can be seen by all other forms and modules in the application. You can declare public variables with the same name in different modules, and differentiate them by using their parent form or module name as a prefix. The main difference between the former global declaration and the new public declaration is that you can also make form-level variables public. This allows you to directly pass or access data between forms and other forms or modules. This is not the same as using a globally declared variable. With a global, you can declare that particular name only once and it is common to all modules and forms. With a public declaration, while it is accessible throughout the program, it is a specific property of the form or module that it is declared in instead of being just a global variable. This means that you can have the same variable name declared as public in several forms or modules. Form1.Mydata is different from Form2.Mydata and Module1.Mydata, but they are all available globally throughout your application.

Variables that are declared as private in the declarations section of an object (form or module) have an object-wide scope. They are available for access from all of the procedures in that object. Variables declared inside of a procedure (sub or function) are by default private to that procedure. Variables declared as public in a class module that is itself declared as a public object are also available to other applications. Visual Basic procedures reside inside of form-, module-, or class module–type objects. You cannot declare procedure-level variables as public, because their scope is always limited to the procedure in which they are declared.

To better understand this arrangement of variable scope, look at the illustration in Figure 14-1. The two outer rectangles represent either form or module objects. Within each object are the three object levels of declaration. The arrows from the module-level public and private rectangles point to the procedure level, indicating that their content is available to the procedure level. The rectangle that crosses the boundaries of the two objects represents the module-level public variables that are commonly available between them. If you have a question as to the scope of a variable, fit it into its place in this illustration, and you can immediately determine its scope.

Procedure-Level Variables

A procedure-level declaration limits the availability of the variable to the procedure. Procedure-level variable names can be freely reused in other procedures, as shown in these examples:

```
Private Sub DoSomething ()
    Dim Myvar as String      'Myvar declared as string and
    MyVar = Form1.Text1.Text 'local to this procedure.
    MsgBox MyVar             'Note that Dim is used instead
End Sub                      'of Public or Private which are
                             'invalid at the procedural level.

Private Sub DoNothing ()
    Dim MyVar as Date        'Same name, different procedure
    MyVar = Now              'declared as Date. They are completely
    MsgBox Myvar             'different unrelated variables.
End Sub
```

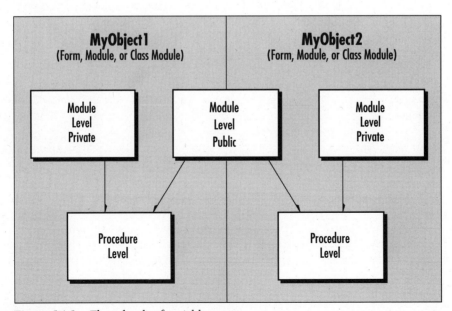

Figure 14-1   Three levels of variable scope

In these examples the variables named MyVar are alive only while the procedures that contain them are active. When the procedures are exited, the data contained in the variables is lost.

In some circumstances you will wish to preserve the value of a procedure-level variable for the lifetime of a form or even the application. To accomplish this, use the Static statement:

```
Private Function StoredItem (Item as String) As String
    Static StoredIt as String    'Creates a Variable whose lifetime
                                 'is for the duration of the object
    If IsNull(Item) Then          it was declared in.
StoredItem = StoredIt    'The function returns whatever is
                                 'stored in StoredIt
    Else                         'if Item contains a Null, else it
                                 'will store whatever
        StoredIt = Item          'is in Item into StoredIt.
End Function
```

This example illustrates a function that acts as an access routine between objects. The StoredIt variable will retain its data as long as the object that contains it remains viable. In a module or a class module, this would be for the lifetime of the application, whereas in a form, the variable's data would be lost if the application set the form to Nothing after unloading it.

Object-Level Variables

The next level of scope is the object-level variable that is declared as Private in the General Declarations section of a form, module, or class module. This type of declaration limits the scope and lifetime of the variable to the object in which it is declared. In the case of a module, this would be for the life of the application. In the case of a class module or form, the variable would be valid as long as an instance of the form or module was in memory. The object instance can be explicitly removed from memory using the Set Object=Nothing statement, thus ending the viability of its storage segment. These examples show variables with object=level scope:

```
Private Type MyUDT                'type definition local to Object
    MyName as String * 40
    MyPlace as String * 40
    MyId as Integer
End Type
Private People() as Myudt         'array of Myudt local to object
Private MyString as string        'string local to object
```

These variables are available only to procedures within the object in which the variables were declared. The lifetime of the data that they contain is limited to the lifetime of the object instance that they belong to.

Application-Level Variables

The application-level variables are also declared in the General Declarations section of their parent objects. In versions of Visual Basic prior to Visual Basic 4.0, this was accomplished with the Global keyword. In Visual Basic 4.0 and 5.0, the Public keyword is used in place of Global, which brings about some subtle changes. One change is that you can declare public variables with the same name as long as they are declared in different objects. Another change is that you now have access to variables in forms from within other forms and modules if those variables are declared Public in the General Declarations section of their form. When you refer to a public variable in a form that is not loaded, just the required code segment is loaded, not the entire form. On the surface, this appears to fulfill the programmer's desire for easy data transfer between objects without the use of globals; but in fact, public variables are still global variables with many of the same pitfalls as their predecessors. A better way to pass data between objects is to use the Property Procedures. The following examples show public variables:

```
Public Type MyUDT                 'type definition global to
                                  'application
    MyName as String * 40
    MyPlace as String * 40
    MyId as Integer
End Type
Public People() as Myudt          'array of Myudt global to
                                  'application
Public MyString as string         'string global to application
```

Systemwide Variables

Yet another level of scope is available in Visual Basic 5.0. If you create an OLE automation server object (Professional Edition only), your public objects (and public variables) can become exposed to external applications. Visual Basic forms are always private class objects, but modules and class modules can be either public or private. This means that other applications can access any members of these objects that are declared Public as well. In the preceding example, MyString would be available to any application that used the qualifying path

```
Msgbox AppName.Module1.MyString     'displays the value of MyString
                                    'in AppName project's Module1
```

To make the scope of an object's public members available only within the parent application, you must use the Option Private Module statement in your modules. Visual Basic is evolving into a much more object-oriented environment, which brings about a whole new set of scope issues to consider. It is a good practice to limit variable scope as much as possible, exposing only those elements that must be exposed. In fact, it is better to use the Property Let, Set, and Get functions to expose data outside the application rather than allow direct access to internal data. You should also adopt a naming convention that clearly identifies the scope of variables at a glance. A good naming convention makes code easier to understand and debug during the development process as well as during subsequent updates or modifications.

Declaring Variables

So far we have discussed assigning a name and a type to an area of storage and referring to that memory location by its assigned name. The actual practice of assigning a name and type to an area of memory is called "declaring" a variable. In most languages a variable must be declared in a program before it can be used. This is done because most compilers need to know how memory will be set up before they can begin compiling the executable code of a program. Although, like other languages, Visual Basic allows you to formally declare a variable before using it, this is not required. Variables in Visual Basic can be declared either implicitly or explicitly. Implicitly declared variables are variables that have been declared "on the fly"—that is, no code needs to be written to specifically set up a memory location for the variable before it is used in the program. An explicitly declared variable is formally declared before it is used in the program. When you explicitly declare a variable, you include code in your program for the express purpose of informing Visual Basic that memory is to be allocated for a variable.

Implicitly Declared Variables

In order to implicitly declare a variable in Visual Basic, you just use it in a line of code. For instance, in the following line of code, a value is assigned to a numeric variable.

```
MyVar = 1
```

If the variable MyVar has not yet been declared, Visual Basic will create storage for that variable. Because assigning a value to a variable is an executable command, implicitly defined variables can only be defined within a procedure. Therefore, all implicit variables are local variables; they cannot be accessed outside of the procedure in which they are used.

By default, when you use a variable that has not been formally declared, Visual Basic assumes that it will be a variant. However, there are two ways you can control the type of an implicitly declared variable. First, by appending a type declaration character to the end of the variable name, you can force Visual Basic to use a specific variable type. If you append a type declaration to a variable name, it becomes part of the variable name and must always be used to refer to that variable. For instance, in the code below, three implicit variables are assigned the numeric value of –1. Each one will store this value differently, based on the type declaration character at the end of its variable name.

```
Var1% = -1
Var2! = -1
Var3# = -1
```

In this example, Var1% is an integer variable, Var2! is a single-precision variable, and Var3# is a double-precision variable.

When strings are declared in an implicit manner, they are always declared as variable-length strings. See Table 14-3 for a list of the type declaration characters and the variable types with which they are used.

The second way to modify the type of an implicit variable is with the Deftype statements. This statement is used in the General Declarations area of a form or module to define a range of letters that indicate a specific variable type. If the first letter of an implicit variable falls within this defined range, that variable will be assigned the data type specified by the Deftype statement. For instance:

```
DefInt A-F
```

In the example above, Visual Basic will assign the integer variable type to any variable that is implicitly declared in the same form or module, as long as the first letter of the variable's name falls into the range A through F. Table 14-3 lists the 11 Deftype statements and the variable types with which they are used.

Table 14-3 Declaration characters and Deftype statements used to implicitly declare variable types

Variable Type	Declaration Character	Deftype Statement
String	$	DefStr
Byte	(none)	DefByte
Boolean	(none)	DefBool
Integer	%	DefInt
Long	&	DefLng
Single	!	DefSng
Double	#	DefDbl
Currency	@	DefCur
Object	(none)	DefObj
Date	(none)	DefDate
Variant	(none)	DefVar

Because you can declare variables implicitly simply by using them, Visual Basic does not generate an error when it comes across a variable name it has not yet encountered. Instead it allocates storage for that variable and proceeds normally. This can cause logic errors in your programs if you are not careful. One of the most frustrating and hard-to-find bugs that can occur in a Visual Basic program is the one that is caused by the programmer accidentally mistyping a variable name. For instance, in the following code fragment, the program is supposed to figure the square root of the number 128, and place it into the variable SqrRoot.

```
ThisNmber = 128          'mis-typed!
SqrRoot = Sqr(ThisNumber)   'Sqr returns the square root of ThisNumber
```

The variable SqrRoot will have the value of 0 assigned to it rather than the expected value of 12 because of the mistyping in the first assignment.

Explicitly Declared Variables

Visual Basic also allows you to declare variables explicitly. Explicitly declared variables are assigned a variable name and data type before they are used. This is the preferred manner of declaring variables, because it makes your programs more readable and less prone to errors. In Visual Basic 5.0, you explicitly declare variables by using the Public, Private, Dim, or Static statements. These statements have different implications for the visibility of the declared variable. Table 14-4 summarizes the statements used to declare constants and variables.

Table 14-4 Statements used to declare variables and constants

Use This...	Type	To Do This...
Const	Statement	Assign a permanent value to a name
Dim	Statement	Explicitly declare a variable within a procedure or function
Private	Statement	Explicitly declare a variable local to a form, module, or class module
Public	Statement	Explicitly declare a variable global to an application
Static	Statement	Explicitly declare a variable within a procedure or function that retains its value

The Public statement is used when you wish to make a variable available throughout your application or, in the case of a public class module, available to other applications. Public variable names can be duplicated as long as they reside in different objects. You differentiate between similarly named public variables by providing the complete path of their origin:

```
Object1.MyVar
Module1.MyVar
Myform3.MyVar
```

In the above case, MyVar represents a different variable in each of these objects despite the identical name. This permits you to reuse names from object to object without having to come up with a unique identifier for globally available variables.

The Private statement is used to declare object-level variables in the General Declarations area of your forms or modules. Private variables are accessible to all the procedures contained in the object in which the variable is declared. In procedures, the Private or Dim statement declares variables that are available only within that procedure's lifetime. These local variables cannot be accessed by other procedures. Private procedure variables are allocated each time the procedure is entered, and deallocated when it is exited. When Visual Basic begins to execute a procedure, it scans the procedure for Private or Dim statements. If there are any in it, it will allocate memory for the variables specified in the procedure. When Visual Basic is through executing the procedure, it deallocates any memory that was assigned to the variables in the procedure that were declared as Private. As a consequence, the values assigned to any variables local to the procedure will not be retained between calls to that procedure.

The Static statement and the Dim statement are used to allocate storage for local variables. Local variables created with the Static statements are often called "static" variables. Unlike local variables that have been declared with the Dim statement, static variables are allocated once, and are not deallocated until the program terminates. This means that static variables retain their value between procedure calls.

To explicitly declare a simple variable, use one of the following forms of syntax:

```
Public VariableName As Type    'use this to declare a public variable
Private VariableName As Type   'use this to declare a module-level or form-level variable
Static VariableName As Type    'use this to declare a procedure-level static variable
Dim VariableName As Type       'use this to declare a procedure-level non-static variable
```

In the VariableName parameter, supply a unique name that complies with the rules that apply to variable names listed earlier. Specify the type as Byte, Boolean, Integer, Single, Double, Currency, Date, String, or String * Length (for fixed-length strings). For example:

```
Private StringVar As String      'declares a string variable called StringVar
Private ByteVar As Byte          'declares a Byte variable called ByteVar
Private BooleanVar As Boolean    'declares a Boolean variable called BooleanVar
Private IntegerVar As Integer    'declares a integer variable called IntegerVar
Private LongVar As Long          'declares a long integer called LongVar
Private SingleVar As Single      'declares a single-precision variable called SingleVar
Private DoubleVar As Double      'declares a double-precision variable called DoubleVar
Private CurrencyVar As Currency  'declares a currency variable called CurrencyVar
Private FixedVar As String * 10  'declares a 10-byte-long fixed-length string called
                                 'FixedVar
Private ObjectVar As Object      'declares an object variable Called ObjectVar
Private DateVar as Date          'declares a date variable called Datevar
Private VariantVar As Variant    'declares a variant variable called VariantVar
```

You can set Visual Basic to require that all variables be explicitly declared. This will significantly reduce bugs and help to make your programs far more readable. Explicitly declaring your variables is a highly recommended practice for large projects. Use the Option Explicit statement in any module to force explicit declarations. You can also set Visual Basic's environment to automatically add this statement to all of your programs. Do this by pulling down the Tools menu, choosing the Environment Options command, and setting the Require Variable Declaration check box.

Converting Data Types

Quite often, you might need to use different data types together in the same code statement. Visual Basic can perform data type conversions on some data types automatically. For other data types, you will have to convert the variable before you can use the value. Converting a data type is necessary when you are passing a variable or value as an argument to a function or procedure, and the procedure is expecting a parameter that is different from the one being passed. If the data type of the passed variable or value is not the same data type the procedure is expecting, you will receive a Type Mismatched error.

Automatic Data Type Conversion

Visual Basic handles converting between data types very well. In many cases, you can just let Visual Basic perform the conversion itself without the use of a conversion function.

Converting to similar data types is automatic, like converting from a numeric data type to another numeric data type (integer to double). You need to be careful when you're converting a larger numeric data type to a smaller data type, because if the value in the variable is larger than the target data type, you will get an Overflow error. You should be cautious of the following larger data type conversions:

- Double to byte

- Double to integer

- Double to long

- Double to single

- Long to byte

- Long to integer

- Single to byte

- Single to integer

Another thing you need to be aware of when converting from one numeric data type to another is how the target data type handles decimal values. Integer and long data types do not accept decimal values; therefore, the decimal value will be rounded to the nearest whole number.

```
Dim iFahrenheit as Integer
Dim dCelsius as Double

dCelsius = 24
iFahrenheit = (dCelsius * 9 / 5) + 32
```

In the above example, the result of the calculation is 75.2, but because the target data type is an integer, the value is rounded to 75.

If a string variable or a control property has the data type of String, like the Text Box's Text property, it can be used as a variable in a numeric statement.

```
If IsNumeric(txtCelsius.Text) Then
    iFahrenheit = (txtCelsius.Text * 9 / 5) + 32
Else
    MsgBox "You entered an invalid Celsius value"
End If
```

In the above example, the IsNumeric function checks the Text property value of txtCelsius. If you performed the calculation without first checking the value of the txtCelsius text box, you would receive a Type Mismatch error. Also, just as with the numeric-to-numeric data type conversion, you need to be careful that the numeric value in the String variable is not larger than the target numeric data type.

Data Type Conversion Functions

Visual Basic provides several data type conversion functions you can use to convert variables or values into a specific data type. For example, to convert a value to the currency data type, you use the CCur function:

```
PayPerWeek = CCur(hours * HourlyPay)
```

Values passed to a conversion function must be valid for the destination data type, or else an error occurs. For example, if you attempt to convert a long to an integer, the long must be within the valid range for the integer data type. Table 14-5 is a list of all the conversion functions you can use to convert data types.

Table 14-5 Data type conversion functions

Use This Function...	To Convert This Data Type...
CBool	Boolean
CByte	Byte
CCur	Currency
CDate (or CVDate)	Date
CDbl	Double
CInt	Integer
CLng	Long
CSng	Single
CStr	String
CVar	Variant
CVErr	Error

> **NOTE**
> The CVDate function provides backward compatibility with older versions of Visual Basic.

User-Defined and Intrinsic Constants

In Visual Basic, a *constant* is a named memory location that stores a fixed value. This value can range from a single byte to a large string. The value of constants remains unchanged throughout your program. With all versions of Visual Basic, you can assign user-defined constants in the General Declarations area of your forms, standard modules, user documents, or class modules. The syntax for declaring a user-defined constant is

```
[Public|Private] Const CONSTANTNAME [As Type] = value
```

The Public keyword is used to give the constant application-wide scope. To make a constant available only within the form or module, declare it as Private. The CONSTANTNAME parameter is a unique name you will use in place of the defined value in your program. The same naming rules for variables apply to user-defined constants. The As Type keyword is optional to let you define what data type the constant will be. In versions of Visual Basic prior to Visual Basic 4.0, it was a common practice to use all uppercase letters when naming constants. In Visual Basic 4.0 and 5.0, the naming convention should perhaps adopt the same format as the intrinsic constants. In the case of the intrinsic constants, the prefix identifies the source, such as *vb* for

Visual Basic. When defining the value in a constant, you can use any valid expression except calls to procedures. The following shows valid constant declarations:

```
Public Const conMyString = "use any text"
Public Const conPI = 3.14
Public Const ConPIx2 = conPI * 2
```

Intrinsic (system-defined) constants are constants that are provided by the Visual Basic programming environment or by application objects that provide their own, such as the DAO (Data Access Objects), Microsoft Excel, and Microsoft Project. Examples of intrinsic constants are as follows:

```
Select Case WeekDay(Now)
    Case vbMonday
        code.....
    Case vbTuesday
        code.....
End Select
```

In the above case, the vbMonday and vbTuesday constants are provided by Visual Basic without your specifically having to declare them. The WeekDay function will return a value that corresponds to these constants. Previous versions of Visual Basic provided text files, such as CONSTANT.TXT, that included many of the constant declarations needed for use with Visual Basic. These files are no longer needed with Visual Basic 4.0 and 5.0, but can still be used for backward compatibility.

Constants are used in your programs to give a meaningful name to a value that might otherwise be ambiguous or hard to remember. For instance, colors in Visual Basic are represented by a long integer number. This number represents a mixture of the electronic primary colors: red, green, and blue. You could set the background color of an object by assigning a color's number to its BackColor property:

```
Text1.BackColor = &hFFFF
```

While this works fine, and causes no confusion to Visual Basic, it can cause you a little extra work in deciphering that the hex value FFFF is the color number for yellow. A better, more readable way to do this is to use the intrinsic constant for the color yellow supplied by Visual Basic. By using the constant vbYellow, which holds the value of the color number for yellow, a much more coherent line of code is produced:

```
Public Text1.Backcolor = vbYellow
```

Changing the value of a constant requires you to change only the line that it's declared in, rather than search through your entire program for every literal value the constant replaces. Note that it's a common programming practice to make all user-defined constants uppercase to distinguish them from variables. Visual Basic and other object library constants use upper- and lowercase characters preceded by a lowercase prefix—for example, vbSomeConstant.

A list of the intrinsic constants defined for Visual Basic is in the Visual Basic object library. This list can be accessed through the Object Browser. The Visual Basic library prefix is vb; in Visual Basic for Applications it is vba; and for the data access objects it is dao. Other applications, such as Microsoft Excel and Microsoft Project, that provide object libraries can also be found here.

User-Defined Data Types

Visual Basic provides all the simple variable types needed to write just about any application. For more complex data types, Visual Basic allows you to set up your own variable types. You can assign meaningful names to these user-defined data types, and then use them to declare variables anywhere in your program. For example, a user-defined data type might be set up to contain employee information, like first and last name, social security number, and salary. User-Defined data types are set up with the Type...End Type statement as follows:

```
Type NameAndSS
    FirstName As String * 25
    LastName As String * 25
    SocialSecurity As Long
End Type
```

Like any variable, they can be defined as both Public and Private in the General Declaration section in standard modules. If you define them within a class module, they can only be defined as Private. You can then assign this type to variables. The following example lets you refer to all elements as one variable:

```
Private Person1 As NameAndSS
Private Person2 As NameAndSS
Person1.FirstName = "Nick"
Person1.LastName = "Scott"
Person1.SocialSecurity = 427859672
Person1 = Person2
```

As you can see, in the last line of the example, the value of one user-defined data type is assigned to another. This copies the contents of all the elements in one user-defined data type to the corresponding elements in the other. However, this can only be done when both user-defined data types are of the same type.

Enumerated Constants

In other development languages, like C/C++, Pascal, and Java, you can define related named constants by grouping them in an enumerator, or Enum. Enum is now available for Visual Basic developers. With the Professional and Enterprise Editions, Enums can be included in an ActiveX component's type library, making them available for use by any developer who uses the component.

An enumeration, or Enum, is a special long integer data type and not really a derived type. It provides developers a convenient way to work with sets of related constants and to associate mnemonic constant values with names. The syntax for declaring an Enum constant is

```
[Public|Private] Enum ENUMNAME
```

The Public keyword is used to give the enumerated constant application-wide scope. To make an enumerated constant available only within the form or module, declare it as Private. The ENUMNAME parameter is a unique name you are assigning to the enumerated group.

The most common example used to illustrate Enum constants is a listing of the days of the week. To make a public Enum for the days of the week, the syntax would be similar to the following:

```
Public Enum Days
    Sunday
    Monday
    Tuesday
    Wednesday
    Thursday
    Friday
    Saturday
End Enum
```

The first constant in the enumeration, by default, is set to the value 0. The following constant values are incremented by one; therefore, Monday would be 1, Tuesday would be 2, and so on. You can specifically assign any integer values, positive or negative, to constants within the enumeration. This is done in the same way you assign a value to any constant:

```
Saturday = 0
```

You can then assign this type to variables. This lets you refer to all elements as one variable. Below is an example of using enumerated values within a procedure.

```
If lstDaysOfWeek.ListIndex = Friday Then
    MsgBox "Thank God its Friday!"
Endif
```

Instead of checking the ListIndex against the enumerated value, Friday, it could have been checked against the value 5, but then you would have to remember that 5 is equal to Friday. Using enumerated constants makes debugging easier and also assists in self-documenting your code.

Operators

Operators are symbols that tell Visual Basic to manipulate data in a specified way. For example, the assignment operator (=) can store a value in a variable, while the addition operator (+) adds two quantities together. There are also operators that compare values, returning a True or False value as the result.

The Assignment Operator

In Visual Basic the assignment operator is used to place values into a variable or property. The assignment operator is the equal sign (=). This operator is used by placing a variable or property to the left of the operator and an expression to the right. This causes the value of the expression to be assigned to the variable or property. For example,

```
Height% = 100
Area! = PI * Radius ^ 2
MyBox.Text = MyPrompt$
```

The first example assigns the numeric literal value 100 to the integer variable Height%. In the second example, the value of the expression PI * Radius ^ 2 is assigned to the single-precision variable Area!. The last example assigns the string MyPrompt$ to the Text property of the object MyBox.

The assignment operator assigns values to both numeric and string variables and properties. If your program assigns a numeric value of one data type to a numeric variable or property of a different data type, Visual Basic will automatically convert the value to the type of the receiving variable or property. For instance, if your program assigns an integer value to a single-precision variable, the value will be converted to a single-precision value before it is assigned to the variable. However, if the value is not within the allowable range for the type of the result data item, an overflow error will occur. For example, your program will cause an error if it assigns a value greater than 32767 or less than –32768 to an integer variable. You cannot assign a string value to a numeric variable or property. This causes a Type Mismatch error. By the same token, you cannot assign a numeric value to a string variable or property. Visual Basic provides the Str$ and Val functions for converting numeric values to strings and strings to numeric values.

Option Statement

The Option statement adjusts module-level settings within Visual Basic. You can use the various forms of the Option statement to set default settings for arrays, strings, and variable declaration. Table 14-6 lists three different module-level options you can use.

Table 14-6 Module-level Option statements

Use This...	To Do This...
Option Base	Declare the default lower bound for array subscripts
Option Compare	Declare comparison method to use when comparing strings
Option Explicit	Force developers to declare all variables explicitly

Some programmers find it more intuitive to work with array subscripts that begin with 1 rather than with 0. Option Base is used to declare the default lower bound for array subscripts. The syntax is

```
Option Base {0 | 1}
```

The default Option Base setting is 0, so this parameter is not required if you want your array base to start at zero. If you want your array base to start at 1, Option Base must appear in a module before any constant or variable arrays are declared.

You use Option Compare to declare the default comparison method to use when string data is compared. The syntax is

```
Option Compare {Binary | Text}
```

The default Option Compare setting is Binary, which means that a string comparison is based on the development system's binary representation of the characters. This results in a case-sensitive comparison. If you set Option Compare to Text, a string comparison will be based on a case-insensitive text sort. This sort is locale sensitive, because the order is determined by the system's country code in the international section of the user's WIN.INI.

Option Explicit forces you to define all variables and constants. The syntax is

```
Option Explicit
```

Setting Option Explicit helps you eliminate bugs caused by spelling errors, because misspelled variable and constant names will trigger a Variable Not Defined error. This option can also help when the scope of a variable is not clear. When a module contains the Option Explicit statement and an error is not triggered, it is safe to assume that a referenced variable is scoped at the project level rather than at the module level. If Option Explicit is not set, all undeclared variables are assumed to be of variant type. You can set Option Explicit either by typing it in the General Declarations section in every form and standard module, or by checking the box labeled Require Variable Declaration in the Environment Options item from the Tools menu.

15

DATA STRUCTURES

In Chapter 14, "Variables," you were introduced to defining variables using simple data types. Variables are useful when dealing with storing information for future use, calculations, and so on. Sometimes it is necessary to define a relationship among different variables or to store and reference variables as a group. For these reasons, you can build data structures composed of simple data types. These data structures can be built up into more complex structures, but ultimately they are composed of simple data types.

This chapter discusses some of the data structures built into Visual Basic, as well as how to create and use your own data structures.

Arrays

The basic purpose of an array is to store an entire series of variables of the same data type and reference them by the same variable name. This is very useful when you are working on several pieces of data that all have the same variable data type and purpose.

Suppose, for example, you need to keep track of an inventory of cars, and you need to separate them by color. You could set up a separate variable for each color, such as RedCars, BlueCars, WhiteCars, and BlackCars. Each of these variables would be declared as an integer. The purpose of each variable is the same: to hold the number of cars that are that color. This presents two problems, however. First, all the cars cannot be referenced by the same name. Therefore, if you need to determine the number of all the cars, you have to add all the variables: AllCars = RedCars + BlueCars + WhiteCars + BlackCars. This makes referring to all the cars an awkward process. Second, if a new color is added, you have to create a new variable to handle it. This means that each time a new color is added, you need to modify the program and recompile it.

A better solution is to use an array to hold the data. Using an array allows you to set up one variable name, Cars, that has a separate storage area for each color. Each of these areas is referred to as an element of the array. When you work with an array, you use an index number (called the subscript) to tell Visual Basic which element you are referencing. To create an array, use the Dim, Private, Public, or Static statements. These statements declare an array's name, variable type, and size. For instance:

```
Private Cars(100) As Integer
Private Colors(100) As String
```

These statements declare two arrays. The first array, Cars, is an integer array. This array can be used to store the number of cars per color. The second array, Colors, is a string array. It can be used to store the names of each of the possible colors.

The argument inside the parentheses of the array declaration specifies the number of the first and last elements in the array. In the previous example, only the number of the last element in the array is specified, so Visual Basic will assume the starting array element is number 0. Therefore, both arrays will have 101 elements, numbered from 0 to 100.

The starting element number of an array can be changed in two ways. First, you may place an Option Base statement in the General Declarations area of a form or module. This allows you to set the default starting element number to 0 or 1 when an array is declared. Second, you can specify the starting element in the array declaration:

```
Private WorkHours(800 To 1700) As String
```

This statement declares an array whose lowest available element is 800 and whose highest is 1700.

After an array is declared, you need some technique for referencing elements in the array. This is done by specifying the desired element number, or subscript, in parentheses following the array name. This code fragment, for instance, assigns a color name to element number 5 of the Colors array:

```
Colors(5) = "Red"
```

Not only can you define the number of elements in an array, but you can also define the number of dimensions. Up to this point, the examples we've used have all been one-dimensional arrays. You can think of one-dimensional arrays in a linear manner. The Cars array from the previous example, for example, can be visualized:

```
Cars(0)    Cars(1)    Cars(2)    ...    Cars(98)    Cars(99)    Cars(100)
```

Visual Basic, however, enables you to set up multidimensional arrays. Multidimensional arrays have more than one set of subscript elements. By creating a two-dimensional array, for example, you define that the array has both length and width. This lets you set up data in a tabular format. The following statement sets up a two-dimensional array:

```
Private Tbl(1 To 5, 1 To 5) As Integer
```

In order to reference an element in a multidimensional array, you need to supply a subscript for each dimension in the array. If you were to visualize the Tbl array, it might look something like this:

```
Tbl(1,1)    Tbl(2,1)    Tbl(3,1)    Tbl(4,1)    Tbl(5,1)
Tbl(1,2)    Tbl(2,2)    Tbl(3,2)    Tbl(4,2)    Tbl(5,2)
Tbl(1,3)    Tbl(2,3)    Tbl(3,3)    Tbl(4,3)    Tbl(5,3)
```

| Tbl(1,4) | Tbl(2,4) | Tbl(3,4) | Tbl(4,4) | Tbl(5,4) |
| Tbl(1,5) | Tbl(2,5) | Tbl(3,5) | Tbl(4,5) | Tbl(5,5) |

Adding a third dimension would give the array depth, as well as length and width. You do not, however, have to stop at just three dimensions. Visual Basic enables you to create arrays that have as many as 60 dimensions. Although this is a neat feature, your mind can get a little boggled when the number of dimensions in an array exceeds three. Large multidimensional arrays can also consume prodigious amounts of memory.

Dynamic Arrays

Dynamic arrays are arrays that can be allocated and deallocated at runtime. This allows you to make your programs more flexible by creating arrays whose size is determined by factors that are unknown at design time, such as the size of a data file.

Dynamic arrays are allocated using the ReDim statement and deallocated with the Erase statement. The most efficient way to set up a dynamic array is to declare it twice. The first declaration is performed in the General Declarations section of a form, module, or class module using the Public or Private specifier depending on the intended scope of the array. However, declare the array without any number inside its parentheses:

```
Private Cars() As Integer
Private Colors() As String
```

This tells Visual Basic that you want to declare an array, but you do not yet know how many dimensions or elements it will contain. You can then place the ReDim statement inside a procedure to define the number of dimensions and elements:

```
Private Sub LoadColors (LastColor As Integer)
    ReDim Colors(LastColor) As String
    ReDim Cars(LastColor) As Integer
    :
    [Place your code here]
    :
End Sub
```

You are not required to use the Private, Public, or Dim statements to originally declare a dynamic array. When Visual Basic allocates storage for a dynamic array at runtime, however, the use of these statements allows it to do so faster and more efficiently. Also, the array's scope will reflect the placement of the original declaration. That is, if the array is declared as Public at the module or form level, its elements will be available as object properties throughout the program. Using this method, however, has the disadvantage of limiting a dynamic array to eight dimensions. Although eight is usually enough dimensions for any application, some programs require that an array have more.

If you wish to declare a dynamic array with more than eight dimensions, or wish it to be a local array (not accessible by any other procedure), do not include a Private or Public statement for the array.

After a dynamic array has been declared, you can again use the ReDim statement any number of times to change the number of elements in the array. Take care when doing this, as redimensioning an array will erase the current contents of the array. The number of dimensions in an array, however, cannot be changed once it has been set.

You can also choose to preserve the contents of a dynamic array rather than erasing them. Use the Preserve keyword:

```
Private Sub LoadColors (LastColor As Integer)
    ReDim Preserve Colors(LastColor) As String
    ReDim Preserve Cars(LastColor) As Integer
    :
    [Place your code here]
    :
End Sub
```

This example preserves the contents of the Colors and Cars arrays during the redimensioning process.

Variant Arrays

Because the variant data type can store many different types of data, a variant array can be used in many situations where you might need to use a user-defined data type. A variant array is actually more flexible than a user-defined type because you can change the type of data stored in each element at any time, and you can make the array dynamic, so you can change its size when necessary. A caveat about variant arrays is that they use more memory than their user-defined counterparts.

To declare an array as variant, define the variable as in the following code:

```
Dim vRows() as Variant
```

There are cases where data retrieved from a method is returned into a variant data structure. When using the Data Access Object 3.5 and the Remote Data Object, the method GetRows stores data in a variant data structure. In the following code example, the GetRows method is used to retrieve a maximum of 10 rows into a variant array. The array is dynamically built as a two-dimensional array in which the first element is the column and the second is the row.

```
Private Sub Form_Load()

    Dim env as rdoEnvironment
    Dim con as rdoConnection
    Dim rs as rdoResultset
    Dim vReturnedRows as Variant
    Dim x as Integer
    Dim y as Integer
    Dim sRowInfo as String

    ' Establish connection to database and create resultset
    Set env = rdoEnvironment(0)
    Set con = env.OpenConnection(dsName:="dsnConnection"")
    Set rs = con.OpenResultSet("Select Lname, Fname, Publisher from tblAuthors")

    ' If there is data in the resultset,
```

```
' retrieve the first 10 rows
If (Not rs.BOF) Then
    vReturnedRows = rs.GetRows(10)
Else
    Exit Sub
End If

' Print the retrieved 10 rows to the Form
For y = 0 to Ubound(vReturnedRows, 2)
    For x = 0 to 2
        SRowInfo = sRowInfo & ", " & vReturnedRows(x, y)
    Next x
    Form1.Print sRowInfo
Next y
End Sub
```

Array Function

Another way to define a variant array is to use the Array function. The Array function is probably one of the most underused functions that Visual Basic has to offer. It enables a user to create an array from a comma-delimited list of values. To use the Array function, your code should look like the following example:

```
Dim DaysOfWeek as Variant
DaysOfWeek = Array("Sun", "Mon", "Tues", "Weds", "Thurs", "Fri", "Sat")

Print DaysOfWeek(2)    ' Displays "Tues"
Print DaysOfWeek(7)    ' Displays "Sat"
```

As it does in all arrays, the Array function builds the array at base 0, unless Option Base 1 is used. If no arguments are specified, an array of zero length is created. A more efficient method of defining arrays is by using enumerated values, which is described in Chapter 14.

Working with the ASCII Character Set

You may sometimes find it useful to be able to determine the ASCII code of a character, or to translate an ASCII code into a character. The Asc and Chr functions handle these duties for you. The Asc function returns the ASCII code for the supplied character. Conversely, the Chr function returns a 1-byte string containing the character that is represented by the supplied ASCII code.

```
Function MakeSecretCode(phrase$) As String
    For i = 1 To Len(phrase$)
        temp = Asc(Mid(phrase$, i, 1))
        Mid(phrase$, i, 1) = Chr(Abs(temp - 255))
    Next i
End Function
```

In the previous example, the function will translate a given phrase into a secret code. It does this by translating each character in the phrase into a different character using a simple transformation, thus effectively scrambling the phrase to casual observers. (Cryptographers would probably laugh at the simplicity of the transformation we use, and could probably break the code in not much more time than it took to write it!)

Comparing Strings

Strings are compared using the same operators (such as =, <, or >) that are used with numbers, in addition to the Like operator, which is used for pattern matching. String comparison was enhanced in Visual Basic 4.0 by the addition of a string comparison option, Option Compare. This statement is placed in the beginning of a form, module, or class module to determine the method used to compare strings. Visual Basic defaults to a binary comparison mode, meaning that comparisons are based on ASCII value and therefore are case sensitive. To explicitly declare binary comparison, use the Option Compare Binary statement. If instead you use the Option Compare Text statement, then string comparisons will be made without regard to case. The difference between these two options is shown here:

```
Option Compare Binary      'case sensitive comparisons
A < B < C < a < b < c      'binary sorted order

Option Compare Text        'not case sensitive.
A = a, B = b, C = c        'text sorted order
```

Using the comparison operators, you can compare strings for many different conditions:

```
If A$ = B$ Then MsgBox "They are equal"
If A$ > B$ Then MsgBox "B$ is alphabetically before A$"
If A$ < B$ Then MsgBox "A$ is alphabetically before B$"
If A$ Like B$ Then MsgBox "A$ is similar to B$"
```

When comparing strings, you must keep in mind that even undisplayed members of a string (such as a space character) are considered. For example:

```
A$ = "Hello"
B$ = "Hello "

'message will not be displayed
If A$ = B$ Then MsgBox "They are equal"
```

A$ is not equal to B$ because of the extra space in the string. Visual Basic provides a way to account for trailing or leading spaces using the functions LTrim, RTrim, and Trim. These functions return a given string with the leading, trailing, or both leading and trailing spaces removed, respectively.

```
A$ = LTrim(" Hello ")      'A$ results in "Hello "
A$ = RTrim(" Hello ")      'A$ results in " Hello"
A$ = Trim(" Hello ")       'A$ results in "Hello"
```

Another situation that can interfere with string comparisons is case (capitalization). This problem arises if you choose not to use the Option Compare Text declaration, or if you are using a version of Visual Basic earlier than Visual Basic 4.0. If two strings that are otherwise identical have different capitalization, the string comparison between them will fail.

```
A$ = "Hello"
B$ = "hello"

If A$ = B$ then MsgBox "They are equal"     'message will not be shown!
```

Although A$ and B$ consist of the same word, the case is different, and Visual Basic will not consider them equal. This type of error can be avoided in all versions of Visual Basic by using the LCase and UCase functions. They will return a string in all lower-case or all uppercase, respectively.

```
A$ = LCase("Hello")        'A$ results in "hello"
A$ = UCase("Hello")        'A$ results in "HELLO"
```

The Like operator enables you to use pattern matching in your string comparisons, searching strings for a pattern that you can specify using pattern symbols. These symbols are shown in Table 15-1.

Table 15-1 Like operator pattern symbols

Symbol	Function
?	Matches any single character
#	Matches any single digit (0 to 9)
*	Matches any sequence of zero or more characters
[charlist]	Matches any single character in [charlist] list of characters
[!charlist]	Matches any single character not in [!charlist] list of characters
[charRange]	Matches any single character in [charRange] range of characters
[!charRange]	Matches any single character not in the [!charRange] range of characters

The [charlist] symbol represents a list of characters enclosed by brackets and separated by commas (A, G, g, l, P). The [charRange] represents a range of characters delineated by a hyphen ([a-g]) and enclosed in brackets. The Like operator returns True or False depending on the success of a pattern match:

```
Private Result as Boolean

Result = "Pattern" Like "Pa??ern"         'Result is True
Result = "Pattern" Like "P*"              'Result is True
Result = "Patton" Like "P*"              'Result is True
Result = "Pattern" Like "PaTT?n"          'Result is False
Result = "Fatten" Like "[F,P]att*n"       'Result is True
Result = "Patton" Like "[F,P]att*n"       'Result is True
Result = "Pattern" Like "[F,P]att*n"      'Result is True
Result = "Pattern" Like "[A-F]att*n"      'Result is False
Result = "Fatten" Like "[A-F]att*n"       'Result is True
```

These simple comparisons give you an idea of the very powerful pattern matching capabilities of Visual Basic. As with the other types of comparisons, the Like operator is affected by the Option Compare statement.

Creating a Series of Characters

Suppose you want to create a string that is 20 bytes long and contains 20 asterisks. To do this, you could assign a string literal of 20 asterisks to a string variable:

```
Asters$ = "********************"
```

Although this works, it is not very elegant. What if you need a 200-byte-long string? You certainly wouldn't want to sit and type 200 asterisks! Or suppose, as with printing checks, you need to be able to print a variable number of asterisks following the written amount on demand? A better alternative is to use the String function. This function enables you to create strings of repeated characters by supplying two arguments that indicate the number and type of character desired. For example:

```
Asters$ = String(200, "*")
Fill$ = String(Remain%, "*")
```

The first line of code assigns 200 asterisks to the variable Asters$, whereas the second statement uses the value of the variable Remain% to determine how many asterisks will be stored in Fill$.

The Space function works in the same manner as the String function, except that it always returns spaces.

```
Blanks$ = Space(100)
```

This line of code assigns 100 spaces to the variable Blanks$.

16

OBJECTS AND COLLECTIONS

Visual Basic 5.0 is an object-oriented language. An *object* contains both information and the methods required to manipulate the information. Programming language objects are usually modeled after real objects. For example, Visual Basic provides predefined objects that help form the user interface. Forms, controls, and menus are all examples of Visual Basic's built-in user interface objects that mimic real objects such as paper, push buttons, or a book's table of contents.

In Visual Basic 5.0, you can also define your own objects. For example, you might define an object to represent a refrigerator. Refrigerators have "information," such as manufacturer, color, size, capacity, temperature, and contents. Some properties of the refrigerator are relatively static, such as manufacturer and color. Some properties are dynamic, and changing them might trigger other actions. For example, raising the temperature would both change the piece of information for "temperature" and affect the state of some of the contents—any contents of type "dairy" might change their state to "spoiled."

This chapter contains an overview of the types of predefined objects in Visual Basic, including the exciting additions in version 5.0. It also explains how to name and use these objects, and discusses the vital topics of object variables, instances, and collections. Finally, the chapter describes what each object is and what it does, including complete tables of all applicable properties, methods, and events.

Properties, Events, and Methods

Each built-in Visual Basic object has a set of *properties* associated with it. These properties (such as Height, BorderStyle, or Caption) determine the appearance and behavior of an object. When you create your application, you set an object's properties during the design phase using the Properties box illustrated in Figure 16-1. In most cases, your program can read or set these properties while it is running. Some properties are read-only at runtime, meaning that you can only set their value when the program is in its design phase. Other properties cannot be set during the design phase; you must make any changes to these properties in the program's code.

Visual Basic also assigns a set of *events* to most objects. These events are Visual Basic sub procedures that trigger when the user performs an action with an object. For instance, GotFocus, Click, MouseMove, and LostFocus are events common to many objects. Double-clicking on an object in design phase displays Visual Basic's code window. From here, you may define the actions to take when a particular event occurs. Refer to Chapters 13, "Program Flow," and 34, "Events," for more information about events and event procedures. Figure 16-2 shows a command button on a form, with an event sub procedure shown in the code window.

Most objects also have associated *methods*. Methods are commands that perform an action with or on an object. They are used like Visual Basic's statements or functions, but their operations act directly on an object when invoked by code. For example, a list box has the Clear method, which clears it of all entries.

Types of Objects

Visual Basic has several different types of objects. The form is one of the most basic objects. A *form* is a window that contains application code and has other objects placed on it to create the user interface. A form may fill the entire screen, have other forms contained within it, or may be a smaller custom dialog box. Chapter 36, "Forms and Menus," discusses forms in detail.

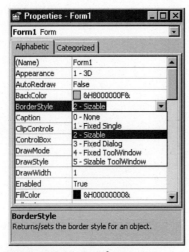

Figure 16-1   Set object properties in the Properties box during the design phase

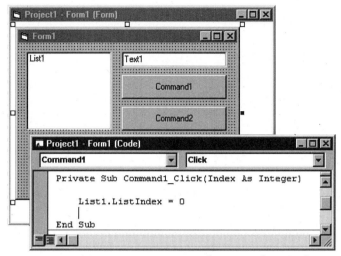

Figure 16-2   React to user actions with event sub procedures

The most familiar objects are the standard user interface objects: command buttons, list boxes, menus, and so forth. These objects are commonly referred to as *controls*. A control object is typically drawn directly on a form, except for the menu control, which is created with the menu design window. You draw controls on the form by selecting the type of control from the tool palette, illustrated in Figure 16-3, and dragging it with the mouse onto the form where you want to place it. Details about controls, and their associated properties, events, and methods, make up the bulk of this book. See Chapter 36 for details about menus.

Visual Basic also has five specialized system objects that let you work with an application's environment. These are the App, Clipboard, Debug, Printer, and Screen objects.

Figure 16-3   Choose control objects from the tool palette

The App object lets your program find out important information about the environment, such as the name of the associated help file and the application's path. The Clipboard object lets your program interact with the Windows Clipboard area. Visual Basic programs can copy text or graphics to and from the Clipboard. Chapter 53, "Using the Clipboard," presents detailed information on how to use the Clipboard object. The Debug object, used only within the Visual Basic environment, can help with the testing and debugging of a program.

The Printer object generates printed output. Since the Windows environment handles the actual printing duties, your Visual Basic program doesn't really send output to the printer. Instead, the Printer object sends that output to the Windows printing routines, which then send the data to the printer. Chapter 52, "Printing," covers the Printer object in detail. The Screen object globally references other objects. Your program can use the Screen object to determine which form or control is active, and how many and what types of fonts are available to the system. Chapter 35, "Accessing Forms and Controls," discusses the Screen object in more detail.

Two very comprehensive objects are also available in Visual Basic Professional and Enterprise Editions. The DBEngine object gives you full access to the Jet database engine. Learning Edition users can gain access to the most important parts of this large object through the data control. The Application object gives a program access to the actual Visual Basic design environment, making it possible to write "add-in" utilities to help you as you program.

Visual Basic can also use objects that other programmers have created. You can purchase third-party OCX controls that plug into the Visual Basic design environment and work just like the built-in controls. These controls have their own properties, methods, and events just as normal controls do. Some are extremely sophisticated, and using an intelligently chosen set of OCX controls can dramatically reduce your coding time. You can also use the older VBX technology pioneered with Visual Basic 1.0, 2.0, and 3.0. VBXs are similar to OCXs, but offer a somewhat limited range of functionality and performance. Visual Basic Learning Edition ships with a few OCXs, such as the Common Dialog control and the DBList, DBCombo, and DBGrid controls. The Professional and Enterprise Editions ship with many more OCXs developed by other companies.

Visual Basic lets you control other applications that offer OLE automation, such as Microsoft Excel or Visio Corporation's Visio. You can create objects defined by these commercial applications and manipulate them just as you would native Visual Basic objects, as described in Chapter 76, "OLE Automation."

Finally, you can create your own objects with Visual Basic's new class modules. You manipulate these objects much as you would any OLE automation object. You can create fully encapsulated OLE automation servers with the Professional and Enterprise Editions, so that any other application that can use OLE automation objects can use the objects you create. Creating objects can dramatically improve your programming style, and will prove especially valuable if you are working on larger programs. Part XVII, "New Object-Oriented Programming," explains how to create and use your own objects.

Naming Conventions

Each Visual Basic object has a name that you use to refer to it in code. Set the name of forms and controls during the design phase with the Name property in the Properties box. The name must start with a letter and may be up to 40 characters long. It may contain the underscore character (although this is not recommended, as it makes event procedures harder to read), but may not contain any other punctuation symbols. Each control or form starts with a default name consisting of the object type plus a unique integer. For example, the first text box is named Text1, the second one Text2; the fourth list box created would be named List4.

The default names work well for smaller applications. Most of the code examples in this book keep the default names for simplicity. Larger applications demand an intelligent and consistent naming practice to make it easier to debug your code. As with variables, you should give objects names that indicate their purpose; for example, PatientName or ShippingMethods.

It's good practice to start any object name with some sort of abbreviation that indicates what kind of object it is. This will help you as you trace your code, and it also groups similar kinds of controls together in the code window (for example, all text box event procedures would be near each other). Microsoft suggests using a three-letter code (such as txt for text box, lst for list box). There are many possible conventions; what is important is that you be consistent. For larger examples and many of the larger projects, this book uses four-letter abbreviations (such as text for text box, list for list box). The examples from the proceeding paragraph might then be named txtPatientName and lstShippingMethods. Chapter 35 includes a table of suggested object prefixes.

The system objects (App, Clipboard, Debug, Printer, and Screen) cannot be renamed. You always refer to them by their default name. The data control's two underlying objects (Database and Recordset) also cannot be renamed.

Refer to an object's properties and methods with the dot operator. This consists of the object's Name property, a period (.), and the property or method. For example:

```
reponse$ = Text1.Text
Clipboard.Clear
Form1.ScaleHeight = 2700
textPatientName.ForeColor = YELLOW
listShippingMethods.AddItem "Federal Express"
```

In versions prior to version 5.0, reference a control on another form with the bang operator. This consists of the form's Name property, an exclamation point (!), and the name of the control:

```
reponse$ = Form2!Text1.Text
Form3!textPatientName.ForeColor = YELLOW
formShip!listShippingMethods.AddItem "Federal Express"
```

You may also use the dot operator in place of the exclamation point. Visual Basic 1.0 used this type of construction exclusively, and Visual Basic 2.0 and 3.0 have retained it to ease compatibility with older applications. The bang operator more clearly differentiates between the name of the control you're referencing, and the property or method of that control.

```
Form2.Text1.Text = "Hello"    'Works but not recommended. Kept for compatibility with VB 1.0
Form2!Text1.Text = "Hello"    'recommended; clearer distinction between name and property
```

In version 5.0, the bang operator is still a valid operator, but is not recommended for use anymore. As the saying goes, "Engineers love to change things." For backward compatibility, the bang can still be used, but it will not work with Visual Basic's IntelliSense features, like Complete Word and QuickInfo. For more information about these features, refer to Chapter 1, "Why Visual Basic?"

Finally, events are usually named with the Name property of the control, an underscore (_), and the name of the event, as in txtPatientName_Click. Forms are the exception; rather than using the name of the form, the event routine uses the keyword Form.

```
Private Sub Command1_Click ()
    MsgBox "You've just clicked Command1!"
End Sub

Private Sub txtPatientName_GotFocus ()
    txtPatientName.BackColor = QBColor(7)
    txtPatientName.ForeColor = QBColor(1)
    txtPatientName.SelLength = Len(txtPatientName.Text)
End Sub

Private Sub Form_Load ()
    List1.AddItem "Red"
    List1.AddItem "Blue"
    List1.AddItem "Green"
End Sub
```

For more information about naming and referring to objects, see Chapter 35.

Object Variables

You can assign most objects to an object variable. This lets you manipulate the object just as easily as you would manipulate any standard variable, such as a string or integer variable. You can pass objects to sub procedures or functions, create arrays of objects, and shorten and simplify your code.

Declare an object variable just as you would declare any standard variable by using the Dim, ReDim, Static, Public, or Private keywords. Table 16-1 lists the available control types and the class names associated with them. The property box lists the class names in the right-hand portion of the top combo box; this is especially helpful for determining the class name of custom controls.

Table 16-1 Class names used for creating object variables

Object Type	Class Name Used in Dim, ReDim, Static, Public, or Private Statements (any object) Object
(any control)	Control
(any form)	Form
(any custom class)	Custom Name property
(custom controls)	Custom control's class name

Object Type	Class Name Used in Dim, ReDim, Static, Public, or Private Statements (any object) Object
(OLE automation server)	Server's class name
Check box	CheckBox
Collection	Collection
Combo box	ComboBox
Command button	CommandButton
Data	Data
DBCombo	DBCombo
DBGrid	DBGrid
DBList	DBList
Directory list box	DirListBox
Drive list box	DriveListBox
File list box	FileListBox
Font	Font (also StdFont to define a new font)
Form	Name property of specific form
Frame	Frame
Grid	Grid
Horizontal scroll	HScrollBar
Image	Image
Label	Label
Line	Line
List	ListBox
MDI Form	MDIForm
Menu	Menu
OLE	OLE
Option	OptionButton
Picture box	PictureBox
Picture	Picture (also StdPicture to define a new picture)
Shape	Shape
Text box	TextBox
Timer	Timer
Vertical scroll	VScrollBar

For example, here is how to declare a variable that can refer to any text box in your application:

```
Dim myTextBoxVariable As TextBox
```

You can then use this variable just as you would use the actual name of the object, and assign an object to it with the Set keyword:

```
Set myTextBoxVariable = Text1
myTextBoxVariable.Text = "Hello"
```

This next example shows how to shorten and simplify your code by using an object variable:

```
Private Sub Command1_Click ()          'without object variable
    newName$ = frmPatientInput.txtPatientName.Text & " (discharged)"
    frmPatientInput.txtPatientName.Text = newName$
    frmPatientInput.txtPatientName.ForeColor = QBColor(3)
End Sub

Private Sub Command1_Click ()          'using object variable to simplify code
    Dim old As TextBox
    Set old = frmPatientInput.txtPatientName
    newName$ = old & " (discharged)"
    old.Text = newName$
    old.ForeColor = QBColor(3)
End Sub
```

You can also declare an object variable to accept any kind of control with the Control class name. This allows you to write generic functions and sub procedures. For example, this code hides or unhides any control that is passed to it:

```
Public Sub Flip (c As Control)
    c.Visible = Not c.Visible
End Sub
```

Some controls may not have the property or method you're trying to use, which would cause an error. For instance, timers don't have the Visible property. You can check for what kind of control an object variable represents with the If TypeOf <control> Is <class name> construction. You can also use the Not operator as part of the If TypeOf statement to reverse the true or false outcome of an If statement. Note that you can only use TypeOf...Is in an If statement; you cannot use it in a Select Case block.

```
Public Sub Flip (c As Control)
    If Not(TypeOf c Is Timer) Then            'timers don't have the Visible property
        c.Visible = Not c.Visible
    End If
End Sub
```

You may also use the Is keyword without TypeOf to check whether two object variables refer to the same object:

```
Public Sub Test (c As Control, d As Control)
    If c Is d Then MsgBox "Controls are the same!"
End Sub
```

Generic object variables declared with the Control class name are flexible, because they can refer to any type of control, but are slower than specific class name variables. You should use specific object variables whenever possible. Visual Basic can create the reference to a specific variable when your program starts up, while generic object variables need to have the reference created each time they are used.

You can have form object variables refer to the generic class of "all forms" by using the Form class name. You may also refer to specific forms by using the form's Name property as its class name; in contrast, regular control variables can never refer to specific controls. For example,

```
Private Sub Command1_Click ()
    Dim f As formPatientForm
    f.Caption = "This is still the formPatientForm"
    f.Text1.Text = "HelLo"
End Sub
```

Instances

Objects are created from classes. Think of a *class* as a blank template, or as a potential but not-yet-created object. A class contains all the information necessary to create an actual object, but it isn't the object. For example, Visual Basic 5.0 lets you define your own classes using class modules. Chapter 104, "Creating Classes and Class Modules," describes exactly how to do this. The class module consists of Visual Basic code you write. This code makes up the definition of the class. If you included the class module in a project, but never referred to the class in the rest of the project's code, no objects would be created from the class.

You build an object from a class by *instantiating* it. For example, if you define a class module called Refrigerator (it simulates a real-world refrigerator), you can create and manipulate an object with this code:

```
Dim downstairsFridge As New Refrigerator
downstairsFridge.Color = beige
downstairsFridge.Temperatune = 38
```

The Dim statement, with the New keyword, is the key to creating the object. An object that's been created, or instantiated, is called an *instance* of the class. In this example, the downstairsFridge object is an instance of the Refrigerator class.

This concept becomes crucial once you have instantiated many different objects from the same class. For example, suppose you're modeling a hotel in which many rooms have a refrigerator. You may have hundreds of instances of the class Refrigerator. Each instance is a separate object. Each of these objects can manipulate itself in the same way as the other instances, but the information inside each object instance is separate. This lets you have dozens of different models, makes, and sizes of refrigerators all based on the same class.

Visual Basic provides a number of built-in classes. You've already seen examples of many of these, such as forms, command buttons, and text boxes. When you draw these control objects on a form, you're creating the class structure or definition, but these control objects don't turn into real objects until you have instantiated them. This generally happens automatically, so you may not be aware of the distinction: Referring to an object's properties on a form (such as a command button's Caption property) automatically instantiates the form and all the controls on that form. All of Visual Basic's built-in objects (or more properly, built-in classes) feature this automatic instantiation.

You may have multiple instances of your program running at one time, and multiple instances of forms within a single application. Recall that an instance means an exact but independent copy of something. Thus, two copies of your program can be running at the same time, without interacting or interfering with each other. As another example, a single application can contain multiple copies of a single form class;

these forms are completely independent. Although they are exact copies of the original "template" form class, their data remains separate from the other forms and they each may be manipulated independently.

This is an important concept used in creating Multiple-Document Interface (MDI) applications, a subject covered in more detail in Chapter 36. In an MDI application, you may have several documents open at one time. For instance, Microsoft Word or Lotus AmiPro lets you have many different files available for editing at once, and you can simultaneously view more than one file at a time.

Your Visual Basic program can do this by creating a single document form with all the user interface elements (such as command buttons, text boxes, and menu structure) plus all the code that is document specific (like repagination or search and replace) during the design phase. This serves as the class from which you create individual instances. Each time the user needs to create a new document, your program creates a new instance of the original form. It retains all the code and user interface of the original, but does not interact with any other open documents based on the original form. This new instance also contains its own data. This coupling of information (say, the actual text of the document) with the means of manipulating the information (the code and user interface you create) is the central foundation of object-oriented programming. Keeping the information, code, and user interface elements together simplifies program design and makes programs easier to maintain.

You may create new instances of forms by using the New keyword in the declaration statement:

```
Private Sub mnuNewDocument_Click ()
    Dim d As New formBlankDocument    'Create a new document form
    d.Show                            'and display it.
End Sub
```

You may think of the original form as a "template" used to create the other instances. Each instance gets its own copy of data, so you cannot use module-level variables to share information between the various instances. You can use global-level variables instead, although it's better to set up a class hierarchy with class functions and properties, as discussed in Chapter 104.

You usually don't need to know what instance of a form or class module is currently being used. Procedure code automatically runs in the appropriate instance. Sometimes, however, you need to distinguish among the various instances. The Me keyword lets you refer to the instance in which the code is running, and is generally useful for avoiding ambiguity and creating self-documenting code:

```
Private Sub Command1_Click ()
    Me.Hide                'hide this form instance
End Sub

Public Sub Unplug()
    'refrigerator is unplugged; set temperature appropriately and decrease power ⇐
consumption
    Me.Temperature = 70
    Me.Watts = 0
End Sub
```

Chapter 35 includes more examples of the Me keyword, which also plays an important role in the project at the end of Chapter 36.

Collections

Many objects contain some arbitrary number of other objects. For example, a form object may contain a number of control objects. The sample Refrigerator class contains a number of objects called "contents," which represent each food item. Visual Basic provides an easy way of working with sets of objects through collections. A *collection* is simply a group of anything—any set of objects, whether similar or not. Collections normally include only one type of object, however, and this is the way you'll probably use them most often. You can create your own collections as well as use Visual Basic's built-in collections.

Built-In Collections

The built-in collections are ordered sets of similarly typed objects. For example, the Forms collection consists of all the loaded forms in your application, and the Controls collections consist of the controls on each form, with each form having its own Controls collection. The data control has several other collections: the TableDefs collection of each table in a database, the Fields collection of each field in a table, and the Indexes collection of each index in a table. The Application object also has many built-in collections.

Each built-in collection is like a zero-based array of objects. The first member of a zero-based array has an ordinal position (index) of 0, not 1. You don't need to declare collections; Visual Basic declares them automatically. Each collection has a Count property, which gives the total number of members in the collection (for example, Form1.Controls.Count gives the total number of controls on Form1).

Collections are particularly useful when you want to iterate through all the loaded instances of the objects. For example, the following few lines of code step through all controls on all forms and put the controls' Tag property into an array for subsequent use:

```
For i = 0 To Forms.Count - 1
    For j = 0 To Forms(i).Controls.Count - 1
        TagArray(i, j) = Forms(i).Controls(j).Tag
    Next j
Next i
```

Combining collections with the TypeOf test lets you perform repeated actions on similar types of controls. This code steps through all controls on all forms, and sets the FontName and ForeColor properties of all text boxes. It also demonstrates the new (and recommended) way of accessing all the elements in a collection, the For Each...Next loop:

```
Dim c As Object, f As Object
For Each f In Forms
    For Each c In f.Controls
        If TypeOf c Is TextBox Then
            c.Font.Name = "Arial"
            c.ForeColor = QBColor(2)
```

continued on next page

continued from previous page

```
            End If
    Next c
Next f
```

Custom Collections

You will most often use custom collections that emulate the structure of the built-in collections when you build custom classes. Many programmer-defined classes will fall naturally into the structure of a general "template" from which many individual instances are built. You'll use a collection to store the instances. For example, you may want to create a Refrigerator object; each refrigerator has a number of different food item objects stored in the Refrigerator object's Contents collection. This example shows how to create a new object and place it in a parent object's collection:

```
'these appear in the Refrigerator class module
Private Contents As New Collection

Public Function CreateFoodItem(newName As String) As Object
    'create a new food item
    Dim newFood As New Food
    newFood.Name = newName
    'add the new food object to the Contents collection
    Contents.Add (item:=newFood, key:=newFood.Name)
    'return the new food object to the calling procedure
    Set CreateFoodItem = newFood
End Function
```

Chapter 104 includes more examples of using a collection to store instances of custom classes.

Collections are marvelously flexible data structures. You can use them for many things other than storing custom classes. The Add method defaults to adding a new member at the end of the collection, but you can specify that you want to add a new member immediately before or after an existing one. This makes it simple to build structures such as heaps and stacks: Let Visual Basic do all the housekeeping for you with the Collection object!

For example, a stack is a common data structure. It lets you put a new item on top of a "stack" of other items. When you read the value of the stack, the value of the *last* item placed on the stack is returned. This is referred to as a LIFO (last in, first out) structure. Programmers commonly call placing an object on a stack "pushing" the stack, and removing an item "popping" the stack. This example shows how simple these processes are with Visual Basic's new Collection object:

```
'This creates a stack
Dim stack As New Collection

'This pushes a new item onto the stack
stack.Add(item:=thingYouWantToAdd, before:= 1)

'This reads the value of the stack
x = stack.Item(1)
```

```
'This pops the stack
stack.Remove(1)
```

This process requires less code than implementing a stack using traditional arrays. You'll still use arrays for most of your data structure needs, particularly when speed is important, but consider taking advantage of the flexibility of collections before you do.

Notice a few potentially troublesome differences between built-in collections and custom collections: The built-in collections are zero-based (the first item in the collection is number 0), and include only one type of object. Custom collections are one-based (the first item in the collection is number 1), and can store any kind of object.

Objects and Collections Summary

Visual Basic's built-in objects and collections are summarized in Table 16-2. Note that the word "object" is used in two senses in Visual Basic. Each of the items in the table is an "object," as described above, but some objects are also "controls." A control, as the name implies, is an object that the user can use to communicate with or control the application. Objects that are not controls are not directly manipulated by the user.

Table 16-2 Visual Basic objects

Use This...	Type	To Do This...
App	Object	Determine environmental settings for the application
CheckBox	Control	Display a choice that the user can turn on or off
ClassModule	Object	Define a new custom class
Clipboard	Object	Copy and paste text or graphics to and from the Windows Clipboard
Collection	Object	Create and manipulate custom collections
ComboBox	Control	Display a list box with a text input area
CommandButton	Control	Display a button that performs a function when the user clicks on it
CommonDialog	Control	Display Open, Save As, Print, Color, and Font dialog boxes
Controls	Collection	Access any loaded control on a form
Data	Control	Connect an application to a database file
DBCombo	Control	Display a list box with a text input area, fill list from a database
DBEngine	Object	Access and manipulate databases
DBGrid	Control	Display a series of rows and columns from a database
DBList	Control	Display a list box filled from a database
Debug	Object	Get help in the development/debugging process of a program
DirListBox	Control	Allow the user to choose a disk directory from a list box
DriveListBox	Control	Allow the user to choose a disk drive from a drop-down list box
Err	Object	Store and retrieve information about runtime errors
FileListBox	Control	Allow the user to choose a file in a specific directory from a list box

continued on next page

continued from previous page

Use This...	Type	To Do This...
Font	Object	Manipulate properties determining how text is displayed
Form	Object	Define a window on the screen on which objects may be placed
Forms	Collection	Access any loaded form in currently running project
Frame	Control	Define an area on a form that can contain several related controls
Grid	Control	Display a series of rows and columns with cells at the intersections
Image	Control	Define an area to display a picture
Label	Control	Place a text label on a form, picture, or frame
Line	Control	Display a horizontal, vertical, or diagonal line
ListBox	Control	Display in a box a list of items from which the user can choose
MDIForm	Object	Define a window to contain MDI child forms
Menu	Control	Define pull-down menus that appear at the top of a form
MSFlexGrid	Control	Display a series of rows and columnswith cells at the intersections. The data can also be bound to database
OLE	Control	Create linked or embedded objects
OptionButton	Control	Define a group of choices where only one choice may be selected
Picture	Object	Manipulate a graphic metafile or bitmap without using a picture box or form
PictureBox	Control	Define an area on a form for displaying graphics
Printer	Object	Generate output to the printer
Printers	Collection	Access any printer installed on the user's computer
Screen	Object	Activate a specific form or control at runtime
Scroll Bars	Control	Provide a visual method for setting a value
Shape	Control	Display a graphical control
TextBox	Control	Define an area on a form for text editing
Timer	Control	Provide a program with timing capabilities
VBE	Object	Provide access to the Visual Basic design environment for add-in utilities

This chapter explores the purposes and uses of each of these objects. Each entry discusses the object's related properties, events, and methods. An accompanying figure shows each object's appearance on the screen, unless the object is not visible. Also, if the object is covered in a later chapter of this book, you will be directed there for an example of how it is used.

A *control* is a type of object. In the entries that pertain to controls, the word "control" refers to the control being discussed; "object" refers to objects in the more general sense. In some cases these two terms may be used interchangeably.

APP OBJECT

Purpose The App object determines environmental settings for the application, such as the path and filename of the application itself and its associated help files.

Properties   Table 16-3 summarizes the properties of the App object; it has no events or methods.

Table 16-3 Properties of the App object

Use This Property...	To Do This...
Comments	Read the value of the Comments set in the Make EXE dialog.
CompanyName	Read the value of the Company Name set in the Make EXE dialog.
EXEName	Determine the filename of the application's executable file.
FileDescription	Read the value of the File Description set in the Make EXE dialog.
HelpFile	Read or set the name of this application's help file.
hInstance	Read the value of the instance handle for this instance of the application.
LegalCopyright	Read the value of the Legal Copyright as set in the Make EXE dialog.
LegalTrademarks	Read the value of the Legal Trademarks as set in the Make EXE dialog.
LogMode	Set a value that determines how logging through the LogEvent method will be done. It is read-only at runtime.
LogPath	Set the path and filename of the file used to capture output from the LogEvent method. It is not available at design time; read-only at runtime.
Major	Read the value of the major release number as set in the Make EXE dialog.
Minor	Read the value of the minor release number as set in the Make EXE dialog.
NonModalAllowed	Set the value that indicates whether a form can be shown modeless. It is not available at design time.
OLERequestPendingMsgText	Read or set the text displayed when an OLE automation server is busy.
OLERequestPendingMsgTitle	Read or set the dialog box title displayed when an OLE automation server is busy.
OLERequestPendingTimeout	Read or set the number of milliseconds before an OLE automation server sends a busy message.
OLEServerBusyMsgText	Read or set the text displayed when an OLE automation server refuses a request.
OLEServerBusyMsgTitle	Read or set the dialog box title displayed when an OLE automation server refuses a request.
OLEServerBusyRaiseError	Read or set whether an OLE automation server raises an error when it refuses a request.
OLEServerBusyTimeout	Read or set the number of milliseconds to retry an operation.
Path	Read the absolute path of the application's executable file.
PrevInstance	Determine whether a previous instance of the application is running.
ProductName	Read the value of the Product Name as set in the Make EXE dialog.
Revision	Read the value of the revision number as set in the Make EXE dialog.
StartMode	Read or set whether the application starts as a standalone program or an OLE automation object.
TaskVisible	Read or set whether the application appears in the Windows Task List.
ThreadID	Read the value of the Win32 ID of the executing thread. Used for Win32 API calls.
Title	Read or set the title of the application as it appears in the Windows Task List.
UnattendedApp	Read the value that determines whether an application will run without any user interface.

Description   Use the App object to set and determine some fundamental information about your application's environment. The Path property gives the full path, including drive letters, to the directory in which the executable file (*.EXE) resides. The EXEName property gives the actual name of the executable file (without path) even if the user has renamed it after the application was compiled. HelpFile specifies the name of the help file associated with this application. PrevInstance lets you determine if another instance of your application is already running. If so, you may want to determine this during the Form_Load event to prevent more than one instance from loading. You may also use the hInstance property to get the handle of the current instance, which is helpful when calling the Windows API.

Visual Basic 5.0 returns a wealth of information that you can set in the Project Properties' Make section. The Comments, CompanyName, FileDescription, LegalCopyright, LegalTrademarks, and ProductName are all text strings that match what you put in the Project Properties' Make section when you compile your application. These are embedded in the executable, and can also be read by other software (such as the Windows 95 or NT Explorer's Properties page.) The Major, Minor, and Revision properties all return the integer values that make up the revision number of the executable.

The StartMode property indicates whether the application starts as a standalone program or as an OLE automation server—automation servers will remain running even if no code is called from their Sub Main procedure. See Chapter 104 for more details about this process. The Title property determines the exact title for your application in the Windows Task Manager, and the TaskVisible property determines whether to display the task in the Task List at all. This is very useful with OLE automation servers, especially those without a visible user interface.

The properties beginning with OLE... determine the behavior of OLE automation servers if they take too long to process a request. The default behavior is for Visual Basic to display a default dialog box, which may not meet your needs. For example, your OLE automation server may not have a visible interface. In this case, displaying the default dialog box won't work, because it has a Switch To command button on it, but your server doesn't have an interface to switch to. Use the OLERequestPending-MsgText and OLEServerBusyMsgText properties to determine the actual text displayed in the dialog box, and the OLERequestPendingMsgTitle and OLEServerBusyMsgTitle properties to determine the caption displayed in the title bar of the dialog box. The OLERequestPendingTimeout and OLEServerBusyTimeout properties determine the number of milliseconds until a pending request is declared busy, or a new request is refused because the server is busy or unavailable. You can also use the OLEServerBusyRaiseError property to raise an error rather than display a dialog box, although no equivalent is available for pending results.

CHECKBOX CONTROL

Purpose   The CheckBox control presents the user with an on/off choice. The user can either select or deselect this control by clicking it. Your program can determine whether the user has selected this control by examining its properties.

Properties, Events, and Methods

Tables 16-4, 16-5, and 16-6 list the properties, events, and methods that relate to the CheckBox control.

Table 16-4 Properties of the CheckBox control

Use This Property...	To Do This...
Alignment	Read or set the alignment of this control
Appearance	Read or set whether the object is drawn with 3D effects
BackColor, ForeColor	Read or set the background and foreground colors of this control
Caption	Assign text to this control
Container	Set or return a reference to the object that contains this object
DataChanged	Determine whether the value displayed in this control has changed
DataField	Read or set the name of the field in the recordset of the data control to which this control is bound
DataSource	Set the name of the data control to which this control is bound
DragIcon	Read or set what displays when this control is dragged
DragMode	Determine whether drag operations are to occur manually or automatically
Enabled	Read or set whether this control can react to events
Font	Set or return a font object that controls the way text displays in this control
FontBold, FontItalic, FontStrikeThru, FontUnderline	Read or set special effects for this control's font
FontName	Read or set the name of this control's font
FontSize	Read or set the size of this control's font
Height	Read or set the height of this control
HelpContextID	Read or set the context number to this control for context-sensitive help
hWnd	Read the handle for this control's window
Index	Uniquely identify an element of a control array
Left	Read or set the left edge position of this control on a picture or form
MaskColor	Read or set a color in a button's picture to be a "mask" or transparent
MouseIcon	Set a custom mouse pointer
MousePointer	Read or set the shape of the mouse pointer when it's over this control
Name	Read or set the name used in code to refer to this control
Parent	Read the name of the form to which the control belongs
Picture	Read or set a graphic to be displayed in a control when the Style setting is set to Graphical
Style	Read or set a value indicating the display type and behavior of the control, read-only at runtime
TabIndex	Read or set the placement of this control within the form's tab order
TabStop	Read or set whether this control is included in the form's tab order
Tag	Read or set any extra string data associated with this control

continued on next page

continued from previous page

Use This Property...	To Do This...
Top	Read or set the coordinate of this control's top edge relative to its container
UseMaskColor	Read or set a value that determines whether the color assigned in the MaskColor property is used as a "mask" for the transparent regions
Value	Read or set the current state of this control
Visible	Read or set whether this control is visible
WhatsThisHelpID	Read or set the context number to this object for context-sensitive help in Windows 95
Width	Read or set the width of this control

Table 16-5 Events of the CheckBox control

Use This Event...	To Do This...
Click	React to the user's clicking this control.
DragDrop	React to the user's dropping another object onto this control.
DragOver	React to the user's dragging another object over this control.
GotFocus	Initiate an action when this control receives the focus.
KeyDown	Initiate an action when the user presses or holds a key down.
KeyPress	React to the user's typing an ASCII character.
KeyUp	Initiate an action when the user releases a key on the keyboard.
LostFocus	Initiate an action when this control loses the focus.
MouseDown	React to the user's pressing any mouse button.
MouseMove	React to the user's moving the mouse over this control.
MouseUp	React to the user's releasing any mouse button.
OLECompleteDrag	A target component reacts to a source component being dropped on it. It is informing the source component that a drag action was either canceled or performed.
OLEDragDown	A target component reacts to a source component being dropped on it.
OLEDragOver	React to one component being dragged over another.
OLEGiveFeedback	Trigger the source component to provide visual feedback to the user.
OLESetData	A source component will react when a target component performs a GetData method, but the data for the specified format has not yet been loaded.
OLEStartDrag	React to a component's OLEDrag method, or when a component initiates an OLE drag-and-drop operation when the OLEDragMode property is set to Automatic.

Table 16-6 Methods of the CheckBox control

Use This Method...	To Do This...
Drag	Control manual dragging of this object
Move	Change the position of this object

Use This Method...	To Do This...
OLEDrag	Cause the OLE drag-and-drop operation
Refresh	Update and repaint this control
SetFocus	Move the focus to the specified object
ShowWhatsThis	Display the What's This help topic pop-up provided by the Windows 95 help system
ZOrder	Place this control at the front or back of the z-order

Description

The CheckBox control presents the user with a choice that has only two possible settings. It consists of a small box, which may be checked or empty, and some accompanying text (see Figure 16-4). When the user clicks this control, the status of the box is reversed; if it was checked before the user clicked it, the box will now be empty; if it was empty, it will now be checked. Unlike option buttons, check boxes on forms, labels, or pictures are independent of all other check boxes; changing the status of one check box does not affect other check boxes.

The program can set or read the current status with the Value property. This property has three possible settings. A setting of 0 indicates the box is currently empty. A setting of 1 means the box is currently checked. A setting of 2 indicates the control is grayed. The Value property can only be set to 2 by your program's code. This allows your programs to have an alternate method for indicating that a check box has been selected. However, setting the value property to 2 does not disable the control. It can still receive the focus, and will still react to the user's activity. If the check box is clicked while in this state, its Value property will be set to 0, and the box will be cleared.

The Caption property defines the text that will accompany the check box. The size and style of this text are defined by the settings of the Font... properties. Including an ampersand (&) underlines the following letter, and the check box may be selected by holding down the ⟨ALT⟩ key and pressing that letter. For instance, if a check box's Caption property is set to &Cash, the displayed text will be Cash and the user can select the box by pressing ⟨ALT⟩+⟨C⟩. Chapter 54, "Application Focus," covers the Caption property in more detail.

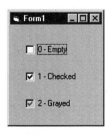

Figure 16-4 The three possible values of the check box

Clicking on this control activates its Click event. Use this event so your program can react immediately to any changes in the setting of the check box. This event also initiates if the user presses the (SPACEBAR) while the check box has the focus or any time the check box's Value property is changed within the program's code.

The Picture and Style properties are used together if you want to use a different type of check box style. Rather than the traditional check box look and feel, you can make the check box more like a toggle button, as illustrated in Figure 16-5.

CLASSMODULE OBJECT

Purpose
The ClassModule object lets you create your own custom classes, complete with custom methods and properties. A custom class is quite similar to a form, but without the visible user interface.

Properties and Events
Tables 16-7 and 16-8 list the properties and events of the ClassModule object. You should be aware that in version 4.0, there was a property called Public. This property has been removed in version 5.0, but it has been encapsulated into the Instancing property.

Table 16-7 Properties of the ClassModule object

Use This Property...	To Do This...
Instancing	Set whether the class can be created outside its own project
Name	Read or set the name of the class

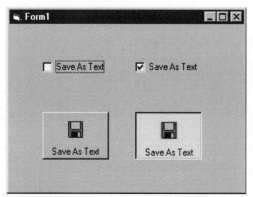

Figure 16-5   The top row illustrates traditional check boxes and the bottom row shows check boxes with the Style property set to Graphical

Table 16-8 Events of the ClassModule object

Use This Event...	To Do This...
Initialize	React when an object is first instantiated from the class
Terminate	React when an instantiated object of the class is about to be destroyed

Description

The ClassModule object lets you create your own classes, and brings Visual Basic 5.0 firmly into the realm of object-oriented languages. Create a new class module by choosing Class Module from the Project menu. This creates a new module in your project that looks just like a standard module. You write code in the class module just as you write code in a standard module or in a form's code window. Since you're defining a class structure, however, you can instantiate individual objects of the class. This lets you solve programming problems from a more abstract perspective than is possible with standard structured programming, and should help you as you write larger, more complex programs. See Chapter 104 and Chapter 105, "Using Classes and Class Modules," for more details about object-oriented analysis and programming and for many examples of how to create and use your own custom classes.

Set the two properties of the class module with the Properties box, just as you would set the properties of a form. The Name property of the class module defines the class name you'll use when referring to the class in code, as in a Dim statement or a parameter in a procedures argument list.

The Instancing property defines where and how the class may be used and is only available when developing ActiveX components. Learning Edition users can ignore these properties; they are only useful for compiled object applications, and only the Professional and Enterprise Editions can compile an object application. Learning Edition users will always include the actual class module in the project that makes use of the class, and the class will always be visible and creatable within that project. Professional and Enterprise Edition users, however, can compile an EXE file that includes all the classes appropriate for a custom OLE automation server, and instantiate the classes without actually including the class modules in the project that uses them.

When developing an ActiveX component, its property defaults to 1, Private, which means that it is only available for use within your component. A class hierarchy normally has only one creatable class that serves as the "root" object, and this root object then creates all other objects in the hierarchy. Chapter 104 explains this concept and includes several examples.

The Initialize and Terminate events let your custom class set any defaults or run any initialization procedures when objects are first created, and perform any necessary cleanup as they're being destroyed. (If you're familiar with other object-oriented languages, these events are similar to constructors and destructors.) Chapter 105 demonstrates the proper use of these events.

Note that the Form object is much like a class module, except that it has a visible interface. Visual Basic 5.0's object-orientation now fully supports the idea of a form as an object, complete with public methods and properties.

CLIPBOARD OBJECT

Purpose   The Clipboard object copies and pastes data to and from the Clipboard area of the Windows environment. This enables you to transfer data between most Windows applications as well as between forms or other objects in the same application.

Methods   Table 16-9 lists the methods that relate to the Clipboard object. This object has no associated properties or events.

Table 16-9 Methods of the Clipboard object

Use This Method...	To Do This...
Clear	Clear the contents of the Clipboard
GetData	Return graphics information from the Clipboard
GetFormat	Return whether or not the Clipboard holds a desired type of data
GetText	Return text information from the Clipboard
SetData	Send graphics information to the Clipboard
SetText	Send text information to the Clipboard

Description   One of the advantages of the Windows operating environment is that all Windows programs can copy and retrieve text and graphics to and from an area in the environment called the Clipboard. The Clipboard is a temporary holding area for data that has been cut or copied from the current or another program.

This Clipboard area is an element of the operating environment, and as such can be used by any program running in the environment. This means you can cut or copy information from one program and paste it into another. All Windows programs can use the Clipboard area.

The Clipboard can hold three types of items. First, it can hold text. Text is any letters, numbers, or characters that can be represented by an ASCII code. Second, it can hold graphics. Windows lets the user cut and paste pictures as well as text. Last, the Clipboard can hold DDE messages sent from one program to another.

The Clipboard can hold only one of each type of these data items at a time. When a program copies an item to the Clipboard, it replaces any item of the same type that previously resided there. The GetText and SetText methods retrieve and send text from and to the Clipboard. GetData and SetData are used to retrieve and send graphics from and to the Clipboard. The GetFormat method tests whether the Clipboard is currently holding a specific type of data.

The Clipboard object is discussed in detail in Chapter 53.

COLLECTION OBJECT

Purpose
The Collection object lets you create and manipulate your own collections of objects. A collection is normally made up of a group of the same type of objects.

Properties and Methods
Tables 16-10 and 16-11 list the properties and methods of the collection object. It has no events.

Table 16-10 Property of the Collection object

Use This Property...	To Do This...
Count	Return the number of members in a collection

Table 16-11 Methods of the Collection object

Use This Method...	To Do This...
Add	Add a new member to a collection
Item	Return the actual object in the collection
Remove	Remove an object from a collection

Description
The Collection object lets you create your own collections, manipulate the collection as a whole, and refer to individual members within the collection. A *collection* is a group of valid Visual Basic objects, such as text boxes, forms, recordsets, variables, user-defined types, or custom classes. You can mix different types of objects in a single collection, but normally collections include similarly typed objects, much like the built-in collections of controls, forms, errors, and printers, and the collections associated with database access and the add-in objects.

Most of the time, you will use custom collections when you emulate the structure of the built-in collections as you build custom classes. Many programmer-defined classes naturally fall into the structure of a general "template" from which many individual "instances" are built. You'll use a collection to store the instances. Chapter 104 includes several examples of using a collection to store instances of custom classes. You can use collections for many other purposes; the "Custom Collections" section at the beginning of this chapter illustrates how to build a stack using a collection.

ComboBox Control

Purpose   The ComboBox control provides three techniques for presenting a list of choices to the user.

Properties, Events,   Tables 16-12, 16-13, and 16-14 list the properties, events, and methods
and Methods   that relate to the combo box.

Table 16-12 Properties of the ComboBox control

Use This Property...	To Do This...
Appearance	Read or set whether the object is drawn with 3D effects
BackColor, ForeColor	Read or set the background and foreground colors of this control
Container	Set or return a reference to the object that contains this object
DataChanged	Determine whether the value has been changed
DataField	Read or set the name of the field in the recordset of the data control to which this control is bound
DataSource	Set the name of the data control to which this control is bound
DragIcon	Read or set what displays when this control is dragged
DragMode	Determine whether drag operations are to occur manually or automatically
Enabled	Read or set whether this control can react to events
Font	Set or return a font object that controls the way text displays in this control
FontBold, FontItalic, FontStrikeThru, FontUnderline	Read or set special effects for this control's font
FontName	Read or set the name of this control's font
FontSize	Read or set the size of this control's font
Height	Read or set the height of this control
HelpContextID	Read or set the context number to this control for context-sensitive help
hWnd	Read the handle for this control's window
Index	Uniquely identify an element of a control array
IntegralHeight	Read or set whether the list displays partial items
ItemData	Read or set an index entry associated with the currently selected item
Left	Read or set the left edge placement of this control relative to its container
List	Read or set the value of a listed item
ListCount	Read the number of items in a list
ListIndex	Read or set the index of the currently selected item in a list

Use This Property...	To Do This...
Locked	Read or set whether a control can be edited or not
MouseIcon	Set a custom mouse pointer
MousePointer	Read or set the shape of the mouse pointer when it's over this control
Name	Read or set the name used in code to refer to this control
NewIndex	Read the index of the item most recently added to this control
OLEDragMode	Read or set whether the component or the programmer handles an OLE drag/drop operation
OLEDropMode	Read or set how a target component handles drop operations
Parent	Read the name of the form to which this control belongs
SelLength	Read or set the number of characters selected in a text box
SelStart	Read or set the starting position of selected text in a text box
SelText	Read or replace the selected text in a text box
Sorted	Read or set whether Visual Basic will automatically sort the list
Style	Read or set the style of the combo box and the behavior of its list
TabIndex	Read or set the placement of this control within the form's tab order
TabStop	Read or set whether this control is part of the form's tab order
Tag	Read or set any extra string data associated with this control
Text	Read or set the text contained in this control
ToolTipText	Read or set a value that explains an object
Top	Read or set the coordinate of this control's top edge relative to its container
TopIndex	Read or set a value that specifies which item is displayed in the topmost position
Visible	Read or set whether this control is visible
WhatsThisHelpID	Read or set the context number to this object for context-sensitive help in Windows 95
Width	Read or set the width of this control

Table 16-13 Events of the ComboBox control

Use This Event...	To Do This...
Change	React to a change in a combo box's text property (Style = 0 or 1).
Click	React to the user's clicking this control.
DblClick	React to the user's double-clicking this control.
DragDrop	React to the user's dragging and dropping an object onto this control.
DragOver	React to the user's dragging another object over this control.
DropDown	React to the user's clicking the down scroll arrow of a combo box.
GotFocus	Initiate an action when this control receives the focus.
KeyDown	Initiate an action when the user presses or holds a key down.
KeyPress	React to the user's typing an ASCII character.
KeyUp	Initiate an action when the user releases a key.
LostFocus	Initiate an action when this control loses the focus.

continued on next page

continued from previous page

Use This Event...	To Do This...
OLECompleteDrag	A target component reacts to a source component being dropped on it. It is informing the source component that a drag action was either canceled or performed.
OLEDragDown	A target component reacts to a source component being dropped on it.
OLEDragOver	React to one component being dragged over another.
OLEGiveFeedback	Trigger the source component to provide visual feedback to the user.
OLESetData	A source component will react when a target component performs a GetData method, but the data for the specified format has not yet been loaded.
OLEStartDrag	React to a component's OLEDrag method, or when a component initiates an OLE drag-and-drop operation when the OLEDragMode property is set to Automatic.
Scroll	React to the user's clicking on the scroll box of the drop-down list.

Table 16-14 Methods of the ComboBox control

Use This Method...	To Do This...
AddItem	Add an item to this control's list
Clear	Clear the contents of this control
Drag	Control manual dragging of this control
Move	Change the position of this control
OLEDrag	Cause the OLE drag-and-drop operation
Refresh	Update and repaint this control
RemoveItem	Delete items from a list
SetFocus	Move the focus to this control
ShowWhatsThis	Display the What's This help topic pop-up provided by the Windows 95 help system
ZOrder	Place this control at the front or back of the z-order

Description

Combo boxes provide a combination of the list box and the text box objects. All combo boxes have an edit area and a list area. The currently selected item is always displayed in the edit area of a combo box. The list area, when visible, appears below the edit area. The user may choose an item from the list portion of a combo box by clicking on it or by using the up and down arrow keys to move the reverse highlight to the desired item and pressing (ENTER). If there are more items in the list than can be displayed in the list portion of the combo box, Visual Basic automatically adds a vertical scrollbar on the right edge of the list. The user can then use this scrollbar to move up or down.

There are three types of combo boxes: the drop-down combo, the simple combo, and the drop-down list box. Setting the Style property determines which type will be used. The Style property can only be set at design time. It is a read-only property at runtime.

Setting the Style property to 0 causes a combo box to become a drop-down combo. The drop-down combo box displays the currently selected item in an edit area similar to a text box (see Figure 16-6). A down scroll arrow displays to the right of the edit area. The list portion of this combo box stays hidden until the user clicks the down scroll arrow. This causes the list of items to drop down. The user may either choose an item from the list, or type an entry in the edit area.

Setting the Style property to 1 causes a combo box to become a simple combo. The simple combo box also has an edit area that displays the currently selected item (see Figure 16-7). The list portion of this combo box is always visible under the edit area. As with the drop-down combo, the user may either choose an item from the list or type an entry in the edit area.

Figure 16-6 The drop-down combo box allows users to type in their own text as well as choose from the list

Figure 16-7 The simple combo box always displays its list

Setting the Style property to 2 causes a combo box to become a drop-down list. The drop-down list box is similar in structure to the drop-down combo box. As with the drop-down combo, the list area stays hidden until the user clicks on the down scroll arrow. However, the user cannot edit the text in the edit area, but can only choose an item from the list portion of the drop-down list (see Figure 16-8).

The Text property reads the text associated with the currently selected list item. If no item is currently selected, this property returns an empty string. The Text property can also be set during runtime for the drop-down and simple combo boxes, but is a read-only property with the drop-down list box.

The List property provides a method for reading and setting a list's contents in a manner similar to accessing and assigning values in an array. The List property is followed by an index number in parentheses that identifies which list entry is being referenced. The index numbering of the list is zero-based. Therefore, if a list contains five items, the first item is index number 0, and the highest index number is 4. The number of items in a list can be determined by using the ListCount property.

The ListCount property determines the number of items that have been added to a combo box. Each time the AddItem method is used on a combo box control, this property is incremented. Using the RemoveItem method decrements it.

The ListIndex property returns the index number of the currently selected item in a list. If no item is currently selected, -1 is returned. If the user enters text in the edit area of the simple or drop-down combo box, and that text does not match a listed item, this property will also return a ListIndex value of -1.

Figure 16-8   The drop-down list box only allows choices from the list

The program may also set the currently selected item of a list by setting this property. When using the ListIndex property to set the currently selected list entry, the program must use an index number that references a currently existing item in the list. For instance, if a list has five items in it, an index number of 0 to 4 must be specified, or an "Invalid property array index" error occurs.

The AddItem and RemoveItem methods add and delete items from a combo box's list, and the new Clear method clears the combo of all items.

Visual Basic 5.0 lets you bind the combo box to a field in a data control's recordset, enabling you to update the field based on the user's selection. Note that the list portion of the combo box is not bound, so you'll still need to use the AddItem method to create the list. See the DBCombo control entry if you'd like to fill the list from the database as well.

This object is discussed in detail in Chapter 59, "DBList and DBCombo."

CommandButton Control

Purpose   The CommandButton control displays a button that performs a function when the user clicks it.

Properties, Events, and Methods   Tables 16-15, 16-16, and 16-17 list the properties, events, and methods that relate to the CommandButton control.

Table 16-15 Properties of the CommandButton control

Use This Property...	To Do This...
Appearance	Read or set whether the object is drawn with 3D effects
BackColor, ForeColor	Read or set the background and foreground colors of this control
Cancel	Assign a command button's Click event to the (ESC) key
Caption	Assign text to this control
Container	Set or return a reference to the object that contains this object
Default	Assign a command button's Click event to the (ENTER) key
DragIcon	Read or set what displays when this control is dragged
DragMode	Determine whether drag operations are to occur manually or automatically
Enabled	Read or set whether this control can react to events
Font	Set or return a font object that controls the way text displays in this control
FontBold, FontItalic, FontStrikeThru, FontUnderline	Read or set special effects for this control's font
FontName	Read or set the name of this control's font
FontSize	Read or set the size of this control's font

continued on next page

continued from previous page

Use This Property...	To Do This...
Height	Read or set the height of this control
HelpContextID	Read or set the context number to this control for context-sensitive help
hWnd	Read the handle for this control's window
Index	Uniquely identify an element of a control array
Left	Read or set the left edge placement of this control relative to its container
MaskColor	Read or set a color in a button's picture to be a mask" or transparent
MouseIcon	Set a custom mouse pointer
MousePointer	Read or set the shape of the mouse pointer when it's over this control
Name	Read or set the name used in code to refer to this control
OLEDragMode	Read or set how the drop operation is handled
Parent	Read the name of the form to which this control belongs
Picture	Read or set a graphic to be displayed in a control when the Style setting is set to Graphical
Style	Read or set a value indicating the display type and behavior of the control
TabIndex	Read or set the placement of this control within the form's tab order
TabStop	Read or set whether this control is part of the form's tab order
Tag	Read or set any extra string data associated with this control
Top	Read or set the coordinate of this control's top edge relative to its container
UseMaskColor	Read or set a value that determines whether the color assigned in the MaskColor property is used as a "mask" for the transparent regions
Value	Determine whether this control is chosen
Visible	Read or set whether this control is visible
WhatsThisHelpID	Read or set the context number to this object for context-sensitive help in Windows 95
Width	Read or set the width of this control

Table 16-16 Events of the CommandButton control

Use This Event...	To Do This...
Click	React to the user's clicking this control.
DragDrop	React to the user's dragging and dropping an object onto this control.
DragOver	React to the user's dragging another object over this control.
GotFocus	Initiate an action when this control receives the focus.
KeyDown	Initiate an action when the user presses or holds a key down.
KeyPress	React to the user's typing an ASCII character.
KeyUp	Initiate an action when the user releases a key.
LostFocus	Initiate an action when this control loses the focus.
MouseDown	React to the user's pressing any mouse button.
MouseMove	React to the user's moving the mouse over this control.
MouseUp	React to the user's releasing any mouse button.

Use This Event...	To Do This...
OLECompleteDrag	A target component reacts to a source component being dropped on it. It is informing the source component that a drag action was either canceled or performed.
OLEDragDown	A target component reacts to a source component being dropped on it.
OLEDragOver	React to one component being dragged over another.
OLEGiveFeedback	Trigger the source component to provide visual feedback to the user.
OLESetData	A source component will react when a target component performs a GetData method, but the data for the specified format has not yet been loaded.
OLEStartDrag	React to a component's OLEDrag method, or when a component initiates an OLE drag-and-drop operation when the OLEDragMode property is set to Automatic.

Table 16-17 Methods of the CommandButton control

Use This Method...	To Do This...
Drag	Control manual dragging of this control
Move	Change the position of this control
OLEDrag	Cause the OLE drag-and-drop operation
Refresh	Update and repaint this control
SetFocus	Move the focus to this control
ShowWhatsThis	Display the What's This help topic pop-up provided by the Windows 95 help system
ZOrder	Place this control at the front or back of the z-order

Description

A *command* button is an object that represents a task to be performed. Pressing the button activates the associated task.

The user can press a button by clicking it, or by pressing ENTER or SPACEBAR while the button has the focus. Doing so initiates the command button's Click event. This event defines the actions to take when the button is pressed.

The Caption property defines the text displayed on the button (see Figure 16-9). The size and style of this text is defined by the settings of the font... properties. Including an ampersand (&) underlines the following letter, and the button can be selected by holding down ALT and pressing that letter. For instance, if the button's Caption property is set to &Cash, the displayed text will be Cash and the user can select the box by pressing ALT+C.

In most cases a form has one command button that performs the default action for that form. The Default property allows you to assign that default action to the ENTER key so that pressing ENTER has the same effect as clicking the command button. This property can either be set to True (-1) or False (0) by you at design time, or by the application during runtime.

Figure 16-9
Normal, default, and
cancel command
buttons

Because only one button on a form may be the default, setting this property to True for one button automatically sets it to False for all the other buttons on the same form.

NOTE

When a command button has focus, regardless of which one is the default, the command button with focus will trigger when the (ENTER) key is pressed.

Sometimes it is necessary to give the user a way to back out of, or cancel, an operation. The Cancel property allows the programmer to assign that cancel action to the (ESC) key. This property can either be set to True (-1) or False (0) by you at design time, or by the application during runtime. When the user presses the (ESC) key, the Click event of the command button whose Cancel property is True will be triggered. Because only one button on a form may be the Cancel button, setting this property to True for one button automatically sets it to False for all the other buttons on the same form.

The Default and Cancel properties are covered in greater detail in Chapter 42.

The Picture and Style properties are used together if you want to use a different type of command button style. Rather than the traditional command button look and feel of just plain text, you can have command buttons with graphics as well, similar to the navigation button on Netscape Navigator or Microsoft Internet Explorer, as illustrated in Figure 16-10.

Figure 16-10 Command
buttons displayed with graphics
and text

CommonDialog Control

Purpose	The CommonDialog control provides an easy way to produce standard dialog boxes such as File Open, File Save, Print, Select Font, and Choose Color.
Properties and Methods	Tables 16-18 and 16-19 list the properties and methods for the CommonDialog control. It has no events.

Table 16-18 Properties of the CommonDialog control

Use This Property...	To Do This...
Action	Specify the type of dialog box to display; now outdated; use the Show... methods instead
CancelError	Determine whether an error is generated upon Cancel
Color	Read or set the selected color
Copies	Read or set the number of copies to be printed
DefaultExt	Set the default extension for the dialog box
DialogTitle	Set the caption of the dialog box's title bar
FileName	Read or set the path and name of the file to open or save
FileTitle	Read the name of the file to open or save
Filter	Set or read the file filter specification in File Open and Save As
FilterIndex	Set or read the default file filter
Flags	Sets various options for each dialog box
FontBold, FontItalic, FontStrikeThru, FontUnderline	Read or set special effects for this object's font
FontName	Read or set the name of this object's font
FontSize	Read or set the size of this object's font
FromPage, ToPage	Read or set the values of the Print From and To input boxes
hDC	Read the Windows device handle for this object
HelpCommand	Set the kind of help requested
HelpContext	Set the context number for context-sensitive help
HelpFile	Set the name of the help file to display
HelpKey	Set the keyword for the help file to search for
Index	Uniquely identify an element of a control array
InitDir	Set the initial file directory
MaxFileSize	Set the maximum length of the filename given in the FileName property
Min, Max	(Font) Set the smallest and largest fonts displayed
Min, Max	(Printer) Set the smallest and largest page numbers to be printed
Name	Read or set the name used in code to refer to this object
Parent	Read the name of the form to which this control belongs
PrinterDefault	Determine whether changes in the Print dialog change default printer settings
Tag	Read or set any extra string data associated with this control

Table 16-19 Methods of the CommonDialog control

Use This Method...	To Do This...
AboutBox	Display the About box for the control
ShowColor	Display the Color common dialog box
ShowFont	Display the Font common dialog box
ShowHelp	Display the Windows Help application
ShowOpen	Display the File Open common dialog box
ShowPrinter	Display the Printer common dialog box
ShowSave	Display the File Save As common dialog box

Description

The CommonDialog control gives you easy access to the most commonly used dialog boxes. This saves you from having to re-create standard dialog boxes for every application. The Show... methods determine which kind of dialog box to display and immediately display it. There are six styles of dialog box: Open, Save As, Color, Font, Printer, and Help. (Visual Basic 2.0 and 3.0 used the Action property to display the various dialog boxes. This property is still supported for compatibility reasons, but should not be used in new programs.)

The Open dialog box has areas for filename, directories, drives, and default file types. The Save As dialog looks identical to Open, except for its caption. The Color dialog allows the user to select a color from a palette or from a custom color-picker. This is the same box as is used in the Windows Control Panel Desktop color choice. The Font dialog displays a list of all available fonts, and shows an example of the selected font. The Printer dialog box allows the user to choose printers, page defaults, and page print ranges.

The ShowHelp method runs WINHELP.EXE rather than calling up a dialog box. This gives you a simple way to call up your custom help file for your application. The HelpFile, HelpKey, HelpCommand, and HelpContext properties let you pass the appropriate information to the Help program to pull up general help, context-sensitive help, or the help Search dialog. Custom help files can be created in the Professional and Enterprise Editions of Visual Basic.

The CancelError property sets whether the dialog box returns an error if the user chooses the Cancel button. Your code can then test for this error and take appropriate action.

See Chapter 25, "CommonDialog Control," for more information on this versatile control.

Controls Collection

Purpose	The Controls collection contains each control on a form.
Properties and Methods	Tables 16-20 and 16-21 list the properties and methods of the Controls collection.

Table 16-20 Properties of the Controls collection

Use This Property...	To Do This...
Count	Return the number of members of the Controls collection
Item	Return a specific member within a Controls collection either by position or by key

Table 16-21 Methods of the Controls collection

Use This Method...	To Do This...
Clear	Clear all property settings
Item	Return a specific member within a Controls collection either by position or by key
Remove	Remove a member from a Controls collection

Description	The Controls collection of a form contains each control on that form. This allows you to iterate through the controls without explicitly naming them. For example, the following procedure disables all controls on the form passed to it:

```
Sub DisableControls(onForm As Form)
    'disables all controls on the form
    On Error Resume Next
    Dim controlNum As Integer
    For controlNum = 0 To onForm.Controls.Count - 1
        onForm.Controls(controlNum).Enabled = False
    Next controlNum
End Sub
```

Data Control

Purpose	The Data control lets you access databases and display the information in bound controls. The data control uses the same database engine that powers Microsoft Access. This gives you the capacity to work with databases in a variety of formats, including Access, Btrieve, dBASE, Paradox, and SQL. The data control exposes two of the objects contained in the DBEngine object: the Database and Recordset objects.

Properties, Events, and Methods Tables 16-22, 16-23, and 16-24 list the properties, events, and methods that relate to the data control.

Table 16-22 Properties of the data control

Use This Property...	To Do This...
Appearance	Read or set whether the object is drawn with 3D effects
Align	Read or set where this control displays on its parent form
BackColor, ForeColor	Read or set the background and foreground colors of this control
BOF Action, EOF Action	Read or set the control behavior when the Recordset's BOF or EOF properties are True
Caption	Assign text to this control
Connect	Read or set information to open or attach to an external database
Database	Reference the associated Database object
DatabaseName	Read or set the name and location of the database
DefaultCursorType	Set the type of cursor driver used on the data connection, used with ODBCDirect only
DefaultType	Read or set the value that determines whether the data source is Jet or ODBCDirect
DragIcon	Read or set what displays when this control is dragged
DragMode	Determine whether drag operations are manual or automatic
EditMode	Read the editing state of the current record
Enabled	Read or set whether this control can react to events
Exclusive	Read or set whether the database is single-user or multiuser
Font	Set or return a font object that controls the way text displays in this control
FontBold, FontItalic, FontStrikeThru, FontUnderline	Read or set special effects for this control's font
FontName	Read or set the name of this control's font
FontSize	Read or set the size of this control's font
Height	Read or set the height of this control
Index	Uniquely identify an element of a control array
Left	Read or set the left edge placement of this control relative to its container
MouseIcon	Set a custom mouse pointer
MousePointer	Read or set the shape of the mouse pointer when it's over this control
Name	Read or set the name used in code to refer to this control
OLEDropMode	Read or set how a target component handles drop operations
Options	Read or set characteristics of the control's Recordset
Parent	Specify the form on which this object is located
ReadOnly	Determine whether the database is opened for read-only access
Recordset	Access the underlying Recordset object
RecordsetType	Read or set the type of recordset to create
RecordSource	Specify the current table, SQL statement, or QueryDef for the recordset
Tag	Read or set any extra string data associated with this control

Use This Property...	To Do This...
Top	Read or set the coordinate of this control's top edge relative to its container
Visible	Read or set whether this control is visible
WhatsThisHelp ID	Read or set the context number to this object for context-sensitive help in Windows 95
Width	Read or set the width of this control

Table 16-23 Events of the data control

Use This Event...	To Do This...
DragDrop	React to the user's dragging and dropping an object onto this control.
DragOver	React to the user's dragging another object over this control.
Error	React to errors in reading data.
MouseDown	React to the user's pressing any mouse button.
MouseMove	React to the user's moving the mouse over this control.
MouseUp	React to the user's releasing any mouse button.
OLECompleteDrag	A target component reacts to a source component being dropped on it. It is informing the source component that a drag action was either canceled or performed.
OLEDragDown	A target component reacts to a source component being dropped on it.
OLEDragOver	React to one component being dragged over another.
OLEGiveFeedback	Trigger the source component to provide visual feedback to the user.
OLESetData	A source component will react when a target component performs a GetData method, but the data format or the specified format has not yet been loaded.
OLEStartDrag	React to a component's OLEDrag method, or when a component initiates an OLE drag-and-drop operation when the OLEDragMode property is set to Automatic.
Reposition	React when a new record becomes current.
Resize	React when an object is first displayed or when the window state changes.
Validate	Initiate an action before a different record becomes current.

Table 16-24 Methods of the data control

Use This Method...	To Do This...
Drag	Control manual dragging of this control
Move	Change the position of this control or form
OLEDrag	Cause the OLE drag-and-drop operation
Refresh	Close and rebuild the recordset
ShowWhatsThis	Display the What's This help topic pop-up provided by the Windows 95 help system
UpdateControls	Retrieve and display the data from the recordset
UpdateRecord	Save the values of the bound controls to the recordset
ZOrder	Place this control at the front or back of the z-order

Description

Many applications work with data. The data control lets your application perform sophisticated database manipulation without writing any code at all. The control inherits the capability to create new records, delete old ones, move from record to record, maintain referential integrity, create virtual query tables (called Recordsets), maintain indexes, and immediately update bound controls. (Visual Basic also includes DATAMGR.EXE, a program that lets you create databases compatible with the data control and Access.)

The data control does all this by using the database engine from Microsoft Access. If you're familiar with Access, you'll find working with the data control very natural. Even if you've never used Access (or any other database), the data control makes working with databases much easier than trying to develop the thousands of lines of code yourself. By using the data control, you can write many simple database applications with virtually no code other than that for the user interface.

To use the data control, set the DatabaseName property to the full path and name of the underlying database. Set the RecordSource property to the name of the table within the database you want to use. Then use any data-aware control (text box, check box, image, label, or picture box) to display and edit the underlying information.

You bind these data-aware controls to the data control by setting their DataSource, DataField, and DataChanged properties. Once bound, each control automatically displays data from the current record for the field indicated by their DataField property. All bound controls are automatically updated each time the data control moves to a new record. Changes made by the user in a bound control are automatically saved in the database when the data control moves to a new record. Figure 16-11 shows the data control and two bound text boxes.

The data control's Database and Recordset properties actually refer to the control's underlying Database object and Recordset object, which are contained in the DBEngine object. Both of these objects have properties and methods of their own that allow you to manipulate your data.

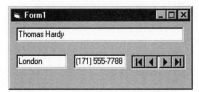

Figure 16-11   The data control lets you easily manipulate external databases

DBCombo Control

Purpose   The DBCombo control has the appearance and power of a normal combo box and can be fully bound to a data control. Rather than filling the control's list with the AddItem method, you specify display and value fields from a data control's recordset to bind to the display list. You can also optionally bind the text box portion to a field in a second data control. This allows you to display and update database information without writing any code.

Properties, Events, Tables 16-25, 16-26, and 16-27 list the properties, events, and methods
and Methods   that relate to the DBCombo control.

Table 16-25 Properties of the DBCombo control

Use This Property...	To Do This...
Appearance	Read or set whether the object is drawn with 3D effects
BackColor, ForeColor	Read or set the background and foreground colors of this control
BoundColumn	Read or set the name of the list's source field in the recordset of the bound data control
BoundText	Read or set the value placed in the DataField during an update
Container	Set or return a reference to the object that contains this object
DataBindings	Read the collection containing the bindable properties
DataChanged	Determine whether the value has been changed
DataField	Read or set the name of the field in the recordset of the data control to which this control is bound
DataSource	Set the name of the data control to which this control is bound
DragIcon	Read or set what displays when this control is dragged
DragMode	Determine whether drag operations are to occur manually or automatically
Enabled	Read or set whether this control can react to events
Font	Set or return a font object that controls the way text displays in this control
Height	Read or set the height of this control
HelpContextID	Read or set the context number to this control for context-sensitive help
Index	Uniquely identify an element of a control array
IntegralHeight	Read or set a value indicating whether the control will display partial items
Left	Read or set the left edge placement of this control relative to its container
ListField	Read or set the name of the field in the bound recordset used to fill the list
MatchedWithList	Return True if the current content of the BoundText property matches one of the records in the list
MatchEntry	Read or set a value indicating how the control performs searches based on user input
MouseIcon	Set a custom mouse icon
MousePointer	Read or set the shape of the mouse pointer when it's over this control
Name	Read or set the name used in code to refer to this control
OLEDragMode	Read or set whether the component or the programmer handles an OLE drag/drop operation

continued on next page

continued from previous page

Use This Property...	To Do This...
OLEDropMode	Read or set how a target component handles drop operations
Parent	Specify the form on which a control is located
RightToLeft	Return a Boolean value that indicates the text display direction for international versions of Windows
RowSource	Set the name of the data control used to fill the list
SelectedItem	Read the bookmark of the selected record
SelLength, SelStart	Read or set the length of or starting point of selected text
SelText	Read or set the string containing the currently selected text
Style	Read or set the style of the combo box and the behavior of its list
TabIndex	Read or set the placement of this control within the form's tab order
TabStop	Read or set a value indicating whether a user can use (TAB) to give the focus to an object
Tag	Read or set any extra string data associated with this control
Text	Return the selected item in a list box
ToolTipText	Read or set a value that explains an object
Top	Read or set the coordinate of this control's top edge relative to its container
Visible	Read or set whether this control is visible
VisibleCount	Read a value indicating how many items are visible in the list
VisibleItems	Return an array of bookmarks for items visible in the list
WhatsThisHelpID	Read or set the context number to this object for context-sensitive help in Windows 95
Width	Read or set the width of this control

Table 16-26 Events of the DBCombo control

Use This Event...	To Do This...
Change	React to a change in the value of the control.
Click	React to the user's clicking this control.
DblClick	React to the user's double-clicking this control.
DragDrop	React to the user's dragging and dropping an object onto this control.
DragOver	React to the user's dragging another object over this control.
DropDown	React to the user's clicking the drop-down button.
GotFocus	Initiate an action when this control receives the focus.
KeyDown	Initiate an action when the user presses or holds a key down.
KeyPress	React to the user's typing an ASCII character.
KeyUp	Initiate an action when the user releases a key.
LostFocus	Initiate an action when this control loses the focus.
MouseDown	React to the user's pressing any mouse button.
MouseMove	React to the user's moving the mouse over this control.
MouseUp	React to the user's releasing any mouse button.

Use This Event...	To Do This...
OLECompleteDrag	A target component reacts to a source component being dropped on it. It is informing the source component that a drag action was either canceled or performed.
OLEDragDown	A target component reacts to a source component being dropped on it.
OLEDragOver	React to one component being dragged over another.
OLEGiveFeedback	Trigger the source component to provide visual feedback to the user.
OLESetData	A source component will react when a target component performs a GetData method, but the data for the specified format has not yet been loaded.
OLEStartDrag	React to a component's OLEDrag method, or when a component initiates an OLE drag-and-drop operation when the OLEDragMode property is set to Automatic.

Table 16-27 Methods of the DBCombo control

Use This Method...	To Do This...
AboutBox	Display the About box for the control
Drag	Control manual dragging of this control
Move	Change the position of this control
OLEDrag	Cause the OLE drag-and-drop operation
Refill	Repaint this object and refill the list
Refresh	Update and repaint this control
SetFocus	Move the focus to the specified object
ShowWhatsThis	Display the What's This help topic pop-up provided by the Windows 95 help system
ZOrder	Place this control at the front or back of the z-order

Description

You can bind two independent data controls to a DBCombo box. One data control fills the list portion of the box, and the other data control contains a database record that can be updated by the control. This gives you substantial flexibility without requiring you to write much code.

Give the name of the data control that supplies values for the display list in the RowSource property. You can now work with two fields within the source data control's recordset: one field to actually display in the list, and one field to serve as the value that will be passed to the other data control for updating the database. Specify the name of the field that will display in the list with the ListField property, and the field that will pass its value with the BoundColumn property.

Give the name of the data control that will receive an updated value in the DataSource property, and the name of the field to receive the value in the DataField property. The value of the BoundColumn property will be placed in this field.

This implementation makes it easy to perform database lookups. Most database implementations store lengthy information (such as SalespersonName) just once, and associate an ID code with that information (for example, SalespersonID) as part of the same record. Any other tables in the database that need to refer to the salesperson would store just the ID rather than the entire name.

In this example, you'd have two data controls: one called dataSalesperson, which has a query that returns the SalespersonName and SalespersonID, and a second called dataTransaction, with a query that returns a set of records that you'd like to update (say, a SalesTransaction record). This second query contains a field for the ID of the person making the sale (perhaps called EmployeeID). You'd specify:

```
RowSource=dataSalesperson
ListField=SalespersonName
BoundColumn=SalespersonID
DataSource=dataTransaction
DataField=EmployeeID
```

This would fill the list with the names of all salespeople and would place the salesperson ID into the transaction record when the user selected a salesperson. You can do all this without writing a single line of code.

Note that specifying a source data control and fields is required, but specifying a data control to receive the data is optional. This allows you to fill the list from your database, but use the return value directly in your code for other purposes. Use the BoundText property to retrieve the value of the bound field if you want to manually process information like this.

The DBCombo control supports advanced searching capabilities. Set the MatchEntry property to vbMatchEntrySimple (=0) to use normal matching, and to vbMatchEntryExtended (=1) for extended matching. Normal matching means that the box jumps to the first entry that begins with the letter just typed. Pressing the same letter advances one selection further down the list if that entry also starts with the typed letter. Extended matching means that typing a word matches the closest entry to that word, as in the Windows Help Search combo box.

DBEngine Object

Purpose

The DBEngine object provides a uniform way of accessing data stored in a variety of different formats. Visual Basic Learning Edition exposes a limited subset of the objects in the DBEngine through the data control's Database and Recordset objects. Visual Basic Professional and Enterprise Editions expose all of the DBEngine objects.

Properties, Methods, and Internal Classes

Tables 16-28, 16-29, and 16-30 list the properties, methods, and internal classes of the DBEngine object.

Table 16-28 Properties of the DBEngine object

Use This Property...	To Do This...
DefaultType	Set or return the type of database workspace to be created
DefaultPassword	Set the default password used when creating new workspaces
DefaultUser	Set the default user name used when creating new workspaces
IniPath	Set or return the full path name of the initialization file for the Jet database engine
LoginTimeout	Set or return the number of seconds that may elapse before an error occurs when logging in to a database
SystemDB	Set or return the path for the current location of the database workgroup information file
Version	Return the version number of the database engine

Table 16-29 Methods of the DBEngine object

Use This Method...	To Do This...
BeginTrans	Use to mark the beginning of a new transaction
CommitTrans	End the current transaction and process the information if no error occurs
CompactDatabase	Copy and compact a database; optionally change database version, sort order, and encryption
CreateWorkspace	Create a new workspace object
Idle	Suspend database processing and allow the database engine to finish any pending tasks
OpenConnection	Open a connection to an ODBC datasource
OpenDatabase	Open a specified database within a workspace and return a reference to the database
RegisterDatabase	Enter connection information about an ODBC datasource
RepairDatabase	Repair a corrupt database
RollBack	Undo changes within a transaction if errors occur
SetOption	Temporarily override the values for the Jet database engine keys in the Windows registry

Table 16-30 Classes contained within the DBEngine object; most also belong to a collection

Use This Class...	To Do This...
Container	Manipulate access privileges and properties of physical database objects
Database	Access physical databases
Document	Manage properties of databases, relationships, and queries
Field	Manipulate an individual column within a database
Group	Manage group accounts
Property	Create and manipulate properties for data access objects
QueryDef	Manage predefined queries within a database
Recordset	Manage records within a database

continued on next page

continued from previous page

Use This Class...	To Do This...
Relationship	Manage relationships between tables and queries
TableDef	Manipulate physical tables within a database
User	Manage user accounts
Workspace	Manage sessions within the DBEngine

Description

The DBEngine object lets you access many different physical databases using a standard, consistent interface. It exposes the internal objects of the Jet database engine and gives the Visual Basic programmer a great degree of power. This power, however, comes at a price: The DBEngine object is large and complex, and takes time to master.

Visual Basic Professional and Enterprise Editions provide complete access to the DBEngine object and all of its internal collections. Programming professionals will want to use the Professional and Enterprise Editions to gain access to the engine's full capabilities. This finer level of control is crucial for successful client/server work. Simple multiuser applications can successfully use Visual Basic Learning Edition, but complex multiuser database applications will become unwieldy with it.

Visual Basic Learning Edition provides limited access to the most important aspects of the DBEngine, and hides much of the complexity within the data control. This is the perfect balance between capability and complexity for most single-user database programs or less complex multiuser programs.

DBGRID CONTROL

Purpose

The DBGrid control in Visual Basic 5.0 is a sophisticated grid that you can bind to a data control. It displays its data in rows and columns, much like a spreadsheet. Rows correspond to individual records in the recordset of the data control, and columns represent the fields within the recordset. The DBGrid control looks like the standard Grid control, but offers far greater control over its runtime appearance and behavior.

Properties, Events, and Methods

Tables 16-31, 16-32, and 16-33 list the properties, events, and methods of the DBGrid control. Its collection, Columns, is discussed under "Description," following the tables.

Table 16-31 Properties of the DBGrid control

Use This Property...	To Do This...
AddNewMode	Return the location of the current cell with respect to the grid's AddNew row
Align	Determine where and how this control appears on form

Use This Property...	To Do This...
AllowAddNew	Read or set whether the user can add new records to the recordset
AllowArrows	Read or set whether arrow keys can be used for navigation
AllowDelete	Read or set whether the user can delete records from the recordset
AllowRowSizing	Read or set whether the user can resize the height of the rows
AllowUpdate	Read or set whether the user can edit fields in the recordset
BackColor, ForeColor	Read or set the background and foreground colors of this control
Bookmark	Read or set a bookmark for the current record in the recordset
BorderStyle	Read or set the style of the border around the control
Caption	Read or set the text displayed as a column heading
Col, Row	Read or set the active cell
ColumnHeaders	Read or set whether to display headings for each column
Columns	Return a column object
Container	Set or return a reference to the object that contains this object
CurrentCellModified	Read or set the modification status of the active cell
CurrentCellVisible	Read or set the visibility of the active cell
DataBindings	Read the collection containing the bindable properties
DataChanged	Read or set a value indicating that the data has been changed by some process other than that of retrieving data from the current record
DataMode	Set whether object is bound or unbound
DataSource	Set the name of the data control to which this control is bound
DefColWidth	Read or set the default column width
DragIcon	Read or set what displays when this control is dragged
DragMode	Determine whether drag operations are to occur manually or automatically
EditActive	Read or set the editing status of the active cell
Enabled	Read or set whether this control can react to events
ErrorText	Return the error message string from the underlying datasource
FirstRow	Read or set the bookmark of the first visible row in the grid
Font	Set or return a font object that controls the way text displays in this control
HeadFont	Set or return a font object that controls the way text displays in the headers
HeadLines	Read or set the number of lines used by the column headers
Height	Read or set the height of this control
HelpContextID	Read or set the context number to this object for context-sensitive help
hWnd	Read the handle of the grid
hWndEditor	Read the unique window handle assigned to the grid's editing window
Index	Uniquely identify an element of a control array
Left	Read or set the left edge placement of this control relative to its container
MarqueeStyle	Read or set the Marquee style for the grid
MarqueeUnique	Read or set whether the marquee is displayed only the current split of the grid
Name	Read or set the name used in code to refer to this control

continued on next page

continued from previous page

Use This Property...	To Do This...
Object	Read the object and/or setting of an object's method or property
Parent	Specify the form on which a control is located
RecordSelectors	Read or set whether to display record selection markers at the far left edge of the grid
RowDividerStyle	Read or set the style of lines displayed between rows
RowHeight	Read or set the height of rows
ScrollBars	Read or set whether to display scrollbars
SelBookmarks	Return an array of bookmarks for selected rows
SelEndCol, SelStartCol	Read or set the starting and ending columns in a selection
SelEndRow, SelStartRow	Read or set the ending and starting rows in a selection
SelLength, SelStart	Read or set the length of or starting point of selected text
SelText	Read or set the string containing the currently selected text
Split	Read or set the index value of the active split
Splits	Read a collection of Split objects
TabAcrossSplits	Read or set how TAB and arrow key of a split border behave
TabAction	Read or set how TAB behaves
TabIndex	Read or set the placement of this control within the form's tab order
TabStop	Read or set a value indicating whether a user can use TAB to give the focus to an object
Tag	Read or set any extra string data associated with this control
Text	Return the selected item in a list box
Top	Read or set the coordinate of this control's top edge relative to its container
ToolTipText	Read or set a value that explains an object
Visible	Read or set whether this control is visible
VisibleCols	Read or set the number of visible columns
VisibleRows	Read the number of visible rows
WhatsThisHelpID	Read or set the context number to this object for context-sensitive help in Windows 95
Width	Read or set the width of this control
WrapCellPointer	Read or set how the arrow keys behave

Table 16-32 Events of the DBGrid control

Use This Event...	To Do This...
AfterColEdit	React after user finishes editing within a cell
AfterColUpdate	React after user has changed the contents of a column's field
AfterDelete	React after user has deleted a record
AfterInsert	React after user has inserted a record
AfterUpdate	React after user has updated one or more fields
BeforeColEdit	React before user enters edit mode of a cell
BeforeColUpdate	React before changes to a field's contents are saved

Use This Event...	To Do This...
BeforeDelete	React before a record is deleted
BeforeInsert	React before a record is inserted
BeforeUpdate	React before changes to a record are saved
ButtonClick	React when the active cell's built-in button is clicked
Change	React to a change in the value of the control
Click	React to the user's clicking this control
ColEdit	React as the first cell enters edit mode when the user starts to type
ColResize	React to the user's changing the size of a column
DblClick	React to the user's double-clicking this control
DragDrop	React to the user's dragging and dropping an object onto this control
DragOver	React to the user's dragging another object over this control
Error	React only as a result of a data access error
GotFocus	Initiate an action when this control receives the focus
HeadClick	React to the user's clicking the head line
KeyDown	Initiate an action when the user presses or holds a key down
KeyPress	React to the user's typing an ASCII character
KeyUp	Initiate an action when the user releases a key
LostFocus	Initiate an action when this control loses the focus
MouseDown	React to the user's pressing any mouse button
MouseMove	React to the user's moving the mouse over this control
MouseUp	React to the user's releasing any mouse button
OnAddNew	React when a user invokes the AddNewoperation
RowColChange	React to the current cell changing to a different cell
RowResize	React when a user resizes a row in the grid
Scroll	React to the user's clicking on the scroll box of ScrollBar control within the grid
SelChange	React to the selection changing
SplitChange	React to the active cell changing to a different cell in a different split
UnboundAddData	Initiate an action within your application to add a new row of data
UnboundDeleteRow	Initiate an action within your application to remove a row of data
UnboundGetRelativeBookmark	React when the grid requires data to be displayed
UnboundReadData	React when the grid requires data to be displayed as a result of the scrollbar's being pressed
UnboundWriteDate	Initiate an action within your application to write modified data to the dataset

Table 16-33 Methods of the DBGrid control

Use This Method...	To Do This...
ClearFields	Restore the grid layout to the default setting
ClearSelCols	Deselect all selected columns in a split

continued on next page

continued from previous page

Use This Method...	To Do This...
ColContaining	Return the column index of a given horizontal coordinate
Drag	Control manual dragging of this control
GetBookmark	Return a bookmark of a row relative to the current row
HoldFields	Set the current row and column layout as the layout the Rebind method will use
Move	Change the position of this control
Rebind	Resync the control to a recordset
Refresh	Update and repaint this control
RowBookmark	Return a bookmark for a given visible row
RowContaining	Return the row number of a given vertical coordinate
Scroll	Scroll the grid
SetFocus	Move the focus to the specified object
ShowWhatsThis	Display the What's This help topic pop-up provided by the Windows 95 help system
SplitContaining	Return the value of the split containing x and y coordinates
ZOrder	Place this control at the front or back of the z-order

Description

The DBGrid control is a data-aware grid. It looks much like the standard Grid control, with a number of columns and rows creating individual cells, as in a spreadsheet. The DBGrid control gets its values to display from the recordset of a data control to which it is bound. You can optionally let the grid automatically update values in the recordset as the user edits cells, adds new records to the recordset, and deletes records from the recordset. There are several options for controlling its behavior and appearance.

Using the grid is easy. First, add it to your project with the Custom Controls command on the Tools menu. (Chapter 8, "Extending the IDE with ActiveX Controls," describes how to add custom controls to your project.) Draw the grid on your form just as you would draw any other control. Set the DataSource property to the name of the data control to bind to, and set the data control's RecordSource property to the table name or SQL query for the records to display. That's it! You don't have to write a single line of code.

The grid has a number of sensible defaults. It automatically displays the name of each field in the recordset as a column header. It automatically adds vertical and horizontal scrollbars if the number of rows or columns exceeds the physical dimensions of the grid. It also has a set of record selector boxes to the left of the first column. It defaults to read-only, so users cannot update, add, or delete records.

Set the AllowUpdate property to True to allow the user to edit and update records. The grid will then automatically allow in-cell editing, much like a text box. Set the AllowAddNew property to True to let the user add new records by adding information to the blank last row of the grid. Set the AllowDelete property to True to enable the user to delete a record by selecting a row (using the record selectors at the left edge of the grid) and pressing the [DELETE] key.

This level of functionality is good enough for simpler applications. To go further with the DBGrid control, you must understand that the grid is really made up of a number of individual columns contained in the grid's Columns collection. You can manipulate properties for the grid as a whole, or for any individual column in the Columns collection.

The grid as a whole supports standard formatting properties, such as BackColor, ForeColor, BorderStyle, Font, and HeadFont. Turn off column headers by setting the ColumnHeaders property to False; set how many lines are displayed in the headers with the HeadLines property. The RowHeight property determines the height of each row; RowDividerStyle determines whether the rows are shown with no divider, a black line (the default), a gray line, a raised or inset line (only effective if BackColor is light gray), or the same as ForeColor. Set the default column width with DefColWidth. Leaving DefColWidth at the default of 0 lets each column automatically size itself to best fit the size of the field.

Set the Col and Row properties to control which cell is active. SelStartCol, SelEndCol, SelStartRow, and SelEndRow let you read or set which cells are selected. The Scroll method allows you to programmatically scroll the grid, and the ColContaining and RowContaining methods let you determine what column or row corresponds to a particular coordinate, such as from the mouse. You can combine this with the Drag method to support drag-and-drop editing of cell contents.

There are many events for the grid. They allow you to finely control grid behavior for individual column updates (AfterColUpdate, BeforeColUpdate) or globally (AfterInsert, BeforeInsert, AfterDelete, BeforeDelete, AfterUpdate, BeforeUpdate). You can respond to user navigation and mouse movements with the standard events such as KeyPress and MouseMove, as well as grid-specific events (ColResize, RowResize, Scroll, RowColChange).

The BeforeColEdit, ColEdit, and AfterColEdit events work together. The ColEdit event immediately follows the BeforeColEdit event only when the latter is not canceled. When the user completes editing within a grid cell, by either tabbing to another column in the same row, pressing the [ENTER] key, or clicking on another cell, the BeforeColUpdate and AfterColUpdate events are executed if the data has been changed. The AfterColEdit event is then performed to indicate that editing is completed.

Access individual columns with the grid's Columns collection. Columns are automatically added to the Columns collection when the grid is populated by the recordset; each field in the recordset corresponds to a column in the Columns collection. The column's Caption property determines what is displayed in the heading line. It defaults to the name of the field in the recordset, and naming your field intelligently in the query is probably the easiest method of setting the Caption. SQL queries are described in detail elsewhere, but here's a quick hint: Use the SQL aliasing capability to name fields whatever you'd like, such as "SELECT EmployeeName AS Employee, DiscPct AS Discount, YearlyTotalVolume AS Total WHERE...." Setting the data control's RecordSource property to this SQL statement would produce column headings of Employee, Discount, and Total. You can set the Caption property directly if modifying the SQL query is impractical.

Columns have a number of other properties that you can set. Standard formatting properties include Alignment, BackColor, ForeColor, HeadBackColor, HeadForeColor, and Font. If you set the AllowSizing property to True, users can change the size of the column using the mouse. You can disable editing in a particular column by setting the Locked property to True. Set the formatting of numbers by supplying a string to the NumberFormat property; the string you supply should be the same as one you'd use with the Format function. You can change the order in which the columns appear with the ColIndex property. This defaults to the same order as the fields returned by the recordset, and is probably more easily controlled by specifying the Select clause of your SQL query intelligently. You can also change the field the column is bound to by setting the DataField property.

You can manipulate columns directly. Add columns with the Insert method, remove them with the Remove method, and access any individual column with the Columns collection's Item method. Note that newly inserted columns have their Visible property set to False; make sure to set this property to True to display the new column. Read the raw (unformatted) value of a cell with the CellValue method, and the formatted value with the CellText method.

There are also easy ways of manipulating the grid directly in the design environment. You can change most of the grid's properties with the property sheet, just as you would change any other control. You can access individual columns by making the grid *UI-active*. By default, the control cannot be changed directly by the developer. UI-active means that you can modify the grid directly, adjusting column sizes, adding or removing columns, and so on. Do this by right-clicking the mouse on the grid, and choosing the Edit command from the pop-up menu. Once the grid is UI-active, select a column by clicking its heading line, and select a group of columns by dragging their heading lines. You can now use the property sheet to manipulate the properties of the selected columns. You can also use the pop-up menu to add new columns, delete existing columns, copy and paste columns to and from the Clipboard, display a dedicated

Properties dialog box, and retrieve the field names and settings from the bound recordset.

The DBGrid is best designed when used with the Data control. The Unbound... events are available so that you can use the DBGrid in an unbound fashion. Using these events will give you greater flexibility over how your data is handled, because frequently when using a data bound control, the control handles all the data manipulation. When building a prototype, letting the bound control handle all your data manipulation is good, but as you start building more complex systems, the bound control might not be handling your data in the most efficient manner. This can cause your application to execute slower.

DBLIST CONTROL

Purpose

The DBList control has the appearance and power of a normal list box and can be fully bound to a data control. Rather than filling the control's list with the AddItem method, you specify display and value fields from a data control's recordset to bind to the display list. You can also optionally bind the selected item to a field in a second data control. This allows you to display and update database information without writing any code.

Properties, Events, and Methods

Tables 16-34, 16-35, and 16-36 list the properties, events, and methods of the DBList control.

Table 16-34 Properties of the DBList control

Use This Property...	To Do This...
Appearance	Read or set whether the object is drawn with 3D effects
BackColor, ForeColor	Read or set the background and foreground colors of this control
BoundColumn	Read or set the name of the list's source field in the recordset of the bound data control
BoundText	Read or set the value placed in the DataField during an update
Container	Set or return a reference to the object that contains this object
DataBindings	Read the collection containing the bindable properties
DataChanged	Determine whether the value has changed
DataField	Read or set the name of the field in the recordset of the data control to which this control is bound
DataSource	Set the name of the data control to which this control is bound
DragIcon	Read or set what displays when this control is dragged
DragMode	Determine whether drag operations are to occur manually or automatically
Enabled	Read or set whether this control can react to events
Font	Set or return a font object that controls the way text displays in this control
Height	Read or set the height of this control
HelpContextID	Read or set the context number to this control for context-sensitive help

continued on next page

continued from previous page

Use This Property...	To Do This...
hWnd	Read the handle of the control
Index	Uniquely identify an element of a control array
IntegralHeight	Read or set a value indicating whether the control will display partial items
Left	Read or set the left edge placement of this control relative to its container
ListField	Read or set the name of the field in the bound recordset used to fill the list
Locked	Read or set whether information in the object can be changed
MatchedWithList	Return True if the current content of the BoundText property matches one of the records in the list
MatchEntry	Read or set a value indicating how the control performs searches based on user input
MouseIcon	Set a custom mouse icon
MousePointer	Read or set the shape of the mouse pointer when it's over this control
Name	Read or set the name used in code to refer to this control
Object	Read the object and/or setting of an object's method or property
OLEDragMode	Read or set whether the component or the programmer handles an OLE drag/drop operation
OLEDropMode	Read or set how a target component handles drop operations
Parent	Specify the form on which a control is located
RightToLeft	Return a Boolean value that indicates the text display direction for international versions of Windows
RowSource	Set the name of the data control used to fill the list
SelectedItem	Read the bookmark of the selected record
TabIndex	Read or set the placement of this control within the form's tab order
TabStop	Read or set a value indicating whether a user can use TAB to give the focus to an object
Tag	Read or set any extra string data associated with this control
Text	Return the selected item in a list box
Top	Read or set the coordinate of this control's top edge relative to its container
ToolTipText	Read or set a value that explains an object
Visible	Read or set whether this control is visible
VisibleCount	Read a value indicating how many items are visible in the list
VisibleItems	Return an array of bookmarks for items visible in the list
WhatsThisHelpID	Read or set the context number to this object for context-sensitive help in Windows 95
Width	Read or set the width of this control

Table 16-35 Events of the DBList control

Use This Event...	To Do This...
Click	React to the user's clicking this control.
DblClick	React to the user's double-clicking this control.
DragDrop	React to the user's dragging and dropping an object onto this control.

Use This Event...	To Do This...
DragOver	React to the user's dragging another object over this control.
GotFocus	Initiate an action when this control receives the focus.
KeyDown	Initiate an action when the user presses or holds a key down.
KeyPress	React to the user's typing an ASCII character.
KeyUp	Initiate an action when the user releases a key.
LostFocus	Initiate an action when this control loses the focus.
MouseDown	React to the user's pressing any mouse button.
MouseMove	React to the user's moving the mouse over this control.
MouseUp	React to the user's releasing any mouse button.
OLECompleteDrag	A target component reacts to a source component being dropped on it. It is informing the source component that a drag action was either canceled or performed.
OLEDragDown	A target component reacts to a source component being dropped on it.
OLEDragOver	React to one component being dragged over another.
OLEGiveFeedback	Trigger the source component to provide visual feedback to the user.
OLESetData	A source component will react when a target component performs a GetData method, but the data for the specified format has not yet been loaded.
OLEStartDrag	React to a component's OLEDrag method, or when a component initiates an OLE drag-and-drop operation when the OLEDragMode property is set to Automatic.

Table 16-36 Methods of the DBList control

Use This Method...	To Do This...
AboutBox	Display the About box for the control
Drag	Control manual dragging of this control
Move	Change the position of this control
OLEDrag	Cause the OLE drag-and-drop operation
Refill	Repaint this control and refill the list
Refresh	Update and repaint this control
SetFocus	Move the focus to the specified object
ShowWhatsThis	Display the What's This help topic pop-up provided by the Windows 95 help system
ZOrder	Place this control at the front or back of the z-order

Description   The DBList control functions almost exactly like the DBCombo box. See the description of DBCombo for more details on how to bind the control to display a list from one data control and update a field in another data control.

DEBUG OBJECT

Purpose The Debug object uses the Print method to send output to the Debug window when a program is run under the Visual Basic environment. This output can help you track down and fix problems with your program.

Methods Table 16-37 lists the methods that relate to the Debug object. This object has no associated properties or events.

Table 16-37 Methods of the Debug object

Use This Method...	To Do This...
Assert	Conditionally suspend execution at the line on which the method you specify appears
Print	Print text on the Debug window

Description The Debug window automatically opens when a program runs under the Visual Basic environment. While in run mode, the program can send text to this window by executing the Print method with the Debug object. This is generally used to check the value of a variable at a specific point in a program. For instance, the following code will send the value of the variable A% to the Debug window:

```
Debug.Print A%
```

See Figure 16-12 for a brief illustration of the object.

DIRLISTBOX CONTROL

Purpose The DirListBox control displays a list box from which the user can navigate through all the directories on the selected disk drive.

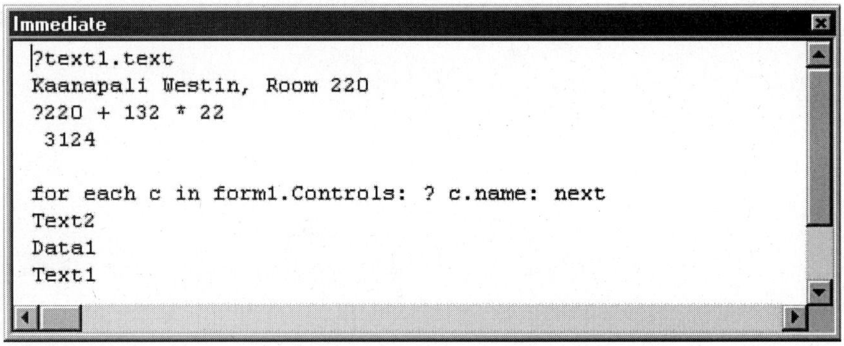

Figure 16-12 The Debug window showing the Immediate pane

Properties, Events, and Methods Tables 16-38, 16-39, and 16-40 list the properties, events, and methods that relate to the DirListBox control.

Table 16-38 Properties of the DirListBox control

Use This Property...	To Do This...
Appearance	Read or set whether the object is drawn with 3D effects
BackColor, ForeColor	Read or set the background and foreground colors of this control
Container	Set or return a reference to the object that contains this object
DragIcon	Read or set what displays when this control is dragged
DragMode	Determine whether drag operations are to occur manually or automatically
Enabled	Read or set whether this control can react to events
Font	Set or return a font object that controls the way text displays in this control
FontBold, FontItalic, FontStrikeThru, FontUnderline	Read or set special effects for this control's font
FontName	Read or set the name of this control's font
FontSize	Read or set the size of this control's font
Height	Read or set the height of this control
HelpContextID	Read or set the context number to this control for context-sensitive help
hWnd	Read the handle for this control's window
Index	Uniquely identify an element of a control array
Left	Read or set the left edge placement of this control relative to its container
List	Read the value of a listed item
ListCount	Read the number of items in a list
ListIndex	Read or set the index of the currently selected item in a list
MouseIcon	Set a custom mouse pointer
MousePointer	Read or set the shape of the mouse pointer when it's over this control
Name	Read or set the name used in code to refer to this control
OLEDragMode	Read or set whether the component or the programmer handles an OLE drag/drop operation
OLEDropMode	Read or set how a target component handles drop operations
Parent	Read the name of the form to which this control belongs
Path	Read or set the currently selected directory path
TabIndex	Read or set the placement of this control within the form's tab order
TabStop	Read or set whether this control is part of the form's tab order
Tag	Read or set any extra string data associated with this control
ToolTipText	Read or set a value that explains an object
Top	Read or set the coordinate of this control's top edge relative to its container
Visible	Read or set whether this control is visible
WhatsThisHelpID	Read or set the context number to this object for context-sensitive help in Windows 95
Width	Read or set the width of this control

Table 16-39 Events of the DirListBox control

Use This Event...	To Do This...
Change	React to the user's choosing a new directory, or a change in the Path property.
Click	React to the user's clicking this control.
DragDrop	React to the user's dragging and dropping an object onto this control.
DragOver	React to the user's dragging another object over this control.
GotFocus	Initiate an action when this control receives the focus.
KeyDown	Initiate an action when the user presses or holds a key down.
KeyPress	React to the user's typing an ASCII character.
KeyUp	Initiate an action when the user releases a key.
LostFocus	Initiate an action when this control loses the focus.
MouseDown	React to the user's pressing any mouse button.
MouseMove	React to the user's moving the mouse over this control.
MouseUp	React to the user's releasing any mouse button.
OLECompleteDrag	A target component reacts to a source component being dropped on it. It is informing the source component that a drag action was either canceled or performed.
OLEDragDown	A target component reacts to a source component being dropped on it.
OLEDragOver	React to one component being dragged over another.
OLEGiveFeedback	Trigger the source component to provide visual feedback to the user.
OLESetData	A source component will react when a target component performs a GetData method, but the data for the specified format has not yet been loaded.
OLEStartDrag	React to a component's OLEDrag method, or when a component initiates an OLE drag-and-drop operation when the OLEDragMode property is set to Automatic.
Scroll	React to the user's clicking on the scroll box of the drop-down list.

Table 16-40 Methods of the DirListBox control

Use This Method...	To Do This...
Drag	Control manual dragging of this control
Move	Change the position of this control or form
OLEDrag	Cause the OLE drag-and-drop operation
Refresh	Update and repaint this control
SetFocus	Move the focus to this control
ShowWhatsThis	Display the What's This help topic pop-up provided by the Windows 95 help system
ZOrder	Place this control at the front or back of the z-order

Description   The DirListBox displays a hierarchical directory tree in a box. Each directory entry displays a small folder icon next to the name of the directory (see Figure 16-13). This object gives the user a method for navigating the DOS file system when used in conjunction with the DriveListBox and FileListBox objects.

The top of the displayed directory tree represents the root directory of the drive currently selected for that directory box. Each subdirectory that is part of the path to the current directory displays underneath the root. The folder icons for these directories display as open folders. Also displayed are all subdirectories that are one level below the current directory. The folder icons for these directories display as closed.

The user may select a different directory by clicking its entry in the box. This sets the ListIndex property to the selected directory. However, this does not change the current directory for the list box. To change the current directory, the user must double-click an entry. This not only changes the ListIndex property for the box, but it also changes the Path property to the new directory. You can also set these properties directly in your code. In that case, the DirListBox visually reflects these changes.

The Path property sets or reads the current drive and path for the DirListBox. Whenever the Path property changes, the DirListBox's Change event activates. This event is used so the program can react to the user's changing the current directory.

See Chapter 47, "File, Directory, and Drive Boxes," for more information on the use of the DirListBox control.

DriveListBox Control

Purpose   The DriveListBox control displays a drop-down list box that allows the user to choose an available disk drive.

Properties, Events,   Tables 16-41, 16-42, and 16-43 list the properties, events, and methods
and Methods   that relate to the DriveListBox control.

Figure 16-13   The DirListBox includes support for long file names in Windows 95 and NT

Table 16-41 Properties of the DriveListBox control

Use This Property...	To Do This...
Appearance	Read or set whether the object is drawn with 3D effects
BackColor, ForeColor	Read or set the background and foreground colors of this control
Container	Set or return a reference to the object that contains this object
DragIcon	Read or set what displays when this control is dragged
DragMode	Determine whether drag operations are to occur manually or automatically
Drive	Read or set the current selected drive
Enabled	Read or set whether this control can react to events
Font	Set or return a font object that controls the way text displays in this control
FontBold, FontItalic, FontStrikeThru, FontUnderline	Read or set special effects for this control's font
FontName	Read or set the name of this control's font
FontSize	Read or set the size of this control's font
Height	Read or set the height of this control
HelpContextID	Read or set the context number to this control for context-sensitive help
hWnd	Read the handle for this control's window
Index	Uniquely identify an element of a control array
Left	Read or set the left edge placement of this control relative to its container
List	Read the value of a listed item
ListCount	Read the number of items in a list
ListIndex	Read or set the index of the currently selected item in a list
MouseIcon	Set a custom mouse pointer
MousePointer	Read or set the shape of the mouse pointer when it's over this control
Name	Read or set the name used in code to refer to this control
OLEDropMode	Read or set how a target component handles drop operations
Parent	Read the name of the form to which this control belongs
TabIndex	Read or set the placement of this control within the form's tab order
TabStop	Read or set whether this control is part of the form's tab order
Tag	Read or set any extra string data associated with this control
ToolTipText	Read or set a value that explains an object
Top	Read or set the coordinate of this control's top edge relative to its container
Visible	Read or set whether this control is visible
WhatsThisHelpID	Read or set the context number to this object for context-sensitive help in Windows 95
Width	Read or set the width of this control

Table 16-42 Events of the DriveListBox control

Use This Event...	To Do This...
Change	React to the user's or code's changing the Drive property.
DragDrop	React to the user's dragging and dropping an object onto this control.
DragOver	React to the user's dragging another object over this control.
GotFocus	Initiate an action when this control receives the focus.
KeyDown	Initiate an action when the user presses or holds a key down.
KeyPress	React to the user's typing an ASCII character.
KeyUp	Initiate an action when the user releases a key.
LostFocus	Initiate an action when this control loses the focus.
OLECompleteDrag	A target component reacts to a source component being dropped on it. It is informing the source component that a drag action was either canceled or performed.
OLEDragDown	A target component reacts to a source component being dropped on it.
OLEDragOver	React to one component being dragged over another.
OLEGiveFeedback	Trigger the source component to provide visual feedback to the user.
OLESetData	A source component will react when a target component performs a GetData method, but the data for the specified format has not yet been loaded.
OLEStartDrag	React to a component's OLEDrag method, or when a component initiates an OLE drag-and-drop operation when the OLEDragMode property is set to Automatic.
Scroll	React to the user's clicking on the scroll box of the drop-down list.

Table 16-43 Methods of the DriveListBox control

Use This Method...	To Do This...
Drag	Control manual dragging of this control
Move	Change the position of this control or form
OLEDrag	Cause the OLE drag-and-drop operation
Refresh	Update and repaint this control
SetFocus	Move the focus to this control
ShowWhatsThis	Display the What's This help topic provided by the Windows 95 help system
ZOrder	Place this control at the front or back of the z-order

Description
The DriveListBox, used in conjunction with the directory and file list boxes, gives the user a way to navigate the DOS file system. It is a drop-down list box in which the current drive displays in the text area (see Figure 16-14). When the user clicks the down scroll arrow of the box, a list of drives available to the user's system drops down. The user may change the current drive by clicking on one of the listed entries.

Figure 16-14 The DriveListBox displays all available drives

When the program starts running, Visual Basic automatically explores the user's system and adds all of the floppy, fixed, and network drives to the list. Drive list items that reflect local fixed disks will also display that disk's label with the drive letter. It also displays the network name of network drives.

The Drive property may be used to set or read the current drive. Changing this property, either by user input or by instructions in the program, activates the Change event.

If the program is being run on a network, the Refresh method can be used to update the entries for this control. This will cause the list entries to reflect changes in shared drives.

See Chapter 47 for more information on the DriveListBox control.

ERR OBJECT

Purpose   The Err object stores information about runtime errors.

Properties and   Tables 16-44 and 16-45 list the properties and methods of the Err
Methods   object.

Table 16-44 Properties of the Err object

Use This Property...	To Do This...
Description	Read or set a description for this error
HelpContext	Read or set the context number ID for this error
HelpContextID	Read or set the string containing the context ID for this error
HelpFile	Read or set the filename of the help file for this error
Number	Read or set the number associated with this error
Source	Read or set the name of the procedure, module, object, or application that caused the error

Table 16-45 Methods of the Err object

Use This Method...	To Do This...
Clear	Clear all properties of the Err object
Raise	Trigger a runtime error

Description   The Err object stores information about runtime errors, and can generate or clear errors as well. The default property of the Err object is Number, which lets existing code that used the old Err statement continue functioning normally without any revision. The Description property stores the text description of the error, much like the Error$ function. You can also set and read the HelpFile and HelpContext properties to provide access to online help for user-generated errors. The Source property allows you to identify what procedure caused the error, which is especially important in an OLE server application.

Use the Clear method to clear the Err object of information. Use the Raise method to trigger a runtime error.

Note that the Err object is similar to, but different from, the Error object of the Errors collection in the DBEngine. The DBEngine's Error object contains the same properties as the Err object, but does not accept the Raise and Clear methods. The Error object contains only those errors generated through the DBEngine, whereas the Err object contains errors generated by any code. For more information on the Error collection and error handling, refer to Chapter 30, "Error Handling."

FILELISTBOX CONTROL

Purpose   The FileListBox control displays a list box that lists the files in a specific directory and allows the user to select a file for further operations.

Properties, Events,   Tables 16-46, 16-47, and 16-48 list the properties, events, and methods
and Methods   that relate to the FileListBox control.

Table 16-46 Properties of the FileListBox control

Use This Property...	To Do This...
Appearance	Read or set whether the object is drawn with 3D effects
Archive	Read or set whether files with their archive bit set will be displayed
BackColor, ForeColor	Read or set the background and foreground colors of this control
Container	Set or return a reference to the object that contains this object

continued on next page

continued from previous page

Use This Property...	To Do This...
DragIcon	Read or set what displays when this control is dragged
DragMode	Determine whether drag operations occur manually or automatically
Enabled	Read or set whether this control can react to events
FileName	Read or set the currently selected file
Font	Set or return a font object that controls the way text displays in this control
FontBold, FontItalic, FontStrikeThru, FontUnderline	Read or set special effects for the font used with this control
FontName	Read or set the name of this control's font
FontSize	Read or set the size of this control's font
Height	Read or set the height of this control
HelpContextID	Read or set the context number to this control for context-sensitive help
Hidden	Read or set whether files with their hidden bit set will be displayed
hWnd	Read the handle for this control's window
Index	Uniquely identify an element of a control array
Left	Read or set the left edge placement of this control relative to its container
List	Read the value of a listed item
ListCount	Read the number of items in a list
ListIndex	Read or set the index of the currently selected item in a list
MouseIcon	Set a custom mouse pointer
MousePointer	Read or set the shape of the mouse pointer when it's over this control
MultiSelect	Determine whether a user can make multiple selections in the list
Name	Read or set the name used in code to refer to this control
Normal	Read or set whether to display files with system and hidden bits off
OLEDragMode	Read or set whether the component or the programmer handles an OLE drag/drop operation
OLEDropMode	Read or set how a target component handles drop operations
Parent	Read the name of the form to which this control belongs
Path	Read or set the currently selected path
Pattern	Read or set the filename pattern
ReadOnly	Read or set whether files with their read-only bits set will be displayed
Selected	Read the selection status of an item in the list
System	Read or set whether files with their system bits set will be displayed
TabIndex	Read or set the placement of this control within the form's tab order
TabStop	Read or set whether this control is part of the form's tab order
Tag	Read or set any extra string data associated with this control
ToolTipText	Read or set a value that explains an object
Top	Read or set the coordinate of this control's top edge relative to its container
TopIndex	Read which item in the list appears in the topmost position

Use This Property...	To Do This...
Visible	Read or set whether this control is visible
WhatsThisHelpID	Read or set the context number to this object for context-sensitive help in Windows 95
Width	Read or set the width of this control

Table 16-47 Events of the FileListBox control

Use This Event...	To Do This...
Click	React to the user's clicking this control.
DblClick	React to the user's double-clicking this control.
DragDrop	React to the user's dragging and dropping an object onto this control.
DragOver	React to the user's dragging another object over this control.
GotFocus	Initiate an action when this control receives the focus.
KeyDown	Initiate an action when the user presses or holds a key down.
KeyPress	React to the user's typing an ASCII character.
KeyUp	Initiate an action when the user releases a key.
LostFocus	Initiate an action when this control loses the focus.
MouseDown	React to the user's pressing any mouse button.
MouseMove	React to the user's moving the mouse over this control.
MouseUp	React to the user's releasing any mouse button.
OLECompleteDrag	A target component reacts to a source component being dropped on it. It is informing the source component that a drag action was either canceled or performed.
OLEDragDown	A target component reacts to a source component being dropped on it.
OLEDragOver	React to one component being dragged over another.
OLEGiveFeedback	Trigger the source component to provide visual feedback to the user.
OLESetData	A source component will react when a target component performs a GetData method, but the data for the specified format has not yet been loaded.
OLEStartDrag	React to a component's OLEDrag method, or when a component initiates an OLE drag-and-drop operation when the OLEDragMode property is set to Automatic.
PathChange	Initiate an action when the current path of a file list box has changed.
PatternChange	Initiate an action when the file pattern of a file list box has changed.
Scroll	React to the user's clicking on the scroll box of the drop-down list.

Table 16-48 Methods of the FileListBox control

Use This Method...	To Do This...
Drag	Control manual dragging of this control
Move	Change the position of this control or form

continued on next page

continued from previous page

Use This Method...	To Do This...
OLEDrag	Cause the OLE drag-and-drop operation
Refresh	Update and repaint this control
SetFocus	Move the focus to this control
ShowWhatsThis	Display the What's This help topic pop-up provided by the Windows 95 help system
ZOrder	Place this control at the front or back of the z-order

Description

The FileListBox, used in conjunction with the drive and directory list boxes, gives the user a way to navigate the DOS file system. This control lists all the files in the directory specified by the control's Path property (see Figure 16-15). The files that are displayed are also limited to those whose filenames match the control's Pattern property and whose attributes match the Archive, Hidden, ReadOnly, and System properties.

The Path property sets or reads the directory path for the files to be displayed. It is not available during design time. At the start of the program, it defaults to the current default directory. If the Path property changes, the PathChange event will be activated.

The Pattern property defines a subset of files within the directory specified by the Path property. This property consists of any full or partial filenames, and can contain the wildcard characters * and ? that match filenames according to the standard rules for DOS.

The currently selected file in a list box may be read or set by using the FileName property. This property is changed anytime the user clicks a new filename within the FileListBox.

The FileListBox control and its related properties, methods, and events are covered in Chapter 47.

Figure 16-15 The FileListBox includes support for long filenames in Windows 95 and NT

Font Object

Purpose	The Font object allows you to read or set attributes for text display. It offers a more convenient and object-oriented way of working with fonts than the outdated FontBold, FontItalic, FontName, FontStrikeThru, and FontTransparent properties.
Properties	Table 16-49 lists the properties of the Font object.

Table 16-49 Properties of the Font object

Use This Property...	To Do This...
Bold	Read or set whether the font is bold
Italic	Read or set whether the font is italic
Name	Read or set the name of the font
Size	Read or set the size (in points) of the font
StrikeThrough	Read or set whether the font has a line through the middle of the characters
Underline	Read or set whether the font is underlined
Weight	Read or set the weight of the font

Description Visual Basic offers fine control over the display and printing of text. Use the Font object contained in many other controls and objects to specify how this text displays.

Many of the properties of the Font object directly replace the outdated (but still supported) formatting properties: Bold replaces FontBold, Italic replaces FontItalic, Name replaces FontName, Size replaces FontSize, StrikeThrough replaces FontStrikeThru, and Underline replaces FontUnderline. The new Weight property will not be useful until new versions of Windows support finer gradations of "boldness." Visual Basic internally converts Weight to 400 for normal or italic text, and to 700 for bold or bold italic text.

The Font object allows a much cleaner and object-oriented coding style than did the old font... properties. You can use the Set statement to set one object's font to equal that of another object, and you can create a new font object with the New keyword. Note that Visual Basic's implementation of creating a new font is rather confusing: You don't use the class name of Font; you use StdFont. Thus, your line would read

```
Dim displayStyle As New StdFont

displayStyle.Bold = True
displayStyle.Italic = False
displayStyle.Name = "Arial"
```

continued on next page

continued from previous page
```
displayStyle.Size = 10
displayStyle.Underline = False

Set formMain.Font = displayStyle
```

FORM OBJECT

Purpose   The Form object defines a visual work area on the Windows desktop on which you can arrange controls. Forms can be used to set up any windows, dialogs, or message boxes that are required for a program.

Properties, Events, and Methods   Tables 16-50, 16-51, and 16-52 list the properties, events, and methods that relate to the Form object.

Table 16-50 Properties of the Form object

Use This Property...	To Do This...
Appearance	Read or set whether the object is drawn with 3D effects
ActiveControl	Return an object for the control that has the focus
AutoReDraw	Read or set whether graphic pictures will be redrawn automatically
BackColor, ForeColor	Read or set the background and foreground colors of this object
BorderStyle	Determine whether this object has a border, and if it does, set its style
Caption	Assign text to the title bar of this object
ClipControls	Determine whether graphic methods repaint the entire object
ControlBox	Determine whether this control box displays on a form
Controls	Read a reference to a collection of controls on the form
Count	Read a number of objects in a collection
CurrentX, CurrentY	Read or set the current graphics position on this object
DrawMode	Read or set the appearance of drawings by graphics methods
DrawStyle	Read or set the style of lines drawn by graphics methods
DrawWidth	Read or set the size of lines drawn by graphics methods
Enabled	Read or set whether this object can react to events
FillColor	Read or set the color used by graphics methods for fill-in effects
FillStyle	Read or set the pattern used by graphics methods for fill-in effects
Font	Set or return a font object that controls the way text displays in this object
FontBold, FontItalic, FontStrikeThru, FontTransparent, FontUnderline	Read or set typestyle effects for this object's font
FontName	Read or set the name of this object's font
FontSize	Read or set the size of this object's font
hDC	Read the Windows device context handle for this object

Use This Property...	To Do This...
Height	Read or set the height of this object
HelpContextID	Read or set the context number to this object for context-sensitive help
hWnd	Read the handle for this object's window
Icon	Read or set the icon used when a form is minimized
Image	Read the Windows device handle for this object's persistent bitmap
KeyPreview	Read or set when form keyboard events are processed
Left	Read or set the left edge placement of this control relative to its container
LinkMode	Read or set whether a DDE conversation is hot, cold, or none
LinkTopic	Read or set the topic of a DDE conversation
MaxButton	Read or set whether a maximize button will appear on a form
MDIChild	Read or set whether a form is an MDIChild form
MinButton	Read or set whether a minimize button will appear on a form
MouseIcon	Set a custom mouse pointer
MousePointer	Read or set the shape of the mouse pointer when it's over this object
Name	Read or set the name used in code to refer to this object
OLEDropMode	Read or set how the form handles drop operations
Picture	Read or assign a graphic image to a picture or form
ScaleHeight	Read or set the number of units that define the height of this object
ScaleLeft	Read or set the coordinates for the left edge of this object
ScaleMode	Read or set the unit of measurement used to place and size objects
ScaleTop	Read or set the coordinates for the top edge of this object
ScaleWidth	Read or set the number of units that define the width of this object
ShowInTaskbar	Read or set whether form appears in the Windows 95 taskbar
Tag	Read or set any extra string data associated with this control
Top	Read or set the coordinate of this control's top edge relative to its container
Visible	Read or set whether this object is visible
WhatsThisButton	Read or set whether a What's This button appears on the title bar in Windows 95
WhatsThisHelp	Read or set whether context-sensitive help uses main help window or a What's This pop-up
Width	Read or set the width of this object
WindowState	Read or set whether a form is maximized, minimized, or normal

Table 16-51 Events of the Form object

Use This Event...	To Do This...
Activate	React when this object becomes activated either by code or by the user.
Click	React to the user's clicking this object.
DblClick	React to the user's double-clicking this object.
Deactivate	React when this object becomes deactivated either by code or by the user.

continued on next page

continued from previous page

Use This Event...	To Do This...
DragDrop	React to the user's dragging and dropping an object onto this object.
DragOver	React to the user's dragging another object over this object.
GotFocus	Initiate an action when this object receives the focus.
Initialize	React when this form first becomes instantiated.
KeyDown	Initiate an action when the user presses or holds a key down.
KeyPress	React to the user's typing an ASCII character.
KeyUp	Initiate an action when the user releases a key.
LinkClose	React to the termination of a DDE conversation.
LinkError	React to an error in a DDE conversation.
LinkExecute	React to a DDE Execute command from a DDE client application.
LinkOpen	React to the initiation of a DDE conversation.
Load	Initiate an action when a form is first loaded.
LostFocus	Initiate an action when this object loses the focus.
MouseDown	React to the user's pressing any mouse button.
MouseMove	React to the user's moving the mouse over this object.
MouseUp	React to the user's releasing any mouse button.
OLECompleteDrag	A target component reacts to a source component being dropped on it. It is informing the source component that a drag action was either canceled or performed.
OLEDragDown	A target component reacts to a source component being dropped on it.
OLEDragOver	React to one component being dragged over another.
OLEGiveFeedback	Trigger the source component to provide visual feedback to the user.
OLESetData	A source component will react when a target component performs a GetData method, but the data for the specified format has not yet been loaded.
OLEStartDrag	React to a component's OLEDrag method, or when a component initiates an OLE drag-and-drop operation when the OLEDragMode property is set to Automatic.
Paint	Initiate an action when a form or picture needs to be redrawn.
QueryUnload	React to an attempt to unload the form.
Resize	Initiate an action when a form is first displayed or its size is changed.
Terminate	React to the last reference to this object being removed from memory.
Unload	Initiate an action when a form is removed from memory.

Table 16-52 Methods of the Form object

Use This Method...	To Do This...
Add	Add a member to a collection of objects
Circle	Create a circle or ellipse on a form or picture box
Cls	Clear graphics and text that have been drawn on the form at runtime

Use This Method...	To Do This...
Hide	Make a form invisible
Line	Draw a line on a form or picture
Move	Change the position of this control or form
OLEDrag	Cause the OLE drag-and-drop operation
PaintPicture	Transfer a graphic from this object to another
Point	Return the color setting of a specified point on a form or picture box
Pop-upMenu	Display a pop-up menu
Print	Print text on a form or picture box
PrintForm	Send a copy of a form to the printer
PSet	Set the color of a specified point on a form or picture box
Refresh	Update and repaint this object
Scale	Define the coordinate system used for the form
ScaleX	Convert a value for the width from one scale mode to another
ScaleY	Convert a value for the height from one scale mode to another
SetFocus	Move the focus to this form
Show	Display a previously hidden form
TextHeight	Return the height of text in this object's font
TextWidth	Return the width of text in this object's font
WhatsThisMode	Cause the mouse pointer to change into the What's This pointer and prepare the application to display What's This Help on the selected object
ZOrder	Place this object at the front or back of the z-order

Description   A form is a special kind of class that defines a window upon which you may place user interface controls. A program can have zero or more forms. Each form represents a window in your program (see Figure 16-16). You can then use Visual Basic's Toolbox to draw controls, such as command buttons, text, and check boxes, on the form (see Figure 16-17). You can create a variety of effects by choosing appropriate controls and manipulating their properties (see Figure 16-18).

Figure 16-16   A blank form

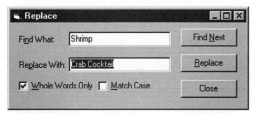

Figure 16-17 A search and replace dialog
box created from a form

Figure 16-18 Visual Basic offers powerful control
over form appearance, as demonstrated by this
splash form

Forms define a logical, as well as visual, portion of your program. Each
form has its own separate code area. Procedures entered into a form's code
area may be local to that form, and so cannot be accessed by routines in
other forms or code modules. Alternatively, they may be public, in which
case the procedures define the "public interface" of the form object and
may be called from any other forms or modules in the project. The code
portion of a form can contain three types of program code: the general
declarations area, programmer-defined procedures, and object-related
events.

A form's general declarations area declares variables, arrays, and constants.
Items declared in this area will be accessible to any program code that also
resides in the code area of the same form. Procedures that are contained in
other forms will not be able to use these variables or constants unless they
have been declared as Public.

Programmer-defined sub procedures and functions are self-contained procedures that you write to handle specific tasks or return certain values.

Note that previous versions of Visual Basic always defined procedures as Private to the form. Visual Basic 5.0 now allows you to create Public procedures, which can dramatically simplify programming if done intelligently. You can define custom properties for your form with the new Property, Let, Get, and Set statements, and custom methods with regular sub procedures. This change makes forms much more object-oriented. See Chapters 104 and 105 for a discussion of object-oriented programming and how to define custom classes. Although those chapters deal primarily with class modules, remember that a form is much like a class module with a visual user interface.

The program code for each of a form's related events is placed in the form's code area. The event procedures for any controls that have been drawn on a form are also placed in the form's code area.

Each form has a name by which it may be referenced. This name is set at design time, and is specified by the Name property. This property is now available at runtime; previous versions of Visual Basic could not read this property while your program was running.

The Load and Unload statements load and erase a form from memory at runtime. Loading a form does not automatically display it. This is done with the Show method. If the Unload statement is used on a form, and that form is the only form remaining in memory for that project, the program ends. The Initialize and Terminate events are also available, as they are with custom classes. Note that accessing non-user-interface components of the form object (say, a custom method or property that doesn't access any of the user interface controls) automatically instantiates the form and triggers the Initialize event, but does not automatically load the form. Accessing any of the user interface controls automatically loads the form.

The Show method will display a form that had been previously hidden or not yet displayed. This method also determines whether a form is to be modal or modeless. A modal form does not allow any other window on the desktop to receive the focus until it is closed. A modeless form places no restrictions on where the focus goes. A form may be hidden with the Hide method.

FORMS COLLECTION

Purpose   The Forms collection contains each of the loaded forms. This collection makes it easy to iterate through each form in a running project.

Property and Method   Tables 16-53 and 16-54 list the property and method of the Forms collection.

Table 16-53 Property of the Forms collection

Use This Property...	To Do This...
Count	Return the number of loaded forms

Table 16-54 Method of the Forms collection

Use This Method...	To Do This...
Item	Return an individual form object (optional; item is the default method of the forms collection)

Description Use the Forms collection to access any loaded form during runtime. This collection makes it easy to iterate through all forms without having to specify a particular form's Name property. Note that the Forms collection only contains forms that are loaded; it is possible to have forms in a project that have not yet been loaded.

FRAME CONTROL

Purpose The Frame control visually groups controls that are functionally related.

Properties, Events, and Methods Tables 16-55, 16-56, and 16-57 list the properties, events, and methods that relate to the Frame control.

Table 16-55 Properties of the Frame control

Use This Property...	To Do This...
Appearance	Read or set whether the object is drawn with 3D effects
BackColor, ForeColor	Read or set the background and foreground colors of this control
Caption	Assign text to this control
ClipControls	Determine whether graphic methods repaint entire control
Container	Set or return a reference to the object that contains this object
DragIcon	Read or set what displays when this control is dragged
DragMode	Determine whether drag operations are to occur manually or automatically
Enabled	Read or set whether this control can react to events
Font	Set or return a font object that controls the way text displays in this control
FontBold, FontItalic, FontStrikeThru, FontUnderline	Read or set special effects for this control's font
FontName	Read or set the name of this control's font
FontSize	Read or set the size of this control's font

Use This Property...	To Do This...
Height	Read or set the height of this control
HelpContextID	Read or set the context number to this control for context-sensitive help
hWnd	Read the handle for this control's window
Index	Uniquely identify an element of a control array
Left	Read or set the left edge placement of this control relative to its container
MouseIcon	Set a custom mouse pointer
MousePointer	Read or set the shape of the mouse pointer when it's over this control
Name	Read or set the name used in code to refer to this control
OLEDropMode	Read or set how a target component handles drop operations
Parent	Read the name of the form to which this control belongs
TabIndex	Read or set the placement of this control within the form's tab order
Tag	Read or set any extra string data associated with this control
ToolTipText	Read or set a value that explains an object
Top	Read or set the coordinate of this control's top edge relative to its container
Visible	Read or set whether this control is visible
WhatsThisHelpID	Read or set the context number to this object for context-sensitive help in Windows 95
Width	Read or set the width of this control

Table 16-56 Events of the Frame control

Use This Event...	To Do This...
Click	React to the user's clicking this control.
DblClick	React to the user's double-clicking this control.
DragDrop	React to the user's dragging and dropping an object onto this control.
DragOver	React to the user's dragging another object over this control.
MouseDown	React to the user's pressing any mouse button.
MouseMove	React to the user's moving the mouse over this control.
MouseUp	React to the user's releasing any mouse button.
OLECompleteDrag	A target component reacts to a source component being dropped on it. It is informing the source component that a drag action was either canceled or performed.
OLEDragDown	A target component reacts to a source component being dropped on it.
OLEDragOver	React to one component being dragged over another.
OLEGiveFeedback	Trigger the source component to provide visual feedback to the user.
OLESetData	A source component will react when a target component performs a GetData method, but the data for the specified format has not yet been loaded.
OLEStartDrag	React to a component's OLEDrag method, or when a component initiates an OLE drag-and-drop operation when the OLEDragMode property is set to Automatic.

Table 16-57 Methods of the Frame control

Use This Method...	To Do This...
Drag	Control manual dragging of this control
Move	Change the position of this control or form
OLEDrag	Cause the OLE drag-and-drop operation
Refresh	Update and repaint this control
ShowWhatsThis	Display the What's This help topic pop-up provided by Windows 95 help system
ZOrder	Place this control at the front or back of the z-order

Description

You may draw a frame on a form, and then draw other controls on the frame. This visually groups the controls together. If the frame is moved to a new location on the form, its controls move with it.

When OptionButton controls are placed on a frame (see Figure 16-19), not only are they visually grouped together, but they become logically grouped as well. When several option buttons share a frame, they become mutually exclusive. That is to say, when one button is selected, all the other buttons in the same frame get unselected. This is how you can create "radio buttons."

If you want to place controls on a frame, the frame must be drawn first. Any controls that are to be within the frame must then be drawn on it. You cannot move an already drawn control onto a frame except by choosing the Edit menu's Cut and Paste commands to paste the control onto the frame.

A title may be displayed at the upper-left corner of the frame by setting its Caption property.

GRID CONTROL

Purpose

The Grid control displays a series of rows and columns, with individual cells at the intersections. Although there is no spreadsheet intelligence built in, the Grid control is very similar to the way a spreadsheet is laid

Figure 16-19 The frame control enclosing three option buttons

out. In Visual Basic 5.0, the Grid control has been replaced with the MSFlexGrid control, described later in this chapter. For backward compatibility, the Grid control is included on your Visual Basic CD-ROM under the Tools/Controls subdirectory. For a full description of the control's properties, events, and methods, refer to the Waite Group's *Visual Basic 4 Objects and Classes SuperBible*, Chapter 3, "Objects and Collections." Many of the properties, events, and methods in MSFlexGrid are compatible with those defined in the Grid control. If you replace the Grid control with MSFlexGrid, you should have no problems adapting it to your application.

IMAGE CONTROL

Purpose   Use the Image control to define an area to display a picture. The Image control repaints faster and uses fewer system resources than the PictureBox control, but only has a subset of the picture control's properties. New to version 5.0, the Image control can also display JPEG and GIF image files. For animated GIF images, like those found on HTML documents on the World Wide Web, you will need to use a third-party control like AccuSoft's ImageGear.

Properties, Events, and Methods   Tables 16-58, 16-59, and 16-60 list the properties, events, and methods that relate to the Image control.

Table 16-58 Properties of the Image control

Use This Property...	To Do This...
Appearance	Read or set whether the object is drawn with 3D effects
BorderStyle	Determine whether this control has a border and, if it does, set its style
Container	Set or return a reference to the object that contains this object
DataChanged	Determine whether the value displayed in this control has changed
DataField	Read or set the name of the field in the recordset of the data control to which this control is bound
DataSource	Set the name of the data control to which this control is bound
DragIcon	Read or set what displays when this control is dragged
DragMode	Determine whether drag operations are to occur manually or automatically
Enabled	Read or set whether this control can react to events
Height	Read or set the height of this control
Image	Read the Windows device handle for a picture's persistent bitmap
Index	Uniquely identify an element of a control array
Left	Read or set the left edge placement of this control relative to its container
MouseIcon	Set a custom mouse pointer
MousePointer	Read or set the shape of the mouse pointer when it's over this control

continued on next page

continued from previous page

Use This Property...	To Do This...
Name	Read or set the name used in code to refer to this control
OLEDragMode	Read or set whether the component or the programmer handles an OLE drag/drop operation
OLEDropMode	Read or set how a target component handles drop operations
Parent	Read the name of the form to which this control belongs
Picture	Read or assign a graphic image to a picture or form
Stretch	Determine whether the picture is resized to fit the control or vice versa
Tag	Read or set any extra string data associated with this control
ToolTipText	Read or set a value that explains an object
Top	Read or set the coordinate of this control's top edge relative to its container
Visible	Read or set whether control is visible
WhatsThisHelpID	Read or set the context number to this object for context-sensitive help in Windows 95
Width	Read or set the width of this control

Table 16-59 Events of the Image control

Use This Event...	To Do This...
Click	React to the user's clicking this control.
DblClick	React to the user's double-clicking this control.
DragDrop	React to the user's dragging and dropping an object onto this control.
DragOver	React to the user's dragging another object over this control.
MouseDown	React to the user's pressing any mouse button.
MouseMove	React to the user's moving the mouse over this control.
MouseUp	React to the user's releasing any mouse button.
OLECompleteDrag	A target component reacts to a source component being dropped on it. It is informing the source component that a drag action was either canceled or performed.
OLEDragDown	A target component reacts to a source component being dropped on it.
OLEDragOver	React to one component being dragged over another.
OLEGiveFeedback	Trigger the source component to provide visual feedback to the user.
OLESetData	A source component will react when a target component performs a GetData method, but the data for the specified format has not yet been loaded.
OLEStartDrag	React to a component's OLEDrag method, or when a component initiates an OLE drag-and-drop operation when the OLEDragMode property is set to Automatic.

Table 16-60 Methods of the Image control

Use This Method...	To Do This...
Drag	Control manual dragging of this control
Move	Change the position of this control or form
OLEDrag	Cause the OLE drag-and-drop operation
Refresh	Update and repaint this control
ShowWhatsThis	Display the What's This help topic pop-up provided by the Windows 95 help system
ZOrder	Place this control at the front or back of the z-order

Description   The Image control lets you display graphical images without the performance and overhead penalties of the PictureBox control. The Image control repaints faster and uses far fewer system resources than does the PictureBox. It does this by restricting its properties, events, and methods to those used to display predefined images and eliminating those dealing with creating graphic images. The Image control also cannot function as a grouping mechanism for other controls (like a frame) the way a PictureBox can, nor can it function in a DDE conversation. For more on the Image control, see Chapter 38, "Graphics Fundamentals."

LABEL CONTROL

Purpose   The Label control labels an area of a frame, form, or picture.

Properties, Events, and Methods   Tables 16-61, 16-62, and 16-63 list the properties, events, and methods that relate to the Label control.

Table 16-61 Properties of the Label control

Use This Property...	To Do This...
Appearance	Read or set whether the object is drawn with 3D effects
Alignment	Align text to the right, left, or center within the control
AutoSize	Determine whether this control is automatically resized to fit its contents
BackColor, ForeColor	Read or set the background and foreground colors of this control
BackStyle	Determine whether the control's background is opaque or transparent
BorderStyle	Determine whether this control has a border and, if it does, set its style
Container	Set or return a reference to the object that contains this object
Caption	Assign text to this control
DataChanged	Determine whether the value displayed in this control has changed
DataField	Read or set the name of the field in the recordset of the data control to which this control is bound
DataSource	Set the name of the data control to which this control is bound

continued on next page

continued from previous page

Use This Property...	To Do This...
DragIcon	Read or set what displays when this control is dragged
DragMode	Determine whether drag operations are to occur manually or automatically
Enabled	Read or set whether this control can react to events
Font	Set or return a font object that controls the way text displays in this control
FontName	Read or set the name of this control's font
FontSize	Read or set the size of this control's font
FontBold, FontItalic, FontStrikeThru, FontUnderline	Read or set typestyle effects for this control's font
Height	Read or set the height of this control
Index	Uniquely identify an element of a control array
Left	Read or set the left edge placement of this control relative to its container
LinkItem	Read or set the item in a DDE conversation
LinkMode	Read or set a DDE conversation to hot, cold, or none
LinkTimeout	Read or set the amount of time before a DDE conversation times out
LinkTopic	Read or set the topic of a DDE conversation
MouseIcon	Set a custom mouse pointer
MousePointer	Read or set the shape of the mouse pointer when it's over this control
Name	Read or set the name used in code to refer to this control
OLEDropMode	Read or set how a target component handles drop operations
Parent	Read the name of the form to which this control belongs
TabIndex	Read or set the placement of this control within the form's tab order
Tag	Read or set any extra string data associated with this control
ToolTipText	Read or set a value that explains an object
Top	Read or set the coordinate of this control's top edge relative to its container
UseMnemonic	Read or set whether an ampersand (&) defines an access key
Visible	Read or set whether this control is visible
WhatsThisHelpID	Read or set the context number to this object for context-sensitive help in Windows 95
Width	Read or set the width of this control
WordWrap	Determine whether the label expands to fit its contents

Table 16-62 Events of the Label control

Use This Event...	To Do This...
Change	React to a change in the control's Caption property.
Click	React to the user's clicking this control.
DblClick	React to the user's double-clicking this control.

Use This Event...	To Do This...
DragDrop	React to the user's dragging and dropping an object onto this control.
DragOver	React to the user's dragging another object over this control.
LinkClose	React to the termination of a DDE conversation.
LinkError	React to an error in a DDE conversation.
LinkNotify	React to a change in the DDE source data.
LinkOpen	React to the initiation of a DDE conversation.
MouseDown	React to the user's pressing any mouse button.
MouseMove	React to the user's moving the mouse over this object.
MouseUp	React to the user's releasing any mouse button.
OLECompleteDrag	A target component reacts to a source component being dropped on it. It is informing the source component that a drag action was either canceled or performed.
OLEDragDown	A target component reacts to a source component being dropped on it.
OLEDragOver	React to one component being dragged over another.
OLEGiveFeedback	Trigger the source component to provide visual feedback to the user.
OLESetData	A source component will react when a target component performs a GetData method, but the data for the specified format has not yet been loaded.
OLEStartDrag	React to a component's OLEDrag method, or when a component initiates an OLE drag-and-drop operation when the OLEDragMode property is set to Automatic.

Table 16-63 Methods of the Label control

Use This Method...	To Do This...
Drag	Control manual dragging of this control
LinkExecute	Send a DDE Execute command to a DDE server application
LinkPoke	Send data from a DDE client to a DDE server
LinkRequest	Ask for data from a DDE server
Move	Change the position of this control or form
OLEDrag	Cause the OLE drag-and-drop operation
Refresh	Update and repaint this control
ShowWhatsThis	Display the What's This help topic pop-up provided by the Windows 95 help system
ZOrder	Place this control at the front or back of the z-order

Description   The Label control places noneditable text on a form, frame, or picture. Most often this control displays a meaningful name that describes the purpose of a text, list, or combo box control. In Figure 16-20 Find What: and Replace With: are such descriptive labels.

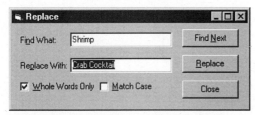

Figure 16-20   Label controls identify the
Find What and Replace With text boxes

The text displayed by a Label control is defined by its Caption property. At
design time this property can be assigned a one-line text string. If needed,
at runtime the program's code may assign this property a string that contains carriage return/line feed pairs to create a multiple-line label. Set the
AutoSize and WordWrap properties to display variable length lines or a
varying number of lines.

LINE CONTROL

Purpose

Use the Line control to display a horizontal, vertical, or diagonal line
directly on the form.

**Properties and
Methods**

Tables 16-64 and 16-65 list the properties and methods of the line
control.

Table 16-64 Properties of the Line control

Use This Property...	To Do This...
BorderColor	Read or set the color of the line
BorderStyle	Read or set the style of the line (for example, solid, dotted, dashed)
BorderWidth	Read or set the width of the line
Container	Set or return a reference to the object that contains this object
DrawMode	Read or set the draw mode (for example, overwrite, inverse, XOR pen)
Index	Uniquely identify an element of a control array
Name	Read or set the name used in code to refer to this control
Parent	Read the name of the form to which this control belongs
Tag	Read or set any extra string data associated with this control
Visible	Read or set whether this control is visible
X1, Y1, X2, Y2	Read or set the coordinates of the end points for the line

Table 16-65 Methods of the Line control

Use This Method...	To Do This...
Refresh	Update this control
ZOrder	Place this control at the front or back of the z-order

Description The Line control draws a line directly on your form during the design phase. This is especially helpful for designing your forms, because you can see the effects immediately. Graphics methods like PSet or Line, in contrast, do not display until runtime and can be difficult to design with. See Chapter 40, "Drawing Shapes," for more on the Line Control.

LISTBOX CONTROL

Purpose The ListBox control displays a box with a list of items from which the user may make a selection.

Properties, Events, Tables 16-66, 16-67, and 16-68 list the properties, events, and methods
and Methods that relate to the ListBox control.

Table 16-66 Properties of the ListBox control

Use This Property...	To Do This...
Appearance	Read or set whether the object is drawn with 3D effects
BackColor, ForeColor	Read or set the background and foreground colors of this control
Container	Set or return a reference to the object that contains this object
Columns	Determine how many columns are displayed
DataChanged	Read or set whether value has been changed
DataField	Read or set the name of the field in the recordset of the data control to which this control is bound
DataSource	Set the name of the data control to which this control is bound
DragIcon	Read or set what displays when this control is dragged
DragMode	Determine whether drag operations are to occur manually or automatically
Enabled	Read or set whether this control can react to events
Font	Set or return a font object that controls the way text displays in this control
FontBold, FontItalic, FontStrikeThru, FontUnderline	Read or set special effects for this control's font
FontName	Read or set the name of this control's font

continued on next page

continued from previous page

Use This Property...	To Do This...
FontSize	Read or set the size of this control's font
Height	Read or set the height of this control
HelpContextID	Read or set the context number to this control for context-sensitive help
hWnd	Read the handle for this control's window
Index	Uniquely identify an element of a control array
IntegralHeight	Read or set whether the list displays partial items
ItemData	Read or set a number associated with the currently selected item
Left	Read or set the left edge placement of this control relative to its container
List	Read or set the value of a listed item
ListCount	Read the number of items in a list
ListIndex	Read or set the index of the currently selected item in a list
MouseIcon	Set a custom mouse pointer
MousePointer	Read or set the shape of the mouse pointer when it's over this control
MultiSelect	Determine whether a user can make multiple selections in the list
Name	Read or set the name used in code to refer to this control
NewIndex	Read the index of the item most recently added to this control
OLEDragMode	Read or set whether the component or the programmer handles an OLE drag/drop operation
OLEDropMode	Read or set how a target component handles drop operations
Parent	Read the name of the form to which this control belongs
SelCount	Read the number of selected items in the list
Selected	Read the selection status of an item in the list
Sorted	Read or set whether Visual Basic will automatically sort the list
Style	Read or set the behavior of the list box, either traditional or check box list box
TabIndex	Read or set the placement of this control within the form's tab order
TabStop	Read or set whether this control is part of the form's tab order
Tag	Read or set any extra string data associated with this control
Text	Read the currently selected item
ToolTipText	Read or set a value that explains an object
Top	Read or set the coordinate of this control's top edge relative to its container
TopIndex	Read which item in the list appears in the topmost position
Visible	Read or set whether this control is visible
WhatsThisHelpID	Read or set the context number to this object for context-sensitive help in Windows 95
Width	Read or set the width of this control

Table 16-67 Events of the ListBox control

Use This Event...	To Do This...
Click	React to the user's clicking this control

Use This Event...	To Do This...
DblClick	React to the user's double-clicking this control.
DragDrop	React to the user's dragging and dropping an object onto this control.
DragOver	React to the user's dragging another object over this control.
GotFocus	Initiate an action when this control receives the focus.
KeyDown	Initiate an action when the user presses or holds a key down.
KeyPress	React to the user's typing an ASCII character.
KeyUp	Initiate an action when the user releases a key.
LostFocus	Initiate an action when this control loses the focus.
MouseDown	React to the user's pressing any mouse button.
MouseMove	React to the user's moving the mouse over this control.
MouseUp	React to the user's releasing any mouse button.
OLECompleteDrag	A target component reacts to a source component being dropped on it. It is informing the source component that a drag action was either canceled or performed.
OLEDragDown	A target component reacts to a source component being dropped on it.
OLEDragOver	React to one component being dragged over another.
OLEGiveFeedback	Trigger the source component to provide visual feedback to the user.
OLESetData	A source component will react when a target component performs a GetData method, but the data for the specified format has not yet been loaded.
OLEStartDrag	React to a component's OLEDrag method, or when a component initiates an OLE drag-and-drop operation when the OLEDragMode property is set to Automatic.
Scroll	React to the user's clicking on the scroll box of the drop-down list.

Table 16-68 Methods of the ListBox control

Use This Method...	To Do This...
AddItem	Add an item to a list box
Clear	Clear the contents of this control
Drag	Control manual dragging of this control
Move	Change the position of this control or form
OLEDrag	Cause the OLE drag-and-drop operation
Refresh	Update and repaint this control
RemoveItem	Delete items from a list
SetFocus	Move the focus to this control
ShowWhatsThis	Display the What's This help topic pop-up provided by the Windows 95 help system
ZOrder	Place this control at the front or back of the z-order

Description   The user may choose an item from a ListBox control by clicking it or by using the up and down arrow keys to move the highlight to the desired item (see Figure 16-21). If there are more items in the list than can be displayed in the area defined for the box, Visual Basic will automatically add a vertical scrollbar on the right edge of the list. The user can then use this scrollbar to move up or down in the list.

An alternative to the traditional method of displaying items in a ListBox control is to place a check box next to the item within the list. This is similar to the Components list box, in which a check box is to the left of the item's caption. Figure 16-22 illustrates this example using the same list as in Figure 16-21.

The List property provides a way to read and set a list's contents in a manner similar to accessing and assigning values in an array. The List property is followed by an index number in parentheses, which identifies which list entry is being referenced. The index numbering of the list is zero-based. Therefore, if a list contains five items, the first item is index number 0 and the highest index number is 4. The number of items in a list can be determined by using the ListCount property.

The ListIndex property returns the index number of the currently selected item in a list. If no item is currently selected, -1 is returned.

The program may also set the ListIndex property directly. When using the ListIndex property to set the currently selected list entry, you must use an index number that references a currently added item in the list. For instance, if a list has five items in it, an index number from 0 to 4 must be specified, or an "Invalid property array index" error will occur.

Figure 16-21   The list box allows users to select one or several choices from a fixed list

Figure 16-22   The list box allows users to mark one or several choices from a list using the check box style

The AddItem and RemoveItem methods add entries to and delete them from a list box control. The Clear method clears the entire control of items.

Visual Basic 5.0 lets you bind the list box to a field in a data control's recordset. This allows you to update the field based on the user's selection. Note that the contents of the list are not bound, so you still need to use the AddItem method to create the list. See the entry on the DBList control if you would like to fill the list from the database as well.

The list box control is discussed in detail in Chapter 46, "List and Combo Boxes."

MDIFORM OBJECT

Purpose	An MDI (Multiple-Document Interface) form is a form that acts as a container for other forms, or *child forms*, and serves as the main background form for your application.
Properties, Events, and Methods	Tables 16-69, 16-70, and 16-71 list the properties, events, and methods of the MDIForm.

Table 16-69 Properties of the MDIForm object

Use This Property...	To Do This...
ActiveControl	Read which control has the focus
ActiveForm	Read which form is active
Appearance	Read or set whether the object is drawn with 3D effects
AutoShowChildren	Read or set whether MDI child forms are displayed when first loaded
BackColor	Read or set the background color for this object
Caption	Assign text to the title bar of this object
Controls	Read a reference to a collection of controls on the form
Count	Read a number of objects in a collection
Enabled	Read or set whether this object can react to events
Height	Read or set the height of this object
HelpContextID	Read or set the context number to this object for context-sensitive help
hWnd	Read the handle for this object's window
Icon	Read or set the icon used when a form is minimized
Left	Read or set the left edge placement of this form
LinkMode	Read or set a DDE conversation to hot, cold, or none
LinkTopic	Read or set the topic of a DDE conversation
MouseIcon	Set a custom mouse pointer

continued on next page

continued from previous page

Use This Property...	To Do This...
MousePointer	Read or set the shape of the mouse pointer when it's over this object
Name	Read or set the name used in code to refer to this object
OLEDropMode	Read or set how the form handles drop operations
Picture	Read or set the picture displayed on form
ScaleHeight	Read or set the number of units that define the height of this object
ScaleWidth	Read or set the number of units that define the width of this object
ScrollBars	Determine whether scrollbars appear in a multiple-line text box
StartUpPosition	Read or set the location where the form first appears
Tag	Read or set any extra string data associated with this control
Top	Read or set the coordinate of this control's top edge relative to its container
Visible	Read or set whether this object is visible
WhatsThisHelp	Read or set whether context-sensitive help uses main help window or a What's This pop-up
Width	Read or set the width of this object
WindowState	Read or set whether a form is maximized, minimized, or normal

Table 16-70 Events of the MDIForm object

Use This Event...	To Do This...
Activate	React when this object becomes activated either by code or by the user.
Deactivate	React when this object becomes deactivated either by code or by the user.
DragDrop	React to the user's dragging and dropping an object onto this object.
DragOver	React to the user's dragging another object over this object.
Initialize	React when this form first becomes instantiated.
LinkClose	React to the termination of a DDE conversation.
LinkError	React to an error in a DDE conversation.
LinkExecute	React to a DDE Execute command from a DDE client application.
LinkOpen	React to the initiation of a DDE conversation.
Load	Initiate an action when a form is first loaded into memory.
OLECompleteDrag	A target component reacts to a source component being dropped on it. It is informing the source component that a drag action was either canceled or performed.
OLEDragDown	A target component reacts to a source component being dropped on it.
OLEDragOver	React to one component being dragged over another.
OLEGiveFeedback	Trigger the source component to provide visual feedback to the user.
OLESetData	A source component will react when a target component performs a GetData method, but the data for the specified format has not yet been loaded.
OLEStartDrag	React to a component's OLEDrag method, or when a component initiates an OLE drag-and-drop operation when the OLEDragMode property is set to Automatic.

Use This Event...	To Do This...
QueryUnload	React to an attempt to unload the form.
Resize	Initiate an action when a form is first displayed or its size is changed.
Unload	Initiate an action when a form is removed from memory.

Table 16-71 Methods of the MDIForm object

Use This Method...	To Do This...
Arrange	Arrange the windows or icons within this MDI form
Hide	Make a form invisible
Move	Change the position of this control or form
OLEDropMode	Read or set how the form handles drop operations
PopUpMenu	Display a pop-up menu
SetFocus	Move the focus to this form
Show	Display a previously hidden form
WhatsThisMode	Cause the mouse pointer to change into the What's This pointer and prepare the application to display What's This Help on the selected object
ZOrder	Place this object at the front or back of the z-order

Description

Make a Visual Basic application MDI capable by creating an MDI form with the Project menu's Add MDI Form command. Then flag other forms as children of the main MDI form by setting their MDIChild property to True. Although there may be only one MDI form per Windows application, you may have many kinds of child forms as well as non-MDI forms. For example, Microsoft Excel has both worksheet and chart child forms in addition to a host of normal dialog boxes. See Figure 16-23 for an example of how Excel can have many documents of several kinds open at once.

A child's menu bar replaces the MDIForm's menu when the child form has the focus. Thus, in the Excel example above, the MDIForm may only have the File and Help menu items; the worksheet child form will display File, Edit, Formula, Format, Data, and so on, while the chart child form will display File, Edit, Gallery, Chart, and so forth.

A child form is totally contained within the MDIForm. When maximized, the child form takes up the entire client area—that is, the area within the MDIForm's borders not taken up with the title bar, menu bar, and any picture controls placed on the top or bottom of the MDIForm. When minimized, the child form appears as an icon within the MDIForm. Multiple child forms may be opened at once, and may be arranged in various ways within the MDIForm.

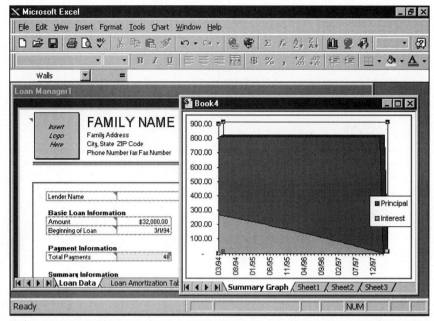

Figure 16-23   The Multiple-Document Interface of a commercial application

The only standard controls that may be directly placed on a MDIForm are the Picture control and Data control. You would typically place picture controls at the top or bottom of the form. Once these picture controls are placed, other controls may be placed on top of them to form toolbars and status bars. Visual Basic 5.0 lets you place a data control directly on a MDIForm, which allows the entire application easy access to a single recordset. This makes many MDI database applications easier to write, because the child forms can all access the MDIForm's data control as a "master" record.

For more information on MDIForms, see Chapter 36.

MENU CONTROL

Purpose   The Menu control defines a pull-down menu system for a form.

Properties and   Tables 16-72 and 16-73 list the properties and events that relate to this
Events   object. There are no methods associated with the Menu control.

Table 16-72 Properties of the Menu control

Use This Property...	To Do This...
Caption	Assign text to this control
Checked	Place or remove a checkmark from a menu item
Enabled	Read or set whether this control can react to events
HelpContextID	Read or set the context number to this control for context-sensitive help
Index	Uniquely identify an element of a control 1array
Name	Read or set the name used in code to refer to this control
NegotiatePosition	Set whether top-level menu item is displayed when a linked or embedded object is active
Parent	Read the name of the form to which this control belongs
ShortCut	Specify a shortcut key
Tag	Read or set any extra string data associated with this control
Visible	Read or set whether this control is visible
WindowList	Display a list of MDI child forms

Table 16-73 The Menu control event

Use This Event...	To Do This...
Click	React to the user's clicking this control

Description

The major functions performed by most Windows programs are accessible with a pull-down menu system (see Figures 16-24 and 16-25). Visual Basic provides you with the Menu Design window with which you can define a menu system. Each menu may have up to four levels of submenus. Each menu, and each option on each menu, is assigned a Name by which you reference it.

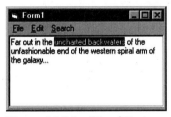

Figure 16-24 Visual Basic makes it easy to create powerful menu systems

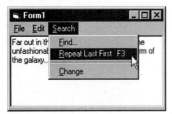

Figure 16-25 The same
form with the Search menu
open

When a user chooses a menu item, that menu's Click event occurs. Code
can be placed in this event to perform the task related to the menu or
option chosen by the user.

The Enabled property may be set to 0 to disable a particular menu or
menu option. Doing so prevents the user from being able to choose that
item. Disabling a menu effectively disables all options under that menu. A
disabled item displays in gray.

The Checked property may have a value of True (-1), meaning checked, or
False (0), meaning not checked. When a menu item's Checked property is
True, a small checkmark will be displayed next to that menu item to show
its current setting. For instance, if a menu option turns a particular function on or off, the Checked property may be used to indicate the current
status of the function.

In the Menu Design window, if a value is assigned to the Index property
for a menu item, that menu item becomes part of a control array. This
gives the program the opportunity to dynamically add and delete menu
options at runtime, by using the Load and Unload statements (see Chapter
36 for more on these statements).

MSFLEXGRID CONTROL

Purpose   The MSFlexGrid control displays a series of rows and columns, with individual cells at the intersections. It provides flexibility with working with
tables that contain string values and images. It can be bound to a data control to provide read-only access to information.

Properties, Events, Tables 16-74, 16-75, and 16-76 list the properties, events, and methods of
and Methods the MSFlexGrid control.

Table 16-74 Properties of the MSFlexGrid control

Use This Property...	To Do This...
AllowBigSelection	Determine whether selecting the entire row or column is possible by clicking the row or column header
AllowUserResizing	Determine whether to allow the user to resize rows or columns
Appearance	Read or set whether the object is drawn with 3D effects
BackColor, ForeColor	Read or set the background and foreground colors of this control
BackColorBkg,	
BackColorFixed,	
BackColorSel	Read or set the color of the control's background, fixed cells, and selected cells
BorderStyle	Determine whether this control has a border and, if it does, set its style
CellAlignment	Read or set the alignment of data within a cell
CellBackcolor, CellForeColor	Read or set the background and foreground colors within a cell
CellFontBold,	
CellFontItalic,	
CellFontStrikeThrough,	
CellFontUnderline	Read or set the special effects for this current cell's fonts
CellFontName	Read or set the font name within the current cell
CellFontSize	Read or set the font size within the current cell
CellFontWidth	Read or set the font width within the current cell
CellHeight, CellLeft,	
CellTop, CellWidth	Read the position and size of the current cell
CellPicture	Read or set an image to be displayed within the current cell or range of cells
CellPictureAlignment	Read or set the alignment of images within the current cell or range of cells
CellTextStyle	Read or set the 3D effect for the text within the current cell or range of cells
Clip	Read or set the contents of the cells in a selected region
Col, Row	Read or set the active cell
ColAlignment	Read or set the alignment of a column's data
ColData, RowData	Read or set an arbitrary value associated with each row and column
CollsVisible	Read a Boolean value that indicates whether a column is visible or not
ColPos	Read the twips between the upper-left corner of the control and the upper-left corner of a specific column
ColPosition, RowPosition	Set the position of a row or column
Cols, Rows	Read or set the total number of columns or rows
ColSel, RowSel	Read or set the start or end row or column for a range of cells
ColWidth	Read or set the width of a column
Container	Set or return a reference to the object that contains this object
DataBindings	Read the collection containing the bindable properties
DataSource	Set the name of the data control to which this control is bound
DragIcon	Read or set what displays when this control is dragged
DragMode	Determine whether drag operations are to occur manually or automatically

continued on next page

continued from previous page

Use This Property...	To Do This...
Enabled	Read or set whether this control can react to events
FillStyle	Read or set how text is assigned to a range of cells
FixedAlignment	Read or set the alignment of data in the fixed cells of a column
FixedCols, FixedRows	Read or set the number of fixed rows or columns on the left and top
FocusRect	Read or set whether a focus rectangle should be displayed around the current cell
FontWidth	Read or set the width of the font
GridColor, GridColorFixed	Read or set the gridline color
Gridlines, GridLinesFixed	Read or set whether the gridlines are visible
GridLineWidth	Read or set the pixel width of the gridlines of the control
Height	Read or set the height of this control
HelpContextID	Read or set the context number to this control for context-sensitive help
HighLight	Read or set whether the selected cells appear highlighted
hWnd	Read the handle for this control's window
Index	Uniquely identify an element of a control array
Left	Read or set the left edge placement of this control relative to its container
LeftCol	Read or set the leftmost visible nonfixed column
MergeCells	Read or set whether the cells with the same content will be grouped in single cell across multiple rows or columns
MergeCol, MergeRow	Read or set which rows or columns should contain the merged contents
MouseCol, MouseRow	Read the current mouse position over the control
MouseIcon	Set a custom mouse pointer
MousePointer	Read or set the shape of the mouse pointer when it's over this control
Name	Read or set the name used in code to refer to this control
Object	Read the object and/or setting of an object's method or property
OLEDropMode	Read or set how a target component handles drop operations
Parent	Read the name of the form to which this control belongs
Picture	Read or assign a graphic image to a cell
PictureType	Read or set the picture cell to display a graphic image in color or monochrome
RowHeight	Read or set the height of the specified row
RowHeightMin	Read or set the minimum row height for the entire control
RowIsVisible	Read the value to determine whether the row is visible or not
RowPos	Read the twips between the upper-left corner of the control and the upper-left corner of a specific row
ScrollBars	Determine whether scrollbars appear in a multiple-line text box
ScrollTrack	Read or set whether the control should scroll the contents while the user moves the scroll box within the scrollbar
SelectionMode	Read or set the controls selection method by cell, rows, or columns
Sort	Set the method to sort selected rows
TabIndex	Read or set the placement of this control within the form's tab order
TabStop	Read or set whether this control is part of the form's tab order
Tag	Read or set any extra string data associated with this control
Text	Read or set the text in a cell or a range of cells

Use This Property...	To Do This...
TextArray	Read or set the text contents of an arbitrary column without changing Col or Row properties
TextMatrix	Read or set the text contents of an arbitrary cell without changing the Col or Row properties
TextStyle, TextStyleFixed	Read or set the three-dimensional style of the regular and fixed cells
ToolTipText	Read or set a value that explains an object
Top	Read or set the coordinate of this control's top edge relative to its container
TopRow	Read or set the topmost nonfixed row
Version	Read the version of this control
Visible	Read or set whether this control is visible
WhatsThisHelpID	Read or set the context number to this object for context-sensitive help in Windows 95
Width	Read or set the width of this control
WordWrap	Read or set whether the text appears on multiple lines within a cell or on the same line

Table 16-75 Events of the MSFlexGrid control

Use This Event...	To Do This...
Click	React to the user's clicking this control.
DblClick	React to the user's double-clicking this control.
DragDrop	React to the user's dragging and dropping an object onto this control.
DragOver	React to the user's dragging another object over this control.
EnterCell	React when the active cell changes.
GotFocus	Initiate an action when this control receives the focus.
KeyDown	Initiate an action when the user presses or holds a key down.
KeyPress	React to the user's typing an ASCII character.
KeyUp	Initiate an action when the user releases a key.
LeaveCell	React when the active cell changes.
LostFocus	Initiate an action when this control loses the focus.
MouseDown	React to the user's pressing any mouse button.
MouseMove	React to the user's moving the mouse over this control.
MouseUp	React to the user's releasing any mouse button.
OLECompleteDrag	A target component reacts to a source component being dropped on it. It is informing the source component that a drag action was either canceled or performed.
OLEDragDown	A target component reacts to a source component being dropped on it.
OLEDragOver	React to one component being dragged over another.
OLEGiveFeedback	Trigger the source component to provide visual feedback to the user.
OLESetData	A source component will react when a target component performs a GetData method, but the data for the specified format has not yet been loaded.
OLEStartDrag	React to a component's OLEDrag method, or when a component initiates an OLE drag-and-drop operation when the OLEDragMode property is set to Automatic.

continued on next page

continued from previous page

Use This Event...	To Do This...
RowColChange	React to the user's changing to a different cell.
Scroll	React to the user's clicking on the scrollbar of this control.
SelChange	React to the user's changing the selection to a different range of cells.

Table 16-76 Methods of the MSFlexGrid control

Use This Method...	To Do This...
AddItem	Add a new row
Clear	Clear the contents of this control
Drag	Control manual dragging of this control
Move	Change the position of this control or form
OLEDrag	Cause the OLE drag-and-drop operation
Refresh	Update and repaint this control
RemoveItem	Remove a row
SetFocus	Move the focus to this control
ShowWhatsThis	Display the What's This help topic pop-up provided by the Windows 95 help system
ZOrder	Place this control at the front or back of the z-order

Description   The MSFlexGrid control allows you to set up display structures similar to a spreadsheet. Rows and columns intersect to form individual cells. These cells may have their contents changed independently, and may be selected individually or as a region. You also have the facility to create fixed rows and columns, which would be familiar to spreadsheet users as Row and Column heads (A1, B3, and so forth).

Although the MSFlexGrid control looks similar to a spreadsheet, it has no inherent calculation properties. It is merely a collection of cells that you may manipulate with code, and that the user may interact with. One vital difference between the MSFlexGrid control and a spreadsheet is that the user may not directly change the contents of a cell. Your program code can change the contents; so with some additional programming, you can simulate most behaviors of a spreadsheet.

The MSFlexGrid control can be used for any task that requires displaying data in rows and columns. Although a spreadsheet is its most familiar format, there are many other possibilities: database tables, general ledger "printouts," and even multiple-column pick lists.

The most direct way of changing the contents of a cell is with its Text property. The Text property applies to whatever cell is at the intersection of the Rows and Cols properties. If the FillStyle property is 1, then the text is applied to all cells whose CellSelected property is True, regardless of the Rows and Cols settings.

Unlike the Grid control that came with previous versions of Visual Basic, the MSFlexGrid control can be bound to a database. If the MSFlexGrid is bound to a database, the information is only for display. You will have to modify your application if you want the modify the grid and the database.

An advanced feature of this control is its ability to merge, or group, information of similar content together to decrease redundancy. For an example of an MSFlexGrid control illustrating its ability to merge similar items together, see Figure 16-26. For more information on the MSFlexGrid control, see Chapter 48.

OLE CONTAINER CONTROL

Purpose   The OLE (object linking and embedding) container control displays data from many different Windows applications and lets the user of your Visual Basic application edit the data in the original program. Compatible applications even let users edit the data from within your Visual Basic application and may expose features and objects that your Visual Basic program can use much as you'd use a custom control.

Properties, Events, and Methods   Tables 16-77, 16-78, and 16-79 list the properties, events, and methods that relate to the OLE container. In these tables "OLE container" refers to the OLE container object. "OLE object" refers to the object that is embedded or linked in the OLE container.

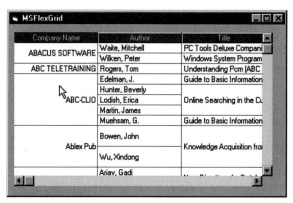

Figure 16-26   The MSFlexGrid control displays data in rows and columns

Table 16-77 Properties of the OLE container

Use This Property...	To Do This...
Action	Perform an OLE action
Appearance	Read or set whether the object is drawn with 3D effects
ApplsRunning	See whether the originating application is running
AutoActivate	Determine how an OLE container is activated
AutoVerbMenu	Determine whether a menu of the OLE object's verbs is automatically displayed
BackColor, ForeColor	Read or set the background and foreground colors of the OLE container
BackStyle	Read or set whether the background of the OLE container is opaque or transparent
BorderStyle	Determine whether the OLE container has a border, and if it does, set its style
Class	Read or set the class name of the embedded OLE object
Container	Set or return a reference to the object that contains this object
Data	Read a handle to a GDI object containing data in the specified format
DataChanged	Determine whether the value displayed in this object has changed
DataField	Read or set the name of the field in the recordset of the data control to which this control is bound
DataText	Read or set a string from the OLE object
DisplayType	Read or set whether the OLE object displays as an icon or the actual contents
DragIcon	Read or set what displays when this control is dragged
DragMode	Determine whether drag operations are to occur manually or automatically
Enabled	Read or set whether this object can react to events
FileNumber	Read or set the file number used when saving or loading an OLE object
Format	Determine the format used when sending or receiving data
Height	Read or set the height of this object
HelpContextID	Read or set the context number to this object for context-sensitive help
HostName	Read the descriptive name of the application that created the OLE object
hWnd	Read the handle for this object's window
Index	Uniquely identify an element of a control array
Left	Read or set the left edge placement of this control relative to its container
lpOLEObject	Set the address of the OLE object for API calls
MiscFlags	Read or set values that determine additional features of the OLE container
MouseIcon	Set a custom mouse icon
MousePointer	Read or set what style of mouse pointer is displayed over this control
Name	Read or set the name used in code to refer to this object
Object	Return the OLE object when using OLE automation
ObjectAcceptFormatsCount	Read the number of formats that can be accepted by the OLE object
ObjectAcceptFormats	Read the list of formats an OLE object can accept
ObjectGetFormatsCount	Read the number of formats that can be returned by the OLE object
ObjectGetFormats	Read the list of formats the OLE object can return
ObjectVerbFlags	Determine the menu state of the object's verbs
ObjectVerbs	List the object's verbs

Use This Property...	To Do This...
ObjectVerbsCount	Count the number of the object's verbs
OLEDropAllowed	Read or set whether the OLE container can be a drop target for an OLE drag-and-drop operation
OleType	Set or determine the type of object (link or embed)
OleTypeAllowed	Determine the types of objects allowed
Parent	Read the name of the form to which this control belongs
PasteOK	Read whether the contents of the Clipboard can be pasted into the OLE container
Picture	Read or assign a graphic image to this object
SizeMode	Set or determine how the object reacts to the OLE container being resized
SourceDoc	Set or determine the filename of the source document
SourceItem	Set the region or subset of data when creating the object
TabIndex	Read or set the placement of this control within the form's tab order
TabStop	Read or set whether this control is part of the form's tab order
Tag	Read or set any extra string data associated with the OLE container
Top	Read or set the coordinate of this control's top edge relative to its container
UpdateOptions	Set or determine how an OLE container reacts to changes
Verb	Set or determine what action an OLE object performs
Visible	Read or set whether this object is visible
WhatsThisHelpID	Read or set the context number to this object for context-sensitive help in Windows 95
Width	Read or set the width of this object

Table 16-78 Events of the OLE container

Use This Event...	To Do This...
Click	React to the user's clicking this object
DblClick	React to the user's double-clicking this object
DragDrop	React to the user's dragging and dropping an object onto this object
DragOver	React to the user's dragging another object over this object
GotFocus	Initiate an action when this object receives the focus
KeyDown	Initiate an action when the user presses or holds a key down
KeyPress	React to the user's typing an ASCII character
KeyUp	Initiate an action when the user releases a key
LostFocus	Initiate an action when this object loses the focus
MouseDown	React to the user's pressing any mouse button
MouseMove	React to the user's moving the mouse over this object
MouseUp	React to the user's releasing any mouse button
ObjectMove	React to the user's moving or resizing the object inside the OLE container
Resize	Initiate an action when the object is first displayed or its size is changed
Updated	React to a modification in the object's data

Table 16-79 Methods of the OLE container

Use This Method...	To Do This...
Close	Close the object and terminate its connection to the application
Copy	Copy the object in the OLE container to the Clipboard
CreateEmbed	Create an embedded object
CreateLink	Create a linked object
Delete	Delete the object and free memory resources
DoVerb	Perform an action on the object
Drag	Control manual dragging of this control
FetchVerbs	Update list of verbs the object supports
InsertObjDlg	Display the Insert Object dialog box
Move	Change the position of this control or form
Paste	Copy an object from the Clipboard
PasteSpecialDlg	Display the Paste Special dialog box
ReadFromFile	Load an object from a data file
Refresh	Update and repaint this object
SaveToFile	Save an object to a data file in OLE 2.0 format
SaveToOle1File	Save an object to a data file in OLE 1.0 format
SetFocus	Move the focus to this control
Update	Retrieve current data for the object
ShowWhatsThis	Display the What's This help topic pop-up provided by the Windows 95 help system
ZOrder	Place this object at the front or back of the z-order

Description

OLE allows your Visual Basic applications to display and manipulate data from many other Windows programs. For example, your application could have a spreadsheet object from Excel, a drawing object from CorelDraw!, a word processor object from AmiPro, and a music sequencer object from Cakewalk. Even though you haven't written any code to do all the things these other applications can, your application can still serve as a front end to tie them all together.

Although OLE and DDE are both ways of sharing data between applications, there are some fundamental differences in their approach. OLE temporarily transfers control to the program that originally created the data to do any data manipulation, while DDE functions solely within your Visual Basic application. OLE also displays the data as the original application would, whereas DDE data displays in whatever way you choose to format it. For example, if the original application is a document created in Word, the OLE control displays its contents exactly as it would appear in Word. Figure 16-27 illustrates how an OLE object retains its formatting.

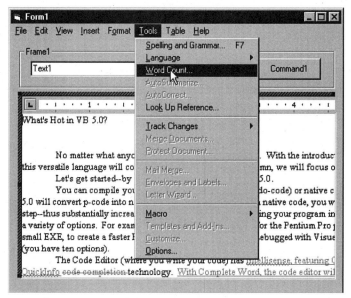

Figure 16-27   A Word document embedded in a Visual Basic form being edited in place. Notice the Word menu that's pulled down from the Visual Basic menu bar

The OLE container lets you create both linked and embedded objects. A linked object is only a placeholder for and pointer to the real data. For example, if you link a drawing into an OLE container, the data for the drawing stays in the original source file. Only an image of the data and a link back to the original data are stored in the OLE container. This makes it possible to access the linked data from several different applications.

An embedded object actually stores the data within the OLE container. You can store the contents of the container in a file, and the file contains the name of the application that produced the object originally, the actual data, and an image of the data for display. When you embed an object in an OLE container, only your application can access the data; no other application can read or write the data directly.

Visual Basic version 3.0 was one of the first applications to support the OLE 2.0 specification. OLE 2.0 allows your Visual Basic application to edit another compatible application's object in-place. Rather than starting the other application in its own window, as in OLE 1.0, the other application lets you edit the object within your Visual Basic application. This makes it look as if your application is doing all the work. Some OLE 2.0–compliant applications also expose a set of objects to your Visual Basic application. This lets you use the other application's features as easily as you would any Visual Basic control through OLE automation.

OptionButton Control

Purpose	The OptionButton control provides a technique for presenting a group of choices where only one choice may be selected. In other words, the OptionButton control is used when the selection of one choice excludes the selection of any other related choices.
Properties, Events, and Methods	Tables 16-80, 16-81, and 16-82 list the properties, events, and methods that relate to the OptionButton control.

Table 16-80 Properties of the OptionButton control

Use This Property...	To Do This...
Alignment	Read or set the alignment of this control
Appearance	Read or set whether the object is drawn with 3D effects
BackColor, ForeColor	Read or set the background and foreground colors of this control
Caption	Assign text to this control
Container	Set or return a reference to the object that contains this object
DisabledPicture	Read or set reference to a picture to display a control when it is disabled
DragIcon	Read or set what displays when this control is dragged
DragMode	Determine whether drag operations are to occur manually or automatically
Enabled	Read or set whether this control can react to events
Font	Set or return a font object that controls the way text displays in this control
FontBold, FontItalic, FontStrikeThru, FontUnderline	Read or set special effects for this control's font
FontName	Read or set the name of this control's font
FontSize	Read or set the size of this control's font
Height	Read or set the height of this control
HelpContextID	Read or set the context number to this control for context-sensitive help
hWnd	Read the handle for this control's window
Index	Uniquely identify an element of a control array
Left	Read or set the left edge placement of this control relative to its container
MaskColor	Read or set a color in a button's picture to be a "mask" or transparent
MouseIcon	Set a custom mouse pointer
MousePointer	Read or set the shape of the mouse pointer when it's over this control
Name	Read or set the name used in code to refer to this control
OLEDropMode	Read or set how a target component handles drop operations
Parent	Read the name of the form to which this control belongs
Picture	Read or set a graphic to be displayed in a control when the Style setting is set to Graphical

Use This Property...	To Do This...
Style	Read or set a value indicating the display type and behavior of the control
TabIndex	Read or set the placement of this control within the form's tab order
TabStop	Read or set whether this control is part of the form's tab order
Tag	Read or set any extra string data associated with this control
Top	Read or set the coordinate of this control's top edge relative to its container
ToolTipText	Read or set a value that explains an object
UseMaskColor	Read or set a value that determines whether the color assigned in the MaskColor property is used as a "mask" for the transparent regions
Value	Read or set whether the option button is selected
Visible	Read or set whether this control is visible
WhatsThisHelpID	Read or set the context number to this object for context-sensitive help in Windows 95
Width	Read or set the width of this control

Table 16-81 Events of the OptionButton control

Use This Event...	To Do This...
Click	React to the user's clicking this control.
DblClick	React to the user's double-clicking this control.
DragDrop	React to the user's dragging and dropping an object onto this control.
DragOver	React to the user's dragging another object over this control.
GotFocus	Initiate an action when this control receives the focus.
KeyDown	Initiate an action when the user presses or holds a key down.
KeyPress	React to the user's typing an ASCII character.
KeyUp	Initiate an action when the user releases a key.
LostFocus	Initiate an action when this control loses the focus.
MouseDown	React to the user's pressing any mouse button.
MouseMove	React to the user's moving the mouse over this control.
MouseUp	React to the user's releasing any mouse button.
OLECompleteDrag	A target component reacts to a source component being dropped on it. It is informing the source component that a drag action was either canceled or performed.
OLEDragDown	A target component reacts to a source component being dropped on it.
OLEDragOver	React to one component being dragged over another.
OLEGiveFeedback	Trigger the source component to provide visual feedback to the user.
OLESetData	A source component will react when a target component performs a GetData method, but the data for the specified format has not yet been loaded.
OLEStartDrag	React to a component's OLEDrag method, or when a component initiates an OLE drag-and-drop operation when the OLEDragMode property is set to Automatic.

Table 16-82 Methods of the OptionButton control

Use This Method...	To Do This...
Drag	Control manual dragging of this control
Move	Change the position of this control or form
OLEDrag	Cause the OLE drag-and-drop operation
Refresh	Update and repaint this control
SetFocus	Move the focus to this control
ShowWhatsThis	Display the What's This help topic pop-up provided by the Windows 95 help system
ZOrder	Place this control at the front or back of the z-order

Description

The OptionButton control consists of a small circle accompanied by text. Generally, the text defines the purpose of the button. Clicking a button causes the circle to be filled in with a solid dot. This happens regardless of whether or not the circle had already been filled in.

Option buttons generally work in groups (see Figure 16-28). A group of option buttons is created when two or more option buttons are drawn on the same form, frame, or picture. When this is the case, all the option buttons in the same group become mutually exclusive. That is, when one button is clicked, it gets selected, and all other buttons in the same group become unselected. Option buttons grouped this way are often called radio buttons.

To create a group of option buttons, first draw the frame or picture on which they will be placed. Then draw the buttons on the frame or picture. To have more than one group of option buttons on the same form, create a frame for each group and then place the buttons in the appropriate frame.

The Caption property defines the text that will accompany the button. The size and style of this text is defined by the settings of the font... properties. Including an ampersand (&) underlines the following letter, and the check box may be selected by holding down ALT and pressing that letter. For instance, if a button's Caption property is set to &Cash, the displayed text will be Cash, and the user can select the button by pressing ALT+C. Chapter 54, "Application Focus," covers the Caption property in more detail.

Figure 16-28 Three option buttons grouped together in a frame

The status of an OptionButton control may be set or read by the program's code by using the Value property. This property will be True (-1) if the button is selected and False (0) if not.

When an option button is selected, its Click event triggers. This allows the program to react immediately to the setting of the button.

The Picture and Style properties are used together if you want to use a different type of check box style. Rather than the traditional check box look and feel, you can display the check box more like a toggle button, as illustrated in Figure 16-29.

PICTUREBOX CONTROL

Purpose   The PictureBox control defines an area on a form, frame, or another picture in which graphics may be displayed. The PictureBox control can also be used much like the Frame control to group together controls that are functionally related based on how they are used in a program. New to version 5.0, the PictureBox control can also display JPEG and GIF graphic files. For animated GIF images, like those found on HTML documents on the World Wide Web, you will need to use a third-party control like AccuSoft's ImageGear.

Properties, Events,   Tables 16-83, 16-84, and 16-85 list the properties, events, and methods
and Methods   that relate to the PictureBox control.

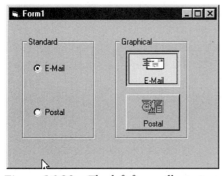

Figure 16-29   The left frame illustrates the traditional option buttons, and the right frame shows option buttons with the Style property set to Graphical

Table 16-83 Properties of the PictureBox control

Use This Property...	To Do This...
Align	Determine where and how the control appears on a form
Appearance	Read or set whether the object is drawn with 3D effects
AutoRedraw	Read or set whether graphic pictures will be redrawn automatically
AutoSize	Read or set whether the size of a picture is controlled by its source file
BackColor, ForeColor	Read or set the background and foreground colors of this control
BorderStyle	Determine whether this control has a border and, if it does, set its style
ClipControls	Determine whether graphic methods repaint the entire control
Container	Set or return a reference to the object that contains this object
CurrentX, CurrentY	Read or set the current graphics position on this control
DataChanged	Determine whether the value displayed in this control has changed
DataField	Read or set the name of the field in the recordset of the data control to which this control is bound
DataSource	Set the name of the data control to which this control is bound
DragIcon	Read or set what displays when this control is dragged
DragMode	Determine whether drag operations are to occur manually or automatically
DrawMode	Read or set the appearance of drawings by graphics methods
DrawStyle	Read or set the style of lines drawn by graphics methods
DrawWidth	Read or set the size of lines drawn by graphics methods
Enabled	Read or set whether this control can react to events
FillColor	Read or set the color used by graphics methods for fill-in effects
FillStyle	Read or set the pattern used by graphics methods for fill-in effects
Font	Set or return a font object that controls the way text displays in this control
FontBold, FontItalic, FontStrikeThru, FontTransparent, FontUnderline	Read or set special effects for this control's font
FontName	Read or set the name of this control's font
FontSize	Read or set the size of this control's font
hDC	Read the Windows device handle for this control
Height	Read or set the height of this control
HelpContextID	Read or set the context number to this control for context-sensitive help
hWnd	Read the handle for this control's window
Image	Read the Windows device handle for a picture's persistent bitmap
Index	Uniquely identify an element of a control array
Left	Read or set the left edge placement of this control relative to its container
LinkItem	Read or set the item in a DDE conversation
LinkMode	Read or set a DDE conversation to hot, cold, or none
LinkTimeout	Read or set the amount of time before a DDE conversation times out
LinkTopic	Read or set the topic of a DDE conversation

Use This Property...	To Do This...
MouseIcon	Set a custom mouse pointer
MousePointer	Read or set the shape of the mouse pointer when it's over this control
Name	Read or set the name used in code to refer to this control
OLEDragMode	Read or set whether the component or the programmer handles an OLE drag/drop operation
OLEDropMode	Read or set how a target component handles drop operations
Parent	Read the name of the form to which this control belongs
Picture	Read or assign a graphic image to a picture or form
ScaleHeight	Read or set the number of units that define the height of this control
ScaleLeft	Read or set the coordinates for the left edge of this control
ScaleMode	Read or set the unit of measurement used to place and size objects
ScaleTop	Read or set the coordinates for the top edge of this control
ScaleWidth	Read or set the number of units that define the width of this control
TabIndex	Read or set the placement of this control within the form's tab order
TabStop	Read or set whether this control is part of the form's tab order
Tag	Read or set any extra string data associated with this control
ToolTipText	Read or set a value that explains an object
Top	Read or set the coordinate of this control's top edge relative to its container
Visible	Read or set whether this control is visible
WhatsThisHelpID	Read or set the context number to this object for context-sensitive help in Windows 95
Width	Read or set the width of this control

Table 16-84 Events of the PictureBox control

Use This Event...	To Do This...
Change	React to a change in the image pointed to by the Picture property.
Click	React to the user's clicking this control.
DblClick	React to the user's double-clicking this control.
DragDrop	React to the user's dragging and dropping an object onto this control.
DragOver	React to the user's dragging another object over this control.
GotFocus	Initiate an action when this control receives the focus.
KeyDown	Initiate an action when the user presses or holds a key down.
KeyPress	React to the user's typing an ASCII character.
KeyUp	Initiate an action when the user releases a key.
LinkClose	React to the termination of a DDE conversation.
LinkError	React to an error in a DDE conversation.
LinkNotify	React to a change in the DDE source data.
LinkOpen	React to the initiation of a DDE conversation.

continued on next page

continued from previous page

Use This Event...	To Do This...
LostFocus	Initiate an action when this control loses the focus.
MouseDown	React to the user's pressing any mouse button.
MouseMove	React to the user's moving the mouse over this control.
MouseUp	React to the user's releasing any mouse button.
OLECompleteDrag	A target component reacts to a source component being dropped on it. It is informing the source component that a drag action was either canceled or performed.
OLEDragDown	A target component reacts to a source component being dropped on it.
OLEDragOver	React to one component being dragged over another.
OLEGiveFeedback	Trigger the source component to provide visual feedback to the user.
OLESetData	A source component will react when a target component performs a GetData method, but the data for the specified format has not yet been loaded.
OLEStartDrag	React to a component's OLEDrag method, or when a component initiates an OLE drag-and-drop operation when the OLEDragMode property is set to Automatic.
Paint	Initiate an action when the control needs to be redrawn.
Resize	Initiate an action when the control is first displayed or its size is changed.

Table 16-85 Methods of the PictureBox control

Use This Method...	To Do This...
Circle	Create a circle or ellipse on a form or picture box
Cls	Clear graphics and text that have been created at runtime
Drag	Control manual dragging of this control
Line	Draw a line on a form or picture
LinkExecute	Send a DDE Execute command to a DDE server application
LinkPoke	Send data from a DDE client to a DDE server
LinkRequest	Ask for data from a DDE server
LinkSend	Send graphic data to a DDE client
Move	Change the position of this control or form
OLEDrag	Cause the OLE drag-and-drop operation
PaintPicture	Transfer an image from this object to another
Point	Return the color setting of a specified point on a form or picture box
Print	Print text on a form or picture box
PSet	Set the color of a specified point on a form or picture box
Refresh	Update and repaint this control
Scale	Define the coordinate system used with the picture box control
ScaleX	Convert a value for the width from one scale mode to another
ScaleY	Convert a value for the height from one scale mode to another

Use This Method...	To Do This...
SetFocus	Move the focus to this control
ShowWhatsThis	Display the What's This help topic pop-up provided by the Windows 95 help system
TextHeight	Return the height of text in this control's font
TextWidth	Return the width of text in this control's font
ZOrder	Place this control at the front or back of the z-order

Description

The PictureBox control is used for two different purposes. Primarily, it displays a graphic image on a form (see Figure 16-30). However, you can also place controls on a PictureBox control in the same manner as placing them on a form or frame. This gives you an alternative to the Frame control for grouping together other controls. This is particularly useful when you need to place controls on the client area of an MDI form, because the PictureBox control is the only standard control that may be placed there.

The Picture property defines the graphic image to be displayed by this control. The PictureBox control can display icons, Windows bitmaps, and Windows metafiles.

The size of the PictureBox control defines how much of a graphic image displays. If a graphic image is too large to be displayed within the boundaries of a PictureBox control, you can use two PictureBox controls, placing one on top of the other, to simulate scrolling of the image. This technique is demonstrated in Chapter 43, "Scrollbars."

If other controls are drawn on a PictureBox control, they work in the same manner as if they'd been drawn on a Frame control. Because the border can be turned off by using the PictureBox control's BorderStyle property, this provides a technique for grouping several controls together without displaying a frame around them.

Figure 16-30 The PictureBox displays graphics

Refer to Chapter 39, "Pictures," for more information on this control and its related properties, events, and methods.

PICTURE OBJECT

Purpose	The Picture object allows you to manipulate metafiles and bitmaps without having to use a PictureBox control or form object.
Properties and Method	Tables 16-86 and 16-87 list the properties and method of the Picture object.

Table 16-86 Properties of the Picture object

Use This Property...	To Do This...
Handle	Read the handle to the graphic contained in the object
Height	Read or set the height of this object
hPal	Read the handle to the palette of the object
Type	Read the type of graphic contained in the object
Width	Read or set the width of this object

Table 16-87 Method of the Picture object

Use This Method......	To Do This...
Render	Draw all or part of the source image to the object

Description	The Picture object provides a convenient means of manipulating a graphics metafile or bitmap without having to use a PictureBox control or form object. It also offers several properties that make it very convenient to work with the Windows API or other DLLs.

The Handle property returns the handle of the graphic; this is frequently needed in calls to the Graphics Device Interface (GDI) of Windows. The hPal property returns the handle to the palette of the graphic. You'll need this less frequently, but if you do, using the hPal property is much easier than the techniques required in previous versions of Visual Basic. The Type property returns the type of graphic contained in the Picture object: bitmap, metafile, or icon.

Note that you can manipulate a Picture object much like any other object. This implies that you can use the Set statement to set one object's Picture property (say, a PictureBox control's Picture property) to reference the picture object. This also implies that you can create an array of Picture objects to store many icons, bitmaps, or metafiles in memory. This is far more efficient than creating a control array of PictureBox controls, and is much easier to work with and more adaptable than using the PicClip control of the Professional and Enterprise Editions.

The Picture object shares the same peculiarity as the Font object: You can declare a variable of type Picture, but to instantiate a new picture object, you must use the class name StdPicture:

```
Dim normalDragIcon As New StdPicture

Set normalDragIcon = LoadPicture("MYICON.ICO")

Dim c As Object
For Each c In Form.Controls
    Set c.DragIcon = normalDragIcon
Next c
```

PRINTER OBJECT

Purpose   The Printer object generates printed output by assembling pages to be sent to the printer.

Properties and Methods   Tables 16-88 and 16-89 list the properties and methods that relate to the Printer object. This object has no associated events.

Table 16-88 Properties of the Printer object

Use This Property...	To Do This...
ColorMode	Read or set whether the printer prints in color or monochrome
Copies	Read or set how many copies are to be printed
CurrentX, CurrentY	Read or set the current graphics position on this object
DeviceName	Read the name of the device a driver supports
DrawMode	Read or set the appearance of graphics methods
DrawStyle	Read or set the style of lines drawn by graphics methods
DrawWidth	Read or set the size of lines drawn by graphics methods
DriverName	Read the name of the driver for the Printer object
Duplex	Read or set whether a page is printed on both sides
FillColor	Read or set the color used by graphics methods for fill-in effects
FillStyle	Read or set the pattern used by graphics methods for fill-in effects
Font	Set or return a font object that controls the way text displays in this object
FontBold, FontItalic, FontStrikeThru, FontTransparent, FontUnderline	Read or set special effects for this object's font

continued on next page

continued from previous page

Use This Property...	To Do This...
FontCount	Read the number of fonts available to the system
FontName	Read or set the name of this object's font
Fonts	Read the names of the fonts available to the system
FontSize	Read or set the size of this object's font
hDC	Read the Windows device handle for this object
Height	Read or set the height of this object
Orientation	Read or set whether document prints in landscape or portrait mode
Page	Read the current output page of the Printer object
PaperBin	Read or set the default paper bin
PaperSize	Read or set the paper size
Port	Read the name of the printer port
PrintQuality	Read or set the printer resolution
ScaleHeight	Read or set the number of units that define the height of this object
ScaleLeft	Read or set the coordinates for the left edge of this object
ScaleMode	Read or set the unit of measurement used to place and size objects
ScaleTop	Read or set the coordinates for the top edge of this object
ScaleWidth	Read or set the number of units that define the width of this object
TrackDefault	Read or set whether the Printer object changes to track the default printer set in the Control Panel
TwipsPerPixelX, TwipsPerPixelY	Read the number of twips per pixel
Width	Read or set the width of this object
Zoom	Read or set the percentage to scale output

Table 16-89 Methods of the Printer object

Use This Method...	To Do This...
Circle	Create a circle or ellipse on the page
EndDoc	End output to the Printer object, and send data to the printer
KillDoc	Immediately terminate the print job
Line	Draw a line on the page
NewPage	End output to the current printer page and begin a new one
PaintPicture	Draw a graphic image on the page
Print	Print text on the page
PSet	Set the color of a specified point on the page
Scale	Define the coordinate system used with the PictureBox control
ScaleX	Convert a value for the width from one scale mode to another

Use This Method...	To Do This...
ScaleY	Convert a value for the height from one scale mode to another
TextHeight	Return the height of text in this object's font
TextWidth	Return the width of text in this object's font

Description

Many programs need to create some sort of printed output. Because the Windows environment handles all printer output, Visual Basic includes the predefined Printer object. This object sends printer output commands from your programs to the Windows routines that in turn send the output to the printer.

Many other languages treat the printer as a sequential output device. Once an item is written to the printer, the print position advances and there can be no going back. With Visual Basic, however, this is not true.

You can think of the Printer object as a form that cannot be viewed until the Visual Basic program tells Windows to print it. This "form" represents one page of printed output. In most cases, until your program instructs Windows to print it, anything can be done to a page of printer output. This is very advantageous, because it allows the program to move the print position anywhere on a page regardless of where it currently resides. This makes printing graphics and special effects very easy.

The program works one page at a time when creating a printed document. All the output for a specific page is first set up by using many of the same methods that work on a form. These include the Circle, Line, Print, PSet, TextHeight, and TextWidth methods. The program determines where these methods write to a page by specifying coordinates on the page as arguments to the method or by setting the page's CurrentX and CurrentY properties. Each of the properties works in the same manner as when it's used on a form, except that printers incapable of printing in color ignore the color argument.

When the program has finished creating the current page, it can use the NewPage method. This ends the current page, saves it in memory, and clears the Printer object's work area for the next page.

As each page is generated, Visual Basic keeps track of the current page number with the Page property, which is specific to the Printer object. This property can never be set (either at design time or runtime), but it can be read and thereby printed on each page.

The EndDoc method sends all the printer output to the Windows printing routines when all printing is finished. Windows then takes care of the chores associated with sending the output to the printer.

Refer to Chapter 52 for more information on this object and its uses.

PRINTERS COLLECTION

Purpose   The Printers collection lets you access any of the installed printers on the user's computer. You can use the Set statement to set the Printer object equal to a member of the Printers collection, so that all future printer method and property settings go to that printer.

Property   Table 16-90 lists the property of the Printers collection.

Table 16-90 Property of the Printers collection

Use This Property...	To Do This...
Count	Read the number of items in the collection

Description   Use the Printers collection to determine what printers are attached to the user's computer, and what capabilities these printers have. Use the Set statement to set the Printer object equal to a member of the Printers collection; this lets you use that printer as the output device for your program. Note that all properties of printers in the Printers collection are read-only; you must set the Printer object to the member before you can set the printer's properties or use its methods.

SCREEN OBJECT

Purpose   The Screen object has four basic purposes. First, it defines the physical height and width of the display. Next, it provides access to screen fonts that are available to the system. Third, it references the currently active form or control. Finally, it sets or reads the current shape of the mouse cursor.

Properties Table 16-91 lists the properties that relate to the Screen object. This object has no associated events or methods.

Table 16-91 Properties of the Screen object

Use This Property...	To Do This...
ActiveControl	Reference the current control with the focus
ActiveForm	Reference the current form with the focus
FontCount	Read the number of fonts available to the system for screen display
Fonts	Read the names of the fonts available to the system for screen display
Height	Read the height of the screen
MouseIcon	Set a custom mouse pointer
MousePointer	Read or set the shape of the mouse pointer for all objects

Use This Property...	To Do This...
TwipsPerPixelX,	
TwipsPerPixelY	Read the number of twips per pixel
Width	Read the width of the screen

Description

The Height and Width properties of the Screen object define the dimensions of the screen in twips. A twip is defined as 1/20 of a point, which equates to 1440 twips per printed inch. This gives the Visual Basic program a method for displaying forms and controls in the proper absolute proportions, regardless of the type of display being used. These properties are discussed in Chapter 33, "Application Appearance."

The FontCount and Fonts properties are used to determine the number and types of fonts available for display on a form or control on the screen. The use of fonts is covered in Chapter 45, "Fonts."

When used with its ActiveControl and ActiveForm properties, the Screen object will reference the control or form that currently has the focus. For more information on referencing forms and controls, see Chapter 35.

Setting the Screen object's MousePointer property overrides the MousePointer property setting for all forms and controls in the program. Setting this property to 0 for the Screen object returns control of this property setting to the individual forms and controls. More discussion on the MousePointer property can be found in Chapter 33.

Scroll Bars Control (VScrollBar and HScrollBar)

Purpose

Scrollbar controls give the user the ability to position text or graphics or set a value by manipulating a visual object. Scrollbars are most commonly used to control the up and down and left to right movement of a graphic viewport or list.

Properties, Events, and Methods

Tables 16-92, 16-93, and 16-94 list the properties, events, and methods that relate to this object.

Table 16-92 Properties of the Scroll Bars control

Use This Property...	To Do This...
Container	Set or return a reference to the object that contains this object
DragIcon	Read or set what displays when this control is dragged
DragMode	Determine whether drag operations are to occur manually or automatically
Enabled	Read or set whether this control can react to events
Height	Read or set the height of this control

continued on next page

continued from previous page

Use This Property...	To Do This...
HelpContextID	Read or set the context number to this control for context-sensitive help
hWnd	Read the handle for this control's window
Index	Uniquely identify an element of a control array
LargeChange	Read or set the amount of change when a user clicks the bar
Left	Read or set the left edge placement of this control relative to its container
Max	Read or set the maximum value possible in a scrollbar
Min	Read or set the minimum value possible in a scrollbar
MouseIcon	Set a custom mouse pointer
MousePointer	Read or set the shape of the mouse pointer when it's over this control
Name	Read or set the name used in code to refer to this control
Parent	Read the name of the form to which this control belongs
SmallChange	Read or set the amount of change when a user clicks an arrow
TabIndex	Read or set the placement of this control within the form's tab order
TabStop	Read or set whether this control is part of the form's tab order
Tag	Read or set any extra string data associated with this control
Top	Read or set the coordinate of this control's top edge relative to its container
Value	Read or set the current value of this control
Visible	Read or set whether this control is visible
WhatsThisHelpID	Read or set the context number to this object for context-sensitive help in Windows 95
Width	Read or set the width of this control

Table 16-93 Events of the Scroll Bars control

Use This eVent...	To Do This...
Change	React to a change in the control's Value property
DragDrop	React to the user's dragging and dropping an object onto this control
DragOver	React to the user's dragging another object over this control
GotFocus	Initiate an action when this control receives the focus
KeyDown	Initiate an action when the user presses or holds a key down
KeyPress	React to the user's typing an ASCII character
KeyUp	Initiate an action when the user releases a key
LostFocus	Initiate an action when this control loses the focus
Scroll	Continuously react to a change in the control's Value property

Table 16-94 Methods of the Scroll Bars control

Use This Method...	To Do This...
Drag	Control manual dragging of this control
Move	Change the position of this control or form
Refresh	Update and repaint this control
SetFocus	Move the focus to this control
ShowWhatsThis	Display the What's This help topic pop-up provided by Windows 95 help system
ZOrder	Place this control at the front or back of the z-order

Description

Scrollbars are primarily used to control scrolling of a form, picture, or a list of items. They can also be used as a graphic technique for setting a particular value. For instance, in the Mouse settings of the Windows Control Panel, the user can set the speed of the mouse by manipulating a horizontal scrollbar.

Scrollbars are graphic objects that consist of a bar with arrows at each end and a button (called a thumb) between the arrows (see Figure 16-31). There are two types of scrollbars: vertical and horizontal.

The thumb's position within the scrollbar directly relates to the value represented by the scrollbar. For horizontal scrollbars, the thumb is in the leftmost position when the value of the scrollbar is at its minimum setting, and at the rightmost position when the value is at its maximum. A minimum value on a vertical scrollbar places the thumb at the top, while the maximum value places the thumb at the bottom. Any value in between places the thumb on the bar in a position proportional to the value represented by the bar.

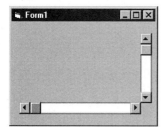

Figure 16-31 Vertical and horizontal scrollbars

The value represented by the scrollbar can be changed in four ways. First, the user can click either arrow. This causes the value represented by the scrollbar to be incremented or decremented by a small amount in the direction of the selected arrow. Second, the user may click the scrollbar on one side of the thumb or the other. This causes the scrollbar's value to be affected similarly to the way it is affected by clicking an arrow, but the amount of change is greater. The user can also click and drag the thumb to a specific position on the bar. This causes the value of the scrollbar to be set according to the position of the thumb. Finally, the value of a scrollbar can be set in the program's code.

The events, methods, and properties that relate to scrollbars are discussed in Chapter 43.

SHAPE CONTROL

Purpose   Use the Shape control to display a graphical control directly on a form.

Properties and Methods   Tables 16-95 and 16-96 list the properties and methods that relate to the Shape control.

Table 16-95 Properties of the Shape control

Use This Property...	To Do This...
BackColor	Read or set the color of this control
BackStyle	Read or set whether text on this control is opaque or transparent
BorderColor	Read or set the color of the line that surrounds this control
BorderStyle	Read or set the style of the line (for example, solid, dotted, dashed)
BorderWidth	Read or set the width of the line
Container	Set or return a reference to the object that contains this object
DrawMode	Read or set the appearance of drawings by graphics methods
FillColor	Read or set the color used by graphics methods for fill-in effects
FillStyle	Read or set the pattern used by graphics methods for fill-in effects
Height	Read or set the height of this control
Index	Uniquely identify an element of a control array
Left	Read or set the left edge placement of this control relative to its container
Name	Read or set the name used in code to refer to this control
Parent	Read the name of the form to which this control belongs
Shape	Read or set the type of shape
Tag	Read or set any extra string data associated with this control
Top	Read or set the coordinate of this control's top edge relative to its container
Visible	Read or set whether this control is visible
Width	Read or set the width of this control

Table 16-96 Methods of the Shape control

Use This Method...	To Do This...
Move	Change the position of this control or form
Refresh	Update and repaint this control
ZOrder	Place this control at the front or back of the z-order

Description The Shape control draws a shape (such as a circle or rectangle) directly on your form during the design phase. This is especially helpful for designing your forms, because you can see the effects immediately. Graphics methods like PSet or Line, in contrast, do not display until runtime and can be difficult to design with. See Chapter 38, "Graphics Fundamentals," for more details.

TextBox Control

Purpose The TextBox control is used for displaying and editing text.

Properties, Events, and Methods Tables 16-97, 16-98, and 16-99 list the properties, events, and methods that relate to the TextBox control.

Table 16-97 Properties of the TextBox control

Use This Property...	To Do This...
Alignment	Read or set the alignment of this control
Appearance	Read or set whether the object is drawn with 3D effects
BackColor, ForeColor	Read or set the background and foreground colors of this control
BorderStyle	Determine whether this control has a border, and if it does, set its style
Container	Set or return a reference to the object that contains this object
DataChanged	Determine whether the value displayed in this control has changed
DataField	Read or set the name of the field in the recordset of the data control to which this control is bound
DataSource	Set the name of the data control to which this control is bound
DragIcon	Read or set what displays when this control is dragged
DragMode	Determine whether drag operations are to occur manually or automatically
Enabled	Read or set whether this control can react to events
Font	Set or return a font object that controls the way text displays in this control
FontBold, FontItalic, FontStrikeThru, FontUnderline	Read or set special effects for this control's font
FontName	Read or set the name of this control's font
FontSize	Read or set the size of this control's font

continued on next page

continued from previous page

Use This Property...	To Do This...
Height	Read or set the height of this control
HelpContextID	Read or set the context number to this control for context-sensitive help
HideSelection	Determine whether selected text is highlighted when the control loses focus
hWnd	Read the handle for this control's window
Index	Uniquely identify an element of a control array
Left	Read or set the left edge placement of this control relative to its container
LinkItem	Read or set the item in a DDE conversation
LinkMode	Read or set a DDE conversation to hot, cold, or none
LinkTimeout	Read or set the amount of time before a DDE conversation times out
LinkTopic	Read or set the topic of a DDE conversation
Locked	Read or set whether user can edit text
MaxLength	Read or set the maximum length of text allowed
MouseIcon	Set a custom mouse pointer
MousePointer	Read or set the shape of the mouse pointer when it's over this control
Multiline	Read or set whether a text box can edit multiple lines or the text stays on one line
Name	Read or set the name used in code to refer to this control
OLEDragMode	Read or set whether the component or the programmer handles an OLE drag/drop operation
OLEDropMode	Read or set how a target component handles drop operations
Parent	Read the name of the form to which this control belongs
PasswordChar	Determine how typed characters appear (used for password entry)
ScrollBars	Determine whether scrollbars appear in a multiple-line text box
SelLength, SelStart	Read or set the starting point or length of selected text
SelText	Read or set the string containing the currently selected text
TabIndex	Read or set the placement of this control within the form's tab order
TabStop	Read or set whether this control is part of the form's tab order
Tag	Read or set any extra string data associated with this control
Text	Read or set the text contained in a text box
ToolTipText	Read or set a value that explains an object
Top	Read or set the coordinate of this control's top edge relative to its container
Visible	Read or set whether this control is visible
WhatsThisHelpID	Read or set the context number to this object for context-sensitive help in Windows 95
Width	Read or set the width of this control

Table 16-98 Events of the TextBox control

Use This Event...	To Do This...
Change	React to a change in the text box control's Text property.
Click	React to the user's clicking this control.

Use This Event...	To Do This...
DblClick	React to the user's double-clicking this control.
DragDrop	React to the user's dragging and dropping an object onto this control.
DragOver	React to the user's dragging another object over this control.
GotFocus	Initiate an action when this control receives the focus.
KeyDown	Initiate an action when the user presses or holds a key down.
KeyPress	React to the user's typing an ASCII character.
KeyUp	Initiate an action when the user releases a key.
LinkClose	React to the termination of a DDE conversation.
LinkError	React to an error in a DDE conversation.
LinkNotify	React to a change in the DDE source data.
LinkOpen	React to the initiation of a DDE conversation.
LostFocus	Initiate an action when this control loses the focus.
MouseDown	React to the user's pressing any mouse button.
MouseMove	React to the user's moving the mouse over this control.
MouseUp	React to the user's releasing any mouse button.
OLECompleteDrag	A target component reacts to a source component being dropped on it. It is informing the source component that a drag action was either canceled or performed.
OLEDragDown	A target component reacts to a source component being dropped on it.
OLEDragOver	React to one component being dragged over another.
OLEGiveFeedback	Trigger the source component to provide visual feedback to the user.
OLESetData	A source component will react when a target component performs a GetData method, but the data for the specified format has not yet been loaded.
OLEStartDrag	React to a component's OLEDrag method, or when a component initiates an OLE drag-and-drop operation when the OLEDragMode property is set to Automatic.

Table 16-99 Methods of the TextBox control

Use This Method...	To Do This...
Drag	Control manual dragging of this control
LinkExecute	Send a DDE Execute command to a DDE server application
LinkPoke	Send data from a DDE client to a DDE server
LinkRequest	Ask for data from a DDE server
LinkSend	Send data to a DDE client
Move	Change the position of this control or form
OLEDrag	Cause the OLE drag-and-drop operation
Refresh	Update and repaint this control
SetFocus	Move the focus to this control
ShowWhatsThis	Display the What's This help topic pop-up provided by the Windows 95 help system
ZOrder	Place this control at the front or back of the z-order

Description   The TextBox control is a rectangle in which the user may enter or edit text. When a TextBox control receives the focus, an insertion point appears in the box. The insertion point is a slim, flashing vertical line that indicates where any new text will be entered within the box. This line can be moved by using the direction keys or by clicking the desired position in the text box with the mouse. A Visual Basic text box automatically inherits all the conventions of a standard Windows text box, including the ability to cut, copy, and paste to and from the Windows Clipboard area.

The Text property sets or reads the text that is currently in a text box. The style and size of the text are determined by the control's font properties.

By default, a text box consists of only one line of text. Setting the MultiLine property to True (-1) will allow the user to enter more than one line of text (see Figure 16-32). If you set the MultiLine property to True, you may want to also set the ScrollBars property to True. This causes either a horizontal scrollbar, vertical scrollbar, or both scrollbars to automatically appear at the right of the text box if the entered text exceeds the screen area defined for the box. See Chapter 32, "Getting User Input," for more information on these properties.

When a TextBox control has the focus, each keystroke can be intercepted by the program with the KeyDown, KeyPress, and KeyUp events. This allows a program to create validity checking on edit fields. For instance, if you want to limit the number of characters entered in a text box, you could use the KeyPress event to determine the current length of the text in a text box before allowing the next keystroke to be added to the text. More information on these events can be found in Chapter 51, "Keyboard Input."

A TextBox control can be used as a client in a dynamic data exchange.

TIMER CONTROL

Purpose   The Timer control runs code at regular intervals.

Properties and Event   Tables 16-100 and 16-101 list the properties and event that relate to the Timer control. This control has no associated methods.

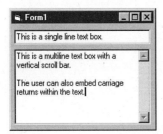

Figure 16-32   Single- and multiple-line text boxes

Table 16-100 Properties of the Timer control

Use This Property...	To Do This...
Enabled	Read or set whether this control can react to events
Index	Uniquely identify an element of a control array
Interval	Read or set the length of time between each call to a Timer event
Left	Read or set the left edge placement of this control relative to its container
Name	Read or set the name used in code to refer to this control
Parent	Read the name of this control's parent form
Tag	Read or set any extra string data associated with this control
Top	Read or set the coordinate of this control's top edge relative to its container

Table 16-101 Event of the Timer control

Use This Event...	To Do This...
Timer	Initiate an action at a regular timed interval

Description

The Timer control is invisible on a form and cannot be manipulated directly by the user (see Figure 16-33). The main purpose for a timer is to define an activity that is to take place at a regular interval. This is useful for writing routines that are to run in the background of an application with no need for user interaction.

The activity to be performed by the timer is defined by placing code in the control's timer event. The timer control's Interval property specifies how often this event is to be executed. This control, its properties, and event are covered in Chapter 23, "Time."

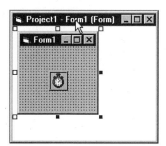

Figure 16-33 The Timer control at design time; it is invisible at runtime

VBE Object (VBA Add-In Object Model)

Purpose　　　　The VBE object gives you access to the Visual Basic IDE (Integrated Development Environment), which lets you write "add-in" programs that alter the design environment or provide additional functionality. This object is available only in the Professional and Enterprise Editions of Visual Basic.

Properties and　Tables 16-102 and 16-103 list the properties and method of the VBE
Method　　　　object.

Table 16-102 Properties of the VBE object

Use This Property...	To Do This...
ActiveCodePane	Return or set a reference to the currently active CodePane object
ActiveVBProject	Return a reference to the currently active project
ActiveWindow	Return a reference to an active window in the development environment
AddIns	Return a reference to the add-ins that can be registered
DisplayModel	Return or set the display model of SDI or MDI
Events	Set references that enable add-ins to be connected to all events within Visual Basic for Applications
FullName	Return full path of where Visual Basic is executed from
LastUsedPath	Read a string indicating the full path used in the last File dialog box
MainWindow	Return the main window of the Visual Basic IDE
Name	Return "Microsoft Visual Basic"
Parent	Return a reference to the Application object
ReadOnlyMode	Return or set how the Visual Basic IDE works with read-only files
SelectedVBComponent	Return selected components from the Project window
TemplatePath	Return the full path name where Visual Basic template files are stored
VBProjects	Return VBProjects collection of all the projects currently open with the Visual Basic IDE
Version	Return the version number of the Visual Basic design environment to which the add-in is connected
Windows	Return a window in the Visual Basic IDE

Table 16-103 Method of the VBE object

Use This Method...	To Do This...
Quit	Attempt to exit Visual Basic

Description　　The VBE object provides you with access to the Visual Basic design environment. You can alter the way you work with Visual Basic by creating add-in modules that use the objects contained within the Application object's collections. Visual Basic Learning Edition can use add-ins, but only the Professional and Enterprise Editions can create them.

The basic idea of add-ins is simple: You write programs that manipulate the actual design environment, using the VBE object to "hook" into the environment. The objects in the VBE object let you determine what form, control, or group of controls are selected, and alter their properties. They also let you react to the user's saving files, alter the design environment's menus, and manage the connection and disconnection of add-ins.

This allows you to write nifty time-saving utilities. You can write add-ins to align controls automatically, renumber the tab order, globally change the name of all selected controls and put them in a control array, create new controls based on an existing "template," manage automatic file back-ups, or interface to version control software, among other things.

The VBE object exposes several key objects that allow you to manipulate the environment. The ActiveVBProject property gives you access to the project itself, in turn giving you access to the forms and controls within the project. The AddIns property gives you access to the Add-In menu bar in the design environment, letting you add menu selections to your add-in.

The LastUsedPath property returns a string that gives the full path used in the last used File dialog box. The Version property returns the version of Visual Basic to which the add-in is connected. The Name property of the VBE object always returns "Microsoft Visual Basic," and the Parent property always returns references to the VBE object itself.

PART II
FUNCTIONS AND STATEMENTS

17

STRING FORMATTING

One of Visual Basic's strongest assets is its string-formatting capabilities. Visual Basic has inherited from previous BASIC languages a rich and powerful array of functions and statements designed to make even the most complicated string operations a snap to perform.

Previous versions of Visual Basic had pairs of functionally similar string handling functions, such as Chr and Chr$. Functions qualified with $ return strings, while functions without $ return variants. In Visual Basic 5.0, string functions qualified with $ are supported for backward compatibility, but their use is no longer recommended.

Starting with the 32-bit version of VB4, Visual Basic treats all strings internally as Unicode. Unicode is a standard means of translating disparate alphabets into one coding style all computers can handle, much like ASCII coding style handles the English alphabet. In Unicode characters are 2 bytes wide, so an ASCII "A" is translated as 0,65, expressed in decimal numbers. The first 127 characters in the Unicode standard are the first 127 characters of the 7-bit ASCII character set with a leading zero added. (In hexadecimal, the ASCII "A" is expressed in Unicode as 0041.) In addition to Unicode, the Asian versions of Windows support the various alphabets using the Double Byte Character Set (DBCS). Both Unicode and DBCS use 2 bytes to represent one character. This can affect your string handling, and Microsoft has provided variations of some of the string handling functions for use with DBCS and Unicode. These functions have a suffix of W or B. The W-suffixed function returns the 2-byte character, and the B-suffixed function returns a single byte, regardless of the actual width of the character.

String Formatting Summary

Table 17-1 lists the string formatting commands available in Visual Basic 5.0. Detailed descriptions follow the table, and at the end of the chapter, a sample project demonstrates their use.

Table 17-1 Functions and statements that format

Use This...	Type	To Do This...
Format	Function	Translate a date variant or a number into formatted string
LCase	Function	Translate all uppercase characters in a string to lowercase
LSet	Function	Left-justify a value in a string or a programmer-defined type
LTrim	Function	Truncate any leading spaces from a string
Mid	Statement	Replace characters at a specific location in a string
MidB	Statement	Assign a byte value to a portion of a byte array or string
RSet	Function	Right-justify a value in a string or a programmer-defined type
RTrim	Function	Truncate any following spaces from a string
Str	Function	Translate a numeric value into an unformatted string
StrConv	Function	Convert a string expression to another style
String	Function	Return a string of characters repeated a specified number of times
Trim	Function	Truncate any leading or trailing spaces from a string
UCase	Function	Translate all lowercase characters of a string into uppercase

FORMAT FUNCTION

Purpose   The Format function takes a string, number, or date variant and returns a formatted number, date, or time. Dates and times are covered in depth in Chapters 22, "Date," and 23, "Time." The Format function is aware of the locale of the Windows installation and uses the appropriate separator, decimal, and currency signs.

Table 17-2 lists the arguments of the Format function, and Table 17-3 lists the different types of formats available for the format parameter.

General Syntax   `Format(expression, "format1; format2", firstdayofweek, firstweekwfyear)`

Table 17-2 Arguments of the Format function

Argument	Description
expression	Data to format.
format1,2, ... (optional)	How to format the Expression.
	Multiple formats are separated by semicolons.
firstdayofweek (optional)	Optional parameter used when formatting dates.
firstweekofyear (optional)	Optional parameter used when formatting dates.

Table 17-3 Formats available

Argument	Description
(0)	Displays a zero or a number.
(#)	Displays a number or nothing.
(.)	Decimal point. Actual decimal point is based on regional settings.
(%)	Percentage. Number is multiplied by 100 and percent sign is shown based on position of % in format.
(,)	Thousands separator. Actual separator depends on regional settings.
(:)	Time separator. Actual separator depends on regional settings.
(/)	Date separator. Actual separator depends on regional settings.
@	Character placeholder. Displays a character or a space.
&	Character placeholder.
	Displays a character or nothing.
<	Force lowercase.
>	Force uppercase.
!	Force left to right fill of placeholders.
(E- E+ e- e+)	Scientific notation.
- + $ ( )	Displays character entered.
(\)	Displays next character, regardless of meaning within the format string.
"General Number"	No thousands separator.
"Currency"	Use thousands separator and display two places to the right of the decimal place.
"Fixed"	Display at least one number to the left of the decimal place and two to the right.
"Standard"	Use thousands separator, one place to the left of the decimal place and two to the right.
"Percent"	Multiplies number by 100 with two places to the right of the decimal place.
"Scientific"	Standard scientific notation.
"Yes/No"	Displays Yes unless the number is 0; then it displays No.
"True/False"	Displays False unless the number is 0; then it displays True.
"On/Off"	Displays On unless the number is 0; then it displays Off.

Example Syntax   The project at the end of the chapter uses the Format function to display numbers in several different formats, as shown below.

```
SFormat = "Currency"

Picture1.Print SFormat & ": "; Tab(30); Format(Val(Text1), SFormat)
SFormat = "######.00"
Picture1.Print SFormat & ": "; Tab(30); Format(Val(Text1), SFormat)
SFormat = "000000.##"
Picture1.Print SFormat & ": "; Tab(30); Format(Val(Text1), SFormat)
SFormat = "Standard"
Picture1.Print SFormat & ": "; Tab(30); Format(Val(Text1), SFormat)
SFormat = "General Number"
Picture1.Print SFormat & ": "; Tab(30); Format(Val(Text1), SFormat)
SFormat = "Fixed"
```

continued on next page

continued from previous page

```
Picture1.Print SFormat & ": "; Tab(30); Format(Val(Text1), SFormat)
SFormat = "Percent"
Picture1.Print SFormat & ": "; Tab(30); Format(Val(Text1), SFormat)
SFormat = "Scientific"
Picture1.Print SFormat & ": "; Tab(30); Format(Val(Text1), SFormat)
```

Description   The Format function has a number of ways to format many different types of things. The format parameter can have more than one part depending on the type of the item to be formatted. For numbers, you can have up to four parts. Part 1 is for positive numbers, part 2 is for negative numbers, part 3 is for 0, and part 4 is for Null. For strings you can have two parts. The first part is for strings with one or more characters and the second part is for zero-length strings ("") or Null.

Comment   If you use user-defined format strings for dates, times, and currencies, your string formatting will not follow the regional settings of the user's computer. This can become a serious issue if your code will be used internationally.

LCASE FUNCTION

Purpose   LCase translates a string of upper- or mixed case into all lowercase. Table 17-4 lists the argument for LCase.

General Syntax   `LCase(string)`

Table 17-4 Argument of the LCase function

Argument	Description
string	The string data to be formatted

Example Syntax   `rs!Description = LCase(txtDescription.Text)`

Description   LCase forces all letters to be lowercase. It is ideal for situations in which you need to be sure a string is all lowercase, such as dealing with data from a form.

LSET FUNCTION

Purpose   LSet moves data from one string or user-defined type (UDT) to another. When LSet is used to move data from one variable to another, the data in the from variable is placed left-justified in the to variable.

General Syntax   `LSet s1 = s2`

Example Syntax   Here is an example of using LSet to move data from one UDT to another.

```
Private Type OneType
    a As String * 10
    b As Integer
    c As Long
End Type

Private Type TwoType
    a As String * 10
    b As Integer
    c As Long

End Type
Private Sub cmndLset_Click()
    Dim ot As OneType
    Dim tt As TwoType

    ot.a = "Hi"
    ot.b = 2
    ot.c = 3

    LSet tt = ot

    Debug.Print tt.a, tt.b, tt.c
End Sub
```

In this example the Debug.Print returns "Hi" 2 3, which is the correct result.

The project at the end of this chapter offers another example.

```
If Len(Text1) < 20 Then
    LSet sLeft = Text1
    Picture1.Print "LSet:"; Tab(30); sLeft
    RSet sRight = Text1
    Picture1.Print "RSet:"; Tab(30); sRight
End If
```

This code shows the difference between LSet and RSet strings.

Description   LSet copies and left-justifies data from a string or UDT into a second string or UDT.

Comment   With care you can use LSet to move data from one user-defined type to another. A serious opportunity for problems is the way Visual Basic aligns the data within the type. The various fields in the UDT are aligned for efficient C usage, which means that great care must be used when using LSet to move data between disparate UDTs.

One proviso to using LSet with user-defined types is that the UDTs can only contain fixed-length strings, not the normal variable-length string.

LTRIM FUNCTION

Purpose   LTrim removes leading spaces from a string or byte array. See Table 17-5 for a description of the single argument of the LTrim function.

General Syntax   LTrim(string)

Table 17-5 Argument of the LTrim function

Argument	Description
string	The string being trimmed

Example Syntax
```
ds!Name = LTrim(txtName.text)
```
Description   LTrim removes all leading spaces from a string or byte array. LTrim is usu-
                     ally used with data entered on a form to make sure no extraneous spaces
                     are stored with the data.

MID, MIDB STATEMENTS

Purpose   The Mid statement allows you to replace the characters at an arbitrary
                     location in a string. Table 17-6 explains the arguments of the Mid and
                     MidB statements.

General Syntax
```
Mid(string1,startpos,length) = string2
MidB(string1,start,length) = string2
```

Table 17-6 Arguments of the Mid, MidB statements

Argument	Description
string1	String to be modified.
string2	String to insert into string1.
startpos	A long that indicates where to insert string2 into string1.
length	The amount of string2 to insert into string1. If string2 is shorter than length, then only len(string2) of string1 is replaced starting at startpos.

Example Syntax   The example syntax below is a function that replaces tabs in a string with
                    single spaces.
```
Private Function Stripped(sInput As String) As String
    Dim j As Integer
    For j = 1 To Len(sInput)
        If Mid(sInput, j, 1) = vbTab Then
            Mid(sInput, j, 1) = " "

        End If

    Next j
    Stripped = sInput
End Function
```

Description   The Mid statement allows you to replace one or more characters at an arbitrary location in a string or byte array. This is different from the Mid function, which returns one or more characters from a string.

You can only use Mid to replace existing characters, not to add or remove characters. For example, you couldn't use Mid(s,1,2) = "ABCD", because you'd only replace the first two characters with AB, with Mid discarding the remaining "CD". Mid(s,1,2) = "A" replaces the first character with A, and leaves the remaining characters as they were.

RSET FUNCTION

Purpose   RSet copies one string into another and right-justifies it. Table 17-7 explains the arguments of the RSet function.

General Syntax

```
RSet string1 = string2
```

Table 17-7 Arguments of the RSet function

Argument	Description
string1	Target string
string2	String to be copied and right-justified

Example Syntax

The project at the end of this chapter demonstrates the effects of RSet with the following code.

```
If Len(Text1) < 20 Then
    LSet sLeft = Text1
    Picture1.Print "LSet:"; Tab(30); sLeft
    RSet sRight = Text1
    Picture1.Print "RSet:"; Tab(30); sRight
End If
```

Description   RSet lets you copy one string into another and right-justify the target string.

Comment   The effect of RSet is most dramatic when the target string is a fixed-length string.

Purpose   The RTrim function removes spaces from the end of a string or byte array. Table 17-8 explains the argument of the RTrim function.

General Syntax

```
RTrim(String)
```

Table 17-8 Argument of the RTrim function

Argument	Description
String	String to be modified

Example Syntax

```
rs!LastName = RTrim(txtLastName.Text)
```

Description	RTrim removes spaces from the end of strings and byte arrays. This makes it useful for doing cleanup prior to editing or saving string data.

STR FUNCTION

Purpose	The Str function converts numeric data into an unformatted string. Table 17-9 explains the arguments of the Str function.

General Syntax

```
str(number)
```

Table 17-9 Arguments of the Str function

Argument	Description
number	Numeric data to convert to a string

Example Syntax

```
s = Str(txtNumber.Text)
```

Description	The Str function translates a number into a string or byte array. Str does no formatting, so if you need commas, thousands separators, and so on, use the Format command.
Comments	Str inserts a leading space for positive or unsigned numbers to act as a placeholder for the sign. To remove the space, you can either use one of the Trim functions or use Format with no formatting.

STRCONV FUNCTION

Purpose	The StrConv function translates a string from one state to another. Table 17-10 explains the arguments of the StrConv function, and Table 17-11 lists the different values of the conversion parameter.

General Syntax

```
StrConv(string, conversion)
```

Table 17-10 Arguments of the StrConv function

Argument	Description
string	String to be modified
conversion	Action(s) to take

Table 17-11 Values of the conversion parameter

Argument	Description
vbUpperCase	Changes value of string to all uppercase
vbLowerCase	Changes value of string to all lowercase
vbProperCase	Capitalizes the first letter of each word
VbWide (DBCS systems only)	Converts ANSI-encoded characters to the equivalent DBCS character
vbNarrow (DBCS systems only)	Converts DBCS encoded characters to the equivalent ANSI character
vbKatakana (DBCS systems only)	Converts Hiragana characters to Katakana
vbHiragana (DBCS systems only)	Converts Katakana characters to Hiragana
vbUnicode	Converts ANSI-encoded characters to the default Unicode code page
vbFromUnicode	Converts Unicode characters to ANSI

Example Syntax

```
StrConv(txtName.Text,vbProperCase)
```

Description   StrConv converts a string from one format to another. It combines several separate functions into one function-of-all-trades, with added functionality. You can use StrConv to replace the UCase and LCase functions. StrConv can also capitalize the first letter of each word in a string. This is the equivalent of the Toggle Case command in Word.

StrConv gives you the ability to convert a string to or from the Unicode and DBCS character encoding schemes. This allows you to read ANSI-formatted data and convert it to the local encoding scheme, or the reverse.

Comments   The DBCS conversion arguments only function in versions of Windows 95 and Windows NT that include the DBCS functionality. Using these parameters in any other system causes a compile-time error.

STRING FUNCTION

Purpose   The String function returns a string of repeating characters. Table 17-12 explains the parameters of the String function.

General Syntax

```
String(number, character)
```

Table 17-12 Parameters of the String function

Argument	Description
number	The number of characters to return
character	The character to return

Example Syntax
```
mySring = String(5, "*"
Print myString
        Prints "*****"
```

Description	The String function is used to fill a string with a specific number of any single character.
Comments	Windows API functions that return do not create string space for you. You must create a string long enough to handle the longest string that the API function could return. The String function is used to meet that requirement, usually sending a string of 255 spaces to the API.
Purpose	Trim removes leading spaces from a string or byte array. See Table 17-13 for a description of the argument of the Trim function.

General Syntax
```
Trim(string)
```

Table 17-13 Argument of the Trim function

Argument	Description
string	The string being trimmed

Example Syntax
```
ds!Name = Trim(txtName.text)
```

Description	Trim removes all leading and trailing spaces from a string or byte array. Trim is usually used with data entered on a form to make sure no extraneous spaces are stored with the data.
Comments	Most often you'll use Trim rather than LTrim or RTrim.

UCase Function

Purpose	UCase translates a string of lower- or mixed case into all uppercase. Table 17-14 describes the argument for UCase.

General Syntax
```
UCase(string)
```

Table 17-14 Argument of the UCase function

Argument	Description
string	The string data to be formatted

Example Syntax

```
rs!Description = UCase(txtDescription.Text)
```

Description   UCase forces all letters to be uppercase. It is ideal for situations in which you need to be sure a string is all uppercase, such as if you're dealing with data from a form.

The Strings Project

Project Overview

The Strings project demonstrates many of the string and number formatting techniques described in this chapter. The project includes a text box into which you can type either numbers or text, and a command button that causes the contents of the text box to be "printed" into a picture box in various formats.

Assembling the Project: frmStrings

1. Make a new form with the objects and properties in Table 17-15. Use Figure 17-1 as a guide to size and placement.

Table 17-15 Elements of the Strings form

Object	Property	Setting
Form	Name	frmStrings
	Caption	String Formatting
CommandButton	Name	Command2
	Caption	E&xit
CommandButton	Name	Command1
	Caption	&Print
TextBox	Name	Text1
	TabIndex	0
PictureBox	Name	Picture1
	BackColor	&H00FFFFFF&
	TabIndex	1
	TabStop	0 'False

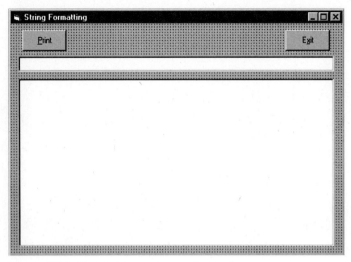

Figure 17-1 The Strings project at design time

2. Add the following code to the GotFocus event of Text1. The code selects the contents of the text box when it receives focus.

```
Private Sub Text1_GotFocus()
    Text1.SelStart = 0
    Text1.SelLength = Len(Text1)
End Sub
```

3. Add the following code to the Click event of Command1. This code determines whether the contents of Text1 are numeric or text, then displays the text in various formats, using the Print method to print it into the picture box.

```
Private Sub Command1_Click()
    Dim SFormat As String, sLeft As String * 20, sRight As String * 20
    Picture1.Cls
    Picture1.Print "Text1: " & Text1
    Picture1.Print
    If Val(Text1) = 0 Then
        Picture1.Print "Upper:"; Tab(30); StrConv(Text1, vbUpperCase)
        Picture1.Print "Lower:"; Tab(30); StrConv(Text1, vbLowerCase)
        Picture1.Print "Proper:"; Tab(30); StrConv(Text1, vbProperCase)
        Picture1.Print "Format Force Lower:"; Tab(30); Format(Text1, "<")
        Picture1.Print "Format Force Upper:"; Tab(30); Format(Text1, ">")
        If Len(Text1) < 20 Then
            LSet sLeft = Text1
            Picture1.Print "LSet:"; Tab(30); sLeft
```

```
            RSet sRight = Text1
            Picture1.Print "RSet:"; Tab(30); sRight
        End If
    Else
        SFormat = "Currency"
        Picture1.Print SFormat & ": "; Tab(30); ⇐Format(Val(Text1), SFormat)
        SFormat = "######.00"
        Picture1.Print SFormat & ": "; Tab(30); ⇐Format(Val(Text1), SFormat)
        SFormat = "000000.##"
        Picture1.Print SFormat & ": "; Tab(30); ⇐Format(Val(Text1), SFormat)
        SFormat = "Standard"
        Picture1.Print SFormat & ": "; Tab(30); ⇐Format(Val(Text1), SFormat)
        SFormat = "General Number"
        Picture1.Print SFormat & ": "; Tab(30); ⇐Format(Val(Text1), SFormat)
        SFormat = "Fixed"
        Picture1.Print SFormat & ": "; Tab(30); ⇐Format(Val(Text1), SFormat)
        SFormat = "Percent"
        Picture1.Print SFormat & ": "; Tab(30); ⇐Format(Val(Text1), SFormat)
        SFormat = "Scientific"
        Picture1.Print SFormat & ": "; Tab(30); ⇐Format(Val(Text1), SFormat)
    End If
End Sub
```

4. Add the following code to the Click event of Command2. The code unloads the form and ends the program.

```
Private Sub Command2_Click()
    Unload Me
    End
End Sub
```

How It Works

The test If Val(Text1) = 0 determines whether Text1 contains a textual string or a numeric string. If the value is zero, the contents are treated as text, and the text is sent to Picture1 in various text formats. If the value is not zero, the contents are sent to the picture box in various numeric formats. Figure 17-2 shows the project displaying text and Figure 17-3 shows the project displaying numeric data.

You can experiment with different formats by changing the format strings in the calls to the Format function.

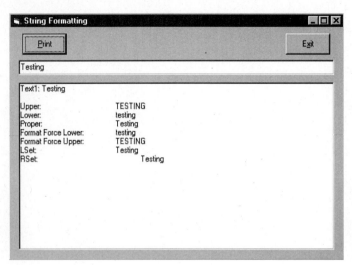

Figure 17-2 The Strings project displaying text

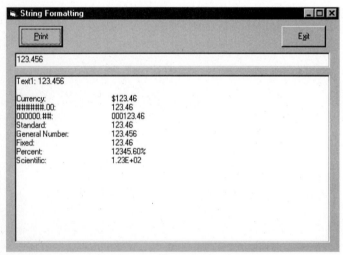

Figure 17-3 The Strings project displaying numbers

18

STRING MANIPULATION

One of the strengths of the BASIC programming language is that a string is a built-in data type. BASIC also provides you with a variety of functions to manipulate strings. These two language features give you convenient tools to deal with strings. In this chapter, you will discover how simple it is in Visual Basic to convert the case of a string, get a specific part of a string, and so on.

String Manipulation Summary

Table 18-1 lists the string functions and statements available to you. These are discussed in detail following the table, and the String project at the end of the chapter demonstrates their use.

Table 18-1 Functions and statements that affect strings

Use This...	Type	To Do This...
Asc	Function	Determine the ANSI value of a string character
AscB	Function	Determine the ANSI value of a single-byte character
AscW	Function	Determine the Unicode value of a string character
Chr	Function	Translate an ANSI value into a string character
ChrB	Function	Translate an ANSI value into a single-byte character
ChrW	Function	Translate a Unicode value into a string character
InStr	Function	Find the character position of one string within another
InStrB	Function	Find the byte position of one string within another
LCase	Function	Translate all uppercase characters in a string to lowercase
Left	Function	Return a specified number of characters of a string starting from the leftmost character
LeftB	Function	Return a specified number of bytes of a string starting from the leftmost byte
Len	Function	Determine the length in characters of a string (or other variable type)
LenB	Function	Determine the length in bytes of a string (or other variable type)
LSet	Statement	Left-justify a value in a string (or a programmer-defined type)

continued on next page

continued from previous page

Use This...	Type	To Do This...
LTrim	Function	Truncate any leading spaces from a string
Mid	Function	Return a specified number of characters of a string by specifying start point and number of characters
MidB	Function	Return a specified number of bytes of a string by specifying start point and number of bytes
Mid	Statement	Assign a value to a portion of a character string
MidB	Statement	Assign a value to a portion of a byte string
Option Compare	Statement	Set binary or text comparison method for strings
Right	Function	Return a specified number of characters of a string starting from the rightmost character
RightB	Function	Return a specified number of bytes of a string starting from the rightmost byte
RSet	Statement	Right-justify a value in a string (or a programmer-defined type)
RTrim	Function	Truncate any following spaces from a string
Space	Function	Return a specified number of spaces
StrComp	Function	Return a value indicating the result of a string comparison
StrConv	Function	Convert a string expression to another style
String	Function	Return a string of characters repeated a specified number of times
Trim	Function	Truncate any leading or trailing spaces from a string
UCase	Function	Translate all lowercase characters of a string into uppercase

Asc, AscB, and AscW Functions

See Also	Chr, ChrB, ChrW
Purpose	The Asc functions return the numeric code of a character. Table 18-2 describes the argument of the Asc functions.

General Syntax

```
Asc(strExpression)
AscB(strExpression)
AscW(strExpression)
```

Table 18-2 Argument of the Asc functions

Argument	Description
strExpression	String for which you want to return the numeric code of the first character

Example Syntax

```
Dim intAnsi as Integer

intAnsi = Asc( Hello )
```

Description This example places the value 72 (the ANSI code for the character "H") in the variable intAnsi.

The Asc function returns the numeric ANSI value of the first character in the supplied string. The range for returns is from 0 to 255 on non-DBCS (Double Byte Character Set) systems, but from -32768 to 32767 on DBCS systems.

The AscB function is used with byte strings. Instead of returning the character code for the first character, AscB returns the first byte. The AscW function returns the Unicode character code except on platforms where Unicode is not supported, when its behavior is identical to the Asc function.

Example The String project at the end of this chapter uses the AscW function to determine whether a character is in lowercase, using the assumption that the ANSI values for the lowercase letters are contiguous.

CHR, CHRB, AND CHRW FUNCTIONS

See Also Asc, AscB, AscW

Purpose The Chr functions return the character that corresponds to the supplied code. Table 18-3 describes the argument of the Chr functions.

General Syntax
```
Chr(intANSICode)
ChrB(intANSICode)
ChrW(intANSICode)
```

Table 18-3 Argument of the Chr functions

Argument	Description
intANSICode	Integer for which you want to return the corresponding character

Example Syntax
```
Dim strDoubleQuote as String
strDoubleQuote = Chr(34)
```

Description The previous example places a double quote in the variable strDoubleQuote.

The Chr function is the complement to the Asc function. It returns the character whose ANSI code is specified as its argument. Normally, the intANSICode argument must be in the range of 0 to 255. However, on DBCS systems, the actual range for intANSICode is -32768 to 32767.

This function is useful for specifying characters that you cannot type at the keyboard, such as special control codes for the printer. Another good use for this function is generating double quote marks in strings. Because Visual Basic uses double quotes to delimit strings, you cannot include a double quote mark in a string directly. You can, however, use Chr(34) to produce a double quote mark within a string.

The ChrB function is used with byte data contained in a string. Instead of returning a character, which may be 1 or 2 bytes, ChrB always returns a single byte. The ChrW function returns a string containing the Unicode character except on platforms where Unicode is not supported, when its behavior is identical to the Chr function.

INSTR AND INSTRB FUNCTIONS

Purpose
The InStr functions return the position of an occurrence of a search string within another string being searched. Table 18-4 summarizes the arguments of the InStr functions.

General Syntax
```
InStr([lngStartPos], strString1, strString2)
InStrB([lngStartPos], strString1, strString2)
```

Table 18-4 Arguments of the InStr functions

Argument	Description
lngStartPos	Position in strString1 from which to start the search for strString2
strString1	String in which to search for strString2
strString2	String to be searched

Example Syntax
```
Dim strBye as String
Dim lngPos1 as Integer, lngPos2 as Integer
strBye = Good Bye

lngPos1 = InStr(strBye, Bye )
lngPos2 = InStr(7, strBye, Bye )
```

The first example assigns the value 6 to the variable lngPos1 because the string "Bye" can be found at the sixth position in strBye. The second example starts the search at position 7; therefore, "Bye" cannot be found. The variable lngPos2 is assigned a value of 0.

Description	The parameter strString1 is the string that will be searched. strString2 is the string that is being searched for. If strString2 is found within strString1, InStr returns the position where the beginning of the search string is found. If the string cannot be found, a 0 is returned. You can optionally use the lngStartpos parameter. This specifies the position in strString1 where you wish the search to start. This is useful for searching one string for multiple occurrences of another. If strString2 is a null string, InStr returns the value of lngStartpos (or 0, if lngStartpos was not specified).
	The InStrB function is used with byte data contained in a string. Instead of returning the character position of the first occurrence of one string within another, InStrB returns the byte position.
Example	The String project at the end of this chapter uses the InStr function to find the token separator (the space) and split a sentence into "words."

LCase Function

See Also	UCase
Purpose	The LCase function returns a copy of a variant or a string in which all uppercase alphabetic characters have been converted to lowercase. Table 18-5 describes the argument of the LCase function.

General Syntax

```
LCase(strExpression)
```

Table 18-5 Argument of the LCase function

Argument	Description
strExpression	String you want converted to lowercase

Example Syntax
```
Dim strCommandLine as String, strLowerCommand as String
strCommandLine = Command
strLowerCommand = LCase(strCommandLine)
```

	This example retrieves the command-line parameters that were used to start the program and converts the entries to lowercase.
Description	The strExpression parameter can be a fixed- or variable-length string, a string constant, a literal string, the result of any function that returns a string, or any other string expression. The UCase function works the same as LCase, but it converts lowercase to uppercase.

This function is very useful for making a non–case-sensitive comparison of two strings. This is helpful when an internal variable is being compared to a user's string input. By using LCase (or UCase), the program can ignore the case of the string that has been entered by the user.

Note that you can use the Option Compare text statement if you prefer to use a non–case-sensitive string comparison throughout a module.

Example   The String project at the end of this chapter uses the LCase fuction to convert uppercase letters to lowercase.

LEFT AND LEFTB FUNCTIONS

See Also   Mid, MidB, Right, RightB

Purpose   The Left functions return a portion of a variant or a string, starting at the first character, of the length specified. Table 18-6 summarizes the arguments of the Left functions.

General Syntax

```
Left(strExpression, lngLength)
LeftB(strExpression, lngLength)
```

Table 18-6 Arguments of the Left functions

Argument	Description
strExpression	String of which you want the lngLength leftmost characters
lngLength	Number of characters of the returned substring

Example Syntax

```
Dim strDolly as String, strHello as String
strDolly =  Hello, Dolly!
strHello = Left(strHello, 5)
```

The previous example assigns the leftmost five characters from strDolly to the variable strHello, giving it a value of "Hello."

Description   The strExpression parameter can be a fixed- or variable-length string, a string constant, a literal string, the result of any function that returns a string, or any other string expression.

The lngLength parameter refers to the number of characters to copy. This value may be in the range of 0 to 2,147,483,647. If the length specified is greater than or equal to the full length of the source string, Left returns an exact copy of the source string. If the length is 0, a null string is returned. If lngLength has a value of less than 0 or greater than 2,147,483,647, an "Illegal function call" error is generated.

The LeftB function is used with byte data contained in a string. Instead of specifying the number of characters to return, lngLength specifies the number of bytes.

LEN AND LENB FUNCTIONS

Purpose

The Len functions return the storage length of a variable. They are most commonly used to find the length of a string. Table 18-7 describes the argument of the Len functions.

General Syntax

```
Len(variable-name)
```

Table 18-7 Argument of the Len functions

Argument	Description
variable-name	The name of the Visual Basic variable for which you want to determine the storage length

Example Syntax

```
Dim strHello as String
Dim lngStrLen as Long
strHello =  Hello
lngStrLen = Len(strHello)
```

Because the string "Hello" is five characters long, this places the value 5 into the variable lngStrLen.

Description

This function returns the amount of data space needed to store a particular variable. Any type of variable may be used, including user-defined variables. Most commonly, Len is used to get the length of a variable-length string so it can be processed with a loop.

LenB returns the length in bytes, while Len returns the length in characters.

Example

The String project at the end of this chapter uses the Len function in various spots, for instance, to determine the length of the parse string.

LSET STATEMENT

See Also

RSet, LTrim

Purpose

The LSet statement left-justifies the contents of a string variable. It can also be used to copy one string or user-defined type to another, starting from the left and working to the right. Table 18-8 summarizes the arguments of the LSet statement.

General Syntax

```
LSet resultvariable = sourcevariable
```

Table 18-8 Arguments of the LSet Statement

Argument	Description
resultvariable	Destination string for the assignment
sourcevariable	String value you want to assign to the destination variable

Example Syntax

```
Dim strSrc As String * 10
Dim strDest As String * 4
strSrc = " 987654321"
strDest = "1234"
LSet strDest = strSrc 'strDest = " 987"
```

Description

The LSet statement assigns to resultvariable the value of sourcevariable. Both variables may be fixed- or variable-length strings or a programmer-defined variable type. The assignment performed by LSet is done byte by byte from the left of sourcevariable to the right. The assignment cannot change the length of resultvariable. If resultvariable is shorter than sourcevariable, the characters that are beyond the length of resultvariable are truncated. If resultvariable is longer than sourcevariable, spaces are used to fill out the balance of resultvariable.

The RSet statement performs the same function, except the copy is executed from right to left.

LTRIM FUNCTION

See Also   RTrim, Trim

Purpose   The LTrim function returns a copy of a string with any leading spaces removed. Table 18-9 describes the argument of the LTrim function.

General Syntax

```
LTrim(strExpression)
```

Table 18-9 Argument of the LTrim function

Argument	Description
strExpression	String of which you want to return a copy without the leading spaces

Example Syntax

```
Dim strString as String
strString = LTrim(   Good Bye")
```

This example assigns the value "Good Bye" to the variable strString.

Description   This is the complement of the RTrim function. It returns a copy of the supplied string expression without any leading spaces.

The strExpression parameter can be a fixed- or variable-length string, a string constant, a literal string, the result of any function that returns a string, any other string expression, or a variant that can evaluate to a string.

MID AND MIDB FUNCTIONS

See Also   Left, LeftB, Right, RightB

Purpose   The Mid functions return the specified portion of a string expression. Table 18-10 summarizes the arguments of the Mid functions.

General Syntax

```
Mid(strExpression, lngStart[, lngLength])
MidB(strExpression, lngStart[, lngLength])
```

Table 18-10 Arguments of the Mid functions

Argument	Description
strExpression	String of which you want to return a substring
lngStart	Starting position for the returned substring
lngLength	Number of characters of the returned substring

Example Syntax

```
Dim strGood as String
Dim strBye as String, strDolly as String
strGood =  Good bye, Dolly
strBye = Mid(strGood, 6, 3)
strDolly = Mid(strGood, 11)
```

This example uses the Mid function to assign the value "bye" to the variable strBye. In the second example, the length parameter is omitted, so the string returned starts where indicated and continues for the balance of the length of strGood. Therefore, the variable strDolly is assigned the value "Dolly".

Description   This function returns the specified substring of a string expression. The strExpression parameter designates the source string and can be a fixed- or variable-length string, a string constant, a literal string, the result of any function that returns a string, or a variant that can evaluate to a string.

The lngStart parameter specifies the position within the source string where the copy will begin. This parameter must be in the range of 1 to 2,147,483,647. If not, an "Illegal function call" will occur. If this parameter is greater than the length of the source string, the returned string will be null.

The lngLength parameter is used to specify how many characters will be copied. This is an optional parameter. If it is not used, the function will return all the characters from lngStart to the end of the source string. The lngLength parameter has a range of 0 to 2,147,483,647. If it is not in this range, an "Illegal function call" will occur. If a 0 is specified, a null string is returned. If it specifies a length beyond the end of the source string, only the characters up to the length of the string are returned.

The MidB function is used with byte data contained in a string. Instead of specifying the number of characters, the arguments specify numbers of bytes.

Example   The String project at the end of this chapter uses the Mid function to retrieve the string that still needs to be parsed and to retrieve each word.

MID AND MIDB STATEMENTS

See Also   Left, LeftB, Right, RightB

Purpose   The Mid statements replace the specified characters of one string with another string. Table 18-11 summarizes the arguments of the Mid statements.

General Syntax

```
Mid(strResultString, lngStart[, lngLength]) = strExpression
MidB(strResultString, lngStart[, lngLength]) = strExpression
```

Table 18-11 Arguments of the Mid statements

Argument	Description
strResultString	String in which you want to replace a substring with another substring
lngStart	Starting position for the replacement
lngLength	Number of characters of the substring to be replaced
strExpression	Replacement value for the substring

Example Syntax

```
Dim strHello as String
strHello =  Hello, Dolly
Mid(strHello, 1, 5) =  Oh my
Mid(strHello, 8) =  Beck
```

The first example replaces the "Hello" in strHello with "Oh my." The second example starts at the eighth position and replaces whatever text is there with "Beck." Because the length is not specified, the replace is effective for the length of "Beck." This makes strHello's final value "Oh my, Becky."

Description

This statement copies the supplied string expression into the specified string. The strResultString parameter must be a variable- or fixed-length string or a variant that can evaluate to a string. This is the string that will receive the characters being copied.

The lngStart parameter specifies where in the result string the characters are to be placed. This parameter must be greater than 0 and cannot exceed the length of the result string. If it is not in this range, an "Illegal function call" will result.

The lngLength parameter is optional, and it specifies how many characters will be replaced. If this parameter is omitted, the length will default to the size of strExpression. Regardless of the value in lngLength and the length of strExpression, the copy never goes beyond the original length of strResultString.

The strExpression parameter specifies the source of the copy. It can be a fixed- or variable-length string, a string constant, a literal string, the result of any function that returns a string, or a variant that can evaluate to a string.

The MidB statement is used with byte data contained in a string. In the MidB statement, lngStart specifies the byte position within strResultString where replacement begins, and lngLength specifies the numbers of bytes to replace.

OPTION COMPARE STATEMENT

See Also   StrComp

Purpose   Use the Option Compare statement to control how string comparisons are made.

General Syntax

```
Option Compare (Binary | Text)
```

Example Syntax

```
Option Compare Text
```

Description

Visual Basic defaults to using a binary comparison method when comparing two strings. Binary comparisons are case sensitive, so "A" does not equal "a". The relative order of characters is determined by their order in the ANSI character set.

Text comparisons are not case sensitive, so "A" does equal "a". Furthermore, the relative order of characters is determined by the international section of WIN.INI.

Place the Option Compare statement in the declarations section of a form or module to control comparisons for code in that form or module.

RIGHT AND RIGHTB FUNCTIONS

See Also   Left, LeftB, Mid, MidB

Purpose   The Right functions return a portion of a string, starting at the last character and working to the left, for the length specified. Table 18-12 summarizes the arguments of the Right functions.

General Syntax

```
Right(strExpression, lngLength)
RightB(strExpression, lngLength)
```

Table 18-12 Arguments of the Right functions

Argument	Description
strExpression	String of which you want the lngLength rightmost characters
lngLength	Number of characters of the returned substring

Example Syntax

```
Dim strHello as String, strDolly as String
strDolly = Hello, Dolly!
strHello = Right(strDolly, 6)
```

The above example assigns the rightmost six characters from strHello to the variable strDolly, giving it a value of "Dolly!".

Description   The strExpression parameter can be a fixed- or variable-length string, a string constant, a literal string, the result of any function that returns a string, or any other string expression. The lngLength parameter refers to the number of characters to copy. This value may be in the range of 0 to 2,147,483,647. If the length specified is greater than or equal to the full length of the source string, Right returns an exact copy of the source string. If the length is 0, a null string is returned. If lngLength has a value of less than 0 or greater than 2,147,483,647, an "Illegal function call" error is generated. The RightB function is used with byte data contained in a string. Instead of specifying the number of characters to return, lngLength specifies the number of bytes.

Example   The String project at the end of this chapter uses the Right function to retrieve the last token of the sentence.

RSET STATEMENT

See Also   LSet

Purpose   The RSet statement copies one string into another, byte by byte, starting at the rightmost character in the source string and working to the left. Table 18-13 summarizes the arguments of the RSet statement.

General Syntax

```
RSet resultvariable = sourcevariable
```

Table 18-13 Arguments of the RSet statement

Argument	Description
resultvariable	Destination string for the assignment
sourcevariable	String value you want to assign to the destination variable

Example Syntax

```
Private strNumberBuffer As String * 12
Dim sngAmount as Single
Dim strAmount as String
sngAmount = 2003.45
strAmount = Format(sngAmount,  #,###,###.#0 )
RSet strNumberBuffer = strAmount
lblBuffer.Caption = strNumberBuffer ' The result is "     2,003.45"
```

This example uses RSet to right-justify the string representation of a number in a label object.

Description   This statement assigns to resultvariable the value of sourcevariable. Both variables may be fixed- or variable-length strings. The assignment performed by RSet is done byte by byte from the right of sourcevariable to the left. The assignment cannot change the length of resultvariable. If resultvariable is shorter than sourcevariable, the characters that are beyond the length of resultvariable are not copied. If resultvariable is longer than sourcevariable, spaces are used to fill out the balance of resultvariable.

RTRIM FUNCTION

See Also   LTrim, Trim

Purpose   The RTrim function returns a copy of a string with any trailing spaces removed. Table 18-14 describes the argument of the RTrim function.

General Syntax

```
RTrim(strExpression)
```

Table 18-14 Argument of the RTrim function

Argument	Description
strExpression	String of which you want to return a copy without the trailing spaces

Example Syntax
```
Dim strString as String
strString = RTrim(   Good Bye   )
```

Description   This example assigns the value "Good Bye" to the variable strString.

This is the complement of the LTrim function. It returns a copy of the supplied string expression without any following spaces.

The strExpression parameter can be a fixed- or variable-length string, a string constant, a literal string, the result of any function that returns a string, or any other string expression.

SPACE FUNCTION

See Also   String

Purpose   The Space function returns a string containing the specified number of spaces. Table 18-15 describes the argument of the Space function.

General Syntax

```
Space(lngNumSpaces)
```

Table 18-15 Argument of the Space function

Argument	Description
lngNumSpaces	Number of spaces in the returned string

Example Syntax
```
Dim strString as String
strString = Space(5)
```

Description   This example gives the variable strString the value of "   " (five spaces).

This function returns a string of the specified number of spaces (ANSI character 32). The lngNumSpaces parameter can be of any numeric type, but it must be a value from 0 to 2,147,483,647. If it is not in this range, an "Illegal function call" will occur.

StrComp Function

Purpose   StrComp compares two strings. Table 18-16 summarizes the arguments and Table 18-17 the possible return values of the StrComp function.

General Syntax

```
StrComp(strString1, strString2 [, compareType%])
```

Table 18-16 Arguments of the StrComp function

Argument	Description
strString1	First string you want to compare
strString2	Second string you want to compare
compareType%	0 for case-sensitive comparison, 1 for non–case-sensitive comparison

Table 18-17 Return values of the StrComp function

Condition	Value
strString1 < strString2	-1
strString1 = strString2	0
strString1 > strString2	1
Either string is Null	Null

Example Syntax

```
hilo=StrComp(in$, old$)
```

Description   StrComp compares two strings and returns one of four values.

You can use the compareType% argument to set how comparisons are made. 0 makes string comparison case sensitive (for example, "A" does not equal "a") and 1 makes it case insensitive ("A" equals "a").

StrConv Function

See Also   LCase, UCase

Purpose   StrConv converts a string into the specified format. Table 18-18 summarizes the arguments of the StrConv function.

General Syntax

```
StrConv(strExpression,conversionType)
```

Table 18-18 Arguments of the StrConv function

Argument	Description
strExpression	String you want converted
conversionType	Constant indicating the conversion type

Example Syntax

```
Dim strOldString as String, strNewString as String
strOldString = "bill GATES"
strNewString = StrConv(strOldString,vbProperCase)       Returns "Bill Gates"
```

Description   Given a string and one of the Visual Basic conversion constants as argu-
ments, StrConv will return the string converted to the specified pattern.
When casing a string, the following ANSI codes are valid word separators:
Null (Chr(0)), horizontal tab (Chr(9)), linefeed (Chr(10)), vertical tab
(Chr(11)), form feed (Chr(12)), carriage return (Chr(13)), space
(SBCS)(Chr(32)). In double-byte character sets, the space character varies
from country to country. Table 18-19 provides a listing of all the valid con-
version constants.

Table 18-19 Constant values for use with StrConv

Constant	Value	Description
vbUpperCase	1	Uppercases the entire string
vbLowerCase	2	Lowercases the entire string
vbProperCase	3	Uppercases the first letter in each word in the string
vbWide*	4	Converts wide (single-byte) characters in the string into narrow (double-byte) characters
vbNarrow*	8	Converts wide (double-byte) characters in the string into narrow (single-byte) characters
vbKatakana**	16	Converts wide Hiragana characters in the string to wide Katakana characters
vbHiragana**	32	Converts wide Katakana characters in the string to wide Hiragana characters
vbUnicode	64	Converts the string to Unicode using the default code page of the system
vbFromUnicode	128	Converts the string from Unicode to the default code page of the system

* Far Eastern locales

** Japanese only

STRING FUNCTION

See Also   Space

Purpose   The String function returns a string containing the specified number of the
requested character. Table 18-20 summarizes the arguments of the String
function.

General Syntax

```
String(lngNumChars, intANSICode)
String(lngNumChars, strCharacters)
```

Table 18-20 Arguments of the String function

Argument	Description
lngNumChars	Number of repeating characters in the returned string
intANSICode	ANSI code of the character to be repeated in the returned string
strCharacters	String where the first character is the character to be repeated in the returned string

Example Syntax

```
Dim strString as String
strString = String(10, "*")
strString = String(10, 42)
```

Description   Because 42 is the ANSI code for the asterisk character, both of these statements return the same value: "**********".

This function returns a string of the requested character of the length specified by lngNumChars. The lngNumChars parameter must be in the range of 0 to 2,147,483,647 or an "Illegal function call" will occur. You may specify which character to have returned either by supplying the ANSI code of the desired character or by supplying a string whose first character is the desired character.

TRIM FUNCTION

See Also   LTrim, RTrim

Purpose   The Trim function removes leading and trailing spaces from a string. Table 18-21 describes the argument of the Trim function.

General Syntax

```
Trim(strExpression)
```

Table 18-21 Argument of the Trim function

Argument	Description
strExpression	String of which you want to return a copy without the leading and training spaces

Example Syntax

```
Dim strClean as String
strClean=Trim(InputBox( Enter your name ))
```

Description	Trim serves as a combination of LTrim and RTrim, removing all spaces from the beginning and ending of strings.

UCASE FUNCTION

See Also	LCase
Purpose	The UCase function returns a copy of a string in which all lowercase alphabetic characters have been converted to uppercase. Table 18-22 describes the argument of the UCase function.

General Syntax

```
UCase(strExpression)
```

Table 18-22 Argument of the UCase function

Argument	Description
strExpression	String you want converted to uppercase

Example Syntax

```
Dim strCommand as String
Dim strUpperCommand as String
strCommand = Command
strUpperCommand = UCase(strCommand)
```

	This example retrieves the command-line parameters that were used to start the program and converts the entries to uppercase.
Description	The strExpression parameter can be a fixed- or variable-length string, a string constant, a literal string, the result of any function that returns a string, or any other string expression. The LCase function works the same as UCase, but it converts uppercase to lowercase.
	This function is very useful for making a non–case-sensitive comparison of two strings. This is helpful when an internal variable is being compared to a user's string input. By using UCase (or LCase), the program can ignore the case of the string that has been input by the user.
Example	The String project at the end of this chapter uses the UCase function to convert lowercase letters to uppercase.

The String Project

Project Overview

The String project performs a complex string manipulation on any sentence you type in a text box. Every word is reversed and the case of all letters is reversed; that is, uppercase becomes lowercase and vice versa.

The following pages discuss the assembly and operation of the String project. The first section deals with the assembly of the only form in the project. Next, there is a listing and explanation of the contents of the only code module of this project. Finally, a How It Works guide to the operation of the project discusses the operation of the code. Please read this information carefully and use the pictures of the form to check your results. When you are finished, run the project and watch how "The quick Brown Fox jumps over the lazy Dog" becomes "EHt KCIUQ NWORb XOf SPMUJ REVO EHT YZAL GOd." You can restore the text to its original form by clicking once more on the Parse button.

Assembling the Project

1. Make a new form with the objects and properties listed in Table 18-23.

Table 18-23 Elements of the main form

Object	Property	Setting
Form	Name	frmMain
	BorderStyle	3 - Fixed Dialog
	Caption	"String Project"
	MaxButton	False
	MinButton	False
TextBox	Name	txtToBeParsed
	Text	Type some text here
CommandButton	Name	cmdDoIt
	Caption	"&Parse"
CommandButton	Name	cmdExit
	Caption	"E&xit"

2. Size the objects on the screen as shown in Figure 18-1.

3. Go to the Form Layout window, right-click on the frmMain form, and select Center Screen as the startup position.

4. Enter the following code in the Click event of the cmdExit button. This unloads the form and terminates the application.

```
Private Sub cmdExit_Click()
    Unload Me
End Sub
```

5. Enter the following code in the Click event of the cmdDoIt button. The text in the Text box is modified by the Parse function implemented in the following code module.

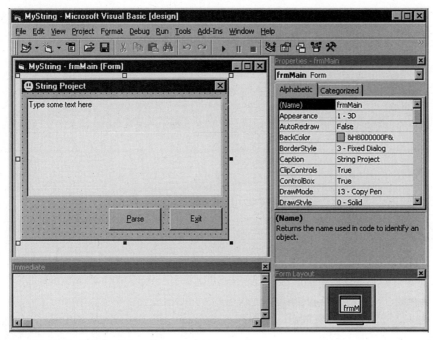

Figure 18-1 The frmMain form in design mode

```
Private Sub cmdDoIt_Click()
    txtToBeParsed.Text = Parse(txtToBeParsed.Text)
End Sub
```

6. Add a code module to the project. Name it modString and add the following code to it. Parse is the function encountered earlier called from the Parse command button. It repeatedly calls GetNextToken to extract every word out of the text. StrReverse reverses the text it is being passed. CaseReverse changes the case of the letters of the text it is being passed, while nonalphabetic characters remain as they are.

```
Public Function Parse(strText As String) As String
    Const cSeparator = " "

    Dim strNewText As String, strToken As String
    Dim lngStartPosition As Long

    lngStartPosition = 1

    While lngStartPosition <= Len(strText)
        strToken = GetNextToken(lngStartPosition, strText, cSeparator)
        strNewText = strNewText & StrReverse(strToken) & cSeparator
    Wend

    Parse = CaseReverse(strNewText)
End Function
```

```
Public Function GetNextToken(lngStartPosition As Long, strText As String, strSeparator ⇐
                    As String) As String

    ' Look for the next separator.
    Dim lngNextSeparatorPosition As Long
    lngNextSeparatorPosition = InStr(lngStartPosition, strText, strSeparator)
    If lngNextSeparatorPosition <> 0 Then        ' Got it!
        GetNextToken = Mid(strText, lngStartPosition, lngNextSeparatorPosition - ⇐
                    lngStartPosition)
        lngStartPosition = lngNextSeparatorPosition + 1
    Else                                    ' No more separators, return remaining
        GetNextToken = Right(strText, Len(strText) - lngStartPosition + 1)
        lngStartPosition = Len(strText) + 1
    End If
End Function

Public Function StrReverse(strText As String) As String
    Dim lngPos As Long

    StrReverse = ""

    For lngPos = Len(strText) + 1 To 1 Step - 1
        StrReverse = StrReverse & Mid(strText, lngPos, 1)
    Next
End Function

Public Function CaseReverse(strText As String) As String
    Dim lngPos As Long

    CaseReverse = ""

    For lngPos = 1 To Len(strText)
        If isLower((Mid(strText, lngPos, 1))) Then
            ' Lower Case
            CaseReverse = CaseReverse & UCase(Mid(strText, lngPos, 1))
        Else
            ' Upper Case or non-alphabetic
            CaseReverse = CaseReverse & LCase(Mid(strText, lngPos, 1))
        End If
    Next
End Function

Public Function isLower(strText As String) As Boolean
    isLower = (AscW(strText) >= AscW("a") And AscW(strText) <= AscW("z"))
End Function
```

7. Run the project. Replace the default text in the text box with "The quick Brown Fox jumps over the lazy Dog." Click on Parse and see the strange result of the text manipulation: "EHt KCIUQ NWORb XOf SPMUJ REVO EHT YZAL GOd." The text can be restored to its original form by clicking on Parse once more.

How It Works

The form delegates all the real work to the functions implemented in the modString module.

As shown in Table 18-24, the isLower function returns True if the first character in the string is a lowercase letter (a–z) and False otherwise (including when the first character is not alphabetic).

Table 18-24 isLower return values

strText Value	isLower Return Value
"wonders"	True
"Wonders"	False
"7 wonders"	False

The CaseReverse function puts all lowercase letters of the string it receives in uppercase and all uppercase letters in lowercase. Nonalphabetic characters are left untouched; for example, CaseReverse("AbC123") returns "aBc123."

The StrReverse function reverses a string; for example, StrReverse("abc") returns "cba."

The GetNextToken function returns the substring between lngStartPosition and the separator. It sets lngStartPosition to the character position following the separator, or past the end of string to indicate that it is done.

The Parse function performs the complex string manipulation. Every word (separated by spaces) is reversed, and the case of all letters is reversed; that is, uppercase becomes lowercase, and vice versa.

19

MATH

One of the primary functions of computers is to relieve the user of the drudgery of having to manually perform mathematical calculations. Visual Basic does a good job of relieving the programmer of these tasks as well. Included in its array of commands are several advanced functions for handling trigonometry, logarithms, and random number generation.

Trigonometric Functions

Trigonometry is a branch of mathematics that involves the measurement of the sides and angles of triangles. Through the use of trigonometric functions, you can determine the length of all sides and the size of all angles in a triangle, given limited information.

Trigonometry depends on two concrete facts about a right triangle. First, by definition, the size of one of the angles in a right triangle is always 90 degrees. Second, the sum of all the angles in a triangle is 180 degrees. Using this information, you can determine the measurements of all sides and angles of a right triangle if you know the length of two of the sides, or the length of one side and the size of one angle (other than the right angle). Figure 19-1 shows a right triangle with the parts labeled. We will refer to this triangle throughout the following discussion.

Visual Basic has four trigonometric functions: Tan, Atn, Sin, and Cos. In order to provide the highest accuracy possible, each of these functions treats angle measurements as radians. Therefore, if your angles are measured in units of degrees, you will need to convert your measurements. You can convert degrees to radians with the following function definition:

```
Public Const PI = 3.14159265358979

Function Deg2Rad(dblDegrees as Double) as Double
     Deg2Rad = dblDegrees * (PI / 180)
End Function
```

The first of the four functions is Tan. This function is based on the trigonometric function tangent. The tangent of an angle is equal to the altitude (A) of the triangle divided by the width (W). Therefore:

```
Tan(R) = A / W    or    W = A / Tan(R)    or    A = W * Tan(R)
```

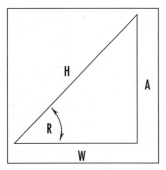

Figure 19-1 A right triangle whose width is W, altitude is A, hypotenuse is H, and angle is R

The following two lines of code use the Tan function to figure the length of the width and altitude of a triangle:

```
dblAltitude  = dblWidth * Tan(dblAngle)
dblWidth = dblAltitude / Tan(dblAngle)
```

The Atn function is used for the trigonometric arctangent function, which is the inverse of the tangent function. It returns the angle for which the supplied argument is the tangent. This allows you to determine the size of the angle when you know the lengths of the width and altitude:

```
Atn(A / W) = R    ' R is the angle, in Radians
```

The following line of code would then determine the angle:

```
dblAngle = Atn(dblAltitude / dblWidth)    ' dblAngle is in Radians
```

The Sin function is based on the trigonometric sine function. The sine of an angle is equal to the altitude divided by the hypotenuse (the hypotenuse is the side that is opposite the right angle). Therefore:

```
Sin(R) = A / H    or    A = Sin(R) * H    or    H = A / Sin(R)
```

The following two lines of code use the Sin function to figure the length of the hypotenuse and altitude of a triangle:

```
dblHypotenuse = dblAltitude / Sin(dblAngle)
dblAltitude = Sin(dblAngle) * dblHypotenuse
```

Finally, the Cos function is used for the trigonometric cosine function. The cosine of an angle is equal to the width divided by the hypotenuse. Therefore:

```
Cos(R) = W / H    or    W = Cos(R) * H    or    H = W / Cos(R)
```

The following two lines of code use the Cos function to figure the length of the hypotenuse and width of a triangle:

```
dblHypotenuse = dblWidth / Cos(dblAngle)
dblWidth = Cos(dblAngle) * dblHypotenuse
```

Your programs can determine the measurements for all sides and angles of a right triangle with only limited information by using these trigonometric functions.

Logarithms

There is a way to reverse the effect of almost every mathematical operation. For example, you can reverse $3 \times 4 = 12$ to $12 \div 4 = 3$. This is a fairly simple operation when applied to addition or multiplication; however, when the arithmetic gets a bit more advanced, reversing the operations gets more complicated.

One of the areas where this applies is in exponentiation. You probably know that the formula $X = Y \char`^ Z$ means multiply Y by itself the number of times indicated by Z and assign the value to X. So far no problem. But what if you have values for X and Y, and need to determine the value of Z?

This is where logarithms come in. Simply put, a logarithm is the exponent required to raise a certain base number so that it matches the target number. In other words, the logarithm of X is Z, as long as the logarithmic base is agreed upon as being Y.

There are two frequently used types of logarithms: common and natural. Common logarithms have a base of 10. Therefore, using the above equation, Y would equal 10, and Z (the logarithm of X) would be the value needed to raise Z so it matched X. Natural logarithms have a base of approximately 2.71828182845905 (referred to as e or Euler's number). Natural logarithms can be used to calculate the logarithm of a number when the desired base is e, and any desired base through the use of a simple formula.

Visual Basic provides two functions that deal with logarithms: Log and Exp. Both of these functions assume a logarithmic base of e (natural log). The Log function returns the natural logarithm of the supplied numeric value. Exp is the inverse of Log. It raises e to the specified power. The following two lines of code are functionally equivalent:

```
dblResult = Exp(5)
dblResult = 2.71828182845905 ^ 5
```

You can use the Log function to return the logarithm of any base. This is done by dividing the natural log of the desired number by the natural log of the desired base. The following function performs this task:

```
Public Function AnyLog(dblLogBase as Double, dblNumber as Double) as Double
    AnyLog = Log(dblNumber) / Log(dblLogBase)
End Function
```

You could also easily write a conversion to a fixed base, as the following example shows:

```
Public Function Log10(dblNumber as Double) as Double

    Log10 = Log(dblNumber) / Log(10#)
End Function
```

This returns the familiar base-10 logarithm.

Random Numbers

In computers, random numbers are not truly random. A series of random numbers must start with a seed number on which to base number generation. This seeding is performed by the Randomize statement. By default, the Randomize statement uses the system timer (which holds the number of seconds elapsed since midnight) as the seed. However, you can optionally specify any other number in the range -2,147,483,648 to 2,147,483,647. It's usually best to use the default, because this creates the closest thing to truly random numbers. If you use a specific number as a seed, the series of random numbers generated will always be the same. This may be suitable for some statistical procedures or for debugging, but would not make for good games.

Randomize must be used before the Rnd function is used. Although it can be used several times throughout a program, it is best if it is used only once. The Randomize statement should be placed in the Main module or in the Load event of the main form of a program.

The Rnd function returns pseudorandom numbers (based on the seed provided by the Randomize statement) in a range between 0 and 1. It is often more convenient to return random numbers in some other specified range. The following function assumes that the Randomize statement has already been executed:

```
Public Function Random(sngLoVal as Single, sngHiVal as Single) as Single
    Dim sngRange as Single
    sngRange = 1 + (sngHiVal - sngLoVal)
    Random = (Rnd * sngRange) + sngLoVal
End Function
```

In the above example, the programmer-defined function Random generates a random number that falls into the range defined by the arguments sngLoVal and sngHiVal. You could also use the Int function to produce random integers:

```
Public Function RandomInt(intLoVal as Integer, intHiVal as Integer) as Integer
    Dim intRange as Integer
    intRange = 1 + (intHiVal - intLoVal)
    RandomInt = Int(Rnd * intRange) + intLoVal
End Function
```

Math Summary

Table 19-1 lists Visual Basic's arithmetic commands. Detailed descriptions of them follow the table, and the project at the end of the chapter demonstrates their use.

Table 19-1 Functions and statements that affect numbers and numeric variables

Use This...	Type	To Do This...
Abs	Function	Return the absolute value of a numeric expression
Atn	Function	Return the arctangent of a numeric expression
Cos	Function	Return the cosine of a numeric expression
Exp	Function	Raise the natural logarithmic base (e) to the specified power
Fix	Function	Truncate the fractional part of a number and convert it to integer format
Int	Function	Return the largest integer that is less than or equal to a number
Log	Function	Return the natural logarithm
Randomize	Statement	Seed the random number generator
Rnd	Function	Return a randomly generated number between 0 and 1
Sgn	Function	Determine the sign of a numeric expression
Sin	Function	Return the sine of a numeric expression
Sqr	Function	Return the square root of a number
Tan	Function	Return the tangent of a number

ABS FUNCTION

See Also   Sgn

Purpose   The Abs function returns the absolute value of a number. Table 19-2 describes the argument of the Asc function.

General Syntax   `Abs(numExpression)`

Table 19-2 Argument of the Abs function

Argument	Description
numExpression	Numeric expression of which you want to return the absolute value

Example Syntax

`aNumber = Abs(aSignedNumber)`

Description   This statement places the absolute value of the variable aSignedNumber into the variable aNumber.

Abs returns the unsigned value of the supplied numeric expression. For instance, both Abs(-299) and Abs(299) return the value of 299. aNumber will have the same data type as aSignedNumber. If aSignedNumber is a variant of variant type 8 (string) that can be converted into a number, then aNumber will be a variant of type 5 (double).

ATN FUNCTION

See Also Cos, Sin, Tan

Purpose The Atn function returns the arctangent of a numeric expression. Table 19-3 describes the argument of the Atn function.

General Syntax

```
Atn(dblExpression)
```

Table 19-3 Argument of the Atn function

Argument	Description
dblExpression	Numeric expression for which you want to return the arctangent

Example Syntax

```
Dim dblAngle as Double, dblRatio as Double
dblAngle = Atn(dblRatio)
```

Description This example places the arctangent of the value of dblRatio in the variable dblAngle.

Atn is a trigonometric function that returns the arctangent of the supplied expression. The arctangent is the inverse of tangent. The arctangent of a number gives the size of the angle for which the number is the tangent. The angle returned by the Atn function is in radians.

COS FUNCTION

See Also Atn, Sin, Tan

Purpose The Cos function returns the cosine of an angle. Table 19-4 describes the argument of the Cos function.

General Syntax

```
Cos(dblAngle)
```

Table 19-4 Argument of the Cos function

Argument	Description
dblAngle	Numeric expression for which you want to return the cosine

Example Syntax

```
A! = Cos(4.93)
```

Description   The cosine of 4.93 is assigned to the variable A!.

The Cos function determines the cosine of an angle. The function expects the angle to be expressed in radians; therefore, if the angle is in degrees, it must first be converted using the formula radians = degrees * pi/180.

If angle is supplied as an integer or a single-precision value, Cos will return a single-precision value; otherwise it returns a double-precision value.

EXP FUNCTION

See Also   Log

Purpose   The Exp function raises the natural logarithmic base e to the specified power. (The natural logarithm, which has a base of about 2.718282, should not be confused with the common logarithm, whose base is 10.) Table 19-5 describes the argument of the Log function.

General Syntax

Exp(dblPower)

Table 19-5 Argument of the Log function

Argument	Description
dblPower	Numeric expression representing the power to which you want to raise the number e

Example Syntax
```
Dim dblNumber as Double, dblResult as Double
dblNumber = 14
dblResult = Exp(dblNumber)
```

Description   This example returns a double-precision number that represents the natural logarithmic base raised to the power of 14.

The logarithm of a number is the power to which the logarithmic base must be raised in order to achieve that number. The natural logarithmic base is referred to by the symbol e, and has an approximate value of 2.718282. Exp performs the inverse operation of a natural logarithm. It raises e to the power specified by the power parameter. Note that the power parameter must not exceed 709.782712893. Doing so will cause an "Overflow" error to occur.

FIX FUNCTION

See Also   CInt, Int

Purpose   The Fix function truncates the fractional part of a numeric expression and
returns the rest as an integer. Table 19-6 describes the argument of the Fix
function.

General Syntax

`Fix(dblExpression)`

Table 19-6 Argument of the Fix function

Argument	Description
dblExpression	Numeric expression of which you want to return the value with the fractional part truncated

Example Syntax
```
Dim dblNumber as Double
Dim intResult as Integer
dblNumber = 54.72
intResult = Fix(dblNumber)
```

Description   This example assigns the value 54 to the variable intResult.

The Fix function returns the whole-number portion of a dblExpression.
All digits to the right of the decimal are truncated. No rounding is performed. Use the CInt or CLng functions to convert to an integer with
rounding.

The Int function performs the same operation as Fix when the argument is
positive, or when there are no digits to the right of the decimal. The difference between the two is how they handle negative values. Int will return
the next whole negative number that is less than the argument. Fix returns
the next whole negative number that is greater than the argument. Table
19-7 compares the effects of Fix versus Int and CInt.

Table 19-7 Return values for the Fix, Int, and CInt functions

Value	Fix(Value)	Int(Value)	CInt(Value)
2.7	2	2	3
2.2	2	2	2
2	2	2	2
-2	-2	-2	-2
-2.2	-2	-3	-2
-2.7	-2	-3	-3

INT FUNCTION

See Also:	C<Type>, Fix
Purpose	The Int function returns the largest integer that is less than or equal to the supplied numeric expression. Table 19-8 describes the argument of the Int function.

General Syntax

```
Int(numExpression)
```

Table 19-8 Argument of the Int function

Argument	Description
numExpression	Numeric expression for which you want to return the largest integer less than or equal to it

Example Syntax

```
A% = Int(-2.86)
B% = Int(2.86)
```

Description

These statements place the value -3 in the variable A%, and the value 2 in the variable B%.

The Int function essentially rounds a numeric expression to the nearest integer. Int performs the same operation as Fix when the argument is positive, or when there are no digits to the right of the decimal. The difference between the two is how they handle negative values with fractions. Int will return the next whole negative number that is less than the argument. Fix returns the next whole negative number that is greater than the argument. Table 19-9 compares the effects of Int, Fix, and CInt.

Table 19-9 Return values for Fix, Int, and CInt functions

Value	Int(Value)	Fix(Value)	CInt(Value)
2.7	2	2	3
2.2	2	2	2
2	2	2	2
-2	-2	-2	-2
-2	2	-3	-2
-2.7	-3	-2	-3

Log Function

See Also	Exp
Purpose	The Log function returns the natural logarithm of a numeric expression. The natural logarithm, which has a base of approximately 2.718282, should not be confused with the common logarithm, whose base is 10. Table 19-10 describes the argument of the Log function.

General Syntax

```
Log(dblExpression)
```

Table 19-10 Argument of the Log function

Argument	Description
dblExpression	Numeric expression for which you want to return the natural logarithm

Example Syntax

```
Dim dblNumber, dblResult as Double
dblNumber = 14
dblResult = Log(dblNumber)
```

Description	This example returns a double-precision number that represents the natural logarithm for 14.
	The logarithm of a number is the power to which the logarithmic base must be raised in order to achieve that number. The natural logarithmic base, also known as Euler's number, is referred to by the symbol e, and has an approximate value of 2.718282.
	The supplied numeric expression may be of any numeric format. It must be a nonzero number. If the expression is zero, an "Illegal function call" error will occur.
	Exp performs the inverse operation of a natural logarithm. It raises e to the power specified by the power parameter.

Randomize Statement

See Also	Rnd, Timer
Purpose	The Randomize statement seeds the random number generator, allowing the generation of a new sequence of random numbers. Table 19-11 describes the argument of the Randomize statement.

General Syntax

```
Randomize [lngSeed]
```

Table 19-11 Argument of the Randomize statement

Argument	Description
lngSeed	Seed number for a sequence of pseudo-random numbers

Example Syntax

```
Function RndInt(intLoNum As Integer, intHiNum As Integer) As Integer
    Static blnSeeded As Boolean
    Dim intRange As Integer
    'seed the random number generator if it has not
    'yet been done.
    If blnSeeded = False Then
        Randomize
        blnSeeded = True
    End If
    intRange = intHiNum - intLoNum + 1
    RndInt = Int(intRange * Rnd + intLoNum)
End Function
```

Description   This example is a function that uses the Randomize statement and Rnd function to return an integer in the range specified by the integer parameters intLoNum and intHiNum. No parameter is used for the Randomize statement, so the value from the Timer function is automatically used for the seed.

The Randomize statement seeds the random number generator. Random numbers can then be returned by the Rnd function. If this statement is not executed before the Rnd function, each time the program is run, the numbers generated will be the same. The lngSeed parameter should be a number in the range of -2,147,483,648 to 2,147,483,647. If it is omitted, Visual Basic will automatically use the value returned by the Timer function as the seed. This default is usually best for applications that require an unpredictable random number sequence. Seeding with a specific integer may be helpful for returning a repeatable set of "random" numbers during debugging.

RND FUNCTION

See Also   Randomize

Purpose   The Rnd function returns a single-precision random number between 0 and 1. Table 19-12 describes the argument of the Rnd function.

General Syntax

```
Rnd[(lngExpression)]
```

Table 19-12 Argument of the Rnd function

Argument	Description
lngExpression	A value determines which number in the pseudo-random sequence to return

Example Syntax

```
Function RndInt(intLoNum As Integer, intHiNum As Integer) As Integer
        Static blnSeeded As Boolean
        Dim intRange As Integer
        'seed the random number generator if it has not
        'yet been done.
        If blnSeeded = False Then
                Randomize
                blnSeeded = True
        End If
        intRange = intHiNum - intLoNum +1
        RndInt = Int(intRange * Rnd + intLoNum)
End Function
```

Description This example is a function that uses the Randomize statement and Rnd function to return an integer in the range specified by the integer parameters intLoNum and intHiNum.

The Randomize statement should be used before the first time the Rnd function is called. This seeds the random number generator. If this is not done, the numbers returned by the Rnd function will be the same every time the program is run.

The lngExpression tells the Rnd function what to return. If lngExpression is omitted, or has a value greater than 0, the next random number is returned. If lngExpression has a value of 0, the previous random number generated is returned. If lngExpression has a negative value, the same number is returned for any given lngExpression for use in debugging your application.

The preceding example shows how to convert the value returned by Rnd to a random integer within a specified range.

Sgn Function

See Also Abs

Purpose The Sgn function evaluates a numExpression and returns a value based on whether the numExpression is negative, positive, or 0. Table 19-13 describes the argument of the Sgn function.

General Syntax

```
Sgn(numExpression)
```

Table 19-13 Argument of the Sgn function

Argument	Description
numExpression	Numeric expresssion for which you want to determine the sign

Example Syntax

`intSign1 = Sgn(100)`	This example sets the variable intSign1 to 1, indicating that the numExpression evaluated was positive.
`intSign2 = Sgn(0)`	This example sets the variable intSign2 to 0, indicating that the numExpression evaluated was 0.
`intSign3 = Sgn(-100)`	This example sets the variable intSign3 to -1, indicating that the numExpression evaluated was negative.
Description	The Sgn function evaluates the supplied numExpression, and returns a -1 if it is negative, 1 if it is positive, and 0 if it equals 0.

SIN FUNCTION

See Also	Atn, Cos, Tan
Purpose	The Sin function returns the sine of an angle. Table 19-14 describes the argument of the Sin function.
General Syntax	

`Sin(dblAngle)`

Table 19-14 Argument of the Sin function

Argument	Description
dblAngle	Numeric expression for which you want to return the sine

Example Syntax

```
Dim dblResult as Double
dblResult = Sin(4.93)
```

Description	In this example, the sine of 4.93 is assigned to the variable dblResult.
	Sin is used to determine the sine of an angle. The function expects the angle to be expressed in radians; therefore, if the angle is in degrees, it must be converted using the formula radians = degrees × pi ÷ 180.

SQR FUNCTION

Purpose	The Sqr function returns the square root of a number. Table 19-15 describes the argument of the Sqr function.

General Syntax

```
Sqr(dblExpression)
```

Table 19-15 Argument of the Sqr function

Argument	Description
dblExpression	Numeric expression of which you want to return the square root

Example Syntax
```
Dim dblResult as Double
dblResult = Sqr(72)
```

Description	This example places the square root of 72 into the variable dblResult, giving it a value of 8.485281.
	This function requires that dblNumericExpression be a nonnegative number of any numeric data type.
Example	The Math project at the end of this chapter uses the Sqr function in the Pythagorean theorem to calculate the third side of a triangle when the lengths of two sides are known.

TAN FUNCTION

See Also	Atn, Cos, Sin
Purpose	The Tan function returns the tangent of an angle. Table 19-16 describes the argument of the Tan function.

General Syntax

```
Tan(dblAngle)
```

Table 19-16 Argument of the Tan function

Argument	Description
dblAngle	Numeric expression for which you want to return the tangent

Example Syntax
```
Dim dblResult as Double
dblResult = Tan(4.93)
```

Description
In this example, the tangent of 4.93 is assigned to the variable dblResult.

Tan is used to determine the tangent of an angle. The function expects the angle to be expressed in radians; therefore, if the angle is in degrees, it must be converted using the formula radians = degrees × pi ÷ 180.

The Math Project

Project Overview

The Math project uses the Pythagorean theorem to calculate the third side of a triangle using the values of the other two sides.

The following pages discuss the assembly and operation of the Math project. The first section deals with the assembly of the only form in the project. Next, there is a listing and explanation of the contents of the subroutines of this project. Finally, a How It Works guide to the operation of the project discusses the operation of the code. Please read this information carefully and use the pictures of the form to check your results. When you are finished, run the project and check out how the third side of the triangle is being calculated.

Assembling the Project

1. Make a new form with the objects and properties listed in Table 19-17.

Table 19-17 Elements of the main form

Object	Property	Setting
Form	Name	frmMain
	BorderStyle	3 - Fixed Dialog
	Caption	"Math Project"
	MaxButton	False
	MinButton	False
Label	Name	lblPythagoras
	Caption	"Pythagoras: C^2 = A^2 + B^2"
Line	Name	linTriangle
	Index	0
Line	Name	linTriangle
	Index	1
Line	Name	linTriangle
	Index	2
Label	Name	lblSide
	Index	0
	Caption	"A"

continued on next page

continued from previous page

Object	Property	Setting
Label	Name	lblSide
	Index	1
	Caption	"B"
Label	Name	lblLength
	Index	2
	Caption	"C"
TextBox	Name	txtLength
	Index	0
	Text	""
TextBox	Name	txtLength
	Index	1
	Text	""
TextBox	Name	txtLength
	Index	2
	Text	""
Label	Name	lblLength
	Index	0
	Caption	"Length of &A"
Label	Name	lblLength
	Index	1
	Caption	"Length of &B"
Label	Name	lblLength
	Index	2
	Caption	"Length of &C"
CommandButton	Name	cmdCalc
	Caption	"&Calculate"
CommandButton	Name	cmdExit
	Caption	"E&xit"

2. Size the objects on the screen as shown in Figure 19-2.

3. Go to the Form Layout window, right-click on the frmMain form, and select Center Screen as the startup position.

4. Add the following code to the declaration section of the Form.

```
Option Explicit

Private Const cAppTitle = "Math Project"
Private Const cNumLengthTextBoxes = 3

Private Const cAltitude = 0
Private Const cWidth = 1
Private Const cHypotenuse = 2
```

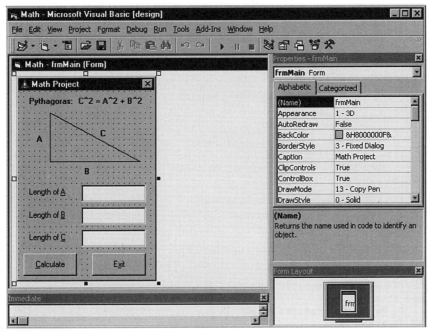

Figure 19-2   The frmMain form in design mode

5. Enter the following code in the Click event of the cmdExit button. This unloads the form and terminates the application.

```
Private Sub cmdExit_Click()
    Unload Me
End Sub
```

6. Enter the following code in the Click event of the cmdCalc button. After you have ensured that exactly two lengths were entered, you ensure that they are positive. If that is the case, you find out which one is missing and calculate its value.

```
Private Sub cmdCalc_Click()
Select Case NumValuesEntered
    Case 3
        ErrMsgBox "Leave the side you want calculated empty!"
    Case 2
        Dim intEmptyTextBox As Integer
        Dim dblHypotenuse As Double, dblAltitude As Double,  dblWidth As Double
        Dim blnAllPositive

        ' Make Sure Lengths are positive
        blnAllPositive = True
        dblAltitude = Val(txtLength(cAltitude).Text)
        blnAllPositive = blnAllPositive And isPositive(dblAltitude, "length A")

        dblWidth = Val(txtLength(cWidth).Text)
```

continued on next page

363

continued from previous page

```
        blnAllPositive = blnAllPositive And isPositive(dblWidth, "Length B")

        dblHypotenuse = Val(txtLength(cHypotenuse).Text)
        blnAllPositive = blnAllPositive And isPositive(dblHypotenuse, "Length C")

        If blnAllPositive Then
            intEmptyTextBox = FindLengthToBeCalculated
            Select Case intEmptyTextBox
            Case cAltitude
                If dblHypotenuse > dblWidth Then
                    txtLength(intEmptyTextBox).Text =  CalcSide(dblHypotenuse, dblWidth)
                Else
                    ErrMsgBox "Hypotenuse must be larger than the Width!"
                End If
            Case cWidth
                If dblHypotenuse > dblAltitude Then
                    txtLength(intEmptyTextBox).Text = ⇐
                    CalcSide(dblHypotenuse, dblAltitude)
                Else
                    ErrMsgBox "Hypotenuse must be larger " &  "than the Altitude!"
                End If
            Case cHypotenuse
                txtLength(intEmptyTextBox).Text = CalcHypotenuse(dblAltitude, dblWidth)
            Case Else
                ErrMsgBox "Unexpected error"
            End Select
        End If
    Case Else
        ErrMsgBox "You need to fill in two lengths!"
    End Select
End Sub
```

7. Add the following functions to the form.

```
Private Function NumValuesEntered() as Integer
    Dim i As Integer

    NumValuesEntered = 0
    For i = 0 To cNumLengthTextBoxes - 1
        If Val(txtLength(i).Text) <> 0 Then
            NumValuesEntered = NumValuesEntered + 1
        End If
    Next
End Function

Private Function FindLengthToBeCalculated() As Integer
    Dim i As Integer

    FindLengthToBeCalculated = -1
    For i = 0 To cNumLengthTextBoxes - 1
        If Val(txtLength(i).Text) = 0 Then
            FindLengthToBeCalculated = i
            Exit For
        End If
    Next
End Function
```

```
Private Function isPositive(dblNumber As Double, strVarName As String)  As Boolean
    isPositive = True

    If Sgn(dblNumber) < 0 Then
        ErrMsgBox "Please fill in a positive for " & strVarName & "!"
        isPositive = False
    End If
End Function

Private Sub ErrMsgBox(strMessage As String)
    MsgBox strMessage, vbOKOnly + vbCritical, cAppTitle
End Sub
```

8. Add a code module to the project. Name it modPythagoras and add the following code to it. These two functions use the Pythagorean theorem to calculate the third side of a triangle when the lengths of two sides are known.

```
Public Function CalcSide(dblHypotenuse As Double, dblOtherSide As Double)  as Double
    CalcSide = Sqr(dblHypotenuse ^ 2 - dblOtherSide ^ 2)
End Function

Public Function CalcHypotenuse(dblAltitude As Double, dblWidth As Double)  as Double
    CalcHypotenuse = Sqr(dblAltitude ^ 2 + dblWidth ^ 2)
End Function
```

How It Works

The core actions occur in the Click event of cmdCalc. NumValuesEntered is called to ensure that exactly two lengths were entered. If this is the case, three successive calls to isPositive ensure that all lengths are positive. If that is also the case, FindLengthToBeCalculated determines which one is missing.

Then, finally, either CalcSide or CalcHypotenuse is called to calculate the missing side. These functions use the well-known trigonometrical theorem discovered by the ancient Greek mathematician Pythagoras.

20

FINANCIAL

Visual Basic provides a series of financial functions to add to your programming arsenal. These functions include sophisticated math formulas optimized for their particular type of output.

These functions provide your applications with extraordinary financial math capabilities with very simple coding. An example of this is using the NPV function to determine the Net present value of an investment:

```
Private dblPeriod(4) As Double, dblRetRate as Double

dblRetRate = .0625
dblPeriod(0) = -10,000      'initial investment
dblPeriod(1) = 3500      'cash flows for given periods
dblPeriod(2) = 3850
dblPeriod(3) = 5500
dblPeriod(4) = 6500
MsgBox Format(NPV(dblRetRate, dblPeriods()),"$#####.00")      'returns NPV in Dollars: ⇐
$6014.31
```

This example illustrates the ease of use the NPV function provides to an application concerned with financial modeling.

Financial Summary

Table 20-1 describes the financial functions provided in Visual Basic. These are discussed in detail following the table, and the Financial project at the end of the chapter demonstrates their use.

Table 20-1 Financial functions provided in Visual Basic

Use This...	Type	To Do This...
DDB	Function	Calculate the depreciation of an asset using the double-declining method
FV	Function	Calculate the Future Value of an annuity
IPmt	Function	Calculate the interest payment for a given period of an annuity
IRR	Function	Calculate the internal rate of return for a series of cash flows

continued on next page

continued from previous page

Use This...	Type	To Do This...
MIRR	Function	Calculate the modified rate of return for a series of cash flows
NPer	Function	Calculate the number of periods for an annuity
NPV	Function	Calculate the net present value of an investment based on a series of periodic cash flows (payments and receipts) and a discount rate
Pmt	Function	Calculate the payment for an annuity
PPmt	Function	Calculate the principle payment for a given period
PV	Function	Calculate the present value of an annuity
Rate	Function	Calculate the interest rate per period for an annuity
SLN	Function	Calculate the straight-line depreciation of an asset for a single period
SYD	Function	Calculate the sum-of-years' digits depreciation of an asset

DDB Function

See Also SLN, SYD

Purpose The DDB function returns the depreciation of an asset based on the double-declining balance method. Table 20-2 summarizes the arguments of the DDB function.

General Syntax

```
DDB(dblCost, dblSalvage, dblLife, dblPeriod, [vntFactor])
```

Table 20-2 Arguments of the DDB function

Argument	Description
dblCost	Initial cost of the asset
dblSalvage	Salvage value of the asset
dblLife	Total life span of the asset
dblPeriod	Period for which you want to determine the depreciation amount of the asset
vntFactor	The rate at which the balance declines

Example Syntax

```
dblPeriodDepreciation = DDB(dblItemValue, 0, 30, dblWhichPeriod)
```

Description Use the DDB function to return the proper depreciation amount for a given item value at a given point in its life span. You can specify the initial cost of the item, the eventual salvage value of the item when finally scrapped, the total life span of the item, and which period you want to calculate for. The period must be in the same units as the life span.

vntFactor specifies the rate at which the balance declines. If this optional parameter is omitted, 2 (double-declining balance method) is assumed. This places the bulk of the depreciation at the beginning of the life span and progressively less at the end. The DDB function uses the following formula to calculate depreciation for a given period:

```
dblPeriodDepreciation / dblPeriod = ((dblCost    dblSalvage) * vntFactor) ⇐ / dblLife
```

FV FUNCTION

See Also	NPV, PV
Purpose	Use the FV function to determine the future value of an annuity based on constant payments and a constant interest rate. Table 20-3 summarizes the arguments of the FV function.

General Syntax

```
FV(dblRate, intNumPeriods, dblPayment, [vntPresentValue, [vntWhenDue]])
```

Table 20-3 Arguments of the FV function

Argument	Description
dblRate	Effective interest rate of the annuity
intNumPeriods	Number of payments
dblPayment	Payment amount of the annuity
vntPresentValue	Starting value of the annuity
vntWhenDue	Number specifying whether the payments are due at the beginning (1) or end of the period (0)

Example Syntax

```
dblAmountSaved = FV(dblInterestRate / 12, intNumberMonths, ⇐
dblAmountInvestedPerMonth, 0, 0)
```

Description   The FV function returns the future value of an annuity, given constant payments and a constant interest rate. You can use this function either for investments (positive payments) or loans (negative payments). The number of periods should be given in the same units of measure as the interest rate. The vntWhenDue argument specifies when the payment is due: at the end of the period (0), or at the beginning of the period (1). The end of the period (0) is assumed if this argument is missing.

The sample syntax shows how the FV function can return the total amount of money accrued in an interest-bearing account, given a constant revenue stream. In this case, the annual percentage interest rate is divided by 12 to obtain a monthly interest, and the number of periods is given in months. The amount put into the account every month is given by dblAmountInvestedPerMonth. Note that the vntPresentValue of the account is given as 0 to indicate this is a new savings account started with a zero balance. Zero balance is also assumed when this optional argument is missing.

IPmt Function

See Also   Pmt, PPmt, Rate

Purpose   The IPmt function returns the interest portion of a payment on an annuity, given constant payments and constant interest rate. Table 20-4 summarizes the arguments of the IPmt function.

General Syntax

```
IPmt(dblRate, dblCurrentPeriod, dblNumberTotalPeriods, [vntPresentValue, [vntFutureValue,
[vntWhenDue]]])
```

Table 20-4 Arguments of the IPmt function

Argument	Description
dblRate	Effective interest rate of the annuity
dblCurrentPeriod	Sequential number representing the current period
dblNumberTotalPeriods	Number of payments
vntPresentValue	Starting value of the annuity
vntFutureValue	Value of the annuity when it is complete
vntWhenDue	Number specifying whether the payments are due at the beginning (1) or end of the period (0)

Example Syntax

```
interest = IPmt(dblRate/12, dblThisMonth, 360, vntLoanAmount, 0, 0)
```

Description   Use the IPmt function to return the interest portion of an annuity payment. The function assumes that payments and interest rates remain constant for the life of the annuity.

Make sure that the interest rate and dblNumberTotalPeriods are in the same units—for example, months or years. The vntPresentValue is the current value of the loan (or starting value of an annuity). A present value of 0 is used if none was supplied. vntFutureValue is the value of the loan or annuity when complete. Loans will generally have a vntFutureValue of $0, while a savings program will have a positive amount, such as $100,000 for a retirement fund. A future value of 0 is used when this argument is missing. The vntWhenDue argument specifies when payments are due: 0 if due at the end of the period, and 1 if the payment is due at the beginning of the period. The end of the period (0) is assumed if this argument is missing.

The sample syntax gives the interest portion of a 30-year home mortgage (dblNumberTotalPeriods = 30 × 12 = 360).

Example   The Financial project at the end of this chapter uses the IPmt function to determine the interest payments in the mortgage amortization schedule.

IRR FUNCTION

See Also   MIRR, Rate

Purpose   Use the IRR function to return the Internal Rate of Return for a series of periodic payments and receipts. Table 20-5 summarizes the arguments of the IRR function.

General Syntax

```
IRR(dblValuesArray( ), [vntGuess])
```

Table 20-5 Arguments of the IRR function

Argument	Description
dblValuesArray	Array of cashflows
vntGuess	Estimate for the IRR used as a starting point in the first iteration

Example Syntax

```
dblMoney(0) = -500000      'first year startup costs
dblMoney(1) = -250000      'second year operation costs
dblMoney(2) = 0            'third year breakeven
dblMoney(3) = 100000       'fourth year profit
dblMoney(4) = 300000
dblMoney(5) = 500000
dblMoney(6) = 2000000      'seventh year cashout
return = IRR(dblMoney(), 0.20) * 100
```

Description   The IRR function can provide the overall rate of return for an investment that has a varying payment and receipt schedule. The dblValuesArray() argument is a one-dimensional array holding the monetary values; it must have at least one negative amount (the payment) and one positive amount (the receipt). As the example syntax shows, you can provide a varying cash flow stream for the function to evaluate. The IRR function uses the vntGuess argument as its starting point in an iterative process that refines the returned value to within 0.00001 percent. If vntGuess is omitted, 0.1 is used. If vntGuess is too different from the actual return, IRR may fail to derive a final figure within 20 iterations and will fail.

IRR evaluates a varying cash flow, while the annuity functions (Pmt, IPmt, FV, NPV, and so on) only work with a steady stream of payments.

The sample syntax shows how IRR can derive the return for a business startup that loses substantial amounts of money in the beginning but pays off handsomely in the end. This "internal rate of return" is analogous to the APR of a loan.

MIRR FUNCTION

See Also   IRR, Rate

Purpose   The MIRR function returns the Modified Internal Rate of Return for a varying series of cash flows. Table 20-6 summarizes the arguments of the MIRR function.

General Syntax

```
MIRR(dblValuesArray( ), dblFinanceInterestRate, dblReinvestmentInternalRate)
```

Table 20-6 Arguments of the MIRR function

Argument	Description
dblValuesArray	Array of cash flows
dblFinanceInterestRate	Interest rate of initial investment
dblReinvestmentInternalRate	Interest rate for reinvested monies

Example Syntax

```
dblMoney(0) = -500000        'first year startup costs
dblMoney(1) = -250000        'second year operation costs
dblMoney(2) = 0              'third year breakeven
dblMoney(3) = 100000         'fourth year profit
dblMoney(4) = 300000
dblMoney(5) = 500000
dblMoney(6) = 2000000        'seventh year cashout
dblFinanceRate = 0.1         'ten percent charged to borrow money
dblReinvestRate = 0.8        'eight percent reinvestment rate
dblReturn = MIRR(dblMoney(), dblFinanceRate, dblReinvestRate) * 100
```

Description   The MIRR function returns the Modified Internal Rate of Return for a varying series of cash flows. The MIRR differs from the IRR in that it accounts for the finance charges associated with borrowing the initial investment (or the "opportunity cost" of not being able to invest the money in other ventures) as well as the interest earned on reinvestment of returns.

The values array can have a varying cash flow, but must have at least one negative value (the investment) and one positive value (the return).

The sample syntax shows how to calculate the MIRR given a cash flow of high startup costs financed at 10% APR and reinvesting the payouts at 8% APR.

NPer Function

See Also   IPmt, Pmt, PPmt, Rate

Purpose   The NPer function calculates the number of periods for an annuity, assuming constant payments and interest rate. Table 20-7 summarizes the arguments of the NPer function.

General Syntax

```
NPer(dblInterestRate, dblPeriodicPayment, vntPresentValue, [vntFutureValue, [vntWhenDue]])
```

Table 20-7 Arguments of the NPer function

Argument	Description
dblInterestRate	Interest rate
dblPeriodicPayment	Periodic payment
vntPresentValue	Starting value of annuity
vntFutureValue	Value of the annuity when it is complete
vntWhenDue	Number specifying whether the payments are due at the beginning (1) or end of the period (0)

Example Syntax

```
dblNumMonths = NPer(0.0975/12, 350.00, -12000, 0, 0)
```

Description   Use the NPer function to determine how many payments must be made on a loan to pay it off, or how many deposits must be made to achieve a savings goal. It assumes the payments are constant and periodic, and the interest rate does not vary. Make sure the interest rate is given in the same units as the number of payments.

vntPresentValue is the current value of the loan. vntFutureValue is the value of the loan when complete. Loans will generally have a vntFutureValue of $0, and this is the value used when this argument is missing. The vntWhenDue argument specifies when payments are due: 0 if due at the end of the period, and 1 if the payment is due at the beginning of the period. The end of the period (0) is assumed if this argument is missing.

The example syntax determines the number of monthly payments necessary to pay off a $12,000 loan (note the negative sign) at 9.75% APR.

NPV Function

See Also   FV, IRR, MIRR, PV

Purpose	The NPV function returns the net present value of a varying series of periodic cash flows (both negative and positive) at a given discount rate. Table 20-8 summarizes the arguments of the NPV function.
General Syntax	

```
NPV(dblDiscountRate!, dblValuesArray( ) )
```

Table 20-8 Arguments of the NPV function

Argument	Description
dblDiscountRate	Discount rate
dblValuesArray	Array of cash flows

Example Syntax

```
dblMoney(0) = -500000        'first year startup costs
dblMoney(1) = -250000        'second year operation costs
dblMoney(2) = 0              'third year breakeven
dblMoney(3) = 100000         'fourth year profit
dblMoney(4) = 300000
dblMoney(5) = 500000
dblMoney(6) = 2000000        'seventh year cashout
dblFinanceRate = 0.1         'ten percent APR
dblReturn = NPV(dblFinanceRate, dblMoney() )
```

Description	Use the NPV function to determine the net present value of a series of varying cash flows. Note that this differs from the PV function in that the payments can vary over time. The values array must have at least one negative and one positive number.

Pmt Function

See Also	IPmt, NPer, PPmt, Rate
Purpose	Use the Pmt function to return the total payment amount (principal and interest) on an annuity, assuming constant periodic payments and a constant interest rate. Table 20-9 summarizes the arguments of the Pmt function.
General Syntax	

```
Pmt(dblInterestRate, intNumberOfPayments, vntPresentValue, [vntFutureValue, [vntWhenDue]])
```

Table 20-9 Arguments of the Pmt function

Argument	Description
dblInterestRate	Interest rate
intNumberOfPayments	Number of payments
vntPresentValue	Starting value of the annuity
vntFutureValue	Value of the annuity when it is complete
vntWhenDue	Number specifying whether the payments are due at the beginning (1) or end of the period (0)

Example Syntax

```
dblTotalPayment = Pmt(dblRate/12, intNumPayments, -dblMortgage, 0, 0)
```

Description　Use the Pmt function to determine the total payment (both interest and principal) on an annuity. The annuity can either be a loan (negative dblPresentValue) or an investment (positive dblPresentValue).

The function assumes a steady stream of unchanging payments, and a nonvarying interest rate. vntPresentValue is the current value of the loan. vntFutureValue is the value of the loan when complete. Loans will generally have a vntFutureValue of $0, and this is the value used when this argument is missing. The vntWhenDue argument determines when the payments are made: 0 indicates the end of the payment period, and 1 the beginning of the payment period. The end of the period (0) is assumed if this argument is missing. Make sure that the dblInterestRate and intNumberOfPayments arguments are in the same units.

Example　The Financial project at the end of this chapter uses the Pmt function to determine the total payments (both principal and interest) in the mortgage amortization schedule.

PPMT FUNCTION

See Also　IPmt, NPer, Pmt, Rate

Purpose　The PPmt function returns the amount of principal payment for an annuity, assuming constant periodic payments and an unvarying interest rate. Table 20-10 summarizes the arguments of the PPmt function.

General Syntax

```
PPmt(dblInterestRate, intWhichPeriod, intTotalPeriods, vntPresentValue, [vntFutureValue,
[vntWhenDue]])
```

Table 20-10 Arguments of the PPmt function

Argument	Description
dblInterestRate	Interest rate
intWhichPeriod	Sequential number representing current period
intTotalPeriods	Total number of periods
vntPresentValue	Starting value of the annuity
vntFutureValue	Value of the annuity when it is complete
vntWhenDue	Number specifying whether the payments are due at the beginning (1) or end of the period (0)

Example Syntax

```
dblPrinicipal = PPmt(dblRate/12, intPeriod, 360, dblMortageAmount, 0, 0)
```

Description   Use PPmt to get the amount of principal paid on a loan or investment for a particular period. The function assumes that payments are periodic and unvarying, and that the interest rate remains constant.

vntFutureValue is the value of the loan when complete. Loans will generally have a vntFutureValue of $0, and this is the value used when this argument is missing. The vntWhenDue argument specifies when payments are due: 0 if due at the end of the period, and 1 if the payment is due at the beginning of the period. The end of the period (0) is assumed if this argument is missing.

The example syntax uses the PPmt function to get the principal on a 30-year (30 years × 12 months = 360) home mortgage. The amount borrowed is given the dblMortgageAmount argument, the interest rate in the dblInterestRate, and the particular period by the periods arguments. This example might be in a For...Next loop to step through each period and print out a principal payment table.

Make sure that the interest rate and the number of periods are in the same units. The example syntax takes a yearly interest rate and divides it by 12 to put it in the same units (months) as the periods arguments.

Example   The Financial project at the end of this chapter uses the PPmt function to determine the principal payments in the mortgage amortization schedule.

PV FUNCTION

See Also   FV, IRR, MIRR, NPV

Purpose   Use the PV function to derive the present value of an annuity, assuming a constant stream of periodic payments and an unvarying interest rate. Table 20-11 summarizes the arguments of the PV function.

General Syntax

```
PV(dblInterestRate, intTotalPeriods, dblPayment, [vntFutureValue, [vntWhenDue]])
```

Table 20-11 Arguments of the PV function

Argument	Description
dblInterestRate	Interest rate
intTotalPeriods	Total number of payments
dblPayment	Amount of payment
vntFutureValue	Value of the annuity when it is complete
vntWhenDue	Number specifying whether the payments are due at the beginning (1) or end of the period (0)

Example Syntax

```
dblPresentValue = PV(dblRate, 360, dblPayout, 0, 0)
```

Description   The PV function returns the present value of an annuity. It assumes a steady stream of unvarying payments and an unvarying interest rate. The annuity may be either a loan (negative present value) or an investment (positive present value).

vntFutureValue is the value of the loan when complete. Loans will generally have a vntFutureValue of $0, and this is the value used when this argument is missing. The vntWhenDue argument specifies when payments are due: 0 if due at the end of the period, and 1 if the payment is due at the beginning of the period. The end of the period (0) is assumed if this argument is missing.

The example syntax calculates how much money you could borrow at a given interest rate given a monthly payment of dblPayout.

RATE FUNCTION

See Also   IPmt, NPer, Pmt, PPmt

Purpose   The Rate function returns the interest rate of an annuity, given a constant periodic series of cash payments and an unvarying interest rate. Table 20-12 summarizes the arguments of the Rate function.

General Syntax

```
Rate(dblTotalPeriods, dblPayment, dblPresentValue, [vntFutureValue, [vntWhenDue,
[vntGuess]]])
```

Table 20-12 Arguments of the Rate function

Argument	Description
dblTotalPeriods	Total number of periods
dblPayment	Periodic payment
vntPresentValue	Starting value of the annuity
vntFutureValue	Value of the annuity when it is complete
vntWhenDue	Number specifying whether the payments are due at the beginning (1) or end of the period (0)
vntGuess	Estimate for the Rate used as a starting point in the first iteration

Example Syntax

```
dblRate = Rate(360, 600, -100000, 0, 0.1) * 12
```

Description   Use the Rate function to determine the interest rate of a loan or investment, given the total number of payments, the payment, and the starting and ending values of the loan. This function assumes that payments will be made regularly, and both payments and interest rate remain unchanging.

The example calculates the interest rate on a 30-year $100,000 loan, given a $600 payment. Note that you need to multiply the result of the Rate function by the number of months per year to derive the yearly interest rate. Loans have negative present values, and investments have positive values.

vntFutureValue is the value of the loan when complete. Loans will generally have a vntFutureValue of $0, and this is the value used when this argument is missing. The vntWhenDue argument specifies when payments are due: 0 if due at the end of the period, and 1 if the payment is due at the beginning of the period. The end of the period (0) is assumed if this argument is missing.

Rate is an iterative function, and uses the vntGuess argument to begin its iterative process. If vntGuess is too far away from the actual interest rate, the function may not converge. If vntGuess is missing, 0.1 is used.

SLN Function

See Also   DDB, SYD

Purpose   Use the SLN function to return the straight-line depreciation of an asset. Table 20-13 summarizes the arguments of the SLN function.

General Syntax

```
SLN(dblInitialCost, dblSalvageValue, dblLifeSpan)
```

Table 20-13 Arguments of the SLN function

Argument	Description
dblInitialCost	Initial cost of the asset
dblSalvageValue	Salvage value of the asset
dblLifeSpan	Total life span of the asset

Example Syntax

```
dblYearlyDepreciation=SLN(50000, 2500, 10)
```

Description   The SLN function returns the depreciation value for an asset. You provide the initial cost of the item, the eventual salvage value (what it is worth after its useful life span), and the total life span. SLN will return the average depreciation.

SYD Function

See Also   DDB, SLN

Purpose   The SYD function returns the sum-of-years' digits depreciation of an asset. Table 20-14 summarizes the arguments of the SYD function.

General Syntax

```
SYD(dblInitialCost, dblSalvageValue, dblLifeSpan, dblPeriod)
```

Table 20-14 Arguments of the SYD function

Argument	Description
dblInitialCost	Initial cost of the asset
dblSalvageValue	Salvage value of the asset
dblLifeSpan	Total life span of the asset
dblPeriod	Sequential number representing current period

Example Syntax

```
For i=1 to 10
     Print SYD(10000, 800, 10, i)
Next i
```

Description   This function returns the depreciation value for a given period using the sum-of-years' digits algorithm. This gives a weighted depreciation schedule, with a greater amount of depreciation in the beginning than that of the SLN depreciation.

You provide the initial cost of the item, the salvage value (what it could be sold for at the end of its life span), the total amount of time it will be in service, and the particular period you need. Note that different periods will yield different depreciation results.

The Financial Project

Project Overview

The Financial project calculates monthly payments and the amortization schedule of a mortgage, based on the amount, principal, and amortization period of the mortgage. It does this for both U.S. and Canadian type mortgages.

The following pages discuss the assembly and operation of the Financial project. The first section deals with the assembly of the only form in the project. Next, there is a listing and explanation of the contents of the subroutines of this project. Finally, a How It Works guide to the operation of the project discusses the operation of the code. Please read this information carefully and use the pictures of the form to check your results.

Assembling the Project

1. Make a new form with the objects and properties listed in Table 20-15.

Table 20-15 Elements of the main form

Object	Property	Setting
Form	Name	frmMain
	BorderStyle	3- Fixed Dialog
	Caption	"Financial Project"
	MaxButton	False
	MinButton	False
Label	Name	lblInput
	Index	0
	Caption	"&Principal Loan Balance:"
Label	Name	lblInput
	Index	1
	Caption	"&Interest Rate (%):"
Label	Name	lblInput
	Index	2
	Caption	"&Length of the Loan (Years):"
TextBox	Name	txtPrincipal
	Text	""
TextBox	Name	txtInterest

Object	Property	Setting
	Text	""
TextBox	Name	txtLengthInYears
	Text	""
OptionButton	Name	optRateType
	Caption	"&Canada"
	Index	0
	Value	False
OptionButton	Name	optRateType
	Caption	"&US"
	Index	1
	Value	True
CommandButton	Name	cmdCalc
	Caption	"C&alculate"
CommandButton	Name	cmdExit
	Caption	"E&xit"

2. Size the objects on the screen as shown in Figure 20-1.

3. Go to the Form Layout window, right-click on the frmMain form, and select Center Screen as the startup position.

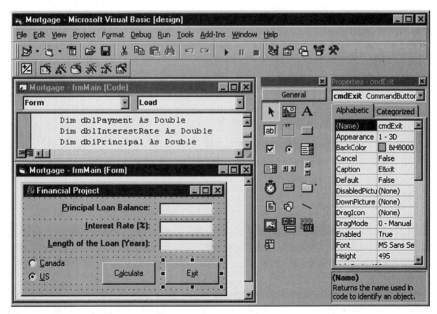

Figure 20-1 The frmMain form in design mode

4. Enter the following code in the form Load event. This sets some default values for the principal, interest rate, and mortgage duration.

```
Private Sub Form_Load()
    txtPrincipal.Text = 100000
    txtInterest.Text = 8
    txtLengthInYears.Text = 30
End Sub
```

5. Enter the following code in the Click event of the cmdExit button. This unloads the form and terminates the application.

```
Private Sub cmdExit_Click()
    Unload Me
End Sub
```

6. Enter the following declaration in the general section of the form, defining a constant for the index of the optRateType control array.

```
Private Const cOptCanadaRate = 0
```

7. Enter the following code in the Click event of the cmdCalc button. This converts the rate to a U.S. rate, if needed, and calculates the monthly payment. Then the amortization is scheduled for each period, giving the choice to stop at each period.

```
Private Sub cmdCalc_Click()
Dim dblPayment As Double
    Dim dblInterestRate As Double
    Dim dblPrincipal As Double

    If optRateType(cOptCanadaRate).Value Then
        dblInterestRate = ConvertToUSRate(Val(txtInterest.Text))
    Else ' US = default
        dblInterestRate = Val(txtInterest.Text)
    End If

    dblPrincipal = Val(txtPrincipal.Text)
    dblPayment = Pmt(dblInterestRate / 1200, Val(txtLengthInYears.Text) * ⇐
12, -dblPrincipal)

    If vbYes = AskYN("Your payment will be " & Money(dblPayment) & " per ⇐
month." & vbCrLf & vbCrLf & _
    "Do you want to see the amortization schedule?") Then
        Amortize dblInterestRate, CInt(txtLengthInYears.Text), dblPrincipal
    End If
End Sub
```

8. Add a class module to the project. Name it modMortgage and add the following code to it. The function you used in the previous section to convert to a U.S. rate is seen here, as is the iterative amortization display routine. Finally, two helper functions are implemented: a function to convert an amount into a formatted string, and a Yes/No message box function wrapper.

```
Private Const cAppTitle = "Financial Project"

Public Function ConvertToUSRate(dblCanadianRate As Double) As Double
    ConvertToUSRate = 1200 * ((1 + dblCanadianRate / 200) ^ (1 / 6) - 1)
End Function

Public Sub Amortize(dblInterestRate As Double, intLengthInYears As Integer, ⇐
dblPrincipal As Double)
    Dim intPaymentCnt As Integer
    Dim dblRemainingPrincipal As Double
    Dim dblPrincipalPayment As Double
    Dim blnMore As Boolean

    intPaymentCnt = 0
    dblRemainingPrincipal = dblPrincipal
    blnMore = True
    While dblRemainingPrincipal > 0 And blnMore
        intPaymentCnt = intPaymentCnt + 1
        dblPrincipalPayment = PPmt(dblInterestRate / 1200, intPaymentCnt, ⇐
intLengthInYears * 12, -dblPrincipal)
        dblRemainingPrincipal = dblRemainingPrincipal - dblPrincipalPayment

        blnMore = (vbYes = AskYN("Payment #" & Trim(intPaymentCnt) & vbCrLf & _
            "Interest Payment = " & Money(IPmt(dblInterestRate / 1200, intPaymentCnt, ⇐
intLengthInYears * 12, -dblPrincipal)) & vbCrLf & _
            "Principal Payment = " & Money(dblPrincipalPayment) & vbCrLf & _
            "Remaining Principal = " & Money(dblRemainingPrincipal) & vbCrLf & vbCrLf & _
            "Continue with the next payment?"))
    Wend
End Sub

Public Function Money(dblAmount As Double) As String
    Money = Format(dblAmount, "$###,###,###,##0.00")
End Function

Public Function AskYN(strQuestion As String) As Integer
    AskYN = MsgBox(strQuestion, vbYesNo + vbExclamation, cAppTitle)
End Function
```

How It Works

American mortgages are calculated monthly and are payable at the start of the period. Canadian mortgages, because of the Interest Act of Canada, are calculated semiannually and are payable at the end of the period. The following formula converts a Canadian interest rate into a U.S. rate:

```
ConvertToUSRate = 1200 * ((1 + dblCanadianRate / 200) ^ (1 / 6) - 1)
```

The Pmt function is used to calculate the monthly payment. Note that the rate is divided by 1200 to determine the monthly rate and the length in years is multiplied by 12 to use the same monthly unit of measurement.

In Amortize, we calculate the interest and principal payment for each period using IPmt and PPmt. We deduct these amounts from the remaining principal and iterate until the last period is reached or the user indicates that enough periods were computed.

21

CONVERSION

Visual Basic has eight numeric formats: Boolean, Byte, Integer, Long, Single, Double, Date, and Currency. Each format is stored in memory in a different manner. There are times in a program when variables of one type must be converted to another type before they can be accurately used. For instance, when a sub procedure is called with arguments, any values passed to the procedure must be of the type that the sub procedure is expecting. If the value you need to pass is not in the correct format, it must be converted before it is passed. If you assign a value to a variable, Visual Basic will automatically handle any conversion needed. Therefore:

```
dblValue = 200.22
sngValue = dblValue
Call Test(sngValue)
```

In this example, the value is automatically converted to single-precision format before it is assigned to the variable sngValue. However, if the only reason you are doing this assignment is to pass the value to a sub procedure or function, it adds an extra line of code to your program and creates an extra variable that is otherwise not needed. A better solution is to use one of the numeric conversion functions: CBool, CByte, CDate, CInt, CLng, CSng, CDbl, or CCur. Each of these functions converts a numeric value from any other type to the type indicated by the function. Using a conversion function eliminates the extra line of code and the extra variable used in the above example:

```
dblValue = 200.22
Call Test(CSng(dblValue))
```

Two more functions are used to convert numeric values. These are the Int and Fix functions. Like the CInt function, these functions convert a numeric value (such as a single- or double-precision decimal) to integer format. Both of these differ slightly from the CInt function in how they treat the fractional portion of the supplied argument. While CInt will round the fractional portion to the nearest whole number, Int returns the next lowest integer value, and Fix simply truncates the fractional portion without doing any rounding, as shown in Table 21-1.

Table 21-1 Return values for the Fix, Int, and CInt functions

Value	Int(Value)	Fix(Value)	CInt(Value)
2.7	2	2	3
2.2	2	2	2
2	2	2	2
-2	-2	-2	-2
-2.2	-3	-2	-2
-2.7	-3	-2	-3

Notice that for a negative number such as -2.7, Fix returns -2 because that is the next lower integer, whereas Int returns -3 because that is the closest integer.

The final conversion function converts a string into a numeric value. This is done with the Val function. Val accepts one string argument, and if that argument contains a readable number, it will return that number's value. Val does this by examining the supplied string from left to right. It begins its translation as soon as it encounters a character that is not a space. The translation ends as soon as it encounters a nonnumeric character. For example:

```
strAddress1 = " 1234 Street"
atrAddress2 = " ThisTown, Ca, 92122"
dblValue1 = Val(atrAddress1)
dblValue2 = Val(atrAddress2)
```

In this example, dblValue1 will be assigned a value of 1234. Because the Val function encounters nonnumeric characters before any numeric characters in strAddress2, dblValue2 will be assigned a value of 0.

Hexadecimal and Octal Notation

By default, numeric values in Visual Basic are decimal (base 10) numbers. However, you can use hexadecimal (base 16) or octal (base 8) notation to specify values. These two forms of notation are sometimes used because they more readily represent the internal organization of computer memory. References to addresses in memory are therefore usually given in hexadecimal. Hexadecimal notation is indicated by preceding a hexadecimal number with the prefix "&H". Octal numbers are preceded by an "&O". For instance:

```
intNum1% = &H100     'assign hexadecimal 100 to intNum1% (hexadecimal 100 = decimal 256)
intNum2% = &O100     'assign octal 100 to intNum2% (octal 100 = decimal 64)
```

Visual Basic also provides a way to translate decimal numbers for display in hexadecimal or octal format with the Hex and Oct functions. Each of these functions requires a numeric argument and returns a string that is the value of the argument in the respective notation.

```
strHexNum = Hex(256)
strOctNum = Oct(64)
```

In this example, the string variable strHexNum will have a value of "100", and strOctNum will also have a value of "100".

Conversion Summary

Table 21-2 lists the conversion functions available to you. These are discussed in detail following the table, and the Conversion project at the end of the chapter demonstrates their use.

Table 21-2 Summary of conversion functions

Use This...	To Do This...
CBool	Convert a numeric or string expression to Boolean
CByte	Convert a numeric or string expression to Byte
CCur	Convert a numeric or string expression to Currency
CDate	Convert a numeric or string expression to Date
CDbl	Convert a numeric or string expression to Double
CDec	Convert a numeric or string expression to Decimal
CInt	Convert a numeric or string expression to Integer
CLng	Convert a numeric or string expression to Long
CSng	Convert a numeric or string expression to Single
CStr	Convert a numeric or string expression to String
CVar	Convert a numeric or string expression to Variant
Format	Format an expression according to a format expression
Hex	Return a string representing the hexadecimal value of a number
Oct	Return a variant (string) representing the octal value of a number
Str	Return a variant (string) representing the decimal value of a number
Val	Return the numbers contained in a string as a numeric value of appropriate type

C<TYPE> (NUMERIC CONVERSION FUNCTIONS)

Purpose   Functions whose names have the form C<Type> convert an expression from any data type into the specified data type. The actual functions used for different data types are shown here.

General Syntax

```
CBool(expression)
CByte(expression)
CCur(expression)
CDate(expression)CDbl(expression)
CDec(expression)
CInt(expression)
CLng(expression)
CSng(expression)
CStr(expression)
CVar(expression)
```

Example Syntax

```
A = CBool(Int%)        'convert from Integer to Boolean
B = CByte(Int%)        'convert from Integer to Byte
C@ = CCur(Dbl#)        'convert from Double to Currency
D = CDate(Dbl#)        'convert from Double to Date
E = CDec(&Hex)         ' convert from Hexadecimal to Decimal
F# = CDbl(Vnt)         'convert from Variant to Double
G% = CInt(Lng&)        'convert from Long to Integer
H& = CLng(Vnt)         'convert from Variant to Long
I! = CSng(Cnc@)        'convert from Currency to Single
     J$ = CStr(Dbl#)       'convert from Double to String
K = CVar(Lng&)         'convert from Long to Variant
```

The previous examples demonstrate the use of the ten data type conversion functions.

Description There are seven numeric data type conversion functions, one date conversion function, one string type conversion function, and one variant type conversion function in Visual Basic. These are CBool (convert to Boolean), CByte (convert to byte), CCur (convert to currency) , CDate (convert to date), CDbl (convert to double), CDec (convert to decimal), CInt (convert to integer), CLng (convert to long), CSng (convert to single), CStr (convert to string), and CVar (convert to variant).

Each method converts an expression from any data type to the type specified by the function. You can generally do the same thing, without the explicit use of the conversion functions, by assigning an expression to a variable of the desired data type, but the explicit use of the conversion functions can make your code clearer and less prone to obscure errors. These functions can also be used to ensure that the correct data type is being passed to a Visual Basic sub procedure or a Windows dynamic link library (DLL).

With the numeric functions, the numeric expression parameter must be within the range of the resultant data type or Visual Basic will issue an overflow error.

Example The Conversion project at the end of this chapter uses the CLong function to convert strings to long integers. These strings are correctly parsed whether they are in decimal, octal or hexadecimal notation merely by using the Clong function.

FORMAT FUNCTION

See Also DateSerial, Now, Str, TimeSerial

Purpose The Format function formats a numeric expression, date type, or string according to a specified pattern. Table 21-3 summarizes the arguments of the Format function.

General Syntax

```
Format(Expression [, editpattern [,FirstDayOfYear [FirstWeekOfYear]]])
```

Table 21-3 Arguments of the Format function

Argument	Description
Expression	Any valid expression
editPattern	A valid format expression
FirstDayOfYear	A constant that specifies the first day of the week
FirstWeekOfYear	A constant that specifies the first week of the year

Example Syntax

```
N! = 545.3
Label1.Caption = Format$(N!, "###.00")
```

This example sets the Caption property of Label1 to "545.30".

```
D# = DateValue("08/22/1964")
Label2.Caption = Format$(D#, "dddd, mmmm dd, yyyy")
```

This example sets the Caption property of Label2 to "Saturday, August 22, 1964".

```
T# = TimeValue("01:02:45")
Label3.Caption = Format$(T#, "h:mm")
```

Description This example sets the Caption property of Label3 to "1:02".

Any number can be converted to a formatted string. For a number, the edit pattern can have one of four styles. The first style supplies one edit pattern, and all numbers are converted using that pattern. The second style has two edit patterns separated by a semicolon. Nonnegative numbers will be formatted according to the first edit pattern, and negative numbers will use the second. The third style has three edit patterns, all separated by semicolons. The first pattern is used to format positive numbers, the second for negative, the third for 0, and the fourth for null values.

Table 21-4 details the numeric formatting characters, and their uses.

Table 21-4 Numeric format symbols

Symbol	Effect of Symbol
0	Zero-digit placeholder. If the number has fewer digits than the edit pattern, the empty digits are 0-filled.
#	Null-digit placeholder. If the number has fewer digits than the edit pattern, the empty digits become null. This placeholder does not blank fill. Therefore, the resultant string may be shorter than the original edit pattern.
%	Percentage placeholder. This symbol returns the result of the number multiplied by 100, and appends a % to it.
.	Decimal placeholder. Indicates where the decimal point is to be placed in the edit string.

continued on next page

continued from previous page

Symbol	Effect of Symbol
,	Thousands separator. This is used to separate every three digits to the left of the decimal to make a long number more readable. Two commas adjacent to each other cause the three digits that would be between them to be ignored. The same effect is created when a comma is used just to the left of the decimal placeholder.
E-, e-	Returns the number in scientific format. This requires that a digit placeholder (0 or #) be placed to the immediate left of the E or e, or an "Illegal function call" error will occur. An appropriate number of digit placeholders should be placed to the right of the - in order to display the exponent. A minus sign will be inserted next to any negative exponents.
E+, e+	Returns the number in scientific notation. Works the same as E- and e-, but a + sign is inserted next to any positive exponents as well as a - sign next to negative exponents.
-, +, $, (,)	These characters will be returned literally and do not affect the format of the number.
\char	This symbol returns the character specified by char. The backslash is not returned.
"string"	Enclosing a string in quotes will return that string literally. Quotation marks can only be inserted into an edit pattern via the use of Chr$(34) and string concatenation.

Dates Dates can be converted to a string with a variety of date formats. Table 21-5 details the date string formatting symbols, and what is returned when a date type for the date 07/04/1995 is used.

Table 21-5 Date format symbols

Symbol	Example	Effect of Symbol
/	/	Date separator
-	-	Date separator
d	4	Returns the day of the month, omitting any leading 0
dd	04	Returns the day of the month with a leading 0, if needed
ddd	Sat	Returns the abbreviated day of the week
dddd	Saturday	Returns the full name of the day of the week
ddddd	07/04/1995	Returns the full date string in Short Date format specified by WIN.INI
dddddd	July 04, 1995	Returns the full date string in Long Date format specified by WIN.INI
w	3	Returns day of week as number (Sunday = 1, Saturday = 7)
ww	34	Returns week of year as number (1–53)
m	7	Returns the number of the month of the year, without a leading 0
mm	07	Returns the number of the month of the year, with a leading 0
mmm	Jul	Returns the abbreviated name of the month
mmmm	July	Returns the full name of the month
q	2	Returns the number of the quarter (1–4)
y	243	Returns the number of the day of the year (1–366)
yy	95	Returns the two-digit year
yyyy	1995	Returns the four-digit year
c		Returns date variant as ddddd ttttt

When using the "w" or "ww" format expressions, you can modify the first day of the week from Sunday to any day of the week by using the FirstDayOfWeek parameter. With the "ww" format expression, you can change the FirstWeekOfYear setting by including the right parameter as well. Table 21-6 shows the different constants that affect these format expressions.

Table 21-6 FirstDayOfWeek and FirstWeekOfYear constants

Constant	Value	Description
FirstDayOfWeek Constants		
vbUseSystem	0	Use NLS API setting as first day of week.
vbSunday	1	Sunday(default) set as first day of week.
vbMonday	2	Monday set as first day of week.
vbTuesday	3	Tuesday set as first day of week.
vbWednesday	4	Wednesday set as first day of week.
vbThursday	5	Thursday set as first day of week.
vbFriday	6	Friday set as first day of week.
vbSaturday	7	Saturday set as first day of week.
FirstWeekOfYear Constants		
vbUseSystem	0	Use NLS API setting as first week of year.
vbFirstJan1	1	Start with week in which January 1 occurs (default).
vbFirstFourDays	2	Start with week that has at least four days in the year.
vbFirstFullWeek	3	Start with first full week of year.

Times

Whereas the whole portion of a date type represents a date, the fractional part can represent a time, which is stored as a fraction of a day. The time returned will be in 24-hour format unless one of the AM/PM format symbols is used. Times can be formatted with the symbols shown in Table 21-7 (the examples are based on a time of 1:05:31 a.m.).

Table 21-7 Time format symbols

Symbol	Example	Effect of Symbol
:	:	Time separator
h	1	Returns the hour, without a leading 0
hh	01	Returns the hour, with a leading 0, if needed
n	5	Returns the minute, without a leading 0
nn	05	Returns the minute, with a leading 0
s	31	Returns the second, without a leading 0

continued on next page

continued from previous page

Symbol	Example	Effect of Symbol
ss	31	Returns the minute, with a leading 0
ttttt	01:05:31	Returns the time in the format specified by the entry "sTime" in the WIN.INI file
c		Returns date variant as ddddd ttttt
AM/PM, am/pm		Returns "AM" for any hour before noon, and "PM" for any hour after
A/P, a/p		Returns "A" for any hour before noon, and "P" for any hour after
AMPM		Uses the AM/PM format specified by the "s1159" and "s2359" entries in the WIN.INI file

Strings   The Format functions can also format string arguments. Table 21-8 summarizes the symbols that control string formatting, with the examples working on the string "Hello."

Table 21-8 String format symbols

Symbol	Example	Effect of Symbol
@	Hello	Placeholder: displays a character, or a space if there is no character
&	Hello	Placeholder: displays a character, or nothing if there is no character
<	hello	Forces lowercase
>	HELLO	Forces uppercase
!	olleH	Forces placeholders to fill from left to right

HEX FUNCTION

See Also   Oct

Purpose   The Hex function converts a decimal numeric expression to a variant or string that represents the value of the numeric expression in hexadecimal format. Table 21-9 describes the argument of the Hex function.

General Syntax

```
Hex(numExpression)
```

Table 21-9 Argument of the Hex function

Argument	Description
numExpression	Numeric expression to be converted to hexadecimal notation

Example Syntax
```
A% = 140
B$ = Hex$(A%)
```

Description   This example places a string with the hexidecimal value "8C" into the variable B$.

Hexadecimal notation is a way of counting using 16 digits. The digits in hexadecimal include 0 through 9 and A through F. Hexadecimal "A" equals a decimal 10, "B" equals 11, and so on. Hexadecimal is often used to display memory addresses because it easily converts back and forth from binary. The Hex$ function provides a method of converting a decimal number into hexadecimal.

The supplied numExpression is rounded to the nearest whole number before conversion is begun. If numExpression is an integer, the string returned by Hex$ will be 4 or fewer bytes long. Otherwise, the return string can be up to 8 bytes long.

Example   The Conversion project at the end of this chapter uses the Hex function to get the hexadecimal representation of the results.

Oct Function

See Also   Hex

Purpose   The Oct function returns a variant or string that represents the supplied numeric expression in octal notation (base 8). Table 21-10 describes the argument of the Oct function.

General Syntax

```
Oct(numExpression)
```

Table 21-10 Argument of the Oct function

Argument	Description
numExpression	Numeric expression to be converted to octal notation

Example Syntax

```
strOctal = Oct(100)
```

Description   This example places the octal number 144 into the string variable strOctal.

Octal notation is a method of counting using only eight digits. This is sometimes used to work with memory addresses because it converts back and forth from binary more easily than decimal, although hexadecimal is more commonly used for this purpose. The Oct function provides a method of converting a decimal number into octal.

The supplied numExpression is rounded to the nearest whole number before conversion begins. It cannot exceed the range defined by the long integer data type. If numExpression is an integer, the string returned by Oct will be 4 or fewer bytes long. Otherwise, the return string can be up to 11 bytes long.

Example
The Conversion project at the end of this chapter uses the Oct function to get the octal representation of the results.

VAL FUNCTION

See Also
Str

Purpose
The Val function returns the numeric value of the supplied string expression. Table 21-11 describes the argument of the Val function.

General Syntax

```
Val(strExpression)
```

Table 21-11 Argument of the Val function

Argument	Description
strExpression	String for which you want to return the numeric value

Example Syntax

```
A! = Val("123")
B! = Val("1 2 3")
C! = Val(" 123doggy")
D! = Val("G")
```

Description
The first three lines of this example assign a value of 123 to their respective variables. The fourth line returns 0.

The Val function is the complement to the Str$ function. It translates the supplied string expression into a double-precision number. Translation begins at the left of the string and works toward the right. Spaces are ignored. Translation ends at the first nonnumeric character or at the end of the string, whichever comes first. The first period encountered in a string is translated as a decimal point, but a second period causes the translation to end. Dollar signs and commas are not recognized as numeric characters.

This function is useful for translating the string representation of hexadecimal or octal values into numeric values. For instance, the following code assigns the value 255 to the variable A%:

```
B$ = Hex(255)          'gives B$ the value "FF"
A% = Val("&H" + B$)    'same as Val("&HFF") which equals 255
```

Str Function

See Also   Val

Purpose   The Str function converts a numeric expression to a string. Table 21-12 describes the argument of the Str function.

General Syntax

Str(numExpression)

Table 21-12 Argument of the Str function

Argument	Description
numExpression	Numeric expression you want to convert to a string

Example Syntax
A$ = Str(100)
B$ = Str(-100)

Description   In this example, the value of A$ becomes "100." A leading space precedes the number where the positive sign is implied. The value of B$ will be "-100". It has no leading space because the negative sign is explicit.

This function returns a string that is an unformatted representation of numExpression. If formatting is desired, use the Format function instead. When a number is converted to a string, the first space of the string is reserved for the sign of the numeric expression. If the numeric expression is positive, the sign is implied, and the string representation of the number is preceded by a space. If it is negative, the string representation of the number is preceded by a minus (-) sign.

The Conversion Project

Project Overview

The Conversion project converts two numbers and their sum from one base (decimal, octal, or hexadecimal) to another.

The following pages discuss the assembly and operation of the Conversion project. The first section deals with the assembly of the only form in the project. Next, there is a listing and explanation of the contents of the subroutines of this project. Finally, a How It Works guide to the operation of the project discusses the operation of the code. Please read this information carefully and use the pictures of the form to check your results.

Assembling the Project

1. Make a new form with the objects and properties listed in Table 21-13.

Table 21-13 Elements of the main form

Object	Property	Setting
Form	Name	frmMain
	BorderStyle	3- Fixed Dialog
	Caption	"Conversion Project"
Frame	Name	fraValues
	Caption	"Values"
OptionButton	Name	optValueNumBase
	Index	0
	Caption	"Decimal"
	Value	True
OptionButton	Name	optValueNumBase
	Index	1
	Caption	"Hexadecimal"
	Value	False
OptionButton	Name	optValueNumBase
	Index	2
	Caption	"Octal"
	Value	False
TextBox	Name	txtValue
	Index	0
	Text	""
Label	Name	lblPlus
	Caption	"+"
TextBox	Name	txtValue
	Index	1
	Text	""
Frame	Name	fraResult
	Caption	"Result"
OptionButton	Name	optResultNumBase
	Index	0
	Caption	"Decimal"
	Value	True
OptionButton	Name	optResultNumBase
	Index	1
	Caption	"Hexadecimal"

Object	Property	Setting
	Value	False
OptionButton	Name	optResultNumBase
	Index	2
	Caption	"Octal"
	Value	False
Label	Name	lblResult
	Caption	"="
CommandButton	Name	cmdCalc
	Caption	"C&alculate"
CommandButton	Name	cmdExit
	Caption	"E&xit"

2. Size the objects on the screen as shown in Figure 21-1.

3. Go to the Form Layout window, right-click on the frmMain form, and select Center Screen as the startup position.

4. Enter the following code in the Click event of the cmdExit button. This unloads the form and terminates the application.

```
Private Sub cmdExit_Click()
    Unload Me
End Sub
```

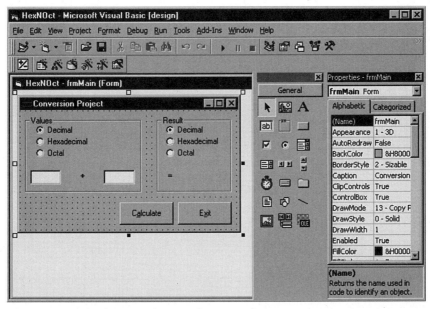

Figure 21-1 The frmMain form in design mode

5. Enter the following definitions in the general declarations section of the form. These constants will make the code a little easier to read.

```
Private Const optCDecimal = 0
Private Const optCHexadecimal = 1
Private Const optCOctal = 2
```

6. Enter the following code in the Load event of the Form. Initial values are provided for the two text boxes.

```
Private Sub Form_Load()
    txtValue(0).Text = 6
    txtValue(1).Text = 10
End Sub
```

7. Enter the following code in the Click event of the cmdCalc button. This code does not check for illegal values, such as 9s in octal values.

```
Private Sub cmdCalc_Click()
    Dim strValue1 As String, strValue2 As String
    Dim lngResult As Long

    ' Interpret values in decimal base?
    strValue1 = txtValue(0).Text
    strValue2 = txtValue(1).Text

    If optValueNumBase(optCHexadecimal).Value Then
            ' Nope, in Hex: add Hex prefix
            strValue1 = "&H" & txtValue(0).Text
            strValue2 = "&H" & txtValue(1).Text
    Else
        If optValueNumBase(optCOctal).Value Then
            ' Nope, in Octal: add Octal prefix
            strValue1 = "&O" & txtValue(0).Text
            strValue2 = "&O" & txtValue(1).Text
        End If
    End If

    lngResult = CLng(strValue1) + CLng(strValue2)

    ' Display result in decimal base?
    lblResult.Caption = "= " & Str(lngResult)

    If optResultNumBase(optCHexadecimal).Value Then
        ' Nope, in Hex!
        lblResult.Caption = "= " & Hex(lngResult)
    Else
        If optResultNumBase(optCOctal).Value Then
            ' Nope, in Octal!
            lblResult.Caption = "= " & Oct(lngResult)
        End If
    End If
End Sub
```

How It Works

Depending on what number base was chosen for the values, nothing (decimal), "&H" (hexadecimal) or "&O" (octal) is prepended to the text entered. Then the CLng function is used to convert the strings to long integers. These two longs are added and the result is displayed in the number base chosen for the result, if needed, by using the Hex or Oct functions.

22

DATE

Sometimes a Visual Basic application needs to keep track of dates. Visual Basic provides a variety of ways to convert to and from a number of different ways of expressing dates. It also offers a complete set of date manipulation functions.

Serial Numbers, and the Date Data Type

In Visual Basic the date and time are expressed with a Date data type, as well as with a Variant variable.

The Variant variable type can store any of the kinds of variable types, be it a string or any of the numeric types. The date variant is a variant of type 7. It is stored internally by Visual Basic as a double-precision number. Use of the variant of VarType 7 is no longer encouraged. Any of the previous functions or statements that returned VarType 7 now return the date in the date data type.

The date data type is stored as an 8-byte floating-point number that represents dates ranging from January 1, 100, to December 31, 9999, and times from 0:00:00 to 23:59:59. Any recognizable literal date values can be assigned to the date data type. Literal dates must be enclosed within number sign characters (#) (for example, #January 1, 1998#, or #1 Jan 98#). When other numeric date types are converted to date data types, values to the left of the decimal represent date information, whereas values to the right of the decimal represent time. Midnight is 0 and midday is .5. Negative whole numbers represent dates before December 30, 1899. The great advantage to using the date data type is that Visual Basic attempts to automatically convert the arguments and results of the functions to whatever format is appropriate. This makes your code simpler to write because you don't have to explicitly convert the variable types.

For instance, the Date statement accepts a date data type, and the Date$ statement only accepts a string of the proper format. Both statements do the same thing: change your computer's system date. The Date$ statement only accepts dates expressed as "08-20-97" or "08/24/1997", whereas the Date statement accepts all formats accepted by the Date$ statement plus expressions such as "August 20, 1997" or "20-Aug-94 12:32 am."

Date Summary

You can convert dates with a series of functions: DateSerial, DateValue, Month, Day, Year, and CDate. Table 22-1 displays the statements and functions that affect date manipulation within a Visual Basic application.

Table 22-1 The functions and statements that affect dates in Visual Basic applications

Use or Set This...	Type	To Do This...
CDate	Function	Convert a string or a number to a date data type
Date, Date$	Function	Return the system date set in the computer
Date, Date$	Statement	Set the system date
DateSerial	Function	Return the date data type that represents a date given in integer format
DateValue	Function	Return the date data type of a date given in string format
Day	Function	Return an integer between 1 and 31 that represents the day of the month
Month	Function	Return the integer between 1 and 12 that represents the number of the month
Now	Function	Return a date value for the current date and time
WeekDay	Function	Return an integer between 1 and 7 that represents the day of the week
Year	Function	Return an integer between 100 and 9999 that represents the year

The following pages investigate in detail the features summarized in Table 22-1. Step-by-step directions at the end of this section describe how to assemble the Date project.

CDATE FUNCTION

Purpose   The CDate function converts a string or numeric expression into a date data type. Table 22-2 shows the argument of the CDate function, and Table 22-3 summarizes how the CDate function handles a variety of inputs.

General Syntax

`CDate(expression)`

Table 22-2 Argument of the CDate function

Argument	Description
expression	String or number that can be evaluated as a legal date or time

Table 22-3 CDate input handling

If expression Is...	The CDate Function Returns...
Numeric, -657434 to 2958465	Date
Numeric, out of range	Error 13 (Type Mismatch)
String that looks like a date	Date
String that looks like a number	Date, if number in range; Error 13 if out of range
Other string expression	Error 13 (Type Mismatch)

Example Syntax

```
Private Sub Form_Load()
    Dim InDate As String, OutDate As Date, Msg, TABSTOP
    TABSTOP = Chr$(9)
    Do
        Msg = "Enter any date and time in any format you like."
        InDate = InputBox(Msg)
        If InDate = "" Then Exit Sub
        If Len(Format(InDate, "mm-dd-yy")) <> 8 ⇐
Or Format(InDate, "mm-dd-yy") = "01-01-00" _
        Or (Len(InDate) = 8 And Val(InDate) = 0) Then
            MsgBox "Invalid date!  Try again.", 48
        Else
            OutDate = CDate(InDate)
            Msg = "You entered: " & TABSTOP & InDate & vbCRLF
            Msg = Msg & "Long Form:    " ⇐
& TABSTOP & Format(OutDate, "mmmm d, yyyy") & vbCRLF
            Msg = Msg & "Long Time:    " ⇐
& TABSTOP & Format(OutDate, "h:mm:ss am/pm") & vbCRLF
            Msg = Msg & "Serial Time: "  & TABSTOP & CStr(CDbl(OutDate))
            MsgBox Msg
        End If
    Loop
End Sub
```

Description

The CDate function converts a variety of input expressions into a valid date data type. This saves you from writing more specific code by letting CDate handle the intricacies of the conversion. The argument must be a string or numeric expression that can be interpreted as a date. If the expression cannot be interpreted as a date, CDate generates runtime error number 13 (Type Mismatch).

CDate handles numbers, strings, and strings that look like numbers differently. If the input is numeric, CDate checks to see whether it is within the range of -657434 to 2958465. If it is, CDate converts it to a date. If not, CDate generates a runtime error. A string expression that looks like a date (such as "April 1, 1994 11:34 pm" or "12/10/98") is converted into a date. A string expression that looks like a number (such as "3456") is first converted to a number, and then validated for regular numeric input. Finally, any other string expression (such as "Foobar" or "April 1st, 1994 at 11:34 in the morning") generates a runtime error, as summarized in Table 22-3.

The preceding example uses the versatile Format function to see if the input is a valid date before passing it to the CDate function. Format handles a variety of input, as does CDate, and is more forgiving of input that cannot be interpreted correctly.

Example The Date project at the end of this chapter uses the CDate function to convert a text string the user types in the txtThen text box to a legal date. It does this in both the cmdCalculate_Click events and the cmdSet_Click events. The conversion process is surrounded by an error trap to trap any strings that aren't legal dates.

DATE, DATE$ FUNCTIONS

Purpose The Date function returns the current system date as a date data type, and the Date$ function returns the current system date as a string. Table 22-4 summarizes the return values of the Date$ function.

Table 22-4 Possible returned settings of the Date$ function

Date	Settings Range
Month (mm)	A number between 01 and 12 inclusive
Day (dd)	A number between 01 and 31 inclusive
Year (yyyy)	A year between 0100 and 9999 inclusive

General Syntax
```
Date
Date$
```

Example Syntax
```
Private Sub Form_Load()
    Dim Msg$
    'default message: date as string
    Msg$ = "Today's date is: " & Date$
    'compare date literal

    If Date = #7/4/97# Then
        'display date as date data type
        Msg$ = "Today is the Fourth of July: " & Date
    'compare part of a date
    ElseIf Format(Now, "mm-dd") = "12-25" Then
        'display formatted date as string
        Msg$ = "Today is Christmas: " & Format(Now, "mm-dd-yyyy")
    End If

    'display result
    MsgBox Msg$
End Sub
```

Description   The Date function returns a date data type value that represents the computer's current system date. If you put the results of the Date function directly into the Text property of a text box, the text box automatically formats the results as m/d/yy. The function has no argument.

The Date$ function returns a value that represents the computer's current system date. It functions almost exactly like the Date function, except in the type of value it returns. The value it returns is a string presented in the form mm-dd-yyyy. In this form, the mm part of the string stands for the current month, which must be between 01 and 12. The dd portion of the returned string is the current day of the month and must be between 01 and 31. This string ends with the yyyy that returns the current year between 0100 and 9999. Table 22-4 lists the meaning of the characters returned by the Date$ function. Thus, the Date$ function would return August 20, 1997 as "08-20-1997" and the Date function would return "8/20/97."

It is recommended that you use the Date function rather than the Date$ function to represent the system date. If your application is attached to a database, the database probably expects the date value to be a date data type; therefore, when you use the Date function, no conversion is needed. The only times you should consider using the Date$ function are when

- Your program is very large and uses a lot of variables.

- You want to detect when your data has been converted from one format to another.

- When you are writing to a data file.

In the example syntax, an If...Then statement checks the current date of the computer to determine a message to display on the screen. Figures 22-1 and 22-2 demonstrate the difference in the way the Date and Date$ functions format their values.

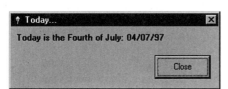

Figure 22-1   The Date function returns the current system date as a date data type

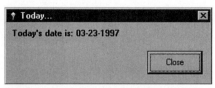

Figure 22-2 The Date$ function
returns the current system date as a
string; note the difference in format
compared to the Date function

The Format Function The Format function, when used with the current date returned by the Now function, produces the same result as the Date$ function. In the example syntax, the Date function checks to see if the day is July 4, 1997, and the Format function looks to see whether the day is December 25. The Format function will work on its date for any year, while the Date function only operates for the current year.

This example demonstrates the trade-off between the flexibility of the Format function and the simplicity of the Date function.

Comments Use the Date statement to change the current system date of the computer.

DATE, DATE$ STATEMENTS

Purpose The Date and Date$ statements enable the user to change the system date of a computer within a Visual Basic application. Table 22-5 summarizes the arguments of the Date and Date$ statements, and Table 22-6 summarizes the possible acceptable contents of the datestring$ argument.

General Syntax
```
Date = expression$
Date$ = datestring$
```

Table 22-5 Arguments of Date and Date$ statements

Argument	Description
datestring$	String that represents the date in the form of "mm-dd-yy" or "mm-dd-yyyy"
expression$	String that represents the date (more generalized than datestring$)

Table 22-6 Possible acceptable contents of the datestring$ argument

datestring$	Possible Settings
mm	A number between 1 and 12 inclusive

datestring$	Possible Settings
dd	A number between 1 and 31 inclusive
yy	A number between 00 and 99 inclusive
yyyy	A number between 1980 and 2079 (on Windows NT; 2099 on Windows 95) inclusive

Example Syntax

```
Private Sub Command1_Click ()
    On Error GoTo BadDate
    Date = Text1.Text
Exit Sub

Bad Date:
    MsgBox "That date is not in an acceptable format!"
Exit Sub

End Sub
```

Description

The Date$ statement enables the user to change the system date of a computer within a Visual Basic application. The Date statement does the same thing, but accepts a much wider variety of formats that it tries to convert to a proper date.

The argument for the Date$ statement must be a string containing a valid date. The valid date formats that the Date$ statement will accept are mm-dd-yy, mm-dd-yyyy, mm/dd/yy, and mm/dd/yyyy. A datestring$ must be a string variable, or else the system will generate an error. In this form, the mm part of the string stands for the current month and must be between 0 and 12, for the 12 months of the year. The dd portion of the returned string is the current day of the month and must be between 1 and 31. This string ends with the yyyy that returns the current year, which must be between 1980 and 2099. (Note that this acceptable date range is considerably smaller than what all of the other date functions accept.) Strings that end in yy represent the last two digits of the familiar year, with 1994 being expressed as 94.

The Date statement accepts a wider variety of formats. It accepts variants of variant type 7 (date) and type 8 (string). The Date statement attempts to convert whatever you pass it to a legal date. It recognizes all the string formats that the Date$ format accepts, plus strings that contain unambiguous month names. For instance, "08-20-97," "8/20/1997," "August 20, 1997," "Aug-20-97," and "20/August/97" are all acceptable. You can also use the date data type returned by other functions, such as the DateSerial function. If the format is not acceptable, the Date statement generates a trappable error.

We recommend that you use the Date statement rather than the Date$ statement to change the system date. Both statements accomplish the same task, but the Date statement allows for a wider variety of formats.

The example syntax gives the user the opportunity to change the system date with a text box entry. Notice that if the user enters a date in any format other than those shown, the system generates an error that we trap to display an explanatory message box. It's a good idea to always set error traps if you allow your user to manually input dates; the range of acceptable input for statements such as Date is quite wide, but not as extensive as what your users will inevitably dream up. Figure 22-3 shows what this might look like.

Example

The Date project at the end of this chapter uses the Date statement to set the system date in the cmndSet_Click event. The user can type any arbitrary date and time in the textThen text box. The cmndSet_Click event first converts the user's input to a valid date with the CDate function. It then sets the system date. The routine also will reset the system date back to normal if the user presses the button a second time.

Comments

For MS-DOS computers, the valid dates are from January 1, 1980, to December 31, 2099. For Microsoft Windows NT computers, the valid dates are from January 1, 1980, to December 31, 2079.

Remember that although 31 is the maximum number allowed for the day argument, not all months have 31 days.

DateSerial Function

Purpose

The DateSerial function converts the numeric values of an indicated date to a Visual Basic date data type. Table 22-7 summarizes the arguments of the DateSerial function.

General Syntax

```
DateSerial(year%, month%, day%)
```

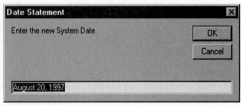

Figure 22-3   The Date statement accepts a variety of date formats to set the system date

Table 22-7 Arguments of the DateSerial function

Argument	Description
year%	A number or expression that evaluates to between 100 and 9999 inclusive
month%	A number or expression that evaluates to between 1 and 12 inclusive
day%	A number or expression that evaluates to between 1 and 31 inclusive

Example Syntax

```
Private Sub Command1_Click ()
    'how many months to add to current date
    monthsToAdd = Val(Combo1.Text)
    thisYear = Year(Now())
    thisMonth = Month(Now())
    thisDay = Day(Now())
    On Error GoTo BadDate
    newDate = DateSerial(thisYear, thisMonth + monthsToAdd, thisDay)
    Text1.Text = Format$(newDate, "###,###")
Exit Sub
BadDate:
    MsgBox "The resultant date is not acceptable!"
Exit Sub

End Sub
```

Description

The DateSerial function returns a date variant that represents the month, day, and year of a date on the calendar, as discussed in the beginning of this chapter. Each of the three arguments of this function represents the numeric values of the year, month, and date. The year% argument variable is a number between 100 and 9999 inclusive. The month% argument stands for the month of a date between 1 and 12, with January being represented by 1 and December by 12. The date% argument represents the day of a month between 1 and 31. Although the range for the date% argument goes up to 31, note that many months don't have that many days.

The example syntax adds on a number of months (as determined by Combo1) to the current date, and displays the results in the text box.

The Month, Day, and Year Functions

The Month, Day, and Year functions are the logical choices to use to obtain the variables for a DateSerial function. In the example syntax, each of these functions provides the necessary values of the date entered by the user. Notice how each function only returns the value that represents the month, day, or year, respectively, of the date. Each function ignores all the other values in the date.

Example

The Date project at the end of this chapter uses the DateSerial function to determine a date, given the mouse's coordinates over a picture box. It scales the mouse's current horizontal position to determine a year, month, and day to use in the DateSerial function.

Comments When the year% argument is between 0 and 99, inclusive, it will be interpreted as the years 1900–1999. For all other year% arguments, you will need to use a four-digit year (for example, 2010).

DateValue Function

Purpose The DateValue function converts a date in the form of a string into a Visual Basic date data type. This function changes differently formatted dates to a universal numerical form. Table 22-8 summarizes the argument of the DateValue function, and Table 22-9 summarizes the valid DateValue formats.

General Syntax

```
DateValue(datestring$)
```

Table 22-8 Argument of DateValue function

Argument	Description
datestring$	String that represents a date for the DateValue function to convert

Table 22-9 A few examples of valid datestring$ argument values for the DateValue function

datestring$
01/01/1994
01/01/94
January 1, 1994
Jan 1, 1994
01-Jan-1994
01 January 94

Example Syntax

```
Private Sub cmdCalculate_Click()
    Dim dtmFirstDate As Date, dtmEndDate As Date
    Dim vntDays As Variant

    On Error GoTo BadDate
    If txtDate(0).Text = "" Or txtDate(1).Text = "" Then
        ErrMsgBox "Please enter a date in each box."
        Exit Sub
    End If

    ' Find date variant of entered Date
    dtmFirstDate = DateValue(txtDate(0).Text)
    ' Find date variant of entered Date
```

```
    dtmEndDate = DateValue(txtDate(1).Text)

    ' Display date variant
    txtDate(0).Text = Str(dtmFirstDate)
    ' Display date variant
    txtDate(1).Text = Str(dtmEndDate)

    ' Find number of days between dates
    vntDays = Abs(dtmEndDate - dtmFirstDate)
    lblDifference.Caption = "Number of days between dates: "  & Trim(vntDays) & " Days."
Exit Sub

BadDate:
    ErrMsgBox "Please enter a valid date."
Exit Sub

End Sub
```

Description

The DateValue function converts a date string to a date data type that represents the month, day, and year of a date on the calendar. There are a number of acceptable date formats for the order of appearance of the month, day, and year in the datestring$. The international section of the WIN.INI file defines the default order of the month, day, and year. If a datestring$ contains the actual name of a month in long or abbreviated form, the DateValue function will also be able to convert it to a date data type. In addition to recognizing 01/01/1994 and 01/01/94, the DateValue function will also be able to convert January 1, 1994, Jan 1, 1994, 01-Jan-1994, and 01 January 94. If the year portion of a datestring$ is omitted, the current year is assumed. All of these combinations will work in the example, so try them out with different date formats for each text box.

In the example syntax, the DateValue function finds the date value of the two dates that the user enters in the Text1 and Text2 text boxes. The difference between the two date values provides the number of days that are between the two entered dates. Figure 22-4 shows what this example might look like on the screen.

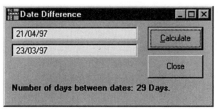

Figure 22-4 The DateValue function converts date strings to date values; you can then easily perform math operations, such as taking the difference between two date values

Example	The Date project at the end of this chapter uses the DateValue function to help build up a representation of the serial number representing the current system time. The timeClock_Timer event triggers several times a second to update the display.
Comments	Although DateValue will not display time information that might be in the text string, invalid time information (such as 89;98) will cause Visual Basic to generate an error.

NOW FUNCTION

Purpose   The Now function provides the current date and time of the computer's system clock-calendar as a date data type.

General Syntax

`Now`

Example Syntax

```
Private Sub Timer1_Time ()
    'sets timer interval
    Timer1.Interval = 100
    'displays the date variant
    Text1.Text = Str$(Now)
    'displays formatted date and time
    Text2.Text = Format$(Now,"mmmm-dd-yy hh:mm:ss")
End Sub
```

Description	The Now function has no arguments. The date returned by the Now function represents the system date and time at the moment the code runs.
	In the example syntax, the Now function serves as a means of displaying the date, time, and date data type on the screen. With this example, the time and date are shown in the Text2 text box, and the variable that produces this information, returned by the Now function, is placed in the Text1 text box. Notice that in both cases, the date variable must be converted to a string prior to defining the Text property of the Text1 and Text2 text boxes.
Example	In the Date project at the end of this chapter, the Now function gives the current system date and time to the Year, Month, Day functions in the cmdCalculate_Click event.

WEEKDAY, MONTH, DAY, AND YEAR FUNCTIONS

Purpose   The Weekday, Month, Day, and Year functions return an integer value representing the day of the week, the month, the day, or the year, respectively. These values can be used to construct or format a date in the usual terms, such as "Thursday, December 15, 1997." Table 22-10 summarizes the arguments of the Weekday, Month, Day, and Year functions. Table 22-11 summaries the settings for the Weekday function. Table 22-12 summarizes the return values associated with the Weekday function.

General Syntax

```
Month(expression$)
Day(expression$)
Year(expression$)
Weekday(expression$, [firstdayofweek])
```

Table 22-10 Arguments of the Weekday, Month, Day, and Year functions

Argument	Description
expression$	Date variant to display in month, day, year, or weekday format.
firstdayofweek	A constant that specifies the first day of the week, as described in Table 22-11. If omitted, vbSunday is assumed.

Table 22-11 Arguments of the firstdayofweek setting

Value	VB.Constants	Description
0	vbUseNLS	Use NLS API setting
1	vbSunday	Sunday
2	vbMonday	Monday
3	vbTuesday	Tuesday
4	vbWednesday	Wednesday
5	vbThursday	Thursday
6	vbFriday	Friday
7	vbSaturday	Saturday

Table 22-12 Return values of Weekday function

Value	VB.Constants	Description
1	vbSunday	Sunday
2	vbMonday	Monday
3	vbTuesday	Tuesday
4	vbWednesday	Wednesday
5	vbThursday	Thursday
6	vbFriday	Friday
7	vbSaturday	Saturday

Example Syntax

```
Private Sub Form_Load ()
    'store current month number
    CMonth% = Month(Now)
    'store current day number
    CDay% = Day(Now)
    'store current year number
    CYear% = Year(Now)
    'store current weekday number
    Week% = Weekday(Now)
    'check if current year is less than 2000
    'or if current year is greater than 1899
    If CYear% < 2000 Or CYear% > 1899 Then
            'stores last two digits of year
            Yr$ = Format$(CYear%, "yy") 'stores last two digits of year
        Else
            'store all four digits of year
            Yr$ = Str$(CYear%)
        End If
    End If

    'check month number to store
    Select Case CMonth%
        Case 1: M$ = "Q1 - January "
        Case 2: M$ = "Q1 - February "
        Case 3: M$ = "Q1 - March "
        Case 4: M$ = "Q2 - April "
        Case 5: M$ = "Q2 - May "
        Case 6: M$ = "Q2 - June "
        Case 7: M$ = "Q3 - July "
        Case 8: M$ = "Q3 - August "
        Case 9: M$ = "Q3 - September "
        Case 10: M$ = "Q4 - October "
        Case 11: M$ = "Q4 - November "
        Case 12: M$ = "Q4 - December "
    End Select

    'check the week number for which week name
    Select Case Week%
        Case vbSunday:    W$ = "Sunday "
        Case vbMonday:    W$ = "Monday "
        Case vbTuesday:   W$ = "Tuesday "
        Case vbWednesday: W$ = "Wednesday "
        Case vbThursday:  W$ = "Thursday "
        Case vbFriday:    W$ = "Friday "
        Case vbSaturday:  W$ = "Saturday "
    End Select
    Text1.Text = W$ & ", " & M$ &  Str$(CDay%) + ", " + Str$(CYear%)
End Sub
```

Description   The Weekday, Month, Day, and Year functions each take a Visual Basic date data type and return the appropriate numeric value for that element of the date.

The Weekday function returns an integer between 1 (Sunday) and 7 (Saturday). The Month function returns the month as an integer between 1 and 12. January is represented by 1 and December by 12. With the Day function, an integer between 1 and 31 inclusive is returned. Because not every month has 31 days, the month of a date data type can reduce the range of possible days. The Year function returns an integer between 100 and 9999 that stands for the year of the date. If the date value is negative, then it represents a year prior to 1900.

In the example syntax, the date data type produced by the Now function works with each of these functions to find the values that represent the present date stored in the computer. A Select Case statement determines the month and weekday names using the Weekday and Year functions. All of this resulting information combines to display the weekday and date in the Text1 text box.

Example   The Date project at the end of this chapter uses these functions in the cmdCalculate_Click event to help determine the difference between the current system date and a date the user types in the txtThen text box. The Year, Month, and Day functions are all used to determine the difference between the two dates.

The Date Project

Project Overview

The Date project outlined in the following pages demonstrates the concept of time in Visual Basic. This example demonstrates the property, event, functions, and statements that directly affect time. By following the examples of the different elements of this project, you will learn how these elements work in Visual Basic.

The following pages discuss the assembly and operation of the Date project. The first section deals with the assembly of the Time form. Next, there is a listing and explanation of the contents of the subroutines of this project. Finally, a guide to the operation of the project discusses the operation of the code. Read this information carefully and use the pictures of the form to check your results.

Assembling the Project

1. Make a new form with the objects and properties listed in Table 22-13.

Table 22-13 Elements of the Date project form

Object	Property	Setting
Form	Name	frmMain
	BorderStyle	3—Fixed Double
	Caption	"Date Project"
Command	Caption	"&Calculate"
	Default	True
	Name	cmdCalculate

continued on next page

continued from previous page

Object	Property	Setting
Command	Caption	"E&xit"
	Name	cmdExit
Command	Caption	"&Set System"
	Name	cmdSet
Label	Caption	"Now (String)"
Label	Caption ·	"Now (Serial)"
Label	Name	lblNow
Label	Name	lblSerial
Label	Name	lblDifference
Text	Name	txtThen

2. Size the objects on the screen as shown in Figure 22-5.

3. Go to the Form Layout window, right-click on the frmMain form, and select Center Screen as the startup position.

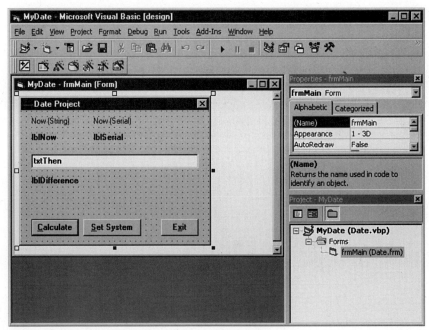

Figure 22-5   The frmMain form in design mode

4. Enter the following code in the Click event of the cmdExit button. This unloads the form and terminates the application.

```
Private Sub cmdExit_Click()
    Unload Me
End Sub
```

5. Enter the following definitions in the general declarations section of the form. These constants make the code a little easier to maintain.

```
Private Const conAppTitle = "Date Project"
Private Const conSetSystem = "&Set System"
Private Const conResetSystem = "&Reset System"
```

6. Enter the following code in the cmdCalculate_Click event. This calculates the difference between the current system date and the value entered by the user in the text box. It first converts the string to a date data type, then calculates the differences. After the differences have been calculated, the event displays the results in the label directly below the text box.

```
Private Sub cmdCalculate_Click ()
    Dim dtmThen As Date, dtmNow As Date
    Dim strYear As String, strMonth As String, strDay As String
    Dim strWeekDay As String, strMessage As String

    'set the trap
    On Error GoTo BadDate
    'convert date the user typed in
    dtmThen = CDate(txtThen.Text)
    'success!
    On Error GoTo 0

    dtmNow = Now
    'difference in years
    strYear = Str$(Year(dtmThen) - Year(dtmNow))
    'difference in months
    strMonth = Str$(Month(dtmThen) - Month(dtmNow))
    'difference in days
    strDay = Str$(Day(dtmThen) - Day(dtmNow))

    'get the day of the week
    strWeekDay = Format(dtmThen, "dddd")

    strMessage = strYear & " years, " & strMonth & " months, " & ⇐
strDay & " days; " & Chr$(10)         'put together the label
    strMessage = strMessage & "The day of the week you gave is a "  & strWeekDay & "."
    lblDifference.Caption = strMessage
Exit Sub

BadDate:
    ErrMsgBox "Please type a date in the correct format."
    txtThen.SetFocus
Exit Sub

End Sub
```

7. Enter the following code in the cmdSet_Click event. This either sets the system clock to the new date and time displayed in the text box, or resets the system time back to the original settings. The two static variables dtmOldSystem and dtmOffset will remember the exact time before and after setting the system clock, so you can calculate the difference when resetting. Note that although it might appear more elegant to replace the Date statement from inside the Select Case block with one set right after it (after all, you're setting the same variable), that would cause a problem if the user entered an unacceptable date. For example, if the user enters a legal date for the CDate function that is before 1980, the Date statement will generate an error. The routine will correctly handle this error as it is written now. The routine resets the system clock by taking the elapsed time between the current time and the time it originally finished setting the system clock, and adding on the original time before it set anything.

```
Private Sub cmndSet_Click ()
    'these allow us to reset the date
    Static dtmOldSystem As Date, dtmOffset As Date
    Dim dtmSetSystem As Date
    'are we setting or resetting?
    Select Case cmdSet.Caption
        'set the system clock
        Case conSetSystem
            'mark the start of the new date
            dtmOldSystem = Now
            'set trap
            On Error GoTo BadSetDate
            'new date
            dtmSetSystem = CDate(txtThen.Text)
            'set the date
            Date = dtmSetSystem
            'successful!
            On Error GoTo 0
            'now indicate need to reset
            cmdSet.Caption = conResetSystem
        'reset date back to where we were
        Case conResetSystem
            'difference between old and new
            dtmSetSystem = dtmOldSystem + Now - dtmOffset
            'set date
            Date = dtmSetSystem
            'reset the caption
            cmdSet.Caption = conSetSystem
    End Select
    'the new date after being set
    dtmOffset = Now
    'display new values
    ShowCurrentDate
Exit Sub

BadSetDate:
    ErrMsgBox "Please type a date in the correct format."
    txtThen.SetFocus
Exit Sub

End Sub
```

8. Enter the following code in the Form_Load event. This just sets the text in some of the controls.

```
Private Sub Form_Load ()
    ShowCurrentDate

    txtThen.Text = "Type a date in me!"
    lblDifference.Caption = "I'll display the difference between " & ⇐
 & "the system date and the date you type above."
End Sub
```

9. Enter the following code in the Form_Unload event. This checks to see if the system clock needs to be set back to the original settings, in case the user forgets to do that manually. If so, it resets the clock by calling the cmdSet_Click event procedure before allowing the form to unload.

```
Private Sub Form_Unload (Cancel As Integer)
    If cmdSet.Caption = conResetSystem Then
        'if we still need to reset the date,
        'do it before unloading
        cmdSet_Click
    End If
End Sub
```

10. Enter the following code in the txtThen_GotFocus event. This selects all the text in the text box.

```
Private Sub txtThen_GotFocus ()
    'select all the text
    txtThen.SelStart = 0
    txtThen.SelLength = Len(txtThen.Text)
End Sub
```

11. Add a private Sub ShowCurrentDate to the form. It is be used to update the labels with the current time.

```
Private Sub ShowCurrentDate()
    'generic function for right now
    lblNow.Caption = Date
    'format as serial numbers, not as date variants!
    lblSerial = Format(Now, "###,##0")
End Sub
```

12. Add a private Sub ErrMsgBox to the form. It is used to display error messages to the user when invalid dates are entered.

```
Private Sub ErrMsgBox(strMessage As String)
    MsgBox strMessage, vbOKOnly + vbCritical, conAppTitle
End Sub
```

How It Works

The Date project does several distinct things. First, it displays the current date in two different formats. The lblNow label displays the current date as returned by the Date function, and the lblSerial label shows you what this looks like as a serial number.

Next, you can type in any date you want in the text box. When you press the ENTER key, or click the Calculate button, the difference between the current system date and the date you entered displays in the label beneath the command buttons.

You can also click the Set System button to set the system clock to whatever date you typed in the text box. Note that you can only set the system clock from 1980 to 2099; even though a far wider range of dates are acceptable to the calculate function, you can't set your system clock to that wide a range. After you set the clock to some arbitrary date, press the button again (now relabeled as Reset System) to reset the date back to normal. The program will automatically reset the date for you if you forget before exiting.

Figure 22-6 shows what the project looks like when running.

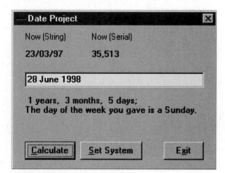

Figure 22-6   The Date project in action

23

TIME

Some Visual Basic applications need to keep track of time. Visual Basic provides a variety of ways to determine the time at which something happened, or should be made to happen. It also offers a wealth of functions to convert to and from a number of different ways of expressing time.

Time in Visual Basic

Visual Basic divides time into units of measure that are familiar to the user, such as the time of day. Time is measured using the hour, minute, and second to pinpoint a specific moment.

The Timer Control

In order for a set of actions to be governed by time, those actions must be connected to a timer control on a Visual Basic form. The timer lets you bypass the normal operation of a program with actions based on time rather than user input. Unless the timer control is disabled, the timer's Timer event triggers each time the amount of time set in the Interval property elapses. Although a Visual Basic application may have as many timer controls as needed, no more than 16 timer controls may be active at any given point. This is a limitation of the Windows environment and not Visual Basic. Timer controls are only visible at design time, not at runtime.

Time Summary

Visual Basic provides several tools that influence the display and manipulation of time. The Interval property of the timer control indicates how much time must pass before the actions in the Timer event are triggered. The Timer function returns the number of seconds that have passed since 12:00 midnight. Obtain the current setting of the time and date in the computer with the Date and Time functions, and modify them with the Date and Time statements.

You can convert times with a series of functions: TimeSerial, TimeValue, Hour, Minute, and Second, and CDate (discussed in Chapter 22, "Date"). Table 23-1 displays the statements, property, event, and functions that affect timing within a Visual Basic application.

Table 23-1 The property, event, functions, and statements that affect timing in Visual Basic applications

Use or Set This...	Type	To Do This...
Hour	Function	Return an integer between 0 and 23 that represents the hour of the day
Interval	Property	Determine the interval of time before processing the Timer event
Minute	Function	Return an integer between 0 and 59 that represents the minute of the day
Now	Function	Return a date value for the current date and time
Second	Function	Return the integer between 0 and 59 that represents the second
Time, Time$	Function	Return the current system time
Time, Time$	Statement	Set the system time
Timer	Event	Determine actions that take place when the Interval has passed
Timer	Function	Return the number of seconds since midnight
TimeSerial	Function	Return the date data type for the indicated time given in numeric format
TimeValue	Function	Convert a time in string format to a date data type

The following pages investigate the features summarized in Table 23-1 in detail. Step-by-step directions at the end of this section describe how to assemble the Time project.

HOUR, MINUTE, AND SECOND FUNCTIONS

Purpose   The Hour, Minute, and Second functions return an integer representing the hour, minute, or second portions of a date value. The Hour function returns an integer that is between 0 (12:00 a.m.) and 23 (11:00 p.m.) inclusive. The Minute and Second functions return an integer between 0 and 59 representing the minute or second portion of the date value. Table 23-2 summarizes the argument of the Hour, Minute, and Second functions.

General Syntax

```
Hour(expression)
Minute(expression)
Second(expression)
```

Table 23-2 Argument of the Hour, Minute, and Second functions

Argument	Description
expression	Variant representing a date and time or a number that can be converted to a serial number

Example Syntax

```
Private Sub Timer1_Timer ()
    'set Interval to 1 Second
    Timer1.Interval = 1000

    'check if time is AM or PM
    If Hour(Now) > 12 Then
        'set Daytime string to PM
        DayTime$ = " PM"
        'change 24hour to 12hour time
        NormalTime = Hour(Now) - 12
    Else
        'set Daytime string to AM
        DayTime$ = " AM"
        'find the current hour
        NormalTime = Hour(Now)
    End If

    'define variable as the current hour
    'minute, and seconds separated by
    'colons.
    Current$ = Str$(NormalTime) + " :"
    Current$ = Current$ + Str$(Minute(Now)) + " :"
    Current$ = Current$ + Str$(Second(Now))
    Current$ = Current$ + DayTime$

    'displays the current time in Text1
    Text1.Text = Current$

End Sub
```

Description   The expression argument of the Hour, Minute, or Second function may represent a date and time between January 1, 0100, and December 31, 9999, inclusive. In a date data type, the digit to the right of the decimal point returns the time of the day. Only the right side of the date value is necessary for the Hour, Minute, and Second functions to produce the time of the day. The part of the date data type on the left side of the decimal point is the date and has no effect on the value returned by the Hour, Minute, and Second functions.

The expression argument may also be any acceptable date and time string expression, such as "12:30 pm" or "August 20, 1997 5:34 AM." See the TimeValue entry for examples of acceptable formats.

In the example syntax, the Hour, Minute, and Second functions work together to display the current time in the Text1 text box on the form. The text "AM" and "PM" also follows the time displayed on the screen.

Current Time and the Now Function   The Now function provides the date data type of the current system date and time. When this function is used with the Hour, Minute, and Second functions, the result is a value that defines the hour, minute, and second. In the example syntax, the Now function provides the date data type for the Hour, Minute, and Second functions to display in the text box. Notice that a space is left for the unseen 0 when the number is a single digit.

The Timer Event and Interval Property   When the Timer event and Interval property are used along with the Hour, Minute, Second, and Now functions, the time may be obtained at intervals specified by the Interval property of the timer control. The accuracy of the time displayed on the screen depends on the Interval property. If you watch the seconds change in the example syntax, you will notice that sometimes certain seconds are skipped. In order to keep this problem from happening, reduce the interval to one-half the needed accuracy. For the example, this may be avoided by changing the interval from 1000 milliseconds (1 second) to 500 milliseconds (1/2 second).

Example   In the Time project at the end of this chapter, the Hour, Minute, and Second functions help display the difference between the current system time and a time the user types in the txtThen text box in the cmdCalculate_Click event. Each function converts the present system time and the date represented by the text box and puts the difference in a variable. The variables are then combined for display in the lblDifference label.

INTERVAL PROPERTY

Objects Affected   Timer

Purpose   The Interval property of a timer control indicates the length of time to wait before processing the Timer event. This property may be changed either at design time or runtime. Each timer control's Interval property is independent of the Interval properties of other timer controls on the same form. Table 23-3 summarizes the arguments of the Interval property of a timer control, and Table 23-4 summarizes its possible settings.

General Syntax

```
[form!]Name.Interval = milliseconds&
```

Table 23-3 Arguments of the Interval property of a timer control

Argument	Description
form	Name property of the form
Name	Name property of the timer control being affected
milliseconds&	Amount of time that must pass between triggerings of the Timer event (as a long integer)

Table 23-4 Possible settings of the Interval property of a timer control

milliseconds&	Effect
0	Disables the timer (default)
1–65535	Milliseconds between triggerings; 1000 = 1 second

Example Syntax

```
Private Sub TextUpdateDisplay_LostFocus ()
    Timer1.Interval = Val(TextUpdateDisplay.Text)
End Sub
```

Description   The Interval property of a timer control indicates the length of time to wait before processing the Timer event. The milliseconds& argument may be any number between 0 and 65,535 milliseconds (65.535 seconds). Even though the measurements are in milliseconds, the system measures the passage of time with 18 ticks per second. For this reason, the interval cannot be guaranteed to pass exactly on time.

The example syntax uses a text box to set the timer interval, perhaps for a procedure that updates a display in real time (anything from system resources to a stock price!).

The Enabled Property   If the Interval property of a timer control is set to 0, then the timer control is disabled and will not process the Timer event. The Enabled property of a timer control indicates whether the control is active or inactive. When the Enabled property of a timer control is False (0), it is disabled, and the countdown to the next Timer event is suspended. For this reason, if either the Enabled property or the Interval property is disabled in this way, the timer control stays inactive until its Interval property is a nonzero value and the Enabled property is True (-1). In the example syntax, the Enabled property is changed at design time to allow the timer control to activate immediately when the program is started.

The Timer Function   Because the Interval property has a maximum possible length of 65,535 milliseconds (a little more than 65 seconds), the Timer function must be used to generate actions that require longer lengths of time before they are triggered. A timer event could be set up on a form to check the amount of time since midnight with the Timer function until the timer returns an amount that is greater than the time specified for the event to take place.

Example   Both of the timers have their Interval property set during the Time project's design phase. The first timer, tmrClock, is set to a quarter second (250 milliseconds) to update the real-time displays. The other timer pauses the display of new times in the picTheWindsOfTime_MouseMove event for 2 1/2 seconds (2500 milliseconds).

Comments   Although the Interval property of one timer control has no effect on another timer control, Windows has a limit of no more than 16 active timer controls at a time.

Now Function

Purpose   The Now function provides the current date and time of the computer's system clock-calendar as a date data type.

General Syntax

```
Now
```

Example Syntax

```
Private Sub Timer1_Time ()
    'set timer interval
    Timer1.Interval = 100
    'display the date variant
    Text1.Text = Str$(Now)
    'display formatted date and time
    Text2.Text = Format$(Now,"mmmm-dd-yy hh:mm:ss")
End Sub
```

Description   The Now function has no arguments. The date returned by the Now function represents the system date and time at the moment the code runs.

In the example syntax, the Now function serves as a means of displaying the date, time, and date data type on the screen. With this example, the time and date are shown in the Text2 text box and the variable that produces this information, returned by the Now function, is placed in the Text1 text box. Notice that in both cases the date variable must be converted to a string prior to defining the Text property of the Text1 and Text2 text boxes.

Example   In the Time project at the end of this chapter, the Now function gives the current system date and time to the Year, Month, Day, Hour, Minute, and Second functions in the cmndCalculate_Click event.

TIME AND TIME$ FUNCTIONS

Purpose   The Time function returns the current system time as a date data type. The Time$ function returns your computer's current system time as a string. Table 23-5 summarizes the possible returned settings of the Time and Time$ functions.

General Syntax

```
Time
Time$
```

Table 23-5 Possible returned values of the Time and Time$ functions

Time	Description
Hour (hh)	A number between 00 and 23 inclusive
Minute (mm)	A number between 00 and 59 inclusive
Second (ss)	A number between 00 and 59 inclusive

Example Syntax

```
Private Sub tmrStopWatch_Timer()
    tmrStopWatch.Interval = 500

    txtNow(0).Text = Time
    txtNow(1).Text = Time$
    txtNow(2).Text = Format(Time, "hh:mm")
End Sub
```

Description   We recommend that you use the Time function rather than the Time$ function to represent the system time. If your application is attached to a database, the database probably expects the time value to be a date data type; therefore, if you use the Date function, no conversion is needed. You should consider using the Time$ function only when

■ Your program is very large and uses a lot of variables.

■ You want to detect when your data has been converted from one format to another.

■ You are writing to a data file.

The example syntax checks the current time of the computer and displays it in three text boxes. The Time function displays the time as a date data type. The Time$ function works like the Format function combined with the Time function to display the current time, and the Format function displays only the hour and minutes of the current time based on a 24-hour clock. Figure 23-1 shows what this example might look like on the screen.

Figure 23-1 The Time function (top text box) displays the current system time like a clock. The Time$ function (middle text box) is a convenient way of displaying the current system time without having to use the Format function (bottom text box)

Comments Use the Time statement to change the current system time of the computer.

TIME AND TIME$ STATEMENTS

Purpose The Time and Time$ statements enable the user to change the system time of a computer within a Visual Basic application. Table 23-6 summarizes the arguments of the Time and Time$ statements. Table 23-7 summarizes the possible acceptable contents of the timestring$ argument of a Time$ statement, and Table 23-8 gives examples of some of the acceptable arguments of the Time statement.

General Syntax

```
Time = expression$
Time$ = timestring$
```

Table 23-6 Arguments of the Time and Time$ statements

Argument	Description
timestring$	Time in string format "hh:mm:ss"
expression$	Acceptable time format (more general than timestring$)

Table 23-7 Possible acceptable contents of the timestring$ of a Time$ statement

timestring$	Possible Settings
hh	A number between 00 and 23 inclusive
mm	A number between 00 and 59 inclusive
ss	A number between 00 and 59 inclusive

Table 23-8 Examples of acceptable time arguments of the Time statement

expression$

2:21

2:21 pm

14:21

August 12, 1995 12:02 am

Example Syntax

```
Private Sub cmdOk_Click()
    Dim intHours As Integer, intMinutes As Integer, intSeconds As Integer

    intHours = Val(txtHours.Text)
    intMinutes = Val(txtMinutes.Text)
    intSeconds = Val(txtSeconds.Text)
    If Len(LTrim(txtHours.Text)) > 0 Then
        If intHours < 0 Or intHours > 23 Then
            ErrMsgBox "Hours not in an acceptable format!"
            txtHours.SetFocus
            Exit Sub
        End If
        If intMinutes < 0 Or intMinutes > 59 Then
            ErrMsgBox "Minutes are not in an acceptable format!"
            txtMinutes.SetFocus
            Exit Sub
        End If
        If intSeconds < 0 Or intSeconds > 59 Then
            ErrMsgBox "Seconds are not in an acceptable format!"
            txtSeconds.SetFocus
            Exit Sub
        End If
        Time$ = Trim(intHours) & ":" & Trim(intMinutes) & ":" & Trim(intSeconds)
    Else
        ' If the text isn't in a valid time
        On Error GoTo BadTime
        ' format, run the BadTime routine, otherwise
        Time = txtTime.Text
        ' set time.
        On Error GoTo 0
    End If
Exit Sub

BadTime:
    ErrMsgBox "That time is not in an acceptable format!"

End Sub
```

Description   The Time and Time$ statements set the computer's internal system clock. They function almost identically, but the Time statement accepts a wider variety of time formats.

The valid time formats that the Time$ statement will accept are hh, hh:mm, and hh:mm:ss. The timestring$ argument must be a string variable, or else the system generates an error. In this form, the hh part of the string stands for the current hour, which must be between 00 and 23. These values represent the 24 hours of the day. The mm portion of the returned string is the minute of the current day, and must be between 00 and 59. This string may end with ss, which returns the current seconds. The seconds must be between 0 and 59. For strings that do not end in mm or ss, these settings represent 0.

The Time statement accepts any string that is recognized as a valid time by the TimeValue function. It accepts the same formats that the Time$ statement does, plus a wide variety of others. Table 23-8 gives a few examples of acceptable formats for the Time statement.

We recommend that you use the Time statement rather than the Time$ statement to change the system time. Both statements accomplish the same task, but the Time statement allows for a wider variety of formats.

The example syntax enables the user the opportunity to change the system date by changing the values in four text boxes. The If...Then statement is used to determine which text boxes to take the input from. If the first three text boxes, labeled hh, mm, and ss, are used, the Time$ statement is used. Notice that if the user enters an incorrect time, the code beeps and doesn't attempt to change the time. If the time entered is valid, the Time$ statement changes the system time to the time entered by the user. If the fourth text box is used, the system time is changed by the Time statement. Notice that if the user enters a time in any format other than those shown in Table 23-8, the system generates an error that we trap, displaying an explanatory message box. It's a good idea to always set error traps if you allow your user to manually input times; the range of acceptable input for the Time statement is quite wide, but not as extensive as what your users will inevitably dream up.

Figure 23-2 shows what this example might look like on the screen.

Figure 23-2 The Time$ statement lets you change the computer's internal clock

Example	In the Time project at the end of this chapter, the Time statement sets the system time in the cmdSet_Click event. The user can type in any date and time in the txtThen text box, and the cmdSet_Click event sets the system date and time to the date in the text box. The routine remembers the original system date and time, and resets them when clicked a second time.
Comments	Computers running DOS versions before 3.3 will not permanently change their time; you'll generally need to use a special machine-specific setup disk to do this. It's probably unlikely, however, that your modern Windows program is running on a machine with a very old versions of DOS.

TIMER EVENT

Objects Affected	Timer
Purpose	The Timer event contains the actions that take place when a time equal to the interval value of the timer control has elapsed. This event triggers every time the interval of time elapses until the timer control is disabled. A timer control is disabled by setting its Enabled property to False, by setting its Interval property to 0, or by unloading the form. Table 23-9 summarizes the arguments of the Timer event.

General Syntax

```
Sub Name_Timer ([Index As Integer])
```

Table 23-9 Arguments of the Timer event

Argument	Description
Name	Name property of the timer.
Index	This argument serves as a reference for the part of a control array.

Example Syntax

```
Private Sub Timer1_Timer ()
    'clear the form
    Cls
    'define Constant PI
    Const PI = 3.14159265
    'define Static variable
    Static Num As Double
    'set form's FillColor
    FillColor = QBColor(1)
    'set form's FillStyle to solid
    FillStyle = 0
    'define as half width of screen
    X% = ScaleWidth / 2
    'define as half height of screen
    Y% = ScaleHeight / 2
    'define as 1/4 of width of screen
```

continued on next page

continued from previous page

```
        Radius% = ScaleWidth / 4
        'draw partial circle on screen
        Circle (X%, Y%), Radius%, , Num, -6.283
        'reduce value of variable
        Num = Num - ((2 * PI) / 60)
        'display setting of variable
        Text1.Text = Str$(Num)

        'check value of variable
        If Abs(Num) >= 6.283 Then
                'redefine variable as zero
                Num = 0
                'disable Timer
                Timer1.Enabled = 0
                'clear screen
                Cls
        End If
End Sub
```

Description	The Timer event lets you take repeated actions at specific time intervals. You might want to periodically update a display or check on changeable values.
	In the example syntax, the Timer event displays a circle on the screen with a line drawn from the center of the circle to the right edge of the circle. Each time the event runs, it draws a circle with a larger and larger slice removed. When the circle disappears from the screen, the timer control's Enabled property is changed to False, ending the timing.
The Interval Property	The Interval property of a timer control indicates how frequently to process the Timer event. This property is measured in milliseconds and may range in value from 0 to 65,535 (a little more than 65 seconds). No matter what the setting of this property, if the Enabled property is False, the Timer event will not be processed. The example syntax might set the Interval property of the Timer1 control to 1000 during the design phase to process the Timer event at once per second. Setting up the Interval property in this way makes the circle graphically display the amount of time left in the minute since the form first loaded.
The Enabled Property	The Enabled property of a timer control determines whether the control is active or inactive. When the timer control's Enabled property is True, the code processes the Timer event at the intervals specified by the Interval property. While the timer control's property is False, the control remains disabled. If the Interval property is 0, the Timer event is not processed. In the example syntax, the Enabled property of the timer control must be True to trigger the Timer event at the loading of the form. An If statement sets this property to False when the circle has disappeared off the screen.
Example	In the Time project at the end of this chapter, the tmrClock_Timer event updates the real-time displays of system time and the stopwatch several times a second. The tmrMouse_Timer disables the tmrMouse timer to re-enable mouse movements displaying the resultant date and time in the picTheWindsOfTime_MouseMove event.

Comments	Timers in a timer control array only trigger a Timer event for the first timer in the array. This makes timer control arrays useless, and they are allowed only to be consistent with the rest of Visual Basic controls. Set up each timer as an independent control.

TIMER FUNCTION

Purpose	The Timer function provides the number of seconds that have elapsed since 12:00 midnight. This function may serve as a reference for determining the number of seconds elapsed between two different uses of the Timer function on the same day.

General Syntax

```
Timer.
```

Example Syntax

```
Private Sub tmrStopWatch_Timer()
    Static dblProgStart As Double
    Dim strMessage As String
    Dim lngElapsed As Long

    tmrStopWatch.Interval = 500
    ' Stores current seconds
    lngElapsed = Int(Timer)
    If dblProgStart = 0 Then
        dblProgStart = lngElapsed
    End If

    txtSinceMidnight.Text = Str(lngElapsed) & " Elapsed seconds since Midnight"
    txtSinceStart.Text = Str(lngElapsed - dblProgStart) & " Seconds since program start"
End Sub
```

Description	The Timer function returns the value that represents the number of seconds elapsed since midnight. This function has no argument, and returns a value between 0 and 86,400 (the number of seconds in one day). If the day changes (that is, the system clock goes past midnight), the difference between two values gained on different days will not return the true number of seconds elapsed.
	The example syntax uses the Timer function to store and display the current number of seconds since midnight and program startup. It finds the difference between the variables produced at program startup and at the current time, and then provides the number of elapsed seconds since program startup. Figure 23-3 shows what the example should look like on the screen.
Example	In the Time Project at the end of this chapter, the Time project's tmrClock_Timer event uses the Timer function to update the lblStopWatch label. The program's Form_Load event puts the Timer value

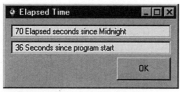

Figure 23-3 The Timer function measures how many seconds have elapsed since midnight, and can be used to time program functions

in the tmrClock's Tag property to use as a baseline. Each triggering of the tmrClock_Timer event then calculates the difference between the baseline and the current Timer value to determine the number of seconds that have elapsed since the program first started.

TimeSerial Function

Purpose

The TimeSerial function converts the values of an indicated time to a Visual Basic date data type. Table 23-10 summarizes the arguments of the TimeSerial function.

General Syntax

```
TimeSerial(hour%, minute%, second%)
```

Table 23-10 Possible arguments of the TimeSerial function

Argument	Description
hour%	A number or expression that evaluates to a number between 0 and 23 inclusive
minute%	A number or expression that evaluates to a number between 0 and 59 inclusive
second%	A number or expression that evaluates to a number between 0 and 59 inclusive

Example Syntax

```
Private Sub Command1_Click ()
Start:
     'Take the time entered in Text box 1 and
     'adds the figures entered in the other text
     'boxes to the Hour, Minute, and Second of the
     'entered Time to obtain a new time.
     On Error GoTo NotTime
     If Text1.Text = "" Then GoTo EnterTime
     BeginTime = TimeValue(Text1.Text)
     BeginHour = Hour(BeginTime)
     EndHour = Val(Text2.Text)
```

```
        BeginMinute = Minute(BeginTime)
        EndMinute = Val(Text3.Text)
        BeginSecond = Second(BeginTime)
        EndSecond = Val(Text4.Text)
        EndTime = TimeSerial(BeginHour + EndHour, BeginMinute + EndMinute, ⇐
                BeginSecond + EndSecond)
        Label1.Caption = Format$(EndTime, "hh:mm:ss")
        Exit Sub
EnterTime:
        MsgBox "Please Enter a value in each box."
        Exit Sub
NotTime:
        If BeginSecond + EndSecond > 60 Then
            EndSecond = EndSecond - 60
            EndMinute = EndMinute + 1
        ElseIf BeginHour + EndHour > 24 Then
            EndHour = EndHour - 24
        ElseIf BeginMinute + EndMinute > 60 Then
            EndMinute = EndMinute - 60
            EndHour = EndHour + 1
        Else
            MsgBox "Please enter a valid Time."
            Text1.Text = ""
        End If
        Resume Start
End Sub
```

Description

The TimeSerial function returns a date data type that represents the hour, minutes, and seconds of a time on the clock. Each of the three arguments of this function represents the numerical values of time. The hour% argument provides the hour of a day expressed as a two-digit number between 01 and 23 inclusive. The minute% argument stands for the minutes of an hour between 0 and 59. The second% argument represents the seconds of a minute between 0 and 59.

In the example syntax, the numbers entered into the text boxes below the date increase the hour, minutes, and seconds of the entered time to produce a new time based on the amount specified in each text box.

An error-checking system in the example syntax enforces the limits of each of these arguments.

The Hour, Minute, and Second Functions

The Hour, Minute, and Second functions are the logical choices to use to obtain the variables for the TimeSerial function. The example syntax uses each of these functions to obtain the necessary values of the time entered by the user. Notice that the function only returns the value of the item specified by the function. For example, the Hour function only provides the value of the hour portion of the time.

Example

The Time project at the end of this chapter uses the TimeSerial function to determine a time, given the mouse's coordinates over a picture box. It scales the mouse's current vertical position to determine an hour, minute, and second to use in the TimeSerial function.

TimeValue Function

Purpose The TimeValue function converts a time in the form of a string into a Visual Basic date data type. Table 23-11 summarizes the argument of the TimeValue function, and Table 23-12 gives some examples of acceptable argument values.

General Syntax

```
TimeValue(timestring$)
```

Table 23-11 Argument of the TimeValue function

Argument	Description
timestring$	Text string to convert that is an acceptable time value

Table 23-12 Some examples of acceptable timestring$ arguments for the TimeValue function

timestring$
3:05
3:05:23
03:05:23
15:05
3:05 pm
3:05 AM
August 12, 1995 3:05 pm

Example Syntax

```
Private Sub Command_Click ()
Start:
    'set error trap to NotTime
    On Error GoTo NotTime
    'check to see if text boxes are blank
    If Text1.Text = "" or Text2.Text = "" Then
        MsgBox "Please Enter a Time in each box."
        Exit Sub
    End If
    'find date variant of entered Time
    FirstTime = TimeValue(Text1.Text)
    'find date variant of entered Time
    EndTime = TimeValue(Text2.Text)
    'display the date variant
    Text1.Text = Str$(FirstTime)
    'display the date variant
```

```
    Text2.Text = Str$(EndTime)
    'find the difference between Times
    T = EndTime - FirstTime
    'find the number of seconds
    Seconds$ = Str$(Int(T * 86400))
    'display the number of seconds
    Label1.Caption = Seconds$ + " seconds"
    'exit subroutine
    Exit Sub
NotTime:
    MsgBox "Please enter a Time only"
    Text1.Text = ""
    Text2.Text = ""
    Resume Start
End Sub
```

Description   A TimeValue function converts a time string to a date data type that represents the hour, minutes, and seconds of a time. There are a number of acceptable time formats for the order of appearance of the hour, minutes, and seconds in the timestring$. The time setting of the international section of the WIN.INI defines the default order of the hour, minutes, and seconds.

      The example syntax demonstrates how to convert date strings of differing formats to date data types. The TimeValue function is used to find the date value of the two times the user enters in the Text1 and Text2 text boxes. When the code finds the difference between the two date data types, the result is the number of days between the two entered times.

Example   The Time project at the end of this chapter uses the TimeValue function to help display the current system time during the tmrClock_Timer event. It displays a representation of the serial number in the lblSerial label.

The Time Project

Project Overview

The Time project outlined in the following pages demonstrates the concept of time in Visual Basic. This example demonstrates the property, event, functions, and statements that directly affect time. By following the examples of the different elements of this project, you will learn how these elements work in Visual Basic.

    The following pages discuss the assembly and operation of the Time project. The first section deals with the assembly of the Time form. Next, there is a listing and explanation of the contents of the subroutines of this project. Finally, a guide to the operation of the project discusses the operation of the code. Read this information carefully and use the pictures of the form to check your results.

Assembling the Project

    1. Make a new form (the Time form) with the objects and properties listed in Table 23-13.

Table 23-13 Elements of the Time project form

Object	Property	Setting
Form	Name	frmMain
	BorderStyle	3–Fixed Double
	Caption	"Time Project"
Command	Name	cmdExit
	Caption	"E&xit"
Command	Name	cmdSet
	Caption	&Set System
Label	Caption	"Now (String)"
Label	Caption	"Now (Serial)"
Label	Name	lblMrMouse
Label	Name	lblNow
Label	Name	lblSerial
Label	BackColor	&H00000000–Black
	BackStyle	1–Opaque
	FontSize	18
	ForeColor	&H0000C000&–Green
	Name	lblStopWatch
Picture	Name	picTheWindsOfTime
Text	Name	txtThen
Timer	Interval	250
	Name	tmrClock
Timer	Interval	2500
	Name	tmrMouse

2. Size the objects on the screen as shown in Figure 23-4.

3. Go to the Form Layout window, right-click on the frmMain form, and select Center Screen as the startup position.

4. Enter the following code in the Click event of the cmdExit button. This unloads the form and terminates the application.

```
Private Sub cmdExit_Click()
    Unload Me
End Sub
```

5. Enter the following definitions in the general declarations section of the form. These constants make the code a little easier to maintain.

```
Private Const conAppTitle = "Time Project"
Private Const conSetSystem = "&Set System"
Private Const conResetSystem = "&Reset System"
```

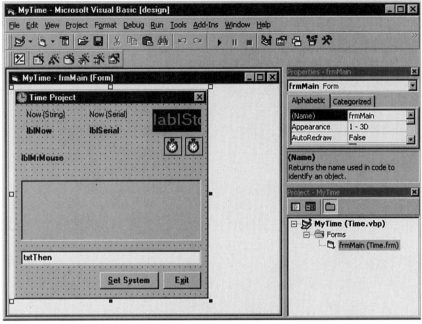

Figure 23-4   The frmMain form in design mode

6. Enter the following code in the cmdSet_Click event. This either sets the system
clock to the new date and time displayed in the text box, or resets the system
time back to the original settings. The two static variables dtmOldSystem and
dtmOffset will remember the exact time before and after setting the system clock,
so you can calculate the difference when resetting. The routine resets the system
clock by taking the elapsed time between the current time and the time it originally finished setting the system clock, and adding on the original time before it
set anything.

```
Private Sub cmdSet_Click ()
 'these allow us to reset the time
 Static dtmOldSystem As Date, dtmOffset As Date
    Dim dtmSetSystem As Date
    'are we setting or resetting?
    Select Case cmdSet.Caption
        'set the system clock
        Case conSetSystem
            'mark the start of the new time
            dtmOldSystem = Now
            'set trap
            On Error GoTo BadSetTime
            'new time
            dtmSetSystem = CDate(txtThen.Text)
            'set the time
            Time = dtmSetSystem
            'successful!
```

continued on next page

continued from previous page

```
                On Error GoTo 0
                'now indicate need to reset
                cmdSet.Caption = conResetSystem

        'reset time back to where we were
        Case conResetSystem
                'difference between old and new
                dtmSetSystem = dtmOldSystem + Now - dtmOffset
                'set time
                Time = dtmSetSystem              'set time
                'reset the caption
                cmdSet.Caption = conSetSystem        'reset the caption
    End Select

    'the new time after being set
    dtmOffset = Now
    ShowCurrentTime
Exit Sub

BadSetTime:
    ErrMsgBox "Please type the time in the correct format."
    txtThen.SetFocus
Exit Sub
End Sub
```

7. Enter the following code in the Form_Load event. This just sets the text in some of the controls. It also sets the ScaleMode for the picture box for ease of calculation in the picTheWindsOfTime_MouseMove event. Finally, it stores the original Timer value so that you can calculate the number of seconds that have elapsed since the program began.

```
Private Sub Form_Load ()
    ShowCurrentTime

    txtThen.Text = "Type a time in me!"

    lblMrMouse.Caption = "I display the mouse position " & "as a date (x) and time (y)"
    'for mouse movement
    picTheWindsOfTime.Scale (0, 0)-(1, 1)
    picTheWindsOfTime.Print
    picTheWindsOfTime.Print "   Click Me!"
    'remember where we start (for stopwatch)
    tmrClock.Tag = Str(Timer)
End Sub
```

8. Enter the following code in the Form_Unload event. This checks to see if the system clock needs to be set back to the original settings, in case the user forgets to do that manually. If so, it resets the clock by calling the cmdSet_Click event procedure before allowing the form to unload.

```
Private Sub Form_Unload (Cancel As Integer)
    'if we still need to reset the time,
    If cmdSet.Caption = conResetSystem Then
        'do it before unloading
        cmdSet_Click
    End If
End Sub
```

9. Enter the following code in the picTheWindsOfTime_Click event. This stops mouse movement from wildly updating the label's display for a few seconds. The picTheWindsOfTime_MouseMove event checks to see if the timer is enabled; if it is, it doesn't update the display.

```
Private Sub picTheWindsOfTime_Click ()
    'stop updating lblMrMouse for a couple of seconds
    tmrMouse.Enabled = True
End Sub
```

10. Enter the following code in the picTheWindsOfTime_MouseMove event. Every time the user moves the mouse over the picture box, this routine updates the label directly above with a date and time related to the mouse's current position. Moving the mouse horizontally from left to right will gradually increase the date; moving it vertically from top to bottom will gradually increase the time. Note that we first check to see if tmrMouse is enabled. If it is, we don't update the display.

```
Private Sub picTheWindsOfTime_MouseMove (Button As Integer, Shift As ⇐
Integer, x As Single, _y As Single)
    Dim yr As Integer, mt As Integer, dy As Integer
    Dim hr As Integer, mn As Integer, sc As Integer
    Dim mouseTime As Date

    'if user hasn't clicked, update lblMrMouse's display
    If tmrMouse.Enabled = False Then
        'keep it to 1997
        yr = 1997
        'horizontal mouse position represents the date
        mt = Int(x * 12)
        dy = Int(x * 365)
        'vertical mouse position represents the time
        hr = Int(y * 24)
        mn = Int(y * 60 * 24) Mod 60
        sc = Int(y * 60 * 24 * 24) Mod 60
        'put together the date and time
        mouseTime = DateSerial(yr, mt, dy) + TimeSerial(hr, mn, sc)
        ' and display it
        lblMrMouse.Caption = Format$(mouseTime, dd, mmmm d, yyyy   h:mm:ss am/pm")
    End If
End Sub
```

11. Enter the following code in the txtThen_GotFocus event. This selects all the text in the text box.

```
Private Sub txtThen_GotFocus ()
    txtThen.SelStart = 0                    'select all the text
    txtThen.SelLength = Len(txtThen.Text)
End Sub
```

12. Enter the following code in the tmrMouse_Timer event. This triggers after the timer has counted down the 2 1/2 seconds since it was first enabled, and turns itself off. The picTheWindsOfTime_MouseMove event checks to see if this timer is enabled before updating the date and time display. If it is enabled, it doesn't update it to give the user a chance to see the display.

```
Private Sub tmrMouse_Timer ()
    tmrMouse.Enabled = False        'start updating lblMrMouse again
End Sub
```

13. Enter the following code in the tmrClock_Timer event. This triggers several times a second to update the real-time displays of the current date and time and the stopwatch.

```
Private Sub tmrClock_Timer ()
    Dim sngStartTime As Single, sngElapsed As Single

    'this is when program started
    sngStartTime = tmrClock.Tag
    'how much time has gone by?
    sngElapsed = Timer - sngStartTime
    'time is measured in base 60
    sngElapsed = (sngElapsed \ 60) * 100 + sngElapsed Mod 60
    'and update the stopwatch
    lblStopWatch = Format(sngElapsed, "00:00")

    ShowCurrentTime
End Sub
```

14. Add a private Sub ShowCurrentDate to the form. It is be used to update the labels with the current time.

```
Private Sub ShowCurrentDate()
    'generic function for right now
    lblNow.Caption = Date
    'format as serial numbers, not as date variants!
    lblSerial = Format(Now, "###,##0")
End Sub
```

15. Add a private Sub ErrMsgBox to the form. It is used to display an error message to the user when invalid dates are entered.

```
Private Sub ErrMsgBox(strMessage As String)
    MsgBox strMessage, vbOKOnly + vbCritical, conAppTitle
End Sub
```

How It Works

The Time project does several distinct things. First, it displays the current time in two different formats. The lblNow label displays the current time as returned by the Time functions, and the lblSerial label shows you what this looks like as a serial number. The stopwatch, next to these labels, displays a count of the amount of time the program has been running.

You can also click the Set System button to set the system clock to whatever time you typed in the text box. After you set the clock to some arbitrary time, press the button again (now relabeled as Reset System) to reset the time back to normal. The program will automatically reset the time for you if you forget before exiting.

Finally, you can move the mouse around the picture box to update the label's display of date and time. Moving the mouse horizontally updates the date, and moving it vertically updates the time. Clicking on the picture box starts up a timer that pauses the updates for a few seconds. Although this might seem a somewhat ridiculous use of the mouse at first glance, consider how natural this would be in a program such as a personal information manager. You could display a nicely rendered bitmap of a calendar or clock, and derive a date or time setting from the position of the mouse when the user clicks on the bitmap.

Figure 23-5 shows what the project looks like when running.

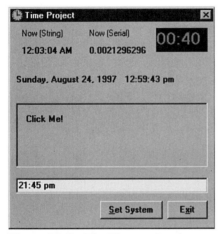

Figure 23-5   The Time project in action

PART III
INTERACTIVE FUNCTIONS AND STATEMENTS

24

DIALOG BOXES

Dialog boxes appear in almost every Windows program. A *dialog box* is a specialized form meant to display or obtain specific information, and is hidden from sight once it has done its work. Some dialog boxes are extremely simple, displaying just a single line of text while the program is performing a lengthy action. Other dialog boxes may be complex, with many controls displaying a variety of information for the user to view or edit.

Most applications have one main window, from which the user directs the program. Although the user will spend most of his or her time working within this window, some of a program's tasks require information that is not part of the main window's user interface. The dialog box created to augment the main window may contain one or more objects, such as text boxes or command buttons, with which the user can interact with the application.

For instance, within the Visual Basic environment, you load a project onto the desktop by selecting Open Project from the File menu. When you do this, Visual Basic needs to determine which project file you wish to open. In order to get your input, Visual Basic displays a dialog box where you can select a project file. Once you've selected your file, the dialog box disappears and you are returned to the main area of the Visual Basic environment.

Visual Basic supplies several kinds of predefined dialog boxes. These make your programming job easier, because one line of code can call up a completed box to display a message or solicit input. At the end of Chapter 25, "CommonDialog Control," is a sample project that covers the material from this chapter and Chapter 25.

Types of Dialog Boxes

There are five basic styles of dialog boxes. Visual Basic provides four styles of predefined dialog boxes. You can use these with just a few lines of code to perform most basic interactions. The fifth style is a custom dialog box you build yourself. It can be as complex as you like.

The first style is the simple message box. This type of dialog box simply displays a message and waits for the user to close the box by clicking a button. The simple message dialog box is used to notify the user of certain information. For instance, when a runtime error occurs in a Visual Basic program, a simple message dialog box is displayed telling you which error caused the program to halt. You can use a simple message box when you need to tell the user what has happened, but don't require anything from the user other than the acknowledgment implied in clicking on the OK button.

The second style of dialog box also displays a simple message. However, more than one command button is displayed on the dialog box so the user can choose among several options. In most Windows programs, if you attempt to exit a program with unsaved files, this type of dialog box appears and asks if you want to save the files before exiting. Generally, such a dialog box will have Yes, No, and Cancel buttons. How the program acts when the dialog box closes is based on the button you choose.

The third style is a simple input box. If you need a quick and easy method to enter a single line of text, you can use a single statement to do this.

The fourth style of dialog box is really a whole family of commonly used dialog boxes. These are fairly complex dialog boxes that let the user choose printer settings, open and save files, change fonts, and select and define colors. These dialogs will be discussed in Chapter 25.

The fifth style of dialog box is a custom dialog box. This is really just another form, but one designed specifically as a dialog box. If none of the four predefined types meets your needs, you'll need to design your own by placing the appropriate controls on a standard form object.

Dialog Box Summary

This chapter discusses the first three types of dialog boxes in detail. Table 24-1 lists the control, functions, and statement that help create dialog boxes.

Table 24-1 The four built-in styles of dialog boxes

Use This...	Type	To Do This...
CommonDlg	Control	Display a custom dialog box
InputBox	Function	Display a box with a message that returns a line of text from the user
MsgBox	Function	Display a message in a box that returns a button choice from the user
MsgBox	Statement	Display a message in a box with just an OK button

INPUTBOX FUNCTION

Purpose   The InputBox function displays a dialog box with a message and a text box in which the user may enter some text. It returns a string containing the text entered by the user. The InputBox function is thus an alternative to designing a form with a text box for simple text input. Table 24-2 summarizes the arguments for the InputBox function.

General Syntax

```
InputBox(Prompt$ [, Title$][, DefaultText$][, Left%, Top%] ⇐
[,HelpFile,Context])
```

Table 24-2 Arguments of the InputBox function

Arguments	Description
Prompt$	Instructions for the user
Title$	The title of the dialog box
DefaultText$	Default entry in the dialog's text box
Left%, Top%	Placement of the dialog box on the HelpFileName of the help file for the Context
	Context number of the appropriate topic in the help file

Example Syntax

```
Private Sub Command1_Click ()
    Title$ = "Greetings"
    Prompt$ = "What is your name?"
    Default$ = ""
    X% = 2000
    Y% = 4000
    N$ = InputBox(Prompt$, Title$, Default$, X%, Y%, "MYAPP.HLP," 356)
End Sub
```

Description   Use the InputBox function when you want to get a line of text from the user. InputBox displays a dialog box that contains an OK button and a Cancel button, a text box for user input, and the text specified by the Prompt$ argument. The Prompt$ argument may be any string expression of up to approximately 255 characters (the exact number of characters allowed is determined by the width of the characters used). If this string is too long to fit on one line in the dialog box, the text will automatically wrap around to the next line. You may force a new line by inserting a carriage return/line feed pair (Chr(13) & Chr(10)) in the prompt string. Visual Basic now defines a global constant for the carriage return/line feed pair. The following lines of code behave identically.

```
N$ = InputBox(PromptLine1$ + Chr(13) + Chr(10) + PromptLine2$ _
    , Title$, Default$, X%, Y%, "MYAPP.HLP," 356)
N$ = InputBox(PromptLine1$ + vbCrLf + PromptLine2$ _
    , Title$, Default$, X%, Y%, "MYAPP.HLP," 356)
```

The Title$ argument specifies the text displayed in the title area of the dialog box. If this argument is not used, the title bar will be empty.

When the dialog box displays, the text specified by the DefaultText$ argument is automatically placed in the dialog's text box. This argument specifies a default entry in the text box; normally, this is what you anticipate will be the most frequently used response. This text is selected, so any new entry will replace it unless the user presses Ⓗ, Ⓩ, Ⓒ, or Ⓢ, or clicks the text box with the mouse. If this argument is not used, the text box will be empty when the dialog box initially displays.

The Left% and Top% arguments specify the position of the dialog box on the screen. They must both be used or both be omitted. The Top% argument indicates the distance between the top of the screen and the top of the dialog box. The Left% argument specifies the distance between the left edge of the screen and the left edge of the dialog box. If these arguments are omitted, the box will be centered horizontally, and placed one-third of the way from the top of the screen. See Chapter 37, "The Coordinate System," for more about screen measurements and positioning objects.

While the dialog box is displayed, the user can type text in its text box. When the user clicks the OK button, or presses the Ⓔ key, the dialog box will disappear and return the string in the text box. Optionally, the user can click the Cancel button, or press the Ⓨ key. This also makes the dialog box disappear, but the string returned is null ("").

The example syntax displays a dialog box with the title Greetings that asks for the user's name, as shown in Figure 24-1.

MsgBox Function

Purpose   The MsgBox function displays a dialog box with a message and an optional icon. Your program instructs the function to display one or more sets of predefined command buttons on the dialog box. When the user selects one of these buttons, this function returns a number based on the selected button. The arguments and values for the MsgBox function are summarized in Tables 24-3, 24-4, 24-5, 24-6, 24-7, 24-8, and 24-9.

General Syntax

```
MsgBox(Message$[, Options%][, BoxName$] [, HelpFile, Context]
```

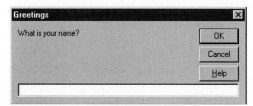

Figure 24-1   Example syntax displays this input box

Table 24-3 Arguments of the MsgBox function

Arguments	Description
Message$	A string expression containing a message to the user
Options%	An integer value specifying which icon (if any) and button set will be used with the dialog box
BoxName$	A string expression that will be used for the title of the dialog box
HelpFile	Name of the help file for the dialog box
Context	Context number of the appropriate topic in the help file

Table 24-4 Values for the buttons displayed with the MsgBox function and statement

Button Value	VB.Constants	Meaning of Value
0	vbOKOnly	(Default) Display an OK button only
1	vbOKCancel	Display OK and Cancel buttons
2	vbAbortRetryIgnore	Display Abort, Retry, and Ignore buttons
3	vbYesNoCancel	Display Yes, No, and Cancel buttons
4	vbYesNo	Display Yes and No buttons
5	vbRetryCancel	Display Retry and Cancel buttons
4000	vbMsgBoxHelpButton	Adds a help button to the other displayed buttons

Table 24-5 Values for the default button setting with the MsgBox function and statement

Default Value	VB.Constants	Meaning of Value
0	vbDefaultButton1	(Default) Sets first button as default
256	vbDefaultButton2	Sets second button as default
512	vbDefaultButton3	Sets third button as default
768	vbDefaultButton4	Sets fourth button as default

Table 24-6 Values for the icons displayed with the MsgBox function and statement

Icon Value	VB.Constants	Displays	Used For
16	vbCritical	Red STOP sign	Critical messages
32	vbQuestion	Question mark in green circle	Queries
48	vbExclamation	Exclamation mark in red circle	Warnings
64	vbInformation	Letter i in blue circle	Informative messages

Table 24-7 Values for the behavior of the MsgBox function and statement

Behavior Value	VB.Constants	Behavior
0	VbApplicationModal	Prevents the user from interacting with the current application until the message box is completed
4096	VbSystemModal	Prevents the user from interacting with any application until the message box is completed
10000	vbMsgBoxSetForeground	Brings the application to foreground if it is not the application in focus

Table 24-8 Values for the appearance of the MsgBox function and statement

Appearance Value	VB.Constants	Appearance
80000	vbMsgBoxRight	Right-justifies the text in the Message$ parameter
100000	vbMsgBoxRtlReading	Displays the text right to left on Hebrew and Arabic systems

Table 24-9 Values returned by the MsgBox function

Return Value	VB.Constants	Button That Was Pressed
1	vbOK	OK
2	vbCancel	Cancel
3	vbAbort	Abort
4	vbRetry	Retry
5	vbIgnore	Ignore
6	vbYes	Yes
7	vbNo	No

Example Syntax

```
Private Sub FileOpen ()
    On Error Goto DinnaOpen
    Open "Zirfgrod.prn" For Input As #1
Exit Sub

DinnaOpen:
    ButtonPressed = MsgBox("Disk Error", vbAbortRetryIgnore,         "Cannot Open File")
    Select Case ButtonPressed
        Case vbAbort, vbIgnore    'Abort, Ignore
            Exit Sub
        Case vbRetry            'Retry
            Resume
    End Select
End Sub
```

Description

The MsgBox function displays a message in a dialog box with an optional icon. Your program specifies a set of buttons to display on the dialog box, and the function returns a value that indicates which button the user clicked on. You use this function to get a decision from the user. Figure 24-2 shows a typical use of the MsgBox function.

The Message$ argument specifies the text that prompts the user. This must be a string expression of up to 1024 characters. Any characters past the 1024-character limit will be truncated. The message will automatically word wrap at the right edge of the box. However, this word wrapping requires that spaces appear somewhere within the text. If no spaces are present, the displayed string is truncated at the 255th character. You may force a new line by inserting a carriage return/line feed pair (Chr(13) & Chr(10)) in the message string. Visual Basic now defines a global constant for the carriage return/line feed pair. The following lines of code behave identically.

```
ButtonPressed = MsgBox("Disk Error" + vbCrLf + ⇐
     "Please call the Help Desk for assistance." ⇐
     , vbAbortRetryIgnore, "Cannot Open File")
ButtonPressed = MsgBox("Disk Error" + Chr(13) + Chr(10) + ⇐
     "Please call the Help Desk for assistance." _
     , vbAbortRetryIgnore, "Cannot Open File")
```

The Options% argument determines the appearance of the dialog box. The value of this argument controls five things: the icon displayed (if any), the command buttons displayed, which command button will be the default, the appearance of the text, and the behavior of the dialog. Tables 24-4 through 24-8 summarize the constants used with the options argument.

Button Types

The MsgBox function has six predefined sets of buttons and the optional Help button that may be displayed on its dialog box. The Options% argument specifies which of these sets are used and whether to include the Help button. Each set provides a group of possible answers to a specific type of question. For instance, one set displays Abort, Retry, and Ignore buttons. You can use this set to give the user a choice of actions to take when the program encounters some sort of hardware error. Another set displays Yes, No, and Cancel buttons. A good use for this set is to ask the user if he or she wishes to save any open files before exiting a program. Table 24-4 summarizes the seven sets of buttons available to the MsgBox

Figure 24-2   Example syntax
displays this message box

function. The Help button can be included with any of the sets of buttons. If no button set is specified, the dialog box displays one OK button.

Default Button

The default button on the dialog box is the button whose value will be returned if the user presses the Ⓔ key. Normally, the leftmost button on the dialog box is set as the default button. However, you may change the default to another button by setting the Options% argument to one of the values defined in Table 24-5. If a dialog box displays a Cancel button, the Cancel button's value will be returned if the user presses the Ⓨ key.

Icon

Placing an icon on the dialog box helps the user understand the nature of the dialog box. For example, suppose the user has instructed your program to delete a file. Knowing that people can make mistakes, you might want to display a message in a dialog box and make the user confirm the action. Displaying the familiar stop sign in the dialog box is a good visual tool to let the user know that a critical operation is about to be performed. Your program uses the Options% argument to specify one of several predefined icons. Table 24-6 summarizes the types of icons available and their values.

Behavior

The default behavior of the MsgBox prevents the user from interacting with the application until the user has dismissed the dialog. A system modal MsgBox keeps the dialog in front of all applications until it has been dismissed. This behavior is good for warning messages in cases where it is imperative to get the user's attention. By setting the foreground option, the application will become the foreground application when the MsgBox function or statement is called; however, the user could still hide the dialog with another application's window.

Combining the Various Options

You specify a combination of the above settings by using the logical OR operator. For instance, to display a critical error dialog box with Yes, No, and Cancel buttons, and the Cancel button as the default, your code would look something like this. Figure 24-3 shows the resulting dialog box.

```
Private Sub Command1_Click ()
    MB_Options = vbYesNoCancel Or vbDefaultButton3 Or vbQuestion
    ButtonPressed = MsgBox("Save open files before exiting?"          , MB_Options)
    Select Case ButtonPressed
        Case vbYes
            SaveFiles
            End
        Case vbNo
            End
        Case vbCancel
            'do nothing
    End Select
End Sub
```

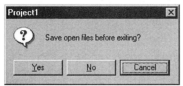

Figure 24-3   Question dialog
box created using multiple
constants to define MsgBox
parameters

Returned Value   When the user chooses a button, the dialog box disappears and the function returns a value indicating which button was chosen. Table 24-9 summarizes the possible values returned by this function.

Dialog Title   Finally, you may specify a title for the dialog box using the BoxName$ argument. This argument must be a string expression, and will be displayed in the title area of the dialog box. If this argument is omitted, the name of the project is displayed. For instance, if your project is named Project1, that is what will be displayed.

MsgBox Statement

Purpose   The MsgBox statement displays a dialog box with a message, an OK button, and an optional icon. The only user action is acknowledging the message by clicking on the OK button. No value is returned to the program. The arguments of the MsgBox statement are the same as those for the MsgBox function; Table 24-3 summarizes the arguments of the MsgBox statement, and Tables 24-4 through 24-9 summarize the values of the Options% argument.

General Syntax

```
MsgBox Message$[, Options%][, BoxName$] [, HelpFile, Context]
```

Example Syntax
```
Form_Load ()
    MsgBox "Greetings!", vbExclamation
End Sub
```

Description   The MsgBox statement behaves the same as the MsgBox function, with the exception that the statement does not return a value indicating which button the user pressed. Therefore, it is useless to specify that any buttons aside from the default OK button or the Help button be displayed on the MsgBox statement's dialog box.

25

COMMONDIALOG CONTROL

The CommonDialog control exposes the dialogs built into Windows. Microsoft has created standard dialogs for many of the common tasks users face, such as choosing printer settings, opening and saving files, changing fonts, and selecting and defining colors. Many commercial applications use these common dialog boxes. Using common dialog boxes saves you a substantial amount of work and lends your programs a professional appearance, giving them a consistency that users have grown to expect.

CommonDialog Control Summary

This chapter describes the CommonDialog control in detail. Table 25-1 describes the common dialogs available from the CommonDialog control.

Table 25-1 Common dialogs

Use This Dialog...	To Do This...
Color	Let the user choose a color
Font	Let the user choose a font
Help	Show the user help
Open	Let the user open a file
Printer	Let the user change the printer settings
Save	Let the user save a file

COMMON DIALOG

Purpose   The CommonDialog control provides an easy way to produce standard dialog boxes such as File Open, File Save, Print, Select Font, and Choose Color.

Properties, Events, and Methods   Table 25-2 lists the properties of the CommonDialog control, and Table 25-3 lists its methods.

Table 25-2 Properties of the CommonDialog control

Use This Property...	To Do This...
Action	Specify the type of dialog box to display
CancelError	Determine whether an error is generated upon Cancel
Color	Read or set the selected color
Copies	Read or set the number of copies to be printed
DefaultExt	Set the default extension for the dialog box
DialogTitle	Set the caption of the dialog box's title bar
FileName	Read or set the path and name of the file to open or save
FileTitle	Read the name of the file to open or save
Filter	Read or set the filter for the kinds of files the file list box displays
FilterIndex	Read or set the index number of the filter for the default pattern
Flags	Set various options for each dialog box
FontBold, FontItalic, FontStrikeThru, FontUnderline	Read or set special effects for this object's font
FontName	Read or set the name of this object's font
FontSize	Read or set the size of this object's font
FromPage, ToPage	Read or set the values of the page range
hDC	Read the Windows device handle for this object
HelpCommand	Set the kind of help requested
HelpContextID	Set the context number for context-sensitive help
HelpFile	Set the name of the help file to display
HelpKey	Set the keyword for the help file to search for
InitDir	Read or set the initial directory to use for File Open
Max, Min	Set the smallest and largest fonts displayed
Max, Min	Set the smallest and largest page numbers to print
MaxFileSize	Set the maximum length of filename used in the FileName property
PrinterDefault	Determine whether changes in the Print dialog change default printer settings

Table 25-3 Methods of the CommonDialog control

Use This Method...	To Do This...
ShowColor	Display the Color dialog box
ShowFont	Display the Font dialog box
ShowHelp	Invoke WINHELP.EXE
ShowOpen	Display the File Open dialog box
ShowPrinter	Display the Printer dialog box
ShowSave	Display the Save As dialog box

Description

The CommonDialog control gives you easy access to the most commonly used dialog boxes. This saves you from having to re-create standard dialog boxes for every application. The Action property determines which kind of dialog box to display and immediately displays it. There are six styles of dialog box: Open, Save As, Color, Font, Printer, and Help.

The Open dialog box has areas for filenames, directories, drives, and default file types. The Save As dialog looks identical to Open, except for its caption. The Color dialog enables the user to select a color from a palette or from a custom color-picker. This is the same box used in the Windows Control Panel Desktop color choice. The Font dialog displays a list of all available fonts and shows an example of the selected font. The Printer dialog box enables the user to choose printers, page defaults, and page print ranges.

The Action setting for Help runs WINHELP.EXE rather than calling up a dialog box. This gives you a simple way to call up your custom help file for your application. The HelpFile, HelpKey, HelpCommand, and HelpContextID let you pass the appropriate information to the Help program to pull up general help, context-sensitive help, or the help Search dialog. Custom help files can be created using a Windows help compiler.

Although the Action property is still supported, the Show... methods provide a better way of using the CommonDialog control. Usually, you expect that methods cause some action to be performed in the application, whereas properties normally change the state of a setting. In other words, using the methods is more intuitive and makes your code more readable and easy to maintain. The six Show... methods precisely duplicate the functionality of the older Action properties. The use of the common dialog methods is demonstrated throughout this chapter, and all six of the methods are used in the Dialog project at the end of the chapter. The methods do not affect backward compatibility to earlier versions of Visual Basic. Because the following pairs of statements are equal, code written using the old CommonDialog.Action property setting will continue to function.

```
CommonDialog1.Action = 1
CommonDialog1.ShowOpen
```

```
CommonDialog1.Action = 2
CommonDialog1.ShowSave

CommonDialog1.Action = 3
CommonDialog1.ShowColor

CommonDialog1.Action = 4
CommonDialog1.ShowFont

CommonDialog1.Action = 5
CommonDialog1.ShowPrinter

CommonDialog1.Action = 6
CommonDialog1.ShowHelp
```

Common Features Although each style of common dialog box has unique settings, the general process of using them is the same for all six types. To use a common dialog box in an application, draw a CommonDialog control on the form. Much like the timer, it will resize itself and is invisible at runtime. You can place it anywhere you want on the form without affecting your application's appearance. A single CommonDialog control can produce any of the common dialog boxes. You need to make sure to distribute the COMMDLG.DLL file along with your program; place this file in the Windows system directory.

At runtime, set the appropriate values for the kind of dialog box you're about to display. For example, set the default drive, path, and pattern for the Open dialog. Then use either the Action property or the appropriate Show method to display the dialog. Table 25-4 summarizes the arguments of the Action property.

Table 25-4 Summarizing the arguments of the Action property

Action Setting	Method	To Do This...
0	n/a	No action taken
1	ShowOpen	Open a file; lists drives, directories, files, and pattern
2	ShowSave	Save a file; lists drives, directories, files, and pattern
3	ShowColor	Set or define colors; shows the color palette and optional color-picker
4	ShowFont	Set the font; shows list of fonts and font example
5	ShowPrinter	Specify print settings; shows the printer options for the selected printer
6	ShowHelp	Invoke WINHELP.EXE

The CancelError property lets you trap for whether or not the user pressed the Cancel button. If CancelError is set to True, pressing Cancel on the dialog box generates error 32755, defined as cdlCancel. You can then trap this error and take appropriate action. This helps prevent errors if your code tries to assign nothing to a property that needs something; for instance, specifying a Null BackColor causes a runtime error. If

CancelError is set to False (the default), then no error occurs; the box just closes and returns a Null. The following example shows a simple implementation of this idea to prevent attempts to set the ForeColor to a nonexistent color:

```
Private Sub menuFormatColor_Click ()
    CMDialog1.Color = QBColor(1)              'default color
     CMDialog1.Flags = cdlCCRGBInit Or cdlCCFullOpen 'rgb style, open with
                                                     'full color-picker
    CMDialog1.CancelError = True              'trap for the cancel button
    On Error GoTo errCancel                   'set the trap
    CMDialog1.ShowColor                       'display the color box
    On Error GoTo 0                           ' turn off error trap
    Text1.Backcolor = CMDialog1.Color         'set the color
Exit Sub                                      'done!
errCancel:                                    'error trap
    If Err <> cdlCancel  Then Stop            'if it wasn't a cancel
                                              ', then we've got a bug!
End Sub
```

Open and Save As   The Open and Save As dialog boxes let the user open or save a file. They have areas for choosing drives, directories, filenames, a list of available files, a list of patterns (file extensions), the option to open the file read-only, and advanced options for opening files on a network. Figure 25-1 shows what the dialog produced by the example syntax looks like, and Tables 25-5 and 25-6 summarize the subset of properties and flag settings that apply to the Open and Save As dialog boxes.

Example Syntax

```
Private Sub Command1_Click ()
    CMDialog1.DefaultExt = '*.BMP'
    CMDialog1.DialogTitle = 'Place Graphics File'
    CMDialog1.Filter = 'Icons|*.ICO|Bitmaps|*.BMP|Metafiles|*.WMF'
    CMDialog1.FilterIndex = 2
    CMDialog1.Flags = cdlOFNHelpButton
    CMDialog1.ShowOpen
    Picture1.Picture = LoadPicture(CMDialog1.FileName)
End Sub
```

Table 25-5 Properties particular to the Open and Save As common dialog boxes

Property	Action
DefaultExt	Sets the default extension for a saved file if no extension is given
DialogTitle	Sets the title displayed in the dialog box's title bar
FileName	Sets or returns the full name and path of the file to open or save
FileTitle	Returns the name only (no path) of the file to open or save
Filter	Sets the filter patterns and names for the box's Type combo box
FilterIndex	Sets the default filter
Flags	Sets a variety of options for the dialog box
InitDir	Sets the initial file directory
MaxFileSize	Sets the maximum length of the filename specified by FileName

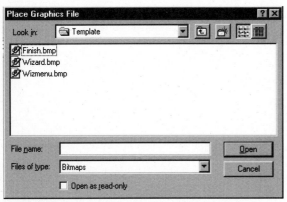

Figure 25-1 Example syntax displays this Open common dialog box

The DefaultExt Property	Use DefaultExt to set the default extension for a Save As box. For example, a word processing application might default to the extension .DOC. If the user enters just the filename with no extension, the DefaultExt is appended to the filename.
The FileName Property	The FileName property sets or returns the name and full path of the file to open or save. When the user selects a file and clicks the box's OK button, the FileName property takes on a value that can be used to save or open the file. Setting this property before the box displays sets the initial name shown in the File Name text box. The FileTitle property is similar, but is read-only and returns just the name of the file without any path.
The Filter Property	The Filter property lets you define a number of filter patterns to display in the File Type combo box. These patterns determine which files in the current directory will be listed. For example, if the filter is *.ICO, then only files with that extension get listed. Specify this as a string that follows this format: the description, the pipe symbol (|), then the actual file pattern. For example,

```
description1|filter1|description2|filter2|description3|filter3
```

```
Dialog1.Filter = 'Icons|*.ico|Bitmaps|*.bmp|Metafiles|*.wmf'
```

The FilterIndex Property	FilterIndex can then be used to set the default pattern filter. In the preceding example, setting the FilterIndex property to 2 makes Bitmaps (*.BMP) the default filter.
The Flags Property	The Flags property sets and returns a number of miscellaneous settings for the dialog box. Table 25-6 summarizes these.

Table 25-6 Settings for Open and Save As flags

Flag	MSComDlg.FileOpenConstants	Meaning
&H200	cdlOFNAllowMultiSelect	File Name list box enables multiple selections
&H2000	cdlOFNCreatePrompt	Box will prompt if user wants to create a file that doesn't exist yet
&H400	cdlOFNExtensionDifferent	Return flag indicates that returned extension is different from default extension
&H1000	cdlOFNFileMustExist	Specifies that user must enter a filename that already exists
&H4	cdlOFNHideReadOnly	Hides the read-only check box
&H10	cdlOFNHelpButton	Box will display the Help button
&H8	cdlOFNNoChangDir	Forces the box to set the current directory to what it was when invoked
&H100000	cdlOFNNoDereferenceLinks	Shows a link's filename instead of the link's target
&H8000	cdlOFNNoReadOnlyReturn	Specifies that the returned file cannot be read-only or in a write-protected directory
&H100	cdlOFNNoValidate	Box will accept invalid characters in the returned filename
&H2	cdlOFNOverWritePrompt	Box will prompt user to confirm overwriting an existing file
&H800	cdlOFNPathMustExist	Specifies user can only enter valid path names
&H1	cdlOFNReadOnly	Read-only box defaults to checked
&H4000	cdlOFNShareAware	Specifies that the SharingViolation error be ignored

The Dialog Box Summary section at the beginning of this chapter explains how to use these flag values. Specify multiple flags by using the OR operator. For example, use this line to specify showing the Help button, not showing the read-only check box, and prompt on overwrite:

```
Dialog1.Flags = cdlOFNHelpButton Or cdlOFNHideReadOnly ⇐
    Or cdlOFNOverWritePrompt
```

Color The Color common dialog box lets the user choose a color from a palette or create new colors. It shows the actual palette colors, and when expanded to enable the creation of new colors, shows the whole color gamut and has input boxes for both HSV (Hue, Saturation, Value) and RGB (Red, Green, Blue) values. The example syntax displays the dialog box shown in Figure 25-2; Tables 25-7 and 25-8 summarize the properties and flags particular to the Color common dialog box.

Example Syntax

```
Private Sub Command1_Click ()
    CMDialog1.Color = QBColor(1)
    CMDialog1.Flags = cdlCCRGBInit Or cdlCCFullOpen
    CMDialog1.ShowColor
    Text1.Backcolor = CMDialog1.Color
End Sub
```

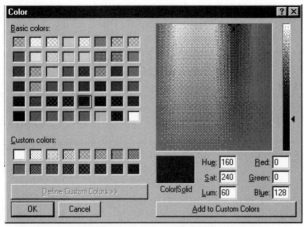

Figure 25-2 Example syntax displays this Color
common dialog box

Table 25-7 Properties unique to the Color common dialog box

Property	Action
Color	Sets or returns the selected color as a long integer; make sure to set the RGBInit flag too
Flags	Sets or returns a number of dialog box options

Table 25-8 Flags of the Color common dialog box

Flag	MSComDlg.ColorConstants	Meaning
&H2	cdlCCFullOpen	Opens the dialog box already showing the custom color-picker
&H8	cdlCCHelpButton	Makes the box display a Help button
&H4	cdlCCPreventFullOPen	Disables the Define Custom Colors command button
&H1	cdlCCRGBInit	Sets the initial value for the dialog box

The Dialog Box Summary section at the beginning of this chapter explains
how to use these flag values. Specify multiple flags by using the OR operator. For example, use this line to specify showing the Help button and
preventing the user from defining custom colors:

```
CMDialog1.Flags = cdlCCPreventFullOpen Or cdlCCHelpButton
```

Fonts   The Font common dialog box lets the user choose a font. It has combo
boxes listing the names of all the available fonts, colors, sizes, and styles
particular to the system the program is running on. It shows the selected
font and attributes in a sample window. The example syntax displays the
Font box illustrated in Figure 25-3, and Tables 25-9 and 25-10 list the
properties and flags particular to the Font box.

Example Syntax

```
Private Sub Command1_Click ()
    CMDialog1.Flags = cdlCFBoth Or cdlCFHelpButton Or cdlCFEffects ⇐
        Or cdlCFTTOnly
    CMDialog1.FontBold = Text1.FontBold
    CMDialog1.FontItalic = Text1.FontItalic
    CMDialog1.FontUnderLine = Text1.FontUnderline
    CMDialog1.FontStrikeThru = Text1.FontStrikethru
    CMDialog1.Color = Text1.ForeColor
    CMDialog1.FontName = Text1.FontName
    CMDialog1.FontSize = Text1.FontSize
    CMDialog1.ShowFont                    'display the Font dialog box
    Text1.FontBold = CMDialog1.FontBold
    Text1.FontItalic = CMDialog1.FontItalic
    Text1.FontStrikethru = CMDialog1.FontStrikeThru
    Text1.FontUnderline = CMDialog1.FontUnderLine
    Text1.ForeColor = CMDialog1.Color
    Text1.FontName = CMDialog1.FontName
    Text1.FontSize = CMDialog1.FontSize
End Sub
```

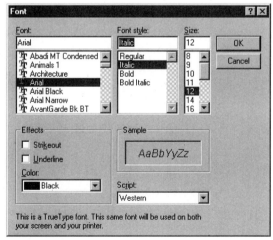

Figure 25-3   Example syntax displays this Font
common dialog box

Table 25-9 Property settings unique to the Font common dialog box

Property	Action
Color	Sets or returns the color of the font
Flags	Sets or returns a number of options
FontBold	Sets or returns the bold status of the font
FontItalic	Sets or returns the italics status of the font
FontStrikethru	Sets or returns the strikethrough status of the font
FontUnderline	Sets or returns the underline status of the font
FontName	Sets or returns the name of the selected font
FontSize	Sets or returns the size of the selected font
Max	Sets the maximum font size displayed in the Size combo box; set LimitSize first
Min	Sets the minimum font size displayed in the Size combo box; set LimitSize first

Some properties need to have flags set before you can use them. Color, FontBold, FontItalic, FontStrikethru, and FontUnderline all need the Effects flag set. Min and Max need LimitSize set before they can take effect. WYSYWIG needs to have both ScreenFonts and PrinterFonts set too. Make sure you set at least one of ScreenFonts, PrinterFonts, or Both before calling the dialog box, otherwise the 'No Fonts Exist' error occurs. Table 25-10 lists the flags of the Fonts dialog box.

Table 25-10 Flags particular to the Font common dialog box

Flag	MSComDlg.FontsConstants	Meaning
&H200	cdlCFApply	Enable the box's Apply button
&H400	cdlCFAnsiOnly	Only allow selection of fonts that use the Windows character set
&H3	cdlCFBoth	List both printer and screen fonts
&H100	cdlCFEffects	Enable strikeout, underline, and color effects
&H4000	cdlCFFixedPitchOnly	Only allow selection of fixed-pitch fonts
&H10000	cdlCFForceFontExist	Make box generate an error if user attempts to select a nonexistent font
&H4	cdlCFHelpButton	Box displays a Help button
&H2000	cdlCFLimitSize	Box will select only sizes between Min and Max
&H1000	cdlCFNoSimulations	Box will not allow GDI font simulations
&H800	cdlCFNoVectorFonts	Box will not allow vector fonts
&H2	cdlCFPrinterFonts	List only printer fonts
&H20000	cdlCFScalableOnly	List only scalable fonts

Flag	MSComDlg.FontsConstants	Meaning
&H1	cdlCFScreenFonts	List only screen fonts
&H40000	cdlCFTTOnly	List only TrueType fonts
&H8000	cdlCFWYSIWYG	List only fonts common to both printer and screen

The Dialog Box Summary section at the beginning of this chapter explains how to use these flag values. Specify multiple flags by using the OR operator. For example, use this line to specify showing only WYSIWYG fonts, which require that the fonts be available to both printer and screen:

```
CMDialog1.Flags = cdlCFWYSIWYG Or cdlCFPrinterFonts Or cdlCFScreenFonts
```

Print   The Print common dialog box lets the user specify how material is to be printed. It has areas that enable input of page ranges, number of copies, print quality, collation, and print to file. It also has command buttons that allow for setting up the current printer or specifying a different printer. Note that the dialog box does not do any actual printing; your code still has to do that. The example syntax displays the Print common dialog box shown in Figure 25-4; Tables 25-11 and 25-12 show the properties and flags for the Print dialog box.

Example Syntax

```
Private Sub Command1_Click ()
    CMDialog1.Copies = 3
    CMDialog1.Flags = cdlPDAllPages Or cdlPDCollate
    CMDialog1.ShowPrinter
End Sub
```

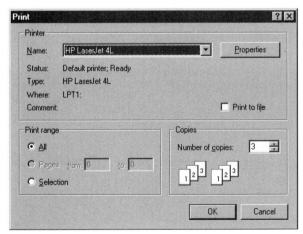

Figure 25-4   Example syntax displays this Print common dialog box

Table 25-11 Properties particular to the Print common dialog

Property	Action
Copies	Sets or returns the number of copies to be printed
Flags	Sets or returns a number of options
FromPage	Sets or returns the value of the Print From text box
hDC	Returns a device context handle for the selected printer
Max, Min	Sets the minimum and maximum allowed values for the print range
PrinterDefault	Changes the printer default to the settings the user makes in Printer Setup
ToPage	Sets or returns the value of the Print To text box

If the default printer is selected, you can print directly to the Visual Basic Printer object. If the user selects another printer in Print Setup, you need to use the hDC property to make Windows API calls to the GDI and do your printing directly. Setting the PrinterDefault property to True avoids this challenge by always making the user's selection the default printer.

Table 25-12 Flags particular to the Print common dialog box

Flag	MSComDlg.PrinterConstants	Meaning
&H0	cdlPDAllPages	Sets or returns the state of the All Pages option button in Print Range
&H10	cdlPDCollate	Sets or returns the state of the Collate check box
&H80000	cdlPDDisablePrintToFile	Disables the Print To File check box
&H100000	cdlPDHidePrintToFile	Hides the Print To File check box
&H800	cdlPDHelpButton	Displays a Help button
&H8	cdlPDNoPageNums	Disables the Print Range option buttons and text boxes
&H80	cdlPDNoWarning	Suppresses a warning message if there is no default printer
&H4	cdlPDNoSelection	Disables the Selection option button in Print Range
&H2	cdlPDPageNums	Sets or returns the state of the Pages option button in Print Range
&H40	cdlPDPrintSetup	Displays the Print Setup dialog box instead of the Print dialog box
&H20	cdlPDPrintToFile	Sets or returns the state of the Print To File check box
&H100	cdlPDReturnDC	Returns a device context for the printer selected in Print Setup
&H200	cdlPDReturnIC	Returns an information context for the printer selected in Print Setup
&H1	cdlPDSelection	Sets or returns the state of the Selection option button in Print Range
&H40000	cdlPDUseDevModeCopies	Disables Copies edit box if printer driver doesn't support multiple copies; stores the requested number of copies in the Copies property if the printer driver does support multiple copies

The Dialog Box Summary section at the beginning of this chapter explains how to use these flag values. Specify multiple flags by using the OR operator. For example, use this line to specify showing the Help button, disabling Print To File, and using the device driver's copies setting:

```
CMDialog1.Flags = cdlPDHelpButton Or cdPDHidePrintToFile ⇐
    Or cdlPDUseDevModeCopies
```

Help The Help common dialog box action doesn't really bring up a dialog box. Instead, it calls WINHELP.EXE and passes it the proper parameters for context-sensitive help, keyword searches, or even help on Help. Tables 25-13 and 25-14 show the properties and arguments of the Help settings.

Example Syntax
```
Private Sub Command1_Click ()
    CMDialog1.HelpFile = "MYAPP.HLP"
    CMDialog1.HelpCommand = vbHelpKey
    CMDialog1.HelpKey = "Graphing"
    CMDialog1.ShowHelp
End Sub
```

Table 25-13 The properties dealing with common dialog Help procedures

Property	Action
HelpCommand	Specifies the type of Help
HelpContext	Specifies the context ID of the Help topic
HelpFile	Specifies the name of the help file
HelpKey	Specifies the keyword for a keyword search

Table 25-14 Visual Basic Help constants

Value	Constant	To Do This...
1	vbHelpContext	Display Help for a topic
2	vbHelpQuit	Quit Help for a specified file
3	vbHelpIndex	Display the index of a help file
3	vbHelpContents	Display the contents topic of the help file
4	vbHelpOnHelp	Display help for using the Help application
5	vbHelpSetIndex	Set the current Help index
5	vbHelpSetContents	Designate a topic as the contents topic
8	vbHelpContextPopup	Display the topic indicated by a context number
9	vbHelpForceFile	Create a help file that displays text in only one font
257	vbHelpKey	Display Help for a keyword
258	vbHelpCommand	Display Help for a command
261	vbHelpPartialKey	Call the Windows Help search engine

The Dialog Box Summary section at the beginning of this chapter explains how to use these values.

Example The Dialog project at the end of this chapter focuses almost entirely on displaying each of these common dialog boxes. Each box is brought up by a menu command after having the appropriate properties and flags set correctly.

Comment You cannot specify where any common dialog box appears on the screen.

The Dialog Project

Project Overview

This project demonstrates each of the built-in kinds of dialog boxes: MsgBox function, MsgBox statement, InputBox$, and each of the common dialog boxes. The main form has a text box to display sample text, and another form serves as a user-defined dialog box.

Assembling the Project: formMain

1. Make a form with the objects and properties listed below in Table 25-15. After placing these controls on the form, start the Menu Editor by selecting Menu Editor on the Tools menu. Use Table 25-16 as a guide to set up the menu structure.

Table 25-15 Property settings of the Dialog project

Object	Property	Setting
Form	BorderStyle	2–Sizable
	Caption	Dialog project
	Name	formMain
CMDialog	Name	cdlgBox
Text	Name	textEntry
	Multiline	−1 True
	Scrollbars	2–Vertical

Table 25-16 Menu settings of formMain

Name	Caption	Property	Setting
menuBar	&File	Index	0
menuFile	&Open	Index	0
menuFile	&Save	Index	1

Name	Caption	Property	Setting
menuFile		Index	2
menuFile	&Print Setup	Index	3
menuFile		Index	4
menuFile	E&xit	Index	5
menuBar	F&ormat	Index	1
menuFormat	&Color	Index	0
menuFormat	&Font	Index	1
menuBar	&Help	Index	2
menuHelp	&VB MsgBox	Index	0
menuHelp	&Search	Index	1
menuHelp		Index	2
menuHelp	&About	Index	3

2. Size and place the objects as shown in Figure 25-5.

3. Place the code below in the menuFormat_Click event. It changes the background color of the text box using the Color common dialog box and changes the font the text displays in. An On Error Goto CancelFormat statement precedes each call to the common dialog box to set an error trap. If the user presses Cancel on the common dialog box, the error routine simply does nothing and exits the procedure.

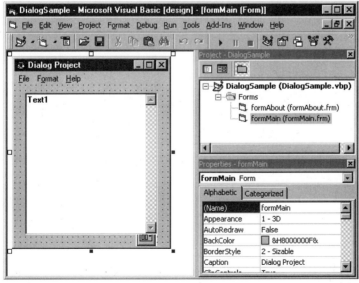

Figure 25-5 The Dialog project during design

The Color command first sets the dialog's color to match the current background of Text1, tells it that we're using RGB values to specify colors, then calls the common dialog box using the Color action constant. All common dialog boxes are modal, so the next line only executes after the user closes the Color dialog box. It sets the background color of Text1 to whatever the user specified.

The Font command will set all the font attributes for Text1 using the Font common dialog box. It first sets all the font parameters for the dialog box to equal what is already in Text1. After calling the Font dialog box, it then sets all the parameters for Text1 to what the user selects in the dialog box.

```
Private Sub menuFormat_Click (Index As Integer)
    Select Case Index
        Case 0 '**************************** color
            cdlgBox.Color = textEntry.BackColor   'default color
            cdlgBox.Flags = RGBInit               'set for rgb values
            'trap for Cancel
            On Error GoTo CancelFormat
            cdlgBox.ShowColor
            On Error GoTo 0
            textEntry.BackColor = cdlgBox.Color   'set the new color
        Case 1 '**************************** font
            'Both printer and screen
            cdlgBox.Flags = cdlCFBoth Or cdlCFEffects
            'set the dialog box's default values to the text box.
            cdlgBox.FontBold = textEntry.FontBold
            cdlgBox.FontItalic = textEntry.FontItalic
            cdlgBox.FontUnderLine = textEntry.FontUnderline
            cdlgBox.FontStrikeThru = textEntry.FontStrikethru
            cdlgBox.Color = textEntry.ForeColor
            cdlgBox.FontName = textEntry.FontName
            cdlgBox.FontSize = textEntry.FontSize
            'trap for user pressing Cancel
            On Error GoTo Cancel
            cdlgBox.ShowFont
            On Error GoTo 0
            'set the text box's properties
            textEntry.FontBold = cdlgBox.FontBold
            textEntry.FontItalic = cdlgBox.FontItalic
            textEntry.FontStrikethru = cdlgBox.FontStrikeThru
            textEntry.FontUnderLine = cdlgBox.FontUnderLine
            textEntry.ForeColor = cdlgBox.Color
            textEntry.FontName = cdlgBox.FontName
            textEntry.FontSize = cdlgBox.FontSize
    End Select
Exit Sub

CancelFormat: 'user pressed Cancel button
    'just exit sub without doing anything
End Sub
```

4. Place the following code in the menuHelp_Click event. The first command calls up the Visual Basic help file on the MsgBox command by using the common dialog box's HelpKey HelpCommand. The Search command uses HelpPartialKey to bring up the Help program's Search dialog box. The About command displays the About custom dialog box.

```
Private Sub menuHelp_Click (Index As Integer)
    Select Case Index
        Case 0 '*********************** VB Help
            cdlgBox.HelpFile = "VB.HLP"    'call up VB help
            cdlgBox.HelpCommand = HelpKey 'search for a keyword
            cdlgBox.HelpKey = "MsgBox"     'ask about MsgBox!
            cdlgBox.ShowHelp               'do it
        Case 1 '*********************** Search
            cdlgBox.HelpFile = "VB.HLP"    'call up VB help
            cdlgBox.HelpCommand = HelpPartialKey 'bring up search box
            cdlgBox.ShowHelp                     'do it
        Case 2 '(separator bar)
        Case 3 '*********************** About
            formAbout.Show 1          'show about box modally
    End Select
End Sub
```

5. Place the code below in the menuFile_Click event. It calls up the Open common dialog box to read a file into Text1, the Save As common dialog box to simulate saving the file, and the Print common dialog box to set up the printer. It also has the Exit command to exit the program. The File Open error-handling routine uses the three other predefined dialog boxes. An On Error Goto CancelFile statement precedes each call to the common dialog box to set an error trap. If the user presses Cancel on the common dialog box, the error routine simply does nothing and exits the procedure.

The File Open command is the most involved routine. Note how we set the filter to read-only text files (*.TXT) but leave the user the option of reading all files (*.*). We set an error trap before attempting to open the file in case something goes wrong (for example, if the user types the name of a nonexistent file into the File Name box). If the file opens correctly, the routine reads in up to 10 lines of text and assigns the text to Text1 before exiting the subroutine.

If an error occurs while opening the file, the DinnaOpen error handler takes over. It first displays a message box asking the user to Abort, Retry, or Ignore. It uses the answer to select which action to take. If the user chooses Abort, then the routine displays a warning message box to confirm that the text has not been altered. If the user chooses Retry, the routine asks the user to type in another filename in an InputBox function. (This, of course, is for demonstrating the InputBox function; a better approach would be to redisplay the Open dialog box.) After getting the user's input, the routine attempts to resume at the Open For Input statement. Ignore simply exits the subroutine.

The Save routine calls up the Save As common dialog box. Note that we don't really save anything to prevent this project from wiping out anything during the demonstration! The default for the Save As dialog box is to warn on overwrite, so experiment with trying to overwrite a file, safe in the knowledge that nothing will happen.

The Print routine simply calls up the Print common dialog box and prints the contents of the text box.

The Exit routine first calls the Help common dialog to close down the help file opened by the Help command. It then ends the program.

```
Private Sub menuFile_Click (Index As Integer)
    Select Case Index
        Case 0 '**************************** Open
            Dim lines As Integer, newLine As String, bigLine As String
            Dim mbType As Integer, buttonPressed As Integer
            Dim Filename As String

            cdlgBox.DialogTitle = "Open Text File"
            cdlgBox.Filter = "Text Files (*.TXT)|*.TXT|All Files (*.*)|*.*"
            cdlgBox.FilterIndex = 1                 'set default to text files
            On Error GoTo CancelFile                'trap for user pressing Cancel
            cdlgBox.ShowOpen                        'show the File Open dialog
            Filename = cdlgBox.Filename             'store the file name

            On Error GoTo DinnaOpen                 'set error trap
            Open Filename For Input As #1           'open up the file
            On Error GoTo 0                         'successful! turn off trap
            Do While (Not EOF(1)) And lines < 10    'read in up to 10 lines
                Line Input #1, newLine              'get the line
                bigLine = bigLine & newLine & Chr$(13) & Chr$(10) 'append the line
                lines = lines + 1
            Loop
            textEntry.Text = bigLine  'assign the line to the text box
            Close                      'close the text file
        Case 1 '**************************** Save
            cdlgBox.DefaultExt = "TXT"
            cdlgBox.DialogTitle = "Save Text File"
            cdlgBox.Filter = ⇐
                "Text Files (*.TXT)|*.TXT|All Files (*.*)|*.*"
            cdlgBox.FilterIndex = 1
            On Error GoTo CancelFile    'trap for user pressing Cancel
            cdlgBox.ShowSave            'show the File Open dialog
            On Error GoTo 0            'didn't press Cancel
                                       'We're not really going
                                       'to write anything.
        Case 2 '(separator bar)
        Case 3 '**************************** Print Setup
            cdlgBox.PrinterDefault = True
            cdlgBox.Flags = ALLPAGES
            On Error GoTo CancelFile    'trap for user pressing Cancel
            cdlgBox.ShowPrinter        'display Print dialog box
            On Error GoTo 0            'user didn't press Cancel
            Printer.Print textEntry.Text
        Case 4 '(separator bar)
        Case 5 '**************************** Exit
            'call up VB help to close down the Help file.
            cdlgBox.HelpFile = "VB.HLP"
            cdlgBox.HelpCommand = QUIT
            cdlgBox.ShowHelp
            End
    End Select
Exit Sub

'user pressed Cancel button
CancelFile:
    Exit Sub
```

```
DinnaOpen:              'oops! bad file name
    mbType = vbAbortRetryIgnore Or vbDefaultButton3 Or vbExclamation
    'what to do?
    buttonPressed = MsgBox("Disk Error", mbType, "Cannot Open File")
    Select Case buttonPressed
        Case vbAbort                    'stop the action
            MsgBox "Text is unchanged"  'confirm nothing happened
            Exit Sub                    'and leave
        Case vbRetry                    'let's do it again!
            'plug in a new file name by hand
            Filename = InputBox("Enter new filename:")
            Resume                      'and try to open it again
        Case vbIgnore                   'no big deal, just ignore it
            Exit Sub                    'and leave
    End Select
End Sub
```

6. Enter the following code in the Form_Load event. This tells the common dialog box to generate a trappable error when the user presses the Cancel button.

```
Private Sub Form_Load ()
    cdlgBox.CancelError = True        'trap for user pressing Cancel
End Sub
```

7. Enter the following code in the Form_Resize event. This resizes the text box to take up the entire form when the form changes size.

```
Private Sub Form_Resize ()
    textEntry.Top = 0                 'make the text box fill the whole form
    textEntry.Left = 0
    textEntry.Height = formMain.ScaleHeight
    textEntry.Width = formMain.ScaleWidth
End Sub
```

Assembling the Project: formAbout

1. Make a form with the objects and properties listed in Table 25-17.

Table 25-17 Elements of formAbout

Object	Property	Setting
Form	BackColor	&H00C0C0C0—Light Gray
	BorderStyle	3—Fixed Double
	Name	formAbout
Object	**Property**	**Setting**
Command	Caption	OK
	Default	True
	Name	cmndOK
Label	AutoSize	–1–True
	Caption	Dialog project
	FontSize	24

2. Position the controls as shown in Figure 25-6.

3. Enter the following code in the Form_Load event. This occurs when the form first loads. It duplicates the existing label twice, then moves the copies very slightly out of position. It colors one white (to serve as a highlight) and the other the same light gray as the form. The original label's color was black; this serves as the shadow. It then brings the light gray one up, to the top of the stack. The result looks like the form has been embossed with the words Dialog Project. This illustrates why the built-in dialog boxes don't work for all occasions—think of how much weaker the MsgBox function would be in this context. The functionality would be identical, but this custom dialog box looks a lot snazzier.

```
Private Sub Form_Load ()
    offset = 14                                 'how deep is offset effect
    Load lablProject(1)                         'create two identical
    Load lablProject(2)                         'label copies to create
                                                'offset
    lablProject(1).ForeColor = QBColor(15)   'White (highlight)
    lablProject(1).Left = lablProject(0).Left - 1.8 * offset
    lablProject(1).Top = lablProject(0).Top - 1.8 * offset
    lablProject(1).Visible = True
    lablProject(2).ForeColor = QBColor(7)    'Light Gray (background)
    lablProject(2).Left = lablProject(0).Left - offset
    lablProject(2).Top = lablProject(0).Top - offset
    lablProject(2).Visible = True
    lablProject(2).ZOrder                        'bring to front of stack
End Sub
```

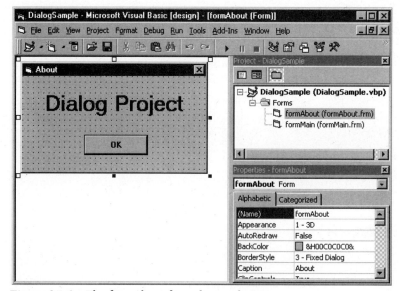

Figure 25-6   The formAbout form during design

4. Enter the following code in the cmndOK_Click event. This just hides the form.

```
Private Sub cmndOK_Click ()
      Hide
End Sub
```

How It Works

As you can see, a small amount of code and form design produces the illusion of a great deal of thought and effort having gone into this project. Using the common dialog boxes, you can give this project the air of a commercial application with hardly any effort. Note that the single common dialog box control brings up all six of the common dialog box types.

The main form calls up each of the six common dialog boxes. Figure 25-7 shows the main form in action, after having set the fonts and colors. The bulk of the code in each subroutine sets up the dialog box parameters before display, then displays the box. As this project demonstrates, using the common dialog boxes with mostly default parameters gives great results. The common dialog boxes have quite a lot of built-in intelligence, and will alter themselves or display warning messages automatically given various user input.

Note that the common dialog box is always modal—that is, your code stops executing until the dialog box closes.

We display the three other types of built-in dialog boxes in the Open error-handling routine. This shows typical examples of specifying parameters for the MsgBoxes and InputBox before and during the box display. Note how we use the returned button value in the MsgBox function to choose which action to take.

Finally, the Help About command brings up a custom dialog box. Although the functionality is the same as the MsgBox statement (single line of text with an OK button), this dialog box does some tricky formatting the MsgBox statement couldn't do. Figure 25-8 shows the About box with its embossed text.

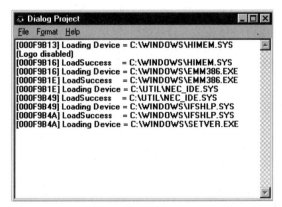

Figure 25-7   The Dialog project in action

Figure 25-8 Sometimes you need to use a customized dialog for a desired effect

26

FILE SYSTEM

Even in today's world of client/server and Web-based applications, it is sometimes necessary to manipulate files on a local storage device. The *file system* is the interface between an application and the local storage on the system.

Visual Basic provides several useful commands for manipulating the file system. These commands include the ability to navigate through the DOS file system, copy and move files and directories, and examine and set attributes and properties of files and directories.

Drives, Directories, and Files

The Visual Basic language includes several commands for performing directory and file management tasks from within your program. You can use the ChDrive and ChDir statements to change the default drive and working subdirectory. You can also use the CurDir function to determine the current default drive and directory.

Visual Basic also has four commands that work with DOS files. The Dir function returns filenames in the current default directory that match a specified pattern. The Kill statement erases files from a disk. The Name statement changes the name of a file. FileCopy copies a file.

GetAttr, SetAttr, FileLen, and FileDateTime retrieve and set a file's properties.

The File System Summary

Table 26-1 lists the Visual Basic commands that deal with the file system. It is followed by a detailed description of those commands.

Table 26-1 Functions and statements dealing with the file system

Use This...	Type	To Do This...
ChDir	Statement	Change the current working directory
ChDrive	Statement	Change the default working drive

continued on next page

continued from previous page

Use This...	Type	To Do This...
CurDir	Function	Retrieve the current working directory
Dir$	Function	Retrieve a directory entry that matches a specified filename pattern
FileCopy	Statement	Copy a file
FileDateTime	Function	Retrieve the creation or last modified date
FileLen	Function	Retrieve the file length in bytes
GetAttr	Function	Retrieve the file properties
Kill	Statement	Remove a file from the disk
MkDir	Statement	Create a subdirectory
Name	Statement	Rename a file on the disk
RmDir	Statement	Remove a subdirectory
SetAttr	Statement	Change the file properties

ChDir Statement

Purpose   The ChDir statement changes the current working directory on the specified drive.

General Syntax

```
ChDir path$
```

path$ must be a string in the format of

```
[drive:][\]dir[\subdir][\subdir...]
```

Example Syntax
```
ChDir "D:\MYDIR"
ChDir "\MAIN\MAILBOX"
```

Description   The first statement changes the current working (default) directory on drive D to MYDIR. The second statement changes the default directory on the default drive to \MAIN\MAILBOX.

The ChDir statement can affect the operation of file-related commands, such as Open and Kill. When the drive and/or directory is not specified, those commands will use the current working, or default, drive and directory.

The ChDir statement changes the setting of the default directory. In this statement, the path$ parameter must be a valid directory on the drive specified and may be no longer than 128 characters. If not, Visual Basic will issue a "Path not found error." If no drive is specified in the path parameter, the default drive is used. If a drive other than the current drive is specified, Visual Basic only changes the default directory on it; it does not change the default drive on the one in the path parameter. Use the ChDrive statement to change the default drive.

ChDrive Statement

Purpose   The ChDrive statement changes the current default drive.

General Syntax

```
ChDrive Drive$
```

Example Syntax
```
ChDrive "A"
ChDrive "C:"
```

Description   The ChDrive statement changes the default working drive for Visual Basic's file-related statements, such as Open and Kill. When the drive or directory is not specified, those commands will use the current working, or default, drive and directory.

The ChDrive statement is used to change the current default drive setting. The drive argument must be a string with a first character corresponding to the letter of a valid DOS drive.

CurDir, CurDir$ Functions

Purpose   The CurDir$ or CurDir function returns the current default directory for the specified drive.

General Syntax
```
CurDir[(drive$)]
CurDir$[(drive$)]
```

Example Syntax
```
Default$ = CurDir
A$ = CurDir("A")
Cdirectory = CurDir("C:")
```

Description   The first example assigns a string containing the default directory path from the default drive to the variable Default$. The second example assigns the default directory on drive A, while the third example assigns the default directory path on drive C to the variant Cdirectory.

DOS always maintains a default directory for each drive in the system. The default directory is the one that will be searched first for a filename if no path is specified. The CurDir$ function returns the default directory of the specified drive. If a drive designation is supplied, only the first character is used. The drive letter can be uppercase or lowercase, and must be a valid drive letter (A through *n*, in which *n* is specified by the Lastdrive parameter in the CONFIG.SYS file; or E if not specified). If the letter is not a valid drive, a "Device unavailable" error occurs. If the first character of the drive parameter is not a letter, Visual Basic generates an "Illegal function call" error. If no drive is specified or the drive parameter is a Null string, the default drive is used.

Since the path returned by CurDir$ includes the drive letter, this function is also useful for determining which drive is currently the default drive.

CurDir returns a variant; CurDir$ returns a string.

DIR, DIR$ FUNCTIONS

Purpose

The Dir and Dir$ functions return a filename that matches the supplied pattern, file attribute, or volume label of a drive. The Dir$ function is retained for backward compatibility.

General Syntax

For the first call to Dir:

```
Dir[(pattern$ [,Attributes])}
```

For each successive call for the same pattern:

```
Dir
```

Example Syntax

```
Temp$ = Dir("*.DOC")              'returns the first match for "*.DOC"
Do Until Temp$ = ""
    i=i+1                         'increments counter
    Docs(i) = Temp$              'stores file name
    Temp$ = Dir                  'returns the next "*.DOC"
Loop
Temp$ = Dir("*.*",vbHidden)      'returns the first hidden file
Temp$ = Dir("c:\",vbDirectory)   'returns the first directory
```

Description

Pattern$ represents a filename, including the path or drive if needed. If there is no match to the supplied pattern, then a Null is returned. The first time that you call Dir, you must include the Pattern$ parameter. The Pattern$ parameter can include a drive specifier, a file path, and a filename. Wildcard characters (? and *) can be used in the filename, following the usual rules of DOS. Subsequent calls to Dir without the parameter will return successive entries that meet the previously declared specifications. The Attributes parameter is optional and further refines the specifications according to a supplied numeric argument or constant. A list of these arguments is provided in Table 26-2.

Table 26-2 Constants used to specify attributes in the Dir function

Constant	Value	Description
vbNormal	0	Normal
vbHidden	2	Hidden
vbSystem	4	System file
vbVolume	8	Volume label; if specified, all other attributes are ignored
vbDirectory	16	Directory

When all matching entries have been retrieved, a Null will be returned indicating that there are no more entries. A subsequent call to Dir without a new pattern after a Null return will cause an "Illegal function call" error. It is not necessary to call Dir until a Null string is returned before you use a new pattern.

Comments Visual Basic does not check to see if the supplied pattern parameter is a valid DOS filename. If the pattern supplied is not a valid filename, Dir just returns a Null string. If the pattern specified a drive that does not exist, a "Device unavailable" error will be returned.

FileCopy Statement

Purpose Use the FileCopy statement to copy a file. This is similar to the DOS COPY command.

General Syntax

```
FileCopy source$, dest$
```

Example Syntax

```
FileCopy "~TEMP.TMP", dataFileName
```

Description This command copies a DOS file. The source$ file may be opened for read-only access, but must not be opened for write access. You may specify a drive and directory in either of the filenames, but may not specify any wildcards. The example syntax copies the file ~TEMP.TMP to the filename specified by the variable dataFileName.

FileDateTime Function

Purpose The FileDateTime function returns a date that indicates the date and time a file was created or last modified.

General Syntax

```
FileDateTime(filename$)
```

Example Syntax

```
lastSaved = CVDate(FileDateTime("DATAFILE.MDB"))
```

Description Use the FileDateTime function to determine when a DOS file was created or last saved. The function returns a date. The example syntax determines when the file DATAFILE.MDB was last modified and converts the returned string to a date variant. The filename$ argument must be a nonambiguous file and may not contain wildcards.

FileLen Function

See Also	FileDateTime, GetAttr
Purpose	The FileLen function returns the total length of a file in bytes.

General Syntax

```
FileLen(filename$)
```

Example Syntax

```
totalBytes = FileLen(Dir())
```

Description Use the FileLen function to determine the size of a DOS file. It returns a long integer indicating the total number of bytes in the file.

GetAttr Function

Purpose The GetAttr function lets you determine a file, directory, or volume label's attributes.

General Syntax

```
GetAttr(fileName$)
```

Example Syntax

```
If GetAttr(fileName$) And vbHidden Then chekHidden.Value = CHECKED
```

Description All files, directories, and volumes have an attribute byte associated with them. This information indicates whether the filename is normal, read-only, hidden, system, a volume label, a directory, or has been modified since the last backup. Table 26-3 summarizes the return values of the GetAttr function.

Table 26-3 Visual Basic intrinsic constants used with the GetAttr function

Constant	Value	Description
vbNormal	0	Normal
vbReadOnly	1	Read-only
vbHidden	2	Hidden
vbSystem	4	System file
vbDirectory	16	Directory
vbArchive	32	File has changed since last backup

Note that the return value can have several different states set simultaneously—for example, a file can be read-only, system, and hidden. Use the AND operator to perform a bitwise test for individual attributes. The example syntax uses the AND operator to test whether a file is hidden or not; if it is (GetAttr(fileName$) And vb.Hidden evaluates to nonzero), then the hidden check box gets checked.

KILL STATEMENT

Purpose
The Kill statement deletes the specified file from the disk.

General Syntax

```
Kill filename$
```

Example Syntax

```
Kill File1.List(File1.ListIndex)
```

Description
This example erases the file that is currently selected in the FileListBox named File1.

The Kill statement erases files from a fixed or floppy disk device. The filename$ parameter specifies the path and file name of the file(s) to be deleted. It may contain the wildcard characters ? and *. The ? wildcard is used to match any single character, and the * matches a full filename or extension. If the drive or path are not specified in the filename$ parameter, the default drive and/or path is used. If the file does not exist on the specified path or the path itself does not exist, Visual Basic will issue a "File not found" error.

Great care should be taken when using this statement. It is a destructive command that can, if not handled properly, cause you grief. Improper use of the Kill statement can cause your programs to inadvertently delete needed files. To prevent this from happening, when debugging a program using this statement, we suggest you preface this statement with a MsgBox$ function that confirms the action. Then, when you are sure the program is deleting the correct file (or files), remove the MsgBox$ function if desired.

MKDIR STATEMENT

Purpose
The MkDir statement creates a subdirectory on the specified drive.

General Syntax

```
MkDir dirname$
```

dirname$ must be in the format of [drive:][\]dir[\subdir][\subdir]...

Example Syntax

```
MkDir "TEST"
MkDir "\TEST"
MkDir "D:\TEST"
```

Description The first example creates the subdirectory "TEST" underneath the default directory on the default drive. The second line creates the subdirectory "TEST" underneath the root directory of the default drive. The last example creates the subdirectory "TEST" underneath the root directory of drive D.

This statement works much like the DOS command of the same name, but cannot be shortened to MD.

MkDir creates the subdirectory specified by the dir-name$ parameter. Unless the full path name is specified, the new subdirectory is created on the default drive, under the default directory. If a full path name is not indicated, and dir-name$ matches a file or directory that resides on the default drive and directory, a "Path file access error" will occur.

NAME STATEMENT

Purpose The Name statement renames a file or directory, or moves a file to another directory.

General Syntax

```
Name oldname As newname
```

Example Syntax

```
Name "Test_1.Dat" As "Test_2.Dat"
```

This example changes the name of the file TEST_1.DAT in the default directory to TEST_2.DAT.

Description The Name statement is very similar to the RENAME (REN) command in DOS. However, unlike the DOS RENAME, this statement allows the program to rename subdirectories as well as files.

The parameters oldname and newname specify the original path, the new path, and the filename. The file specified by oldname must exist. If it does not, a "File not found" error will occur. Conversely, the file specified by newname must not exist or a "File already exists" error is issued. If the drive is specified, the same drive must be used in both oldname and newname, or a "Rename across disks" error will occur. However, Visual Basic does not require the paths of the two parameters to match. This creates the useful side effect of being able to move files from one directory to another. For instance,

```
Name "C:\Temp\Test1.Dat" As "C:\Test1.Dat"
```

will move the file TEST1.DAT from the C:\TEMP subdirectory to the root directory.

This statement cannot be used if the file specified by either oldname or newname is currently open. Doing so causes a "File already open" error.

RmDir Statement

Purpose

The RmDir statement removes a subdirectory from a disk.

General Syntax

`RmDir dirname$`

dirname$ must be in the format of [drive:][\]dir[\subdir][\subdir]...

Example Syntax

```
RmDir "TEST"
RmDir "\TEST"
RmDir "D:\TEST"
```

Description

The first example removes the subdirectory "TEST" underneath the default directory on the default drive. The second example removes the subdirectory "TEST" underneath the root directory of the default drive. The last example removes the subdirectory "TEST" underneath the root directory of drive D.

This statement works much like the DOS command of the same name, but cannot be shortened to RD.

RmDir removes the subdirectory specified by the dir-name$ parameter. If the drive and/or full path name are not specified in dir-name$, the default drive and/or path are used. If the directory to be removed does not exist, a "Path not found" error will occur. The directory specified must be an empty directory, with no child subdirectories. Attempting to remove a directory that is not empty will also generate a "Path not found" error.

SetAttr Statement

Purpose

The SetAttr statement sets the attribute information for DOS files.

General Syntax

`SetAttr fileName$, attrbuteBits%`

Example Syntax

`SetAttr "MYFILE.TMP", vbReadOnly + vbSystem`

Description

All files, directories, and volumes have an attribute byte associated with them. This information indicates whether the filename is normal, read-only, hidden, system, a volume label, a directory, or has been modified since the last backup. You can add the values to set multiple bits, as the usage example shows. Table 26-4 summarizes the bit values of the SetAttr statement.

Table 26-4 Constants of the SetAttr statement

Constant	Value	Description
vbNormal	0	Normal file (default)
vbReadOnly	1	Read-only file
vbHidden	2	Hidden file
vbSystem	4	System file
vbArchive	32	File has changed since last backup

27

SEQUENTIAL AND RANDOM ACCESS FILES

Visual Basic puts a complete set of file manipulation commands at your disposal. In addition to relational file elements, Visual Basic offers a number of statements and functions for working with nonrelational disk files.

Opening a File

The Open statement initiates processing on a file. A file must be opened before you can do anything else with it. This statement tells Visual Basic the path and name of the file you want to open, how you want to process the file, and what number you wish to use in order to refer to this file in subsequent operations. This is an example of a typical Open statement:

```
Open "TEST.DAT" For Random As #1 Len = 128
```

This example opens the file TEST.DAT and specifies that it will be processed in random input/output mode. This file is opened as file number 1. The file number is how this particular file will be referenced by other file operations as long as it is open. No two open files can use the same file number simultaneously. Visual Basic tracks which file numbers are currently in use. You can use the FreeFile function to assign the next available unused file number to a variable. Then you use that variable to reference the file in all subsequent file operations:

```
Public TestFile As Integer      Declare public so Testfile can be accessed
                                from anywhere in the program.
TestFile = FreeFile             get next available unused file number
Open "TEST.DAT" For Random As #TestFile Len = 128      open the file
```

Sequential Access Files

Sequential files are processed from beginning to end, line-by-line. When opened, the file pointer is placed at the beginning of the file (except when opened for Append, which places the pointer at the end of the file). Each read or write moves the file pointer forward. Under normal circumstances, the file pointer never goes back; it only moves forward.

Sequential files can be opened in one of three modes: Output, Append, or Input. When you open a sequential output file, Visual Basic searches the specified directory. If the filename you specified in the Open statement does not exist, it will be created. If it does exist, the current file is erased, and a new one is created. You can then write data to the file with the Print # and Write # statements. Both of these statements write ASCII characters to the file. The difference between the two is that the Print # statement does not automatically format the data (although you could add in delimiters yourself), while the Write # statement automatically adds comma delimiters between each value written to the file.

When you open a sequential file for appending, Visual Basic searches the specified directory for the specified filename. If the file is not found, an error occurs. However, if the file is found, the file pointer is placed at the end of the file. From that point on, the file is treated as if it were a sequential output file, and the data you write is added to the file.

When you open a sequential file for input, Visual Basic searches the specified directory for the specified filename. If the file is not found, an error occurs. If the file is found, you may use the Input #, Input, and Line Input # statements to read data from the file. You must be careful not to read past the end of the file, as this causes an error. You can prevent this by using the EOF function to test for the end of the file. The following example reads a sequential file one line at a time until the end is reached.

```
Open "TEST.DAT" For Input As #TestFile
Do Until EOF(TestFile)
     Line Input #TestFile, A$
Loop
```

Random Access Files

Random access files are both input and output files. Random access files are record-based. In other words, they are made up of a group of the same-sized records. The size of a random access record is defined in the file's Open statement with the Len clause. Unlike sequential files, this type of access mode enables you to move directly to any record position in the file.

Records are read with the Get # statement. The Get # statement enables you to specify which record you wish to read, as well as a record variable as the target of the operation. Visual Basic will read data from the indicated record and copy it to the record variable. Each time a read is done, a full record is read, regardless of the size of the record variable used. In other words, if you specify a record length of 128 bytes in the Open statement, then 128 bytes will be read with each Get # statement, no matter how large or small the record variable is. Records are most often defined with the Type...End Type structure in the general declarations section of a module or form:

```
Type NameAndAddress
    First As String * 25          'first name
    Middle As String * 1          'middle initial
    Last As String * 25           'last name
    Address As String * 100       'Address
End Type

Private NaddrsRecord As NameAndAddress   'declare record variable
RecordLen% = Len(NaddrsRecord)           'get length of record
NaddrsFile% = FreeFile                   'get a file number
Open "NADDRS.DAT" For Random As #NaddrsFile% Len = RecordLen%
    'open the file
Get #NaddrsFile%, 100, NaddrsRecord
```

This example opens the random file NADDRS.DAT and reads record number 100 into the record variable NaddrsRecord. See Chapter 15, "Data Structures," for information about using record variables.

The LSet statement can be used to copy the contents of one record variable to another. For example,

```
Private Person1, Person2 As NameAndAddress
LSet Person1 = Person2
```

copies all the information for Person2 into the Person1 record. Note that if the two records are of different user-defined types, only the number of bytes contained in the shorter of the two record types will be copied.

Writing records to a random file is very similar to reading them. Instead of the Get statement, you use the Put statement. Plus, you can specify a record number on which the operation will take place, just as you would in the Get statement. Again, the record size indicated by the Open statement dictates how many bytes are written to the file.

```
Put #NaddrsFile%, 100, NaddrsRecord
```

This will add a new record to the file at the 100th position or update the existing contents of the 100th record.

Binary Files

Like random files, binary files are also input/output files. However, whereas random files are record-oriented, binary files are byte-oriented. This means that the records in a binary file can be variable size. Binary files also use the Get # and Put # statements to read and write to files. Instead of specifying a record position in the file, however, when used on binary files these statements specify a byte position. The length of the read or write is determined by the length of the record variable used.

Getting Information About an Open File

Visual Basic provides several commands that report on the current condition of an open file. One of these is the FileAttr function. Depending on which you request, this function returns one of two pieces of information. The first of the two is a code that indicates which mode the file was opened under: Input, Output, Append, Random, or Binary. This function can also return a value that equals the DOS file handle assigned to the file by the operating system. This number is sometimes needed in order to access this file from a DLL (dynamic link library). The following example uses both aspects of the FileAttr function:

```
VB_OpenMode% = FileAttr(1, 1)          'get the open mode of file #1
DOS_Handle% = FileAttr(1, 2)           'get the handle number of file #1
```

Another useful function is the LOF (length of file) function. This function returns the length of a file in bytes. It is most useful for determining the end of a binary file or the number of records in a random file. The following example figures the number of 128-byte-long records in a random file opened using file number 1.

```
NumberOfRecords& = LOF(1) / 128
```

The Seek function returns a value that indicates the current position of the file pointer. When used on random files, the value returned by this function indicates a record number. With all other file types, this value represents a byte position within the file. You can also use Seek as a statement to move the file pointer to a specific position in a file.

The final function that returns file information is the Loc function. This function is very similar to the Seek function. Whereas the Seek function returns the current position of the file pointer, Loc returns the position of the file pointer at the time of the last read or write. For random files, the value returned is a record number. For binary files, the value is a byte position. For sequential files, the value is the current byte position divided by 128. This makes Loc useless with sequential files.

Working in a Networked Environment

When working in a networked environment, special attention must be paid to how files are accessed. Because several users may have access to the same data in the same file simultaneously, you need to write your programs so that they prevent any possible corruption of data. Most often, this is done by restricting multiple accesses to the file or portions of the file at specific times.

To start with, the Open statement has two clauses that control the access to a file: Access and Lock. The Access clause tells the operating system what type of access your program is requesting from the file. You can request read, write, or both read and write privileges. The success or failure of the file open depends on the access you request and any restrictions other users have previously placed on the file.

The Lock clause tells the operating system what privileges your program will allow other users after it has opened the file. Your program can specify that other users be allowed full access, or it can restrict read access, write access, or both read and write access.

Requesting access and restricting privileges in the Open statement are file locking measures. In other words, such measures affect the entire file. However, if several users need simultaneous access to a file, you should not restrict access to the entire file.

Instead, you should only restrict access to those portions of the file currently being worked on by your program. This is done with the Lock and UnLock statements. With the Lock statement, you specify a portion of a file (one or more records for random files, or one or more bytes for binary files) to which no other users may have access. This restriction stays in effect until you reverse it with the UnLock statement.

Sequential and Random Access Files Summary

Table 27-1 lists the file-related functions and statements in Visual Basic that are not specific to using the Jet database engine and data control.

Table 27-1 Functions and statements of file operations

Use This...	Type	To Do This...
Close	Statement	Close an open file
EOF	Function	Determine if the end of a file has been reached
FileAttr	Function	Retrieve system information about an open file
FreeFile	Function	Retrieve an unused file number
Get	Statement	Read data from a binary or random access file
Input	Statement	Read data from a sequential access input file
Input	Function	Read a specified number of bytes from a file
Line Input #	Function	Read one line of data from a sequential access input file
Loc	Function	Retrieve the current location of the file pointer in a file
Lock...UnLock	Statements	Restrict multiple-user access to a portion of a file
LOF	Function	Retrieve the length (in bytes) of an open file
Open	Statement	Initiate processing of a file
Print #	Statement	Write undelimited data to a sequential access output file
Put	Statement	Write data to a binary or random access file
Reset	Statement	Close all open files
Seek	Function	Return the actual position of the file pointer
Seek	Statement	Move the file pointer to a specified position in a file
Width #	Statement	Define the width of a line in a sequential access output file
Write #	Statement	Write delimited data to a sequential access output file

CLOSE STATEMENT

Purpose   Closes an open file channel.

General Syntax

```
Close [#][filenumber%][, [#]filenumber%]
```

Example Syntax
```
Close
Close #1
Close 1, 5, 10
```

Description   In the preceding examples, the first example closes all the open files. The second example closes the file opened as file number 1. The last example closes the files opened as file numbers 1, 5 and 10. Notice that the # sign is optional.

The Close statement closes a file previously opened by the Open statement. The Close statement also flushes the buffers associated with the file and writes any remaining data in them to disk. If the file number supplied is not a currently open file, Visual Basic will ignore this statement and continue with the next statement. Although Visual Basic will automatically close all open files at program termination, it is good programming practice to close each open file before the program ends.

After a file has been closed, the file number cannot be referenced by any other file-related statements (such as Get or Put) until an Open statement has been issued with the file number.

EOF Function

Purpose   The EOF function returns the end of file status of an open file. It is important to check the end of file status to avoid reading past the end of a file, which causes an error.

General Syntax

```
EOF(file-number)
```

Example Syntax
```
Do Until EOF(1)
     Line Input #1, A$
Loop
```

Description   For sequential files, the EOF function returns True (-1) if the last Input, or Line Input, statement caused the program to reach the end of the file. For random access and binary files, this function returns True (-1) if the last Get attempted to read a record beyond the length of the file.

The file number must be a currently open file. If not, Visual Basic generates a "Bad file name or number" error.

FileAttr Function

Purpose   The FileAttr function returns system information about an open file.

General Syntax

```
FileAttr(filenumber%, infotype%)
```

Example Syntax

```
Open "Test" For Input As #1
VBOpenMode% = FileAttr(1, 1)
DOSHandle% = FileAttr(1, 2)
```

Description   The filenumber% parameter must be a currently open file. If not, Visual Basic issues a "Bad file name or number" error.

The infotype% parameter indicates the type of information being requested. If infotype% is 1, FileAttr returns a number that refers to the mode the file was opened under. Table 27-2 lists the open modes and the codes returned.

Table 27-2 Return values of the FileAttr function

Open Mode	Return Value
Input	1
Output	2
Random	4
Append	8
Binary	32

When infotype% is 2, FileAttr returns the DOS file handle assigned to this file.

FREEFILE FUNCTION

Purpose   The FreeFile function returns an unused file number that you can use to open a file.

General Syntax

```
FreeFile
```

Example Syntax

```
FileNo% = FreeFile
Open "Test.Dat" For Random As #FileNo% Len = 32
```

Description   When opening a file, you must supply a number (ranging from 1 to 511) by which the file will be referenced throughout the program. Visual Basic will issue a "File already open" error if you attempt to open a file using a file number assigned to an already open file. FreeFile eliminates the need for you to keep track of which file numbers have and have not been used.

The number returned by the FreeFile function does not change until you open a file with the returned number, and repeated calls to FreeFile will return the same value. Therefore it is a good idea to open a file with the returned number immediately after using this function.

GET STATEMENT

Purpose The Get statement reads a block of data from a disk file into a predefined record buffer.

General Syntax

```
Get [#]filenumber%,[position&], recordbuffer
```

Example Syntax

```
Type Rolodex
    Name as String * 20
    Number as Long
    Address as String * 100
End Type

Private PhoneCard as Rolodex
Open "Cards.Dat" For Random As #1 Len = 128
Get #1, 129, PhoneCard

Type Rolodex
    Name as String * 20
    Number as Long
    Address as String * 100
End Type

Private PhoneCard as Rolodex
Open "Cards.Dat" For Binary As #1
Get #1, 129, PhoneCard
```

Description The first example opens a file for random access and reads the 129th record into the user-defined variable PhoneCard. The size of the data read is 128 bytes, as defined by the Len keyword in the Open statement. Because PhoneCard is only 124 bytes long and the file was opened for random access, the extra bytes read are discarded. The second example opens a file for binary access and reads the file beginning at the 129th byte. Because the file was opened for binary access, the length of the data read is 124 bytes, as defined by the length of the PhoneCard variable.

The Get statement reads data from a disk file into a previously defined record area. The filenumber% parameter indicates which file will be read from. This must be a currently open file. If it is not, a "Bad file name or number" error is generated. The file must have been opened in either Random access or Binary mode. If not, Visual Basic will issue a "Bad file mode" error.

If the position& parameter is omitted, the commas must still be used. If position& specifies an area beyond the length of the file, the record buffer will be empty. Visual Basic does not check to see if a Get is being attempted past the length of the file. This task is left to you. Use the LOF function to determine the length of an open file.

The recordbuffer parameter refers to the area in which the data from the read will be stored. It can be of any data type. Most often, it is of a type defined by you (using the Type statement), with fields matching those of the file's record structure.

Reading Random Access Files

The position parameter for random access files represents the desired record number. If this parameter is omitted, the next record in the file is read. For instance, if no records have been read, a Get without the position specified will read record number 1. The next Get will read record number 2, and so on. The largest possible valid record number is 2,147,483,647.

The variable used for the recordbuffer must be of a length less than or equal to the length specified in the Open statement. Using a variable whose length is too long results in a "Bad record length" error.

Reading Binary Files

The position parameter for binary files refers to the byte position in the file where reading will start. The first byte in the file is position 1, the second is 2, and so on.

The size of the read is determined by the size of the record buffer. This enables a file to have variable record lengths.

INPUT AND INPUT$ FUNCTIONS

Purpose

The Input$ or Input function reads a string of characters from a file, assigning no special meaning to carriage returns and line feeds.

General Syntax

```
Input$(inputlength%,[#]filenumber%)
```

Example Syntax

```
A$ = Input$(100, 1)
```

Description

The preceding example reads 100 characters from the file opened as number 1. The Input$ function returns a string of the length specified by inputlength% from a data file. The file can be opened under Input, Random, or Binary mode. If it is a Random file, the maximum inputlength% is the record length specified in the Open statement with the Len parameter. For Input and Binary files, the maximum length is 32,767 bytes. However, any attempt to read past the length of the file will cause an "Input past end of file" error to occur. You should therefore use the LOF function or some other means to check for the end of the file before reading.

Input$ assigns no special meaning to commas, quotes, spaces, carriage returns, or linefeeds, so the string returned may contain these characters.

Input returns a variant; Input$ returns a string.

Line Input # Statement

Purpose The Line Input # statement reads from a sequential file until a carriage return/linefeed pair or the end of the file is reached.

General Syntax

```
Line Input #filenumber%, variable
```

Example Syntax
```
SeqFile% = FreeFile
Open "Notes.Txt" For Input As #SeqFile%
Line Input #SeqFile%, A$
```

Description The preceding example reads one line from NOTES.TXT into the variable A$. The filenumber% parameter must be a currently open file that was opened under the Input mode. If it is not, Visual Basic issues a "Bad file name or number" error.

The variable parameter must be a string variable or variant. This should normally be a variable-length string. If a fixed-length string is used and the length of the data read is shorter than the string, the balance of the variable will be filled with spaces. If the read length is longer than the string, any characters read beyond the length of the string are lost.

Unlike the Input # statement, Line Input # treats commas, spaces, and quotes no differently than any other characters. This makes it useful for reading ASCII files. A read ends when a carriage return/linefeed pair is encountered, resulting in reading one complete line of text. The carriage return/linefeed pair is then skipped and the next read continues from the first character after them. A read also ends when the end of the file is reached.

Loc Function

Purpose The Loc function returns the current position of the pointer for an open file, which indicates where the next read or write operation will occur. The meaning of the number returned depends on the mode under which the file was opened.

General Syntax

```
Loc(filenumber%)
```

Example Syntax

```
A% = Loc(1)
```

Description   The example places a number representing the current position in the file opened as #1 in the variable A%. The filenumber% parameter must be a currently open file. If it is not, Visual Basic issues a "Bad file name or number" error.

Visual Basic defaults to a 128-byte file buffer for sequential files. When a read or write is done to a sequential file, it does so 128 bytes at a time. Internally, this is much like reading and writing records with 128-byte lengths. The value returned by the Loc function for a sequential file is the result of the current byte position divided by 128 (which is the *record number* of the last internal read or write). You can open sequential files with a different size of buffer by using the Len= parameter in the Open statement. This does not change the result of Loc; it always divides by 128 no matter what the physical size of the buffer.

For random access files, this function returns the record number of the last Get or Put statement. If no Get or Put statement has yet been executed, the Loc function returns a 0.

Because binary files are byte-oriented, the number returned corresponds to the last byte read or written to the file. Again, if no read or write has been performed, Loc returns a 0.

Lock...UnLock Statements

Purpose   The Lock statement restricts multiuser access to a specified area of a file. The UnLock statement releases the restrictions placed on an area of a file by a previously issued Lock statement. This only applies to files opened with the Open statement; it does not apply to Microsoft Access databases.

General Syntax

```
Lock [#]filenumber%[,startpos&][ To endpos&]
      :
[statements]
      :
UnLock [#]filenumber%[,startpos&][ To endpos&]
```

Example Syntax

```
Lock #1
    :
UnLock #1

Open "TEST.DAT" For Random As #1 Len = 32
Lock #1, 100
    :
UnLock #1, 100

Open "TEST.DAT" For Binary As #1
Lock #1, 10 To 20
```

continued on next page

continued from previous page
```
        :
UnLock #1, 10 To 20

Open "TEST.DAT" For Binary As #1
Lock #1, To 300
        :
UnLock #1, To 300
```

Description

The first example restricts other users from accessing the entire file. When the file processing is finished, the restrictions are released with the UnLock statement. The second example locks and unlocks access to the 100th record in the random access file TEST.DAT. The third example locks and unlocks access to byte positions 10 through 20 of the binary file TEST.DAT. The final example locks and unlocks access to byte positions 1 through 300 of the binary file TEST.DAT.

The Lock and UnLock statements are used for controlling multiuser access to files in a networked or multitasking environment. Because more than one user may have access to the same file simultaneously, such environments present special problems when it comes to maintaining data integrity. For instance, let us suppose two users, Bob and Mary, are on a network working on the same file. Bob reads a record from the file, and a copy of its contents is placed in the memory of his computer. If the program that Bob is using does not restrict access to the record, Mary can also read the record into her own computer's memory. This in itself causes no problems. However, if Bob updates the record, and Mary also updates the record, Mary's update will be written over Bob's. By using the Lock and UnLock statements, Bob's program could restrict Mary's access to the record until Bob is finished with it. This ensures that when Mary reads the record, it will reflect any changes Bob has made to it.

The filenumber% parameter must be the file number of a currently open file. If the file number does not match that of a currently open file, Visual Basic issues a "Bad file name or number" error.

The area within the file to be locked may be specified with the startpos& and endpos& parameters. If endpos& is omitted, the To keyword must also be omitted. This will cause the statement to affect only the position specified by startpos&. If the startpos& parameter is not used, the range affected will be from the beginning of the file to the position specified by endpos&. If both parameters are omitted, the entire file is affected.

When used on a file that has been opened under Random mode, Lock and UnLock affect the records that fall into the range specified by startpos& and endpos&.

For files opened under the Binary mode, these statements affect a range of bytes specified by the startpos& and endpos& parameters.

When used on a file opened under Input or Output modes, the Lock and UnLock statements restrict access to the entire file. If a range has been specified, it is ignored.

Use the UnLock statement to release the restrictions placed on a file by the Lock statement. The parameters in the UnLock statement must match the parameters in the related Lock statement exactly. Not doing so will result in a "Permission denied" error. Failing to unlock the locked portions of a file before closing it can cause unpredictable results.

When a Lock is placed on a file, the specified portion of the file is not accessible to any other process. This includes other programs running on the same computer. If a Visual Basic program tries to read a portion of a file that has been locked by a different process, a "Permission denied" error will occur. This error will also occur if the program attempts to lock a portion of a file that has already been locked by another process.

Comments   The Lock and UnLock statements depend on the operating system to take care of the details involved with restricting access to files. These capabilities are provided by running SHARE.EXE under a DOS version 3.1 or higher.

LOF FUNCTION

Purpose   The LOF function returns the length, in bytes, of an open file.

General Syntax

```
LOF([#]filenumber%)
```

Example Syntax

```
Function NumberOfRecords(FileNo%, RecordLength%) As Long
    Dim FileLength As Integer
    FileLength = LOF(FileNo%)
    NumberOfRecords = FileLength \ RecordLength%
End Function
```

Description   The above example uses the LOF function to calculate the number of records in a random access file.

This function returns the number of bytes in a file, regardless of the mode under which it was opened.

The filenumber% parameter must be a valid open file. If the file number does not match that of a currently open file, Visual Basic issues a "Bad file name or number" error.

OPEN STATEMENT

Purpose   The Open statement enables input and output operations on a file.

General Syntax

```
Open filename$ [For mode] [Access access] [locktype] As [#]filenumber [Len=recordlength]
```

Example Syntax

```
Type RecordType
      Type NameAndAddress_1
      Name As String * 20
      Number As Long
      Address As String * 75
End Type

Private TestRec As RecordType
TestFile% = FreeFile
Open "Test.Dat" For Random Access Read Write Shared As #TestFile% Len = Len(TestRec)

Open "TEST.TXT" For Input As #1
```

Description   The first example opens a random access file for reading and writing. The Shared locktype parameter enables the file to be opened by other processes. It is opened under the file number specified by TestFile%. The Len keyword is used along with the Len function to define the length of each record. The second open statement opens the file TEST.TXT for sequential input.

Before any input or output operations may be performed on a file, it must first be opened. Opening a file causes Visual Basic to allocate a buffer area for the file. Because physically reading from and writing to a file is a slow process, this buffer area is set up, and acts as a way station for the file's data. Visual Basic generally reads large blocks of data from a file into this buffer area. When a Get, Input #, Line Input #, or Put statement is executed, the Input/Output (I/O) is done from the buffer, not the disk. This reduces the number of physical reads and writes, thereby speeding up file access.

The filename$ parameter can be any type of string expression that contains a valid DOS filename. The drive and path may be specified explicitly. However, if left out, the default drive and/or directory is used.

PRINT # STATEMENT

Purpose   The Print # statement writes unformatted data to a sequential file that has been opened under Output or Append modes.

General Syntax

```
Print #filenumber, [[{Spc(n)|Tab(m)}]expression[{;|,}]...]
```

Example Syntax

```
Print #1, "Hello world"

Print #1, 100, A$;
```

Description The first example writes the string literal "Hello world" to the file opened under file number 1. A carriage return/line feed pair is then written to the file. The second example writes the number 100 and the value of A$ to the file. The comma after the number 100 causes A$ to be written at the next print zone. The semicolon after A$ causes Visual Basic to suppress the printing of the carriage return/linefeed pair.

This statement prints one or more numeric or string expressions to the file indicated by the supplied file number. This is most commonly used to output ASCII text files. If the file number does not match that of a currently open file, Visual Basic issues a "Bad file name or number" error. Also, the file must have been opened under either the Output, or Append modes, or a "Bad file mode" error occurs.

More than one expression may be written at a time. The expressions may be separated by either semicolons or commas. If a semicolon is used, the next expression is written at the very next byte position in the file. If a comma is used, the expression is written at the next print zone. Print zones occur at every 14th byte position in the record.

By default, the Print # statement appends a carriage return/linefeed pair to the end of each record written. This can be suppressed by placing a semicolon after the last expression in the Print # statement.

The Spc and Tab functions can be used to insert n spaces or to write at the nth column.

You can have multiple uses of Spc, Tab, and expression. For instance,

```
Print #1, Spc(2); "Hello"; Tab(20); A$; B$; Spc(2); "Seattle", C, Tab(50); E$
```

PUT STATEMENT

Purpose The Put statement writes data to a file that has been opened under Random or Binary mode.

General Syntax

```
Put [#]filenumber%,[position&], variablename
```

Example Syntax

```
Type Rolodex
    Name as String * 20
    Number as Long
    Address as String * 100
End Type

Dim PhoneCard as Rolodex
Open "CARDS.DAT" For Random As #1 Len = Len(PhoneCard)
    :
    :
    :
Put #1, 129, PhoneCard
```

Description

The example writes the data that is in the record variable PhoneCard to the 129th record in CARDS.DAT. The Put statement is used to write data to a disk file from a previously defined record variable. The filenumber% parameter indicates the file to which the data will be written. This number must be a currently open file. If it is not, a "Bad file name or number" error is generated. The file must have been opened in either Random or Binary mode. If not, Visual Basic will issue a "Bad file mode" error.

If the position parameter is omitted, the commas must still be used. If position specifies an area beyond the length of the file, the file length is extended to that position. Visual Basic does not check to see if a Put is being attempted past the current length of the file. This task is left to you. Use the LOF function to determine the length of an open file.

The recordbuffer parameter refers to a variable containing the data that will be written to the file. It can be of any data type. Most often, it is of a type defined by you (using the Type statement) whose fields match those of the file's record structure.

Positioning in Random Access Files

The position& parameter for random access files specifies the desired record number. If this parameter is omitted, the write occurs at the position currently pointed to by the file pointer. When a Random file is opened, this pointer is set to 1. Each Get or Put sets the file pointer to the next record after the Get or Put. This file pointer may be read using the Seek function or set by using the Seek statement. The largest valid record number can be 2,147,483,647.

The variable used for the recordbuffer must be of a length less than or equal to the length specified in the Open statement. Using a variable whose length is too long results in a "Bad record length" error. If the recordbuffer is a variable length string, a 2-byte string descriptor is also written; therefore, these 2 bytes should be accounted for in the length. If the recordbuffer is shorter than the length specified in the Open statement, only the bytes in the variable will be written.

Positioning in Binary Files

The position& parameter for binary files refers to the byte position in the file where writing will start. The first byte in the file is position 1, the second is 2, and so on. If this parameter is omitted, the write occurs at the position currently pointed to by the file pointer. When a Binary file is opened, this pointer is set to 1. Each Get or Put sets the file pointer to the next byte position after the Get or Put. This file pointer may be read using the Seek function, or set by using the Seek statement.

The size of the write is determined by the size of the record buffer. This allows a file to have variable record lengths.

RESET STATEMENT

Purpose   The Reset statement writes all data residing in open file buffers to the appropriate disk files, then closes all open disk files.

General Syntax

```
Reset
```

Example Syntax

```
Reset
```

Description   This performs the same task as using the Close statement with no parameters.

SEEK FUNCTION AND STATEMENT

Purpose   As a function, Seek returns the current position of the file pointer for any open file. As a statement, Seek moves the file pointer to the specified position in any open file.

General Syntax

As a function:

```
Seek(filenumber%)
```

As a statement:

```
Seek [#]filenumber%, position&
```

Example Syntax

```
Open "TEST.DAT" For Random As #1 Len = 32
Get #1, 25, TestRec
CurrentRec& = Seek(1)
Seek #1, 100
```

Description   The example first uses the Seek function to save the position of the file pointer after the file is read. This assigns the value 26 (the next record after the Get statement is executed) to the variable CurrentRec&. The Seek statement is then used to move the file pointer to record number 100.

The filenumber% parameter indicates the file to which Seek is referring. This number must be a currently open file. If it is not, a "Bad file name or number" error is generated.

The Seek Function   For files opened under Random mode, this function returns the current record number. For all other files, the number returned is the current byte position of the file pointer. The position is returned as a long integer, greater than or equal to 1.

The Seek Statement   For files opened under Random mode, this statement moves the file pointer to the record number specified by the position& parameter. For all other files, the position& parameter specifies the byte position to move the file pointer to. The position specified must be a number between 1 and 2,147,483,647.

WIDTH # STATEMENT

Purpose The Width # statement defines the width of a sequential file's output line.

General Syntax

```
Width #filenumber, width%
```

Example Syntax

```
Width #1, 80
```

Description The example sets the output line width for file number 1 to 80 columns. When printing to an ASCII text file, it is sometimes necessary to define a maximum output length for each line. This statement defines the width of an output line. The filenumber parameter must be a currently open file that was opened in either Output or Append modes.

The width parameter can be a value of from 0 to 255 columns. Specifying a column width of 0 sets an infinite output width. The default width for a file when it is open is 0.

WRITE # STATEMENT

Purpose The Write # statement formats and writes data to a sequential file that has been opened in Output or Append modes.

General Syntax

```
Write #filenumber[, var1][, var2][, var3]..
```

Example Syntax

```
Write #1, A$, B%, C!, D#
```

Description The example writes the specified variables to the file opened under number 1. This statement writes a comma-delimited list of the supplied variables to the indicated file. Double quotes are placed around any strings, and a newline character is written to the file after each write is finished. If no variables are indicated, only the newline character is written to the file.

28

ENVIRONMENT

Visual Basic exposes several commands to query and manipulate the environment from within an application. There are commands to examine how the application was started, retrieve environment variables like PATH and TEMP, sound the speaker, and start and activate other applications.

Command-line Parameters and Environment Variables

The *command line* is the text used to launch an application from the Windows environment. It always includes the path and name of the program's executable file. This command line can also include one or more parameters that, when read by the application, direct it to behave in a certain manner on startup. The syntax and meaning of these parameters, sometimes called *switches*, are defined by the application that reacts to them. You can design your programs to react to command-line switches by reading the string returned by the Command function. This function returns all text that appears on the command line following the program's executable filename. You would normally specify this in the Program Manager's File Run dialog box or in the Command Line item in the Program Item Properties dialog box.

One common use for the Command function is to specify the name of a file to automatically load when the program starts up. The following example reads the string returned by the Command function, and if a valid filename is specified, calls a procedure to load it:

```
fName$ = Command              get the command line parameter
If Len(fName$) > 0 Then       if file specified, check to see if exists
     fName$ = Dir(fName$)
End If
If Len(fName$) > 0 Then       if fName$ is not null, it exists, so load it
     Call LoadFile(fName$)
End If
```

Another useful function for obtaining information from the system is the Environ function. DOS contains an internal table that holds miscellaneous strings. These strings are called *environment variables* and most often hold information regarding the setup of the particular system your program is running on.

Environment variables follow a specific format. The name of the environment variable precedes an equal sign, which is then followed by the value of the variable, as in

```
variable_name=variable_value
```

For example, this AUTOEXEC.BAT file sets the TEMP environment variable to the TEMPDIR subdirectory:

```
@echo off
prompt $p$g
path c:\windows;c:\dos;c:\winword;c:\bat;c:\utils
loadhigh doskey
rem the next line sets environment variable
set temp=c:\TEMPDIR
cls
```

The Visual Basic Environ function lets your programs read these variables in one of two possible ways. First, you can read a variable by specifying its name in the Environ function:

```
A$ = Environ("TEMP")
```

This will copy the value of the TEMP variable to the string variable A$. If this example line were run after the above-mentioned AUTOEXEC.BAT file, A$ would contain the string "C:\TEMPDIR". (If this variable does not exist, A$ will be given a Null value.) Notice that DOS returns environment variables as all uppercase, even if they were typed in lowercase. The second method for retrieving environment variables involves using a number to indicate the position of the desired variable in the environment table. When this method is used, the variable name as well as its value is returned. This example reads all of a system's environment variables into a list box:

```
Ctr = 1                         'initialize counter variable
Do
      'add environment variable name and value into list box
      List1.AddItem Environ(Ctr)
      'point to next environment variable
      Ctr = Ctr + 1
'when Environ returns null, all variables have been read
Loop Until Len(Environ(Ctr)) = 0
```

Environment variables are set with the DOS SET command. Each computer system will probably have a different set of environment variables with different values. As a matter of fact, it's a fair bet that no two computers have exactly the same group of environment variable settings. However, there are a few environment variables that can be found on most computers. One of these variables is the PATH variable. This variable lists all drives and directories that should be searched when trying to locate an executable file. Another is the COMSPEC variable. This variable lists the drive and path in which the DOS command-line processor (COMMAND.COM) can be found. Finally, when Windows starts, it adds its own variable, called windir. Unlike all other environment variable names, which are in uppercase letters, this entry is in lowercase letters. The windir variable contains the path to the Windows directory.

Executing Other Programs

The Shell function executes other programs. Specify the path and filename of the executable file you wish to run. This file can be a DOS command (such as CHKDSK) or some other program on the disk. You can also specify the status of the program when it begins to control whether the new program will run in windowed or full screen mode, and whether it will immediately receive the focus. Shell automatically searches the DOS path for the executable file. If the file is found and it executes without error, the Shell function will return the Windows task ID of the executing program.

You can also use the AppActivate statement to direct Windows to give the focus to a specific application. This application must already be running before the AppActivate statement executes.

Environment Summary

Table 28-1 lists the Visual Basic commands that deal with the environment. A detailed description of each item follows.

Table 28-1 Functions and statements dealing with the environment

Use This...	Type	To Do This...
AppActivate	Statement	Give the focus to a running Windows application
Beep	Statement	Sound a tone on the system speaker
Command	Function	Retrieve command-line parameters used to launch the program
Environ	Function	Retrieve entries from DOS's environment variable table
Shell	Function	Initiate execution of a program

AppActivate Statement

Purpose
The AppActivate statement activates a running Windows program and gives it the current focus. It does not change the WindowState property (minimized or maximized) of the program.

General Syntax

```
AppActivate programtitle$[, wait]
```

Example Syntax
```
AppActivate "Paintbrush — (Untitled)"
```
```
AppActivate "Paintbrush — (Untitled)", True
```

Description
The first example will give the Paintbrush application the focus, assuming it is already running and has no file loaded. Note that the exact title as it appears in the program's window must be used, although case is disregarded. The second example works the same as the example above, except it

will wait until the calling application has the focus. If the calling application already has the focus, then the Paintbrush application will activate immediately.

The AppActivate statement changes the focus from the current application to the application with a caption matching the programtitle$ parameter. If there are no matches an "Invalid procedure call or argument" error is generated. If there are multiple matches, then AppActivate will arbitrarily pick one to activate.

The wait parameter is Boolean and indicates whether the application should activate immediately or wait until the calling application gets the focus.

BEEP STATEMENT

Purpose   The Beep statement causes the computer's speaker to produce a short tone.

General Syntax

```
Beep
```

Example Syntax

```
If ErrorNumber% > 0 Then Beep
```

Description   The example beeps the speaker if the variable ErrorNumber is set. The Beep statement causes the computer to send a short tone to the speaker. You can control neither the tone nor the duration; however, issuing several beep commands consecutively can create the effect of a longer beep.

The Beep statement won't do anything if sound is turned off in the sound section of the Windows Control Panel application.

COMMAND, COMMAND$ FUNCTIONS

Purpose   The Command and Command$ functions return a variant or string that contains any command-line parameters used when Visual Basic or the Visual Basic environment program was started.

General Syntax

```
CommandCommand$
```

Example Syntax

```
Params$ = Command$
```

Description   The example stores command-line parameters for the current program into the string Params$. These functions return any text that followed the /CMD parameter on the command line. The string returned by the Visual Basic environment can be modified by choosing the Properties... option from the Project menu. When used with a Visual Basic program, Command$ returns any text that followed the executable filename on the command line. This function is useful for providing a way for the user to set up different options at runtime. (Note that unlike the case with DOS command-line parameters, the name of the program file is not included in the parameter string.)

Command returns a variant, Command$ returns a string.

Environ, Environ$ Functions

Purpose   The Environ and Environ$ functions return settings from the operating system's environment table.

General Syntax

```
Environ({entry_name$ | entry_position%})
Environ$({entry_name$ | entry_position%})
```

Example Syntax

```
A$ = Environ("Path")
A$ = Environ(1)
```

Description   The first example places the current path into the variable A$. The second example places the current setting for the first environment table entry into the variable A$.

DOS maintains a table of values called environment variables. Values in the environment table typically store information about such things as the current drive and path, the location of the command processor, or special settings needed by various programs.

The Environ and Environ$ functions allow the program to read the current setting of the operating system's environment table. Entries in the environment table are set by using the DOS command syntax SET entry_name = entry_value. See a DOS reference manual for more information on the SET command. Environ allows you to specify either the name or position of the entry to be retrieved.

If you specify a table entry name, it must match exactly (including capitalization) one of the entry names in the environment table, or a Null string is returned. If the supplied string does match an entry name, Environ returns only the text assigned to that entry.

You can also specify an entry number as the parameter to Environ. This number corresponds to the position of an entry in the environment table. For example, if a numeric argument of 2 is used, Environ returns the second line in the environment table. If the number specified is 0, Visual Basic generates an "Illegal function call" error. If the number specified is greater than the number of lines in the table, a Null string is returned.

Using a valid numeric argument causes the entire corresponding entry to be returned in the format entry name = entry value.

Environ returns a variant; Environ$ returns a string.

SHELL FUNCTION

Purpose   The Shell function runs a specified .EXE, .COM, .BAT, or .PIF program.

General Syntax

```
Shell(program-name$[, mode%])
```

Example Syntax

```
A% = Shell("WINWORD.EXE")

B% = Shell("C:\WORD\WINWORD.EXE", 3)
```

Description   The first example loads and runs the program file WINWORD.EXE. It assumes the file is in the default directory or in a directory specified by the path statement. Since the mode is not specified, it uses the default mode of 2 (minimized with focus). The second example explicitly declares the drive and path of the program file. The program is executed in mode 3 (maximized with focus).

The Shell function loads an executable file into the Windows environment and returns the task ID number that Windows assigns to each running program. The program-name$ parameter must be a string expression that contains a valid executable filename. If the desired program file is not in the default directory on the default drive or in a directory in the DOS PATH, the drive and path must be specified or a "File not found" error will occur. Specifying a file that does not have an extension of .EXE, .COM, .BAT, or .PIF will cause an "Illegal function call" error.

The mode% parameter determines how the program will be loaded into the Windows environment. It specifies the window style and whether the program is to receive the focus immediately. Table 28-2 details the settings of mode%.

Table 28-2 Shell function constants of the mode% parameter

Constant	Value	Description
vbHide	0	Window is hidden with focus
vbNormalFocus	1	Window has focus and is restored to its original size and position
vbMinimizedFocus	2	Window is minimized with focus
vbMaximizedFocus	3	Window is maximized with focus
vbNormalNoFocus	4	Window is restored to its original size and position without focus
vbMinimizedNoFocus	6	Window is minimized without focus

This parameter is optional. If omitted, the new program will be loaded as if mode 2 were specified. The full effect of the mode% parameter can only be taken advantage of by Windows programs. For DOS programs, the mode values 1, 2, and 4 work the same as mode 3.

You could run the DOS command processor by specifying the program COMMAND.COM.

29

DLLS AND THE WINDOWS API

The Microsoft Windows environment defines more than 500 separate functions that programs can use to interact directly with the operating environment, and third-party DLLs expose thousands more. Traditional Windows program development involves making calls to many of these functions, usually from programs written in the C language.

Visual Basic provides built-in features that make it unnecessary to use the API functions in most applications. There may be times, however, when you want to accomplish something that is not directly supplied by Visual Basic. For example, the project at the end of this chapter demonstrates how you can read and write the profile strings in .INI files. Visual Basic lets you access any API function directly from your program, putting all the power of Windows at your disposal.

Declaring Windows API Functions

Before a Windows API function can be used in Visual Basic, it must be declared. Declarations for Windows API functions should be located in module-level code, which basically means putting it in the Declarations section of any module or form. The exact format of a Windows API function declaration is determined by which function you use. Not all Windows API functions are declared as functions. The few Windows API functions that do not return a value should be declared as subroutines. Visual Basic expects you to specify the type of the value that will be returned by a Windows API function. This is not true for a subroutine declaration. For a thorough list of predefined Windows API function declarations, consult the WIN32API.TXT in the \WINAPI subdirectory of the main Visual Basic directory (Professional Edition of Visual Basic only). This text file contains declarations for all the Windows API functions you are likely to need. The file is lengthy, so do not attempt to load the entire file into your project. Instead, cut the declaration lines you need from the file and paste them into your project. You can also use the API Viewer provided with the Professional Edition of Visual Basic 5.0 to selectively import constants, declarations, and types via the Clipboard.

Figure 29-1 shows a sample Text API Viewer screen. The Declare statement for the GetCurrentDirectory function has already been added to the Selected Items list using the Add button. Other declarations can be added or deleted from the Selected Items list. Once the desired declarations have been added to the Selected Items list, they can be copied to the Clipboard by choosing Copy from the Edit menu. The declarations can then be pasted directly into a Visual Basic source code module.

TIP

The API Text Viewer is quicker if you Convert Text to Database. This function, available under the file menu, saves all the information for the APIs in an Access Database. The next time you use the API Text Viewer, load the database instead of the text file. After you have converted it to a database, you can create a shortcut that automatically loads the Windows API database using this command line: C:\VB\Winapi\APILOAD.EXE /D Win32api.MDB; in which C:\VB is the installation directory for Visual Basic.

To declare an API function, use the following syntax:

```
[Private|Public] Declare Function APIFunctionName Lib  LibName" _
    [Alias AliasName] [(ArgumentList)] As APIFunctionType
```

To declare an API subroutine, use the following syntax:

```
[Private|Public] Declare Sub APIFunctionName Lib  LibName" _
    [Alias AliasName] [(ArgumentList)]
```

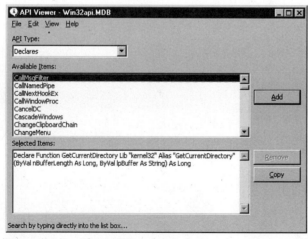

Figure 29-1   The API Viewer window

Here are some examples of actual Windows API function and subroutine declarations:

```
Declare Function CloseMetaFile Lib "gdi32" (ByVal hMF As Long) As Long

Declare Function InvalidateRgn Lib "user32" _
    (ByVal hwnd As Long, ByVal hRgn As Long, ByVal bErase As Long) As Long
```

There are a few items worth noting about the preceding declarations. First, notice that you can use the Private or Public keyword to define whether this API declaration is available to all modules or just the one in which it resides. Next, notice the use of As APIFunctionType in the first declaration. Because we are declaring a function that will return a value, we must tell Visual Basic what type of value will be returned. Second, each declaration requires the name of the Windows API function that will be used. This argument, noted above as APIFunctionName, can be located in any Windows API function reference. For example, you can use the Windows 95 SDK help file that comes with the professional edition of Visual Basic. In addition, a Windows API function reference should detail which dynamic link library (DLL) the function is imported from. Although DLLs frequently have the .DLL extension, this is not a requirement. In fact, .DLL and .EXE are extensions that may indicate a dynamic link library. LibName is the string containing the name of the DLL from which to import the specified function. The three DLLs that contain the bulk of the Windows API functions are USER32.EXE, GDI32.EXE, and KERNEL32.EXE. Since .EXE is the default extension for specified DLLs, it is therefore not required in the LibName argument string. For example, Lib "USER32" is sufficient to indicate use of the USER32.EXE dynamic link library. Finally, notice that ArgumentList, which contains a list of any variables to be passed to the function and the data type of each, is optional in some cases. Certain Windows API functions need no arguments.

Instead of using the As keyword to define the type of a function return value and the types of the variables in the argument list, you can use the Visual Basic shorthand notation of following a variable or function with a type-identifier character. You can use the %, &, and $ characters in place of As Integer, As Long, and As String, respectively. To see an example, examine the following two Declare statements, which are functionally equivalent.

```
Declare Function SetViewportExtEx Lib "gdi32" _
    (ByVal hdc As Long, ByVal nX As Long, ByVal nY As Long, _
    lpSize As SIZE) As Long

Declare Function SetViewportExtEx& Lib "gdi32" _
    (ByVal hdc&, ByVal nX&, ByVal nY& _
    , lpSize As SIZE)
```

Although the latter method of using the Declare statement with the Visual Basic type-identifier characters is more concise, modern programming practice prefers the more explicit form. This book presents the Windows API function declarations using the former method for clarity.

The Proper Use of Alias

One of the more confusing portions of the Windows API function declaration has to do with the use of the Alias keyword. Using Alias, you can tell Visual Basic that you will be calling a Windows API function by a name other than the function's given name in the stated library. APIFunctionName should contain the name that will be used to reference the Windows API function in the Visual Basic program. AliasName is the function's actual name as defined by the library in which it resides. At first, reading this may not seem intuitively correct, so be careful.

As an example of using the Alias keyword, assume that you have already defined a function in your program by the name GetBkColor. If you now want to use the Windows API function GetBkColor, you must use the Alias keyword in order to avoid a name conflict. The following Declare statement would declare the GetBkColor Windows API function, but because of the use of Alias, this function would be referred to as GetBkgndColor throughout your Visual Basic program. Here is the declaration:

```
Declare Function GetBkgndColor Lib "gdi32" Alias "GetBkColor" (ByVal hdc As Long) As Long
```

Remember to always define the APIFunctionName portion of the declaration as the name you will be using to call the function throughout your Visual Basic code. In addition, any time you define APIFunctionName as something other than the function name defined in the stated library, you must use the Alias keyword to give the actual name (AliasName in the previous declarations) of the Windows API function.

Even though Visual Basic lets you reference a Windows API function by any name you choose using the Alias keyword, it is wise to use the given function name in almost every case. Look at the following two Declare statements:

```
Declare Function GetFileSize Lib "kernel32" _
    (ByVal hFile As Long, lpFileSizeHigh As Long) As Long

Declare Function GFS Lib "kernel32" Alias "GetFileSize" _
    (ByVal hFile As Long, lpFileSizeHigh As Long) As Long
```

The first declaration uses the standard Windows API function name GetFileSize. The second example muddles the true meaning of the function by referring to it as GFS throughout the Visual Basic code.

On the other hand, there are cases in which it is absolutely necessary to use the Alias keyword in the declaration of a Windows API function. In these instances, the Windows API function name may contain an illegal character (such as an underscore), or the Windows API function name may be identical to a Visual Basic reserved word or a function already being used in your code. The Windows API function SetFocus, for instance, has the same name as the Visual Basic SetFocus method. To use the Windows API function SetFocus in your programs, you must use the Alias keyword in the declaration to change the name used to call this function. For example, you might use the following Declare statement:

```
Declare Function SetFocusAPI Lib "user32" Alias "SetFocus" _
    (ByVal hwnd As Long) As Long
```

With this declaration in place, you can call this Windows API function with the new name SetFocusAPI.

The Alias keyword also becomes useful when you wish to use a function that can accept multiple argument types. More often than not, this situation arises when a Windows API function expects an address that points to data rather than the data itself. In this situation, the Windows API function will often accept a Null value (zero) in place of the address of some data in order to indicate the lack of such an address. This situation is discussed further in the section "Passing by Reference Versus Passing by Value."

In addition to referencing a Windows API function by name, you can identify each function in a DLL by a unique ordinal number. If you know the ordinal number for the function you wish to use, you can use the Alias keyword to declare the function, as in this example:

```
Declare Function GetWinFlags Lib "Kernel" Alias "#132" As Long
```

You may experience slightly better performance from DLL routines declared in this manner, and they will consume less memory in your final application. Still, most programmers simply reference DLL functions by name rather than ordinal number.

Passing Information to the Windows API Functions

Many Windows API functions require a list of arguments (see ArgumentList in the preceding declarations). You state this argument list much like you state a standard Visual Basic function or subroutine. You supply an argument name, followed by the As keyword, followed by the type of the argument. Table 29-1 contains a list of useful standard Visual Basic types. When arrays or user-defined types are required by a Windows API function, a pointer or long pointer to the array or user-defined type structure is passed. As amazing as it may seem, the Windows API functions use only integer math. Therefore, you should never have to pass a variable declared as Single or Double to a Windows API function.

Table 29-1 Sample type declarations of the Declare statement

Sample Variable Type	Explanation	Size
ByVal n As Integer	signed integer	2 bytes
ByVal w As Integer	unsigned integer	2 bytes
ByVal p As Integer	pointer	2 bytes
ByVal h As Integer	window handle	2 bytes
ByVal l As Long	signed long integer	4 bytes
ByVal lw As Long	unsigned long integer	4 bytes
ByVal lp As Long	long pointer	4 bytes
ByVal c As Byte	byte	1 byte

continued on next page

continued from previous page

Sample Variable Type	Explanation	Size
ByVal c As String	string of character bytes	1 byte per character
Single	not used	
Double	not used	
Currency	not used	
Variant	not used	

The window handle is a frequently required parameter. A *window handle* is a unique identifier that Windows associates with each window. Because Visual Basic forms and many Visual Basic controls are windows, the hWnd property can be taken from these forms and controls and passed to a Windows API function requiring a window handle. In a 32-bit environment, a window handle is a 4-byte integer.

Arguments from the argument list are placed on the stack before a call to a Windows API function. For this reason, the size (in bytes) of the arguments in the list is very important. If the size (in bytes) of the arguments passed to a Windows API function does not match the size required by the function, a "Bad DLL Calling Convention" error occurs. But if the size (in bytes) of the arguments passed to the Windows API function is correct, this error does not occur, even if the arguments are not the correct type or if they specify illegal values. For example, because the Long data type requires 4 bytes and the Single data type requires 4 bytes, you could pass a variable declared As Single to a Windows API function that expects a variable declared As Long. The "Bad DLL Calling Convention" error will not occur, but the function will most likely fail because the internal representation of a single-precision variable will probably not present valid data to the function. The results of such an experiment are unpredictable, and a system lockup or a General Protection Fault could result. For this reason, you must carefully identify the type of each argument to the Windows API functions in the Declare statement using the As keyword. In addition, you should avoid using the As Any type identifier, which allows you to pass any variable type to a specified Windows API function. If your variable types are accurate in the Declare statements, you can catch many errors from the Visual Basic environment itself, and these are much more friendly than errors that manifest themselves at the Windows API level.

When the Windows API function requires a value, rather than the address of a value, use the ByVal keyword within the function declaration. This is true for all the standard Visual Basic types (Integer, Long, String, Byte). When a Windows API function requires an array of values or a user-defined type structure of values, do not use the ByVal keyword, for reasons explained in the following section.

Retrieving Information from the Windows API Functions

As mentioned, some Windows API functions return a value (Declare as Function) and some do not (Declare as Sub). Those that return a value can be used in the same manner as a standard Visual Basic function. You might retrieve some system information, as in the following code section:

```
Dim heapSize As Long

heapSize = GetFreeSpace(fFlags%)
```

Of course, for this to work correctly, the GetFreeSpace Windows API function has to have been declared previously. This method is an easy way to retrieve small amounts of information from a Windows API function. But what happens when more information, such as an array of values, is expected from a Windows API function? In these cases, the array is passed to the Windows API function, and the Windows API function modifies this array directly. When control is returned to Visual Basic and the array contents are analyzed, any changes made by the Windows API function are reflected. For this to work correctly, the address of the array in memory must be passed to the Windows API function. A similar case exists for strings and user-defined types.

Passing by Reference Versus Passing by Value

If a Windows API function requires that a simple value be passed—such as the handle to a window or an integer graphics coordinate—the ByVal keyword should precede this value in the argument list. When the ByVal keyword appears within the argument list, it tells Visual Basic that any argument—whether a constant, a variable, or an expression—at this location in the argument list should be evaluated and this value should be passed to the Windows API function. In programming terminology, this is referred to as *passing an argument by value*. Alternatively, leaving out the ByVal keyword or explicitly using the ByRef keyword causes Visual Basic to pass the address of the associated variable rather than the value. This is referred to as *passing by reference*. Visual Basic defaults to passing by reference, so the ByRef keyword is not needed, although it may make your function declarations more readable. In contrast, the C/C++ language defaults to passing by value. Figure 29-2 illustrates the difference between passing a variable by reference and passing it by value.

In some cases involving arrays, strings, and user-defined types, a Windows API function will require the address of the data rather than the data itself. When an array is passed to a Windows API function, for example, the whole array is not actually passed to the function. Instead, the address in memory of the beginning of the array is passed to the function. Similarly, when a Windows API function requires a user-defined type, the address to the location in memory of the user-defined type structure is passed rather than the whole structure itself. In each of these cases, the ByVal keyword is omitted, and the default method of passing by reference is used.

The Windows API functions use C language-style Null-terminated strings exclusively. *C language-style Null-terminated strings* consist of a string of character bytes terminated by the Null character, Chr$(0). When passing a string to a Windows API function, be sure to include the ByVal keyword. This informs Visual Basic that the string will be automatically converted into a Null-terminated string before being passed to the Windows API function. Frequently, you will have to create a string ahead

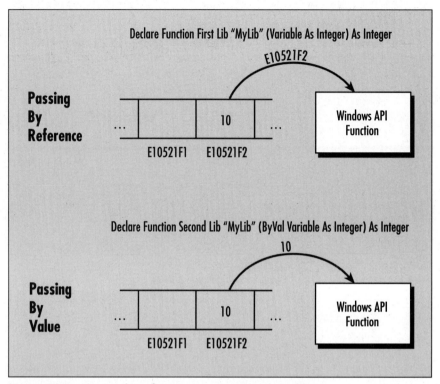

Figure 29-2   Passing by reference versus passing by value

of time that can then be passed to the Windows API function and be modified. Be careful to create a string large enough to hold the data expected from the Windows API function. You can do this either by passing a fixed-length string or by setting a variable-length string to a string of spaces (using the Space$ function). Some Windows API functions also request the size of the string being passed to ensure that only a specified number of bytes are written to the string. When calculating the string size required for a Windows API function, be sure to account for the extra byte needed by the Null terminator. Errors involving incorrectly sized strings can often result in a General Protection Fault.

Some Windows API functions that accept string arguments also allow the Null value to be passed. Exercise great care when dealing with such function arguments. If you attempt to pass "" (Null string) as a function argument of this type, you are not passing the Null value. Rather, you are passing the pointer to a zero-length string. The correct way to pass the Null value to such a function is by specifying 0 (zero). Because zero is an integer and not a string, you cannot create your function declaration with the As String type specifier. Instead, Visual Basic provides the As Any type specifier, which tells Visual Basic that any variable type is acceptable at this argument position. Although this may seem advantageous, it actually defeats one of the only lines of defense when dealing with errors in code that calls Windows API functions. Visual

Basic would not warn us if we tried to pass a Single or Double argument in this position, because any variable type is acceptable. A better solution to the problem of passing either a Null value or a string is to use the Alias keyword to define two separate function declarations, both of which represent the same Windows API function, but with different argument types. Examine these two declarations:

```
Declare Function LoadCursor Lib "User" (ByVal hInstance As Integer, _
    ByVal lpCursorName As Long) As Integer

Declare Function LoadCursorStr Lib "User" Alias LoadCursor _
    (ByVal hInstance As Integer, ByVal lpCursorName As String) _
    As Integer
```

After these two declarations are made, we can call the first Windows API function, LoadCursor, if we wish to pass the Null value to the function, or we can call the second Windows API function, LoadCursorStr, if we wish to pass a valid string. In this manner, we have still enabled some type checking by not allowing any argument other than an integer or a string, respectively.

Passing Function Pointers

Visual Basic 5.0 introduces the ability to pass function pointers. A function pointer allows an API call to *call back* your application by calling a function in it. In fact, the function pointer passed to an API function is typically referred to as a *callback function*. Before Visual Basic 5.0, there were many parts of the Windows API and third-party DLLs that were unavailable to Visual Basic programmers because Visual Basic could not pass a function pointer. The following bit of code uses the EnumChildWindows API call to change the captions or move the position of all the child windows of a form:

```
Private Declare Function EnumChildWindows Lib "user32" _
    (ByVal hWndParent As Long, ByVal lpEnumFunc As Long _
    , ByVal lParam As Long) As Long

Private Sub cmdCaption_Click()
    Dim lRet As Long
    lRet = EnumChildWindows(hwnd, AddressOf EnumChildProc, gcSetCaption)
End Sub

Private Sub cmdMove_Click()
    Dim lRet As Long
    lRet = EnumChildWindows(hwnd, AddressOf EnumChildProc, gcSetPos)
End Sub
```

The following code would be in a module elsewhere. The callback function must be in a BAS module; it cannot be part of a class or form.

```
Declare Function SetWindowText Lib "user32" Alias "SetWindowTextA" _
    (ByVal hwnd As Long, ByVal lpString As String) As Long
Declare Function SetWindowPos Lib "user32" (ByVal hwnd As Long, _
    ByVal hWndInsertAfter As Long, ByVal x As Long, ByVal y As Long, _
    ByVal cx As Long, ByVal cy As Long, ByVal wFlags As Long) As Long
Declare Function GetWindowRect Lib "user32" (ByVal hwnd As Long, _
```

continued on next page

continued from previous page

```
        lpRect As Rect) As Long

Global Const gcSetCaption = 1
Global Const gcSetPos = 2

Type Rect
        Left As Long
        Top As Long
        Right As Long
        Bottom As Long
End Type

Public Function EnumChildProc(ByVal hwnd As Long, ByVal lParam As Long) _
      As Boolean
      Dim R As Rect
      Select Case lParam
            Case gcSetCaption

                SetWindowText hwnd, "New Caption"

            Case gcSetPos
                If GetWindowRect(hwnd, R) Then
                        SetWindowPos hwnd, 0, R.Left + 20, R.Top + 20, _
                                R.Right - R.Left, R.Bottom - R.Top, 0
                End If

      End Select
      EnumChildProc = True
End Function
```

A callback function must be declared in the format expected by the calling API. In the sample above, if the hwnd parameter was an Integer instead of a Long, the behavior could be unexpected and could crash the application. Most often the specification for the callback function can be found with the documentation of the API. This is where the techniques presented in the "Passing Information to the Windows API Functions" and "Using Third-Party DLL Routines" sections of this chapter can come in handy. Typically, you will have to figure out how to convert the specification for a C function in the documentation to a Visual Basic function.

If you need to store the function pointer, you may do so by creating a function that takes a Long as a parameter and immediately returns the parameter's value. The function below uses a similar strategy to save the value of the function pointer into the target user-defined type. Once the function pointer has been passed to a function, it may copied in the same way as any other Long value.

```
Sub FillType (pTarget as MyType, ByVal plFunctionPointer As Long, plOptions as Long)
      pTarget.CallbackFunction = plFunctionPointer
      pTarget.Options = plOptions
End Function
```

API Programming Pitfalls

As mentioned, you should not use the As Any type specifier in your Windows API function declarations if at all possible. Using As Any is appropriate only when a

Windows API function requires so many different declaration forms (using the Alias keyword) that it's impractical to include them all. In this case, it is acceptable to use As Any to specify only one Windows API function declaration.

Using Third-Party DLL Routines

There are some third-party DLLs specifically for Visual Basic. DLLs created to work with Visual Basic may incorporate the use of variable types outside the realm of those normally used with Windows API function calls (Integer, Long, String, and Byte). You may find DLLs that make use of Single, Double, or even Currency data types. When using these DLLs, follow the accompanying instructions for creating a Declare statement to take advantage of the available routines. Often there is a separate text file containing declaration statements for every available function in the DLL. This allows you to simply cut and paste the declarations you need into your Visual Basic program. This is similar to the technique for incorporating Microsoft's declarations for Windows API calls from WIN32API.TXT.

Many DLLs were not specifically made to interface with Visual Basic. Most available DLLs are designed to be used with the C/C++ language. Fortunately, you can still use many of the routines in these DLLs by simply preparing the appropriate Visual Basic Declare statement for each routine you need. Because so many DLLs are written with the C/C++ programmer in mind, a little knowledge about converting from C/C++ type declarations to Visual Basic declarations is very helpful. Table 29-2 lists many C/C++ type declarations and their Visual Basic counterparts. You can use this list to create your own declarations for DLL routines geared toward C/C++ rather than Visual Basic.

Table 29-2 Converting C/C++ types to Visual Basic types

C/C++ Type Declaration	Use in Visual Basic Declare Statement
Boolean	ByVal variable As Boolean
Pointer to a string	ByVal variable As String
Pointer to an integer	variable As Integer
Pointer to a long integer	variable As Long
Pointer to a structure	variable As UserDefinedType
Integer	ByVal variable As Integer
Handle (16-bit)	ByVal variable As Integer
Handle (32-bit)	ByVal variable As Long
Long	ByVal variable As Long
Pointer to array of integers	variable As Integer
Pointer to a void	variable As Any
Void	Sub procedure
Null	As Any
Char	ByVal variable As Byte
Pointer to a char	variable As Byte

Comments

The Windows API is an extremely powerful set of functions at the disposal of every Visual Basic programmer. But along with the added functionality of the Windows API functions comes a great deal of responsibility. Beyond the reaches of the relatively friendly Visual Basic environment lie potential General Protection Faults, system lock-ups, and terse error messages. To protect your code, be sure to save your projects before running them. This is always a good idea, but is an even better idea when your project makes use of Windows API function calls. Let Visual Basic help you out by choosing Save Before Run from the Environment menu.

If you spend any amount of time using the Windows API functions from Visual Basic, you are destined to run into some of the problems just mentioned. When you do lock up the system or generate a General Protection Fault, simply reset and carefully examine your Windows API function declarations, paying particular attention to the variable types used. If you can recover from an error, but subsequently experience inexplicable problems, you may want to reset your machine to clear things out. Errors generated by faulty Windows API function calls sometimes introduce subtle bugs that only become apparent much later than the original error. Two excellent reference sources for Windows API functions are *The Windows API Bible* (Waite Group Press, 1992) and *The Windows API New Testament* (Waite Group Press, 1993). These references describe every Windows 3.0 API function and newer Windows 3.1 API functions, respectively.

DLLs and the Windows API Summary

Table 29-3 summarizes DLLs and the Windows API. Detailed descriptions of entries follow.

Table 29-3 DLLs and Windows API summary

Use This...	Type	To Do This...
Declare	Statement	Specify a reference to an external DLL
AddressOf	Operator	Return an address of a function or subroutine

DECLARE STATEMENT

Purpose The Declare statement is used to specify a reference to a Sub or Function in an external DLL. Table 29-4 lists the arguments of the Declare statement.

General Syntax
```
[Public | Private] Declare Sub name Lib "libraryname" Alias "aliasname" _
    ([argumentlist])
[Public | Private] Declare Function name Lib "libraryname" Alias _
    "aliasname" ([argumentlist])
```

Table 29-4 Arguments of the Declare statement

Argument	Description
name	The name of the call as it is referenced in code
libraryname	The name of the DLL
aliasname	The name of the call as it is internal to the DLL
arglist	A list of arguments for the call

Example Syntax

```
Declare Function SetFocus Lib "user32" Alias "SetFocus" _
    (ByVal hwnd As Long) As Long
Declare Function GetWindowRect Lib "user32" Alias "GetWindowRect" _
    (ByVal hwnd As Long, lpRect As RECT) As Long
Declare Sub DebugBreak Lib "kernel32" Alias "DebugBreak" ()
```

Description   The argumentlist parameter follows the same format as a normal Visual Basic Sub or Function. In addition, parameters may be of the Any type.

By default, declarations are public if the Private keyword is not used. You may only declare a public DLL call in a module. You must use the Private keyword when specifying a declaration in a class or form.

ADDRESSOF OPERATOR

Purpose   The AddressOf Operator returns the address of a Function or Sub it precedes. Table 29-5 shows the argument of the AddressOf operator.

General Syntax

```
AddressOf suborfunctionname
```

Table 29-5 Argument of the AddressOf operator

Argument	Description
suborfunctionname	A module level Sub or Function

Example Syntax

```
lRet = EnumChildWindows(hwnd, AddressOf MyCallbackFunction, 0)
```

Description   The AddressOf operator can only be used as a parameter to a Function or Sub. The following code is invalid.

```
Dim lFunctionAddress As Long
lFunctionAddress = AddressOf MyCallbackFunction
```

If you need to save the value returned by an AddressOf operator, use the following function:

```
Function GetAddress(ByVal plAddr As Long)
    GetAddress = plAddr
End Function
'call like this
lFunctionAddress = GetAddress(AddressOf MyCallbackFunction)
```

The API Project

Project Overview

The API project demonstrates how to incorporate Windows API calls into a Visual Basic application. You will learn how to use API calls in Visual Basic applications with an easy and useful set of functions that let you read and write to the WIN.INI file.

Assembling the Project

1. Make a new form with the object and property in Table 29-6.

Table 29-6 Setting of the main form in the API project

Object	Property	Setting
Form	Name	Form1

2. Enter the following code in the General Declarations section. This code defines the API functions to be used in the API project.

```
Private Declare Function GetProfileInt Lib "kernel32" _
    Alias "GetProfileIntA" (ByVal lpAppName As String, _
    ByVal lpKeyName As String, ByVal nDefault As Long) As Long
Private Declare Function GetProfileString Lib "kernel32" _
    Alias "GetProfileStringA" (ByVal lpAppName As String, _
    ByVal lpKeyName As String, ByVal lpDefault As String, _
    ByVal lpReturnedString As String, ByVal nSize As Long) As Long
Private Declare Function WriteProfileString Lib "kernel32" _
    Alias "WriteProfileStringA" (ByVal lpszSection As String, _
    ByVal lpszKeyName As String, ByVal lpszString As String) As Long
Const APPNAME = "Waite Group - Chapter 29"
Dim MyColor As Integer
```

3. Enter the following code in the Form_Load event subroutine. This code triggers at program startup. This code reads the appropriate setup values from the WIN.INI file. It sets the form's size, position, and background color to the last saved values. Note how we carefully declare each variable to exactly match the types given in the declarations in step 2. The GetProfileString function places the return value in the temp variable. (The value of the function, which is assigned to junk, is *not* the value of the string; rather, it is the length of the string passed to the temp variable.) Notice how we initialize the temp variable to be 16 Null characters (ASCII 0) long. This properly sets it up for use as a buffer.

```
Private Sub Form_Load ()

    Dim temp As String * 16
    Dim junk As Integer

    temp = String$(16, 0)
    junk = GetProfileString(APPNAME, "Left", "1000", temp, 16)
    Me.Left = Val(temp)

    temp = String$(16, 0)
    junk = GetProfileString(APPNAME, "Top", "1000", temp, 16)
    Me.Top = Val(temp)

    temp = String$(16, 0)
    junk = GetProfileString(APPNAME, "Width", "5000", temp, 16)
    Me.Width = Val(temp)

    temp = String$(16, 0)
    junk = GetProfileString(APPNAME, "Height", "3000", temp, 16)
    Me.Height = Val(temp)

    Me.BackColor = QBColor(GetProfileInt(APPNAME, "Color", 1))

End Sub
```

4. Enter the following code in the Form_Unload event subroutine. This code triggers when the form is unloaded from memory and saves the settings of the form's size, position, and background color.

```
Private Sub Form_Unload (Cancel As Integer)

    Dim junk As Integer

    junk = WriteProfileString(APPNAME, "Left", Str$(Me.Left))
    junk = WriteProfileString(APPNAME, "Top", Str$(Me.Top))
    junk = WriteProfileString(APPNAME, "Width", Str$(Me.Width))
    junk = WriteProfileString(APPNAME, "Height", Str$(Me.Height))
    junk = WriteProfileString(APPNAME, "Color", Str$(MyColor))

End Sub
```

5. Enter the following code in the Form_Click event. This increments the form's background color.

```
Sub Form_Click ()
    MyColor = (MyColor + 1) Mod 15
    Me.BackColor = QBColor(MyColor)

End Sub
```

How It Works

This project demonstrates the use of API calls with a simple but useful set of functions. Many programs need to save certain settings from session to session. The Windows API provides several functions that save you from having to write tedious ASCII file parsing routines.

These functions read and write to .INI files. The three functions illustrated in this project (WriteProfileString, GetProfileString, and GetProfileInt) all read from and write to the WIN.INI file. This file is in the Windows directory and serves as a master initialization file for many applications. You may also wish to use three related functions to read and write to a separate, private .INI file: WritePrivateProfileString, GetPrivateProfileString, and GetPrivateProfileInt.

All .INI files share a common format. They are all ASCII text, and can be edited and viewed by simple text editors and utilities, as well as by Windows programs. Each .INI file can have multiple sections, with many different named parameters in each section. Each section has a header enclosed in square brackets, and the section continues until the end of the file or until a new section header is encountered. Each parameter is identified by a keyword, followed by an equal sign. The actual data lies to the right of the equal sign. The following listing shows the individual section written and read by this chapter's project:

```
[Waite Group -- Chapter 29]
Left= 6108
Top= 5040
Width= 1056
Height= 2436
Color= 3
```

The section header [Waite Group--Chapter 29] uniquely identifies this section within the much larger WIN.INI file. The five parameters specify the position, size, and background color of the application's form.

When you start the application for the first time, there is no section in your WIN.INI file. The Form_Load event attempts to read the parameters from the file and, not finding the section at all, returns the default values set in the GetProfileString statements.

Once the form is open, click on it to color the background, resize it, and reposition it. Close it by double-clicking its control box (or by pressing (ALT)+(F4)). Start the application again, and notice how it retains the size, position, and color you last gave it. This happens because the Form_Unload event saves the settings to the WIN.INI file. When the form loads again during program startup, it can successfully read the last saved parameters.

30

ERROR HANDLING

An unfortunate fact of the development process is that runtime errors will inevitably occur. Although careful design and testing can eliminate many potential errors, there is, in fact, no way to provide for every eventuality. From illegal drive specifications to running out of memory or resources, there are literally thousands of situations that may generate errors during program execution. For this reason, Visual Basic provides the Err object and its associated properties and methods to determine the cause of runtime errors and assist in choosing a proper course of action.

Designing an Error Handler

There are two basic methods of dealing with errors in your Visual Basic program: *exception error handling* and *inline error handling*. When an error occurs, exception error handling forces program execution to jump to a specific section of code that deals with errors. This section of code is typically referred to as an *error handler*, and this type of scheme is referred to as *error trapping*. Inline error handling, on the other hand, does not force program execution to jump to a specific error handler. Instead, it allows execution to continue as if nothing happened, and you, the programmer, are responsible for checking the properties of the Err object at any point in the program where errors are likely to occur (such as after attempting to open a specific file for input). If the properties of the Err object do indicate that an error has occurred, your program should be capable of taking appropriate action. We will deal with exception error handling first because it is most often associated with Visual Basic programming. Inline error handling is often associated with a language like C or C++, so it may seem more intuitive to programmers familiar with those languages.

Exception Error Handling

There are three basic steps to designing an exception error handler:

1. Enable error trapping with On Error Goto

2. Write an error-handling routine

3. Decide how to exit the error-handling routine

First, the On Error Goto statement is the statement that tells Visual Basic to actually activate error trapping. It is entirely possible to have an error-handling routine within the code that is not used because it has not been activated with the On Error Goto statement. In fact, because only one error handler can be active at a time, there are frequently several different error-handling routines that coexist and several different On Error Goto statements to activate separate error handlers for separate parts of the program. An error trap is only active until the currently executing procedure (the one in which the error trap resides) is exited, but if you need to disable error trapping before the procedure is exited, use On Error Goto 0, which is a special case of the On Error Goto statement.

Once you have activated an error-handling routine with the On Error Goto statement, Visual Basic will automatically set the properties of the Err object and will immediately begin executing the statements in the error-handling routine when a runtime error occurs. Figure 30-1 displays the general flow of program execution when a runtime error is encountered while an error handler is active.

Here are some examples of various On Error Goto statements:

```
On Error Goto ErrorHandler    'jump to the ErrorHandler label

On Error Goto DiskError       'jump to the DiskError label

On Error Goto 0               'disable error handling
```

Once you have activated error handling with the On Error Goto statement, you must design the routine that will actually handle the errors. Here is an example of an error-handling routine that will handle a variety of file errors:

```
Private Sub Command1_Click()
Dim fileName As String

fileName = CStr(Text1.Text) 'get the file name from a text box
On Error Goto FileError 'activate our error handler
Open fileName For Input As #1 'attempt to open the file
Close #1 'and close it
Exit Sub 'exit this routine (skipping the error handler)

FileError: 'an error would force execution to this statement
Select Case Err.Number
Case 52 'bad file name or number error
MsgBox  "Your file name is invalid."
Resume Next
Case 53 'file not found error
MsgBox  "Cannot find the file."
Resume Next
Case 57 'device I/O error
MsgBox  "An I/O device error has occurred."
Resume Next
Case Else
Beep
MsgBox Err.Description, vbCritical
Stop
End Select
End Sub
```

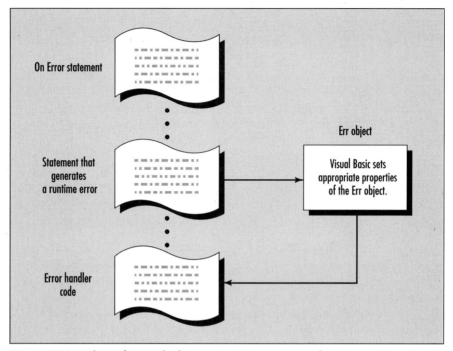

On Error statement

Statement that
generates
a runtime error

Err object

Visual Basic sets
appropriate properties
of the Err object.

Error handler
code

Figure 30-1 Flow of control when an error is encountered

This listing shows an error handler to the Command1_Click routine. When the user clicks the Command1 command button, we turn on error handling with the On Error Goto statement, open the file, close the file, and exit the routine. If an error occurs while attempting to open or close the file, the code beginning at the FileError label will begin executing. This routine contains a simple Select Case statement to display an error message for several specific errors. If the error is not one of the specific errors we are testing for, the Case Else code is executed, printing a warning message to the user and stopping execution. It is always a good idea to put an Else case in your error handler, because you cannot possibly trap for every specific error that may occur. Using an Else case and displaying the Description property of the Err object is a way to ensure that all types of errors will be handled.

You cannot enable an error-handling routine that does not exist, so the second necessary step in the design of an error handler is writing the actual routine to handle errors that may occur at runtime. In general, the error handler is placed just before the End Sub or End Function statement, and an Exit Sub or Exit Function statement precedes the error handler to prevent the procedure execution from falling through to the error handler. Either the Select...Case or the If...Then...Else construct is useful within the error-handling routine to select an appropriate course of action based on the generated error code. This error code can be obtained from the Number property of the Err object.

Finally, once the error handler is written and an On Error Goto statement is used to activate it, a proper method for exiting the error handler must be decided upon. In general, the two most popular ways to leave the error handler are to use the Resume statement or the Resume Next statement. The Resume statement will attempt to continue execution at the point where the error occurred originally. Alternatively, the Resume Next statement will attempt to continue execution at the statement immediately following the statement that generated the original error. Which statement to use depends entirely on the situation within the error handler and what you are trying to accomplish. If the error can be corrected, then the Resume statement can be used to try an operation again. On the other hand, Resume Next is useful when the error cannot be corrected and you simply want to move on to other sections of the program or re-initialize it. Figures 30-2 and 30-3 demonstrate the use of Resume and Resume Next.

Inline Error Handling

In place of the On Error Goto statement, you may use the On Error Resume Next statement to handle errors. The On Error Resume Next statement forces Visual Basic to continue execution at the statement immediately following any statement in which an error occurs. In effect, this bypasses the typical Visual Basic error-handling scheme and gives you, the programmer, responsibility for monitoring the properties of the Err object at any point in the program where an error is likely to occur. Examine the Err.Number property. If it contains a number other than zero, then an error has occurred. This method of handling errors is known as inline error handling.

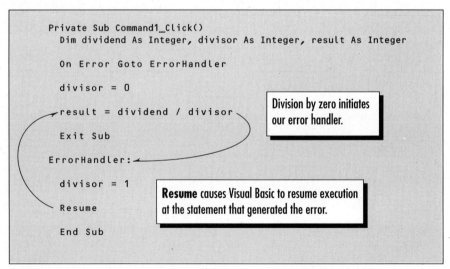

Figure 30-2   Program flow of error handler using the Resume statement

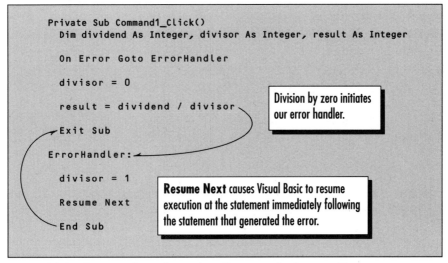

Figure 30-3   Program flow of error handler using the Resume Next statement

The following function uses inline error handling to check for an overflow error (which would occur if you attempted to store too large a value in an integer variable):

```
Private Function Square(x As Integer) As Integer
Dim result As Integer

On Error Resume Next activate inline error handling
result = x * x 'attempt to square the argument x
If Err.Number = 6 Then 'did we cause an overflow error?"
Beep
MsgBox  "The number passed to the Square function was too large."
Stop
Else 'if not, return value should be fine
Square = result
End If
End Function
```

Error Handling Summary

Tables 30-1 lists the properties and methods that relate to the Err object. This object has no associated events.

Table 30-1 Properties and methods of the Err object

Use This Property...	Type	To Do This...
Clear	Method	Clear the Err object after an error has been handled
Description	Property	Get a string containing a description of the error
HelpContext	Property	Display a help topic from a specified help file
HelpFile	Property	Specify a help file to display if the user presses Help
LastDLLError	Property	Return an error from the last DLL call
Number	Property	Return or set a numeric value specifying an error
Raise	Method	Generate a runtime error using the Err object
Source	Property	Return or set the name of the object that generated an error

When an error occurs during the execution of your Visual Basic program, you can examine the Err object to determine the cause of the error. The Number property contains a unique error number that identifies the runtime error, and the Description property contains a string expression that briefly describes the cause of the error.

You will normally use the Err object to decide a proper course of action to take inside an error-handling routine. After an On Error Goto statement has been used to establish error trapping, execution will jump to the specified line if a runtime error occurs. In this section of code (the error handler), you can examine the Err object to determine the cause of the error, and the Err object can display a brief description of the error and provide resources for obtaining help from a help file.

After an error has been appropriately handled, use the Clear method to reset the state of the Err object. If you wish to generate an error of your own during program execution, use the Raise method. Generating an error in this manner is a good way to test your error handler.

The remainder of this chapter contains a more thorough discussion of each property and method of the Err object.

CLEAR METHOD

Objects Affected   Err

Purpose   The Clear method clears all the property settings of the Err object. After an error has been handled, use this method to reset the properties of the Err object, so that future errors will be handled correctly.

General Syntax

```
Err.Clear
```

Example Syntax

```
Private Sub Command1_Click ()
On Error Resume Next 'use deferred error handling
Open  "TEMP.DAT"  For Input As #1 'attempt to open a file for input
Input #1, st 'get some input from the file
```

```
Close #1 'and close the file

If Err.Number <> 0 Then 'if an error occurred, then display a message box
MsgBox Err.Description, vbCritical,  "Error Opening File"
Err.Clear 'the Err object must be explicitly cleared
End if
End Sub
```

Description   When a runtime error occurs, the Err object properties are set according to that error. Number, Description, and Source will all contain information about the runtime error. In the following instances, the Clear method will be called automatically: upon execution of any type of Resume statement; upon execution of an Exit Sub, Exit Function, or Exit Property statement; or upon execution of an On Error statement.

    One instance in which you may need to execute the Clear method explicitly occurs during deferred error handling. If the On Error Resume Next statement is used to continue execution at the next program line when an error occurs, the Err object properties will not be reset and the Clear method must be used to explicitly clear these properties.

Example   The Clear method is executed upon execution of a standard Resume or Resume Next statement. But when inline error handling is used (by utilizing the On Error Resume Next statement), the Err object maintains its properties until the Clear method is called explicitly. (See the Error project at the end of this chapter for an example of this.)

DESCRIPTION PROPERTY

Objects Affected   Err

Purpose   When a runtime error occurs, the Description property can be used to obtain a string expression that contains a text description of the nature of the error. Alternatively, the Raise method can set the Description property to any error description that fits the needs of your project.

General Syntax

```
Err.Description
```

Example Syntax

```
Private Sub Command1_Click ()
On Error Goto ErrorHandler 'turn on error trapping
Open  "TEMP.DAT" For Input As #1 'attempt to open a file for input
Input #1, st$ 'get some input from the file
Close #1 'and close the file
Exit Sub 'do not fall through to the error handler

ErrorHandler:
If Err.Number = 53 Then 'if file is not found, then continue as normal
Err.Clear 'clear the Err object
Resume Next 'continue execution at the next statement
```

continued on next page

continued from previous page

```
Else
MsgBox Err.Description, vbCritical,  "Error Opening File"  'critical error
Err.Clear 'clear the Err object
Resume Next 'continue execution at the next statement
End If
End Sub
```

Description   When a runtime error occurs, a short description of the error should be found in the Description property of the Err object. If the error is not a Visual Basic error, but rather one that you have defined in your program, you might wish to set the Description property to identify the nature of the error. If Description is not filled in and the error number corresponds to a Visual Basic runtime error, Visual Basic will fill the Description property with a description that corresponds to the error number. The string placed in the Description property is the same string that would be returned by the Error function.

Example   In the example project at the end of this chapter, the Description property is used within message boxes to display a description of an error that was generated. In three special cases, I have chosen to use an error description of my own, but in order to handle all other possible error codes, I use the Description property to display a brief account of the error in question.

HELPCONTEXT PROPERTY

Objects Affected   Err

Purpose   If a specific help file has been set using the HelpFile property of the Err object, the HelpContext property can be used to provide the context ID for a topic in this help file. In addition, the current help context ID can be obtained by examining the HelpContext property. Table 30-3 explains the HelpContext property argument.

General Syntax

```
Err.HelpContext [= ContextID]
```

Table 30-3 Argument of the HelpContext property

Argument	Description
ContextID	Identifier for a help topic within a specified help file

Example Syntax

```
Private Sum Command1_Click()
Dim j As Integer
```

```
On Error Goto ErrorHandler 'activate error trapping
j = Int(Rnd(1) * 600) + 1
Err.Raise j 'generate a random error
Exit Sub

ErrorHandler:
MsgBox  "Error Trapped:"   & Err.Description, ,  "Error #"  & Err.Number, ⇐
Err.HelpFile, _   Err.HelpContext
Resume Next
End Sub
```

Description   A specific help file and help context ID can be designated using the
HelpFile and HelpContext properties, respectively. In the example above,
Visual Basic will use the default HelpFile and HelpContext properties of
the Err object because the error numbers fall in the range of error codes
defined by Visual Basic (0 to 600). When an error occurs during the execution of your Visual Basic program, it may be desirable to allow the user
to bring up Windows Help in order to better understand the meaning and
causes of the error. Using the HelpContext property, the help file can be
set up to display its appropriate section. If you haven't established a specific help file using the HelpFile property, the HelpContext property is
assumed to refer to the standard Visual Basic help file, which documents
most runtime errors.

Example   In the example at the end of this chapter, pressing [F1] from specific message box dialogs will open Visual Basic Help and display the correct help
topic. We are able to accomplish this by passing the values of the HelpFile
and HelpContext properties to the message box function.

HELPFILE PROPERTY

Objects Affected   Err

Purpose   You use the HelpFile property to specify a help file that will be used in reference to any runtime errors. HelpFile should contain the full path and
filename of the desired help file. In addition, you may obtain the currently
selected help file by examining the value of the HelpFile property. Table
30-4 explains the HelpFile property argument.

General Syntax

```
Err.HelpFile [= PathName]
```

Table 30-4 Argument of the HelpFile property

Argument	Description
PathName	Full path and filename of the Windows help file

Example Syntax

```
Private Sub Command1_Click()
On Error Goto ErrorHandler 'activate error trapping
Err.Number = 700 'outside range 0 to 600 is a user-defined error
Err.Description =  "This error is specific to our application." ⇐
 'define our own description
Err.HelpFile =  c:\thisapp\thisapp.hlp  'use our own help file
Err.HelpContext = 1000700 'and a specific context within the help file
Err.Raise 700 'now generate the error
Exit Sub

ErrorHandler:
MsgBox  "Error Trapped:"   & Err.Description, ,  "Error #"  & Err.Number, ⇐
Err.HelpFile,   Err.HelpContext
Resume Next
End Sub
```

Description   When a user presses the Help button or F1 from within an error message dialog box, the HelpFile and HelpContext properties of the Err object are examined. If a help file is specified in the HelpFile property, that Windows help file is called. In the preceding example, for instance, the help file that Visual Basic attempts to use is C:\THISAPP\THISAPP.HLP. Additionally, if a context ID is specified in the HelpContext property, that topic is automatically displayed. If no path and filename string is specified in the HelpFile property, the Visual Basic help file is used as the default.

Example   In the example at the end of this chapter, pressing F1 from specific message box dialogs will open Visual Basic Help and display the correct help topic. We are able to accomplish this by passing the values of the HelpFile and HelpContext properties to the message box function.

LastDLLError Property

Objects Affected   Err

Purpose   The LastDLLError property is a read-only property that returns the error code from the last DLL call.

General Syntax

```
Err.LastDLLError
```

Example Syntax

```
Private Declare Function SetFileAttributes Lib "kernel32" Alias _
     "SetFileAttributesA" (ByVal lpFileName As String, _
     ByVal dwFileAttributes As Long) As Long
Private Const FILE_ATTRIBUTE_READONLY = &H1
Private Const FILE_ATTRIBUTE_SYSTEM = &H4

Private Sub Command1_Click()
     If SetFileAttributes("c:\text.txt", _
          FILE_ATTRIBUTE_READONLY Or FILE_ATTRIBUTE_SYSTEM) = False Then
          MsgBox Err.LastDllError
     End If
End Sub
```

Description	The LastDLLError property is used to return errors from the last DLL call. Typically, a DLL called from Visual Basic will return a value indicating success or failure. If the DLL function returns a failure, then you can check the LastDLLError property for an error code indicating the reason why.
	The sample above displays the error code if the API call to SetFileAttributes fails. If there is no c:\text.text file, the code above will show a message box containing a 2. That is the system error code for "The system cannot find the file specified."

NUMBER PROPERTY

Objects Affected	Err
Purpose	The Number property returns the unique error number for any runtime errors that occur. You may also set this property to a long integer value representing an error number. The argument of the Number property is explained in Table 30-5.
General Syntax	

```
Err.Number [= ErrorNumber]
```

Table 30-5 Argument of the Number property

Argument	Description
ErrorNumber	Long integer identifying a Visual Basic error value

Example Syntax
```
Private Sub Command_Click ()
If Val(txtIntValue.Text) > 32767 Then 'examine user-provided value. If too large ⇐
Err.Raise 6 'for integer, set error number of  "Overflow"
Else
Call ProcessInt(Val(txtIntValue.Text)) 'otherwise, process the value
End If
End Sub
```

Description	The Number property is the default property of the Err object. Therefore, any existing code that simply refers to Err will, by default, refer to Err.Number. The Number property contains a long integer that identifies a Visual Basic error value. You can set this value at runtime, or you can examine it after the occurrence of an error to determine the cause of the error. Although both the Number and Description properties will be set when an error occurs, the text contained in the Description property is not guaranteed to stay constant; therefore, it is a good practice to rely on the value in the Number property to determine the nature of the error.

You can use the constant vbObjectError to determine if an error number corresponds to a Visual Basic object-generated error or to a standard Visual Basic runtime error. If the result of subtracting vbObjectError from Err.Number is within the range of 601 to 65,535, then the error is a Visual Basic object-generated error. If the result falls in the range 0 to 600, then the error is a standard Visual Basic runtime error. If the value falls outside the range 0 to 65,535, the error is generated by an object other than the standard Visual Basic objects. Table 30-6 explains the one constant value that relates to the Number property of the Err object.

Table 30-6 Constant value of object-generated errors in the Err object's Number property

Value	Constants
vbObjectError	-2147221504

Example   The Number property is used in the project at the end of this chapter in order to understand what particular error has been generated. The Select...Case structure within the error handler relies on the Number property to decide its course of action.

RAISE METHOD

Objects Affected   Err

Purpose   The Raise method can be used to generate a runtime error in your Visual Basic program. Table 30-7 explains the Raise method arguments.

General Syntax

```
Err.Raise(Number[,Source] [,Description] [,HelpFile] [,HelpContext])
```

Table 30-7 Arguments of the Raise method

Argument	Description
Number	Number that identifies the nature of the error
Source	String expression that specifies which object or application generated the error
Description	String expression that gives a text description of the error
HelpFile	Path and filename of the help file in which help on this error can be found
HelpContext	Context ID to identify the topic within the specified help file that describes this error

Example Syntax

```
Private Sub Command1_Click()
Err.Number = 660 'set up some of our own error numbers
Err.Description =  "ID Number Too Large."  'and descriptions...
```

```
Err.Number = 670
Err.Description =  "ID Number Not Evenly Divisible By 2."

On Error Goto ErrorHandler 'activate the error handler
If MemberID > MAXID Then 'is the ID number too large?
Err.Raise 660
ElseIf MemberID Mod 2 <> 0 Then 'is it not evenly divisible by 2?
Err.Raise 670
End if
Exit Sub

ErrorHandler:
Select Case Err.Number 'print an appropriate message and resume
Case 660
MsgBox  "You must enter a Member ID smaller than"   & Format$(MAXID) &  "."
Resume Next
Case 670
MsgBox  "The Member ID number must be even!"
Resume Next
Case Else 'or halt if error is not one of ours
Beep
MsgBox Err.Description, vbCritical
Stop
End Select
End Sub
```

Description   The Raise method allows you to generate a runtime error within your program. It is often advantageous to write a single error-handling routine for a given subroutine or function. Within such a subroutine or function, you can use the Raise method to begin executing the error handler when something within your program code is not quite right. Although the condition you detect might not normally generate an error, you can use the Raise method to force generation of an error. In the example syntax, a member ID number that is too large will cause an error to be generated. In this way, the error is handled by a single error-handling routine within the subroutine.

Example   We use the Raise method as the core functionality of the project at the end of the chapter. When the user clicks a command button, an appropriate error-handling method is established and the Raise method is used to generate an error.

SOURCE PROPERTY

Objects Affected   Err

Purpose   The Source property is used to determine the object or application that generated an error. In addition, you can set the Source property at runtime to relay this same information to the Err object. Table 30-8 explains the Source property argument.

General Syntax

```
Err.Source [=StringExpression]
```

Table 30-8 The Source property argument

Argument	Description
StringExpression	String representing the object or application that generated an error

Example Syntax

```
Private Sub Command1_Click()
Dim j As Integer

On Error Goto ErrorHandler 'activate error trapping
j = Int(Rnd(1) * 600) + 1
Err.Raise j 'generate a random error
Exit Sub

ErrorHandler:
MsgBox  "Error: "  & Err.Description & Chr$(13) &  "Source:"   & Err.Source
Resume Next
End Sub
```

Description   When an error occurs in an object that has been accessed by your Visual Basic code, the Source property will be set to identify the object that generated the error. The Source property generally contains the class name of the guilty object. In the example above, the Source property will be displayed as "Project1" (or whatever happens to be the name of the currently executing Visual Basic project). If an error occurs during the use of an accessed object, it may be helpful to relay the name of the offending object to the user. This name is obtained from the Source property. If an error occurs outside a standard Visual Basic object, the error code returned in the Number property will not match the standard Visual Basic error codes. Therefore, do not try to determine the type of error of another object by comparing the Number property of the Err object to the standard Visual Basic error codes. Errors generated in objects other than standard Visual Basic objects are outside the 0 to 65,535 range (after the vbObjectError constant is subtracted from Err.Number).

Example   In the project at the end of this chapter, the Source property is displayed in a message box so the user can see the name of the application that generated an error. (For our purposes, the application that generates the error will always be the project itself.)

The Error Project

Project Overview

The following project details the use of the Err object, its methods, and its properties. This project attempts to present in a clear and concise way several different approaches to error handling. After completing this project, you should be able to create your own error handler, enable error trapping, investigate and manipulate the Err object, and use inline error handling.

Assembling the Project: The Error Form

1. Create a new form (the Error form) and place on it the controls specified in Table 30-9.

Table 30-9 Settings and properties of the Error project

Object	Property	Setting
Form	Name	Form1
	Caption	Error Project
Label	Name	Label1
	Caption	Generate Error:
Command Button	Name	Command1
	Caption	Out of Memory
Command Button	Name	Command2
	Caption	File Not Found
Command Button	Name	Command3
	Caption	Disk Full
Command Button	Name	Command4
	Caption	(Random Error)
Check Box	Name	Check1
	Caption	Enable Error Trapping
	Value	1
Check Box	Name	Check2
	Caption	Inline Error Handling

2. Check the appearance of your form against Figure 30-4.

3. Enter the following line into the General Declarations section of your form. This line defines the three constants that we will use in the project. Each of these constants represents a Visual Basic error number.

```
Private Const ERROUTOFMEMORY = 7, ERRFILENOTFOUND = 53, ERRDISKFULL = 61,
```

4. Enter the following code into the Command1_Click() event. This event occurs when the user clicks the button marked Out of Memory.

```
Private Sub Command1_Click()
Dim retValue As Integer

retValue = ProcessError(ERROUTOFMEMORY)
If retValue <> 0 Then
MsgBox  "Inline Error #"  & retValue
End If
End Sub
```

5. Enter the following code into the Command2_Click() event. This event occurs when the user clicks the button marked File Not Found.

```
Private Sub Command2_Click()
Dim retValue As Integer

retValue = ProcessError(ERRFILENOTFOUND)
If retValue <> 0 Then
MsgBox  "Inline Error #"  & retValue
End If
End Sub
```

6. Enter the following code into the Command3_Click() event. This event occurs when the user clicks the button marked Disk Full.

```
Private Sub Command3_Click()
Dim retValue As Integer

retValue = ProcessError(ERRDISKFULL)
If retValue <> 0 Then
MsgBox  "Inline Error #"  & retValue
End If
End Sub
```

7. Enter the following code into the Command4_Click() event. This event occurs when the user clicks the button marked (Random Error).

```
Private Sub Command4_Click()
Dim rndError As Integer
Dim retValue As Integer
Randomize Timer
 'Pick a random error that is not one of the
 'errors we specifically look for in our handler.
Do
rndError = Int(Rnd(1) * 600) + 1
Loop While rndError = ERROUTOFMEMORY Or rndError = ERRFILENOTFOUND ⇐
Or rndError = _ ERRDISKFULL

retValue = ProcessError(rndError)
If retValue <> 0 Then
MsgBox  "Inline Error #"  & retValue
End If
End Sub
```

8. To insert the following function, select Procedure from the Visual Basic Insert menu, choose the Function option, and type the name ProcessError. This function contains the actual error handler, and when each of the command buttons is clicked, it simply passes an error value to this function. Whether or not an error handler will be installed and what type of handler (inline or exception) will be used is determined by the state of the two check boxes on the form. The error handler in this function handles three particular errors and considers the rest critical, displaying an error message and halting execution.

```
Private Function ProcessError(errorNum As Integer) As Integer
 'See if we are handling error trapping  "inline"
 'or if error trapping is on at all.
If Check1.Value = 1 Then
If Check2.Value = 1 Then
On Error Resume Next
Else
On Error Goto ErrorHandler
End If
End If

Err.Raise errorNum generate the appropriate error

 'For the Out of Memory error only, we will clear the
 'error object so the error never makes it back to the
 'calling procedure, even when the Inline Error Handling
 'box is checked (see explanation later).
If Err.Number = ERROUTOFMEMORY Then
MsgBox  "Handling inline error: Out of Memory"
Err.Clear
End If

ProcessError = Err.Number 'return any inline error number

Exit Function

ErrorHandler:
 'we have picked three particular errors to handle specifically
Select Case Err.Number
Case ERROUTOFMEMORY
If MsgBox( "Error Trapped: Not enough memory."  & Chr$(13) & _
       "Source: "  & _  Err.Source, vbExclamation + vbOK, _
       , Err.HelpFile, Err.HelpContext) = vbOK Then
Resume
Else
Resume Next
End If
Case ERRFILENOTFOUND
If MsgBox( "Error Trapped: Can't find the file."  & Chr$(13) & _
       "Source:"   & _ Err.Source, vbExclamation + vbOK, _
       , Err.HelpFile, Err.HelpContext) = vbOK Then
Resume
Else
Resume Next
End If
Case ERRDISKFULL
If MsgBox( "Error Trapped: Not enough space on disk."  & Chr$(13) & _
       "Source:"   & _ Err.Source, vbExclamation + vbOK, _
       , Err.HelpFile, Err.HelpContext) = vbOK Then
Resume
Else
Resume Next
End If
Case Else
Beep
MsgBox  "Unexpected Error #"  & Err.Number &  " - "  & Err.Description, _
       vbCritical _ + vbOK, , Err.HelpFile, Err.HelpContext
Stop
End Select
End Function
```

How It Works

This example program demonstrates some of the different ways of setting up an error-handling routine. The command buttons each generate a different error, and the check boxes allow you to disable error trapping or try out inline error handling. If error trapping is disabled, pressing the buttons will result in a runtime error. At design time, you will have the option to debug the application. At runtime, the application will simply present a message box that, once acknowledged, will let the application terminate.

When each command button is pressed, an appropriate error code is passed to the ProcessError function. The ProcessError function begins by examining the settings of the two check boxes. If error handling is enabled, then the check box for inline error handling is examined. Inline error handling is achieved using the On Error Resume Next statement. This tells Visual Basic to set all the appropriate properties in the Err object when an error occurs, but then simply continue executing at the next line rather than jumping to an error handler. If we do not choose inline error handling, then the On Error Goto ErrorHandler statement is executed, and subsequent errors will cause the program to jump to our error-handling routine. When error handling is enabled, pressing F1 while a message box dialog is active will cause Visual Basic Help to appear with the correct error message displayed. This happens because we pass the Err.HelpFile and Err.HelpContext properties to the message box function in the error handler.

The error handler uses a Select...Case statement to determine if the Err.Number property contains one of the three error codes we have chosen to handle specially. If so, the error is handled by the appropriate section of the Select...Case statement, and a simple message box is displayed with our own wording of a description of the error, the Err.Source property, and both the OK and Cancel buttons. If the user selects OK, the program will attempt to Resume and will fail because execution continues on the same line that caused the error (in this case, the line in question contains a call to the Err.Raise method, thereby generating the same error each time execution is resumed there). If the user selects Cancel, the program will attempt to Resume Next, which will be successful because execution continues with the line immediately following the line that generated the error.

If the user selects the (Random Error) button, an error will be generated that is not one of the three errors for which there is a special case in the Select...Case statement. Here, the Case Else case is executed, a message box appears, declaring that a critical error has occurred, and execution stops.

One final consideration is the ability to use inline error handling. As mentioned in the chapter introduction, Visual Basic handles errors in an exception fashion rather than in an inline fashion (like the C language). If the Inline Error Handling box is checked, the On Error Resume Next statement will allow execution to continue to the next line automatically when an error occurs. But even though execution continues as normal, the values in the Err object properties are preserved so they can be examined later. In this case, we simply return the value in the Err.Number property as the value for our function. Since the Resume and Resume Next statements used in our exception-oriented error handling will automatically execute the Err.Clear method, we know that any function return value other than 0 indicates that inline error handling is currently active and the error code has been returned as the function's value. In the particular case of the Out of Memory button, we handle the inline error within the ProcessError procedure and subsequently illustrate the use of the Err.Clear method. Because we issue the Err.Clear method, the Err object properties are reset, and we never execute the code in the Command1_Click() event procedure that displays a message box if the return value of the ProcessError function is nonzero.

31

DEBUGGING

Even the best-written programs will have a few bugs or programming errors. The better you become at isolating and fixing these bugs, the better a programmer you will become. Fortunately, Visual Basic has been steadily improving its debugging features with each new release, and Visual Basic 5.0 offers one of the best debugging environments available. Although Visual Basic cannot diagnose programming errors for you, it does provide tools that enable you to analyze the order of program statement execution and track the values of variables and property settings. This chapter will describe the tools available in Visual Basic 5.0 for finding and fixing bugs.

Compile Errors

There are basically three kinds of programming errors: compile errors, runtime errors, and logic errors. Of the three, compile errors are by far the easiest to fix. A *compile error* is usually the result of incorrect syntax, such as an incorrect or missing keyword, a missing parenthesis, or a function call that is missing an argument. For example, you can cause a compile error by typing any of the following three statements in a Visual Basic subroutine:

```
Load The File        'error: this makes no sense to Visual Basic

Fore j = 1 To 100    'error: the keyword For is misspelled

firstName$ = Left(nameString$)
                     'error: the Left function requires two arguments
```

The first statement is completely foreign to Visual Basic. The problem with the second statement is that the Visual Basic keyword For has been misspelled as Fore. In the third statement, only one argument has been specified for the Left function, which requires two arguments. Errors in which you misspell or incorrectly use a keyword or attempt to pass an incorrect number of arguments to a function are commonly called *syntax errors*.

Visual Basic prevents most syntax errors from becoming compile errors. It does this by checking the code as you type it, beeping and displaying an error message as soon as a syntax error is detected. It is, after all, much easier to fix an error when you make it than to have to go back and find it later. (If you do want to enter all your code before dealing with errors, you can go to the Editor tab from the Options choice of the Tools menu and turn Auto Syntax Check off.)

A compile error could also take the form of the following:

```
Private Sub Command1_Click()
    Dim k As Integer

    While k < 30
        Form1.Print k
End Sub
```

In this subroutine the keywords have been used correctly, but the While statement is missing a corresponding Wend statement. This type of error is not a syntax error because no keywords or functions have been misused. Visual Basic will not catch this error until you attempt to run the program or create an .EXE file. Another example of a compile error that is not the result of a syntax error is attempting to allocate an object that is larger than the limits defined by Visual Basic. Again, you will receive an explanatory error message if you make this type of compile error.

Runtime Errors

Runtime errors are usually fairly easy to fix. One common runtime error is the type mismatch, in which the kind of data you supply as a subprocedure or function argument is different from the kind the procedure or function expects. For example, the statement

```
N$ = Str$(A$)
```

will cause a runtime error because the Str$ function expects a numeric value, not a string.

Another common runtime error is caused by an attempt to reference a nonexistent array element. If MyArray has 100 elements, and the variable Current gets set to 101, then a reference to MyArray(Current) will generate a runtime error. This kind of error sometimes requires a closer examination of your program logic, such as the boundaries defined in a loop.

Logic Errors

The sometimes sad reality of computers is that they always do what you tell them, even if it's not what you wanted. This is why logic errors happen. A *logic error* occurs when a portion of an application, although free of syntax and compile errors, is not performing the way you want. Logic errors are the hardest kind of error to fix because Visual Basic cannot detect them and cannot give you a helpful error message. You must examine the symptoms, make a diagnosis, fix the problem, then test your code to make sure you really *have* fixed the problem. The process of locating and repairing logic errors is called *debugging*.

The design of a program determines the amount of debugging it will need. When designing an application, remember the five P's: Proper planning prevents poor performance. An application that is well planned from the outset will be much less likely to encounter unexpected results than one designed on the fly. The more complicated an application, the more chance of a logic error occurring, and the more planning you will need to do.

Even the best-planned project is destined to have some logic errors. Visual Basic provides several tools for ferreting out these errors. Beginning with version 2.0, Visual Basic added a number of powerful features to the debugging suite, like the ability to *watch* variables, set *breakpoints*, and *trace* the execution of a program. These features and other related ones are discussed in the upcoming sections of this chapter.

Table 31-1 details the tools available to you for debugging your Visual Basic programs.

Table 31-1 Tools used to debug a Visual Basic program

Use This...	Type	To Do This...
Break	Command	Halt program execution
Call Stack	Command	Display a list of all active procedure calls
Clear All Breakpoints	Command	Cancel any breakpoints that have been set in the program
Debug	Object	Send debug information directly to the Immediate window
Immediate window	Object	Execute Visual Basic functions, statements, and methods in real time
Quick Watch	Command	Check the value of an expression
Run To Cursor	Command	Execute to the current cursor position
Set Next Statement	Command	Set the next executing statement to a different line of code
Show Next Statement	Command	Display the next executing statement in the Code window
Step Into	Command	Step through code, branching into sub and function calls
Step Out	Command	Step out of the current sub or function
Step Over	Command	Step through code, treating sub and function calls as a single step
Stop	Statement	Halt execution from within the program's code
Toggle Breakpoint	Command	Set a breakpoint in a program on or off
Watch	Command	Set or edit a watch expression

Program Modes

At any given time, Visual Basic is in one of three modes: design mode, run mode, or break mode. The current mode is always displayed in the title bar.

As the name suggests, *design mode* is used for creating screen objects and writing code. When you type code in design mode, Visual Basic traps syntax errors and gives you appropriate feedback. The debugging tools and features discussed in this chapter are not available in design mode, except for setting breakpoints.

Once you run a program (such as by selecting Start or Restart from the Run menu), Visual Basic is in *run mode*. During run mode, if a runtime error occurs, the program will stop and an appropriate error message will be given. You can also suspend program execution by selecting Break from the Run menu or the toolbar (or pressing the CTRL-BREAK key combination). Note that the Run menu will not be available if the program is waiting for input (such as in a modal dialog box).

When you have executed a break, the program is in *break mode*. All the debugging tools described in this chapter are available in break mode. In addition, you can use the Watches and Immediate windows to examine data or make changes to code in the Code window. You can step through code (executing one statement at a time), continue execution of the program at the next statement, or restart the program from the beginning. Figure 31-1 shows the Debug toolbar.

The Immediate and Watches Windows

You can often correct a programming logic error by analyzing the program's data and observing how it changes during the program. The Immediate window, which can be displayed by selecting the View|Immediate Window menu item, gives you the ability to execute Visual Basic commands at runtime. Figure 31-2 shows the Immediate window. The Watches window, which can be displayed by selecting the View|Watches Window, can be used to monitor or modify your program's data. Figure 31-3 shows the Watches window.

The Immediate window can be used to enter Visual Basic statements directly. You can, for example, assign values to various properties and variables by typing normal assignment statements in the Immediate window. You can also use the Print statement to display the values of various properties and variables. Generally, any statement or group of statements (such as a loop) can be entered in the Immediate window, as long as it can be placed on a single line (with multiple statements separated by colons). In

Figure 31-1 The Debug toolbar

Figure 31-2 The Immediate window

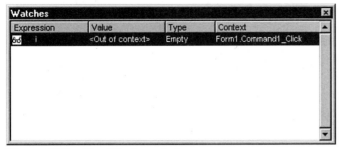

Figure 31-3   The Watches window

addition, the output from the Print method of the Debug object (which will be covered later in this chapter) appears in the Immediate window. For example, the following statement would display its output in the Immediate window:

```
Debug.Print "myVar ="; myVar
```

The Watches window is used to monitor the values of various variables and expressions. You select which variables and expressions (if any) you want Visual Basic to monitor by adding them to the list of *watch expressions*. The current watch expressions are then displayed in the Watches window. You add to the list of watch expressions using the Add Watch option of the Debug menu. The Quick Watch choice of the Debug Menu, which shows you the current value of a highlighted variable or expression, also gives you the option of adding to the list of watch expressions. To edit a watch expression, select Edit Watch from the Debug menu.

The Code window displays the program code and highlights its current execution point. You can use the scrollbars on the side of the Code window to display other sections of your code. Using the tools for *stepping* through your code (described later) will cause the highlighted statement in the Code window to advance to the next executed statement.

Dealing with Runtime Errors

When a runtime error occurs in your code, Visual Basic highlights the statement causing the error, your program ceases to execute, and a dialog box appears similar to the one shown in Figure 31-4. This dialog box offers four options (some of which may appear dimmed to indicate they are not currently available): Continue, End, Debug, and Help.

If you are able to modify the highlighted statement to correct the error, you can select Continue to continue program execution with the highlighted statement. There are certain changes to your code that will force Visual Basic to restart your program rather than continue. When this is the case, Visual Basic will present a dialog box describing the situation and asking if you want to accept the changes anyway. If you decide to accept your new changes, you will be forced to restart your program, but if you decide not to accept them, the changes you have made will be lost. Generally, it is not a tragedy to restart your program, so you will want to accept the changes.

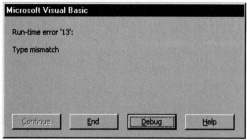

Figure 31-4   An example runtime error

The End option will end your program execution. Visual Basic will revert to design mode, and you will have to restart your program rather than continue execution. Although the Debug option is useful for minor program revisions, major revisions will require you to use the End option.

Choosing Debug will bring up the Debug window to allow you to examine code, properties, variables, and expressions, and to make changes as detailed earlier in the section about the Debug window.

Finally, choosing Help will bring up Windows Help with any available information on the runtime error that has occurred. Errors are classified according to their numbers and have a corresponding description.

Watch Expressions

As discussed earlier, you choose which variables or expressions will be watched by adding them to the list of *watch expressions*. When a variable or expression is added to the list of watch expressions, its value can be monitored in the Watches window.

To add a variable or expression to the list of watch expressions, select Add Watch from the Debug menu. You will be presented with the Add Watch dialog box, as shown in Figure 31-5. The Procedure and Module fields under Context are used to distinguish variables or expressions that may appear locally in different sections of your code. If, for example, you declare the variable i as an integer variable in several different subroutines, you would identify which instance of the i variable you want to watch by specifying the appropriate subroutine name in the Procedure field and the appropriate module name in the Module field.

To edit or delete a watch expression, highlight that watch expression in the Watches window of the Debug window and select Edit Watch from the Tools menu, or press [CTRL]-[W]. The Edit Watch dialog box is very similar to the Add Watch dialog box. The only difference is the addition of a Delete button to remove a variable or expression from the list of watch expressions. You may also delete the watch through the context-sensitive menu brought up by the right mouse click on a watch.

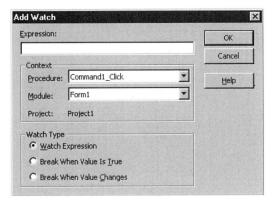

Figure 31-5   The Add Watch dialog box

In addition to simply monitoring the value of a watch expression, you have the option of causing the program to break when the value of a watch expression becomes True or changes. These options are available from the Add Watch and Edit Watch dialog boxes.

Finally, you can use Quick Watch (also under the Debug menu), or SHIFT-F9, to obtain the current value of a variable or expression. The variable or expression must be highlighted (dragged over or clicked with the mouse) before Quick Watch can be used. After you display the current value of the variable or expression using Quick Watch, Visual Basic gives you the option to add that variable or expression to your list of watch expressions. Choosing Add Watch will bring up the familiar Add Watch dialog box shown in Figure 31-5.

Breakpoints

You can use a *breakpoint* to halt execution at a specific point in your program. Frequently, you will be able to guess which section of your program might contain logic errors. By setting a breakpoint at the beginning of such a section of code, you can examine the values of variables, expressions, and properties, and you can step through the code using the tools described a little later in this chapter.

You set a breakpoint by positioning the cursor on a specific statement within the Code window and selecting Toggle Breakpoint from the Run menu or the toolbar, or by pressing F9. Similarly, you can use the same method to deselect a line that has been previously marked as a breakpoint. To clear all the breakpoints, select the Clear All Breakpoints choice in the Run menu, or press CTRL-SHIFT-F9. Visual Basic will highlight any statements marked as breakpoints so you can distinguish them from other program statements.

As an alternative to using a breakpoint, you may use the Stop statement. Placing a Stop statement within your code will halt program execution at that point and place Visual Basic in break mode just like setting a breakpoint. Unlike breakpoints, however, Stop statements will remain in your code when you create an .EXE file, so be sure to remove any Stop statements before you attempt to create an .EXE file or use the conditional compilation feature of Visual Basic (discussed later in this chapter and detailed in Chapter 92, "Conditional Compilation").

Stepping Through Code

After program execution has been halted and Visual Basic enters break mode through any of the previously described methods, you can selectively execute program statements one at a time using the single-step debugging features of Visual Basic. By creating watch expressions and stepping through program statements one at a time, you can observe exactly how the data in your program is changing.

From break mode, you can use the Step Into or Step Over options in the Debug menu to execute the next program statement. (You can also use the Step Into and Step Over buttons on the toolbar, or press F8 or SHIFT-F8, respectively.) Step Over differs from Step Into by treating a procedure call as a single statement. Alternatively, Step Into will attempt to execute each statement of any procedures encountered.

There may be certain sections of code, such as loops, that would take too long to step through one statement at a time. In these cases, you can use the Step To Cursor option on the Debug menu (or press CTRL-F8). Step To Cursor will cause execution to continue until the statement at which the cursor is currently located in the Code window is reached. For example, you could place the cursor on the statement immediately following a long loop and choose Step To Cursor to execute the entire loop and once again halt execution at the current cursor location.

You may also want to use the Step Out option. Step Out will execute until it leaves the current sub or function. Select the Step Out item on the Debug menu or press CTRL-SHIFT-F8, and execution start and stop, leaving you at the line of code immediately after the point where the current sub or function was called.

Finally, you may not want the statements in your program to execute in the order in which they are placed. For instance, if a section of code contains a known error, you may choose to skip this section of code until you have had a chance to fix the bug. By using the Set Next Statement option from the Run menu (or pressing CTRL-F9), you can tell Visual Basic which program statement should be executed next when program execution is continued or when the Step Into or Step Over debugging tools are used. The Show Next Statement option of the Run menu identifies which statement is currently set to be executed next.

The Call Stack Dialog Box

Large applications that use many subroutines will typically make use of nested procedures. A *nested procedure* is a subroutine or function that is called from another subroutine or function. In the following example, Main calls SubA, which calls SubB, which, in turn, calls SubC.

```
Private Sub Main()
     Call SubA
End Sub

Private Sub SubA()
     Call SubB
End Sub

Private Sub SubB()
     Call SubC
End Sub

Private Sub SubC()
     Form1.Print "SubC activated."
     Stop
End Sub
```

In order to keep track of how procedures are interacting with one another, Visual Basic provides the Call Stack dialog box. The Call Stack dialog box can be accessed from the View menu, with the Call Stack button on the toolbar, or by pressing CTRL-L. The Call Stack dialog box generated when the procedures above are executed is presented in Figure 31-6.

The Call Stack dialog box lists procedures in chronological order, with the most recently called procedures at the top. Notice that SubC, which was executing when the Stop statement was encountered, is located at the top of the list. Main, which was executed first, appears at the bottom of the list. You can select a procedure from the list and use the Show button in the top-right corner of the dialog box to display the code for that procedure.

Command-line Arguments

Sometimes a program may be written to operate on command-line arguments specified after the application name when launching the program from the Windows Program Manager. For example, the following might be entered in the Run dialog box to launch a program named Display and pass a command-line argument:

```
Display hello
```

The Command function returns a string containing any arguments passed to your Visual Basic program from the command line. If Command returns an empty string,

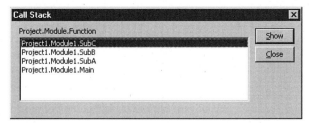

Figure 31-6   The Call Stack dialog box

then no arguments have been passed. If the following statement was placed in the program named Display and the line above was used to launch the Display program, the word "hello" would be printed:

```
Form1.Print Command
```

To test code you have written requiring command-line arguments, select Properties from the Project menu. Place any command-line arguments in the Command Line Arguments field on the Make tab, and they will be available to the Command function as if they had been passed from the Start Button's Run dialog box.

Conditional Compilation

Sometimes you need statements or sections of code only during the debugging process, and you must later remove these statements before you create an .EXE file. Fortunately, Visual Basic 5.0 has the capability to perform *conditional compilation,* which enables you to include certain sections of code only if a specified expression evaluates to True. The format of a conditional compilation block closely resembles the standard Visual Basic If-Then-End If block. A pound sign (#) precedes both the If and the End If statements of a conditional compilation block, as in the following example:

```
Private Function ProcA(x As Integer, y As Integer) As Integer
    Dim result As Integer

    result = x + y
# If debug Then
        result = 100
# End If

    ProcA = result
End Sub
```

In this example, the function ProcA will always return the value 100 while we are debugging. This might be helpful because you would know for certain the result of this function, and you could rely on this return value while debugging other parts of your program.

For a complete discussion of conditional compilation, see Chapter 92.

Debugging Events

One final note about debugging concerns the actions of certain events in a debugging environment. When you break execution during a MouseDown, Keydown, GotFocus, or LostFocus procedure using a breakpoint or CTRL-BREAK, the results may be unpredictable. Here are some things to watch for while breaking execution during these event procedures:

■ If you break execution during a MouseDown procedure, Visual Basic will assume the mouse button is still pressed when the program execution is resumed. Because of this, you may not receive a corresponding MouseUp event as expected.

■ If you break execution during a KeyDown procedure, the same warning applies: A corresponding KeyUp event may not be generated.

■ If you break execution during a GotFocus or LostFocus procedure, the results may be unpredictable. It is best not to set a breakpoint within a GotFocus or LostFocus event procedure.

BREAK COMMAND

Purpose The Break command begins the debugging process. It is used while a program is in run mode to temporarily halt execution so that the program's code and the values of its variables may be examined or modified.

Selection The Break command can be selected from the Run menu or the toolbar, or can be executed by pressing (CTRL)-(BREAK).

Description The Break command makes all Visual Basic's debugging commands available. While your program is in run mode, you may select this command to halt the program. When you do this, Visual Basic goes into break mode, and both the Code and Immediate windows appear. If the program was inactive (waiting for an event to occur), the Immediate window is given the focus. However, if your program was executing code, the Code window is given the focus, and a box is placed around the next line of code to be executed.

While in break mode, you can perform any of the other Debug commands (Toggle Breakpoint, Step Into, Step Over, Set Next Statement, and so on), and you may enter Visual Basic commands into the Immediate window. You can even make changes to your code, thereby changing the way your program executes. In most cases after making a change, you can cause the program to continue where it left off, without having to restart it from the beginning. However, some changes will require that the program be restarted. Visual Basic will inform you of this when you make such a change, and enable you to choose whether you wish to continue with the change and restart the program from the beginning, or to undo the change.

There are three ways to exit break mode. First, you can choose the Continue option from the Run menu (or press (F5)). This allows the program to continue at the statement surrounded by the box indicating that it is the next command to be executed. Second, you can choose the Restart option (or press (SHIFT)-(F5)) from the Run menu. This causes the program to restart from the beginning. Finally, you can choose the End option from the Run menu. This causes the program to terminate, and you are returned to design mode.

CALL STACK COMMAND

Purpose The Call Stack command displays all current procedure calls in the Call Stack dialog box.

Selection	Select the Call Stack command from the View menu or the toolbar or by pressing CTRL-L.
Description	Complex programs often have many procedures running at the same time. You can display a list of all active procedures (procedures that were begun but have not yet ended) to help trace program execution. This can be particularly helpful in nested procedures, in which one procedure calls another, which calls yet another procedure.
	The Call Stack dialog box places the most recent procedure at the top of the list and works backward through all procedures to the bottom of the list.

CLEAR ALL BREAKPOINTS COMMAND

Purpose	The Clear All Breakpoints command is used when all known errors in a program have been found and repaired. This command cancels all breakpoints set throughout a program. Except for those instances in which a halt is coded into the program (as with the Stop statement), issuing this command allows the program to proceed without further interruptions.
Selection	Execute this command by choosing the Clear All Breakpoints option from the Debug menu or by pressing CTRL-SHIFT-F9.
Description	Breakpoints are placed in your code with the Toggle Breakpoint command. These are used to halt program execution at specified points in your program. The Clear All Breakpoints command searches your program and cancels any breakpoints that have been set.

DEBUG OBJECT

Purpose	The Debug object sends output directly to the Immediate Window or stops execution based on an evaluated expression.
Selection	The Debug object can only be accessed from within the code of your program. The syntax for using the Debug object is

```
Debug.Print [expression-list]
```

or

```
Debug.Assert expression
```

Description	The Debug object is used with the Print method to send output directly to the Immediate window. This object provides an alternative technique for setting up watch variables. A watch variable is a variable whose value is displayed each time it is changed. The use of watch variables is very helpful, because it allows the programmer to see exactly what is being assigned to a variable and when the variable's value changes. Visual Basic provides a

direct way of setting watch variables (see the Watch command entry to learn how to do this).

If you need to do more than simply watch the value of a single variable, printing to the Debug object might still make sense. For instance, in the following code fragment, we want to keep tabs on the values of a two-dimensional array:

```
Private Sub Button1_Click ()
    .
    .
    .
    For i = 1 to 4
        For j = 1 to 4
            Debug.Print watchedArray(i, j);
        Next j
        Debug.Print
    Next i
    .
    .
    .
End Sub
```

In this example, the values held by watchedArray will be displayed each time you click on the Command button named Button1. This would have been much harder to do with watch variables.

The Assert Method

Purpose   The Assert method acts as a Stop command based on the value of the expression. If the expression is True, execution is not interrupted. If the expression is False, execution stops on the Assert call.

Immediate Window Object

Purpose   Use the Immediate window object to execute Visual Basic functions, statements, and methods in real time, and as an output area for the Debug object.

Selection   The Immediate window automatically appears when execution breaks through use of the Break command or Stop statement. If the Immediate window is not showing, it can also be selected by choosing the Immediate window option from Visual Basic's View menu or by pressing CTRL-G. However, real time commands can only be entered into this window while the Visual Basic environment is in break mode.

Description   When a program is halted due to a Break command, a breakpoint, the execution of a Stop statement, or the occurrence of an untrapped error, the Immediate window is opened. Before the Immediate window can be used, it must be given the focus. If you have issued a Break command while your program was idle (waiting for an event), the Immediate window will automatically be given the focus. Otherwise, you must give it the focus by selecting it with one of the procedures described earlier.

While in the Immediate window, you may enter any valid Visual Basic commands. This includes reading and setting the values of any variables accessible from the section of the program at which execution was halted. In other words, variables accessible to the Immediate window are those that have been declared: (1) in the global module, (2) in the General Declarations area of the form with the focus, and (3) in the procedure in which execution was halted. For instance, given the following code:

```
Public GlobalVar As Integer    this variable is declared in the global routine
Private ModuleVar As Integer ⇐
this variable is declared in the General Declarations area

Private Sub Button1_Click ()
    Dim ThisVar1 As Integer
    ThisVar1 = Int(34.54)    there is a breakpoint at this line
End Sub

Private Sub Button2_Click ()
    Dim ThisVar2 As Integer
    ThisVar2 = Sqr(254)
End Sub
```

when Visual Basic encounters the line in Button1_Click in which the breakpoint is set, execution will halt and the Immediate window will be given the focus. At that time, you would be able to read and set the values of the variables GlobalVar, ModuleVar, and ThisVar1. However, you would not be able to access ThisVar2 because it is defined in a different procedure from the one where execution was halted.

You can examine variable contents by printing them out with the Print keyword. Type in Print and whatever variable list you'd like to examine. You might wish to abbreviate the keyword Print with a question mark (?) when examining the contents of variables. This can save quite a bit of typing in a lengthy debugging session!

The Immediate window is also used as an output area for the Debug object. This allows you to display information about how a program is running by strategically placing Debug.Print commands in your code. For an example of how to do this, see the entry for the Debug object in this chapter.

QUICK WATCH COMMAND

Purpose   Use the Quick Watch command to check the value of an expression during break mode.

Selection	Select an expression in the Code window or in the Immediate window, and choose the Quick Watch command from the Debug menu. You may also press [SHIFT]-[F9].
Description	Use the Quick Watch command to check the value of an expression for which you have not defined a regular watch expression. Select an expression in the Code window or in the Immediate window, and then choose Quick Watch from the Debug menu. The results of the expression are displayed in the dialog box. You can click the Add Watch button to add this expression as a regular watch expression.

RUN TO CURSOR COMMAND

Purpose	The Run To Cursor command executes your code up to the source line at which you currently placed the cursor.
Selection	Execute this command by choosing Run To Cursor from Visual Basic's Debug menu, or by pressing [CTRL]-[F8].
Description	Although the Step Into and Step Over commands can be used to step through the execution of your program, it may take a good deal of time for program execution to reach a certain position in the code. As an alternative to setting a breakpoint to halt execution at a specified line, you can choose the Run To Cursor option to make the program execute up to the program line you indicate, by placing the cursor within the source code.

SET NEXT STATEMENT COMMAND

Purpose	The Set Next Statement command is used while in break mode to tell Visual Basic which line of code to execute next.
Selection	This command executes by selecting the Set Next Statement option from the Debug menu or by pressing [CTRL]-[F9].
Description	When Visual Basic enters break mode, it places a box around the statement to be executed next. You can use the Set Next Statement command to move this box to a different line of code. However, the line of code you choose must reside in the same procedure or function as the original Next statement. You set the next statement to be executed by placing the insertion point on the desired line of code, then selecting the Set Next Statement command.
	There are two situations in which this command is most commonly used. First, because Visual Basic enables you to change your code while in break mode, you may wish to immediately test how the changes will execute. This can be done by setting up the first line of your change to be the next statement executed. You can then use the Step Into or Step Over commands to test how the new coding changes will work.

The second common use for this command is to recover from an untrapped error. Any time an error occurs that you have not trapped in your program's code, the program halts, Visual Basic displays an error message, and the Immediate window is displayed. Sometimes this can happen because a variable is not set to the correct value. For instance, in the following code fragment, an attempt is made to open a file:

```
FileNumber = Free_File
Open "TEST.DAT" For Random As #FileNumber
```

In this example, it seems as though the programmer intended to get a free file number from Visual Basic's FreeFile function. Unfortunately, our programmer mistyped the function name and included an underscore. As a result, Visual Basic creates a variable called Free_File and assigns it the default value of 0. When Visual Basic encounters the line that assigns a value to the variable FileNumber, the assigned value will also be 0. This will cause the Open statement on the next line to issue a "Bad file name or number" error.

When this happens, you can fix the code immediately by changing the line above the file open. The new code fragment would look like this:

```
FileNumber = FreeFile
Open "TEST.DAT" For Random As #FileNumber
```

You would then use the Set Next Statement command to tell Visual Basic to continue execution at the line where the FileNumber variable is assigned a value from the FreeFile function. Not only have you fixed the error, but you have also saved yourself from having to restart the program from the beginning.

SHOW NEXT STATEMENT COMMAND

Purpose   The Show Next Statement command locates the next statement that will be executed and displays it in the Code window.

Selection   This command executes by selecting the Show Next Statement option from the Debug menu.

Description   Visual Basic enables you to edit your program's code while in break mode. When Visual Basic enters break mode, the currently executing procedure is displayed in the Code window. However, you can edit other procedures in the program while in break mode. Doing so causes the current procedure to be replaced in the Code window by the procedure you wish to edit. If you need to edit several procedures, you could forget in which procedure the execution was halted. The Show Next Statement command provides a technique for you to quickly set the focus to the Code window where the program halt occurred. When this command executes, Visual

Basic locates the line of code to be the next executed statement and loads its procedure into the Code window. The next line to be executed is displayed in the center of the window, with a box around it.

STEP INTO COMMAND

Purpose The Step Into command steps through your code one line at a time. When a function or procedure call is encountered, this command will load the function or procedure into the Code window and execute its statements one line at a time.

Selection Execute this command by choosing the Step Into option from Visual Basic's Debug menu or the toolbar, or by pressing F8.

Description It is often useful to execute your program one line at a time so that you can view exactly which steps are taken throughout the program's execution. This helps you determine where bugs in your program may occur. Portions of your code that you are stepping through may include several calls to functions or procedures you have written. If you have not yet debugged these functions and procedures, you may wish to step through each line of code in them when they are called. When this is the case, you can use the Step Into command. This command will step through code one line at a time. When Step Into encounters a function or procedure call, it will load that function or procedure into the Code window and execute its code one line at a time. When execution reaches an Exit Function, End Function, Exit Sub, or End Sub statement, it will load into the Code window the parent function or procedure that made the call to the current function or procedure, and continue execution there one step at a time.

Comment If you want to step through a main program but not the procedures or functions it calls, use the Step Over command instead of Step Into.

STEP OUT COMMAND

Purpose The Step Out command executes your code until it leaves the current sub or function.

Selection This command executes by choosing the Step Out option from the Debug menu or the toolbar, or by pressing CTRL-SHIFT-F8.

Description Sometimes when stepping through a sub or function, you may decide you have all the information you need from this run. The Step Out command quickly returns you to the calling routine. Execution will break again at the line of code immediately after the line that called the current sub or function.

STEP OVER COMMAND

Purpose   The Step Over command steps through your code, executing one line at a time. A whole function or procedure is considered to be a single step.

Selection   This command executes by choosing the Step Over option from the Debug menu or the toolbar, or by pressing (SHIFT)-(F8).

Description   It is often useful to execute your program one line at a time so that you can see exactly which steps are taken throughout the execution. This helps you determine where bugs in your program may occur. Portions of your code that you are stepping through may include several calls to functions or procedures you have written. If you have already debugged these functions and procedures and know they work correctly, there is no reason for you to step through each line when they are called. When this is the case, you can use the Step Over command, which will step through code one line at a time. However, when Step Over encounters a function or procedure call, it will execute the entire function or procedure as one step. This saves you the hassle of stepping through all the lines of code in that procedure or function.

Comment   If you want to step through every program statement, including code in procedures or functions, use the Step Into command rather than Step Over.

STOP STATEMENT

Purpose   The Stop statement halts the execution of a program.

Selection   The Stop statement is placed in your code. The syntax for this statement is simply:

`Stop`

Description   The Stop statement is used much like a breakpoint in your code. Unlike a breakpoint, which marks a particular line of code, this command is placed inside your code as an executable statement. The effect of a Stop statement is exactly the same as if you had issued a Break command while executing the line of code with the Stop statement on it. When this command executes, Visual Basic is placed into break mode. Both the Code and Immediate windows appear, and the Code window has the focus. Although it will have already been executed, the line of code with the Stop statement will be surrounded with a box, indicating it is the next statement to be executed. However, performing Single Step or Procedure Step at this time will not execute the Stop statement again; it will just set the next statement to the line following the Stop statement.

Most commonly, the Stop statement halts execution when a certain condition occurs. For instance, imagine you have a variable in your program that can be set to True or False. For some reason, you may wish to examine the program when that variable becomes False. Using the following line of code, you can cause the program to halt when this is the case:

```
If ThisVar = False Then Stop
```

This sets a conditional breakpoint in a program. You must be careful if you use the Stop statement in the debugging of your program. If you do not remove all Stop statements in your program before creating an .EXE file, they will be compiled into the executable version of your program. Then if the executable program comes across a Stop statement, it will terminate, and a "Stop statement encountered" message will be displayed. This is a guaranteed way to make the user of the program very unhappy. Therefore, if you ever place a Stop statement in your program, always do a global search for the word "Stop" and remove every Stop statement before creating an .EXE file.

TOGGLE BREAKPOINT COMMAND

Purpose   The Toggle Breakpoint command sets or clears a flag that marks a point in the program at which execution will be halted. This command works like a toggle switch. If a line of code is not yet a breakpoint, choosing this command makes it one; otherwise, it cancels the breakpoint for this line of code.

Selection   This command can be selected by choosing the Toggle Breakpoint option from Visual Basic's Debug menu or the toolbar, or by pressing F9.

Description   A breakpoint is a line of code in your program at which you wish execution to be halted. The effect of a breakpoint is exactly the same as if you had issued a Break command while executing the line of code just prior to the breakpoint. In other words, the program is halted before the line with the breakpoint executes. When a breakpoint is encountered, Visual Basic is placed into break mode. Both the Code and Immediate windows appear, and the Code window will have the focus. The line of code with the breakpoint will be surrounded with a box, indicating it is the next statement to be executed.

Breakpoints are used to halt program execution just prior to a portion of code that you wish to step through, or to examine before it executes. A breakpoint can also be used to check the results of a particular routine after it has executed.

WATCH COMMAND

Purpose   Use the Watch command to add, delete, or edit a watch expression. Watch statements let you monitor expressions during program execution.

Selection   Add a new watch statement using the Debug menu's Add Watch command. Edit or delete existing watch statements with the Debug menu's Edit Watch command.

Description   Watch expressions help you discover problems that occur only when a variable or property assumes a certain value. Setting watch expressions lets you monitor the behavior of a variable or of an expression throughout a procedure.

Visual Basic automatically monitors each watch expression for you, and updates their values every time the program enters break mode. These values are displayed in the top of the Debug window in the Watches window. If the Watches window is not visible in the upper part of the Debug window, you can click the Watch button to make it visible.

You can also set watch expressions to halt program execution when an expression reaches a certain value. This can be a handy adjunct to setting breakpoints. Breakpoints always halt execution whenever program flow executes that statement; watch expressions can let program flow execute a statement repeatedly (as in a loop) and only halt when the condition you specify is met.

Use the Add Watch dialog box to add a new watch expression. You can enter any valid expression (variable, property, function call, or a complex expression combining all these) into the Expression text box. Use the Context settings to indicate what the scope of expression will be—procedure, module, or project. The Watch Type group lets you set what action to take when the expression is evaluated. You can have Visual Basic display the results of the expression (Watch Expression), break when the expression evaluates to True (Break When Value Is True), or break any time the expression changes value (Break When Value Changes).

Use the Edit Watch dialog box to edit or delete existing watch expressions. Select whatever expression you'd like (either with the mouse or the arrow keys) and choose Edit to change the expression or Delete to delete it. Clicking the Add command button brings up the Add Watch dialog box.

The results of the watch expressions are displayed in the Watches window.

PART IV
BUILDING USER INTERFACES

32

GETTING USER INPUT

Visual Basic's text box control lets you easily get text input from the user. The text box control inherits a number of powerful features that make it simple to let your user select, cut, and copy text. The text box also automatically follows Windows conventions with the movement keys like ARROW-LEFT and ARROW-RIGHT, as well as the HOME and END keys. You can tell the text box to automatically create scrollbars for you, and Visual Basic even lets you specify a password character to use in a password entry routine.

The text box control lets the user enter or edit text. When a text box control receives the focus, an insertion point appears in the box. The *insertion point* is a slim flashing vertical line that indicates where any new text will be entered within the box. Although the proper Windows terminology for this line is *caret*, most people commonly refer to it as the *cursor*. The cursor can be moved by using the direction keys, using the HOME and END keys, or clicking at the desired position in the text box with the mousepointer. The default behavior for the mousepointer is to change to an I-beam when held over a text box, in order to facilitate precise positioning. See Chapter 33, "Application Appearance," for more about the MousePointer property.

The text box's primary property is the Text property. This property is a string value containing any text that has been entered into the text box. The value of the Text property can be modified in one of four ways: user input, your program's code, dynamic data exchange (DDE) messages, or a change in the record of an underlying database record if the text control has been bound to a database. Any time the text changes, the text box's Change event occurs (see Chapter 35, "Accessing Forms and Controls," for more about the Change event).

Editing in a Text Box

A Visual Basic text box gives the user all the standard Windows editing capabilities. It automatically inherits all the conventions of a standard Windows text box, including the ability to cut, copy, and paste to and from the Windows Clipboard area. A user can select text for these functions by holding down SHIFT and pressing ARROW-LEFT or

ARROW-RIGHT, or by clicking and dragging the mouse over the desired text. This highlights the selected text.

Once text has been selected, the user may perform several operations on it. Pressing DELETE eliminates the selected text from the text box. Pressing SHIFT-DELETE or CTRL-X copies the selected text to the Clipboard, then deletes it from the text box. This is commonly called *cutting* text. The user can also *copy* selected text to the Clipboard without deleting it by pressing CTRL-INS or CTRL-C. Pressing SHIFT-INS or CTRL-V will *paste* any text currently stored on the Clipboard into the text box at the position specified by the insertion point. You can control these functions in your program using the SelText, SelStart, and SelLength properties. For more information on how to interact with the Windows Clipboard, see Chapter 53, "Using the Clipboard."

Multiline Text Boxes

By default, a text box consists of only one line of text. You can allow the user to enter more than one line of text by setting the MultiLine property to True. If you've set the MultiLine property to True, you may also wish to set the ScrollBars property. This allows you to place scrollbars on the left and bottom edges of the text box, enabling the user to quickly scroll through the text.

Rich Text Boxes

The rich text box control, available in the professional and enterprise versions of Visual Basic, adds advanced formatting, such as font selection and indentation, to the capabilities of the regular text box. It can read and write to text and .RTF files and has drag-and-drop support. Refer to Chapter 44, "Text Boxes," for more information on the rich text box.

Combo Boxes

The combo box control has two styles, DropDown combo and Simple combo, both of which include an edit area very similar to the text box control. These two styles of combo boxes share the SelLength, SelStart, SelText, and Text properties with the text box control. Refer to Chapter 46, "List and Combo Boxes," for more information on combo boxes.

Getting User Input Summary

Table 32-1 lists the properties that relate to the text box control and their uses. Each of these properties is explained in detail in this chapter. At the end of the chapter, an example project demonstrates how to combine all these elements.

Table 32-1 The properties governing the appearance and behavior of a text box control

Use or Set This...	Type...	To Do This...
Alignment	Property	Set or determine the text alignment
HideSelection	Property	Set or determine whether selected text appears highlighted when a control loses the focus
Locked	Property	Set or determine whether editing is allowed
MaxLength	Property	Set or determine the maximum numbers of characters that can be entered
MultiLine	Property	Set up a text box to accept multiline input
PasswordChar	Property	Set or determine if text box displays actual text or a placeholder
ScrollBars	Property	Set up horizontal or vertical scrollbars (or both) for a text box
SelLength	Property	Set or read the length of the currently selected text (if any)
SelStart	Property	Set or read the starting position of the currently selected text (if any)
SelText	Property	Replace or read the currently selected text string
Text	Property	Set or read the text contained in a text box

Constant Values

It is usually best to use named constants rather than numeric values when developing software. Named constants make your code more readable and easier to maintain.

Table 32-2 lists the values of the constants relevant to this chapter, mentions their names, and briefly describes what they mean. These constants can be viewed in the VB Constants module using the Object Browser. It is not necessary to explicitly add these objects to your project. For more information on using object library constants, see Chapter 16, "Objects and Collections"; for information on constant naming conventions, see Chapter 35.

Table 32-2 Constant values of text input

Value	VB.Constants	Meaning
Alignment property		
0	vbLeftJustify	The text will be left-aligned (default)
1	vbRightJustify	The text will be right-aligned
2	vbCenter	The text will be centered
ScrollBars property		
0	vbDefault	The text box will have no scrollbars, and text will wrap automatically (default)
1	vbHorizontal	A horizontal scrollbar appears at the bottom edge of the text box with no word wrapping
2	vbVertical	A vertical scrollbar appears at the right edge of the text box with automatic word wrapping
3	vbBoth	Vertical and horizontal scrollbars appear with automatic word wrapping

ALIGNMENT PROPERTY

Objects Affected	CheckBox, Column, Label, OptionButton, TextBox
Purpose	The Alignment property is used to specify how the text of a multiline text box is aligned. Table 32-3 summarizes the arguments of the Aligment property. The MultiLine property in a text box control must be set to True for the Alignment property to work correctly. If the MultiLine property setting of a text box control is False, the Alignment property is ignored. Table 32-4 shows the possible Alignment settings for multiline textboxes.

General Syntax

```
[form!]Name.Aligment = [value]
```

Table 32-3 Arguments of the Alignment property

Argument	Description
form	Name property of the parent form
Name	Name property of the control
value	Alignment library constant

Table 32-4 Possible settings of the Alignment property for multiline text box controls

Value	VB.Constants	Meaning
0	vbLeftJustify	The text is left-aligned (default)
1	vbRightJustify	The text is right-aligned
2	vbCenter	The text is centered

Example Syntax

```
Private Sub Command1_Click ()
    Text1.Alignment = vbRightJustify
End Sub
```

Description	By default, the text in a multiline text box is left-aligned. You can change this by setting the Alignment property to vbRightJustify or vbCenter.
Example	You may want to right-justify the text in a text box used in a calculator. In this case, you may be forced to use a multiline text box even if you do not foresee more than one line of text being entered.

HideSelection Property

Objects Affected   ListView, Masked Edit, RichTextBox, TextBox, TreeView

Purpose   The HideSelection property determines whether the selected text remains highlighted when the control loses the focus. Table 32-5 summarizes the arguments of the HideSelection property.

General Syntax

```
[form!]Name.HideSelection [ = True | False ]
```

Table 32-5 Arguments of the HideSelection property

Argument	Description
form	Name property of the parent form
Name	Name property of the control

Example Syntax

```
Private Sub cmdSpellCheck_Click ()
    Text1.HideSelection = False
    SpellCheck Text1.Text
End Sub
```

Description   By default, the selected text does not appear highlighted when the text box control loses focus. By setting the HideSelection to False, you can change this behavior.

Example   In a spell check dialog box, you may want to keep an incorrectly spelled word in a text box highlighted.

Locked Property

Objects Affected   Column, DBCombo, DBList, Split, RichTextBox, TextBox

Purpose   The Locked property determines whether editing of the text in the text box is allowed. Table 32-6 summarizes the arguments of the Locked property.

General Syntax

```
[form!]Name.Locked [ = True | False ]
```

Table 32-6 Arguments of the Locked property

Argument	Description
form	Name property of the parent form
Name	Name property of the control

Example Syntax

```
Private Sub Command1_Click ()
    Text1.Locked = True
End Sub
```

Description	By default, the text in a text box can be edited. By setting the Locked property of a text box to True, you can prohibit editing. The text can still be highlighted and scrolled. The text can also still be changed from code through the Text property.
Example	You may want to prevent users from editing text in a text box used in a calculator by setting the Locked property to True.

MAXLENGTH PROPERTY

Objects Affected	Masked Edit, RichTextBox, TextBox
Purpose	The MaxLength property indicates whether there is a maximum number of characters the text box control can hold and, if there is, specifies the maximum number of characters. Table 32-7 summarizes the arguments of the MaxLength property.

General Syntax

```
[form!]Name.MaxLength = [lngValue]
```

Table 32-7 Arguments of the MaxLength property

Argument	Description
form	Name property of the parent form.
Name	Name property of the control.
lngValue	Any number greater than 0 indicates the maximum number of characters. 0 indicates no maximum other than the maximum created by memory constraints on the user's system.

Example Syntax

```
Private Sub Form_Load ()
    Text1.MaxLength = 16
End Sub
```

Description	The default for the MaxLength property is 0, indicating the maximum allowed is determined only by the memory on the user's system for single-line text box controls and is approximately 32K for multiline text box controls. Any number greater than 0 indicates the maximum number of characters. Changing this property doesn't affect the current contents of the text box, but will affect any subsequent changes to the contents.
	If text that exceeds the MaxLength property setting is assigned to a text box from code, only the maximum number of characters is assigned to the Text property and extra characters are truncated. No runtime error occurs.
Example	In the TextBox project, the MaxLength for txtPassword is set to 10 at design time.

MULTILINE PROPERTY

Objects Affected	RichTextBox, TextBox
Purpose	The MultiLine property sets up a text box control to enter multiple lines of text. This property can only be set at design time, although your program can read its value at runtime. Table 32-8 summarizes the arguments of the MultiLine property.

General Syntax

```
[form!]Name.MultiLine
```

Table 32-8 Arguments of the MultiLine property

Argument	Description
form	Name property of the parent form
Name	Name property of the control

Example Syntax

```
Private Sub Command1_Click ()
    MultiLineStatus = Text1.MultiLine
End Sub
```

Description	By default, the MultiLine property is set to False (0), causing the associated text box to be a single-line text box. However, you may wish to set this property to True (–1) at design time to create a multiline text box. A multiline text box allows the user to enter more than one line in the text box.
	If the ScrollBars property is set to 0 (none) or 2 (vertical only), a multiline text box will automatically wrap text over to the next line when it exceeds the width of the box. If the ScrollBars property is set to 1 (horizontal) or 3

(both horizontal and vertical), it is up to the user to create new lines. If there is no button on the same form with its Default property set to True, the user can create new lines by pressing ENTER. If there is a default button on the form, the user must press CTRL-ENTER to create a new line.

The example syntax reads the value of the MultiLine property for the text box Text1. It could be used in an If statement to determine whether to format multiline text.

Example   In the TextBox project at the end of this chapter, the edit area of the mini-text editor is a multiline text box.

PASSWORDCHAR PROPERTY

Objects Affected   TextBox

Purpose   Use the PasswordChar property to set up a text box for password entry. By default, this property displays the characters that the user types. If you set this property to anything other than an empty string, it will display the first character contained in the property setting instead of the character typed by the user. This gives the user visual feedback for each character typed without displaying the actual characters. Tables 32-9 and 32-10 summarize the arguments of the PasswordChar property.

General Syntax

```
[form!]Name.PasswordChar [ = string$]
```

Table 32-9 Arguments of the PasswordChar property

Argument	Description
form	Name property of the parent form
Name	Name property of the control
string$	Read or set the password character

Table 32-10 Meaning of the string$ argument in the PasswordChar property

string$	Meaning
empty string	Echo characters typed by the user (default)
nonempty string	Echo the first character in the string (other characters ignored)

Example Syntax

```
Private Sub Form_Load ()
    Form2.Caption = "Enter Your Password"
```

```
        Form2!Text1.PasswordChar = "*"
        Form2.Show vbModal
        If Form2!Text1.Text = Form1.Tag Then
            LoadMainProgram
        Else
            MsgBox "Incorrect Password!"
            End
        End If
End Sub
```

Description   Use the PasswordChar property to convert an ordinary text box into a password entry box. Passwords typically should not be displayed as they are typed in, to minimize the risk of prying eyes discovering someone's password. Most Windows programs use the asterisk (*) character as a placeholder for password characters. Figure 32-1 shows what a typical password entry dialog box looks like.

Set the PasswordChar property to a string to make it display the placeholder in the text box. Only the first character of the string is significant; subsequent characters are ignored. The example syntax assigns the asterisk as the placeholder character. Set PasswordChar to an empty string ("") to disable the password setting and display normal text.

The text box will always contain the actual characters, no matter what the PasswordChar property is set to. This lets you check the Text property to determine if the user typed the right password, as the example syntax shows.

Example   The TextBox project at the end of this chapter uses the PasswordChar property to set up a password entry dialog box. The File New command asks for the password before clearing the editing area.

SCROLLBARS PROPERTY

Objects Affected   DBGrid, MDI Form, MSFlexGrid, RichTextBox, Split, Text Box, UserDocument

Purpose   The ScrollBars property is set at design time to determine what types of scrollbars, if any, will appear at the edges of a text box (or a grid or MDI Form). Scrollbars allow the user to read text that is too wide (or has too many lines) to fit in the window. This property is read-only at runtime.

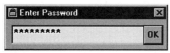

Figure 32-1   The PasswordChar property lets you easily set up password input dialog boxes

The arguments of the ScrollBars property are summarized in Table 32-11, while Table 32-12 lists the possible values for this property and their effects.

General Syntax

```
[form!]Name.ScrollBars [ = value ]
```

Table 32-11 Arguments of the ScrollBars property

Argument	Description
form	Name property of the parent form
Name	Name property of the control

Table 32-12 Possible settings for the ScrollBars property

Value	VB.Constants	Meaning
0	vbDefault	The text box will have no scrollbars, and text will wrap automatically (default)
1	vbHorizontal	A horizontal scrollbar appears at the bottom edge of the text box with no word wrapping
2	vbVertical	A vertical scrollbar appears at the right edge of the text box with automatic word wrapping
3	vbBoth	Vertical and horizontal scrollbars appear, with automatic word wrapping

Example Syntax

```
Private Sub Form_Load ()
    ScrollBarStatus = Text1.ScrollBars
End Sub
```

Description   The ScrollBars property is only useful when the MultiLine property is set to True (−1). This property has no effect in text boxes when the MultiLine property is False. *Scrollbars* are graphic objects that consist of a bar with arrows at each end and a button (called a *thumb*) between the arrows. Scrollbars give the user the ability to quickly scroll through text with the mouse. There are two types of scrollbars, vertical and horizontal.

The scrollbar's thumb indicates the relative position of the text box's text. The user can move the thumb by clicking and dragging it, by clicking on the bar itself, or by clicking on one of the arrows at either end of the scrollbar. Moving the button on the scrollbar causes the text within the text box to scroll in proportion to the amount it is moved.

The example syntax stores the current value of the ScrollBars property of form Text1 in the variable ScrollBarStatus. It could be used in an If statement to test for the presence of scrollbars.

If the ScrollBars property is set to 0 (none) or 2 (vertical only), a multiline text box will automatically wrap text over to the next line when it exceeds the width of the box. Otherwise, it is up to the user to create new lines. If there is no button on the same form with its Default property set to True, the user can create new lines by pressing E. If there is a default button on the form, the user must press Q-E to create a new line.

Example   In the TextBox project at the end of this chapter, the ScrollBars property for the edit portion of the mini-text editor is set to 2 (vertical scrollbars) at design time.

SELLENGTH PROPERTY

Objects Affected   Combo, DBCombo, Masked Edit, RichTextBox, Slider, TextBox

Purpose   The SelLength property is used to set or return the number of selected characters within a text or combo box. Characters can be selected (highlighted) by the user, usually for an editing operation. Your program can also select a portion of the text in the text box. This property can be set and read at runtime only. The arguments for the SelLength property are summarized in Table 32-13.

General Syntax

```
[form!]Name.SelLength [ = NumChars&]
```

Table 32-13 Arguments of the SelLength property

Argument	Description
form	Name property of the parent form
Name	Name property of the control
NumChars&	Reads or sets the number of selected characters

Example Syntax

```
Private Sub Text1_MouseUp (Button As Integer, Shift As Integer, X As Single, Y As Single)
    SaveSelLength = Text1.SelLength      'save the length of the selected text
    Text2.Text = Str(SaveSelLength)
End Sub
```

Description   The SelLength property is used in conjunction with the SelStart and SelText properties to work with text selected by the user in a text or combo box. A user can select text for these properties by holding down SHIFT and pressing LEFT-ARROW or RIGHT-ARROW, or by clicking and dragging the mouse over the desired text. This highlights the selected text. Your program can then read the settings of these properties and perform operations on the selected text. The SelStart property determines the starting point of the selected text within a text or combo box. The SelLength property determines the number of characters selected. SelText is a string property that contains the selected text.

The SelLength property is a long integer that may be used to set or return the number of selected characters in the text. If no characters are selected, this property returns 0.

Setting the SelLength property within a program's code has no effect, unless the text box has the focus when the property is set. If the text box does have the focus, assigning SelLength a value causes that number of characters to be selected in the text box, starting at the position indicated by the SelStart property and counting from left to right. If the program assigns SelLength a value that exceeds the length of the text in the text box, only the existing characters are selected and the SelLength property is adjusted to reflect this. Setting this property to a value less than 0 causes an "Invalid property value" error to occur at runtime.

The example syntax saves the length of the current text selection to a variable for future use. Figure 32-2 shows a text box with selected text.

Example

In the TextBox project at the end of this chapter, the SelLength and SelStart properties are saved in the txtDocument_KeyDown event. This is done to enable the Undo function of the mini-text editor.

Comments

This property also applies to combo boxes and DBCombo boxes whose Style property has been set to 0 (DropDown Combo) or 1 (Simple Combo).

SELSTART PROPERTY

Objects Affected   Combo, DBCombo, Masked Edit, RichTextBox, Slider, TextBox

Purpose   The SelStart property is used to set or return the starting position of selected text within a text or combo box. Text may be selected by the user or the program and is highlighted in the text box. If there is no selected text, this property sets or returns the position of the box's insertion point. The arguments of the SelStart property are summarized in Table 32-14.

Figure 32-2   Example syntax shows text box with selected text; the other text box shows SelLength

General Syntax

```
[form!]Name.SelStart [ = StartPos&]
```

Table 32-14 Arguments of the SelStart property

Argument	Description
form	Name property of the parent form
Name	Name property of the control
StartPos&	Reads or sets the character position of the insertion point or the start of selected text

Example Syntax

```
Private Sub Text1_MouseUp (Button As Integer, Shift As Integer, X As Single, Y As Single)
    SaveSelStart = Text1.SelStart        'get the start of the selected text
    Text2.Text = Str$(SaveSelStart)
End Sub
```

Description   The SelStart property is used in conjunction with the SelLength and SelText properties to work with text selected in a text or combo box by the user. A user can select text for these properties by holding down [SHIFT] and pressing [LEFT-ARROW] or [RIGHT-ARROW], or by clicking and dragging the mouse over the desired text. This highlights the selected text (see Figure 32-3). Your program can then read the settings of these properties and perform operations on the selected text. The SelStart property determines the starting point of the selected text within a text or combo box. SelLength determines the number of characters selected. SelText is a string property that contains the selected text.

The SelStart property is a long integer value that indicates the starting position of the selected characters in a text or combo box. The value of SelStart is zero-based. This means the first selected character is the position after the value of SelStart. For instance, if the value of SelStart is 1 and the value of SelLength is 2, the second and third characters in the text are selected. If there is no text currently selected, SelStart will return the position of the text box's insertion point.

Figure 32-3   Example syntax shows text box with selected text; the other text box shows the SelStart

You may set the SelStart property by assigning a long integer value to it. This value must be a nonnegative number or an "Invalid property value" error will occur during runtime. If this value is greater than the length of the text in the text or combo box, SelStart is set to a value equal to the length of the text. Assigning a value to the SelStart property automatically sets the SelLength property to 0 and moves the insertion point in the text box to the specified position.

The example syntax saves the starting position of the selected text in a variable for future use.

Example

In the TextBox project at the end of this chapter, the SelLength and SelStart properties are saved in the txtDocument_KeyDown event. This is done to enable the Undo function of the mini-text editor.

Comments

This property also applies to combo boxes and DBCombo boxes with the Style property set to 0 (DropDown Combo) or 1 (Simple Combo).

SELTEXT PROPERTY

Objects Affected Combo, DBCombo, Masked Edit, RichTextBox, Slider, TextBox

Purpose The SelText property replaces or returns the currently selected text within a text or combo box. Users can select text (typically by dragging with the mouse), or text may be selected by program action. The arguments for the SelText property are summarized in Table 32-15.

General Syntax

```
[form!]Name.SelText [ = NewText$]
```

Table 32-15 Arguments of the SelText property

Argument	Description
form	Name property of the parent form
Name	Name property of the control
NewText$	A string that can be placed at the text box's insertion point; NewText$ replaces any selected text

Example Syntax

```
Private Sub Text1_MouseUp (Button As Integer, Shift As Integer, X As Single, Y As Single)
    Clipboard.SetText Text1.SelText      'save the start of the selected text
    Text2.Text = Text1.SelText
End Sub
```

Description The SelText property is used in conjunction with the SelLength and SelStart properties to work with text selected in a text or combo box by the user. A user can select text for these properties by holding down F and pressing ⟨◁⟩ or ⟨▷⟩, or by clicking and dragging the mouse over the desired text. This highlights the selected text. Your program can then read the settings of these properties and perform operations on the selected text. The SelStart property determines the starting point of the selected text within a text or combo box. SelLength determines the number of characters selected. SelText is a string property that contains the selected text.

The SelText property returns a string copy of the selected characters from the text or combo box. This string can be used by your programs to cut and paste to the Windows Clipboard. If no characters are currently selected, this property will return a Null string.

Assigning a string value to this property can cause one of two things to happen. If there is any text selected when the assignment is made, the selected text in the text or combo box is replaced by the assigned text. If no text is selected, the new text is inserted into the text or combo box's text at the box's insertion point.

Figure 32-4 displays a text box with selected text. In this example, the value of the SelStart property is 8, SelLength is 4, and SelText is "some".

The example syntax copies the selected text to the Clipboard by assigning the value of the SelText property of the text box to the SetText method of the Clipboard, then copies the selected text to Text2.

Comments   This property also applies to combo boxes and DBCombo boxes with the Style property set to 0 (DropDown Combo) or 1 (Simple Combo).

TEXT PROPERTY

Objects Affected   AxisTitle, Column, ComboBox, DBCombo, DBList, ListBox, TextBox

Purpose   The Text property reads or sets the text contained in a text box or grid cell, or reads the selected item in a list or combo box. This property can also be set when used with a combo or DBCombo box whose Style property is set to 0 (Drop-Down Combo) or 1 (Simple Combo). The arguments of the Text property are summarized in Table 32-16.

Figure 32-4   Example syntax shows text box with selected text; the other text box shows the SelText

General Syntax

```
[form.]Name.Text [= TextString$]
```

Table 32-16 Arguments of the Text property

Argument	Description
form	Name property of the parent form
Name	Name property of the control
TextString$	A string that can be assigned to this property, thereby replacing all text in the text box

Example Syntax

```
Command1_Click ()
    Text1.Text = TxtBeforeChange$        'assigns a string to the text box Text1
    SelectedItem$ = List1.Text           'assigns the value of a list box's selected item to a
string
End Sub
```

Description

The Text property is a string that allows your program to access the contents of the edit area of a text or combo box, or the contents of a grid cell. It also can represent a chosen item in a list box.

The Text property also allows you to access and manipulate the text inside a text box. This property is a string representation of the contents of the box, and can be manipulated by any of Visual Basic's string functions and statements such as Left, Mid, and Right. Any operations performed on this property are reflected by the text inside a text box.

You may assign a string to the Text property. This replaces the text in the box with the assigned string. The user can also directly edit the text represented by the Text property. Any time a box's Text property is modified, it triggers the box's Change event.

This property can contain a string up to approximately 32K characters if MultiLine is True and has no limits, except for the available memory if MultiLine is False. However, assigning large numbers of characters to this property greatly degrades the performance of the box. In other words, the longer the value of the Text property, the slower the text box will react to user input.

The first example syntax assigns a string to the Text property of text box Text1. This text would then appear in the text box. The second example syntax assigns the text in list box List1 to a string for future use.

Combo and List Boxes and the Grid Control

The Text property is also used with the Combo, DBCombo, DBList, and list box controls. When used on the DropDown (Style = 0) and Simple (Style = 1) combo box styles, this property works in the exact same manner as described previously. When used with the list box control or a DropDown list (combo box with Style set to 2), the Text property is read-only and returns the string value of the selected item in the list.

Individual grid cells also have a Text property (although the grid control itself does not). You cannot directly manipulate grid cells, so the Text property needs to be set with your code. You would typically have a text box accept the input, then assign the text box's Text property to the grid cell's Text property. Refer to Chapter 46 and Chapters 47, "File, Directory, and Drive Boxes," and 48, "Grid Controls," for more information on lists, combos, and grids.

Example In the TextBox project at the end of this chapter, a multiline text box is used to edit text. The Text property of this box is manipulated in several procedures. The length of the Text property is determined in the Change event for the text box, so the number of characters typed can be displayed. In the mnuFile(0)_Click event, the Text property is set to an empty string. In the txtDocument_KeyDown event, the value of the Text property is saved in a string variable, so that it can be restored by the user. When the Undo option is chosen from the Edit menu, the EditUndo_Click event occurs. This event assigns the value of the previously saved string variable to the Text property, thereby restoring its original state.

The TextBox Project

Project Overview

The project outlined in the following pages demonstrates the concepts behind the text box control. This project uses each of the properties covered in this chapter and demonstrates how they work together. By following the examples in this project, you should be able to get a firm grasp on the concepts behind text boxes.

This project makes use of the KeyDown event. This event occurs when the user presses any key on the keyboard. More information on the KeyDown event can be found in Chapter 51, "Keyboard Input." There are also some methods used with the Clipboard object in this project. These methods send or receive text from the Clipboard area of Windows. Refer to Chapter 53, for more on this subject.

Assembling the Project: frmMain

1. Create a new form (the TextBox form) and place on it the following controls. Use Table 32-17 to set the properties of the form and each control.

Table 32-17 Elements of the TextBox form

Object	Property	Setting
Form	Name	frmMain
	Caption	"Text Box Project"
Label	Name	lblStatus
	Caption	" 0 Characters"
Text Box	Name	txtDocument
	Text	"" (Null)
	Multiline	True (–1)
	ScrollBars	2–Vertical

2. Using the Menu Design window, create a menu with the settings in Table 32-18. (Choose the Menu Design window option from Visual Basic's Window menu.)

Table 32-18 Menu settings for the TextBox project

Name	Caption	Property	Setting
mnuBar	&File	Index	0
mnuFile	&New	Index	0
mnuFile		Index	1
mnuFile	E&xit	Index	2
mnuBar	&Edit	Index	1
mnuEdit	&Undo	Index	0
mnuEdit		Index	1
mnuEdit	Cu&t	Index	2
mnuEdit	&Copy	Index	3
mnuEdit	&Paste	Index	4
mnuEdit	&Delete	Index	5

3. Check the appearance of your form against Figure 32-5.

4. Enter the following code into the General Declarations area of the form. Three module-level variables are created for later use in the program. If the user changes the text in the box, these variables save the contents of the text box just prior to the changes. This information can then be used to later restore the text box to its value before the changes were made. We also define enumerated constants used for menu processing. If you add more items to the menus, all you need to do is ensure these enumerations are correct.

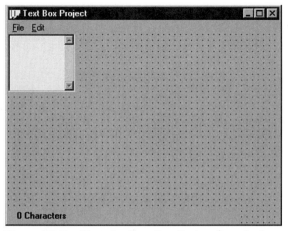

Figure 32-5   How the Text Box Project form looks during design

```
Option Explicit
Private Const conAppTitle = "TextBox Project"

Private mTextBeforeChange As String
Private mPosBeforeChange As Integer
Private mLenBeforeChange As Integer

Enum BarMenuIndex
    enmBarFile = 0
    enmBarEdit = 1
End Enum

Enum FileMenuIndex
    enmFileNew = 0
    enmFileSep1 = 1
    enmFileExit = 2
End Enum

Enum EditMenuIndex
    enmEditUndo = 0
    enmEditSep1 = 1
    enmEditCut = 2
    enmEditCopy = 3
    enmEditPaste = 4
    enmEditDelete = 5
End Enum
```

    5. Enter the following code into the Form_Resize event. This event occurs when the user changes the size of the form. It adjusts the size of the edit area to match the size of the form.

```
Private Sub Form_Resize()
    txtDocument.Height = frmMain.ScaleHeight - 250
    txtDocument.Width = frmMain.ScaleWidth
    lblStatus.Top = txtDocument.Height
    lblStatus.Height = 250
    lblStatus.Width = frmMain.ScaleWidth
End Sub
```

6. Enter the following code in the mnuBar_Click event. This event occurs whenever the user clicks on the top-level menu choices (File and Edit), and completes its processing before the menu is actually pulled down. No special processing occurs for the File menu, but the Edit menu needs to be set properly depending on whether text has been selected or text is available on the Clipboard. The routine first disables all the menu choices (note that mnuEdit(1) is a separator bar). It then checks to see if there is any information stored in the undo buffer mTextBeforeChange. If so, it enables the Undo command. It then checks to see if any text has been selected. If so, the Cut, Copy, and Delete commands are enabled. It then checks the Clipboard to see if there is anything there in text format. If so, the Paste command is enabled.

```
Private Sub mnuBar_Click(Index As Integer)
    Select Case Index
        Case enmBarFile
        Case enmBarEdit
            mnuEdit(enmEditUndo).Enabled = False
            mnuEdit(enmEditCut).Enabled = False
            mnuEdit(enmEditCopy).Enabled = False
            mnuEdit(enmEditPaste).Enabled = False
            mnuEdit(enmEditDelete).Enabled = False
            If Len(mTextBeforeChange) > 0 Then mnuEdit(enmEditUndo).Enabled = True
            If txtDocument.SelLength > 0 Then
                mnuEdit(enmEditCut).Enabled = True
                mnuEdit(enmEditCopy).Enabled = True
                mnuEdit(enmEditDelete).Enabled = True
            End If
            If Clipboard.GetFormat(vbCFText) Then mnuEdit(enmEditPaste).Enabled = True
    End Select
End Sub
```

7. Place the following code in the mnuEdit_Click command. This event occurs whenever the user chooses a menu choice from the Edit menu. Note that we don't have to worry about inappropriate actions (such as attempting to cut text when there is none selected), because the mnuBar_Click routine disables inappropriate menu choices before the menu pulls down.

The Undo command simply resets the Text, SelStart, and SelLength properties back to their old values as set in the Text_Change event. The Cut command places the selected text on the Clipboard, then sets the selected text to an empty string to delete it. The Copy command places the selected text on the Clipboard (just like the Cut command) but doesn't do anything to the selected text in the text box. The Paste command places whatever text is on the Clipboard into the selected text in the text box. If no text is selected, it places the new text at the insertion point. Finally, the Delete command sets the selected text to an empty string.

```
Private Sub mnuEdit_Click(Index As Integer)
    Select Case Index
        Case enmEditUndo
            txtDocument.Text = mTextBeforeChange
            txtDocument.SelStart = mPosBeforeChange
            txtDocument.SelLength = mLenBeforeChange
        Case enmEditCut
            Clipboard.SetText txtDocument.SelText
            txtDocument.SelText = ""
        Case enmEditCopy
            Clipboard.SetText txtDocument.SelText
        Case enmEditPaste
            txtDocument.SelText = Clipboard.GetText(1)
        Case enmEditDelete
            txtDocument.SelText = ""
    End Select
End Sub
```

8. Place the following code in the mnuFile_Click event. This event triggers when the user selects a command from the File menu. Note that mnuFile(1) is a separator bar. The New command brings up a password protection dialog box before blanking out the text in the text box (to protect the valuable document you're creating?). It first blanks out any old text in the password text box, then shows the dialog box. Note that we specify Modal in the Show method; this prevents the rest of the code from continuing until the user closes the dialog box. We've set txtPassword's PasswordChar property to an asterisk (*) at design time. Once the user closes the dialog box, we check the password to see if it's acceptable. We've made it especially difficult for hackers to break our security here, as the only acceptable password is…anything! If the user has somehow managed to divine our devious password strategy, the routine clears txtDocument's text for a new document. If the user falls into our trap and simply presses ENTER in the password box, the routine calls itself again to force another attempt at the password entry. The Exit command ends the program.

```
Private Sub mnuFile_Click(Index As Integer)
    Select Case Index
        Case enmFileNew
            frmPassword!txtPassword.Text = ""
            frmPassword.Show vbModal
            If frmPassword!txtPassword.Text <> "" Then   'all passwords work!
                txtDocument.Text = ""
            Else                                   'user didn't even try, so
                ErrMsgBox "Invalid Password"       'tell'm to ...
                mnuFile_Click False                'try again!
            End If
        Case enmFileExit
            Unload Me
    End Select
End Sub
```

9. Enter the following code into the txtDocument_Change event. This event determines the number of characters in the text box and displays that information by assigning a string to the Caption property of the label control named lblStatus.

```
Private Sub txtDocument_Change()
    Dim strTemp As String

    strTemp = Format$(Len(txtDocument.Text), "  ##,###,##0")
    strTemp = strTemp + " character"
    If Len(txtDocument.Text) <> 1 Then strTemp = strTemp + "s"
    lblStatus.Caption = strTemp
End Sub
```

10. Enter the following code into the txtDocument_KeyDown event. This event saves the current settings of the text box before changes are made. The values of the Text, SelStart, and SelLength properties are assigned to the variables defined in the general declarations area of the form. The Shift argument is tested to determine whether the user has pressed CTRL or ALT. The properties are only saved if the Shift argument indicates these have not been pressed. More information can be found on the KeyDown event in Chapter 51.

```
Private Sub txtDocument_KeyDown(KeyCode As Integer, Shift As Integer)
    If Shift < vbCtrlMask Then
        mTextBeforeChange = txtDocument.Text
        mPosBeforeChange = txtDocument.SelStart
        mLenBeforeChange = txtDocument.SelLength
    End If
End Sub
```

11. Add the following Sub to the form. It pops up a Message box to inform the user that an error occurred.

```
Private Sub ErrMsgBox(strMessage As String)
    MsgBox strMessage, vbOKOnly + vbCritical, conAppTitle
End Sub
```

Assembling the Project: Password Form

1. Create a new form (the Password form) and place on it the following controls. Use Table 32-19 to set the properties of the form and each control.

Table 32-19 Elements of frmPassword

Object	Property	Setting
Form	Border	3–Fixed Double
	Caption	"Enter Password"
	Name	frmPassword

Object	Property	Setting
Command	Caption	"OK"
	Default	True
	Name	cmdOK
Text Box	FontSize	12
	MaxLength	10
	Name	txtPassword
	PasswordChar	*(asterisk)

2. Size and position the controls as in Figure 32-6.

3. Enter the following code in the cmdOK_Click event. This simply hides the dialog box. Note that we don't unload it, as the File New routine in the main form needs to access the txtPassword's Text property to determine if the user entered the correct password.

```
Sub cmdOK_Click ()
     frmPassword.Hide
End Sub
```

How It Works

The program created by this project is a simple text editor. The txtDocument control is the text entry area of the form. This control is a multiline (MultiLine = True) text box with a vertical scrollbar (ScrollBars = 2) on the right edge of the text area. The user can edit text in this control. Portions of text may be selected by pressing (SHIFT)-(ARROW-RIGHT) or by dragging the mouse over the text. The selected text may be cut by pressing (SHIFT)-(DELETE), copied to the Clipboard by pressing (CTRL)-(INSERT), deleted by pressing (DELETE), or replaced by text from the Clipboard by pressing (SHIFT)-(INSERT).

The mnuBar control array processes the user's menu clicks before the submenus are pulled down. The File menu doesn't need any further processing, but the Edit menu needs to have its options properly set. The routine first checks to see if any text has been selected; if so, it enables the Cut, Copy, and Delete commands. Paste is enabled if there is any text on the Clipboard, and Undo is enabled if there is anything in the Undo variables.

Figure 32-6   The password entry dialog box frmPassword during design

Choosing the New option from the mnuFile menu first calls up a password protection dialog box before clearing txtDocument. Note that we set the PasswordChar property of the txtPassword text box at design time. Choosing Exit causes the program to end.

The mnuEdit menu control array provides the editor with the normal Windows edit commands. The Undo option restores the text in the text box to the state it was in before the last time it was changed. For instance, if the user selects and deletes some text, the Undo option can restore the text to its value before the deletion.

The rest of the mnuEdit options provide alternative methods for working with the Clipboard. The Cut, Copy, and Delete options are all disabled unless the user has selected some text in the text box. The Cut and Delete options both remove the selected text from the text box. However, Cut copies the selected text to the Clipboard before removing it. The Copy option copies any selected text to the Clipboard. The Paste option on the mnuEdit menu copies any text that resides on the Clipboard object into the text box. This option is only enabled if the Clipboard contains text.

Figure 32-7 shows the project in action, with some text selected and the Edit menu pulled down.

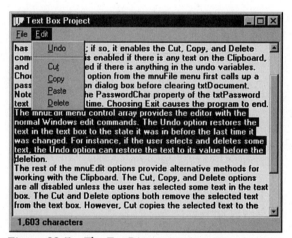

Figure 32-7   The TextBox project in action

33

APPLICATION APPEARANCE

Poorly designed screens impair the overall usefulness of even the most cleverly written program. A screen with clashing colors annoys users; command buttons placed in haphazard fashion can confuse and frustrate. Unnecessarily complex control arrangements also create difficulties. Users always notice these kinds of problems, if only on a subconscious level. Such problems reduce the chance that people will bother to work with a program. A user does not see cleverly written code; a user reacts to the way the program looks and behaves.

Compare the two functionally equivalent interfaces shown in Figures 33-1 and 33-2. Which would you rather use?

Windows provides menus, dialog boxes, and other objects that operate in a standard way and usually have a common look and feel. The Microsoft Windows environment thus represents an attempt to simplify the operation of computers and computer software. Windows provides a universal interface that a user theoretically can apply to new programs. Well-designed Windows programs are consistent in the way interface elements respond to the user. For example, most menu bars start with File and Edit, and end with Window and Help. Double-clicking an item in most list boxes is the same as single-clicking an item, then clicking on an associated command button.

Hundreds of these conventions, when appropriately applied, make learning Windows programs easy. When you've learned how to use one DOS program, you've learned how to use one DOS program. But when you've learned how to use one Windows program, you've learned much of what you need to know to operate any Windows program.

This chapter covers some of the key elements that make up an application's appearance.

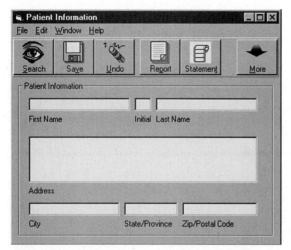

Figure 33-1 Harmonious and effective interface design

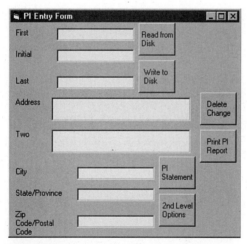

Figure 33-2 Functionally equivalent to Figure 33-1, yet ineffective

Color

People respond to the color of the elements on the screen. For example, red usually represents danger or warning (at least in most Western cultures). Red text stands out on a screen full of black text. This powerful visual tool augments the appearance of forms and controls on the screen.

In designing a form interactively with Visual Basic, you can use the onscreen color palette to make color choices (see Figure 33-3).

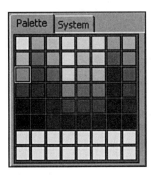

Figure 33-3   The color palette lets you easily choose colors for your application

The BackColor and ForeColor properties control an object's color. Colors are represented by a 4-byte integer number that indicates a mixture of the three electronic primary colors: red, blue, and green. One way to set a color value is to set this number directly. The first byte of this number is ignored. The second, third, and fourth bytes represent how much blue, red, and green, respectively, will be used in the color mixture. Each color can be assigned a value between 0 and 255 (or 0 to FF in hexadecimal notation), which indicates that color's intensity in the mixture. You can also assign a color value with the RGB function. This function lets you supply a decimal number between 0 and 255 for each electronic primary color and returns a color number based on these values. Still another way to assign a color value uses the QBColor function. This function lets you select one of 16 colors from a palette in a way familiar to QuickBASIC programmers.

Appearance of Screen Objects

Forms have four possible border styles: none, sizable, fixed single, and fixed double. The BorderStyle property of a form determines which type of border appears around it. A form with no border also has no Maximize button, Minimize button, or control box. This border style is a popular choice for warning boxes, which usually do not need these options. The user can change the size of sizable forms with the mouse, just as the name suggests. Both the fixed single and fixed double borders disable the mouse's ability to change their sizes. However, the user can still maximize or minimize the form.

Each object has a height and a width. The numbers representing the object's height and width depend on the type of measurement. The value of a height is different if expressed in inches or centimeters (although the object's actual height does not change). For example, objects that are 1 inch in height are also 2.54 centimeters high. Visual Basic determines the height and width of objects with the Height and Width properties of the object in the measurement system set in the ScaleMode property.

Each object on the screen is a certain distance from the edges of another object. A control on a form positions itself in terms of the left and top edges of the form, whereas forms on the screen locate themselves in terms of the left and top edges of the screen. Visual Basic returns the distance from the left and top edges with the Left and Top properties of the object in the measurement system set in the ScaleMode property.

Icons and Pointers

A minimized form becomes an icon that represents the form. This icon reminds the viewer that the form still resides in the operating memory of the computer. Visual Basic lets you modify this icon either at runtime or design time. At design time the properties box provides a list of the icons available. Access this list by selecting the Icon property in the properties box and double-clicking (Icon).

Figures 33-4 and 33-5 show what the properties box and list look like in the default Visual Basic setup. You can also change the icon of the mousepointer to reflect the current function of the program. Some pointer shapes have become traditional for Windows programs. When activity takes place in the background such that the user must wait before continuing work, an hourglass can replace the normal arrow. If the cursor is over a text box, the cursor can change to an I-beam so the user can manipulate the text box's contents. In Visual Basic, the MousePointer property determines the type of cursor that appears over an application's forms and controls.

Finally, an object's visibility determines whether or not the user sees it on the screen. (Don't confuse an invisible object with one that is covered by another window or application.)

Figure 33-4   Properties box showing Icon line

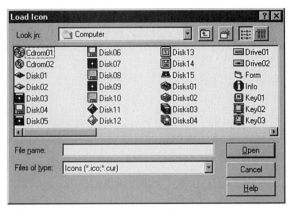

Figure 33-5   Load Icon dialog box

Application Appearance Summary

Table 33-1 summarizes the properties that affect the appearance of forms and controls.

Table 33-1 Properties dealing with the general appearance of a form or control

Use or Set This...	Type	To Do This...
Appearance	Property	Add 3D look to form or control automatically
BackColor	Property	Adjust the background color of a form or control
BackStyle	Property	Determine whether the background of a label or shape is transparent
BorderStyle	Property	Adjust the edges of a form and some controls
Caption	Property	Indicate what text will appear on a form or control
ForeColor	Property	Adjust the color of the text of a form or control
Height	Property	Adjust the vertical size of a form or control
Icon	Property	Determine the icon to display for a minimized form
Left	Property	Adjust the position of a form in relation to the left edge
MouseIcon	Property	Custom mousepointer
MousePointer	Property	Determine the icon to display when a mouse is over a form or control
Top	Property	Adjust the position of a form in relation to the top edge
Visible	Property	Determine whether a form is visible to the user
Width	Property	Adjust the horizontal size of a form or control

Constant Values

It is usually best to use named constants rather than numeric values when developing software. Named constants make your code more readable and easier to maintain.

Table 33-2 lists the values of the constants relevant to this chapter, mentions their names, and briefly describes what they mean. These constants can be viewed in the VB.Constants module (or, in some cases, in other object libraries) using the Object Browser. It is not necessary to explicitly add these objects to your project. For more information on using object library constants, see Chapter 16, "Objects and Collections"; for information on constant naming conventions, see Chapter 35, "Accessing Forms and Controls."

Table 33-2 Constant values for application appearance

Value	VB.Constants	Meaning
BackColor and ForeColor		
&H0	vbBlack	Black
&HFF	vbRed	Red
&HFF00	vbGreen	Green
&HFFFF	vbYellow	Yellow
&HFF0000	vbBlue	Blue
&HFF00FF	vbMagenta	Magenta
&HFFFF00	vbCyan	Cyan
&HFFFFFF	vbWhite	White
BackStyle		
0	vbTransparent	Background color and graphics visible behind object
1	vbSolid	Object's BackColor obscures any color or graphics (default)
BorderStyle (forms)		
0	NONE	None (no border, control box, Maximize button, or Minimize button)
1	vbFixedSingle	Fixed single (nonsizable, with Maximize and Minimize buttons)
2	vbSizable	Sizable (sizable border, with Maximize and Minimize buttons) (default)
3	vbFixedDouble	Fixed double (nonsizable border, without Maximize and Minimize buttons)
BorderStyle (labels, images, picture boxes, text boxes, OLE)		
0	NONE	None
1	vbFixedSingle	Fixed single
BorderStyle (lines and shapes)		
0	vbTransparent	Transparent
1	vbSolid	Solid
2	vbDash	Dash
3	vbDot	Dot
4	vbDashDot	Dash-Dot
5	vbDashDotDot	Dash-Dot-Dot
6	vbInsideSolid	Inside solid
MousePointer		
0	vbDefault	Default for this control
1	vbArrow	Arrow

Value	VB.Constants	Meaning
2	vbCrosshair	Cross-hair pointer
3	vbIbeam	Text entry I-beam
4	vbIconPointer	Square within a square
5	vbSizePointer	Four-directional cross; arrows facing up, down, left, and right
6	vbSizeNESW	Two-directional diagonal arrow (northeast to southwest)
7	vbSizeNS	Two-directional vertical arrow (north to south)
8	vbSizeNWSE	Two-directional diagonal arrow (northwest to southeast)
9	vbSizeEW	Two-directional horizontal arrow (east to west)
10	vbUpArrow	Arrow pointing up
11	vbHourglass	Hourglass
12	vbNoDrop	No drop (circle with line through it)
13	vbCustom	Custom pointer specified by MouseIcon property

The following pages investigate these properties in detail. At the end of this section, step-by-step directions describe how to assemble the Appearance project that demonstrates each of these properties.

APPEARANCE PROPERTY

Objects Affected CheckBox, ComboBox, CommandButton, Data, DBCombo, DBGrid, DBList, DirListBox, DriveListBox, FileListBox, Form, Forms Collection, Frame, Image, Label, ListBox, MDIForm, OLE Container, OptionButton, PictureBox, PropertyPage, RemoteData, TextBox, UserControl, UserDocument

Purpose The Appearance property gives you the ability to automatically have 3D effects in your Visual Basic application without using any of the 3D custom controls. Appearance automatically gives the CheckBox, ComboBox, Databound Combobox, Databound Grid, Databound Listbox, Frame, ListBox, OptionButton, and TextBox controls a 3D appearance. Table 33-3 shows the different arguments of the Appearance property. Table 33-4 shows the possible values for the Appearance property.

General Syntax

```
[Name.]Appearance [= style%]
```

Table 33-3 Arguments of the Appearance property

Argument	Description
Name	Name property of affected object
Style%	Set whether the control is 3D or flat in appearance

Table 33-4 Available settings of the Appearance property

Style%	VB.Constants	Effect
0	vbFlat	Flat
1	vb3D	Standard 3D appearance

Example Syntax

```
Private Sub Form_Load
        If Form1.Appearance = vbFlat Then
                Label1.Caption = Name & " is not using 3D effects"
        Else
                Label1.Caption = Name & " is standard Windows 95 appearance"
        End If
End Sub
```

Description The Appearance property gives you the ability to add a 3D appearance to your Visual Basic application very easily. Using this property ensures compatibility with Windows 95, with only minimal coding changes.

The Appearance property can be set only at design time and is read-only at runtime.

Example Figure 33-6 shows a form with Appearance set to 1. Figure 33-7 shows the same form with Appearance set to 0. Appearance automatically changes the background color to the color of the command button from the Windows Control Panel.

Comments Windows 95 has a 3D appearance. The Appearance property will give your forms and standard Visual Basic controls running under Windows 3.1 the same appearance. Any third-party controls will have to supply their own 3D look and feel.

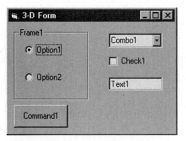

Figure 33-6 Form with 3D appearance

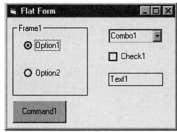

Figure 33-7 Form with flat appearance

BackColor Property

Objects Affected AmbientProperties, Animation, CheckBox, ComboBox, CommandButton, Data, DBCombo, DBGrid, DBList, DirListBox, DriveListBox, FileListBox, Form, Forms Collection, Frame, ImageList, Label, ListBox, ListView, Masked Edit, MDIForm, MSFlexGrid, OLE Container, OptionButton, PictureBox, Printer, Printers Collection, PropertyPage, RemoteData, RichTextBox, Shape, SSTab, TextBox, UserControl, UserDocument

Purpose The BackColor property defines or determines the background color of a form or control. Table 33-5 summarizes the arguments of the BackColor property, and Table 33-6 lists the values of the color& argument.

General Syntax

```
[form.]BackColor [ = color&]
[form!]Name.BackColor [ = color&]
```

Table 33-5 Arguments of the BackColor property

Argument	Description
form	Name property of the form; changes or references current form if not specified
Name	Name property of the control
color&	Value of the color defined with hexadecimal number, RGB function, or QBColor function

Table 33-6 Values of common colors in RGB, hexadecimal, and QBColor formats

Color	VB.Constants	Red Value	Green Value	Blue Value	Hexadecimal	QBColor
Black	vbBlack	0	0	0	&H0	0
Red	vbRed	255	0	0	&HFF	4

continued on next page

continued from previous page

Color	VB.Constants	Red Value	Green Value	Blue Value	Hexadecimal	QBColor
Green	vbGreen	0	255	0	&HFF00	2
Yellow	vbYellow	0	255	255	&HFFFF	6
Blue	vbBlue	0	0	255	&HFF0000	1
Magenta	vbMagenta	255	0	255	&HFF00FF	5
Cyan	vbCyan	0	255	255	&HFFFF00	3
White	vbWhite	255	255	255	&HFFFFFF	15
Light gray	n/a	192	192	192	&H00C0C0C0	7
Dark gray	n/a	128	128	128	&H00808080	8

Example Syntax

```
Private Sub Form_Resize
    If WindowState = 2 Then              'if the window is maximized
        BackColor = RGB(0, 0, 255)     ⇐
'changes the form's background to blue
    Else
        BackColor = RGB(255, 255, 255) ⇐
'changes the form's background to white
    End If
End Sub
```

Description   The BackColor property changes the Windows environment's default settings for the background color of a form or control. (The default setting of a form's BackColor is the color chosen in the control panel for the Windows background.) Each BackColor property expression begins with the name of the object whose background is being changed. The Name property uniquely identifies a control or form. If no name precedes an expression, the code references or changes the BackColor property of the current form.

The color& argument of a BackColor expression must be a hexadecimal value. An explicit hexadecimal number, the RGB function, or the QBColor function defines the hexadecimal value of color&. In the example syntax, the background color of the form changes according to its present size. The background of a maximized form is blue; a normalized form is white.

Setting the Color& Argument   You may set the color& argument in several different ways. Table 33-6 summarizes the settings of the color& argument.

The most direct method uses the hexadecimal number of the color. A valid hexadecimal value ranges from 0 to 16,777,215 (&HFFFFFF). This is the format that Visual Basic uses if you read the color's property during runtime. Note that the Visual Basic object library constants hold these hexadecimal values.

You may also obtain the hexadecimal value of any of the 16 standard Windows colors with the QBColor function by specifying the integer color number as used in Quick BASIC (and other versions of Microsoft BASIC).

The RGB function returns the hexadecimal equivalent given the arguments red, green, and blue. Each argument ranges from 0 to 255; customized colors result from the adjustment of the values of these three variables.

The ForeColor Property

The BackColor and ForeColor properties of a form combine to produce the colors that you see when the form displays. Whenever you change one of these properties, you should consider how the new color combination will work together. If the foreground and background colors clash, it might make your program harder to use and might detract from its effectiveness. For example, setting the BackColor property to blue and the ForeColor property to bright red is objectionable to most users.

Example

In the Appearance project at the end of this chapter, the BackColor property of the formAppear and formWarning forms is gray (&H00C0C0C0). You will set this property at design time to simplify the process. Notice how the BackColor property of the form has no effect on the setting of the control's background color. Each control has its own separate BackColor property, independent of the settings of the form's BackColor property.

Comments

The BackColor property of a form or control is an effective way to highlight certain controls to attract the user's attention or to make something more visible. For instance, to emphasize list boxes on a form with a gray background, set the BackColor property of the list boxes to white.

BACKSTYLE PROPERTY

Objects Affected   Label, OLE Container, Shape, UserControl

Purpose   The BackStyle property determines whether a label or shape's background is opaque or transparent. Tables 33-7 and 33-8 summarize the arguments of the BackStyle property.

General Syntax

```
[form!]Name.BackStyle [ = style%]
```

Table 33-7 Arguments of the BackStyle property

Argument	Description
form	Name property of the form the control is on
Name	Name property of the shape or label control
style%	Sets the transparency of the background

Table 33-8 Settings of the style% argument in the BackStyle property

style%	VB.Constants	Setting
0	vbTransparent	Background color and graphics visible behind object
1	vbSolid	Object's BackColor obscures any color or graphics (default)

Example Syntax

```
Private Sub Command1_Click ()
    Label1.BackStyle = Abs(Label1.BackStyle - 1)     ⇐
'flips transparency of label
    Label1.Caption = Choose(Label1.BackStyle + 1, "Transparent", "Opaque")
End Sub
```

Description   The BackStyle property lets you determine whether to obscure the background when you place a label or shape on top of another object. Setting a label's BackStyle to Transparent (0) lets the background color of its container show through. This may be helpful if you use colored backgrounds, as you don't have to set each label's background color independently. You might also need to label a set of graphics. If you leave BackStyle at the default of Solid (1), you run the risk of obscuring the graphics you're trying to label.

The example syntax shows how the label obscures the background when its BackStyle property is set to 1 and how it lets the background color of the form show through when its BackStyle property is set to 0. Figures 33-8 and 33-9 show how the example syntax might look.

Example   The Appearance project sets the BackStyle of the labels to Transparent. This makes form design and upkeep easier.

Comment   If the BackStyle property is set to Transparent (0), the BackColor property has no effect.

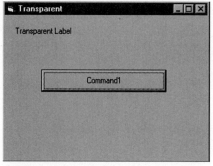

Figure 33-8   Label1 with transparent BackStyle

Figure 33-9 Label1 with opaque
BackStyle

BORDERSTYLE PROPERTY

Objects Affected   DBGrid, Form, Forms Collection, Frame, Image, Label, Line, ListView,
Masked Edit, MSChart, MSFlexGrid, MCI, OLE Container, PictureBox,
ProgressBar, RichTextBox, Shape, Slider, TextBox, ToolBar, TreeView,
UserControl

Purpose   The BorderStyle property determines the appearance of a border for a
form, grid, image, label, line, OLE container, picture box, shape, or text
box. This property is modifiable at design time only for forms and text
boxes. Tables 33-9 through 33-12 summarize the different settings of the
BorderStyle property's arguments.

General Syntax

```
[form.]BorderStyle [ = setting%]
[form!]Name.BorderStyle [ = setting%]
```

Table 33-9 Arguments of the BorderStyle property

Argument	Description
form	Name property of the form
Name	Name property of the text box, label, or picture box
setting%	Value representing the type of border

Table 33-10 Settings for the BorderStyle property of a form

setting%	VB.Constants	Description
0	NONE	None (no border, control box, Maximize button, or Minimize button).
1	vbFixedSingle	Fixed single (nonsizable, with Maximize and Minimize buttons).
2	vbSizable	Sizable (sizable border, with Maximize and Minimize buttons) (default).
3	vbFixedDialog	Fixed dialog (nonsizable border, without Minimize or Maximize buttons)
4	vbFixedToolWindow	Fixed ToolWindow: In Windows 3.1 and NT 3.51, acts like vbFixedSingle; in Windows 95, displays only a Close button, along with shortening the title bar and a smaller title bar font. Forms with this border style don't appear on the Win95 task bar.
5	vbSizableToolWindow	Sizable ToolWindow: In Windows 3.1 and NT 3.51, acts like vbSizable; in Windows 95, displays only a Close button, along with a shortened title bar and a smaller title bar font. Forms with this border style don't appear on the Win95 task bar.

Table 33-11 Settings for the labels, images, picture boxes, text boxes, and OLE containers

setting%	VB.Constants	Description	Controls That Default to This Style...
0	NONE	None	label, image
1	vbFixedSingle	Fixed single	picture box, text box, OLE container

Table 33-12 Settings for the BorderStyle property of shapes and lines

setting%	VB.Constants	Description	Controls That Default to This Style...
0	vbTransparent	Transparent	
1	vbSolid	Solid	shape, line
2	vbDash	Dash	
3	vbDot	Dot	
4	vbDashDot	Dash-Dot	
5	vbDashDotDot	Dash-Dot-Dot	
6	vbInsideSolid	Inside solid	

Example Syntax

```
Sub SetBackground (Name As Form)
    Select Case Name.BorderStyle        'obtains border of indicated form
        Case vbNone                     'no border
            Name.BackColor = vbBlue         'blue background
            Name.ForeColor = vbWhite        'white text
        Case vbFixedSingle              'fixed single border
            Name.BackColor = vbWhite        'white background
            Name.ForeColor = vbBlue         'blue text
        Case vbSizable                  'sizable border
            Name.BackColor = vbBlue         'blue background
            Name.ForeColor = vbYellow       'yellow text
```

```
            Case vbFixedDouble              'fixed double border
                  Name.BackColor = vbCyan      'cyan background
                  Name.ForeColor = vbBlack     'black text
        End Select
End Sub
```

Description   Use the BorderStyle property at design time to set the appearance of the
edges of a form, text box, label, or picture box. The border chosen at
design time affects a form's control box, Maximize button, and Minimize
button at runtime. (At design time the control box, Maximize button, and
Minimize button are always visible.) The BorderStyle property of a form
also affects the user's ability to change the form's size. When the
BorderStyle property of a text box, picture box, or label changes, the single
border line around the object appears or disappears.

Forms   BorderStyle applies to both forms and various controls. The settings for
these two groups, although similar, differ enough that we'll cover them
separately, discussing forms first.

Sizable Border   The default setting for the BorderStyle property of a form is 2 (sizable). A
sizable border has no effect on the display of the control box, Maximize
button, and Minimize controls. Figure 33-10 displays how a form with a
sizable border appears on the screen. Corresponding values for these properties (ControlBox, MaxButton, MinButton) are True (-1) by default.
Changing one of these properties does not affect the other two properties.
When a form retains the default border style, the user can change the size
of the form at runtime.

No Border   A form with the BorderStyle set to 0 will not have a border or any of the
objects normally associated with a border. For this reason the Maximize
button, Minimize button, and control box will not appear on the form,
regardless of the settings of the ControlBox, MaxButton, or MinButton
properties. The title bar of the form will also not appear. When a form's
BorderStyle property is 0, the form may not be resized or minimized. You
may wish to use this kind of border for warning or informational dialog

Figure 33-10   BorderStyle 2 (the
default) gives a sizable border

boxes. For example, this style might be used with an application's first
screen (splash screen), which quickly displays while the application loads

the rest of the forms into memory. Figure 33-11 shows what a form with no border looks like.

Figure 33-11   BorderStyle 0 gives no border

Fixed Single Border

If the BorderStyle of a form is 1 (fixed single), then the border is a single line around the form. Figure 33-12 demonstrates the appearance of a form with a fixed single border. The Maximize button, Minimize button, and control box may appear on the form, depending on the setting of the MaxButton, MinButton, and ControlBox properties. A form with this border style may have its size changed only by maximizing or minimizing it. The user maximizes or minimizes this kind of form with either the command options on the control box or the icon buttons.

Fixed Dialog Border

When a form's BorderStyle property is 3 (fixed dialog), Minimize and Maximize buttons do not appear, regardless of the settings of the MaxButton and MinButton properties. A control box appears on the form, provided that the ControlBox property is True. Both the Maximize and Minimize command buttons will be options on the Control Box menu unless the MaxButton and MinButton properties are False. Users cannot adjust the size of the form at runtime by dragging the borders with the mouse. Only the WindowState property—or the maximize, minimize, or restore options on the control box—can change the size of a form with this kind of border style. Forms with a menu bar never display as a fixed double border; Visual Basic automatically displays fixed double forms as fixed single forms if there is a menu. Figure 33-13 shows what a form with a fixed dialog border looks like on the screen.

Fixed Tool Window

When a form's BorderStyle is 4 (fixed ToolWindow), the title bar is shorter, and the title font is smaller than the title bar and title fonts in styles 1, 2, and 3. There are no Minimize, Maximize, and ControlBox buttons, regardless of the settings of the MaxButton, MinButton, and ControlBox properties. Users cannot adjust the size of the window by dragging the borders. The programmer can change the size of the window by changing the Width, Height, or WindowState property or using the form's Move method.

Sizable Tool Window

When a form's BorderStyle is 4 (fixed ToolWindow), the title bar is shorter, and the title font is smaller than the title bar and title fonts in styles 1, 2, and 3. There are no Minimize, Maximize, or ControlBox buttons, regardless of the settings of the MaxButton, MinButton, and ControlBox properties. Users can adjust the size of the window by dragging the borders.

The programmer can change the size of the window by changing the Width, Height, or WindowState property or using the form's Move method.

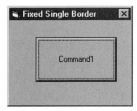

Figure 33-12   BorderStyle 1 gives a fixed single border

Figure 33-13   BorderStyle 3 gives a fixed dialog border

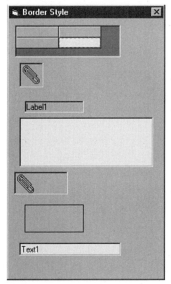

Figure 33-14   Borders around grid, image, label, OLE container, picture box, shape, and text box

Text Boxes, Labels, and Picture Boxes

Every grid, image, label, OLE container, picture box, shape, and text box has a BorderStyle property. Figure 33-14 demonstrates the appearance of the border around each of these controls. Unlike the setting of a form's property, the BorderStyle property of a label, text box, or picture box has an effect only if there is a border. This border appears around the indicated control. If the value of this property is True, then a single line appears around the bounds of the label, image, picture box, and text box. A border does not appear around one of these controls with a False (0) BorderStyle property. The line and shape controls have a variety of border styles.

Example

In the Appearance project at the end of this chapter, the BorderStyle property removes the border of formWarning. This removes the control box, Maximize button, and Minimize button from the user's view. The BorderStyle property of both the label boxes on the Warning forms remains at the default value of 0. As a result, no border appears around either of these labels. FormAppear begins with its border set to fixed single.

Comments

Make sure to choose the correct border for each form in a program. The default sizable setting is not always appropriate. In many cases, giving the user the ability to change the size of the form might cause errors. Many forms look bad when maximized—all the controls remain stuck in the upper-left corner, with wide expanses of blank form covering the screen. Strongly consider one of the fixed border styles, unless you write special code in the Resize event (covered in Chapter 36, "Accessing Forms and Menus") to resize and reposition a form's controls.

CAPTION PROPERTY

Objects Affected

Button, CheckBox, CommandButton, Data, DBGrid, Form, Forms Collection, Frame, Label, MDIForm, Menu, OptionButton, PropertyPage, RemoteData, SSTab

Purpose

The Caption property indicates what label is displayed in a control or form. A form's Caption property appears in its title bar, between the control box and the Minimize and Maximize buttons. Text in the Caption property of a label, data control, or command button appears on the control. Option buttons or check boxes place the contents of their Caption property to the right of the control. A frame's Caption property displays on the upper-right corner of the frame. All these controls' Caption properties are both read and write at either design time or runtime. Table 33-13 summarizes the arguments of the Caption property.

General Syntax

```
[form.]Caption [ = textString$]
[form!]Name.Caption [ = textString$]
```

Table 33-13 Arguments of the Caption property

Argument	Description
form	Name property of the form
Name	Name property of the control
textString$	Text to place in or on the control or form indicated

Example Syntax

```
Private Sub Commmand1_Click
    If  Command1.Caption = "Print" Then  ⇐
'Alternates between displaying the word "Display"
        Command1.Caption = "Display"    ⇐
'and "Print" each time the user presses Command1.
    Else
        Command1.Caption = "Print"
    End If
End Sub
```

Description   The Caption property defines or determines the text that appears on a command button, option box, check box, data control, frame, label, menu, or form. You can set this property at design time with the properties box. You can also set the Caption property of a form or control at runtime. The textString$ argument contains the string of text to redefine the Caption property with. If the textString$ argument is blank, then the text on the form or control is blank. In the example, the Caption property of the Command1 command button changes with each clicking of the command button.

Forms   The Caption displays in a form's title bar. The *title bar* is the region between the control box and the Minimize and Maximize buttons. If the BorderStyle of a form is 0 (no border), then there is no title bar and the Caption property (if any) is ignored. Remember that the Caption property of a form is for visually cueing the user, not for identifying the form in your code. Figure 33-15 shows how the Caption property appears at the top of Form1.

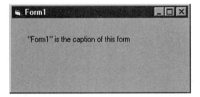

Figure 33-15   Caption property text appears on form's title bar

Labels   Text entered into the Caption property of a label displays on the form in the label's position. A label's Caption property is alterable either at design time or runtime. If the label's AutoSize property is True (-1), then the label's size automatically increases or decreases to fit with each change. For example, the label below a picture box containing a Trashcan icon could change from Delete to Disabled whenever the user turns the delete feature off. In this case, the AutoSize property allows the label to expand or contract to accommodate the different word lengths. Figure 33-16 shows where the Caption property of the Label1 label box appears on the label control.

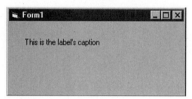

Figure 33-16   Caption property text appears in label

Command Buttons The Caption property for a command button places the text in the middle of the command button. A command control's Caption property is modifiable either at design time or runtime. You can also use the Caption property to assign an access key to a command button. Place an ampersand (&) before the letter in the caption that you wish to make the access key. For example, Ⓟ would become the access key for a command button with a Caption property of &Print. The user can then hold down Ⓐ and press Ⓟ to trigger the command button's Click event. This change appears in text on the command button shown with the access letter underlined. If you need to include an ampersand literal within your caption, use double ampersands: For example, &UPS && Airborne becomes U̲PS & Airborne. Figure 33-17 indicates the location where the Caption property displays on the Command1 command button.

Figure 33-17   Caption property text appears inside a command button

Option Buttons and Check Boxes Option buttons and check boxes have their Caption property contents placed on the right of the graphic objects. These properties are modifiable at both design time and runtime but do not possess the AutoSize feature of the label box. Make sure you provide enough space for any changes to the captions of these controls. Figure 33-18 demonstrates the place where the Caption properties of the Option1 option box and Check1 check boxes appear on the screen.

Example The Appearance project at the end of this chapter uses the Caption property several times. It is set at design time to label various elements used in the program, and the Caption property of formAppear changes to identify what number is being dialed.

Comments A form's Caption property does not appear when the form's BorderStyle is 0.

FORECOLOR PROPERTY

Objects Affected AmbientProperties, Animation, CheckBox, ComboBox, CommandButton, Data, DBCombo, DBGrid, DBList, DirListBox, DriveListBox, FileListBox, Form, Forms Collection, Frame, ImageList, Label, ListBox, ListView, Masked Edit, MDIForm, MSFlexGrid, OLE Container, OptionButton, PictureBox, Printer, Printers Collection, PropertyPage, RemoteData, RichTextBox, Shape, SSTab, TextBox, UserControl, UserDocument

Purpose The ForeColor property reads or sets the foreground color of a form or control. Tables 33-14 and 33-15 list the arguments and values of the ForeColor property.

General Syntax

```
[form.]ForeColor [ = color&]
[form!]Name.ForeColor [ = color&]
```

Figure 33-18 Caption property text of option and check boxes appears next to the box or button

Table 33-14 Arguments of the ForeColor property

Argument	Description
form	Name property of the form; no name means the current form
Name	Name property of the control
color&	Value of the color defined with hexadecimal number, RGB function, or QBColor function

Table 33-15 Values of common colors in RGB, hexadecimal, and QBColor formats

Color	VB.Constants	Red Value	Green Value	Blue Value	Hexadecimal	QBColor
Black	vbBlack	0	0	0	&H0	0
Red	vbRed	255	0	0	&HFF	4
Green	vbGreen	0	255	0	&HFF00	2
Yellow	vbYellow	0	255	255	&HFFFF	6
Blue	vbBlue	0	0	255	&HFF0000	1
Magenta	vbMagenta	255	0	255	&HFF00FF	5
Cyan	vbCyan	0	255	255	&HFFFF00	3
White	vbWhite	255	255	255	&HFFFFFF	15
Light gray	n/a	192	192	192	&H00C0C0C0	7
Dark gray	n/a	128	128	128	&H00808080	8

Example Syntax

```
Private Sub Form_Load ()
    If  ForeColor = RGB(0,0,0) Then
        BackColor = RGB(255,255,255)
    End If
End Sub
```

Description   The ForeColor property changes the Windows environment's default settings for the foreground color of a form or control. (The default setting of the ForeColor of a form is the color chosen in the control panel for the Windows text.) Each ForeColor property expression begins with the name of the object whose foreground is being changed. The Name property uniquely identifies a control or form. If no name precedes an expression, the code references or changes the ForeColor property of the current form.

The color& argument of a ForeColor expression must be a hexadecimal value. Either an explicit hexadecimal number, the RGB function, or the QBColor function defines the hexadecimal value of color&. In the example syntax, the foreground color of the form changes according to its present size. The foreground of a maximized form is blue; a normalized form is white.

Setting the Color& Argument

You may set the color& argument in several different ways. Table 33-15 summarizes the settings of the color& argument. The most direct method uses the hexadecimal number of the color. A valid hexadecimal value ranges from 0 to 16,777,215 (&HFFFFFF). This is the format that Visual Basic uses if you read the color's property during runtime. Note that the Visual Basic object library constants hold these hexadecimal values.

You may also obtain the hexadecimal value of any of the 16 standard Windows colors with the QBColor function by specifying the integer color number as used in Quick BASIC (and other versions of Microsoft BASIC).

The RGB function returns the hexadecimal equivalent given the arguments red, green, and blue. Each argument ranges from 0 to 255; customized colors result from the adjustment of the values of these three variables.

The BackColor Property

The ForeColor and BackColor properties of a form combine to produce the colors that you see when the form displays. Whenever you change one of these properties, you should consider how the new color combination will work together. If the background and foreground colors clash, it may make your program harder to use and may detract from its effectiveness. For example, setting the ForeColor property to blue and the BackColor property to bright red is objectionable to most users.

Example

In the Appearance project at the end of this chapter, the ForeColor property of the FormAppear and Warning forms changes to blue (&HFF000). This property change occurs at design time for both forms to simplify the process. Modifications are also possible at runtime.

Comments

The ForeColor property of a form or control is an effective means of highlighting certain controls to get the user's attention or to make it easier for the user to see something. For instance, red text on an otherwise black-and-white screen will draw the user's attention.

HEIGHT PROPERTY

Objects Affected

Animation, Button, CheckBox, Column, ColumnHeader, ColumnHeaders Collection, ComboBox, CommandButton, Data, DirListBox, DriveListBox, FileListBox, Form, Forms Collection, Frame, HScrollBar, VScrollBar, Image, Label, ListBox, ListItem, ListItems Collection, ListView, Masked Edit, MCI, MDIForm, MSChart, MSFlexGrid, OLE Container, OptionButton, Panel, Pen, Picture, PictureBox, PictureClip, Printer, Printers Collection, ProgressBar, PropertyPage, RemoteData, RichTextBox, Screen, Shape, Slider, SSTab, StatLine, StatusBar, Tab, TabStrip, TextBox, Toolbar, TreeView, UpDown, UserControl, UserDocument, Wall, WebBrowser

Purpose

The Height property defines or determines the vertical size of a form or control on the screen, form, picture box, or Printer object. Forms, Printer objects, and Screen objects are always measured in twips. A control's size uses the units of measurement set in the ScaleMode property of the current form or picture box. Table 33-16 summarizes the arguments of the Height property, and Table 33-17 outlines measurement types.

General Syntax

```
[form.]Height [ = height!]
[form!]Name.Height [ = height!]
Printer.Height [ = height!]
Screen.Height [ = height!]
```

Table 33-16 Arguments of the Height property

Argument	Description
form	Name property of the form
Name	Name property of the control
Printer	'Printer' for Printer object
Screen	'Screen' for Screen object
height!	Vertical height of the object

Table 33-17 Possible measurement types in relation to 1 inch

Measurement	Size
Twip	1440 twips = 1 inch
Point	72 points = 1 inch
Pixels	Varies, depending on system being used
Characters	12 characters horizontally and 6 vertically = 1 inch
Millimeters	254 millimeters = 1 inch
Centimeters	2.54 centimeters = 1 inch

Example Syntax

```
Private Sub Form_Load
    Form1.Height = (Command1.Height * 5)    ⇐
'Defines height and width of the form as 5
    Form1.Width = (Command1.Width * 5)      ⇐
'times the height and width of command button.
End Sub
```

Description

The Height property of an object measures the vertical height of the object. You can enter this value at design time by manually sizing the object with the mouse or by entering the value at the properties box. You can modify the Height property of a control or form either at design time or runtime. In contrast, you can only set the Height properties of the

Figure 33-19 The left side of the toolbar shows the Left, Top, Width, and Height properties

Printer and Screen objects at runtime. A setting must be between 0 and a maximum value specified by the system itself. Visual Basic automatically adjusts itself to the resolution of the screen or printer. You should ensure that your objects are not too large for the most common 640×480 and 800×600 resolution screens to display.

Left, Top, Width, and Height Properties

When you create a form or control in Visual Basic, the Left, Top, Width, and Height properties display in the far left side of the toolbar. Figure 33-19 shows what the toolbar looks like on the screen.

The first two numbers, separated by a comma, represent the left and top position of the control or form. A form's Height property provides the maximum visible height for the controls placed on it. (Note that it is possible to have a control larger than the form it is on; only part of the control would display.) Similarly, the value of the Height property of the screen sets the maximum value of a form's property. This varies from system to system, according to the resolution of the monitor. The width and the height of the object appear to the right of these numbers, separated by an ×. If the object is a control, then the numbers shown are in the units of measurement specified by the ScaleMode property of the current form. A form's Height property is measured in twips. This difference allows for variances in the resolution of screens used for each computer. For example, a system with an 800×600 display shows more on the screen than a 640×480 display. See Chapter 37, "The Coordinate System," for more information.

Screen and Printer

The Height property returns the height of the screen or page available based on the resolution of the computer screen or printer being used. The Height property of the screen and printer objects is not available at design time and is read-only at runtime.

Scale Mode

The ScaleMode property of a form directly controls the meaning of the value of the Height property. When the ScaleMode property changes at design time from one measurement to another, Visual Basic recalculates the value of the Height property in this new type of measurement. As the ScaleMode property is not modifiable at runtime, the meaning of the value of the Height property does not change while the program is running. For example, no matter what size a command box becomes based on changes in the size of the parent form, the Height property will remain the same.

**ScaleHeight
Property**

The ScaleHeight property divides the height of a form, picture box, or Printer object into the number of units set in the property. For example, when a form's ScaleHeight property changes to 100, the height of the form is divided into 100 equal units. (Changing the ScaleHeight property of the form to a new value does not change the actual size of the control.) This unit changes in size as the form's height changes. Increasing the height of the form thus has the effect of increasing the size of one of these units (the height remains divided into 100 units that are now larger in size). The size of the control adjusts based on the changes in height to the form.

These units define the upper and lower limits of the possible height of controls on this form. For example, a Resize event might adjust the Height property of a command box of a form by triggering a move statement that always ensures the command box is one-fourth the size of the form. In this example, the ScaleHeight property of the form is 100, and the Height property of the Command1 command button is 25 (one-fourth the height of the form). Figures 33-20 and 33-21 display this concept visually.

Example

The Appearance project at the end of this section sets the Height property of the forms and controls at design time. This is done either by dragging the control's edges with the mouse or by entering the value into the properties box.

ICON PROPERTY

Objects Affected   Form, MDI Form

Purpose   The Icon property defines the icon displayed on the screen when a form is in a minimized window state. This property is only available for a form, and the file must be in the standard icon format (.ICO). Table 33-18 summarizes the argument of the Icon property.

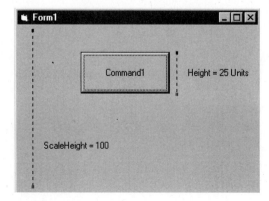

Figure 33-20   Height and ScaleHeight compared at start...

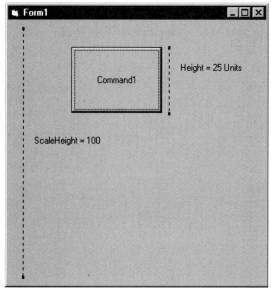

Figure 33-21   ...and after resizing; note that the
Height of the command button is the same number
of relative units, although it is physically larger

General Syntax

```
[form.]Icon [= LoadPicture (stringexpression)]
```

Table 33-18 Argument of the Icon property

Argument	Description
form	Name property of the form

Example Syntax

```
Private Sub Form_Resize ()
    If WindowState = 0 Then                           ⇐
'checks if form is minimized
        If Form1.Caption = "Dialing Number" Then  ⇐
'checks if form reads this text
            Form1.Icon = LoadPicture("\VB\ICONS\COMM\PHONE04.ICO")  ⇐
'Off Hook phone
        ElseIf Form1.Caption = "Hanging Up" Then  ⇐
'checks if form reads this text
            Form1.Icon = LoadPicture("\VB\ICONS\COMM\NET3.ICO")    ⇐
'knife cutting
        Else
            Form1.Icon = LoadPicture("\VB\ICONS\COMM\PHONE01.ICO")  ⇐
'regular phone
    End If
End Sub
```

Description	A form's Icon property defines the default icon to display when a form appears minimized on the screen. At creation time, a form's Icon property defaults to the Visual Basic Icon. A form's Icon property may be modified either at design time or runtime. In this way, you can temporarily change an icon at runtime to reflect changes in the functioning of the program. In the example above, the main form of a communications program's Icon property changes for different functions. An open phone symbol appears for a dialing operation, a knife cutting a cable for a phone hang-up operation, and a phone for an inactive program.
Design Time Setting	At design time, you can choose an icon on the properties box. Select the Icon property and click (Icon). Use the File list box to find the directory containing the icon you want, then select the icon. Any of the icons included with the Visual Basic package will work well for this property.
	Setting a form's Icon during design time lets Visual Basic make the icon part of the executable file. This relieves you from needing to supply an external icon file with your application.
The LoadPicture Function	Use the LoadPicture function to change the Icon property of a form at run time. In the example above, the original setting for the form's Icon property is the PHONE01.ICO icon. This displays if the text on the communications program is neither Dialing Number nor Hanging Up.
Example	In the Appearance project at the end of this chapter, the Icon property of frmAppear begins as PHONE01.ICO. This is the icon that appears at the bottom of the screen when the dialer is not running. The Minimize button is on frmAppear so that the user may take a look at this default icon.
	Pressing tmrDial activates the tmrDial_Timer, which uses the LoadPicture function to change the Appearance form's Icon property to the PHONE04.ICO icon. The program then minimizes frmAppear, and the user sees an icon with the receiver off the hook at the bottom of the computer screen.
	After pressing the Cancel command button, the Icon property of frmAppear becomes the former icon. This is a graphic means of indicating the completion of the dialing operation. This way, the icons constantly inform the user what operations (if any) are taking place.
Comments	Give every form that can be minimized a different kind of icon rather than leaving the default icon on. This enables the user to differentiate between the icons at the bottom of the screen.

LEFT PROPERTY

Objects Affected	Button, CheckBox, Column, ColumnHeader, ColumnHeaders Collection, ComboBox, CommandButton, CommonDialog, Data, DBCombo, DBGrid, DBList, DirListBox, DriveListBox, FileListBox, Form, Forms Collection, Frame, HScrollBar, Image, Label, ListBox, ListItems Collection, ListView,

Masked Edit, MCI, MDIForm, MSChart, MSFlexGrid, OLE Container, OptionButton, Panel, PictureBox, ProgressBar, RemoteData, RichTextBox, Shape, Slider, SSTab, StatusBar, Tab, TabStrip, TextBox, Timer, ToolBar, TreeView, UpDown, VScrollBar, WebBrowser

Purpose   The Left property defines or determines the distance of a form or control from the left edge of its container. An object's distance is measured in the units indicated by the ScaleMode property of its container. Tables 33-19 and 33-20 summarize the different arguments of the Left property and the possible measurement types.

General Syntax

```
[form.]Left [ = left!]
[form!]Name.Left [ = left!]
```

Table 33-19 Arguments of the Left property

Argument	Description
form	Name property of the form
Name	Name property of the control
left!	Horizontal left distance of the object

Table 33-20 Possible measurement types in relation to 1 inch

Measurement	Converts To...
Twip	1440 twips = 1 inch
Point	72 points = 1 inch
Pixels	Varies, depending on system being used
Characters	12 characters horizontally and 6 vertically = 1 inch
Millimeters	254 millimeters = 1 inch
Centimeters	2.54 centimeters = 1 inch

Example Syntax

```
Public Sub LeftDistance (Ctl As Control, Name As Form)
'all of the following values equal one inch
    Select Case Name.ScaleMode        'Based on Control's ScaleMode
        Case vbUser                   'User-Defined Measurement
            Ctl.Left = Ctl.ScaleLeft  'distance equals ScaleLeft
        Case vbTwips                  'measure in twips
            Ctl.Left = 1440
        Case vbPoints                 'measure in Points
            Ctl.Left = 72
        Case vbPixels                 'measure in Pixels
            Ctl.Left = 1000
        Case vbCharacters             'measure in Characters
```

continued on next page

continued from previous page

```
            Ctl.Left = 12
    Case vbInches                  'measure in Inches
            Ctl.Left = 1
    Case vbMillimeters             'measure in Millimeters
            Ctl.Left = 254
    Case vbCentimeters             'measure in Centimeters
            Ctl.Left = 2.54
    End Select
End Sub
```

Description	The Left property of an object measures the horizontal distance from the left edge of its container, be it a form, screen, or picture box. You can enter this value at design time by manually moving the object with the mouse or by directly entering the value in the properties box. You can modify the Left property of a control or form either at design time or at runtime. Visual Basic automatically adjusts itself to the resolution of the screen. You should ensure that your objects are not too far from the edges for the most common 640×480 and 800×600 resolution screens to display.
	The example syntax outlines a sub procedure named LeftDistance, which sets a control's distance from the left side of the screen. This change references the ScaleMode property of the form. This shows the use of a generic procedure that applies to more than one control in a program.
Left, Top, Width, and Height Properties	When you create a form or control in Visual Basic, the Left, Top, Width, and Height properties display in the far right side of the toolbar. See the discussion of the toolbar in the Height property entry in this chapter. A form's Left property is measured in twips.
The ScaleMode Property	The ScaleMode property of a form directly controls the meaning of the value of the Left property. When the ScaleMode property changes from one measurement to another at design time, Visual Basic recalculates the value of the Left property in this new type of measurement. As the ScaleMode property is not modifiable at runtime, the meaning of the value of the Left property does not change while the program is running. For example, no matter what size a command box becomes, based on changes in the size of the parent form, the Left property will remain the same.
Example	The Appearance project at the end of this chapter sets the Left property of the forms and controls at design time. This is done either by dragging the control's edges with the mouse or by entering the value into the properties box.
Comments	Remember that changes to the ScaleLeft property of a form alter only the value of the Left property of a control and not the actual distance.

MOUSEICON PROPERTY

Objects Affected	CheckBox, ComboBox, CommandButton, Data, DBCombo, DBList, DirListBox, DriveListBox, FileListBox, Form, Forms Collection, Frame, HScrollBar, VScrollBar, Image, Label, ListBox, ListView, Masked Edit,

MDIForm, MSFlexGrid, OLE Container, OptionButton, PictureBox, ProgressBar, PropertyPage, RichTextBox, Screen, Slider, SSTab, StatusBar, TabStrip, TextBox, Toolbar, TreeView, UserControl, UserDocument

Purpose   The MouseIcon property lets you add a custom mouse cursor to your application. This gives you the ability to use more visual feedback for confirmation when you use MousePointer=vbCustom to select the custom cursor. Refer to Table 33-21 for the arguments of the MouseIcon property.

General Syntax

```
[Name].MouseIcon [= LoadPicture(stringexpression)]
```

Table 33-21 Arguments of the MouseIcon property

Argument	Description
Name	Name property of Control, Form, or MDIForm
Stringexpression	Filename of .ICO file to load into Control, Form, or MDIForm

Example Syntax

```
Private Sub Form_Load
        'load the phone icon as a custom mouse cursor
          Form1.MouseIcon = LoadPicture(app.path & "\phone.ico")
End Sub
```

Description   See Chapter 38, "Graphics Fundamentals," for an explanation of the LoadPicture function.

Visual Basic 4.0 added the new property MouseIcon and a new value to the MouseCursor property to allow you to select the custom cursor. The example syntax shows how to load the CustomCursor property dynamically using LoadPicture and an icon stored in the application's working directory. You also can load an icon at design time by double-clicking on the property in the Properties list.

Using a custom cursor is a good example of how to use the graphical environment to provide feedback to the user.

Example   The Appearance project at the end of this chapter loads a custom Phone icon and uses it to tell the user he or she can dial. This visual feedback confirms the user's selection of a name to dial and activates the dialing code.

Comments   Visual Basic will sometimes cause the mouse cursor to flip back and forth between the default Arrow or Hourglass cursor and any custom cursor you've loaded using MouseIcon, due to the way it handles cursors internally. This is particularly common when you use DoEvents to share time with the rest of Windows during long running processes.

MousePointer Property

Objects Affected	CheckBox, ComboBox, CommandButton, Data, DBCombo, DBGrid, DBList, DirListBox, DriveListBox, FileListBox, Form, Forms Collection, Frame, HScrollBar, Image, Label, ListBox, ListView, Masked Edit, MDIForm, MSChart, MSFlexGrid, OLE Container, OptionButton, PictureBox, ProgressBar, PropertyPage, RichTextBox, Screen, Slider, SSTab, StatusBar, TabStrip, TextBox, ToolBar, TreeView, UserControl, UserDocument, VScrollBar
Purpose	The MousePointer property of a form or control sets which cursor displays when the mousepointer is over the object. Set this property either at design time or runtime. A mousepointer can take many forms, including the arrow, hourglass, and I-beam. Table 33-22 shows the different arguments of the MousePointer property. Table 33-23 shows the possible values of the MousePointer property.

General Syntax

```
[form.]MousePointer [ = setting%]
[form!]Name.MousePointer [ = setting%]
Screen.MousePointer [ = setting%]
```

Table 33-22 Arguments of the MousePointer property

Argument	Description
form	Name property of the form
Name	Name property of the control
Screen	'Screen' for Screen object
setting%	Value indicates what style of mousepointer to use

Table 33-23 Possible values of the MousePointer property

setting	VB.Constants	Description
0	vbDefault	Default for this control
1	vbArrow	Arrow
2	vbCrosshair	Cross-hair pointer
3	vbIbeam	Text entry I-beam
4	vbIconPointer	Square within a square
5	vbSizePointer	Four-directional cross; arrows facing up, down, left, and right
6	vbSizeNESW	Two-directional diagonal arrow (northeast to southwest)
7	vbSizeNS	Two-directional vertical arrow (north to south)
8	vbSizeNWSE	Two-directional diagonal arrow (northwest to southeast)

setting	VB.Constants	Description
9	vbSizeEW	Two-directional horizontal arrow (east to west)
10	vbUpArrow	Arrow pointing up
11	vbHourGlass	Hourglass
12	vbNoDrop	No drop (circle with line through it)
13	vbCustom	Custom icon assigned by MouseIcon property

Example Syntax

```
Private Sub Command1_GotFocus ()
     Form1.MousePointer = 11     ⇐
'changes the MousePointer to an hourglass
End Sub

Private Sub Command1_LostFocus ()
     Form1.MousePointer = 0      ⇐
'changes the MousePointer back to the default
End Sub
```

Description   The MousePointer property determines what cursor to display on the screen when the mousepointer is over a control or form. Set this property for either the entire form or individual controls. Any form or control may have its MousePointer property changed at runtime. When you modify the Screen object's MousePointer property, the MousePointer property changes for all objects. When you modify a form's MousePointer property, any special settings for individual controls on the form similarly alter. To restore the settings for individual forms or controls, set the MousePointer property of the screen or form to 0. For example, when the user clicks the command button labeled Print, the mousepointer of the screen becomes an hourglass. The cursor will remain an hourglass until the property is restored to the default value of 0.

Outline Pointer   Every control begins with the outline of itself as the default mousepointer. This mousepointer only appears on the screen during a mouse operation such as a drag operation. You can use this outline to guide the user during a drag operation. Since this property is the default value for a control, it is not necessary to change it for a drag operation. Figure 33-22 shows what the outline mousepointer looks like.

Arrow Pointer   One of the most familiar mousepointers is the left-pointing arrow cursor. Figure 33-23 shows how the arrow mousepointer appears on the screen. This is the cursor most frequently used in Windows to select items and activate programs. When a form's MousePointer property has this value, the user can easily select command buttons, check boxes, and option boxes by placing the arrow's small point directly on the desired object. The horizontal and vertical scrollbars also function well with the arrow mousepointer.

Figure 33-22 The default mouse
pointer takes the shape of the
object's outline

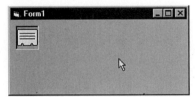

Figure 33-23 The familiar arrow
cursor

Figure 33-24 The I-beam
cursor, particularly useful for text
selection

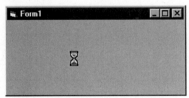

Figure 33-25 The hourglass
cursor indicates the user needs to
wait

I-Beam Cursor　　The I-beam cursor gives the user a guide in selecting and entering text on
the screen. Figure 33-24 shows how the I-beam cursor appears over a text
box. The I-beam mousepointer allows easy manipulation of text. Changing

to this cursor makes it easier to move in between different characters for editing and selecting text. The I-beam is the best choice for working with text.

Hourglass Cursor An hourglass is also a familiar symbol to the Windows user (particularly those with older, slower systems!). Figure 33-25 shows an hourglass cursor. This cursor normally reminds the user that the computer is working and cannot process any further commands until it finishes with its current action. When you plan to stop the user from taking further actions, change the MousePointer property of the screen to the hourglass cursor. In this case the cursor will not change, no matter which form or control the mousepointer moves over.

Sizing Cursors All the sizing cursors, which have values between 5 and 9, are also familiar to Windows users. Figure 33-26 shows each of these cursors. These cursors appear when the user changes the size of a window on the screen. Each cursor consists of arrows pointing toward the parts of the window that the resizing changes.

Custom Cursors You can use the Custom setting to assign a custom cursor to your form or control. This allows you to use a specific cursor for specific events, such as a phone icon for a phone dialer. The custom cursor is stored in the MouseIcon property of the form. You can load MouseIcon at runtime to change the mousepointer dynamically.

Example In the Appearance project at the end of this section, the MousePointer property of the screen changes when the user clicks either timeDial on formAppear or the Redial command button on formWarning. This tells the user that no other actions may take place while the dial operation is under way. The MousePointer property of the screen overrides the settings of the various controls of both the FormAppear and Warning forms. Until the MousePointer property returns to 0, the only MousePointer that displays is the hourglass.

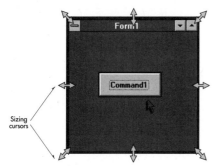

Figure 33-26   The eight sizing cursors

Comments   You can use nonstandard cursors in your program by loading an .ICO file into the MouseIcon property and setting the MousePointer property to 13, vbCustom. Waite Group's *Visual Basic How-To, 2nd Edition* also discusses ways to use the Windows API to reset the mouse cursor. If you give your program a custom cursor using the MouseIcon and MousePointer properties, you should be aware that Visual Basic may cause the mouse cursor to flicker between the default cursor icon and your custom icon as your program processes, particularly if you use DoEvents to share time with other Windows applications.

TOP PROPERTY

Objects Affected   CheckBox, Column, ComboBox, CommandButton, CommonDialog, Data, DBCombo, DBGrid, DBList, DirListBox, DriveListBox, FileListBox, Form, Forms Collection, Frame, HScrollBar, Image, Label, ListBox, MDIForm, OLE Container, OptionButton, PictureBox, RemoteData, Shape, TextBox, Timer, VScrollBar

Purpose   The Top property defines or determines the distance of a form or control from the top edge of its container. A control's distance is measured in the units indicated by the ScaleMode property of the container. Forms are always measured in twips. Tables 33-24 and 33-25 summarize the different arguments of the Top property and the possible measurement types.

General Syntax
```
[form.]Top [ = top!]
[form!]Name.Top [ = top!]
```

Table 33-24 Arguments of the Top property

Argument	Description
form	Name property of the form
Name	Name property of the control
top!	Vertical top distance of the object

Table 33-25 Possible measurement types in relation to 1 inch

Measurement	Converts To...
Twip	1440 twips = 1 inch
Point	72 points = 1 inch
Pixels	Varies, depending on system being used
Characters	12 characters horizontally and 6 vertically = 1 inch

Measurement	Converts To...
Millimeters	254 millimeters = 1 inch
Centimeters	2.54 centimeters = 1 inch

Example Syntax

```
Public Sub ResetForm (Name As Form)
    If Name.ScaleMode <> 0 Then        ⇐
'checks if ScaleMode is set to user-defined
        Name.Top = 1                   ⇐
'form's distance from top placed at 1
        Name.Left = 1                  ⇐
'form's distance from left placed at 1
    Else
        Name.Top = Name.ScaleTop       ⇐
'Form's distance from left and top made equal
        Name.Left = Name.ScaleLeft ⇐
'to the value of the ScaleLeft & ScaleTop properties.
    End If
End Sub
```

Description

The Top property of an object measures the vertical distance from the top of its container. You can enter this value at design time by manually moving the object with the mouse or by entering the value at the properties box. The Top property of a control or form is modifiable either at design time or runtime. You should ensure that your objects are not too far from the edges for the most common 640×480 and 800×600 resolution screens to display.

The example syntax outlines a sub function named ResetForm, which sets a form's distance from the left and top sides of the screen. If the ScaleMode property is user-defined, the Left and Top properties are set to the values of the ScaleLeft and ScaleTop properties. This is another excellent example of the use of a generic function to apply to all the forms in a program.

The Left, Top, Width, and Height Properties

When you create a form or control in Visual Basic, the Left, Top, Width, and Height properties display in the far left side of the toolbar. See the discussion of the toolbar in the Height property entry in this chapter. A form's Top property begins with a measurement in twips.

The ScaleMode Property

The ScaleMode property of a form directly controls the meaning of the value of the Top property. When this property changes at design time from one measurement to another, Visual Basic recalculates the value of the Top property in this new type of measurement. Because the ScaleMode property is not modifiable at runtime, the meaning of the value of the Top property does not change while the program is running. For example, no matter what size a command box becomes, based on changes in the size of the parent form, the Top property will remain the same.

Example

In the Appearance project at the end of this chapter, set the Top property of the forms and controls at design time. This is done either by dragging the control's edges with the mouse or by entering the value into the properties box.

Comments   Remember that changes to the ScaleTop property of a form only alter the value of the Top property of a control and not the actual distance.

VISIBLE PROPERTY

Objects Affected   Animation, AxisTitle, Button, CheckBox, Column, ComboBox, CommandButton, Data, DBCombo, DBGrid, DBList, DirListBox, DriveListBox, Extender, FileListBox, Form, Forms Collection, Frame, HScrollBar, Image, Label, Line, ListBox, ListView, Location, Marker, Masked Edit, MSChart, MSFlexGrid, MCI, MDIForm, Menu, Node, Nodes Collection, OLE Container, OptionButton, Panel, PictureBox, ProgressBar, RemoteData, RichTextBox, Shape, Slider, SSTab, StatusBar, TabStrip, TextBox, ToolBar, TreeView, UpDown, VScrollBar, WebBrowser, Window

Purpose   The Visible property defines whether a form or control is visible to the user. Tables 33-26 and 33-27 summarize the arguments of the Visible property.

General Syntax

```
[form.]Visible [ = boolean%]
[form!]Name.Visible [ = boolean%]
```

Table 33-26 Arguments of the Visible property

Argument	Description
form	Name property of the form
Name	Name property of the control
boolean%	Indicates whether the object is visible or invisible to the user

Table 33-27 Available settings for the Visible property

boolean%	Effect
0	False; makes an object invisible to the user
-1	True; makes an object visible to the user (default)

Example Syntax

```
Private Sub Form_Load ()
    Load "AddressBook"          'places an invisible form in memory
    Form2.Show                  'places a visible form in memory
        Form2.Visible = False   'makes it invisible
End Sub
```

```
Public Sub Change (ControlName As Form, Control)  ⇐
'flips the visibility of an object
    If ControlName.Visible = False Then
        ControlName.Visible = True    'makes indicated control visible
    Else
        ControlName.Visible = False   'makes indicated control invisible
    End If
End Sub
```

Description   The Visible property lets you show or hide a control or form on the screen. There are two possible settings for the Visible property of a form or control: True (-1) and False (0). A form or control with a False Visible property disappears from the user's sight. While its Visible property is False, a form or control remains in memory and quickly returns to the screen when needed. When the Visible property of a form or control is True (-1), the form or control is visible to the user. A Show method, Hide method, or Load statement directly affects this value. In the example syntax, the Form_Load event changes the Visible property of Form2 to False.

The Show Method   When a Show method brings a form up on the screen, it automatically sets the Visible property of the form to True. The Show method loads the form into memory if necessary. Setting a form's Visible property directly loads it into memory if it isn't already there and makes it visible. The main difference is that the Show method has two modes of operation. A form opened with the Modeless Show method will behave in the same way as a form opened by setting the Visible property directly. However, if a form loads with a Modal Show method, then the form has full control of the program until hidden or unloaded from memory. Any code that follows a Modal Show method executes only after the hiding or closing of the modal form. See Chapter 36 for more details on modal and modeless forms.

The Hide Method   The Hide method changes the Visible property of a form to False and removes it from view. Unlike the Show method, this element of the language is indistinguishable from the Visible property if applied to a form. Unlike the Hide and Show methods, the Visible property is available for either a form or a control. This makes it flexible for more generic functions. In the example function above, any kind of control or form can be made visible or invisible.

The Load Statement   A Load statement brings a form into memory and sets its Visible property to False. Using this statement differs from directly setting the Visible property in only one way. The Visible property works on both controls and forms, but the Load statement will only work on forms. Table 33-28 outlines the different ways that the Hide method, Show method, and Load statement interact with the Visible property.

Table 33-28 The effects and differences of various language elements on the Visible property

Element	Effect On	Visible Property Differences
Show method	Changes	Visible property to True (-1) Modal mode
Hide method	Changes	Visible property to False (0); affects only forms
Load statement	Changes	Visible property to False (0); affects only forms

Example   In the Appearance project at the end of this chapter, the Visible property removes the Results label box from view. This keeps the contents of the Caption property available for reference for the next time the user presses the Redial command button. This way, the Results label box disappears from the user's sight to prevent confusion about what is presently taking place in the program. If the Results label box were not hidden in this fashion, then the user might be confused with the contents of that box when it is no longer needed.

Comments   The Visible property will work on either a form or control. It is a more flexible element of the language than the Hide and Show methods, which can be used only on forms.

WIDTH PROPERTY

Objects Affected   CheckBox, Column, ComboBox, CommandButton, Data, DirListBox, DriveListBox, FileListBox, Form, Forms Collection, Frame, HScrollBar, Image, Label, ListBox, MDIForm, OLE Container, OptionButton, Picture, PictureBox, Printer, Printers Collection, PropertyPage, RemoteData, Screen, Shape, TextBox, UserControl, UserDocument, VScrollBar

Purpose   The Width property defines or determines the horizontal size of a form or control on the screen, form, picture box, or Printer object. Forms, Printer objects, and Screen objects are always measured in twips. A control's size uses the units of measure indicated by the ScaleMode property of the current form or picture box. Table 33-29 summarizes the different arguments of the Width property. Table 33-30 summarizes the possible measurement settings of the Width property.

General Syntax

```
[form.]Width [ = width!]
[form!]Name.Width [ = width!]
Printer.Width [ = width!]
Screen.Width [ = width!]
```

Table 33-29 Arguments of the Width property

Argument	Description
form	Name property of the form
Name	Name property of the control
Printer	'Printer' for Printer object
Screen	'Screen' for Screen object
width!	Horizontal width of the object

Table 33-30 Possible measurement types in relation to 1 inch

Measurement	Converts To...
Twip	1440 twips = 1 inch
Point	72 points = 1 inch
Pixels	Varies, depending on system being used
Characters	12 characters horizontally and 6 vertically = 1 inch
Millimeters	254 millimeters = 1 inch
Centimeters	2.54 centimeters = 1 inch

Example Syntax

```
Private Sub Form_Resize
    Form1.Width = (Picture1.Width * 2)       ⇐
'Width and height of form made twice the
    Form1.Height = (Picture1.Height * 2)      'size of Picture 1.
    Picture1.Move (Me.ScaleWidth / 2) - _
        (Picture1.Width / 2), _
        (Me.ScaleHeight / 2) - _
        (Picture1.Height / 2)
End Sub
```

Description
The Width property of an object measures the horizontal width of a form, screen, or picture box. You can enter this value at design time by manually moving the object with the mouse or by entering the value in the properties box. You can modify the Width property of a control at runtime or design time. In contrast, you can only set the Width properties of both the Printer and Screen objects at runtime. A setting must be between 0 and a maximum value specified by the system itself. Visual Basic automatically adjusts itself to the resolution of the screen or printer. You should ensure that your objects are not too large for the most common 640×480 and 800×600 resolution screens to display.

In the example syntax, Picture1's Width and Height are set to half of Form1's ScaleWidth and Height. This demonstrates how easily you can resize and move controls. Figure 33-27 shows how this example might look.

Figure 33-27   The example syntax centers Picture1, no matter what the form's size or shape

The Left, Top, Width, and Height Properties

When you create a form or control in Visual Basic, the Left, Top, Width, and Height properties display in the far left side of the toolbar. See the discussion of the toolbar in the Height property entry in this chapter. A form's Width property begins with a value that represents a measurement in twips.

Screen and Printer

The Width property returns the width of the screen or page available, based on the resolution of the computer screen and printer used. With this property, the code determines the amount of usable space available on the printed page or screen. The Width property of the Screen and Printer objects is not available at design time and is read-only at runtime. The value of this property normally serves as a reference and is not changeable at runtime.

The ScaleMode Property

The ScaleMode property of a form directly controls the meaning of the value of the Width property. When the ScaleMode property changes at design time from one measurement to another, Visual Basic recalculates the value of the Width property in this new type of measurement. As the ScaleMode property is not modifiable at runtime, the meaning of the value of the Width property does not change while the program is running. For example, no matter what size a command box becomes, based on changes in the size of the parent form, the Width property will remain the same. See Chapter 37 for more information about the ScaleMode property.

The ScaleWidth Property

The ScaleWidth property divides the width of a form, picture box, or Printer object into the number of units set in the property. When a form's ScaleWidth property changes to 100, the width of the form is divided into 100 equal units. (Changing the ScaleWidth property of the form to a new value does not change the actual size of the control.)

This unit changes in size as the form's height changes. Increasing the width of the form has the effect of increasing the size of one of these units. (The width remains divided into 100 units that are now larger in size.) These units define the upper and lower limits of the possible width of controls on this form.

With the Move statement, the size of the control adjusts based on the changes in width to the form. For example, a Resize event might adjust the Width property of a form's command box by triggering a Move statement that always ensures the command box is one-fourth the size of the form. In this example, the ScaleWidth property of the form is 100, and the Width property of the Command1 command button is 25 (one-fourth the width of the form). Figures 33-28 and 33-29 display this concept visually.

Example   The Appearance project at the end of this chapter sets the Width property of the forms and controls at design time. This is done either by dragging

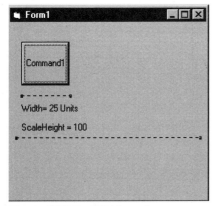

Figure 33-28   Width and ScaleWidth compared at start...

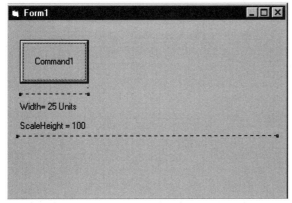

Figure 33-29   ...and after resizing; note that the Width of the command button is the same number of relative units, although it is physically larger

the control's edges with the mouse or by entering the value into the properties box.

Comments   Remember that changes to the ScaleWidth property of a form only alter the value of a control's Width property and not the actual width.

The Appearance Project

Project Overview

The Appearance project demonstrates the properties of the Visual Basic language that influence the appearance of a program's forms and controls. Assembling the different forms and functions of this project will teach you how to change the appearance of forms and controls on the screen. This project has three sections. The first section assembles frmAppear and its associated functions. The second section constructs frmWarning and its associated functions. The third section discusses how the project works.

Assembling the Project: frmAppear

1. Make a new form (frmAppear) with the objects and properties in Table 33-31.

Table 33-31 Settings for frmAppear

Object	Property	Setting
Form	BorderStyle	1—Fixed single
	Caption	"Appearance Project"
	Name	frmAppear
	Icon	C:\Program Files\DevStudio\VB\Graphics\Icons\Comm\Phone01.ICO
	MaxButton	False
	MouseIcon	C:\Program Files\DevStudio\VB\Graphics\Icons\Comm\Phone01.ICO
Command	Caption	"&Dial"
	Name	cmdDial
	MousePointer	12—no drop
Command	Caption	"E&xit"
	Name	cmdExit
ListBox	Name	listPhone
	Sorted	True
Timer	Name	tmrDial
	Enabled	False
	Interval	2500

2. Size the objects on the screen, as shown in Figure 33-30. Figure 33-31 shows how frmAppear will look when running.

3. Enter the following code in the Form_Load event subroutine. This code adds the items to the phone list and disables the timer.

```
Private Sub Form_Load()
    tmrDial.Enabled = False                 ⇐
'Make sure dialing timer is disabled
'   lstPhone.AddItem "517-555-1212     John Doe"    ⇐
'Fill list box with fake-o numbers
    lstPhone.AddItem "908-789-8901     Jane Mazurski"
    lstPhone.AddItem "313-531-7909     Fred Dopfler"
    lstPhone.AddItem "206-908-8973     Alan Goodson"
End Sub
```

4. Enter the following code in the cmdDial_Click event subroutine. This code executes when the user clicks the cmdDial command button. We first check to make sure we have a number to dial (if the cursor is still vbNoDrop, the user hasn't picked a name from the list). Assuming we've got a number to dial, tell the user we'll be a while by setting the cursor to an hourglass. Set the title bar of frmWarning to indicate whom we're dialing, change the icon of frmAppear to indicate an off-hook phone, and minimize it. Enable the tmrDial timer to simulate dialing.

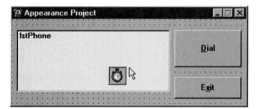

Figure 33-30   frmAppear during design

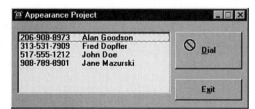

Figure 33-31   frmAppear in action; note the No Drop cursor because we haven't chosen a number to dial yet

```
Private Sub cmdDial_Click()
    If cmdDial.MousePointer <> vbNoDrop Then          ⇐
'Make sure we're supposed to dial
        Screen.MousePointer = vbHourglass             ⇐
'Tell user we've got to wait
        frmWarning.Caption = "Dialing " + lstPhone.List(lstPhone.ListIndex)
        'you might need to change the path in loadpicture ⇐
to fit your system
        frmAppearance.Icon = LoadPicture⇐
("C:\Program Files\DevStudio\VB\Graphics\Icons\Comm\Phone12.ICO")  ⇐
'Phone Handset
        frmAppearance.WindowState = vbMinimized     'Minimize Appear form
        tmrDial.Enabled = True                      'Turn on dialing timer
    End If
End Sub
```

5. Enter the following code in the tmrDial_Timer event subroutine. The timer delay simulates making a call. When the call fails (after all, we don't even try!), display frmWarning. Note that because of the vbModal argument, the code after the Show method doesn't continue executing until that form is closed or hidden. When control returns from the Warning dialog, we reset the mouse cursor, deselect the phone number list box, and set timeDial's mousepointer back to vbNoDrop to signal that a call couldn't be made.

```
Private Sub tmrDial_Timer()
    frmWarning.Show vbModal                      'Let the Dialer form take over
    frmAppearance.Caption = "Appearance Project"  'Reset caption
    Screen.MousePointer = vbDefault              'Set cursor to normal
    lstPhone.ListIndex = -1                       'Deselect list
    cmdDial.MousePointer = vbNoDrop              'We can't dial now...
    frmAppearance.MousePointer = vbDefault
    tmrDial.Enabled = False                       'Turn off dialing timer
End Sub
```

6. Enter the following code in the cmdExit_Click event subroutine. This closes all forms and exits.

```
Private Sub cmdExit_Click()
    Unload Me
End Sub
```

7. Enter the following code in the PhoneList_Click event. This simply resets the Dial button's mousepointer to the default (which tells the cmdDial_Click event that it's okay to dial now).

```
Private Sub lstPhone_Click()
    cmdDial.MousePointer = vbCustom               ⇐
'We've selected number to dial; OK to push dial button
    frmAppearance.MousePointer = vbCustom
End Sub
```

Assembling the Project: frmWarning

1. Make a new form (frmWarning) with the objects and properties in Table 33-32.

Table 33-32 Settings for frmWarning

Object	Property	Setting
Form	BackColor	&H00C0C0C0& 'light gray
	ForeColor	&H00000000& 'black
	Name	frmWarning
	BorderStyle	3–Fixed double
Label	Alignment	2–Centered
	BackStyle	0–Transparent
	Name	lblDial
Label	Alignment	2–Centered
	BackStyle	0–Transparent
	Name	lblResults
Command	Caption	"ReDial"
	Name	cmdRedial
Command	Caption	"Cancel"
	Name	cmdCancel
Timer	Name	tmrDialing
	Enabled	False
	Interval	1000
Timer	Name	tmrResults
	Enabled	False
	Interval	1000

2. Size the objects on the screen, as shown in Figure 33-32. Figure 33-33 shows what frmWarning looks like when running and after the user has clicked redial three times.

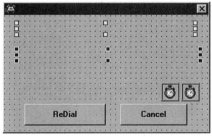

Figure 33-32   frmWarning during design (note the two labels without captions)

Figure 33-33   frmWarning in action
after the third click

3. Enter the following code in the cmdCancel_Click event. This resets both labels, unloads the form, resets the main form's icon, and restores the main form from its minimized state.

```
Private Sub cmdCancel_Click()
    lblDial.Caption = ""                  'Blank out Dialing label
    lblResults.Caption = ""               'and Results label
    Unload frmWarning                     'Unload the form
    'you might need to change the path in loadpicture to fit your system
    frmAppearance.Icon = ⇐
LoadPicture("C:\Program Files\DevStudio\VB\Graphics\Icons⇐
\Comm\Phone01.ICO")
    frmAppearance.WindowState = vbNormal       'and put back the main form
End Sub
```

4. Enter the following code in the tmrResults_Timer event. This simulates making another redial attempt. It redisplays the results label, and chooses what to display next by looking at what it displayed last time. Note that as we continue to get negative dialing results, we change the BackStyle from transparent to opaque to add greater emphasis to the label. The cursor goes back to normal now that the program has "called."

```
Private Sub tmrResults_Timer()
    lblResults.Visible = True             'Display the results box
    Select Case lblResults.Caption        'Determine message based on
                                          '   what we've already done
        Case ""                           'First time through...
            lblResults.Caption = "No Response"
        Case "No Response"                'Second time through...
            lblResults.Caption = "Sorry, No Response"
        Case "Sorry, No Response"              'Third time through...
            lblResults.Caption = "Sorry, Still No Response"
            lblResults.BackStyle = vbSolid
            lblResults.BackColor = vbYellow
        Case Else                         'Pretty persistent, eh?
            lblResults.Caption = ⇐
"Hey what do you expect? This is a demonstration!"
            lblResults.BackColor = vbRed
            lblResults.ForeColor = vbYellow
    End Select
```

```
    Screen.MousePointer = vbDefault              ⇐
'Done dialing, OK for user to go on
    tmrResults.Enabled = False                   'Turn off the results loop
End Sub
```

5. Enter this code into the tmrDialing_Timer event. This timer just delays by a second, simulating dialing. It turns itself back off and reenables the tmrResults timer.

```
Private Sub tmrDialing_Timer()
    tmrDialing.Enabled = False          'Done with dialing delay...
    tmrResults.Enabled = True           'Turn on results loop
End Sub
```

6. Enter this code into the Form_Load event. It turns on the tmrDialing to simulate making a call.

```
Private Sub Form_Load()
    tmrDialing.Enabled = True           'Simulate a "dialing" delay
    tmrResults.Enabled = False          'turn off the results loop
End Sub
```

7. Enter this code into the cmdRedial_Click event. It tells the user to wait by setting the cursor to an hourglass, hides the results box (just in case we have a call that connects?), and displays an appropriate message in lblDial. Note that after the third attempt we add greater emphasis to the label by setting its BackStyle to opaque and making the box red to attract attention.

```
Private Sub cmdRedial_Click()
    Screen.MousePointer = vbHourglass            ⇐
'Tell user we're going to be a while...
    lblResults.Visible = False                   ⇐
'Hide the results box (to simulate dialing)

    Select Case lblDial.Caption                  ⇐
'Determine the proper message from what
                                        '     we've already got
        Case ""                         'First time through...
            lblDial.Caption = "Redialing Number"
        Case "Redialing Number"              'Second time through...
            lblDial.Caption = "Redialing Number Again!"
        Case Else                            'Third time through...
            lblDial.Caption = "Redialing Number one more time!"
            lblDial.BackStyle = vbSolid
            lblDial.BackColor = vbRed
            lblDial.ForeColor = vbYellow
    End Select
    tmrDialing.Enabled = True                    ⇐
'Set the time to simulate a "dialing" delay
End Sub
```

How It Works

The Appearance project opens by displaying a list of phone numbers in a list box on frmAppear. When the user selects one of these numbers from the list and presses Dial, frmWarning displays on the screen. While frmWarning appears on the screen, frmAppear is minimized at the bottom of the screen. FrmWarning displays the results of the attempt to dial. (Note: This example does not actually dial the number.) Each time the user presses the Redial button on frmWarning, new messages appear on the screen. The user presses the Cancel command button to exit frmWarning.

Running the Appearance Project

When the user selects a number from the phone list, the mousepointer for the Dial button changes back to the default pointer from its original value of No Drop. This lets the user click on the Dial command button to trigger the cmdDial_Click event. The screen's mousepointer changes to an hourglass to reflect that the program is busy. Setting the screen's mousepointer overrides any settings of the other controls.

Next, the Caption property of frmWarning is modified to read "Dialing" and show the name and number of the person being dialed. The Caption is displayed in the title bar of frmWarning, which is an easy and natural place to show this.

The cmdDial_Click event ends by changing the Icon property of frmAppear to a picture of an off-hook phone. It then minimizes frmAppear and enables the tmrDial timer event. The first command in the timeDial timer shows frmWarning. Note that because frmWarning displays modally, the code does not continue to run in the tmrDialing event until frmWarning closes.

At this point, the tmrDialing_Timer and tmrResults_Timer events trigger. The tmrResults event makes the Results label box (below the Dial box) visible to the user and then changes its message, based on the current setting. Next, the screen's MousePointer property is restored to the default value of 0, which restores the mouse-pointer settings of the controls and forms of the program. In this case, the hourglass changes back to the standard arrow.

Each time the user clicks the Redial command button, the screen's mousepointer changes back to an hourglass and the Dial label box's caption changes. This command button changes the messages on the label boxes to reflect how many times the Redial command button has been pressed. The Redial routine then triggers the tmrDialing_Timer event, which in turn triggers the tmrResults_Timer event. Note how we change the appearance of the labels as well as their messages. Setting the BackStyle property to opaque and setting their BackColor properties attract attention to the later messages.

When the user clicks the Cancel button, frmWarning is unloaded from memory and the Icon property of frmAppear changes back to its original setting with a LoadPicture function. This displays a hung-up phone briefly on the bottom of the screen, until formAppear is placed back up on the screen.

Notice that the last portion of the tmrDial_Timer event is processed as soon as frmWarning is removed. This changes frmAppear's Caption property back to the original Appearance project text. To exit the program, press the command button labeled Exit.

34

EVENTS

Visual Basic is an event-driven language. An *event* is an action recognized by a form or control, such as a mouse click or a keystroke. Event-driven languages like Visual Basic let the user control program flow. The application spends most of its time idle, waiting for the user to act on it. When the user does something (or the system causes an event, such as a shutdown message), the program responds to that action. This is the essence of a graphical user interface: Create a flexible environment that the user can control.

Contrast this approach with traditional programming methods. A traditional program starts at the beginning and controls all aspects of program flow. The user can certainly give the program input, but cannot alter program flow other than in limited, narrowly defined ways. Traditional programming languages have usually had inflexible user interfaces because of this approach.

Each object in Visual Basic has a number of specific events it recognizes. You can make your application respond to events by writing code in an event procedure. Much like regular sub procedures, event procedures contain code that performs specific actions. For example, clicking a command button with the mouse triggers its Click event; the code you write for this event procedure might confirm that the user wants to end the application. Although each control recognizes a predefined set of events, you determine if they respond to those events by writing code in the event procedures. Each object has its own set of event procedures independent of any other objects in the application.

Visual Basic 5.0 recognizes 200 different intrinsic events. This chapter summarizes those events and gives details on the Change event, not covered elsewhere in this book. Visual Basic 5.0 introduces the capability to add events to forms and classes. This chapter covers adding events to forms, while adding events to classes is covered in Chapter 105, "Using Classes and Class Modules."

Event Procedures

A reference to an event begins with the name of the object that triggers the event, followed by an underscore (_) and the name of the event:

```
Private Sub Command1_Click ()
    MsgBox "You've just clicked Command1"
End Sub

Private Sub textPatientName_GotFocus ()
    textPatientName.BackColor = QBColor(7)
    textPatientName.ForeColor = QBColor(1)
    textPatientName.SelLength = Len(textPatientName.Text)
End Sub
```

Forms are the exception: Rather than using the name of the form, the event subroutine uses the keyword Form (or MDIForm for the main MDI form of an application).

```
Private Sub Form_Load ()
    List1.AddItem "Red"
    List1.AddItem "Blue"
    List1.AddItem "Green"
End Sub

Private Sub MDIForm_Load ()
    Form1.Load
    Form2.Load
    Form3.Show
End Sub
```

Many events pass arguments to the procedure that your code can use. For example, the MouseDown event passes information about which mouse button was pressed, which control keys (if any) were held down, and exactly where the mouse is positioned.

```
Private Sub Picture1_MouseDown (Button As Integer, Shift As Integer, X As Single, Y As ⇐
Single)
    If Button = LEFT_BUTTON Then          'button argument checks which mouse button
        Picture1.Line (x1!, y1!)-(X, Y)    'X and Y are current mouse position
    End If
End Sub
```

Control arrays have just one event procedure for the entire array. This makes it easy to write generic code that applies to related controls grouped in the array. Event procedures in control arrays always have an Index argument that determines which control in the array triggered the event. This next example shows a menu control array with four elements. The Select Case uses the Index property to take appropriate action depending on which menu choice the user clicked.

```
Private Sub mnuWindowArrange_Click (Index As Integer)
    Select Case Index
        Case 0: MDIForm1.Arrange vbCascade
        Case 1: MDIForm1.Arrange vbTileHorizontal
        Case 2: MDIForm1.Arrange vbTileVertical
        Case 3: MDIForm1.Arrange vbArrangeIcons
    End Select
End Sub
```

Visual Basic Events

Visual Basic 5.0 has 200 intrinsic events. Some events are recognized by many objects, some by only a few or even just one object. These events are covered in detail in various chapters throughout this book; this chapter covers the Change event. Table 34-1 lists the events and their meaning. To locate the reference section that covers a specific event, refer to the jump tables or the index of this book.

Table 34-1 Visual Basic events

Event	Meaning
AccessKeyPressed*	Control's access key has been pressed
Activate	Form just received focus
AfterAddFile	File added to current project
AfterChangeFileName	Filename changed
AfterCloseFile	File closed
AfterColEdit*	Editing is completed in grid cell
AfterColUpdate*	Cell data was moved to the copy buffer
AfterDelete*	Selected record in a grid was deleted
AfterInsert*	Record was inserted in a grid
AfterLabelEdit*	Currently selected Node or ListItem was edited in a TreeView or ListView
AfterRemoveFile	File removed from project
AfterUpdate*	Changed data in grid was written to the database
AfterWriteFile	File saved
AmbientChanged*	Ambient property value changed
ApplyChanges*	OK or Apply pressed on a property page
Associate*	New connection associated with resultset
AsyncReadComplete*	Container completed an asynchronous rad request
AxisActivated*	Chart axis just got double-clicked
AxisLabelActivated*	Chart axis label just got double-clicked
AxisLabelSelected*	Chart axis label just got clicked
AxisLabelUpdated*	Chart axis label just got changed
AxisSelected*	Chart axis just got clicked
AxisTitleActivated*	Chart axis title just got double-clicked
AxisTitleSelected*	Chart axis title just got clicked
AxisTitleUpdated*	Chart axis title just got changed
AxisUpdated*	Chart axis just got changed
BeforeClick*	Tab got clicked in TabStrip
BeforeColEdit*	Before edit mode is entered in a grid
BeforeColUpdate*	Before data is moved from a grid's cell, but after the cell edit
BeforeConnect*	Before the RDO connection establishes a connection to the server

continued on next page

continued from previous page

Event	Meaning
BeforeDelete*	Before the selected record in a grid is deleted
BeforeInsert*	Before new records are inserted in a grid
BeforeLabelEdit*	Before the label of the currently selected ListItem or Node in a ListView or TreeView is edited
BeforeLoadFile	Before a File is added
BeforeUpdate*	Before grid data is moved to the copy buffer
BeginTrans*	After the RDO BeginTrans method has completed
ButtonClick*	Button was clicked in a toolbar, grid cell, or Multimedia MCI control
ButtonCompleted*	Multimedia MCI command activated by a control button has finished
ButtonGotFocus*	Multimedia MCI control button has the focus
ButtonLostFocus*	Multimedia MCI control button lost the focus
Change	Control's value just changed
ChartActivated*	Chart control just got double-clicked
ChartSelected*	Chart control just got clicked
ChartUpdated*	Chart control has changed
Click	Control just got clicked
Close*	The remote computer has closed the WinSock connection
ColEdit*	DBGrid cell enters edit mode
Collapse*	Node in a TreeView just got collapsed
ColResize*	DBGrid column was resized
ColumnClick*	ColumnHeader in a ListView in Report View mode just got clicked
CommitTrans*	After the RDO CommitTrans method has completed
Compare*	The sort property for a MSFlexGrid Control has been set to Custom Sort
ConfigChangeCancelled*	Change to the hardware profile was canceled
ConfigChanged*	The hardware profile on the system has changed
Connect*	RDO connection to the server has been established
ConnectAddIn	AddIn added to Visual Basic
ConnectionRequest*	TCP server received connection request
DataArrival*	New data just arrived
DataChanged*	The value of a rdoColumn has changed
DataUpdated*	The chart data grid has changed
DblClick	Control just got double-clicked
Deactivate	Form just lost focus
DeviceArrival*	New device is added to the system
DeviceOtherEvent*	Notification event that does not map onto general events
DeviceQueryRemove*	Device is about to be removed from the system
DeviceQueryRemoveFailed*	The removal of a device was canceled by code in the DeviceQueryRemove event
DeviceRemoveComplete*	Device has been removed from the system
DeviceRemovePending*	All applications have given approval to remove a device, and the device is about to be removed
DevModeChange*	The device mode settings have been changed

Event	Meaning
Disconnect*	rdoConnection has been closed
DisconnectAddIn	AddIn removed from Visual Basic
DisplayChanged*	The system screen resolution has been changed
Dissociate*	The rdoResultset has been dissociated from its connection
DoGetAddFileName	User selected Add File
DoGetNewFileName	User saving file or project
DoGetOpenProjectName	User opening a new project
Done*	MCI command has finished
DonePainting*	MSChart has been redrawn
DownClick*	Down or left arrow button on an UpDown control has been clicked
DragDrop	Control just got dropped
DragOver	Another control just got dragged over this control
DropDown	User clicked the down arrow on combo box
EditProperty*	The developer pressed the ellipsis button to edit a property
EnterCell*	The currently active cell of a MSFlexGrid changes to a different cell
EnterFocus*	Focus enters the object
Error	Externally caused error
ExitFocus*	Focus leaves the object
Expand*	The node in a TreeView control was expanded
FootnoteActivated*	The MSChart footnote just got double-clicked
FootnoteSelected*	The MSChart footnote just got clicked
FootnoteUpdated*	The MSChart footnote just got changed
GotFocus	Control just received the focus
HeadClick*	The header for a column of a DBGrid control just got clicked
Hide*	Visible property was changed to False
InfoMessage*	Informational message was added to the rdoErrors collection
Initialize	Object created
InitProperties*	New instance of an object was created
ItemActivated*	Component just got double-clicked in the Project window
ItemAdded*	Reference was added
ItemCheck*	Item's check box in a ListBox was selected or cleared
ItemClick*	ListItem object in a ListView control was clicked
ItemReloaded*	Component was reloaded
ItemRemoved*	Reference was removed from a project
ItemRenamed*	Project, control, or component was renamed
ItemSelected*	Component was clicked
KeyDown	User just pressed a key
KeyPress	User just pressed a key
KeyUp	User just released a key

continued on next page

continued from previous page

Event	Meaning
LeaveCell*	The currently active cell in a MSFlexGrid changes to a different cell
LegendActivated*	The legend in a MSChart just got double-clicked
LegendSelected*	The legend in a MSChart just got clicked
LegendUpdated*	The legend in a MSChart just got changed
LinkClose	DDE Link just closed
LinkError	DDE Link has an error
LinkExecute	DDE Link just received an external command
LinkNotify	DDE Link data has changed in a Notify style link
LinkOpen	DDE Link has just opened
Load	Form has just loaded
LostFocus	Control just lost focus
MouseDown	User just pressed mouse button
MouseMove	User just moved mouse
MouseUp	User just released mouse button
NodeClick*	Node in TreeView just got clicked
ObjectMove	OLE object moved or resized
OLECompleteDrag*	Drag action just performed or canceled
OLEDragDrop*	Source component was dropped onto a target component
OLEDragOver*	Component was dragged over another component
OLEGiveFeedback*	A OLEDragOver event just fired
OLESetData*	The data for a GetData call has not yet been loaded
OLEStartDrag*	OLEDrag is performed for a component with Automatic OLEDragMode
OnAddNew*	User invoked an AddNew operation on a DBGrid control
OnComm*	Communication event or error occurred
Paint	Control just got uncovered
PathChange	Path property just changed
PatternChange	Pattern property just changed
PlotActivated*	MSChart plot just got double-clicked
PlotSelected*	MSChart plot just got clicked
PlotUpdated*	MSChart plot just got changed
PointActivated*	MSChart data point just got double-clicked
PointLabelActivated*	MSChart data point label just got double-clicked
PointLabelSelected*	MSChart data point label just got clicked
PointLabelUpdated*	MSChart data point label just got changed
PointSelected*	MSChart data point just got clicked
PointUpdated*	MSChart data point just got changed
PowerQuerySuspend*	System power is about to be suspended
PowerResume*	System just came out of suspend mode
PowerStatusChanged*	The power status of the system just changed

Event	Meaning
PowerSuspend*	The system is about to go into suspend mode
QueryChangeConfig*	Request is made to change the current hardware profile
QueryComplete*	The query of a rdoResultset just returned the first resultset
QueryCompleted*	The query of a rdoResultset generated by a RemoteData control just returned the first resultset
QueryTimeout*	Query execution time just exceeded the value of the QueryTimeout property of the rdoConnection
QueryUnload	Form is about to unload
ReadProperties*	Old instance of an object with a saved state was just loaded
Reposition	Current record just changed
RequestChangeFileName	User specified new filename
RequestWriteFile	Prompt before project saved
Resize	Form just changed size
ResultsChanged*	A new result was made available by the MoreResults method
RollbackTrans*	After the RDO RollbackTrans method has completed
RowColChange	Grid's active cell just changed
RowCurrencyChange*	The resultset just got repositioned
RowResize*	Row in DBGrid just got resized
RowStatusChanged*	An edit, delete, or insert has just changed the data state of the current row in an rdoResultSet
Scroll	Scrollbar thumb just moved
SelChange	New cell selected in grid
SelectionChanged*	The selection of controls on the form just changed
SendComplete*	The send operation just completed
SendProgress*	Data is being sent
SeriesActivated*	MSChart series just got double-clicked
SeriesSelected*	MSChart series just got clicked
SeriesUpdated*	MSChart series just got changed
SettingChanged*	System-wide parameter just got changed
Show*	Visible property was changed to True
SplitChange*	The current cell in a DBGrid changed to a different cell in another split
StateChanged*	State just got changed in a Microsoft Internet Transfer Control connection
StatusUpdate*	The UpdateInterval in a Multimedia MCI control just elapsed
SysColorsChanged*	System color settings just changed
Terminate	Object was destroyed
TimeChanged*	System time just changed
Timer	Timer interval finished
TitleActivated*	MSChart title just got double-clicked
TitleSelected*	MSChart title just got clicked
TitleUpdated*	MSChart title just got changed
UnboundAddData*	A new row just got added to an unbound DBGrid
UnboundDeleteRow*	A new row just got deleted from an unbound DBGrid

continued on next page

continued from previous page

Event	Meaning
UnboundGetRelativeBookmark*	Unbound DBGrid requires data for display
UnboundReadData*	Unbound DBGrid requires data for display
UnboundWriteData*	Entire row of modified data in an unbound DBGrid is ready to be written
Unload	Form unloading
UpClick*	Up or right arrow button on an UpDown control has been clicked
Updated	OLE object changed
Validate	Current record about to change
ValidationError*	Masked Edit received invalid input
WillAssociate*	New connection is about to be associated with rdoResultset
WillChangeData*	Data is about to be changed in rdoColumn
WillDissociate*	rdoResultset connection is about to be set to Nothing
WillExecute	Query is about to be executed
WillUpdateRows*	Database is about to be updated
WriteProperties*	Instance of User object is about to be saved

* = New in Visual Basic version 5.0

CHANGE EVENT

Objects Affected ComboBox, DBCombo, DBGrid, DirListBox, DriveListBox, HScrollBar, Label, Picture Box, TextBox, VScrollBar

Purpose The Change event initiates an action when the user changes the value of an object's primary property, for example, by making a selection or entering data. Table 34-2 summarizes the arguments used for the Change event.

General Syntax

```
Sub Name_Change ([Index As Integer])
```

Table 34-2 Arguments of the Change event

Argument	Description
Name	Name of the control
Index	An integer that uniquely identifies an element of a control array

Example Syntax
```
Public OldText As String

Private Sub Text1_Change ()
      OldText = Text1.Text      'update ThisText any time the text in Text1 is changed
End Sub
```

Description

Many of the objects in Visual Basic have a primary property. For instance, the text box control's primary property is the Text property. Use the Change event to respond to any changes in an object's primary property. This event occurs regardless of the manner in which the property is changed: It initiates if the property changes by a user action, the program's code, or DDE events. The Change event doesn't trigger if you assign a value to an object's primary property that is the same as its current setting.

Table 34-3 lists all the objects that use the Change event, and the properties on which they are based.

Table 34-3 Objects that activate the Change event and their primary properties

Use Change with This Object...	To React to a Change in This Property...
ComboBox	Text
DBCombo	Text
DBGrid	Value
DirListBox	Path
DriveListBox	Drive
FileListBox	Path (use the PathChange event)
FileListBox	Pattern (use the PatternChange event)
HScrollBar	Value
Label	Caption
Picture	Picture
VScrollBar	Value
TextBox	Text

Be careful not to code circular Change events. Writing code in one control's Change event that triggers a change in another control's primary property, which in turn changes the original control's primary property, leads to an uncontrollable series of Change events that only end when Windows gives an error message after it runs out of stack space. For instance, imagine a program that has two labels, with the following Change events:

```
Private Sub Label1_Change ()
      Label2.Caption = Str(Val(Label1.Caption) + 1)
End Sub

Private Sub Label2_Change ()
      Label1.Caption = Str(Val(Label2.Caption) + 1)
End Sub
```

The Label1_Change event modifies the Caption property of the Label2 object. This causes Label2's Change event to occur. That event modifies Label1's Caption property, which will again cause its Change event to occur. As you can see, this will result in both events calling each other endlessly.

Combo Boxes and Data Bound Combo Boxes

Changes made to a combo box's Text property trigger its Change event. The Text property only applies when a combo box's Style property is set to 0 or 1 (drop-down or simple combo). Therefore, the Change event can only occur with these styles. If a combo box's Style property is set to 2, no Change event could ever be initiated.

Users may change the Text property of a combo box by doing one of two things. First, they can type text directly in the edit portion of a combo box. Since the text changes with each keystroke, the Change event occurs every time the user presses another key. For example, if the user types the word "Hello," the Change event will be called five times, once for each keystroke. Second, the user can change this property by selecting any of the list entries in the combo box. A list entry is selected any time the user presses the up or down arrow keys, or clicks on one of the entries with the mouse.

Setting the combo box's Text property within a program's code also triggers the Change event. For instance,

```
Combo1.Text = "Hello"
```

In the above line of code, the Text property of a combo box is set to "Hello." After this is performed, Visual Basic initiates the combo box's Change event. When that event has finished, execution will resume at the line following this one. Chapter 46, "List and Combo Boxes," contains more detailed information about combo boxes.

DBGrid

The primary property for the DBGrid control is Value. The Change event will occur any time this property changes. You must set the AllowUpdate property of the DBGrid to True to allow users to change DBGrid data. Once AllowUpdate is set to True, users may then update data directly in the grid triggering the Change event. You can also change the Value property via code. See Chapter 61, "DBGrid Behavior," for more information on the DBGrid control.

Directory, Drive, and File List Boxes

The primary property for the directory list box is the Path property. The Change event will occur any time this property changes. The user may change this property by double-clicking on any entry listed in the directory box. This sets the Path property to the path specified by the entry the user chose. Setting the Path property to a new value within a program's code also causes the Change event to occur.

The primary property for the Drive list box is the Drive property. This property can be changed by choosing a new drive letter from the object's drop-down list or by assigning a value to the property within the program's code.

The File list box has two primary properties: Path and Pattern. Because of this, it also has two Change events: PathChange and PatternChange. The PathChange event occurs when the Path property of a File list box has been changed. The PatternChange property occurs when its Pattern property has been modified. Both these events are explained in detail in Chapter 47, "File, Directory, and Drive Boxes."

Label

The primary property for the Label object is the Caption property. The Caption property can be changed by assigning it a string value within your program's code, or it can be changed as the result of a DDE operation.

Picture Boxes

The primary property for the Picture object is the Picture property. The Picture property can be changed by assigning it a value within your program's code, or it can be changed as the result of a DDE operation.

Scroll Bars

The primary property for the Scroll Bars object is the Value property. This property indicates the relative position of a scrollbar's thumb on the bar. The Value property of a scrollbar can be changed in four ways. First, the user can click on either arrow. This causes the Value property to increment or decrement by the amount indicated by the scrollbar's SmallChange property. Second, clicking the gray area of the scrollbar updates the Value property in a manner similar to clicking an arrow, but the amount of change is indicated by the scrollbar's LargeChange property. Third, the user can click and drag the thumb to a specific position on the scrollbar. This causes the Value property to be set according to the position of the thumb on the scrollbar. Finally, your code can directly set the Value. Chapter 43, "Scrollbars," uses the Change event with the Scroll Bars object in its example project.

Text Boxes

When used with the Text Box object, the Change event occurs when any change is made to the box's Text property. Since the text changes with each keystroke, the Change event occurs every time the user presses a key that generates an ASCII character. For example, if the user types the word "Hello," the Change event happens five times, once for each keystroke. Assigning a string value to this property within your program will also initiate a Change event. A DDE conversation may also create a change in a text box, causing a Change event.

Chapter 32, "Getting User Input," uses the Change event along with the Text Box object.

Example   The Change project at the end of this chapter uses the Change event to trigger an event when the user types a character, and another event if that character is a space. This allows you to count the characters and spaces typed in a text box.

Comments   Although some objects do not have an associated Change event, you may code your program to react to a change in their primary properties by using other events for the same purpose. For example, the Click event may be used to react to a change in the check box, option button, and list box objects.

Adding Events to a Form   Visual Basic 5.0 now allows you to add your events to forms and classes. Since adding events to forms is only a special case of class events, we will limit our coverage to outlining the steps needed to add an event to a form. You will find the remaining details in Chapter 105, in which adding events to classes is covered in depth. The object and routine names in parentheses refer to the Change project at the end of this chapter.

1. Create a Form (frmMain).

2. Create a Class (CFormEventHandler).

3. Write a Form property to the event handler class to provide access to a private form variable (Get/Set EventForm).

4. Add an Event name to the Form (CharsAdded).

5. Add a private instance of the event handler class to the Form (mFormEventHandler).

6. Add the private form variable to the event handler class referenced in the Get and Set methods, declaring it to be WithEvents (mForm).

7. Write code in the newly created event procedure in the event handler class.

8. In the Form Load procedure, instantiate the event handler class and set the form property of the event handler class to Me.

9. Where appropriate in the Form, fire the event you have created with RaiseEvent.

The Change Project

Project Overview

The Change project demonstrates the use of the Change event. In this project, you will create a form with a text box control and a label control. The text box's Change event will be used to display the number of characters in the box. Although this project uses only one of the controls that has a Change event, the concept behind using the Change event is similar for all other controls. You will also add an event to the form. The event will be fired when characters are added in the text box and will, for simplicity's sake, ignore character deletions. It will display how many spaces have been typed. The event handling code will be encapsulated in a class.

Assembling the Project

1. Create a new form (the Change form) and place on it the controls specified in Table 34-4.

Table 34-4 Property settings for the Change project

Object	Property	Setting
Form	BorderStyle	3–Fixed Double
	Caption	"Change Project"
	Name	frmMain
Text Box	BorderStyle	0–None
	Name	txtEditor
	Height	1605
	Left	0
	MultiLine	True
	ScrollBars	2–Vertical
	Text	(No text)
Label	BackColor	Light Sray–&H00C0C0C0
	BorderStyle	1–Fixed Single
	Caption	"No characters"
	Name	lblCharCount
Label	BackColor	Light Gray–&H00C0C0C0
	BorderStyle	1–Fixed Single
	Caption	"No characters"
	Name	lblSpaceCount

2. Check the appearance of your form against Figure 34-1.

3. On the Project menu, select Add Class Module to add a class module to the project. Name the class CFormEventHandler in the Property window. Place the following code in the Declarations section of CFormEventHandler:

```
Option Explicit

Private WithEvents mForm As frmMain
Private mlngSpacesCount
```

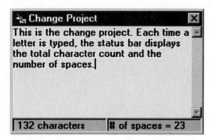

Figure 34-1 The Change project

4. Add the EventForm property to CFormEventHandler. This property exposes the mForm private WithEvents variable to the class users.

```
Public Property Get EventForm() As frmMain
    Set EventForm = mForm
End Property

Public Property Set EventForm(ByVal theMain As frmMain)
    Set mForm = theMain
End Property
```

5. Add the following code to the Initialize section of CFormEventHandler. The space count is initialized to 0.

```
Private Sub Class_Initialize()
    mlngSpacesCount = 0
End Sub
```

6. Add the following code to the Declarations section of frmMain. The class that will handle the CharsAdded event is declared.

```
Option Explicit

Private mFormEventHandler As CFormEventHandler
Event CharsAdded()
```

7. Add the following code in the Load event of frmMain. We instantiate the CFormEventHandler class and set the form property of the event handler class to Me.

```
Private Sub Form_Load()
    Set mFormEventHandler = New CFormEventHandler
    Set mFormEventHandler.EventForm = Me
End Sub
```

8. Add the following event handler to CFormEventHandler. This rather naïve subroutine does not handle text deletion by assuming text is only added. It displays the number of spaces in the text.

```
Private Sub mForm_CharsAdded()
    If Right(mForm!txtEditor.Text, 1) = " " Then
        mlngSpacesCount = mlngSpacesCount + 1
    End If
    mForm!lblSpaceCount.Caption = "# of spaces = " & Trim$(mlngSpacesCount)
End Sub
```

9. Enter the following code into the txtEditor_Change event. In this event, the number of characters that reside in the text box is determined with the Len function. The last line raises the CharsAdded event and fires the mForm_CharsAdded routine in the mFormEventHandler class instance.

```
Private Sub txtEditor_Change()
    Dim lngCharCount As Long
    Dim strCountMsg As String

    lngCharCount = Len(txtEditor.Text)
    Select Case lngCharCount
        Case 0
            strCountMsg = " no characters"
        Case 1
            strCountMsg = " one character"
        Case Else
            strCountMsg = Format$(lngCharCount, " ### ")
            strCountMsg = strCountMsg & "characters"
    End Select
    lblCharCount.Caption = strCountMsg
    RaiseEvent CharsAdded
End Sub
```

Running the Change Project

Run the project and type some text in the text box. Notice how the application keeps track of the number of characters being typed. (As stated in the introduction to this project, this simple application is not smart enough to deal with character deletions.) As you type spaces, you will also notice that they are counted.

How It Works

When the user enters some text in the text box, the Change event triggers. The Caption property of lblCharCount is set in the txtEditor_Change event's code, based on the number of characters found. Because this event occurs any time a change is made to the text in txtEditor, the label caption gets updated immediately. The number of spaces is also displayed because of the CharsAdded event being raised in the txtEditor_Change event's code.

35

ACCESSING FORMS AND CONTROLS

Every object in Visual Basic has a unique name that identifies it. You use this name to work with the object's properties, methods, and events. This chapter covers the details of accessing objects directly through the Name property, indirectly through several other useful properties, and gives suggested naming conventions to create clean, self-documenting code.

Naming Conventions

Each Visual Basic object has a name that you use to refer to it in code. Set the name of forms and controls during the design phase with the Name property in the properties box. The name must start with a letter and may be up to 40 characters long. It may contain the underscore character (although it is not recommended, as it creates hard to read Event subroutines), but may not contain any other punctuation symbols. Each control or form starts with a default name consisting of the object type plus a unique integer. For example, the first text box is named Text1, the second one Text2; the fourth list box created would be named List4.

For smaller applications, the default names work well. Many of the code examples in this book keep the default names for simplicity. Larger applications demand intelligent and consistent naming practices to help debug your code. Just as with any variable, you should name an object with something that indicates its purpose, for example, PatientName or ShippingMethods.

A very helpful practice is to start any object name with some sort of abbreviation that indicates what kind of object it is. This creates self-documenting names, as you can tell at a glance what each object is. This will save time as you trace your code. It also has the advantage of grouping similar kinds of controls together in the code window (for example, all text box event procedures would be near each other). There are many possible conventions; what is important is that you're consistent. For larger examples and many of the larger projects, this book uses the three-letter abbreviations suggested by Microsoft (such as txt for text box, lst for list box). The examples given in the last paragraph might then be named txtPatientName and lstShippingMethods. Tables 35-1 and 35-2 list the prefixes used in this book.

Table 35-1 Use Name prefixes to help create self-documenting code

Object	Prefix	Example
3D panel	pnl	pnlPatientInfo
Animated button	ani	aniRecycle
Check box	chk	chkShipNextDay
Combo box	cbo	cboStates
Command button	cmd	cmdExit
Common dialog	dlg	dlgPrinter
Communications	com	comOutbox
Control of unknown type	ctr	ctrGeneric
Data control	data	dataMain
Data bound combo	dbcbo	dbcboCustomer
Data bound list	dblst	dblstStatus
Data bound grid control	dbgrd	dbgrdBrowseDB
Dir list box	dir	dirCurrent
Drive list box	drv	drvCurrent
File list box	fil	filCurrent
Form	frm	frmMain
Frame	fra	fraChooseOption
Gauge	gau	gauProgress
Grid	grd	grdDataSheet
Horizontal scrollbar	hsb	hsbPictureView
Image	img	imgIcon
Image list	ils	ilsIcons
Key status	key	keyIndicator
Label	lbl	lblResults
Line	lin	linHorizontal
List box	lst	lstContinent
List view	lvw	lvwFiles
MAPI message	mpm	mpmMessage
MAPI session	msm	msmSession
MCI	mci	mciPlayer
MDI child	mdi	mdiChild
MDI form		Not essential, as there can only be one MDI form
Menu	mnu	mnuWindow

Object	Prefix	Example
MS flex grid	msg	msgBrowseDB
MS tab	mst	mstOptions
OLE container	ole	oleLinkToExcel
Option button	opt	optFederalExpress
Outline	out	outChapters
Pen BEdit	bed	bedPen
Pen Hedit	hed	hedPen
Pen Ink	ink	inkPen
Picture box	pic	picMain
Picture clip	clp	clpMain
Progress bar	prg	prgStatus
Report	rpt	rptSales
Rich text box	rtf	rtfDocument
Shape	shp	shpCircularInfinityWheel
Slider	sld	sldMain
Status bar	sta	staMain
Spin	spn	spnAge
Tab strip	tab	tabStartupOptions
Text box	txt	txtMainEntry
Timer	tmr	tmrClockStart
Toolbar	tlb	tlbGeneral
TreeView	tre	treChapters
UpDown	upd	updAge
Vertical scroll	vsb	vsbSliderValue

Table 35-2 Name prefixes for Data Access Objects

Object	Prefix	Example
Container	con	conSalesDocuments
Database	db	dbSales
DBEngine	dbe	dbeMain
Document	doc	docSalesSummary
Field	fld	fldPrimaryKey
Group	grp	grpAdministrators
Index	idx	idxPrimaryKey
Parameter	prm	prmSalesAgent
QueryDef	qry	qryWeeklySales
RecordSet	rec	recWeeklySales

continued on next page

continued from previous page

Object	Prefix	Example
Relation	rel	relForeignKey
TableDef	tbd	tbdWeeklySales
User	usr	usrCurrent
WorkSpace	wsp	wspMain

The system objects (App, Clipboard, Debug, Err, Printer, and Screen) cannot be renamed. You always refer to them by their default name. The data control has two properties (Database and Recordset) that function as system objects; you cannot rename these either, and always refer to them by their default name.

Naming Conventions for Variables

Declaring all variables reduces the number of uncaught typos (for example, aTmpUserName versus sTmpUserName versus sTempUserName). On the Editor tab of the Options dialog, check the Require Variable Declaration option. This causes an Option Explicit statement to be inserted in every new code component you create. You'll need to add this statement to existing code components.

It is also a generally accepted practice to prefix variables to indicate their data type. For large programs, this prefix may be extended to indicate the scope of the variable. Table 35-3 lists recommended prefixes for each variable type and scope.

Table 35-3 Name prefixes for variables

Data Type	Prefix	Example
Boolean	bln	blnProcessClicks
Byte	byt	bytStatusType
Collection object	col	colWidgets
Currency	cur	curPrice
Date time	dtm	dtmSetSystem
Double	dbl	dblStdDeviation
Error	err	errLoop
Integer	int	intItemCount
Long	lng	lngResult
Object	obj	objThingamajig
Single	sng	sngElapsed
String	str	strQuestion
User-defined type	udt	udtWidget
Variant	vnt	vntResult
Constant	cst	cstAppTitle
Enumerations	enm	enmIndex

Scope	Prefix	Example
Global	g	gstrUserName
Module	m	mblnProcessClicks
Local	none	strQuestion

Naming Conventions for Custom Objects

Visual Basic gives you the ability to create your own objects, such as a NameAndAddress object or a GeneralLedgerAccount object. See Chapter 16, "Objects and Collections," for more information about objects, and Chapter 104, "Creating Classes and Class Modules," for details on creating your own objects. Instances of objects should be prefixed with an abbreviation of the class name, much like controls are prefixed with the type of control. For example, an instance of the NameAndAddress object might be naadCustomer.

Naming Conventions for Custom Collections

Visual Basic gives you the ability to create your own collections of objects, much like the Data Access Objects have collections of databases, tables, and fields, or your program has a collection of forms. See Chapter 16 for more information about collections. Although a collection can contain many different types of objects, collections will normally contain objects of the same type. Collections of similar objects should be named the plural of the object name. For example, a collection of NameAndAddress objects should be called NameAndAddresses.

All user-created collections are 1-based, while the system collections are 0-based. (1-based means that the index of the first element is 1, while the index of the first element of a 0-based collection is 0.) When appending items to a collection, you can give the item a unique key in addition to the subscript assigned to it by its position in the collection. For instance, in the NameAndAddresses collection, each NameAndAddress item added to the collection could be given a key that matches the primary key of the person the NameAndAddress object represents. For example,

```
NameAndAddresses.Add Item:=naadCustomer, Key:=naadCustomer.CustID
```

Naming Conventions for Constants

Many of the constants and variables used by Visual Basic are now incorporated into the Visual Basic environment itself. There are two sources of constants:

- System-defined constants provided by applications and controls
- Symbolic, or user-defined, constants declared by using the Const statement

System-defined constants are called *object libraries,* and you can view them through the Object Browser. In versions of Visual Basic before Visual Basic 4.0, user-defined constants were capitalized with underscores instead of spaces, for example, USER_DEFINED. This method still works in Visual Basic 5.0, but for consistency you are encouraged to upgrade your naming standards. The new naming standard for constants is as followed: Qualify by prefix or qualify by Library Reference. Qualifying by prefix appears in mixed-case format with a two character prefix indicating the object library that defines the constant. For example,

```
vbUserDefined
dbAppendOnly
xlDialogBorder
```

The vb prefix means that the constant belongs to the object library of Visual Basic or Visual Basic, Applications Edition. The db prefix represents a data access object library constant. The xl constant prefix means the constant belongs to a Microsoft Excel object library.

When you use constants with custom controls, the syntax is as follows.

```
[libname.][modulename.]constname
```

The libname is the name of the type library that defines the constant. A *type library* is a component or file within another file that contains OLE automation standard descriptions. The modulename is the name of the module in which the type library is defined. The constname is the name defined for the constant in the type library. An example would be

```
Threed.LeftJustify
```

One important exception to this new convention is the Windows API declarations and constants. They are still in the old style format, but may someday migrate into the more modern style discussed here.

Object Properties and Methods

Refer to an object's properties and methods with the dot operator. This consists of the object's name, a period (.) and the property or method. For example,

```
response$ = Text1.Text
Clipboard.Clear
Form1.ScaleHeight = 2700
txtPatientName.ForeColor = YELLOW
ListShippingMethods.AddItem "Federal Express"
```

Refer to a control on another form with the *exclamation operator*. This consists of the form's name, an exclamation point (!), and the name of the control.

You also use the dot operator to refer to controls on forms. Visual Basic 2.0 and 3.0 recommended using the exclamation operator (!), but Visual Basic 4.0 has reverted back to the dot operator for all property or method qualification, except data access objects. However, Visual Basic 4.0 supports both the dot and exclamation method of qualification for compatibility.

Object Events

A reference to an event begins with the Name of the object that triggers the event, followed by an underscore (_) and the name of the event:

```
Private Sub Command1_Click ()
    MsgBox "You've just clicked Command1"
End Sub

Private Sub txtPatientName_GotFocus ()
    txtPatientName.BackColor = QBColor(7)
    txtPatientName.ForeColor = QBColor(1)
    txtPatientName.SelLength = Len(txtPatientName.Text)
End Sub
```

Forms are the exception: Rather than using the name of the form, the event subroutine uses the keyword Form.

```
Private Sub Form_Load ()
    List1.AddItem "Red"
    List1.AddItem "Blue"
    List1.AddItem "Green"
End Sub
```

See Chapter 34, "Events," for more about event procedures.

Modules

Place code that applies to controls and properties of more than one form in a module. To create a new module, select the Module command on the Visual Basic Insert menu (see Figure 35-1). In order to create a sub procedure or function in this module, simply type the code into its General Declarations section, or choose the Procedure option from the Insert menu. Modules allow you to define common behavior for a number of different forms without duplicating code. When you define subs or functions you should include either the Public or Private keyword before Sub or Function. It is better to explicitly define access to procedures rather than relying on default behavior.

Figure 35-1 How to create a new module

Object Arrays

An *object array* is a group of one or more objects that share the same Name property. Each form or control in an array has an index value that distinguishes it from the other objects in the object array. The first object in an object array has an index value of 0. Each new object in the object array receives a successively higher index value. This way, the next object has an index value of 1, the next 2, and so on. This value appears in between parentheses after the Name of the object array. For example, if you have an array of text boxes, you can specify the loading of the nth text box as follows.

```
Load TextBoxes(n)
```

A form may also be used in an object array. Do this by declaring a variable of type YourForm and simply dimensioning an array of them. MDI child forms are often created this way. For a more detailed discussion of this, see Chapters 16, and 36, "Accessing Forms and Menus." The example at the end of Chapter 36 shows the details of creating an arbitrary and dynamic number of child forms. The following example gives you a quick idea of how to create a form array:

```
Dim formNewInfo(10) as New formGetInfoMaster
```

Note that control arrays are different from the collections discussed in Chapter 16.

Forms and Controls Collections

Visual Basic has several built-in collections for forms in a project and controls on a form. The *Forms collection* refers to all the forms in a project. The *Controls collection* refers to all the controls on a form. The Forms collection is the ideal way to make global changes to all your forms. For example, to maximize all the forms in your project you'd use the following code:

```
Dim F As Form

For Each F In Forms
F.WindowState = vbMaximize
Next F
```

The Controls collection for a form works like the Forms collection for an application. You can use the Controls collection to loop through all the controls on a form and set any and all properties available at runtime. You can use the If TypeOf construct to determine the type of object in each element in the collection. For instance, if you wanted to print all the text values from the TextBox controls on a form, you'd use the following code:

```
Dim C As Control

For Each C In formThis.Controls
    If TypeOf C Is TextBox
        Debug.Print C.Text
    End If
Next C
```

Both the Forms and Controls collections have the Count property, which tells you how many forms or controls are in the collection.

See Chapter 16 for a detailed explanation of Objects and Collections.

Parents, Names, Tags, and Me

In Visual Basic every control is on one of the program's forms. This form is the *parent form* of the control. Each control has a Parent property at runtime that identifies its parent form. This property enables the code to reference the properties of the parent form without using the parent's Name property.

```
Private Sub Command1_Click ()
    Text1.Parent.WindowState = 2    'maximizes the form that Text1 is on
End Sub
```

You can use the Name property of a form or control to identify it at runtime. This feature was introduced with Visual Basic 4.0. In previous versions of Visual Basic you used the Tag property or a form-level variable. For instance, a generic module might need to identify a specific control to set properties:

```
Public Sub SetInsertion (ctrControl As Control)

   If it's the first name, position the insertion point at the
   'beginning of the text.
   If ctrControl.Name = "FirstName" Then
      ctrControl.SelStart = 1
   Else
   'otherwise, position it at the end of the text
      ctrControl.SelStart = Len(ctrControl)
   End If

End Sub
```

If you need to identify specific members of a control array or specific forms or controls loaded at runtime, you may want to use the Tag property, because the Name property for control arrays or a dynamically loaded object is the same as the Name property for the base object. The following code demonstrates one possible way to use Tag when Name isn't different enough.

```
Dim frmMyForm As New frmName

Load frmName
Load frmMyForm

frmName.Tag = "frmName"
frmMyForm.Tag = "frmMyForm"

If frmMyForm.Name = frmName.Name Then ' Condition is always true,
                                      ' because MyForm and Name share the same ancestor
   debug.print "always true, because MyForm and Name share the same ancestor"
End If

If frmMyForm.Tag = frmName.Tag Then   ' Condition is never true,
                                      ' because we set them that way
   debug.print "never true, because we set them that way."
End If
```

The Tag property provides a means of identifying forms and controls with descriptive text. Changing a form or control's Tag property has no effect on its appearance or any other property. The Tag property is for identification purposes only. The example project at the end of Chapter 36 uses the Tag property to refer back to an index of child forms. As another example of how to use the Tag property, you may wish to store a text box's value in its Tag property so you can easily undo any changes made by the user:

```
Text1.Tag = Text1.Text       'store old text value
...                           '....intervening code changes value
Text1.Text = Text1.Tag        'undo changes
```

Sometimes you need to refer to the object where code is currently running. For instance, in an MDI application with multiple child document windows, it may not be clear which child form is making a procedure call or triggering an event. Use the special Me object to refer to the currently running object.

You usually don't need to know what instance of a form is currently being used. Event code runs in the appropriate instance automatically. Sometimes, however, you may need to use a method or property that refers explicitly to a particular instance. The Me keyword lets you refer to the instance in which the code is running. Use Me just as if it were the Name property of the object:

```
Private Sub Command1_Click ()
    Me.Hide                            'hide this form instance
End Sub
```

Active Objects

The *active object* is the currently selected form or control on the screen. Visual Basic identifies the currently active control with the Form or Screen object's ActiveControl property. Windows displays different colors of title bars and borders for active and inactive forms. (Set these colors in the appearance tab of the display in the Windows control panel.) Use the Screen object's ActiveForm property to refer to the active form if you don't know the name of the active form. This technique can be useful for writing general purpose procedures to deal with whatever object is active at a particular time. Note that the Me implicit object refers to the form that's had its code run most recently and may not indicate the active form—for instance, if the user has clicked a different form's title bar and shifted focus.

Accessing Forms and Controls Summary

Table 35-4 lists the properties involved in referencing forms or controls in Visual Basic.

Table 35-4 Properties referencing forms and controls

Use or Set This...	Type	To Do This...
ActiveControl	Property	Access the attributes of the active control
ActiveForm	Property	Access the attributes of the active form
Index	Property	Identify a control in a control array
Name	Property	Word that identifies an object in code
Parent	Property	Identify the form that a form is positioned on
Tag	Property	Identify a control or form with a unique value

The following pages investigate these properties in detail. At the end of this chapter, step-by-step directions explain how to assemble the Reference project, which illustrates a variety of techniques for referencing objects in code.

ACTIVECONTROL PROPERTY

Objects Affected   Form, Forms Collection, MDIForm, PropertyPage, Screen, UserControl, UserDocument

Purpose   The ActiveControl property returns the currently active control on the screen or form. The active control is the control that has the focus and will receive subsequent user input. You can examine or change a property of the active control by referring to Screen.ActiveControl[.property]. Table 35-5 gives the arguments of the ActiveControl property.

General Syntax

```
Screen.ActiveControl[.property|method]
Form.ActiveControl[.property|method]
```

Table 35-5 Arguments of the ActiveControl property

Argument	Description
Screen	'Screen' refers to the Screen object
Form	Name of the form or MDIForm referenced
method	Name of the method used
property	Name of the property referenced

Example Syntax

```
Private Sub Form_Click ()
    Select Case Screen.ActiveControl.Name        'checks active control's Name property
        Case "Command1"
            Form1.BackColor = RGB(255, 0, 0)     'changes form's background to red
```

continued on next page

continued from previous page

```
        Case "Command2"
            Form1.BackColor = RGB(0, 255, 0)        'changes form's background to green
        Case "Command3"
            Form1.BackColor = RGB(0, 0, 255)        'changes form's background to blue
    End Select
End Sub

Private Sub CheckControl ()
    If TypeOf Screen.ActiveControl Is CommandButton Then
        Screen.ActiveControl.Visible = False        'makes command button invisible
    ElseIf TypeOf Screen.ActiveControl Is TextBox Then
        StoredText = Screen.ActiveControl.Text        'stores contents of text box
    End If
End Sub
```

Description   The ActiveControl property is a substitute for the name of the control on the screen or form that has the focus. A control has the focus when selected on the screen by the user. This property is only accessible at runtime and will not work at design time. In the example syntax, a Select Case statement determines the background color of the form based on which command button has the focus.

Ineligible Controls You cannot use the ActiveControl property to reference controls ineligible for focus. A control may be ineligible for receiving focus for a number of reasons, such as when the control's Visible property is False. Some controls can never receive the focus, such as the Timer and the Label controls.

The Name Property The Name property can be used to identify the active control. You set the property at design time, and it is read-only at runtime. For controls that are dynamically loaded or are part of a control array, the Name property will be the same, so you may need to use the Tag or Index property to uniquely identify a control. In the example syntax, the Name property is used as the basis for the Select Case statement that sets the background color.

The Tag Property   When none of a control's properties are appropriate for use in an ActiveControl expression, the Tag property can differentiate between the various controls on a form. The Tag property of a control can be assigned a unique text string that you can use to identify the control when necessary. For example, each of the controls on a data entry form can receive a unique Tag property text string in the Form_Load event of the form. This string then identifies the controls. See the Tag property section later in this chapter for more details.

Example   The Reference project at the end of this chapter uses the ActiveControl property at several points in the code to read and set various properties, as well as use methods.

Comments   The word Screen or a form name must appear before ActiveControl or an error occurs.

ACTIVEFORM PROPERTY

Objects Affected   Form, Forms Collection, MDIForm, Screen

Purpose   The ActiveForm property refers to the currently active form. At runtime you can read the value of this property to determine which form has the focus or to set that form's properties. This property is accessible at runtime only and will not work at design time. Table 35-6 lists the arguments of the ActiveForm property.

General Syntax

```
Screen.ActiveForm[.Property]
Form.ActiveForm[.Property]
```

Table 35-6 Arguments of the ActiveForm property

Argument	Description
Screen	'Screen' refers to the Screen object
Form	Name property of the MDIForm
Property	Name of the property to reference

Example Syntax

```
Private Sub FormPosition ()

If Screen.ActiveForm.Name = "Splash" then
        Screen.ActiveForm.Height = Screen.Height / 2    'make form's height half of screen
    Else
        Screen.ActiveForm.Height = Screen.Height        'make form's height equal screen
    End If
        Screen.ActiveForm.Width = (Screen.Width / 2)    'make form's width half of screen
        Screen.ActiveForm.Top = 0                       'place form at top
        Screen.ActiveForm.Left = 0                      'place form on left margin
End Sub
```

Description   The ActiveForm property returns which form on the screen or within an MDI form has the focus. A form has the focus when it is the selected or active form on the screen; its title bar and border colors are usually different than inactive forms to visually cue the user. (The colors for active and inactive forms are set by the Windows Control Panel.) The example syntax shows the ActiveForm property setting the form's size and position without explicitly referring to the form's Name.

Ineligible Forms   The ActiveForm property cannot reference forms that are ineligible for focus. A form may be ineligible for receiving focus for a number of reasons. When a form's Visible property is False, that control may not have the focus or reference it with the ActiveForm property. In order to change the size of a hidden or invisible form, use an alternate property, such as Name.

The Name Property The Name property can be used to identify the active form. You set the property at design time, and it is read-only at runtime. For forms loaded using the New keyword, the Name property will be the same as the base object, so you may need to use the Tag property or a public variable to uniquely identify the form. In the example syntax, the Name property is used to determine how to size the form.

The Tag Property When none of a form's properties is appropriate for use in an ActiveForm expression, the Tag property serves as one possible method for differentiating between the various forms of a program. The Tag property of an object can be assigned a unique text string that you can use to refer to the object when necessary. A Select Case statement might then determine the Tag property of the active form. In the next example, the active form's background color changes from white to blue.

```
Private Sub ChangeBackground ()
    Select Case Screen.ActiveForm.Tag                    'checks Tag property of form
        Case "Main Form"
            Screen.ActiveForm.BackColor = RGB(255,255,255)  'white background
        Case "Secondary Form"
            Screen.ActiveForm.BackColor = RGB(0,0,255)      'blue background
    End Select
End Sub
```

Example In the Reference project at the end of this chapter, the cmndPrint_Click event uses the ActiveForm property to print the letter on the formLetter form. The ActiveForm property determines to which form the GenerateLetter function prints the contents of the letter. Notice that the ActiveForm is the formLetter form and not the Reference form. Even though the cmndPrint_Click event is a subroutine of the Reference form, the active form is the one currently selected on the screen.

Comments Either the word Screen or the Name of the MDIForm must precede each ActiveForm property statement, or it will not work properly. General procedures using the ActiveForm property should be placed in a module so that form-level code can still access these more general routines.

INDEX PROPERTY

Objects Affected Animation, Brush, CheckBox, ComboBox, CommandButton, CommonDialog, Data, DBCombo, DBList, DirListBox, DriveListBox, FileListBox, Frame, HScrollBar, Image, Label, Line, ListBox, ListView, MAPIMessages, MAPISession, Masked Edit, Menu, MSComm, MSFlexGrid, OLE Container, OptionButton, PictureBox, PictureClip, ProgressBar, RemoteData, RichTextBox, Shape, Slider, Split, StatusBar, TabStrip, TextBox, Timer, Toolbar, TreeView, UpDown, VScrollBar

Purpose The Index property determines the referenced element of an object array. When an object is not part of an object array, its Index property has no value. Objects that are part of a control array may have index values of 0

to 32,767. This value may be set at design time and is read-only at run-time. Any reference to an object in an object array must include its Index property value. Table 35-7 lists the arguments of the Index property.

General Syntax

```
[form!]object[(i%)].Index
```

Table 35-7 Arguments of the Index property

Argument	Description
form	Name property of the parent form
object	Shared Name of the object array
i%	Index value of the form or control

Example Syntax

```
Private Sub mnuPrinterChoices_Click (Index As Integer)
    Select Case mnuPrinterChoices(Index).Index    'see which choice was clicked
        Case 0                          'control menuPrinterChoices(0)
            txtPrinter.Text = "HP LaserJet III"
        Case 1                          'control menuPrinterChoices(1)
            txtPrinter.Text = "HP LaserJet 4 MX"
        Case 2                          'control menuPrinterChoices(2)
            txtPrinter.Text = "HP LaserJet 4 SI"
    End Select
End Sub
```

Description   The Index property uniquely identifies an instance of the object within the object array. An Index expression normally consists of the object's Name property followed by the value of the index placed in parentheses. Programs with multiple forms require preceding this with the Name of the form. Forms may also be included in an object array, although the mechanism for doing so differs from creating an object array of controls. The Index property may be modified at design time only.

Note that Event sub procedures pass the control's Index value as an argument for use in the subroutine. Using the control's Index property is functionally identical to using the event's Index variable.

Option Buttons, Check Boxes, and Menu Controls   Option buttons, check boxes, and menus can usually be handled most easily as part of an object array. Each control's index property differentiates it from the other controls in the control array, and each control in the array shares the code in common with the other controls. In the example syntax, a Select Case statement uses the Index property of the control array mnuPrinterChoices to indicate what name will appear in the text box txtPrinter. Note that we could also have used the Index variable passed to the array's event. The following code is functionally equivalent to the example syntax:

```
Sub mnuPrinterChoices_Click (Index As Integer)
    Select Case Index                    'see which choice was clicked
        Case 0                           'control menuPrinterChoices(0)
            txtPrinter.Text = "HP LaserJet III"
        Case 1                           'control menuPrinterChoices(1)
            txtPrinter.Text = "HP LaserJet 4 MX"
        Case 2                           'control menuPrinterChoices(2)
            txtPrinter.Text = "HP LaserJet 4 SI"
    End Select
End Sub
```

The Load and Unload Statements

When used in conjunction with the Load and Unload statements, the Index property of an object array allows the creation of new objects. First, create a single object with an index value of 0. Next, change its Visible property to False (0). At runtime, load a new member of the object array using an unused index value. When no longer needed, you can destroy these objects with the Unload statement. For example, create an option control box with an index value of 0. Each time another option box becomes necessary, load it with the Load statement. This allows your pro gram to dynamically respond to different user needs.

Many programs, for example, place the last four saved files on the bottom of the File menu. When the program starts for the first time, there are no saved files, so no filenames should appear. Each additional file saved adds one more element to the menu.

Creating Multiple Forms in an Array

Forms may also form an object array. To do so, simply assign a form to a variable:

```
Dim InputForm(10) as New Form1
```

MDI child forms typically use an object array. You usually don't know how many instances of the form the user will open, so declare the array without explicitly dimensioning it. Each time the user wishes to create a new MDI child form, redimension the array with the Preserve keyword. This creates a new form without affecting the contents of the forms already open.

```
Sub MDIForm_Load()
    Dim InputForm() as New Form1                   'create the form "template"
End Sub

Sub menuFileNew_Click ()
    InputFormCount = UBound(InputForm)             'count number of child forms open
    ReDim Preserve InputForm(InputFormCount + 1)   'create new child form
    InputForm(InputFormCount + 1).Show             'display new child form
End Sub
```

For a much more thorough discussion of creating multiple instances of forms using form arrays, see Chapters 16 and 36.

Example

The Reference project at the end of this chapter sets the Index property for each of the three object arrays in this program. On the Reference form, the object arrays are optLetter and chkLetter. The frmEntry form has the txtEntry object array.

The Index property serves as a reference at several points in the Reference project. In the optLetter_GotFocus event, the Index property determines which part of the code to process. The identification of the chkLetter array control to be enabled or disabled includes its Index property in this event subroutine. The chkLetter_Click event uses the Index property to indicate exactly which control the user pressed.

Comments   The data control has a completely unrelated Index property associated with the TableDefs collection in addition to this usage of Index. Note that collections (discussed in Chapter 16) also have an index completely unrelated to this Index property.

NAME PROPERTY

Objects Affected   Animation, Brush, CheckBox, ComboBox, CommandButton, CommonDialog, Data, DBCombo, DBList, DirListBox, DriveListBox, Extender, FileListBox, Font, Form, Forms Collection, Frame, HScrollBar, Image, ImageList, Label, Line, ListBox, ListView, MAPIMessages, MAPISession, Masked Edit, MDIForm, Menu, MSComm, MSFlexGrid, OLE Container, OptionButton, PictureBox, PictureClip, ProgressBar, PropertyPage, RemoteData, RichTextBox, Shape, Slider, SSTab, StatusBar, TabStrip, TextBox, Timer, ToolBar, TreeView, UpDown, UserControl, UserDocument, VScrollBar

Purpose   The Name property identifies each control and form in a program. You then refer to the form or control with its Name in your code. This property is only modifiable at design time; it is read-only at runtime. Table 35-8 lists the argument of the Name property.

General Syntax

```
[Name.]Property
```

Table 35-8 Argument of the Name property

Argument	Description
Name	Name used to identify the form or control in code

Example Syntax
```
Sub Form1_Click
    If TextBox(0).Text = "Background is blue" Then    'This subroutine checks the
        Form1.BackColor = RGB(255,255,255)            'contents of the first part of
        Form1.ForeColor = RGB(0,0,255)                'the TextBox Control array for
```
continued on next page

continued from previous page

```
        TextBox(0).Text = "Background is white"          'which color to set the
        TextBox(1).Text = "Foreground is blue"           'foreground and background of
    ElseIf TextBox(0).Text = "Background is white" Then  'the form. 'Clicking' the form
        Form1.BackColor = RGB(0,0,255)                   'changes background and
        Form1.ForeColor = RGB(255,255,255)               'foreground from blue to white.
        TextBox(0).Text = "Background is blue"
        TextBox(1).Text = "Foreground is white"
    End If
End Sub
```

Description

A form or control's Name property may be up to 40 characters in length and must begin with a letter of the alphabet. It may contain underscores (_), but no other punctuation or spaces. Although you may use a reserved word (like If or Select), this can create confusion and potentially subtle bugs. A newly created object's default Name property is the name of the object type and an integer. For example, the default Name for the first text box is Text1. With each addition of another object of the same type, the integer at the end of the Name increments by 1. For example, the second text box on a form has a default Name property of Text2.

Your code uses an object's Name property to refer to that object. This name is either the default setting or a user-defined choice. The Name of an object normally serves as a part of any expression that directly affects the object.

Using a prefix to indicate the type of control can help make your code be self-documenting and reduce errors. For example, txtPatientName refers to a text box, while picEmployeMugShot refers to a picture control. See Naming Conventions at the beginning of this chapter for more details.

The ActiveControl Property

The ActiveControl property can substitute for the name of whatever control is currently active (selected). In this case, the ActiveControl property identifies the control with the focus. For example, a sub procedure can change the BackColor and ForeColor property of the selected control. This enables the program to visually emphasize the selected control. See ActiveControl property for more information.

The ActiveForm Property

The ActiveForm property can substitute for the name of the active form. For example, a module sub procedure can change the size and position of the currently selected form. This might enable the program to standardize the appearance of the forms that appear on the screen.

Object Arrays

When more than one object of the same type on the same form has the same name, these objects are part of an object array. You can only create an object array at design time. (Visual Basic asks if this is what you wish to do in order to prevent accidental creation.) Any number of control objects can belong to an object array, provided that they are of the same object type. Each object has a unique Index property number corresponding to the order of creation. You may, however, modify the object's Index property in the Property Box. The first object in an object array defaults to 0; that is, the first object created has an Index of 0, not 1. The Index values in an object array do not need to be sequential, and you can skip numbers. For instance, if you had an object array of option buttons for modem speeds, you could assign them Index values of 300, 1200, 2400, and so on. The Index value helps to reference that object and appears in parentheses after the shared name. For example, the second control of the Assist object array appears as Assist(1), or the option button representing 2400 baud would be optBaud(2400).

Object arrays can simplify writing code for similar objects, because all the objects in the array can share the same code. For example, you may have a Validation routine that you'd like to run on every Change event for 10 different text boxes. Simply create an object array of txtInput(0) to txtInput(9) and put the validation code in the txtInput_Change event.

```
Sub txtInput_Change (Index as Integer)
    If txtInput(Index).Text = "" Then
        MsgBox "You need to enter some text.  Please retry"
    End If
End Sub
```

Notice that events for control arrays always have the Index argument. This lets you determine which object in the array caused the event. For example, suppose you wanted to place some default text into txtInput(5) and txtInput(7) when they got the focus:

```
Sub txtInput_GotFocus (Index as Integer)
    Select Case Index
        Case 5: txtInput(Index) = "Seattle"      'default city
        Case 7: txtInput(Index) = "WA"           'default state
    End Select
End Sub
```

Example   All the objects of the Reference Project receive names that identify them during the program's operation.

Comment   Visual Basic 1.0 used the CtlName and FormName properties to refer to controls and forms. Later versions of Visual Basic replace these two properties with the single Name property, which refers to both controls and forms.

PARENT PROPERTY

Objects Affected   Animation, CheckBox, ComboBox, CommandButton, CommonDialog, Data, DBCombo, DBGrid, DBList, DirListBox, DriveListBox, Extender, FileListBox, Frame, HScrollBar, Image, ImageList, Label, Line, ListBox, ListView, MAPIMessages, MAPISession, Masked Edit, Menu, MSComm, MSFlexGrid, OLE Container, OptionButton, PictureBox, PictureClip, ProgressBar, RemoteData, RichTextBox, Shape, Slider, SSTab, StatusBar,

TabStrip, TextBox, Timer, ToolBar, TreeView, UpDown, UserDocument, VScrollBar

Purpose   Each control belongs to a form. A control's Parent property identifies the control's form. Each Parent property expression must contain the Name of the control being accessed. This property is not available at design time and is read-only at runtime. Using the Parent property lets you design generic subroutines and functions that apply for any control passed to it. Table 35-9 lists the argument of the Parent property.

General Syntax

```
[control.]Parent
```

Table 35-9 Argument of the Parent property

Argument	Description
control	Name property of the control

Example Syntax

```
Private Sub RestorePointer (Source As Control)
    If TypeOf Source Is TextBox Then          'checks if control is a text box
        Source.Parent.MousePointer = 3        'I-Bar mouse pointer
    Else If TypeOf Source Is PictureBox Then  'checks if control is picture box
        Source.Parent.MousePointer = 4        'Icon mouse pointer
    Else                                      'All other controls are given an
        Source.Parent.MousePointer = 1        'Arrow mouse pointer.
    End If
End Sub
```

Description   The Parent property of a control makes its form's properties and methods available. The Parent property in a subroutine or function can affect the forms of controls on many different forms. Do this with the use of a separate module that holds the function so any code in any form or module can refer to your generic subroutine or function. In the example syntax for this property, the function RestorePointer changes the MousePointer property of the form to a special type based on the named control in the expression. Note the use of the TypeOf and Is keywords to identify the control type. See Chapter 16 for more information about these two keywords.

The ActiveControl Property   You can create a very general function by combining ActiveControl with the Parent property. The ActiveControl property refers to the control with the focus. Depending on which type of control has the focus, different actions can be taken with the properties and methods of the Parent form. The next example changes the Icon property of the form based on the selected control. This pairing of the ActiveControl and Parent property works best when placed within a separate module so that the function or routine operates on more than one form.

```
Private Sub ChooseIcon ()
    If TypeOf Screen.ActiveControl Is TextBox Then
        Screen.ActiveControl.Parent.Icon=LoadPicture("C:\VB\ICONS\MISC\FACE02.ICO")
    ElseIf Screen.ActiveControl Is CommandButton Then
        Screen.ActiveControl.Parent.Icon=LoadPicture("C:\VB\ICONS\MISC\FACE01.ICO")
    End If
End Sub

Private Sub Form_Resize ()
    ChooseIcon
End Sub
```

Example   In the Reference project at the end of this chapter, formEntry's Load event sets the form's caption by using textEntry's Parent property.

Comments   The Parent property works best when placed within an external module, but also works within a form's subroutines.

TAG PROPERTY

Objects Affected   CheckBox, ComboBox, CommandButton, CommonDialog, Data, DBCombo, DBList, DirListBox, DriveListBox, FileListBox, Form, Forms Collection, Frame, HScrollBar, Image, Label, Line, ListBox, MDIForm, Menu, MSChart, MSFlexGrid, OLE Container, OLEObject, OptionButton, PictureBox, PropertyPage, RemoteData, Shape, TextBox, Timer, UserControl, UserDocument, VScrollBar

Purpose   The Tag property is a variant that has no direct affect on its object. It is typically used to attach a text string to a form or control. In versions of Visual Basic before Visual Basic 4.0, the Tag property of a form was used as a means of accessing a variable related to the form outside the form's scope. This is no longer needed, since form-level variables may now be declared as Public. The Tag property still has many uses and can be a great problem solver in your code, such as when form or control objects are loaded dynamically at runtime. The Tag property of each object can be assigned a unique value used to distinguish between identically named objects. This property may be changed at design time or runtime. Table 35-10 lists the arguments of the Tag property.

General Syntax

```
[form.]Tag[ = string$]
[form!]control.Tag[ = string$]
```

Table 35-10 Arguments of the Tag property

Argument	Description
form	Name of the form
control	Name of the control
string$	Contains the identifying string of text

Example Syntax

```
Private Sub Form_Resize ()
    If Form1.Tag = "" Then              'checks if the form's tag property is blank
        Form1.Tag = "Loaded"            'changes tag property to "Loaded"
    ElseIf Form1.Tag = "Loaded" Then    'checks if the form's tag property is "Loaded"
        Form1.Tag = "Changed"           'changes tag property to "Changed"
    End If
End Sub
```

Description   The Tag property serves as a method for differentiating between the various controls of a form, storing information unique to that form or control, or relating the form or control to something else.

A form or control's Tag property can receive a text string (string$) that refers to anything you want. Visual Basic does not use or modify the Tag, so you have complete flexibility in how you use it. You may wish to store a control's old value in the Tag, an entry that relates it to a variable array's index, or perhaps track a control's state. In the example syntax, the Tag property of a form changes to flag when modifications to the size of the form occur.

Every object has a Tag property (except for the system objects App, Clipboard, Debug, Printer, and Screen). It is the *only* property all objects have that can be read and written at runtime. This makes it a valuable problem solver, especially when writing generic functions that are supposed to work on more than one type of control.

Example   In the Reference project that follows, the Tag property of the txtEntry control array contains the appropriate caption to display on the entry form.

The Reference Project

Project Overview

The Reference project demonstrates the properties used to access a program's controls and forms. Following the examples of the different forms and subroutines of this project will give you a good understanding of how to reference forms and controls in Visual Basic.

The Reference project consists of three forms: frmMain, frmLetter, and frmEntry. Each of these forms has a section with step-by-step instructions on how to put the form and its controls together. A table lists the different elements of the form's controls, and a figure shows how the form looks with these controls. Then we cover the actual code used on each form. We wrap the project up with the module-level code and follow that with a complete explanation of the project.

Assembling the Project: Reference Form

1. Make a new form (the Reference form) with the objects and properties in Table 35-11. Notice that all the CheckBox controls have the same Name property of chkLetter. Similarly, all the option button controls share the Name property optLetter. These indicate that the controls make up a control array. When you create the second control of the same type and Name, Visual Basic asks if you'd like to create a control array. Answer yes to this question.

Table 35-11 Settings for frmMain form

Object	Property	Setting
Form	BackColor	Light Gray—&H00C0C0C0
	BorderStyle	1—Fixed Single
	Caption	"Reference Project"
	Name	frmMain
Frame	BackColor	Light Gray—&H00C0C0C0
	Caption	"Letter Type"
	Name	fraType
Option	BackColor	Light Gray—&H00C0C0C0
	Caption	"&Introduction Letter"
	Name	optLetter
	Index	0
Option	BackColor	Light Gray—&H00C0C0C0
	Caption	"&Acceptance Letter"
	Name	optLetter
	Index	1
Option	BackColor	Light Gray—&H00C0C0C0
	Caption	"Ge&neral Letter"
	Name	optLetter
	Index	2
Frame	BackColor	Light Gray—&H00C0C0C0
	Caption	"Letter Options"
	Name	fraOptions
Check	BackColor	Light Gray—&H00C0C0C0
	Caption	"&Return Address"
	Name	chkLetter
	Index	0

continued on next page

continued from previous page

Object	Property	Setting
Check	BackColor	Light Gray—&H00C0C0C0
	Caption	"A&ddressee"
	Name	chkLetter
	Index	1
Check	BackColor	Light Gray—&H00C0C0C0
	Caption	"&Greeting"
	Name	chkLetter
	Index	2
Check	BackColor	Light Gray—&H00C0C0C0
	Caption	"&Body"
	Name	chkLetter
	Index	3
Check	BackColor	Light Gray—&H00C0C0C0
	Caption	"&Closing"
	Name	chkLetter
	Index	4
Check	BackColor	Light Gray—&H00C0C0C0
	Caption	"&Enclosure List"
	Name	chkLetter
	Index	5
Check	BackColor	Light Gray—&H00C0C0C0
	Caption	"Carbon Copy &List"
	Name	chkLetter
	Index	6
Command	Caption	&Print Letter
	Name	cmdPrint
Command	Caption	"E&xit"
	Name	cmdExit

2. Size the objects on the screen as shown in Figure 35-2.

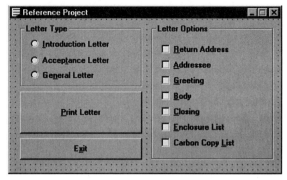

Figure 35-2   How the frmMain form looks when completed

3. Enter the following code into the general declarations section of the form. The
module variable mblnProcessClicks is a flag used to distinguish between user-
generated and code-generated click events. We use the LetterType enumeration to
make the code in this form easier to maintain.

```
Option Explicit

Private mblnProcessClicks As Boolean      'Used to track if we're actively  changing letter
                                          'type

Private Enum LetterType                   'These are the three different letter types
    INTRODUCTION = 0
    ACCEPTANCE = 1
    GENERIC = 2
End Enum
```

4. Enter the following code in the cmdExit_Click event. This ends the program by
unloading all the forms in the Forms collection.

```
Private Sub cmdExit_Click()
    Dim i As Integer

    'loop through Forms collection and unload each form as we go
    For i = Forms.Count - 1 To 0 Step -1
        'note: as we unload a form, all the other forms move down 1
        'in the collection.
        Unload Forms(i) 'unload form
    Next i
End Sub
```

5. Enter the following code in the Form_Load event. This loads the other two forms
used in the project so they display more quickly when needed.

```
Private Sub Form_Load()
    Load frmEntry
    Load frmLetter
End Sub
```

6. Enter the following code in the chkLetter_Click event. This routine happens whenever the user changes which letter option he or she wants. It first checks the module variable mblnProcessClicks to see if the Click event was caused by the code in the optLetter_GotFocus event. The code there checks or grays the check boxes; doing so creates a Click event here, which we need to filter out. If mblnProcessClicks is True, that means it's a real user-induced click and we need to respond to it. The routine then sets the LetterOptionType property to indicate which option the user chose, and opens up the frmEntry form.

```
Private Sub chkLetter_Click(Index As Integer)
    If mblnProcessClicks = True Then
        frmEntry.LetterOptionType = Index
        If chkLetter(Index).Value Then
            ' Get entry
            frmEntry.Show
        Else
            ' Clear previous entry
            frmEntry!txtEntry(Index).Text = ""
        End If
    End If
End Sub
```

7. Enter this code in the optLetter_GotFocus event. This event occurs whenever the user changes the letter type. It first highlights the choice in blue, using Screen.ActiveControl to pass the correct name to the HiLite subroutine. It then flags mblnProcessClicks to make sure the chkLetter_Click event doesn't try to handle any check box clicks.

We then use the ActiveControl argument again to check which letter option the user chose. The Select Case statements enable or disable the appropriate check boxes and unhighlight the other letter types.

The For Next loop cycles through the Controls collection looking for the chkLetter check box controls. When it finds them it grays out any that are disabled but checked, and places a check in any that were grayed out previously and are now enabled. The last line of the routine sets the mblnProcessClicks flag to show that we're done manipulating the check boxes with code.

```
Private Sub optLetter_Click(Index As Integer)
    Dim x As Integer

    HiLite Screen.ActiveControl
    mblnProcessClicks = False               'Flag that we're setting type
    Select Case Screen.ActiveControl.Index
        Case INTRODUCTION
            chkLetter(GREETING).Enabled = False
            chkLetter(BODY).Enabled = False
            chkLetter(CLOSING).Enabled = False
            chkLetter(ENCLOSURE).Enabled = False
            chkLetter(CARBON).Enabled = False
            UnHiLite optLetter(ACCEPTANCE)
            UnHiLite optLetter(GENERIC)
```

```
        Case ACCEPTANCE
            chkLetter(GREETING).Enabled = True
            chkLetter(BODY).Enabled = True
            chkLetter(CLOSING).Enabled = False
            chkLetter(ENCLOSURE).Enabled = False
            chkLetter(CARBON).Enabled = False
            UnHiLite optLetter(INTRODUCTION)
            UnHiLite optLetter(GENERIC)
        Case GENERIC
            chkLetter(GREETING).Enabled = True
            chkLetter(BODY).Enabled = True
            chkLetter(CLOSING).Enabled = True
            chkLetter(ENCLOSURE).Enabled = True
            chkLetter(CARBON).Enabled = True
            UnHiLite optLetter(INTRODUCTION)
            UnHiLite optLetter(ACCEPTANCE)
    End Select
    For x = 0 To Me.Controls.Count - 1  'Gray out checked boxes that are now disabled
        ' use name property of Controls collection to
        ' verify a control is one of the checkboxes
        If Me.Controls(x).Name = "chkLetter" Then
            If Me.Controls(x).Enabled = False And Me.Controls(x).Value = vbChecked Then
                Me.Controls(x).Value = vbGrayed
                frmEntry!txtEntry(Me.Controls(x).Index).Text = ""
            End If                          'Check boxes that are grayed out but now enabled
            If Me.Controls(x).Enabled = True And Me.Controls(x).Value = vbGrayed Then
                Me.Controls(x).Value = vbUnchecked
            End If
        End If
        DoEvents
    Next x
    mblnProcessClicks = True
End Sub
```

8. Place this code in the cmdPrint Click event. When the user clicks this, we simulate printing the letter by hiding the reference form and entry form, generating the letter, and showing the completed letter with the Letter form. Note that because we show the Letter form modally, the rest of the code doesn't run until the user closes that form.

```
Private Sub cmdPrint_Click()
    frmEntry.Hide
    frmMain.Hide
    GenerateLetter
    frmLetter.Show vbModal
    frmLetter.Hide
    frmMain.Show
End Sub
```

Assembling the Project: Letter Form

1. Make a new form with the objects and properties in Table 35-12.

Table 35-12 Settings for frmLetter form

Object	Property	Setting
Form	BackColor	White—&H00FFFFFF
	BorderStyle	1—Fixed Single
	Caption	<blank out caption>
	ControlBox	False
	Name	frmLetter
	MaxButton	False
	MinButton	False
Command	Cancel	-1—True
	Caption	"&Close"
	Default	-1—True
	Name	cmdClose
Text	BackColor	White—&H00FFFFFF
	BorderStyle	1—Single
	Name	txtPage
Text	BorderStyle	0—None
	FontBold	0—False
	FontName	Times New Roman
	FontSize	7.8
	MultiLine	-1—True
	Name	txtPrintout
Text	BackColor	Black—&H80000008
	BorderStyle	1—Single
	Name	txtShadow

2. Size the objects on the screen, as shown in Figure 35-3.

3. Enter the following code in the Close Click event. This just hides the form.

```
Private Sub cmdClose_Click()
    frmLetter.Hide                'Hide the letter display form
End Sub
```

Assembling the Project: frmEntry Form

1. Make a new form with the objects and properties in Table 35-13.

Figure 35-3 How the frmLetter form looks: Note that txtPage contains txtPrintOut; the illustration shows txtPrintOut with a gray outline for clarity

Table 35-13 Settings for frmEntry form

Object	Property	Setting
Form	BorderStyle	1—Fixed Single
	ControlBox	False
	Name	frmEntry
	MaxButton	False
	MinButton	False
Text	Index	0
	MultiLine	-1—True
	Name	txtEntry
	ScrollBar	2—Vertical
	Text	\<blank out text\>
Command	Caption	"&Close"
	Name	cmdClose

2. Size the objects on the screen, as shown in Figure 35-4.

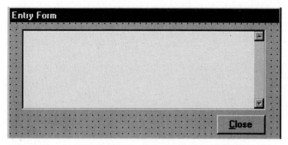

Figure 35-4 How the frmEntry form looks

3. Enter the following code into the general declarations section of the form. The module variable mltrCurrentType will hold the type of letter selected in the chkLetter check box control array. You will expose this variable via a public property.

```
Option Explicit

Private mltrCurrentType As LetterOption
```

4. Enter the following code in the form's Activate event. This event occurs whenever the form receives the focus. It starts by placing the correct text box (as defined by LetterOptionType, which the chkLetter check box control array defines) at the front of the stack of text boxes with the Z-order method. It then sets the title bar of the form using the tags stored in each text box, and resets the tab order correctly.

```
Private Sub Form_Activate()
    txtEntry(LetterOptionType).ZOrder  'Place the correct Text box in the front of the
                                       '"stack"
    txtEntry(LetterOptionType).Parent.Caption = txtEntry(LetterOptionType).Tag 'Label the
                                                                               'form
    txtEntry(LetterOptionType).TabIndex = 0 'Make the current text box first in the tab
                                            'order,
    cmdClose.TabIndex = 1                    'And the close button next
End Sub
```

5. Enter the following code in the Form Load event. This first creates an object array of text boxes to hold the entries for each letter option. It then sets the tag for each of these text boxes to a description of that text box. We use this tag to properly identify the frmEntry form.

```
Private Sub Form_Load()
    Dim x As LetterOption

    For x = ADDRESSEE To CARBON              'We defined the "template" text box
                                             'as txtEntry(RTN_ADDRESS)
        Load txtEntry(x)                     'Now create all the other text boxes
        txtEntry(x).Visible = True           'And make sure they're visible
    Next x
    txtEntry(RTN_ADDRESS).Tag = "Return Address"    'The tags of each text box hold
                                                    'descriptive text that we
```

```
txtEntry(ADDRESSEE).Tag = "Addressee"      'use to label the data entry
txtEntry(GREETING).Tag = "Greeting"        'Title Bar
txtEntry(BODY).Tag = "Body Text"
txtEntry(CLOSING).Tag = "Closing"
txtEntry(ENCLOSURE).Tag = "Enclosures"
txtEntry(CARBON).Tag = "Carbon Copies"
End Sub
```

6. Now enter the following code in the form's Paint event. Any time the form repaints itself, we set the focus to the text box so the user may easily make entries. Note that we can't perform this in the Activate event, as the form is only in the process of activating and isn't yet capable of giving a control the focus.

```
Private Sub Form_Paint()
    txtEntry(LetterOptionType).SetFocus      'Ready for user to enter text
End Sub
```

7. Enter the following code in the cmdClose Click event. This simply hides the frmEntry form.

```
Private Sub cmdClose_Click()
    frmEntry.Hide            'Hide the entry box; back to reference form
End Sub
```

8. Add the following property to the form. It exposes the mltrCurrentType to frmMain, so that clicking chkLetter in frmMain can trigger an appropriate change in the txtEntry form.

```
Public Property Get LetterOptionType() As LetterOption
    LetterOptionType = mltrCurrentType
End Property

Public Property Let LetterOptionType(ByVal ltrCurrentType As LetterOption)
    mltrCurrentType = ltrCurrentType
End Property
```

Assembling the Project: Module

1. Enter the following code into a new module. Start with the general declarations of constants and global enumerations.

```
Option Explicit

Public Enum LetterOption         'These are the seven different letter options
    RTN_ADDRESS = 0
    ADDRESSEE = 1
    GREETING = 2
    BODY = 3
    CLOSING = 4
    ENCLOSURE = 5
    CARBON = 6
End Enum

Private Const BLANK = vbCrLf & vbCrLf         'Two CR LF combos
```

2. Now create the following subroutines. The GenerateLetter subroutine generates the final letter from the input the user has given. It simply appends each bit of text onto a temporary string, making a few decisions along the way of what to include. Note the syntax of how to refer to the text in each text box, with the form name coming before anything else. The last line of this routine assigns the value of the temporary variable to the final printout.

```
Public Sub GenerateLetter()
    Dim strLetter As String

    strLetter = ""                                              'Erase the letter
    strLetter = strLetter & frmEntry!txtEntry(RTN_ADDRESS).Text & BLANK 'Add return address
    strLetter = strLetter & frmEntry!txtEntry(ADDRESSEE).Text & BLANK    'Add Addressee
    If frmEntry!txtEntry(GREETING).Text = "" Then               'If there is no greeting,
        strLetter = strLetter & "To Whom it may concern:" & BLANK  'Add a default greeting
    Else                                                        '...otherwise
        strLetter = strLetter & frmEntry!txtEntry(GREETING).Text & BLANK 'Add user's
                                                                'greeting
    End If
    strLetter = strLetter & frmEntry!txtEntry(BODY).Text & BLANK      'Add body text
    strLetter = strLetter & frmEntry!txtEntry(CLOSING).Text & BLANK    'Add the closing
                                                                'statement
    If frmEntry!txtEntry(ENCLOSURE).Text <> "" Then            'If there are enclosures
        strLetter = strLetter & "Encl: " & frmEntry!txtEntry(ENCLOSURE).Text & BLANK'Add
                                                                'them
    End If
    If frmEntry!txtEntry(CARBON).Text <> "" Then                'If there are Carbon Copies
        strLetter = strLetter & "CC:   " & frmEntry!txtEntry(CARBON).Text  'Add them
    End If
    frmLetter!txtPrintOut.Text = strLetter                     'Transfer letter for display
End Sub
```

3. Enter the following code to highlight text by changing its color. Note that this routine is generic, and that it will work with any control that has a ForeColor property.

```
Public Sub HiLite (controlName As Control)
    controlName.ForeColor = vbBlue                  'make ForeColor text blue
End Sub
```

4. Enter the following code to unhighlight the control by setting its ForeColor property back to the default Black.

```
Public Sub UnHiLite (controlName As Control)
    controlName.ForeColor = vbBlack                 'make ForeColor text back to default
Black
End Sub
```

How It Works

The Reference project demonstrates referencing through the creation of different kinds of letters. When the project opens, the user sees a list of the possible types of letters to create: introduction letter, acceptance letter, and general letter. The user chooses the type of letter, then selects the different letter options to include in the letter from the check boxes in the Letter Options frame. Each time the user selects one of these check boxes, Visual Basic asks for the required information. Once the user has selected all the required options and entered the information, he or she presses the Print Letter command button to display the letter on the screen. Figures 35-5, 35-6, and 35-7 show the project in action, with all three forms displayed.

Each element of the Reference project receives an identification name referenced throughout the program. Each form has its Name changed from the generic Form1, Form2, and Form3 to the more descriptive choices of frmMain, frmLetter, and frmEntry. Likewise, each control takes a more descriptive Name during the design phase.

When the program starts, frmMain displays on the screen, triggering the Form_Load event. This event loads the other two forms into memory, but does not display them. The frmEntry's Form_Load event creates an object array of seven txtEntry boxes to hold the seven parts of the letter. It uses the original txtEntry box as a template.

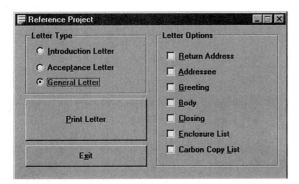

Figure 35-5 Reference form

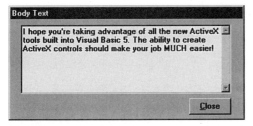

Figure 35-6 Data Entry form

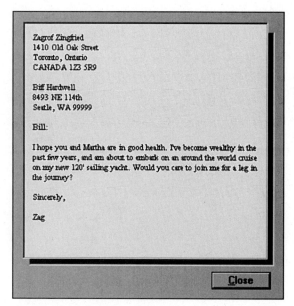

Figure 35-7   frmLetter form showing final product

When the user clicks a Letter Type option button, the option is highlighted by the HiLite subroutine. Note that we pass the control argument to the subroutine using the Screen.ActiveControl. The optLetter_Click event then enables or disables the appropriate check boxes in the Letter Options frame. After setting the check boxes, it grays out the check boxes that were checked but are now disabled, and checks those that were grayed out but are now enabled using the Controls collection.

Pressing any of the check boxes brings up frmEntry to begin data entry. (Note that we first test to see if the Click event was caused by the code in optLetter_Click setting and resetting the check boxes; if it was we ignore the click.)

Displaying frmEntry triggers the Form_Activate event, and we use that to bring the appropriate txtEntry box to the front of the stack with the Z-order method. See Chapter 38, "Graphics Fundamentals," for more information about the Z-order method. The caption of the parent form gets set with the Parent property. We then set the tab stops appropriately.

After the letter sections are properly filled in, clicking the cmdPrint button prints the letter. This just goes through each txtEntry box and adds its entry to the end of a temporary string. Note how we reference txtEntry's Text property by its complete name, frmEntry!txtEntry(Index).Text. Whenever you reference a control on another form, you need to use the complete specification with the form's name.

36

ACCESSING FORMS AND MENUS

Designing forms and menus visually and interactively is the heart of Visual Basic programming. Visual Basic 1.0 revolutionized Windows programming by letting you "paint" the entire user interface without writing any code. Visual Basic, versions 2.0 and 3.0, lets you easily design complex structures, such as a Multiple Document Interface (MDI), pop-up menus, and toolbars. Visual Basic 4.0 added the capability to hide an MDI child form using the AutoShowChildren property, Initiate and Terminate events that fire when forms and objects are created and destroyed, and fuller support for OLE objects and OLE automation using the various Negotiate properties. Visual Basic 5.0 adds a collection of templates that make adding the most commonly used forms automatic.

Prior to the release of Microsoft Visual Basic in May of 1991, form setup frequently required several pages of code. This made the process of setting up the forms and menus used by Windows applications a tedious chore. Languages like C need many hundreds of lines of code statements invoking functions with complex syntax to set up an application's forms. Even the familiar Hello World window required at least three pages of code. This complexity effectively placed Windows programming out of the reach of most users. Visual Basic replaced this complexity with its elegant simplicity.

This chapter covers the basics of forms and menus. It explores the properties, events, methods, and statements used with the two most critical elements of the user interface.

Forms and Form Setup

Most applications have several different forms that make up the foundation of the user interface. For example, databases have data entry, query, and report forms. A communications program might have a form with a list of phone numbers, and another to alert the user to problems. Many programs allow multiple documents at the same time. For instance, a spreadsheet might allow the user to have several macro sheets, spreadsheets, and charts open at once. The user interacts with each of these forms in specified ways.

Forms must be *loaded* into memory before they can be used. You can *unload* forms from memory when no longer needed, which frees memory for other operations. A loaded form must be explicitly *shown* to be made visible on the screen; the form will be automatically loaded into memory if it's not already present. A form can be *hidden* to make it disappear from the screen. Hidden forms still remain in memory, ready for reuse.

Setting up a form requires decisions about five major elements: the maximize button, the minimize button, the control box, the border, and the form's MDI status. These elements directly affect the ways the user will be able to manipulate the form. You can attach a menu structure to a form to allow the user to easily choose a variety of program functions. Finally, modern programs often place toolbars and status bars on a form to provide shortcuts for commonly used commands and status information on the program's operation.

Maximize and Minimize Buttons

Like a standard window, a Visual Basic form can be minimized to an icon, restored to its previous size, or maximized to the full screen. To maximize a form, press the maximize button in the upper-right corner of the form. To minimize a form, press the minimize button in the upper-right corner of the form. You control whether buttons appear on the form with the MinButton and MaxButton properties; both default to True, thus making them visible. Figure 36-1 shows a window's minimize button (on the left) and maximize button (on the right).

Control Box

The control box contains the commands that manipulate the basic appearance and position of the form. Set the form's ControlBox property to True to give a form a control box. The control box is a drop-down menu that Windows activates when the user presses the (SPACEBAR) or clicks on the control box in the upper-left corner of the form. The control box can have a combination of the following commands: Restore, Move, Size, Maximize, Minimize, Close, and Switch To.

The Maximize and Minimize options appear in the control box when their buttons are in the right corner of the form. Choosing one of these command options from the control box has the same effect as pressing the buttons. The Size option lets the user manually change the form's size. The Move option lets the user change the position of the form on the screen without using the mouse. The Close option removes the form from the screen and memory. The Switch To option brings Window's task switch box up on the screen. A typical control box is shown in Figure 36-2.

 Figure 36-1 The minimize and maximize buttons

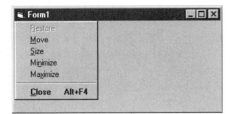

Figure 36-2 A Visual Basic form, showing the control box

Borders

Forms have four possible border styles: none, sizable, fixed single, and fixed double. A form with no border has no maximize button, minimize button, or control box. This border style is a popular choice for warning boxes, which do not need these options. Users can change the size of sizable forms, just as the name suggests. Both the fixed single and fixed double borders disable the user's ability to change the form's size with the mouse; however, the user can still minimize and maximize the form. Use the BorderStyle property to specify what kind of border the form will have.

MDI (Multiple Document Interface)

Windows programs such as Excel or Word can open multiple documents at the same time. Each new document (a spreadsheet, chart, text file, or formatted word processing file) is contained in and managed within the application. This gives the user the ability to cut and paste between documents, compare versions, or cut up large projects into smaller, more manageable pieces.

This feature is called the *Multiple Document Interface*, or *MDI*, and is available in Visual Basic starting with version 2.0. As you'll see in this chapter, MDI is simply an extension of the object variables discussed in Chapter 16, "Objects and Collections," and is surprisingly easy to manage. You'll learn how to create a complete MDI application, including an MDI-specific Window menu, a toolbar, and a status bar.

A Visual Basic application becomes MDI-capable by creating an MDI form with the Project menu's command Add MDI form. The MDI form functions as a container for multiple *child* forms. Each child form contains a single document type (such as unformatted text or a graphical chart) that you define using whatever controls you place on the child form. Specify other forms as children of the main MDI form by setting their MDI child property to True in the Properties box. Although there may be only one MDI form per application, you may have many kinds of child forms as well as regular non-MDI forms. For example, Excel has both worksheet and chart child forms in addition to a host of normal dialog boxes.

Create new child document forms by creating new instances as discussed in Chapter 16.

Display of Child Forms and Regular, Non-MDI forms

A regular, non-MDI form may display anywhere on the screen. A child form displays completely within the *client area* of the MDI form. The client area is inside the MDI form's borders, not including items like the menu bar, scrollbars, toolbars, or status bars. The user can move and resize the child form, but the child form is restricted to the client area.

When a child form is minimized, its icon appears at the bottom of the client area rather than at the bottom of the desktop as it does for a normal, non-MDI form. A maximized child form fills the entire client area and combines its caption with that of the MDI form, displaying it in the MDI form's title bar. A maximized regular, non-MDI form fills the entire screen.

During the design process, child forms are treated like other Visual Basic forms. This lets you move and resize child forms without restriction anywhere on the desktop. You write code, add controls, and set properties, as with any other form. Indeed, they are just regular forms with the one difference of having the MDI child property set to True.

You can tell if a form is a child form either by looking at the MDI child property in the Property window, or by looking at the Project window. Child forms have a special icon, shown in Figure 36-3.

Forms as Objects

Visual Basic considers forms objects. You can create multiple instances of forms and use any variables and functions that you declare Public in the form as if they were properties and methods of the form object. Once a form is added to the project, it appears in the Object Browser, along with any variables and functions that you declare Public. You can Dim generic form variables or Dim variables as specific forms, and you can create an instance of a form using the New statement, as shown in the code below.

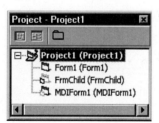

Figure 36-3 The Project window, showing a non-MDI form, an MDI child form, and an MDI form. Note the different icons for each.

```
Option Explicit

Dim frmForm As Form
Dim frmName As formName

Sub CreateForms ()
    Set frmForm = New formMisc 'create a new instance of formMisc
    Set frmName = New formName 'create a new instance of formName
    Load frmForm ' load the forms
    Load frmName
End Sub
```

The first Dim creates a generic form variable. The second Dim creates a variable of type formName. The variable frmForm can hold any type of form, while frmName can only be assigned forms of type formName. In the CreateForms sub, each variable is assigned a new instance of a form, formMisc for frmForm and formName for frmName. Once these objects are created, you can load them, make them visible, and generally treat them as forms, because they are forms. When you are finished with your form variables, you should set them to Nothing.

```
Sub DestroyForms ()
    Unload frmForm          'unload the form
    Set frmForm = Nothing 'free its resources
    Unload frmName
    Set frmName = Nothing
End Sub
```

This allows Visual Basic to free up the resources allocated to the forms you created in the CreateForms sub.

Initialize Event

The first time a form is loaded, Visual Basic fires the Initialize event. Visual Basic fires the Initialize event only when a form is created, so if you load and unload a form more than once, you only get one Initialize event. If you're using a form directly, Initialize fires the first time you load the form and never again. If you're using form variables, setting a form variable to Nothing destroys the form, so each time you create and load a new instance of a form you cause Visual Basic to fire the Initialize event.

Terminate Event

Terminate is to Initialize as Unload is to Load. Each time you destroy a form by setting it to Nothing, you cause the Terminate event to fire. Unlike the Unload or QueryUnload events, you have no way of causing Terminate to not unload the form, so Terminate is final. Like Initialize, Terminate only fires once, when the form is set to Nothing, and Terminate is always the last form event to fire.

Forms Collection

Each Visual Basic application has a Forms collection. This collection gives you access to each loaded form and all its controls, methods, and properties. You can use the For Each...Next statement to look at all the loaded forms easily. The Forms collection is covered in depth in Chapter 16 and in Chapter 35, "Accessing Forms and Controls."

Menus

Most Windows applications have a menu structure. A menu allows the user to access a number of different functions of the program. Typical menu systems have at least two levels: The top level displays on the menu bar, and the second level displays as a drop-down menu. A particular menu structure is always attached to an associated form. Each form may have its own unique menu structure.

Some menu structures have submenus branching off the second level; these allow further refinement of the actions available to the user. Visual Basic allows up to four levels of submenus. Be aware that deeply nested menu structures with many sublevels will confound the user and make your program hard to learn. If you find the need to have many choices available to the user, a dialog box usually makes for a clearer implementation.

Creating a Menu Structure

You create menus by clicking on the form with which you'd like to associate a menu and then choosing Menu Editor from the Tools menu (shortcut key: CTRL-E), by clicking the Menu Edit icon on the toolbar, or right-clicking on the form and selecting Menu Editor from the pop-up menu that appears. The options on the Menu Editor dialog box are explained in the sections that immediately follow. Figure 36-4 shows how to access the Menu Editor dialog box; Figure 36-5 shows the Menu Editor dialog box itself.

Caption

Caption indicates the text that appears on the menu. Place an ampersand in front of one of the caption's letters, indicating an accelerator key. For instance, Visual Basic's Tools menu has an ampersand placed in front of the T, which makes it read Tools, and makes ALT-T directly access the menu. Entering a hyphen (-) in the Caption text box places a *separator bar* in that menu position. Separator bars are thin lines that stretch across the width of the open menu to visually separate groups of related functions.

Name

Name refers to the Name property of the menu item, and serves as the name used in your code.

Figure 36-4 Accessing the Menu Editor from the Tools menu

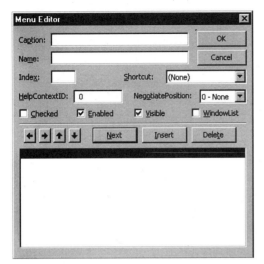

Figure 36-5 The Visual Basic 5.0 Menu Editor

Index

Use Index if you want to create a control array for the menu. You would use this if more than one menu item has the same name. There is an example of this in the Forms project at the end of this chapter.

Checked, Enabled, and Visible

Checked, Enabled, and Visible define the default state of the menu item you're creating. A *checked* menu option has a checkmark placed in front of it to indicate its on/off state. Use the Checked property to turn the check on and off in your application's code.

NegotiatePosition

Use NegotiatePosition with OLE objects to determine the placement of your program's menu items and an embedded OLE object's menus.

WindowList

WindowList creates an automatic list of all open MDI child windows. See "MDI Child Form Menus" later in this chapter for more details.

Shortcut

Shortcut defines a shortcut key (like CTRL-Q) associated with this menu entry, and HelpContextID lets you associate the entry with context-sensitive help.

The actual structure of the menu shows as indentation levels in the bottom window. No indentation is a top-level menu that displays on the title bar; each further indentation indicates one deeper level of submenu. You can easily control the level of indentation by highlighting the menu item and clicking on the arrows immediately above the Menu Editor's main window.

Using the Menu Structure

A Click event occurs when the user selects a menu item. Place any code you'd like to execute in the Click event procedure. For example:

```
Private Sub menuPatFileNew_Click ()
     'This routine sets up a new patient
     PatEntry.Show MODAL        'Show the entry dialog
End Sub
```

Pop-Up Menus

Visual Basic lets you use *pop-up menus* in your applications. A pop-up menu typically appears when the user clicks the nondefault (usually right) mouse button. Pop-ups are usually context sensitive, and will display options appropriate for the object the user was pointing to. For instance, a word processor may pop up a menu listing font choices, sizes, and styles when the user is editing text, and a different menu listing row height or column width adjustments when the user is editing a table.

Pop-up menus display when you use the PopupMenu method on a form. You specify what menu you want to display, and give the method optional parameters for exactly where it displays and how it behaves. The menu name can be either an existing menu that appears on a menu bar, or a custom menu designed specifically for that context. The menu you use must have at least one sublevel of menus; it is the sublevels that display in the pop-up.

Pop-up display routines are typically written in the MouseDown event. The program checks the Button parameter to see if the right mouse button is pressed before displaying the menu. The following example shows the menuWindow menu being popped up:

```
Private Sub Text1_MouseDown (Button As Integer, Shift As Integer, X As Single, Y As Single)
     If Button = vbRightButton Then
          PopupMenu menuWindow, 2  'pop up menu, OK to choose item w/right mouse button
     End If
End Sub
```

For more information about MouseDown, see Chapter 49, "Mouse Events." For more about the exact usage of the PopupMenu method, see its entry later in this chapter.

MDI Child Form Menus

Child forms display menus slightly differently from non-MDI forms. The child form's menus display on the parent MDI form's menu bar rather than on the child form. If no children are loaded (or the loaded children have no menus), then the MDI form displays its own menu.

Place menu controls that apply to a child form on the child form. If your application has more than one kind of document, create different child forms to perform the different functions, and supply each child form with its own menu.

An MDI application should have a special Window menu. This typically displays the captions of all child forms and lets the user rearrange the display with commands like Cascade, Tile, and Arrange Icons, as discussed in the Arrange method's entry and shown in Figure 36-6.

Although any menu control on an MDI form or child form can display the list of child forms, common Windows programming practice puts this list on the MDI form's Window menu. To display the list, simply set the WindowList property of that menu control to True. Visual Basic then automatically manages and displays the list of open child forms for you. It displays the captions of each child and places a checkmark next to the one that had the focus most recently. The WindowList property applies only to MDI forms and child forms; it has no effect on standard forms.

Toolbars and Status Bars

Many Windows applications contain toolbars, progress bars, control bars, and status bars. These provide easy access to commonly used commands and let you monitor the status of the application.

Visual Basic 5.0 includes toolbars, progress bars, and status bars. You will have to add Microsoft Windows Common Controls 5.0 in the Custom Controls dialog under the Project Menu to place them in the VB5 Toolbox.

To use one of these controls, place it on a regular non-MDI form, or the MDI form if you are creating an MDI application. The control box will automatically stretch to fill the width of the form. You can only place controls that support the Align property and controls that have no visible interface on an MDI form. The controls listed above and a few others, including the picture box, the DBGrid, and the data control, have that property. (Some third-party controls also support the Align property.) The Align property may be set to Top (=1) or Bottom (=2). (Left, Right, and None are included, but, as of this writing, do not work correctly.)

Use the property pages (Custom... in the properties window) to add buttons to a toolbar. If you plan to use images on the button faces, you must first add an ImageList control to the form and place the images in the list. If you want to use other controls on an MDI form, start by adding a picture box to the form. Place any controls you'd like on the picture box.

Figure 36-6 A typical Window menu

Toolbars are typically at the top of the form, and status bars are typically at the bottom. Figure 36-7 shows the example application for this chapter with these elements noted.

The coding for toolbars is usually very simple, as they most often repeat commands accessible from other areas of your application. When you have several different ways of executing a command (such as by a main menu, a child menu, a toolbar, and a dialog box) you can place the common code in its own sub procedure in a code module. For example:

```
Public Sub FileClose ()
    'This procedure is placed in a code module, and is called from several
    'different areas.
    Unload DocumentForm
End Sub

Private Sub menuMDIFileClose_Click ()
    FileClose
End Sub

Private Sub menuChildFileClose_Click ()
    FileClose
End Sub

Private Sub Toolbar1_ButtonClick(ByVal Button as ComctlLib.Button)
    Select Case Button.Key
        Case Is "Close"
            FileClose
        ' other buttons here
    End Select
End Sub

Private Sub cmndDialogFileClose_Click ()
    FileClose
End Sub
```

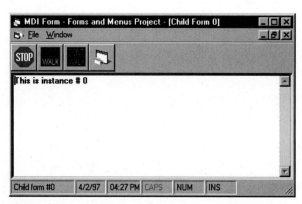

Figure 36-7 ToolBar and StatusBar on an MDI form

Forms and Menus Summary

Table 36-1 displays the methods, statements, events, and properties that control the basic setup of a form. Detailed descriptions of these elements follow Table 36-2.

Table 36-1 Methods, statements, properties, and events dealing with setting up a form

Use or Set This...	Type	To Do This...
Arrange	Method	Arrange MDI child forms within the MDI form
AutoShowChildren	Property	Control how MDI child forms are displayed
ControlBox	Property	Determine whether the control box appears on a form
Hide	Method	Make a form invisible on the screen
Initialize	Event	React when a form is created
Load	Event	React when a form loads into memory
Load	Statement	Load a form into memory but do not make it visible
MaxButton	Property	Determine whether the form has a maximize button
MDI child	Property	Determine whether a form is a child of the MDI form
MinButton	Property	Determine whether the form has a minimize button
PopupMenu	Method	Display a pop-up menu
QueryUnload	Event	React before a form is removed from memory
Resize	Event	React when a form's size changes
Show	Method	Make a form visible, and if necessary, load it into memory first
StartUpPosition	Property	Specify the initial position of a form when it is loaded
Terminate	Event	React when a form is set to Nothing
Unload	Event	React when a form is removed from memory
Unload	Statement	Remove a form from memory
WindowState	Property	Read or set whether a form is minimized, maximized, or normal

Constant Values

It is best to use named constants rather than numeric values when developing software. Named constants make your code more readable and easier to maintain.

Table 36-2 lists the values of the constants relevant to this chapter, mentions their names, and briefly describes what they mean. These constants can be viewed in the VB Constants module (or, in some cases, in other object libraries) using the Object Browser. It is not necessary to explicitly add these objects to your project. For more information on constant naming conventions, see Chapter 35.

Table 36-2 Constant values for forms and menus

Value	VB.Constants	Meaning
		Arrange Method
0	vbCascade	Cascade all nonminimized MDI child forms.
1	vbTitleHorizontal	Tile all nominimized MDI child forms horizontally.
2	vbTileVertical	Tile all nonminimized MDI child forms vertically.
3	vbArrangeIcons	Arrange the icons of all minimized MDI child forms.
		AutoShowChildren Property
-1	True	(Default) Automatically show MDI child forms when they're loaded.
0	False	Only show MDI child forms when Visible property is set to True.
		PopupMenu Method
0	vbPopupMenuLeftAlign	(Default) The left side of the pop-up menu is at x.
4	vbPopupMenuCenterAlign	The pop-up menu is centered at x.
8	vbPopupMenuRightAlign	The right side of the pop-up menu is at x.
0	vbPopupMenuLeftButton	(Default) The pop-up menu responds to the left mouse button only.
2	vbPopupMenuRightButton	The pop-up menu responds to both the left and right mouse buttons.
		UnloadMode Argument in QueryUnload Event
0	vbFormControlMenu	User chose the Close command from the control box.
1	vbFormCode	Unload event invoked in code.
2	vbAppWindows	Windows is ending.
3	vbAppTaskManager	Task Manager is closing the application.
4	vbFormMDIForm	MDI child form closing because the MDI form is closing.
		Show Method
0	vbModeless	(Default) Code after the Show method runs normally.
1	vbModal	Code after the Show method runs after the form closes.
		WindowState Property
0	vbNormal	Restores the form to the previous size.
1	vbMinimized	Reduces the form to an icon.
2	vbMaximized	Fills the screen (or client area for an MDI child) with the form.

ARRANGE METHOD

Objects Affected   MDI form

Purpose   Use the Arrange method on an MDI form to automatically arrange all MDI child forms contained within it. Tables 36-3 and 36-4 summarize the arguments of the Arrange method.

General Syntax

```
[Name.]Arrange setting%
```

Table 36-3 Arguments of the Arrange method

Argument	Description
Name	Name property of the MDI form
setting%	A value that specifies how to arrange the windows or icons

Table 36-4 Meanings of the setting% argument in the Arrange method

Value	VB.Constants	Meaning
0	vbCascade	Cascade all nonminimized MDI child forms.
1	vbTitleHorizontal	Tile all nonminimized MDI child forms horizontally.
2	vbTileVertical	Tile all nonminimized MDI child forms vertically.
3	vbArrangeIcons	Arrange the icons of all minimized MDI child forms.

Example Syntax

```
Private Sub menuWindow_Click (Index As Integer)
    Select Case Index
        Case 0: MDIForm.Arrange vbCascade
        Case 1: MDIForm.Arrange vbTileHorizontal
        Case 2: MDIForm.Arrange vbTileVertical
        Case 3: MDIForm.Arrange vbArrangeIcons
    End Select
End Sub
```

Description   An MDI application should have a special Window menu, which displays the captions of all child forms and lets the user rearrange the display with commands like Cascade, Tile, and Arrange Icons using the MDIForm's Arrange method. The Arrange method takes a numerical argument that determines how Windows will arrange the child windows. Note that only the MDIForm has the Arrange method; regular forms do not.

Common Windows programming practice puts the arrangement choices on their own Window menu, along with a list of all the open child forms. Set the menu's WindowList property to True to have Visual Basic automatically create and track a list of these child forms for you.

Example   The Forms project at the end of the chapter shows how to build a typical Window menu. It includes all four arrangement methods.

AutoShowChildren Property

Objects Affected	MDI form
Purpose	The AutoShowChildren property indicates whether an MDI child form may be hidden when it is loaded. Visual Basic 5.0 has the capability to load but not show an MDI Child form. Tables 36-5 and 36-6 describe the arguments and settings of the AutoShowChildren property.
General Syntax	

```
[Name].AutoShowChildren [= boolean%]
```

Table 36-5 Arguments of the AutoShowChildren property

Argument	Description
boolean%	An optional boolean expression that specifies whether MDI child forms are automatically visible. If not included, defaults to True.
Name	Name property of MDIForm.

Table 36-6 Meanings of the boolean% argument in the AutoShowChildren property

Setting	VB.Constants	Meaning
-1	True	(default) MDI forms are automatically displayed when loaded.
0	False	MDI child forms aren't automatically displayed when loaded.

Example Syntax

```
Private Sub Form_Load
    MDIForm1.AutoShowChildren = True
End Sub
```

Description	AutoShowChildren = False allows you to preload MDI child forms just as you can normal forms. This speeds up the appearance of the form when you finally display it and gives you the ability to keep a form in memory without losing any setting information or loaded controls. Forms hidden in this manner can still respond to coded events and any property changes or DDE conversations.
Comments	Forms loaded into memory use scarce Windows resources, and speed gains should be balanced against resources used.

CONTROLBOX PROPERTY

Objects Affected   Form

Purpose   The ControlBox property governs whether a control box appears in the top-left corner of a form. This property is read-only at runtime. Tables 36-7 and 36-8 summarize the meaning of the argument of the ControlBox property and the property's possible values.

General Syntax

```
[form.]ControlBox
```

Table 36-7 Argument of the ControlBox property

Argument	Description
form	Name property of the form (if no name is specified, then references the current form's ControlBox property)

Table 36-8 Possible values of ControlBox property

Value	Description
True, -1	(Default) Displays the control box
False, 0	Does not display the control box

Example Syntax

```
Public Sub SetColor (FormName As Form)
    If FormName.ControlBox=0 Then          'tests for disabled ControlBox on the form
        FormName.BackColor=RGB(192,192,192) 'form's background changes to gray
    Else
        FormName.BackColor=RGB(0,128,0)     'form's background changes to green
    End If
End Sub
```

Description   The ControlBox property manages the user's access to a drop-down command menu that contains options for sizing, closing, or moving the window. The control to access the menu can be selected with the mouse or keyboard. The control box is in a form's upper-left corner, as shown in Figure 36-2. A form's ControlBox property can only be set at design time. Any attempt to change the ControlBox property of a form at runtime will generate an error. You can, however, refer to the ControlBox property at runtime. In the example syntax, a sub procedure named SetColor uses the ControlBox property setting to decide the background color of a form.

BorderStyle, MaxButton, and MinButton Properties	The commands displayed on the control box include the familiar Restore, Move, Size, Minimize, Maximize, Close, and Switch To. Several properties affect the display of the control box when the ControlBox property is True. When the BorderStyle property of the form is 0 (none), the control box will not be displayed. If the MaxButton and MinButton properties of that form are False, then those commands will not appear on the control box. When the BorderStyle property of a form is 1 (fixed single) or 3 (fixed double), Size does not appear in the control box. As long as the ControlBox property of a form is True, both the Restore and Move commands will appear on the control box.
Example	The Forms project at the end of this chapter shows the difference between forms with and without the control box. The modal dialog box displays without the control box; all the other forms have a control box.
Comments	Notice that the control box can always be seen on a form at design time. It is only at runtime that you can see the effects of a ControlBox property set to False. This makes it easier to manipulate the forms while you're designing them.

HIDE METHOD

Objects Affected	Form, Forms collection, MDIForm
Purpose	The Hide method makes an active and visible form disappear from the screen and is the same as setting the form's Visible property to False (0). Table 36-9 summarizes the single argument of the Hide method.
General Syntax	

```
[form.]Hide
```

Table 36-9 Argument of the Hide method

Argument	Description
form	Name property of the form

Example Syntax

```
Private Sub Form1_Load ()
    Form2.Hide                      'hide form2
    Form2.BackColor = RGB(0,255,0)  'set background color of form2 to light green
    Form2.ForeColor = RGB(0,0,255)  'set the text color of form2 to blue
    MsgBox "Press OK to see form2"  'display MsgBox indicating press OK to see form2
    Form2.Show                      'unhide Form2
End Sub
```

Description	The Hide method reduces clutter by removing a form from the screen without removing it from memory. Any forms not initially needed can be loaded and hidden until desired. The Show method displays a hidden form on the screen. Hidden forms take a little more time to load at program startup, but can then be displayed very quickly. For example, a personal information manager might load up the address book, scheduler, and to-do list at program startup. This allows the user to switch quickly between the information found in each form. With this approach, each form displays in a fraction of the time necessary to load it.
	Hidden forms reside in the operating memory of the computer. A form's Visible property changes to False when the form is hidden with the Hide method. This method disconnects the form from user input. A hidden form can still respond to coded events and any resulting property changes or DDE (dynamic data exchange) communication. For example, a law firm's client data entry system could begin with the primary name and address form visible and the case detail form hidden. Events could place the information the user enters (such as a name) into the corresponding fields of the hidden data entry form.
The Show Method	The Hide method shares an inverse relationship with the Show method. Hide removes the form from sight and Show restores it. In the example syntax, the two methods work together to make a form invisible while its colors change. After making modifications, the Show method restores it to view. This technique also can be used for a warning dialog box that displays context-sensitive messages. If the form is not loaded, the Show method loads it into memory.
The Visible Property	When the Hide method makes a form invisible, the Visible property of the form becomes False. The difference between using the Hide method and directly changing the setting of the Visible property lies in the types of objects affected. The Hide method can only be used on a form. In contrast, the Visible property can be used on any of the objects in Visual Basic. This difference can be used in generic functions and procedures to limit an effect to forms, or to apply it to all objects.
Example	The Forms project at the end of this chapter demonstrates the Hide method several times. When the user closes either of the dialog boxes, the Hide method removes the form from the screen. A Hide method expression keeps the form in memory while taking it out of the user's view. In this case the Hide method is better than the Unload statement because it saves time displaying the form when it is needed again.
Comments	A hidden form or control can still have its properties changed or referenced. The amount of available operating memory determines the number of forms that can be hidden.

INITIALIZE EVENT

Objects Affected   ClassModule, Form, MDI form

Purpose   The Initialize event fires when a form, MDI form, or Class is first loaded into memory. Table 36-10 describes the arguments of the Initialize event.

General Syntax

```
Sub Form_Intialize()
Sub MDIForm_Intialize()
Sub Class_Initialize()
```

Table 36-10 Arguments of the Initialize event

Argument	Description
Form	'Form' (literal, not the Name property of the form) specifies the normal or MDI child form.
MDIForm	'MDIForm' (literal, not the Name property of the MDI form) specifies the MDI form.
Class	'Class' (literal, not the Name property of the class) specifies the class.

Example Syntax

```
Private Sub Form_Intialize
   'Initialize the database
   me!data1.DatabaseName = "C:\NADDB\NAD.MDB"
   me!data1.datasource = "Name and Addresses"
   redim NADTable(1 to 10)  'start out with 10 names and addresses
End Sub
```

Description   The Initialize event fires when a form is loaded into memory using a Load statement, when the startup form for a project is loaded, or when an instance of an object is loaded with the New keyword. The Initialize event is used to initialize any information used by a form or object. Initialize occurs before Load, and occurs only once during the lifetime of a form or object.

The Terminate Event The Terminate and Initialize events have an inverse relationship. Where the Initialize event occurs when a form or object is created, the Terminate event occurs when a form or object is destroyed. You destroy a form or object by setting it to Nothing, which you do after unloading it in the case of a form. Terminate is the last event in the lifetime of an object. Terminate occurs after Unload.

LOAD EVENT

Objects Affected   Form, MDI form

Purpose   The Load event loads a form into memory and specifies what actions occur when it loads. Table 36-11 summarizes the arguments of the Load event.

General Syntax

```
Private Sub Form_Load ()
Private Sub MDIForm_Load ()
```

Table 36-11 Arguments of the Load event

Argument	Description
Form	'Form' (literal, not the Name property of the form) specifies the normal or MDI child form.
MDIForm	'MDIForm' (literal, not the Name property of the MDIForm) specifies the MDI form.

Example Syntax

```
Private Sub Form_Load ()
     Dir1.Path = "\WINWORD"        'sets the initial path to the Winword directory
     File1.Path = Dir1.Path        'makes File box's path same as Directory box
     File1.FileName = "*.DOC"          'Limits the types of files displayed to the⇐
                                        "DOC" extension
     Text1.Text = File1.Path       'displays current path in the text window
End Sub
```

Description   The Form_Load event procedure initializes the form and any related variables when the form loads. Text boxes may have their initial information inserted. List and combo boxes can be given their lists for the user to choose from. A letter-writing program might prompt the user to select a name from its database. Any option or check box controls may be set to their initial values. The drive, directory, and file boxes get their default Path and FileName properties in the Form_Load event of the example syntax. This relieves the user of changing to the correct drive and directory. In the example syntax, the File1 file box displays only files with the .DOC extension. Figure 36-8 shows what this form and its controls might look like.

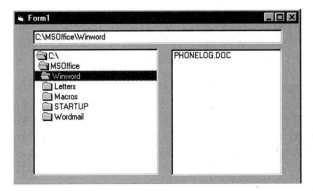

Figure 36-8 Appearance of the example syntax in Form_Load event

A loaded form is in memory but cannot be seen by the user. A form's Load event takes place in three ways. First, any forms loaded at program startup initiate a Form_Load event. Second, Visual Basic generates a Form_Load event when a form is loaded programmatically, using a Load statement. Third, any change or reference made to a property of an "unloaded" control or form loads the form and triggers the Form_Load event. For example, a calculator might have a Form_Load event that changes the Text property of the readout text box to 0. When the user presses a command button labeled Tape, a second form might be loaded below the calculator on the screen. The second form's Load event places the last few calculations made in its display text window.

The Load, Resize, Paint, and GotFocus Events

If more than one event is attached to a particular control, the events are processed in the following order: Load, Resize, Paint, and GotFocus. This is an important point to keep in mind if any of the actions that take place in one event depend upon the result of actions in another event. For example, a data entry form for an address book would have problems if the Load event disabled the Address1 text box, and the GotFocus event tried to use it.

The Unload Event

The Load event shares an inverse relationship with the Unload event. While the Load event affects the form when opened, the Unload event takes place when it is closed. Both events can depend on each other. For example, the Load event might set up the form to initiate some action. The Unload event could either restore the form to its preloaded settings or process the actions that took place. The address book, for example, might use the Load event to insert the last accessed information into the edit screen. An Unload event might save the information entered into the fields to the database.

Initialize Event

The Initialize event occurs once during the life of a form, when the form is first loaded. You should use the Initialize event to perform housekeeping routines such as initializing variables, opening data access objects, or building any dynamic arrays you might need during your form's lifetime. For example, you can get the database name from an .INI file or the system registry, and initialize a Data Access Object used by the form. The Initialize event occurs before the Load event when Visual Basic first loads the form into memory.

Terminate Event

The Terminate event shares an inverse relationship with the Initialize event. While the Initialize event occurs when a form is first loaded into memory, the Terminate event occurs when a form is finally removed from memory. The Terminate event occurs when a form is destroyed by setting it to Nothing, or when a program ends. Unlike the Unload or QueryUnload events, the Terminate event cannot be canceled to cause a form to remain in memory. Use the Terminate event for final cleanup, such as saving .INI or registry information.

Example   •   The Forms project at the end of the chapter demonstrates the Load event. When the MDI form loads at program startup, the Load event defines the current contents of the program variables and sets up the child forms. This initialization works best here because the Load event is always the first event to be processed when more than one event is called at the same time.

LOAD STATEMENT

Objects Affected   Form, MDI form, or any control

Purpose   The Load statement directly places a form or control into memory without making it visible to the user. Table 36-12 summarizes the meaning of the object argument.

General Syntax

```
Load object
```

Table 36-12 Argument of the Load statement

Argument	Description
object	Name property of the item to be loaded

Example Syntax

```
Private Sub Form_Load ()            'form1's load event
    Load Form2                      'Load form2, but don't display
End Sub

Private Sub Command1_Click ()       'created on Form1
    Form2.Visible = True            'display Form2 now
End Sub

Private Sub Form_Load ()
    optnAuto(0).Caption = "GM"      'existing control created at design time
    optnAuto(0).Top = 200
    Load optnAuto(1)                'create new control in array at runtime
    optnAuto(1).Caption = "Ford"
    optnAuto(1).Top = 600
    optnAuto(0).Visible = True      'Display these option
    optnAuto(1).Visible = True      'buttons on the screen.
End Sub
```

Description   The Load statement loads forms and controls into memory without displaying them. Once a form loads into memory, you can quickly unhide it by changing the Visible property of the form or control to True (-1) or using the Show method. While a form is in memory, its properties can be accessed and changed. The second example listed in the example syntax uses the Load statement to create new controls for the optnAuto control array. Figure 36-9 shows this form at design time, and Figure 36-10 shows the additional option button created in the code at runtime.

The single argument used for this statement is the object. An object argument can be the Name property of a form, control, or control array. A form or control remains in memory until taken out by an Unload statement or until the program or parent form closes.

The Show Method   The Load statement and the Show method have similar functions for Visual Basic forms, but the difference between them is very important. The Load statement does not make the forms that it brings into memory visible to the user. The Show method loads the form into memory, if it hasn't already been loaded, and makes it visible to the user. A Load statement allows you to preload a form without displaying it. The amount of time required to bring up new screens can be reduced by loading all the necessary forms before they are needed.

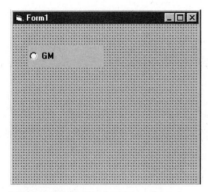

Figure 36-9   Single object forms a "template" for a control array

Figure 36-10   Multiple objects in control array loaded into memory

Example

In the Forms project at the end of this chapter, the Load statement loads the two dialog boxes into memory at program startup. In this case the Load statement is a better choice than a Show method because it does not make the form visible on the screen. This reduces screen clutter and makes it less likely for the user to be confused when confronted with two forms at once.

Comments

Multiple instances of a particular control can be made visible on a form by setting up a control array and giving each control a unique array number. This is useful for standardizing the events for a particular type of control. For example, an option box can be set up and loaded initially as a control array. Each instance of the control array can be made visible, and can have a different label.

When you use the Load statement to load a control, there must already be at least one such control on the form, and it must be part of a control array. The new control is invisible and positioned atop the "pattern" control. Change the new control's Top (and perhaps Left) property before you change its Visible property.

MAXBUTTON PROPERTY

Objects Affected Form

Purpose The MaxButton property controls whether the maximize icon button appears in the top-right corner of a form at runtime. Clicking this button maximizes the form, making it fill the entire screen. The MaxButton property is read-only at runtime. Table 36-13 summarizes the argument of the MaxButton property. Figure 36-11 shows the MaxButton of a form that is normalized. Figure 36-12 shows the MaxButton of a maximized form.

General Syntax

```
[form.]MaxButton
```

Figure 36-11 The maximize button of a normalized form. Pressing it maximizes the form.

Figure 36-12 The maximize button of a maximized form. Pressing it restores the form to its normal size.

Table 36-13 Argument of the MaxButton property

Argument	Description
form	Name property of the form (if no name is specified, then references the current form's MaxButton property)

Example Syntax

```
Private Sub WindowLoad (FormName As Form)
    If FormName.MaxButton = True Then      'checks for enabled Maximize button
        FormName.WindowState = 2           'maximizes the specified form
    Else
        FormName.WindowState = 0           'normalizes the specified form
    End If
End Sub
```

Description	The MaxButton property of a form controls whether a form displays a maximize button in the top-right corner. A form's MaxButton property can only be set at design time. Any attempt to change the MaxButton property of a form at runtime generates an error. You can, however, read the MaxButton property at runtime. The example syntax uses a form's MaxButton setting to determine whether to maximize or normalize a form. This is a generic procedure that can be used on more than one form of a program. The MaxButton property defaults to True. Note that an MDIForm always has a maximize button, and does not have the MaxButton property. Figures 36-11 and 36-12 show what the maximize buttons of maximized and normalized forms look like.
The BorderStyle and WindowState Properties	The BorderStyle property of a form also affects the appearance of the maximize control. If the BorderStyle of a form is either 0 (none) or 3 (fixed double), then the maximize button will not display with either setting. With BorderStyle 3, if the MaxButton property is True, then the Maximize command will appear in the control box of the form even though there is no maximize button. No matter what the settings of the MaxButton and BorderStyle properties are, you can still maximize a form using the WindowState property, as shown in the example syntax. A form's BorderStyle property has no effect on the form's capability to be maximized.
Example	The Forms project at the end of this chapter shows the difference between a form with and without the maximize button. The modal dialog box displays without a maximize button, while other forms have one.
Comments	Remember that the absence of the maximize button on a form does not prevent the form from being maximized by the user if the maximize option appears in the control box menu.

MDI CHILD PROPERTY

Objects Affected   Form

Purpose   The MDI child property defines whether a form is a regular, non-MDI form or an MDI child form. The MDI child property is read-only at run-time. Tables 36-14 and 36-15 describe the argument and settings of the MDI child property.

General Syntax

```
[Form.]MDI child
```

Table 36-14 Argument of the MDI child property

Argument	Description
Form	Name property of the form

Table 36-15 Settings of the MDI child property

Setting	Description
True	The form is an MDI child form.
False	The form is a normal, non-MDI form.

Example Syntax

```
Private Sub MDIForm_Load ()
    Dim childForm as New Form1          'set Form1's MDI child property to True
    childForm.Show                      'display the newly created Child form
    If childForm.MDI child = True Then
        MsgBox "This is a child form"   'always true if Form1.MDI child is True
    End If
End Sub
```

Description   The MDI parent form functions as a container for multiple child forms. Flag other forms as children of the main MDI form by setting their MDI child property to True. Although there may be only one MDI form per application, you may have many kinds of child forms, as well as normal, non-MDI forms. For example, Excel has both worksheet and chart child forms, as well as a host of normal dialog boxes.

A regular, non-MDI form may display anywhere on the screen. A child form displays completely within the client area of the MDI form. The client area is inside the MDI form's borders, not including items like the menu bar, scrollbars, toolbars, or status bars. The user can move and resize the child form, but it is restricted to the client area. When a child form is minimized, its icon appears at the bottom of the client area rather than at the bottom of the desktop as it would for a normal, non-MDI form. A maximized child form fills the entire client area, combines its caption with the MDI form's, and displays it in the MDI form's title bar. In contrast, a maximized regular, non-MDI form fills the entire screen.

Minimizing the MDI parent form puts its icon at the bottom of the desktop just as with any application. All child forms are contained within the MDI form, so there are no additional icons on the desktop for them.

A regular, non-MDI form's menu (if it has one) displays directly below its title bar. A child form's menus display on the MDI form's menu bar. The only time the MDI form's own menus display is when there are no child forms open. For example, closing all documents in Excel removes most menus and leaves only an abbreviated File menu and Help menu. This is the MDI parent form's menu. Switching between a worksheet and chart changes the menus to reflect the choices available in the two different child forms. See the sections on menus at the beginning of this chapter for more on menu design.

During the design process, child forms are treated like other Visual Basic forms. You write code, add controls, and set properties as with any other form. Indeed, they are just regular forms, with the one difference of having the MDI child property set to True. One of the few exceptions to this is that MDI child forms cannot be modal—they are always modeless.

Create a new MDI child form by declaring it in a Dim statement as in the example syntax. This creates an MDI child form using Form1 as a template, assuming Form1 has its MDI child property set to True. The example project at the end of this chapter shows a more complete method of creating and tracking MDI child forms. Note that the MDI child property is read-only at runtime.

Borders, Positioning, and Control

If a child form's borders are sizable (BorderStyle=2), Windows determines the height and width based on the size of the parent MDI form. If the child's StartPostion property is -'0' - vbStartUpManual, Windows also determines the form's position; otherwise, the start position is determined by the StartPostion property. If a child's borders are fixed (BorderStyle=0, 1, or 3), then it is loaded with the Height and Width of its design-time properties.

You can disable the child form's control box, minimize button, and maximize button by setting these properties to False. The control box and sizing buttons will still appear on the form even though they won't respond to user clicks. A disabled control box can still drop down (using ALT -) but won't have the Close and Next Window commands available.

Loading and Unloading

Loading and unloading child forms is somewhat more involved than loading a regular, non-MDI form. Loading a child form automatically loads its parent MDI form. However, loading the parent MDI form does not automatically load any children. If you want to automatically load a blank document into your application, specify the child form as the default start up form.

If a child form's borders are sizable (BorderStyle=2), Windows determines the height and width based on the size of the parent MDI form. The only way to exactly size a child form is by using the Width and Height properties discussed in Chapter 33, "Application Appearance," after the form is loaded. If a child's borders are fixed (BorderStyle=0, 1, or 3), then it is loaded with the Height and Width of its design-time properties.

A child form unloads when it is closed from its control box, an Unload command is performed on it, or its parent MDI form closes. The parent MDI form may be closed for a variety of reasons: it might be closed by its control box, within code triggered by a File Exit command, by the Windows Task Manager, or by Windows shutting down.

Use the QueryUnload event to perform any cleanup necessary before unloading a child form. This event is invoked before the form unloads (in the event of the MDI form or application being closed) and provides a means of stopping the whole unloading process. A typical use for this is to let the user save changes to a document. The following example uses the global variable ChangedText to check whether to prompt the user to save before closing:

```
Private Sub Form_QueryUnload (Cancel As Integer, UnloadMode As Integer)
    If ChangedText Then                     'ChangedText flags changes to this child's data
        Msg = "Document has changed.  Save Changes?"
        SaveChange = MsgBox(Msg, vbexclamation + vbYesNoCancel)
        Select Case SaveChange
        Case vbCancel                           'user chooses cancel; stop unloading process
            Cancel = True
        Case vbYes                              'save the file and continue unloading
            FileSave                            'save the document!
            Cancel = False
        Case vbNo                               'user chooses no save; continue unloading
            Cancel = False
        End Select
    End If
End Sub
```

Example   The Forms project at the end of the chapter uses MDI child forms in addition to normal, non-MDI forms. A button on the main MDI form's toolbar lets you create multiple instances of the MDI child form.

MinButton Property

Objects Affected   Form

Purpose   The MinButton property controls whether the minimize button will appear in the top-right corner of a form at runtime. The MinButton property is read-only at runtime. Table 36-16 summarizes the form argument of the MinButton property.

General Syntax

```
[form.]MinButton
```

Table 36-16 Argument of the MinButton property

Argument	Description
form	Name property of the form (if no name is specified, then references the current form's MinButton property)

Example Syntax

```
Private Sub FormSize (FormName As Form)
    If FormName.MinButton = True Then        'checks for enabled Minimize button
        FormName.WindowState = 1             'minimizes the specified form
    Else
        FormName.WindowState = 0             'normalizes the specified form
    End If
End Sub
```

Description The MinButton property of a form determines whether a form displays its minimize control button in the top-right corner of the form. A form's MinButton property can only be set at design time. Any attempt to change the MinButton property of a form at runtime will generate an error. You can, however, refer to the MinButton property at runtime. The example above uses the setting of the MinButton property of a form to determine whether the form will appear in normal or minimized size. This function is generic so that it can be used for all the forms of a program to establish a standard setup.

Figure 36-13 shows how the minimize button appears on a form. There are two possible settings for the MinButton property: True (-1) and False (0). True is the default value for all forms.

The presence of the MinButton control determines whether the user will be able to use the minimize button to reduce the size of the form down to the icon symbol designated for it. The MinButton property is a useful tool for removing this ability from the user in cases where minimizing the form would be inappropriate.

The BorderStyle and WindowState Properties The BorderStyle property of a form also affects the appearance of the minimize control. If the BorderStyle of a form is either 0 (none) or 3 (fixed double), then the minimize button will not be displayed with either setting. As long as the MinButton property is True and the BorderStyle of the

Figure 36-13 The minimize button.
Pressing it minimizes the form

form is 3 (fixed double), the Minimize command will still appear in the control box of a form. No matter what the setting for the MinButton or BorderStyle properties is, a form can still be minimized using the WindowState property, as shown in the example syntax. A form's BorderStyle property has no effect upon the form's capability to be mini mized. For example, a form with a MinButton property set to False (0) and a BorderStyle of 3 (fixed double) can still be minimized using this statement:

```
Form.WindowState = 2
```

Example   The Forms project at the end of the chapter demonstrates the differences between forms with and without the minimize button. The modal dialog box does not have a minimize button, while all other forms do.

Comments   Remember that the absence of the MinButton on a form does not prevent the user from minimizing a form if the Minimize command appears in the control box menu.

POPUPMENU METHOD

Objects Affected   Form

Purpose   The PopupMenu method displays a *pop-up menu*. These menus can appear anywhere on the form, and are generally context sensitive. Most applications display them when the right mouse button is clicked. Tables 36-17 and 36-18 show the arguments and values for the PopupMenu method.

General Syntax

```
[form.]PopupMenu menuName[, flags%[, x![, y!]]]
```

Table 36-17 Arguments of the PopupMenu method

Arguments	Description
form	Name property of the form.
menuName	Name property of the menu to display.
flags%	Defines the general location and behavior of the menu.
x!, y!	Defines the exact location of the menu.
0	vbPopupMenuLeftAlign(default). The left side of the pop-up menu is at x.
4	vbPopupMenuCenterAlign. The pop-up menu is centered at x.
8	vbPopupMenuRightAlign. The right side of the pop-up menu is at x.

Table 36-18 Values for the flags% argument in the PopupMenu method

flags%	VB.Constants	Meaning
0	vbPopupMenuLeftButton	(Default) The pop-up menu responds to the left mouse button only.
2	vbPopupMenuRightButton	The pop-up menu responds to both left and right mouse buttons.

Example Syntax

```
Private Sub Text1_MouseDown (Button As Integer, Shift As Integer, X As Single, Y As Single)
    If Button = vbRightButton Then
        PopupMenu menuWindow, vbPopupMenuRightButton
    End If
End Sub
```

Description   A pop-up menu typically appears when the user clicks the nondefault (usually right) mouse button. Pop-ups are usually context sensitive, and display options appropriate for the object the user clicked. For instance, a word processor may pop up a menu listing font choices, sizes, and styles when the user is editing text, and a different menu listing row height or column width adjustments when the user is editing a table.

Pop-up menus are modal. No code executes, nor can the focus shift from the menu until the user selects a menu item or dismisses the menu with (ESC) or by clicking outside of the menu. If the user selects a menu option, the code in that menu's Click event runs before returning control to the routine that called PopupMenu.

Pop-up menus display when you use the PopupMenu method on a form. You specify what menu you want to display, and give the method optional parameters for exactly where it displays and how it behaves. The menu name you give can be either an existing menu that appears on a menu bar, or a custom menu designed specifically for that context. The name you give must have at least one sublevel of menus; it is the sublevels that actually display in the pop-up.

Define a custom menu structure for your pop-ups by making a standard menu structure and setting each menu element's Visible property to False. (See the sections that discuss menus at the beginning of this chapter for more about defining a menu structure.) This prevents the custom menus from displaying on the menu bar along with the normal menus. PopupMenu ignores the Visible property, and will still display your custom pop-up menus.

You typically write a pop-up display routine in the MouseDown event, and display the menu if the right mouse button is pressed. The example syntax shows this, and Figure 36-14 illustrates what this example might look like. For more information about MouseDown, see Chapter 49.

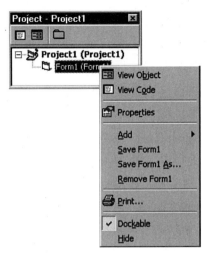

Figure 36-14 Pop-up menus are typically activated by a right mouse click, and are context sensitive

The default position of the pop-up menu is with the menu's top-left corner placed at the current mouse position. You can modify this behavior in a general way and you can also set very specific placement. The flags% argument specifies left alignment (the default), centered, or right alignment. You can also specify the exact location with the x! and y! arguments. These are in the ScaleMode of the form. For more detail about ScaleMode, see Chapter 37, "The Coordinate System." See the section "Forms and Menus Summary" at the beginning of this chapter for instructions on how to use the built-in Visual Basic constants.

Pop-ups default to accepting only the left (or default) mouse button clicks just as regular menus do. If you pop the menu up with a right mouse click, as most applications do, it's more convenient for the user to enable either the right or the left mouse buttons for choosing menu items. Specify vbPopupMenuRightButton in the flags% argument to allow the menu to respond to either button.

Example   The Forms project at the end of this chapter uses the PopupMenu method to display a pop-up menu that helps manage the MDI child documents.

Comments   Context-sensitive pop-up menus have become a feature of many commercial programs that users have come to expect. The PopUpMenu method gives you the ability to easily add this user-friendly feature to your programs when needed.

QUERYUNLOAD EVENT

Objects Affected   Form, MDI form

Purpose   The QueryUnload event lets you react to an attempt to Unload a form. This allows you to perform any necessary cleanup (like saving unsaved data) and possibly query the user before any form is Unloaded. Tables 36-19 and 36-20 show the arguments and settings for the QueryUnload event.

General Syntax

```
Sub Form_QueryUnload(Cancel as Integer, UnloadMode as Integer)
Sub MDIForm_QueryUnload(Cancel as Integer, UnloadMode as Integer)
```

Table 36-19 Arguments of the QueryUnload event

Argument	Description
Form	'Form' (literal, not the Name property of the form) specifies the normal or MDI child form.
MDIForm	'MDIForm' (literal, not the Name property of the MDIForm) specifies the MDI form.
Cancel	Set this to True to stop the QueryUnload event for all loaded forms.
UnloadMode	Shows the reason for the QueryUnload event.

Table 36-20 Values of the UnloadMode argument

Value	VB.Constants	Description
0	vbFormControlMenu	User chose the Close command from the control box.
1	vbFormCode	Unload event invoked in code.
2	vbAppWindows	Windows is ending.
3	vbAppTaskManager	Task Manager is closing the application.
4	vbFormMDIForm	MDI child form closing because the MDI form is closing.

Example Syntax

```
Private Sub Form_QueryUnload (Cancel As Integer, UnloadMode As Integer)
    Dim Msg, SaveChange
    If ChangedText Then                       'Use Global variable to flag changes to document
        Msg = "Document has changed.  Save Changes?"
        SaveChange = MsgBox(Msg, vbexclamation + vbYesNoCancel)
        Select Case SaveChange
        Case vbCancel                         'user chooses cancel; stop unloading process
            Cancel = True
        Case vbYes                            'save the file and continue unloading
            FileSave                          'save the document!
            Cancel = False
        Case vbNo                             'user chooses no save; continue unloading
            Cancel = False
```

```
        End Select
    End If
End Sub
```

Description The Form_QueryUnload and MDIForm_QueryUnload events specify what actions take place when an attempt is made to close a form. All forms close automatically at the end of the program, and closing an MDI form closes all child forms. An Unload statement can also close a form. Use this event to give the user a final chance to prevent ending the program or to ask about cleanup procedures. In the example syntax, a MsgBox statement in the QueryUnload event asks the user if he or she wants to save files before exiting.

There is an advantage to placing certain routines in a QueryUnload event rather than linking them to a command button or placing them in the Unload event. Using a QueryUnload event provides users with a safety net that will prevent them from forgetting to save a file or forgetting to enter important information in a data entry field. In MDI applications, using the QueryUnload event rather than the Unload event gives the user a chance to stop the entire unloading process before any forms are unloaded, which might be important if there are multiple child forms.

The UnloadMode argument gives the reason for the event. You may want to take different actions, depending on the reason that the form is unloading. Visual Basic defines these values; see "Constant Values" at the beginning of this chapter for instructions on how to use the Visual Basic constant values.

Setting Cancel to True will cancel the Unload event for all forms. If the user cancels the Unload operation, then all forms remain open as they were before the QueryUnload. Contrast this with putting the same cleanup code in the Unload event: Some forms might be unloaded before the user cancels the process. This is particularly critical for MDI applications.

Example The Forms project at the end of the chapter uses a QueryUnload event for each child form. This event presents a message box asking whether the user wishes to save any changed documents.

Comments The QueryUnload event occurs first in an MDI form and then in all other forms. If no form cancels the QueryUnload event, all other forms are unloaded before the MDI form.

RESIZE EVENT

Objects Affected Data, Form, Forms collection, MDIForm, OLE container, PictureBox, UserControl, UserDocument

Purpose The Resize event specifies what actions take place when the user resizes a form or picture box, or when the form or picture box first becomes visible. This event can be triggered by anything that brings the object into the user's sight or changes its size. Table 36-21 shows the arguments of the Resize event.

General Syntax

```
Sub Form_Resize ()
Sub MDIForm_Resize ()
```

Table 36-21 Arguments of the Resize event

Argument	Description
Form	'Form' (literal, not the Name property of the form) specifies the normal or MDI child form.
MDIForm	'MDIForm' (literal, not the Name property of the MDIForm) specifies the MDI form.

Example Syntax

```
Private Sub Form_Load ()
    For i = 1 To 40           'generates 40 line items in the List1 list box
        List1.AddItem "Line " + Str$(i)
    Next i
End Sub

Private Sub Form_Resize ()
    List1.Move 25, 25, ScaleWidth-50 ,ScaleHeight-25 'fill Form1 with List1
End Sub
```

Description   When your program changes the WindowState, Visible, Height, or Width properties of a form, Visual Basic triggers a Resize event. This event is also triggered any time a form loads with the Load or Show statements. The user can also trigger this event by changing the size of the form with the mouse. You can use the Resize event to adjust the position of controls on a form after the form's size has changed. Sometimes changes to the WindowState, Visible, Height, and Width properties make it necessary to adjust the position of controls on the same form. In the syntax example, each time the Form1 form's height or width changes, the Form_Resize event adjusts the height and width of the List1 list box. This makes List1 fill the surface of the form. Figures 36-15 and 36-16 illustrate how this might look.

Example   The Resize event in the Forms project at the end of this chapter controls the size and placement of the Text1 control within the child form. When the form's size changes, the Resize event adjusts the size of the text box to completely fill the internal area of the child form. This shows how a form's controls can be adjusted to compensate for changes in the form's size.

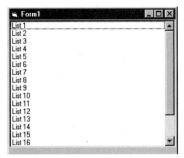

Figure 36-15 Form1 with List1 list box filling it after the Resize event

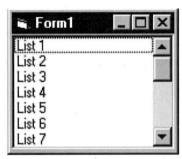

Figure 36-16 Form1 and List1 made smaller. Note that List1 still fills Form1.

The ScaleWidth and ScaleHeight Properties

The ScaleWidth and ScaleHeight properties of a form serve as references. Each control's size is a fraction of the values of the ScaleWidth and ScaleHeight properties. In the example syntax, the Move statement refer ences these properties to change the size of a control. This is a very basic example of this technique; the Forms project at the end of this chapter shows this process in further detail. The ScaleWidth and ScaleHeight properties are the *usable* area of a form or other object. The difference between the Width property, for example, and the ScaleWidth property is the border width of the object.

Comments

The Resize event takes place every time a form loads, resizes, or displays on the screen.

STARTUPPOSITION PROPERTY

Objects Affected   Form

Purpose   The StartUpPosition property specifies where a form is shown on the screen when it is first loaded. Table 36-22 shows the arguments of the property, and Table 36-23 lists the settings for StartUpPosition.

General Syntax

```
object.StartUpPosition = p!
```

Table 36-22 Arguments of the StartUpPosition property

Argument	Description
object	The Form to be positioned
p!	An integer specifying the desired position

Table 36-23 Values of the p! argument of the StartUpPosition property

Argument	Description
'0' - vbStartUpManual	Windows decides where to position the form (default)
'1' - vbStartUpOwner	Center in the object to which the form belongs
'2' - vbStartUpScreen	Center on the screen
'3' - vbStartUpWindowsDefault	Positions the form in the upper-left corner

Example Syntax

```
frmMsg.StartUpPosition = vbStartUpScreen
```

Description   The example syntax programatically sets the StartUpPosition of frmMsg to the center of the screen. Usually, you will set the StartUpPosition during design time rather than in code.

Example   In the Forms project at the end of this chapter, the modal form's StartUpPosition is set to '2' - vbStartUpScreen at design time.

Comments   If you use the Form Layout window after setting a form's StartUpPosition property, the property will be changed back to '0' - vbStartUpManual. Although the property is visible in the Properties window of MDI child forms, the only legal value is '0' - vbStartUpManual. If you attempt to change it in your code, an error will be raised.

The Load, Resize, Paint, and GotFocus Events   If there is more than one event attached to a particular control, they are processed in the following order: Load, Resize, Paint, and GotFocus. This is an important point to keep in mind if any of the actions that take place in one event are based upon actions in another event. For example, a data entry form for an address book will have problems if the Form_Load event disables the Address1 text box. If the Form_GotFocus event subsequently attempts to define the Address1 text box's contents, this raises an error. See Chapter 54, "Application Focus," for more on GotFocus and LostFocus events.

SHOW METHOD

Objects Affected   Form , Forms collection, MDIForm

Purpose   The Show method loads a form into memory and displays it on the screen. Tables 36-24 and 36-25 summarize the arguments of the Show method.

General Syntax

```
[form.]Show [style%]
```

Table 36-24 Arguments of the Show method

Argument	Description
form	Name property of the form
style%	Value representing whether to load the form in modal or modeless format

Table 36-25 Possible settings of the style% argument of the Show method

style%	VB.Constants	Description
0	vbModeless	(Default) Code after the Show method runs normally
1	vbModal	Code after the Show method runs after the form closes

Example Syntax

```
Private Sub Command1_Click ()
    Form1.Show vbModeless        'display modeless form
    Text1.Text = ""              'change text property of Text1 to blank
    Form1.Hide                   'hide DataForm
    Show vbModal                 'show current form modally
End Sub
```

Description   The Show method lets you load and display a form on the screen, or display an already loaded form. A form remains in memory until it is removed using an Unload statement or until the program ends. For example, a data entry program could load all of its secondary forms into memory when the program starts. Later the program's main menu could use the Show method to quickly display a form that is needed.

A Show method statement can begin with the Name property of the form. If Show does not specify a form, then the current form appears. A Show method has either a modeless or modal style. The default setting is modeless. Modal forms block the execution of any code until you remove a form from sight. (This also has the effect of preventing the user from changing the focus to another form.) Forms shown in modeless style will allow other code to run.

Modeless Versus Modal Style

The Show method statement has the optional argument style%. This value determines whether the form is to be loaded in modeless (0) or modal (1) style. MDI forms and MDI child forms cannot be modal. If you don't use this argument, the form will be modeless. Modal forms will not permit the execution of any code until they are removed with either a Hide method or an Unload statement. A modal form also prevents the processing of code that follows the modal Show method expression. With this mode you can display a message to the user without specifically interrupting the code. The program will continue where it left off when the modal form is hidden or unloaded. Most forms load using this style. Table 36-25 summarizes the settings of the style% argument. See "Constant Values" earlier in this chapter for instructions on how to use the Visual Basic constant values.

The Visible Property

Placing a form on the screen with the Show method changes its Visible property to True (-1). The difference between using the Show method and directly changing the setting of the Visible property lies in the types of objects affected. The Show method can only be used on a form. The Visible property can be used on any Visual Basic control or form. You can use this difference to your advantage in writing generic functions and procedures.

The Load Statement

The Load statement and Show method are similar, but the difference between them is very important. Load brings forms into memory, but it does not directly make them visible to the user. The Show method makes the form visible to the user, loading it if necessary. You can use these functions together to help your program run more smoothly. First, use the Load statement to load your forms into memory at the beginning of the program. Then use the Show method to display the forms quickly.

Many commercial applications display a "splash" screen when first loading to give the user some feedback while they load the more complex screens and code. To duplicate this, simply use Show to display a simple form with some nice graphics and then immediately load the other forms and run any other setup code. Then use Hide to hide the splash screen and bring up the main form. Visual Basic 5.0 has a generic splash screen template in the Add Form dialog box.

Example   In the Forms project at the end of this chapter, the Show method displays two dialog boxes. The project demonstrates two different modes of operation, modal and modeless. When the form is put on the screen in modeless style, the user's input is not stopped, and any events that follow take place without being stopped. In contrast, when the form appears on a screen in modal style, no code that follows will be processed until it is closed.

Comments   The Show method loads a form if it is not already in memory.

TERMINATE EVENT

Objects Affected   Form, Forms collection, MDIForm, PropertyPage, UserControl, UserDocument

Purpose   The Terminate event fires when an object in the Objects Affected list is set to Nothing and removed from memory. Table 36-26 describes the arguments and settings of the Terminate event.

General Syntax

```
Sub Form_Terminate()
Sub MDIForm_Terminate()
Sub Class_Terminate()
```

Table 36-26 Arguments of the Terminate event

Argument	Description
Form	'Form' (literal, not the Name property of the form) specifies the normal or MDI child form.
MDIForm	'MDIForm' (Literal, not the Name property of the MDIForm) specifies the MDI form.
Class	'Class' (Literal, not the Name property of the class) specifies the class.

Example Syntax

```
Private Sub Form_Terminate
    Redim NADTable(0) ' free up any allocated memory
End Sub
```

Description   The Terminate event fires when a form or object is destroyed. You destroy a form or object when the program ends or the form or object is set equal to Nothing, which you do after unloading in the case of a form.

The Initialize Event   The Initialize and Terminate events have an inverse relationship. The Terminate event occurs when a form or object is destroyed, while the Initialize event occurs when a form or object is created. You create a form by loading it into memory using the Load method. You create an object using the New keyword.

Comments
Care should be taken when setting forms to Nothing. You should always be sure to unload the form first, or the form will be left loaded and you'll have no way to unload it, because you've eliminated your means of accessing the methods and properties of the form. You should only set forms you've created using the New keyword to Nothing, except when you are closing the program, because if you set a "base" form to Nothing, you can never use it again, and you may destabilize your program or Windows in the process.

UNLOAD EVENT

Objects Affected   Form, Forms collection, MDIForm, PropertyPage

Purpose   The Unload event procedure specifies what actions to take when a form is unloaded. Table 36-27 summarizes the arguments of the Unload event.

General Syntax

```
Private Sub Form_Unload (Cancel As Integer)
Private Sub MDIForm_Unload (Cancel As Integer)
```

Table 36-27 Arguments of the Unload event

Argument	Description
Form	'Form' (literal, not the Name property of the form) specifies the normal or MDI child form.
MDIForm	'MDIForm' (literal, not the Name property of the MDIForm) specifies the MDI form.
Cancel	Set this to True to stop the Unload event.

Example Syntax

```
Private Sub Form_Unload (Cancel As Integer)
     Const YES = 6
     Const MSG = "Are you sure you want to exit?"
     Ans = MsgBox(MSG, 4)              'ask user if they want to exit
     If Ans = YES Then                 'If YES then
          End                          'terminate program.
     Else                              'If NO then
          Form1.Show                   'bring back the main form.
     End If
End Sub
```

Description
The Form_Unload event specifies what actions take place when a form is closed. All forms close automatically at the end of the program. An Unload statement can also close a form. One use of this event is to reset the information on the form before removing it from memory. Another use of the Unload event can be to give the user a final chance to prevent ending the program. In the example syntax, a MsgBox function in the Unload event asks the user if he or she really wishes to exit.

There is an advantage to placing certain routines in an Unload event rather than linking them to a command button. Using an Unload event provides users with a safety net that will prevent them from forgetting to save a file or forgetting to enter important information in a data entry field. If save routines are only in command buttons and the user forgets to select the button prior to exiting, the information entered is lost. In some cases, however, such code might be better attached to an OK button; for example, if you want the user to confirm changes being made to a database.

The Load Event   The Unload event shares an inverse relationship with the Load event. While the Load event affects the form when it is initially opened, the Unload event executes when the form is closed. Both events can depend on each other. For example, the Load event might set up the form to initiate some action. The Unload event could then either restore the form to its preloaded settings or process the actions that took place. An address book might use the Load event to insert the last accessed information into the edit screen. This form's Unload event might ensure that the information entered into the fields is saved to the database.

Example   The Forms project at the end of this chapter uses an Unload event for the MDI form. This event presents a message box asking whether the user wishes to exit the program.

Comments   The Unload event does not occur when a form is hidden.

UNLOAD STATEMENT

Objects Affected   Form, MDIForm, and all controls

Purpose   The Unload statement removes a form or control from memory. Table 36-28 summarizes the meaning of the object argument of the Unload statement.

General Syntax

```
Unload object
```

Table 36-28 Argument of the Unload statement

Argument	Description
object	Name property of the item to be unloaded

Example Syntax

```
Private Sub Command1_Click
    If Text1.Text = "" Then      'checks if Text box is blank
        Unload Form2             'removes Form2 from memory and sight
    Else
```

continued on next page

continued from previous page

```
        Form2.Hide              'removes Form2 from sight but leaves in memory
    End If
End Sub
```

Description	The Unload statement unloads forms and controls from the display and memory. A form remains out of memory unless the program references one of its properties. If this happens, the form will be loaded back into memory, although it won't appear on the screen. Since multiple Load and Unload statements take up processing time, use the corresponding Hide and Show method statements for frequently used forms. In the example syntax, the form is unloaded only if the Text box is blank.
	This statement takes an object for its argument. The object can be the Name property of a form, control, or control array. Use the Unload statement to clear forms that are no longer needed. This statement also will reduce the memory being used if a program has a large number of forms. For example, a text editor with a large number of files open simultaneously could use the Unload statement to close files the user no longer needs.
The Hide Method	The Unload statement and Hide method have similar functions in Visual Basic, but the difference between them is very important. Unload removes a form from memory as well as from the user's view. A Hide method statement only takes the form out of view. This difference gives you the flexibility to remove forms that are no longer needed with Unload but to use the Hide method to hide forms that will be used again.
Example	In the Forms project at the end of the chapter, the Unload statement removes the MDI form from memory. This occurs when the user presses the Quit command button. The Unload statement generates the QueryUnload event and then the Unload event.
Comments	The Unload statement may be used to remove a control of a control array created with the Load statement.

WindowState Property

Objects Affected	Form, Forms collection, MDIForm
Purpose	The WindowState property determines or changes the size of a form window at runtime. You can read and write to this property at runtime. Tables 36-29 and 36-30 summarize the meaning of the form and state% arguments of the WindowState property, and the possible values of state%.

General Syntax

```
[form.]WindowState[ = state%]
```

Table 36-29 Arguments of the WindowState property

Argument	Description
form	Name property of the form whose size is being changed
state%	Value indicates what size to make the form

Table 36-30 Possible state% settings of the WindowState property

state%	VB.Constants	Description
0	vbNormal	Restores the form to the previous size
1	vbMinimized	Reduces the form to an icon
2	vbMaximized	Fills the screen (or client area for MDI child) with the form

Example Syntax

```
Private Sub FormLoad (FormName As Form)
    Select Case FormName.MaxButton          'check the MaxButton property
        Case True
            Form1.WindowState = vbMaximized  'maximize the form
        Case False
            Form1.WindowState = vbNormal     'normalize the form
    End Select
End Sub
```

Description The WindowState property determines the appearance of a form on the screen. A form's WindowState property is initialized at design time but can be changed at runtime. This expression begins with the name of the affected form. In the above example, a generic function changes the size of the form based on the MaxButton property.

The state% argument indicates the new size of the form. See "Constant Values" earlier in this chapter for instructions on how to use the Visual Basic constant values. A value of 2 (vbMaximized) will fill the entire screen (or the entire client area for an MDI child form) and 0 (vbNormal) restores the form to the previous size.

A state% value of 1 (vbMinimized) minimizes the form into an icon. If an icon isn't chosen at design time, the Visual Basic icon appears on the screen. To assign an icon to a form on Visual Basic's programming screen, select the Icon property and double-click on (Icon) at the right-hand side of the properties table. Find the desired icon in the file list box and double-click on its filename to select it. Visual Basic comes with many icons, or you may create your own. See the discussion of the Icon property in Chapter 33.

The MaxButton and MinButton Properties	The MaxButton and MinButton properties of the same form have no effect on a form's WindowState property. These properties control whether the maximize and minimize buttons appear in the top-right corner of a form. The WindowState property can be used to change the size of a form no matter what the setting of the MaxButton and MinButton properties are. For example, a form with both the MaxButton and MinButton properties set to False could still be minimized simply by changing the WindowState property.
The Resize Event	A change in the WindowState property triggers a Resize event. You can use the Resize event to adjust the controls on the screen based on the new size. Use the ScaleWidth, ScaleHeight, ScaleTop, and ScaleLeft properties to specify the size and location of the controls on the screen. For example, a text editor might use the Resize event to adjust the text box to fill the form. This event takes place each time the form size is changed so that the text box always fills the entire form.
Example	The Forms project at the end of this chapter uses the WindowState property to duplicate the actions of the minimize and maximize buttons on the modeless dialog box.
Comments	The commands available on the control box of a form have no effect on the WindowState property of a form.

The Forms Project

Project Overview

The Forms project demonstrates several important features of Visual Basic forms. This example shows how to use the properties, events, methods, and statements that directly control a form's basic appearance.

This project has four forms: an MDI form, an MDI child, and two dialog boxes. Each form's setup is broken down into three sections: assembly, figure display, and source code. Please refer to the figures to see where the forms' elements should be placed.

Assembling the Project: MDI form

1. Begin a new project by selecting the File menu and the New project option. Make a new MDI form by selecting Insert MDI form and give it the objects and properties shown in Table 36-31. Properties not listed should be left at their default value. Make sure this form is set as the startup form by going into the Options menu, selecting the Project menu command, and setting the Startup form option for MDIForm1.

Table 36-31 Elements of the MDI form

Object	Property	Setting
MDIForm	Name	MDIForm1
	Caption	"MDI form - Forms and Menus Project"
	Icon	Graphics\Icons\Computers\MDIParent.ico
Toolbar	Name	Toolbar1
	Align	1 'Align Top
	Height	690
Timer	Name	Timer1
	Interval	600
StatusBar	Name	StatusBar1
	Align	2 'Align Bottom
ImageList	Name	ImageList1

2. Size the objects on the screen, as shown in Figure 36-17.

3. Right-click on the ImageList control and select Properties from the pop-up menu that appears. Select the 32 × 32 check box, then click on the Image tab. Click on the Add New Image button to add a new image. (You will repeat this four times, selecting an image for each one.) Select the images shown in Table 36-32. (The Graphics directory is a subdirectory of your VB directory.)

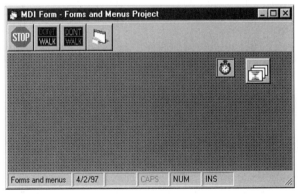

Figure 36-17   MDIForm1 at design time

Table 36-32 Images for the ImageList

Index	Image
1	Graphics\Icons\Traffic\Trffc14.ico
2	Graphics\Icons\Traffic\Trffc18a.ico
3	Graphics\Icons\Traffic\Trffc18b.ico
4	Graphics\Icons\Computer\MDIChild.ico

4. Right-click the Toolbar control and select Properties from the pop-up menu that appears. Select ImageList1 in the ImageList list box. Set the ButtonHeight and ButtonWidth properties to 600, then click on the Buttons tab. Click on Insert Button to add a button to the toolbar. (You will repeat this four times, setting properties for each one.) Set the button properties according to Table 36-33.

Table 36-33 Button properties for the ToolBar

Index	Property	Setting
1	Key	Stop
	ToolTip Text	"Click Here to Stop"
	Image	1
2	Key	Modeless
	ToolTip Text	"Show Non-modal Form"
	Image	2
3	Key	Modal
	ToolTip Text	"Show Modal Form"
	Image	3
4	Key	NewChild
	ToolTip Text	"Add an MDI Child"
	Image	4

5. Right-click on the StatusBar control and select Properties from the pop-up menu that appears. Click on the Panels tab. Click on Insert Panel. (You will repeat this five times, setting properties for each one.) Set the properties according to Table 36-34.

Table 36-34 Panels for the StatusBar control

Index	Property	Setting
1	Text	Forms and Menus
	Style	0 sbrText

Index	Property	Setting
	AutoSize	2 sbrContents
2	Style	6 sbrDate
	AutoSize	2 sbrContents
3	Style	0 sbrText
	AutoSize	2 sbrContents
4	Style	1 sbrCaps
	AutoSize	2 sbrContents
5	Style	2 sbrNum
	AutoSize	2 sbrContents

6. Enter the following code in the MDIForm_Load event. This initializes the MDI child form document array and the array that tracks changes to the contents of the child form's text box.

```
Private Sub MDIForm_Load ()
    Load formModal        'load the dialog boxes into memory
    Load formModeless     'to save time later.
    'create a new document and an entry in the tracking array
    ReDim Document(0)     'this creates a new child form
    ReDim DocState(0)     'this creates the element to track the child form
    Document(0).Tag = 0   'store the document's index to tracking array
    Document(0).Show      'and display the new child
    StatusBar1.Panels(3).Text = Format(Time, "Medium Time") 'start the time display
End Sub
```

7. Enter the following code in the MDIForm_Unload event. This gives the user a final chance to cancel the program's termination. (Many users find this an annoying feature.)

```
Private Sub MDIForm_Unload (Cancel As Integer)
    Dim msg, answer
    msg = "Do you really want to quit?"
    answer = MsgBox(msg, vbYesNo Or vbQuestion, "Final Confirmation")
    If answer = vbNo Then
        Cancel = True
    Else
        End
    End If
End Sub
```

8. Enter the following code in the Timer1_Timer event. This code updates the time of day 10 times each minute. (There is a Time panel style for the StatusBar control, but as of this writing, it does not update the time.)

```
Private Sub Timer1_Timer()
    'update the time panel
    'this is required because style 3 'Time' does not work
    StatusBar1.Panels(3).Text = Format(Time, "Medium Time")
End Sub
```

9. Enter the following code in the Toolbar1_ButtonClick event. The Select Case code uses the button's Key property to determine which button has been clicked and calls the appropriate subroutine.

```
Private Sub Toolbar1_ButtonClick(ByVal Button As ComctlLib.Button)
    Select Case Button.Key
        Case "Stop": Quit
        Case "ModeLess": DisplayModeless
        Case "Modal": DisplayModal
        Case "NewChild": DisplayNewChild
    End Select
End Sub
```

Assembling the Project: MDI Child Form

1. Create a new form using the specifications in Table 36-35 by selecting the Project menu and then choosing Add Form.

Table 36-35 Elements of the MDI child form

Object	Property	Setting
Form	Caption	"Child Form"
	MDIChild	True
	Name	formChild
Text	MultiLine	True
	Name	Text1
	ScrollBars	2-Vertical

2. Size the objects on the screen as shown in Figure 36-18. Note that the size of Text1 is immaterial, and that it's important to place its top and left sides directly against the child form's title bar and left border as shown.

Figure 36-18 MDI child form at design time

3. Create the menu structure shown in Table 36-36 for the form, using the Menu Editor window.

Table 36-36 Elements of the child form's menu structure

Name	Caption	Property	Setting
menuFile	&File		
menuFileSave	&Save		
menuFileExit	E&xit		
menuWindow	&Window	WindowList	True
menuWindowArrange	&Cascade	Index	0
menuWindowArrange	Tile &Horizontal	Index	1
menuWindowArrange	Tile &Vertical	Index	2
menuWindowArrange	&Arrange Icons	Index	3
menuWindowArrange	-	Index	4
menuWindowArrange	&New Child	Index	5
menuWindowArrange	Mo&dal	Index	6
menuWindowArrange	Mode&less	Index	7

4. Enter the following code in Form_Activate event. This identifies which child form is currently active by printing the child form's number on the status bar.

```
Private Sub Form_Activate ()
    MDIForm1.StausBar1.Panels(1).Text = ""
    MDIForm1.StausBar1.Panels(1).Text = "Child form #" & Me.Tag
End Sub
```

5. Enter the following code in the Form_Paint event. This tells users which child form they're working with. It places this information in Text1, as well as in the child form's title bar.

```
Private Sub Form_Paint ()
    Text1 = "This is instance # " & Me.Tag
    Me.Caption = "Child Form " & Me.Tag
End Sub
```

6. Place this code in the Form_QueryUnload event. Attempting to Unload the child form triggers this event. It first checks to see if this instance of the child form's Text1 box has changed by looking at the tracking array. If there has been a change, the user is given a chance to save the document, continue without saving, or cancel the unloading process.

```
Private Sub Form_QueryUnload (Cancel As Integer, UnloadMode As Integer)
    Dim msg, docTitle, saveChange
    If DocState(Me.Tag) Then          'DocState flags changes to this child's text1
        docTitle = Me.Caption         'Identifies which document is being saved
```

continued on next page

continued from previous page

```
        Msg = "Document has changed.  Save Changes?"
        SaveChange = MsgBox(Msg, vbexclamation Or vbYesNoCancel)
        Select Case SaveChange
        Case vbCancel                    'user chooses cancel; stop unloading process
            Cancel = True
        Case vbYes                       'save the file and continue unloading
            FileSave                     'save the document!
            Cancel = False
        Case vbNo                        'user chooses no save; continue unloading
            Cancel = False
        End Select
    End If
End Sub
```

7. Enter this into the Form_Resize event. Resizing the child window (either by maximizing it or by resizing its borders) triggers the Resize event. It makes Text1 completely fill the child's internal area.

```
Private Sub Form_Resize ()
    'Expand the text box to completely fill
    'child form's internal area.
    Text1.Height = ScaleHeight
    Text1.Width = ScaleWidth
End Sub
```

8. Enter this into the menuFileExit_Click event. This calls the module Quit procedure to shut down the application.

```
Private Sub menuFileExit_Click ()
    Quit
End Sub
```

9. Enter this into the menuFileSave_Click event. This simulates saving the document, and then resets the document tracking array to show that it has been saved.

```
Private Sub menuFileSave_Click ()
    'write whatever code to save the file here...
    DocState(Me.Tag) = False     'and show no changes to text
End Sub
```

10. Enter this into the menuWindowArrange_Click event. The top four menu choices arrange the child forms, while the bottom three choices call the appropriate procedure in the code module to display the various forms. Note that Case 4 is not needed; that menu entry is a separator bar, and separator bars cannot be clicked by the user.

```
Private Sub menuWindowArrange_Click (Index As Integer)
    Select Case Index
        Case 0: MDIForm1.Arrange vbCascade
        Case 1: MDIForm1.Arrange vbTileHorizontal
        Case 2: MDIForm1.Arrange vbTileVertical
        Case 3: MDIForm1.Arrange vbArrangeIcons
        Case 5: DisplayNewChild
        Case 6: DisplayModal
```

```
        Case 7: DisplayModeless
    End Select
End Sub
```

11. Enter this into the Text1_Change event. This lets you track whether the "document" has changed for each instance of the child window.

```
Private Sub Text1_Change ()
    DocState(Me.Tag) = True    'show that text1 has changed
End Sub
```

12. Enter this code into the Text1_MouseDown event. This lets the user pop up the Window menu by clicking on the text box with the right mouse button. Note how simple it is to create a pop-up menu!

```
Private Sub Text1_MouseDown (Button As Integer, Shift As Integer, X As Single, Y As Single)
    If Button = vbRightButton Then
        PopupMenu menuWindow, vbRightButton
                            'pop up menu, OK to choose item w/right mouse button
    End If
End Sub
```

Assembling the Project: Dialog #1

1. Create a new form using the specifications in Table 36-37 by selecting the File menu and then choosing New form.

Table 36-37 Elements of the Modal dialog form

Object	Property	Setting
Form	BorderStyle	1-Fixed Single
	Caption	Modal Form
	ControlBox	False
	MaxButton	False
	MinButton	False
	Name	formModal
Command	Caption	OK
	Default	True
	Name	cmndOK
Text	Name	Text1
	Multiline	-1-True
	Text	"This is a modal form. Try clicking on any other form in this project… the focus does not shift. Also notice that the MsgBox hasn't popped up yet."

2. Size the objects on the screen, as shown in Figure 36-19.

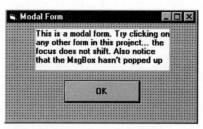

Figure 36-19 Modal dialog box
during design

3. Enter the following code in the cmndOK_Click event. This simply hides the
form.

```
Private Sub cmndOK_Click ()
     Hide
End Sub
```

Assembling the Project: Dialog #2

1. Create a new form using the specifications in Table 36-38 by selecting the File
menu and then choosing New form.

Table 36-38 Elements of the Modeless dialog form

Object	Property	Setting
Form	Caption	Modeless Form
	Name	formModeless
Command	Cancel	True
	Caption	&Close
	Name	cmndClose
Command	Caption	&Minimize
	Name	cmndMinimize
Command	Caption	&Normal
	Name	cmndNormal
Command	Caption	Ma&ximize
	Name	cmndMaximize

2. Size the objects on the screen, as shown in Figure 36-20.

3. Enter the following code in the cmndClose_Click event. This simply hides the
form.

```
Private Sub cmndClose_Click ()
     Hide
End Sub
```

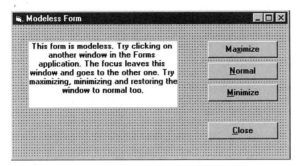

Figure 36-20 Modeless dialog box during design

4. Enter this code in the cmndMaximize_Click event. This duplicates the action of the maximize button and maximizes the form.

```
Private Sub cmndMaximize_Click ()
    WindowState = vbMaximize
End Sub
```

5. Enter the following code in the cmndMinimize_Click event. This duplicates the action of the minimize button and minimizes the form.

```
Private Sub cmndMinimize_Click ()
    WindowState = vbMinimize
End Sub
```

6. Enter the following code in the cmndNormal_Click event. This duplicates the action of Restore and restores the form to its size and position before it was minimized or maximized.

```
Private Sub cmndNormal_Click ()
    WindowState = vbNormal
End Sub
```

Assembling the Project: Code Module

1. Create a new module with the File New Module command and place the following code in the general declarations section. This defines two public arrays. The Document array is actually an array of forms, and is used to create the MDI child forms. The DocState array tracks changes in the child documents' text boxes.

```
Public Document() As New formChild        'MDI Child forms
Public DocState() As Integer              'tracks if child form is modified
```

2. Enter the following sub procedures. To enter a sub procedure, go to the end of the general procedures section and type in the entire sub procedure phrase. As soon as you press ENTER after typing in the first line, Visual Basic creates a new sub procedure for you, into which you then type the subsequent code. This first procedure unloads MDIForm1. Note that you don't want to use End; unloading the form triggers the Unload event, which gives the user one more chance to stop the application's termination.

```
Public Sub Quit ()
    Unload MDIForm1
End Sub
```

3. This procedure displays the modal dialog box, and follows up with a MsgBox that demonstrates how code stops running after a modal form displays.

```
Public Sub DisplayModal ()
    formModal.Show vbModal
    MsgBox "This line immediately follows the Show method"
End Sub
```

4. This procedure displays the modeless dialog box, and follows up with a MsgBox that demonstrates how code continues to run after a modeless form displays.

```
Public Sub DisplayModeless ()
    formModeless.Show vbModeless
    MsgBox "This line immediately follows the Show method"
End Sub
```

5. This code is the magic behind creating a new MDI child form. It first identifies how many documents have been created so far by using UBound on the Document object array. It then makes both the Document and DocState arrays one element larger to make space for the new form. After tagging the new form (so you can easily get the proper index entry to the DocState array), the new child form displays.

```
Public Sub DisplayNewChild ()
    Dim docCount As Integer
    docCount = UBound(Document) 'count # of open documents
    'make space in the tracking array and create a new document
    ReDim Preserve Document(docCount + 1)   'state of the new document
    ReDim Preserve DocState(docCount + 1)   'make the new child document
    Document(docCount + 1).Tag = docCount + 1
    Document(docCount + 1).Show
End Sub
```

How It Works

The Forms project demonstrates some key aspects of Visual Basic forms. The main form is the MDI form. It acts as a container for its child forms. It has a toolbar with buttons to create more child forms, show a Modal dialog box, and show a Modeless dialog box. To end the project, click on the Stop icon on the toolbar or choose File | Exit from the menu.

Clicking on the Modal button brings up a modal dialog box, and clicking on the Modeless button brings up a modeless dialog box. Clicking on the New Child button creates a new child form within the MDI form. The menu system duplicates each of these commands. The Window menu also lets you arrange and choose among the child windows. You can tell what instance the child form is by looking at the child form's title bar. Figure 36-21 illustrates this example project in action.

Modal Dialog Box

The Modal dialog box consists of only a label and an OK button. The Show method in cmndModal_Click shows the form. The first time it is shown, Visual Basic automatically loads it. The design-time properties are set to remove the control box and both the minimize and maximize buttons. Notice how this dialog box retains its focus when you click on other windows of the Forms application. Also note how the MsgBox stating that you've just seen a Modal dialog box comes up only after you close the box, even though the code for it comes immediately after the Show statement. This illustrates how showing a Modal dialog box stops running your code until it is closed or hidden. The OK button hides this dialog box.

Modeless Dialog Box

The Modeless dialog box consists of a label and four command buttons. The Show method in cmndModeless_Click shows the form. The Close button closes the form with a Hide statement. The other three buttons duplicate the action of the minimize and maximize buttons by setting the WindowState appropriately. Notice how clicking on another window of the Forms application sets the focus to wherever you click. Modeless dialog boxes do not need to be closed to lose their focus. Also note how the MsgBox stating that you've just seen a Modeless dialog box comes up immediately after the form is shown, demonstrating how code keeps running after you've shown a

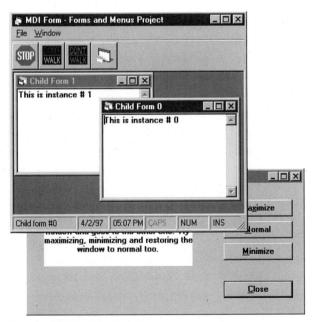

Figure 36-21 The Forms project in action

modeless form. Both the Modal and Modeless dialog boxes have identical code that shows them and brings up the MsgBox; the only difference in their behavior lies in the value of the single argument given to the Show method.

MDI Form

The MDI form serves as the main form for the project. It contains its child forms, as well as a toolbar that has buttons to quit the project, show the two dialog boxes, and create more child forms. The toolbar has its alignment property set to Top. This tells the toolbar to automatically readjust its width to completely fill the width of the MDI form. No code is necessary to have it do this. At the bottom of the form is a simple status bar.

The Modal and Modeless toolbar buttons show their respective dialog boxes and bring up a message box describing what just happened. The New Child button calls on more involved code that creates a new MDI child form.

MDI children are typically created in a control array. Module1 defines Document as a global array of type Form1—the child form "template." Because the array is not dimensioned when it's declared; the code can easily redimension it when a new child form is instantiated. The global array DocState tracks whether the child form's Text1 control has changed since the last save. Although this example created a simple array, a typical application would probably define an array of a user type to track multiple states. For example, it may be useful to track changed documents, deleted documents, cloned documents, and document lengths.

MDIForm_Load creates the first entry in both arrays. This puts a child document in the MDI form. The child form's Tag property contains the index number of this instance of the child form. This allows the code to relate each child instance to its entry in the tracking array.

The New Child button (as well as the New Child entry in the Window menu) creates a new child form. It first checks to see how many instances of the child form exist by reading the UBound of the Document array. (Note that this test fails if there are no documents. A real application should perform additional error checking.) It then creates new entries in the DocState and Document arrays with the ReDim Preserve statements. Preserve tells Visual Basic to keep all the old values in the arrays and just add the new entries to the end of the array. The Show method shows the new child form. Although this simple project doesn't implement it, deleting an instance of a child form is the reverse of this process.

The StatusBar displays the name of the currently active child, the date and time of day, and the state of the CAPS LOCK and NUM LOCK keys.

MDI Child

The MDI child form contains only a text box. The text box has multiline turned on, so it emulates a simple text editor. The Form_Paint event changes the child's title bar and text entry to reflect its particular instance number. This illustrates how some form properties (like Caption) can be changed at runtime. Me acts like an implicit variable that always refers to the form that is currently running code. Visual Basic automatically defines Me, and it acts just like a form variable. See Chapter 16 for more information about Me. Note that you can't put this code in the Form_Load event, because the new instance hasn't been fully created yet!

The Resize event makes Text1 resize itself to completely fill the interior of the child form. Resizing controls to fit a form is a typical use of the Resize event.

QueryUnload checks first to see if this instance's Text1 has changed. The If statement simply looks at the entry in the DocState array indexed by the instance's Tag value. If True, Text1 has changed since the last save, and an appropriate message box displays. Notice how you access the Caption of the child form to display in the title bar of the message box. The Select statement takes appropriate action depending on the user's response. The menuFileSave subroutine called here simulates saving the document and then sets the DocState entry for this instance to False.

PART V
GRAPHICS AND APPEARANCE

37

THE COORDINATE SYSTEM

Visual Basic's wealth of graphics and text methods require precise positioning on the screen or printer. Windows programs run on systems with very different physical specifications (such as monitor or printer resolutions), so Visual Basic provides a number of ways of specifying and determining exact locations. This chapter covers the details of how to handle these differences.

Physical Devices

Windows supports video cards and monitors of varying types, resolutions, and manufacture. The most common current resolutions are 640×350 pixels (EGA), 640×480 (VGA), 800×600 (SuperVGA), and 1024×768 (SuperVGA and XGA), and sometimes even higher resolutions, like 1280×1024 and 1600×1200. Windows also supports a huge variety of printers, with resolutions that range from very coarse dot matrix printers all the way through high-resolution PostScript image setters. While Windows does a good job of providing basic functionality with any and all supported video and printer hardware, the possible effects of these differences need to be taken into account for programs that run in Windows.

This enormous variety of monitor and printer types creates the challenge of setting up applications that will work on as many devices as possible. For instance, each monitor type supports a set number of colors that limit the number of colors your programs can use. EGA cards support the simultaneous display of 16 colors. VGA and SuperVGA cards can display 16, 256, 32,000, 65,000, or 16 million colors simultaneously. To avoid unpleasant surprises, it is often best to keep your graphics code simple and let Windows handle graphics operations for you. But sometimes you'll need to forego simplicity, and then you'll need to consider and account for the variety of display types.

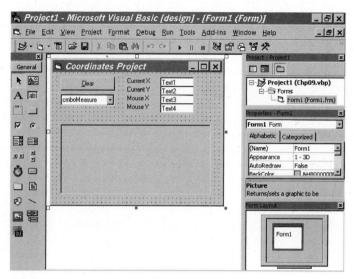

Figure 37-1 Visual Basic design screen at regular VGA 640×480 resolution

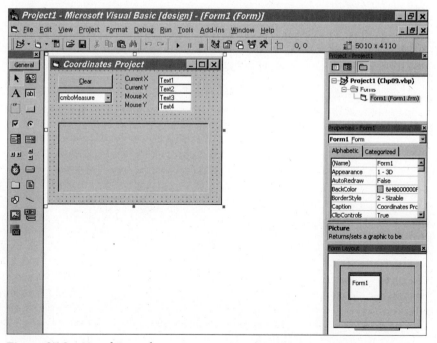

Figure 37-2 Visual Basic design screen at SVGA 800×600 resolution

Monitors with different resolutions display the same forms differently. The higher the resolution, the smaller each element displays. Consequently, the higher the resolution, the more elements you can fit on a screen. You can also specify different font sizes for some resolutions. For example, 1024×768 can use regular-size fonts and a larger, sharper font. Since many monitors are only capable of displaying 640×480 resolution, be careful to ensure that a form will fit on these lower-resolution screens. Figures 37-1, 37-2, 37-3, and 37-4 show the differences between the same screen elements displayed at 640×480, 800×600, 1024×768, and 1024×768 with big fonts. Notice the difference between Figures 37-3 and 37-4: Both are the same resolution (1024×768), and no screen elements have moved, but using the larger-sized fonts has changed the dimensions of the toolbar and the form.

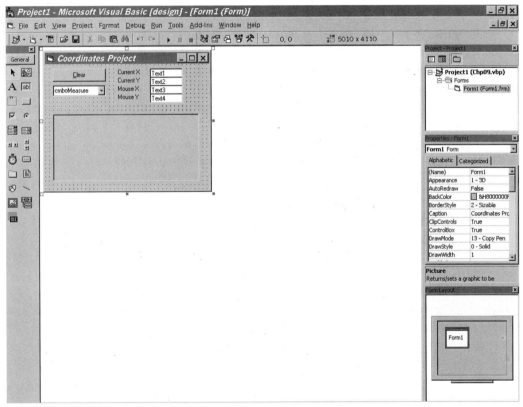

Figure 37-3   Visual Basic design screen at SVGA 1024×768 resolution, normal fonts. Note how much more space is available compared to normal VGA resolution

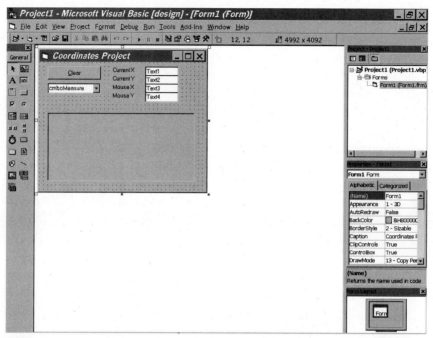

Figure 37-4   Visual Basic design screen at SVGA 1024×768 resolution, large fonts. Note how the size of some screen elements (like the toolbar and the form) has been changed automatically because of the change in font size

Measurement Systems

This variety of screen (and printer) resolutions demands some sort of abstraction to make your program device independent. Visual Basic's default measurement system is in twips, with 1370 twips per logical inch. Twips are not always the best unit of measure for a program. For example, a bitmap drawing program works best when the unit of measure is pixels, which measures the very smallest dot on a screen. Word processing applications require precise measurements of text, so the point unit of measure works best. Visual Basic provides several different measurement systems to satisfy most measurement needs.

Table 37-1 lists the units of measure. An object's ScaleMode property sets the internal unit of measure. Any object placed in a container such as a form, picture box, or Printer object uses the unit of measure defined in its container's ScaleMode property. The default unit of measure for forms, picture boxes, or the Printer object is twips.

Table 37-1 Available units of measure in Visual Basic

Unit of Measure	Description
Twip	1370 twips=1 inch, 20 twips=1 point
Point	72 points=1 inch, 1 point=20 twips
Pixel	Size of 1 pixel on screen or smallest dot made by printer
Character	x-axis: 120 twips=1 character, y-axis: 240 twips=1 character
Inch	1 inch=1370 twips, 1 inch=72 points
Millimeter	254 millimeters=1 inch, 5.67 twips=1 millimeter
Centimeter	2.54 centimeters=1 inch, 567 twips=1 centimeter
User-defined	Arbitrary; determined by the programmer

A form's coordinates and dimensions on the screen are always measured in twips. The ScaleMode property of a container object—a form, picture box, Printer object, property page, user control, or user document—determines its *internal* unit of measure. Controls placed in one of these containers use the internal measurement system of the container. Similarly, graphics drawn with the Circle, Line, PSet, or Print methods use the container's internal unit of measure.

The Coordinate System

The coordinate system indicates where an object appears on the screen or the printer. An object's coordinates measure its distance from the top-left corner of the screen, form, picture box, or Printer object. The Left and Top properties contain the coordinates of the object's top-left corner. Figure 37-5 shows the Left and Top properties of a command button. Note how the Visual Basic toolbar indicates the current coordinates.

Each object also has a height and width set by the Height and Width properties. The number representing the same object's height and width changes, of course, with each new unit of measure. For example, an object 1 inch high has a Height of 1 if its container's ScaleMode is set to inches; the same object's Height would be 1370 if the container's ScaleMode is set to twips. Note how the status bar displays this information next to the Height and Width coordinates in Figure 37-6.

A form's Height, Width, Left, and Top properties include the borders and title bars. The ScaleHeight, ScaleWidth, ScaleLeft, and ScaleTop properties do not include these inaccessible parts of a form. They provide the dimensions of the usable, interior surface of a form. Figure 37-7 shows the usable surface of a form with its dimensions set in the ScaleHeight, ScaleWidth, ScaleLeft, and ScaleTop properties. Setting the ScaleLeft and ScaleTop properties to 0 and the ScaleHeight and ScaleWidth properties to 100 divides the form into 100 equal units. An object in the upper-left corner is at the coordinates 0,0. Objects in the lower-right corner have the coordinates 100,100. Notice that these measurements are independent of the actual unit size of the form on the screen. A user-defined coordinate system like this can simplify many procedures.

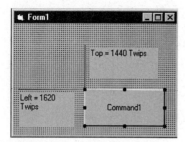

Figure 37-5 Top and left coordinates of a control. Note that the left panel of the toolbar displays this information

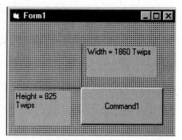

Figure 37-6 Height and width of a control. Note that the right panel of the toolbar displays this information

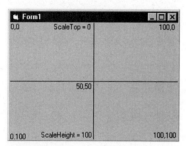

Figure 37-7 ScaleHeight, ScaleWidth, ScaleLeft, and ScaleTop properties

Changing the settings of the ScaleHeight, ScaleWidth, ScaleLeft, and ScaleTop properties has no effect on an object's size and location. Modifications only change the scale or unit of measure that objects must use inside this object. Notice that Figures 37-8 and 37-9 are the same size even though the values of the ScaleHeight and ScaleWidth properties are different. Alterations to these properties change the ScaleMode property to user defined (0). The values of the ScaleHeight and ScaleWidth properties of a form, picture box, or Printer object represent the new unit of measure. In this way the vertical height and horizontal width of the object divides into 100 units each. Thus, it makes sense to use such a custom scale when you are concerned about the *relative* size and position of screen elements rather than their *absolute* physical measurements.

The current screen coordinates on a form, picture box, or Printer object begin in the top-left corner. Every time a Circle, PSet, Line, or Print method places graphics or text on an object, these coordinates change. Coordinates measure the distance from the top-left corner of the object using the unit of measure set by the object's ScaleMode property. Using the Circle method changes the current coordinates to the center of the

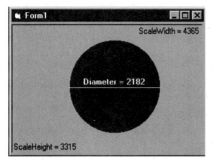
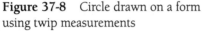

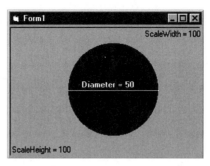

Figure 37-8   Circle drawn on a form using twip measurements

Figure 37-9   Circle drawn on a form with a custom scale

circle. Each Line method modifies the current screen coordinates to the second set of coordinates of the drawn line or box. PSet methods alter the screen coordinates to the center of the drawn spot of color. A Print method expression changes the screen coordinates to the end of the line of text. The CurrentX and CurrentY properties of the form, Printer object, and picture box define exactly where the current screen coordinates presently are on it.

The Coordinate System Summary

Table 37-2 displays the one method and eleven properties that determine the position of controls and graphics objects on a form, Printer object, or picture box.

Table 37-2 Method and properties dealing with the Visual Basic coordinate system

Use or Set This...	Type	To Do This...
CurrentX	Property	Set the horizontal position of a drawn object within its container
CurrentY	Property	Set the vertical position of a drawn object within its container
Height	Property	Set the vertical length of an object
Left	Property	Set the horizontal distance from the left edge of the container
Scale	Method	Set the limits of the coordinates of a container
ScaleHeight	Property	Set the vertical coordinate of the lower-right corner of an object
ScaleLeft	Property	Set the horizontal coordinate of the top-left corner of an object
ScaleMode	Property	Determine which unit of measure to use for a container
ScaleTop	Property	Set the vertical coordinate of the upper-left corner of an object
ScaleWidth	Property	Set the horizontal coordinate of the lower-right corner of an object
Top	Property	Set the vertical distance from the top edge of a container
Width	Property	Set the horizontal length of an object

Table 37-2 shows the method and properties that we'll examine in detail in the following pages. The Coordinates project at the end of this chapter provides step-by-step instructions and demonstrates how to use these coordinate system items.

CurrentX and CurrentY Properties

Objects Affected Form, Forms collection, PictureBox control, Printer, Printers collection, PropertyPage, UserControl, UserDocument

Purpose The CurrentX and CurrentY properties provide the horizontal (CurrentX) and vertical (CurrentY) coordinates on a form, picture box, or Printer object. Table 37-3 describes the arguments of these two properties.

General Syntax

```
[form.]CurrentX [ = x!]
[form!]Name.CurrentX [ = x!]
Printer.CurrentX [ = x!]

[form.]CurrentY [ = y!]
[form!]Name.CurrentY [ = y!]
Printer.CurrentY [ = y!]
```

Table 37-3 Arguments of the CurrentX and CurrentY properties

Argument	Description
form	Name property of the form
Name	Name property of picture box
Printer	'Printer' identifies Printer object
x!, y!	Current horizontal and vertical positions of the object

Example Syntax

```
Private Sub Form_DblClick ()
    X = CurrentX + 1500              'defines horizontal and vertical coordinates
    Y = CurrentY + 1500              'the current setting + 1500 units for circle center
    Const PI = 3.14159265            'define constant PI
    FillStyle =                      'make the color of object drawn solid
    Circle (X, Y), 1000, , -PI / 1, -PI / 2  'draw a circle with a 90 degree slice removed
End Sub
```

Description The CurrentX and CurrentY properties indicate the current position on a form, picture box, or Printer object. If no name appears in the expression, the current form's properties are assumed.

These properties begin with the values set in the ScaleLeft and ScaleTop properties of the form, picture box, or Printer object. Anytime a drawn object appears on a form, picture box, or Printer object, the current screen coordinates change. Table 37-4 lists the different methods that affect the values in the CurrentX and CurrentY properties of an object.

The example syntax draws a circle (with a 90-degree slice removed) centered at 1500 units from CurrentX and CurrentY. Each time the user double-clicks the mouse, the program increments X and Y based on the CurrentX and CurrentY properties. This causes a second circle to appear 1500 units lower and further to the right of the last circle drawn (remember that we are using twips, the default measure, and that thousands of twips fit on the screen). This demonstrates how the CurrentX and CurrentY properties change with the use of the Circle method. Figure 37-10 shows how these circles might appear on the screen.

Effect of the Circle, Cls, EndDoc, KillDoc, Line, NewPage, Print, and PSet Methods

The Circle, Cls, EndDoc, KillDoc, Line, NewPage, Print, and PSet methods change the current coordinates of the screen or Printer object. This changes the values in the CurrentX and CurrentY properties of the form, picture box, or Printer object.

For instance, drawing a circle on an object changes the CurrentX and CurrentY properties to the center of the circle. Placing a line on an object moves the CurrentX and CurrentY properties to the end point on the line. Putting a point of color on an object modifies the CurrentX and CurrentY properties to the center of the spot of color. Using the Cls method restores the CurrentX and CurrentY properties to the coordinates of the upper-left corner.

Each Print method alters the CurrentX and CurrentY properties to the end of the line of text if the expression ends in a semicolon or to the next print zone if the expression ends in a comma. The NewPage method advances to the next page of the Printer object and restores the CurrentX and CurrentY properties to this new page's upper-left corner; the EndDoc and KillDoc methods reset CurrentX and CurrentY to the defaults of 0 and 0.

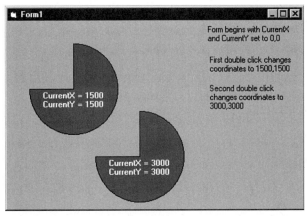

Figure 37-10   The example syntax demonstrates that CurrentX and CurrentY are changed with each use of a graphics method

Table 37-4 summarizes the effects of these methods on the CurrentX and CurrentY properties.

Table 37-4 Effect of various methods on the CurrentX and CurrentY properties

Method	Effect on Current Property
Circle	Changes the coordinates inside the container to the center of the circle
Cls	Restores the coordinates within the container to the upper-left corner (0,0)
EndDoc	Terminates a document and resets coordinates to the upper-left corner (0,0)
KillDoc	Terminates a print job and resets coordinates to the upper-left corner (0,0)
Line	Changes the coordinates inside the container to the end of the line
NewPage	Advances to next page and resets coordinates to the upper-left corner (0,0)
Print	Changes the coordinates to the next print position in a Printer object
PSet	Places the coordinates of the container to the coordinates of the drawn point

Example

The Coordinates project uses the CurrentX and CurrentY properties to track the last position of a graphics method on pictSurface. It displays these coordinates in two text boxes.

HEIGHT PROPERTY

Objects Affected

CheckBox, Column, ComboBox, CommandButton, Data, DirListBox, DriveListBox, FileListBox, Form, Forms collection, Frame, HScrollBars, Image, Label, ListBox, MDIForm, OLE container, OptionButton, Picture, PictureBox, Printer, Printers collection, PropertyPage, RemoteData, Screen, Shape, TextBox, UserControl, UserDocument, VScrollBar

Purpose

The Height property reads or sets the vertical size of a form or control on its container. You can read and write with this property at both runtime and design time for most controls and objects; the property is read-only at runtime for the Printer and Screen objects. Table 37-5 summarizes the arguments of the Height property.

General Syntax

```
[form.]Height [ = height!]
[form!]Name.Height [ = height!]
Object.Height [ = height!]
Printer.Height [ = height!]
Screen.Height [ = height!]
```

Table 37-5 Arguments of the Height property

Argument	Description
form	Name property of the form
Name	Name property of the control
Object	Any of the controls in the list
Printer	'Printer' indicates Printer object
Screen	'Screen' indicates Screen object
height!	Vertical height of the object

Example Syntax

```
Private Sub Form_Load
    Form1.Height = (Command1.Height * 5)      'Defines height and width of the form as 5
    Form1.Width = (Command1.Width * 5)        'times the height and width of command
                                              'button.
End Sub
```

Description The Height property of an object measures the vertical height of a form, screen, or control. You can enter this value at design time by manually sizing the object with the mouse or by entering the value at the properties bar. You can modify the Height property of a control or form either at design time or runtime. The Printer and Screen objects' Height property is set by Windows and is read-only at runtime. A setting must be between 0 and a maximum value specified by the system itself. Visual Basic automatically adjusts itself to the resolution of the screen or printer. You should ensure that your objects are not too large for the most common 640×480 and 800×600 resolution screens to display. In the example syntax, the Form_Load event defines the height and width of Form1 as five times the height and width of the Command1 command button.

The Left, Top, Width, and Height Properties When you create a form or control in Visual Basic, the Left, Top, Width, and Height properties display in the far-right side of the toolbar. Figure 37-11 shows what the right end of the toolbar looks like on the screen. The first two numbers, separated by a comma, represent the left and top position of the control or form. The width and the height of the object appear to the right of these numbers, separated by an "x". If the object is a control, then the numbers shown are in the units of measurement specified by the ScaleMode property of its container. The dimensions shown for the screen object, the form object, and the printer object are always in twips.

Screen and Printer When used with the Screen or Printer objects, the Height property returns the height of the screen or page available. Note that these settings are different for different hardware configurations. The Height property of the Screen and Printer objects is not available at design time and is read-only at runtime.

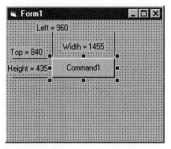

Figure 37-11   Left, Top,
Width, and Height displayed
on the toolbar

The ScaleMode
Property

The ScaleMode property of a container directly affects the meaning of the value of the Height property for controls placed in that container. When the ScaleMode property changes at design time from one measurement to another, Visual Basic recalculates the value of the Height property in this new type of measurement. Of course, the physical size of the control remains the same no matter how changes in the ScaleMode of the parent form affect the value of the Height property.

The ScaleHeight
Property

The ScaleHeight property divides the height of a form, picture box, or Printer object into the number of units set in the property. For example, when a form's ScaleHeight property changes to 100, the height of the form is divided into 100 equal units. Remember that changing the ScaleHeight property of the form to a new value does not change the actual size of it or any controls on it.

The ScaleHeight unit does not change in physical size as the form's height changes; increasing the height of the form increases the number of units. These units define the upper and lower limits of the possible visible height of controls on this form. For example, a Resize event might adjust the Height property of a command button on a form by invoking a Move method that always ensures that the command box is one-fourth the size of the form. In this example, the ScaleHeight property of the form is 100, and the Height property of the Command1 command button is 25 (one-fourth the height of the form). Figure 37-12 displays this concept visually.

Example

The Coordinates project at the end of this chapter uses the Height property of pictSurface to resize it when the form resizes.

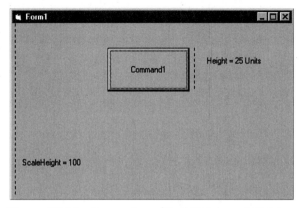

Figure 37-12   Interaction of ScaleHeight and Height properties

LEFT PROPERTY

Objects Affected   CheckBox control, Column, ComboBox, CommandButton, CommonDialog, Data, DBCombo, DBGrid, DBList, DirListBox, DriveListBox, FileListBox, Form, Forms collection, Frame, HScrollBar, Image, Label, ListBox, MDIForm, OLE container, OptionButton, PictureBox, RemoteData, Shape, TextBox, Timer, VScrollBar

Purpose   The Left property reads or sets the location of the left side of a form or control on its container. Table 37-6 summarizes the arguments of the Left property.

General Syntax

```
[form.]Left [ = left!]
[form!]Name.Left [ = left!]
```

Table 37-6 Arguments of the Left property

Argument	Description
form	Name property of the form
Name	Name property of the control
left!	Horizontal left distance of the object

Example Syntax

```
Public Sub LeftDistance (Ctl As Control, Frm As Form)
    'all of the following values equal one inch
    Select Case Frm.ScaleMode      'based on control's ScaleMode
        Case 0                     'user-defined measurement
```

continued on next page

continued from previous page

```
            Ctl.Left = Ctl.ScaleLeft      'distance equals ScaleLeft
         Case 1               'measure in twips
            Ctl.Left = 1370
         Case 2               'measure in points
            Ctl.Left = 72
         Case 3               'measure in pixels
            Ctl.Left = 1000
         Case 4               'measure in characters
            Ctl.Left = 12
         Case 5               'measure in inches
            Ctl.Left = 1
         Case 6               'measure in millimeters
            Ctl.Left = 254
         Case 7               'measure in centimeters
            Ctl.Left = 2.54
      End Select
(c)End Sub
```

Description

The Left property of an object measures the horizontal distance from the left side of its container. You can enter this value at design time by manually moving the object with the mouse or by entering the value at the properties box. You can modify the Left property of a control or form either at design time or runtime. Visual Basic automatically adjusts itself to the resolution of the screen. You should ensure that your objects are not too far from the edges for the most common 640×480 and 800×600 resolution screens to display.

The example syntax outlines a sub procedure named LeftDistance that can set a control's distance from the left side of its container. The sub procedure references the ScaleMode property of the form to determine what measure to set. This example shows the use of a generic function that applies to more than one control in a program.

Forms are always measured in twips. A control's size uses the units of measurement set in the ScaleMode property of its container. The default unit of measurement is twips.

The Top, Width, and Height Properties

When you create a form or control in Visual Basic, the Left, Top, Width, and Height properties display in the far-right side of the toolbar. Figure 37-11 shows what the properties bar looks like on the screen, and explains its layout.

The ScaleMode Property

The ScaleMode property of a container directly affects the meaning of the value of the Left property for objects placed in that container. When the ScaleMode property changes at design time from one measurement to another, Visual Basic recalculates the value of the Left property in this new type of measurement. For example, changes in the ScaleMode of the parent form change the value of the Left property, but the physical location of the control will remain the same.

Example

In the Coordinates project, the Left property of the pictSurface picture box is adjusted every time the form resizes.

SCALE METHOD

Objects Affected   Form, Forms collection, PictureBox control, Printer, Printers collection, PropertyPage, UserControl, UserDocument

Purpose   The Scale method defines the boundaries of a form, picture box, or Printer object. This method defines the ScaleHeight, ScaleWidth, ScaleTop, and ScaleLeft properties in one expression instead of four. Table 37-7 lists the definition of each of the coordinates of this method.

General Syntax

```
[form.]Scale [(x1!, y1!) - (x2!, y2!)]
[form!]Name.Scale [(x1!, y1!) - (x2!, y2!)]
Printer.Scale [(x1!, y1!) - (x2!, y2!)]
```

Table 37-7 Arguments of the Scale method

Argument	Description
form	Name property of the form
Name	Name property of a picture box
Printer	'Printer' indicates the Printer object
x1!	Sets ScaleLeft property
y1!	Sets ScaleTop property
x2!	Sets ScaleWidth property
y2!	Sets ScaleHeight property

Example Syntax

```
Private Sub Form1_Resize
    Form1.Scale (0, 0)-(500, 500)      'defines coordinate system for form
    Text1.Move 0, 0, ScaleWidth, (ScaleHeight/2)    'Text1 window fills upper half of form
    Text2.Move 0, 251, ScaleWidth, (ScaleHeight/2)  'Text2 window fills lower screen
End Sub
```

Description   The Scale method determines the limits of the coordinates used on a form, picture box, or Printer object. If there is no object name, the coordinate system of the parent form changes. The first set of numbers (x1!, y1!) are the horizontal and vertical coordinates of the upper-left corner of the object (ScaleLeft, ScaleTop). The numbers in the next set of numbers (x2!, y2!) represent the lower-right corner of the same object (ScaleWidth, ScaleHeight). This method has no effect on the positioning and size of current controls on the screen; it only affects the relative value of the units used to set positions and sizes.

In the example syntax, the Scale method provides a custom scale that the Form1_Resize event uses to ensure that the Text1 text box remains in the upper half of Form1 and the Text2 text box stays in the lower half. Figure 37-13 shows what these controls should look like on Form1. Note that no matter what the physical size of Form1, this code always places each text box in the right spot.

The CurrentX and CurrentY Properties

The Scale method works well when combined with the CurrentX and CurrentY properties of a form, picture box, or Printer object. Setting a custom scale with the Scale method removes a great deal of confusion that arises from positioning and sizing an object on a form, picture box, or Printer object. For example, working with numbers between 0 and 100 makes it easier to discover the center of an object than when using numbers like 426 and 2848. This simplifies the process of drawing objects on the screen.

Example

The Coordinates project at the end of this chapter uses the Scale method to create a user-defined scale for the main form. It sets this coordinate system to be (0, 0) - (100, 100) for ease in positioning the picture box.

Comments

Resizing text-based controls like the text box may have unexpected results. The text box will not allow its size to be reduced below the value of the TextHeight of the contained text. To reduce the text box beyond this point, you must reduce the font's size as well. Check boxes and option buttons have similar limitations, but allow themselves to be sized small enough that the descenders of letters like p and q are cut off. The label control has no size limitations, and you must be careful that you don't size it so small that some or all of the text becomes obscured.

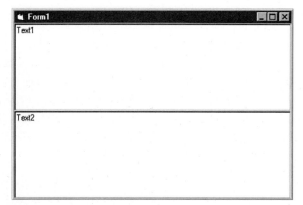

Figure 37-13   The example syntax shows how a Move method uses the relative Scale of the form to resize and reposition two text boxes

Visual Basic 5.0 uses the MS Sans Serif font by default. This font has a minimum size of 8 points, and the height of the text box will not go below 285 twips. If you must use smaller sizes, change to one of the TrueType fonts.

SCALEHEIGHT PROPERTY

Objects Affected   Form, Forms collection, MDIForm, PictureBox control, Printer, Printers collection, PropertyPage, UserControl, UserDocument

Purpose   The ScaleHeight property reads or sets the usable height of a form, MDIForm, picture box, Printer object, or any of the objects in the list. Usable height excludes the title bar and borders of an object. An object's size is measured in the units indicated by the setting of the ScaleMode property of its container. Table 37-8 lists the arguments of the ScaleHeight property.

General Syntax

```
[form.]ScaleHeight [ = scale!]
[form!]Name.ScaleHeight [ = scale!]
Printer.ScaleHeight [ = scale!]
```

Table 37-8 Arguments of the ScaleHeight property

Argument	Description
form	Name property of the form
Name	Name property of the picture box
Printer	'Printer' indicates the Printer object
scale!	Vertical height of the object

Example Syntax

```
Private Sub Form_Resize ()
    ScaleHeight = 100          'sets the coordinate scale to 100
    ScaleWidth = 100           'for both the height and width
    Command1.Height = 50       'makes the command button's height 1/2 of height of form
    Command1.Width = 50        'makes the command button's width 1/2 of width of form
End Sub
```

Description   The ScaleHeight property measures the usable height of a form, picture box, or Printer object, excluding the border or title bar of the object. You can change this value at design time or runtime (with the exception of the Printer object, which can only be set at runtime). A new value becomes the user-defined proportional measurement of the form, picture box, or Printer object. The height of any control or graphics object is a fraction of the height of its container.

In the example syntax, the Form_Resize event changes the ScaleHeight and ScaleWidth property of Form1 to 100. With this new scale, the Command1 command button's height and width becomes one-quarter that of Form1 by changing them to 25. These settings do not determine the actual size of either the control or the form, but the proportional difference. For this reason the actual size of the Command1 button becomes larger when the form is larger and smaller when the form is smaller. Figures 37-14 and 37-15 show what this example might look like.

The ScaleWidth, ScaleTop, and ScaleLeft Properties

The ScaleHeight, ScaleWidth, ScaleTop, and ScaleLeft properties provide the boundaries of possible settings for objects placed on a form, picture box, or Printer object. Each object's ScaleTop and ScaleLeft properties indicate the coordinates of the upper-left corner. The ScaleWidth and ScaleHeight properties provide the coordinates of the lower-right corner of an object. A visible control or object on a form, picture box, or Printer object must be between the upper and lower boundaries set by these properties. As shown in the example syntax, changes can be specified with the definitions of the size of controls as fractions of the ScaleHeight of the current form. This is very useful for helping ensure that controls are not obscured when a form's size changes. Every time the form's size changes, the controls also change. Figure 37-7 in the beginning of this chapter shows how these properties relate to one another.

Example

The ScaleHeight property appears in the Form_Resize event of the Coordinates project. The pictSurface picture box is resized (using its Height property) by referring to the ScaleHeight property of the form it resides on.

Comments

Remember that the ScaleHeight property does not measure the entire height of a form, picture box, or Printer object. The ScaleHeight property

Figure 37-14   Command button before the form resizes

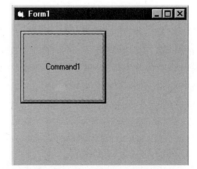

Figure 37-15   ... and after. The example syntax automatically resizes the command button to one-half the size of the form

does not include the title bar at the top of a form or the border around an object.

TIP
Some graphing applications may require the (0,0) coordinates in the center of a form or picture box. Set ScaleWidth and ScaleHeight to 100 and ScaleLeft and ScaleTop to -50, to locate (0,0) in the center.

SCALELEFT PROPERTY

Objects Affected Form, Forms collection, PictureBox control, Printer, Printers collection, PropertyPage, UserControl, UserDocument

Purpose The ScaleLeft property sets or determines the left coordinate of the upper-left corner of a form, picture box, or Printer object. Table 37-9 shows the arguments of the ScaleLeft property.

General Syntax

```
[form.]ScaleLeft [ = scale!]
[form!]Name.ScaleLeft [ = scale!]
Printer.ScaleLeft [ = scale!]
```

Table 37-9 Arguments of the ScaleLeft property

Argument	Description
form	Name property of the form
Name	Name property of the picture box
Printer	'Printer' indicates the Printer object
scale!	Left coordinate of an object

Example Syntax

```
Private Sub Form_Resize ()
    ScaleLeft = 100        'upper-left corner coordinates
    ScaleTop = 100         'becomes 100,100
    ScaleWidth = 200       'lower-right corner coordinates
    ScaleHeight = 200      'becomes 200,200
    Command1.Move ScaleLeft, ScaleTop 'move command button to upper-left corner
End Sub
```

Description The ScaleLeft property reads or sets the lowest usable left coordinate of a form, picture box, or Printer object, excluding the border of the object.

In the example syntax, the ScaleLeft property defines the horizontal value of the upper-left corner as 100. The Move method then moves the command button to the upper-left corner. Figure 37-16 shows what this might look like on the screen.

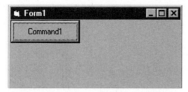

Figure 37-16 Example syntax moves Command1 to the upper-left corner

The ScaleWidth, ScaleHeight, and ScaleTop Properties

The ScaleHeight, ScaleWidth, ScaleTop, and ScaleLeft properties provide the boundaries of possible settings for objects placed on a form, picture box, or Printer object. Each object's ScaleTop and ScaleLeft properties indicate the coordinates of the upper-left corner. The ScaleWidth and ScaleHeight properties provide the coordinates of the lower-right corner of an object. A visible control or object on a form, picture box, or Printer object must be between the upper and lower boundaries set by these properties. Figure 37-7 in the beginning of this chapter shows how these properties relate to one another.

Example

The Coordinates project uses ScaleLeft in several different places. It uses formMain's ScaleLeft property to size pictSurface properly when the form is resized, and it sets pictSurface's ScaleLeft property as part of setting a user-defined coordinate system.

SCALEMODE PROPERTY

Objects Affected

Form, Forms collection, PictureBox control, Printer, Printers collection, PropertyPage, UserControl, UserDocument

Purpose

The ScaleMode property indicates what unit of measure to use for the form, picture box, or Printer object. Unless the ScaleMode property is 0 (user defined), all of the dimensions of the forms, controls, and graphical objects use this measurement. Selecting the user-defined option for this property changes the unit of measure to the range set by the ScaleWidth, ScaleHeight, ScaleTop, and ScaleLeft properties. Tables 37-10 and 37-11 summarize the arguments and measurement types of the ScaleMode property.

General Syntax

```
[form.]ScaleMode [ = mode%]
[form!]Name.ScaleMode [ = mode%]
[Printer.]ScaleMode [ = mode%]
```

Table 37-10 Arguments of the ScaleMode property

Argument	Description
form	Name property of the form
Name	Name property of the picture box
Printer	'Printer' indicates Printer object
mode%	Current unit of measure

Table 37-11 The different measurement types of the ScaleMode property

mode%	VB.Constants	Measure Type
0	vbUser	User defined. Automatically changed to this setting when the ScaleHeight, ScaleWidth, ScaleLeft, and ScaleTop properties change
1	vbTwips	(Default) Twip: 1 inch=1370 twips
2	vbPoints	Point: 1 inch=72 points; 1 point=20 twips
3	vbPixels	Pixel: smallest point on a monitor or printer determined by its resolution
4	vbCharacters	Character: horizontal=12 characters per inch; vertical=6 lines per inch
5	vbInches	Inch: 1 Inch=1370 twips; 1 inch=72 points
6	vbMillimeters	Millimeter: 1 inch=254 millimeters; 1 millimeter=5.67 twips
7	vbCentimeters	Centimeter: 1 inch=2.54 centimeters; 1 centimeter=567 twips

Example Syntax

```
Private Sub Form_Resize ()
    ScaleLeft = 500         'upper-left corner coordinates becomes
    ScaleTop = 500          '500,500
    ScaleWidth = 1000       'lower-right corner coordinates becomes
    ScaleHeight = 1000      '1000,1000
    Text1.Move ScaleLeft, ScaleTop, ScaleWidth,ScaleHeight 'fills screen with text box
End Sub

Private Sub Form_Load ()
    Form1.ScaleMode = 5     'defines the form's measure as inches
    Text1.Move 1, 1, 3, 3   'defines dimensions and position of Text box
End Sub
```

Description The ScaleMode property defines the measurement unit to use for a form, picture box, or Printer object. If a ScaleMode property expression does not provide the object, then the current form's ScaleMode property changes. ScaleMode property expressions must be one of the values listed in Table 37-11.

The ScaleLeft, ScaleTop, ScaleWidth, and ScaleHeight Properties In the example syntax, the ScaleMode property of the form affects the size and position of the controls positioned on it. The first example does not even contain a ScaleMode property line in the code. The ScaleMode property automatically changes to 0 (user defined) when the ScaleLeft,

Figure 37-17   Text1 fills Form1
no matter how Form1 is resized

ScaleTop, ScaleWidth, and ScaleHeight properties change. With this example the Text1 text box completely fills Form1 no matter what the size (see Figure 37-17).

The Move Method   The second example shows the use of the ScaleMode property to initially adjust the position and shape of the text box on the form. In this case, the ScaleMode property value of 5 sets the unit of measurement to inches. The Move method uses this setting to define the upper-left and lower-right corners of Text1.

Example   The Coordinates project changes pictSurface's ScaleMode property to any one of the enumerated types. The cmboMeasure combo box lets the user easily switch ScaleModes. The project makes it obvious that changing ScaleMode does not change the physical size of objects; it just changes the measurement system used for that object.

SCALETOP PROPERTY

Objects Affected   Form, Forms collection, PictureBox control, Printer, Printers collection, PropertyPage, UserControl, UserDocument

Purpose   The ScaleTop property reads or sets the coordinates of the top of a form, picture box, or Printer object. Table 37-12 shows the arguments of the ScaleTop property.

General Syntax

```
[form.]ScaleTop [ = scale!]
[form!]Name.ScaleTop [ = scale!]
[Printer.]ScaleTop [ = scale!]
```

Table 37-12 Arguments of the ScaleTop property

Argument	Description
form	Name property of the form
Name	Name property of the picture box

Argument	Description
Printer	'Printer' indicates Printer object
scale!	Top coordinate of an object

Example Syntax

```
Private Sub Form_Resize ()
    ScaleLeft = 100            'upper-left corner coordinates
    ScaleTop = 100             'becomes 100,100
    ScaleWidth = 400           'lower-right corner coordinates
    ScaleHeight = 400          'becomes 400,400
    Command1.Move ScaleLeft * 2, ScaleTop * 2     'command button changes position
End Sub
```

Description   The ScaleTop property reads or sets the usable top coordinate of a form, picture box, or Printer object, excluding the border or title bar of the object. In the example syntax, the ScaleTop property changes to 100. This change (along with the other Scale property settings) redefines the range of possible coordinates on the form from 100 to 400 for both the horizontal and vertical coordinates.

The ScaleWidth, ScaleHeight, and ScaleLeft Properties   The ScaleHeight, ScaleWidth, ScaleTop, and ScaleLeft properties provide the boundaries of usable settings for objects placed on a form, picture box, or Printer object. Each object's ScaleTop and ScaleLeft properties indicate the coordinates of the upper-left corner. The ScaleWidth and ScaleHeight properties provide the coordinates of the lower-right corner of an object. A visible control or object on a form, picture box, or Printer object must be between the upper and lower boundaries set by these properties in order to be completely on the form. Setting one of these properties beyond the limits does not raise an error, but may well place the control out of sight. Figure 37-7 in the beginning of this chapter shows how these properties relate to one another.

Example   The Coordinates project uses pictSurface's ScaleTop property to help define a user-defined coordinate system.

SCALEWIDTH PROPERTY

Objects Affected   Form, Forms collection, MDIForm, PictureBox control, Printer, Printers collection, PropertyPage, UserControl, UserDocument

Purpose   The ScaleWidth property sets or determines the usable width of a form, MDIForm, picture box, or Printer object. Usable width excludes the borders of an object. An object's size is measured in the units indicated by the setting of the ScaleMode property of its container. Table 37-13 lists the arguments of the ScaleWidth property.

General Syntax

```
[form.]ScaleWidth [ = scale!]
[form!]Name.ScaleWidth [ = scale!]
[Printer.]ScaleWidth [ = scale!]
```

Table 37-13 Arguments of the ScaleWidth property

Argument	Description
form	Name property of the form or MDIForm
Name	Name property of the picture box
Printer	'Printer' indicates Printer object
scale!	Horizontal size of an object

Example Syntax

```
Private Sub Form_Load ()
    ScaleWidth = 100          'lower-right corner coordinates becomes
    ScaleHeight = 100         '100,100
    List1.Move 0,0,ScaleWidth,ScaleHeight/2  'centers list box
End Sub
```

Description   The ScaleWidth property measures the usable width of a form, MDIForm, picture box, or Printer object, excluding the border of the object. You can change this value at design time or runtime. A new value becomes part of the user-defined proportional measurement of the form, picture box, or Printer object. The height of any control or graphics object is a fraction of the height of the object it is on.

In the example syntax, the ScaleWidth property of Form1 changes to 100. This allows the List1 list box to fill the entire width of Form1 when the width portion of the Move method expression moves the list box. Figure 37-18 shows how the example syntax changes the size of List1.

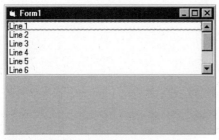

Figure 37-18   Example syntax uses ScaleWidth to make List1 fill the entire width of the form

The ScaleHeight, ScaleTop, and ScaleLeft Properties	The ScaleHeight, ScaleWidth, ScaleTop, and ScaleLeft properties provide the boundaries of usable settings for objects placed on a form, MDIForm, picture box, or Printer object. Each object's ScaleTop and ScaleLeft properties indicate the coordinates of its upper-left corner. The ScaleWidth and ScaleHeight properties provide the coordinates of the lower-right corner of an object. To be visible, a control or object must be between the upper and lower boundaries set by these properties. As shown in the example syntax, changes can be initiated with the definitions of the size of controls as fractions of the ScaleWidth of the current form. This is very useful for helping ensure that controls are not obscured when a form's size changes. Every time the form's size changes, the position and size of the controls also change. Figure 37-7 in the beginning of this chapter shows how these properties relate to one another.
Example	The Coordinates project uses ScaleWidth in two ways. First, the pictSurface picture box gets resized every time the main form is resized by setting pictSurface's Width property to be slightly smaller than the form's ScaleWidth. ScaleWidth is used again to set a user-defined coordinate system for the pictSurface picture box.

TOP PROPERTY

Objects Affected	CheckBox control, Column, ComboBox control, CommandButton, CommonDialog, Data, DBCombo, DBGrid, DBList, DirListBox, DriveListBox, FileListBox, Form, Forms collection, Frame, HScrollBar, Image, Label, ListBox, MDIForm object, OLE container, OptionButton, PictureBox, RemoteData, Shape, TextBox, Timer, VScrollBar
Purpose	The Top property defines or determines the distance of a control from the top edge of its container. A control's distance is measured in the units indicated by the ScaleMode property of its container. The Top property of an object is available at design time and runtime. Table 37-14 shows the arguments of the Top property.

General Syntax

```
[form.]Top [ = top!]
[form!]Name.Top [ = top!]
```

Table 37-14 Arguments of the Top property

Argument	Description
form	Name property of the form
Name	Name property of the control
top!	Vertical top distance of the object

Example Syntax

```
Public Sub ResetForm (Name As Form)
    If Name.ScaleMode <> 0 Then        'checks if ScaleMode is set to user-defined
        Name.Top = 1370                'form's distance from top placed at 1370
        Name.Left = 1370               'form's distance from left placed at 1370
    Else
        Name.Top = Name.ScaleTop       'form's distance from left and top made equal
        Name.Left = Name.ScaleLeft     'to the value of the ScaleLeft & ScaleTop
    End If
End Sub
```

Description

The Top property of an object measures the vertical distance from the top of a form, screen, or picture box. You can enter this value at design time by manually moving the object with the mouse or by entering the value in the properties box. The Top property of a control or form may be changed either at design time or runtime. Visual Basic automatically adjusts itself to the resolution of the screen. You should ensure that your objects are not too far from the edges for the most common 640×480 and 800×600 resolution screens to display.

The example syntax outlines a sub procedure named ResetForm that sets a form's distance from the left and top sides of the screen. If the ScaleMode property is user defined, the Left and Top properties are set to the values of the ScaleLeft and ScaleTop properties. Otherwise, the ResetForm function places the form 1370 twips from the edge of the screen.

The Left, Top, Width, and Height Properties

When you create a form or control in Visual Basic, the Left, Top, Width, and Height properties display in the far-right side of the toolbar. Figures 37-10 and 37-11 show what the properties bar looks like on the screen, and explain its layout.

The ScaleMode Property

The ScaleMode property of a container directly affects the meaning of the value of the Top property for objects placed in that container. When the ScaleMode property changes at design time from one measurement to another, Visual Basic recalculates the value of the Top property in this new type of measurement. No matter what the Top property of a control becomes based on changes in the ScaleMode of the parent form, the physical location of the control will remain the same.

Example

The Coordinates project at the end of this chapter uses the pictSurface picture box's Top property to help properly position and size it when the form it's on is resized by the user.

Comments

Remember that changes to the ScaleTop property of a form only alter the value of the Top property of a control and not the actual distance.

WIDTH PROPERTY

Objects Affected   CheckBox control, Column, ComboBox control, CommandButton, Data, DirListBox, DriveListBox, FileListBox, Form, Forms collection, Frame, HScrollBar, Image, Label, ListBox, MDIForm, OLE container, OptionButton, Picture, PictureBox, Printer, Printers collection, PropertyPage, RemoteData, Screen, Shape, TextBox, UserControl, UserDocument, VScrollBar

Purpose   The Width property reads or sets the horizontal size of a form or control on the screen, form, picture box, or Printer object. This property is measured in the measurement system defined by the container's ScaleMode property. You can read and write with this property at runtime and design time for most controls and objects; the property is read-only at runtime for the Printer and Screen objects. Table 37-15 shows the arguments for the Width property.

General Syntax
```
[form.]Width [ = width!]
[form!]Name.Width [ = width!]
Printer.Width [ = width!]
Screen.Width [ = width!]
```

Table 37-15 Arguments of the Width property

Argument	Description
form	Name property of the form
Name	Name property of the control
Printer	'Printer' indicates the Printer object
Screen	'Screen' indicates the Screen object
width!	Horizontal width of the object

Example Syntax
```
Private Sub Form_Load ()
    Form1.Width = (Picture1.Width * 2)      'Width and height of form made twice the size
    Form1.Height = (Picture1.Height * 2)    'of the width and height of picture box.
End Sub
```

Description   The Width property of an object measures its horizontal width. You can enter this value at design time by manually sizing the object with the mouse or by entering the value in the properties box. You can modify the Width property of a control at runtime or design time. The Printer and Screen objects' Width property is set by Windows and is read-only at runtime. A setting must be between 0 and a maximum value specified by the system itself. Visual Basic automatically adjusts itself to the resolution of the screen or printer. You should ensure that your objects are not too large for the most common 640×480 and 800×600 resolution screens to display.

The example syntax sets Form1's Width property to twice the size of the setting of the Picture1 picture box. This demonstrates the ways in which this property can change the measurements of other objects.

The Left, Top, and Height Properties

When you create a form or control in Visual Basic, the Left, Top, Width, and Height properties display in the far-right side of the toolbar. Figure 37-11 shows what the properties bar looks like on the screen, and explains its layout. The first two numbers, separated by a comma, represent the left and top position of the control or form. The width and the height of the object appear to the right of these numbers separated by an "x". If the object is a control, then the numbers shown are in the units of measurement specified by the ScaleMode property of its container. The Screen and Printer objects, as well as forms, are always measured in twips.

Screen and Printer

When used with the Screen or Printer objects, the Width property returns the width of the screen or page available. Note that these settings are different for different hardware configurations. The Width property of the Screen and Printer objects is not available at design time and is read-only at runtime.

The ScaleMode Property

The ScaleMode property of a container directly affects the meaning of the value of the Width property for controls placed in that container. When the ScaleMode property changes at design time from one measurement to another, Visual Basic recalculates the value of the Width property in this new type of measurement. No matter what Width a control becomes based on changes in the ScaleMode of the parent form, the physical size of the control will remain the same.

The ScaleWidth Property

The ScaleWidth property divides the Width of a form, picture box, or Printer object into the number of units set in the property. For example, when a form's ScaleWidth property changes to 100, the Width of the form is divided into 100 equal units. Remember that changing the ScaleWidth property of the form to a new value does not change the actual size of it or any controls on it.

This unit does not change in size as the form's Width changes. These units define the upper and lower limit of the possible Width of controls on this form. For example, a Resize event might adjust the Width property of a command button on a form by triggering a Move statement that always ensures that the command box is one-fourth the size of the form. In this example, the ScaleWidth property of the form is 100, and the Width property of the Command1 command button is 25 (one-fourth the width of the form). Figure 37-19 displays this concept visually.

Example

In the Coordinates project at the end of this chapter, the Width property of the pictSurface picture box changes when the form is resized to fit the picture box to the width of the form.

Comments

Remember that changes to the ScaleWidth property of a form only alter the value of the Width property of a control and not the actual width.

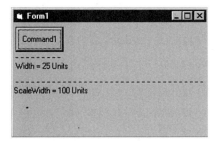

Figure 37-19   Interaction of the
ScaleWidth and Width properties

The Coordinates Project

Project Overview

The Coordinates project demonstrates the concepts of the coordinate system in Visual
Basic. It lets you define your own coordinate system or use one of the predefined ones,
and gives you immediate feedback on how these coordinate systems differ.

Assembling the Project: Coordinates Form

1. Make a new form with the objects and properties listed in Table 37-16.

Table 37-16 Settings for formMain

Object	Property	Setting
Form	Caption	"Coordinates Project"
	Name	formMain
Combo	Name	cmboMeasure
Command	Caption	"Clear"
	Name	cmndClear
Label	Caption	"Current X"
Label	Caption	"Current Y"
Label	Caption	"Mouse X"
Label	Caption	"Mouse Y"
Picture	Name	pictSurface
Text	Name	textCurrentX
Text	Name	textCurrentY
Text	Name	textMouseX
Text	Name	textMouseY

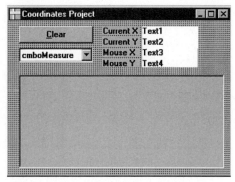

Figure 37-20 formMain at design time

2. Size the objects on the screen as shown in Figure 37-20.

3. Enter the following code in the cmndClear_Click event. This simply clears the picture box of all the drawn lines.

```
Private Sub cmndClear_Click ()
    pictSurface.Cls                          'clear the picture
End Sub
```

4. Enter the following code in the cmboMeasure_Click event. This triggers when the user chooses a different coordinate system in the combo box. It tests to see if the user wants to specify a user-defined coordinate system. If so, it pops up a dialog box to get the information, then goes on to set the scaling factors appropriately for ScaleTop, ScaleLeft, ScaleHeight, and ScaleWidth for the picture box. If the user chooses one of the standard formats, it sets the Picture1's ScaleMode directly.

```
Private Sub cmboMeasure_Click()
  'We need to define coordinate system
  If cmboMeasure.Text = "User Defined" Then
    'Show modal input box
    formGetUserDefined.Show 1
    pictSurface.ScaleTop = Val(formGetUserDefined!textTop.Text)
    pictSurface.ScaleLeft = Val(formGetUserDefined!textLeft.Text)
    pictSurface.ScaleWidth = Val(formGetUserDefined![TextWidth].Text)
    pictSurface.ScaleHeight = Val(formGetUserDefined![TextHeight].Text)
  Else
    'items were added to combo box in order, so index is ScaleMode
    pictSurface.ScaleMode = cmboMeasure.ListIndex
  End If
  'update display when scaleMode changes
  textCurrentX.Text = Format$(pictSurface.CurrentX, "####0.00")
  textCurrentY.Text = Format$(pictSurface.CurrentY, "####0.00")
End Sub
```

5. Enter the following code in the Form_Load event. This sets up the form, and loads the combo box with the scale mode selections. It then chooses twips as the default starting scale mode.

```
Private Sub Form_Load()
    'custom coordinate system for form
    formMain.Scale (0, 0)-(100, 100)
    'scaleMode choices into combo box
    'note that we add these in the
    'correct order, so that listIndex
    'indicates correct ScaleMode
    cmboMeasure.AddItem "User Defined"
    cmboMeasure.AddItem "Twips"
    cmboMeasure.AddItem "Points"
    cmboMeasure.AddItem "Pixels"
    cmboMeasure.AddItem "Characters"
    cmboMeasure.AddItem "Inches"
    cmboMeasure.AddItem "Millimeters"
    cmboMeasure.AddItem "Centimeters"
    'set initial ScaleMode to twips
    cmboMeasure.ListIndex = 1
End Sub
```

6. Enter the following code in the Form_Resize event. This triggers any time the
form changes size (including startup). This sizes the picture box so it fills the
entire bottom part of the form, leaving enough room on top for the controls and
a small border on the sides and bottom.

```
Private Sub Form_Resize()
    'leave room for controls on top
    pictSurface.Move 0, 40
    'fill rest of form, less a small border
    pictSurface.Left = formMain.ScaleLeft + 2
    pictSurface.Width = formMain.ScaleWidth - 4
    pictSurface.Height = formMain.ScaleHeight - 4 - pictSurface.Top
End Sub
```

7. Enter the following code in the pictSurface_MouseDown event. This draws lines
on the picture box and updates the text box displays to show your current position. The line drawing can be in either one of two modes: starting to draw a line
(first click) or finishing drawing a line (second click). The static variable named
drawing tracks which part of the process you're in, and x1! and y1! remember
where the line is supposed to start.

```
Private Sub pictSurface_MouseDown _
    (Button As Integer, Shift As Integer, X As Single, Y As Single)
    'drawing is a flag; x1 and y1 are old positions
    Static drawing As Integer, x1!, y1!
    'if user's already clicked once, draw the line
    'and get a fresh start next click
    If drawing = True Then
        pictSurface.DrawWidth = 1
        pictSurface.Line (x1!, y1!)-(X, Y)
        drawing = False
    Else
    '....otherwise, start the line draw by:
        pictSurface.DrawWidth = 3
        'make a dot where user is starting the line
```

continued on next page

continued from previous page

```
    pictSurface.PSet (X, Y)
    'remember our starting coordinates
    x1! = X
    y1! = Y
    'and flag that we're drawing
    drawing = True
  End If
  'update display box
  textCurrentX.Text = _
    Format$(pictSurface.CurrentX, "####0.00")
  'update display box
  textCurrentY.Text = _
    Format$(pictSurface.CurrentY, "####0.00")
End Sub
```

8. Enter the following code in the MouseMove event for pictSurface. This triggers anytime the mouse moves when it's over pictSurface. This simply updates the MouseX and MouseY display boxes.

```
Private Sub pictSurface_MouseMove(Button As Integer, _
  Shift As Integer, X As Single, Y As Single)
  'update MouseX box
  textMouseX.Text = Format$(X, "####0.00")
  'update MouseY box
  textMouseY.Text = Format$(Y, "####0.00")
End Sub
```

Assembling the Project: Form

1. Make a new form with the objects and properties listed in Table 37-17.

Table 37-17 Settings for the Coordinates form

Object	Property	Setting
Form	BorderStyle	3–Fixed Double
	Caption	User Defined
Form	Name	formGetUserDefined
Label	Caption	Top
Label	Caption	Left
Label	Caption	Height
Label	Caption	Width
Text	Name	textTop
Text	Name	textLeft
Text	Name	textHeight
Text	Name	textWidth

Figure 37-21
formGetUserDefined
at design time

2. Size the objects on the screen, as shown in Figure 37-21.

3. Enter the following code in Command1's Click event. This simply hides the form. Note that you only hide it (rather than unload it), because you need to access the information in the text boxes from the other form.

```
Private Sub Command1_Click ()
      Hide
End Sub
```

How It Works

When the program first starts, the combo box gets filled with an entry for each ScaleMode measurement system. Note that they are added to the combo box in the correct order, so the combo box's ListIndex property refers to the corresponding ScaleMode setting. Form_Load also sets a user-defined coordinate system for the form. This lets you easily move and resize the elements on the form in the form's Resize event.

The Resize event triggers when the form first loads, and every time the user resizes the form. This sets the pictSurface picture box's size and position to almost fill the lower half of the form. It uses the form's ScaleLeft, ScaleWidth, and ScaleHeight properties to set its own Left, Width, and Height properties; Top is set to a predetermined spot underneath the controls in the top part of the form.

Moving the mouse around on pictSurface immediately updates the displays of the current coordinates of the mouse. Clicking the mouse sets a point on pictSurface to signal the start of a drawing operation; the second click finishes the drawing operation by drawing a line connecting the starting and ending points. Each click updates the display of CurrentX and CurrentY.

Choosing a new measurement system in the combo box resets the ScaleMode property of pictSurface. Note how nothing visibly changes; only the measurement system changes, which is illustrated in the four text boxes displaying the coordinates.

If the chosen measurement system is user defined, then a dialog box pops up that allows the user to enter the appropriate values for the top, left, width, and height of the measurement system.

Finally, clicking the Clear button clears pictSurface to begin a new drawing. Double-click the control box (or pull down the Control Box menu and choose Close) to end the program. Figure 37-22 shows the project in action.

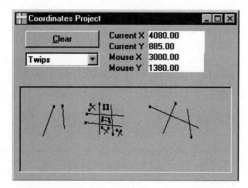

Figure 37-22 The Coordinates project in action

38

GRAPHICS FUNDAMENTALS

Visual Basic provides a variety of ways to create and manipulate graphics with ease. Because of this flexibility, generating special effects on the screen becomes a simpler task than in many other languages. Users expect and demand graphics of Windows programs. Databases now show pictures instead of just words, spreadsheets have sophisticated drawing functions, and word processors support advanced graphics handling.

Graphics elements in Visual Basic applications fall into three main categories: displaying existing graphics, drawing new graphics, and using graphic elements in form design. Forms, picture boxes, user controls, user documents, and the image control can all display existing graphics. Check boxes, option buttons, and command buttons also have a picture property, and can display existing images within the constraints of their control function. You can create new graphics by drawing on forms, user controls, user documents, picture boxes, property pages, and the printer. The line and shape controls let you easily add graphics elements to forms and other containers during design.

This chapter covers the fundamentals of graphics in Visual Basic, focusing on those language elements common to all three graphics categories and providing an overview of how to use graphics in your applications. Chapter 39, "Pictures," covers the intricacies of using existing images, and Chapter 40, "Drawing Shapes," goes into detail on how to draw graphics using both the graphics methods and the graphics controls.

Graphics Overview

Forms, picture boxes, the image control, user controls, user documents, check boxes, option buttons, and command buttons can all display existing graphics files. Use the Picture property to load the graphics file. A loaded file may be in icon (.ICO),

Windows metafile (.WMF), Windows extended metafile (.EMF), device independent bitmap (.DIB), bitmap (.BMP), Graphical interchange format (.GIF), or Joint Photographic Experts Group (.JPG) format. To display a file, first select the object that will display the picture. Choose the Picture property in the Properties window. Double-click on (picture) on the right side of Properties box. Select the file from the File→Open dialog box and click on OK to load it. Figure 38-1 shows a picture box displaying the contents of a file.

You normally set the contents of forms, picture boxes, and image controls at design time. This way, the loaded file becomes a part of the executable file of the program. You may also load them during runtime, if the picture needs to change during program execution, by using the LoadPicture function. You can clear an object of a loaded picture by using LoadPicture with no argument. To clear a loaded picture from an object at design time, highlight the Picture property value of the object with your mouse and press the [DELETE] key.

Forms and picture boxes handle more complex graphics operations than the image control. The image control is like a stripped-down picture box: It can display existing graphics files, but cannot employ graphics methods to create new graphics. It uses fewer system resources than the picture box, and displays faster.

A variety of graphics methods can act on forms and picture boxes. Drawn graphics are any shapes produced with the Circle, Line, or PSet graphics methods. The Circle method creates curved objects, including circles, ellipses (ovals), and arcs. The Line method generates lines or box objects, including straight lines, squares, rectangles, and triangles. The PSet method makes spots of varying size and color. Each of these methods produces graphics at runtime. Graphics drawn with these methods can appear on forms, picture boxes, property pages, user controls, and user documents. Use the Cls method to clear the object of any drawn graphics. Figure 38-2 displays a drawn circle, triangle, and box.

You may want to incorporate graphics elements like lines or rectangles directly in your form design. Whether you use an existing graphics file or graphics drawn at runtime, the line and shape controls let you do it more easily. You can draw these controls

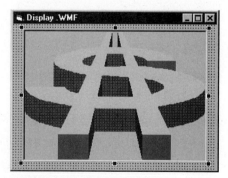

Figure 38-1   A picture box
displaying a Windows metafile

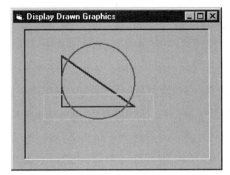

Figure 38-2   Drawn graphics on a form

directly on the form, just as you would with other controls, such as command buttons and text boxes. This lets you see exactly how the graphics elements look during the design process.

Color

Color affects the ways people respond to the elements on the screen. For example, red usually represents danger or warning (at least in most Western cultures). If a warning message is red, and all other text on the screen is black, your user's eye will naturally be drawn to the warning. Color can be a powerful agent in creating a beautiful and effective user interface. Careful and sparing use of color can help increase your user's comprehension and enjoyment; overuse of color elements can create a busy jumble that actually detracts from your application.

Each Visual Basic color has a unique hexadecimal code. Finding a particular color's code involves one of several possible methods. The color palette helps you interactively set color properties at design time. Double-clicking on a color property setting in the properties box brings up a "mini-palette" that you can use to quickly pick out common colors. Figure 38-3 shows this palette in the ForeColor property.

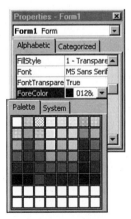

Figure 38-3   This mini-color palette pops up in the Properties window to help you set color properties

Figure 38-4   The system colors selections

Windows users often like to set their own color schemes. Visual Basic 5.0 makes it easy to adopt your user's system colors. Then, if the user changes his or her computer's color scheme, your program's colors will change to match. When you click on a color property setting, select the System tab instead of the Palette tab and choose your colors accordingly. Figure 38-4 shows the system colors option in the ForeColor property.

An object's colors can change at runtime. The RGB and QBColor functions provide the necessary settings for the BackColor and ForeColor properties, and you may also specify hexadecimal numbers directly, or use the constants defined in the Visual Basic object library.

Visual Basic, starting with version 2.0, provides support for 256-color palettes. Standard VGA adapters only allow 16 colors, which make for unrealistic renderings of complex graphics. The availability of 256 colors greatly enhances image quality. Visual Basic's implementation of this is really quite simple.

To use the extended palette, simply load a bitmap that contains the palette you'd like into a form, picture box, or image control. This bitmap can be quite small; even a single pixel will suffice. Three palettes ship with Visual Basic: RAINBOW.DIB, PASTEL.DIB, and BRIGHT.DIB. Table 38-1 summarizes this.

Table 38-1 Standard 256-color palettes that ship with Visual Basic

Device Independent Bitmap (.DIB)	Description
RAINBOW.DIB	Standard range of all colors
PASTEL.DIB	Lighter colors, with lots of blues
BRIGHT.DIB	Bright colors

Once the picture control contains the palette, Windows attempts to match any requested color to the closest available color in the palette. Thus, if a line specifies ultramarine blue, and the nearest color is dark blue, then dark blue gets drawn.

Note that there may be many palettes competing for priority. More than 16 million colors are possible, but only 256 can be displayed at any time. The window with the focus generally gets the highest priority from Windows, so its colors are truest. Other windows may look strangely colored if they don't have the focus.

Graphical Layering

Graphical controls and the graphics methods appear on separate layers in a container. Think of a container (say, a form) as having three superimposed transparent layers. The topmost layer, the one closest to the user, contains nongraphical controls like command buttons, check boxes, or file controls. Underneath this is a middle layer containing the graphical controls (Line, Shape, and Image) as well as Labels. Finally, in the back layer, lies the drawing space for the container. All the graphical methods (Line, Circle, Cls, PSet, and so on) apply to this back layer. Objects on the front layers obscure whatever lies behind them. Figure 38-5 illustrates the normal layering arrangement. This means that both graphical and nongraphical controls will obscure graphics methods.

This normal layering may change with different settings of the AutoRedraw and ClipControls properties interacting with the Paint event. Setting AutoRedraw to True always produces normal layering. Although this makes your life simpler, it may also reduce performance due to the large amounts of memory consumed by AutoRedraw. Setting ClipControls to False can speed up the display time for forms. Setting both AutoRedraw and ClipControls to False can have unpredictable results. See Table 38-2 for a summary of layering interactions. As you can see, keeping your graphics methods confined to Paint events always produces predictable, normal layering.

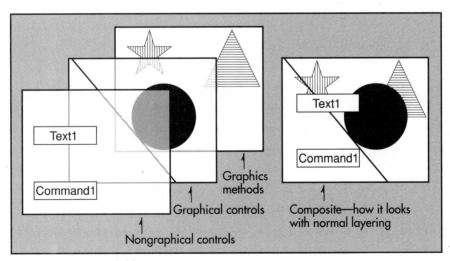

Figure 38-5   Normal layering

Table 38-2 The possible layering interactions

AutoRedraw	ClipControls	Paint Event	Layering Behavior
True	True	N/A	Normal layering
True	False	N/A	Normal layering
False	True	Graphics during Paint	Normal layering
		Graphics out of Paint	Middle and back layers mixed
False	False	Graphics during Paint	Normal layering
		Graphics out of Paint	All three layers mixed

PicClip Professional Edition Control

Sometimes you need to store many pictures on a form. The PictureBox is a resource-intensive control, so it isn't a good choice when you need many pictures. If your pictures are all the same size, you can put them in the PicClip control. The PicClip control gives you the ability to store one large bitmap and pick parts of it to load into other picture or image controls. For instance, you could store the up and down images of toolbar buttons or command buttons in a PicClip control and load the appropriate segments of the picture in the MouseDown and MouseUp events of the PictureBox. The PicClip control is limited to 16-color bitmaps.

Graphics Fundamentals Summary

Table 38-3 displays the properties, methods, functions, statements, and events that influence the basic display of graphics in Visual Basic.

Table 38-3 Methods, properties, events, functions, and statements dealing with graphics

Use or Set This...	Type	To Do This...
AutoRedraw	Property	Determine whether a drawn object redisplays after uncovering it
ClipControls	Property	Determine what parts of a newly exposed object are repainted
Cls	Method	Wipe the surface of a picture box or form of all drawn objects
Image	Property	Determine the Microsoft Windows handle name assigned to an object
LoadPicture	Function	Change the graphics contents of a picture box or form
Paint	Event	Trigger when a portion of a form or picture box uncovers
PaintPicture	Method	Paint a .BMP, .WMF, .DIB, or .ICO on a form, picture box, or printer object
Picture	Property	Determine the graphics object that initially appears in a form or picture box
Point	Method	Discover the RGB colors of a particular point on a form or picture box
PSet	Method	Change the RGB colors of a particular point on a form or picture box
QBColor	Function	Determine the RGB values of a specified color
RGB	Function	Define the RGB values of an object in an expression

Use or Set This...	Type	To Do This...
SavePicture	Statement	Save any graphical object on a form or picture box to a specified filename
Stretch	Property	Set or determine how the image control displays graphics
ZOrder	Method	Place an object in front of or in back of other objects

The following pages investigate these items in detail. At the end of this section, step-by-step directions explain how to assemble the Graphics project.

AUTOREDRAW PROPERTY

Objects Affected   Form, PictureBox, PropertyPage, UserControl, UserDocument

Purpose   The AutoRedraw property indicates whether the drawn graphical objects on a form or picture box automatically redisplay when uncovered. Forms with the AutoRedraw property set to True automatically have their graphics redrawn when uncovered by another overlapping window or form, or when resized or restored to normal from being minimized. AutoRedraw may be set at design time or runtime. Table 38-4 lists the arguments of the AutoRedraw property.

General Syntax

```
[form.]AutoRedraw [ = boolean%]
[form!]Name.AutoRedraw [ = boolean%]
```

Table 38-4 Arguments of the AutoRedraw property

Argument	Description
form	Name of the form
Name	Name of the picture box
boolean%	True or False value indicating the property's new setting

Example Syntax

```
Private Sub Form_Click ()
    'Displays a circle while the AutoRedraw property is True
    'and a triangle while AutoRedraw is False. If the form is
    'minimized and then restored on the screen, only the circle
    ScaleMode = 5
    AutoRedraw = True
    FillStyle = 0
    FillColor = RGB(0, 0, 255)   'reappears.
    Circle (1, 1), .5
    AutoRedraw = False
    ForeColor = RGB(255, 0, 0)
    Line (0.5 , 0.5)-(2, 1)
    Line -(2, 2)
    Line -(0.5, 0.5)
End Sub
```

Description

The AutoRedraw property specifies whether a drawn object on a form or picture box redraws after being uncovered on the screen. A *drawn object* is an object produced with the Circle, Line, or PSet methods. There are two possible settings for this property, True (-1) and False (0). By default, AutoRedraw is set to False.

An AutoRedraw property expression begins with the name of the picture box or form affected. If a Redraw property expression does not begin with the name of the picture box or form, then the active form's property changes. The example syntax provides no name for the object being drawn on, so the circle and triangle appear on the form and the AutoRedraw of the form changes.

The example syntax demonstrates this difference between the two settings of the AutoRedraw property. First, the Circle method draws a circle with the AutoRedraw property set to True (-1). Next, three Line method expressions create a triangle with the AutoRedraw property set to False (0). Figure 38-6 shows what this example should look like. Minimizing and then normalizing the form erases the triangle and restores the circle. Figure 38-7 shows what Form1 looks like without the triangle.

The Cls Method and BackColor Property

The Cls method and BackColor property of a form or picture box change their effects depending on the setting of the AutoRedraw property. Calling the Cls method or changing the BackColor property will remove any graphics that were generated with the AutoRedraw property of the picture box or form set to False (0). Graphics created with the AutoRedraw property set to True (-1) are erased only by changing the BackColor property; the Cls method does not affect these graphics. This distinction might prove useful when you'd like to have persistent graphics (say, grid lines on a graph) and still retain the capacity to have nonpersistent graphic elements (the actual graph) that can be erased and redrawn at will.

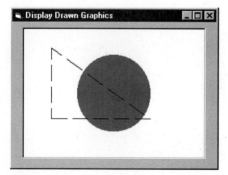

Figure 38-6 Example syntax graphics before minimizing the form

Figure 38-7 Example syntax graphics after minimizing and then normalizing the form, showing how an object drawn with AutoRedraw = False does not reappear

The Paint Event

The Paint event of a form and the AutoRedraw property of a form or picture box have similar effects. Both redraw graphic elements whenever a form or picture box is normalized, maximized, or uncovered. In fact, if the AutoRedraw property was True when the graphics were drawn, no Paint events are needed—Visual Basic handles the redrawing for you.

The ClipControls Property

Normal layering may change with different settings of the AutoRedraw and ClipControls properties interacting with the Paint event. Setting AutoRedraw to True always produces normal layering. Although this makes your life simpler, it may also reduce performance due to the large amounts of memory consumed by AutoRedraw. Setting ClipControls to False can speed up the display time for forms. Setting both AutoRedraw and ClipControls to False can have unpredictable results. Refer to Table 38-2 for a summary of layering interactions.

The Refresh Method

When a form's AutoRedraw property is False, the Refresh method clears whatever graphics are on the screen. If the AutoRedraw property is True, then the Refresh property only removes those elements of the screen generated while the AutoRedraw property was False.

Example

The Graphics project at the end of this chapter adjusts the AutoRedraw property of the image control imagIcon and forms formGraphics and formScreen. The AutoRedraw property of both formGraphics and the image control imagIcon are set to True. This allows any graphics placed on either formGraphics or imagIcon to redisplay after being temporarily obscured. In order to allow periodic removal of the graphics on formScreen, formScreen's AutoRedraw property is set to False (0).

ClipControls Property

Objects Affected   Form, Frame, PictureBox, UserControl, UserDocument

Purpose   The ClipControls property determines if Windows repaints the entire object, or only newly exposed parts. Tables 38-5 and 38-6 summarize the arguments of the ClipControls property.

General Syntax

```
[form.]ClipControls [ = boolean%]
[form!]Name.ClipControls [ = boolean%]
```

Table 38-5 Arguments of the ClipControls property

Argument	Description
form	Name property of the form
Name	Name property of the control
boolean%	True/False

Table 38-6 Meanings of the boolean% argument in the ClipControls property

boolean%	Meaning
True	(Default.) Graphics methods in Paint events repaint the entire object; a clipping region is created.
False	Graphics methods in Paint events repaint only newly exposed areas; no clipping region is created.

Example Syntax

```
Private Sub Command1_Click ()
    Picture1.ClipControls = Not Picture1.ClipControls
End Sub
```

Description   The ClipControls property determines whether graphics methods in a Paint event repaint the entire object, or just those parts of the object that are newly exposed. It also determines whether a *clipping region* is created for the object. A clipping region is like a mask that Windows keeps in memory that corresponds to the area covered by nongraphical controls like text boxes and command buttons. Setting ClipControls to False can speed up the display and repainting of forms.

The AutoRedraw Property   Normal layering may change with different settings of the AutoRedraw and ClipControls properties interacting with the Paint event. Setting AutoRedraw to True always produces normal layering. Although this makes your life simpler, it may also reduce performance due to the large amounts of memory consumed by AutoRedraw. Setting ClipControls to

False can speed up the display time for forms. Setting both AutoRedraw and ClipControls to False can have unpredictable results. Refer to Table 38-2 for a summary of layering interactions.

Example   The ClipControls property of the forms in the Graphics project are both set to False to increase performance.

Cls Method

Objects Affected   Form, PictureBox, PropertyPage, UserControl, UserDocument

Purpose   The Cls method removes drawn graphics or text from an object on the screen. Table 38-7 explains the arguments of the Cls method.

General Syntax

```
[form.]Cls
[form!]Name.Cls
```

Table 38-7 Arguments of the Cls method

Argument	Description
form	Name property of the form
Name	Name property of the picture box; if not specified, then acts on current form

Example Syntax

```
Private Sub Form_Click ()
     'objects placed on the screen will contain crosshatch lines
    FillStyle = 6
    'color inside a drawn object will be red
    FillColor = QBColor(4)
    'X and Y place the circle in the center of the form
    X = ScaleWidth / 2
    Y = ScaleHeight / 2
     'Radius defined as one quarter of width of form
    Radius = ScaleWidth / 4
    'prints this text on screen
    Print "Demo Text"
    'draws Circle
    Circle (X, Y), Radius
    'displays message
    Select Case AutoRedraw
        Case True
            MsgBox "Effects of Cls with AutoRedraw set to True."
        Case False
            MsgBox "Effects of Cls with AutoRedraw set to False."
    End Select
    AutoRedraw = Not AutoRedraw 'flip AutoRedraw status
    Cls                              'clears the form
End Sub
```

Description	The Cls method clears drawn text and graphics on a form or picture box. If a Cls method begins with the Name of a picture box, only the contents of the indicated picture box change. Cls method expressions that begin with no name or the Name of the form only affect the contents of a form. The example syntax doesn't specify an object, so the properties and methods in the sample apply to the currently active form.
	This method clears all the objects drawn with AutoRedraw set to False. The Cls method has no effect on a form's controls and their contents. Loaded pictures do not disappear when the Cls method removes the drawn graphics on a form or picture box. Similarly, a Cls statement directed to the form has no effect on graphics placed on a picture box. Using the Cls method on a picture box has no effect on the graphics on the form containing the picture box.
The CurrentX and CurrentY Properties	The Cls method changes the CurrentX and CurrentY properties of a form or picture box to 0. Graphics created on a form or picture box with the AutoRedraw property set to True (-1) remain unaffected.
The Picture Property	The use of the Cls method has no effect on a picture box's Picture property. The Cls method only affects drawn graphics. However, the Cls method clears any drawn graphics within a picture box that also has a loaded picture.
The BackColor Property and AutoRedraw Property	The Cls method and BackColor property of a form or picture box have different effects depending on the setting of the AutoRedraw property. Calling the Cls method or changing the BackColor property will both remove any graphics that were generated with the AutoRedraw property of the picture box or form set to False (0). Graphics created with the AutoRedraw property at True (-1) are erased only by a change to the BackColor property; the Cls method does not affect these graphics. This distinction might prove useful when you'd like to have persistent graphics (say, gridlines on a graph) and still retain the capacity to have nonpersistent graphic elements (the actual graph lines) that can be erased and redrawn at will.
Example	In the Graphics project at the end of this chapter, the Cls method clears formScreen of all drawn graphics when formScreen is double-clicked.

IMAGE PROPERTY

Objects Affected	Form, PictureBox, UserControl, UserDocument, PropertyPage
Purpose	The Image property defines the value that Microsoft Windows automatically gives to an image on a picture box or form; it serves as a pointer to the memory position that contains the image. Windows sets the value returned by the Image property. It is not available at design time, and is read-only at runtime. Table 38-8 lists the arguments for the Image property.

General Syntax

```
[form.]Image
[form!]Name.Image
```

Table 38-8 Arguments of the Image property

Argument	Description
form	Name property of the affected form
Name	Name property of the affected picture box

Example Syntax

```
Private Sub Command1_Click ()
     AutoRedraw = -1              'makes form1's AutoRedraw property True
     FillStyle = 0                'defines the object to be drawn as solid
     FillColor = QBColor(4)       'defines the object to be drawn as red
     ScaleMode = 5          'defines dimensions as being measured in inches
     Print "This is a red circle"'prints test in top left corner of window
     Circle (1, 1), .5            'draws a red circle on the form
     FillColor = QBColor(1)       'defines the object to be drawn as blue
     Circle (3, 1), .5            'draws a blue circle on the form
     Form2.Show                   'displays second form on the screen
     Form2.AutoRedraw = -1        'makes Form2's AutoRedraw property True
     Form2.Picture = Form1.Image  'gives Form2 the same images as Form1
End Sub
```

Description

The Image property provides the value that Microsoft Windows uses to identify the text and generated graphics on a form or picture box. This value references all the graphics and text that appear on the object. You can use this value in API calls, as well as in saving graphics to disk or transferring graphics images from one control to another.

In the example syntax, the Image property transfers all the graphics on Form1 to Form2 by setting Form2's Picture property equal to Form1's Image property. This shows that the Image property identifies all the graphics on a form, not just one individual part of the graphics. Because the Windows environment sometimes changes the value returned by the Image property, another variable should never store this value for later reference. Figure 38-8 shows what Form1 and Form2 might look like on the screen.

The Picture Property

The Picture property of a form or picture may be set equal to the Image property of another form or picture. This reproduces the same graphics on both forms and picture boxes. In the example syntax, the Picture property of Form2 is assigned the Image property of Form1, thus making the same graphics appear on both forms. Notice that this change has no effect on the other properties of Form2. As a result, the actual image that appears on Form1 appears on Form2 without changes to Form2's ScaleMode, FillColor, and FillStyle properties.

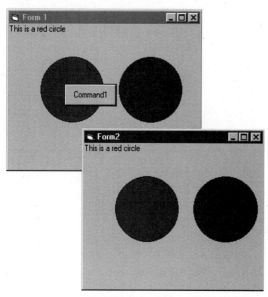

Figure 38-8   The Image property of Form1 was
used to transfer a graphical image to Form2

Example   In the Graphics project at the end of this chapter, the Image property
serves as a means of saving the current graphics image on the screen.
When the user clicks the form, the Form_Click event prompts the user to
save the current image to a file. If the user responds Yes, then the
SavePicture statement accesses the Image property of formScreen to determine the Windows handle value. The code then uses this value to save the
current contents of the screen to the bitmap file ~TEMP.BMP.

Comments   The Image property of a form or picture box may change during program
execution. Do not define variables with this value.

LoadPicture Function

Purpose   The LoadPicture function places pictures in forms, image controls, and
picture boxes. Table 38-9 explains the stringexpression$ argument.

General Syntax

```
LoadPicture(stringexpression$)
```

Table 38-9 Argument of the LoadPicture function

Argument	Description
stringexpression$	Path and filename of the graphics file to load

Example Syntax

```
Private Sub Picture1_MouseDown (Button As Integer, Shift As Integer, _
    X As Single, Y As Single)
    Picture1.Picture = _
      LoadPicture("\VB\ICONS\OFFICE\FILES03B.ICO") 'open file cabinet
    Picture1.DragIcon = _
      LoadPicture("\VB\ICONS\OFFICE\FILES04.ICO") 'hand taking file out
    Form1.Icon = _
      LoadPicture("\VB\ICONS\MISC\FACE03.ICO")           'happy face
End Sub
```

Description

The LoadPicture function loads a graphical image into a form, image, or picture box. The loaded picture must be in bitmap (.BMP), device independent bitmap (.DIB), icon (.ICO), run-length encoded (.RLE), Windows metafile (.WMF), Windows extended metafile (.EMF), Graphical interchange format (.GIF), or Joint Photographic Experts Group (.JPG) format. The argument stringexpression$ is the name of the picture file, with or without the extension. If the file is in the current search path or the same directory, then the extension is not necessary. In the example syntax, the icons appear with their full paths because none of the icons are in the path and would otherwise generate an error. To avoid confusion, use the extension. Use LoadPicture without stringexpression$ (that is, load nothing) to clear the contents of the object.

```
Set Picture1.Picture = LoadPicture("")
```

The Icon, DragIcon, and Picture properties are all definable at runtime with this function. This function overrides the initial setting of these properties.

In the example syntax, the LoadPicture function redefines all three of these properties to signify the beginning of a drag operation. The picture box becomes an open file cabinet to signify the beginning of a drag operation. See Figure 38-9 for a picture of what the form produced by the example syntax should look like.

The DragIcon Property

Define the DragIcon of a control at runtime with a LoadPicture function similar to the one in the example syntax. This icon displays from the time a drag operation begins until the drag operation ends. This permits the program to signify to the user the type of operation taking place. For example, the DragIcon changes to an open file folder or a disk to signify when a file or an entire disk is being copied from one place to another. Chapter 50, "Dragging-and-Dropping," goes into this in more detail.

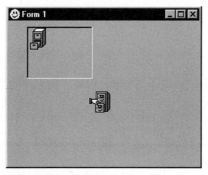

Figure 38-9   The LoadPicture
function lets you change graphics at
runtime

The Icon Property   Define the Icon property of a control at runtime with a LoadPicture function similar to the one used in the example syntax. This icon represents a
minimized form. Changing the Icon property of a form might specify what
type of operation is taking place. For example, a communications program
might change the Icon property of a dialer directory form to a phone off
the hook when the dialer dials a number.

**The Picture
Property**   The LoadPicture function defines the Picture property of a form, picture
box, or image control at runtime in the same way as the example syntax.
Either the AutoRedraw of the form or the Picture must be True, or the
changes must occur within a Paint event for it to be immediately apparent.
For example, the icon displayed in the Picture1 control box does not
change unless the AutoRedraw property is True. Note that the grid control
also has a Picture property that lets you load graphics images into individ
ual cells.

Example   In the Graphics project at the end of this chapter, the LoadPicture function
loads in all the icons to represent the different kinds of screen blankers.
The Form_Load event first creates a control array of image controls, then
LoadPicture reads in the appropriate icons.

PAINT EVENT

Objects Affected   Form, PictureBox, UserControl, UserDocument, PropertyPage

Purpose   The Paint event defines what actions take place when uncovering a previously obscured part of a form or picture box. Either restoring a minimized
form or uncovering an obscured form triggers a Paint event. This event
only applies to generated graphics and does not affect the appearance of
the controls on a form. Table 38-10 gives the arguments of the Paint event.

General Syntax

```
Sub Form_Paint ()
Sub Name_Paint ([Index As Integer])
```

Table 38-10 Arguments of the Paint event

Argument	Description
Form	'Form' indicates the paint event of the current form
Name	Name property of the affected picture box

Example Syntax

```
Private Sub Form_Click ()
    Refresh                      'triggers the Paint event
End Sub

Private Sub Form_Paint ()
    Static Num As Integer        'retain value of Num
    X = ScaleWidth / 2           'define X as half of width of form
    Y = ScaleHeight / 2          'define Y as half of height of form
    Radius = ScaleWidth / 4      'define Radius as 1/4 of width of form
    FillStyle = 0                'objects drawn will be solid
    Num = Num + 1                'increment the variable Num
    Select Case Num
        Case 1
            'FillColor is black
            FillColor = QBColor(0)
            'draw part of a circle
            Circle (X, Y), Radius, , -6.283, -1.571
        Case 2
            'FillColor is blue
            FillColor = QBColor(1)
            'draw part of a circle
            Circle (X, Y), Radius, , -1.571, -3.142
        Case 3
            'FillColor is green
            FillColor = QBColor(2)
            'draw part of a circle
            Circle (X, Y), Radius, , -3.142, -4.713
        Case 4
            'FillColor is cyan
            FillColor = QBColor(3)
            'draw part of a circle
            Circle (X, Y), Radius, , -4.713, -6.283
        Case 5
            'FillColor is red
            FillColor = QBColor(4)
            'draw a red circle
            Circle (X, Y), Radius
        Case 6
            'reset Num for the next round
            Num = 0
    End Select
End Sub
```

Description	The Paint event may contain actions that place graphics objects on the screen. A Paint event triggers when the form loads, at the uncovering of a form, or when a minimized form changes to normalized or maximized. This event normally reproduces the same graphic image or images on a form or picture box. In some cases, however, it can produce a totally new graphics image. In the example syntax, triggering the Paint event with each click on the form produces a new portion of a circle on the screen.
Graphics from the Circle, Line, PSet, and Print Methods	The Paint event directly affects the production of the graphics and text effects produced by the Circle, Line, PSet, and Print methods. With the AutoRedraw property of a form or picture box set to False, the Paint event reproduces any expressions that place graphics or text on the form or picture box. Otherwise, hidden portions of drawn graphics on forms and controls do not reappear when uncovered.
The AutoRedraw Property	The AutoRedraw property and Paint event share similar tasks. Both determine what happens to a form when the form is loaded or uncovered. The example syntax demonstrates one very important difference. A form with its AutoRedraw property set to True (-1) only reproduces the portions of the screens drawn while that property was True. This is in direct contrast to the example syntax showing that the Paint event can process actions that produce entirely different graphics with each triggering of the Paint event.
The ClipControls Property	Normal layering may change with different settings of the AutoRedraw and ClipControls properties interacting with the Paint event. Setting AutoRedraw to True always produces normal layering. Although this makes your life simpler, it may also reduce performance due to the large amounts of memory consumed by AutoRedraw. Setting ClipControls to False can speed up the display time for forms. Setting both AutoRedraw and ClipControls to False can have unpredictable results. Refer to Table 38-2 for a summary of layering interactions.
The Refresh Method	The Refresh method triggers the Paint event of a form. This method represents a means of activating a Paint event when it is necessary without the normal criteria for generating one. In the example syntax, the Refresh method is in the Form_Click event so that the Paint event triggers with each clicking of the form. With this setup, the image on the form changes under the control of the user.
The Load, Resize, Paint, and GotFocus Events	If there is more than one event attached to a particular control, they process in the following order: Load, Resize, Paint, and GotFocus. This is an important point to keep in mind if any of the actions that take place in one event depend on actions in another event. For example, a data entry form for an address book will cause an error if the Load event disables the Address1 text box and the GotFocus event tries to use it.

Example The Graphics project at the end of this chapter demonstrates the operation of the Paint event as part of formScreen's Click event. When the Form_Click event triggers, the Refresh method activates the Paint event of formScreen.

PICTURE PROPERTY

Objects Affected CheckBox, CommandButton, Form, Image control, MDIForm, OLE container, OptionButton, PictureBox, PropertyPage, UserControl, UserDocument

Purpose The Picture property indicates what image appears on a form or in one of the other affected objects. This property is definable at design time or runtime and defaults to display nothing. Table 38-11 summarizes the arguments of the Picture property.

General Syntax

```
[form.]Picture [ = picture]
[form!]Name.Picture [ = picture]
```

Table 38-11 Arguments of the Picture property

Argument	Description
Name	Name property of the form, image, OLE client, or picture box
Picture	Picture property setting

Example Syntax

```
Private Sub Picture1.Click
    Picture1.AutoRedraw = True        'objects redrawn when uncovered
    X = Picture1.ScaleWidth /2        'X equals width of picture box
    Y = Picture1.ScaleHeight / 2      'Y equals height of picture box
    Radius = Picture1.ScaleWidth /4   'Radius equals picture box's width
    Picture1.FillStyle = 0            'solid FillStyle
    Picture1.Fillcolor = QBColor(4)   'fill color is red
    If Command1.Caption = "Icon" Then 'if the caption is "Icon"
        Picture1.Picture = LoadPicture("C:\PROGRAM FILES\⇐
        DEVSTUDIO\VB\GRAPHICS\ICONS\MISC\FACE03.ICO") 'smiling face
        Command1.Caption = "Circle"
    ElseIf Command1.Caption = "Circle" Then  'if the caption is "Circle"
        Picture1.Circle (X, Y),Radius        'draw a circle
        Command1.Caption = "Square"
    ElseIf Command1.Caption = "Square" Then  'if the caption is "Square"
        Picture1.Line(500,500) - Step (1000,1000), , BF  'draw a square
        Command1.Caption = "Other"
    ElseIf Command1.Caption = "Other" Then   'if the caption is "Other"
        Picture2.Picture = Picture1.Image    'copies to Picture2 box
        Command1.Caption = "Icon"
    End If
End Sub
```

Description   The Picture property determines the graphic image that displays on a form or picture box. A loaded picture must be in bitmap (.BMP), icon (.ICO), run-length encoded (.RLE), Windows metafile (.WMF), Windows extended metafile (.EMF), Graphical interchange format (.GIF), or Joint Photographic Experts Group (.JPG) format. A Picture property contains the full path of the picture file, with or without its extension. If the file is in the current search path or the same directory, then the extension is not necessary. In the example syntax, the picture box displays a circle, a square, or an icon, changing with each click on the picture. This demonstrates the full range of graphics that may be displayed on a picture box or form.

The Image Property   In order to copy a picture from one picture box into another, redefine the Picture property of the destination picture box with the Image property of the source picture box. Microsoft Windows gives every graphic image in Visual Basic a unique value that is returned by the Image property of the picture box or form. In the example syntax, the Picture property of Picture2 is set to equal the Image property of Picture1. This has reproduced all of the graphic images of Picture1 in the Picture2 picture box.

Example   In the Graphics project at the end of this chapter, the Picture property of the image control imagIcon changes according to the currently selected blanker option on screen.

POINT METHOD

Objects Affected   Form, PictureBox, UserControl, UserDocument, PropertyPage

Purpose   The Point method returns the RGB hexadecimal value of the color of a specified point on a form or picture box. This method only works at runtime. Table 38-12 displays the arguments of the Point method.

General Syntax

```
[form.]Point(x!, y!)
[form!][Name.]Point(x!, y!)
```

Table 38-12 Arguments of the Point method

Argument	Description
form	Name property of the form
Name	Name of picture box; if not given, defaults to current form
x!	Horizontal coordinate of the point on the object
y!	Vertical coordinate of the point on the object

Example Syntax

```
Private Sub Form_Click ()
    'sets form's AutoRedraw property to True
    AutoRedraw = True
    'sets drawn object to solid
    FillStyle = 0
    'sets drawn object to black
    FillColor = QBColor(0)
    'sets X equal to half of the width of the form
    X = ScaleWidth / 2
    Y = ScaleHeight / 2
    'sets Radius equal to 1/4 of the width of the form
    Radius = ScaleWidth / 4
    'draws a circle on the form
    Circle (X, Y), Radius
End Sub

Private Sub Command1_Click
    'changes the background color to circle's color
    BackColor = Point (CurrentX, CurrentY)
End Sub
```

Description

The Point method returns the color of a place on a form or picture box. Both the x and y coordinates represent values of measurements according to the ScaleMode measurement system of the container. If x! or y! lies outside the bounds of the object, the Point method returns -1.

In the example syntax, the background color of the form changes to match the circle's color when the user presses the command button. The Point method finds the color of the current coordinates on the form in the center of the black circle. This results in changing the background color of the form to black. With no Name provided, the color of the form changes.

The CurrentX and CurrentY Properties

The combination of the Point method and the CurrentX and CurrentY properties provides the color of the current coordinates on a form or picture box. The current coordinates begin in the upper-left corner of the form or picture box. Each drawn object changes the coordinates based on where the object appears. As shown in the example syntax, the CurrentX and CurrentY properties directly define the x and y coordinates of the Point method. Since the CurrentX and CurrentY coordinates are already in the center of the drawn circle, the coordinates do not change. This returns the color of the circle in the center of the form.

Example

In the Graphics project at the end of this section, the timeBlanker event uses the Point method to reset the BackColor property of formScreen. This is done with a Point method expression that uses the CurrentX and CurrentY coordinates to determine the color of the current point on the form. Since the BackColor property of the form is already white, the background remains white. Although there is no change to the color of the background of the form, the redefinition of the BackColor of the form erases all of the graphics images on the screen. If the AutoRedraw property of the form is True, then the graphics image is unaffected.

PSET METHOD

Objects Affected   Form, PictureBox, UserControl, UserDocument, Printer, PropertyPage

Purpose   The PSet method sets the color of a point on a form, picture box, or Printer object. The DrawWidth property of the form, picture box, or Printer object determines the size of this point. This method only works at runtime. Table 38-13 lists the arguments of the PSet method.

General Syntax

```
[form.]PSet [ Step ] (x!, y!) [ , color&]
[form!]Name.PSet [ Step ] (x!, y!) [ , color&]
Printer.PSet [ Step ] (x!, y!) [ , color&]
```

Table 38-13 Arguments of the PSet method

Argument	Description
form	Name property of the form
Name	Name of picture box
Printer	'Printer' for Printer object
Step	x and y coordinates measure relative distance from the current coordinates on the object
x!, y!	Horizontal and vertical distance from upper-left corner of the object or the current coordinates
color&	Hexadecimal value representing the created point's color

Example Syntax

```
Private Sub Timer1_Timer ()
    'set timer's interval to something other than zero
    'remember the last color we drew
    Static Color As Integer
    'If we haven't run out of QB colors,
    If Color <> 15 Then
        'cycle up to the next color.
        Color = Color + 1
    Else
        'back to black
        Color = 0
    End If
    X = Int((ScaleWidth - (ScaleWidth / 20)) * Rnd + _
      (ScaleWidth / 20))        'random X
    Y = Int((ScaleHeight - (ScaleHeight / 20)) * Rnd + _
      (ScaleHeight / 20))  'random Y
    DrawWidth = 20                      'big dot
    PSet (X, Y), QBColor(Color)         'now plot the big random dot
End Sub
```

Description   The PSet method places a point of color (in RGB hexadecimal format) on a specified point of a form, picture box, or Printer object. If there is no specified object, then the point of color appears on the current form. This method requires both the x! and y! coordinates in single precision.

The Step option makes x! and y! a relative distance from the last plotted point, rather than an absolute coordinate. Without Step, the x! and y! coordinates measure the distance from the upper-left corner of the object. In the example syntax, the PSet method places points with differing colors at absolute, random locations on the screen.

The example syntax uses the QBColor function to redefine the color of the point with each generation of the Timer1 event. A static variable named Color keeps the last value in the QBColor function between each generation of the Timer1 event. This value increments by one with each execution of the Timer1 event until it reaches 15. See Figure 38-10 for an illustration of this example.

The RGB and QBColor Functions   Set the color of a PSet method expression with either the RGB or QBColor functions. For specialized color combinations, use the RGB function. The RGB function provides the ability to set the red, green, and blue elements of a color to produce its hexadecimal value. If one of the standard colors is acceptable, then the QBColor function provides a simple means of setting the color with one value. Set a QBColor function with a value between 0 and 15 as used in QuickBASIC and other versions of Microsoft BASIC.

The DrawMode and DrawWidth Properties   The PSet method also produces points of varying sizes and colors with changes to DrawMode and DrawWidth properties. These properties control the size and effect of the graphics generated with the PSet method. The next example varies the size of the circles by scaling DrawWidth to a random value. Figure 38-11 shows what this example might look like.

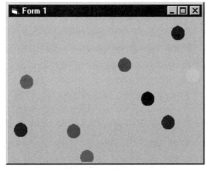

Figure 38-10   The PSet method plots individual points

Figure 38-11   What the DrawWidth
and DrawMode example should look
like: random-sized dots

```
Private Sub Timer1_Timer ()
'set timer's interval to something other than zero
     'remember the last color we drew
     Static Color As Integer
     'If we haven't run out of QB colors,
     If Color <> 15 Then
     'cycle up to the next color.
          Color = Color + 1
     Else
     'back to black
          Color = 0
     End If
     X = Int((ScaleWidth - (ScaleWidth / 20)) * Rnd + _
       (ScaleWidth / 20))      'random X
     Y = Int((ScaleHeight - (ScaleHeight / 20)) * Rnd + _
       (ScaleHeight / 20))   'random Y
     DrawMode = Int((16 - (1)) * Rnd + (1))         'random mode and
     DrawWidth = Int((100 - (20)) * Rnd + (20))    'random dot size
     PSet (X, Y), QBColor(Color)             'now plot the truly random dot
End Sub
```

**The CurrentX and
CurrentY
Properties**

The CurrentX and CurrentY properties are useful replacements for the x!
and y! arguments of the PSet method. These properties return the current
horizontal and vertical position on the form, picture box, or Printer object.
When a form loads, the default position is in the upper-right corner of the
form, picture box, or Printer object. This position changes with the use of
the Circle, Line, PSet, and Cls methods according to the new coordinates
that they set. Using CurrentX and CurrentY lets you continue drawing
where the previous graphics method left off.

Example

In the Graphics project at the end of this chapter, the PSet method generates
spots of color on the screen with the Spots option selected on formGraphics.
A spot of color appears on the screen based on the random setting of the x

and y coordinate variables and the Color variable. The random setting of the DrawWidth property determines the size of the spot. A series of color spots of random size appears on the screen at random locations.

QBColor Function

Purpose   The QBColor function helps define the color of an object on the screen. An object defined with this function is one of 16 possible colors. These colors simulate the 16 standard colors of older DOS-based programming languages. Table 38-14 lists each possible value and the color it defines.

General Syntax

```
QBColor(qbcolor%)
```

Table 38-14 Colors returned by QBColor

qbcolor%	Color
0	Black
1	Blue
2	Green
3	Cyan
4	Red
5	Magenta
6	Yellow
7	White (Light Gray)
8	Gray
9	Light Blue
10	Light Green
11	Light Cyan
12	Light Red
13	Light Magenta
14	Light Yellow
15	Bright White

Example Syntax

```
Private Sub Form_Click ()
    AutoRedraw = True        'makes sure graphics are drawn immediately
    Cls                      'clears the screen
    ScaleHeight = 4          'divides height of form into four parts
    ScaleWidth = 4           'divides width of form into four parts
    Color = 0                'start with black
```

continued on next page

continued from previous page

```
      For H = 0 To 3        'Draw a grid of 16 colors, 4 high
         For W = 0 To 3     'by 4 wide.
            Line (W, H)-(W + 1, H + 1), QBColor(Color), BF
            Color = Color + 1 'next color
         Next W
      Next H
End Sub
```

Description   The QBColor function returns the hexadecimal color code of a specified
                         number. Each number specified in a QBColor function must be between 0
                         and 15. These numbers represent preset color combinations of RGB values
                         that may be assigned to properties, methods, and statements that use
                         color. In the example syntax, the QBColor function provides the colors of
                         the boxes drawn with the Line method.

                         Every color is a combination of RGB color values that makes up its hexa-
                         decimal value. In the example syntax, all 16 of the possible color choices
                         appear in a 16-box grid. Each color displays in numerical order from left
                         to right and top to bottom.

The FillColor,   The QBColor function can provide the hexadecimal color for the FillColor,
BackColor, and   BackColor, and ForeColor properties. In the next example, the
ForeColor   background color of a form changes to blue. The code references the new
Properties   property setting with the next clicking of the form to change the color
                         back to white.

```
Private Sub Form_Click
    If BackColor = QBColor(15)        'checks if BackColor is white
          BackColor -=QBColor(1)      'backColor is blue
    ElseIf BackColor = QBColor(1)     'checks if BackColor is blue
          BackColor = QBColor(15)     'backColor is white
    End If
End Sub
```

Example   In the Graphics project at the end of this chapter, the QBColor function
                         sets the BackColor and ForeColor properties of the forms and the color of
                         spots, circles, squares, and lines. The Form_Click and Form_Paint events
                         of formScreen resets its BackColor property to white.

RGB FUNCTION

Purpose   The RGB function provides a means of defining the color of an object on
                         the screen. Each value in an RGB function expression represents the
                         amount of red, green, and blue contained in the displayed color. Table
                         38-15 lists some common colors with the corresponding red, green, and
                         blue arguments.

General Syntax

```
RGB(red%, green%, blue%)
```

Table 38-15 Values of common colors in RGB format

Color	Red Value	Green Value	Blue Value
Black	0	0	0
Red	255	0	0
Green	0	255	0
Yellow	0	255	255
Blue	0	0	255
Magenta	255	0	255
Cyan	0	255	255
White	255	255	255
Light Gray	192	192	192
Dark Gray	128	128	128

Example Syntax

```
Private Sub Timer1_Timer ()
    AutoRedraw = True          'makes sure graphics are drawn immediately
    Cls                        'clears the screen
    ScaleHeight = 4            'divides height of form into four parts
    ScaleWidth = 4             'divides width of form into four parts
    For H = 0 To 3             'Draw a grid of 16 colors, 4 high
        For W = 0 To 3                   'by 4 wide.
            red = Int(256 * Rnd)         'random red, 0-255
            green = Int(256 * Rnd)       'random green, 0-255
            blue = Int(256 * Rnd)        'random blue, 0-255
            Color = RGB(red, green, blue) 'make the color
            Line (W, H)-(W + 1, H + 1), Color, BF
        Next W
    Next H
End Sub
```

Description   The RGB function returns the hexadecimal value of the combination of three color values. Each of the numbers in an RGB function is between 0 and 255. Thus, there are 256×256×256 possible color combinations, or a total of 16,777,216 possible distinct colors. Many video cards do not support this many colors directly. Windows handles this for you by automatically dithering the available onscreen colors to approximate the actual color you specify. See the ForeColor and BackColor entries in Chapter 33, "Application Appearance," for more details and a comparison of using the RGB function with QBColor or directly setting the color values with a hexadecimal number or a constant.

In the example syntax, the RGB function defines the color argument of the Line method expression that generates the squares of colors on the screen. Each box has completely random settings for the red, green, and blue components of its color. Make sure the timer interval is set to something other than 0 to make the colors cycle properly.

Example   The Graphics project at the end of this chapter uses the RGB function with the selection of the option box labeled Blank Screen. In this case the timeBlanker event changes the BackColor of the form to black with an RGB function definition.

SavePicture Statement

Objects Affected   Form, Image, PictureBox

Purpose   The SavePicture statement saves a picture drawn on a picture box, image control, or form to a new file. If the picture was loaded as a bitmap, icon, or metafile, it is saved in the same format. GIF and JPG image files and drawn graphics are always saved in bitmap (.BMP) format. Table 38-16 lists the arguments of the SavePicture statement.

General Syntax

```
SavePicture picture, stringexpression$
```

Table 38-16 Arguments of the SavePicture statement

Argument	Description
picture	Picture or Image property of the object
stringexpression$	Path and filename of the file to save

Example Syntax

```
Private Sub Command1_Click ()
    AutoRedraw = True          'ensures that graphics remain on the form
    ScaleWidth = 4             'draws a square on the screen
    ScaleHeight = 4
    X = 1
    Y = 1
    Line (X, Y)-(X + 2, Y + 2), QBColor(1), BF
    SavePicture Image, "C:\VB\SQUARE.BMP"    'save the picture
End Sub
```

Description   The SavePicture statement saves the current graphic of an object or control to a file. If the picture to save comes from a loaded file, and was a bitmap, icon, or metafile, SavePicture saves the file in its original format. If the picture to save comes from drawn graphics, a GIF or JPG file, or is from the image control, then the picture is always saved as a bitmap (.BMP). The path of the file is optional. If no path is specified, the file will be saved in the current directory.

A SavePicture statement's picture argument identifies exactly which graphics to save with the Image property of the form or picture box. The example syntax saves the current contents of the form to the file SQUARE.BMP.

Example   In the Graphics project at the end of this chapter, the SavePicture statement saves the drawn graphics on the screen. Until the user clicks the
form with the mouse, the screen either remains black or keeps generating
spots, circles, squares, or lines on the screen. Clicking the form displays a
message box that asks whether to save the current image on the screen to a
file. If the user responds Yes, then the SavePicture statement uses the
Image property of formScreen to determine the Windows handle value.
Using this value, the SavePicture statement saves the current picture to the
bitmap file ~TEMP.BMP.

Comments   If you use the SavePicture statement to save the Image of a form, it does
not include any of the controls on the form.

Stretch Property

Objects Affected   Image

Purpose   The Stretch property determines whether the image control stretches to fit
the picture or the picture stretches to fit the image control. You can read
and write with this property at both runtime and design time. Tables
38-17 and 38-18 summarize the arguments of the Stretch property.

General Syntax

```
[form!]Name.Stretch [ = boolean%]
```

Table 38-17 Arguments of the Stretch property

Argument	Description
form	Name property of the form
Name	Name property of the image control
boolean%	True/False

Table 38-18 Meanings of the boolean% argument in the Stretch property

boolean%	Meaning
True	Picture resized to fit the image control
False	(Default) Image control resized to fit the picture

Example Syntax

```
Private Sub Check1_Click ()
    If Check1.Value = 0 Then
        Image1.Stretch = True
```

continued on next page

continued from previous page

```
    Else
          Image1.Stretch = False
    End IF
End Sub
```

Description   The Stretch property determines whether the image control stretches to fit the picture or the picture stretches to fit the image control. If Stretch is True, then resizing the image control also resizes the picture.

Stretching Windows metafiles (.WMF) does not adversely affect the image quality, because these images are based on vectors and can be arbitrarily resized. Stretching a bitmap graphic (like a .BMP) can degrade the image quality. Windows will attempt the smoothest stretch it can, but you will often have moiré patterns and excessive "jaggies" if the stretch is by something other than an exact multiple of the original image size.

Example   The chapter project uses an image control to display one of several icons. Stretch is set to True in order to enlarge the small icon.

ZOrder Method

Objects Affected   Animated Button, Check, Combo, Command, Data, DBCombo, DBList, DBGrid, Dir, Drive, File, Form, Frame, Grid, Image, Label, Line, List, ListView, MDIForm, Masked Edit, MSFlexGrid, Progress Bar, OLE, Option, PictureBox, Remote Data, Shape, Slider, StatusBar, TabStrip, TextBox, ToolBar, TreeView, UpDown, Scroll, Shape, Text

Purpose   The ZOrder method places an object in front of or behind other objects within its graphical level. You can read and write with this method at both design time and runtime. Tables 38-19 and 38-20 summarize the arguments of the ZOrder method.

General Syntax

```
[form.]ZOrder order%
[form!]Name.ZOrder order%
```

Table 38-19 Arguments of the ZOrder method

Argument	Description
form	Name property of the form
Name	Name property of the control
order%	Bring to front or send to back

Table 38-20 Meanings of the order% argument in the ZOrder method

order%	VBConstants	Meaning
0	vbBringToFront	(Default.) Place this control or form in front of all others.
1	vbSendToBack	Place this control or form in back of all others.

Example Syntax

```
Private Sub Timer1_Timer
    'remember what iteration we're on
    Static I As Integer
    'flip through the image control array stack
    Image1(I).ZOrder vbBringToFront
    'increment which image will display next time...
    I = I + 1
    '10 images; reset if cycled through all 10
    If I = 10 Then I = 0
End Sub
```

Description
The ZOrder method lets you control the way in which controls layer. Each object has x and y coordinates (that is, Left and Top); the ZOrder method takes this to the third dimension of a z coordinate. If several different controls or forms overlap each other in the x-y plane, you can use ZOrder to determine which displays in front of the other. You can set the ZOrder of a control at design time by using the Edit menu's Bring To Front or Send To Back commands.

The example syntax rotates through a stack of image controls, using the ZOrder method. If each image control had a slightly different picture in it, this would produce a simple animation.

ZOrder will only change the order of the controls on the layer to which they belong. All graphics controls (shapes, lines, image controls, and labels) exist on the second layer; all nongraphical controls (like command buttons and text boxes) exist on the front layer. The front layer will always obscure the second layer, and both the front and second layers will always obscure the third layer, where the graphics methods operate. ZOrder will arrange the controls on each layer but not between layers. See the section "Graphical Layering" at the beginning of this chapter for more details.

The ZOrder method rearranges the display order of MDI child forms. You can control which child is at the front or back of the workspace with ZOrder. You can also apply ZOrder to the MDIForm or any regular form. This arranges the forms on the screen. Thus you can use ZOrder to send a form to the back of the screen without hiding it.

Example
The Graphics project at the end of this chapter uses ZOrder to rotate through a stack of image controls. Each image control contains an icon that represents what kind of screen blanker will run. Clicking on the

option buttons chooses the blanker type, and uses the Index argument of the control array to send the appropriate image control to the front of the stack.

The Graphics Project

Project Overview

The Graphics project demonstrates the properties of the Visual Basic language that affect basic graphics on a form or picture box. Following the examples of the different forms and subroutines of this project will teach you how to change basic graphics on a picture box or form.

The first section deals with the assembly of the controls and subroutines of formGraphics. The next section discusses the construction of the controls and subroutines of formScreen. Each of these sections includes step-by-step instructions on how to put together the form and its controls. A section on how the program works follows these two sections. Read this information carefully and use the pictures of the forms as guides while you assemble this project.

Assembling the Project: formGraphics

1. Make a new form (formGraphics) with the objects and properties listed in Table 38-21. Notice that all of the option box controls have the Name property of optnBlanker. The second control created with the same name generates a message asking you whether you want to create a control array; respond Yes. If you want to avoid this, simply change the first control's index property to 0. This creates a control array without the message.

Table 38-21 Properties and controls of formGraphics in the Graphics project

Object	Property	Setting
Form	BorderStyle	1–Fixed Single
	Caption	Graphics Project
	ClipControls	0, False
	Name	formGraphics
	MaxButton	False
	MinButton	True
Frame	Caption	Blanker Options
	Name	framBlanker
Option	Caption	Blank Screen
	Name	optnBlanker
	Index	0
	TabIndex	0

Object	Property	Setting
Option	Caption	Color Spots
	Name	optnBlanker
	Index	1
	TabIndex	1
Option	Caption	Circles
	Name	optnBlanker
	Index	2
	TabIndex	2
Option	Caption	Squares
	Name	optnBlanker
	Index	3
	TabIndex	3
Option	Caption	Lines
	Name	optnBlanker
	Index	4
	TabIndex	4
Image	BorderStyle	None
	Index	0
	Name	imagIcon
	Stretch	True
Command	Caption	&Activate
	Name	cmndActivate
Command	Caption	E&xit
	Name	cmndQuit

2. Size the objects on the screen. Note that the image control should be exactly square; set the width equal to the height directly in the properties box.

3. Enter the following code in the declarations section of formGraphics. This public variable will be referenced by formScreen to determine what type of graphics to display.

```
'BlankerType is set here and referenced by formBlanker
'as an attribute of this form — formGraphics.BlankerType.
Public BlankerType As Integer
```

4. Enter the following code in the cmndActivate_Click event procedure. This code triggers when the user presses the command button labeled Activate. This routine hides formGraphics from the user's view, displays formScreen on the screen, and activates the timer that does the actual drawing.

```
Private Sub cmndActivate_Click ()
    formGraphics.Hide
    formScreen.Show
    formScreen!timeBlanker.Enabled = True
End Sub
```

5. Enter the following code in the optnBlanker_GotFocus event procedure. This routine activates when one of the controls of the control array optnBlanker receives the focus. The imagIcon control that contains the proper icon is brought to the front of the stack using the ZOrder method, the form's Icon property is set to display the same icon, and you place the type of screen blanker in the public variable BlankerType.

```
Private Sub optnBlanker_GotFocus (Index As Integer)
    imagIcon(Index).ZOrder vbBringToFront
    Icon = imagIcon(Index).Picture
    BlankerType = Index
End Sub
```

6. Enter the following code in the cmndQuit_Click event procedure. This code triggers when the user presses the command button labeled Exit. When this is done, the End statement closes the program.

```
Private Sub cmndQuit_Click ()
    End
End Sub
```

7. Enter the following code in the Form_Load event procedure. This creates a control array of the imagIcon controls. Then it reads in the appropriate icons into each member of the array using the LoadPicture function.

```
Private Sub Form_Load ()
    Dim I As Integer
    For i = 1 To 4                'create a control array of image controls
        Load imagIcon(i)
        imagIcon(i).Visible = True
    Next I
'   Note that if your image directory is not at this path, you must
'   change the program lines below
    imagIcon(0).Picture = LoadPicture("\VB\ICONS\ELEMENTS\MOON01.ICO")
    imagIcon(1).Picture = LoadPicture("\VB\ICONS\ELEMENTS\MOON05.ICO")
    imagIcon(2).Picture = LoadPicture("\VB\ICONS\MISC\MISC38.ICO")
    imagIcon(3).Picture = LoadPicture("\VB\ICONS\MISC\MISC36.ICO")
    imagIcon(4).Picture = LoadPicture("\VB\ICONS\MISC\MISC22.ICO")
End Sub
```

Assembling the Project: formScreen

1. Make a new form with the objects and properties listed in Table 38-22.

Table 38-22 Properties and controls of formScreen in the Graphics project

Object	Property	Setting
Form	AutoRedraw	-1–True
	BorderStyle	0–None
	Caption	""
	ClipControls	0–False
	ControlBox	0–False
	DrawMode	14 `Merge Pen Not
	Name	formScreen
	MaxButton	False
	MinButton	False
Timer	Name	timeBlanker
	Enabled	False
	Interval	1

2. Size the objects on the screen as shown in Figure 38-12.

3. Enter the following code in the timeBlanker event procedure. This routine triggers when the Enabled property of the Blanker timer changes to True and processes at intervals of 1 millisecond. Depending on the selected option box on formGraphics, a blank screen, series of colored spots, circles, squares, or lines appear on the screen. These graphics continue to generate on the screen until the user clicks the form.

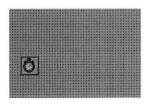

Figure 38-12 What formScreen should look like

```
Private Sub timeBlanker_Timer()
    Static Color As Integer 'stores color from previous timer triggering
    Dim X As Single, X1 As Single
    Dim Y As Single, Y1 As Single
    Dim Radius As Single
    Randomize 'Seed the random number generator from the system clock
    X = Int((ScaleWidth - (ScaleWidth / 20)) * Rnd + _
            (ScaleWidth / 20))
    Y = Int((ScaleHeight - (ScaleHeight / 20)) * Rnd + _
            (ScaleHeight / 20))
    DrawWidth = Int((100 - (20)) * Rnd + (20))
    Select Case formGraphics.BlankerType
        Case 0 'blank screen
            formScreen.BackColor = QBColor(0) ' black
        Case 1 'spots
            formScreen.PSet (X, Y), QBColor(Color)
        Case 2 'circles
            Radius = Int((ScaleWidth / 2 - (ScaleWidth / 20)) * Rnd + _
                (ScaleWidth / 20))
            Circle (X, Y), Radius, QBColor(Color)
        Case 3 'squares
            X1 = Int((ScaleWidth - (ScaleWidth / 20)) * Rnd + _
                (ScaleWidth / 20))
            Y1 = Int((ScaleHeight - (ScaleHeight / 20)) * Rnd + _
                (ScaleHeight / 20))
            Line (X, Y)-(X1, Y1), QBColor(Color), BF
        Case 4 'lines
            X1 = Int((ScaleWidth - (ScaleWidth / 20)) * Rnd + _
                (ScaleWidth / 20))
            Y1 = Int((ScaleHeight - (ScaleHeight / 20)) * Rnd + _
                (ScaleHeight / 20))
            Line (X, Y)-(X1, Y1), QBColor(Color)
    End Select
    If formGraphics.BlankerType <> 0 Then
        If Color <> 15 Then
            Color = Color + 1
        Else
            Color = 0
            BackColor = QBColor(Rnd * 16)
        End If
    End If
End Sub
```

4. Enter the following code in the Form_Click event procedure. This routine processes when the user clicks the form with the mouse. This prompts the user to save the bitmap on the screen. It then clears the form of all drawn graphics, hides itself, and brings up the main control form.

```
Private Sub Form_Click()

    Dim msg As String
    Dim Title As String
    Dim Ans As Integer

    timeBlanker.Enabled = False
    msg$ = "Would you like to save this image?"
    Title$ = "Graphics Project"
```

```
    Ans = MsgBox(msg$, vbYesNo, Title$)
    If Ans = 6 Then
        MousePointer = vbHourglass
        'the savepicture line will not work if the
        '\vb directory doesn't exist
        On Error Resume Next
        SavePicture formScreen.Image, "C:\VB\~TEMP.BMP"
        MousePointer = vbDefault
    End If
    formScreen.Cls
    formScreen.Hide
    formGraphics.Show

End Sub
```

5. Enter the following code in the Form_Load event procedure. This code triggers when formScreen displays on the screen. This code maximizes the form. Because there is no border or title bar, the drawing surface of the form takes up the entire screen.

```
Private Sub Form_Load ()
    WindowState = vbMaximize
End Sub
```

6. Enter the following code in the Form_Paint event procedure. This code activates whenever the form displays. The background of formScreen changes to white with this event.

```
Private Sub Form_Paint ()
    BackColor = RGB(255, 255, 255)' white background
End Sub
```

How It Works

The Graphics project opens with a configuration form that allows the user to select which kind of blanker to display on the screen (see Figure 38-13). Each time the user selects a new option from the list of options boxes, a new icon appears on the configuration screen. This icon represents the type of blanker chosen by the user. Note that because the Stretch property is set to True, the image control magnifies the small icon and displays it as large as you make the control on the form.

To display the blanker on the screen, the user presses the Activate command button. The chosen graphics continue to display on the screen until the user clicks the screen with the mouse. At this point the system asks the user whether to stop the program, and whether to save the current graphics on the screen. Press the Quit button on the configuration screen to exit.

Startup

The AutoRedraw of the image control imagIcon and forms formGraphics and formScreen receive initial adjustments at design time. The AutoRedraw property of both forms and the image control imagIcon are set to True. This allows any graphics placed on either form or the image control to redisplay every time they are obscured

Figure 38-13   The Graphics project lets you save graphics like this to disk

and revealed. You also set formGraphics ClipControls property to False, because you're not going to draw directly on the form and you can save some system overhead this way.

When the program starts, formGraphics displays on the screen. The topmost control of the optnBlanker control array receives the initial focus, triggering the optnBlanker_GotFocus event. This event uses a Select Case statement to set the appropriate icon in imagIcon.

After determining the icon to display in the image control imagIcon, the Icon property of the Graphics form becomes the same icon. A simple expression makes the Icon property equal to imagIcon.Picture. In this way the Picture property of the image control defines the property of another element of the project.

Running the Graphics Project

Pressing the Activate command button triggers the timeBlanker_Timer event on formScreen. This event displays a series of graphics images on the form in colors defined with the RGB and QBColor functions.

The QBColor function sets the color of each of the spots, circles, squares, and lines that appear on the screen. Each QBColor definition has the variable Color placed in the parentheses that follow the QBColor name. This variable increments by one each time the Timer event triggers until the value reaches 15. The value represents a color displayed in the indicated spot, circle, square, or line. At that point the Color variable changes to 0 and the process begins again.

The PSet method draws spots of differing sizes and colors on the screen. Based on the random setting of the x and y coordinate variables and the Color variable, a spot of color appears on the screen. The DrawWidth property determines the size of the spot on the form. In this way a series of spots of random size and color appear on the screen.

Until the user clicks the form with the mouse, the screen keeps generating the indicated graphics. Clicking the form displays a message that asks the user whether he or she wants to save the current image on the screen to a file. If the user responds Yes, then the SavePicture statement accesses the Image property of formScreen to determine the Windows handle value. Using this value, the code saves the current contents of the screen to the bitmap file ~TEMP.BMP.

39

PICTURES

Visual Basic 5.0 provides a variety of ways to create and manipulate graphics easily. Graphics elements in Visual Basic applications fall into three main categories: displaying existing graphics, drawing new graphics, and using graphic elements in form design.

Forms, PictureBoxes, and the image control can all display existing graphics. Visual Basic 5.0 also adds graphics capability to several controls that are not commonly thought of as graphical controls, such as command buttons, check boxes, and option buttons. This chapter covers the fundamentals of using existing graphics in Visual Basic.

You can display pictures directly on a form, in a PictureBox control, or in an image control.

PictureBox Control

Purpose   The PictureBox control defines an area on a form, frame, or another picture in which graphics may be displayed. The PictureBoxPictureBox control can also be used as a container, much like the frame control, to group together controls that are functionally related based on how they are used in a program.

Properties,   Table 39-1 lists the properties that relate to the PictureBoxPictureBox control.
Events, and
Methods

Table 39-1 Properties of the PictureBoxPictureBox control

Use This Property...	To Do This...
Align	Determine where and how the control appears on a form
Appearance	Read or set whether the object is drawn with 3D effects
AutoRedraw	Read or set whether graphic pictures will be redrawn automatically
AutoSize	Read or set whether the size of a picture is controlled by its source file

continued on next page

continued from previous page

Use This Property...	To Do This...
BackColor, ForeColor	Read or set the background and foreground colors of this control
BorderStyle	Determine whether this control has a border and, if it does, set its style
ClipControls	Determine whether graphics methods repaint the entire control
Container	Set or return a reference to the object that contains this object
CurrentX, CurrentY	Read or set the current graphics position on this control
DataChanged	Determine if the value displayed in this control has changed
DataField	Read or set the name of the field in the recordset of the data control to which this control is bound
DataSource	Set the name of the data control to which this control is bound
DragIcon	Read or set what displays when this control is dragged
DragMode	Determine whether drag operations are to occur manually or automatically
DrawMode	Read or set the appearance of drawings by graphics methods
DrawStyle	Read or set the style of lines drawn by graphics methods
DrawWidth	Read or set the size of lines drawn by graphics methods
Enabled	Read or set whether this control can react to events
FillColor	Read or set the color used by graphics methods for fill-in effects
FillStyle	Read or set the pattern used by graphics methods for fill-in effects
Font	Set or return a font object that controls the way text displays in this control
FontBold, FontItalic, FontStrikeThru, FontTransparent, FontUnderline	Read or set special effects for this control's font
FontName	Read or set the name of this control's font
FontSize	Read or set the size of this control's font
hDC	Read the Windows device handle for this control
Height	Read or set the height of this control
HelpContextID	Read or set the context number to this control for context-sensitive help
hWnd	Read the handle for this control's window
Image	Read the Windows device handle for a picture's persistent bitmap
Index	Uniquely identify an element of a control array
Left	Read or set the left edge placement of this control relative to its container
LinkItem	Read or set the item in a DDE conversation
LinkMode	Read or set a DDE conversation to hot, cold, or none
LinkTimeout	Read or set the amount of time before a DDE conversation times out
LinkTopic	Read or set the topic of a DDE conversation
MouseIcon	Set a custom mouse pointer
MousePointer	Read or set the shape of the mouse pointer when it's over this control
Name	Read or set the name used in code to refer to this control

Use This Property...	To Do This...
OLEDragMode	Read or set whether the control handles OLE drag/drop operations
OLEDropMode	Read or set whether the control accepts drop operations
Parent	Read the name of the form to which this control belongs
Picture	Read or assign a graphic image to a picture or form
ScaleHeight	Read or set the number of units that define the height of this control
ScaleLeft	Read or set the coordinates for the left edge of this control
ScaleMode	Read or set the unit of measurement used to place and size objects
ScaleTop	Read or set the coordinates for the top edge of this control
ScaleWidth	Read or set the number of units that define the width of this control
TabIndex	Read or set the placement of this control within the form's tab order
TabStop	Read or set whether this control is part of the form's tab order
Tag	Read or set any extra string data associated with this control
Top	Read or set the coordinate of this control's top edge relative to its container
Visible	Read or set whether this control is visible
WhatsThisHelpID	Read or set the context number to this object for context-sensitive help in Windows 95
Width	Read or set the width of this control

Table 39-2 lists the events of the PictureBoxPictureBox control.

Table 39-2 Events of the PictureBoxPictureBox control

Use This Event...	To Do This...
Change	React to a change in the image pointed to by the Picture property
Click	React to the user clicking this control
DblClick	React to the user double-clicking this control
DragDrop	React to the user dragging and dropping an object onto this control
DragOver	React to the user dragging another object over this control
GotFocus	Initiate an action when this control receives the focus
KeyDown	Initiate an action when the user presses or holds a key down
KeyPress	React to the user typing an ASCII character
KeyUp	Initiate an action when the user releases a key
LinkClose	React to the termination of a DDE conversation
LinkError	React to an error in a DDE conversation
LinkNotify	React to a change in the DDE source data
LinkOpen	React to the initiation of a DDE conversation
LostFocus	Initiate an action when this control loses the focus
MouseDown	React to the user pressing any mouse button
MouseMove	React to the user moving the mouse over this control
MouseUp	React to the user releasing any mouse button

continued on next page

continued from previous page

Use This Event...	To Do This...
OLECompleteDrag	React to a source component being dropped onto the control
OLEDragDrop	Reacts when a source component is dropped onto the control if a drop can occur
OLEDragOver	Reacts when a component is dragged over the control
OLEGiveFeedback	Allows the control to give the user visual feedback when a component is dragged over the control
OLESetData	Reacts to the GetData method of another component
OLEStartDrag	Reacts to the OLEDrag method. Specifies the data formats and drop effects
Paint	Initiate an action when the control needs to be redrawn
Resize	Initiate an action when the control is first displayed or its size is changed

Table 39-3 lists the methods of the PictureBoxPictureBox control.

Table 39-3 Methods of the PictureBoxPictureBox control

Use This Method...	To Do This...
Circle	Create a circle or ellipse on a form or PictureBoxPictureBox
Cls	Clear graphics and text that have been created at runtime
Drag	Control manual dragging of this control
Line	Draw a line on a form or picture
LinkExecute	Send a DDE Execute command to a DDE server application
LinkPoke	Send data from a DDE client to a DDE server
LinkRequest	Ask for data from a DDE server
LinkSend	Send graphic data to a DDE client
Move	Change the position of this control or form
OLEDrag	Initiate an OLE drag/drop operation
PaintPicture	Transfer an image from this object to another
Point	Return the color setting of a specified point on a form or PictureBox
Print	Print text on a form or PictureBox
PSet	Set the color of a specified point on a form or PictureBox
Refresh	Update and repaint this control
Scale	Define the coordinate system used with the PictureBox control
ScaleX	Convert a value for the width from one scale mode to another
ScaleY	Convert a value for the height from one scale mode to another
SetFocus	Move the focus to this control
ShowWhatsThis	Display the What's This help topic pop-up provided by the Windows 95 help system
TextHeight	Return the height of text in this control's font
TextWidth	Return the width of text in this control's font
ZOrder	Place this control at the front or back of the z-order

Description	The PictureBox control is used for two different purposes. Primarily, it displays a graphical image on a form (see Figure 39-1). However, you can also place controls on a picture control in the same manner as placing them on a form or frame. This gives you an alternative to the frame control for grouping together other controls. This is particularly useful when you need to place controls on the client area of an MDI form, because the PictureBox control is the only standard control that may be placed there.

If other controls are drawn on a PictureBox control, they work in the same manner as if they'd been drawn on a frame control. Because the border can be turned off by using the PictureBox control's BorderStyle property, this provides a technique for grouping several controls together without displaying a frame around them.

IMAGE CONTROL

Purpose	Use the image control to define an area to display a picture. The image control repaints faster and uses fewer system resources than the PictureBox control, but only has a subset of the picture control's properties.
Properties, Events, and Methods	Table 39-4 lists the properties of the image control.

Table 39-4 Properties of the image control

Use This Property...	To Do This...
Appearance	Read or set whether the object is drawn with 3D effects
BorderStyle	Determine whether this control has a border and, if it does, set its style
Container	Set or return a reference to the object that contains this object
DataChanged	Determine if the value displayed in this control has changed
DataField	Read or set the name of the field in the recordset of the data control to which this control is bound
DataSource	Set the name of the data control to which this control is bound
DragIcon	Read or set what displays when this control is dragged
DragMode	Determine whether drag operations are to occur manually or automatically
Enabled	Read or set whether this control can react to events
Height	Read or set the height of this control
Image	Read the Windows device handle for a picture's persistent bitmap
Index	Uniquely identify an element of a control array
Left	Read or set the left edge placement of this control relative to its container
MouseIcon	Sets a custom mouse pointer
MousePointer	Read or set the shape of the mouse pointer when it's over this control
Name	Read or set the name used in code to refer to this control
OLEDragMode	Read or set whether the control handles OLE drag/drop operations
OLEDropMode	Read or set whether the control accepts drop operations
Parent	Read the name of the form to which this control belongs

continued on next page

continued from previous page

Use This Property...	To Do This...
Picture	Read or assign a graphic image to a picture or form
Stretch	Determine if the picture is resized to fit the control or vice versa
Tag	Read or set any extra string data associated with this control
Top	Read or set the coordinate of this control's top edge relative to its container
Visible	Read or set whether control is visible
WhatsThisHelpID	Read or set the context number to this object for context-sensitive help in Windows 95
Width	Read or set the width of this control

Table 39-5 lists the events of the image control.

Table 39-5 Events of the image control

Use This Event...	To Do This...
Click	React to the user clicking this control
DblClick	React to the user double-clicking this control
DragDrop	React to the user dragging and dropping an object onto this control
DragOver	React to the user dragging another object over this control
MouseDown	React to the user pressing any mouse button
MouseMove	React to the user moving the mouse over this control
MouseUp	React to the user releasing any mouse button
OLECompleteDrag	React to a source component being dropped onto the control
OLEDragDrop	React when a source component is dropped onto the control if a drop can occur
OLEDragOver	React when a component is dragged over the control
OLEGiveFeedback	Allow the control to give the user visual feedback when a component is dragged over the control
OLESetData	React to the GetData method of another component
OLEStartDrag	React to the OLEDrag method. Specifies the data formats and drop effects

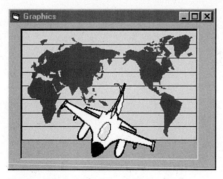

Figure 39-1   The PictureBox displays graphics

Table 39-6 lists the methods of the image control.

Table 39-6 Methods of the image control

Use This Method...	To Do This...
Drag	Control manual dragging of this control
Move	Change the position of this control or form
OLEDrag	Initiate an OLE drag/drop operation
Refresh	Update and repaint this control
ShowWhatsThis	Display the What's This help topic pop-up provided by the Windows 95 help system
ZOrder	Place this control at the front or back of the z-order

Description

The image control is a "lightweight" control that can also be used to display existing images. It uses considerably fewer of the computer's resources. The image control lets you display graphical images without the performance and overhead penalties of the PictureBox control. The image control repaints faster and uses far fewer system resources than does the PictureBox. It does this by restricting its properties, events, and methods to those used to display predefined images and eliminating those dealing with creating graphical images. The image control also cannot function as a grouping mechanism for other controls (like a frame) the way a PictureBox can, nor can it function in a DDE conversation.

The Stretch property is unique to the image control. If you set Stretch to True, the picture resizes itself to fit the control. If the control is resized, the image is resized with it. Figure 39-2 shows the same image in a PictureBox on the left and an image control on the right. Both controls are the same size, but the image control has its Stretch property set to True.

Figure 39-2 A PictureBox and an image control displaying the same picture

Adding the Picture

Forms, PictureBoxes, and the image control can all display existing graphics files. Use the Picture property to load the graphics file. A loaded file may be in icon (.ICO), Windows metafile (.WMF), Windows Extended Metafile (.EMF), device independent bitmap (.DIB), bitmap (.BMP), CompuServe's Graphical Interchange Format (.GIF), or Joint Photographic Experts Group (JPEG, or .JPG) format. To display a file, first select the form, PictureBox, or other control that will display the picture. Choose the Picture property in the properties box. Double-click on (picture) on the right side of properties box. Select the file from the File→Open dialog box and press ENTER to display it on the screen.

You normally set the contents of forms, PictureBoxes, and image controls at design time. This way, the loaded file becomes a part of the executable file of the program. You may also load them during runtime, if the picture needs to change during program execution, by using the LoadPicture function. You can clear an object of a loaded picture by using LoadPicture with no argument. To clear a loaded picture from an object at design time, use your mouse to select the Picture property value of the object with your mouse and press the DELETE key. The following code fragment illustrates using the LoadPicture function to clear an image from one control and load an image into another.

```
' Clear Picture1
Set Picture1.Picture = LoadPicture("")
' Display Clouds in Picture2
Set Picture2.Picture = LoadPicture("C:\Windows\Clouds.Bmp")
```

Forms and PictureBoxes handle more complex graphics operations than does the image control. The image control is like a stripped-down PictureBox: It can display existing graphics files, but cannot employ the graphics methods of Chapter 40 to create new graphics. It uses fewer system resources than the PictureBox, and displays faster.

PAINTPICTURE METHOD

Objects Affected Form, PictureBox, Printer, PropertyPage, UserControl, UserDocument

Purpose The PaintPicture method gives you the ability to quickly copy a picture or portion of a picture from one graphics object to any location on another graphics object. For instance, you can copy a form or a portion of a form to the Printer object for printing. You can use the PaintPicture method to invert the picture you're copying horizontally or vertically. The PaintPicture method only works with a loaded object and it only copies from the drawing layer, so PaintPicture won't copy controls that have been loaded on a form or a picture control. The PaintPicture method uses the ScaleMode of the source and destination objects for the x and y coordinates. Table 39-7 summarizes the arguments of the PaintPicture method.

General Syntax

```
[form.]PaintPicture [object.]Picture,tox,toy,towidth,toheight,fromx,fromy,fromwidth,_
fromheight,OpCode
[form!]Name.PaintPicture [object.]Picture,tox,toy,towidth,toheight,fromx,fromy,
_fromwidth,fromheight,OpCode
Printer.PaintPicture [object.]Picture,tox,toy,towidth,toheight,fromx,fromy,
_fromwidth,fromheight,OpCode
```

Table 39-7 Arguments of the PaintPicture method

Argument	Description
form	Name property of form.
Name	Name property of PictureBox.
Printer	Printer indicates the Printer object.
object	Name of the source object.
tox	X coordinate to copy picture to.
toy	Y coordinate to copy picture to.
towidth	Width of copied picture. It can be smaller or larger than original picture. A negative value inverts the picture.
toheight	Height of copied picture. It can be smaller or larger than original picture. A negative value inverts the picture.
fromx	X coordinate to start copying from.
fromy	Y coordinate to start copying from.
fromwidth	Width of picture to copy.
fromheight	Height of picture to copy.
OpCode	How to merge the source and destination pictures.

Table 39-8 shows some of the values of the OpCode argument in the PaintPicture method.

Table 39-8 Values of the OpCode argument in the PaintPicture method

OpCode Name	Value	Description
BLACKNESS	&H42&	Destination is painted black.
DSTINVERT	&H550009	Invert destination colors.
MERGEPAINT	&HBB0226	Source colors are inverted and ORed with destination colors.
SRCAND	&H8800C6	Destination colors and source colors are ANDed together.
SRCCOPY	&HCC0020	Destination colors are set to source colors.
SRCERASE	&H440328	Destination colors inverted and ANDed with source colors.
SRCINVERT	&H660039	Destination colors are XORed with source colors.
SRCPAINT	&HEE0086	Destination colors are ORed with source colors.
WHITENESS	&HFF0062	Destination is painted white.

Example Syntax

```
Private Sub CmndCopyInverted_Click

    Picture2.PaintPicture Picture1.Image, _
    Picture2.ScaleWidth - 1, Picture2.ScaleHeight - 1, _
    -(Picture2.ScaleWidth), -(Picture2.ScaleHeight)

End Sub
```

Description   The PaintPicture method offers another way to load pictures into a graphics object. The PaintPicture method copies a graphical image or portion of an image from one control or form to another. You can resize or invert the image if you'd like. PaintPicture copies as much of the image as you specify using the starting coordinates and the starting width and height. PaintPicture resizes or inverts based on the destination starting coordinates and the destination width and height. If you specify a smaller or larger width or height, PaintPicture stretches the picture accordingly. If you specify a negative width or height, PaintPicture reverses the image. You may skip an argument in the middle of the syntax, but you must include a comma (,) for each argument excluded.

The starting coordinates tox and toy are not optional. The towidth and toheight arguments are optional, and they default to the height and width of the source picture. The fromx and fromy coordinates are optional and default to the upper-left corner of the source object. The fromwidth and fromheight arguments are also optional and default to the source picture's width and height. OpCode is optional, and if OpCode is left out, PaintPicture copies the source picture to the destination picture (SRCCOPY). Don't end PaintPicture with a comma.

The example syntax shows an example of a PaintPicture that takes the picture in one Picture control and copies it upside down and backwards into a second PictureBox. Figure 39-3 shows the original picture in the left-hand PictureBox and the results of the PaintPicture method in the right-hand PictureBox.

OpCode   The OpCode parameter of PaintPicture applies only to bitmap pictures. It defines the raster operation used to copy the source picture into the destination picture. The values of OpCode listed in Table 39-8 are not defined in the Object Browser. The best way to understand the meaning of each OpCode value is to experiment with it. If you attempt to use OpCode with a picture other than a bitmap, the method raises an error.

Example   In the Pictures project at the end of this chapter, the PaintPicture method may be used to copy a section of any of four different picture sources into a PictureBox.

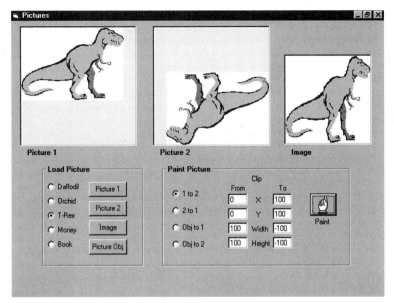

Figure 39-3   PaintPicture can invert the picture

PICTURE OBJECT

Purpose   The Picture object allows you to store images without using a PictureBox control. This means that you can create dynamic arrays to hold pictures. You can use these arrays, for example, to implement an undo feature in a drawing program. You can also use Picture objects as parameters to functions, which enables you to pass the Picture property of a PictureBox control to a function and set a Picture object equal to the value of the Picture property. Table 39-9 lists the properties of the Picture object.

Table 39-9 Properties of the Picture object

Use This Property...	To Do This...
Handle	Read the handle to the graphic contained in the object
Height and Width	Read or set the height and width of this object
hPal	Read the handle to the palette of the object
Type	Read the type of graphic contained in the object

Description

Visual Basic 4.0 introduced the Picture object as part of the Standard OLE objects library. The Picture object is part of the Standard OLE objects library, so you must reference the Standard OLE objects library as part of your project, using the References dialog box. The Picture object can hold a bitmap, Windows metafile, Windows extended metafile, GIF, JPG, or icon. You can set a Picture object to hold the value of the Picture property of a form or PictureBox control, and you can also set the value of the Picture property using a Picture object. Picture objects are compatible with the Picture property of form and PictureBoxes, so you can use a generic subroutine to deal with all three objects. You can define arrays of Picture objects, or use them as part of a collection. An array or collection gives you the ability to store a series of images without using hidden controls.

Note that you can manipulate a Picture object in the same way as any other object. You can use the Set statement to set one object's Picture property (say, a PictureBox control's Picture property) to reference the Picture object. The Picture object shares the same peculiarity as the Font object: You can declare a variable of type Picture, as shown here:

```
Dim X As Picture
Set X = LoadPicture("PARTY.BMP")
Set Picture1.Picture = X
```

But to instantiate a new Picture object, you must use the class name StdPicture, as shown here:

```
Dim normalDragIcon As New StdPicture
Set normalDragIcon = LoadPicture("MYICON.ICO")
Dim c As Object
For Each c In Form.Controls
    Set c.DragIcon = normalDragIcon
Next c
```

The Pictures Project

Project Overview

The Pictures project demonstrates the methods and properties that directly affect the display of images. The project uses PictureBoxes, image controls, and a Picture object. It demonstrates the LoadPicture function and the PaintPicture method as well as loading pictures at design time.

The following pages discuss the assembly and operation of the Pictures project. The first section deals with the assembly of the controls on the Pictures form. Following this is a discussion that shows and briefly explains the contents of the subroutines of this project. Finally, there is a How It Works guide to the operation of the project. Read this information carefully and use the pictures of the form as guides in the process of assembling the project.

Assembling the Project: frmPix

1. Make a new form with the objects and properties in Table 39-10. The graphical controls need to be precisely positioned by directly entering their position properties in the properties box.

Table 39-10 Elements of the Pictures form

Object	Property	Setting
Form	Name	frmPix
	Caption	Pictures
	ScaleMode	1 'Twips
	WindowState	2 'Maximized
PictureBox	Name	Picture1
	BackColor	&H0080FFFF&
	Height	3000
	Left	240
	ScaleHeight	100
	ScaleMode	0 'User
	ScaleWidth	100
	TabStop	0 'False
	Top	120
	Width	3000
PictureBox	Name	Picture2
	BackColor	&H0080FFFF&
	Height	3000
	Left	3660
	ScaleHeight	100
	ScaleMode	0 'User
	ScaleWidth	100
	TabStop	0 'False
	Top	120
	Width	3000
Image Control	Name	Image1
	BorderStyle	1 'Fixed Single
	Height	2250
	Left	7020
	Stretch	−1 'True
	Top	840
	Width	2250

2. Add a frame to the frmPix. Place a control array of five option buttons into the frame. Place a control array of four command buttons into the frame. Set the properties according to Table 39-11.

Table 39-11 Elements of the Load Picture frame

Object	Property	Setting
Frame	Name	fraLoad
	Caption	Load Picture
	Height	2535
	Left	810
	TabIndex	27
	Top	3600
	Width	2595
OptionButton	Name	optLoadPic
	Caption	Daffodil
	Height	255
	Index	0
	Left	120
	TabIndex	0
	Top	420
	Width	855
OptionButton	Name	optLoadPic
	Caption	Orchid
	Height	255
	Index	1
	Left	120
	TabIndex	1
	Top	780
	Width	855
OptionButton	Name	optLoadPic
	Caption	T-Rex
	Height	255
	Index	2
	Left	120
	TabIndex	2
	Top	1140
	Width	855
OptionButton	Name	optLoadPic
	Caption	Money
	Height	255

Object	Property	Setting
	Index	3
	Left	120
	TabIndex	3
	Top	1500
	Width	855
OptionButton	Name	optLoadPic
	Caption	Book
	Height	255
	Index	4
	Left	120
	TabIndex	4
	Top	1860
	Width	855
CommandButton	Name	cmdLoad
	Caption	Picture 1
	Height	375
	Index	0
	Left	1200
	TabIndex	5
	Top	420
	Width	975
CommandButton	Name	cmdLoad
	Caption	Picture 2
	Height	375
	Index	1
	Left	1200
	TabIndex	6
	Top	900
	Width	975
CommandButton	Name	cmdLoad
	Caption	Image
	Height	375
	Index	2
	Left	1200
	TabIndex	7
	Top	1380
	Width	975
CommandButton	Name	cmdLoad
	Caption	Picture Obj.
	Height	375

continued on next page

continued from previous page

Object	Property	Setting
	Index	3
	Left	1200
	TabIndex	8
	Top	1860
	Width	975

3. Add a second frame to the frmPix. Place a control array of four option buttons into the frame. Place two controls arrays of four text boxes each into the frame. Place a command button in the frame. Set the properties according to Table 39-12. Note that you must use the path on your computer to the Graphics directory.

Table 39-12 Elements of the Paint Picture frame

Object	Property	Setting
Frame	Name	fraPaint
	Caption	Paint Picture
	Height	2535
	Left	3900
	Top	3600
	Width	4815
OptionButton	Name	optPaint
	Caption	1 to 2
	Height	255
	Index	0
	Left	240
	TabIndex	9
	Top	600
	Width	855
OptionButton	Name	optPaint
	Caption	2 to 1
	Height	255
	Index	1
	Left	240
	TabIndex	10
	Top	1020
	Width	855

Object	Property	Setting
OptionButton	Name	optPaint
	Caption	Obj to 1
	Height	255
	Index	2
	Left	240
	TabIndex	11
	Top	1440
	Width	855
OptionButton	Name	optPaint
	Caption	Obj to 2
	Height	255
	Index	3
	Left	240
	TabIndex	12
	Top	1860
	Width	855
TextBox	Name	txtFrom
	Height	285
	Index	0
	Left	1680
	TabIndex	13
	Top	720
	Width	495
TextBox	Name	txtFrom
	Height	285
	Index	1
	Left	1680
	TabIndex	14
	Top	1080
	Width	495
TextBox	Name	txtFrom
	Height	285
	Index	2
	Left	1680
	TabIndex	15
	Top	1440
	Width	495
TextBox	Name	txtFrom
	Height	285
	Index	3
	Left	1680

continued on next page

continued from previous page

Object	Property	Setting
	TabIndex	16
	Top	1800
	Width	495
TextBox	Name	txtTo
	Height	285
	Index	0
	Left	2820
	TabIndex	17
	Top	720
	Width	495
TextBox	Name	txtTo
	Height	285
	Index	1
	Left	2820
	TabIndex	18
	Top	1080
	Width	495
TextBox	Name	txtTo
	Height	285
	Index	2
	Left	2820
	TabIndex	19
	Top	1440
	Width	495
TextBox	Name	txtTo
	Height	285
	Index	3
	Left	2820
	TabIndex	20
	Top	1800
	Width	495
CommandButton	Name	cmdPaint
	Height	555
	Left	3780
	Picture	Graphics\Icons\Arrows\Point05.Ico
	Style	1 'Graphical
	TabIndex	21

Object	Property	Setting
	Top	720
	Width	675
Label	Name	Label4
	Alignment	2 'Center
	Caption	From
	Height	255
	Left	1680
	Top	480
	Width	495
Label	Name	Label5
	Alignment	2 'Center
	Caption	To
	Height	255
	Left	2820
	Top	480
	Width	495
Label	Name	Label6
	AutoSize	-1 'True
	Caption	X
	Left	2400
	Top	780
Label	Name	Label7
	AutoSize	-1 'True
	Caption	Y
	Left	2400
	Top	1140
Label	Name	Label8
	AutoSize	-1 'True
	Caption	Width
	Left	2280
	Top	1500
Label	Name	Label9
	AutoSize	-1 'True
	Caption	Height
	Left	2280
	Top	1860
Label	Name	Label10
	AutoSize	-1 'True
	Caption	Clip
	Left	2280

continued on next page

continued from previous page

Object	Property	Setting
	Top	240
Label	Name	Label11
	AutoSize	-1 'True
	Caption	Paint
	Left	3900
	Top	1320

4. Use Figure 39-4 as a guide to sizing and positioning the objects on the screen.

5. Add the following global declarations to the General section of the code window.

```
Private sPix As String
Private objPix As Picture
Private nSource As Integer, nDest As Integer
Private nFromX As Integer, nFromY As Integer
Private nFromWidth As Integer, nFromHeight As Integer
Private nToX As Integer, nToY As Integer
Private nToWidth As Integer, nToHeight As Integer
```

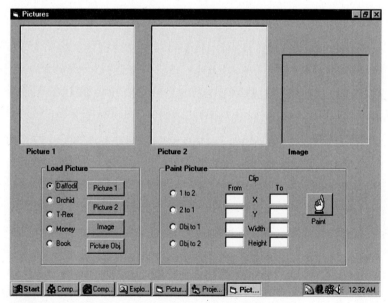

Figure 39-4 The Pictures project at design time

6. Add the following code to the optLoadPic_Click subroutine. This code fires when a user selects a picture to load. Note that the variable sPath uses App.Path, which requires the pictures to be in the same directory as the program files. When a user selects one of the option buttons, the global variable sPix is set to the path and filename of the selected picture.

```
Private Sub optLoadPic_Click(Index As Integer)
    Dim sPath As String
    sPath = App.Path
    ' Check for backslash (is there if path is root)
    If Right(sPath, 1) <> "\" Then
        sPath = sPath & "\"
    End If
'   Build the path\filename of the selected picture
    Select Case Index
        Case 0 ' Daffodil
            sPix = sPath & "Daffodil.gif"
        Case 1 ' Orchid
            sPix = sPath & "Orchid.gif"
        Case 2 ' T-Rex
            sPix = sPath & "T-rex.gif"
        Case 3 ' Money
            sPix = sPath & "Money1.gif"
        Case 4 ' Book
            sPix = sPath & "Book1.gif"
    End Select
End Sub
```

7. Add the following code to the cmdLoad_Click subroutine. The code is fired when a user clicks on one of the cmdLoad buttons. The code calls the LoadPix subroutine and passes the command button's index to it.

```
Private Sub cmdLoad_Click(Index As Integer)    LoadPix Index
End Sub
```

8. Add a new procedure to the program. Declare it as a public procedure with the name LoadPix.

9. Add the following code to the LoadPix procedure. The code is triggered by cmdLoad_Click. It uses the command button's index to determine where to place the selected picture. This code demonstrates the use of the LoadPicture function.

```
Public Sub LoadPix(iPixCmd As Integer)
    'Be sure a picture is selected
    If sPix = "" Then
        MsgBox "Must select a picture.", _
            vbOKOnly Or vbInformation, _
            "No Picture"
        Exit Sub
    End If
    ' OK -- now load the selected picture into a control
    Select Case iPixCmd
        Case 0 ' Picture 1
            Set Picture1 = LoadPicture(sPix)
        Case 1 ' Picture 2
```

continued on next page

continued from previous page

```
            Set Picture2 = LoadPicture(sPix)
        Case 2 ' Image Control
            Set Image1 = LoadPicture(sPix)
        Case 3 ' Picture Control
            Set objPix = LoadPicture(sPix)
    End Select
End Sub
```

10. Add the following code to the optPaint_Click subroutine. This code is fired when a user selects one of the option buttons in the Paint Picture frame. The code sets the global variables nSource and nDest, which are used to set the source and destination for PaintPicture. Since the Picture object has no size, the txtFrom text boxes are disabled when the Picture object is selected as the picture source.

```
Private Sub optPaint_Click(Index As Integer)
    Select Case Index
        Case 0 ' 1 to 2
            nSource = 1
            nDest =2
            EnableFrom
        Case 1 ' 2 to 1
            nSource = 2
            nDest = 1
            EnableFrom
        Case 2 ' Obj to 1
            nSource = 3
            nDest = 1
            DisableFrom
        Case 3 ' Obj to 2
            nSource = 3
            nDest = 2
            DisableFrom
    End Select
End Sub
```

11. Add a new private procedure, named EnableForm, to the program, and add the following code to the procedure. This code is called by the optPaint_Click procedure to enable the txtFrom text boxes.

```
Private Sub EnableFrom()
    Dim i As Integer
    For i = 0 To 3
        txtFrom(i).Enabled = True
    Next i
End Sub
```

12. Add a new private procedure, named DisableForm, to the program, and add the following code to the procedure. This code is called by the optPaint_Click procedure to disable the txtFrom text boxes when the Picture object is selected as the picture source.

```
Private Sub DisableFrom()
    Dim i As Integer
```

```
    For i = 0 To 3
        txtFrom(i).Enabled = False
    Next i
End Sub
```

13. Add the following code to the txtFrom_GotFocus subroutine. The code is triggered when one of the txtFrom text boxes gets the focus. The code selects the text that is in the active text box.

```
Private Sub txtFrom_GotFocus(Index As Integer)
    txtFrom(Index).SelStart = 0
    txtFrom(Index).SelLength = Len(txtFrom(Index).Text)
End Sub
```

14. Add the following code to the txtFrom_KeyPress procedure. The code is fired when a user types in the text box. This code allows only numbers and the BACKSPACE key to register in the text box. All other keys are rejected.

```
Private Sub txtFrom_KeyPress(Index As Integer, KeyAscii As Integer)
    ' Limit to 0 - 9 and backspace
    If (KeyAscii < vbKey0 Or KeyAscii > vbKey9) And _
        KeyAscii <> vbKeyBack Then
        KeyAscii = 0
    End If
End Sub
```

15. Add the following code to the txtTo_GotFocus subroutine. The code is triggered when one of the txtTo text boxes gets the focus. The code selects the text that is in the active text box.

```
Private Sub txtTo_GotFocus(Index As Integer)
    txtTo(Index).SelStart = 0
    txtTo(Index).SelLength = Len(txtTo(Index).Text)
End Sub
```

16. Add the following code to the txtTo_KeyPress procedure. The code is fired when a user types in the text box. This code allows only numbers, the minus sign, and the BACKSPACE key to register in the text box. All other keys are rejected.

```
Private Sub txtTo_KeyPress(Index As Integer, KeyAscii As Integer)
    ' Limit to 0 - 9, backspace and minus sign
    If (KeyAscii < vbKey0 Or KeyAscii > vbKey9) And _
      KeyAscii <> vbKeyBack And _
      Chr(KeyAscii) <> "-" Then
        KeyAscii = 0
    End If
End Sub
```

17. Add the following code to the cmdPaint_Click subroutine. The code is triggered when a user clicks on the Paint button. It selects the source picture and the destination picture from the global variables. Because a user could leave one of the From or To text boxes empty, the code assigns default values to empty text boxes. Because a user might attempt to paint a picture from an empty PictureBox, an error handler is included.

```
Private Sub cmdPaint_Click()
    On Error GoTo Error_Handler
    Select Case nSource
        Case 1
            If Val(txtTo(2)) = 0 Then txtTo(2).Text = Picture1.ScaleWidth
            If Val(txtTo(3)) = 0 Then txtTo(3) = Picture1.ScaleHeight
            If Val(txtFrom(2)) = 0 Then txtFrom(2) = Picture1.ScaleWidth
            If Val(txtFrom(3)) = 0 Then txtFrom(3) = Picture1.ScaleHeight
                Set Picture2 = LoadPicture("")
                Picture2.PaintPicture Picture1.Picture, _
                    Val(txtTo(0)), Val(txtTo(1)), Val(txtTo(2)), _
                    Val(txtTo(3)), Val(txtFrom(0)), Val(txtFrom(1)), _
                    Val(txtFrom(2)), Val(txtFrom(3))
        Case 2
            If Val(txtTo(2)) = 0 Then txtTo(2).Text = Picture2.ScaleWidth
            If Val(txtTo(3)) = 0 Then txtTo(3) = Picture2.ScaleHeight
            If Val(txtFrom(2)) = 0 Then txtFrom(2) = Picture2.ScaleWidth
            If Val(txtFrom(3)) = 0 Then txtFrom(3) = Picture2.ScaleHeight
                Set Picture1 = LoadPicture("")
                Picture1.PaintPicture Picture2.Picture, _
                    Val(txtTo(0)), Val(txtTo(1)), Val(txtTo(2)), _
                    Val(txtTo(3)), Val(txtFrom(0)), Val(txtFrom(1)), _
                    Val(txtFrom(2)), Val(txtFrom(3))
        Case 3
            If nDest = 1 Then
                If Val(txtTo(2)) = 0 Then txtTo(2).Text = _
                    Picture1.ScaleWidth
                If Val(txtTo(3)) = 0 Then txtTo(3) = Picture1.ScaleHeight
                    Set Picture1 = LoadPicture("")
                    Picture1.PaintPicture objPix, _
                        Val(txtTo(0)), Val(txtTo(1)), Val(txtTo(2)), _
                        Val(txtTo(3))
            Else
                If Val(txtTo(2)) = 0 Then txtTo(2).Text = _
                    Picture2.ScaleWidth
                If Val(txtTo(3)) = 0 Then txtTo(3) = Picture2.ScaleHeight
                    Set Picture2 = LoadPicture("")
                    Picture2.PaintPicture objPix, _
                        Val(txtTo(0)), Val(txtTo(1)), Val(txtTo(2)), _
                        Val(txtTo(3))
            End If
    End Select
Error_Handler:
    MsgBox "PaintPicture error " & Error, vbOKOnly, "Sorry"
End Sub
```

How It Works

The Pictures project displays a form with two PictureBoxes, an image control, and several option buttons and command buttons. The user can select a picture from the Load Picture list and load it into either of the PictureBoxes, into the image control, or into a picture object. Since the Picture object is not visible, the user will not see anything happen if the picture is loaded into it until he or she uses the PaintPicture dialog.

The PaintPicture frame offers several choices. The user begins by selecting the source and destination for the PaintPicture method. If the Paint button is clicked at that time, the program copies the source picture into the destination PictureBox on a one-for-one basis.

The user can also select a clipping region from the source picture by entering values into the From text boxes. The x and y values select the top-left corner, and the width and height properties determine the bottom-right corner. Both PictureBoxes have their ScaleWidth and ScaleHeight properties set to 100 to make clipping simpler.

By typing values into the To text boxes, the user can select the destination location and size. Entering a negative number for Width flips the picture horizontally, and a negative number for Height flips the picture vertically. There is a catch to negative values for width or height. If the width is set to a negative number, the value in To X must be greater than zero or the picture is painted to the left of the PictureBox and is invisible. The same constraints apply to negative height values.

Figure 39-5 shows the Pictures project when running.

Running the Pictures Project

When the program starts, both PictureBoxes and the image control are blank and the picture Object is empty. The user can select from the five pictures and load the picture into any of the destinations.

Once one of the PictureBoxes or the picture object contains a picture, the user can test the PaintPicture method to copy all or part of a picture into one of the PictureBoxes.

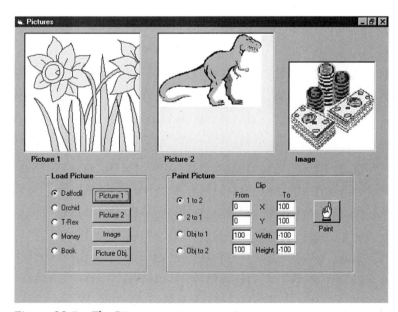

Figure 39-5   The Pictures project at runtime

40

DRAWING SHAPES

Many programs benefit from the use of graphics. Chapter 38, "Graphics Fundamentals," covers the basics of using graphical elements, and Chapter 39, "Pictures," provides the details of displaying existing graphics files. However, you'll often need to create your own graphics rather than using existing files. You might need to highlight an area of your form, create animation, graph data, or even set up a complete drawing application. This chapter covers the intricacies of drawing shapes. The Shapes project at the end of the chapter also demonstrates how to store and retrieve your drawn images using the Picture object.

Another interesting feature in Visual Basic is the ability to pass controls and standard objects as parameters. For instance, you can pass a Printer object, Form object, or picture control to one of the graphics methods to draw or print on the passed object. This makes adding print preview functions much simpler, because you can use the same functions to draw on a generic object rather than having separate functions for drawing on the printer and on a visual object.

Shapes are graphical images drawn on the surface of an object. You can use the Shape and Line controls to draw shapes directly on your form, on a PictureBox, on the printer, or on one of several other objects. You can use the graphics methods to draw with curved lines to produce arcs, circles, and ellipses, or use the Line method to produce lines, squares, rectangles, triangles, and other polygons.

A drawn shape may contain any combination of curved or straight lines. You can define both color and patterns to fill solid (enclosed) shapes. The lines that make up a shape can be solid, dashed, or dotted. You can make the line around a shape any color, or even invisible. When an image appears, it can cover or be covered by the other objects on the screen.

Controls and Methods

Visual Basic provides several controls and methods for specifying the appearance of shapes on a form, PictureBox, or Printer object. The Circle method places a curved shape on the indicated portion of a screen. The Line method produces any kind of shape that consists of straight lines. Two controls, the Shape and Line controlsLine control, let you draw graphical controls on your form at design time. Although there are some fundamental differences between the graphical controls and the graphics methods, many of the concepts in this chapter apply to both.

Graphical Controls

The line and shape controls prove especially useful for creating graphics at design time. The immediate feedback of seeing the line or shape on your form saves valuable time otherwise spent tinkering with code for the graphics methods. In many cases you can simply draw the graphical controls with no code whatsoever. Graphical controls also use significantly fewer system resources than the graphics methods, which improves your program's performance.

LINE CONTROL

Purpose	Use the Line control to display a horizontal, vertical, or diagonal line directly on the form, or in a PictureBox or frame.
Properties and Methods	Tables 40-1 and 40-2 list the properties and methods of the Line control.

Table 40-1 Properties of the Line control

Use This Property...	To Do This...
BorderColor	Read or set the color of the line
BorderStyle	Read or set the style of the line (for example, solid, dotted, dashed)
BorderWidth	Read or set the width of the line
Container	Set or return a reference to the object that contains this object
DrawMode	Read or set the draw mode (for example, overwrite, inverse, XOR pen)
Index	Uniquely identify an element of a control array
Name	Read or set the name used in code to refer to this control
Parent	Read the name of the form to which this control belongs
Tag	Read or set any extra string data associated with this control
Visible	Read or set whether this control is visible
X1, Y1, X2, Y2	Read or set the coordinates of the end points for the line

Table 40-2 Methods of the Line control

Use This Method...	To Do This...
Refresh	Update this control
ZOrder	Place this control at the front or back of the z-order

Description	The Line control draws a line directly on your form during the design phase. This is especially helpful for designing your forms, because you can see the effects immediately. Graphics methods like PSet or Line, in contrast, do not display until runtime and can be difficult to design with.

Note that there is no Move method for the Line control. It can be moved and resized at runtime by changing its X1, X2, Y1, and Y2 properties with your code.

SHAPE CONTROL

Purpose	Use the shape control to display a graphical control directly on a form, or in a PictureBox or frame, or on the printer object.
Properties and Methods	Tables 40-3 and 40-4 list the properties and methods that relate to the shape control.

Table 40-3 Properties of the shape control

Use This Property...	To Do This...
BackColor	Read or set the color of this control
BackStyle	Read or set whether text on this control is opaque or transparent
BorderColor	Read or set the color of the line that surrounds this control
BorderStyle	Read or set the style of the line (for example, solid, dotted, dashed)
BorderWidth	Read or set the width of the line
Container	Set or return a reference to the object that contains this object
DrawMode	Read or set the appearance of drawings by graphics methods
FillColor	Read or set the color used by graphics methods for fill-in effects
FillStyle	Read or set the pattern used by graphics methods for fill-in effects
Height	Read or set the height of this control
Index	Uniquely identify an element of a control array
Left	Read or set the left-edge placement of this control relative to its container
Name	Read or set the name used in code to refer to this control
Parent	Read the name of the form to which this control belongs
Shape	Read or set the type of shape
Tag	Read or set any extra string data associated with this control
Top	Read or set the coordinate of this control's top edge relative to its container
Visible	Read or set whether this control is visible
Width	Read or set the width of this control

Table 40-4 Methods of the shape control

Use This Method...	To Do This...
Move	Change the position of this control or form
Refresh	Update and repaint this control
ZOrder	Place this control at the front or back of the z-order

Description   The shape control draws a shape directly on your form during the design phase. This is especially helpful for designing your forms, because you can see the effects immediately. Available shapes are rectangle, square, oval, circle, rounded rectangle, and rounded square.

Several of the graphics properties (like FillColor and DrawStyle) let you customize the appearance of the shape controls. You can also manipulate the size and shape of the controls through your program code, although they are placed on the form at design time, and are normally left where they were placed.

Example   The Shapes project at the end of this chapter uses the line and shape controls to dress up the user interface. One shape control serves as a "shadow" behind a picture control to give it more definition, and another shape control lies behind the command buttons to visually group them. This second shape control has two Line controls carefully positioned next to it to help create the three-dimensional illusion of being inset, or carved into the form.

Graphics Methods

The graphics methods, Line, Circle, and PSet, offer more flexibility and control than the line and shape controls. You can paint individual pixels, draw partial arcs, and create repeating graphics (such as gridlines) more easily with the graphics methods. You can use the PaintPicture method to copy a picture or portion of a picture from one Picture property to another and resize or invert it in the process.

LINE METHOD

Objects Affected   Form, PictureBox, Printer, PropertyPage, UserControl, UserDocument

Purpose   The Line method draws a line or box shape on an object on the screen or printer. This method can create a number of shapes, including straight lines, squares, rectangles, polygons, and triangles. The object drawn on may be a Form, PictureBox, Printer, PropertyPage, UserControl, or UserDocument. Shapes drawn on a form have no effect on the controls placed on the form. Table 40-5 lists the different arguments of the Line method.

General Syntax

```
[form.]Line [[Step] (x1!, y1!)] - [Step] (x2!, y2!) [, [color&], B [F]]]
[form!]Name.Line [[Step] (x1!, y1!)] - [Step] (x2!, y2!) [, [color&], B [F]]]
Printer.Line [[Step] (x1!, y1!)] - [Step] (x2!, y2!) [, [color&], B [F]]]
```

Table 40-5 Arguments of the Line method

Argument	Description
form	Name property of the form
Name	Name of the object
Step	If first 'Step' is present, makes start coordinates relative to CurrentX and CurrentY
x1!, y1!	The horizontal and vertical coordinates of the start of the line
Step	If second 'Step' is present, makes end coordinates relative to start coordinates
x2!, y2!	The horizontal and vertical coordinates of the end of the line
color&	The RGB color of the outline of the shape; if not specified, then use current ForeColor
B	This argument creates a box with the indicated coordinates serving as the opposite corners
F	If 'B' argument present, then 'F' fills the box with the color specified by the color& argument

Example Syntax

```
Private Sub Picture1_Click ()
    'lines will draw in black
    Clr = QBColor(0)
    'clear picture
    Picture1.Cls
    'divides picture's width into 20 parts
    Picture1.ScaleWidth = 20
    'divides picture's height into 20 parts
    Picture1.ScaleHeight = 20
    Picture1.Line (1, 1)-(4, 4), Clr          'straight line
    Picture1.Line (10, 1)-(14, 4), Clr, B     'draws a box
    Picture1.Line (1, 10)-(4, 14), Clr, BF    'draws a filled in box
    Picture1.Line (13, 11)-(14, 14), Clr      'draws a triangle
    Picture1.Line (14, 14)-(11, 13), Clr      'second leg of triangle
    Picture1.Line (11, 13)-(13, 11), Clr      'completes triangle
    'increases the size of the DrawWidth
    Picture1.DrawWidth = Picture1.DrawWidth + 1
End Sub
```

Description   The Line method produces a line or box on a form, PictureBox, or Printer object. When a Line method expression does not include the object's name, the method applies to the current form.

The Line method coordinates (x1!, y1!) and (x2!, y2!) represent the positions of the start and end points on a line, or the upper-left and lower-right corners of a box. The x1! and x2! coordinates represent the horizontal positions; the y1! and y2! coordinates define the vertical positions. If the Step keyword precedes (x1!, y1!), then the coordinates are relative to the values of the CurrentX and CurrentY properties. If Step precedes (x2!, y2!), then the ending coordinates are relative to the starting coordinates (x1!, y1!). When Step does not appear in either the first or second instance, the appropriate set of coordinates are absolute references relative to the top-left corner of the object.

The color& argument sets the color of the line, and defaults to the ForeColor property. This argument contains a hexadecimal number that you may specify with an RGB function, a QBColor function, or by directly giving a hexadecimal number.

You may skip an argument in the middle of the syntax, but must include the comma (,) for each argument skipped. Don't end a Line method with a comma. Look at the Line method expressions in the example syntax for some examples.

In the example syntax, the Line method draws a line, a rectangle, a filled-in rectangle, and a triangle. Each Line method expression demonstrates the proper operation of this method with different results. The creation of the triangle involves the integration of three different Line method expressions. Figure 40-1 shows what each of these shapes looks like on the screen.

The B and F Arguments

When the B and F arguments are in a Line method expression, a box appears instead of a line. In this case the start point (x1!, y1!) coordinates represent the top-left corner of the box and the end point (x2!, y2!) defines the bottom-right corner. If the F argument appears, the interior of the box is the color indicated by the color& argument. With the FillStyle set to the default setting of one (1=transparent), the F argument has no apparent effect; set FillStyle to another setting to see the interior fill. In the example syntax, the B argument and then the B and F arguments produce

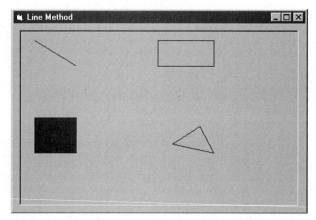

Figure 40-1 The Line method draws all of these shapes

Example

a square on the PictureBox. When the B argument is alone, an unfilled square displays. With both the B and F arguments, a square appears filled with the color specified by the color& argument.

In the Shapes project at the end of this chapter, the Line method draws lines, squares, rectangles, and triangles on the pictSurface PictureBox. The command buttons labeled Line, Square, Box, and Triangle all contain Line methods to produce the indicated object on the Draw PictureBox. When the Line method appears without the B or F arguments in the cmndDrawLine_Click event, a line is drawn between the randomly indicated points. By adding the B argument to the Line method in the cmndDrawBox_Click event, a rectangle of varying size and location displays instead of a line. Three Line methods work together in the cmndDrawTriangle_Click event to produce the three sides of the triangle on the Draw PictureBox.

Comments

The Line method can create polygons or any other type of straight-line shape by making the starting point of one line begin at the same point as another line's end point. If you just need a square or rectangle, it's easier to use the B option.

CIRCLE METHOD

Objects Affected   Form, PictureBox, Printer, PropertyPage, UserControl, UserDocument

Purpose   The Circle method generates a curved shape on an indicated object on the screen or printer. This method can create a variety of curved objects including circles, ellipses (ovals), and arcs. The object on the screen to be drawn on is a form, PictureBox, or Printer object. Table 40-6 summarizes the arguments of the Circle method.

General Syntax

```
[form.]Circle [Step] (x!, y!), radius![, [color&][, [start!][, [end!][, aspect!]]]]
[form!]Name.Circle [Step] (x!, y!), radius![, [color&][, [start!][, [end!][, aspect!]]]]
Printer.Circle [Step] (x!, y!), radius![, [color&][, [start!][, [end!][, aspect!]]]]
```

Table 40-6 Arguments of the Circle method

Argument	Description
form	Name property of the form
Name	Name property of the object that the shape is drawn on. If not specified, the form is assumed
Printer	'Printer' indicates the Printer object
Step	If 'Step' is present, makes center coordinates relative to CurrentX and CurrentY
(x!,y!)	The horizontal and vertical coordinates of the shape's center

continued on next page

continued from previous page

Argument	Description
radius!	The radius (distance from center to edge) of the circle or arc
color&	The RGB color of the outline of the shape; if not specified, then use current ForeColor
start!, end!	Indicates the beginning and ending position, in radians, of a partial circle or arc
aspect!	The aspect ratio of the shape; <1 is horizontal ellipse, =1 is a circle, >1 is vertical ellipse

Example Syntax

```
Private Sub Command1_Click ()
    'Draws a circle with a slice taken out.
    'This slice grows larger each time the user
    'presses the Command1 command button.
    Static Start As Double          'defines a static variable
    Cls                             'clears the form
    Aspect! = 1                     'aspect = 1:1; a circle
    FillColor = QBColor(7)          'changes color to white
    FillStyle = 0                   'makes all objects solid
    x! = ScaleWidth / 2             'defines x as half ScaleWidth
    y! = ScaleHeight / 2            'defines y as half ScaleHeight
    R = ScaleWidth / 3              'defines r as 1/3 ScaleWidth
    'checks if Start is greater than 6.283
    If Abs(Start) > 6.283 Then
        Start = 0                   'defines Start as 0
    End If
    Circle (x!, y!), R, QBColor(0), Start, -6.283, Aspect!
    Start = Start - .785            'reduces Start value
End Sub
```

Description

The Circle method produces a curved shape on a form, PictureBox, or Printer object with several arguments that modify the shape's appearance.

If the keyword Step follows the word Circle, then the x! and y! coordinates are relative to the values of the CurrentX and CurrentY properties. Omitting the word Step means that x! and y! are relative to the top-left corner of the object. The values of the x! (horizontal) and y! (vertical) coordinates define the position of the center of the shape. The radius! argument defines the curve's radius. All of these measurements are made in the unit of measure defined by the container's ScaleMode property.

The color& argument sets the color of the line that surrounds a curved shape and defaults to the ForeColor property when left blank. Define this argument with either an RGB hexadecimal number, RGB function, or QBColor function. Colors are covered in more detail in the FillColor entry later in this chapter. To skip an argument in the middle of the syntax, include the comma (,) for each argument excluded. Don't end a Circle method with a comma.

Using Pi

A circle is a line whose points are all the same distance from a point on a surface. The total length of this line is called the circumference. The distance between the line and the center point is the radius; the distance between each side of the line through the center point is called the diameter and is twice the radius. The ratio of the circumference to the diameter is a number called pi π. This is approximately equal to 3.1415926535.

Although most of us have forgotten more of our high school geometry than we still remember, using pi can make your computations for the Circle method much easier. If you're using the Circle method, define a constant called PI and use the constant in your code. There are also many formulas that use PI. This chapter includes a few examples of its use. A few formulas are given in Table 40-7.

Table 40-7 Circle formulas

Formula	Description
2 * pi * radius	A circle's circumference
Pi * (radius)^2	A circle's area
4 * atn(1)	Finds the value of PI
Degrees * pi / 180	Radian
Radian * 180 / pi	Degree

The start! and end! Arguments The start! and end! arguments of the Circle method define the dimensions of a partial circle or arc. Each partial circle's start! and end! arguments are expressed in radians. A radian equals (degrees * π / 180). This formula returns a value between 0 and 6.283 representing the degrees of a circle from 0 to 360 degrees. All start! and end! arguments have a value between -2π radians (–6.283) and 2π radians (6.283). In Visual Basic, the 360-degree point on a circle is at the three o'clock position on the circle. Table 40-8 displays the values to use for possible positions on a circle from 45 to 360 at intervals of 45 degrees. Figure 40-2 visually displays these positions on a circle.

Table 40-8 Approximate values for start! and end! positions on a circle

Degrees	Approximate Value	Formula
360	6.283	360 * PI/180
315	5.498	315 * PI/180
270	4.712	270 * PI/180
225	3.927	225 * PI/180
180	3.142	180 * PI/180
135	2.356	135 * PI/180
90	1.571	90 * PI/180
45	0.785	45 * PI/180
0	0.000	0 * PI/180

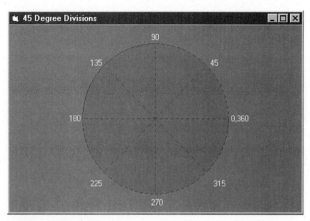

Figure 40-2 Degrees on a circle. Note the 0 degree position at three o'clock.

In the example syntax, the start! argument changes each time the command button is pressed. This reflects a larger and larger slice removed from the circle. Note that the circles drawn by the pressing of the Command1 command button appear behind the button, since drawn graphics are always placed under existing controls. This obscures any parts of the circles that are in the same position as the command button. Figures 40-3 and 40-4 show what these examples might look like.

Partial Circles and Arcs Using the start! and end! arguments in a Circle method produces partial circles. The part of the circle displayed appears between the boundaries of the degrees indicated. When start! and end! are positive, only the outer

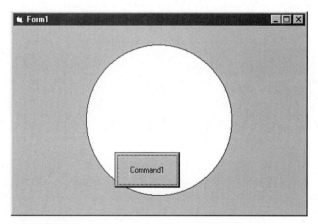

Figure 40-3 Example syntax shows full circle. The command button in front of the circle demonstrates normal layering.

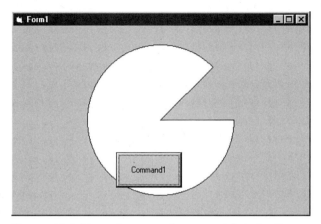

Figure 40-4 Example syntax shows partial circle after
Command1 is pressed

line on the circumference of the circle is drawn. When the values of the
start! and end! arguments are negative numbers, a radius appears from the
center of the circle to the edge of the drawn arc. Figure 40-5 displays some
example arcs. In the example syntax, the end! argument reduces in size
with each pressing of the Command1 command button. This produces a
smaller visible portion of the circle on the screen.

Experiment with the example syntax. Change the minus signs in the last
two lines to plus signs. Change Aspect! to numbers greater or smaller than
one. A few moments of experimentation instantly clarifies these concepts.

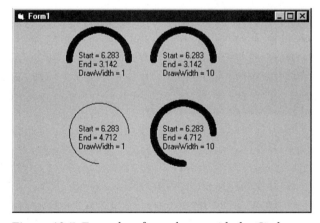

Figure 40-5 Examples of arcs drawn with the Circle
method

Ellipses   The value of the aspect! argument of a Circle method defines the aspect ratio, or whether a circle is a perfect circle or elongated. When the aspect! argument is 1, the horizontal and vertical distances from the edge of the circle to the center are each equal to the radius. If the value is less than one, then the circle is elongated horizontally. Setting the aspect! argument to a value greater than one creates a vertical ellipse. A value specified in the aspect! argument defines the ratio of difference between the horizontal and vertical dimensions of the ellipse. The aspect! argument also affects arcs. Figure 40-6 shows the effects of the aspect! on the drawing of a circle.

The FillColor and FillStyle Properties   The FillColor and FillStyle properties affect the contents of a shape drawn with the Circle method. A shape contains the color indicated by the FillColor property of the form, PictureBox, or Printer object. Depending on the setting of the FillStyle property, the shape contains a solid or pattern form of the color set in the FillColor property.

The DrawWidth Property   The DrawWidth property defines the width of the line that surrounds a shape drawn with the Circle method. If the start! and end! arguments of the Circle method have positive values, then the DrawWidth property defines the width of the line drawn to the center of the circle.

Example   The Shapes project at the end of the chapter uses the Circle method to draw circles on the pictSurface PictureBox. Pressing the cmndDrawCircle command button draws the circle, using the appropriate settings in the combo boxes.

Comments   A curved shape may only be filled with a color or pattern when it is completely bounded by a line on all sides. Otherwise, the shape is empty no matter what the settings of the properties that affect a shape's interior.

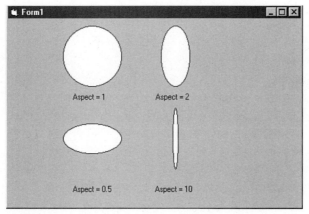

Figure 40-6 The effect of the aspect ratio on circles

PSet Method

Objects Affected   Form, PictureBox, Printer, PropertyPage, UserControl, UserDocument

Purpose   The PSet method is covered in Chapter 38. Refer to that chapter for general syntax and arguments. It is included here to demonstrate its use with the Line method in generating a graph.

Example Syntax

```
Private Sub Form_Click()
    Dim x As Single
    Dim y As Single
    DrawWidth = 1
    ScaleWidth = 100
    ScaleHeight = 100
    ' Draw Grid
    For x = 10 To ScaleWidth Step 10
        ' Draw center lines in bright blue
        If x = 50 Then
            ForeColor = QBColor(9)
        Else
            ' all other lines in black
            ForeColor = 0
        End If
        ' Horizontal lines
        Line (0, x)-(ScaleWidth, x)
        ' Vertical lines
        Line (x, 0)-(x, ScaleHeight)
    Next x
    ' Make PSet spots a little bigger
    DrawWidth = 2
    ' Draw a sine wave for 720 degrees (two fill cycles)
    ' 100 * 7.2 = 720 degrees
    For x = 0 To 100 Step 0.5
        ' convert to radians for VB
        y = Sin(x * 7.2 * 3.14159 / 180)
        ' y is multiplied by 20 to make waveform bigger
        ' Add 50 to draw line around the center horizontal axis
        PSet (x, (y * 20) + 50)
    Next x
End Sub
```

Description   Figure 40-7 shows the output of the example syntax. Note that an offset was added to the y coordinate to center it on the grid and that the y coordinate was scaled to make the plot large enough to see clearly. This example demonstrates how to draw curves with the PSet method and how to create graphs from scratch.

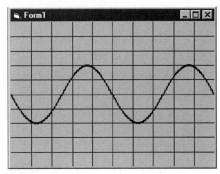

Figure 40-7 The example syntax draws this graph

Drawing Shapes Summary

Once you have designed a shape, there are a number of ways you can alter its appearance. The FillColor property determines the color to place within an enclosed shape (or you can make it transparent). You can also use the FillStyle property to specify a pattern to fill a closed shape; a shape can have both a pattern and a fill color. Setting the DrawMode property of a form or control affects how the shape's colors interact on the screen. This property indicates whether a newly drawn shape covers the existing graphic objects on the screen.

Shapes are also tied to the characteristics of their form or control. Each form or control determines the width of the line around a shape with the DrawWidth property. The DrawStyle property indicates the format of the line that surrounds a shape (solid, dashed, dotted, or even nonexistent). Table 40-9 summarizes these properties and methods. Detailed descriptions and examples follow the table.

Table 40-9 Methods and properties dealing with drawing shapes

Use or Set This...	Type	To Do This...
Circle	Method	Draw a circle, ellipsis, or arc on the form, PictureBox, or printer
DrawMode	Property	Define the appearance of drawn shapes
DrawStyle	Property	Define the outside line around a shape
DrawWidth	Property	Define the width of the line on the edge of a shape
FillColor	Property	Set the color to fill circles and boxes created with Line and Circle methods
FillStyle	Property	Set the pattern to fill circles and boxes
Line	Method	Draw a line, square, or rectangle on a form, PictureBox, or printer
PaintPicture	Method	Copy and optionally resize a picture from one control or form to another
PSet	Method	Paint a single point on the screen a specific color

DRAWMODE PROPERTY

Objects Affected   Form, Line, PictureBox, Printer, Shape, UserControl, UserDocument

Purpose   The DrawMode property determines what happens to a shape's colors when the shape appears on the screen. This property modifies the colors of the FillColor, ForeColor, and BackColor properties of a form, PictureBox, or Printer object to produce differing results. You can read and write this property at both runtime and design time. Tables 40-10 and 40-11 summarize the arguments of the DrawMode property.

General Syntax

```
[object.]DrawMode [ = mode%]
[object!]Name.DrawMode [ = mode%]
Printer.DrawMode [ = mode%]
```

Table 40-10 Arguments of the DrawMode property

Argument	Description
object	Name property of object
Name	Name property of the control
Printer	'Printer' indicates Printer object
mode%	Value representing the appearance of new shapes

Table 40-11 Possible settings and effects of the DrawMode property

mode%	VB.Constants	Effect
1	vbBlackness	All shapes are black.
2	vbNotMergePen	Colors are the inverse of Merge Pen.
3	vbMaskNotPen	Colors are a mixture of the BackColor and inverse of the FillColor.
4	vbNotCopyPen	Colors are the inverse of the FillColor.
5	vbMaskPenNot	Colors are a mixture of the FillColor and the inverse of the BackColor.
6	vbInvert	Output is inverse of the BackColor property.
7	vbXorPen	Colors are a mixture of the FillColor and BackColor.
8	vbNotMaskPen	Colors are the inverse of Mask Pen.
9	vbMaskPen	Colors are the common ones between the BackColor and FillColor.
10	vbNotXorPen	Colors are the inverse of the Xor Pen colors.
11	vbNop	Output remains unmodified.
12	vbMergeNotPen	Colors are a mixture of BackColor and inverse of FillColor.
13	vbCopyPen	(Default) FillColor.
14	vbMergeNotPen	Colors are a mixture of the FillColor and inverse of BackColor.
15	vbMergePen	Colors are a mixture of the FillColor and BackColor.
16	vbWhiteness	All shapes are white.

Example Syntax

```
Public Sub DisplayColor (Num As Integer, Con As Control)
     If Num = 0 Then Con.Text = "Black"
     If Num = 1 Then Con.Text = "Blue"
     If Num = 2 Then Con.Text = "Green"
     If Num = 3 Then Con.Text = "Cyan"
     If Num = 4 Then Con.Text = "Red"
     If Num = 5 Then Con.Text = "Magenta"
     If Num = 6 Then Con.Text = "Yellow"
     If Num = 7 Then Con.Text = "White"
     If Num = 8 Then Con.Text = "Gray"
     If Num = 9 Then Con.Text = "Light Blue"
     If Num = 10 Then Con.Text = "Light Green"
     If Num = 11 Then Con.Text = "Light Cyan"
     If Num = 12 Then Con.Text = "Light Red"
     If Num = 13 Then Con.Text = "Light Magenta"
     If Num = 14 Then Con.Text = "Light Yellow"
     If Num = 15 Then Con.Text = "Bright White"
End Sub


Private Sub Form_Click ()
     Static Color As Integer
     'defines temporary variable
     Cls                                      'clears form of graphics
     FillColor = QBColor(Color)               'defines the color
     FillStyle = 0                            'graphics are solid
     DrawWidth = 5
       'drawn lines are 5 pixels in width
     ForeColor = QBColor(1)                   'foreColor is blue
     If DrawMode = 16 Then                    'checks if DrawMode is 16
          DrawMode = 1                        'changes DrawMode to 1
     Else
          DrawMode = DrawMode + 1             'increments DrawMode by 1
     End If
     Text1.Text = Str$(DrawMode)
     'display the current DrawMode setting
     DisplayColor Color, Text2                'calls sub procedure
     X = ScaleWidth / 2
     'defines X as half the width of screen
     Y = ScaleHeight / 2
     'defines Y as half the height of screen
     R = ScaleWidth / 4
     'defines R as 1/4 the width of screen
     Circle (X, Y), R                         'draws a circle
     If Color = 15 Then                       'checks if Color is 15
          Color = 0                           'changes Color to black
     Else
          Color = Color + 1                   'increments Color by 1
     End If
     FillColor = QBColor(Color)               'changes FillColor
     DisplayColor Color, Text3
     'calls sub function DisplayColor
     X = 2 * ScaleWidth / 3
     'defines X as 2/3 the width of screen
     Y = 2 * ScaleHeight / 3
     'defines Y as 2/3 the width of screen
     Circle (X, Y), 1000
     'draws a circle
End Sub
```

Description   The DrawMode property affects the color of shapes drawn on the screen. When the DrawMode property does not refer to a specific object, the form's DrawMode property changes. The mode% argument determines which DrawMode setting subsequent graphics actions take. Each object starts with a default DrawMode property set to 13 (Copy Pen). This setting draws the shape normally.

Visualizing these modes without actually seeing them can be challenging. The example syntax demonstrates each of these settings, changing with each click of the form; this should help you get a feel for how each mode works. Notice that sometimes nothing displays. Try changing the BackColor property to another color and see how this affects each of these settings. As noted earlier, the ForeColor and BackColor properties remain unchanged. Although the FillColor property changes, its alteration is independent of the settings of the DrawMode property. Figures 40-8 and 40-9 illustrate two samples created with the example syntax.

Xor Pen   Although each pen has its uses, the Xor Pen can be a particular problem solver for you. If you draw the exact same graphic twice in a row with the Xor Pen, it resets everything back to how it was originally. Thus, you can produce simple animation by drawing the object with the Xor Pen, then drawing it again with the Xor Pen in the same position. This erases the graphic. Increment the position and start the process over again to produce the illusion of movement.

Example   In the Shapes project at the end of this chapter, the DrawMode property determines how the indicated colors display on the pictSurface

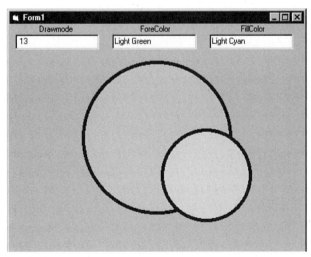

Figure 40-8 Example syntax shows the effects of the DrawMode property

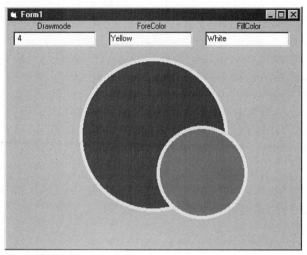

Figure 40-9 Another illustration produced by the example syntax

PictureBox. The cmboPickPen combo box lists the possible settings of the DrawMode property. The form loads with the default DrawMode set to Copy Pen.

Comments   This property has no effect on previously drawn shapes, unless they are covered by a newly drawn shape.

DrawStyle Property

Objects Affected   Form, PictureBox, Printer, PropertyPage, UserControl, UserDocument

Purpose   The DrawStyle property controls the appearance of the line surrounding a drawn shape on a form, PictureBox, or Printer object. An object's DrawStyle property defaults to producing a solid line. Using the other possible settings of the DrawStyle property, the line might change to a dashed line, dotted line, dash-dot line, or dash-dot-dot line. When the DrawStyle property is invisible, the line around a shape does not appear. This property only affects a shape when it is being drawn. Any changes made to this property have no effect on those images that have already been drawn. Table 40-12 summarizes the arguments for the DrawStyle property, and Table 40-13 summarizes the possible values for this property.

General Syntax

```
[form.]DrawStyle [ = style%]
[form!]Name.DrawStyle [ = style%]
Printer.DrawStyle [ = style%]
```

Table 40-12 Arguments of the DrawStyle property

Argument	Description
form	Name property of form
Name	Name property of PictureBox
Printer	'Printer' indicates the Printer object
style%	Value representing the appearance of lines around shapes

Table 40-13 Possible settings of the DrawStyle property

style%	VB.Constants	Example
0	vbSolid	_____
1	vbDash	_ _ _ _ _ _
2	vbDot	....
3	vbDashDot	_._._._
4	vbDashDotDot	_.._.._
5	vbInvisible	
6	vbInsideSolid	_____

Example Syntax

```
Private Sub Form_Click()
    Dim x, y, r
    '10 units for each circle, plus 5 to grow on
    ScaleWidth = 145
    ScaleHeight = 145
    x = 72.5 ' 145 / 2 - center circle
    y = 72.5 ' 145 / 2 - in form
    'each circle is 10 units out from
    'the previous circle
    r = (DrawStyle + 1) * 10
    Circle (x, y), r
    'drawstyle rolls over at 6
    If DrawStyle = 6 Then
        DrawStyle = 0
    Else
        DrawStyle = DrawStyle + 1
    End If
End Sub
```

Description   The DrawStyle property sets the type of line placed around a shape. When a DrawStyle expression does not include an object, the DrawMode property of the current form changes. The style% argument sets the DrawStyle. Each object starts with a default DrawStyle property set to Solid (0). With this setting, the line around a shape displays as a solid line.

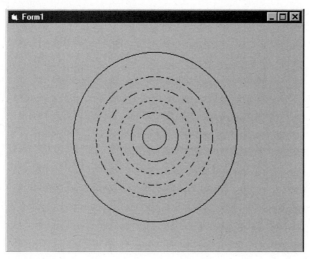

Figure 40-10 Different settings of the DrawStyle property

The example syntax shows results of each of the possible settings of the style% variable inside the circle. Each of these line patterns display on the screen in successively smaller circles. Figure 40-10 displays what this example might look like on your screen.

The DrawWidth Property

The DrawWidth property defines the thickness of the line around a drawn shape. Changing the value of the DrawWidth property to greater than 1 pixel in width makes the line around the shape solid when the DrawStyle property is a solid line, dashed line, dotted line, dash-dot line, or dash-dot-dot line (values 0 through 4). When this happens, the actual setting of the DrawStyle property remains unchanged. If the DrawWidth property of the form in the example syntax changes to a value greater than one, the first settings produce four circles with solid lines. This demonstrates the interaction of the DrawWidth and DrawStyle properties. The radius of the circle or arc is measured from the center of the drawn line, which is noticeable when DrawWidth becomes relatively large.

Example

In the Shapes project at the end of this chapter, the DrawStyle property determines how the indicated lines display on the pictSurface PictureBox. The cmboPickLine combo box lists the possible settings of the DrawStyle property. The form loads with the default choice set to Solid.

Comments

The ForeColor property sets the color of the line around a shape.

DrawWidth Property

Objects Affected   Form, PictureBox, Printer, PropertyPage, UserControl, UserDocument

Purpose   The DrawWidth property sets the width of lines drawn on a form, PictureBox, or Printer object. A value given to the DrawWidth property represents the thickness of the line in pixels. When this property's value increases, the border around a drawn shape such as a circle or square thickens. Table 40-14 summarizes the arguments of the DrawWidth property.

General Syntax

```
[form.]DrawWidth [ = size%]
[form!]Name.DrawWidth [ = size%]
Printer.DrawWidth [ = size%]
```

Table 40-14 Arguments of the DrawWidth property

Argument	Description
form	Name property of form
Name	Name property of PictureBox
Printer	'Printer' indicates Printer object
size%	Value representing the width of lines around shapes in pixels

Example Syntax

```
Private Sub Form_Click ()
    Static Y As Integer
    'remember the Y coordinate from click to click...
    CX = ScaleWidth / 500     'define the horizontal plotting increment
    CY = ScaleHeight / 10     'define the vertical plotting increment
    DrawWidth = DrawWidth + 1 'increments DrawWidth
    X = CX                    'starting point
    Y = Y + CY
    'starting line (incremented up from last click...)
    For L = 1 To 499
        X = X + CX
        'move over by the horizontal plotting increment
        PSet (X, Y)           'draws a point on a form
    Next L
End Sub
```

Description   The DrawWidth property sets the thickness of a line drawn on a form, PictureBox, or Printer object. When a DrawWidth property expression doesn't specify an object to act on, the form's DrawWidth property changes. The size% argument sets the DrawWidth. Each object begins with a default DrawWidth property set to 1, drawing lines that are 1 pixel thick.

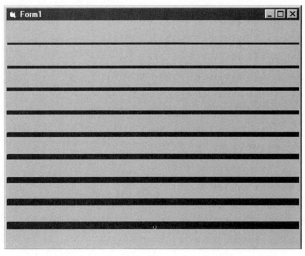

Figure 40-11 DrawWidth affects the thickness of drawn lines and points

In the example syntax, the DrawWidth property of the form increases by one with each click of the form. Notice that each line created by the PSet method is successively thicker. Figure 40-11 shows what this example might look like on your screen.

The DrawStyle Property

If the DrawWidth property changes to greater than 1, a DrawStyle property of 1, 2, 3, or 4 has no effect on the appearance of a drawn line, which will be solid. With the DrawWidth property set to 1, the DrawStyle property changes the line or lines in a drawn shape from a solid line to dashes, dots, or a combination of the two depending on that property's value. When the DrawWidth property is larger than 4, a line drawn by either the Circle or Line method is solid. This has no effect on the actual setting of the DrawStyle property.

Example

In the Shapes project at the end of this chapter, the DrawWidth property determines how the indicated lines display on the pictSurface PictureBox. The cmboPickWidth combo box lists some of the possible settings of the DrawWidth property.

FILLCOLOR PROPERTY

Objects Affected Form, PictureBox, Printer, PropertyPage, UserControl, UserDocument

Purpose The FillColor property sets the color of the interior of circles and boxes drawn in a container. Define an object's FillColor property either directly (with a hexadecimal number) or with the QBColor or RGB functions.

Changes made to the FillColor property have no effect on the colors of previously drawn shapes already on the object. This property works in conjunction with the FillStyle property to choose what will fill the interior of circles and boxes. Table 40-15 lists the arguments of the FillColor property, and Table 40-16 lists the values of some common colors.

General Syntax

```
[form.]FillColor [ = color&]
[form!]Name.FillColor [ = color&]
Printer.FillColor [ = color&]
```

Table 40-15 Arguments of the FillColor property

Argument	Description
form	Name property of form
Name	Name property of the control
Printer	'Printer' indicates Printer object
color&	Value representing the interior color of drawn shapes

Table 40-16 Values of common colors in RGB, hexadecimal, and QBColor formats

Color	VB.Constants	Red Value	Green Value	Blue Value	Hexadecimal	QBColor
Black	vbBlack	0	0	0	&H0	0
Red	vbRed	255	0	0	&HFF	4
Green	vbGreen	0	255	0	&HFF00	2
Yellow	vbYellow	0	255	255	&HFFFF	6
Blue	vbBlue	0	0	255	&HFF0000	1
Magenta	vbMagenta	255	0	255	&HFF00FF	5
Cyan	vbCyan	0	255	255	&HFFFF00	3
White	vbWhite	255	255	255	&HFFFFFF	15
Light Gray	n/a	192	192	192	&H00C0C0C0	7
Dark Gray	n/a	128	128	128	&H00808080	8

Example Syntax

```
Private Sub Form_Click ()
    AutoRedraw = True          'make sure graphics are drawn immediately
    Cls                        'clears the form
    ScaleWidth = 4
    'divides the width of the form into four parts
    ScaleHeight = 4
    'divides the height of the form into four parts
    DrawWidth = 5              'defines thickness as 5 pixels
```

continued on next page

continued from previous page

```
      FillStyle = 0              'defines FillStyle as solid
      ForeColor = QBColor(0)
      'defines ForeColor as black (for the box borders)
      LineColor = 0
      'this will be the FillColor; start with black
      For H = 0 To 3
      'draws 16 colored boxes on the screen with the
            For W = 0 To 3       'fillColor property and Line method.
                  FillColor = QBColor(LineColor)
                  Line (W, H)-(W + 1, H + 1), , B
                  LineColor = LineColor + 1'increment to the next color
            Next W
      Next H
End Sub
```

Description The FillColor property defines the interior color of drawn circles and boxes on forms, PictureBoxes, or Printer objects. If a FillColor property expression does not include the object's name, then the current form's FillColor property changes. The FillColor property defaults to black. The color& variable refers to the Long value given to the FillColor property. This integer must be in hexadecimal form. You can set this property with either the RGB or QBColor functions, or by directly specifying a hexadecimal number. Table 40-16 lists some common color values.

In the example syntax, the FillColor property changes each time a new box is drawn on the screen. The program increments the value used with the QBColor function by one to get the next color. This results in the division of the form into 16 equal parts, one for each of the 16 possible colors

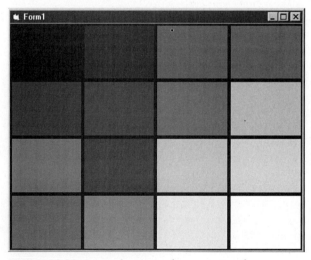

Figure 40-12 Example syntax demonstrates the FillColor property

of the QBColor function. Figure 40-12 shows what this example might look like.

The RGB and QBColor Functions

Both the RGB and QBColor functions provide a means of defining the color of the FillColor property without using the confusing hexadecimal RGB codes. If standard colors like red, green, blue, and cyan are accepta ble, then the QBColor function works very well. When you require a special mix of RGB values, the RGB function allows you to specify any one of more than 16 million colors. Be careful not to give this property a color that matches the background color of the form or PictureBox, or else you won't be able to see the graphics shape you've just drawn. Table 40-16 lists the most common settings of the RGB and QBColor functions. In the example syntax, the QBColor function serves as a means of defining the color of each of the boxes as it appears on the screen. Notice that the color of each square is unaffected by the changes made to the FillColor property for the subsequent squares. Once a shape appears on the screen or printer, its attributes are permanent.

The FillStyle Property

The FillStyle property works in conjunction with the FillColor property to define the pattern and color inside drawn circles and boxes. If the FillStyle of a form, PictureBox, or Printer object is left at the default value of 1 (Transparent), then any drawn objects appear empty. When the FillStyle property is 0 (Solid), the drawn circles and boxes contain the color indicated by the FillColor property. Since the default value of the FillColor property is 0 (Black), the default output is a black circle or box (provided the FillStyle property is set to Solid). With the FillStyle property set to a value between 2 and 7 inclusive, the FillColor property determines what color to give the patterns drawn inside the circle or box. In the example syntax, the FillStyle property is 0 to indicate that each of the boxes drawn contains solid styles of the colors indicated by the FillColor property.

Example

In the Shapes project at the end of this chapter, the FillColor property determines what color the shapes get filled with on the pictSurface PictureBox. The cmboPickColor combo box lists some of the possible settings of the FillColor property, and the QBColor function provides the actual color setting. The form loads with the default choice set to Black.

Comments

Remember to change the FillStyle property from the default setting of 1 (Transparent); otherwise, the FillColor property has no effect on any shapes drawn with the Line or Circle methods.

FILLSTYLE PROPERTY

Objects Affected

Form, Grid, PictureBox, PropertyPage, Printer, Shape, UserControl, UserDocument

Purpose

The FillStyle property defines the pattern of the interior of a drawn shape on a form, PictureBox, shape, or Printer object. An object's FillStyle property is a value between 0 and 7 inclusive. This property works in conjunction with the FillColor property to specify what fills the interior of circles and boxes. Tables 40-17 defines the arguments used with the FillStyle property, and Table 40-18 lists its possible settings.

General Syntax

```
[form.]FillStyle [ = style%]
[form!]Name.FillStyle [ = style%]
Printer.FillStyle [ = style%]
```

Table 40-17 Arguments of the FillStyle property

Argument	Description
form	Name property of form
Name	Name property of the control
Printer	'Printer' indicates the Printer object
style%	Value representing the style to place in the interior of drawn shapes

Table 40-18 Possible settings of the FillStyle property

style%	VB.Constants	Description
0	vbSolid	Solid fill
1	vbTransparent	(Default) Transparent, no fill
2	vbHorizontalLine	Horizontal lines
3	vbVerticalLine	Vertical lines
4	vbUpwardDiagonal	Upward diagonal lines (from upper left to lower right)
5	vbDownwardDiagonal	Downward diagonal lines (from lower left to upper right)
6	vbCross	Crosshatch
7	vbDiagonal	Diagonal crosshatch

Example Syntax

```
Private Sub Form_Click ()
    AutoRedraw = True          'makes sure graphics are drawn immediately
    Cls                        'clears the form
    ScaleWidth = 2
    'divides the width of the form into two parts
    ScaleHeight = 4
    'divides the height of the form into four parts
    FillColor = QBColor(0)     'defines Color as Black
    FillStyle = 0              'start with solid fill
    For H = 0 To 3
    'Draws 8 patterned boxes on the screen with the
        For W = 0 To 1
```

```
        'FillColor property and Line method.
              Line (W, H)-(W + 1, H + 1), , B
              If FillStyle = 7 Then Exit Sub
    'exit if we've done them all
              FillStyle = FillStyle + 1              'next fill style
        Next W
    Next H
End Sub
```

Description

The FillStyle property defines the interior pattern style of drawn shapes. If a FillStyle property expression does not include the object's name, the current form's FillStyle property changes. Each form, PictureBox, and Printer object begins with the FillColor property set to Transparent. With its default Transparent setting, the FillStyle property prevents the display of the color set in the FillColor property. Setting the FillStyle property to 0 produces the solid color indicated by the FillColor property. The other settings, as listed in Table 40-18, give various patterns.

In the example syntax, the FillStyle property increments for each box drawn to display the different possible settings. Figure 40-13 shows each one of the eight possible FillStyles.

The FillColor Property

The FillStyle property works in conjunction with the FillColor property to define the pattern and color inside drawn circles and boxes. If the FillStyle of a form, PictureBox, or Printer object is left at the default value of 1 (Transparent), then any drawn objects appear empty no matter what the FillColor property is. When the FillStyle property is 0 (Solid), the drawn circles and boxes contain the color indicated by the FillColor property.

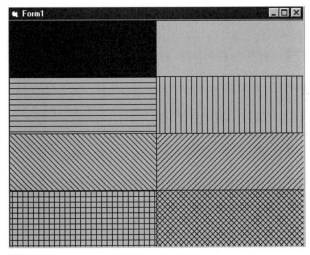

Figure 40-13 The eight different FillStyles

Since the default value of the FillColor property is 0 (Black), the default output is a black circle or box. With the FillStyle property set to a value between 2 and 7 inclusive, the FillColor property determines what color to give the patterns drawn inside the circle or box.

Example

In the Shapes project at the end of this chapter, the FillStyle property determines what style the shapes get filled with on the pictSurface PictureBox. The cmboPickPattern combo box lists all the possible settings of the FillStyle property. The form loads with the default choice set to Solid.

Comments

The grid control and the MSFlexGrid control also have a FillStyle property. Their use of this property is totally different from the usage explained above. See Chapter 48, "Grid Controls," for more information about the Grid control.

Constant Values

It is usually best to use named constants rather than numeric values when developing software. Named constants make your code more readable and easier to maintain.

Table 40-19 lists the values of the constants relevant to this chapter, lists their names, and briefly describes what they mean. These constants can be viewed in the VB Constants module using the Object Browser. It is not necessary to explicitly add these objects to your project.

Table 40-19 Constant values used with drawing shapes

Value	VB.Constants	Meaning
		DrawMode Property
1	vbBlackness	All shapes are black.
2	vbNotMergePen	Colors are the inverse of Merge Pen.
3	vbMaskNotPen	Colors are a mixture of the BackColor and inverse of the FillColor.
4	vbNotCopyPen	Colors are the inverse of the FillColor.
5	vbMaskPenNot	Colors are a mixture of the FillColor and the inverse of the BackColor.
6	vbInvert	Output is inverse of the BackColor property.
7	vbXorPen	Colors are a mixture of the FillColor and BackColor.
8	vbNotMaskPen	Colors are the inverse of Mask Pen.
9	vbMaskPen	Colors are the common ones between the BackColor and FillColor.
10	vbNotXorPen	Colors are the inverse of the Xor Pen colors.
11	vbNop	Output remains unmodified.
12	vbMergeNotPen	Colors are a mixture of BackColor and inverse of FillColor.
13	vbCopyPen	(Default) FillColor.
14	vbMergeNotPen	Colors are a mixture of the FillColor and inverse of BackColor.

Value	VB.Constants	Meaning
15	vbMergePen	Colors are a mixture of the FillColor and BackColor.
16	vbWhiteness	All shapes are white.

DrawStyle Property

Value	VB.Constants	Meaning
0	vbSolid	_____
1	vbDash	_ _ _ _ _
2	vbDot	. . . .
3	vbDashDot	_ . _ . _ . _
4	vbDashDotDot	_ . . _ . . _
5	vbInvisible	
6	vbInsideSolid	_____

FillColor Property

Value	VB.Constants	Meaning
&H0	vbBlack	Black
&HFF	vbRed	Red
&HFF00	vbGreen	Green
&HFFFF	vbYellow	Yellow
&HFF0000	vbBlue	Blue
&HFF00FF	vbMagenta	Magenta
&HFFFFFF	vbWhite	White

FillStyle Property

Value	VB.Constants	Meaning
0	vbSolid	Solid fill
1	vbTransparent	(Default) Transparent, no fill
2	vbHorizontalLine	Horizontal lines
3	vbVerticalLine	Vertical lines
4	vbUpwardDiagonal	Upward diagonal lines (from upper left to lower right)
5	vbDownwardDiagonal	Downward diagonal lines (from lower left to upper right)
6	vbCross	Crosshatch
7	vbDiagonal	Diagonal crosshatch

The Shapes Project

Project Overview

The Shapes project demonstrates the methods and properties that directly affect the drawing of shapes. Using the Line and Circle methods, the Shapes project places circles, lines, squares, rectangles, and triangles on the PictureBox. By manipulating the settings of the FillColor, FillStyle, DrawMode, DrawStyle, and DrawWidth properties, the Shapes project visually displays how these properties affect the interaction between different drawn shapes.

The following pages discuss the assembly and operation of the Shapes project. The first section deals with the assembly of the controls on the Shapes form. Following this is a discussion that shows and briefly explains the contents of the subroutines of this project. Finally, there is a How It Works guide to the operation of the project. Read this information carefully and use the pictures of the form as guides in the process of assembling the project.

Assembling the Project: formShapes

1. Make a new form with the objects and properties in Table 40-20. The graphical controls need to be precisely positioned by directly entering their position properties in the properties box.

Table 40-20 Elements of the Shapes form

Object	Property	Setting
Form	BorderStyle	1–Fixed Single
	Caption	Shapes Project
	MaxButton	False
Combo	Name	cmboPickWidth
	Style	2–Dropdown List
	TabIndex	1
Combo	Name	cmboPickColor
	Style	2–Dropdown List
	TabIndex	3
Combo	Name	cmboPickLine
	Style	2–Dropdown List
	TabIndex	5
Combo	Name	cmboPickPen
	Style	2–Dropdown List
	TabIndex	7
Combo	Name	cmboPickPattern
	Style	2–Dropdown List
	TabIndex	9
Command	Caption	&Circle
	Name	cmndDrawCircle
	TabIndex	10
Command	Caption	&Line
	Name	cmndDrawLine
	TabIndex	11

Object	Property	Setting
Command	Caption	&Square
	Name	cmndDrawSquare
	TabIndex	12
Command	Caption	&Box
	Name	cmndDrawBox
	TabIndex	13
Command	Caption	&Triangle
	Name	cmndDrawTriangle
	TabIndex	14
Command	Caption	"" {set it to nothing}
	Name	cmndClearScreen
	TabIndex	15
Label	Caption	&Width
	TabIndex	0
Label	Caption	C&olor
	TabIndex	2
Label	Caption	Lin&e
	TabIndex	4
Label	Caption	&Pattern
	TabIndex	6
Label	Caption	Pe&n
	TabIndex	8
PictureBox	Height	3660
	Left	120
	Name	pictSurface
	TabIndex	16
	Top	1200
	Width	5385
Shape	BorderColor	&H00FFFFFF&, White
	BorderWidth	2
	Height	615
	Left	135
	Name	Shape1
	Top	5130
	Width	5415

continued on next page

continued from previous page

Object	Property	Setting
Line	BorderColor	&H00000000&, Black
	BorderWidth	2
	Name	Line1
	X1	135
	X2	135
	Y1	5145
	Y2	5720
Line	BorderColor	&H00000000&, Black
	BorderWidth	2
	Name	Line2
	X1	135
	X2	5517
	Y1	5130
	Y2	5130

2. Size and position the objects on the screen as shown in Figure 40-14.

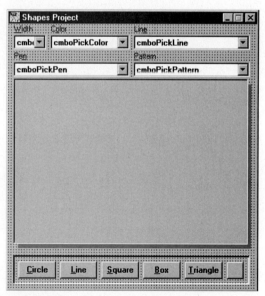

Figure 40-14 What the Shapes form should look like

3. Enter the following code in the cmboPickColor_Click event subroutine. This code triggers when the user selects a new color in the Color combo box. When this code activates, the Draw form's FillColor property changes to the new color.

```
Private Sub cmboPickColor_Click ()
    pictSurface.FillColor = QBColor(cmboPickColor.ListIndex)
End Sub
```

4. Enter the following code in the cmboPickLine_Click event subroutine. When the user clicks one of the options in the Line combo box, the index value of the chosen option redefines the setting of the DrawStyle property of the pictSurface PictureBox.

```
Private Sub cmboPickLine_Click ()
    pictSurface.DrawStyle = cmboPickLine.ListIndex
End Sub
```

5. Enter the following code in the cmboPickPattern_Click event subroutine. When the user selects an option in the Pattern combo box, the FillStyle property of the pictSurface PictureBox changes to the new setting.

```
Private Sub cmboPickPattern_Click ()
    pictSurface.FillStyle = cmboPickPattern.ListIndex
End Sub
```

6. Enter the following code in the cmboPickPen_Click event subroutine. When the user selects an option in the Pen combo box, the DrawMode property of the pictSurface PictureBox changes to the new setting.

```
Private Sub cmboPickPen_Click ()
    pictSurface.DrawMode = cmboPickPen.ListIndex + 1
End Sub
```

7. Enter the following code in the cmboPickWidth_Click event subroutine. When the user selects an option in the Width combo box, the DrawWidth property changes to the new setting.

```
Private Sub cmboPickWidth_Click ()
    pictSurface.DrawWidth = cmboPickWidth.ListIndex + 1
End Sub
```

8. Enter the following code in the cmndDrawBox_Click event subroutine. When the user clicks the Box command button, this code draws a rectangle of random size and location.

```
Private Sub cmndDrawBox_Click ()
    X1 = Int((75 - (1)) * Rnd + (1))          'pick starting coordinates
    Y1 = Int((75 - (1)) * Rnd + (1))
    X2 = Int((50 - (1)) * Rnd + (1))          'pick ending coordinates
    Y2 = Int((50 - (1)) * Rnd + (1))
    pictSurface.Line (X1, Y1)-Step(X2, Y2), , B    'draw the box
End Sub
```

9. Enter the following code in the cmndDrawCircle_Click event subroutine. When the user clicks the Circle command button, this code draws a circle of random size and location.

```
Private Sub cmndDrawCircle_Click ()
    X = Int((100 - 1) * Rnd + 1)              'pick center coordinates
    Y = Int((100 - 1) * Rnd + 1)
    R = Int((25 - 1) * Rnd + 1)               'pick radius
    pictSurface.Circle (X, Y), R              'draw circle
End Sub
```

10. Enter the following code in the cmndDrawLine_Click event subroutine. When the user clicks the Line command button, this code draws a line of random length and location.

```
Private Sub cmndDrawLine_Click ()
    X1 = Int((100 - 1) * Rnd + 1)             'pick starting coordinates
    Y1 = Int((100 - 1) * Rnd + 1)
    X2 = Int((100 - 1) * Rnd + 1)             'pick ending coordinates
    Y2 = Int((100 - 1) * Rnd + 1)
    pictSurface.Line (X1, Y1)-(X2, Y2)        'draw box
End Sub
```

11. Enter the following code in the cmndDrawSquare_Click event subroutine. When the user clicks the Square command button, this code draws a square of random size and location.

```
Private Sub cmndDrawSquare_Click ()
    X1 = Int((50 - 1) * Rnd + 1)              'pick starting coordinates
    Y1 = Int((50 - 1) * Rnd + 1)
    X2 = Int((50 - 1) * Rnd + 1)              'pick ending coordinates
    Y2 = X2
    pictSurface.Line (X1, Y1)-Step(X2, Y2), , B    'draw square
End Sub
```

12. Enter the following code in the cmndDrawTriangle_Click event subroutine. When the user clicks the Triangle command button, this code draws a triangle of random size and location.

```
Private Sub cmndDrawTriangle_Click ()
    X1 = Int((100 - 1) * Rnd + 1)             'pick one corner
    Y1 = Int((100 - 1) * Rnd + 1)
    X2 = Int((100 - 1) * Rnd + 1)             'pick another corner
    Y2 = Int((100 - 1) * Rnd + 1)
    X3 = Int((100 - 1) * Rnd + 1)             'pick third corner
    Y3 = Int((100 - 1) * Rnd + 1)
    pictSurface.Line (X1, Y1)-(X2, Y2)        'draw triangle
    pictSurface.Line (X2, Y2)-(X3, Y3)
    pictSurface.Line (X3, Y3)-(X1, Y1)
End Sub
```

13. Enter the following code in the Form_Load event subroutine. This code processes when the program starts. At that time, the code adds the choices to all five of the combo boxes, sets their values to the normal defaults, and sets the default values of the pictSurface PictureBox.

```
Private Sub Form_Load ()
    'fill Width pick list with possible widths
    For i = 1 To 10
        cmboPickWidth.AddItem Str$(i)
    Next i
    'fill Color pick list with possible colors
    cmboPickColor.AddItem "Black"
    cmboPickColor.AddItem "Blue"
    cmboPickColor.AddItem "Green"
    cmboPickColor.AddItem "Cyan"
    cmboPickColor.AddItem "Red"
    cmboPickColor.AddItem "Magenta"
    cmboPickColor.AddItem "Yellow"
    cmboPickColor.AddItem "White"
    cmboPickColor.AddItem "Gray"
    cmboPickColor.AddItem "Light Blue"
    cmboPickColor.AddItem "Light Green"
    cmboPickColor.AddItem "Light Cyan"
    cmboPickColor.AddItem "Light Red"
    cmboPickColor.AddItem "Light Magenta"
    cmboPickColor.AddItem "Light Yellow"
    cmboPickColor.AddItem "Bright White"
    'fill Pattern pick list with patterns
    cmboPickPattern.AddItem "Solid"
    cmboPickPattern.AddItem "Transparent"
    cmboPickPattern.AddItem "Horizontal Line"
    cmboPickPattern.AddItem "Vertical Line"
    cmboPickPattern.AddItem "Upward Diagonal"
    cmboPickPattern.AddItem "Downward Diagonal"
    cmboPickPattern.AddItem "Cross"
    cmboPickPattern.AddItem "Diagonal Cross"
    'fill Pen pick list with possible pens
    cmboPickPen.AddItem "Blackness"
    cmboPickPen.AddItem "Not Merge Pen"
    cmboPickPen.AddItem "Mask Not Pen"
    cmboPickPen.AddItem "Not Copy Pen"
    cmboPickPen.AddItem "Mask Pen Not"
    cmboPickPen.AddItem "Invert"
    cmboPickPen.AddItem "Xor Pen"
    cmboPickPen.AddItem "Not Mask Pen"
    cmboPickPen.AddItem "Mask Pen"
    cmboPickPen.AddItem "Not Xor Pen"
    cmboPickPen.AddItem "Not"
    cmboPickPen.AddItem "Merge Not Pen"
    cmboPickPen.AddItem "Copy Pen"
    cmboPickPen.AddItem "Merge Pen Not"
    cmboPickPen.AddItem "Merge Pen"
    cmboPickPen.AddItem "Whiteness"
    'fill Line pick list with possible pens
    cmboPickLine.AddItem "Solid"
    cmboPickLine.AddItem "Dash"
    cmboPickLine.AddItem "Dot"
    cmboPickLine.AddItem "Dash-Dot"
    cmboPickLine.AddItem "Dash-Dot-Dot"
    cmboPickLine.AddItem "Invisible"
    cmboPickLine.AddItem "Inside Solid"
    '1    (these are all set to defaults)
    cmboPickWidth.ListIndex = 0
```

continued on next page

continued from previous page

```
      cmboPickColor.ListIndex = 0          'black
      cmboPickPattern.ListIndex = 0        'solid
      cmboPickPen.ListIndex = 13           'copy pen
      cmboPickLine.ListIndex = 0           'solid
      'set up an easy custom scale
      pictSurface.ScaleHeight = 100
      pictSurface.ScaleWidth = 100
      'make sure graphics redrawn immediately
      pictSurface.AutoRedraw = True
End Sub
```

14. Enter the following code in the pictSurface_DblClick event and cmndClearScreen_Click event procedures. This code triggers when the user double-clicks on the PictureBox or clicks the blank command button. When this happens the pictSurface PictureBox clears of all the drawn shapes.

```
Private Sub pictSurface_DblClick ()
      pictSurface.Cls
End Sub

Private Sub cmndClearScreen_Click ()
      pictSurface.Cls
End Sub
```

15. Enter the following code in the Form_Unload event. This code ends the program.

```
Private Sub Form_Unload
End
End Sub
```

Assembling the Project: formCopyShapes

1. Make a new form with the objects and properties in Table 40-21.

Table 40-21 Elements of the Copy Shapes form

Object	Property	Setting
Form	BorderStyle	1 - Fixed Single
	Caption	Copy Shapes
	MaxButton	False
Command	Caption	&Copy Shape
	Name	cmndCopyShape
	TabIndex	1
ComboBox	Name	cmboChoosePicture
	Style	2 'Dropdown List
	TabIndex	2
PictureBox	Name	pictCopy
	TabIndex	3

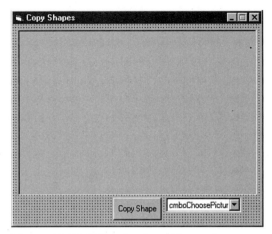

Figure 40-15 What the Copy Shapes form should look like

2. Size the objects on the screen as shown in Figure 40-15.

3. Enter the following code in the General section of formCopyShapes. This defines the constant and collection used to store pictures.

```
Private collSavePictures As New Collection
Private Const MAX_PICTURES = 10
```

4. Enter the following code in the cmndCopyShape_Click event subroutine. This code triggers when the user clicks the command button. It copies the picture in the pictSurface PictureBox into the pictCopy PictureBox. This sub also loads the collSavePictures collection using the AddToArray sub.

```
Private Sub cmndCopyShape_Click()
    'Note: to use a picture object, choose
    'Tools/Reference menu item and click on the
    'Standard OLE Types reference.
    Dim opicPicture As Picture
    'copy the entire picture from pictSurface
    'do this the easy way, take the defaults
    pictCopy.PaintPicture Form1!pictSurface.Image, 0, 0
    'Once you capture it, put it in the picture
    'object collection.
    Set opicPicture = pictCopy.Image
    AddtoArray opicPicture
    Set opicPicture = Nothing
 End Sub
```

5. Enter the following code in the pictCopy_Click event subroutine. This code causes the cmndCopyShape command button to click, firing its Click event.

```
Private Sub pictCopy_Click()
    'fire the cmndCopyShape click event
    cmndCopyShape = True
End Sub
```

6. Enter the following code in the Form_Unload event subroutine. This event fires when the user closes the form, ending the program.

```
Private Sub Form_Unload(Cancel As Integer)
    'Neatness counts! Clean up any defined objects.
    Set collSavePictures = Nothing
    End
End Sub
```

7. Enter the following code in the cmboChoosePicture_Click event subroutine. This event fires when the user chooses an item from the combo box.

```
Private Sub cmboChoosePicture_Click()
    Dim opicPicture As Picture
    If cmboChoosePicture.ListIndex = -1 Then
        'nothing chosen
        Exit Sub
    End If
    Set opicPicture = _
        collSavePictures.Item(cmboChoosePicture.ListIndex + 1)
    pictCopy.Picture = opicPicture
End Sub
```

8. Add the following subroutine. AddToArray updates the picture collection that holds the last ten pictures copied to this form. It is passed a picture object and stores it in a collection. If there are more than MAX_PICTURES, the first item is removed. If the cmboChoosePicture object has fewer than MAX_PICTURES items, a new item is added.

```
Private Sub AddtoArray(opicPicture As Picture)
    'Note: to use a picture object, choose
    'Tools/Reference menu item and click on the
    'Standard OLE Types reference.
    If collSavePictures.Count >= MAX_PICTURES Then
        collSavePictures.Remove 1
    End If
    'Store the passed picture object in the collection.
    collSavePictures.Add Item:=opicPicture
    If cmboChoosePicture.ListCount < MAX_PICTURES Then
        cmboChoosePicture.AddItem "Picture " & _
            Format(collSavePictures.Count)
    End If
End Sub
```

How It Works

The Shapes project displays a form with a PictureBox. There are several command buttons along the form's bottom edge. Each time the user presses one of these command buttons, a graphics image of random size appears in a random location on the PictureBox. The text on the command button determines what type of graphics appears. For example, a circle appears when the user presses the command button labeled Circle.

To change the way that the graphics get drawn, the user selects a new option in one of the Shapes form's combo boxes. These selections represent all the possible settings of the properties that affect the appearance of graphics. The user clearly sees the ways that these properties interact by changing these properties.

The graphical Shape and Line controlsLine control add some pizzazz to the user interface. The Shape1 lies behind the command buttons to visually group them. Notice how the default layering leaves the standard controls like command buttons layered on top of the graphical shape control. We could have used a frame or PictureBox control as a container for the command buttons, but the shape control uses fewer Windows resources. In Windows 95, resources are plentiful but still limited, so you should conserve where you can.

This second shape control has two Line controls carefully positioned on the top and left to help create the appearance of being inset, or carved into the form. This illusion is created by setting the shape's border color to white, and then layering the black lines on the top and left. All standard controls (like command buttons) have the "light" coming from the top-left corner, so the black lines create the inset "shadow" and the shape control's white border creates the inset "highlight." Although this is a bit more work than the 3D controls that come with the Professional Edition of Visual Basic, it does show that you can create effective user interface touches like these with just the standard controls.

The Copy Shapes form is a very simple form that takes advantage of the default values of the PaintPicture method to make a copy of the pictSurface picture on the pictCopy picture.

Startup

When the program starts, both the ScaleHeight and ScaleWidth properties of the pictSurface PictureBox get set to 100. This divides the available space on the pictSurface PictureBox into 100 equal units. The AutoRedraw property of the pictSurface PictureBox is True to ensure that layering is normal, and that any graphics are automatically redrawn if obscured (for instance, another form or window opening on top of the Shapes project window).

All the combo boxes get filled with the appropriate value names. Note that we fill the combo boxes so that the name of the value corresponds directly with its ListIndex property. This makes changing the appropriate property very simple. Finally, all the combo boxes get set to the normal default values for the properties they represent.

Running the Shapes Project

The actual code is easy to follow. The Click event for each combo box simply sets the appropriate graphic property using the combo box's ListIndex property. The Click event for each button draws the appropriate shape at a random spot on the PictureBox, using whatever settings for the graphics properties the user has set with the combo boxes. Figure 40-16 shows how the project looks when running.

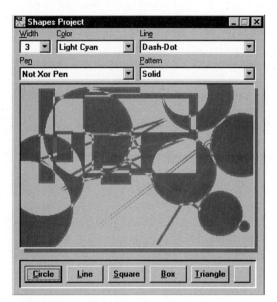

Figure 40-16 The Shapes project at runtime, showing the effects of graphics methods and properties

41

DISPLAYING TEXT

Windows offers tremendous flexibility in the ways it displays text. Some controls, such as text boxes, command buttons, and labels, display text using their Text or Caption properties. Although convenient, these properties don't offer the fine control you can achieve by using Visual Basic's Print method.

The Print method places text directly on a form, picture box, or Printer object. The font properties of these objects define the font, size, and appearance of text strings. Drawing text on an object in this way produces graphics rather than text, and lets you precisely specify placement. After a text string prints on an object, it becomes part of the background of the object and may be saved to a graphics file. Text strings drawn on a form, picture box, or Printer object are not editable. Once a text string is on an object, this text behaves in the same ways as other graphics on the object.

This flexibility lets programs mix a variety of text styles on an object. For example, the word processor used to write this book displays different typefaces in different styles and a variety of sizes all at the same time. This ability to display text in the same way it will print is commonly called WYSIWYG (pronounced wizzywig), or What You See Is What You Get. Figure 41-1 shows an example of mixing a variety of text styles on the screen. The properties and methods discussed in this chapter are the means of doing this.

Drawing Text in Visual Basic

Text in Windows can print and display in a variety of fonts and point sizes. You cannot assume that all text will have the same size characters, 80 characters to a line, in the time-honored format of teletypes and text-based DOS programs. Your program must be able to dynamically scale and position text according to the font, size, and object being used.

Chapter 45, "Fonts," discusses several properties that affect the appearance of text strings. The Font object that is associated with a form or picture control sets the font style to format text strings. The Size property of the Font object sets the size of a text string. The Bold, StrikeThrough, and Underline properties of the Font object change the actual appearance of the text to bold, strikethrough, or underline. You can use the FontTransparent property of the form or picture control to make the text string either overwrite or show the graphics placed under it.

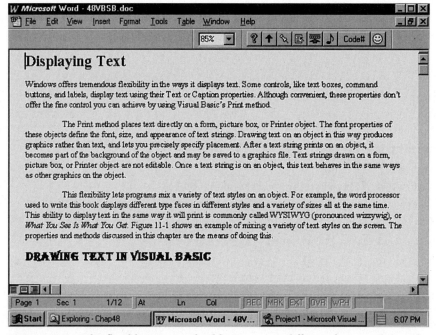

Figure 41-1   The flexible Print method lets you mix different fonts, styles, and sizes to produce WYSIWYG output

Beginning with Visual Basic 4.0, the Font object provides some additional functionality to the Font properties found in previous versions of Visual Basic. Probably the most useful new feature is the ability to use the Font object of one form or picture control to directly update the Font object of another form or picture control. All the available fonts for the screen or any printer defined in Windows are gathered into the Fonts collection for that object. Although the Font properties of forms or picture controls have been left in the language for compatibility with previous versions, the preferred method for controlling fonts is the Font object. For more information on the Font object and the Fonts collection, see Chapter 16, "Objects and Collections." See Chapter 45 for a discussion of fonts and how they are used.

This chapter discusses the methods, properties, and functions that let you precisely position the text on an object after you've determined the font size and style. The TextHeight method returns the amount of vertical space needed to display a specified text string in the current font and size, and the TextWidth method determines the amount of horizontal space necessary to show the text string. Each text string is actually placed on a form, picture box, or Printer object with the Print method. The Spc and Tab functions let you insert a precise number of spaces or print at a specific column.

Displaying Text Summary

Table 41-1 summarizes the methods and functions used for displaying text.

Table 41-1 Methods dealing with drawing text

Use or Set This...	Type	To Do This...
Print	Method	Place a text string or numeric value on the object
Spc	Function	Insert a given number of spaces
Tab	Function	Move to a specified column position
TextHeight	Method	Determine the amount of vertical space needed for a string
TextWidth	Method	Determine the amount of horizontal space needed for a string

The following pages investigate the methods in Table 41-1 in detail. The Text project at the end of the chapter includes step-by-step directions to assemble a demonstration of drawing text.

PRINT METHOD

Objects Affected   Debug, Form, PictureBox, Printer

Purpose   The Print method places text on the debug window, a form, picture box, or Printer object. Each text string prints at the position on the object indicated by the CurrentX and CurrentY properties (current screen or printer coordinates). Since there is no text wrap feature, any strings that are larger than the space allowed will be cut short on the right. A text string displays on the screen in the font and point size set in the FontName and FontSize property. (In Visual Basic 5.0, you can use the Font object to set the font and font size.) The form, picture box, or Printer object's ForeColor property determines the text's color. Once a text string prints on an object with the Print method, the content and format of the text cannot be changed.

The Debug object uses the Print method to help trace the execution of your programs for debugging purposes. Table 41-2 summarizes the arguments of the Print method.

General Syntax

```
[form.]Print [{Spc(n) | Tab(m)}][expressionlist][{;|,}]
[form!]Name.Print [{Spc(n) | Tab(m)}][expressionlist][{;|,}]
Printer.Print [{Spc(n) | Tab(m)}][expressionlist][{;|,}]
Debug.Print [{Spc(n) | Tab(m)}][expressionlist][{;|,}]
```

Table 41-2 Arguments of the Print method

Argument	Description
form	Name property of the form
Name	Name property of the picture box
Printer	'Printer' indicates the Printer object
Debug	'Debug' indicates the Debug object
Spc(n)	Insert n number of spaces; multiple use permitted
Tab(m)	Print at column m; multiple use permitted
expressionlist	A number or text string for the Print method to print on the object; multiple use permitted
;	Places the text cursor immediately after the last character; multiple use permitted
,	Places the text cursor in the next print zone; multiple use permitted

Example Syntax

```
Private Sub Timer1_Timer ()
    'makes sure graphics refresh immediately
    AutoRedraw = True
    'color will remember the last used color
    Static PrintColor As Integer
    Display$ = "Warning"               'stores text string
    Font.Name = "Arial"                'indicates Arial font
    Font.Size = 30                     'indicates 30pt. font
    'defines X as half of Text width
    X = TextWidth(Display$) / 2
    'defines Y as half of Text height
    Y = TextHeight(Display$) / 2
    CurrentX = (ScaleWidth / 2) - X    'Sets current position so that
    CurrentY = (ScaleHeight / 2) - Y   'the text appears in the center.
    'Alternates the color between black 'and red with the
    'triggering of the timer event.
    If PrintColor = 0 Then
        PrintColor = 4
    Else
        PrintColor = 0
    End If
    ForeColor = QBColor(PrintColor)
    Print Display$                     'prints warning on the form
End Sub
```

Description

The Print method puts a string of text or a numeric value at an object's current position. Each Print method identifies the object to place the string on by preceding it with the Name property of the form or picture box, or Printer or Debug for the Printer or Debug objects. If a Print method does not include an object, then the text prints on the current form. A Print method may contain multiple expressions separated by Spc(n), Tab(m), commas, and semicolons.

In the example syntax, the Print method places the text string "Warning" in the center of the form in the color, point size, and font indicated by the property settings of the form. Notice that the CurrentX and CurrentY properties control the actual position where the Print method puts the text string as modified by the values calculated by the TextHeight and TextWidth methods. Figure 41-2 illustrates what this example might look like.

Positioning Text with the Commas, Semicolons, Spc(n), and Tab(m)

Print method expressions may have commas and semicolons placed between the expressions to print, or at the end of the entire expression. If a Print method ends without a comma or semicolon, the current position is set to the beginning of the next line. Commas change the current screen or printer coordinates to the next print zone away from the displayed text on the same line. A print zone is 14 average character widths in the current font and point size. Semicolons change the current screen or printer coordinates to the next character position on the same line directly after the text. The current screen or printer position determines where the next text appears on a form, picture box, or Printer or Debug objects. Figure 41-3 shows how the following code example demonstrates the difference between the comma and semicolon:

```
Private Sub Form_Click ()
    'note the comma at the end of the line
    Print "This text ", "has commas ",
    'nothing at end of line; go to next line
    Print "embedded in it"
    'print blank line
    Print
    'note semicolon at the end of the line
    Print "This text "; "has semicolons ";
    'nothing at end of line; go to next line
    Print "embedded in it"
    Print "Done!"
End Sub
```

Figure 41-2   Example syntax shows how to position text precisely

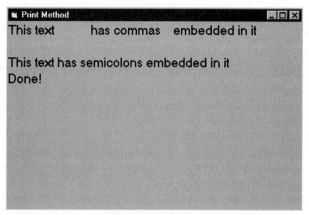

Figure 41-3 The difference between semicolons and commas

The Spc(n) and Tab(m) functions let you insert a certain number of spaces in printed expressions, or let you specify which column to print at. Each font's space size is determined by taking the average width of all characters in that font; each font and size of font will have differently sized spaces. The Spc(n) function places n spaces in the printed output. Tab(m) puts the current print position at column m, where a column is defined as one space. Thus, Spc(n) is relative to the last print position and Tab(m) is relative to the leftmost position on the current line. The following example, illustrated in Figure 41-4, shows the use of the Spc(n) and Tab(m) functions:

```
Private Sub Form_Click ()
    Dim j As Integer
    For j = 1 To 10
        Print Spc(j); "this is"; Tab(30 - j); "some text"
    Next j
End Sub
```

Positioning Text with the TextWidth and TextHeight Methods

The TextWidth and TextHeight methods calculate the amount of horizontal and vertical space necessary to display the specified text string in the currently set font and point size. Values returned by these methods use the unit of measure indicated by the ScaleMode property of the form, picture box, or Printer object. These values serve as a reference for positioning the text on the form, picture box, or Printer object. In the example syntax, the TextWidth and TextHeight methods change the current position to print the text in the center of the form.

Positioning Text with the CurrentX, CurrentY, ScaleWidth, and ScaleHeight Properties

The CurrentX and CurrentY properties work well with the ScaleWidth and ScaleHeight properties to determine where a text string prints on a form, picture box, or Printer object. The ScaleWidth and ScaleHeight properties define the units of measurement for the usable horizontal and vertical surface of an object (Height and Width less the borders and title and menu bars). Defining the CurrentX and CurrentY properties as fractions of the

ScaleWidth and ScaleHeight properties lets you precisely position the text no matter where the last Print method ended. In the example syntax at the beginning of this item entry, these properties find the center of the form by dividing the ScaleWidth and ScaleHeight properties in half and defining the CurrentX and CurrentY properties with the returned values.

Print Method with the Debug Object   The Print method may also be used with the Debug object. In fact, Print is the only method that can be used with Debug. You can use this method to print the contents of variables or messages on the Immediate pane of the Debug window during the debugging process. Although you have no control over font name, font size, and font color, the semicolon and comma, as well as the Spc(n) and Tab(m) functions, work just as described above. You can also directly type Print methods on the Immediate pane when your program is in Break mode.

Example   The Text project at the end of this chapter uses the Print method in all three of its examples. The first example demonstrates TextWidth and TextHeight, the second example demonstrates the Spc and Tab functions, and the third example demonstrates how to place text inside of a box or above a line.

Comments   Visual Basic treats text produced with the Print method as graphics. Displayed text is then subject to the normal effects of graphics operations. If you have AutoRedraw set to False, the Print method prints on top of graphical controls such as the Image and Shape controls.

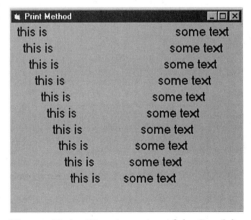

Figure 41-4   Demonstration of the Spc (n) and Tab (m) functions

SPC FUNCTION

Purpose   The Spc function skips a specified number of spaces in the Print method. Table 41-3 shows the single argument of the Spc function.

> **TIP**
>
> When you are using the Print method with the Printer object, you may have to "wake up the printer" in order to change the font or font attributes. This varies from printer to printer. The following code shows frequent uses of Printer.Print, which ensures that the font changes are registered. Note that this needs to be done once per page. Subsequent font changes and font attribute changes on the same page are registered correctly.
>
> ```
>     ' Start the wakeup
> Printer.Print
> Printer.ScaleMode = 5 ' Inches
> Printer.Print
> Printer.FontName = "Arial"
> Printer.Print
> Printer.FontSize = 14
> Printer.Print
> Printer.FontBold = True
> Printer.Print
> ' Move back to the top
> Printer.CurrentY = 0
> ```

General Syntax

```
Spc(number%)
```

Table 41-3 Argument of the Spc function

Argument	Meaning
number%	Number of spaces to skip; a "space" is the average width of all characters in the current font.

Example Syntax

```
Private Sub Command1_Click ()
    Print Spc(10); "Ten spaces in, and now "; Spc(Int(Rnd * 20)); "random!"
End Sub
```

Description

Embed the Spc function in a Print method (or Print # statement) to skip the specified number of spaces, anywhere from 0 to 32767. A *space* is defined as the average width of all characters in the current font, size, and style. Note that the space size will vary depending on your choice of font and appearance. The semicolon is optional. Omitting it results in Visual Basic's inserting the semicolon for you.

The Spc function always inserts spaces from the last print position. This makes it relative to the last printed character. The Tab function, in contrast, is an absolute position from the leftmost character of the current line. See the Print method entry for an example comparing Spc and Tab.

Example

The second example in the Text project at the end of the chapter demonstrates the use of the Spc function. The project inserts a progressively larger number of spaces in a line of text, moving the printed text over each time. It also iterates different sizes of fonts, thus demonstrating that different font sizes have differently sized spaces.

Tab Function

Purpose

Use the Tab function to move to a particular character position on the current line. Table 41-4 summarizes the argument of the Tab function.

General Syntax

```
Tab[(column%)]
```

Table 41-4 Argument of the Tab function

Argument	Meaning
column%	Number of the next print column to use. If omitted, the next print will start at the beginning of the next print zone.

Example Syntax

```
Private Sub Command1_Click ()
    For j = 1 To 20
        Print Tab(j); "Test"; Tab(60 - 2 * j); "case"
    Next j
End Sub
```

Description

Embed the Tab function in a Print method (or Print # statement) to print at the specified column position, anywhere from 0 to 32767. A *column position* is defined as the size of a space, which in turn is defined as the average width of all characters in the current font, size, and style. Note that the space size (and thus the column width) will vary depending on your choice of font and appearance. The leftmost column position is position 1. The semicolon is optional. Omitting it results in Visual Basic's inserting the semicolon for you. If the column position is beyond the width of the object, Visual Basic *wraps* to the next line.

The Tab function is an absolute position from the leftmost character of the current line. The Spc function, in contrast, inserts spaces from the last print position, making it relative to the last printed character. See the Print method entry for an example comparing Spc and Tab.

Example

The second example in the Text project at the end of the chapter illustrates the Tab function. It prints out text both left- and right-justified. The left justification uses just the Tab function; the right justification uses Tab to set the initial position, which is then modified with the returned value of the TextWidth method.

Comments

If you need to align currency or other numeric values at the decimal point, switch to a fixed-width font such as Courier New before printing the numbers. The third example in the Text project at the end of this chapter illustrates decimal alignment.

TextHeight and TextWidth Methods

Objects Affected   Form, PictureBox, Printer, PropertyPage, UserControl, UserDocument

Purpose   The TextHeight and TextWidth methods help you position text on a form, picture box, or Printer object by telling you what the height and width of the text string would be if displayed using the current font and point size. A value returned by the TextHeight and TextWidth methods represents the size of the text string using the unit of measure specified in the ScaleMode property. Both of these methods are available at runtime only. Table 41-5 lists the arguments for these properties

General Syntax

```
[form.]TextHeight(expression$)
[form!]Name.TextHeight(expression$)
Printer.TextHeight(expression$)

[form.]TextWidth(expression$)
[form!]Name.TextWidth(expression$)
Printer.TextWidth(expression$)
```

Table 41-5 Arguments of the TextHeight and TextWidth methods

Argument	Description
form	Name property of the form
Name	Name property of the picture box
Printer	'Printer' indicates the Printer object
expression$	Text string to determine the width or height necessary to display

Example Syntax

```
Private Sub Form_Resize()
    Cls
    'make sure graphics update immediately
    AutoRedraw = True
    'defines the font
    Font.Name = "Arial"
    'defines the point size
    Font.Size = 8.25
    'defines text variable
    display$ = "A string for demonstration"
    Do While TextWidth(display$) < ScaleWidth - TextWidth(" ")
        Font.Size = Font.Size + 0.5
    Loop
    'Defines X and Y as the space needed to display
    X = TextWidth(display$)
    Y = TextHeight(display$)          'the Display$ text string.
    'is displayed horizontally and vertically.
    EndY = Abs(ScaleHeight / Y) + 1
    For H = 1 To EndY                 'fill the form with the text string
        Print display$;
```

```
        CurrentY = CurrentY + Y      'go to next print line
        CurrentX = 0
    Next H
End Sub
```

Description   The TextHeight and TextWidth methods determine the amount of space needed to display the expression$ on an object. An object consists of the Name property of the picture box or form, or Printer for the Printer object. Each expression$ must be a string variable and may not be a numeric value, or else an error occurs. Note that the Print method can print numeric expressions; convert these to strings with the Str$ function before using them with TextHeight and TextWidth.

In the example syntax, the TextWidth method is used to adjust the size of the font so that the text string, "A string for demonstration," fills the screen horizontally. The TextHeight method is used to calculate the amount of vertical space needed to display the string such that it is repeated enough times to fill the screen. Figure 41-5 shows what this example might look like on the screen.

Positioning with the CurrentX and CurrentY Properties   Both the CurrentX and CurrentY properties serve as means of controlling where a text string appears on a form, picture box, or Printer object. Since the ScaleHeight and ScaleWidth properties return the current height and width of the object, fractions of these properties help you position text on an object. For example, to place the letter T in the center of a form, change the values of the CurrentX property to half the ScaleWidth and the CurrentY property to half the ScaleHeight property. Then modify the resulting values by subtracting half of the values returned by the TextHeight and TextWidth methods. This places the letter T in the center

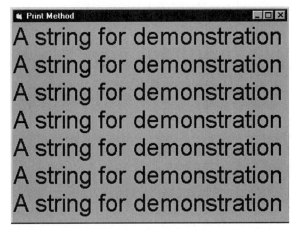

Figure 41-5   The example syntax fills the form with the text string, whatever the size of the form

of the form. In the example syntax, the ScaleHeight and ScaleWidth properties work in conjunction with the TextWidth and TextHeight methods to determine how many times the text appears if printed from top to bottom and left to right. CurrentX and CurrentY are discussed more thoroughly in Chapter 37, "The Coordinate System."

Example   The first two examples in the Text project at the end of the chapter use TextWidth, and the first example uses both TextWidth and TextHeight. The third example uses TextHeight to position the text relative to a box and line drawn on the form. They are used to modify the CurrentX and CurrentY positions to properly center or right-align text, or to place text above or below a line.

The Text Project

Project Overview

The Text project shows how text prints on a form, picture box, or Printer object. These methods calculate the amount of space needed to place the indicated text on the form. This information lets you control exactly where the text appears on the form, and gives the basis for you to do things like creating center- and right-aligned tab stops as well as the traditional left-aligned ones. It also shows you how to place text in a box or above a line, which is often useful for printed output in business applications. Finally, it demonstrates using a fixed-width font to align dollar amounts on the decimal point.

The following pages discuss the assembly and operation of the Text project. The first section deals with the assembly of the Text form. Next, there is a listing and explanation of the contents of the subroutines of this project. Finally, a "How It Works" guide to the operation of the project discusses the operation of the code. Please read this information carefully and use the pictures of the form to check your results.

Assembling the Project

1. Make a new form with the objects and properties listed in Table 41-6.

Table 41-6 Elements of the Text form

Object	Property	Setting
Form	BorderStyle	2–Sizable
	Caption	Text Project

2. Size the form to approximately the size and shape of the form shown in Figure 41-6. The form should appear with the default text shown in Figure 41-6.

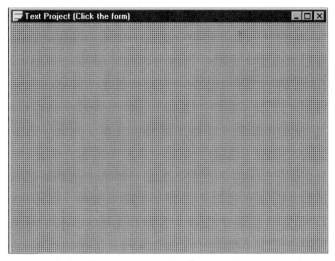

Figure 41-6 The Text project at design time

3. Enter the following code in the Form_Click event subroutine. When the user clicks the form, the next example runs. This routine just alternates among the three examples.

```
Private Sub Form_Click()
    Static example As Integer        'track which example to show
    If example = 0 Then example = 1   'start at the first example
    If example = 1 Then
        Example1                      'demonstrate TextHeight and
                                      'TextWidth
        example = 2                   'next time will be example2
    ElseIf example = 2 Then
        Example2                      'demonstrate Spc() and Tab()
        example = 3                   'next time will be example3
    Else
        Example3                      'demonstrate text in a box
                                      'above a line, and decimal align
        example = 1                   'next time will be example1
    End If
End SubEnd Sub
```

4. Enter the following code in the General section of the code window. This subroutine places text in the upper-left, center, and bottom-right of the form. Note the use of TextHeight and TextWidth to justify the text properly.

```
Private Sub Example1()
    Const MSG1 = "Top Left"          'define the text to display
    Const MSG2 = "Center Center"
    Const MSG3 = "Bottom Right"
    Cls                              'clear the form
    AutoRedraw = True                'graphics automatically repaint
    Me.Font.Name = "Arial"           'select the font
    Me.Font.Size = 20                'select the font size
```

continued on next page

continued from previous page

```
    Print MSG1                      'This goes in upper left corner
    CurrentX = (ScaleWidth / 2) - (TextWidth(MSG2) / 2)    'position
                                                           'this exactly
    CurrentY = (ScaleHeight / 2) - (TextHeight(MSG2) / 2) 'in the center
    Print MSG2
    CurrentX = ScaleWidth - TextWidth(MSG3)      'position this flush
                                                 'right and
    CurrentY = ScaleHeight - TextHeight(MSG3)    'flush bottom
    Print MSG3
End Sub
```

5. Place this code in the general section in the code window. This example shows the use of the Spc and Tab functions. Note how we use TextWidth to help create a right-justified tab stop. The num$ variable lets us build a variable-length string to help demonstrate the left and right tab stops.

```
Private Sub Example2 ()
    Cls                             'Clear the form
    AutoRedraw = True               'graphics automatically⇐ repaint
    Me.Font.Name = "Times New Roman"  'Select font
    For Size = 8 To 20 Step 4       'step through font sizes
      'will contain a variable length string
        num$ = ""
        Me.Font.Size = Size         'Set the font size
        For j = 1 To 5              'five examples at each font⇐ size
            'demonstrate spc()
            Print Spc(j); "Space1"; Spc(j * 2); "Space2";
            'build up the variable length string
            num$ = num$ & "*"
            'print at the tab stop
            Print Tab(35); "Left Tab" & num$;
            y = CurrenlY              'remember what line we're on
            'set the print position to column 65
            Print Tab(65); "";
            CurrentX = CurrentX - TextWidth("Right Tab" & num$)
                                     'right justify at column 65
            CurrentY = y             'reset us back to the correct⇐ line
            Print "Right Tab" & num$ 'and print the text
        Next j
    Next Size
End Sub
```

6. Place this code in the general section in the code window. This example shows how to place text in a box or above or below a line. It also shows how to align numeric values on the decimal point.

```
Private Sub Example3()
    'Demonstrates printing in a box
    'And on a line
    ScaleMode = 5 ' inches
    Dim nOldy As Single
    Dim sCash As String * 8
    Const nAmt1 = 98.98
    Const nAmt2 = 998.98
    ' Clear the screen
    Cls
```

```
AutoRedraw = True    'graphics automatically repaint
Font.Name = "Arial"
Font.Bold = False
Font.Size = 12
Print "In a box -- on a line"
' Draw a box
CurrentX = 1
CurrentY = 1
nOldy = CurrentY     ' Remember where you are
Line -(CurrentX + 1.5, CurrentY + 0.3), , B
CurrentY = nOldy
Font.Name = "Arial"
Font.Size = 6
CurrentX = 1 + 1 / 16
Print "Company Name"
CurrentX = 1 + 1 / 16
Font.Size = 10
Font.Bold = True
Print "Waite Group Press"
' Draw a line
CurrentX = 1
CurrentY = 1.5
nOldy = CurrentY ' Remember where you are
Line -(CurrentX + 2, CurrentY)
CurrentX = 1 + 1 / 16
' Position below the line
Font.Size = 6
Font.Bold = False
Print "Title"
CurrentX = 1 + 1 / 16
' Position above the line
Font.Size = 10
Font.Bold = True
CurrentY = nOldy - TextHeight("I")
Print "Visual Basic 5 Super Bible"
Print
Print
Font.Size = 12
Font.Bold = False
Print "Decimal Alignment"
Print
Font.Size = 10
Print "Amount 1";
Font.Name = "Courier New"
RSet sCash = Format(nAmt1, "#####.##")
CurrentX = 2
Print "$"; sCash
Font.Name = "Arial"
Print "Amount 2";
RSet sCash = Format(nAmt2, "#####.##")
Font.Name = "Courier New"
CurrentX = 2
Print "$"; sCash
Font.Name = "Arial"
Print "Total";
Font.Name = "Courier New"
CurrentX = 2
Line -(CurrentX + 1, CurrentY)
```

continued on next page

continued from previous page

```
    RSet sCash = Format(Str(nAmt1 + nAmt2), "#####.##")
    CurrentX = 2
    Print "$"; sCash
End Sub
```

How It Works

This simple project demonstrates how to use TextHeight and TextWidth to precisely position text. Text always prints with its upper-left corner at CurrentX and CurrentY. For most common operations, this default position works well.

Many applications need more precise positioning. The text box control allows for left, center, and right alignment, yet there is no equivalent in the Print method—it is always left-aligned. Although this might seem to make the text box more convenient than the Print method, it doesn't allow for mixing of fonts, sizes, or alignments. TextHeight and TextWidth provide the key for this more precise positioning using the flexible Print method.

Example1 illustrates three common vertical and horizontal positions: left, center, and right; top, middle, and bottom. You could expand the code to allow for multiple fonts, sizes, and alignments to create a full-featured word processor.

Example1 defines the three text strings, calculates the proper position, and prints them. The Top Left setting doesn't need any special calculations, because CurrentX and CurrentY automatically default to 0,0. The Center setting simply takes half the ScaleHeight and ScaleWidth of the form, and subtracts half of the TextHeight and TextWidth of the message. This exactly centers the printed text. Likewise, the Bottom Right setting simply subtracts the TextWidth and TextHeight of the message from the ScaleWidth and ScaleHeight of the form to properly position its text. Figure 41-7 illustrates what this example looks like when running.

Notice that Top Left still leaves a little room at the top. This is because TextHeight measures the height of the text including the "leading," or the white space between lines of text. This leading makes TextHeight approximately 120% of the actual height of the text.

Example2 demonstrates the use of the Spc and Tab functions. This subprocedure cycles through its sample code in several different point sizes. As Figure 41-8 shows, different point sizes have different sizes of the space used in the Spc and Tab functions. The only tricky part of this example lies in creating the right tab stop. We use the same idea as in Example1 to right-justify the text by subtracting its TextWidth from the CurrentX position. Note that we have to reset CurrentY back to the original line; if we don't, "Right Tab" will print on the next line. Figure 41-8 illustrates this example. Note that you may have to expand the form to see all the text. Note also that when text is printed at an absolute Tab position, some of the text may be cut off by the edge of the form, picture box, or Printer object.

Example3 demonstrates how to place text in a box, how to place it above or below a line, and how to decimal-align numeric values. Note that when Visual Basic draws a

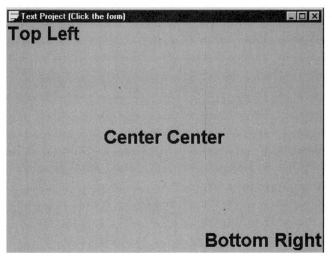

Figure 41-7 Example1 of the Text project, showing several text alignments using TextWidth and TextHeight

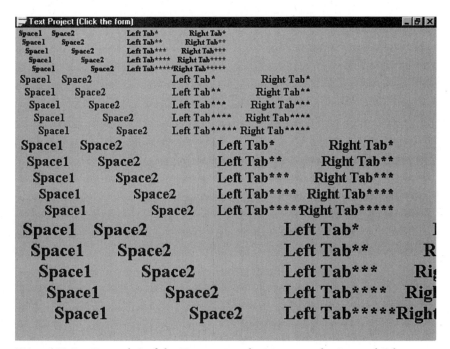

Figure 41-8 Example2 of the Text project demonstrates the Spc and Tab functions

line, the CurrentY position is set just below the line. It is not immediately obvious, but the CurrentY property for text is the *top* of the text, not the bottom. Also note the font switching needed for decimal alignment. Try remarking out the Font.Name = "Courier New" lines to see the effect of proportional fonts on the decimal alignment example. Figure 41-9 illustrates this example.

You can modify this example to use the Print method with the Printer object. Change the Print statements to Printer.Print, add the same Printer. reference to CurrentX and CurrentY statements, and add the Line method in Example3 so that references to CurrentX, for instance, are changed to Printer.CurrentX.

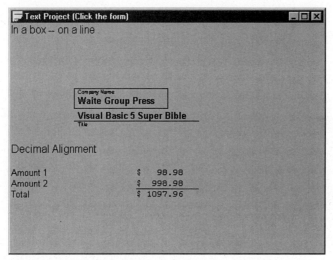

Figure 41-9 Example3 of the Text project shows how to place text in boxes, above and below lines, and how to decimal-align numeric data

PART VI
INTERACTIVE AND TEXT CONTROLS

42

BUTTONS

Check boxes, option buttons, and command buttons are among the simplest and most commonly used controls in the Windows graphical interface. These controls enable users to interact with and provide information to the Windows application. Without a doubt, you'll want to add many instances of these controls to your application.

There are three types of controls that are considered to be "buttons:" check boxes, option buttons, and command buttons. A form with each of these types is shown in Figure 42-1. Each one of these button types has its own look and behavior and is used in an application to serve particular needs.

Operating Check Boxes

The check box (CheckBox) is used to allow the user to select between one of two choices. As shown in Figure 42-1, the check box consists of a box (that can be either checked, unchecked, or grayed) and a text label indicating what the box represents. By clicking on the box, the user can toggle the box between a checked and an unchecked state. Some applications support a third state, grayed, which is often used to indicate some state that is either unknown or neither checked nor unchecked. Because there are three possible states that a check box can be in, you can set it to be unchecked, checked, or grayed.

Operating Option Buttons

Like the check box, the option button (OptionButton) also allows the user to select between one of two choices. However, unlike the check box, the option button consists of a circle (which can be either filled or unfilled) and a text label indicating what the circle represents. By clicking on the circle, the user can toggle the option button between a filled and an unfilled state, depending on whether that option is wanted or not.

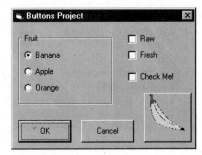

Figure 42-1 A form with buttons of all types

Although technically you can almost use option buttons and check boxes interchangeably within your application, the Microsoft Windows user interface guidelines recommend that you use a set of option buttons to give the user a choice of one of several options. In many applications, you will see a set of option buttons grouped together in a frame with only one selected, as shown in Figure 42-1. Because only one of these options can be selected at a time, when the user selects an unselected option in the frame, the one that is currently selected becomes unselected and the new one becomes the selected option.

As a result, a set of option buttons become a means of allowing the user to select one option from a set of mutually exclusive options. You might be interested to know that if you do any Windows development in C or C++, option buttons are called "radio buttons." So, like the buttons on your car radio, which enable you to select one of several radio stations, option buttons give you the choice of one of a set of possible options.

Sets of option buttons are often used as control arrays in Visual Basic. So, rather than writing code that handles the selection of each option button, you can write one handler that handles the entire set of option buttons. You can create a control array of option buttons by giving each option the same name (through the Name property) and a unique numerical index value. When in a control array, you can write a single handler for the Click event and reference each option button uniquely using this index value.

Operating Command Buttons

When you think of a button on the Windows user interface, you probably have a mental picture of OK and Cancel buttons. These buttons are called command buttons (CommandButton) in Visual Basic. Applications use command buttons to enable the user to tell the application when to do something, such as OK to accept the current input or Cancel to ignore the current input. The user interacts with a command button by simply moving the mouse over to it and selecting it (which visually and temporarily pushes it in).

Often in a Visual Basic form, one of the command buttons is set up to handle the case in which the user presses the (ENTER) key. This command button is called the "default" command button and is drawn with a dark border. In Figure 42-1, the OK button is the default command button. As you design your application's forms, keep in mind which command button it makes the most sense to have as the default command button to make it easiest for the user.

Like the default command button, you can define another of the command buttons on a form to be the "cancel" button. This command button's Click method is invoked when the user presses the (ESC) key, which gives the user an easy way of canceling that form.

Buttons Summary

Table 42-1 displays the properties and events that control the operation of check boxes, option buttons, and command buttons.

Table 42-1 Properties and events that affect the operation of buttons

Use or Set This...	Type	To Do This...
Cancel	Property	Set or return whether or not a command button is the "cancel" button (CommandButton)
Click	Event	Invoked when the user selects a button
DblClick	Event	Invoked when the user double-clicks a button (OptionButton)
Default	Property	Set or return whether or not a command button is the default button (CommandButton)
DisabledPicture	Property	Set or return the graphic to be displayed when the button is disabled
DownPicture	Property	Set or return the graphic to be displayed when the button is selected
Picture	Property	Set or return the graphic to be displayed when the button is not selected
Style	Property	Set or return whether a button is text based or graphical
Value	Property	Set or return the value represented by the button

Constant Values

It is usually best to use named constants rather than numeric values when developing software. Named constants make your code more readable and easier to maintain.

Table 42-2 lists the values of the constants relevant to this chapter, mentions their names, and briefly describes what they mean. These constants can be viewed using the Object Browser. It is not necessary to explicitly add these objects to your project.

Table 42-2 Constants module values for check boxes

Value	VB.Constants	Meaning
0	vbUnchecked	(Default) The check box is not checked.
1	vbChecked	The check box is checked.
2	vbGrayed	The check box is in a grayed state.

These properties and events are explored in the next section. The Buttons project at this end of the chapter puts buttons to use in a sample application.

CANCEL PROPERTY

Objects Affected   CommandButton

Purpose   The Cancel property sets or returns whether or not the command button is clicked when the user presses the (ESC) key. This property can be set at design time, and set or read at runtime. Table 42-3 summarizes the arguments of the Cancel property.

General Syntax

```
[form!]Name.Cancel [ = boolean%]
```

Table 42-3 Arguments of the Cancel property

Argument	Description
form	Name of the parent form
Name	Name of the command button control
boolean%	True means this is the form's cancel button

Example Syntax

```
Private Sub Form_Load ()
    If Button1.Cancel = True Then
        Text1.Text = "Button1 is the cancel button"
    End If
End Sub
```

Description   The Cancel property sets or returns whether or not the specified command button is the one clicked when the user presses the (ESC) key to cancel the current form. You will most often set this property to True for the Cancel command button on your form.

The example syntax shows the checking of the Cancel property value for Button1. When Button1 is the cancel button, text is placed into Text1 stating this fact.

Example   In the Buttons project at the end of this chapter, the Cancel property is set to True at design time. This causes the control cmndCancel to be clicked when the user presses the (ESC) key.

Comments   Only one command button on a form can have the Cancel property set to True.

CLICK EVENT

Objects Affected   CheckBox, ComboBox, CommandButton, DBCombo, DBGrid, DBList,
DirListBox, FileListBox, Form, Frame, Grid, Image, Label, ListBox,
ListView, MDIForm, Menu, OLE Container, OptionButton, PictureBox,
ProgressBar, PropertyPage, Slider, StatusBar, TabStrip, TextBox, Toolbar,
TreeView, UserControl, UserDocument

Purpose   Use the Click event to react to the user's clicking a check box, command
button, or option button. Table 42-4 summarizes the arguments of the
Click event.

General Syntax

```
Sub Name_Click([Index As Integer])
```

Table 42-4 Arguments of the Click event

Argument	Description
Name	Name property of the control
Index	Uniquely identifies an element of a control array

Example Syntax
```
Private Sub Button1_Click()
    Text1.Text = "Button1 has been clicked."
End Sub
Private Sub Button2_Click(Index as Integer)
    Dim Message As String
    Message = "This is index number"
    Message = Message + Format$(Index, "###")
    Message = Message + " of the Button2 control array."
    Button2(Index).Caption = Message
End Sub
```

Description   The Click event is defined in a sub procedure that is named using the control name. An index variable is included if the sub procedure is written to
handle a control array.

This event initiates when the user selects a check box, command button,
or option button. The example sets the text contained in the Text1 control
to a message indicating that Button1 has been clicked.

Control Array   The Index argument is only used if the related control is part of a control
array. This Index specifies which element of the array is the one that activated the event. When referencing the control, the element being
referenced must be specified by placing the index number between parentheses just after the control name, and before the property name (for
example, Name(Index).Property).

Example In the Buttons project at the end of this chapter, the Click event for a control array is processed, causing the image within a graphical button to change to the image corresponding to the selected option.

DblClick Event

Objects Affected ComboBox, DBCombo, DBGrid, DBList, FileListBox, Form, Frame, Grid, Image, Label, ListBox, ListView, MDIForm, OLE Container, OptionButton, PictureBox, PropertyPage, StatusBar, TextBox, Toolbar, TreeView, UserControl, UserDocument

Purpose Use the DblClick event to react to the user's pressing the left or right mouse button twice in quick succession (known as a *double-click*) over an option button. Depending on the design of the application, a double-click on an option button could be an alternative to clicking on an OK button or pressing ENTER to execute the default action. Table 42-5 summarizes the arguments of the DblClick event.

General Syntax

```
Sub Name_DblClick([Index As Integer])
```

Table 42-5 Arguments of the DblClick event

Argument	Description
Name	Name property of the control
Index	Uniquely identifies an element of a control array

Example Syntax

```
Private Sub Button1_DblClick()
    Text1.Text = "Button1 has been double-clicked."
End Sub
Private Sub Button2_DblClick(Index as Integer) 'automatically clicks an OK button
    cmndOK_Click Index                          'when the list item is double-clicked on
End Sub
```

Description The DblClick event is defined in a sub procedure that is named using the control name, followed by an underscore and DblClick(). If the referenced control is part of a control array, the term DblClick is followed by an index variable within parentheses, as in the second syntax example. An index variable is included if the sub procedure is written to handle a control array.

The DblClick event occurs when the user presses and releases the left or right mouse button twice in quick succession. The period of time in which two clicks must occur to be considered a double-click is defined in the mouse settings area of the Windows Control Panel. If the mouse is clicked twice, but not in the time defined by the Control Panel, two separate Click events occur.

The first syntax example sets the text in the Text1 control when the user double-clicks on Button1. The second example syntax calls the Click event for the OK button whenever any list box in the control array is double-clicked. This makes double-clicking an alternative way for the user to provide the confirmation represented by the OK button.

Event Order If you have both Click and DblClick event procedures for a single control, the Click procedure always activates before the DblClick procedure unless you create some special trapping code. Windows automatically sends out the Click message immediately after a click to keep performance high—after all, most programs respond to many more clicks than double-clicks. If it waited to see if the user double-clicked before sending out the first Click message, overall performance would suffer.

Control Array The Index argument is only used if the related control is part of a control array. This Index specifies which element of the array is the one that activated the event. When referencing the control, the element being referenced must be specified by placing the index number between parentheses just after the control name and before the property name (for example, Name(Index).Property).

Example In the Buttons project at the end of this chapter, the DblClick event for a control array is processed, causing the OK command button click event to be triggered.

Default Property

Objects Affected CommandButton

Purpose The Default property sets or returns whether or not the command button is clicked when the user presses the (ENTER) key. This property can be set at design time, and set or read at runtime. Table 42-6 summarizes the arguments of the Default property.

General Syntax

```
[form!]Name.Default [ = boolean%]
```

Table 42-6 Arguments of the Default property

Argument	Description
form	Name of the parent form
Name	Name of the command button control
boolean%	True means this button is the default command button

Example Syntax
```
Private Sub Form_Load ()
    If Button1.Default = True Then
        Text1.Text = "Button1 is the Default button"
    End If
End Sub
```

Description	The Default property sets or returns whether or not the specified command button is the one clicked when the user presses the (ENTER) key to accept the current form. You will most often set this property to True for the OK command button on your form.
	The example syntax shows the checking of the Default property value for Button1. When Button1 is the default button, text is placed into Text1 stating this fact.
Example	In the Buttons project at the end of this chapter, the Default property is set to True at design time. This causes the control cmndOK to be clicked when the user presses the (ENTER) key.
Comments	Only one command button on a form can have the Default property set to True.

DISABLEDPICTURE PROPERTY

Objects Affected	CheckBox, CommandButton, OptionButton
Purpose	The DisabledPicture property sets or returns the current graphic associated with the graphical style button when it is disabled. This property can be set at design time, and set or read at runtime. Table 42-7 summarizes the arguments of the DisabledPicture property.

General Syntax

```
[form!]Name.DisabledPicture [ = picture]
```

Table 42-7 Arguments of the DisabledPicture property

Argument	Description
form	Name of the parent form
Name	Name of the button control
picture	DisabledPicture property setting

Example Syntax
```
Private Sub Form_Load ()
    Button1.DownPicture = LoadPicture("down.bmp")
    Button1.DisabledPicture = LoadPicture("disabled.bmp")
    Button1.Picture = LoadPicture("normal.bmp")
End Sub
```

Description   The DisabledPicture property sets or returns the graphical image that is displayed when the button is disabled. The button must have its Style property equal to Graphical (1) for this property to take effect. Otherwise, only the button's caption is displayed.

The example syntax shows the setting of the three properties associated with graphical buttons: DownPicture, DisabledPicture, and Picture. The Picture property represents the graphical image that is shown when the button is in its unselected state. The DownPicture represents the graphical image that is shown when the button is in its selected state. Finally, the DisabledPicture property represents the graphical image that is shown when the button is disabled.

Example   In the Buttons project at the end of this chapter, a graphical button is shown that changes images, based upon the option button setting.

DownPicture Property

Objects Affected   CheckBox, CommandButton, OptionButton

Purpose   The DownPicture property sets or returns the current graphic associated with the graphical style button when it is selected. This property can be set at design time, and set or read at runtime. Table 42-8 summarizes the arguments of the DownPicture property.

General Syntax

`[form!]Name.DownPicture [ = picture]`

Table 42-8 Arguments of the DownPicture property

Argument	Description
form	Name of the parent form
Name	Name of the button control
picture	DownPicture property setting

Example Syntax
```
Private Sub Form_Load ()
    Button1.DownPicture = LoadPicture("down.bmp")
    Button1.DisabledPicture = LoadPicture("disabled.bmp")
    Button1.Picture = LoadPicture("normal.bmp")
End Sub
```

Description   The DownPicture property sets or returns the graphical image that is displayed when the button is selected. For command buttons, this occurs when the user depresses the button. For option buttons and check boxes, this occurs when the control is in a selected or checked state. The button must have its Style property equal to Graphical (1) for this property to take effect. Otherwise, only the button's caption is displayed.

The example syntax shows the setting of the three properties associated with graphical buttons: DownPicture, DisabledPicture, and Picture. The Picture property represents the graphical image that is shown when the button is in its unselected state. The DownPicture represents the graphical image that is shown when the button is in its selected state. Finally, the DisabledPicture property represents the graphical image that is shown when the button is disabled.

Example In the Buttons project at the end of this chapter, a graphical button is shown that changes images, based upon the option button setting.

PICTURE PROPERTY

Objects Affected CheckBox, CommandButton, OptionButton

Purpose The Picture property sets or returns the current graphic associated with the graphical style button when it is not selected. This property can be set at design time, and set or read at runtime. Table 42-9 summarizes the arguments of the Picture property.

General Syntax

```
[form!]Name.Picture [ = picture]
```

Table 42-9 Arguments of the Picture property

Argument	Description
form	Name of the parent form
Name	Name of the button control
picture	Picture property setting

Example Syntax

```
Private Sub Form_Load ()
    Button1.DownPicture = LoadPicture("down.bmp")
    Button1.DisabledPicture = LoadPicture("disabled.bmp")
    Button1.Picture = LoadPicture("normal.bmp")
End Sub
```

Description The Picture property sets or returns the graphical image that is displayed when the button is not selected. For command buttons, this occurs when the button is in its normal, undepressed state. For option buttons and check boxes, this occurs when the control is in an unselected or unchecked state. The button must have its Style property equal to Graphical (1) for this property to take effect. Otherwise, only the button's caption is displayed.

The example syntax shows the setting of the three properties associated with graphical buttons: DownPicture, DisabledPicture, and Picture. The Picture property represents the graphical image that is shown when the button is in its unselected state. The DownPicture represents the graphical image that is shown when the button is in its selected state. Finally, the DisabledPicture property represents the graphical image that is shown when the button is disabled.

Example   In the Buttons project at the end of this chapter, a graphical button is shown that changes images, based upon the option button setting.

STYLE PROPERTY

Objects Affected   CheckBox, CommandButton, OptionButton

Purpose   The Style property sets or returns the current appearance of the button. Buttons can either be Standard (0), where only a caption is displayed, or Graphical (1), where a program-defined image is displayed. Table 42-10 summarizes the arguments of the Style property for buttons. Table 42-11 summarizes the constants that may be set or returned from this property.

General Syntax

```
[form!]Name.Style [ = style%]
```

Table 42-10 Arguments of the Style property

Argument	Description
form	Name of the parent form
Name	Name of the button control
Style%	The button style setting

Table 42-11 Constants for the Style property

Value	VB.Constants	Meaning
0	vbButtonStandard	(Default) Caption is in plain text.
1	vbButtonGraphical	Graphical images are drawn for the button.

Example Syntax

```
Private Sub Form_Load ()
    If Button1.Style = vbButtonGraphical Then
        Button1.Picture = LoadPicture("normal.bmp")
        Button1.DownPicture = LoadPicture("down.bmp")
    End If
End Sub
```

Description	The Style property sets or returns the button's style, which is either Standard (0) or Graphical (1). For standard buttons, simply the Caption property text is drawn. For graphical buttons, an image is drawn from the Picture, DownPicture, or DisabledPicture property setting based on the current state of the button.
	The syntax example shows the setting of the graphical properties for Button1 based on the Style property setting of the button. In this case, only the Picture and DownPicture graphical images are defined for the button.
Example	In the Buttons project at the end of this chapter, a graphical button has been designed on the form that has its image set depending on which option button is selected.

VALUE PROPERTY

Objects Affected	AsyncProperty, Button, CheckBox, Column, CommandButton, HScrollBar, OptionButton, ProgressBar, RowBuffer, Slider, VScrollBar
Purpose	The Value property sets or returns the current state of the button. All buttons support a selected and an unselected state. Check boxes additionally support a grayed state. Table 42-12 summarizes the arguments of the Value property for buttons. Table 42-13 summarizes the constants that may be set or returned from this property for check boxes.

General Syntax

```
[form!]Name.Value [ = value%]
```

Table 42-12 Arguments of the Value property

Argument	Description
form	Name of the parent form
Name	Name of the button control
value%	The button value setting

Table 42-13 Constants for the Value property for check boxes

Value	VB.Constants	Meaning
0	vbUnchecked	(Default) The check box is not checked.
1	vbChecked	The check box is checked.
2	vbGrayed	The check box is in a grayed state.

Example Syntax

```
Private Sub Button1_Click()
    Select Case Button1.Value
        Case vbChecked
            Button1.Caption = "Checked"
        Case vbUnchecked
            Button1.Value = "Unchecked"
        Case vbGrayed
            Button1.Caption = "Grayed"
    End Select
End Sub
```

Description   The Value property sets or returns the current state of the button. For a command button, this property contains the states in which the button is depressed (True) or not depressed (False). For option buttons, this property contains the states in which the button is selected (True) or unselected (False). For check boxes, this property contains the state where the button is unchecked (0), checked (1), or grayed (2).

The grayed state of check boxes is usually displayed to indicate that either the answer is unknown or that the value that it represents may be partially true and partially false.

The syntax example shows how to respond to the value of a check box. Note that when the button is clicked, the current state determines the new caption of the check box.

Example   In the Buttons project at the end of this chapter, a check box is displayed that shows its current state in its caption. When the graphical button is pressed, the state of this check box becomes grayed.

The Buttons Project

Project Overview

The project outlined in the following pages demonstrates the concepts behind the use of buttons. You will learn how to use check boxes, command buttons, and option buttons using the Click and DblClick events and the Cancel, Default, Picture, Style, and Value properties by experimenting with the project.

Assembling the Project

> **1.** Create a new form (the Buttons form) and place on it the following controls. Use Table 42-14 to set the properties of the form and each control.

Table 42-14 Property settings for the Buttons project

Object	Property	Setting
Form	Name	formButtons
	Caption	"Buttons Project"
	BorderStyle	3 - Fixed Dialog
Frame	Name	Frame1
OptionButton	Name	optFruit
	Caption	"Banana"
	Index	0
OptionButton	Name	optFruit
	Caption	"Apple"
	Index	1
OptionButton	Name	optFruit
	Index	2
CheckBox	Name	chkRaw
	Caption	"Raw"
CheckBox	Name	chkFresh
	Caption	"Fresh"
CheckBox	Name	chkRotate
	Caption	"Check Me!"
CommandButton	Name	cmndOK
	Caption	"OK"
	Default	True
CommandButton	Name	cmndCancel
	Caption	"Cancel"
	Cancel	True
CommandButton	Name	cmndReset
	Style	1 - Graphical

2. Check the appearance of your form against Figure 42-2.

3. Enter the following code into the Form_Load event. This event sets the initial state of the form.

```
Private Sub Form_Load()
    optFruit(0).Value = True
    cmndReset.Picture = LoadPicture("banana.bmp")
End Sub
```

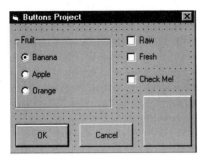

Figure 42-2 How the Buttons form should look when complete

4. Enter the following code into the optFruit_Click event. This event handles the change in value for any of the option buttons in the Fruit frame.

```
Private Sub optFruit_Click(Index As Integer)
    Select Case Index
        Case 0
            cmndReset.Picture = LoadPicture("banana.bmp")
        Case 1
            cmndReset.Picture = LoadPicture("apple.bmp")
        Case 2
            cmndReset.Picture = LoadPicture("orange.bmp")
    End Select
End Sub
```

5. Enter the following code into the optFruit_DblClick event. This invokes the OK command button event to accept the current entry.

```
Private Sub optFruit_DblClick(Index As Integer)
    cmndOK_Click
End Sub
```

6. Enter the following code in the cmndOK_Click event. This ends the program.

```
Private Sub cmndOK_Click()
    End
End Sub
```

7. Enter the following code in the cmndCancel_Click event. This prompts the user, asking whether he or she wants to leave before ending the program.

```
Private Sub cmndCancel_Click()
    If MsgBox("Are you sure you want to cancel?", vbYesNo, "Buttons Sample") = vbYes Then
        End
    End If
End Sub
```

8. Enter the following code in the cmndReset_Click event. This resets the values of the check boxes.

```
Private Sub cmndReset_Click()
    chkRaw.Value = vbUnchecked
    chkFresh.Value = vbUnchecked
    chkRotate.Value = vbGrayed
End Sub
```

9. Enter the following code in the chkRotate_Click event. This displays the appropriate text based upon the current value of the chkRotate check box.

```
Private Sub chkRotate_Click()
    Select Case chkRotate.Value
        Case vbUnchecked
            chkRotate.Caption = "Unchecked"
        Case vbGrayed
            chkRotate.Caption = "Grayed"
        Case vbChecked
            chkRotate.Caption = "Checked"
    End Select
End Sub
```

How It Works

This project creates a program that displays a list of fruit options for the user. Because the user may choose only one of the available fruit options, a control array of option buttons is used. When a fruit option is selected, the graphical button (cmndReset) displays an image of the specified fruit.

When the cmndReset graphical button is pushed, the values of the chkRaw and chkFresh check boxes are set to unchecked (0), and the chkRotate is set to grayed (2). Whenever the chkRotate check box's state is changed, it displays a caption that identifies its current state.

The cmndOK command button is designed to be the default command button. As a result, you can press ENTER to exit the dialog. Note that the OK command button is drawn with a thick, dark border, indicating to the user that it is the default. Likewise, the cmndCancel command button is designed to be the cancel command button. This means that you can press ESC to cause the cmndCancel_Click event to be invoked.

43

SCROLLBARS

You'll most commonly see scrollbars being used to move, or *scroll*, through long text entries. Clicking on the scrollbar lets you move up and down or left and right through text that is too large to display in the window. It's as though you had a small viewport that could be moved around to view a larger world beyond.

This analogy becomes more compelling when scrollbars control a graphics viewport. Imagine a graphical image of a map that's too large to display in the window. Scrolling would let you "fly" over the map to expose whatever area you wanted.

Scrollbars can also graphically represent numeric values. Let's say you have a number that represents magnification of your map image. Rather than forcing users to take their hands off the mouse to manually enter numbers for the amount of magnification, you could set up a scrollbar so they could directly manipulate the value. This would also provide a graphic representation of how the present magnification relates to the minimum and maximum values. Now they can both fly over the map and dive into it.

Scrollbars are ubiquitous features in Windows programs. Visual Basic, as usual, makes it simple to use these powerful tools.

Operating Scrollbars

Scrollbars consist of a bar with arrows at each end and a button (called the *thumb*) between the arrows. There are two types of scrollbars: vertical (VScrollBar) and horizontal (HScrollBar). Figure 43-1 illustrates the two kinds of scrollbars.

The thumb's position directly relates to the value represented by the scrollbar. For horizontal scrollbars, the thumb is all the way to the left when the value of the scrollbar is at its minimum setting and all the way to the right when the value is at its maximum. A minimum value on a vertical scrollbar places the thumb at the top, while the maximum value places the thumb at the bottom. Any value in between places the thumb on the bar in a position proportional to the value represented by the scrollbar.

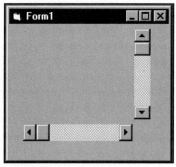

Figure 43-1   Scrollbars can be
either vertical or horizontal

The value represented by a scrollbar can be changed in four ways. First, the user can click on either arrow. This causes the value represented by the scrollbar to increment or decrement by a small amount in the direction of the selected arrow. Second, the user may click the scrollbar on one side of the thumb or the other. This causes the scrollbar's value to increment or decrement also, but the amount of change is greater. The user can also click and drag the thumb to a specific position on the bar. This causes the value of the scrollbar to be set according to the position of the thumb. Finally, the user can set the value of a scrollbar in the program's code.

Scrollbars Summary

Table 43-1 displays the properties that control the operation of scrollbars.

Table 43-1 Properties that affect the operation of a scrollbar

Use or Set This...	Type	To Do This...
LargeChange	Property	Set or return the amount changed when the user clicks on the bar
Max	Property	Set or return the maximum value represented by the scrollbar
Min	Property	Set or return the minimum value represented by the scrollbar
SmallChange	Property	Set or return the amount changed when the user clicks on an arrow
Value	Property	Set or return the value represented by the scrollbar

These five properties are explored in the next section. The Scroll Bars project at the end of the chapter puts scrollbars to use in a sample application.

LARGECHANGE PROPERTY

Objects Affected   HScrollBar, Slider, VScrollBar

Purpose   The LargeChange property sets or returns the amount of change that occurs when the user clicks on the bar portion of a scrollbar. This property can be set at design time, and set or read at runtime. Table 43-2 summarizes the arguments of the LargeChange property.

General Syntax

```
[form!]Name.LargeChange [ = amount%]
```

Table 43-2 Arguments of the LargeChange property

Argument	Description
form	Name of the parent form
Name	Name of the scrollbar control
amount%	An integer value indicating the amount of change made when the user clicks on the bar

Example Syntax

```
Private Sub Form_Load ()
    HScroll2.LargeChange = 100
    Text1.Text = Str(VScroll1.LargeChange)
End Sub
```

Description   The LargeChange property sets or returns the amount of change that occurs in a scrollbar's value when the user clicks on the bar portion of a scrollbar. Clicking on the bar portion of the scrollbar adjusts the Value property of the scrollbar by the amount defined by the LargeChange property. For instance, if the LargeChange property is set to 100, clicking below the thumb on the bar portion of a vertical scrollbar will add 100 to the scrollbar's Value property.

Any value you assign to this property must be an integer whose value is within the range defined by the Min and Max properties of the same control. If the program tries to assign a value that is not in this range, an "Invalid property value" error occurs.

The first statement in the example syntax sets the LargeChange value for the scrollbar control HScroll2 to 100. This is the amount by which the scrollbar's Value property will change when the user clicks on the bar between the thumb and one of the arrows. The second statement simply displays the LargeChange property of the scrollbar VScroll1 in Text1.

Example	In the Scroll Bars project at the end of this chapter, the LargeChange property is set to 100 at design time. This causes the control Picture2 to be scrolled 100 twips at a time.
Comments	The SmallChange property defines a smaller amount of change for when the user clicks one of the arrows at either end of the bar.

MAX PROPERTY

Objects Affected	HScrollBar, ProgressBar, Slider, VScrollBar
Purpose	The Max property sets or returns the maximum value of a scrollbar. This property can be set at design time, and set or read at runtime. Table 43-3 summarizes the arguments of the Max property.

General Syntax

```
[form!]Name.Max [ = value%]
```

Table 43-3 Arguments of the Max property

Argument	Description
form	Name of the parent form
Name	Name of the scrollbar control
value%	An integer expression indicating the value at the high end of the scrollbar

Example Syntax

```
Private Sub Form_Load ()
    HScroll1.Max = 1000            'sets the maximum value for the scroll bar to 1000
End Sub
```

Description	The Max property defines the value represented by a vertical scrollbar when the thumb is at its bottom position, or by a horizontal scrollbar when its thumb is at its farthest right position. This is an integer value in the range -32,768 to 32,767. Along with the Min property, Max defines the acceptable range of values for a scrollbar. By default, this property is set to 32,767.
	You may expect the Max property to always be a value greater than the Min property. However, this is not always true. Visual Basic will accept a Max property that is less than the Min property for the same control. This causes changes to the value of the scrollbar that are the opposite of what normally occurs. For instance, if the Max property is less than the Min property, clicking on the top arrow of a vertical scrollbar would add to the scrollbar's value instead of subtracting from it.

The example syntax sets the maximum value for scrollbar HScroll1 to 1000. Since this is a horizontal scrollbar, it will have the value 1000 when the thumb is all the way to the right.

Example In the Scroll Bars project at the end of this chapter, the Max property of the horizontal and vertical scrollbars is set in the Form_Load event. The value placed in the Max property is an arithmetic equation that figures out values for the Picture2.Top and Picture2.Left properties that would allow the right and bottom edges of the control Picture2 to be displayed.

MIN PROPERTY

Objects Affected HScrollBar, ProgressBar, Slider, VScrollBar

Purpose The Min property sets or returns the minimum value of a scrollbar. This property can be set at design time, and set or read at runtime. Table 43-4 summarizes the arguments of the Min property.

General Syntax

```
[form!]Name.Min [ = value%]
```

Table 43-4 Arguments of the Min property

Argument	Description
form	Name of the parent form
Name	Name of the scrollbar control
value%	An integer expression indicating the value at the low end of the scrollbar

Example Syntax

```
Private Sub Form_Load ()
    HScroll1.Min = 100                 'sets the minimum value for the scroll bar to 100
End Sub
```

Description The Min property defines the value represented by a vertical scrollbar when the thumb is at its top position, or for a horizontal scrollbar when the thumb is at its farthest left position. This is an integer value in the range -32,768 to 32,767. Along with the Max property, Min defines the acceptable range of values for a scrollbar. By default, this property is set to 0.

One would expect the Min property to always be a value less than the Max property. However, this is not always true. Visual Basic will accept a Min property that is greater than the Max property for the same control. This causes changes to the value of the scrollbar that are the opposite of what normally occurs. For instance, if the Min property is greater than the Max property, clicking on the top arrow of a vertical scrollbar would add to the scrollbar's value instead of subtracting from it.

In the example syntax, the minimum value of the horizontal scrollbar HScroll1 is set to 100. This is the value the scrollbar will have when the thumb is all the way to the left.

Example   In the Scrollbars project at the end of this chapter, the Min property of the horizontal and vertical scrollbars is set to 0 in the Form_Load event.

SMALLCHANGE PROPERTY

Objects Affected   HScrollBar, Slider, VScrollBar

Purpose   The SmallChange property sets or returns the amount of change that occurs when the user clicks on one of the arrows at either end of a scrollbar. This property can be set at design time and set or read at runtime. Table 43-5 summarizes the arguments of the SmallChange property.

General Syntax

```
[form!]Name.SmallChange [ = amount%]
```

Table 43-5 Arguments of the SmallChange property

Argument	Description
form	Name of the parent form
Name	Name of the scrollbar control
amount%	An integer value indicating the amount of change made when the user clicks on one of the bar's arrows

Example Syntax

```
Private Sub Form_Load ()
    HScroll1.SmallChange = 10          'the value of the will be changed in increments of 10
    L% = VScroll1.SmallChange          'assigns the SmallChange value to L%
End Sub
```

Description   The SmallChange property sets or returns the amount of change that occurs when the user clicks on one of the arrows at either end of a scrollbar. Clicking on one of the arrows adjusts the value of the scrollbar by the amount defined by the SmallChange property.

The SmallChange property is an integer whose range must be between the values defined by the Min and Max properties of the same control. If the program tries to assign a value that is not in this range, an "Invalid property value" error occurs.

In the example syntax, the SmallChange property for the HScroll1 scroll-bar is set to 10. This is the amount the value of the scrollbar will increase or decrease when the user clicks on the arrows at the ends of the scrollbar.

Example   In the Scroll Bars project at the end of this chapter, the SmallChange property is set to 10 at design time. This causes the control Picture2 to be scrolled 10 twips at a time when the user clicks an arrow.

Comments   The LargeChange property defines a larger change for when the user clicks on the scrollbar itself.

VALUE PROPERTY

Objects Affected   AsyncProperty, Button, CheckBox, Column, CommandButton, HScrollBar, OptionButton, ProgressBar, RowBuffer, Slider, VScrollBar

Purpose   The Value property sets or returns the value currently represented by a scrollbar. This property can be set at design time, and set or read at run-time. Table 43-6 shows the arguments of the Value property.

General Syntax

`[form!]Name.Value [ = value%]`

Table 43-6 Arguments of the Value property

Argument	Description
form	Name of the parent form
Name	Name of the scrollbar control
value%	An integer expression indicating a position on the scrollbar

Example Syntax

```
Private Sub Form_Load ()
    V% = VScroll1.Value              'assigns the value from the scroll bar to V%
End Sub
```

Description   The Value property contains a value that is proportional to the current position of the thumb on the scrollbar relative to the values specified by the Min and Max properties. For instance, if the thumb is three-quarters of the way across a horizontal scrollbar, and the Min and Max properties are set to 0 and 100, respectively, the Value property will have a value of 75. Conversely, if the Value property for the same scrollbar is set to 25, the thumb will be moved to a position one-fourth of the distance across the bar.

If the program sets this property, it must be within the range defined by the Min and Max properties, or an "Invalid property value" error will occur. When read, this property returns an integer within the same range. The maximum range for Min and Max is -32,768 to 32,767, so the Value property for a scrollbar control is always within this range.

This property can be changed in four ways. First, the user can click on the arrow at either end of the scrollbar. This causes the Value property to be incremented or decremented by the amount defined by the SmallChange property in the direction of the selected arrow. Second, the user may click the scrollbar on one side of the thumb or the other. This also increments or decrements the value, but the amount of change is that defined by the LargeChange property. The user can also click and drag the thumb to a specific position on the bar. This causes the Value of the scrollbar to be set according to the position of the thumb in proportion to the Min and Max properties. Finally, the value of a scrollbar can be set in the program's code.

The example syntax saves the current value of the scrollbar VScroll1 in the integer variable V%.

Example

In the Scroll Bars project at the end of this chapter, the Value property is read in the HScroll1_Change and VScroll1_Change events. In these events this property is used to set the position of Picture2.

This property is set by each of the Click events for all the thumbs on the form. By setting the Value property, each of these thumbs positions Picture2 at a different corner.

Comments

The Value property is also used for the check box, command button, and option button controls. For command and option buttons, the possible values for the Value property are True and False, meaning the button is or is not selected. Check boxes can have the values 0 (not checked), 1 (checked), or 2 (grayed).

The Scroll Bars Project

Project Overview

The project outlined in the following pages demonstrates the concepts behind the use of scrollbars. You will learn how to use the LargeChange, Min, Max, SmallChange, and Value properties by experimenting with the project.

Assembling the Project

1. Create a new form (the Scroll Bars form) and place on it the following controls. Use Table 43-7 to set the properties of the form and each control.

   Note: When you create the Picture2 control, first make sure Picture1 has the focus. Then double-click on the picture control icon. This creates Picture2 as a child of Picture1, which is necessary for this program to operate correctly.

Table 43-7 Property settings for the Scroll Bars project

Object	Property	Setting
Form	Name	Scroll
	Caption	"Scroll Bars Project"
PictureBox	Name	Picture1
PictureBox	Name	Picture2
	AutoSize	True
	Picture	(Bitmap) WAITE.BMP
CommandButton	Name	cmndBottomLeft
	Caption	Bottom Left
CommandButton	Name	cmndBottomRight
	Caption	Bottom Right
CommandButton	Name	cmndTopLeft
	Caption	Top Left
CommandButton	Name	cmndTopRight
	Caption	Top Right
HScrollBar	Name	HScroll1
	LargeChange	100
	SmallChange	10
VScrollBar	Name	VScroll1
	LargeChange	100
	SmallChange	10

2. Check the appearance of your form against Figure 43-2.

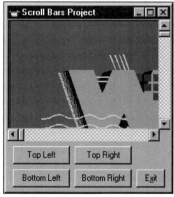

Figure 43-2   How the Scroll Bars form should look when complete

3. Enter the following code into the HScroll1_Change and VScroll1_Change events. These events set the coordinates for the upper-left corner of Picture2.

```
Private Sub HScroll1_Change ()
    Picture2.Left = -HScroll1.Value
End Sub

Private Sub VScroll1_Change ()
    Picture2.Top = -VScroll1.Value
End Sub
```

4. Enter the following code into the Form_Load event. This event sets the minimum and maximum values for the HScroll1 and VScroll1 scrollbar controls.

```
Private Sub Form_Load ()
    HScroll1.Max = (Picture2.Width - Picture1.Width)
    VScroll1.Max = (Picture2.Height - Picture1.Height)
    HScroll1.Min = 0
    VScroll1.Min = 0
End Sub
```

5. Enter the following code into the Click events for the four thumbs. These routines set the coordinates for the Picture2 picture control. By choosing one of these thumbs, the picture gets set to the respective corner.

```
Private Sub cmndTopLeft_Click ()
    HScroll1.Value = HScroll1.Min
    VScroll1.Value = VScroll1.Min
End Sub

Private Sub cmndTopRight_Click ()
    HScroll1.Value = HScroll1.Max
    VScroll1.Value = VScroll1.Min
End Sub

Private Sub cmndBottomLeft_Click ()
    HScroll1.Value = HScroll1.Min
    VScroll1.Value = VScroll1.Max
End Sub

Private Sub cmndBottomRight_Click ()
    HScroll1.Value = HScroll1.Max
    VScroll1.Value = VScroll1.Max
End Sub
```

6. Enter the following code in the cmndExit_Click event. This ends the program.

```
Private Sub cmndExit_Click ()
    End
End Sub
```

How It Works

This project creates a program that displays the WAITE.BMP bitmap. However, the area for displaying the picture is smaller than the picture itself. Therefore, we need to provide a method for the user to "scroll" the picture to the left and right, and up and down.

The picture control Picture1 defines the viewing area for the bitmap. Picture2 is placed as a child of Picture1, with its AutoSize property set to True. Although Picture2 is larger than Picture1, because it is a child, the displayed portion of Picture2 cannot overlap the area defined by Picture1.

We can now determine which portion of Picture2 is displayed by changing its Left and Top properties. Initially, the Left and Top properties are set to 0. These properties are changed in the HScroll1_Change and VScroll1_Change events, which occur whenever the user changes the value of either the horizontal or vertical scrollbars. The minimum and maximum values for the scrollbars are defined in the Form_Load event. In this event the minimum for each bar is set to 0, while the maximum is set to a value that will reflect the Left and Top values of Picture2 when the bottom right-hand corner of the picture is being displayed.

Each of the Click routines sets the Value property of the scrollbars. Doing so also causes the Change events for the scrollbars to occur, thereby changing the Top and Left coordinates of Picture2.

44

TEXT BOXES

Visual Basic's text box control lets you easily get text input from the user. The text box control inherits a number of powerful features that make it simple to let your user select, cut, and copy text. The text box also automatically follows Windows conventions with the movement keys like the left, right, up, and down arrow keys. You can tell the text box to automatically create scrollbars for you, and Visual Basic even lets you specify a password character to use in a password entry routine.

The text box control lets the user enter or edit text. When a text box control receives the focus, an insertion point appears in the box. The insertion point is a slim flashing vertical line that indicates where any new text will be entered within the box. Although the proper Windows terminology for this line is *caret*, most people commonly refer to it as the *cursor*. This cursor can be moved by using the direction keys, the Ⓗ and Ⓩ keys, or by clicking at the desired position in the text box with the mouse pointer. The default behavior for the mouse pointer is to change to an I-beam when over a text box, to facilitate precise positioning.

The text box's primary property is the Text property. This property is a string value that contains any text that has been entered into the text box. The value of the Text property can be modified in one of four ways: user input, your program's code, DDE (dynamic data exchange) messages, or a change in the record of an underlying database record if the text control has been bound to a database. Anytime the text changes, the text box's Change event occurs.

Editing in a Text Box

A Visual Basic text box gives the user all the standard Windows editing capabilities. It automatically inherits all the conventions of a standard Windows text box, including the ability to cut, copy, and paste to and from the Windows Clipboard area. A user can select text for these functions by holding down the Ⓕ key and pressing Ⓒ or Ⓓ, or by clicking and dragging the mouse over the desired text. This highlights the selected text.

Once text has been selected, the user may perform several operations on it. Pressing the Ⓖ key deletes the selected text from the text box. Pressing Ⓕ-Ⓖ or Ⓠ-Ⓧ copies the selected text to the Clipboard, and then deletes it from the text box. This is commonly called *cutting* text. The user can also *copy* selected text to the Clipboard without deleting it by pressing the Ⓠ-Ⓘ or Ⓠ-Ⓒ key combinations. Pressing Ⓕ-Ⓘ or Ⓠ-Ⓥ will *paste* any text currently stored on the Clipboard into the text box at the position specified by the text box's insertion point. You can control these functions in your program using the SelText, SelStart, and SelLength properties. For more information on how to interact with the Windows Clipboard, see Chapter 53, "Using the Clipboard."

MultiLine Text Boxes

By default, a text box consists of only one line of text. You can allow the user to enter more than one line of text by setting the MultiLine property to True. If you've set the MultiLine property to True, you may also wish to set the ScrollBars property. This allows you to place scrollbars on the right and bottom edges of the text box, enabling the user to quickly scroll through the text.

Combo Boxes

The combo box control has two styles, drop-down combo and simple combo, both of which include an edit area that is very similar to the text box control. These two styles of combo boxes share the SelLength, SelStart, SelText, and Text properties with the text box control. Refer to Chapter 46, "List and Combo Boxes," for more information on combo boxes.

Text Boxes Summary

Table 44-1 lists the properties that relate to the text box control, and their uses. Each of these properties is explained in detail in this chapter. At the end of the chapter, an example project demonstrates how to combine all of these elements.

Table 44-1 The properties that govern the appearance and behavior of a text box control

Use or Set This Property...	To Do This...
Alignment	Set up or read the position of the text relative to the text box
HideSelection	Set or read whether a selection is removed when focus is lost
MultiLine	Set up a text box to accept multiple-line input
PasswordChar	Set or determine if text box displays actual text or a placeholder
ScrollBars	Set up horizontal or vertical scrollbars (or both) for a text box
SelLength	Set or read the length of the currently selected text (if any)
SelStart	Set or read the starting position of the currently selected text (if any)
SelText	Replace or read the currently selected text string
Text	Set or read the text contained in a text box

Constant Values

It is usually best to use named constants rather than numeric values when developing software. Named constants make your code more readable and easier to maintain.

Table 44-2 lists the values of the constants relevant to this chapter, mentions their names, and briefly describes what they mean. These constants can be viewed in the VB Constants module using the Object Browser. It is not necessary to explicitly add these objects to your project.

Table 44-2 Constant values for text input

Value	VB.Constants	Meaning
Alignment Property		
0	vbLeftJustify	(Default) The text is aligned with the left edge of the text box.
1	vbRightJustify	The text is aligned with the right edge of the text box.
2	vbCenter	The text is centered within the text box.
ScrollBars Property		
0	vbDefault	(Default) The text box will have no scrollbars, and text will wrap automatically.
1	vbHorizontal	A horizontal scrollbar appears at the bottom edge of the text box with no word wrapping.
2	vbVertical	A vertical scrollbar appears at the right edge of the text box with automatic word wrapping.
3	vbBoth	Vertical and horizontal scrollbars with automatic word wrapping.

ALIGNMENT PROPERTY

Objects Affected	CheckBox, Column, ColumnHeader, Label, OptionButton, Panel, TextBox
Purpose	The Alignment property sets the location at which the text within a text box is displayed. This property can only be set at design time, although your program can read its value at runtime. Table 44-3 summarizes the arguments of the Alignment property, and Table 44-4 lists the possible values for this property and their effects.
General Syntax	

```
[form!]Name.Alignment
```

Table 44-3 Arguments of the Alignment property

Argument	Description
form	Name property of the parent form
Name	Name property of the control

Table 44-4 Constant values for the Alignment property

Value	VB.Constants	Meaning
0	vbLeftJustify	(Default) The text is aligned with the left edge of the text box.
1	vbRightJustify	The text is aligned with the right edge of the text box.
2	vbCenter	The text is centered within the text box.

Example Syntax

```
Private Sub Command1_Click ()
    TextAlignment = Text1.Alignment
End Sub
```

Description   The Alignment property is only useful when the MultiLine property is set to True. This property has no effect in text boxes when the MultiLine property is False. Single-line text boxes always display their text along their left edge (that is, with a vbLeftJustify alignment).

By default, the Alignment property is set to vbLeftJustify, causing the associated text box to display text along the left edge. However, you may wish to set this property to vbCenter or vbRightJustify at design time to either center text or display text along the right edge.

Example   In the Text Box project at the end of this chapter, the edit area of the mini-text editor is a multiple-line text box that is left-justified.

HIDESELECTION PROPERTY

Objects Affected   ListView, TextBox, TreeView

Purpose   The HideSelection property instructs a text box control whether or not to only show the selection when the text box has focus. This property can only be set at design time, although your program can read its value at runtime. Table 44-5 summarizes the arguments of the HideSelection property.

General Syntax

```
[form!]Name.HideSelection
```

Table 44-5 Arguments of the HideSelection property

Argument	Description
form	Name property of the parent form
Name	Name property of the control

Example Syntax

```
Private Sub Command1_Click ()
    HideSelectionStatus = Text1.HideSelection
End Sub
```

Description   By default, the HideSelection property is set to True, causing the associated text box to only display its selection when it has focus. However, you may wish to set this property to False at design time to allow the text box to always display its selection. You would choose to do this if it is important for the user to see the current selection when working with other controls.

Example   In the Text Box project at the end of this chapter, the edit area of the mini-text editor does not hide its selection.

MultiLine Property

Objects Affected   TextBox

Purpose   The MultiLine property sets up a text box control for entry of multiple lines of text. This property can only be set at design time, although your program can read its value at runtime. Table 44-6 summarizes the arguments of the MultiLine property.

General Syntax

```
[form!]Name.MultiLine
```

Table 44-6 Arguments of the MultiLine property

Argument	Description
form	Name property of the parent form
Name	Name property of the control

Example Syntax

```
Private Sub Command1_Click ()
    MultiLineStatus = Text1.MultiLine
End Sub
```

Description   By default, the MultiLine property is set to False, causing the associated text box to be a single-line text box. However, you may wish to set this property to True at design time to create a multiple-line text box. A multiple-line text box allows the user to enter more than one line in the text box.

If the ScrollBars property is set to 0 (none) or 2 (vertical only), a multiple-line text box will automatically wrap text over to the next line when it exceeds the width of the box. If the ScrollBars property is set to 1 (horizontal) or 3 (both horizontal and vertical), it is up to the user to create new lines. If there is no button on the same form with its Default property set to True, the user can create new lines by pressing the E key. If there is a default button on the form, the user must use the Q-E key combination to create a new line.

The example syntax reads the value of the MultiLine property for the text box Text1. It could be used in an If statement to determine whether to format multiline text.

Example
In the Text Box project at the end of this chapter, the edit area of the mini-text editor is a multiple-line text box.

PASSWORDCHAR PROPERTY

Objects Affected   TextBox

Purpose
Use the PasswordChar property to set up a text box for password entry. By default, this property displays the characters that the user types. If you set this property to anything other than an empty string, it will display the first character contained in the property setting instead of the character typed by the user. This gives the user visual feedback for each character typed without displaying the actual characters. Tables 44-7 and 44-8 summarize the arguments of the PasswordChar property.

General Syntax

```
[form!]Name.PasswordChar [ = string$]
```

Table 44-7 Arguments of the PasswordChar property

Argument	Description
form	Name property of the parent form
Name	Name property of the control
string$	Read or set the password character

Table 44-8 Meaning of the string$ argument in the PasswordChar property

string$	Meaning
empty string	(Default) Echo characters typed by the user
nonempty string	Echo the first character in the string (other characters ignored)

Example Syntax

```
Private Sub Form_Load ()
    Form2.Caption = "Enter Your Password"
    Form2!Text1.PasswordChar = "*"
    Form2.Show vbModal
```

```
        If Form2!Text1.Text = Form1.Tag Then
            LoadMainProgram
        Else
            MsgBox "Incorrect Password!"
            End
        End If
End Sub
```

Description   Use the PasswordChar property to convert an ordinary text box into a password entry box. Passwords typically should not be displayed as they are typed in, to minimize the risk of prying eyes discovering someone's password. Most Windows programs use the asterisk (*) character as a placeholder for password characters. Figure 44-1 shows what a typical password entry dialog box might look like.

Set the PasswordChar property to a string to make it display the placeholder in the text box. Only the first character of the string is significant; subsequent characters are ignored. The example syntax assigns the asterisk as the placeholder character. Set PasswordChar to an empty string ("") to disable the password setting and display normal text.

The text box will always contain the actual characters, no matter what the PasswordChar property is set to. This lets you check the Text property to determine if the user typed the right password, as the example syntax shows.

Example   The Text Box project at the end of this chapter uses the PasswordChar property to set up a password entry dialog box. The File New command asks for the password before clearing the editing area.

SCROLLBARS PROPERTY

Objects Affected   DBGrid, Grid, MDIForm, Split, TextBox, UserDocument

Purpose   The ScrollBars property is set at design time to determine what types of scrollbars, if any, will appear at the edges of a text box (or a grid or MDI form). Scrollbars allow the user to read text that is too wide (or has too many lines) to fit in the window. This property is read-only at runtime. The arguments for the ScrollBars property are summarized in Table 44-9, and Table 44-10 lists the possible values for this property and their effects.

General Syntax

```
[form!]Name.ScrollBars
```

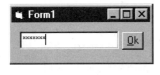

Figure 44-1   The PasswordChar property lets you easily set up password input dialog boxes

Table 44-9 Arguments of the ScrollBars property

Argument	Description
form	Name property of the parent form
Name	Name property of the control

Table 44-10 Possible settings for the ScrollBars property

Value	VB.Constants	Meaning
0	vbDefault	(Default) The text box will have no scrollbars, and text will wrap automatically.
1	vbHorizontal	A horizontal scrollbar appears at the bottom edge of the text box with no word wrapping.
2	vbVertical	A vertical scrollbar appears at the right edge of the text box with automatic word wrapping.
3	vbBoth	Vertical and horizontal scrollbars with automatic word wrapping.

Example Syntax

```
Private Sub Form_Load ()
    ScrollBarStatus = Text1.ScrollBars
End Sub
```

Description   The ScrollBars property is only useful when the MultiLine property is set to True. This property has no effect in text boxes when the MultiLine property is False. Scrollbars are graphic objects that consist of a bar with arrows at each end and a button (called a thumb) between the arrows. Scrollbars give the user the ability to quickly scroll through text with the mouse. There are two types of scrollbars: vertical and horizontal.

The scrollbar's thumb indicates the relative position of the text box's text. The user can move the thumb by clicking and dragging it, by clicking on the bar itself, or by clicking on one of the arrows at either end of the scrollbar. Moving the button on the scrollbar causes the text within the text box to scroll in proportion to the amount it is moved.

The example syntax stores the current value of the ScrollBars property of form Text1 in the variable ScrollBarStatus. It could be used in an If statement to test for the presence of scrollbars.

If the ScrollBars property is set to 0 (none) or 2 (vertical only), a multiple-line text box will automatically wrap text over to the next line when it exceeds the width of the box. Otherwise, it is up to the user to create new lines. If there is no button on the same form with its Default property set to True, the user can create new lines by hitting the E key. If there is a default button on the form, the user must use the Q-E key combination to create a new line.

Example   In the Text Box project at the end of this chapter, the ScrollBars property
for the edit portion of the mini-text editor is set to 2 (vertical scrollbars) at
design time.

SELLENGTH PROPERTY

Objects Affected   ComboBox, DBCombo, DBGrid, Slider, TextBox

Purpose   The SelLength property is used to set or return the number of selected
characters within a text or combo box. Characters can be selected (highlighted) by the user, usually for an editing operation. Your program can
also select a portion of the text in the text box. This property can be set
and read at runtime only. The arguments for the SelLength property are
summarized in Table 44-11.

General Syntax

```
[form!]Name.SelLength [ = NumChars&]
```

Table 44-11 Arguments of the SelLength property

Argument	Description
form	Name property of the parent form
Name	Name property of the control
NumChars&	Reads or sets the number of selected characters

Example Syntax

```
Private Sub Text1_MouseUp (Button As Integer, Shift As Integer, X As Single, Y As Single)
    SaveSelLength = Text1.SelLength      'save the length of the selected text
    Text2.Text = Str(SaveSelLength)
End Sub
```

Description   The SelLength property is used in conjunction with the SelStart and
SelText properties for working with text that has been selected by the user
in a text or combo box. A user can select text for these properties by holding down the Ⓕ key and pressing < or >, or by clicking and dragging the
mouse over the desired text. This highlights the selected text. Your program can then read the settings of these properties and perform operations
on the selected text. The SelStart property determines the starting point of
the selected text within a text or combo box. The SelLength property
determines the number of characters selected. SelText is a string property
that contains the selected text.

The SelLength property is a long integer that may be used to set or return
the number of selected characters in the text. If no characters are selected,
this property returns 0.

Setting the SelLength property within a program's code has no effect unless the text box has the focus when the property is set. If the text box does have the focus, assigning SelLength a value causes that number of characters to be selected in the text box, starting at the position indicated by the SelStart property and counting from left to right. If the program assigns SelLength a value that exceeds the length of the text in the text box, only the existing characters are selected, and the SelLength property is adjusted to reflect this. Setting this property to a value less than 0 causes an "Invalid property value" error to occur at runtime.

The example syntax saves the length of the current text selection to a variable for future use. Figure 44-2 shows a text box with selected text.

Example In the Text Box project at the end of this chapter, the SelLength and SelStart properties are saved in the Text1_KeyDown event. This is done to enable the Undo function of the mini-text editor.

Comments This property also applies to combo boxes and DBCombo boxes whose Style property has been set to 0 (drop-down combo) or 1 (simple combo).

SELSTART PROPERTY

Objects Affected ComboBox, DBCombo, DBGrid, Slider, TextBox

Purpose The SelStart property is used to set or return the starting position of selected text within a text or combo box. Text may be selected by the user or the program, and is highlighted in the text box. If there is no selected text, this property sets or returns the position of the box's insertion point. The arguments for the SelStart property are summarized in Table 44-12.

General Syntax

```
[form!]Name.SelStart [ = StartPos&]
```

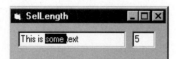

Figure 44-2 Text box with selected text; the other text box shows SelLength

Table 44-12 Arguments of the SelStart property

Argument	Description
form	Name property of the parent form
Name	Name property of the control
StartPos&	Reads or sets the character position of the insertion point or the start of selected text

Example Syntax

```
Private Sub Text1_MouseUp (Button As Integer, Shift As Integer, X As Single, Y As Single)
    SaveSelStart = Text1.SelStart        'save the start of the selected text
    Text2.Text = Str$(SaveSelStart)
End Sub
```

Description

The SelStart property is used in conjunction with the SelLength and SelText properties for working with text that has been selected in a text or combo box by the user. A user can select text for these properties by holding down the Ⓕ key and pressing < or >, or by clicking and dragging the mouse over the desired text. This highlights the selected text (see Figure 44-2). Your program can then read the settings of these properties and perform operations on the selected text. The SelStart property determines the starting point of the selected text within a text or combo box. SelLength determines the number of characters selected. SelText is a string property that contains the selected text.

The SelStart property is a long integer value that indicates the starting position of the selected characters in a text or combo box. The value of SelStart is zero based. This means the first selected character is the position after the value of SelStart. For instance, if the value of SelStart is 1, and the value of SelLength is 2, the second and third characters in the text are selected. If there is no text currently selected, SelStart will return the position of the text box's insertion point.

You may set the SelStart property by assigning a long integer value to it. This value must be a nonnegative number, or else an "Invalid property value" error will occur during runtime. If this value is greater than the length of the text in the text or combo box, SelStart is set to a value equal to the length of the text. Assigning a value to the SelStart property automatically sets the SelLength property to 0, and moves the insertion point in the text box to the specified position.

The example syntax saves the starting position of the selected text in a variable for future use.

Example

In the Text Box project at the end of this chapter, the SelLength and SelStart properties are saved in the Text1_KeyDown event. This is done to enable the Undo function of the mini-text editor.

| Comments | This property also applies to combo boxes and DBCombo boxes whose Style property has been set to 0 (drop-down combo) or 1 (simple combo). |

SELTEXT PROPERTY

| Objects Affected | ComboBox, DBCombo, DBGrid, TextBox |
| Purpose | The SelText property replaces or returns the currently selected text within a text or combo box. Users can select text (typically by dragging with the mouse), or text may be selected by program action. The arguments for the SelText property are summarized in Table 44-13. |

General Syntax

```
[form!]Name.SelText [ = NewText$]
```

Table 44-13 Arguments of the SelText property

Argument	Description
form	Name property of the parent form.
Name	Name property of the control.
NewText$	A string that can be placed at the text box's insertion point. NewText$ replaces any selected text.

Example Syntax

```
Private Sub Text1_MouseUp (Button As Integer, Shift As Integer, X As Single, Y As Single)
    Clipboard.SetText Text1.SelText      'save the start of the selected text
    Text2.Text = Text1.SelText
End Sub
```

| Description | The SelText property is used in conjunction with the SelLength and SelStart properties for working with text that has been selected in a text or combo box by the user. A user can select text for these properties by holding down the Ⓕ key and pressing < or >, or by clicking and dragging the mouse over the desired text. This highlights the selected text. Your program can then read the settings of these properties and perform operations on the selected text. The SelStart property determines the starting point of the selected text within a text or combo box. SelLength determines the number of characters selected. SelText is a string property that contains the selected text. |
| | The SelText property returns a string copy of the selected characters from the text or combo box. This string can be used by your programs to cut and paste to the Windows Clipboard. If no characters are currently selected, this property will return a null string. |

Assigning a string value to this property can cause one of two things to happen. If there is any text selected when the assignment is done, the selected text in the text or combo box is replaced by the assigned text. If no text is selected, the new text is inserted into the text or combo box's text at the box's insertion point.

Figure 44-2 displays a text box with some selected text. In this example, the value of the SelStart property is 8, SelLength is 4, and SelText is "some".

The example syntax copies the selected text to the Clipboard by assigning the value of the SelText property of the text box to the SetText method of the Clipboard, and then copies the selected text to Text2.

Comments   This property also applies to combo boxes and DBCombo boxes whose Style property has been set to 0 (drop-down combo) or 1 (simple combo).

TEXT PROPERTY

Objects Affected   Column, ColumnHeader, ComboBox, DBCombo, DBGrid, DBList, Grid, ListBox, ListItem, Node, Panel, TextBox

Purpose   The Text property reads or sets the text contained in a text box or grid cell, or reads the selected item in a list box or combo box. This property can also be set when used with a combo box or DBCombo box whose Style property is set to 0 (drop-down combo) or 1 (simple combo). The arguments for the Text property are summarized in Table 44-14.

General Syntax

```
[form.]Name.Text [= TextString$]
```

Table 44-14 Arguments of the Text property

Argument	Description
form	Name property of the parent form
Name	Name property of the control
TextString$	A string that can be assigned to this property, and thereby replaces all text in the text box

Example Syntax

```
Command1_Click ()
    Text1.Text = TxtBeforeChange$      'assigns a string to the text box Text1
    SelectedItem$ = List1.Text         'assigns the value of a list box's selected item to a
string
End Sub
```

Description   The Text property is a string that allows your program to access the contents of the edit area of a text or combo box, or the contents of a grid cell. It also can represent a chosen item in a list box.

The Text property also allows you to access and manipulate the text inside a text box. This property is a string representation of the contents of the box, and can be manipulated by any of Visual Basic's string functions and statements, such as Left, Mid, and Right. Any operations performed on this property are reflected by the text inside a text box.

You may assign a string to the Text property. This replaces the text in the box with the assigned string. The user can also directly edit the text represented by the Text property. Anytime a box's Text property is modified, it triggers the box's Change event.

The first example syntax assigns a string to the Text property of text box Text1. This text would then appear in the text box. The second example syntax assigns the text in list box List1 to a string for future use.

Combo and List Boxes and the Grid Control

The Text property is also used with the ComboBox, DBCombo, DBList, and ListBox controls. When used on the drop-down (Style = 0) and simple (Style = 1) combo box styles, this property works in the exact same manner as described previously. When used with the ListBox control or a drop-down list (combo box with Style set to 2), the Text property is read-only, and returns the string value of the selected item in the list.

Individual grid cells also have a Text property (although the grid control itself does not). You cannot directly manipulate grid cells, so the Text property needs to be set with your code. You'd typically have a text box accept the input and then assign the text box's Text property to the grid cell's Text property. Refer to Chapter 46 for more information on list boxes and combo boxes and to Chapter 48, "Grid Controls," for information on grids.

Example

In the Text Box project at the end of this chapter, a multiple-line text box is used to edit text. The Text property of this box is manipulated in several procedures. The length of the Text property is determined in the Change event for the text box, so the number of characters typed can be displayed. In the menuFile(0)_Click event, the Text property is set to an empty string. In the Text1_KeyDown event, the value of the Text property is saved in a string variable, so that it can be restored by the user. When the Undo option is chosen from the Edit menu, the EditUndo_Click event occurs. This event assigns the value of the previously saved string variable to the Text property, thereby restoring its original state.

The Text Box Project

Project Overview

The project outlined in the following pages demonstrates the concepts behind the text box control. This project uses each of the properties covered in this chapter and demonstrates how they work together. By following the examples in this project, you should be able to get a firm grasp on the concepts behind text boxes.

This project makes use of the KeyDown event. This event occurs when the user presses any key on the keyboard. More information can be found on the KeyDown event in Chapter 51, "Keyboard Input." There are also some methods used with the Clipboard object in this project. These methods send or receive text from the Clipboard area of Windows. Refer to Chapter 53 for more on this subject.

Assembling the Project: formMain

1. Create a new form (the Text Box form), and place on it the following controls. Use Table 44-15 to set the properties of the form and each control.

Table 44-15 Elements of the Text Box form

Object	Property	Setting
Form	Name	formMain
	Caption	"Text Box Project"
Label	Name	lablStatus
	Caption	" 0 Characters"
TextBox	Name	textDocument
	Text	"" (Null)
	HideSelection	False
	MultiLine	True
	ScrollBars	2–Vertical

2. Using the Menu Editor window, create a menu with the settings in Table 44-16 (choose the Menu Editor window option from Visual Basic's Tools menu).

Table 44-16 Menu settings for the Text Box project

Name	Caption	Property	Setting
menuBar	&File	Index	0
menuFile	&New	Index	0
menuFile		Index	1
menuFile	E&xit	Index	2

Name	Caption	Property	Setting
menuBar	&Edit	Index	1
menuEdit	&Undo	Index	0
menuEdit		Index	1
menuEdit	Cu&t	Index	2
menuEdit	&Copy	Index	3
menuEdit	&Paste	Index	4
menuEdit	&Delete	Index	5

3. Check the appearance of your form against Figure 44-3.

4. Enter the following code into the General Declarations area of the form. Three module-level variables are created for later use in the program. If the user changes the text in the box, these variables save the contents of the text box just prior to the changes. This information can then be used to later restore the text box to the value it had before the changes were made.

```
Private TxtBeforeChange As String
Private PosBeforeChange As Integer
Private LenBeforeChange As Integer
```

5. Enter the following code into the Form_Resize event. This event occurs when the user changes the size of the form. It adjusts the size of the edit area to match the size of the form.

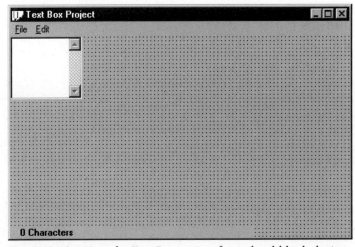

Figure 44-3 How the Text Box project form should look during design

```
Private Sub Form_Resize ()
    textDocument.Height = formMain.ScaleHeight - 250
    textDocument.Width = formMain.ScaleWidth
    lablStatus.Top = textDocument.Height
    lablStatus.Height = 250
    lablStatus.Width = formMain.ScaleWidth
End Sub
```

6. Enter the following code in the menuBar_Click event. This event occurs whenever the user clicks on the top-level menu choices (File and Edit), and completes its processing before the menu is actually pulled down. No special processing happens for the File menu, but the Edit menu needs to be set properly, depending on if text has been selected or if text is available on the Clipboard. The routine first disables all the menu choices (note that menuEdit(1) is a separator bar). It then checks to see if there is any information stored in the undo buffer TxtBeforeChange. If so, it enables the Undo command. It then checks to see if any text has been selected. If so, the Cut, Copy, and Delete commands are enabled. It then checks the Clipboard to see if there is anything there in text format. If so, the Paste command is enabled.

```
Private Sub menuBar_Click (Index As Integer)
    Select Case Index
    Case 0  ' File
    Case 1  ' Edit
        menuEdit(0).Enabled = False      'undo
        menuEdit(2).Enabled = False      'cut
        menuEdit(3).Enabled = False      'copy
        menuEdit(4).Enabled = False      'paste
        menuEdit(5).Enabled = False      'delete
        If Len(TxtBeforeChange) > 0 Then menuEdit(0).Enabled = True 'undo
        If textDocument.SelLength > 0 Then
            menuEdit(2).Enabled = True 'cut
            menuEdit(3).Enabled = True 'copy
            menuEdit(5).Enabled = True 'delete
        End If
        If Clipboard.GetFormat(1) Then menuEdit(4).Enabled = True     'paste
    End Select
End Sub
```

7. Place the following code in the menuEdit_Click command. This event occurs whenever the user chooses a menu choice from the Edit menu. Note that you don't have to worry about inappropriate actions (such as attempting to cut text when there is none selected), because the menuBar_Click routine disables inappropriate menu choices before the menu pulls down.

The Undo command simply resets the Text, SelStart, and SelLength properties back to their old values as set in the Text_Change event. The Cut command places the selected text on the Clipboard, and then sets the selected text to an empty string to delete it. The Copy command places the selected text on the Clipboard (just like the Cut command) but doesn't do anything to the selected text in the text box. The Paste command places whatever text is on the Clipboard into the selected text in the text box. If no text is selected, it places the new text at the insertion point. Finally, the Delete command sets the selected text to an empty string.

```
Private Sub menuEdit_Click (Index As Integer)
    Select Case Index
        Case 0 'undo
            textDocument.Text = TxtBeforeChange
            textDocument.SelStart = PosBeforeChange
            textDocument.SelLength = LenBeforeChange
        Case 2 'cut
            Clipboard.SetText textDocument.SelText
            textDocument.SelText = ""
        Case 3 'copy
            Clipboard.SetText textDocument.SelText
        Case 4 'paste
            textDocument.SelText = Clipboard.GetText(1)
        Case 5 'delete
            textDocument.SelText = ""
    End Select
End Sub
```

8. Place the following code in the menuFile_Click event. This event triggers when the user selects a command from the File menu. Note that menuFile(1) is a separator bar. The New command brings up a password protection dialog box before blanking out the text in the text. It first blanks out any old text in the password text box, and then shows the dialog box. Note that we specify Modal in the Show method; this prevents the rest of the code from continuing until the user closes the dialog box. We've set textPassword's PasswordChar property to an asterisk (*) at design time. Once the user closes the dialog box, we check the password to see if it's acceptable. We've made it especially difficult for hackers to break our security here, as the only acceptable password is anything! If the user has somehow managed to divine our devious password strategy, the routine clears textDocument's text for a new document. If the user falls into our trap and simply presses the Ⓔ key in the password box, the routine calls itself again to force another attempt at the password entry. The Exit command ends the program.

```
Private Sub menuFile_Click (Index As Integer)
    Select Case Index
        Case 0 'new
            formPassword!textPassword.Text = ""
            formPassword.Show 1                         'modal
            If formPassword!textPassword.Text <> "" Then
                                                        'all passwords work!
                textDocument.Text = ""
            Else                                        'User didn't even try, so
                Beep                                    'Bronx cheer.
                menuFile_Click False                    'bad password, try again
            End If
        Case 2 'exit
            End
    End Select
End Sub
```

9. Enter the following code into the textDocument_Change event. This event determines the number of characters in the text box, and displays that information by assigning a string to the Caption property of the label control named lablStatus.

```
Private Sub textDocument_Change ()
    temp = Format$(Len(textDocument.Text), "  ##,###,##0")
    temp = temp + " Character"
    If Len(textDocument.Text) <> 1 Then temp = temp + "s"
    lablStatus.Caption = temp
End Sub
```

10. Enter the following code into the textDocument_KeyDown event. This event saves the current settings of the text box before changes are made. The values of the Text, SelStart, and SelLength properties are assigned to the variables defined in the General Declarations area of the form. The Shift argument is tested to determine whether the user has pressed the Ⓒ or Ⓐ keys. The properties are only saved if the Shift argument indicates that these keys have not been pressed. More information on the KeyDown event can be found in Chapter 51.

```
Private Sub textDocument_KeyDown (KeyCode As Integer, Shift As Integer)
    If Shift < 2 Then
        TxtBeforeChange = textDocument.Text
        PosBeforeChange = textDocument.SelStart
        LenBeforeChange = textDocument.SelLength
    End If
End Sub
```

Assembling the Project: Password Form

1. Create a new form (the TextBox form), and place on it the following controls. Use Table 44-17 to set the properties of the form and each control.

Table 44-17 Elements of formPassword

Object	Property	Setting
Form	BorderStyle	3–Fixed Dialog
	Caption	"Enter Password"
	Name	formPassword
CommandButton	Caption	"OK"
	Default	True
	Name	cmndOK
TextBox	Font	MS Sans Serif, Regular, 12
	Name	textPassword
	PasswordChar	"*" (asterisk)

2. Size and position the controls as shown in Figure 44-4.

Figure 44-4 The password entry dialog box formPassword during design

3. Enter the following code in the cmndOK_Click event. This simply hides the dialog box. Note that we don't unload it, because the File New routine in the main form needs to access the textPassword's Text property to determine if the user entered the correct password.

```
Sub cmndOK_Click ()
      formPassword.Hide
End Sub
```

How It Works

The program created by this project is a simple text editor. The textDocument control is the text entry area of the form. This control is a multiple-line (MultiLine = True) text box with a vertical scrollbar (ScrollBars = 2) on the right edge of the text area. The user can edit text in this control. Portions of text may be selected with the F-S key combination, or by dragging the mouse over the text. The selected text may be cut with F-G, or copied with Q-Ins to the Clipboard, may be deleted G, or may be replaced by text from the Clipboard with F-Ins.

The menuBar control array processes the user's menu clicks before the submenus are pulled down. The File menu doesn't need any further processing, but the Edit menu needs to have its options properly set. The routine first checks to see if any text has been selected; if so, it enables the Cut, Copy, and Delete commands. Paste is enabled if there is any text on the Clipboard, and Undo is enabled if there is anything in the undo variables.

Choosing the New option from the menuFile menu first calls up a password protection dialog box before clearing textDocument. Note that we set the PasswordChar property of the textPassword text box at design time. Choosing Exit causes the program to end.

The menuEdit menu control array provides the editor with the normal Windows edit commands. The Undo option restores the text in the text box to the state it was in before the last time it was changed. For instance, if the user selects and deletes some text, the Undo option can restore the text to its value before the deletion.

The rest of the menuEdit options provide alternative methods for working with the Clipboard. The Cut, Copy, and Delete options are all disabled unless the user has selected some text in the text box. The Cut and Delete options both remove the selected text from the text box. However, Cut copies the selected text to the Clipboard before removing it. The Copy option copies any selected text to the Clipboard. The Paste option on the menuEdit menu copies any text that resides on the Clipboard object into the text box. This option is only enabled if the Clipboard contains text.

Figure 44-5 shows the project in action, with some text selected and the Edit menu pulled down.

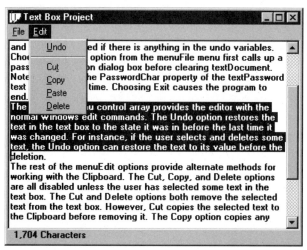

Figure 44-5   The Text Box project in action

45

FONTS

A specific character style, or font, determines the overall appearance of text. Windows comes with a standard set of fonts, and you and your users may obtain additional fonts from a variety of sources. Windows makes all installed fonts available transparently to each program.

Most traditional DOS programs do not allow you to see text on the screen formatted the way it will look when printed. In the Microsoft Windows environment, however, fonts can look exactly the same when printed on any printer as they do when they are displayed on the screen. This WYSIWYG—What You See Is What You Get—feature is one of the major advantages provided by Windows.

Screen and Printer Fonts

There are two general types of fonts in Microsoft Windows: screen and printer fonts. Screen fonts affect the appearance of text on the screen. The Microsoft Windows environment ships with several screen fonts, such as MS Sans Serif, MS Serif, Symbol, and System. Windows may have more screen fonts available if other applications have added them. For instance, Small Fonts and Fences commonly appear on systems with Microsoft application products.

Printer fonts control the look of printed text. A printer font can be either a resident or soft font. Resident fonts are contained in the printer. Soft fonts are located on the computer, and then downloaded to the printer. These older fixed fonts are actually bitmaps representing each character. Although this limits your choice of size, each individual size of bitmap font is hand-tuned to look as perfect as possible in that particular size.

Scalable Fonts

An important group of fonts works equally well on the screen and on the printer. These include the TrueType fonts of Windows (Arial, Courier, Times New Roman, and WingDings), a variety of add-on TrueType fonts, and a multitude of other fonts and font technologies from a variety of vendors like Adobe, BitStream, and Agfa.

These font technologies can scale their fonts to any arbitrary size. Screen and printer fonts, in contrast, come in only specific sizes.

The newer scalable fonts are actually mathematical descriptions of the outline of each character that is then *rasterized* (or converted into a bitmap) and *anti-aliased* (all the "jaggies" have been removed) when needed. This gives Windows the capability to create sharp-looking text at any size on any output device at any resolution. It also makes displayed text look almost exactly the same as printed text.

Points and Font Size

Printing professionals and graphic artists traditionally measure text in points. The point size of a font determines how large or small a text string is on a screen or printed page.

The size of a font is the distance between the top of a capital letter and the bottom of a lowercase descender (see Figure 45-1). Note that different fonts have different visual "weights," which may make them look larger or smaller than the actual size indicates. This is simply an optical illusion. Also note that almost all fonts are proportionally spaced, which means that different letters take up different amounts of horizontal space. For instance, a W takes up more space than an I (see Figure 45-2).

There are 72 points per inch, and 20 twips per point. One of the ScaleMode settings (ScaleMode=2) makes the measurement system points. This may be useful in text-intensive applications, because it allows you to measure in the same units you use to specify text size.

Figure 45-1   The size of a font is the distance between the top of a capital letter and the bottom of a descender

Figure 45-2   Characters in proportionally spaced fonts have different widths

Fonts in Visual Basic

In Visual Basic, you can set the appearance of the text on the screen or the printer to any font and point size available on the system on which the application is running. In versions of Visual Basic prior to Visual Basic 4.0, fonts and font attributes (such as bold and italic) were set in properties attached to objects that display text (such as forms, text boxes, and the Printer object). In Visual Basic 4.0 and later, font attributes are set in the StdFont object, which is accessed through the Font property of objects that display text. To change the Bold property of Form1's StdFont object, for example, you can use this statement:

```
Form1.Font.Bold = True
```

Shared StdFont Objects

Visual Basic gives you the powerful capability of using shared StdFont objects. You can use the Set statement to set one StdFont object equal to another, as shown here:

```
Set Text1.Font = Form1.Font   'make Text1 use the Form1 StdFont object
Form1.Font.Bold = True        'change the bold attribute of both Form1 and Text1
```

This gives you the convenience of setting the font attributes of a number of objects in a single StdFont object. If you set the StdFont objects of a set of objects equal to a shared StdFont object, you can then control the font attributes of all the objects in a single location. The example in the Font property reference entry in this chapter shows you how to do this.

Creating New StdFont Objects

You can use the New keyword to create StdFont objects. You might use a new StdFont object to hold the original settings of the printer object, or to control more than one object's font properties. Here is an example:

```
Dim displayStyle As New StdFont

displayStyle.Bold = True
displayStyle.Italic = False
displayStyle.Name = "Arial"
displayStyle.Size = 10
displayStyle.Underline = False

Set formMain.Font = displayStyle
```

StdFont Properties

The Name and Size properties of the StdFont object determine the font and size of text on a form, control, or Printer object. The Bold, Italic, StrikeThrough, Underline, and Weight properties of the StdFont object add typestyle effects to the text. The Charset property is used to set the types of characters that are displayed.

The Fonts and FontCount properties of the Printer and Screen objects return the names of the fonts and the total number of fonts available for the screen or the printer.

The FontTransparent property determines whether text printed on a form, picture control, or Printer object allows the underlying graphics to show through the text. The FontTransparent property applies to a form, control, or Printer object, and not to the StdFont object.

Fonts Summary

Table 45-1 lists the properties of the StdFont object. Table 45-2 lists the font-related properties of objects that display text.

Table 45-1 Properties of the StdFont object

Use This Property...	To Do This...
Bold	Set or read whether text is boldface
Charset	Set or read the type of characters to display
Italic	Set or read whether text is italic
Name	Set or read the name of the current font
Size	Set or read the point size of the font
StrikeThrough	Set or read whether text has a line drawn through it
Underline	Set or read whether text is underlined
Weight	Set or read the weight (thickness) of the current font

Table 45-2 Font-related properties of objects that display text

Use This Property...	To Do This...
Font	Return an object representing the current font
FontCount	Return the number of fonts available for the screen or active printer
Fonts	Return the names of the fonts available for the screen or active printer
FontTransparent	Set or read whether text includes the background graphics

The following pages examine the properties in Tables 45-1 and 45-2 in detail. The Font project at the end of this chapter pulls all of these items together in a comprehensive demonstration of how to use them.

BOLD PROPERTY

Objects Affected   StdFont

Purpose   The Bold property determines whether the text controlled by a StdFont object is boldface. When it is boldface, the text appears thicker and darker. Properties of a StdFont object may be modified at runtime or at design time (using the Font dialog box). Figure 45-3 shows the Font dialog box. Any changes made to the Bold property of a StdFont object associated with a form, picture box, or Printer object only affect the appearance of text drawn after the alteration. Any changes made to the Bold property of a StdFont object associated with a control always alter the appearance of any text placed within the control's Caption or Text properties. Tables 45-3 and 45-4 list the arguments and settings of the Bold property.

General Syntax

```
[form.]Font.Bold [ = state%]
[form!]Name.Font.Bold [ = state%]
Printer.Font.Bold [ = state%]
FontObject.Bold [ = state%]
```

Table 45-3 Arguments of the Bold property

Argument	Description
form	Name property of the form
Name	Name property of a control
FontObject	Name property of a StdFont object
Printer	Printer indicates the Printer object
state%	Current setting of Bold property

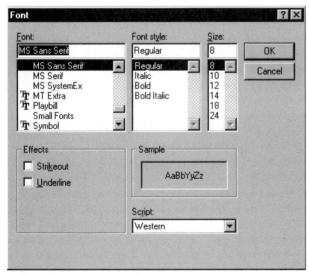

Figure 45-3   Font dialog box

Table 45-4 Settings of the state% variable of the Bold property

state%	Description
True	Text on the indicated object is bold.
False	Text on the indicated object is not bold.

Example Syntax

```
Private Sub Form_Load ()

    Dim objFont As New StdFont      'create a StdFont object

    Set Font = objFont              'set the form StdFont object = ObjFont

    AutoRedraw = True               'property is redrawn each time it is uncovered
    objFont.Size = 8                'initial setting of text is 8-pt
    objFont.Name = "Arial"          'defines name of font
    ForeColor = QBColor(0)          'black text
    BackColor = QBColor(15)         'white background
    For i = 1 To 10                 'generate the following code 10 times
        objFont.Bold = Not objFont.Bold 'toggle the Bold property
        If objFont.Bold = False Then     'checks if Bold is False
            t$ = "Normal"           'defines text string
            objFont.Size = objFont.Size + 1.8      'increments point size by 1.8
        Else
            t$ = "Bold"                 'defines text string
        End If
        mess$ = "This is " + Font.Name + " "       'displays the text on the screen
        mess$ = mess$ + Str$(Font.Size)
        mess$ = mess$ + "pt " + t$
        Print mess$
    Next i

    Set objFont = Nothing 'clear the object

End Sub
```

Description   The Bold property of a StdFont object affects the appearance of the text on any object associated with that StdFont object. StdFont objects can exist independently of any control or form, so setting Bold to a StdFont object that is not associated with an object will have no effect until the StdFont object is used. The Bold expression ends with a Boolean expression of either True or False. This property defaults to False, meaning that text is not bold, but normal weight text. True can have two possible effects. On forms, picture boxes, and Printer objects, the True setting makes only new text bold. Text contained in the Caption and Text properties of controls is immediately affected by changes made to the Bold property of a StdFont object.

In the example syntax, text is printed on the form in both normal and bold format. Figure 45-4 shows approximately what should display on your screen.

Figure 45-4 Example syntax
demonstrates difference between bold
and normal fonts

**Italic,
StrikeThrough,
and Underline**

There are three other special effect font properties in Visual Basic. These
properties are Italic, StrikeThrough, and Underline. More than one of
these properties may be set in the same object, combining the typestyle
effects.

Example

The Font project at the end of this chapter demonstrates the use of the
Bold property. When the check box labeled Bold is clicked with the
mouse, the chekBold_Click event triggers. Each time this event is
processed, the text on the textSample text box is switched from bold to
normal or from normal to bold.

Comments

Notice that a bold text string needs a larger display space. Be careful to
ensure that enough space is provided for bold as well as normal text. Also
note that some font families do not include a bold font. If this is the case,
setting Bold to True does not change the displayed or printed font.

CHARSET PROPERTY

Objects Affected StdFont

Purpose The Charset property determines the character set used to display the text
controlled by a StdFont object. The character set in an integer value that
may indicate that the characters to be displayed are standard Windows
characters, symbol characters, Double Byte Character Set characters
(DBCS), or other sets of characters supported by the font. Any changes
made to the Charset property of a StdFont object associated with a form,
picture box, or Printer object only affect the appearance of text drawn after

the alteration. Any changes made to the Charset property of a StdFont object associated with a control always alter the appearance of any text placed within the control's Caption or Text properties. Tables 45-5 and 45-6 list the arguments and settings of the Charset property.

General Syntax

```
[form.]Font.Charset [ = charSetID%]
[form!]Name.Font.Charset [ = charSetID%]
Printer.Font.Charset [ = charSetID%]
FontObject.Charset [ = charSetID%]
```

Table 45-5 Arguments of the Charset property

Argument	Description
form	Name property of the form
Name	Name property of a control
FontObject	Name property of a StdFont object
Printer	Printer indicates the Printer object
charSetID%	Current setting of character set property

Table 45-6 Common settings of the charSetID% variable of the CharSet property

charSetID%	Description
0	Standard Windows characters
2	Symbol characters
128	DBCS characters (used in Far Eastern versions of Windows)
255	MS-DOS Extended ASCII characters
other integer	Font-supported character set value

Example Syntax

```
Private Sub Form_Load ()

    Dim objFont As New StdFont        'create a StdFont object

    Set Font = objFont                'set the form StdFont object = ObjFont

    AutoRedraw = True                 'property is redrawn each time it is uncovered
    objFont.Size = 8                  'initial setting of text is 8-pt
    objFont.Name = "Arial"            'defines name of font
    ForeColor = QBColor(0)            'black text
    BackColor = QBColor(15)           'white background

    objFont.Charset = 0               'Windows characters
    Print "These are Windows characters:";
```

```
For i=128 to 192
    Print Chr$(i);
Next i
Print

objFont.Charset = 255            'MS-DOS characters
Print "These are MS-DOS characters:";

For i=128 to 192
    Print Chr$(i);
Next i
Print

Set objFont = Nothing 'clear the object

End Sub
```

Description The Charset property of a StdFont object affects the appearance of the text on any object associated with that StdFont object. StdFont objects can exist independently of any control or form, so setting Charset to a StdFont object that is not associated with an object will have no effect until the StdFont object is used. The Charset expression ends with an integer value representing the character set with which the font is to be drawn. This property defaults to 0, meaning that text is drawn using the standard Windows character set. On forms, picture boxes, and Printer objects, setting the Charset property of its associated Font makes only new text be drawn with the new character set. Text contained in the Caption and Text properties of controls is immediately affected by changes made to the Charset property of a StdFont object.

FONT PROPERTY

Objects Affected AmbientProperties, CheckBox, ComboBox, CommandButton, Data, DBCombo, DBGrid, DBList, DirListBox, DriveListBox, FileListBox, Form, Frame, Grid, Label, ListBox, ListView, OptionButton, PictureBox, Printer, PropertyPage, StatusBar, TabStrip, TextBox, TreeView, UserControl, UserDocument

Purpose The Font property returns the StdFont object associated with a form, control, or the Printer object. Properties of the StdFont object associated with a form or control may be set at runtime or at design time using the Font dialog box. Figure 45-3 shows the Font dialog box. Any changes made to any property of a StdFont object associated with a form, picture box, or Printer object only affect the appearance of text drawn after the alteration. Any change made to any property of a StdFont object associated with a control always changes the appearance of any text placed within the control's Caption or Text properties. Table 45-7 lists the arguments of the Font property.

You can control the font attributes of a set of objects by setting the properties of a StdFont object shared by the set of objects. When you change the properties of the shared StdFont object, the font attributes of all the objects that share the StdFont object will change.

General Syntax

```
[form.]Font [ = FontObject]
[form!]Name.Font [ = FontObject]
Printer.Font [ = FontObject]
```

Table 45-7 Arguments of the Font property

Argument	Description
form	Name property of the form
Name	Name property of a Control
FontObject	Name property of a StdFont object
Printer	Printer indicates the Printer object

Example Syntax

```
Private Sub Form_Load()
'load all the font names for the screen
'into the listbox
For I = 0 To Screen.FontCount - 1
    lstFont.AddItem Screen.Fonts(I)
Next I

'using the controls collection, update the
'controls in the form to share the form's font
'object
For Each cntl In Form5.Controls
    Set cntl.Font = Me.Font
Next
'NOTE: using the controls collection makes
'updating each control easy. Generally, you'd
'want to verify the control you're updating
'is a valid control for what you're doing

End Sub

Private Sub lstFont_Click()
'set the form font's name to the name selected
'in the listbox.  Note that all the controls on
'the form switch to that font, because the form and
'all the controls are sharing the form's StdFont object


Font.Name = lstFont.List(lstFont.ListIndex)
Caption = Font.Name 'show the current font name
End Sub
```

Description   The Font property of a form, control, or Printer object sets or returns a StdFont object that affects the appearance of the text on that object. Setting the Font property (or setting properties of the StdFont object returned by the Font property of a form, picture box, or the Printer object), only affects text written on the object after the Font property has been changed. For controls other than the picture box, setting the Font property (or properties of the StdFont object returned by the Font property) affects the text on the control immediately.

In the example syntax, a list box is loaded with all the fonts for the screen. The Font property of all controls on the screen are set to the Font property of the parent form. As fonts are selected in the list box, the Name property of the form's StdFont object is set to that font name. Because all the controls on the form and the form itself share one StdFont object, all the control's fonts are changed along with the form's font. Figure 45-5 shows approximately what should display on your screen.

The StdFont Object
The Font property returns a StdFont object that controls all the font characteristics of the parent object. The Font property and StdFont object are new additions to the language. All changes to font characteristics should be made through the StdFont object's properties.

Example
The Font project at the end of this chapter demonstrates the use of the Font property. When a font is selected from the combo box that holds the list of fonts, the Name property of formMain's Font property is set to the selected font.

FONTCOUNT PROPERTY

Objects Affected   Printer, Screen

Purpose   The FontCount property indicates the number of printer or screen fonts available, depending on whether you specify the Screen or Printer object. For screen fonts, the value returned encompasses all the Windows screen fonts as well as scalable fonts. For the printer, the value specifies the

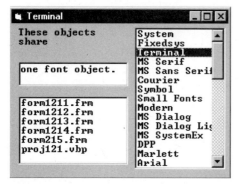

Figure 45-5   Example syntax demonstrates one way to use the Font property

number of fonts that may be placed on a Printer object, including all resident and soft fonts as well as scalable fonts. You may only access the FontCount property at runtime, not design time. Used together, the FontCount and Fonts properties produce a list of the names of the possible fonts. Table 45-8 lists the arguments of the FontCount property.

General Syntax

```
Printer.FontCount
Screen.FontCount
```

Table 45-8 Arguments of FontCount property

Argument	Description
Printer	Printer indicates the Printer object
Screen	Screen indicates the Screen object

Example Syntax

```
Private Sub Form_Load ()
    lblPrinterFonts = "There are " & Printer.FontCount & " Printer fonts"
    lblScreenFonts = "There are " & Screen.FontCount & " Screen Fonts"
End Sub
```

Description

The FontCount property indicates the number of fonts available on the system where the application is running. If a FontCount property is preceded by the word Screen, then this property provides the number of screen fonts and scalable fonts. With the word Printer, the value calculated by the FontCount property includes all of the resident and soft fonts as well as scalable fonts. This property, available for reference at runtime only, will only change if fonts are added or removed. Most system configurations have a different number of fonts available for the screen and printer.

In the example syntax, the FontCount property provides the number of fonts available for the screen and the printer. These numbers are then printed in the Text1 and Text2 text boxes. Figure 45-6 shows what this form might look like on the screen. The actual number of fonts depends on your setup, and be aware that the numbers may not match.

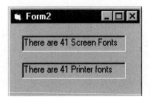

Figure 45-6 Sample screen and printer font count

Fonts Property	Using the Fonts and FontCount properties together provides a list of the names of the available fonts. The FontCount property provides the total number of font names that the Fonts property returns. Each value between 0 and (FontCount-1) will provide the name of one of the fonts available for the screen or printer. Remember not to mix the results from the screen and printer, or the list may not be accurate.
Example	In the Font project at the end of this chapter, the Fonts property generates a list of the fonts available on the system. The FontCount property works with the Fonts property to provide the names of the fonts in string format. At program startup, these properties function together to fill the contents of the cmboFont combo list box. Pressing the command button labeled Display Fonts produces a list of the system fonts on the formFontList form.
Comments	In some configurations, a list of screen or printer fonts may include more than one entry for a particular font.

FONTS PROPERTY

Objects Affected	Printer, Screen
Purpose	The Fonts property provides the name of one of the available fonts of the screen or printer, depending on which of these objects you specify and which font number you use. Exactly which value stands for which font is determined by the system. This property may change whenever the active printer is changed to another printing device with different fonts or a new font is added to the system with the Windows Control Panel. A combination of the FontCount and Fonts properties produces a list of the names of the possible fonts. Table 45-9 lists the arguments of the Fonts property.

General Syntax

```
Printer.Fonts(index%)
Screen.Fonts(index%)
```

Table 45-9 Arguments of Fonts property

Argument	Description
Printer	Printer indicates the Printer object
Screen	Screen indicates the Screen object
index%	Value that represents a screen or printer font

Example Syntax

```
Private Sub Form_Load ()
    AutoRedraw = -1                         'turns on AutoReDraw
    For I = 0 To (Screen.FontCount - 1)     'displays all of the fonts
        FontName = Screen.Fonts(I)          'changes font
        Print Screen.Fonts(I)               'prints the font name
    Next I
End Sub
```

Description

The Fonts property provides the names of an available system font specified by the index number, which must be between 0 and one less than the value of the FontCount property. The FontCount property indicates the total number of fonts available for either the Screen or Printer object. Using Screen with the Fonts property returns all screen and scalable fonts; using Printer returns all soft and resident printer fonts as well as scalable fonts. This property is only available for reference at runtime and will only change if fonts are added to or removed from the system. Most configurations provide a different font name for the same number used with the Screen and Printer objects.

In the example syntax, the Fonts property serves as a means of printing the names of the available screen fonts on the form. A For loop controls the repeated invocation of the Fonts property for each font number from 0 to one less than the value of the FontCount property. These font names are printed in the font indicated by the font name. Figure 45-7 shows what this list might look like. If the Screen object is changed to Printer, this list may be different.

FontCount Property

Using the Fonts and FontCount properties together provides a list of the names of the available fonts. The FontCount property returns the total number of fonts available. Each Fonts index value between 0 and (FontCount-1) will provide the name of one of the fonts available for the display or printer. Remember not to mix up the results from the screen and printer, or the list may not be accurate. In the example, the FontCount property provides the maximum number of screen fonts available.

Example

In the Font project at the end of this chapter, the Fonts property gives a list of the names of the fonts available on the system. The FontCount property works with the Fonts property to provide the names of the fonts in string format. At program startup, these properties function together to fill the contents of the cmboFont combo list box. Pressing the command button labeled Display Fonts produces a list of the system fonts on the pictList picture box.

Comments

With some system configurations, a list of screen or printer fonts may include more than one entry for a particular font.

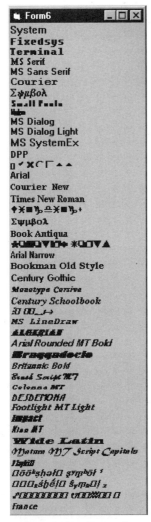

Figure 45-7 Example syntax shows list of available screen fonts

FontTransparent Property

Objects Affected   Form, PictureBox, Printer, PropertyPage, UserControl, UserDocument

Purpose   The FontTransparent property indicates how the text on a form, picture box, or Printer object interacts with the graphics beneath it. When it is made transparent, the graphics show through underneath the text. When text is nontransparent, a block of the background color surrounds the text, obscuring portions of the graphics beneath. This property can be modified at either design time or runtime. Any changes made to the FontTransparent property of a form or Printer object only affect the appearance of text drawn after the change. Tables 45-10 and 45-11 list the arguments of the FontTransparent property.

General Syntax

```
[form.]FontTransparent [ = state%]
[form!]Name.FontTransparent [ = state%]
Printer.FontTransparent [ = state%]
```

Table 45-10 Arguments of FontTransparent property

Argument	Description
form	Name property of the form.
Name	Name property of the picture box.
Printer	Printer indicates the Printer object.
state%	Current setting of FontTransparent property.

Table 45-11 Settings of the state% variable of the FontTransparent property

state%	Description
True	Text on the object lets underlying graphics show through.
False	Underlying graphics are obscured by the space around the text.

Example Syntax

```
Private Sub Picture1_Click ()

    Picture1.Font.Name = "Arial"                        'use Arial font
      Picture1.Font.Size = 20                           'sets the font size to 20
    Picture1.Print "Text on graphics"                   'prints message on the
                                                        'picture box
    Picture1.FontTransparent = Not Picture1.FontTransparent 'toggles the setting
End Sub
```

Description

The FontTransparent property determines what happens when graphics and text share the same space on a form or Printer object. If an object name is not provided, the parent form is assumed.

A FontTransparent property statement ends with a Boolean value of either False or True. This property defaults to False, which indicates that the text placed on the object obscures the underlying graphics. True means that underlying graphics show through the background of the text. Changing this property does not affect any previously placed text.

In the example syntax, the text either obscures or becomes part of the underlying graphics each time the user clicks the form. Figure 45-8 shows what the two options look like.

Example   The Font project at the end of this chapter demonstrates the FontTransparent property's effects. The Display Fonts command button brings up a form with the pictList picture box on it. A list of all available screen fonts gets drawn on the list over a gray box that was previously drawn on the picture box. Clicking the picture box toggles the FontTransparent property back and forth to demonstrate its effects.

Comments   The FontTransparent property controls the appearance of the background around the text, not the text itself. Note that FontTransparent is associated directly with a form, picture box, or Printer object. It is not a property of the StdFont object.

ITALIC PROPERTY

Objects Affected   StdFont

Purpose   The Italic property determines whether the text controlled by a StdFont object appears as italic type. When it is italic, the text is slanted, or script-like. Properties of a StdFont object can be modified at runtime, or at design time using the Font dialog box. Figure 45-3 shows the Font dialog box. Changes made to the Italic property of a StdFont object associated with a form, picture box, or Printer object only affect the appearance of text drawn after the property has changed. However, any change made to the Italic property of a StdFont object associated with a control always

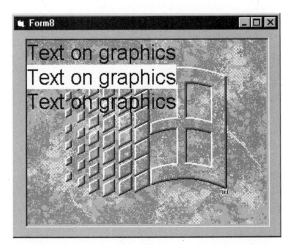

Figure 45-8   Example syntax shows transparent and opaque text backgrounds

changes the appearance of any text placed in the control's Caption or Text properties. Tables 45-12 and 45-13 list the arguments and settings of the Italic property.

General Syntax

```
[form.]Font.Italic [ = state%]
[form!]Name.Font.Italic [ = state%]
Printer.Font.Italic [ = state%]
FontObject.Italic [ = state%]
```

Table 45-12 Arguments of the Italic property

Argument	Description
form	Name property of the form
Name	Name property of a control
FontObject	Name property of a StdFont object
Printer	Printer indicates the Printer object
state%	Current setting of Italic property

Table 45-13 Settings of the state% variable of the Italic property

state%	Description
True	Text on the indicated object is italic.
False	Text on the indicated object is not italic.

Example Syntax

```
Private Sub Form_Load()
Font.Size = 12 'make the printing bigger

AutoRedraw = True   'turn on AutoRedraw
Font.italic = True 'Turn on Italic for the form's
                   'font object.
Print "This is Italic " & Font.Name

Font.italic = False 'turn italic off
Print "This is Normal " & Font.Name

End Sub
```

Description

The Italic property of a StdFont object affects the appearance of the text on any object associated with that StdFont object. StdFont objects can exist independently of any control or form, so setting Italic on a StdFont object that is not associated with a control, form, or Printer object will have no visible effect until the StdFont object is used. The Italic expression ends with a Boolean expression of either True or False. This property defaults to False, meaning that text is not italic. True can have two possible effects.

On forms, picture boxes, and Printer objects, the True setting makes only new text italic. Text contained in the Caption and Text properties of a control is immediately affected by changes made to the Italic property of the StdFont object.

In the example syntax, text is printed on the form in both normal and italic. Figure 45-9 shows approximately what should appear on your screen.

Bold, StrikeThrough and Underline   There are three other special effect font properties in Visual Basic. These properties are Bold, StrikeThrough, and Underline. More than one of these properties may be set to the same object, combining the effects. For instance, when the Bold and Italic properties are both True, the text on the object is bold and italic.

Example   The Font project at the end of this chapter demonstrates the use of the Italic property. When the check box labeled Italic is clicked with the mouse, the chekItalic_Click event is fired. Each time this event is processed, the text on the textSample text box is switched from italic to normal or from normal to italic.

Comments   Some fonts are unaffected by the Italic property, either because there is no italic version of the font, or because the font is inherently italic (like Zapf Chancery).

NAME PROPERTY

Objects Affected   StdFont

Purpose   The Name property determines the font used by the StdFont object. Any text displayed on the object uses the font specified by the Name property of the StdFont object. Properties of a StdFont object can be modified at runtime, or at design time using the Font dialog box. Figure 45-3 shows the Font dialog box. Any changes made to the Name property of a StdFont object associated with a form, picture box, or Printer object only affect the appearance of text drawn after the property has changed. Changes made to the Name property of a StdFont object associated with a control always affect the appearance of any text placed within the control's Caption or Text properties. Table 45-14 lists the arguments of the Name property.

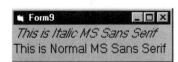

Figure 45-9   Example syntax demonstrates difference between italic and normal fonts

General Syntax

```
[form.]Font.Name [ = font$]
[form!]Control.Font.Name [ = font$]
Printer.Font.Name [ = font$]
FontObject.Name [ = font$]
```

Table 45-14 Arguments of the Name property

Argument	Description
form	Name property of the form
Control	Name property of a control
FontObject	Name property of a StdFont object
Printer	Printer indicates the Printer object
Name	Name of the font displayed
font$	Current setting of Name property

Example Syntax

```
Private Sub Form_Load()

Dim i% ' build a work variable
    AutoRedraw = True    'turn on AutoRedraw

    'load the list box with the screen fonts
    For i = 0 To Screen.FontCount - 1
        list1.AddItem Screen.Fonts(i)
    Next i

    Label1.Caption = Label1.Font.Name & " currently displaying"
End Sub

Private Sub list1_Click()

    Label1.Font.Name = list1.List(list1.ListIndex)
    Label1.Caption = Label1.Font.Name & " currently displaying"

End Sub
```

Description   The Name property of a StdFont object sets or returns the font associated with the StdFont object. StdFont objects can exist independently of any control or form, so setting Name on a StdFont object that is not associated with a control, form, or Printer object will have no visible effect until the StdFont object is used. Each form, control, and Printer object can have its own font, so you can associate different fonts with different objects. You can easily share StdFont objects between different controls and forms by setting the StdFont object of each control or form to the same StdFont object. Once you've done that, when you change the shared StdFont object, all controls, forms, and Printer objects that share the StdFont object will reflect the change.

In the example syntax, all the screen fonts are loaded into List1. As you click List1, Label1's StdFont object is changed to reflect the selected font. Figure 45-10 shows approximately what should display on your screen.

Example   In the Font project at the end of this chapter, the Name property modifies the appearance of an object's text. Selecting a new font name from the cmboFont combo box triggers the cmboFont_Click event, which then sets the Name property of the StdFont object of the textSample text box. Pressing the Display Fonts command button changes the Name property of the StdFont object associated with the pictList picture box for each line of the font list.

SIZE PROPERTY

Objects Affected   StdFont

Purpose   The Size property of the StdFont object determines the point size of text controlled by the StdFont object. Properties of a StdFont object can be modified at runtime or at design time using the Font dialog box. Figure 45-3 shows the Font dialog box. Changes made to the Size property of a StdFont object associated with a form, picture box, or Printer object only affect the appearance of text drawn after the property has changed. However, any change made to the Size property of a StdFont object associated with a control always changes the appearance of any text placed in the control's Caption or Text properties. Each system's configuration controls the default setting of the Size property. If you set the Size property to an invalid size for the current font, Windows will reset the Size property to

Figure 45-10   Example syntax demonstrates selecting a font from the screen fonts

the closest valid size. Third-party font generators, such as the Adobe Type Manager, can also change the default setting of the FontSize property. Table 45-15 lists the arguments of the Size property.

General Syntax

```
[form.]Font.Size [ = points!]
[form!]Name.Font.Size [ = points!]
Printer.Font.Size [ = points!]
FontObject.Size [ = points!]
```

Table 45-15 Arguments of the Size property

Argument	Description
form	Name property of the form
Name	Name property of a control
FontObject	Name property of a StdFont object
Printer	Printer indicates the Printer object
points!	Value that represents the size of letters on an object

Example Syntax

```
Private Sub Form_Load()

    AutoRedraw = True
    Font.Name = "Arial" 'change to a prettier font

    'print the size and font on the form
    Print "Printing "; Font.Name & " at " & _
        Format$(Font.Size) & " Points"

End Sub

Private Sub HScroll1_Change()

    Font.Size = HScroll1.Value 'set the size
    Cls ' clear the form

    'update the form
    Print "Printing "; Font.Name & " at " _
        & Format$(Font.Size) & " Points"

End Sub
```

Description

The Size property of the StdFont object changes the size of text. Define Size expressions with a single-precision number up to 2048, which indicates the size of the text in points. The display device chooses the point size closest to the one you selected to display the font.

It usually makes no difference in what order you set the Name, Bold, Italic, and Size properties. TrueType fonts smaller than 8 points should be handled in a specific order, however. Windows actually uses a different font (internally) for these small TrueType fonts, so specify Size first, then Name, then set the size again with Size.

In the example syntax, the Size property of the StdFont object of Form1 gets set as the scrollbar is dragged back and forth. The form is cleared, and the current Size and Name properties of the StdFont object are printed on the form. Notice that Figure 45-11 shows 15.75 points, even though the scrollbar only returns integer values in HScroll1.Value.

Example   In the Font project at the end of this chapter, the Size property modifies the size of an object's text. When a new point size is chosen from the combo box cmboSize, the cmboSize_Click event changes the Size property of the textSample text box. This changes the text on the text box to the new size.

Comments   Any change to the Size property of a control immediately affects the existing text set with the Text or Caption properties. This means that all the text in the Text or Caption properties must be the same point size.

STRIKETHROUGH PROPERTY

Objects Affected   StdFont

Purpose   The StrikeThrough property determines whether the text controlled by a StdFont object appears with a line drawn through it. Legal documents often use strikethrough text to indicate superseded or eliminated language. Strikethrough is also used to indicate editorial deletions. Properties of a StdFont object may be modified at runtime or at design time using the Font dialog box. Figure 45-3 shows the Font dialog box. Any changes made to the StrikeThrough property of a StdFont object associated with a form, picture box, or Printer object only affect the appearance of text drawn after the alteration. Any change made to the StrikeThrough property of a StdFont object associated with a control always changes the appearance of text placed within the control's Caption or Text properties. Tables 45-16 and 45-17 list the arguments and settings of the StrikeThrough property.

General Syntax

```
[form.]Font.StrikeThrough [ = state%]
[form!]Name.Font.StrikeThrough [ = state%]
Printer.Font.StrikeThrough [ = state%]
FontObject.StrikeThrough [ = state%]
```

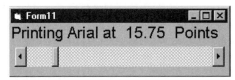

Figure 45-11   Example syntax demonstrates the Size property

Table 45-16 Arguments of the StrikeThrough property

Argument	Description
form	Name property of the form.
Name	Name property of a control.
FontObject	Name property of a StdFont object.
Printer	Printer indicates the Printer object.
state%	Current setting of StrikeThrough property.

Table 45-17 Settings of the state% variable of the StrikeThrough property

state%	Description
True	Text on the indicated object is StrikeThrough.
False	Text on the indicated object is not StrikeThrough.

Example Syntax

```
Private Sub Form_Load()
    Font.Size = 12 'make the printing bigger

    AutoRedraw = True   'turn on AutoRedraw
    Font.StrikeThrough = True 'Turn on StrikeThrough for the Form's
                              'font object.
    Print "This is StrikeThrough " & Font.Name

    Font.StrikeThrough = False 'turn StrikeThrough off
    Print "This is Normal " & Font.Name
End Sub
```

Description The StrikeThrough property of a StdFont object affects the appearance of the text on any object associated with that StdFont object. StdFont objects can exist independently of any control or form, so setting the StrikeThrough property on a StdFont object that is not associated with a control, form, or Printer object will have no visible effect until the StdFont object is used. The StrikeThrough expression ends with a Boolean expression of either True or False. This property defaults to False, meaning that text is not strikethrough. True can have two possible effects. On forms, picture boxes, and Printer objects, the True setting makes only new text strikethrough. Text contained in the Caption and Text properties of controls is immediately affected by changes made to the StrikeThrough property of a StdFont object.

In the example syntax, text is printed on the form in both normal and strikethrough. Figure 45-12 shows approximately what should appear on your screen.

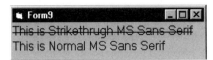

Figure 45-12   Example syntax demonstrates difference between strikethrough and normal fonts

Bold, Italic, and Underline   There are three other special effect font properties in Visual Basic: Bold, Italic, and Underline. More than one of these properties can be set in the same object, combining the typestyle effects.

Example   The Font project at the end of this chapter demonstrates the use of the StrikeThrough property. When the check box labeled StrikeThrough is clicked with the mouse, the chekStrikeThrough_Click event triggers. Each time this event is processed, the text on the textSample text box is switched from strikethrough to normal or from normal to strikethrough.

UNDERLINE PROPERTY

Objects Affected   StdFont

Purpose   The Underline property determines whether the text controlled by a StdFont object is underlined. Properties of a StdFont object can be modified at runtime or at design time using the Font dialog box. Figure 45-3 shows the Font dialog box. Any changes made to the Underline property of a StdFont object associated with a form, picture box, or Printer object only affect the appearance of text drawn after the property has changed. However, any change made to the Underline property of a StdFont object associated with a control always changes the appearance of any text placed within the control's Caption or Text properties. Tables 45-18 and 45-19 list the arguments and settings of the Underline property.

General Syntax

```
[form.]Font.Underline [ = state%]
[form!]Name.Font.Underline [ = state%]
Printer.Font.Underline [ = state%]
FontObject.Underline [ = state%]
```

Table 45-18 Arguments of the Underline property

Argument	Description
form	Name property of the form
Name	Name property of a control
FontObject	Name property of a StdFont object
Printer	Printer indicates the Printer object
state%	Current setting of Underline property

Table 45-19 Settings of the state% variable of the Underline property

state%	Description
True	Text on the indicated object is underlined.
False	Text on the indicated object is not underlined.

Example Syntax

```
Private Sub Form_Load()
    Font.Size = 12 'make the printing bigger

    AutoRedraw = True  'turn on AutoRedraw
    Font.Underline = True 'Turn on Underline for the form's
                          'font object.
    Print "This is Underline " & Font.Name

    Font.Underline = False 'turn Underline off
    Print "This is Normal " & Font.Name
End Sub
```

Description
The Underline property of a StdFont object affects the appearance of the text on any object associated with that StdFont object. StdFont objects can exist independently of any control or form, so setting the Underline property on a StdFont object that is not associated with a control, form, or Printer object will have no visible effect until the StdFont object is used. The Underline expression ends with a Boolean value of either True or False. This property defaults to False, meaning that text is not underlined. True can have two possible effects. On forms, picture boxes, and Printer objects, the True setting makes only new text underlined. Text contained in the Caption and Text properties of controls is immediately affected by changes made to the Underline property of a StdFont object.

In the example syntax, text is printed on the form in both normal and underline. Figure 45-13 shows approximately what will appear on your screen.

Bold, Italic, and StrikeThrough
There are three other special effect font properties in Visual Basic. These properties are Bold, Italic, and StrikeThrough. More than one of these properties may be set in the same object, combining the typestyle effects.

Example
The Font project at the end of this chapter demonstrates the use of the Underline property. When the user clicks the check box labeled

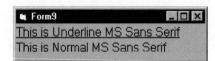

Figure 45-13 Example syntax demonstrates difference between underline and normal fonts

Underline, the chekUnderline_Click event is fired. Each time this event is processed, the text on the textSample text box is switched from underline to normal or from normal to underline.

Comments   The Underline property underlines all characters, including blank spaces.

WEIGHT PROPERTY

Objects Affected   StdFont

Purpose   The Weight property determines how dark the text controlled by a StdFont object appears. The Weight properties of a StdFont object can be modified only at runtime. Depending on the weights supported by a particular font, you can set Weight to a value from 0 to 1000. The weight for normal and italic text is 400, and for bold and bold italic text is 700. For some fonts, if you set the Weight property to a value other than 400 or 700, then Weight will reset itself to 400 or 700—whichever is closer to the value you specified. Any changes made to the Weight property of a StdFont object associated with a form, picture box, or Printer object affect the appearance of text drawn only after the property has changed. However, any change made to the Weight property of a StdFont object associated with a control always affects the appearance of any text placed in the control's Caption or Text properties. Table 45-20 lists the arguments of the Weight property.

General Syntax

```
[form.].Font.Weight [ = weight%]
[form!]Name.Font.Weight [ = weight%]
Printer.Font.Weight [ = weight%]
FontObject.Weight [ = weight%]
```

Table 45-20 Arguments of the Weight property

Argument	Description
form	Name property of the form
Name	Name property of a control
FontObject	Name property of a StdFont object
Printer	Printer indicates the Printer object
weight%	Current setting of Weight property

Example Syntax

```
Private Sub Form_Load()
Font.Name = "Arial"
Font.Size = 12

End Sub
```

continued on next page

continued from previous page

```
Private Sub HScroll1_Change()
Font.Weight = HScroll1.VALUE
Cls
Print "Printing "; Font.Name; " at "; Font.Weight; " Points"
End Sub
```

Description   The Weight property of a StdFont object affects the appearance of the text on any object associated with that StdFont object. StdFont objects can exist independently of any control or form, so setting the Weight property on a StdFont object that is not associated with a control, form, or Printer object will have no visible effect until the StdFont object is used. The Weight property only takes on valid values as set by the display system. If you attempt to use an invalid value, Windows resets Weight to the nearest valid value. Text contained in the Caption and Text properties of controls is immediately affected by changes made to the Weight property of a StdFont object.

In the example syntax, a horizontal scrollbar is used to set the Weight property. Although the scrollbar ranges from 0 to 1000, Weight will only take on the values of 400 or 700. 400 is the default weight for a normal or italic font, and 700 is the normal weight for a bold or bold italic font. Figure 45-14 shows approximately what should appear on your screen.

Bold, Italic,   There are four special effect font properties in Visual Basic. These proper-
Underline, and   ties are Bold, Italic, Underline, and StrikeThrough. More than one of these
StrikeThrough   properties can be set in the same object, combining the typestyle effects.

Example   The Font project at the end of this section demonstrates the use of the Weight property. When the check box labeled Weight is clicked with the mouse, the chekWeight_Click event triggers. Each time this event is processed, the Weight of the text on the textSample text box is switched from 700 to 400 or from 400 to 700.

The Font Project

Project Overview

The Font project demonstrates the properties that affect the appearance of text in Visual Basic. This example will show the interaction of the properties affecting the

Figure 45-14   Example syntax demonstrates setting the Weight property

text's appearance. By manipulating the different controls of this project, you will see all of the fonts available for your system. Exactly what you will see depends upon what fonts you have installed in your system.

This project has two sections, corresponding to the two forms that comprise the Font project. The first section deals with the assembly of the controls and subroutines of the Font form. The second section explains the formFontList form's subroutine. Each of these sections includes step-by-step instructions on how to put the form and its controls together and the different elements of code to enter. After both forms are explained, there is a How It Works guide to the operation of the project. Please read this information carefully and use the pictures of the forms as guides in the process of assembling this project.

Assembling the Project: The Font Project Form

1. Make a new form (the Font form) with the objects and properties shown in Table 45-21.

Table 45-21 Elements of the Font form

Object	Property	Setting
Form	BorderStyle	1–Fixed Single
	Caption	"Font Project"
	MaxButton	False
	Name	formMain
	FontTransparent	False
TextBox	Name	textSample
ComboBox	Name	cmboFont
	Sorted	True
ComboBox	Name	cmboSize
Frame	Caption	"Special Effects"
	Name	framEffects
CheckBox	Caption	&Bold
	Name	chekBold
	Value	0–Unchecked
CheckBox	Caption	&Italic
	Name	chekItalic
	Value	0–Unchecked
CheckBox	Caption	&StrikeThrough
	Name	chekStrikethru
	Value	0–Unchecked
CheckBox	Caption	&Underline
	Name	chekUnderline

continued on next page

continued from previous page

Object	Property	Setting
	Value	0—Unchecked
CommandButton	Caption	&Display Fonts
	Name	cmndDisplay
CommandButton	Caption	E&xit
	Name	cmndExit

2. Size the objects on the screen as shown in Figure 45-15.

3. Enter the following code in the chekBold event subroutine. This code triggers when the user clicks the check box labeled Bold. When the check box has a check in it, the text in the text box textSample changes to bold. Otherwise, the text in the text box is normal.

```
Private Sub chekBold_Click ()
   textSample.Font.Bold = Not textSample.Font.Bold
End Sub
```

4. Enter the following code in the chekItalic_Click event subroutine. This code triggers when the user clicks the check box labeled Italic. When there is an X in the check box, the text in the text box textSample is changed to italics. Otherwise, the text in the text box is normal.

```
Private Sub chekItalic_Click ()
   textSample.Font.Italic = Not textSample.Font.Italic
End Sub
```

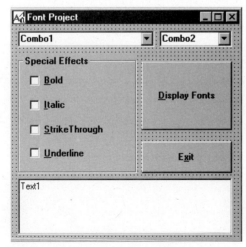

Figure 45-15   What the formMain form should look like when completed

5. Enter the following code in the chekStrikethrough_Click event subroutine. This code triggers when the user clicks the check box labeled StrikeThrough. When there is an X in the check box, the text in the text box textSample has a line placed through it. Otherwise, the text in the text box is normal.

```
Private Sub chekStrikethru_Click ()
    textSample.Font.Strikethrough = Not textSample.Font.Strikethrough
End Sub
```

6. Enter the following code in the chekUnderline_Click event subroutine. This code triggers by the clicking of the check box labeled Underline. When there is an X in the check box, the text in the text box textSample is underlined. Otherwise, the text in the text box is normal.

```
Private Sub chekUnderline_Click ()
    textSample.Font.Underline = Not textSample.Font.Underline
End Sub
```

7. Enter the following code in the cmboFont_Click event subroutine. This code triggers when the user selects another choice in the combo box cmboFont. The FontName property of the textSample text box is modified to match the font selected in the combo box, and changes the text to the name of the font.

```
Private Sub cmboFont_Click ()
    textSample.Font.Name = cmboFont.Text
    textSample.Text = cmboFont.Text
End Sub
```

8. Enter the following code in the cmboSize_Click event subroutine. This code activates when the user changes the number displayed in the cmboSize combo box. The FontSize property of the textSample text box changes to match the point size indicated in the combo box. Note that it then resets the combo box to exactly display the correct size of the font, which is often very slightly different from what is specified.

```
Private Sub cmboSize_Click ()
    textSample.Font.Size = Val(cmboSize.Text)
    cmboSize.Text = Str(textSample.Font.Size)
End Sub
```

9. Enter the following code in the cmndDisplay_Click event subroutine. This code activates when the user presses the cmndDisplay command button. After the user presses this button, formMain is hidden and formFontList is displayed. Note that we first load formFontList; this gives it time to build and print the font list before actually displaying it.

```
Private Sub cmndDisplay_Click ()
    formMain.Hide           'hide this form
    Load formFontList       'load the font list form, don't display
    formFontList.Show       'and display after the form has had a chance to create list
End Sub
```

10. Enter the following code in the cmndExit_Click event subroutine. This code triggers when the user presses the Exit command button.

```
Private Sub cmndExit_Click ()
    End
End Sub
```

11. Enter the following code in the Form_Load event subroutine. The Form_Load event is processed at program startup. This code places the names of all of the fonts available in the present system into the cmboFont combo box. The cmboSize combo box displays a list of the possible point sizes between 4 and 36.

```
Private Sub Form_Load ()
    For F = 0 To (Screen.FontCount - 1)      'iterate through all screen fonts
        cmboFont.AddItem Screen.Fonts(F)     'add the font name to the combo box
    Next F
    For P = 4 To 36                          'iterate through some common point sizes
        cmboSize.AddItem Str$(P)             'and add point size to the combo box
    Next P
    cmboFont.Text = textSample.Font.Name     'set the combo box to the default font
    cmboSize.Text = Str(textSample.Font.Size) 'make combo box read the correct font size
End Sub
```

Assembling the Project: The formFontList Form

1. Make a new form with the objects and properties listed in Table 45-22.

Table 45-22 Elements of the formFontList form

Object	Property	Setting
Form	BorderStyle	3–Fixed Dialog
	Caption	"Font List"
	Name	formFontList
	ScaleMode	2–Point
Label	Caption	"Transparent"
	Name	lablTransparent
Picture	Name	pictContainer
	Appearance	0–Flat
	ScaleMode	2–Point
Picture	Name	pictList
	Appearance	0–Flat
	ScaleMode	2–Point
VScroll	Name	scrlUpDown
CommandButton	Name	cmndClose
	Caption	Close

2. Size the objects on the screen as shown in Figure 45-16. Note that pictList must be drawn completely within pictContainer to make it a child of pictContainer.

3. Enter the following code in the cmndClose_Click event subroutine. When the user clicks the mouse button over the formFontList form, the formFontList form is hidden and the formMain form is displayed.

```
Private Sub cmndClose_Click ()
    formFontList.Hide          'hide this form
    formMain.Show              'show the main form again
End Sub
```

4. Enter the following code in the Form_Load event subroutine. This code triggers when the formFontList form first loads. This routine first sets the pointer to an hourglass (processing the font list will take a while!). It then sets the dimensions of pictList to completely fill pictContainer, and makes it tall enough to fit the entire font list. Then it sets the scrollbar properties to enable the scrolling of the entire list. It then draws a gray box on pictList to help demonstrate the FontTransparent property later. Finally, it iterates through all screen fonts and displays them on pictList.

```
Private Sub Form_Load ()
    Screen.MousePointer = 11                      'hourglass
    pictList.Font.Size = 18                       '18 points
    fontsLength = Screen.FontCount * pictList.TextHeight("Test")    'height of entire font
                                                  'list
    pictList.Top = 0                              'make list flush with container's top
    pictList.Left = 0                             'make list flush with container's left
    pictList.Width = pictContainer.ScaleWidth     'make list flush with container's right
    pictList.Height = fontsLength                 'make list as long as entire font list
    scrlUpDown.Min = 0                            'display top of list
    scrlUpDown.Max = pictList.Height - pictContainer.Height    'length of entire list
    scrlUpDown.LargeChange = scrlUpDown.Max / 50  '1/50th of total list
    scrlUpDown.SmallChange = scrlUpDown.Max / 250 '1/250th of total list
    pictList.Cls                                  'clear the list
    pictList.FillStyle = vbSolid                  'solid fill
    pictList.FillColor = QBColor(7)               'light gray
    pictList.AutoRedraw = True                    'repaint automatically when uncovered
    pictList.Line (0, 0)-(pictList.ScaleWidth, pictList.ScaleHeight), _ QBColor(7), BF
    pictList.CurrentX = 0                         'reset coordinates to left
    pictList.CurrentY = 0                         '  ""      ""      top
    For I = 0 To Screen.FontCount - 1             'iterate through all screen fonts
        pictList.Font.Name = Screen.Fonts(I)      'change list's font
        pictList.Print Screen.Fonts(I)            'and print the name of the font
    Next I
    Screen.MousePointer = vbNormal                'set hourglass back to normal
            End Sub
```

5. Enter the following code in the pictList_Click event. This event flips the transparency setting of the list, and resets the label accordingly. It then scrolls to the top of the list, and calls the Form_Load procedure to redraw the list.

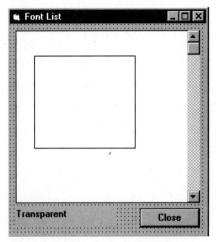

Figure 45-16   What formFontList
should look like during design

```
Private Sub pictList_Click ()
    pictList.FontTransparent = Not pictList.FontTransparent 'switch transparency setting
    If pictList.FontTransparent = True Then      'and tell user what the setting is
        lablTransparent = "Transparent"
    Else
        lablTransparent = "Opaque"
    End If
    scrlUpDown.Value = 0                         'go to top of the list
    Form_Load                                    'and redraw the list
End Sub
```

6. Enter the following code in the scrlUpDown_Change event. This event triggers
whenever the scrollbar changes value, whether it be by the user moving the
thumb, clicking the arrows, clicking the gray areas, or by code setting the value.
It scrolls pictList up and down. The pictContainer picture box contains pictList,
and clips the much longer pictList.

```
Private Sub scrlUpDown_Change ()
    pictList.Top = -scrlUpDown.Value          'scroll the list up or down
End Sub
```

How It Works

This program provides a form that allows the user to see how the different fonts of a
system look. The text displayed in the textSample text box changes according to the
settings of the cmboFont and cmboSize combo boxes. Each of the check boxes labeled
Bold, Italic, StrikeThrough, and Underline define whether the text appears with these
special effects. Pressing the command button labeled Display Fonts produces a list of
the available system screen fonts.

When the program loads, the Form_Load event uses the FontCount property to find how many fonts are available in the system. The FontCount property and Fonts property provide the values to place the names of the system's fonts in the cmboFont combo box. Notice that the Sorted property changes the order in which the names appear in this combo box. This is helpful, because the list returned by the multiple use of the Fonts property is not in alphabetical order. (You can see the actual order of the fonts in the Display Fonts dialog box brought up by the Display Fonts command button.)

The Size property is the default setting of the cmboSize combo box. This shows the point size of the text in the textSample text box. If this is not done, then the combo box cmboSize would be initially blank. Notice that many of the values of the Size property are fractions.

Running the Program

The settings of the check boxes marked Bold, Italic, StrikeThrough, and Underline reflect the appearance of the textSample text box. When a check box is checked, the format of the text in the textSample text box changes. These instructions are contained within the Click event subroutine of each check box.

Each time the user selects a new font or point size, the text in the text box changes to this new setting. This shows the ways in which the point size and font interact with each other. Figure 45-17 shows what the main form looks like when running.

The Fonts, FontCount, and Name properties are all accessed to display a list of fonts when the user presses the command button Display Fonts. This list prints on the pictList on the formFontList form. Each font name appears in the font that it names. For some fonts, such as all-symbol fonts like WingDings, this makes the font name unreadable. The pictList picture box is contained within the pictContainer picture box. That means that no matter how big pictList is, it will always be clipped at the

Figure 45-17   What the main form will look like when running

boundaries of pictContainer. That lets you scroll pictList up and down very easily with the scrollbar scrlUpDown.

The pictList picture box has a gray background drawn on it. Each time pictList is clicked, the FontTransparent property changes and the list is regenerated. When the FontTransparent property is True (as it is initially), the text displays directly on the gray background, as Figure 45-18 illustrates. When FontTransparent is False, each font name has an opaque background that obscures the gray background, as Figure 45-19 illustrates.

Figure 45-18   What formFontList looks like with FontTransparent set to True

Figure 45-19   What formFontList looks like with FontTransparent set to False

PART VII
LISTS

46
LIST AND COMBO BOXES

Visual Basic provides several powerful controls for presenting lists from which users can choose options such as colors, styles, fonts, or even data records. Selection lists can even be combined with text input to give the user the choice of selecting a listed item or typing in the name of some other choice. One style of list box, three styles of combo boxes, and the powerful grid control provide you with a variety of tools for presenting a list of choices or displaying information to the user. The Grid control is described in further detail in Chapter 48, "Grid Controls."

Visual Basic lets you bind list and combo boxes to a data control. The standard list box and combo box controls have DataSource and DataField properties so you can bind their values to a database through a data control. Also, Visual Basic includes additional DBList and DBCombo controls that provide enhanced data awareness, beyond the features offered by the standard controls. You should understand the differences between the various data aware controls when choosing which features are important to a particular application. Although the standard controls can be bound, they have much more limited binding features than the new data bound controls. However, if an application requires that you use lists or combos in an unbound manner, the standard controls discussed in this chapter are the appropriate choices.

List Boxes

The list box contains a list of items that have been defined by the program. The user may choose an item from a list box by clicking on it, or by using the up and down arrow keys to move the highlight bar to the desired item and then pressing E. If there are more items in the list than can be displayed in the list box, Visual Basic will automatically add a scrollbar on the right edge of the list box. The user can then scroll up and down the list quickly with the mouse or the PAGEUP and PAGEDN keys.

Combo Boxes

Combo boxes, as the name implies, provide a combination of the list box and the text box objects. All combo boxes have an edit area and a list area. The currently selected item from the list displays in the edit area of a combo box. The list area appears below the edit area, and when visible, acts in the same manner as a list box. There are three styles of combo boxes: the drop-down combo, the simple combo, and the drop-down list.

The drop-down combo box displays the currently selected item in an edit area similar to that of a text box. A down arrow is displayed to the right of the edit area. The list portion of this combo box stays hidden until the user clicks the down arrow, causing the list of items to drop down. The user may either choose an item from the list, or type an entry in the edit area.

The simple combo box also has an edit area in which the currently selected item is displayed. The list portion of this combo box is always visible under the edit area. As with the drop-down combo, the user may either choose an item from the list or type an entry in the edit area.

The drop-down list box is similar in structure to the drop-down combo box. As with the drop-down combo, the list area stays hidden until the user clicks on the down arrow. However, the user cannot edit the text in the edit area, but can only choose an item from the list portion of the drop-down list.

The types of list and combo boxes are summarized in Table 46-1.

Table 46-1 Types of list and combo boxes

Use This Type of Box...	To Do This...
Simple list box	Present a list of items for selection
Drop-down combo	Let user type in a selection, or open a list from which to make a selection
Simple combo	Let user type in a selection, or select from a list that is always visible
Drop-down list box	Let user accept displayed selection, or open a list for a different selection

Using List and Combo Boxes

List and combo boxes are quite similar to work with. When you first create a list or combo box, there are no items in the control's list. Items need to be added to a control's list from within your program's code. This is done with the AddItem method. Visual Basic keeps track of how many items have been added to a list, and places that number in the ListCount property. Items may be deleted from a list with the RemoveItem method. When this is done, the ListCount property is automatically updated to reflect that an item has been removed.

The lists of these controls are quite similar to one-dimensional string arrays. Each entry is assigned an index number when it is added to the list. Your program can specify the index number of an item when it is added, or Visual Basic can automatically assign the index number. The string value of each listed entry can be read by your program with the List property. Your program supplies an index number to this property, which returns a string copy of the listed item specified by the index. Note that multi-column list boxes are still a one-dimensional array. The data snakes from column to column; the list box does not have different kinds of information in each column. Use the grid control for that.

A list or combo box allows your program to determine the user's choice from a list of items. The ListIndex and Text properties are used to determine which item in the list the user has selected. The ListIndex property returns the index number of the selected item, while the Text property returns a string copy of the selected item. The Selected property lets you determine if a list item is selected in a multiple-selection list box.

The standard list box and combo box controls allow you to use the DataSource and DataField properties to bind the control to a properly initialized data control. Unlike the DBList and DBCombo controls, the standard controls only allow for the controls' selection to be bound to the data source. The contents of the lists are formed using the AddItem method. The list contents cannot be obtained from the data control. The DataSource and DataField properties of the list box and combo box controls work much like those of the other standard data aware controls such as text boxes and labels.

List and Combo Boxes Summary

Table 46-2 displays the methods, events, and properties that influence the settings and effects of the list box and combo box controls. For information on Grid controls, refer to Chapter 48.

Table 46-2 Methods, events, and properties dealing with list and combo boxes

Use or Set This...	Type	To Do This...
AddItem	Method	Add items to the list or combo box
Change	Event	Invoked when the contents of a combo box's text box have changed
Clear	Method	Clear all items from a list or combo box
Column	Property	Set or return the number of columns in a list box
DataChanged	Property	Read or set whether the data has changed within the list or combo box
DataField	Property	Specify the field in a record set to which the list box or combo box is bound
DataSource	Property	Specify the data control to which a list box or combo box is bound
DropDown	Event	Initiate an action when a drop-down box is opened
IntegralHeight	Property	Read or set whether the list or combo box displays partial items
ItemCheck	Event	Invoked when an item within a list box with check box items has been checked or unchecked
ItemData	Property	Read or set an associated data item with the list entry
List	Property	Set or return the text in a list entry in a list or combo box
ListCount	Property	Return the number of items in a list or combo box
ListIndex	Property	Set or return the index number of the selected item in a list or combo box
MultiSelect	Property	Set or return if a list box allows for multiple selections
NewIndex	Property	Determine the ListIndex value of the newest added item in a list or combo box
RemoveItem	Method	Remove an item from a list, combo box, or grid

continued on next page

continued from previous page

Use or Set This...	Type	To Do This...
SelCount	Method	Return the number of selected items in a MultiSelect list box
Selected	Property	Return the selection status of listed items in a MultiSelect list box
SelLength	Property	Return the number of characters selected in a combo box's text box
SelStart	Property	Return the starting position of the selected text in a combo box's text box
SelText	Property	Return the selected text in a combo box's text box
Sorted	Property	Sort the items in a list or combo box
Style	Property	Set the style of a combo box
Text	Property	Return the selected item in a list or combo box
TopIndex	Property	Read or set the topmost row which is visible to the user

Constant Values

It is usually best to use named constants rather than numeric values when developing software. Named constants make your code more readable and easier to maintain.

Tables 46-3 and 46-4 list the values of the constants relevant to this chapter, mentions their names, and briefly describes what they mean. These constants can be viewed using the Object Browser. It is not necessary to explicitly add these objects to your project.

Table 46-3 Constants module values for list boxes

Value	Constant Name	Meaning
0	vbListBoxStandard	The standard list box with text items
1	vbListBoxCheckbox	A list box containing text items with check boxes

Table 46-4 Constants module values for combo boxes

Value	Constant Name	Meaning
0	vbComboDropDown	Lets user type in a selection, or open a list from which to make a selection
1	vbComboSimple	Presents a list of items for selection
2	vbComboDropDownList	Lets user accept displayed selection, or open a list for a different selection

The following pages describe the use of the methods, events, and properties that enable you to set up and manage the various types of list and combo boxes. The Lists and Combos project at the end of the chapter demonstrates how these list management techniques are used together.

ADDITEM METHOD

Objects Affected   ComboBox, Grid, ListBox

Purpose   The AddItem method adds an item to the list of a list or combo box. Table 46-5 summarizes the arguments of the AddItem method.

General Syntax

`[form!]Name.AddItem Item$ [, Index%]`

Table 46-5 Arguments of the AddItem method

Argument	Description
form	Name of the control's parent form
Name	Name of the list or combo box
Item$	A string expression containing the value that is being added to the list
Index%	An optional index number specifying the placement of the new item in the list

Example Syntax

```
Private Sub Form_Load ()
    List1.AddItem "Red"        'add color names to a list box
    List1.AddItem "Blue"
    List1.AddItem "Yellow"
    List1.AddItem "Green"
    List1.AddItem "Purple"
End Sub
```

Description   When the list box and combo box objects first display, no items are assigned to the list. You must use the AddItem method to create list entries. When the AddItem method executes, the value of the string expression specified by the Item$ argument is added to the list.

You can specify the exact placement of the new item in the list by providing the Index% argument. If you supply the index number, Visual Basic will add one to the index number of the item that currently holds the specified index, and all those items that follow it. The new item is then added to the list at the specified index (see Figure 46-1). Supplying an index number inserts the new item at that position in the list. It does not replace the item that is currently at that position.

If you supply the index number, it must be no less than 0 and no greater than the value of the ListCount property. If the index specified is not in this range, Visual Basic issues an Illegal function call error.

The index numbering of the list is zero-based. Therefore, if a list contains five items, the first item is index number 0, and the highest index number is 4. Most often, the AddItem method is used in the Form_Load event of the parent form to initialize the list entries. This ensures the list is loaded before the user has access to the list or combo box.

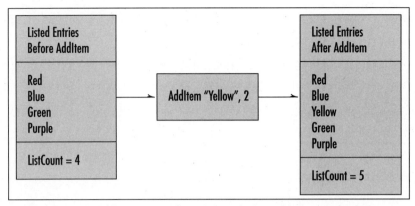

Figure 46-1   Specifying a specific index with the AddItem method

If you omit the index argument, Visual Basic assigns the next available index number to the new item. In other words, if there are five items in the list, the highest index number will be 4. Therefore the next available index number will be 5.

The example syntax adds five color names to a list box. Assuming nothing was added previously, "Red" will have index 0, "Blue" index 1, and so on. Figure 46-2 shows how this list box looks when loaded.

Example   The Form_Load event in the Lists and Combos project uses the AddItem method to initialize several combo boxes with their settings. Each time the user specifies a new financial scenario, the combIncome_DropDown event adds the new scenario to the combo box. Finally, for each new set of values, the NewValues subroutine adds a record of the calculation to the listHistory list box.

Comments   It is recommended that the Index% argument of the AddItem method not be used with a list or combo box that has the Sorted property set to True. This may cause the sort order of the list to be corrupted.

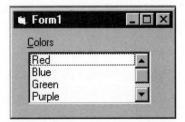

Figure 46-2   Example syntax uses the AddItem method to load the list box

CHANGE EVENT

Objects Affected	ComboBox, DBCombo, DBGrid, DirListBox, DriveListBox, HScrollBar, Label, PictureBox, Slider, TextBox, Toolbar, VScrollBar
Purpose	The Change event is triggered when the contents of a combo box are changed either from user interaction or the program changing the Text property of the combo box. Table 46-6 summarizes the argument of the CellSelected property.

General Syntax

```
Sub Name_Change ()
```

Table 46-6 Argument of the Change event

Argument	Description
Name	Name property of the combo box control

Example Syntax

```
Private Sub Combo1_Change ()
    Text1.Text = Combo1.Text
End Sub
```

Description	Handle the change event for a combo box if you need notification of whenever the value in the combo box's text box has changed. You can retrieve the string contained within the combo box using its Text property. Note: Only combo boxes which have a Style property equal to vbComboDropDown (0) or vbComboSimple (1) will generate this event. To capture the change of selection within a combo box that has a Style property equal to vbComboDropDownList (2), use the Click event.

CLEAR METHOD

Objects Affected	Buttons, Clipboard, ColumnHeaders, ComboBox, DataObject, DataObjectFiles, ErrObject, ListBox, ListImages, ListItems, Nodes, Panels, Tabs
Purpose	The Clear method clears all the items from a list or combo box using a statement. The Clipboard also has a Clear method, which is discussed in more detail in Chapter 53, "Using the Clipboard." Table 46-7 gives the arguments of the Clear method.

General Syntax

```
[form!]Name.Clear
```

Table 46-7 Arguments of the Clear method

Argument	Description
form	Name of the parent form
Name	The name of the combo box or list box

Example Syntax

```
Private Sub Command1_Click ()
    List1.Clear
End Sub
```

Description The Clear method gives you an easy way to completely clear a list box or combo box. Using the Clear method also saves time compared to removing each item individually and makes your application perform better.

COLUMNS PROPERTY

Objects Affected DBGrid, ListBox, Split

Purpose The Columns property lets you scroll a list box horizontally rather than vertically. Note that the list box is still a one-dimensional array; use the grid control if you need a two-dimensional array. Columns defaults to 0 (vertical scrolling). Numbers greater than 0 make it scroll horizontally, with the number indicating the number of columns. Entries will snake automatically from column to column. Table 46-8 summarizes the arguments of the Columns property.

General Syntax

```
[form!]Name.Columns [= number%]
```

Table 46-8 Arguments of the Columns property

Argument	Description
form	Name of the parent form
Name	Name of the list box
number%	Number of columns

Example Syntax

```
Private Sub Form_Load ()
    numFonts = Screen.FontCount            'how many fonts?
    numColumns = Int((numFonts + 25) / 25) 'break into reasonable # of columns
    List1.Columns = numColumns             'make enough columns
    For i = 0 To numFonts                  'and fill list box
        List1.AddItem Screen.Fonts(i)      'horizontally scrolling
        List2.AddItem Screen.Fonts(i)      'vertically scrolling
    Next i
End Sub
```

Description The Columns property lets you scroll a list box horizontally rather than vertically if you wish. It defaults to 0, meaning you get a familiar vertically scrolling list box. Setting number% to something greater than 0 gives that many columns. The width of each column is automatically set to the width of the list box divided by the number of columns. Items snake from column to column, filling each column in sequence from left to right.

The number of columns may not change from 0 to anything else, or from anything else to 0 at runtime. That is, you can never convert a vertically scrolling list box into a horizontally scrolling list box. However, you may change the number of columns in a horizontally scrolling list box, as the example syntax shows. Figure 46-3 compares a horizontally and vertically scrolling list box.

Example The Lists and Combos project at the end of this chapter uses vertically scrolling list boxes (columns = 0).

DATACHANGED PROPERTY

Objects Affected CheckBox, Column, ComboBox, DataBinding, DBCombo, DBGrid, DBList, Image, Label, ListBox, OLE Container, PictureBox, TextBox

Purpose The DataChanged property is used to indicate whether or not the data within a combo box or list box has changed. This property is both readable and writable at runtime. It is not available at design time. Table 46-9 summarizes the arguments of the Columns property.

General Syntax

```
[form!]Name.DataChanged [= boolean%]
```

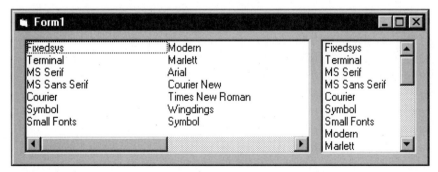

Figure 46-3 Example syntax compares horizontally and vertically scrolling list boxes

Table 46-9 Arguments of the Columns property

Argument	Description
form	Name of the parent form
Name	Name of the control
boolean%	A Boolean indicating whether or not the data has changed

Example Syntax
```
Private Sub Command1_Click ()
    If Combo1.DataChanged Then
        Text1.Text = Combo1.Text
    End If
End Sub
```

Description   The DataChanged property is used to indicate whether or not the data within a control has changed. You typically use it to determine whether a control's data has changed or to force the updating of a bound control. When you set the DataChanged property to True, controls that are bound to this control are automatically notified of the change.

DataField Property

Objects Affected   CheckBox, Combo, DBCombo, DBGrid, DBList, Image, Label, ListBox, OLE Container, PictureBox, TextBox

Purpose   The DataField property specifies what field a particular control will bind to in the database. The developer sets the DataSource property to bind the control to an appropriately initialized data control. The DataField property then specifies which field in the specified data control's RecordSet will be displayed in the bound control. This property is available both read and write at runtime or design time.

General Syntax

```
Combo1.DataField = sFieldName$
```

Example Syntax
```
Private Sub SetDataSettings()

    Data1.Databasename = "C:\MSACCESS\CLIENT.MDB"
    Data1.RecordSource = "Customers"

    'set the list box to display the customer name data from the data control
    List1.DataSource = Data1
    List1.DataField = "CustomerName"

    Data1.Refresh

End Sub
```

Description   The DataField property is always used in conjunction with the DataSource property to bind a data aware control to a data control on a form. The data control must reside on the same form as the object being bound and must be properly initialized to allow for binding. Initializing consists of setting a valid database name and a valid record source for the data control. At runtime you may need to use the data control's Refresh method to establish the link to the database and activate the binding of the data aware controls.

If the DataSource and DataField properties are not set for the data aware control, the control can be used unbound. You can use both list boxes and combo boxes in applications without binding them to the data control. Often, even in database applications, developers choose to not use the data control. In such cases, the list box and combo box controls remain valuable user interface elements. They are available read and write at runtime so you can use them with data access objects or other means of data storage.

DATASOURCE PROPERTY

Objects Affected   CheckBox, ComboBox, DataBinding, DBCombo, DBGrid, DBList, Image, Label, ListBox, MaskedEdt, PictureBox, ProgressBar, RichTextBox

Purpose   The DataSource property specifies the data control to which the bound control is attached. The DataField property then specifies which field in the specified data control's record set is displayed in the bound control. Both properties are available both read and write at runtime or design time.

```
General Syntax
Combo1.DataSource = Data1
```

Description   The DataSource property is always used in conjunction with the DataField property to bind a data aware control to a data control on a form. The data control must reside on the same form as the object being bound and must be properly initialized to allow for binding. Initializing consists of setting a valid database name and a valid record source for the data control. At runtime, you may need to use the data control's Refresh method to establish the link to the database and activate the binding of the data aware controls.

If the DataSource and DataField properties are not set for the data aware control, the control can be used unbound. You can use both list boxes and combo boxes in applications without binding them to the data control. Often, even in database applications, developers choose to not use the data control. In such cases, the list box and combo box controls remain valuable user interface elements. They are available read and write at runtime to allow for use with data access objects or other means of data storage.

DROPDOWN EVENT

Objects Affected	ComboBox, DBCombo
Purpose	The DropDown event specifies what actions will be taken when the user opens the list portion of a drop-down combo box. This provides your program with an opportunity to tailor the list entries based on information that may not have been available at an earlier time, such as the activity the user is performing or preferences previously expressed by the user. Table 46-10 summarizes the arguments of the DropDown event.

General Syntax

```
Sub Name_DropDown([Index As Integer])
```

Table 46-10 Arguments of the DropDown event

Argument	Description
Name	Name of the control
Index	A unique number that identifies a specific element in a control array

Example Syntax

```
Private Sub Title_DropDown()
    If UserSecurity > 100 then          'if this is a high level user
        If Title.ListCount = 4 then
            Title.AddItem "Manager"     'add Manager title to list if not yet added
        End if
    End If
End Sub
```

Description	The combo box control used with the DropDown event must be either a drop-down combo box (Style = 0) or drop-down list box (Style = 2). In drop-down boxes, the list portion of the control is not visible until the user opens it by clicking on its scroll arrow. When this happens, the control's DropDown event triggers. The code in this event executes before the user can choose from the items in the list.
	The example syntax adds an item (the title "Manager") to the list box if the user's security level is high enough. This is an example of how the DropDown event can be used to tailor the choices offered by the program to the circumstances of the user.
Control Array	The Index argument is only used if the related control is part of a control array. This index specifies which element of the array is the one that activated the event. When referencing the control, the element being referenced must be specified by placing the index number between parentheses just after the control name, and before the property name (that is, Name(Index).Property).

INTEGRALHEIGHT PROPERTY

Purpose   The IntegralHeight property lets you allow a list box or combo box to display partial rows within its list. Table 46-11 summarizes the arguments of the ItemData property.

General Syntax

```
[form!]Name.IntegralHeight [= boolean%]
```

Table 46-11 Arguments of the IntegralHeight property

Argument	Description
form	Name property of the form
Name	Name property of the list or combo box
boolean%	True indicates the list will only display full rows; False indicates that it will display partially visible rows

Example Syntax

```
Private Sub Form_Load ()
    List1.IntegralHeight = False 'Allow display of partially visible rows
End Sub
```

Description   You can use the IntegralHeight property to set whether or not a list box or combo box can display partially visible rows. If IntegralHeight is set to True, the list box may resize itself in the vertical direction to only display full rows within it. This property is available at design time and is readable and writable at runtime.

Example   The Lists and Combos project at the end of this chapter uses the IntegralHeight property to allow the list and combo boxes to display partially visible rows.

ITEMCHECK EVENT

Objects Affected   ListBox

Purpose   The ItemCheck event is triggered when a check box associated with a list box row in a checkbox list box has changed its check value. Table 46-12 summarizes the arguments of the ItemCheck event.

General Syntax

```
Sub Name_ItemCheck (Item As Integer)
```

Table 46-12 Arguments of the ItemCheck event

Argument	Description
Name	Name property of the list box control
Item	The row number of the item whose check box has changed

Example Syntax

```
Private Sub List1_ItemCheck (Item As Integer)
    If List1.Selected(Item) == True Then
        Text1.Text = "Row #" & Item & " checked"
    Else
        Text1.Text = "Row #" & Item & " unchecked"
    End If
End Sub
```

Description   Handle the ItemCheck event for a list box if you need notification of whenever the value in the list box row's check box has changed. You can determine whether a particular item is checked or unchecked via the Selected property. The example syntax demonstrates the handling of this event and checking whether or not the specified list box item is checked or unchecked.

ITEMDATA PROPERTY

Purpose   The ItemData property lets you associate a numeric item of data with a displayed value in a list. This can save you the step of having to create an array to hold the data items. Table 46-13 summarizes the arguments of the ItemData property.

General Syntax

```
[form!]Name.ItemData(index%) [ = expression&]
```

Table 46-13 Arguments of the ItemData property

Argument	Description
form	Name property of the form
Name	Name property of the list or combo box
index%	Unique identifier of the item's list index position
expression&	Value to associate with the list item

Example Syntax

```
Private Sub Form_Load ()
    Combo1.AddItem "No Growth"
    Combo1.ItemData(Combo1.NewIndex) = 0
    Combo1.AddItem "Good Growth"
```

```
    Combo1.ItemData(Combo1.NewIndex) = 3
    Combo1.AddItem "Great Growth"
    Combo1.ItemData(Combo1.NewIndex) = 8
End Sub
```

Description   You can use the ItemData property to associate a number with a displayed
value in a list. This might save you from having to create an array to store
the associated values. The example syntax associates various numeric
growth rates with a displayed description of that growth rate.

Note the use of the NewIndex property in the example syntax. Items in a
sorted list may be added anywhere in the list to keep it sorted. The
NewIndex property returns the index position of the last added item.

LIST PROPERTY

Objects Affected   ComboBox, DirListBox, DriveListBox, FileListBox, ListBox

Purpose   The List property has two functions. First, it can set the value of a list
entry in a list or combo box—that is, specify an item to be displayed on a
list. Second, it can read the current value (contents) of a list entry from a
list or combo box. This property cannot be set at design time.

The List property is also used with the drive, directory, and file list box
controls. For a description of how this property is used with these controls, please refer to Chapter 47, "File, Directory, and Drive Boxes."

Table 46-14 summarizes the arguments of the List property.

General Syntax

```
[form!]Name.List(Index%) [= Value$]
```

Table 46-14 Arguments of the List property

Argument	Description
form	Name of the control's parent form
Name	Name of the list or combo box
Index%	The index number of the desired list entry
Value$	A string expression that can be assigned to the list entry

Example Syntax

```
Private Sub Command1_Click ()
    List1.List(1) = "Hello there"      'assigns the string to list entry #1
    FirstItem$ = List1.List(0)         'assigns value of the first listed item to a string
End Sub
```

Description	The List property sets or returns a list's contents in a manner similar to accessing values from and assigning values to an array. The List property begins with the name of the affected list or combo box control. It is followed by an index number in parentheses, which identifies which list entry is being referenced. Optionally, an equal sign and a value can be added to assign the specified value to the list entry.

The index numbering of the list is zero-based. Therefore, if a list contains five items, the first item is index number 0, and the highest index number is 4. The number of items in a list can be determined by using the ListCount property.

When using the List property to assign text to a list entry, the program must use an index number that references an item currently in the list. For instance, if a list has five items in it, the program can only use an index number from 0 to 4 when assigning a value to a list entry, or an "Invalid property array index" error will occur. Your program can determine the highest current index number by subtracting 1 from the value of the ListCount property.

When you use the List property to read list entries, the contents of the list entry specified by the index are returned. Specifying an index that is out of the range of added entries will return a null string.

In the example code, the first statement assigns the string "Hello there" to item 1 in the list for box List1. Note that 1 is actually the second item in the list. The second statement assigns the value of the first item listed in the list (which is index 0) to the string variable FirstItem$.

LISTCOUNT PROPERTY

Objects Affected	ComboBox, DirListBox, DriveListBox, FileListBox, ListBox
Purpose	The ListCount property is read at runtime to determine the number of listed items in a list or combo box. This is a read-only property, and cannot be set by the program at design time or runtime.

The ListCount property is also used with the drive, directory, and file list box controls. For a description of how this property is used with these controls, please refer to Chapter 47.

Table 46-15 summarizes the arguments of the ListCount property.

General Syntax

```
[form!]Name.ListCount
```

Table 46-15 Arguments of the ListCount property

Argument	Description
form	Name of the parent form
Name	Name of the list or combo box

Example Syntax

```
Private Sub Command1_Click ()
    For i = 0 to List1.ListCount - 1
        Printer.Print List1.List(i)
    Next i
End Sub
```

Description   The ListCount property returns the number of items in a list. Each time the AddItem method is used on a list control, this property automatically increments. Using the RemoveItem method decrements it.

The ListCount property is most commonly used for bounds checking. When working with a list or combo box, you can check possible index values against this property to make sure your program does not reference a list entry that does not exist. Keep in mind, however, that the index numbering of a list is zero-based, and that the value of the ListCount property is not the same as the highest index number. In other words, if a list has five items in it, the value of ListCount will be 5, while the highest index number in that list will be 4. Thus you could have a test like this:

```
If Index >  MyBox.ListCount - 1      'bounds error, index too large for list
```

The example syntax uses a For-Next loop with a maximum value of ListCount -1 to print out the contents of a list box.

Example   The Lists and Combos project at the end of this chapter uses ListCount in the cmndRemove event to step through each list item in a MultiSelect list to delete the entries.

LISTINDEX PROPERTY

Objects Affected   ComboBox, DirListBox, DriveListBox, FileListBox, ListBox

Purpose   The ListIndex property returns the index number of the selected item in a list. The selected item is the one that has been previously set by the program, or highlighted by the user by using the arrow keys or by clicking on the item. Assigning a value to the ListIndex property changes the selected item to the entry at the specified index. This property cannot be set at design time.

The ListIndex property is also used with the drive, directory, and file list box controls. For a description of how this property is used with these controls, refer to Chapter 47.

Table 46-16 summarizes the arguments of the ListIndex property.

General Syntax

```
[form!]Name.ListIndex [= Index%]
```

Table 46-16 Arguments of the ListIndex property

Argument	Description
form	Name of the parent form
Name	Name of the list or combo box
Index%	An index number of an item that is currently in the list

Example Syntax

```
Private Sub Command1_Click ()
    L% = List1.ListIndex        'assigns to L% the index number of the selected item
    List1.ListIndex = 0         'sets the selected item in List1 to the first entry
End Sub
```

Description

Specify the ListIndex property by beginning with the name of the list box or combo box control to be affected. When read, this property returns the index number of the currently selected item in a list. If no item is currently selected, a -1 is returned. If the user enters text in the edit area of the simple or drop-down combo box, and that text does not match a listed item, this property will also return a ListIndex value of -1.

The program may also change the currently selected item of a list by setting this property. When using the ListIndex property to set the currently selected list entry, the program must use an index number that references an item currently in the list. For instance, if a list has five items in it, an index number from 0 to 4 must be used or an "Invalid property array index" error will occur.

In the first statement of the example syntax, the ListIndex property returns the index number of the currently selected item in List1, and assigns it to the variable L%. The second statement in the example syntax sets the selected item on List1 to the item with the index value 0: that is, the first item on the list.

Example

The Form_Load event sets the ListIndex property of the cmboSubject, cmboVerb, and cmboObject combo boxes to their default values.

Comments

With list and combo boxes, using the statement Name.List(ListIndex) gives the same result as Name.Text.

MultiSelect Property

Objects Affected FileListBox, ListBox, ListView

Purpose The MultiSelect property lets the user choose more than one item at a time from a list box. Its three possible states include no multiple selection allowed, simple multiple selection, and extended multiple selection. Tables 46-17 and 46-18 list the arguments of the MultiSelect property.

General Syntax

```
[form!]Name.Multiselect
```

Table 46-17 Arguments of the MultiSelect property

Argument	Description
form	Name of the parent form
Name	Name of the list box

Table 46-18 Possible settings for the MultiSelect property

Setting	Description
0	(Default) Single selection only; multiple selection not allowed.
1	Simple multiple selection. Multiple items selected by clicking or by pressing the [SPACEBAR].
2	Extended multiple selection. Whole domains selected with [F], individual items with [Q].

Example Syntax

```
Private Sub ShowList (listBox as Control)
    Select Case listBox.MultiSelect
        Case 0                                   'no multiple selection
            Text1.Text = listBox.Text
        Case 1, 2                                'multiple selections
            For i = 0 to listBox.ListCount - 1
                If listBox.Selected(i) Then
                    bigLine = bigLine & listBox(i).List & Chr(13) & Chr(10)
                End If
            Next i
            Text1.Text = bigLine
    End Select
End Sub
```

Description MultiSelect lets the user choose more than one item from a list box. This lets a user perform batch operations (like moving a group of items) instead of repeating several steps over and over for each item to be operated on.

You'll generally set MultiSelect at design time and write your code to either expect a multiple selection or a single selection. It is possible to read (but not set) MultiSelect at runtime, so you could write a generic procedure that can handle either, as in the above example syntax.

The default setting, 0, means that only single selections may be made in the list box. Selecting a new item deselects any previous item. A setting of 1 means that the user can perform a simple multiple selection. The (SPACEBAR), or single mouse click, selects or deselects individual items from the list. The user can scroll up or down through the list with the usual movement keys and the scroll bars. A setting of 2 means the user may use extended multiple selection. (F)-clicking or (F) used in combination with any arrow key extends the selection from the previously selected item to the current item. (Q)-clicking selects or deselects individual items in the list. The Selected property is set to True whenever the user selects an item. The example syntax loops through the list entries looking for selected items. Figure 46-4 shows a list with multiple selections.

Example The Lists and Combos project at the end of this chapter uses a MultiSelect list, listSentences, to keep a record of each sentence created.

NewIndex Property

Purpose Use the NewIndex property to determine where the newest addition to a sorted list was actually added. Not available at design time, read-only at runtime. Table 46-19 summarizes the arguments of the NewIndex property.

General Syntax

```
[form!]Name.NewIndex
```

Figure 46-4 The MultiSelect property lets your list boxes process multiple selections

Table 46-19 Arguments of the NewIndex property

Argument	Description
form	Name property of the form
Name	Name property of the list box or combo box control

Example Syntax

```
Private Sub Form_Load ()
    Combo1.AddItem "No Growth"
    Combo1.ItemData(Combo1.NewIndex) = 0
    Combo1.AddItem "Good Growth"
    Combo1.ItemData(Combo1.NewIndex) = 3
    Combo1.AddItem "Great Growth"
    Combo1.ItemData(Combo1.NewIndex) = 8
End Sub
```

Description   Adding items to a sorted list puts them in an unpredictable position. You can use the NewIndex property to determine where in the list a new item was added. ItemData returns the index number of the last added item, or −1 if there are no items on the list or if an item has been deleted since the last addition.

This property is particularly helpful with the ItemData property, as shown above.

REMOVEITEM METHOD

Objects Affected   ComboBox, Grid, ListBox

Purpose   The RemoveItem method deletes an item from the list in a grid, list, or combo box. Table 46-20 summarizes the arguments of the RemoveItem method.

General Syntax

```
[form!]Name.RemoveItem Index%
```

Table 46-20 Arguments of the RemoveItem method

Argument	Description
form	Name of the parent form
Name	Name of the grid, list, or combo box
Index%	An integer value specifying the index number of the list item to be removed

Example Syntax

```
Private Sub List1_DblClick ()
    L% = List1.ListIndex
    List1.RemoveItem L%
End Sub
```

Description   The RemoveItem method is the complement to the AddItem method. The RemoveItem method deletes from a list or combo box's list the entry indicated by the Index% argument. Begin the specification of the RemoveItem method with the name of the list or combo box to be affected.

When an item is removed from the list, the index number of each entry in the list that followed the removed item is decremented. The ListCount property for the control is also decremented. Figure 46-5 graphically illustrates this process.

Care should be taken when removing items from a list. If your program specifies an index value that is greater than that of the highest current item, Visual Basic will issue an "Illegal function call" error. To be safe, always check the ListCount property before using the RemoveItem method. The index numbering of the list is zero-based. If a list contains five items, the first item has an index of 0, and the highest index number is 4. Therefore the value of the supplied index should always be less than the value of the ListCount property.

The example code uses List1's DblClick event to remove the currently selected item from the list.

Example   The cmndRemove_Click event uses the RemoveItem method to remove highlighted entries from the list. It iterates through the list, checks to see if the item is highlighted, and removes it if it is. Notice that the routine steps through the list from end to beginning rather than from beginning to end: Removing an item from the list reorders the list, which would cause problems if we iterated through the list in the normal beginning to end manner.

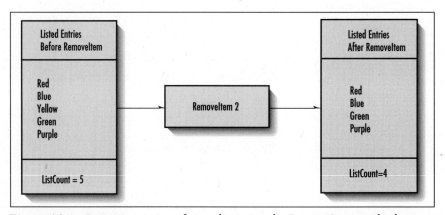

Figure 46-5   Removing an item from a list using the RemoveItem method

SELECTED PROPERTY

Objects Affected   FileListBox, ListBox

Purpose   The Selected property lets you determine which items in a multiple-selection list are selected. This property is an array of True and False values, with one entry for each item in the list. Table 46-21 summarizes the arguments for the Selected property.

General Syntax

```
[form!]Name.Selected(Index%) [= boolean%]
```

Table 46-21 Arguments for the Selected property

Argument	Description
form	Name of the parent form
Name	Name of the list box
Index%	Index in the array; corresponds to ListIndex
boolean%	True (-1) if selected; False (0) if not selected

Example Syntax

```
Private Sub Command1_Click ()
    For i = 0 to listBox.ListCount - 1
        If listBox.Selected(i) Then
            bigLine = bigLine & listBox(i).List & Chr(13) & Chr(10)
        End If
    Next i
    Text1.Text = bigLine
End Sub
```

Description   The Selected property lets you determine which items in a multiple-selection list box are selected. Using ListIndex in a multiple selection will only return the number of the item if the highlight bar is on; it will not indicate whether that item is selected.

The Selected property returns an array of Boolean values with a one-to-one correspondence to the ListIndex property of the list. Stepping through the array, as in the example syntax, is an easy way to check each item for its selected status.

Example   The Lists and Combos Project uses the Selected property to remove multiple items from the listSentences list box in the cmndRemove_Click event.

SELLENGTH PROPERTY

Objects Affected ComboBox, DBCombo, DBGrid, MaskedEdt, RichTextbox, Slider, TextBox

Purpose The SelLength property is used to set or return the number of selected characters within a combo box. Characters can be selected (highlighted) by the user, usually for an editing operation. Your program can also select a portion of the text in the text box. This property can be set and read at runtime only. The arguments for the SelLength property are summarized in Table 46-22.

General Syntax

`[form!]Name.SelLength [ = NumChars&]`

Table 46-22 Possible settings for the SelLength property

Arguments	Description
form	Name property of the parent form
Name	Name property of the control
NumChars&	Reads or sets the number of selected characters

Example Syntax

```
Private Sub Combo1_MouseUp (Button As Integer, Shift As Integer, X As Single, Y As Single)
    SaveSelLength = Combo1.SelLength        'save the length of the selected text
    Text1.Text = Str(SaveSelLength)
End Sub
```

Description The SelLength property is used in conjunction with the SelStart and SelText properties for working with text that has been selected by the user in a combo box whose style property is dropdown combo (0) or simple combo (1). A user can select text for these properties by holding down the F key and pressing ⊂ or ⊃, or by clicking and dragging the mouse over the desired text. This highlights the selected text. Your program can then read the settings of these properties and perform operations on the selected text. The SelStart property determines the starting point of the selected text within a text or combo box. The SelLength property determines the number of characters selected. SelText is a string property that contains the selected text.

The SelLength property is a long integer that may be used to set or return the number of selected characters in the text. If no characters are selected, this property returns 0.

Setting the SelLength property within a program's code has no effect unless the combo box has the focus when the property is set. If the combo box does have the focus, assigning SelLength a value causes that number of characters to be selected in the text box, starting at the position indicated by the SelStart property and counting from left to right. If the program assigns SelLength, a value that exceeds the length of the text in the text box, only the existing characters are selected, and the SelLength property is adjusted to reflect this. Setting this property to a value less than 0 causes an "Invalid property value" error to occur at runtime.

The example syntax saves the length of the current text selection to a variable for future use. Figure 46-6 shows a combo box with selected text.

SelStart Property

Objects Affected   ComboBox, DBCombo, DBGrid, MaskedEdt, RichTextBox, Slider, TextBox

Purpose   The SelStart property is used to set or return the starting position of selected text within a combo box whose style property is dropdown combo (0) or simple combo (1). Text may be selected by the user or the program, and is highlighted in the text box. If there is no selected text, this property sets or returns the position of the box's insertion point. The arguments for the SelStart property are summarized in Table 46-23.

General Syntax

```
[form!]Name.SelStart [ = StartPos&]
```

Table 46-23 Arguments of the SelStart property

Arguments	Description
form	Name property of the parent form
Name	Name property of the control

StartPos&   Reads or sets the character position of the insertion point or the start of selected text.

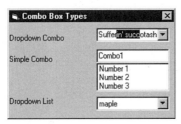

Figure 46-6   Selected text within a drop-down combo box

Example Syntax

```
Private Sub Combo1_MouseUp (Button As Integer, Shift As Integer, X As Single, Y As Single)
    SaveSelStart = Combo1.SelStart        'save the start of the selected text
    Text1.Text = Str$(SaveSelStart)
End Sub
```

Description

The SelStart property is used in conjunction with the SelLength and SelText properties for working with text that has been selected in a combo box whose style property is dropdown combo (0) or simple combo (1) by the user. A user can select text for these properties by holding down the Ⓕ key and pressing ◁ or ▷, or by clicking and dragging the mouse over the desired text. This highlights the selected text (see Figure 46-6). Your program can then read the settings of these properties and perform operations on the selected text. The SelStart property determines the starting point of the selected text within a combo box. SelLength determines the number of characters selected. SelText is a string property that contains the selected text.

The SelStart property is a long integer value that indicates the starting position of the selected characters in a combo box. The value of SelStart is zero-based. This means the first selected character is the position after the value of SelStart. For instance, if the value of SelStart is 1, and the value of SelLength is 2, the second and third characters in the text are selected. If there is no text currently selected, SelStart will return the position of the combo box's insertion point.

You may set the SelStart property by assigning a long integer value to it. This value must be a nonnegative number, or an "Invalid property value" error will occur during runtime. If this value is greater than the length of the text in the text or combo box, SelStart is set to a value equal to the length of the text. Assigning a value to the SelStart property automatically sets the SelLength property to 0, and moves the insertion point in the text box to the specified position.

SelText Property

Objects Affected   ComboBox, DBCombo, DBGrid, MaskedEdt, RichTextBox, Slider, TextBox

Purpose   The SelText property replaces or returns the currently selected text within a combo box whose style property is dropdown combo (0) or simple combo (1). Users can select text (typically by dragging with the mouse), or text may be selected by program action. The arguments for the SelText property are summarized in Table 46-24.

General Syntax

```
[form!]Name.SelText [ = NewText$]
```

Table 46-24 Arguments of the SelText property

Arguments	Description
form	Name property of the parent form.
Name	Name property of the control.
NewText$	A string that can be placed at the text box's insertion point. NewText$ replaces any selected text.

Example Syntax

```
Private Sub Combo1_MouseUp (Button As Integer, Shift As Integer, X As Single, Y As Single)
    Clipboard.SetText Combo1.SelText      'save the start of the selected text
    Text1.Text = Combo1.SelText
End Sub
```

Description

The SelText property is used in conjunction with the SelLength and SelStart properties for working with text that has been selected in a combo box by the user. This property is valid only for ones whose style property is dropdown combo (0) or simple combo (1). A user can select text for these properties by holding down the F key and pressing < or >, or by clicking and dragging the mouse over the desired text. This highlights the selected text. Your program can then read the settings of these properties and perform operations on the selected text. The SelStart property determines the starting point of the selected text within a text or combo box. SelLength determines the number of characters selected. SelText is a string property that contains the selected text.

The SelText property returns a string copy of the selected characters from the text or combo box. This string can be used by your programs to cut and paste to the Windows Clipboard. If no characters are currently selected, this property will return a null string.

Assigning a string value to this property can cause one of two things to happen. If there is any text selected when the assignment is done, the selected text in the text or combo box is replaced by the assigned text. If no text is selected, the new text is inserted into the text or combo box's text at the box's insertion point.

Figure 46-6 displays a combo box with some selected text. In this example the value of the SelStart property would be 8, SelLength would be 4, and SelText would be "some".

The example syntax copies the selected text to the Clipboard by assigning the value of the SelText property of the text box to the SetText method of the Clipboard, and then copies the selected text to Text2.

SORTED PROPERTY

Objects Affected	ComboBox, ListBox
Purpose	The Sorted property specifies at design time whether or not the items in the list or combo box are to be automatically sorted by Visual Basic. Table 46-25 summarizes the arguments of the Sorted property.

General Syntax

```
[form!]Name.Sorted
```

Table 46-25 Arguments of the Sorted property

Argument	Description
form	Name of the parent form
Name	Name of the list or combo box

Example Syntax

```
If Combo1.Sorted = True then      'if the items in the combo box are sorted
    Call BinarySearch(Search$)    'use a binary search,
Else
    Call LinearSearch(Search$)    'otherwise search one item at a time.
End If
```

Description The Sorted property is a great time-saving feature of list and combo boxes. When you set the Sorted property to True (-1), Visual Basic automatically attends to all the chores associated with keeping the list sorted alphabetically. If this property is set to False, no sorting of any kind is performed on the list. This property may only be set at design time, but it may be checked during runtime as a Boolean value.

To keep items sorted, Visual Basic changes the index numbers of the items in a list as necessary. Because of this, Visual Basic needs absolute control over how the index numbers are assigned when items are added. Therefore, using the Index% argument of the AddItem method is not recommended for a list or combo box that has the Sorted property set to True. You can determine where Visual Basic added the item to the list with the NewIndex property.

The example syntax checks the Sorted property of the box Combo1 to determine whether to do a binary search (which is very fast but works only on a sorted list) or a linear search (which is much slower, but can work on an unsorted list).

STYLE PROPERTY

Objects Affected	ComboBox, DBCombo
Purpose	The Style property sets the style of a combo box or list box. A combo box can be one of three styles: drop-down combo, simple combo, or drop-down list. A list box can be one of two styles: standard or check box. Table 46-26 summarizes the arguments of the Style property.
General Syntax	

```
[form!]Name.Style
```

Table 46-26 Arguments of the Style property

Argument	Description
form	Name of the parent form
Name	Name of the list or combo box

Example Syntax

```
If Combo1.Style = 0 Then Text1.Text = "Drop-Down Combo"
If Combo1.Style = 1 Then Text1.Text = "Simple Combo"
If Combo1.Style = 2 Then Text1.Text = "Drop-Down List"
```

Description	Three settings are available for the Style property for combo boxes: 0 for drop-down combo, 1 for simple combo, and 2 for drop-down list. Two settings are available for the Style property for list boxes: 0 for standard list box and 1 for checkbox list box. This property can only be set at design time, but it may be checked at runtime as an integer value.
	Specify the Style property starting with the name of the combo box or list box control to be affected. The example code simply determines what type of combo box Combo1 is, and sets the text accordingly.
Drop-Down Combo Box	The drop-down combo box consists of three areas: the edit area, the down arrow, and the list area. The edit area allows users to enter text as they would in a text box. The down arrow is displayed just to the right, but separated from the edit area. The list area of the drop-down combo box stays hidden from view until the user clicks on the down arrow associated with the box, or presses A-. Either action causes the list area to drop down below the edit area. The list area closes as soon as the user selects an tem. Because the user can enter text, or choose from a list of items, this style provides a useful tool for data entry fields that may have some often used values, yet cannot be restricted to a limited number of choices. Figure 46-7 shows both a closed and dropped-down combo box.

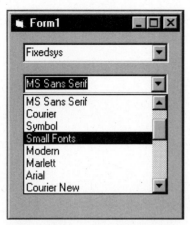

Figure 46-7   Drop-down combo
box closed and dropped down

Simple Combo Box The simple combo box is much like a drop-down combo box that has its
list area always open. Again, its value can be set by user input in the edit
area, or by the user clicking on the desired list item. The default setting for
the Height property of this object will display only the edit area. Therefore, it's a good idea to increase the Height property at design time in order
to let the items in the list be viewed. Because the list area of this style is
constantly open, it uses more screen space than the drop-down combo
box. Figure 46-7 shows a simple combo box.

**Drop-Down
List Box** The drop-down list box is almost identical to the drop-down combo box.
The major functional difference is that the drop-down list box requires the
user to choose an item from the list area. While the selected item appears
in the edit area, nothing can be typed there by the user. This style is used
for data entry fields that have a limited number of valid values. Figure 46-8
shows both a closed and opened drop-down list box.

Standard List Box The standard list box is a simple list box which is prevalent in many
Windows applications. It consists of a set of rows of text of which one
or more rows may be selected. It provides a vertical scroll bar to allow
the user to display rows contained within the list box which may not be
visible.

Checkbox List Box The checkbox list box is almost identical to the standard list box. The
major functional and visual difference is that the checkbox list box
includes a check box at the start of each row of the text. When the row is
selected, the check box on that row is checked. When it is not selected,
the check box is not checked. In checkbox list boxes, the ItemCheck event
is invoked whenever a row's checked status is changed. Use this style to
provide a way for the user to select one of several items. Figure 46-8
shows a checkbox style of list box.

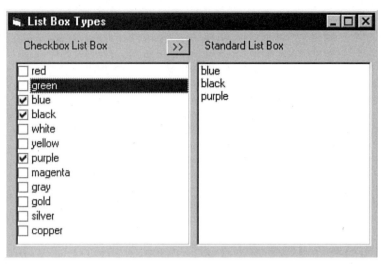

Figure 46-8 Types of list boxes

Example   The Lists and Combos project at the end of this chapter uses both drop-down lists and drop-down combos.

Comments   In styles 0 and 1, if the user enters text in the edit area of the combo box that does not match any items in the control's list, the value of that combo box's ListIndex will be -1.

TEXT PROPERTY

Objects Affected   ComboBox, DBCombo, DBGrid, DBList, Grid, ListBox, TextBox

Purpose   The Text property is used to read the text of the selected item in a list or combo box, or a cell entry in a grid. Additionally, the Text property can be used to set the selected item in combo boxes whose Style property is set to 0 (drop-down combo) or 1 (simple combo). Table 46-27 summarizes the arguments of the Text property when used with a list box or combo box.

General Syntax

```
[form!]Name.Text [= TextString$]
```

Table 46-27 Arguments of the Text property when used with a list box or combo box

Argument	Description
form	Name of the parent form
Name	Name of the list, combo box, or grid control
TextString$	Assigned to the edit area of the drop-down and simple combo box styles or cell of a grid

Example Syntax
```
Private Sub Command1_Click ()
    SelectedItem$ = List1.Text    'assigns the value of a list box's selected item to a ⇐
string
    Combo1.Text = "Hello"         'assigns a string to the edit area of a simple combo box
End Sub
```

Description   When used with list and combo boxes, the Text property returns a string copy of the currently selected item in the control's list. If no item has yet been selected, this property will return a null string.

This is an alternative to using the List and ListIndex properties together. For instance, in most cases the following two lines of code are functionally equivalent:

```
A$ = List1.List(List1.ListIndex)
A$ = List1.Text
```

The only difference between these two examples occurs when the user has not yet selected an item in the list. When this is the case, the first line in the example would generate an error (because ListIndex would have a value of -1). The second line of code would not. Instead, the variable A$ would be assigned a null value.

When used with the grid control, the Text property reads or sets the contents of the active cell. The active cell is set with the Row and Col properties.

In the example syntax, the first statement stores the text of the currently selected item for List1 in the string variable SelectedItem$. The second statement assigns the string "Hello" to the selected item in Combo1. This causes the word "Hello" to appear in the edit area of this combo box.

Drop-Down and Simple Combos   As discussed at the beginning of this chapter, the drop-down combo and simple combo box styles allow the user to edit text in the edit area of the control. Because of this, the Text property takes on a somewhat different meaning when used with these combo box styles.

When used on drop-down or simple combo boxes, the Text property is a string representation of the contents of the edit area of the control. By default, this is the selected item from the list; thus, in the default case, the Text property has the same meaning as with non-combo list boxes. However, since the user can type text into the edit area of a combo box, the Text property can sometimes contain such an input item, probably not matching any item on the list.

You can manipulate the contents of the edit area by assigning it a value, or by using it as an argument with any of Visual Basic's string functions and statements such as Left, Mid, and Right. Any operations performed on this property are reflected by the text inside the edit area.

You may assign a string to the Text property. This causes the text in the box to be replaced by the assigned string. The user can also directly edit the text represented by the Text property. Any time a combo box's Text property is modified, it causes the combo box's Change event to occur.

TopIndex Properties

Objects Affected   ComboBox, DirListBox, DriveListBox, FileListBox, ListBox

Purpose   The TopIndex property reads or sets the topmost visible row in a list box or the list box part of a combo box. This property allows you to programatically determine what rows in a list box are visible. This property is not available at design time and is readable and writable at runtime. Table 46-28 summarizes the arguments of the TopIndex property.

General Syntax

```
[form!]Name.TopIndex [ = row%]
```

Table 46-28 Arguments of the TopIndex property

Argument	Description
form	Name property of the form
Name	Name property of the control
row%	Row number of topmost visible row

Example Syntax

```
Private Sub List1_LostFocus ()
    List1.List(5) = "new data"
    List1.TopRow = 5  'move the list box back to the changed row
End Sub
```

Description   Use the TopIndex property to programatically scroll the list box. This property determines the topmost visible row. You may have code that alters a row's data when that row is not visible. Setting these properties to the row of the altered row brings that changed data into view, as in the example syntax.

The Lists and Combos Project

Assembling the Project

1.   Assemble the controls summarized in Table 46-29 on a blank form.

Table 46-29 Controls for the Lists and Combos project

Object	Property	Setting
Form	BorderStyle	3 - Fixed Dialog
	Caption	"Lists and Combos Project"
	Name	formMain
ComboBox	Name	cmboSubject
	Style	0 - Dropdown Combo
ComboBox	Name	cmboVerb
	Style	2 - Dropdown List
ComboBox	Name	cmboObject
	Style	2 - Dropdown List
CommandButton	Caption	"&Add"
	Name	cmndAdd
CommandButton	Caption	"&Remove"
	Name	cmndRemove
Label	Caption	0 items selected
	Name	lablSelectedCount
ListBox	MultiSelect	2 - Extended
	Name	listSentences

2. Position and size the controls, as shown on Figure 46-9.

3. Enter the following code in the cmboSubject_KeyPress event. This triggers when the user presses E after typing in the combo box's text box. It saves the text which was typed in the list associated with the combo box.

```
Private Sub cmboSubject_KeyPress(KeyAscii As Integer)
    If KeyAscii = 13 And cmboSubject.text <> "" Then
        cmboSubject.AddItem cmboSubject.text
    End If
End Sub
```

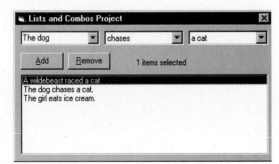

Figure 46-9 Lists and Combos Project at runtime

4. Enter the following code in the cmndAdd_Click event. This builds a sentence from the selected combo box entries and adds it to the list box.

```
Private Sub cmndAdd_Click()
    txt$ = cmboSubject.text & " " & cmboVerb.text & " " & cmboObject.text & _ "."
    listSentences.AddItem (txt$)
End Sub
```

5. Enter the following code in the cmndRemove_Click event. This removes the sentences which are currently selected in the sentence list box.

```
Private Sub cmndRemove_Click()
    For i% = listSentences.ListCount - 1 To 0 Step -1
        If listSentences.Selected(i%) = True Then
            listSentences.RemoveItem (i%)
        End If
    Next i%

    lblSelectedCount.Caption = listSentences.SelCount & " items selected"
End Sub
```

6. Enter the following code in the listSentences_Click event. This triggers the updating of the item selected count label.

```
Private Sub listSentences_Click()
    lblSelectedCount.Caption = listSentences.SelCount & " items selected"
End Sub
```

7. Enter the following code in the Form_Load event. This function initializes all the combo boxes and selects an initial item.

```
Private Sub Form_Load()
    cmboSubject.AddItem ("The girl")
    cmboSubject.AddItem ("A wildebeast")
    cmboSubject.AddItem ("The dog")
    cmboSubject.AddItem ("A car")
    cmboSubject.ListIndex = 0

    cmboVerb.AddItem ("likes")
    cmboVerb.AddItem ("eats")
    cmboVerb.AddItem ("chases")
    cmboVerb.AddItem ("raced")
    cmboVerb.ListIndex = 0

    cmboObject.AddItem ("pizza")
    cmboObject.AddItem ("the train")
    cmboObject.AddItem ("a cat")
    cmboObject.AddItem ("ice cream")
    cmboObject.ListIndex = 0
End Sub
```

How It Works

This project allows the user to build simple sentences using a set of predefined words. These words are contained within three combo boxes: one containing possible subjects of the sentence, one containing possible verbs of the sentences, and one containing possible objects of the sentence. Note that because the subject combo box is a drop-down combo box, you can enter your own text into the text box area of the combo box. If you press (ENTER) while focus is on this combo box, the word is saved in the list.

The list box contains the history of sentences which have been created. Whenever you press the Add command button, a new sentence is created and added to the end of this list. If you want to remove entries from the list, you can select them and press the Remove command button.

47

FILE, DIRECTORY, AND DRIVE BOXES

Windows users will expect your application to provide the same easy access to the file system through point-and-click navigation as the commercial applications to which they're accustomed. In addition to the Common Dialog control, Visual Basic provides the Drive, Directory, and File list boxes for you to use in providing the interface that lets the user move around the logical structure of the DOS files system. These controls take most of the work out of dealing with selecting drives, directories, and files. This lets you concentrate on the main work of the application.

File-Oriented List Boxes

For the user and the programmer, the list boxes that present the file system work much like the List Box and Combo Box controls described in Chapter 46, "List and Combo Boxes." In fact, the file-related list boxes share the List, ListCount, ListIndex, MultiSelect, and Selection properties with the list and combo boxes. These properties are discussed again in this chapter because there are some differences that need to be taken into account when they're used with the file-related list boxes. Here, however, your program does not have to add or remove items from the lists of the file-related list boxes. Visual Basic automatically reads the structure of the disk, builds the lists of directories and files, and updates the list when the user adds or removes files.

The Drive List Box

The Drive list box is like a drop-down list box that lets the user choose from any of the available drives on the system. Visual Basic automatically explores the user's system, and adds all the floppy, fixed, and network drives to the list. Drive list items that reflect local fixed disks will also display that disk's label with the drive letter. For network drives, the network name is displayed. Figure 47-1 shows a Drive list box with the drop-down list open.

Figure 47-1   The
Drive list box

The Directory List Box

The Directory list box is like a simple list box that lets the user choose a directory on a disk drive. Clicking once on any of the listed directories moves the selection bar; double-clicking on a directory entry changes the current directory for the directory list box. Figure 47-2 shows the Directory list box.

The File List Box and File Attributes

The File list box is like a standard list box, except that it is automatically filled with the available files in the directory. A single click selects each individual file. Visual Basic has added the ability to select multiple files if the MultiSelect property is set to either 1 (simple MultiSelect) or 2 (extended MultiSelect). Figure 47-3 shows the File list box.

In the FAT and NTFS file systems, each entry for a file in a directory includes four attributes: archive, hidden, system, and read-only. The File list box has several properties that enable you to select which files are displayed in the box based on the settings of these bits. These are the Archive, Hidden, Normal, ReadOnly, and System properties. When the File list box control scans a directory, it selects files for display based on the settings of these properties. If more than one of these properties is set on, then the files selected will reflect a combination of the set properties.

Figure 47-2   The
Directory list box

Figure 47-3   The File
list box

File System Controls Summary

In this chapter we will be discussing the properties, events, and methods specific to these file-related controls. They are summarized in Table 47-1. At the end of the section, the Drive project demonstrates the use of each of these controls and their properties, events, and methods.

Table 47-1 The properties, events, and methods that pertain to Drive, Directory, and File list boxes

Use or Set This...	Type	To Do This...
Archive	Property	Set or read whether archive files are shown in a File list box
Drive	Property	Set or read the current drive selected in a Drive list box
FileName	Property	Set or read the current file selected in a File list box
Hidden	Property	Set or read whether hidden files are shown in a File list box
List	Property	Return an item from a Drive, Directory, or File list box's list
ListCount	Property	Return the number of items in a Drive, Directory, or File list box's list
ListIndex	Property	Return the index of the selected item in a Drive, Directory, or File list
MultiSelect	Property	Enable the user to select more than one file at a time
Normal	Property	Set or return whether normal files are displayed in a File list box
Path	Property	Set or return the current path for a Directory or File list box
PathChange	Event	Initiate an action when the Path property of a File list box is changed
Pattern	Property	Set or return the current file pattern for a File list box
PatternChange	Event	Initiate an action when a File list box's Pattern property is changed
ReadOnly	Property	Set or return whether read-only files are displayed in a File list box
Refresh	Method	Reset the list entries in a Drive, Directory, or File list box
Selected	Property	Determine which files are selected in a multiple selection
System	Property	Set or return whether System files are displayed in a File list box

Constant Values

It is usually best to use named constants rather than numeric values when developing software. Named constants make your code more readable and easier to maintain.

Table 47-2 lists the values of the constants relevant to this chapter, mentions their names, and briefly describes what they mean. These constants can be viewed using the Object Browser. It is not necessary to explicitly add these objects to your project.

Table 47-2 Constants for list boxes

Value	Constant Name	Meaning
0	vbMultiSelectNone	(Default). Single selection only, multiple selection not allowed
1	vbMultiSelectSimple	Simple multiple selection. Multiple items selected by clicking or by pressing the SPACEBAR
2	vbMultiSelectExtended	Extended multiple selection. Whole domains selected with SHIFT, individual items with CONTROL

ARCHIVE PROPERTY

Objects Affected   FileListBox

Purpose   The Archive property sets or returns a value that determines whether or not files with their archive bit set on will be displayed in a File list box. Files with the archive bit set have been copied by the command line XCOPY or BACKUP commands, or similar programs. Setting this property to False will thus suppress the display of files that have been backed up, which can be helpful for file management. The Archive property can be set at design time and set or read at runtime. Table 47-3 summarizes the arguments of the Archive property.

General Syntax

```
[form!]Name.Archive [= boolean%]
```

Table 47-3 Arguments of the Archive property

Argument	Description
form	Name of the parent form
Name	Name of the File list box
boolean%	A True or False indicating whether archive files will be selected or not

Example Syntax

```
Private Sub ArchiveCheck_Click ()
    File1.Archive = -ArchiveCheck.Value       'check box on the dialog box or form
End Sub

Private Sub Form_Load ()
    ArchiveBit = Abs(File1.Archive)           'read the Archive property setting
    ArchiveCheck.Value = ArchiveBit           'set the check box to reflect it
End Sub
```

Description   The FAT and NTFS file systems set aside one byte in the directory entry of each file for attribute information. Five properties can be used to select files for display in a File list box based on the setting of the attribute byte. These are the Archive, Hidden, Normal, ReadOnly, and System properties. The set of files that are displayed in a File list box is based on the combination of these properties.

One of the bits in the attribute byte is the archive bit. This bit is set on automatically by the operating system every time a file is modified. Certain programs (such as XCOPY and BACKUP) can then set this bit off when a file is backed up. This allows the system to make incremental backups based on whether a file has been modified since the last backup.

The Archive property selects files based on the setting of the archive bit. Specify this property by starting with the name of the file list box control to be affected. This property has two possible values: True or False. It defaults to True.

Interaction of the Archive Property and Other Properties

The files selected when the Archive property is True are a subset of the files selected by the Normal property. Setting the Archive property to True has no effect unless the Normal property is set to False. In that case, any files whose archive bit is set on, but with no other attribute bits set other than read-only, will be selected for display. However, if a file's archive bit is on, but its hidden or system bits are also set on, it will not be selected unless the Hidden or System properties are also True.

Table 47-4 lists all the possible combinations for the attribute byte, and which of those combinations will be displayed when the Archive property is True. This table lists only the files that will be selected with the archive bit as the basis. Other files may be selected for the same File list box by setting the ReadOnly, Hidden, or System properties.

Table 47-4 Files displayed when the Archive property is True, but System, Hidden, and ReadOnly are False

Attribute Value	Select This File?
Archive	Yes
Archive, ReadOnly	Yes
— anything else —	Any other combination will not display the file

Example

In the File System Controls project at the end of this chapter, the Archive property is first read in the Form_Load event. The value returned sets the ArchiveCheck check box. In the ArchiveCheck_Click event, this property is set to reflect the status of the check box. When the check box is checked, the Archive property is set to True. This code is also shown in the example syntax. Note that the Abs function must be used to change the True value to the value of one needed to set a check box. A False value is not affected.

DRIVE PROPERTY

Objects Affected DriveListBox

Purpose The Drive property reads or sets the drive currently selected in a Drive list box. Directories on the selected drive can be displayed by an associated Directory list box. With proper coding, a File list box can, in turn, display the files in the current directory on the new drive. This property is helpful for responding when the user changes the current drive. The arguments for the Drive property are summarized in Table 47-5.

General Syntax

```
[form!]Name.Drive [= drive$]
```

Table 47-5 Arguments of the Drive property

Argument	Description
form	Name of the parent form
Name	Name of the Drive list box
drive$	A string whose first letter is that of a valid file system drive

Example Syntax

```
Private Sub Drive1_Change ()
    Dir1.Path = CurDir(Drive1.Drive)        'uses the Drive property to set path
End Sub

Private Sub Command1_Click ()
    Drive1.Drive = "A:\"                     'sets the selected drive for the Drive list
End Sub
```

Description

The Drive property can be read at runtime to find out which drive is currently selected in a Drive list box. For all types of drives, a two-byte drive designation string is returned with the letter of the drive followed by a colon (for example, D:). When the selected drive is a local fixed disk, the two-byte drive string is followed by the drive's label, if any. For instance, if the fixed disk C: has the label MASTER, this property will return the string "C: [MASTER]". Network drives return the name of the network connection for this drive. For instance, if the shared drive \\SERVER\MAIN is mounted as logical drive D:, this property will return the string "D: [\\SERVER\MAIN]".

Specify the Drive property by starting with the name of the Drive list box control to be affected. You can set the value for this property by assigning a string with a drive letter to it. Only the first character of the string is used. For instance, in the preceding example, although the supplied string is three characters long, only the character A is used to set the Drive property. The balance of the string is ignored. The supplied character must reflect a valid drive on the system, otherwise an error occurs.

When the Drive property sets the selected drive in a Drive list box, it refreshes the list and activates the Drive_Change event. You can include code for this event to do such things as setting a new default path. If this property is not set at design time, it is set to the current process's default drive as recognized by Windows 95 or Windows NT.

The first sub procedure in the example syntax reacts to a change in the current drive by using the CurDir function together with the Drive property to get the current directory for the new drive. This directory path is then used to set the current path for the Dir1 Directory list box. The second example sub procedure simply sets the current drive for drive list box Drive1 to "A:\".

Example   In the File System Controls project at the end of this chapter, the Drive property is set in the Form_Load event to the current drive. In the Drive1_Change event, the Drive property sets the Path property of the Dir1 directory list box control.

Comments   The Refresh method can be used with the Drive list box to update any network drive changes.

FILENAME PROPERTY

Objects Affected   CommonDialog, FileListBox

Purpose   The FileName property enables your program to read the filename that is currently selected in a File list box, or to set a new current filename. This property can only be set or read at runtime. Table 47-6 summarizes the arguments of the FileName property.

General Syntax

```
[form!]Name.FileName [= path$]
```

Table 47-6 Arguments of the FileName property

Argument	Description
form	Name of the parent form
Name	Name of the File list box
path$	A string containing a path or filename pattern

Example Syntax

```
Private Sub File1_Click ()
    Text1.Text = File1.FileName          'set the text box to the currently selected file
End Sub

Private Sub Command1_Click ()
    oldFileName$ = File1.FileName         'change the selected file
    On Error Resume Next
    File1.FileName = Text1.Text
    If Err > 0 Then MsgBox "Invalid File Name Specified", 48
End Sub
```

Description   FileName property enables your program to read the filename that is currently selected in a File list box, or to set a new current filename. The string returned by the FileName property does not specify the drive or path of the file. Use the Path property to determine that information. If no file is selected, a null string is returned.

When setting this property in your program, you can use a drive, path, and filename. The filename can contain wildcard characters ("*" and "?"). When your program supplies the drive or path, the File list box's Path property gets changed to the drive and path specified, and a PathChange event occurs. If the supplied filename contains wildcard characters, the file list box's Pattern property gets changed to the file pattern specified and a PatternChange event occurs. This makes the FileName property perfect for allowing the user to change the path and file search pattern by using a text box.

The first sub procedure in the example syntax activates when the user clicks on the File list box. When this happens, the Text property for the text box is set to the file returned by the FileName property. This makes the selected filename appear in the text box, which is the typical behavior for this control. The second sub procedure, activated when the user clicks on the OK button, sets the FileName property to whatever text is in the text box and then checks for any error involving the filename. This procedure can thus handle the user typing in a filename not on the current list.

Example   In the File System Controls project at the end of this chapter, the FileName property is read to set the Text property of the TextSelected text box control in the File1_PathChange, File1_PatternChange, and File1_Click events. In the cmndOK_Click event, the FileName property is set to the value of the Text property of the TextSelected text box control.

Comments   When setting this property, make sure to check the string you're about to assign to make sure it specifies a valid drive and path. Note that the common dialog box also has a FileName property; the common dialog box is covered in detail in Chapter 25, "CommonDialog Control."

HIDDEN PROPERTY

Objects Affected   FileListBox

Purpose   The Hidden property sets or returns a value that determines whether or not hidden files will be displayed in a File list box. (Under Windows 95 and Windows NT, hidden files are not normally displayed in directory listings.) This property can be set at design time, and set or read at runtime. Table 47-7 summarizes the arguments of the Hidden property.

General Syntax

```
[form!]Name.Hidden [= boolean%]
```

Table 47-7 Arguments of the Hidden property

Argument	Description
form	Name of the parent form
Name	Name of the File list box
boolean%	A True or False indicating whether hidden files will be selected

Example Syntax

```
Private Sub HiddenCheck_Click ()
    File1.Hidden = -HiddenCheck.Value        'sets the Hidden property of File1 list box
End Sub

Private Sub Form_Load ()
    HiddenBit = Abs(File1.Hidden)            'read the Hidden property setting
    chekHidden.Value = HiddenBit             'set the check box to reflect it
End Sub
```

Description
The FAT and NTFS file systems set aside one byte in the directory entry of each file for attribute information. Five possible properties select files for display in a File list box based on the setting of this attribute byte. These are the Archive, Hidden, Normal, ReadOnly, and System properties. The set of files displayed in a File list box is based on the combination of these properties.

One of the bits in this attribute byte is the hidden bit. This bit hides files from the user. When this bit is set on, the related file is invisible to DIR, COPY, and most other Windows command line commands, as well as to most programs. This provides a very limited security scheme for certain files. The Window file manager enables users to view such files.

The Hidden property selects files based on the setting of the hidden attribute bit. Specify this property by beginning with the name of the File Box control to be affected. This property has two possible values: True or False. If this property is not changed at design time, its value will be False when the program begins.

Setting this property to True selects files with their hidden bit set on to be displayed, regardless of the setting of the archive and read-only bits. However, if a file also has its system bit set on, it will only be displayed if the System property is also set to True. Setting this property to False prevents all files whose hidden bit is set on from being excluded from the File list box, regardless of the settings of the other four attribute properties. Omitting the setting returns the current value of the Hidden property.

Table 47-8 lists all the possible combinations for the attribute byte, and which of those combinations will be displayed when the Hidden property is True. This table only lists those files that will be selected with the hidden bit as the basis. Other files may be selected for the same File list box by setting the Archive, Normal, ReadOnly, or System properties.

Table 47-8 Displayed files when the Hidden property is True and Archive, ReadOnly, and System are False

Attribute Value	Select This File?
Archive, Hidden	Yes
Archive, Hidden, ReadOnly	Yes
Hidden	Yes
Hidden, ReadOnly	Yes
— anything else —	Any other combination will not display the file

Example

In the File System Controls project at the end of this chapter, the Hidden property is first read in the Form_Load event. The value returned sets the HiddenCheck check box. In the HiddenCheck_Click event, this property is set to reflect the status of the check box. When the check box is checked, the Hidden property is set to True. This code is also shown in the example syntax given earlier. Note the Abs function must be used to change the True value to the value of one needed to set a check box. A False value is, of course, not affected.

List Property

Objects Affected ComboBox, DirListBox, DriveListBox, FileListBox, ListBox

Purpose The List property can be used with a Drive, Directory, or File list box to read the name of a drive designation, directory name, or filename, respectively. The designation or name to be read is specified using an index to its position in the list. This property is read-only, and cannot be set at design time or runtime. Table 47-9 summarizes the arguments for the List property.

General Syntax

```
[form!]Name.List(Index%)
```

Table 47-9 Arguments of the List property

Argument	Description
form	Name of the parent form
Name	Name of the control
Index%	An integer that identifies a particular list entry

Example Syntax

```
Private Sub Command1_Click ()
    ThisFile$ = File1.List(1)        'puts second file name in List in ThisFile$
End Sub
```

Description   The List property works in the same general way with Drive, Directory, and File list boxes, differing only in the meaning of the item retrieved. (Note that directory boxes use a different index numbering system than other types of list boxes; see "Directory List Boxes" later in this chapter.)

Specify the List property starting with the name of the Drive, Directory, or File list box to be affected. The List property is followed by an index number in parentheses designating the position of the item in the list to be read.

Note that the List property is also used with generic list boxes and combo boxes. See Chapter 46 for details.

Drive List Boxes   A Drive box's List property can be read at runtime to determine which drives are in the list and thus presumably available for use. The desired list item is specified by referencing the List property with an index number in a manner similar to using an array. The drives are listed in alphabetical order, and the index numbering starts at 0. So if a system has drives A:, B:, C:, and D:, drive A: has an index number of 0, and drive D: has an index number of 3. If the supplied index is greater than the highest list item's index number, a null string is returned.

For all types of drives, a two-byte drive designation string is returned with the letter of the drive followed by a colon (for example, "D:"). When the listed drive is a local fixed disk, the two-byte drive string is followed by the drive's label, if any. For instance, if the fixed disk C: has the label MASTER, this property will return the string "C: [MASTER]". Network drives return the name of the network connection for this drive. For instance, if the shared drive \\SERVER\MAIN is mounted as logical drive D:, this property will return the string "D: [\\SERVER\MAIN]".

Directory List Boxes   A Directory box's List property can be read to determine the names of all the directories that are currently being displayed in the Directory list box. The desired list item is specified by referencing the List property with an index number in a manner similar to using an array.

The current open directory is set to index number -1. The index number is incremented once for each subdirectory under the current directory, and decremented for each parent directory over it. For instance, Figure 47-4 shows three Directory list boxes, all with different current directories in the same directory tree.

In the first Directory box, the range for the index numbers in the list is -2 to 0. The current open directory is VB, therefore it is assigned an index

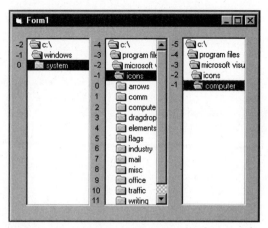

Figure 47-4 Index number assignment for Directory list boxes

value of -1. The "C:\" directory is 1 above it, so it is assigned index -2. The ICONS directory is assigned index 0 because it is the first subdirectory under the first-level VB directory. The second directory box begins the index assignment at the icons directory, giving it an index of -1. The directories VB and "C:\" are assigned index numbers -2 and -3, respectively. As you can probably now guess, the range of index numbers in the third Directory box is -4 to -1.

The string returned when the List property is used with the Directory box contains the full path name from the root directory to the directory in the specified list item.

File List Boxes   A File list box's List property can be read at runtime to find out all the files that match the current Archive, Hidden, Normal, Pattern, ReadOnly, and System properties. The filename returned by this property does not include the file's full path. The latter can be obtained using the Path property with the File list box.

The desired list item is specified by referencing the List property with an index number in a manner similar to using an array. The first file in the list is index 0. The last file has an index number equal to one less than the number of files in the list. If the supplied index is greater than the highest list item's index number, a null string ("") is returned.

The example syntax assigns the name of the second file in the file list to the variable ThisFile$. Notice that the meaning of the index value 1 would be different if a directory list box were used: In that case 1 would mean the second filename listed below the current directory.

LISTCOUNT PROPERTY

Objects Affected   ComboBox, DirListBox, DriveListBox, FileListBox, ListBox

Purpose   The ListCount property is read at runtime to determine the number of listed items in a Drive, Directory, or File list box. This is a read-only property and cannot be set at design time or runtime. Table 47-10 summarizes the arguments of the ListCount property.

General Syntax

```
[form!]Name.ListCount
```

Table 47-10 Arguments of the ListCount property

Argument	Description
form	Name of the parent form
Name	Name of the control

Example Syntax

```
Private Form_Load ()
    NumberOfFiles% = File1.ListCount
    NumberOfSubDirs% = Dir1.ListCount
End Sub
```

Description   When used with Drive and File list boxes, the ListCount property returns the number of items in the list. When used with a Directory list box, the property returns the number of subdirectories under the current directory entry.

Specify the ListCount property beginning with the name of the Drive, Directory, or File list control to be affected.

The example syntax uses the ListCount property to obtain the number of files and subdirectories, respectively. These numbers are assigned to variables for future use.

Note that the ListCount property is also used with generic list and combo boxes. See Chapter 46 for details.

Example   The ListCount property is used in several of the events in the File System Controls project at the end of this chapter. In each of these events, the File1.ListCount property updates the Caption property of the lablCount label. This label displays to the user the number of files contained in the File list box.

Comments   The property returns the number of items in a list, not the index number of the last listed item. Because the index numbers in a list are zero-based, the index number of the last listed item is always ListCount -1.

LISTINDEX PROPERTY

Objects Affected   ComboBox, DirListBox, DriveListBox, FileListBox, ListBox

Purpose   The ListIndex property returns or sets the index number of the selected item in a Drive, Directory, or File list box. This property cannot be set at design time. Table 47-11 summarizes the arguments of the ListIndex property.

General Syntax

```
[form!]Name.ListIndex [= Index%]
```

Table 47-11 Arguments of the ListIndex property

Argument	Description
form	Name of the parent form
Name	Name of the control
Index%	Identifies a particular entry in the control's list

Example Syntax

```
Private Sub Command1_Click ()
    File1.ListIndex = 0      'sets the selected item to the first item in the list
    L% = File1.ListIndex     'assigns L% the index of the selected item in File1
End Sub
```

Description   The ListIndex property can be used to read the index number of the selected item in a Drive, Directory, or File list box. Specifying an index sets the currently selected item to the item in that position on the list, keeping in mind that the first item is referenced with index number 0.

When the program begins, the ListIndex for a drive list box is assigned the value that corresponds to the current default drive. For a Directory list box, the program begins with ListIndex set to -1, indicating the current open directory. For File list boxes, the ListIndex property begins at -1, indicating that no file has been selected yet. When used on a Directory list box, keep in mind that the selected directory can be different from the current directory in the box. Clicking on a directory entry once selects it; double-clicking an entry opens it. To determine the current open directory entry, use the List property with a -1 index value.

The ListIndex property can also be assigned a value in order to change the selected item in a Drive, Directory, or File list box. The value assigned to the ListIndex property must be within the range of the list or an "Invalid property array index" error will occur.

The first statement in the example syntax sets the currently selected file in file list box File1 to the first item on the displayed list. The second example statement saves the index number of the currently selected file in File list box File1 in the variable L%.

MultiSelect Property

Objects Affected   FileListBox, ListBox

Purpose   The MultiSelect property lets the user choose more than one file at a time from the File list box. Its three possible states include no multiple select allowed, simple multiple select, and extended multiple select. Tables 47-12 and 47-13 list the arguments and possible settings of the MultiSelect property.

General Syntax

```
[form!]Name.Multiselect
```

Table 47-12 Arguments of the MultiSelect property

Argument	Description
form	Name of the parent form
Name	Name of the list box

Table 47-13 Possible settings for MultiSelect

Value	Constant Name	Meaning
0	vbMultiSelectNone	(Default). Single selection only, multiple selection not allowed
1	vbMultiSelectSimple	Simple multiple selection. Multiple items selected by clicking or by pressing the [SPACEBAR]
2	vbMultiSelectExtended	Extended multiple selection. Whole domains selected with [SHIFT], individual items with [CONTROL]

Example Syntax

```
Private Sub DeleteFiles (ListBox As Control)
    Select Case listBox.MultiSelect
        Case vbMultiSelectNone          'no multiple selection
            Kill listBox.FileName
        Case vbMultiSelectSimple, vbMultiSelectExtended  'multiple selections
            For i = 0 to listBox.ListCount - 1
                If listBox.Selected(i) Then
                    Kill listBox.FileName
                End If
            Next i
    End Select
End Sub
```

Description   MultiSelect lets the user choose more than one item from a list box. This lets a user perform batch operations (such as moving or deleting a group of files) instead of repeating several steps over and over for each file to be operated on. Note that a regular list box also has the MultiSelect property.

You'll generally set MultiSelect at design time and write your code to either expect a multiple selection or a single selection. It is possible to read (but not set) MultiSelect at runtime, so you could write a generic procedure that can handle either, as in the preceding example syntax.

The default setting, vbMultiSelectNone, means that only single selections may be made in the list box. Selecting a new file deselects any previous file. A setting of vbMultiSelectSimple means that the user can perform a simple multiple selection. The SPACEBAR, or single mouse click, selects or deselects individual files from the list. The user can scroll up or down through the list with the usual movement keys and the scrollbars. A setting of vbMultiSelectExtended means the user may use extended multiple selection. SHIFT-clicking or SHIFT-up or down arrow extends the selection from the previously selected file to the current file. CONTROL-clicking selects or deselects individual files in the list.

Example   The File list box in the File System Controls project at the end of this chapter uses MultiSelect to allow for batch operations.

Normal Property

Objects Affected   FileListBox, ListView, TreeView

Purpose   The Normal property sets or returns a value that determines whether or not normal files will be displayed in a File list box. Normal files are those that do not have the hidden or system attribute set. This property can be set at design time, and set or read at runtime. Table 47-14 summarizes the arguments of the Normal property.

General Syntax

```
[form!]Name.Normal [= boolean%]
```

Table 47-14 Arguments of the Normal property

Argument	Description
form	Name of the parent form
Name	Name of the File list box
boolean%	A True or False indicating whether normal files will be selected

Example Syntax

```
Private Sub NormalCheck_Click ()
    File1.Normal = -NormalCheck.Value        'sets the Normal property of File1
End Sub

Private Sub Form_Load ()
    NormalBit = Abs(File1.Normal)            'read the Normal property setting
    NormalCheck.Value = NormalBit            'set the check box to reflect it
End Sub
```

Description

The FAT and NTFS file systems set aside one byte in the directory entry of each file for attribute information. Five properties select files for display in a File list box based on the setting of this attribute byte: the Archive, Hidden, Normal, ReadOnly, and System properties. The set of files displayed in a File list box is based on the combination of these properties. Normal files are defined as all files whose hidden and system bits are not set on, regardless of the settings of the archive and read-only bits.

The Normal property has two possible values: True or False. If the Normal property is not changed at design time, its value will be True when the program begins.

Setting this property to True selects all files whose hidden and system bits are set off, regardless of the settings of the archive and read-only bits. In essence, this makes normal files a superset of the files selected with the Archive and ReadOnly properties, combined with all files that have no attribute bits set on. When this property is set to False, the File list box excludes any files that have none of the attribute bits set on. Any other files may be selected by setting the other four attribute properties.

Table 47-15 lists all the possible combinations for the attribute byte, and which of those combinations will be selected when the Normal property is True. This table lists only those files that will be selected when the hidden and system bits are off. Other files may be selected by setting the Hidden and System properties.

Table 47-15 Displayed files when the Normal property is True and System and Hidden are False

Attribute Value	Select This File?
none set	Yes
Archive	Yes
Archive, ReadOnly	Yes
ReadOnly	Yes
— anything else —	Any other combination will not display the file

Example

In the File System Controls project at the end of this chapter, the Normal property is first read in the Form_Load event. The value returned sets the NormalCheck check box. In the NormalCheck_Click event, this property is set to reflect the status of the check box. When the check box is checked, the Normal property is set to True. This code is also shown in the preceding example syntax. Note that the Abs function must be used to turn a regular True value into the one value needed to set a check box.

PATH PROPERTY

Objects Affected   App, DirListBox, FileListBox, InternetExplorer

Purpose   The Path property sets or reads the currently opened directory path in a Directory list box, or the current directory in a File list box. At design time, this property is set to the current default directory, and cannot be changed. However, this property can be set or read at runtime. Table 47-16 summarizes the arguments of the Path property.

General Syntax

```
[form!]Name.Path [= path$]
```

Table 47-16 Arguments of the Path property

Argument	Description
form	Name of the parent form
Name	Name of the File or Directory list box
path$	A string containing a valid path name

Example Syntax

```
Private Sub Dir1_Change ()          'Read the Dir list box Path to set the
    File1.Path = Dir1.Path          'File list box Path property and
    ChDir Dir1.Path                 'change the current directory.
End Sub

Private Sub File1_PathChange ()
    Dir1.Path = File1.Path          'Change the Dir list box Path to the
    Drive1.Drive = File1.Path       'Path from the File list box.
End Sub
```

Description   Specify the Path property by beginning with the name of the Directory or File list box to be affected. To set this property, specify a string containing a valid path name.

The operation of the Path property in Directory list boxes is somewhat different than in File list boxes, so the two controls will be discussed separately.

Directory List Boxes   A user can select a directory entry in a Directory list box by clicking on it. However, this does not open the directory; it merely moves the highlight bar to it and changes the ListIndex property to reflect the selected directory. When a user double-clicks on a directory entry, that entry is opened, and any subdirectories underneath it are displayed.

The Path property returns the directory path of the currently open directory in a Directory list box. The full path is returned, including the drive letter.

You can also assign a string to this property from within your program's code. This string must contain the valid path name of an existing directory on the system on which your program is run. This causes the open directory in the Directory list box to be changed to the path specified in the string.

Any time the Path property of a Directory list box is changed, either by the user or by the program, the Directory list box's Change event is triggered.

File List Boxes   The Path property of the File list box control specifies the directory from which the box is to select its files. Reading this property returns the full path of the File list box's current directory, including the drive letter.

You can change the current directory path for a File list box by assigning a string to this property from within your program's code. This string must contain the valid path name of an existing directory on the system on which your program is run. This causes the current directory of a File list box to be changed to the path specified in the string.

Any time the Path property of a File list box is changed, the File list box's PathChange event is triggered.

Example   The Path property for the File1 list box is set in the Form_Load and Dir1_Change events. For the Dir1 list box, it is set in the Form_Load and File1_PathChange events. Whenever the user changes the path in the Directory list or File list box, the other's property is set to reflect the change. This code is also shown in the previous example syntax.

Comments   Some sort of validity checking should be in place to ensure the string being assigned to the Path property is a valid drive and path. If the path is not valid, an error will occur.

PATHCHANGE EVENT

Objects Affected   FileListBox

Purpose   The PathChange event specifies the actions to take when the current path of a File list box changes. The arguments for the PathChange event are summarized in Table 47-17.

General Syntax

```
Name_PathChange ([Index As Integer])
```

Table 47-17 Arguments of the PathChange event

Argument	Description
Name	Name of the File list box
Index	Uniquely identifies an element of a control array

Example Syntax

```
Private Sub File1_PathChange ()
    Dir1.Path = File1.Path          'When the File list box's path is changed,
    Drive1.Drive = File1.Path       'change the path in the Dir & Drive list boxes.
End Sub
```

Description   The PathChange event activates any time the current path for a File list box changes. This can happen by assigning a new value to the Path property or by assigning a value that includes a path to the FileName property of the File list box.

This event is mostly used so the program can change the Path or Drive properties for any Directory or Drive list boxes that are on the same form. The example syntax shows how to update the path for a Drive and a Directory list box when a file box's path is changed somewhere in the code.

Control Array   The index argument is only used if the related control is part of a control array. This index specifies which element of the array is the one that activated the event. When referencing the control, the element being referenced must be specified by placing the index number between parentheses just after the control name, and before the property name (for example, Name(Index).Property).

Example   In the File System Controls project at the end of this chapter, the Path property of the Directory list box control, Dir1, can be changed by the user when a directory entry is clicked on. This causes the Dir1_Change event to occur. In this event, the Path property of Dir1 is assigned to the Path property of the File list box control, File1. This causes the current directory for File1 to be changed to the directory opened by the user. When File1.Path is assigned the value of Dir1.Path, the listed entries in File1 are updated to reflect the files in the opened directory.

Comments   Directory list boxes do not have a PathChange event. This function is covered by using their Change event.

PATTERN PROPERTY

Objects Affected   FileListBox

Purpose   The Pattern property sets or reads the currently selected file-matching pattern in a File list box. Only files that match the Pattern property are displayed in the File list box. This property can be set at design time, and set or read at runtime. Table 47-18 lists the arguments for the Pattern property.

General Syntax

```
[form!]Name.FileName [= pattern$]
```

Table 47-18 Arguments of the Pattern property

Argument	Description
form	Name of the parent form
Name	Name of the File list box
pattern$	Full or partial filename pattern

Example Syntax

```
Private Sub Text1_LostFocus ()
     File1.Pattern = Text1.Text
End Sub
```

Description   The setting of the Pattern property determines which files will be displayed in the File list box. Begin the specification of this property with the name of the File list box to be affected. Follow the property name with an equal sign and a string containing a valid DOS file pattern. The pattern can have no more than eight characters for a name, a period, and up to three characters for the extension. The wildcard characters ("*" and "?") can be (and most often are) used in the pattern. The "?" wildcard matches all characters that share the same position in the filename. The "*" wildcard matches all files that share the same pattern up to the position held by it. The Pattern property cannot specify a drive or path. When this property is changed by a program, it activates the PatternChange event for that File list box.

When the Pattern property is read, it returns the current pattern setting for the specified File list box.

The example code assigns the string "*.DAT" to the Pattern for the File1 File list box. The list will change to show only those files that end in the .DAT extension. (What is displayed is also subject to the settings of the attribute properties.)

Example   In the File System Controls project at the end of this chapter, the Pattern property for the File1 list box is set at design time to display all the files ("*.*").

Comments   Some sort of validity checking should be in place to ensure the string being assigned to the Pattern property is a valid pattern. If the pattern is not valid, an error will occur. Note that you can specify a drive and path as well as a pattern by using the FileName property rather than the Pattern property.

PatternChange Event

Objects Affected   FileListBox

Purpose   The PatternChange event specifies the actions to take when the Pattern property of a File list box changes. The Pattern property specifies a pattern (including wildcard characters) that specifies which filenames will be listed in a file list box. The arguments for the PatternChange event are summarized in Table 47-19.

General Syntax

```
Name_PatternChange ([Index As Integer])
```

Table 47-19 Arguments of the PatternChange property

Argument	Description
Name	Name of the File list box
Index	Uniquely identifies an element of a control array

Example Syntax

```
Private Sub File1_PatternChange ()
    Pattern.Text = File1.Pattern
End Sub
```

Description   The PatternChange event activates any time the display pattern for a File list box changes. This happens when a new value is assigned to the Pattern property or the FileName property of the File list box.

The example syntax responds to a change in the file pattern by assigning the new pattern to the text for the Pattern text box, displaying it as the default text in the text entry area.

Control Array   The index argument is only used if the related control is part of a control array. This index specifies which element of the array is the one that activated the event. When referencing the control, the element being referenced must be specified by placing the index number between parentheses just after the control name, and before the property name (for example, Name(Index).Property).

Example   In the File System Controls project at the end of this chapter, the PathChange event for File list box File1 is coded so that it shows the number of matching files in the box's caption, and also updates the display of the selected file in the TextSelected text box.

Comments	Directory list boxes do not have a PathChange event. This function is covered by using the Change event.

READONLY PROPERTY

Objects Affected	Data, FileListBox
Purpose	The ReadOnly property sets or returns a value that determines whether or not files with their read-only bit on will be displayed in a File list box. Read-only files cannot be changed or deleted, but only examined. Making files read-only thus offers a measure of protection for important files. The ReadOnly property can be set at design time, and set or read at runtime. The arguments for the ReadOnly property are summarized in Table 47-20.

General Syntax

```
[form!]Name.ReadOnly [= boolean%]
```

Table 47-20 Arguments of the ReadOnly property

Argument	Description
form	Name of the parent form
Name	Name of the File list box
boolean%	A True or False indicating whether read-only files will be selected

Example Syntax

```
Private Sub ReadOnlyCheck_Click ()
    File1.ReadOnly = -ReadOnlyCheck.Value        'sets the ReadOnly property of File1
End Sub

Private Sub Form_Load ()
    Dim ReadOnlyBit
    ReadOnlyBit = Abs(File1.ReadOnly)            'read the ReadOnly property setting
    ReadOnlyCheck.Value = ReadOnlyBit            'set the check box to reflect it
End Sub
```

Description	The FAT and NTFS file systems set aside one byte in the directory entry of each file for attribute information. Five properties can be used to select files for display in a File list box based on the setting of this attribute byte: the Archive, Hidden, Normal, ReadOnly, and System properties. The set of files displayed in a File list box is based on the combination of these properties.
	One of the bits in this attribute byte is the read-only bit. When this bit is set on, the file system enables the related file to be read from, but not written to or deleted. This prevents users from inadvertently changing or erasing sensitive files.

The ReadOnly property selects files based on the setting of the read-only bit. You can assign a value to the ReadOnly property, or obtain the current value of this attribute.

The ReadOnly property has two possible values: True or False. If the ReadOnly property is not changed at design time, its value will be True when the program begins.

The files selected when this property is True are a subset of the files selected by the Normal property. In other words, setting this property to True has no effect unless the Normal property is set to False. In that case, any files whose read-only bit is set on will be selected for display, regardless of the setting of the archive bit. However, if a file's read-only bit is on, but its hidden or system bits are also set on, it will not be selected unless the Hidden or System properties are also True.

Table 47-21 lists all the possible combinations for the attribute byte, and which of those combinations will be displayed when the ReadOnly property is True. This table lists only the files that will be selected with the ReadOnly bit as the basis. Other files may be selected for the same File list box by setting the Archive, Hidden, or System properties.

Table 47-21 Displayed files when the ReadOnly property is True, and Archive, System, and Hidden are False

Attribute Value	Select This File?
Archive, ReadOnly	Yes
ReadOnly	Yes
— anything else —	Any other combination will not display the file

Example   In the File System Controls project at the end of this chapter, the ReadOnly property is first read in the Form_Load event. The value returned sets the ReadOnlyCheck check box. In the ReadOnlyCheck_Click event, this property is set to reflect the status of the check box. When the check box is checked, the ReadOnly property is set to True (-1). This is also shown in the example syntax. Note that the Abs function must be used to turn a True value into the value of 1 needed to set the check box.

Comment   The data control also has a ReadOnly property that is completely different than the file system ReadOnly property discussed here.

REFRESH METHOD

Objects Affected   CheckBox, ComboBox, CommandButton, Data, DBCombo, DBGrid, DBList, DirListBox, DriveListBox, FileListBox, Form, Frame, Grid,

HScrollBar, Image, InternetExplorer, Label, Line, ListBox, ListView, MaskEdBox, MSFlexGrid, OLE Container, OptionButton, PictureBox, PropertyPage, RichTextBox, Shape, Slider, StatusBar, TabStrip, TextBox, ToolBar, TreeView, UserControl, UserDocument, VScrollBar, WebBrowser

Purpose

The Refresh method forces any changes affecting a control to be reflected in its status or display immediately. Table 47-22 summarizes the arguments for the Refresh property.

General Syntax

```
[form!]Name.Refresh
```

Table 47-22 Arguments of the Refresh method

Argument	Description
form	Name of the parent form
Name	Name of the control

Example Syntax

```
Private Sub Timer1_Timer ()
     File1.Refresh              'refresh the file list box in case of network activity
End Sub
```

Description

The Refresh method is useful in two situations. First, because Windows is a multitasking program, it is possible to make a change to a control that is not reflected on the screen because background processing is in progress. Using the Refresh method causes any changes to the specified control to be reflected immediately.

Second, the Refresh method can be used to cause the Drive, Directory, and File list boxes to update their lists. These controls only read their information from the disk when the user chooses an item from their list. This can cause problems if the files or directories have changed since the information was read. For instance, if a program uses the File list box to delete a file, unless the Refresh method is invoked, that filename stays in the File list box after the user deletes it. These controls may also need to be refreshed on a regular basis if the user is working in a networked environment, where the file information can change without notice.

Specify the Refresh method by beginning with the name of the control (such as a Drive, Directory, or File list box) to be affected.

In the example syntax, the control File1 (presumably a file list box) is refreshed. Any files that have been added to or deleted from the directory displayed by the file list box (perhaps by another running process on a network) will now be reflected in the file list.

Example	In the File System Controls project at the end of this chapter, the Refresh method is used in the File1_Click event. This causes any changes that have been made to the drive and file information by any other programs to be updated in this program.
Comments	Other than the File-related list boxes, most controls will automatically refresh as fast as needed without using the Refresh method.

SELECTED PROPERTY

Objects Affected	FileListBox, ListBox, ListItem, Node, Tab
Purpose	The Selected property lets you determine which items in a multiple selection list are selected. This property is an array of True and False values, with one entry for each item in the list. Table 47-23 summarizes the arguments for the Selected property.

General Syntax

```
[form!]Name.Selected(Index%) [= boolean%]
```

Table 47-23 Arguments for the Selected property

Argument	Description
form	Name of the parent form
Name	Name of the list box
Index%	Index in the array; corresponds to ListIndex
boolean%	True if selected; False if not selected

Example Syntax

```
Private Sub Command1_Click ()
    For i = 0 to File1.ListCount - 1        'For each item in list box File 1
        If File1.Selected(i) Then           'if the item is selected then
            Kill File1.FileName             'delete the corresponding file.
        End If
    Next i
End Sub
```

Description	The Selected property lets you determine which files in a multiple selection list box are selected. Using ListIndex in a multiple selection will only return the number of the file the highlight bar is on; not whether or not that file is selected.
	The Selected property returns an array of Boolean values with a one-to-one correspondence to the ListIndex property of the list. Stepping through the array, as in the example syntax, is an easy way to check each file for its selected status.

Example
The File System Controls project at the end of the chapter uses the Selected property to move multiple files from a list box to a combo box.

SYSTEM PROPERTY

Objects Affected FileListBox

Purpose
The System property sets or returns a value that determines whether or not files with their system bit set on will be displayed in a File list box. The System bit is used by Windows file systems to designate files that are of special importance to the system, and thus should be hidden from sight and protected from deletion. The System property can be set at design time, and set or read at runtime. Table 47-24 summarizes the arguments of the System property.

General Syntax

```
[form!]Name.System [= boolean%]
```

Table 47-24 Arguments of the System property

Argument	Description
form	Name of the parent form
Name	Name of the File list box
boolean%	A True or False indicating whether system files will be selected

Example Syntax

```
Private Sub SystemCheck_Click ()
    File1.System = -SystemCheck.Value      'set the System property of File1
End Sub

Private Sub Form_Load ()
    Dim SystemBit
    SystemBit = Abs(File1.System)          'read the System property setting
    SystemCheck.Value = SystemBit          'set the check box to reflect it
End Sub
```

Description
The FAT and NTFS file systems set aside one byte in the directory entry of each file for attribute information. Five properties can select files for display in a File list box based on the setting of this attribute byte: the Archive, Hidden, Normal, ReadOnly, and System properties. The set of files displayed in a file list box is based on the combination of these properties.

The system attribute bit normally designates a file as one of the DOS kernel or BIOS files. However, this bit can be set for other nonsystem files, such as the Windows permanent swap file or a disk doubler's hidden volume. As with the read-only attribute bit, files with the system bit set cannot be deleted.

The System property selects files based on the setting of the system attribute bit. This property has two possible values: True or False. If the System property is not changed at design time, its value will be False when the program begins.

Setting this property to True selects files with their system bit set on to be displayed, regardless of the setting of the archive and read-only bits. However, if a file also has its hidden bit set on, it will only be displayed if the Hidden property is also set to True. Setting this property to False prevents all files whose system bit is set on to be excluded from the File list box, regardless of the settings of the other four attribute properties.

Table 47-25 lists all the possible combinations for the attribute byte, and which of those combinations will be displayed when the System property is True. This table only lists those files that will be selected with the system bit as the basis. Other files may be selected for the same File list box by setting the Archive, Hidden, Normal, or ReadOnly properties.

Table 47-25 Displayed files when the System property is True, and Archive, ReadOnly, and Hidden are False

Attribute Value	Select This File?
Archive, ReadOnly, System	Yes
Archive, System	Yes
ReadOnly, System	Yes
System	Yes
— anything else —	Any other combination will not display the file

Example

In the File System Controls project at the end of this chapter, the System property is first read in the Form_Load event. The value returned sets the SystemCheck check box. In the SystemCheck_Click event, this property is set to reflect the status of the check box. When the check box is checked, the System property is set to True. This code is also shown in the example syntax. Note that the Abs function must be used to turn the True value into the value of 1 needed to set the check box.

The File System Controls Project

Project Overview

This project creates a program that lets the user explore the drives, directories, and files on a system. It uses each of the properties and events discussed in this chapter. By following the examples in this project, you should be able to learn the principles of Drive, Directory, and File list boxes.

Assembling the Project

1. Create a new form (the File System Controls form), and place on it the following controls. Use Table 47-26 to set the properties of the form and each control.

Table 47-26 Property settings for the File System Controls project

Object	Property	Setting
Form	BorderStyle	3–Fixed Dialog
	Caption	File System Controls Project
	Name	formMain
CheckBox	Caption	Archive
	Index	0
	Name	chekAttrib
CheckBox	Caption	Hidden
	Index	1
	Name	chekAttrib
CheckBox	Caption	Normal
	Index	2
	Name	chekAttrib
CheckBox	Caption	Read Only
	Index	3
	Name	chekAttrib
CheckBox	Caption	System
	Index	4
	Name	chekAttrib
TextBox	Name	textSelected
	Text	*.*
FileListBox	Name	File1
	Pattern	*.*
Label	Name	lablCount
Label	Name	lablBytes
DriveListBox	Name	Drive1
DirListBox	Name	Dir1
CommandButton	Caption	&OK
	Default	True
	Name	cmndOK

continued on next page

continued from previous page

CommandButton	Caption	&Refresh
	Name	cmndRefresh
CommandButton	Caption	E&xit
	Name	cmndExit

2. Check the appearance of your form against Figure 47-5.

3. Enter the following code into the Form_Load event. This event uses the CurDir function to set the starting paths for the Drive1, Dir1, and File1 list boxes. It also reads the default attribute settings from the File1 File list box control, and sets the values of the chekAttrib control array. Check boxes are set on with a value of 1, while the attribute properties of a File list box return a 0 or a -1. Therefore, the Abs (absolute value) function changes the -1 to a 1.

```
Private Sub Form_Load ()
    Drive1.Drive = CurDir
    Dir1.Path = CurDir
    File1.Path = CurDir
    chekAttrib(0).Value = Abs(File1.Archive)
    chekAttrib(1).Value = Abs(File1.Hidden)
    chekAttrib(2).Value = Abs(File1.Normal)
    chekAttrib(3).Value = Abs(File1.ReadOnly)
    chekAttrib(4).Value = Abs(File1.System)
    textSelected.Text = ParseFileName()
End Sub
```

4. Enter the following code into the chekAttrib_Click event. This event uses the value of the control array member's check box Value property to set the corresponding attribute property of the File1 File list box. They also update the label lablCount to reflect the number of files displayed in the File1 File list box.

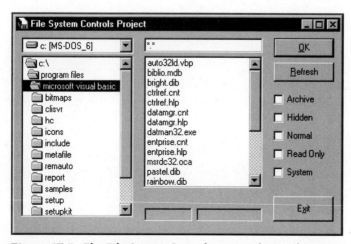

Figure 47-5 The File System Controls project during design

```
Private Sub chekAttrib_Click (Index As Integer)
    Select Case Index
        Case 0' attrib
            File1.Archive = -chekAttrib(0).Value
        Case 1' hidden
            File1.Hidden = -chekAttrib(1).Value
        Case 2' normal
            File1.Normal = -chekAttrib(2).Value
        Case 3' read only
            File1.ReadOnly = -chekAttrib(3).Value
        Case 4' system
            File1.System = -chekAttrib(4).Value
    End Select
    lablCount.Caption = Format(File1.ListCount, "##,###") + " Files"
End Sub
```

5. Enter the following code into the Dir1_Change event. This event does two things. First it updates the Path property of the File1 File list box to reflect the change made to this directory's path. If the new path is different from the old, doing this also causes the File1_PathChange event to be activated. Second, it changes the current directory to the one specified by the new path.

```
Private Sub Dir1_Change ()
    File1.Path = Dir1.Path
    ChDir Dir1.Path
End Sub
```

6. Enter the following code into the File1_Change event. This event first updates the Path property of the Dir1 Directory list box. If the new path is different from the old, doing this also causes the Dir1_Change event to occur. It also sets the Drive property of the Drive1 drive list box. Again, if this changes the current Drive setting, the Drive1_Change event will be activated. The event then updates the text in the TextSelected text box control by making a call to the ParseFileName function. Finally, the number of files displayed in the File1 File list box is updated.

```
Private Sub File1_PathChange ()
    lablCount.Caption = Format(File1.ListCount, "##,##0") + " Files"
    textSelected.Text = ParseFileName()
    Dir1.Path = File1.Path
    Drive1.Drive = File1.Path
    lablBytes.Caption = ""
End Sub
```

7. Enter the following code into the File1_PatternChange event. This event occurs when the user changes the FileName property by editing the text in the TextSelected text box.

```
Private Sub File1_PatternChange ()
    lablCount.Caption = Format(File1.ListCount, "##,##0") + " Files"
    textSelected.Text = ParseFileName()
End Sub
```

8. Enter the following text into the Drive1_Change event. This event sets the Path property of the Dir1 Directory list box. If this changes the current path for the Directory list box, the Dir1_Change event will be initiated.

```
Private Sub Drive1_Change ()
    Dir1.Path = CurDir(Drive1.Drive)
End Sub
```

9. Enter the following code into the File1_Click event. Clicking on a file places its name in the TextSelected text box.

```
Private Sub File1_Click ()
    textSelected.Text = File1.FileName
End Sub
```

10. Enter the following code in the File1_MouseUp event. This steps through the files in the File list box and adds up the total number of bytes for the selected files.

```
Private Sub File1_MouseUp (Button As Integer, Shift As Integer, X As Single, Y As Single)
    For i = 0 To File1.ListCount - 1
        If File1.Selected(i) Then
            bytes = bytes + FileLen(File1.Path & "\" & File1.List(i))
        End If
    Next i
    lablBytes.Caption = Format(bytes, " ###,###,##0") & " Bytes"
End Sub
```

11. Enter the following text for the command buttons. The cmndOK_Click event sets the FileName property of the File1 File list box to the text that is in the TextSelected text box control. If this text specifies a path or pattern that is different than that currently in use by the File1 File list box, it causes the File1_PathChange, or File1_Pattern_Change events to occur.

The cmndRefresh_Click event refreshes File1 to update its list in case of any background changes.

The cmndExit_Click event simply ends the program.

```
Private Sub cmndOK_Click ()
    File1.FileName = TextSelected.Text
End Sub

Private Sub cmndRefresh_Click ()
    File1.Refresh
End Sub

Private Sub cmndExit_Click ()
    End
End Sub
```

12. Enter the following code in the General Declarations area of the form. After the first line is complete (Function...) Visual Basic will give this function its own window. This function reads the current File1.Path and File1.FileName properties and, based on these, parses together the full path and filename of the selected file(s).

```
Function ParseFileName () As String
    Dim tempFile As String
    Dim tempDir As String

    tempDir = File1.Path
    tempFile = File1.Pattern
    If tempFile = "" Then tempFile = "*.*"
    If Right(tempDir, 1) <> "\" Then tempFile = "\" + tempFile
    ParseFileName = tempDir + tempFile
End Function
```

How It Works

This very simple program enables the user to explore the disk drives, directories, and files on the system on which it is run. The user can select drives, directories, and files by clicking or double-clicking on the desired lists. Clicking on the attribute (Archive, Hidden, Normal, Read Only, and System) check boxes causes the selection of the files in the File1 File list box to be limited to those that match the checked boxes.

The selected files for display in the File1 File list box can also be modified by entering a new path or pattern in the TextSelected text box control and clicking the OK button (or pressing the E key, since the Default property of the cmndOK control is set to True). For instance, placing the text *.EXE will cause only the files in the selected directory that have an extension of EXE to be displayed in the file list box.

Selecting a file or multiple files in File1 also updates the total bytes label. The routine steps through each file in the list box and if it has been selected, it adds the length of the file in bytes to the running total.

Regardless of where a change is made, that change is reflected by all the related controls. For instance, if the current directory is changed by double-clicking on the Dir1 directory list box, the files in the File1 File list box are updated. Figure 47-6 shows the program in action.

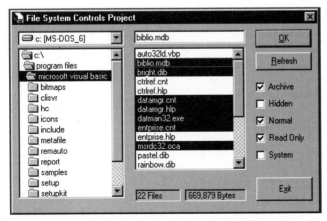

Figure 47-6   The File System Controls project in action

48

GRID CONTROLS

The versatile grid control gives you the power of a two-dimensional list box with many additional features. This control allows you to set up display structures similar to a spreadsheet. Rows and columns intersect to form individual cells. These cells may have their contents changed independently, and may be selected individually or as a region. You also have the facility to create fixed rows and columns, which would be familiar to spreadsheet users as row and column heads (A1, B3, and so on). Both text and graphics may be placed in the cells.

Although the grid control looks similar to a spreadsheet, it has no inherent calculation properties. It is merely a collection of cells that you may manipulate with code, and that the user may interact with. One vital difference between the grid control and a spreadsheet is that the user may not directly change the contents of a cell. Much like a list box, the grid needs all its values set by program code.

The grid control can be used for any task that requires displaying data in rows and columns. Although a spreadsheet is the most familiar metaphor, other possibilities include database tables, general ledger "printouts," and even multicolumn pick lists.

Using Grids

The name of the grid control to use is an ActiveX control called Microsoft FlexGrid control. You can use this grid control by first adding the FlexGrid component to your Visual Basic project. To do this, from the main Visual Basic development window, choose the "Project" pulldown menu and the "Components" menu item. In the Components dialog, check "Microsoft FlexGrid Control" and press OK. At this point, the control has been added to your project, and an MSFlexGrid icon appears at the bottom of your Toolbox window.

Once the control has been added to your project, you can size it with the Rows and Cols properties to set the number of rows and columns in the grid. You can change these properties at will to dynamically resize your grid control. You can then set individual column widths and row heights as well as specify if data is to be left-aligned, right-aligned, or centered.

You can use the AddItem method to add new data to a grid, much like a list or combo box. More commonly, though, you'll either select a region and assign a group of values to the selection with the Clip property, or activate an individual cell with the Row and Col properties to assign its Text or Picture properties.

Grids Summary

Table 48-1 displays the methods, events, and properties that influence the settings and effects of the grid controls.

Table 48-1 Methods, events, and properties dealing with grid controls

Use or Set This...	Type	To Do This...
AddItem	Method	Add items to a grid
AllowBigSelection	Property	Read or set whether an entire row or column can be selected by clicking on its header
AllowUserResizing	Property	Read or set whether the user can resize rows and columns
BackColor, BackColorBkg, BackColorFixed, BackColorSel, CellBackColor	Property	Read or set the background color of grid elements
CellAlignment	Property	Read or set the alignment of the text within a cell
CellHeight, CellLeft, CellTop, CellWidth	Property	Read the size and location of a cell
CellPicture	Property	Read or set the picture contained within a cell
CellPictureAlignment	Property	Read or set the alignment of a picture contained within a cell
Clear	Method	Clear the text, pictures, and formatting in a grid
Clip	Property	Read or set a selected region in a grid
Col, Row, ColSel, RowSel	Property	Read or set the active and selected cells in a grid
ColAlignment	Property	Read or set the alignment of a column's data in a grid
ColData, RowData	Property	Read or set a user-defined value for a row or column in a grid
ColIsVisible, RowIsVisible	Property	Read whether a row or column is visible in a grid
ColPos, RowPos	Property	Read the twip position of the left side of a column or the top of a row in a grid
Cols, Rows	Property	Read or set the total number of columns or rows in a grid
ColWidth, RowHeight	Property	Read or set the width of a column or the height of a row in a grid
FillStyle	Property	Read or set whether the active cell or the selected cells are affected by cell formatting
FixedAlignment	Property	Read or set the alignment of the text in the fixed rows or columns
FixedCols, FixedRows	Property	Read or set the number of grid's fixed rows or columns on the left and top
ForeColor, ForeColorFixed, ForeColorSel, CellForeColor	Property	Read or set the foreground color of grid elements
GridLines, GridLinesFixed	Property	Read or set whether the grid lines are visible
GridLineWidth	Property	Read or set the pixel width of the grid lines
GridLineWidth	Property	Read or set the width of the lines in a grid
HighLight	Property	Read or set whether the selected cells appear highlighted in a grid

Use or Set This...	Type	To Do This...
LeftCol, TopRow	Property	Read or set the leftmost visible nonfixed column or topmost visible nonfixed row in a grid
MouseCol, MouseRow	Property	Read the location of the mouse pointer in the grid
Redraw	Property	Read or set whether the grid can redraw itself
RemoveItem	Method	Remove an item from a grid
RowColChange	Event	React to a new cell becoming active in a grid
SelChange	Event	React to a new selection in a grid
SelectionMode	Property	Read or set the allowable selection types
Text	Property	Return the selected item in a grid cell
TextStyle, TextStyleFixed, CellTextStyle	Property	Read or set the style of the text in cells
WordWrap	Property	Read or set whether the item text wraps within a cell

The following pages describe the use of the methods, events, and properties that enable you to set up and manage grids. The Grid project at the end of the chapter demonstrates how these grid management techniques are used together.

AddItem Method

Objects Affected   ComboBox, ListBox, MSFlexGrid

Purpose   The AddItem method adds an item to the list of a grid. Table 48-2 summarizes the arguments of the AddItem method.

General Syntax

```
[form!]Name.AddItem Item$ [, Index%]
```

Table 48-2 Arguments of the AddItem method

Argument	Description
form	Name of the control's parent form
Name	Name of the grid
Item$	A string expression containing the value that is being added to the list
Index%	An optional index number specifying the placement of the new item in the list

Example Syntax

```
Private Sub Form_Load()
    For i% = 0 To (MSFlexGrid1.Cols - 1)
        MSFlexGrid1.ColWidth(i%) = MSFlexGrid1.Width / 2
    Next
    MSFlexGrid1.AddItem "Red" & Chr$(9) & "RGB = 255,0,0", 0
'add color names to a gridlist box
    MSFlexGrid1.AddItem "Green" & Chr$(9) & "RGB = 0,255,0", 1
```

continued on next page

continued from previous page

```
    MSFlexGrid1.AddItem "Blue" & Chr$(9) & "RGB = 0,0,255", 2
    MSFlexGrid1.AddItem "Yellow" & Chr$(9) & "RGB = 255,255,0", 3
    MSFlexGrid1.AddItem "Purple" & Chr$(9) & "RGB = 255,0,255", 4
End Sub
```

Description

When the grid object first displays, no items are assigned to it. You can use the AddItem method to create grid entries. When the AddItem method executes, the value of the string expression specified by the Item$ argument is added to the grid.

You can specify the exact placement of the new item in the grid by providing the Index% argument. If you supply the index number, Visual Basic will add one to the index number of the item that currently holds the specified index, and all those items that follow it. The new item is then added to the list at the specified index. Supplying an index number inserts the new item at that position in the list. It does not replace the item that is currently at that position.

If you supply the index number, it must be no less than 0 and no greater than the value of the Rows property. If the index specified is not in this range, Visual Basic issues an Illegal function call error.

The index numbering of the list is zero-based. Therefore, if a grid contains five items, the first item is index number 0, and the highest index number is 4. Most often, the AddItem method is used in the Form_Load event of the parent form to initialize the grid entries. This ensures the grid is loaded before the user has access to the grid.

If you omit the index argument, Visual Basic assigns the next available index number to the new item. In other words, if there are five items in the list, the highest index number will be 4. Therefore the next available index number will be 5.

You can add data to more than one column within the same row by using the tab character (Chr$(9)) to delimit each column's data. This means that if you want "column1" to appear in column one and "column2" to appear in column two, you should add the string "column1" & Chr$(9) & "column2" to the grid using the AddItem method. The example syntax demonstrates this use.

The example syntax adds five color names and their respective RGB values to a grid. Figure 48-1 shows how this list box looks when loaded.

Comments

A more effective way of changing the data within a grid is to use its Text property. When you set the Text property, the cell specified by the Col and Row properties is changed to contain this text.

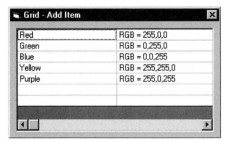

Figure 48-1   Example syntax uses the AddItem method to load the grid

ALLOWBIGSELECTION PROPERTY

Objects Affected   MSFlexGrid

Purpose   The AllowBigSelection property reads or sets whether an entire row or column can be selected by clicking on its header. Tables 48-3 and 48-4 summarize the arguments of the AllowBigSelection property.

General Syntax

```
[form!]Name.AllowBigSelection [ = boolean%]
```

Table 48-3 Arguments of the AllowBigSelection property

Argument	Description
form	Name property of the form
Name	Name property of the grid control
boolean%	True/False value indicating if big selection is allowed or not

Table 48-4 Meanings of the boolean% argument in the AllowBigSelection property

boolean%	Meaning
True	(Default) The user can select an entire row or column by clicking on its header
False	The user must select an entire row or column by sweeping the mouse across the range of cells

Example Syntax

```
Private Sub Form_Load()
    MSFlexGrid1.AllowBigSelection = True        'Allow selection of full rows and columns
End Sub
```

Description   When the grid object first appears, the AllowBigSelection property is set to True by default. This means that the user can click on any fixed column or row cells to select the entire row or column. If the grid does not have any fixed rows or columns, then this property has no effect since there is no header row or column on which to click.

ALLOWUSERRESIZING PROPERTY

Objects Affected   MSFlexGrid

Purpose   The AllowUserResizing property reads or sets whether the user can resize rows and columns. Tables 48-5 and 48-6 summarize the arguments of the AllowUserResizing property.

General Syntax

```
[form!]Name.AllowUserResizing [ = sizing%]
```

Table 48-5 Arguments of the AllowUserResizing property

Argument	Description
form	Name property of the form
Name	Name property of the grid control
sizing%	Value indicating which combinations of rows and columns may be resized

Table 48-6 Meanings of the sizing% argument in the AllowUserResizing property

sizing%	Meaning
flexResizeNone	(Default) Neither rows nor columns may be resized by the user
flexResizeColumns	Allow the user to resize the columns only
flexResizeRows	Allow the user to resize the rows only
flexResizeBoth	Allow the user to resize both the rows and the columns

Example Syntax

```
Private Sub Form_Load()
    MSFlexGrid1.AllowUserResizing = flexResizeBoth
'Allow both rows and columns to be resized by the user
End Sub
```

Description   You would typically allow the user to resize the grid's rows or columns if the data that is put in each cell of the grid may be larger than that which can be displayed. When user resizing is on for the grid's rows or columns, the user can resize that row or column by moving the mouse pointer to the header area and dragging the gridline which needs to be moved.

Note that you can programmatically resize a row or column using the RowPos, ColPos, RowPosition, and ColPosition properties. In addition, you can obtain the dimensions of the current cell using the CellHeight, CellLeft, CellTop, and CellWidth properties.

BackColor, BackColorBkg, BackColorFixed, BackColorSel, CellBackColor Properties

Objects Affected   MSFlexGrid

Purpose   Use the BackColor, BackColorBkg, BackColorFixed, BackColorSel, CellBackColor properties to read or set the background color of grid elements. The BackColor, BackColorBkg, BackColorFixed, and BackColorSel properties are all available at design time. The CellBackColor property is only available at runtime. Tables 48-7 and 48-8 summarize the arguments of the BackColor, BackColorBkg, BackColorFixed, and BackColorSel properties.

General Syntax

```
[form!]Name.BackColor [ = color%]
[form!]Name.BackColorBkg [ = color%]
[form!]Name.BackColorFixed [ = color%]
[form!]Name.BackColorSel [ = color%]
[form!]Name.CellBackColor [ = color%]
```

Table 48-7 Arguments of the BackColor, BackColorBkg, BackColorFixed, BackColorSel, and CellBackColor properties

Argument	Description
form	Name property of the form
Name	Name property of the grid control
color%	Contains the Visual Basic color constant or an RGB value

Table 48-8 Meanings of the color% argument in the BackColor, BackColorBkg, BackColorFixed, BackColorSel, and CellBackColor properties

color%	Meaning
vbBlack	Black (&H000000)
vbBlue	Blue (&HFF0000)
vbCyan	Cyan, a light blue (&HFFFF00)
vbGreen	Green (&H00FF00)

continued on next page

continued from previous page

color%	Meaning
vbMagenta	Magenta, a purplish red (&HFF00FF)
vbRed	Red (&H0000FF)
vbWhite	White (&HFFFFFF)
vbYellow	Yellow (&H00FFFF)
&H*BBGGRR* or RGB(r,g,b)	Arbitrary RGB color value

Example Syntax

```
Private Sub Command1_Click ()
    MSFlexGrid1.BackColor = vbWhite            'Grid background is white
    MSFlexGrid1.BackColorSel = &HC0C0C0        'Grid selection color is gray
    MSFlexGrid1.BackColorBkg = RGB(0,0,255)    'Nongrid background is blue
    MSFlexGrid1.BackColorFixed = vbCyan        'Fixed row backgrounds are cyan

    MSFlexGrid1.Col = 2                        'Set the current column
    MSFlexGrid1.Row = 2                        'Set the current row
    MSFlexGrid1.CellBackColor = vbYellow       'Set the background of (2,2) to yellow
End Sub
```

Description   Use the BackColor, BackColorSel, BackColorBkg, and BackColorFixed properties when you want to customize the background colors of the various parts of the grid. The BackColor property sets the background color of the main nonfixed grid cells. The BackColorSel property sets the background color of the selection. The BackColorBkg property sets the background color of the area behind the grid which may only be visible when you scroll all the way to the right or to the bottom. The BackColorFixed property sets the background color of the fixed (heading) rows and columns of the grid.

Unlike the previously mentioned properties which affect general areas of cells in the grid, you can use the CellBackColor property to change the background color of the current cell. The current cell is the cell indicated by the current setting of the Row and Col properties.

If you need to change the text color (foreground color) of the cells, refer to the ForeColor, ForeColorFixed, ForeColorSel, and CellForeColor properties.

CELLALIGNMENT PROPERTY

Objects Affected   MSFlexGrid

Purpose   Use the grid's CellAlignment property to read or set the alignment of the active cell's data. This property is not available at design time; read and write at runtime. Tables 48-9 and 48-10 summarize the arguments of the CellAlignment property.

General Syntax

```
[form!]Name.CellAlignment [ = alignment%]
```

Table 48-9 Arguments of the CellAlignment property

Argument	Description
form	Name property of the form
Name	Name property of the grid control
alignment%	Expression indicating left-, right-, or center-aligned

Table 48-10 Meanings of the alignment% argument in the grid's ColAlignment property

alignment%	Meaning
flexAlignLeftTop(Default)	Align text along the left and top of the cell
flexAlignLeftCenter	Align text along the left side and centered vertically in the cell
flexAlignLeftBottom	Align text along the left and bottom of the cell
flexAlignCenterTop	Center text horizontally and align along the top of the cell
flexAlignCenterCenter	Center text both horizontally and vertically in the cell
flexAlignCenterBottom	Center text horizontally and align along the bottom of the cell
flexAlignRightTop	Align text along the right and top of the cell
flexAlignRightCenter	Align text along the right side and centered vertically in the cell
flexAlignRightBottom	Align text along the right and bottom of the cell
flexAlignGeneral	Center text vertically and align numeric data on the left and string data on the right

Example Syntax

```
Private Sub Form_Load ()
    Combo1.AddItem "Left-Top"
    Combo1.AddItem "Left-Center"
    Combo1.AddItem "Left-Bottom"
End Sub

Private Sub MSFlexGrid1_Click ()
    MSFlexGrid1.Col = 0
    MSFlexGrid1.Row = 0
    MSFlexGrid1.CellAlignment = Combo1.ListIndex    'set current cell's alignment
End Sub
```

Description Each cell in a grid may have its own alignment—left-, right-, or center-aligned in both the horizontal and vertical directions. The CellAlignment property lets you read or set the alignment of individual cells. Choose one of the ten possible alignments, as summarized in Table 48-10.

This property only affects the active cell designated by the Row and Col properties. A grid may have both fixed and nonfixed rows. Fixed rows are typically used for headings like "1998," "1999," "2000," and so on. Use the FixedAlignment property to set the alignment of cells in fixed rows and the ColAlignment property to set the alignment of cells in nonfixed rows.

The example syntax uses a combo box that has been filled with the alignment possibilities in the correct order. It uses the combo box's ListIndex property to set the alignment of the column with the active cell.

CellHeight, CellLeft, CellTop, CellWidth Properties

Objects Affected   MSFlexGrid

Purpose   Use the CellHeight, CellLeft, CellTop, and CellWidth properties to read the size or position of the current cell. This property is not available at design time and is read-only at runtime.

General Syntax

```
[form!]Name.CellHeight [as Integer]
[form!]Name.CellLeft [as Integer]
[form!]Name.CellTop [as Integer]
[form!]Name.CellWidth [as Integer]
```

Example Syntax

```
Private Sub MSFlexGrid1_Click()
    Text1.Left = MSFlexGrid1.CellLeft + MSFlexGrid1.Left
'Set TextBox location to current cell
    Text1.Top = MSFlexGrid1.CellTop + MSFlexGrid1.Top
    Text1.Width = MSFlexGrid1.CellWidth
'Set TextBox size to match cell
    Text1.Height = MSFlexGrid1.CellHeight

    Text1.Visible = True
    Text1.Text = MSFlexGrid1.Text
    Text1.SetFocus
End Sub
```

Description   Use the CellLeft, CellTop, CellWidth, and CellHeight properties to read the size and position of the current cell. The current cell is the cell currently referenced by the Row and Col properties.

The example syntax makes use of the CellLeft, CellTop, CellWidth, and CellHeight properties to position a text box over the cell to allow the user to edit its contents. In this way, you can provide editing capabilities within your grid control.

CellPicture Property

Objects Affected   MSFlexGrid

Purpose   Use the CellPicture property to read or set the image contained within the current cell in the grid. This property is not available at design time. Table 48-11 summarizes the arguments of the CellPicture property.

General Syntax

```
[form!]Name.CellPicture [ = picture]
```

Table 48-11 Arguments of the CellPicture property

Argument	Description
form	Name property of the form
Name	Name property of the grid control
picture	Contains picture to display

Example Syntax

```
Private Sub Form_Load()
    MSFlexGrid1.Col = 3
' Set current row and column to (3,3)
    MSFlexGrid1.Row = 3
    MSFlexGrid1.CellPictureAlignment = flexAlignTopLeft
    Set MSFlexGrid1.CellPicture = LoadPicture("e:\apple.bmp")
' Load a picture from a bitmap file
End Sub
```

Description   Use the CellPicture property to read or set the image contained within the current cell. The current cell is the cell referenced by the setting of the Col and Row properties. The image can either be loaded from a file using the LoadPicture function or by referencing another control's Picture property. The location of the Picture relative to the cell can be controlled by the CellPictureAlignment property.

CELLPICTUREALIGNMENT PROPERTY

Objects Affected   MSFlexGrid

Purpose   Use the CellPictureAlignment property to read or set the alignment of the picture within a cell. The CellPictureAlignment property is not available at design time. Tables 48-12 and 48-13 summarize the arguments of the CellPictureAlignment property.

General Syntax

```
[form!]Name.CellPictureAlignment [ = alignment%]
```

Table 48-12 Arguments of the CellPictureAlignment property

Argument	Description
form	Name property of the form
Name	Name property of the grid control
alignment%	Contains the alignment type

Table 48-13 Meanings of the alignment% argument in the CellPictureAlignment property

alignment%	Meaning
flexAlignLeftTop	(Default) Align picture along the left and top of the cell
flexAlignLeftCenter	Align picture along the left side and centered vertically in the cell
flexAlignLeftBottom	Align picture along the left and bottom of the cell
flexAlignCenterTop	Center picture horizontally and align along the top of the cell
flexAlignCenterCenter	Center picture both horizontally and vertically in the cell
flexAlignCenterBottom	Center picture horizontally and align along the bottom of the cell
flexAlignRightTop	Align picture along the right and top of the cell
flexAlignRightCenter	Align picture along the right side and centered vertically in the cell
flexAlignRightBottom	Align picture along the right and bottom of the cell
flexAlignGeneral	Center picture vertically and align numeric data on the left and string data on the right

Example Syntax
```
Private Sub Form_Load()
     MSFlexGrid1.Col = 3
' Set current row and column to (3,3)
     MSFlexGrid1.Row = 3     MSFlexGrid1.CellPictureAlignment = flexAlignTopLeft  ⇐
' Align picture along the top and left of the cell
     Set MSFlexGrid1.CellPicture = LoadPicture("e:\apple.bmp")
' Load a picture from a bitmap file
End Sub
```

Description   Use the CellPictureAlignment property to specify the alignment of the picture within the current cell. The picture within the current cell can be specified using the CellPicture property. The current cell is the one indicated by the Row and Col properties.

If you need to specify the alignment of the text within a cell, use the ColAlignment or the FixedAlignment property.

CLEAR METHOD

Objects Affected   Clipboard, ComboBox, DataObject, DataObjectFiles, ErrObject, ListBox, MSFlexGrid

Purpose   The Clear method clears all text, pictures, and formatting within a grid. Table 48-14 summarizes the arguments of the Clear method.

General Syntax

```
[form!]Name.Clear
```

Table 48-14 Arguments of the Clear method

Argument	Description
form	Name of the control's parent form
Name	Name of the grid

Example Syntax

```
Private Sub Form_Load()
    MSFlexGrid1.Clear                          ' Clear the grid
End Sub
```

Description   If you need to clear all the text, pictures, and formatting within a grid, call the Clear method. Note that this method does not reset any foreground or background properties of the grid and only affects the data within the cells.

CLIP PROPERTY

Objects Affected   MSFlexGrid

Purpose   Use the Clip property to read or set the contents of the cells in a selected region. This is the most efficient method of reading or setting large areas of a grid control. This property is not available at design time. Table 48-15 summarizes the arguments of the Clip property.

General Syntax

```
[form!]Name.Clip [ = expression$]
```

Table 48-15 Arguments of the Clip property

Argument	Description
form	Name property of the form
Name	Name property of the grid control
expression$	Contains delimited values to place in selected cells

Example Syntax

```
Private Sub Command1_Click ()
    MSFlexGrid1.Rows = UBound(Addresses, 1)    '# of rows in array (Option Base 1)
    MSFlexGrid1.Cols = UBound(Addresses, 2)    '# of columns in array
    MSFlexGrid1.Col = 1                         'Select the entire grid
    MSFlexGrid1.Row = 1                         'of nonfixed cells.
    MSFlexGrid1.ColSel = MSFlexGrid1.Cols - 1
    MSFlexGrid1.RowSel = MSFlexGrid1.Rows - 1
    For i = 1 To MSFlexGrid1.Rows               'step through each array row
        For j = 1 To MSFlexGrid1.Cols           'step through each array column
```

continued on next page

continued from previous page

```
            data$ = data$ & Addresses(i, j)        'add data value to string
            If j <> MSFlexGrid1.Cols Then          'If not at end of row,
                data$ = data$ & Chr$(9)            'add item delimiter.
            End If
        Next j
        data$ = data$ & Chr$(13)                   'new row; add row delimiter
    Next i
    MSFlexGrid1.Clip = data$                       'put the data into the grid
End Sub
```

Description   Use the Clip property to read or set large regions of the grid control. The string expression this property uses delimits each entry with a tab character (Chr$(9)) and each row with a carriage return (Chr$(13)). The Clip property uses values like this:

```
value TAB value TAB value CR value TAB value TAB value CR value TAB value TAB value CR
R1C1       R1C2       R1C3      R2C1       R2C2       R2C3      R3C1       R3C2       R3C3
```

The example syntax builds up a string expression from a two-dimensional array. It iterates through each item of the array, adding the data value to the string expression, and adding a tab character if it's not at the end of a row, and a carriage return character if it is at the end of a row.

The Clip property only operates on a selected region. If no cells are selected, it returns a null string; if you attempt to assign a string expression to a grid with no selected cells, the string is ignored. If the selected region is smaller than the number of items in the string expression, extra entries are ignored. If the selected region is larger than the number of items in the string expression, then the unassigned cells get set to a null string.

Example   The Grid project at the end of this chapter uses the Clip property to save and restore the contents of the grid to a file. Both cmndOpen_Click and cmndSave_Click use the Clip property to do this. cmndSave_Click is the simplest: It just writes the entire Clip property to disk without modification. The cmndOpen_Click event reads in the contents of the file one line at a time and reassembles the string by appending each line plus a carriage return. It then assigns the built up string to the Clip property to restore the grid's contents.

Comment   The graph control in the Professional Version of Visual Basic uses this same format for its QuickData property. You can assign the contents of a grid to the graph with a single line of code.

```
Graph1.QuickData = MSFlexGrid1.Clip
```

COL, ROW, COLSEL, ROWSEL PROPERTIES

Objects Affected   MSFlexGrid

Purpose   Use the Col, Row, ColSel, and RowSel properties to determine or set the active cell and range of selected cells in a grid. Once an active cell is set, you can use other properties on that cell, such as Text and CellPicture. This property is not available at design time and is readable and writable at runtime. Table 48-16 summarizes the arguments of the Col, Row, ColSel, and RowSel properties.

General Syntax

```
[form!]Name.Col [ = column%]
[form!]Name.Row [ = row%]
[form!]Name.ColSel [ = column%]
[form!]Name.RowSel [ = row%]
```

Table 48-16 Arguments of the Col, Row, ColSel, and RowSel properties

Argument	Description
form	Name property of the form
Name	Name property of the grid control
column%	Column number of active cell or last column selected
row%	Row number of active cell or last row selected

Example Syntax

```
Private Sub Command1_Click ()
    MSFlexGrid1.Rows = UBound(Addresses, 1)      '# of rows in array (Option Base 1)
    MSFlexGrid1.Cols = UBound(Addresses, 2)      '# of columns in array
    For i = 1 To MSFlexGrid1.Rows                'step through each nonfixed grid row
        For j = 1 To MSFlexGrid1.Cols            'step through each nonfixed grid ⇐
column
            MSFlexGrid1.Col = j                  'set active cell's column
            MSFlexGrid1.Row = i                  'set active cell's row
            MSFlexGrid1.Text = Addresses(i, j)   'place data in cell
        Next j
    Next I
    ' Select the entire grid with (1, 1) as the active cell
    MSFlexGrid1.Col = 0
    MSFlexGrid1.Row = 0
    MSFlexGrid1.ColSel = Cols - 1
    MSFlexGrid1.RowSel = Rows - 1
End Sub
```

Description

A grid control consists of a two-dimensional array of cells. Each cell belongs to a specific row and column. The Col and Row properties set the active cell using the column and row numbers. You can use other properties (like Text or CellPicture) once you've set the active cell. The current select starts at the active cell and extends to the column and row specified by the ColSel and RowSel properties.

Grids are zero-based—that is, the first column's number is 0 and the first row is 0. The Cols and Rows properties (*not* the same as the Col and Row properties we're discussing here!) set the total number of columns and rows in a grid.

The example syntax steps through each nonfixed row and column of the grid and assigns it the value contained in the array. The Col and Row properties set which cell to update. When this is complete, the entire grid is selected starting at column 0, row 0 and extending to the last row and column.

Example   The Grid project at the end of this chapter uses Col, Row, ColSel, and RowSel many times to both set the active cell and to determine which cell is active. You'll find Col and Row in the Form_Load, gridSheet_RowColChange, and NewValues procedures.

COLALIGNMENT PROPERTY

Objects Affected   MSFlexGrid

Purpose   Use the grid's ColAlignment property to read or set the alignment of a column's data. This property is not available at design time; read and write at runtime. It is only available for nonfixed columns; use the FixedAlignment property to set the alignment for fixed columns. Tables 48-17 and 48-18 summarize the arguments of the ColAlignment property.

General Syntax

```
[form!]Name.ColAlignment(column%) [ = alignment%]
```

Table 48-17 Arguments of the ColAlignment property

Argument	Description
form	Name property of the form
Name	Name property of the grid control
column%	Number of the column (starting from the far left, column%=0)
alignment%	Expression indicating left-, right-, or center-aligned

Table 48-18 Meanings of the Alignment% argument in the grid's ColAlignment property

alignment%	Meaning
flexAlignLeftTop	(Default) Align text along the left and top of the cell
flexAlignLeftCenter	Align text along the left side and centered vertically in the cell
flexAlignLeftBottom	Align text along the left and bottom of the cell
flexAlignCenterTop	Center text horizontally and align along the top of the cell
flexAlignCenterCenter	Center text both horizontally and vertically in the cell
flexAlignCenterBottom	Center text horizontally and align along the bottom of the cell

alignment%	Meaning
flexAlignRightTop	Align text along the right and top of the cell
flexAlignRightCenter	Align text along the right side and centered vertically in the cell
flexAlignRightBottom	Align text along the right and bottom of the cell
flexAlignGeneral	Center text vertically and align numeric data on the left and string data on the right

Example Syntax

```
Private Sub Form_Load ()
    Combo1.AddItem "Left"
    Combo1.AddItem "Right"
    Combo1.AddItem "Center"
End Sub

Private Sub Combo1_Click ()
    'Combo has the alignments in the correct order
    MSFlexGrid1.ColAlignment(MSFlexGrid1.Col) = Combo1.ListIndex    'set current column's⇐
alignment
End Sub
```

Description   Each column in a grid may have its own alignment—left-, right-, or center-aligned in both the horizontal and vertical directions. The ColAlignment property lets you read or set the alignment of individual columns. Choose one of the ten possible alignments, as summarized in Table 48-18.

This property only affects cells in nonfixed rows. A grid may have both fixed and nonfixed rows. Fixed rows are typically used for headings like "1998," "1999," "2000," and so on. Use the FixedAlignment property to set the alignment of cells in fixed rows.

The example syntax uses a combo box that has been filled with the alignment possibilities in the correct order. It uses the combo box's ListIndex property to set the alignment of the column with the active cell.

Example   The Grid project at the end of this chapter uses a combo box, as in the example syntax above, to set the grid's alignment. The cmboAlign_Click event does this.

COLDATA, ROWDATA PROPERTIES

Objects Affected   MSFlexGrid

Purpose   Use the ColData and RowData properties to read and set a user-defined value associated with a column, row, or cell. This property is not available at design time. Table 48-19 summarizes the arguments of the ColData and RowData properties.

General Syntax

```
[form!]Name(column%).ColData = value%
[form!]Name(row%).RowData = value%
```

Table 48-19 Arguments of the ColData and RowData properties

Argument	Description
form	Name property of the form
Name	Name property of the grid control
column%	Column number
row%	Row number
value%	User-defined value associated with the row or column

Example Syntax
```
Private Sub Form_Load()
    MSFlexGrid1.ColData(0) = 1234        ' Associate 1234 with column 0
    MSFlexGrid1.RowData(0) = 5678        ' Associate 5678 with row 0
End Sub
```

Description   Use the ColData and RowData properties to associate a hidden numeric value with a column or row. This is most useful if you have an array of items which you insert into a grid, one per row or column. By associating the array index of the item with the row or column, your program can always know the actual array item corresponding to a row or column— even if the rows or columns may get rearranged because of sorting or user editing.

COLISVISIBLE, ROWISVISIBLE PROPERTIES

Objects Affected   MSFlexGrid

Purpose   Use the ColIsVisible and RowIsVisible properties to determine whether a specified column is visible to the user. This property is not available at design time and is read-only at runtime. Table 48-20 summarizes the arguments of the ColIsVisible and RowIsVisible properties.

General Syntax
```
[form!]Name.ColIsVisible(column%)

[form!]Name.RowIsVisible(row%)
```

Table 48-20 Arguments of the ColIsVisible and RowIsVisible properties

Argument	Description
form	Name property of the form
Name	Name property of the grid control
column%	Column number of cell to check
row%	Row number of cell to check

Example Syntax

```
Private Sub txtRow_LostFocus()
    If MSFlexGrid1.RowIsVisible(txtRow.text) = False Then
        MSFlexGrid1.TopRow = Val(txtRow.text)
    End If
End Sub

Private Sub txtColumn_LostFocus()
    If MSFlexGrid1.ColIsVisible(txtColumn.text) = False Then
        MSFlexGrid1.LeftCol = Val(txtColumn.text)
    End If
End Sub
```

Description   Use the ColIsVisible and RowIsVisible properties to find out if a specified row or column is visible to the user. Note that if any part of the specified row or column is visible, these properties will be equal to True.

The example syntax shows using the RowIsVisible and ColIsVisible properties in coordination with the TopRow and LeftCol properties. If the row specified in the txtRow text box is not visible, then that row is made to be the top row of the grid. Similarly, if the column specified in the txtColumn is not visible, then that column is made to be the leftmost column of the grid.

COLPOS, ROWPOS PROPERTIES

Objects Affected   MSFlexGrid

Purpose   Use the ColPos and RowPos properties to find the position of the left side of a specific column or the top of a row. The value returned is in twips units. Table 48-21 summarizes the arguments of the ColIsVisible and RowIsVisible properties.

General Syntax

```
[form!]Name.ColPos(column%)
```

```
[form!]Name.RowPos(row%)
```

Table 48-21 Arguments of the ColPos and RowPos properties

Argument	Description
form	Name property of the form
Name	Name property of the grid control
column%	Column number of cell to check
row%	Row number of cell to check

Example Syntax

```
Private Sub Command1_Click()
    Text1.Text = Str(MSFlexGrid1.ColPos(4)) ' get the left pos of column 5 (zero-based 4)
    Text2.Text = Str(MSFlexGrid2.RowPos(4)) ' get the top pos of row 5 (zero-based 4)
End Sub
```

Description   Use the ColPos and RowPos properties to find the actual location (in twip units) of the left side of a column or the top of a row. The value returned from the property is relative to the grid control itself, where (0, 0) is the upper-left corner of the control. This means that you may get position values outside the control if the grid of cells is larger than the control itself. For example, if the top row of a grid is 5 (and you don't have any fixed rows), the row position of row zero will be negative.

The example syntax shows using the ColPos and RowPos properties to display the current twip position of row 5 and column 5. Note in the example, column 5 is specified using the value 4, because column and row numbers are zero-based.

Cols, Rows Properties

Objects Affected   MSFlexGrid

Purpose   Use the Cols and Rows properties to read or set the total number of columns or rows in a grid. This property is not available at design time and is readable and writable at runtime. Table 48-22 summarizes the arguments of the Cols and Rows properties.

General Syntax

```
[form!]Name.Cols [ = columns%]
[form!]Name.Rows [ = rows%]
```

Table 48-22 Arguments of the Cols and Rows properties

Argument	Description
form	Name property of the form
Name	Name property of the grid control
columns%	Number of columns in a grid, including any fixed columns
rows%	Number of rows in a grid, including any fixed rows

Example Syntax

```
Private Sub Command1_Click ()
    MSFlexGrid1.Rows = UBound(Addresses, 1)        '# of rows in array (Option Base 1)
    MSFlexGrid1.Cols = UBound(Addresses, 2)        '# of columns in array
    For i = 1 To MSFlexGrid1.Rows                  'step through each nonfixed grid row
        For j = 1 To MSFlexGrid1.Cols              'step through each nonfixed grid ⇐
column
            MSFlexGrid1.Col = j                    'set active cell's column
            MSFlexGrid1.Row = i                    'set active cell's row
            MSFlexGrid1.Text = Addresses(i, j)     'place data in cell
        Next j
    Next i
End Sub
```

Description   Use the Cols and Rows properties to read or set the total number of rows and columns in a grid. The example syntax shows how the grid is set up to include each entry of a two-dimensional array. The Cols and Rows properties set up the grid with enough cells to include the entire array.

You may dynamically change the number of rows and columns in a grid to account for changes in your data. If you expand a grid's size, all existing values contained in the grid are maintained. If you make a grid smaller, data in the remaining cells remains unaffected; data in the now-nonexistent cells disappears.

Note that certain properties which relate to the active cell can also relate to a selected range of cells depending on the current setting of the FillStyle property.

Example   The Grid project at the end of this chapter assigns the Cols and Rows properties in the Form_Load event to initially dimension the grid. It also reads the Cols and Rows properties several times to set the selection range, as in the cmndOpen_Click and cmndClose_Click events.

Comment   The Cols and Rows properties are not the same as the Col and Row properties. Cols and Rows set the total number of columns and rows; Cols and Rows determine the active cell.

COLWIDTH AND ROWHEIGHT PROPERTIES

Objects Affected   MSFlexGrid

Purpose   The ColWidth property reads or sets the width of a column in a grid; the RowHeight property reads or sets the height of a row in a grid. Not available at design time; read and write at runtime. Table 48-23 summarizes the arguments of the ColWidth and RowHeight properties.

General Syntax

```
[form!]Name.ColWidth(column%) [ = width&]
[form!]Name.RowHeight(row%) [ = height&]
```

Table 48-23 Arguments of the ColWidth and RowHeight properties

Argument	Description
form	Name property of the form
Name	Name property of the grid control
column%	Number of the column; leftmost column is 0
row%	Number of the row; topmost row is 0
width&	Width of the column in twips
height&	Height of the row in twips

Example Syntax

```
Private Sub Form_Load ()
    MSFlexGrid1.Rows = 10                'set number of rows
    MSFlexGrid1.Cols = 10                'set number of cols
    MSFlexGrid1.ColWidth(0) = 500
    For i = 1 to MSFlexGrid1.Rows - 1    'set row heights
        MSFlexGrid.RowHeight(i) = 300
    Next i
End Sub
```

Description   Use the ColWidth and RowHeight properties to read or set the width and height of your grid's columns and rows. The user may also adjust the sizes with the mouse by clicking and dragging the grid lines of a fixed row or column.

The sizes are always expressed in twips, with 1440 twips per inch. See Chapter 45, "Fonts," for more information about the twips measurement system. You may wish to use the TextHeight and TextWidth properties discussed in Chapter 45 to help determine the correct settings for the particular font and text you're displaying.

Example   The Grid project at the end of this chapter uses ColWidth and RowHeight in the Form_Load event to help initialize the grid. The user can also click and drag on the grid lines to manually reset these properties.

FILLSTYLE PROPERTY

Objects Affected   Form, MSFlexGrid, PictureBox, Printer, PropertyPage, Shape, UserControl, UserDocument

Purpose   Use the FillStyle property to indicate whether any properties which affect the active cell also affect all selected cells. Tables 48-24 and 48-25 summarize the arguments of the FillStyle property.

General Syntax

```
[form!]Name.FillStyle [ = style%]
```

Table 48-24 Arguments of the FillStyle property

Argument	Description
form	Name property of the form
Name	Name property of the grid control
style%	Value indicating that the active cell or the selected range is affected

Table 48-25 Meanings of the style% argument in the grid's FillStyle property

style%	Meaning
flexFillSingle	(Default) Only affect the active cell
flexFillRepeat	Repeat action across all selected cells

Example Syntax

```
Private Sub Form_Load ()
    MSFlexGrid1.FillStyle = flexFillRepeat ' Affect all selected cells
    MSFlexGrid1.Col = 0
    MSFlexGrid1.Row = 0
    MSFlexGrid1.ColSel = MSFlexGrid1.Cols - 1
    MSFlexGrid1.RowSel = MSFlexGrid1.Rows - 1
    MSFlexGrid1.Text = "in each cell"
End Sub
```

Description   The FillStyle property allows you to quickly and easily repeat the setting of a single cell property across a range of selected cells. Once set to flexFillRepeat, setting any single cell-specific properties (such as CellPicture or Text) will occur among all of the cells between the active cell and the end of the selection. The active cell is designated by the Col and Row properties. The end of the selection range is designated by the ColSel and RowSel properties.

FIXEDALIGNMENT PROPERTY

Objects Affected   MSFlexGrid

Purpose   Use the FixedAlignment property to read or set the alignment of data in the fixed cells of a grid's column. Not available at design time; read and write at runtime. Tables 48-26 and 48-27 summarize the arguments of the FixedAlignment property.

General Syntax

```
[form!]Name.FixedAlignment(column%) [ = alignment%]
```

Table 48-26 Arguments of the FixedAlignment property

Argument	Description
form	Name property of the form
Name	Name property of the grid control
column%	Number of the column (starting from the far left, column%=0)
alignment%	Expression indicating left-, right-, center-aligned; or use ColAlignment setting

Table 48-27 Meanings of the alignment% argument in the grid's FixedAlignment property

alignment%	Meaning
flexAlignLeftTop	(Default) Align text along the left and top of the cell
flexAlignLeftCenter	Align text along the left side and centered vertically in the cell
flexAlignLeftBottom	Align text along the left and bottom of the cell
flexAlignCenterTop	Center text horizontally and align along the top of the cell
flexAlignCenterCenter	Center text both horizontally and vertically in the cell
flexAlignCenterBottom	Center text horizontally and align along the bottom of the cell
flexAlignRightTop	Align text along the right and top of the cell
flexAlignRightCenter	Align text along the right side and centered vertically in the cell
flexAlignRightBottom	Align text along the right and bottom of the cell
flexAlignGeneral	Center text vertically and align numeric data on the left and string data on the right

Example Syntax

```
Private Sub Form_Load ()
    MSFlexGrid1.Rows = 10
    MSFlexGrid1.Cols = 10
    For i = 0 to MSFlexGrid1.Cols - 1
        MSFlexGrid1.ColAlignment(i) = AlignRightCenter
        MSFlexGrid1.FixedAlignment(i) = AlignCenterCenter
    Next i
End Sub
```

Description   The FixedAlignment property determines the alignment for grid cells in a fixed column. This alignment may be different from the ColAlignment setting, so the grid's column headings may be aligned differently than the actual data.

Example   The Grid project at the end of this chapter uses the Form_Load event to set the fixed column's alignment to right-aligned.

FIXEDCOLS, FIXEDROWS PROPERTIES

Objects Affected   MSFlexGrid

Purpose   Use the FixedCols and FixedRows properties to read or set the number of fixed rows or columns on the left and top of a grid. Fixed rows and columns are typically used for row and column headings. Not available at design time; read and write at runtime. Table 48-28 summarizes the arguments of the FixedCols and FixedRows properties.

General Syntax

```
[form!]Name.FixedCols [ = columns%]
[form!]Name.FixedRows [ = rows%]
```

Table 48-28 Arguments of the FixedCols and FixedRows properties

Argument	Description
form	Name property of the form
Name	Name property of the grid control
columns%	Number of fixed columns; defaults to 1
rows%	Number of fixed rows; defaults to 1

Example Syntax

```
Private Sub Form_Load ()
    MSFlexGrid1.Rows = 10
    MSFlexGrid1.Cols = 10
    MSFlexGrid1.FixedRows = 2
    MSFlexGrid1.FixedCols = 2
End Sub
```

Description   You may wish to give your grid headings for the rows and columns. The FixedCols and FixedRows properties let you define stationary rows and columns to put these headings in. Fixed rows and columns are always visible even if the user scrolls the nonfixed cells away from the edges. This means that heading information you put into the fixed rows and columns is always available to help the user locate their data.

Fixed rows and columns display in gray, and can be changed using the ForeColorFixed and BackColorFixed properties. They can have their own alignment separate from the nonfixed cells by using the FixedAlignment property. The user may manually change the ColWidth and RowHeight properties by clicking and dragging the grid lines in fixed rows and columns.

You may have any number of fixed rows and columns from zero to one less than the total number of rows or columns (Rows -1) or (Cols - 1). This means that a grid will always have at least one nonfixed cell. These properties default to one fixed row or column.

Example   The Grid project at the end of this chapter uses the default of one fixed row and column.

ForeColor, ForeColorFixed, ForeColorSel, CellForeColor Properties

Objects Affected   MSFlexGrid

Purpose   Use the ForeColor, ForeColorFixed, ForeColorSel, CellForeColor properties to read or set the text (foreground) color of grid elements. The ForeColor, ForeColorFixed, and ForeColorSel properties are all available at design time. The CellForeColor property is only available at runtime. Tables 48-29 and 48-30 summarize the arguments of the ForeColor, ForeColorFixed, and ForeColorSel properties.

General Syntax

```
[form!]Name.ForeColor [ = color%]
[form!]Name.ForeColorFixed [ = color%]
[form!]Name.ForeColorSel [ = color%]
[form!]Name.CellForeColor [ = color%]
```

Table 48-29 Arguments of the ForeColor, ForeColorFixed, ForeColorSel, and CellForeColor properties

Argument	Description
form	Name property of the form
Name	Name property of the grid control
color%	Contains the Visual Basic color constant or an RGB value

Table 48-30 Meanings of the color% argument in the ForeColor, ForeColorFixed, ForeColorSel, and CellForeColor properties

color%	Meaning
vbBlack	Black (&H000000)
vbBlue	Blue (&HFF0000)
vbCyan	Cyan, a light blue (&HFFFF00)
vbGreen	Green (&H00FF00)
vbMagenta	Magenta, a purplish red (&HFF00FF)
vbRed	Red (&H0000FF)
vbWhite	White (&HFFFFFF)
vbYellow	Yellow (&H00FFFF)
&H*BBGGRR* or RGB(r,g,b)	Arbitrary RGB color value

Example Syntax

```
Private Sub Command1_Click ()
    MSFlexGrid1.ForeColor = vbWhite              'Grid foreground is white
    MSFlexGrid1.BackColorSel = &HC0C0C0          'Grid selection text color is gray
MSFlexGrid1.BackColorFixed = RGB(0,0,255)    'Fixed row foregrounds are blue

    MSFlexGrid.Col = 2                           'Set the current column
    MSFlexGrid.Row = 2                           'Set the current row
    MSFlexGrid1.CellForeColor = vbYellow         'Set the background of (2,2) to yellow
End Sub
```

Description   Use the ForeColor, ForeColorSel, and ForeColorFixed properties when you want to customize the text (foreground) colors of the various parts of the grid. The ForeColor property sets the text color of the main nonfixed grid cells. The ForeColorSel property sets the text color of the selection. The ForeColorFixed property sets the background color of the fixed (heading) rows and columns of the grid.

Unlike the previously mentioned properties which affect general areas of cells in the grid, you can use the CellForeColor property to change the text color of the current cell. The current cell is the cell indicated by the current setting of the Row and Col properties.

If you need to change the background color of the cells, refer to the BackColor, BackColorFixed, BackColorSel, and CellBackColor properties.

GridLines, GridLinesFixed Properties

Objects Affected   MSFlexGrid

Purpose   Use the GridLines and GridLinesFixed properties to read or set the style of a grid's grid lines in the nonfixed and fixed cells. Grid lines are the light gray lines that visually separate individual cells. This property is available at design time and is readable and writable at runtime. Tables 48-31 and 48-32 summarize the arguments of the GridLines and GridLinesFixed property.

General Syntax

```
[form!]Name.GridLines [ = linestyle%]
[form!]Name.GridLinesFixed [ = linestyle%]
```

Table 48-31 Arguments of the GridLines and GridLinesFixed properties

Argument	Description
form	Name property of the form
Name	Name property of the grid control
linestyle%	The line style of the grid lines

Table 48-32 Meanings of the linestyle% argument in the GridLines and GridLinesFixed properties

linestyle%	Meaning
flexGridNone	No grid lines
flexGridFlat	(Default) Flat grid lines
flexGridInset	Three-dimensional engraved grid lines
flexGridRaised	Three-dimensional raised grid lines

Example Syntax

```
Private Sub Check1_Click ()
    If MSFlexGrid1.GridLines <> flexGridNone Then
        MSFlexGrid1.Gridlines = flexGridNone
    Else
        MSFlexGrid1.GridLines = flexGridFlat
    EndIf
End Sub
```

Description

Grid lines are the light gray lines that visually separate cells in the grid. You can use the GridLines property to set the style of the grid lines (including turning them off). The default is to display flat grid lines. The GridLines property affects the nonfixed cells, whereas the GridLinesFixed property affects the fixed cells.

Grid lines make it easier for the user to navigate around your grid and give visual feedback for the size and location of individual cells. There may be times, however, when you'd like to display the data without the grid lines. For example, a nicely formatted onscreen report would look better without them.

Example

The cmboGridlines combo box sets the Gridlines property on and off. The combo box is first loaded with the two list items "Gridlines" and "No Gridlines," and its ItemData property is set with the correct value for each choice. The cmboGridlines_Click event then simply assigns the ItemData property to the grid's Gridlines property to set the grid line state.

GridLineWidth Property

Objects Affected   MSFlexGrid

Purpose   Use the GridLineWidth property to set the size of lines between the grid cells in a grid.

This property is available at design time and is readable and writable at runtime. Table 48-33 summarizes the arguments of the GridLineWidth property.

General Syntax

```
[form!]Name.GridLineWidth = width%
```

Table 48-33 Arguments of the GridLineWidth property

Argument	Description
form	Name property of the form
Name	Name property of the grid control
width%	The width (in pixels) of the grid lines

Example Syntax

```
Private Sub Command1_Click ()
    MSFlexGrid1.GridLineWidth = 5
End Sub
```

Description

Use the GridLineWdith property to read or set the size in pixels of the lines drawn between the cells in the grid. By default, the lines are one pixel wide. If you want wider lines, set this property to a larger value.

HighLight Property

Objects Affected   MSFlexGrid

Purpose   The grid's HighLight property reads or sets whether the selected cells appear highlighted. This property is available at both design time and runtime. Tables 48-34 and 48-35 summarize the arguments of the HighLight property.

```
General Syntax
[form!]Name.HighLight [ = highlight%]
```

Table 48-34 Arguments of the HighLight property

Argument	Description
form	Name property of the form
Name	Name property of the grid control
highlight%	The way in which highlighting appears

Table 48-35 Meanings of the highlight% argument in the HighLight property

highlight%	Meaning
flexHighlightNever	No cell highlighting
flexHighlightAlways	(Default) Cell highlighting always on
flexHighlightWithFocus	Cell highlighting on only when grid has focus

Example Syntax

```
Private Sub menuFileSave ()
    Open "SAVEFILE.TMP" For Output As #1          'file to save grid data in
    MSFlexGrid1.HighLight = flexHightlightNever   'turn off highlighting
    MSFlexGrid1.Col = 0                           'select entire grid
    MSFlexGrid1.Row = 0
    MSFlexGrid1.ColSel = MSFlexGrid1.Cols - 1
    MSFlexGrid1.RowSel = MSFlexGrid1.Rows - 1
    Print #1, MSFlexGrid1.Clip                    'save the data
    MSFlexGrid1.HighLight = flexHighlightAlways   'back to normal
    Close #1
End Sub
```

Description   The HighLight property determines whether selected cells appear highlighted. The default is flexHighLightAlways, as this gives users visual feedback during a select operation. Like flexHighLightAlways, flexHighLightWithFocus provides visual feedback, but only if the grid control has focus. If HighLight is flexHighLightNever, then the user can't tell what cells are selected.

You may want to turn off highlighting when your code manipulates the grid. In the example syntax, the entire grid must be selected for the Clip property to work. Highlighting the grid during the select operation would annoy the user, so we turn off highlighting for the duration of the operation, and then turn it back on when finished.

Example

The cmndOpen and cmndSave click events both call the NoHighlight procedure to turn the grid lines on and off when saving the file. The save routines use the Clip property, which requires that there be a selected range.

LEFTCOL, TOPROW PROPERTIES

Objects Affected   MSFlexGrid

Purpose

The LeftCol property reads or sets the leftmost visible nonfixed column in a grid. The TopRow property reads or sets the topmost visible nonfixed row in a grid. These properties let you programatically determine what parts of the grid are visible. Not available at design time; read and write at runtime. Table 48-36 summarizes the arguments of the LeftCol and TopRow properties.

General Syntax

```
[form!]Name.LeftCol [ = column%]
[form!]Name.TopRow [ = row%]
```

Table 48-36 Arguments of the LeftCol and TopRow properties

Argument	Description
form	Name property of the form
Name	Name property of the grid control
column%	Column number of leftmost visible nonfixed column
row%	Row number of topmost visible nonfixed row

Example Syntax

```
Private Sub Text1_LostFocus ()
    MSFlexGrid1.Text = Text1.Text
    MSFlexGrid1.LeftCol = MSFlexGrid1.Col
    MSFlexGrid1.TopRow = MSFlexGrid1.Row
End Sub
```

Description

Use the LeftCol and TopRow properties to programmatically scroll the grid. These properties determine the leftmost and topmost visible column and row. You may have code that alters a cell's data when that cell is not visible. Setting these properties to the row and column of the altered cell brings that cell into view, as in the example syntax.

Fixed rows and columns are always in view, so the LeftCol and TopRow properties only scroll to nonfixed cells.

Example   The NewValues procedure in the Grid project at the end of this chapter always brings R1C1 back into view when it finishes recalculating a new scenario.

MOUSECOL, MOUSEROW PROPERTIES

Objects Affected   MSFlexGrid

Purpose   Use the MouseCol and MouseRow properties to read the cell the mouse pointer is currently over. These properties are not available at design time and are readable at runtime. Table 48-37 summarizes the arguments of the MouseCol and MouseRow properties.

General Syntax

```
[form!]Name.MouseCol [ = columns%]
[form!]Name.MouseRow [ = rows%]
```

Table 48-37 Arguments of the MouseCol and MouseRow properties

Argument	Description
form	Name property of the form
Name	Name property of the grid control
columns%	The grid column that the mouse is over
rows%	The grid row that the mouse is over

Example Syntax

```
Private Sub MSFlexGrid1_Click ()
    Label1.Text = "Row " & MSFlexGrid1.Row
    Label2.Text = "Col " & MSFlexGrid1.Col
End Sub
```

Description   Use the MouseCol and MouseRow properties to read the current row and column that the mouse pointer is currently over. This can be useful if you need to perform some special action based upon the location of the mouse pointer over the grid.

REDRAW PROPERTY

Objects Affected   MSFlexGrid

Purpose   The Redraw property reads or sets whether the grid is allowed to repaint itself. Tables 48-38 and 48-39 summarize the arguments of the Redraw property.

General Syntax

```
[form!]Name.Redraw [ = boolean%]
```

Table 48-38 Arguments of the Redraw property

Argument	Description
form	Name property of the form
Name	Name property of the grid control
boolean%	True/False value indicating if the grid is allowed to redraw itself

Table 48-39 Meanings of the boolean% argument in the Redraw property

boolean%	Meaning
True	The grid is allowed to redraw itself
False	The grid is not allowed to redraw itself

Example Syntax

```
Private Sub Form_Load()
    MSFlexGrid1.Redraw = False          ' Turn off redrawing

    For i = 1 To MSFlexGrid1.Rows
'step through each nonfixed grid row
        For j = 1 To MSFlexGrid1.Cols
'step through each nonfixed grid column
            MSFlexGrid1.Col = j                 'set active cell's column
            MSFlexGrid1.Row = i                 'set active cell's row
            MSFlexGrid1.Text = "lotsa data"     'place data in cell
        Next j
    Next i

    MSFlexGrid1.Redraw = True           ' Turn on redrawing
End Sub
```

Description   Use the grid's Redraw property to temporarily disable the grid from redrawing itself when adding a large amount of data to it. Doing this can dramatically improve the graphical performance of the grid. In addition, the user will see a single refresh of data, rather than row-by-row insertion of data.

The example syntax demonstrates the disabling and enabling of the grid's Redraw property so a large amount of data can be inserted.

REMOVEITEM METHOD

Objects Affected   ComboBox, MSFlexGrid, ListBox

Purpose   The RemoveItem method deletes an item from the list in a grid. Table 48-40 summarizes the arguments of the RemoveItem method.

General Syntax

```
[form!]Name.RemoveItem Index%
```

Table 48-40 Arguments of the RemoveItem method

Argument	Description
form	Name of the parent form
Name	Name of the grid, list, or combo box
Index%	An integer value specifying the index number of the list item to be removed

Example Syntax

```
Private Sub MSFlexGrid1_DblClick ()
     MSFlexGrid1.RemoveItem MSFlexGrid1.Row
End Sub
```

Description   The RemoveItem method is the complement to the AddItem method. The RemoveItem method deletes the row indicated by the Index% argument from a grid. Begin the specification of the RemoveItem method with the name of the grid to be affected.

When an item is removed from the grid, the index number of each entry in the list that followed the removed item is decremented. The Rows property for the control is also decremented.

Care should be taken when removing items from a grid. If your program specifies an index value that is greater than that of the highest current item, Visual Basic will issue an "Illegal function call" error. To be safe, always check the Rows property before using the RemoveItem method. The index numbering of the grid rows is zero-based. If a grid contains five items, the first item has an index of 0, and the highest index number is 4. Therefore the value of the supplied index should always be less than the value of the Rows property.

The example code uses MSFlexGrid1's DblClick event to remove the currently selected row from the list.

RowColChange Event

Objects Affected   DBGrid, MSFlexGrid

Purpose   Use the RowColChange event to react to the user changing to a different cell. Table 48-41 summarizes the arguments of the RowColChange event.

General Syntax

```
Name_RowColChange ([Index As Integer])
```

Table 48-41 Arguments of the RowColChange event

Argument	Description
Name	Name property of the grid control
Index	Uniquely identifies member of a control array

Example Syntax

```
Private Sub MSFlexGrid1_RowColChange ()
    Label1.Caption = "Row " & MSFlexGrid1.Row & " , Column " & MSFlexGrid1.Col
End Sub
```

Description	Use the RowColChange event to react to the user changing to a different cell. This event is triggered by both user actions (such as using the arrow keys or clicking with the mouse) and by program actions, such as setting the Row and Col properties.
	The example syntax updates a label that displays the current coordinates. It gets updated every time the active cell changes.
	The SelChange event also triggers when a user clicks on a new cell, but does not trigger when the program changes the active cell.
Example	The Grid project at the end of this chapter uses the RowColChange event to update two labels and lablActive to display the active cell.

SELCHANGE EVENT

Objects Affected	DBGrid, MSFlexGrid
Purpose	Use the SelChange event to react to the user or the program changing the selection to a different range of cells in a grid. Table 48-42 summarizes the arguments of the SelChange event.
General Syntax	

```
Name_SelChange ([Index As Integer])
```

Table 48-42 Arguments of the SelChange event

Argument	Description
Name	Name property of the grid control
Index	Uniquely identifies member of a control array

Example Syntax

```
Private Sub MSFlexGrid1_SelChange ()
    numRows = Abs(MSFlexGrid1.RowSel - MSFlexGrid1.Row)    'calculate nbr of rows
    numCols = Abs(MSFlexGrid1.ColSel - MSFlexGrid1.Col)    'calculate nbr of cols
    If numRows + numCols > 0 Then                          'set captions
```

```
        Label1.Caption = "Selection: ⇐" & numRows & " x " & numCols & " cells"
    Else
        Label1.Caption = ""
    End If
End Sub
```

Description   Use the SelChange event to react to a new selection range. This event triggers both by the user selecting cells or by the program using the Row, Col and SelRow, and SelCol properties. It triggers multiple times if the user clicks and drags to create a new selection. It does not trigger if the active cell changes because of new settings to the Row and Col properties.

The RowColChange event also triggers if the user clicks on a cell. The RowColChange event does not trigger if the selection changes by program code, and only triggers once if the user clicks and drags to create a new selection.

Example   The Grid project at the end of this chapter uses the SelChange event to update one label: lablSelection.

SELECTIONMODE PROPERTY

Objects Affected   MSFlexGrid

Purpose   The SelectionMode property reads or sets whether any cell range can be selected; only rows can be selected, or only columns can be selected. Tables 48-43 amd 48-44 summarize the arguments of the SelectionMode property.

General Syntax

```
[form!]Name.SelectionMode [ = mode%]
```

Table 48-43 Arguments of the SelectionMode property

Argument	Description
form	Name property of the form
Name	Name property of the grid control
mode%	Value indicating the allowable selection types in the grid

Table 48-44 Meanings of the mode% argument in the SelectionMode property

mode%	Meaning
flexSelectionFree	(Default) Any range of cells may be selected
flexSelectionByRow	Only row selection is permitted
flexSelectionByColumn	Only column selection is permitted

Example Syntax

```
Private Sub Form_Load()
    MSFlexGrid1.SelectionMode = flexSelectionByColumn   'Only allow full column selection
End Sub
```

Description   Use the SelectionMode property to restrict the types of selection allowed with a grid. You can allow free selection (which allows the user to select any range of cells), or restrict the selection to rows or columns only.

TEXT PROPERTY

Objects Affected   ComboBox, DBCombo, DBGrid, DBList, ListBox, MSFlexGrid, TextBox

Purpose   The Text property is used to read the text of the current cell entry in a grid. Table 48-45 summarizes the arguments of the Text property when used with a list box or combo box.

General Syntax

```
[form!]Name.Text [= TextString$]
```

Table 48-45 Arguments of the Text property when used with a grid

Argument	Description
form	Name of the parent form
Name	Name of the grid control
TextString$	Assigned to the cell of a grid

Example Syntax

```
Private Sub Command1_Click ()
    MSFlexGrid1.Col = 2
    MSFlexGrid1.Row = 2
    MSFlexGrid1.Text = "Hello"              'assigns a string to row 2, column 2 of the grid
End Sub
```

Description   When used with the grid control, the Text property reads or sets the contents of the active cell. The active cell is set with the Row and Col properties.

Example   The Grid project at the end of this chapter uses the Text property several times. The cmboIncome_DropDown statement uses it to check the contents of the cmboIncome combo box. The grid's Text property is both read and set in the Form_Load and NewValues procedures.

TEXTSTYLE, TEXTSTYLEFIXED, CELLTEXTSTYLE PROPERTIES

Objects Affected   MSFlexGrid

Purpose   Use the TextStyle, TextStyleFixed, and CellTextStyle properties to read or set the style of the text within a grid's cells. Tables 48-46 and 48-47 summarize the arguments of the GridLines and GridLinesFixed property.

General Syntax

```
[form!]Name.TextStyle [ = textstyle%]
[form!]Name.TextStyleFixed [ = textstyle%]
[form!]Name.CellTextStyle [ = textstyle%]
```

Table 48-46 Arguments of the TextStyle, TextStyleFixed, and CellTextStyle properties

Argument	Description
form	Name property of the form
Name	Name property of the grid control
textstyle%	The text style to set

Table 48-47 Meanings of the textstyle% argument in the TextStyle, TextStyleFixed, and CellTextStyle properties

textstyle%	Meaning
flexTextFlat	(Default) Normal text
flexTextRaised	Three-dimensional raised text
flexTextInset	Three-dimensional engraved text
flexTextRaisedLight	Light three-dimensional raised text
flexTextInsetLight	Light three-dimensional engraved text

Example Syntax

```
Private Sub Check1_Click ()
    MSFlexGrid1.TextStyle = flexTextRaised        ' Set the nonfixed text style
    MSFlexGrid1.TextStyleFixed = flexTextInset    ' Set the fixed text style

    MSFlexGrid1.Row = 0
    MSFlexGrid1.Col = 0
    MSFlexGrid1.CellTextStyle = flexTextFlat      ' Set the text style of (0,0)
End Sub
```

Description   Use the TextStyle, TextStyleFixed, and CellTextStyle properties to change the appearance of the text within the cells. The TextStyle property affects all nonfixed rows. The TextStyleFixed property reads or sets the style of all fixed rows. The CellTextStyle property reads or sets the style of the active cell designated by the Col and Row properties.

WORDWRAP PROPERTY

Objects Affected   Label, MSFlexGrid

Purpose The WordWrap property reads or sets whether the text within the active cell should wrap within the cell if it's longer than the cell is wide. Tables 48-48 and 48-49 summarize the arguments of the WordWrap property.

General Syntax

```
[form!]Name.WordWrap [ = boolean%]
```

Table 48-48 Arguments of the WordWrap property

Argument	Description
form	Name property of the form
Name	Name property of the grid control
boolean%	True/False value indicating if word wrapping is on

Table 48-49 Meanings of the boolean% argument in the WordWrap property

boolean%	Meaning
True	Word wrapping is on
False	Word wrapping is off

Example Syntax

```
Private Sub Form_Load()
    MSFlexGrid1.Row = 0
    MSFlexGrid1.Col = 0
    MSFlexGrid1.WordWrap = True                    ' Word wrapping is on for (0,0)
    MSFlexGrid1.Text = "This is a very long string"
End Sub
```

Description In some cases you may want the text to wrap within a cell, whereas in other cases you may not want this behavior. The WordWrap property allows you to set the behavior as you desire it. If word wrapping is on, you can force wrapping to occur by including carriage returns Chr(13) in your text strings at the places you want wrapping to occur.

The Grid Project

Assembling the Project

1. Add support for the Microsoft FlexGrid Control by choosing the "Project" file menu and then "Components". Under the "Controls" tab, make sure that the "Microsoft FlexGrid Control" item is checked. Press the "OK" command button to close the Components dialog.

2. Assemble the controls summarized in Table 48-50 on a blank form.

Table 48-50 Controls for the Grids project

Object	Property	Setting
Form	BackColor	&H00C0C0C0 (Light Gray)
	BorderStyle	3 - Fixed Dialog
	Caption	"Grids Project"
	Name	formGrid
ComboBox	Name	cmboIncome
	Sorted	True
	TabIndex	0
ComboBox	Name	cmboInflation
	TabIndex	1ComboBox
	Name	cmboGridlines
	Style	2 - (Dropdown List)
ComboBox	Name	cmboAlign
	Style	2 - (Dropdown List)
CommandButton	Caption	"&Open"
	Name	cmndOpen
CommandButton	Caption	"&Save"
	Name	cmndSave
CommandButton	Caption	"E&xit"
	Name	cmndExit
ListBox	Font	Fixedsys, Regular, 8 pt.
	MultiSelect	2 - (Extended)
	Name	listHistory
MSFlexGrid	Name	gridSheet
Label	Name	lablActive
Label	Name	lablSelection

3. Position and size the controls, as shown on Figure 48-2.

4. Enter the following code in the cmboAlign_Click event. This triggers when the user clicks on a list item, or presses E after selecting an item. It iterates through each selected column and sets the column alignment.

```
Private Sub cmboAlign_Click ()
    For i = gridSheet.Col To gridSheet.ColSel
'Iterate through selected columns
        gridSheet.ColAlignment(i) = cmboAlign.ItemData(cmboAlign.ListIndex)⇐ 'and set
alignment.
    Next i
End Sub
```

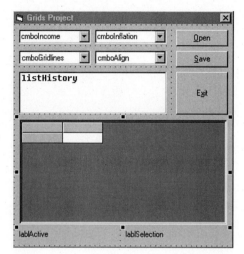

Figure 48-2   The Grids Project during design

5. Enter the following code in the cmboGridlines_Click event. This turns the grid lines on and off.

```
Private Sub cmboGridlines_Click ()
    gridSheet.GridLines = cmboGridlines.ItemData(cmboGridlines.ListIndex) 'set grid lines
End Sub
```

6. Enter the following code in the cmboIncome_DropDown event. The procedure first checks to see if the scenario (that is, the income and inflation rate combination) has already been entered into the list. If it has, we exit the procedure. If not, we add the new scenario to the list, and also add an entry for the inflation rate in the ItemData property.

```
Private Sub cmboIncome_DropDown ()
    If InStr(cmboIncome.Text, "  ") Then
'If this is a previously formatted entry
        value = clean(Left(cmboIncome.Text, InStr(cmboIncome.Text, "  ")))
    Else                                     'otherwise
        value = clean((cmboIncome.Text))
'income value is all there is.
    End If
    value = Format(value, "$###,###,###")        'pretty up the value
    display = value & Space(12 - Len(value) - Len(cmboInflation.Text))⇐
& cmboInflation.Text
    For i = 0 To cmboIncome.ListCount - 1
'run through the existing list
        If display = cmboIncome.List(i) Then
'If we've already got this scenario,
            Exit Sub                              'leave.
        End If
    Next i
     cmboIncome.AddItem display                        'new scenario,so 'add it to⇐
list
```

```
    cmboIncome.ItemData(cmboIncome.NewIndex) = cmboInflation.Text 'remember inflation rate
    cmboIncome.ListIndex = cmboIncome.NewIndex    'and set box to this newest entry
End Sub
```

7. Enter the following code in the cmboIncome_GotFocus event. This triggers every time the Income combo box gets the focus, and highlights the text in the combo box's edit area.

```
Private Sub cmboIncome_GotFocus ()
    cmboIncome.SelLength = Len(cmboIncome.Text) 'highlight the whole entry
End Sub
```

8. Enter the following code in the gridSheet_GotFocus procedure. Whenever the user moves into the MSFlexGrid control (either by clicking with the mouse or by pressing the ⊤ key) this event recalculates the scenario. It first makes sure the income text is properly formatted by calling the cmboIncome_DropDown event procedure; then it extracts the income and the inflation rate. It then calls NewValues to do the actual computation.

```
Private Sub gridSheet_GotFocus ()
    cmboIncome_DropDown               'force the display's update
    bucks = clean(Left(cmboIncome.Text, InStr(cmboIncome.Text, " ")))  'Take income
    inflation = 1 + Val(cmboIncome.ItemData(cmboIncome.ListIndex)) / 100 ⇐
'& inflation
    NewValues bucks, inflation         'and compute new scenario.
End Sub
```

9. Enter the following code in the cmndExit_Click procedure. This simply ends the program.

```
Private Sub cmndExit_Click ()
    End                      'end the program
End Sub
```

10. Enter the following code in the cmndOpen_Click event procedure. This opens up a data file saved by the cmndSave procedure. It first opens up the data file (providing an error trap in the process). Then it reads in each line of the file. The Clip property used to save the file embeds carriage returns at the end of each row; we need to put the carriage returns back in, as the Line Input statement reads up to, but not including, a carriage return. Once we've read the data in, we turn off the highlighting and select the entire grid so we can use the Clip property to assign the saved values back to the grid. We end by resetting the highlighting and selection.

```
Private Sub cmndOpen_Click ()
    On Error GoTo badopen                    'set error trap
    Open "chp48.tmp" For Input As #1         'open the data file
    On Error GoTo 0                          'success!
    Do While Not EOF(1)                      'while there's still data,
    Line Input #1, rawdata$                  'get a line
    clipdata$ = clipdata$ & rawdata$ & Chr(13)
'add the carriage return back in
    Loop
    Close                                    'close data file
```

continued on next page

continued from previous page

```
     NoHilite True
'Turn off highlighting, select whole grid
     gridSheet.Clip = clipdata$
'and put the saved data in the grid.
     NoHilite False
'turn on highlighting, select whole grid
Exit Sub

badopen:                                   'oops! bad file
     MsgBox "Failed to open"               'inform user
Exit Sub                                   'and leave

End Sub
```

11. Enter the following code in the cmndSave_Click event. This saves the grid data so the cmndOpen procedure can read it back in. We first open up the save file (setting up an error trap along the way). We then turn off highlighting and select the entire grid. The single Print #1 line is all we need to save the entire contents of the nonfixed grid cells! We then turn on the highlighting and reset the selection.

```
Private Sub cmndSave_Click ()
     On Error GoTo badsave                 'set error trap
     Open "chp48.tmp" For Output As #1     'open data file
     On Error GoTo 0                       'success!
     NoHilite True
'turn off highlighting, select entire grid
     Print #1, gridSheet.Clip              'save the grid's data
     NoHilite False
'turn on highlighting, select old selection
     Close                                 'close data file
Exit Sub                                   'done

badsave:                                   'oops! bad file
     MsgBox "Failed to save"               'inform user
Exit Sub                                   'leave

End Sub
```

12. Enter the following code in the Form_Load procedure. This sets up the grid and the various combo boxes.

```
Private Sub Form_Load ()
     gridSheet.Rows = 21                              'dimension grid
     gridSheet.Cols = 5
     gridSheet.RowHeight(0) = gridSheet.RowHeight(1) * 1.3 'make top row a bit bigger
     gridSheet.Row = 0                                'add in the labels
     gridSheet.Col = 1
     gridSheet.Text = "Yearly"
     gridSheet.Col = 2
     gridSheet.Text = "Monthly"
     gridSheet.Col = 3
     gridSheet.Text = "Weekly"
     gridSheet.Col = 4
     gridSheet.Text = "Hourly"
     For i = 1 To gridSheet.Cols - 1
'set column widths and alignments
     gridSheet.ColWidth(i) = 950
```

```
        gridSheet.ColAlignment(i) = flexAlignRightCenter    'right align
        gridSheet.FixedAlignment(i) = flexAlignRightCenter 'right align
    Next i
    cmboGridlines.AddItem "No Gridlines"            'set up grid lines combo box
    cmboGridlines.ItemData(0) = flexGridNone        'associate correct settings
    cmboGridlines.AddItem "Flat Gridlines"          'with the displayed items
    cmboGridlines.ItemData(1) = flexGridFlat
    cmboGridlines.AddItem "Inset Gridlines"
    cmboGridlines.ItemData(2) = flexGridInset
    cmboGridlines.AddItem "Raised Gridlines"
    cmboGridlines.ItemData(3) = flexGridRaised
    cmboGridlines.ListIndex = 1
'set the default to "Flat Gridlines
    cmboAlign.AddItem "Left Align"
'add alignment options in correct order
    cmboAlign.ItemData(0) = flexAlignLeftCenter
    cmboAlign.AddItem "Right Align"
    cmboAlign.ItemData(1) = flexAlignRightCenter
    cmboAlign.AddItem "Center Align"
    cmboAlign.ItemData(2) = flexAlignCenterCenter
    cmboAlign.ListIndex = 1
'set default alignment to right align
    For i = 2 To 20                                 'set up inflation box with
      cmboInflation.AddItem i                       'inflation rates from 2 to 20
    Next i
    cmboInflation.ListIndex = 4                     'set default inflation rate
    gridSheet_RowColChange
'force update the active cell label
    cmboIncome.Text = "$75,000"                     'put in default value
    cmboIncome_DropDown                             'force update the displayed value
End Sub
```

13. Enter the following code in the gridSheet_RowColChange event. This triggers every time the active cell moves. It puts the cell's coordinates in a label beneath the grid control.

```
Private Sub gridSheet_RowColChange ()
    currentRow$ = "Row " & gridSheet.Row
'Update the label every time
    currentCol$ = "Column " & gridSheet.Col
'a new cell becomes active
    lablActive.Caption = currentRow$ & " " & currentCol$
End Sub
```

14. Enter the following code in the gridSheet_SelChange procedure. This triggers any time the user (or code) changes the selection. It first computes and displays the size of the selection, and then checks to see if the active cell is selected.

```
Private Sub gridSheet_SelChange()
    numRows = Abs(gridSheet.RowSel – gridSheet.Row) + 1
'num selected rows
    numCols = Abs(gridSheet.ColSel – gridSheet.Col) + 1
'num selected columns
    If numCols + numRows = 0 Then
'If there is no selection
      lablSelection.Caption = "(no selection)"          'say so
    Else                                                'otherwise
```

continued on next page

continued from previous page

```
        lablSelection.Caption = numRows & " x " & numCols
'display selection size.
    End If
End Sub
```

15. Enter the following code in the listHistory_DblClick event. This deletes all entries from the history list.

```
Private Sub listHistory_DblClick ()
    listHistory.Clear                    'clear all history entries
End Sub
```

16. Enter the following code in the listHistory_MouseDown event. This triggers whenever the user presses a button over the list box. This goes through the list and checks to see if the user has selected any items. It deletes them from the list if it finds any.

```
Private Sub listHistory_MouseDown (Button As Integer, Shift As Integer, X As
Single, Y As Single)
    If Button = 2 Then                           'right mouse button
      For i = (listHistory.ListCount - 1) To 0 Step -1
'step through from last to first
            If listHistory.Selected(i) Then
'If user selected item,
                listHistory.RemoveItem i                 'delete it.
            End If
      Next i
    End If
End Sub
```

17. Enter the following code in the General Declarations section. This routine is the main engine of the program. It displays the calculated values of taking the amount of income specified in the cmboIncome combo box, and calculating out over 20 years what inflation will do. Once it's finished, it builds a summary statement involving the initial parameters and the result in the tenth year.

```
Private Sub NewValues (bucks, inflation)
    For years = 1 To 20
'figure out values for the next 20 years
        gridSheet.Row = years              'go to the correct row
        gridSheet.Col = 0                  'Go to label column
        gridSheet.Text = Str$(1996 + years)    'and create label.
        gridSheet.Col = 1                  'go to yearly income column
        If years = 1 Then                  'first year?
            gridSheet.Text = Format$(Val(bucks), "$###,###,###") <=
'just give it base figure
        Else                               'otherwise
            gridSheet.Row = gridSheet.Row - 1  'get last year's data
            oldVal = clean((gridSheet.Text))   'clean it up
            gridSheet.Row = gridSheet.Row + 1  'go back to current year
            gridSheet.Text = Format$(oldVal * inflation, "$###,###,###")
        End If
        newBucks = clean((gridSheet.Text))     'this year's inflated value
        gridSheet.Col = 2                  'monthly wage
        gridSheet.Text = Format$(newBucks / 12, "$###,###,###")
        gridSheet.Col = 3                  'weekly wage
```

```
                gridSheet.Text = Format$(newBucks / 52, "$###,###,###")
                gridSheet.Col = 4                      'Hourly wage
                gridSheet.Text = Format$(newBucks / 2000, "$###,###,###.00")
            Next years
            gridSheet.Col = 1                      'yearly wage
            gridSheet.Row = 10                     'for year 10
            year10 = gridSheet.Text
            listHistory.AddItem cmboIncome.Text & Space$(14 -Len(year10))⇐
& year10 'Add in history
                    gridSheet.TopRow = 1                    'and scroll to the top
                    gridSheet.LeftCol = 1                   'left corner of the grid.
                End Sub
```

18. Add the following code to the General Declarations section. This procedure
selects the entire grid so the Clip property in the calling procedure can open or
save a file. It first determines if we're turning the highlighting on or off. If we're
turning it off, it stores the current selection in the four static variables for use in
the next call to the procedure. It then turns off the highlighting and selects the
entire grid. When it's called to turn on the highlighting again, it restores the previously selected area and turns on the highlighting.

```
Private Sub NoHilite(onOff As Integer)
    Static sCol%, sRow%, eCol%, eRow%
'will remember current selection
        If onOff = True Then                       'turn highlight off
          sCol% = gridSheet.Col                    'remember current selection
          sRow% = gridSheet.Row
          eCol% = gridSheet.ColSel
          eRow% = gridSheet.RowSel
          gridSheet.HighLight = False              'turn off highlight
          gridSheet.Col = 1                        'and select entire grid
          gridSheet.Row = 1
          gridSheet.ColSel = gridSheet.Cols - 1
          gridSheet.RowSel = gridSheet.Rows - 1
        Else                                       'back to normal
          gridSheet.Col = sCol%                    'reset old selection
          gridSheet.Row = sRow%
          gridSheet.ColSel = eCol%
          gridSheet.RowSel = eRow%
          gridSheet.HighLight = True               'and turn on highlighting
        End If
    End Sub
```

19. Add in the following code to the General Declarations section. This routine
cleans up a number, removing any extraneous characters (like dollar signs and
commas), and then converts the clean string to a number.

```
Function clean (number As Variant) As Single
    'this cleans up a number, removing garbage like commas and dollar ⇐
signs
        On Error GoTo woops                        'just in case .
        For i = 1 To Len(number)
'iterate through entire string
        If InStr("1234567890", Mid(number, i, 1))  = 0 Then
'if character isn't a number,
            Mid$(number, i, 1) = " "
'replace with an inoffensive blank
```

continued on next page

continued from previous page

```
        End If
      Next i
      clean = Val(number)
'and make string into a number
Exit Function                              'done

woops:                                     'something went wrong
        clean = 0                          'so fake it
Exit Function                              'and leave

End Function
```

How It Works

This project displays a list of figures showing the effects of inflation on your earning power. You enter a dollar figure in one combo box, and an inflation rate in another. The program then uses a grid control to display how that initial dollar figure grows over time. The grid has columns for yearly, monthly, weekly, and hourly wages needed to stay even. Although the results may prompt you to find ways to increase your income (You mean I have to earn an extra $40,000 just to break even?!), the project does illustrate each of the properties, events, and methods detailed in the chapter. Figure 48-3 shows the project in action.

Enter a figure in the upper-left combo box. It's set to default to $50,000. Set the inflation rate in the combo box on the right. After you tab out of this combo box, the grid control gets updated to display the results. You can scroll up and down with the scrollbar, and can move the active cell and select cells. The labels at the bottom of the grid are updated to show cell and selection status.

The large list box contains a history of what "scenarios," or combinations of income and inflation rate, you've displayed. It lists the starting parameters plus the amount of money you'd need after ten years to just break even. You can clear the entire history by double-clicking on it, or you can delete selected lines by selecting them and then clicking with the right mouse button. The list box is set up as a MultiSelect box, so you can select more than one item.

The bottom two combo boxes let you turn the grid lines on and off and set the alignment of selected columns.

The Save command button saves the grid data to a file, and the Open command button retrieves the information from the file. Exit, of course, exits the program.

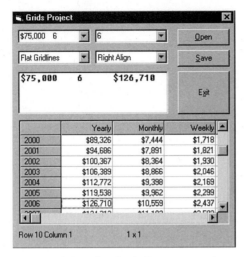

Figure 48-3   The Grids Project in action